STANDARD 9: Geometry and Spatial Sense

In grades K-4, the mathematics curriculum should include two- and three-dimensional geometry so that students can—

* describe, model, draw, and classify shapes;
* Investigate and predict the results of combining, subdividing, and changing shapes;
* develop spatial sense;
* relate geometric ideas to number and measurement ideas;
* recognize and appreciate geometry in their world.

STANDARD 10: Measurement

In grades K-4, the mathematical curriculum should include measurement so that students can—

* understand the attributes of length, capacity, weight, area, volume, time, temperature, and angle;
* develop the process of measuring and concepts related to units of measurement;
* make and use estimates of measurement;
* make and use measurements in problem and everyday situations.

STANDARD 11: Statistics and Probability

In grades K-4, the mathematics curriculum should include experiences with data analysis and probability so that students can—

* collect, organize, and describe data;
* construct, read, and interpret displays of data;
* formulate and solve problems that involve collecting and analyzing data;
* explore concepts of chance.

STANDARD 12:

In grades K-4, the ma... fractions and decimal...

* develop concepts ... ...cimals;
* develop number sense for fractions and decimals;
* use models to relate fractions to decimals and to find equivalent fractions;
* use models to explore operations on fractions and decimals;
* apply fractions and decimals to problem situations.

STANDARD 13: Patterns and Relationships

In grades K-4, the mathematics curriculum should include the study of patterns and relationships so that students can—

* recognize, describe, extend, and create a wide variety of patterns;
* represent and describe mathematical relationships;
* explore the use of variables and open sentences to express relationships.

CURRICULUM STANDARDS FOR GRADES 5-8

STANDARD 1: Mathematics as Problem Solving

In grades 5-8, the mathematics curriculum should include numerous and varied experiences with problem solving as a method of inquiry and application so that students can—

* use problem-solving approaches to investigate and understand mathematical content;
* formulate problems from situations within and outside mathematics;
* develop and apply a variety of strategies to solve problems, with emphasis on multistep and nonroutine problems;
* verify and interpret results with respect to the original problem situation;
* generalize solutions and strategies to new problem situations;
* acquire confidence in using mathematics meaningfully.

STANDARD 2: Mathematics as Communication

In grades 5-8, the study of mathematics should include opportunities to communicate so that students can—

* model situations using oral, written, concrete, pictorial, graphical, and algebraic methods;
* reflect on and clarify their own thinking about mathematical ideas and situations;
* develop common understandings of mathematical ideas, including the role of definitions;
* use the skills of reading, listening, and viewing to interpret and evaluate mathematical ideas;
* discuss mathematical ideas and make conjectures and convincing arguments;
* appreciate the value of mathematical notation and its role in the development of mathematical ideas.

STANDARD 3: Mathematics as Reasoning

In grades 5-8, reasoning shall permeate the mathematics curriculum so that students can—

* recognize and apply deductive and inductive reasoning;
* understand and apply reasoning processes, with special attention to spatial reasoning and reasoning with proportions and graphs;
* make and evaluate mathematical conjectures and arguments;
* validate their own thinking;
* appreciate the pervasive use and power of reasoning as a part of mathematics.

Curriculum Standards for Grades 5-8 are continued on inside back cover.

A Problem Solving Approach to

Mathematics for Elementary School Teachers

Sixth Edition

A Problem Solving Approach to

Mathematics for Elementary School Teachers

Sixth Edition

Rick Billstein
University of Montana
Missoula, Montana

Shlomo Libeskind
University of Oregon
Eugene, Oregon

Johnny W. Lott
University of Montana
Missoula, Montana

▲ **ADDISON-WESLEY**

An imprint of Addison Wesley Longman, Inc.

Reading, Massachusetts • Menlo Park, California • New York • Harlow, England
Don Mills, Ontario • Sydney • Mexico City • Madrid • Amsterdam

Senior Editor • *Bill Poole*

Editorial Project Manager • *Christine O'Brien*

Editorial Production Services • *Jennifer Bagdigian, Sandra Rigney*

Text Designer • *Rebecca Lemna, Lloyd Lemna Design*

Marketing Manager • *Michelle Babinec*

Senior Manufacturing Manager • *Roy Logan*

Manufacturing Coordinator • *Evelyn Beaton*

Prepress Buyer • *Caroline Fell*

Cover Designer • *Barbara Atkinson*

Composition/Prepress Services • *Typo-Graphics, Inc.*

Illustrations • *Typo-Graphics, Inc., James A. Bryant*

Library of Congress Cataloging-in-Publication Data

Billstein, Rick.
    A problem solving approach to mathematics for elementary school
teachers / Rick Billstein, Shlomo Libeskind, Johnny W. Lott.—6th
ed.
        p.   cm.
    Sixth ed. also published under title: A problem solving approach
to mathematics.
    Includes index.
    ISBN 0-201-56649-4 (hardcover)
    1. Mathematics — Study and teaching (Elementary)   2. Problem
solving.   I. Libeskind, Shlomo.   II. Lott, Johnny W., 1944 –
III. Billstein, Rick.   Problem solving approach to mathematics. 6th
ed.   IV. Title.
QA135.5.B49   1996b
372.7— dc20   96-26205
                                                        CIP

Reprinted with corrections, June 1998

Copyright © 1997 by Addison Wesley Longman, Inc.

    5 6 7 8 9 10 - DOW - 9998

In memory of Lee Yunker, a former student, colleague, and friend whose enthusiasm and hard work has left math education much richer.

RWB

In memory of my father Mendel, my uncles Janek and Moshe, and my aunt Chancia.

SL

To Thomas J. Brieske, who helped shape my personal vision as a teacher; to my co-authors, Rick and Shlomo, who share with me a cooperative vision of mathematics; to the Montana Council of Teachers of Mathematics for broadening my vision of mathematics education; and to the National Council of Teachers of Mathematics for providing a vision of mathematics education for the new century.

JWL

Preface

The sixth edition of *A Problem Solving Approach to Mathematics for Elementary School Teachers* continues to focus on the goals of the previous editions, but extends its reach to meet the expectations for mathematics education for elementary teachers in the next century.

Standards of the NCTM

In the sixth edition, we continue to focus on two National Council of Teachers of Mathematics (NCTM) publications, the 1989 *Curriculum and Evaluation Standards of School Mathematics* (hereafter referred to as the *Standards*), and the 1991 *Professional Standards for Teaching Mathematics* (hereafter referred to as the *Teaching Standards*). Of primary importance to us is the standards (*Standards*, p. 253): "Prospective teachers must be taught in a manner similar to how they are to teach—by exploring, conjecturing, communicating, reasoning, and so forth." In addition, "all teachers need an understanding of both the historical development and current applications of mathematics. Furthermore, they should be familiar with the power of technology." In particular, the *Teaching Standards* (p. 3) emphasize the need for the following shifts in the teaching of mathematics.

- Toward logic and mathematical evidence as verification—away from the teacher as the sole authority for right answers;
- Toward mathematical reasoning—away from merely memorizing procedures;
- Toward conjecturing, inventing, and problem solving—away from an emphasis on mechanistic answer-finding;
- Toward connecting mathematics, its ideas, and its applications—away from treating mathematics as a body of isolated concepts and procedures.

To achieve the aforementioned shifts, the sixth edition allows instructors a variety of approaches to teaching, encourages discussion and collaboration among students and with their instructors, allows for the integration of projects into the curriculum, and promotes discovery and active learning.

Continuing Goals

In the sixth edition our goals remain

- To present appropriate mathematics in an intellectually honest and mathematically correct manner.
- To use the heuristic of problem solving as an integral part of mathematics.
- To present the topics in the context of the *Standards*.
- To approach mathematics in a sequence that instills confidence, then challenges students.
- To identify and use the various problem solving strategies.

New Goals

For this edition, we have additional goals:

- To provide opportunity for alternate forms of teaching and learning, such as discovery methods, and group interaction and open-ended problem solving.

- To provide and expand communication problems so that future teachers can develop writing skills and practice the explanation of their thinking.
- To allow for additional integration of technology tools where appropriate.
- To revise the coverage of several topics, in order to make them more accessible.
- To provide core mathematics for prospective elementary teachers in a way that they are challenged to determine why mathematics is done as it is.
- To provide core mathematics that allows instructors to use methods integrated with content.

Problem Solving in the Sixth Edition

We showcase problem solving skills by:

- Devoting Chapter 1 entirely to problem solving skills, and expanding coverage in the sixth edition to place added emphasis on deductive versus inductive reasoning.
- Using a four-step problem solving process to solve problems in each chapter.
- Beginning each chapter with a preliminary problem that poses a question students can answer with the skills mastered from that particular chapter.

We encourage teachers to point out and discuss the preliminary problem at the beginning of each chapter to show how the techniques therein are necessary to solve the problem.

Features Retained in this Edition

Wherever possible, we present topics in ways that could be used in actual classrooms. Further, we have incorporated various study aids and features to facilitate learning.

- **Historical Notes** add context and humanize the mathematics.
- **Brain Teasers** provide a different avenue for problem solving. They are solved in the Instructor's Guide, and may be assigned or used by the teacher to challenge students.
- **Laboratory Activities** are integrated throughout the book to provide hands-on learning exercises. In each non-optional geometry section, van Hiele-type laboratory activities are included.
- **Cartoons** teach or emphasize important material and add levity.
- **Key Terms** are presented in the margins for quick review.
- **Definitions** are either set off in text or presented as key terms in the margin for quick review.
- **Review Problems** are included at the end of each non-optional section.
- **Optional Sections** as well as problems based on these sections are marked with an asterisk (*); more difficult problems are marked with a star (★). Problems numbered in color have answers at the back of the book.
- **Questions from the Classroom** have been continued. We strongly recommend that instructors use these questions posed by actual students in actual classrooms when building a course syllabus. Instructors may require students to write two answers to the questions—one mathematical and one pedagogical—using student texts and professional journals for research.
- **Chapter Outlines** at the end of each chapter help students review the chapter.
- **Chapter Reviews** at the end of each chapter allow students to test themselves.
- **Selected Bibliographies** have been updated and revised. They are at the end of each chapter.
- **Problem Solving Strategies** are often highlighted in italics, and indicated by ⬒.
- **Relevant Quotes** from the *Standards* and *Teaching Standards* are incorporated throughout the text, and marked by the standard icon ◆.

- In view of the *Standards'* emphasis on communicating mathematical ideas, problem sets contain numerous problems in which students are asked to explain or justify their answers.
- **Full Color** has been used for pedagogical reasons and to help students visualize concepts. Figures are more modern, attractive, and easy to follow. All of the pages taken from elementary mathematics texts are presented in full color.

Features New to this Edition

- **Problem Sets** now contain six different types of problems, (1) on-going assessment, (2) communication, (3) open-ended, (4) cooperative learning, (5) technology, and (6) review. **Communication, Open-ended,** and **Cooperative Learning** are new problem sections introduced to conform with the major points stressed in the *Standards.*
- **More Relevant and Realistic Problems** have been added to the problem sets to appeal to and be more accessible to students of diverse backgrounds.
- **Technology Corners** now replace the feature formerly called "Computer Corners," and have been expanded and enhanced to include use of Logo, spreadsheets, both graphing and scientific calculators, Geometer's Sketchpad, and computer activities.
- **Investigations** appear throughout each chapter, and are intended to help students become actively involved in their learning, to facilitate the development and improvement of their critical thinking and problem solving skills, and to stimulate both in-class and out-of-class discussion.

Content

The sixth edition has been slightly reorganized and streamlined, with some new content added.

Chapter 1   An Introduction to Problem Solving

Chapter 1 has been expanded and reorganized. More emphasis is placed on inductive versus deductive reasoning. The calculator section has been expanded to include fraction calculators.

Chapter 2   Sets, Functions, and Logic

Section 2-3 on functions has been rewritten from a more concrete and application-oriented point of view. Relations are introduced in the problem set as generalizations of functions. In the optional section on logic (Sec. 2-4), more emphasis is placed on the understanding of conditionals and biconditionals through concrete examples and analogy between these concepts and set inclusion.

Chapter 3   Numeration Systems for the Ages

In Chapter 3, numeration systems and other number bases have been combined into one coherent package; students can now see where other number bases are actually used.

Chapter 4   Integers and Number Theory

Chapters 4 and 5 from the previous edition have been combined into one chapter. The section on solving equations (previously Sec. 4-3) has been reworked and is now found in the new Chapter 7.

Chapter 5   Rational Numbers as Fractions

Chapter 5 has been shortened and reorganized. The topic of comparing rational numbers has been placed at the beginning of the chapter. In addition, this chapter contains more pictures to help describe the concepts and to assist students with visualization. The presentation of division of rationals has been modified. The sections on ratio and proportion and exponents have been moved to later chapters.

Chapter 6   Exponents and Decimals

Chapter 6 now provides a full treatment of positive and negative integer exponents immediately before they are needed for the development of decimals.

Chapter 7   Applications of Mathematics

Besides a commitment to increased applications in the examples and problem sets throughout the text, the sixth edition has a new chapter with emphasis on applications. Much of the material is new. Coordinate systems are introduced in Section 7-3 and used in subsequent sections. Section 7-4 on ratio and proportion (previously in Chap. 5) includes new topics such as scale drawing, direct and inverse variation, and levers.

Chapter 9   Statistics: An Introduction

Coverage in Chapter 9 has been expanded to include an introduction on different types of graphs, such as double bar graphs. There is more material on box plots and additional uses for box plots. The section on abuses of statistics is no longer marked "optional."

Chapter 10   Introductory Geometry

Section 10-3 on linear measure and circumference of a circle is new, although some of the material in this section appeared in Chapter 13 of the previous edition. Section 10-4, More about Angles, has been completely rewritten from a more intuitive, application-oriented approach.

Chapter 11   Constructions and Similarity

Chapter 11 includes a reorganized discussion of constructions. The separate section on circles and spheres has been eliminated and the material moved into other sections. Some material on coordinate geometry has been moved into a section on similarity to show how slope is developed. A new section on trigonometry ratios via similarity has also been added.

Chapter 12   More Concepts of Measurement

Linear measure, previously covered in this chapter, has been moved to Chapter 10 (Sec. 10-3) as it was needed earlier. (Chap. 12 was previously Chap. 13.)

Chapter 13   Motion Geometry and Tessellations

In Section 13-1, coordinate representation of translations is a new topic. In addition, slopes of perpendicular lines are investigated as an application of rotations. In Section 13-2, reflections in a coordinate system, a topic not presented in the previous edition, is introduced. New coverage also includes treatment of light reflecting from a surface. In Section 13-3, new material includes applications of size transformations, such as perspective drawing and photography.

Appendices

Three new appendices have been added to the sixth edition, including

- Graphing Calculators,
- Geometry Utility (based on Geometer's Sketchpad), and
- Using a Spreadsheet (based on Microsoft Excel).
- The Logo Turtle Graphics appendix has been streamlined and shortened from two sections to one section.

Calculator Usage

As prescribed in the *Standards,* coverage of calculators is necessary and timely. Calculators are introduced in Chapter 1, and a discussion of the use of scientific/fraction calculators appears in that chapter. The use of the graphing calculator is presented, where relevant, in the new Technology Corners, and problems involving the use of both scientific/fraction and graphing calculators appear in the problem sets.

Supplements for the Student

Student's Solutions Manual, by Louis Levy and Edward Fritz, contains detailed solutions to all odd-numbered exercises.

Activities Manual — *Mathematics Activities for Elementary School Teachers: A Problem Solving Approach, Third Edition,* by Daniel Dolan, Jim Williamson, and Mary Muri. This revised edition features activities that can be used to develop, reinforce, and/or apply mathematical concepts. The activities for each concept are ordered by developmental level within each chapter.

Supplements for the Instructor

Instructor's Resource Guide includes: Answers to all problems in the text; two forms of chapter assessments with answers for each chapter; suggested answers to Questions from the Classroom; Solutions to the Brain Teasers, and suggested answers to the Chapter Investigations.

Instructor's Solutions Manual, by Louis Levy and Edward Fritz, contains detailed solutions to all exercises.

Instructor's Guide to *Mathematics Activities for Elementary School Teachers: A Problem Solving Approach, Third Edition,* by Daniel Dolan, Jim Williamson, and Mary Muri, contains answers for all activities, as well as additional teaching suggestions for some activities.

OmniTest[3] is available in DOS-based and Macintosh formats. This new version of this easy-to-use software was developed for Addison-Wesley by ips Publishing, a leader in computerized testing and assessment.

- DOS-based and Macintosh formats.
- The Macintosh format makes full use of the Macintosh graphical user interface.

- DOS user interface is easy to learn and operate. Its Windows look-alike structure lets you easily choose and control the items as well as the format for each test.
- You can quickly and easily create make-up exams, customized homework assignments, and multiple test forms.
- OmniTest[3] is algorithm driven—meaning the program can automatically insert new numbers into the same equation—creating hundreds of variations of that equation.
    - The numbers are constrained to keep answers reasonable, so that you can create a virtually endless supply of parallel versions of the same test.
    - With this new version of OmniTest you can "lock in" the values shown in the model problem, if you wish.
- OmniTest[3] is keyed section by section to the text, allowing you to select questions that test individual objectives from that section.
- You can also enter your own questions by way of OmniTest[3]'s sophisticated editor—complete with mathematical notation.

Acknowledgments

Reviewers of This and Previous Editions

The authors wish to thank the following for their helpful comments and suggestions for this and previous editions of the text.

Leon J. Ablon
G. L. Alexanderson
Bernadette Antkoviak
Jane Barnard
Joann Becker
Cindy Bernlohr
James Bierden
Jim Boone
Sue Boren
Beverly R. Broomell
Maurice Burke
David Bush
Laura Cameron
Louis J. Chatterley
Phyllis Chinn
Donald J. Dessart
Ronald Dettmers
Jackie Dewar
Amy Edwards
Margaret Ehringer
Albert Filano
Marjorie Fitting
Michael Flom
Martha Gady
Sandy Geiger
Glenadine Gibb
Elizabeth Gray
Alice Guckin
Boyd Henry
Alan Hoffer
E. John Hornsby, Jr.
Judith E. Jacobs
Jerry Johnson
Wilburn C. Jones
Robert Kalin

Herbert E. Kasube
Sarah Kennedy
Steven D. Kerr
Leland Knauf
Margret F. Kothmann
Hester Lewellen
Ralph A. Liguori
Don Loftsgaarden
Stanley Lukawecki
Barbara Moses
Charles Nelson
Glenn Nelson
Dale Oliver
Keith Peck
Barbara Pence
Glenn L. Pfeifer
Jack Porter
Edward Rathnell
Helen R. Santiz
Jane Schielack
Barbara Shabell
M. Geralda Shaefer
Gwen Shufelt
Ron Smit
Joe K. Smith
William Sparks
Virginia Strawderman
Viji Sundar
C. Ralph Verno
Hubert Voltz
John Wagner
Virginia Warfield
Mark F. Weiner
Grayson Wheatley
Jerry L. Young

BRIEF CONTENTS

Solution to the cover puzzle follows the index.

CONTENTS

Solution to the cover puzzle follows the index.

*indicates optional section

1

AN INTRODUCTION
TO PROBLEM SOLVING

Female bees are born from fertilized eggs, and male bees are born from unfertilized eggs. This means that a male bee has only a mother, while a female bee has a mother and a father. If the ancestry of a male bee is traced 10 generations back, how many bees are there in all 10 generations?

School mathematics has been associated with performing computations and learning isolated facts, while devoting little time to reasoning and communication skills. Textbook problems typically give students practice with the content presented in a lesson. Such practice problems are often *exercises* involving routine procedures for finding solutions. To perform an exercise, you normally repeat a method illustrated in the book. For example, $4 \times 12 = ?$ is an exercise for most sixth graders. The situation becomes only slightly harder if it is put in some context such as *if each of four students has 12 marbles, how many marbles are there all together.* In most elementary books, this exercise or the contextual problem would be found in a section on multiplying a two-digit number by a single-digit number. In this setting, students know that the question involves multiplication. If the contextual situation was presented to first grade students, this might not be an exercise.

Exercises serve a purpose in learning mathematics, but problem solving must be the focus of school mathematics. *Problem solving has been described as what you do when you don't know what to do.* Your mathematical experience often determines whether situations are *problems* or *exercises*. In the cartoon below, Peppermint Patty tries to substitute another kind of exercise for a problem. How would you react to Patty's problem?

The National Council of Teachers of Mathematics (NCTM) publication *Curriculum and Evaluation Standards for School Mathematics* (1989), hereafter referred to as the *Standards,* addresses *problem solving* at the K–4, 5–8, and 9–12 grade levels. For example, in Standard 1 for grades K–4 (p. 23) we find the following:

 Problem solving should be the central focus of the mathematics curriculum. As such, it is a primary goal of all mathematics instruction and an integral part of all mathematical activity. Problem solving is not a distinct topic but a process that should permeate the entire program and provide the context in which concepts and skills can be learned.

In this text, you will have many opportunities to solve problems. Each chapter opens with a problem that can be solved by using the concepts developed in the chapter. The solution is presented at the end of each chapter using a four-step problem-solving process. You may wish to read only enough of the solution to get a hint of it and then try to complete the problem.

Throughout the text, there will be numerous problems solved using the four-step process and others solved using other formats. At the end of each section, there is a series of exercises and problems labeled *Ongoing Assessment*. Many of the problems require the use of the problem-solving skills developed in this chapter. One portion of the *Ongoing*

Assessment is labeled as *Open-ended.* In this section, the problems usually can have more than one answer or more than one way of arriving at an answer. Your solutions to these problems should discuss what was done to solve the problem and why it was done. The solutions may be written using the four-step process discussed later in this chapter or in paragraph form where the ideas of the four-step process are included.

Working with other students to solve problems can enhance your problem-solving ability and communication skills. In this text, we encourage *cooperative learning* and encourage students to work in groups on problems whenever possible. In the NCTM publication *Professional Standards For Teaching Mathematics,* hereafter referred to as the *Teaching Standards* (1991) (p. 58), is the following:

Students' learning of mathematics is enhanced in a learning environment that is built as a community of people collaborating to make sense of mathematical ideas. . . . Classroom structures that can encourage and support the collaboration are varied: Students may at times work independently, conferring with others as necessary; at other times students may work in pairs or in small groups. Whole class discussions are yet another profitable format. No single arrangement will work at all times; teachers should use these arrangements flexibly to pursue their goals.

To encourage group work and help identify when cooperative learning might be best used, we identify *Cooperative Learning* activities in the problem sets. These activities might involve tasks where it would be helpful to have several people gathering data, or the problems might be such that group discussions might lead to strategies for solving the problem.

Cooperative learning occurs when groups of students are formed to interact in a setting of mutual respect and helpfulness. Each student in a group is accountable for exploring, developing, and discussing ideas that contribute to a solution to a common problem. Each student must be willing to help anyone who asks and must be willing to ask for help when needed.

Students in a group or individually may use strategies explained in the remaining sections of this chapter. One problem-solving strategy, *looking for a pattern,* is used so often that it is discussed alone in the next section. A separate section is also devoted to choosing and using a calculator, an indispensable tool in performing computations and an invaluable aid in many problem-solving situations.

Section 1-1 Explorations with Patterns

Mathematics has been described as the study of patterns. We see patterns everywhere: in wallpaper, tiles, traffic, and even television schedules. Police investigators study case files to find the modus operandi, or pattern of operation, when a series of crimes is committed. Their discovery of it, sometimes aided by a computer, does not necessarily find the criminal, but it may provide clues to do so. Scientists look for patterns in order to isolate variables so that they can reach valid conclusions in their research. The importance of patterns is emphasized in the *Standards* (p. 60):

Patterns are everywhere. Children who are encouraged to look for patterns and to express them mathematically begin to understand how mathematics applies to the world in which they live. Identifying and working with a wide variety of patterns help children develop the ability to classify and organize information.

Patterns can be surprising and aesthetically pleasing. For example, consider the following:

$$1 \cdot 9 + 2 = 11$$
$$12 \cdot 9 + 3 = 111$$
$$123 \cdot 9 + 4 = 1111$$
$$1234 \cdot 9 + 5 = 11111$$
$$12345 \cdot 9 + 6 = 111111$$

Does this pattern continue? Why or why not?

Working with patterns can help you develop number sense and communication skills. Once the pattern is discovered, you should describe it and try to show it always works. Try to solve Example 1-1 before reading the solution.

Example 1-1

A miner finally struck gold, taking 1 oz of gold the first week, 2 oz the second week, and 4 the third week. If this pattern continues, how many ounces of gold will be taken out the tenth week?

Solution   The number of ounces of gold can be written as a numerical sequence 1, 2, 4, . . . and you are to find the 10th term, as shown in Table 1-1.

Table 1-1

Week	1	2	3	4	5	6	7	8	9	10
Gold (oz)	1	2	4							?

If you noticed that the difference between the 1st and 2nd terms is 1 and the difference between the 2nd and 3rd terms is 2, you might say that the difference between the 3rd and 4th terms is 3, the difference between the 4th and 5th terms is 4, and so on. If we use this strategy, then this pattern would give the following sequence for the first 10 terms:

$$1, 2, 4, 7, 11, 16, 22, 29, 37, 46$$

Therefore the amount of gold taken out on the tenth day is 46 oz.

However, if you noticed that the second term is twice the first and the third term is twice the second, then this pattern would give the following sequence for the first 10 numbers:

$$1, 2, 4, 8, 16, 32, 64, 128, 256, 512$$

Based on this pattern, the amount of gold taken out on the tenth day is 512 oz.

Which answer in Example 1-1 is correct? With the given information, we have no way of knowing. Both are possible, since both satisfy the conditions of the problem and a valid argument was given showing how each answer was obtained. It is evident that more than one pattern is possible based on the limited information. Many people say that in mathematics, there is only one correct answer. This example shows that this is not the case.

Patterns do not always have to be numerical, as shown in Investigation 1-1.

I N V E S T I G A T I O N   1 - 1

● **a.** Explain how to find the next three terms to complete a pattern:

o, Δ, Δ, o, Δ, Δ, o, _____ , _____ , _____

b. Complete the following pattern in at least two ways. Explain your rules.

f, s, s, _____ , _____   ●

Inductive Reasoning

inductive reasoning

Scientists make observations and propose general laws based on observations and patterns. Statisticians use patterns when they form conclusions based on collected data. This process is **inductive reasoning,** the method of making generalizations based on observations and patterns. While inductive reasoning may lead to new discoveries, its weakness is that conclusions are drawn only from the collected evidence. If not all cases have been checked, the possibility exists that another case will prove the conclusion false. Inductive reasoning may

conjecture

lead to a **conjecture,** a statement thought to be true but not yet proved true or false. For example, considering only that $0^2 = 0$ and that $1^2 = 1$, a conjecture might be that *every number squared is equal to itself.* When we find an example that contradicts the conjecture, we

counterexample

have provided a **counterexample.** To show that the above conjecture is not true, it is enough to exhibit only one counterexample, for example, $2^2 = 4$. Sometimes finding a counterexample is difficult, but the lack of finding a counterexample does not automatically make a conjecture true.

An example of inductive reasoning is found on the student page on page 6, from *Addison-Wesley Mathematics,* Grade 7, 1993. Patterns and inductive reasoning are used in the example, but a *counterexample* is found to show that pattern 1 fails for age 2. Note that this does not prove that pattern 2 works for all cases. Investigate to see if it works for other cases.

The following discussion illustrates the danger of making a conjecture based on a few cases. In Figure 1-1, we choose points on a circle and connect them to form distinct, nonoverlapping regions. In this figure, 2 points determine 2 regions, 3 points determine 4 regions, and 4 points determine 8 regions. What is the maximum number of regions that would be determined by 10 points?

Figure 1-1

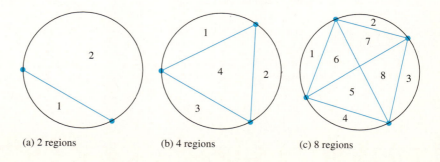

(a) 2 regions   (b) 4 regions   (c) 8 regions

Inductive Reasoning
Discovering Number Patterns

EXPLORE   **Analyze the Situation**

The picture to the right shows how you
might find the number of games to be
played in a round-robin checkers
tournament.

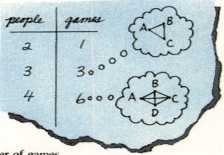

TALK ABOUT IT

1. Do you see a pattern that shows how the number of games
   depends on the number of players? What does your pattern
   indicate for 5 people? 6 people? 20 people? n people?

When you discover a pattern that you think works, try it in
several cases. If the pattern works for those cases, then you
might conclude that it will work for all cases. This is called
inductive reasoning.

Example   At birth Kristy got $100. Each birthday thereafter
she got $100 more than the last. How much will she
have in all at age 20?

Solution   A table can help. Try different patterns.

age	amount ($100s)	total ($100s)	pattern 1	pattern 2
0	1	1	$0 + 1$	$(1 \cdot 2) \div 2$
1	2	3	$1 + 2$	$(2 \cdot 3) \div 2$
2	3	6	$2 + 3$	$(3 \cdot 4) \div 2$
. . .	. . .	. . .	. . .	. . .
n	$n + 1$	?	$n + (n + 1)$	$(n + 1)(n + 2) \div 2$

Both patterns work for ages 0 and 1, but pattern 1 fails for age 2.
It seems that $(n + 1)(n + 2) \div 2$ gives the total saved by age n.
For $n = 20$, the total would be $21 \cdot 22 \div 2 = 231$. So, Kristy
would have 231 hundred dollars or $23,100.

1. How many dots would
   be in the 50th picture?

The data from Figure 1-1 are recorded in Table 1-2. It appears that each time we increase the number of points by 1, we double the number of regions. If this were true, then for 5 points we would have 16, or 2^4, regions; for 6 points we would have 32, or 2^5, regions; and so on. If we base our solution on this pattern, we could conjecture that for 10 points, we would have 512, or 2^9, regions.

Table 1-2

Number of Points	2	3	4	5	6	$\cdots$	10
Maximum Number of Regions	$2 = 2^1$	$4 = 2^2$	$8 = 2^3$				?

Figure 1-2

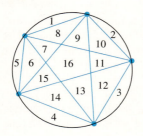

Before reading on, check to see whether we obtain 16 regions for 5 points. We obtain a figure similar to that in Figure 1-2, and our guess of 16 regions is verified. For 6 points, the pattern predicts that the number of regions will be 32. Choose the points so that they are not equally spaced and count the regions carefully. You should obtain 31 regions and not 32 regions as predicted. No matter how the points are located on the circle, the guess of 32 regions is not correct. Therefore the pattern breaks down, and the conjecture of 512 regions for 10 points that is based on this pattern is probably incorrect. This may be shocking to those of us who put our faith in the continuation of a pattern once we have been fortunate enough to discover it.

Arithmetic Sequences

sequence A **sequence** is an ordered arrangement of numbers, figures, or objects. A sequence has items or terms identified as *1st, 2nd, 3rd,* and so on. Often, sequences can be classified by their properties. For example, what property do the following first three sequences have that the fourth does not?

a. 1, 2, 3, 4, 5, 6, . . .
b. 0, 5, 10, 15, 20, 25, . . .
c. 2, 6, 10, 14, 18, 22, . . .
d. 1, 11, 111, 1111, 11111, 111111,

In each of the first three sequences, each term — starting from the second — is obtained from the preceding one by adding a fixed number. In other words, the difference between consecutive numbers in the sequences is always the same. In part (d), the difference between the first two terms is $11 - 1$, or 10; the second difference is $111 - 11$, or 100; the third difference is $1111 - 111$, or 1000; and so on. Sequences such as the first three are

arithmetic sequences arithmetic sequences. An **arithmetic sequence** is one in which each successive term is obtained from the previous term by the addition or subtraction of a fixed number, the

difference **difference.** The difference in part (c) is 4 because 4 is the fixed number that is added each time to obtain the next number.

Neither sequence that was discovered in Example 1-1 about the miner was an arithmetic sequence because there was no fixed term that was added or subtracted each time. Numerical sequences can be generated from objects, as shown in Example 1-2.

Example 1-2 Find a pattern in the number of matchsticks required to continue the pattern shown on the following page in Figure 1-3.

Figure 1-3

Solution   Assume the matchsticks are arranged so that each figure has one more square than the preceding figure. The number of matchsticks required to make the successive figures are 4, 7, 10, and 13. As seen next, each term after the first is 3 units greater than the previous term:

$$\text{Sequence} \quad 4 \quad 7 \quad 10 \quad 13 \quad —$$

$$\text{Difference} \quad \ \ 3 \quad 3 \quad \ \ 3 \quad \ \ 3$$

If this pattern continues, the number of matchsticks in each of the next three terms will be 16, 19, and 22, respectively. We can show that these answers are correct by demonstrating that this pattern of adding 3 each time continues. Observe that the addition of another square requires 3 matchsticks to be added to form the 3 sides of the right-most square. The fourth side is determined by an existing matchstick. Thus the sequence is an arithmetic sequence with a difference of 3.

• • •

Suppose you want to find the number of matchsticks in the 100th figure in Example 1-2 or a general rule for finding the number of matchsticks when given the number of the term. The problem-solving strategy of *making a table* is helpful here. Table 1-3 shows the sequence in Example 1-2. The column headed Number of Term refers to the order of the term in the sequence. The column headed Term lists the sequence terms. An *ellipsis,* denoted by three dots, indicates that the sequence continues in the same manner.

Table 1-3

Number of Term	Term
1	4
2	$7 = 4 + 3 = 4 + 1 \cdot 3$
3	$10 = 4 + 3 + 3 = 4 + 2 \cdot 3$
4	$13 = 4 + 3 + 3 + 3 = 4 + 3 \cdot 3$
.	.
.	.
.	.

In the table, the 2nd term is 3 more than the 1st term; the 3rd term is 3 more than the 2nd, or two 3's more than the first; and so on. In general, the *n*th term, where *n* is any natural number, should be 3 more than the $(n-1)$st term or $(n-1) \cdot 3$'s more than the first term. Therefore the *n*th term should be $4 + (n-1) \cdot 3$. To find the 200th term, let $n = 200$ and you have $4 + (200 - 1) \cdot 3$, or $4 + 199 \cdot 3$, or 601.

A different approach might be as follows: If the matchstick figure has 100 squares, we could find the total number of matchsticks by adding together the number of horizontal and vertical sticks. There are $2 \cdot 100$ placed horizontally. Why? Notice that in the first figure, there are 2 matchsticks placed vertically; in the second, 3; and in the third, 4. In the one hundredth figure, there should $100 + 1$ vertical matchsticks. Altogether there will be

$2 \cdot 100 + (100 + 1)$, or 301 matchsticks in the one hundredth figure. Similarly, in the *n*th figure, there would be $2n$ horizontal and $(n + 1)$ vertical matchsticks for a total of $3n + 1$. This discussion is summarized in Table 1-4.

Are the *n*th terms generated by using both techniques equivalent? That is, does $4 + (n - 1) \cdot 3 = 3n + 1$?

If we were given the value of the term, we could use the formula for the *n*th term in Table 1-4 to work backward to find the number of the term. For example, given the term 1798, we know that $3n + 1 = 1798$. Therefore $3n = 1797$ and $n = 599$. Consequently, the 599th term is 1798. We could obtain the same answer by solving $4 + (n - 1) \cdot 3 = 1798$.

Table 1-4

Number of Term	Number of Matchsticks Horizontally	Number of Matchsticks Vertically	Total
1	2	2	4
2	4	3	7
3	6	4	10
4	8	5	13
.	.	.	.
.	.	.	.
.	.	.	.
100	200	101	301
.	.	.	.
.	.	.	.
n	$2n$	$n + 1$	$2n + (n + 1) = 3n + 1$

INVESTIGATION 1-2

● Could 621 be a total number of matchsticks in Table 1-4? Explain why or why not. ●

deductive reasoning

Deductive reasoning is another method of drawing conclusions from ideas we accept as true. Proving a generalization or generating new examples based on the generalization uses deductive reasoning. For example, when we reason that the 1000th term in the matchstick problem is $3(1000) + 1 = 3001$, we accept the general rule $3n + 1$ as true, and from this rule we *deduce* that the 1000th term is 3001. In Example 1-3, we will use deductive reasoning to find terms assuming the rule for finding the *n*th term.

Example 1-3

Find the first four terms of a sequence whose *n*th term is given by the following:

a. $4n + 3$ **b.** $n^2 - 1$

Solution   **a.** To find the 1st term, substitute $n = 1$ in the formula $4n + 3$ to obtain $4 \cdot 1 + 3$, or 7. Similarly, substituting $n = 2, 3, 4$, we obtain, respectively, $4 \cdot 2 + 3$, or 11;

$4 \cdot 3 + 3$, or 15; and $4 \cdot 4 + 3$, or 19. Hence, the first four terms of the sequence are 7, 11, 15, and 19, and hence this sequence is arithmetic.

b. Substituting $n = 1, 2, 3, 4$ in the formula $n^2 - 1$, we obtain, respectively, $1^2 - 1$, or 0; $2^2 - 1$, or 3; $3^2 - 1$, or 8; and $4^2 - 1$, or 15. Thus the first four terms of the sequence are 0, 3, 8, and 15. This sequence is not arithmetic.

• • •

I N V E S T I G A T I O N   1 - 3

● If you have an arithmetic sequence with the 2nd term 11 and the 5th term 23, find the 100th term. ●

It is possible to generalize our work with arithmetic sequences. Suppose the 1st term in an arithmetic sequence is a and the difference is d. The strategy of *making a table* can be used to investigate the general term for the sequence $a, a + d, a + 2d, a + 3d, \ldots$, as shown in Table 1-5. *The nth term of any sequence with first term a and difference d is given by $a + (n - 1)d$.* For example, in the arithmetic sequence 5, 9, 13, 17, 21, 25, ..., the 1st term is 5 and the difference is 4. Thus the nth term is given by $a + (n - 1)d = 5 + (n - 1)4$. Simplifying algebraically, we obtain $5 + (n - 1)4 = 5 + 4n - 4 = 4n + 1$.

Table 1-5

Number of Term	Term
1	a
2	$a + d$
3	$a + 2d$
4	$a + 3d$
5	$a + 4d$
.	.
.	.
.	.
n	$a + (n - 1)d$

• • •

Example 1-4   The diagrams in Figure 1-4 show the molecular structure of *alkanes,* a class of hydrocarbons. C represents a carbon atom and H a hydrogen atom. A connecting segment shows a chemical bond.

Figure 1-4

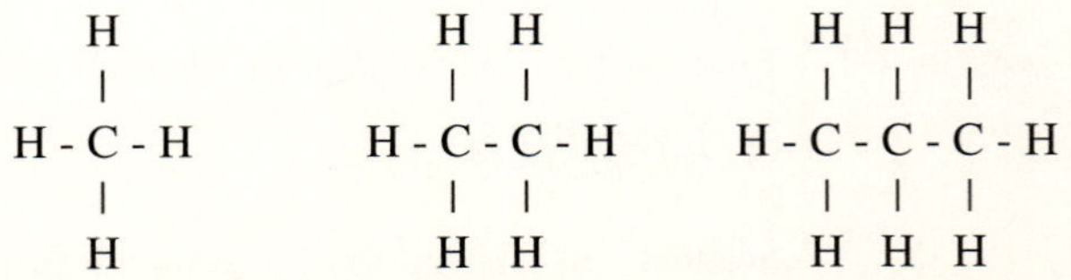

```
      H                  H  H                H  H  H
      |                  |  |                |  |  |
   H - C - H          H - C - C - H       H - C - C - C - H
      |                  |  |                |  |  |
      H                  H  H                H  H  H
```

methane (CH_4)   *ethane* (C_2H_6)   *propane* (C_3H_8)

a. Hectane is an alkane with 100 carbon atoms. How many hydrogen atoms does it have?

b. Write a general rule for alkanes C_nH_m showing the relationship between m and n.

Solution   **a.** To determine the relationship between the number of carbon and hydrogen atoms, study the drawing of the alkanes and disregard the extreme left and right hydrogen atoms in each. We can see that for every carbon atom, there are two hydrogen atoms. Therefore there are twice as many hydrogen atoms as carbon atoms plus the two hydrogen atoms at the extremes. For example, when there are 3 carbon atoms, there are $(2 \cdot 3) + 2$, or 8, hydrogen atoms. This notion is summarized in Table 1-6. If you extend the table for 4 carbon atoms, you get $(2 \cdot 4) + 2$, or 10, hydrogen atoms. For 100 carbon atoms, there are $(2 \cdot 100) + 2$, or 202, hydrogen atoms.

Table 1-6

No. of Carbon Atoms	No. of Hydrogen Atoms
1	4
2	6
3	8
.	.
.	.
.	.
100	?
.	.
.	.
.	.
n	m

b. In general, for n carbon atoms you would have n hydrogen atoms attached above, n attached below, and 2 more attached on the sides. Hence, the total number of hydrogen atoms would be $2n + 2$. Because the number of hydrogen atoms was designated by m, it follows that $m = 2n + 2$.

• • •

• • •

Example 1-5   A theater is set up in such a way that there are 20 seats in the first row and 4 additional seats in each consecutive row. The last row has 144 seats. How many rows are there in the theater?

Solution   We could start writing an arithmetic sequence starting at 20 with the *difference, d,* equal to 4, stop when 144 is reached, and count the number of rows. A calculator could be used to accomplish this task. However, this technique is cumbersome and would be even more so if the numbers were greater. In an arithmetic sequence, the nth term is $a + (n-1)d$, where a is the first term, d is the difference, and n is the number of the term. In this case, $a = 20$ and $d = 4$. Therefore

$$a + (n-1)d = 20 + (n-1)4.$$

We now want to find the number of the term, *n,* when the *n*th term, $20 + (n - 1)\,4$, is equal to 144. Therefore

$$20 + (n - 1)4 = 144$$
$$(n - 1)4 = 124$$
$$n - 1 = 31$$
$$n = 32.$$

This tells us that when $n = 32$, the value of the term is 144. This implies that there are 32 rows in the theater. Instead of using a formula, we could have made a table and looked for a pattern.

• • •

Geometric Sequences

A child has 2 biological parents, 4 grandparents, 8 great grandparents, 16 great-great grand-parents, and so on. The number of ancestors form the **geometric sequence** 2, 4, 8, 16, 32, ... Each successive term of a geometric sequence is obtained from its predecessor by multiplying by a fixed number, the **ratio.** In this example, both the 1st term and the ratio are 2. To find the *n*th term, examine the pattern in Table 1-7.

Table 1-7

Number of Term	Term
1	$2 = 2^1$
2	$4 = 2 \cdot 2 = 2^2$
3	$8 = (2 \cdot 2) \cdot 2 = 2^3$
4	$16 = (2 \cdot 2 \cdot 2) \cdot 2 = 2^4$
5	$32 = (2 \cdot 2 \cdot 2 \cdot 2) \cdot 2 = 2^5$
.	.
.	.
.	.

When the given term is written as a power of 2, the number of the term is the exponent. Following this pattern, the 10th term is 2^{10}, or 1024, the 100th term is 2^{100}, and the *n*th term is 2^n. Thus the number of ancestors in the *n*th previous generation is 2^n.

Finding the *n*th term for a Geometric Sequence

It is possible to find the *n*th term of any geometric sequence when given the first term and the ratio. If the 1st term is *a* and the ratio is *r*, then the terms are as listed in Table 1-8. The *n*th term is ar^{n-1}. For $n = 1$, we have $ar^{1-1} = ar^0$. Because the 1st term is *a*, then $ar^0 = a$. This implies that $r^0 = 1$. This is true for all numbers $r \neq 0$, as discussed in Chapter 6. Thus when $n = 1$ and $r \neq 0$, we have $ar^0 = a(1) = a$. For the geometric sequence 3, 12, 48, 192, . . . , the 1st term is 3 and the ratio is 4, and so the *n*th term is given by $ar^{n-1} = 3 \cdot 4^{n-1}$.

Table 1-8

Number of Term	Term
1	a
2	ar
3	ar^2
4	ar^3
5	ar^4
.	.
.	.
.	.
n	ar^{n-1}

INVESTIGATION   1 - 4

a. Two bacteria are in a dish. The number of bacteria triples every hour. Following this pattern, find the number of bacteria in the dish after 10 hours and after n hours.

b. Suppose that instead of increasing geometrically as in part (a), the number of bacteria increases arithmetically, that is, it increases by 3 each hour. Compare the growth after 10 hr and after n hours. Comment on the difference in growth of a geometric sequence versus an arithmetic sequence.

Other Sequences

figurate numbers

Figurate numbers provide examples of sequences that are neither arithmetic nor geometric. Such numbers can be represented by dots arranged in the shape of certain geometric figures. The number 1 is the beginning of most patterns involving figurate numbers. The array in Figure 1-5 represents the first four terms of the sequence of **triangular numbers.**

triangular numbers

Figure 1-5

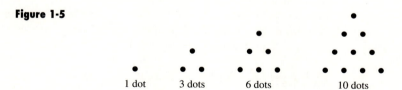

1 dot   3 dots   6 dots   10 dots

The triangular numbers can be written numerically as 1, 3, 6, 10, 15, . . . The sequence 1, 3, 6, 10, 15, . . . is not an arithmetic sequence because there is no common difference, as seen in Figure 1-6.

Figure 1-6

(First difference)

$$\begin{array}{ccccccccc} 1 & & 3 & & 6 & & 10 & & 15 \\ & \vee & & \vee & & \vee & & \vee & \\ & 2 & & 3 & & 4 & & 5 & \end{array}$$

However, the sequence of differences 2, 3, 4, 5, . . . is an arithmetic sequence with difference 1, as seen in Figure 1-7.

Figure 1-7

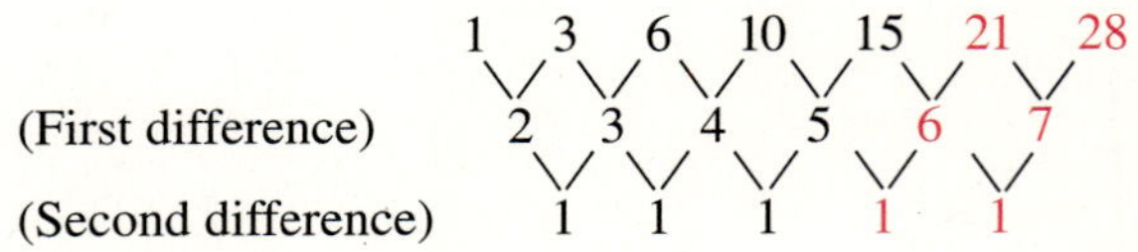

$$\begin{array}{ccccccc}
1 & 3 & 6 & 10 & 15 & 21 & 28
\end{array}$$

(First difference)   2   3   4   5   6   7

(Second difference)   1   1   1   1   1

Successive terms for the original sequence are shown in color.

Table 1-9 suggests a pattern for finding the next terms and the *n*th term for the triangular numbers. The second term is obtained from the first term by adding 2; the third term is obtained from the second term by adding 3; and so on. In general, because the *n*th triangular number has *n* dots in the *n*th row, it is equal to the sum of the dots in the previous triangular number (the $(n-1)$st one) plus the *n* dots in the *n*th row. Following this pattern, the 10th term is $1 + 2 + 3 + 4 + 5 + 6 + 7 + 8 + 9 + 10$, or 55, and the *n*th term is $1 + 2 + 3 + 4 + 5 + \ldots + (n-1) + n$.

Table 1-9

Number of Term	Term
1	1
2	$3 = 1 + 2$
3	$6 = 1 + 2 + 3$
4	$10 = 1 + 2 + 3 + 4$
5	$15 = 1 + 2 + 3 + 4 + 5$
.	.
.	.
.	.
10	$55 = 1 + 2 + 3 + 4 + 5 + 6 + 7 + 8 + 9 + 10$

Next consider the first four **square numbers** in Figure 1-8. These square numbers, 1, 4, 9, 16, . . . , can be written as 1^2, 2^2, 3^2, and 4^2. The number of dots in the 10th array is 10^2; the number of dots in the 100th array is 100^2; and the number of dots in the *n*th array is n^2. Notice that the sequence of square numbers is neither arithmetic nor geometric.

Figure 1-8

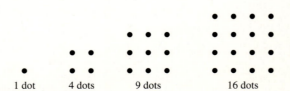

1 dot   4 dots   9 dots   16 dots

• • •

Example 1-6 Assuming that the pattern you discover continues, find the seventh term in each of the following sequences:

a. 5, 6, 14, 29, 51, 80, . . .
b. 2, 3, 9, 23, 48, 87, . . .

Solution **a.** Following is the sequence of first differences:

$$5 \quad 6 \quad 14 \quad 29 \quad 51 \quad 80$$

(First difference)   1   8   15   22   29

To discover a pattern for the original sequence, we try to find a pattern for the sequence of differences 1, 8, 15, 22, 29, ... This sequence is an arithmetic sequence with fixed difference 7:

$$5 \quad 6 \quad 14 \quad 29 \quad 51 \quad 80$$

(First difference)   1   8   15   22   29

(Second difference)   7   7   7   7

Thus the 6th term in the first difference row is 29 + 7, or 36, and the 7th term in the original sequence is 80 + 36, or 116. What number follows 116?

b. Because the second difference is not a fixed number, we go on to the third difference, as shown:

$$2 \quad 3 \quad 9 \quad 23 \quad 48 \quad 87$$

(First difference)   1   6   14   25   39

(Second difference)   5   8   11   14

(Third difference)   3   3   3

The third difference is a fixed number; therefore the second difference is an arithmetic sequence. The 5th term in the second-difference sequence is 14 + 3, or 17; the 6th term in the first-difference sequence is 39 + 17, or 56; and the 7th term in the original sequence is 87 + 56, or 143.

• • •

When asked to find a pattern for a given sequence, first look for some easily recognizable pattern. If none exists, determine whether the sequence is either arithmetic or geometric. If a pattern is still unclear, taking successive differences may help. *It is possible that none of the methods described reveal a pattern.*

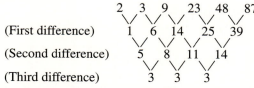

BRAIN TEASER Find the patterns in each of the following:

a. Find the next three terms in the following sequence:

O, T, T, F, F, S, S, E, _____, _____, _____

b. Determine a pattern for placing letters above or below the horizontal line in the following diagram:

A   EF HI KLMN   T   VWXYZ
_____
BCD   G   J   OPQRS U

Ongoing Assessment 1-1

1. For each of the following sequences of figures, determine a possible pattern and draw what figure would be next according to that pattern:

a.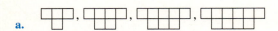

b.

c.

d.

2. In each of the following, list terms that continue a possible pattern. Which of the following sequences are arithmetic, which are geometric, and which are neither?

  a. 1, 3, 5, 7, 9
  b. 0, 50, 100, 150, 200
  c. 3, 6, 12, 24, 48
  d. 10, 100, 1000, 10,000, 100,000
  e. 9, 13, 17, 21, 25, 29
  f. 1, 8, 27, 64, 125

3. Find the 100th term and the *n*th term for each of the sequences in Problem 2.

4. Use a traditional clock face to determine the next three terms in the following sequence:

$$1, 6, 11, 4, 9, \ldots$$

5. Observe the following pattern:

$$1 + 3 = 2^2$$
$$1 + 3 + 5 = 3^2$$
$$1 + 3 + 5 + 7 = 4^2$$

  a. Use inductive reasoning to state a generalization based on this pattern.
  b. Based on your generalization in (a), find

$$1 + 3 + 5 + 7 + \ldots + 35.$$

6. Following is a pattern of circular shapes:

If you make this pattern until you have 10 black circles in a row, how many of each shape will you need?

7. Fill in the following circles by making use of the patterns in a calendar:

a.   **b.**

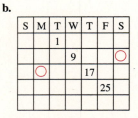

8. The following geometric arrays suggest a sequence of numbers:

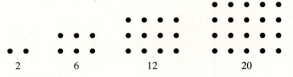

  a. Find the next three terms.
  b. Find the 100th term.
  c. Find the *n*th term.

9. In the following pattern, one hexagon takes 6 toothpicks to build, two hexagons take 11 toothpicks to build, and so on. How many toothpicks would it take to build (a) 10 hexagons? (b) *n* hexagons?

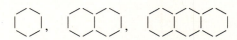

10. The first windmill takes 5 squares to build, the second takes 9 squares to build, and the third takes 13 squares to build, as shown. How many squares will it take to build (a) the 10th windmill? (b) the *n*th windmill?

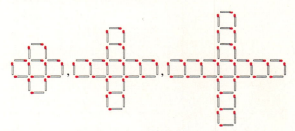

11. Each of the following figures is made of smaller triangles like the first one in the sequence. (The second figure is made of 4 triangles.) Make a conjecture concerning the number of smaller triangles needed to make (a) the 100th figure and (b) the *n*th figure.

12. In the following sequence, the figures are made of cubes that are glued together. If the exposed surface needs to be painted, how many squares will be painted in (a) the 10th figure? (b) the *n*th figure?

13. The school population for a certain school was predicted to increase by 50 students a year for the next 10 yrs. If the current enrollment is 700 students, what will the enrollment be after 10 yrs?

14. A tank contains 15,360 L of water. At the end of each day, half of the water is removed and not replaced. How much water is left in the tank after 10 days?

15. A well driller charges $10 a foot for the first 10 ft, $10.50 a foot for the next 10 ft, $11 a foot for the next 10 ft, and so on, increasing the price by 50¢ for each 10 ft. What is the cost of drilling a 100-ft well?

16. An employee is paid $1200 at the end of the first month on the job. Each month after that, the worker is paid $20 more than in the preceding month.
    a. What is the employee's monthly salary at the end of the second year on the job?
    b. How much will the employee have earned after 6 mo?
    c. After how many months will the employee's monthly salary be $3240?

17. A commuter train picks up passengers at 7:30 A.M. If 1 person gets on at the first stop, 3 at the second stop, 5 at the third stop, and so on in this manner, how many people get on at the tenth stop?

18. Joe's annual income has been increasing each year by the same amount. The first year his income was $24,000, and the ninth year his income was $31,680. In which year was his income $45,120?

19. The first difference of a sequence is 2, 4, 6, 8, ... Find the first six terms of the original sequence in each of the following cases:
    a. The 1st term of the original sequence is 3.
    b. The sum of the first two terms of the original sequence is 10.
    c. The 5th term of the original sequence is 35.

20. List the next three terms to continue a pattern in each of the following. (Finding differences may be helpful.)
    a. 5, 6, 14, 32, 64, 115, 191   b. 0, 2, 6, 12, 20, 30, 42
    ★c. 10, 8, 3, 0, 4, 20, 53

21. How many terms are there in each of the following sequences?
    a. 51, 52, 53, 54, . . . , 151   b. 1, 2, 2^2, 2^3, . . . , 2^{60}
    c. 10, 20, 30, 40, . . . , 2000
    d. 9, 13, 17, 21, 25, . . . , 353
    e. 1, 2, 4, 8, 16, 32, . . . , 1024

22. Find the first five terms of the sequence whose *n*th term is as follows:

    a. $n^2 + 2$ b. $5n - 1$ c. $10^n - 1$ d. $3n + 2$

23. The number of petals on many flowers generates the following sequence:

$$1, 1, 2, 3, 5, 8, 13, 21, . . . ,$$

which is a **Fibonacci sequence.** This sequence is named after the great Italian mathematician Leonardo Fibonacci, who lived in the twelfth and thirteenth centuries.
    a. Write the first 12 terms of the sequence.
    b. Notice that the sum of the first three terms in the sequence is one less than the fifth term of the sequence. Does a similar relationship hold for the sum of the first four terms, five terms, and six terms?
    c. Guess the sum of the first 10 terms of the sequence.
    ★d. Make a conjecture concerning the sum of the first *n* terms of the sequence.

24. The Fibonacci sequence defined in Problem 23 can start with arbitrary first and second terms. If the 1st term is 2 and the 2nd is 4, then the sequence is 2, 4, 6, 10, 16, 26, 42, ... Answer the questions in Problem 23 for this sequence.

25. Consider the following sequences:
    a. 300, 500, 700, 900, 1100, 1300, . . .
    b. 2, 4, 8, 16, 32, 64, . . .
    Find the number of the term in which the geometric sequence becomes greater than the arithmetic sequence.

26. Start with a piece of paper. Cut it into 5 pieces. Take any one of the pieces and again cut it into 5 pieces, and so on.
    a. What number of pieces can be obtained in this way?
    b. What is the number of pieces obtained in the *n*th cut?

27. The sequence 32, *a*, *b*, *c*, 512 is a geometric sequence. Find *a*, *b*, *c*.

28. Each box in the following row had a number written in it such that the sum of any three numbers in succession in the row was 15. Many of the numbers were erased. Determine the missing numbers for each square.

6							4		

Communication

29. Explain how to show that each of these statements is false:
    a. All rectangles have diagonals that are perpendicular.
    b. The sum of two even numbers is divisible by 4.

30. Elsa met 3 university students from Montana, and they all wore cowboy boots. Elsa generalized that all Montana university students wear cowboy boots. How could you show that her generalization is false?

31. Give two examples of how inductive reasoning might be used in your everyday life. Is a conclusion based on inductive reasoning certain?

32. a. If a fixed number is added to each term of an arithmetic sequence, is the resulting sequence an arithmetic sequence? Justify your answer.

b. If each term of an arithmetic sequence is multiplied by a fixed number, will the resulting sequence always be an arithmetic sequence? Justify your answer.

Open-ended

33. Patterns can be used to count the number of dots on the Chinese checkerboard; two patterns are shown below. Determine several other patterns to count the dots.

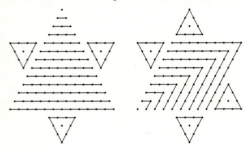

$1 + 2 + 3 + \ldots + 13 + 3(10)$ $1 + 3 + 5 + 7 + \ldots + 17 + 4(10)$

34. Make up a pattern involving *figurate numbers* and find a formula for the 100th term. Describe your pattern and how you found the 100th term.

Cooperative Learning

35. Each person in the group follows this set of directions:
Pick a number.

Multiply by 3.
Add 6.
Divide by 3.
Subtract your original number.

a. Compare your answers and make a generalization based on your results.

b. What type of reasoning did you use in making your generalization?

c. Make up a number puzzle in your group where the answer is always 17 and write an explanation of why your puzzle works.

d. Write another number puzzle; try it with another group.

36. If the pattern below continued indefinitely, the resulting figure would be called the *Sierpinski triangle,* or *Sierpinski gasket.*

In a group, determine each of the following. Discuss different counting strategies.

a. How many black triangles are in the fourth figure?

b. How many white triangles are in the fourth figure?

c. If the pattern is continued for *n* figures, how many black triangles will there be?

d. If the pattern is continued for *n* figures, how many white triangles will there be?

TECHNOLOGY CORNER

A *spreadsheet* is valuable for working with number patterns and finding rules. Spreadsheets are discussed in Appendix IV. The following table is not a spreadsheet, but it will help prepare you for working with spreadsheets. The number in each column is determined by performing some operation(s) on the numbers in the *x*- and *y*-columns. For example, Column A is the result of adding 3 to the number in the *x*-column. The first entry in the A-column is 4 because $1 + 3 = 4$. The value 4 is said to be located in a cell. A **cell** is a location where a column and row intersect. The value 4 is located in cell A1 because it is located in **column A** and **row 1.** We can see that directly under the 4 in cell A1, the value of cell A2 is 5 because $2 + 3 = 5$. The rules for other columns involve both *x* and *y*. Determine these rules and enter them where the question marks appear.

	x	*y*	A (*x* + 3)	B ?	C ?	D ?	E ?	F ?	G ?
1	1	2	4	3	1	2	8	4	3
2	2	3	5	5	1	6	10	7	7
3	3	4	6	7	1	12	12	10	13
4	5	5	8	10	0	25	16	15	26
5	8	0	11	8	−8	0	22	16	1
6	0	−2	3	−2	−2	0	6	−2	1
7	−2	5	1	3	7	−10	2	1	−9

Section 1-2 Mathematics and Problem Solving

George Polya, a late Stanford University mathematician, described the experience of problem solving in his book, *How to Solve It* (p. v):

 A great discovery solves a great problem, but there is a grain of discovery in the solution of any problem. Your problem may be modest; but if it challenges your curiosity and brings into play your inventive facilities, and if you solve it by your own means, you may experience the tension and enjoy the triumph of discovery.

To solve a problem, we must first understand both the task and the given information. Next, it is helpful to determine a strategy to accomplish the task. Once we arrive at a solution, we should determine whether the solution makes sense and is reasonable. This process of problem solving can be described using a four-step process similar to the one developed by George Polya.

Four-step Problem-solving Process

1. Understanding the problem
   a. Can you state the problem in your own words?
   b. What are you trying to find or do?
   c. What are the unknowns?
   d. What information do you obtain from the problem?
   e. What information, if any, is missing or not needed?

2. Devising a plan
   The following list of strategies, although not exhaustive, is very useful:
   a. Look for a pattern.
   b. Examine related problems and determine if the same technique applied to them can be applied here.
   c. Examine a simpler or special case of the problem to gain insight into the solution of the original problem.
   d. Make a table.
   e. Make a diagram.
   f. Write an equation.
   g. Use guess and check.
   h. Work backward.
   i. Identify a subgoal.
   j. Use indirect reasoning.

3. Carrying out the plan
   a. Implement the strategy or strategies in step 2 and perform any necessary actions or computations.
   b. Check each step of the plan as you proceed. This may be intuitive checking or a formal proof of each step.
   c. Keep an accurate record of your work.

4. Looking back
  a. Check the results in the original problem. (In some cases, this will require a proof.)
  b. Interpret the solution in terms of the original problem. Does your answer make sense? Is it reasonable? Does it answer the question that was asked?
  c. Determine whether there is another method of finding the solution.
  d. If possible, determine other related or more general problems for which the techniques will work.

These and other general mathematics problem-solving strategies, or rules of thumb for successful problem solving, are called *heuristics*.

Using the Problem-solving Process

If you approach problems in only one way, you risk forming a mind-set. For example, consider the following. Spell the word "spot" three times out loud. "S-P-O-T! S-P-O-T! S-P-O-T!" Now answer the question, "What do you do when you come to a green light?" Write your answer. If you answered "Stop," you may be guilty of forming a mind-set. You do not stop at a *green* light.

Consider the following problem: "A shepherd had 36 sheep. All but 10 died. How many lived?"

Did you answer "10"? If you did, you are catching on and are ready to try some problems. If you did not answer "10," then you did not understand the question. *Understanding the problem* is the first step in the four-step problem-solving process. Using the four-step process does not guarantee a solution to a problem, but it does provide a systematic means of attacking problems. In the various steps of the process, we follow the recommendations of the *Teaching Standards*. In *Teaching Standard 5* (p. 23), it is pointed out that

Teachers should engage students in mathematical discourse about problem solving. This includes discussing different solutions and solution strategies for a given problem, how solutions can be extended and generalized, and different kinds of problems that can be created from a given situation.

Step 1: Understanding the Problem

Understanding the problem involves not only applying the skills necessary for literary reading but determining what is being asked, what information is known, what information is extraneous, and what information is missing or not known. An example follows:

Thanksgiving was on November 24, 1991. December 2 was on Saturday. Memorial Day was on May 28, 1992. How many days were there between the two holidays?

In this problem, there is one piece of extraneous information but additional information is needed. We must know how many days there are in the months of November, December, January, February, March, and April. In addition, we must recognize that 1992 was a leap year and that February has an additional day in a leap year. Finally, we must know what *between* means. In mathematics, *between* is not inclusive, which means in this case that we do not count November 24 and May 28.

Step 2: Devising a Plan

Devising a plan involves finding a strategy to aid in solving a problem. In his book, *How to Solve It,* Polya emphasized the importance of this step when he wrote, "The main achievement in the solution of a problem is to conceive the idea of a plan."

Which strategy should we use for a specific problem? There is no definite answer to this question. However, being aware of and practicing general strategies for problem solving should be helpful in determining an appropriate strategy for a particular problem. A specific strategy is learned by practicing it. Once learned, strategies are simply tools to aid in the problem-solving process. The notion here is similar to that contained in the following ancient proverb:

If you give a person a loaf of bread, you feed the person for a day;
If you teach the person to bake, you feed the person for a lifetime.

Step 3: Carrying Out the Plan

Carrying out the plan involves attempting to solve a problem with some chosen strategy. If the chosen strategy does not work, we try to devise a new strategy. Here we also perform any necessary arithmetic or algebraic computations. An important tool for performing these operations is the calculator.

Step 4: Looking Back

The looking back step is where we check the solution in terms of the original problem. We begin by asking if the answer is reasonable and if it answers the required question or questions. In this step, we also consider related problems and other ways to solve the problem.

Strategies for Problem Solving

Strategies are tools that might be used in discovering or constructing the means to achieve a goal. For each strategy described next, a problem is given that can be solved with that strategy. Read each problem and try to solve it before reading the solution. If you need a hint, read only enough of the solution to help you get started. After you have solved the problem, compare your solution with the one in the text. Often, problems can be solved in more than one way. Your own strategy may be different from that in the text. This is all right.

Strategy — Look for a Pattern

The strategy of looking for a pattern was examined in the previous section, where we concentrated on sequences of numbers. We continue that investigation here.

Problem 1

When the famous German mathematician Carl Gauss was a child, his teacher required the students to find the sum of the first 100 natural numbers. The teacher expected this problem to keep the class occupied for some time. Gauss gave the answer almost immediately. Can you?

natural numbers   ***Understanding the Problem.***   The **natural numbers** are 1, 2, 3, 4, ... Thus the problem is to find the sum $1 + 2 + 3 + 4 + \ldots + 100$.

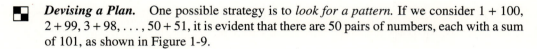

Devising a Plan.   One possible strategy is to *look for a pattern.* If we consider $1 + 100$, $2 + 99, 3 + 98, \ldots, 50 + 51$, it is evident that there are 50 pairs of numbers, each with a sum of 101, as shown in Figure 1-9.

Figure 1-9

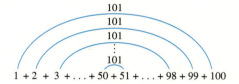

Carrying Out the Plan.   There are 50 pairs, each with the sum 101. Thus the total can be found by multiplying 50(101), or 5050.

Looking Back.   The method is mathematically correct because addition can be performed in any order, and multiplication is repeated addition. A more general problem is to find the sum of the first n numbers, $1 + 2 + 3 + 4 + 5 + \ldots + n$, where n is any natural number. We use the same plan as before and notice the relationship in Figure 1-10. If n is an even natural number, there are $n/2$ pairs of numbers. The sum of each pair is $n + 1$. Therefore the sum $1 + 2 + 3 + \ldots + n$ is given by $(n/2)(n + 1)$. How would you find the sum if $n = 101$ and, in general, if n is odd? Does the same formula work if n is odd?

Figure 1-10

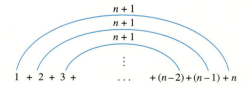

A different strategy for finding the sum $1 + 2 + 3 + \ldots + n$ involves *making a diagram* and thinking of the sum geometrically as a stack of blocks. To find the sum, consider the stack in Figure 1-11(a) and a stack of the same size placed differently, as in Figure 1-11(b). The total number of blocks in the stack in Figure 1-11(b) is $n(n + 1)$, which is twice the desired sum. Thus the desired sum is $n(n + 1)/2$.

Figure 1-11

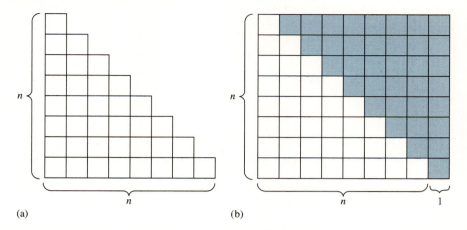

(a)   (b)

Notice that this problem is *connected* to the problems in the previous section that involved triangular numbers.

• • •

Strategy — Make a Table

A table can be used to summarize data or to help us see a pattern. It also can help us to consider all possible cases in a given problem.

Problem 2

How many ways are there to make change for a quarter using only dimes, nickels, and pennies?

Understanding the Problem.   There are no special limits on the number of coins that may be used to make change for a quarter. Nickels, dimes, and pennies need not all be used; that is, 25 pennies is an acceptable answer, as is 2 dimes and 1 nickel.

Devising a Plan.   In this problem, the strategy of *making a table* is used to keep a record of all possibilities as they are examined.

Carrying Out the Plan.   First, consider the possibilities when the number of nickels and dimes is zero and the number of pennies is 25. Continue the chart by trading nickels for pennies, as shown in Table 1-10. Are there other combinations? What about dimes? To finish

Table 1-10

D	N	P
0	0	25
0	1	20
0	2	15
0	3	10
0	4	5
0	5	0

(6 ways using 0 dimes)

the problem, consider all possibilities using dimes. Start with combinations using one dime. With one dime, the greatest number of pennies possible is 15. Next, trade nickels for pennies, as shown in Table 1-11. The last case to consider is possibilities with 2 dimes. Proceeding as before, we obtain Table 1-12. Thus there are $6 + 4 + 2 = 12$ ways to make change for a quarter using only dimes, nickels, and pennies.

Table 1-11

D	N	P
1	0	15
1	1	10
1	2	5
1	3	0

(4 ways using 1 dime)

Table 1-12

D	N	P
2	0	5
2	1	0

(2 ways using 2 dimes)

Looking Back. Check each row of each table to confirm that it shows change for a quarter. The systematic listing used in the tables shows that all cases have been considered. The problem can be extended easily by starting with an initial amount other than one quarter.

• • •

INVESTIGATION 1 - 5

● Jean wants to build a rectangular picture frame that has an area of 120 cm² (square centimeters). She wants the length and width to be natural numbers, {1, 2, 3, 4, . . .}. What dimensions give the least perimeter? ●

Strategy — Examine a Simpler Case

Sometimes it is possible to devise a strategy for solving a complex problem by first *examining a simpler case* of the problem.

Problem 3

In a portion of a large city, the streets divide the city into square blocks of equal size, as shown in Figure 1-12. Eugene drives his taxi daily from the train depot (T) to the bus depot (B). One day, he drove due east from the train depot to the courthouse (C) along First Street and then due north to the bus depot along Seventh Avenue, covering a distance of 11 blocks in all. To avoid boredom, Eugene varies his route, but to save gas he does not want to travel any unnecessary distance. How many possible routes are there from the train depot to the bus depot?

Understanding the Problem. To travel the minimum distance, Eugene should go only north (upward) and east (to the right). Two routes are shown in Figure 1-13. For each route, the total length of the horizontal segments is 6 blocks. Similarly, the total length of the vertical segments is 5 blocks. Thus the length of each of the taxi driver's routes from T to B equals 11 blocks.

Figure 1-12   **Figure 1-13**

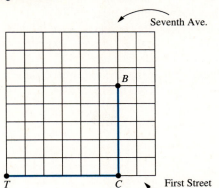
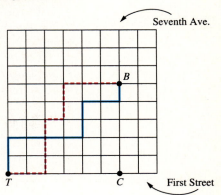

Devising a Plan. One way to solve the problem is by drawing all possible routes from *T* to *B* and counting them. Because this is a difficult task, we examine some *simpler cases.* In Figure 1-14, there is only one possible route from *T* to *D* and only one route from *T* to *F*. In fact, all points due east or all points due north of *T* can be reached by only one (shortest) route.

Figure 1-14

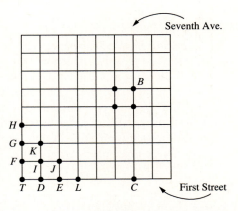

Next, we examine the routes from *T* to *I*. Only two are possible: *T-D-I* and *T-F-I*. From *T* to *J*, there are three routes: *T-D-I-J*, *T-D-E-J*, and *T-F-I-J*. Similarly, the number of routes to various points from *T* can be counted. Figure 1-15 shows the number of possible routes to various points, starting from *T*.

Figure 1-15

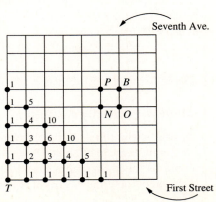

It appears that the number of routes to any given point from T is the sum of the number of routes to each of its two neighboring points, one immediately to the left and the other immediately below. If this pattern continues, it would be easy to work from point to point until we reach point B.

Carrying Out the Plan.   Following the discovered pattern, we can see that the number of routes from T to B is 462, as shown in Figure 1-16.

Figure 1-16

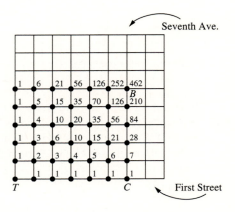

Looking Back.   The pattern can be justified as follows. Any route from T to B in Figure 1-15 must pass through either O or P. The number of routes from T to B that pass through P is the same as the number of routes that pass from T to P because for each route from T to P, there is one single route to B that passes through P. Similarly, the number of routes from T to B that pass through O is the same as the number of routes that pass from T to O. Thus the number of routes from T to B is the sum of the routes from T to P and from T to O. A related problem is to find the number of shortest routes from T to B that must pass through a given intersection point.

• • •

INVESTIGATION   1 - 6

● Nikki is setting up tables for a noon luncheon in the gym. She has 25 small square tables that hold one person to a side. She plans to put 25 of these tables in a row to make one long rectangular table that is only one table wide. If 60 people will be attending the lunch, will she have enough space to seat them all using this plan? If she placed all 25 tables in the form of a big square, how many people could she seat? ●

Strategy — Identify a Subgoal

In your attempt to devise a plan for solving some problems, it may become apparent that the problem could be solved if the solution to a somewhat easier or more familiar problem could be found. In such a case, finding the solution to the easier problem may become a subgoal of the primary goal of solving the original problem. Problem 4 shows an example of this.

Problem 4

Arrange the numbers 1 through 9 into a square subdivided into nine smaller squares like the one shown in Figure 1-17 so that the sum of every row, column, and main diagonal is the same. (The result is called a *magic square.*)

Figure 1-17

Understanding the Problem. We need to put each of the nine numbers 1, 2, 3, . . . , 9 in the small squares, a different number in each square, so that the sum of the numbers in each row, in each column, and in each of the two diagonals is the same.

Devising a Plan. If we know the fixed sum of the numbers in each row, column, and diagonal, we would have a better idea of which numbers can appear together in a single row, column, or diagonal. Thus our *subgoal* is to find that fixed sum. The sum of the nine numbers, $1 + 2 + 3 + \ldots + 9$, equals 3 times the sum in one row. Consequently, the fixed sum is obtained by dividing $1 + 2 + 3 + \ldots + 9$ by 3. Because $45 \div 3 = 15$, the sum in each row, column, and diagonal must be 15. Next, we need to decide what numbers could occupy the various squares. The number in the center space will appear in 4 sums, each adding to 15 (two diagonals, the second row, and the second column). Each number in the corners will appear in three sums of 15. (Do you see why?) If we write 15 as a sum of three different numbers 1 through 9 in all possible ways, we could then count how many sums contain each of the numbers 1 through 9. The numbers that appear in at least four sums are candidates for placement in the center square, whereas the numbers that appear in at least three sums are candidates for the corner squares. Thus our new *subgoal* is to write 15 in as many ways as possible as a sum of three different numbers from the set $\{1, 2, 3, \ldots, 9\}$.

Carrying Out the Plan. The sums of 15 can be written systematically as follows:

$$9 + 5 + 1$$
$$9 + 4 + 2$$
$$8 + 6 + 1$$
$$8 + 5 + 2$$
$$8 + 4 + 3$$
$$7 + 6 + 2$$
$$7 + 5 + 3$$
$$6 + 5 + 4$$

Notice that the order in each sum is not important. (Do you see why?) Hence, $1 + 5 + 9$ and $5 + 1 + 9$, for example, are counted as the same. Notice that 1 appears in only two sums, 2 in three sums, 3 in two sums, and so on. Table 1-13 summarizes this pattern.

Table 1-13

Number	1	2	3	4	5	6	7	8	9
Number of Sums Containing the Number	2	3	2	3	4	3	2	3	2

The only number that appears in four sums is 5; hence, 5 must be in the center of the square. (Do you see why?) Because 2, 4, 6, and 8 appear three times each, they must go in the corners. Suppose we choose 2 for the upper left corner. Then 8 must be in the lower right corner. (Why?) This is shown in Figure 1-18(a). Now we could place 6 in the lower left corner or upper right corner. If we choose the upper right corner, we obtain the result in Figure 1-18(b). The magic square can now be completed, as shown in Figure 1-18(c).

Figure 1-18

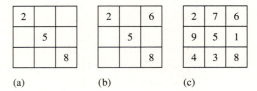

(a)   (b)   (c)

Looking Back.   We have seen that 5 was the only number among the given numbers that could appear in the center. However, we had various choices for a corner, and hence it seems that the magic square we found is not the only one possible. Can you find all the others?

Another way to see that 5 must be in the center square is to consider the sums $1 + 9$, $2 + 8$, $3 + 7$, $4 + 6$, as shown in Figure 1-19. We could add 5 to each to obtain 15.

Figure 1-19

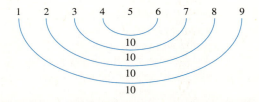

I N V E S T I G A T I O N   1 - 7

● Five friends decided to give a party and split the costs equally. Al spent $4.75 on invitations, Betty spent $12 for drinks and $5.25 on vegetables, Carl spent $24 for pizza, Dani spent $6 on paper plates and napkins, and Ellen spent $13 on decorations. Determine who owes money to whom and how the money can be paid. ●

Strategy — Examine a Related Problem

Sometimes a problem is similar to a previously encountered problem. If so, it is often possible to apply a similar approach to solve the new problem. Such is the case in Problem 5.

Problem 5

Ryan is building matchstick square sequences, as shown in Figure 1-20. He used 67 matchsticks to form the last figure in his sequence. How many matchsticks will he use for the entire project?

Figure 1-20

Understanding the Problem. From your experience with patterns, you can recognize the sequence generated by the matchsticks as 4, 7, 10, 13, . . . , 67. The last number is 67 because Ryan used 67 matchsticks to form the last figure in the sequence. This is an arithmetic sequence with difference 3. You are to find the sum of the numbers in this sequence.

Devising a Plan. A *related problem* is Gauss's problem of finding the sum $1 + 2 + 3 + 4 + \ldots + 100$. In that problem, we paired 1 with 100, 2 with 99, 3 with 98, and so on, and observed that there were 50 pairs of numbers, each with a sum of 101. A similar approach in the present problem yields a sum of 71. To find the total, we need to know the number of pairs in Figure 1-21.

Figure 1-21

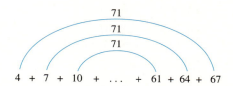

To find the number of pairs, we need the number of terms in the sequence. Thus we have identified a *subgoal,* which is to find the number of terms in the sequence. From the discussion after Example 1-2, we see the *n*th term of this sequence is $4 + (n - 1)3$. To find the number of the term corresponding to 67, we solve the equation $4 + (n - 1)3 = 67$ and obtain $n = 22$. Thus there are 22 terms in the given sequence.

Carrying Out the Plan. Because the number of terms is 22, we have 11 pairs of matchstick figures whose sum is 71 matchsticks each. Therefore the total is 11×71, or 781 matchsticks.

Looking Back. Using the outlined procedure, we should be able to find the sum of any arithmetic sequence in which we know the first two terms and the last term.

• • •

I N V E S T I G A T I O N   1 - 8

● Tonya is building a staircase in the pattern shown in Figure 1-22. The blocks are 1-in. cubes. She wants the last step to be 33 in. tall. How many cubes does she need? ●

Strategy — Write an Equation

A problem-solving strategy commonly used in algebra consists of *writing an equation*. We discuss how to write and solve equations in Chapter 7. An example of this strategy is given on the following student page from *Addison-Wesley Mathematics,* Grade 7, 1993. It is important after solving an equation that you check the answer in the original context rather than substitute into the equation. This is because there could be a mistake in setting up the equation. For example, we should check that the answer on the student page of $42,000 times 2.5 really gives $105,000. This is part of the Looking Back step. Solve the two problems on the bottom of the student page to practice the strategy.

Strategy — Draw a Diagram

It has often been said that a picture is worth a thousand words. This is particularly true in problem solving. In geometry, drawing a picture often provides the insight necessary to solve a problem. A nongeometric problem that can be solved by drawing a diagram is offered in Problem 6.

Problem 6

On the first day of math class, 20 people are present in the room. To become acquainted with one another, each person shakes hands just once with everyone else. How many handshakes take place.

Understanding the Problem.   It takes 2 people for 1 handshake; that is, if Maria shakes hands with John and John shakes hands with Maria, this counts as 1 handshake, not 2. The problem is to find the number of handshakes that take place if 20 people are in the room.

Devising a Plan.   One strategy is to take 20 people and *act it out*. Although this plan provides a solution, it would be nice to find one less elaborate. One way to investigate this problem is to use the strategy of *drawing a diagram*. A diagram showing a handshake between persons A and B can be indicated by a line segment connecting A and B.

Diagrams showing handshakes for 3, 4, and 5 people are given in Figure 1-23. From the diagrams, we can see that the problem becomes one of counting the different line segments needed to connect various numbers of points. In looking at the problem for 5 people (Figure 1-23c), we see that A shakes hands with B, C, D, and E (4 handshakes). Also, B shakes hands with A, C, D, and E (4 handshakes). In fact, each person shakes hands with 4 other people. Therefore it appears that there are $5 \cdot 4$, or 20, handshakes. However, notice that the handshake between A and B has been counted twice. This dual counting occurs for all 5 people. Consequently, each handshake was counted twice; thus to obtain the answer, we must divide by 2. The answer is $(5 \cdot 4)/2$, or 10. This approach can be generalized for any number of people.

Figure 1-23

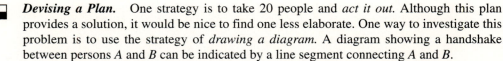

(a)   (b)   (c)

Problem Solving
Using the Strategies

UNDERSTAND
ANALYZE DATA
PLAN
ESTIMATE
SOLVE
EXAMINE

LEARN ABOUT IT

Some problems can be solved using the
strategy **Write an Equation.**

> Find the average price of a home 8 years
> ago for the city described in the newspaper
> article at the right.

Newspaper Reports House-Prices

Bloomington - A local real estate agent was
quoted as saying that the average house price
today in this growing midwestern city is 2.5
times greater than what it was just about 8
years ago. The average price of a house today
is $105,000.

Answer these questions to help you represent a real-world
situation by an equation.

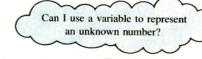

Can I use a variable to represent
an unknown number?

Let p = average price 8 years ago

Can I represent other conditions in terms
of the variable?

$2.5p$ is the price of a home today

What things are equal in the problem.

$2.5p$ must equal $105,000

Can I write and solve an equation?

$2.5p = 105,000$ $p = 42,000$

The average price of a home in this city 8 years ago was $42,000.

TRY IT OUT

Write and solve an equation for each problem.

1. Keisha saw a sign that said "Los
   Angeles—475 miles." Several hours
   later, she saw another sign giving the
   distance as 290 miles. How many miles
   had she traveled between these signs?
   (Let d be the distance between the signs.)

2. A run-for-life campaign made $35,784.
   The money was shared equally among 6
   charities. How much did each charity
   receive? (Let m be the amount each
   charity received.)

Carrying Out the Plan.   Using the outlined strategy, we can see that with 20 people there are $(20 \cdot 19)/2$, or 190, handshakes.

Looking Back.   The answer can be checked by solving the problem by means of a different strategy. Try the strategy of *looking at a simpler problem*. With 1 person in the room, there are no handshakes. If a second person enters the room, there is 1 handshake (remember, 2 people shaking hands counts as 1 handshake). If a third person enters the room, he or she shakes hands with each of the other persons present, so there are 2 additional handshakes, for a total of $1 + 2$. If a fourth person enters the room, he or she shakes hands with each of the other three members present, so there are 3 more handshakes for a total of $1 + 2 + 3$. If a fifth person enters the room, an additional 4 handshakes take place.

Table 1-14

Number of People	Number of Handshakes
1	0
2	1
3	$3 = 1 + 2$
4	$6 = 1 + 2 + 3$
5	$10 = 1 + 2 + 3 + 4$

In Table 1-14, the number of handshakes is recorded. Notice that the last number in the expression $1 + 2 + 3 + 4$ is one less than the number of people shaking hands. Following this pattern, the answer for 20 people is given by $1 + 2 + 3 + 4 + \ldots + 19$. A *related problem* used by Gauss (Problem 1) to find sums of consecutive natural numbers is very useful in completing the problem. Applying this technique, you get the following:

$$1 + 2 + 3 + \ldots + 19 = \frac{19(20)}{2} = 190.$$

• • •

INVESTIGATION 1-9

●   An elevator stopped at the middle floor of a building. It then moved up 4 floors and stopped. It then moved down 6 floors, and then moved up 10 floors and stopped. The elevator was now three floors from the top floor. How many floors does the building have? ●

Strategy — Guess and Check

In the strategy of *guess and check,* we first guess at a solution using as reasonable a guess as possible. Then we check to see if the guess is correct. If not, the next step is to learn as much as possible about the solution based on the guess before making the next guess. This strategy can be regarded as a form of trial and error, where the information about the error helps us choose what trial to make next.

The guess and check strategy is often used when a student does not know how to solve the problem more efficiently or if the student does not yet have the tools to solve the problem in a faster way. The guess and check strategy is demonstrated in Problem 7.

Problem 7

Marques mailed 32 postcards and letters. The bill at the post office was $8.20. He mailed postcards for $.20 each and letters for $.32 each. How many of each kind did he mail?

Understanding the Problem.   The total bill for postage for 32 postcards and letters was $8.20. Postcards cost $.20 to mail and letters cost $.32. We are to determine how many postcards and how many letters were mailed.

Devising a Plan.   When we have a problem with a limited number of possible answers, *guess and check* is a possible strategy. We can make a guess and then see how close our guess is to the correct answer. Then this information can be used to make a better guess the next time. Suppose we guess that the number of postcards is 10. This implies that the number of letters is $32 - 10$, or 22. If this were true, then the total bill would be

$$(10 \cdot \$.20) + (22 \cdot \$.32) = \$9.04.$$

This answer tells us that with 10 postcards and 22 letters, Marques spent too much money and that the next guess should involve more postcards and fewer letters. Suppose the next guess is 20 postcards and therefore 12 letters. Then the amount spent is

$$(20 \cdot \$.20) + (12 \cdot \$.32) = \$7.84.$$

This amount is less than the required $8.20, but you are getting closer. At this point, we know that the correct number of postcards is between 10 and 20. We also know that the number of postcards is closer to 20 than to 10. Why? We can continue guessing and checking to find the correct answer.

Carrying Out the Plan.   If we continue guessing and checking in this manner, we will find that

$$(17 \cdot \$.20) + (15 \cdot \$.32) = \$8.20.$$

Therefore the number of postcards is 17 and the number of letters is 15.

Looking Back.   Remember to check the answer in terms of the original conditions in order to see if the solution is correct. Is the answer found the only answer possible?

Strategy — Work Backward

In some problems, it is easier to start with the final result and to work backward. This is demonstrated on the following student page from *Addison-Wesley Mathematics,* Grade 8, 1993. Note that Heather solved the problem using the *guess and check* strategy while Roberto used the *work backward* strategy. Try the problems on the bottom of the student page. Indicate which strategy you used.

Problem Solving
Using the Strategies

UNDERSTAND
ANALYZE DATA
PLAN
ESTIMATE
SOLVE
EXAMINE

LEARN ABOUT IT

This problem can be solved using different strategies. Heather used **Guess and Check.** Roberto used the strategy **Work Backward.**

> Jamal saved some money to buy CDs and a CD changer. He spent $420 for a 6 disc player and $9 each for 5 CDs. After he received a $40 rebate on the player, he had $65 left. How much money had Jamal saved?

Heather's solution:

Try $500	$500 - 420 = 80$	$80 - 5 \cdot 9 = 35$	$35 + 40 = \$75$ too much
Try $475	$475 - 420 = 55$	$55 - 5 \cdot 9 = 10$	$10 + 40 = \$50$ not enough
Try $490	$490 - 420 = 70$	$70 - 5 \cdot 9 = 25$	$25 + 40 = \$65$ correct!

Roberto's solution:

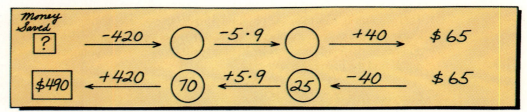

Jamal had saved $490.

TRY IT OUT

1. Nicole is giving away some old records. She gave half of them to her brother. Then she gave half of the remaining records to a friend. Her cousin took the last 5 records. How many records did Nicole give away?

2. Andy, Clara, and Mike sold tickets for a band concert. Clara sold half of the tickets. Andy sold $\frac{1}{3}$ as many tickets as Clara. Mike sold twice as many as Andy. If Mike sold 36 tickets, how many tickets did Andy, Clara, and Mike sell altogether?

Strategy — Use Indirect Reasoning

To show that a statement is true, it is sometimes easier to show that it is impossible for the statement to be false. This can be done by showing that if the statement were false, something contradictory or impossible would follow. This approach is useful when it is difficult to start a direct argument and, when negating the given statement, gives us something tangible with which to work. An example follows.

Problem 8

In Figure 1-24, you are given a checkerboard with the two squares on opposite corners removed and a set of dominoes such that each domino can cover 2 adjacent squares on the board. Can the dominoes be arranged in such a way that all the remaining squares on the board can be covered with no dominoes hanging off the board? If not, why not?

Figure 1-24

Understanding the Problem.   Two red spaces on opposite corners were removed from the checkerboard in Figure 1-24. We are asked whether it is possible to cover the remaining 62 squares with dominoes the size of 2 squares.

Devising a Plan.   If we try to cover the board in Figure 1-24 with dominoes, we will find that the dominoes do not fit and some squares will remain uncovered. To show that there is no way to cover the board with dominoes, we use *indirect reasoning*. If the remaining 62 squares could be covered with dominoes, it would take 31 dominoes to accomplish the task. We want to show that this implies something impossible.

Carrying Out the Plan.   Each domino must cover 1 black and 1 red square. Hence, 31 dominoes would cover 31 red and 31 black squares. This is impossible, however, because the board in Figure 1-24 has 30 red and 32 black squares. Consequently, our assumption that the board in Figure 1-24 can be covered with dominoes is wrong.

Looking Back.   The counting of black and red squares implies that if we remove any number of squares from a checkerboard so that the number of remaining red squares differs from the number of remaining black squares, the board cannot be covered with dominoes. (Do you see why?) We could also investigate what happens when two squares of the same color are removed from an 8-by-7 board and other sized boards. Also, is it always possible to cover the remaining board if two squares of opposite colors are removed?

● ● ●

Puzzle Problems

In addition to the types of problems you have been solving, you will occasionally run across problems that are based on a hidden assumption or trick. These are called *puzzle problems*. An occasional puzzle can enliven a mathematics class and can generate interesting discussions. Before you attempt the problems in the problem set, try the following puzzles. These puzzles have been around in one form or another for many years. They should help you begin to think and to understand what is really being asked in the problem and to make you think about what is given.

1. How much dirt is in a hole 2 ft long, 3 ft wide, and 2 ft deep?
2. Two U.S. coins have a total value of 30¢. One coin is not a nickel. What are the two coins?
3. Walter had a dozen apples in his office. He ate all but 4. How many are left?
4. Sal owns 20 blue and 20 brown socks, which he keeps in a drawer in complete disorder. What is the minimum number of socks he must pull out of the drawer on a dark morning to be sure he has a matching pair?
5. You have 8 sticks. Four of them are exactly half the length of the other 4. Enclose exactly 3 squares of equal size with them.
6. Suppose you have only one 5-L container and one 3-L container. How can you measure exactly 4 L of water if neither container is marked for measuring?
7. What is the minimum number of pitches possible for a pitcher to make in a major league baseball game, assuming he plays the entire 9-inning game and the game is not called prior to completion?
8. Consider the following banking transaction. Deposit $50 and withdraw it as follows:

Withdraw	$20	Leaving	$30
Withdraw	15	Leaving	15
Withdraw	9	Leaving	6
Withdraw	6	Leaving	0
	$50		$51

Where did the extra dollar come from? To whom does it belong?

9. Jane bought 4 pieces of solid-gold chain, each consisting of 3 links.

She wanted to keep them as an investment but felt that joined together they would make a lovely necklace. A jeweler charges $10.50 to break a link and $10.50 to rejoin it. What is the minimum charge possible to form a necklace using all the pieces?

10. Two people played 5 games of checkers. Each won 3 games. How is that possible?
11. How many animals of each species did Adam take with him on the ark?
12. There are four volumes of Shakespeare's collected works on a shelf. The volumes are in order from left to right. The pages of each volume are exactly 2 in. thick. The covers are each $\frac{1}{6}$ in. thick. A bookworm started eating at page 1 of Volume I and ate through to the last page of Volume IV. What is the distance the bookworm traveled?

Ongoing Assessment 1-2

1. Use Gauss's approach in Problem 1 to find the following sums (do not use formulas):
   a. $1 + 2 + 3 + 4 + \ldots + 99$
   b. $1 + 2 + 3 + 4 + \ldots + n$ where n is odd
   c. $1 + 3 + 5 + 7 + \ldots + 1001$

2. How many cuts does it take to divide a log into
   a. 5 equal-sized pieces?
   b. 6 equal-sized pieces?
   c. n equal-sized pieces?

3. A baseball league has 8 teams. Each team must play each other team 4 times. How many games take place?

4. Cookies are sold singly or in packages of 2 or 6. How many ways can you buy a dozen cookies?

5. The sign says you are leaving Missoula, Butte is 120 miles away, and Bozeman is 200 miles away. There is a rest stop half way between Butte and Bozeman. How far is the rest stop from Missoula?

6. Alabama, Bubba, Cory, and Dandy are in a horse race. Bubba is the slowest, Cory is faster than Alabama but slower than Dandy. Name the finishing order of the horses.

7. Frankie and Johnny began reading a novel on the same day. Frankie reads 8 pages a day and Johnny reads 5 pages a day. If Frankie is on page 72, what page is Johnny on?

8. How many different squares are in the following figure?

9. What is the largest sum of money — all in coins and no silver dollars — that you could have in your pocket without being able to give change for a dollar, a half-dollar, a quarter, a dime, or a nickel?

10. How many different ways can you make change for a $50 bill using $5, $10, and $20 bills?

11. How many four-digit numbers have the same digits as 1993?

12. Looking out in the backyard one day, John saw an assortment of boys and dogs. Counting heads, he got 22. Counting feet, he got 68. How many boys and how many dogs were in the yard?

13. A compass and a ruler together cost $4. The compass costs 90¢ more than the ruler. How much does the compass cost?

14. A cat is at the bottom of an 18-ft well. Each day it climbs up 3 ft, and each night it slides back 2 ft. How long will it take the cat to get out of the well?

15. Two houses on the same street are separated by a large, empty field. The first house is numbered 29, and the other is numbered 211. An architect is designing 13 new houses to be built between the two existing houses.

   a. What should the numbers of the new houses be if along with the existing houses, the numbers need to form an arithmetic sequence?
   b. What is the difference of this sequence?

16. Same-sized cubes are glued together to form a staircaselike sequence of solids as shown:

   All of the faces of the cubes not glued together need to be painted. How many squares will need to be painted in **(a)** the 100th solid? **(b)** the nth solid?

17. Marc goes to the store with exactly $1.00 in change. He has at least one of each coin less than a half-dollar coin, but he does not have a half-dollar coin.
   a. What is the least number of coins he could have?
   b. What is the greatest number of coins he could have?

18. A farmer needs to fence a rectangular piece of land. She wants the length of the field to be 80 ft longer than the width. If she has 1080 ft of fencing material, what should the length and the width of the field be?

19. Find a 3-by-3 magic square using the numbers 3, 5, 7, 9, 11, 13, 15, 17, and 19.

20. There were 20 people at a round table for dinner, each of whom shook hands with the person on his or her immediate right and left. At the end of the dinner, each person got up and shook hands with everybody except the people who sat to his or her immediate right or left at dinner. Find the number of handshakes that took place after dinner.

21. A student has a sheet of $8\frac{1}{2}$- by 11-in. paper. She needs to measure exactly 6 in. Can she do it using the sheet of paper?

22. Find the following sums:
   a. $2 + 4 + 6 + 8 + 10 + \ldots + 1020$
   b. $1 + 6 + 11 + 16 + 21 + \ldots + 1001$
   c. $3 + 7 + 11 + 15 + 19 + \ldots + 403$

★ 23. **a.** Using the existing lines on the checkerboard shown below, how many different squares are there?

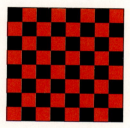

   b. If the number of rows and columns of the checkerboard is doubled, is the number of different squares doubled? Justify your answer.

24. Use the strategy of *indirect reasoning* to justify these:
    a. If the product of two positive numbers is greater than 82, then at least one of the numbers is greater than 9.
    b. If the product of two positive numbers is greater than 81, then at least one of the numbers is greater than 9.

Communication

25. Give an example of how you might use Polya's four-step problem-solving process outside the classroom.
26. In the *Standards,* how is the standard for problem solving for grades K–4 different from the standard for problem solving for grades 5–8?
27. A different version of the story of Gauss's computing $1 + 2 + 3 + \ldots + 100$ reports that he simply listed the numbers in the following way to discover the sum:

$$
\begin{array}{rrrrrrrrr}
1+ & 2+ & 3+ & 4+ & 5+ & \ldots+ & 98+ & 99+ & 100 \\
100+ & 99+ & 98+ & 97+ & 96+ & \ldots+ & 3+ & 2+ & 1 \\
\hline
101+ & 101+ & 101+ & 101+ & 101+ & \ldots+ & 101+ & 101+ & 101
\end{array}
$$

Does this method give the same answer? Discuss the advantages of this method over the one described in the text.
28. Explain why it is impossible to have a 3-by-3 magic square with numbers 1, 3, 4, 5, 6, 7, 8, 9, and 10.
29. Eight marbles look alike, but one is slightly heavier than the others. Using a balance scale, explain how you can determine the heavier one in exactly
    a. 3 weighings.   b. 2 weighings.

Open-ended

30. How many breaths do you take in a year?
31. Examine different elementary textbook series and list the various problem-solving strategies used at each grade level.
32. Choose a problem-solving strategy and make up a problem that would use this strategy. Write the solution using Polya's four-step approach.
33. Construct an extension to one of the problems in the problem set and find the solution to the extension.

Cooperative Learning

34. In your group, make a deck of cards numbered 1 through 10. In what order should the cards be arranged in the deck so that when they are placed on the table according to the following procedure, the pile of cards on the table is in the correct numerical order 1 through 10?

    Place the top card on the table.

    Place the second card on the bottom of the deck.

    Place the third card on the table.

    Place the fourth card on the bottom of the deck, and so on, until all cards are on the table.

    One person should deal the cards and another should record the results of the various investigations.

★ 35. Ten women are fishing all in a row in a boat. One seat in the center of the boat is empty. The 5 women in the front of the boat want to change seats with the 5 women in the back of the boat. A person can move from her seat to the next empty seat or she can step over one person without capsizing the boat. What is the minimum number of moves needed for the 5 women in front to change places with the 5 in back?

Review Problems

36. List three more terms to complete possible patterns:
    a. 3, 6, 9, 12, 15, 18, _____, _____, _____
    b. 1, 2, 3, 2, 9, 2, 27, 2, 81, 2, _____, _____, _____
37. Find the *n*th term for the sequence 22, 32, 42, 52, ...
38. How many terms are in the sequence 3, 7, 11, 15, 19, . . . , 83?
39. Find the sums of the terms in the sequence in Problem 38.
40. Examine the following:

$$
\begin{array}{ll}
2 \cdot 9 = 18 & 5 \cdot 9 = 45 \\
3 \cdot 9 = 27 & 6 \cdot 9 = 54 \\
4 \cdot 9 = 36 &
\end{array}
$$

a. What patterns do you see? Check to see if your patterns work for $7 \cdot 9$, $8 \cdot 9$, $9 \cdot 9$, and $10 \cdot 9$.
b. Explain how the patterns you noticed might be helpful in remembering the basic multiplication table for 9s.

BRAIN TEASER   What day follows the day before yesterday if 2 days from now it will be Sunday?

LABORATORY ACTIVITY   Place a half-dollar, quarter, and nickel in position *A* as shown in the following figure. Try to move these coins, one at a time, to position *C*. At no time may a larger coin be placed on a smaller coin. Coins may be placed in position *B*. How many moves does this take? Now add a penny to the pile and see how many moves this takes. This is a simple case of the famous Tower of Hanoi problem, in which ancient Brahman priests were required to move a pile of 64 disks of decreasing size, after which the world would end. How long will this take at a rate of one move per second?

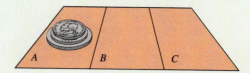

Using a Calculator as a Problem-solving Tool

In the NCTM *Standards* we find the following:

◆ *Because technology is changing mathematics and its uses, we believe that appropriate calculators should be available to all students at all times.* (p. 8)

We also find the following statements for particular grade levels:

◆ *The K–4 curriculum should make appropriate and ongoing use of calculators and computers. Calculators must be accepted at the K–4 level as valuable tools for learning mathematics.* (p. 19)

◆ *[In Grades 5–8,] all students will have a calculator with functions consistent with the tasks envisioned in the curriculum. Calculators should include the following features: algebraic logic . . . ; computation in decimal and common fraction form; constant function . . . ; and memory, percent, square root, exponent, reciprocal, and +/– keys.* (p. 68)

While the *Standards* calls for availability and use of calculators, it is also important to note the following:

◆ *Calculators do not replace the need to learn basic facts, to compute mentally, or [to] do reasonable paper-and-pencil computation. Classroom experience indicates that young children take a commonsense view about calculators and recognize the importance of not relying on them when it is more appropriate to compute in other ways.* (p. 19)

The remainder of this section is spent exploring some common features of a calculator for elementary students.

Recommended Features for Calculators

The calculators described in the *Standards* for grades 5–8 are *scientific calculators*. In this text, we assume a scientific calculator capable of working with fractions is available at all times. We recommend a solar-powered calculator so that batteries are not a problem. Various features listed are discussed next.

Algebraic Logic

Entering a computation as written into a calculator may or may not produce a correct result. The order in which operations are done in mathematics is very important, and it is important that you understand the order in which your calculator performs operations. Many inexpensive four-function calculators process operations in the order in which they are entered. For example,

$$\boxed{2}\boxed{+}\boxed{3}\boxed{\times}\boxed{4}\boxed{=}$$

would be evaluated as

$$5 \times 4 = 20.$$

order of operations

algebraic operating system (AOS)

algebraic logic

However, multiplications and divisions should be done in order from left to right before additions and subtractions. This process is called the **order of operations.** The correct answer using *order of operations* for $2 + 3 \times 4$ is $2 + 12 = 14$. Calculators that have this order of operations feature are said to have an **algebraic operating system (AOS).** Most scientific calculators have an algebraic operating system, and this is what the *Standards* means when it calls for a calculator with **algebraic logic.** If a calculator does not have order of operations built in, but does have parentheses, the above computation can be performed correctly as $2 + (3 \times 4)$.

I N V E S T I G A T I O N   1 - 1 0

● Predict the results for each of the following for a calculator (i) with order of operations; (ii) without order of operations.
a. $2 + 4 \times 5 - 4 \div 2 =$
b. $1 \div 2 + 1 \div 4 =$
c. $(3 + 5) \times 6 \div 3 =$
Check your predictions using a calculator.

Notice that in part (b), if $\frac{1}{2} + \frac{1}{4}$ were entered using division symbols on a calculator without order of operations, then an incorrect answer would be obtained. Later we will see how to enter $\frac{1}{2} + \frac{1}{4}$ using a fraction calculator. ●

Decimal and Fraction Form

We should be aware of how a calculator rounds decimals, if it does. For example, when $\boxed{1}\boxed{\div}\boxed{3}\boxed{=}$ is pressed, we cannot tell if the calculator rounds. (Why?) If we press $\boxed{2}\boxed{\div}\boxed{3}\boxed{=}$, the display will show 0.6666666 or 0.6666667. If the display shows 0.6666667, the rounding is apparent. If the display reads 0.6666666, then we multiply by 3 and observe the result, which may be either 1.9999998, 1.9999999, or 2. If 1.9999998 appears, then the calculator truncated (cut off) all the digits that did not appear on the display and no rounding took place. If 1.9999999 or 2 appears, there is an internal round off. Preferably $(2 \div 3) \times 3$ will display 2 as the answer, since this is consistent with noncalculator computation.

When considering decimal notation, we should determine whether scientific notation is available. Input and output on a calculator may be limited by the number of places on the display. When a number becomes too great for the display, some calculators indicate that there is an error. Most scientific calculators will automatically express the answer in **scientific notation.** That is, they will display the number as the product of a decimal number greater than or equal to 1 but less than 10 and a power of 10. For example, $12,345,678 \times 12,345,678$ would be expressed as 1.52416 14, which means 1.52416×10^{14}. Scientific notation is discussed later in the text.

scientific notation

Many calculators can work with fractions. They can perform the four basic operations of fractions, change decimals to fractions, and convert improper fractions to mixed numbers and back. Fraction calculators usually have either a $\boxed{/}$ or $\boxed{b/c}$ key for entering fractions. For example, to compute $\frac{1}{4} + \frac{3}{8}$, press

$$\boxed{1}\ \boxed{/}\ \boxed{4}\ \boxed{+}\ \boxed{3}\ \boxed{/}\ \boxed{8}\ \boxed{=} \qquad \text{or} \qquad \boxed{1}\ \boxed{b/c}\ \boxed{4}\ \boxed{+}\ \boxed{3}\ \boxed{b/c}\ \boxed{8}\ \boxed{=}$$

Fraction-Decimal key

and the calculator will display 5/8. To convert the fraction to a decimal, press the **Fraction-Decimal key,** $\boxed{F \leftrightarrow D}$, and 0.625 will be displayed. Press this key again, and a fraction is displayed.

Simplify key

Fractions can be simplified using the **Simplify key,** $\boxed{\text{SIMP}}$. Suppose $\frac{625}{1000}$ is displayed. Press the $\boxed{\text{SIMP}}$ key followed by the $\boxed{=}$ key and $\frac{125}{200}$ is displayed. (On some calculators, you need not press the $\boxed{=}$ key.) On the left on the display you will see a message, N/D → n/d (or SIMP), which indicates the fraction can be further simplified. If the factor is not flashed on the display, pressing $\boxed{x \leftrightarrow y}$ will show that a factor of 5 has been removed. Pressing this key again will return you to $\frac{125}{200}$. We can continue in this manner until the fraction's simplest form, $\frac{5}{8}$, is obtained. We can tell when the fraction is in simplest form because the message is no longer visible. On some calculators, it is possible to specify the factor to be taken out directly. For example, if we have $\frac{125}{200}$ on the display we could press $\boxed{\text{SIMP}}\ \boxed{2}\ \boxed{5}\ \boxed{=}$ and the display will read $\frac{5}{8}$.

mixed number key

To convert improper fractions to mixed numbers, we use the **mixed number key,** $\boxed{Ab/c}$. For example, if we enter $\boxed{1}\ \boxed{2}\ \boxed{/}\ \boxed{1}\ \boxed{0}$ and then press $\boxed{Ab/c}$ the display will read 1⌴2/10, which represents $1\frac{2}{10}$. On some calculators, the display will read $1\frac{1}{5}$ directly. Mixed numbers can also be simplified using the $\boxed{\text{SIMP}}$ key. To enter mixed numbers, we enter the whole number and then press the $\boxed{\text{Unit}}$ (or $\boxed{a}$) before entering the fraction part. For example, to enter $2\frac{3}{8}$ we press $\boxed{2}\ \boxed{\text{Unit}}\ \boxed{3}\ \boxed{/}\ \boxed{8}$ (or $\boxed{2}\ \boxed{a}\ \boxed{3}\ \boxed{b/c}\ \boxed{8}$). Different brands of fraction calculators may have keys that are slightly different. Operations involving calculators and fractions are discussed throughout the text as they are needed.

Constant Function

automatic constant

Many calculators have an **automatic constant.** This allows us to perform repeated operations. For example, on a machine with an automatic constant if we want to keep adding 2 each time, we press $\boxed{2}\ \boxed{+}\ \boxed{=}\ \boxed{=}\ \boxed{=}\ \boxed{=}\ \boxed{=}$ . . . and the multiples of 2 are displayed. On other calculators, we would accomplish this by pressing $\boxed{0}\ \boxed{+}\ \boxed{2}\ \boxed{=}\ \boxed{=}\ \boxed{=}\ \boxed{=}$ . . . or $\boxed{2}\ \boxed{+}\ \boxed{+}\ \boxed{=}\ \boxed{=}\ \boxed{=}\ \boxed{=}$ . . . .

Raising numbers to natural number powers can be done by replacing the addition sign with a multiplication sign. Some calculators have specific constant keys. If you are not sure how the constant feature on your calculator works, consult your owner's manual.

Other Functions

percent key

Another frequently used key is the **percent key,** $\boxed{\%}$. This key may operate in various ways depending on the calculator. On some calculators, it changes a percent to a decimal. For example, pressing $\boxed{3}\,\boxed{\%}$ would give 0.03 on the display. On others, pressing $\boxed{2}\,\boxed{\times}\,\boxed{3}\,\boxed{\%}$ yields 0.06 without your having to press the $\boxed{=}$ key. If $\boxed{=}$ is used, the display might read 2.06, which is 2 + 2(3%). You should carefully check how the $\boxed{\%}$ key works on your calculator.

change of sign key

Another key is the **change of sign** key, $\boxed{+\!/\!-}$. This key allows the entry of negative numbers. For example, pressing $\boxed{3}\,\boxed{+\!/\!-}$ changes 3 to $^-3$. It is desirable that the negative sign immediately precede a number to denote a negative number, rather than leaving a space between the sign and the number, as is done on some calculators. If the sign on the number is negative, as in $^-5$, then pressing the $\boxed{+\!/\!-}$ key will cause the number to change sign and become positive.

y-to-the-x-power key

For work in this text, the **y-to-the-x-power key,** $\boxed{y^x}$, is very important. It raises y to the power of x. For example, pressing $\boxed{2}\,\boxed{y^x}\,\boxed{1}\,\boxed{0}\,\boxed{=}$ yields 1024, which is 2^{10}. To perform 2^{-3}, press $\boxed{2}\,\boxed{y^x}\,\boxed{3}\,\boxed{+\!/\!-}\,\boxed{=}$.

square root key
reciprocal key

Other keys that are needed include the **square root key,** $\boxed{\sqrt{}}$. To compute, for example, $\sqrt{4}$, press $\boxed{4}\,\boxed{\sqrt{}}$. Some models of calculators allow you to enter $\boxed{\sqrt{}}\,\boxed{4}$. The **reciprocal key,** $\boxed{1/x}$, computes the reciprocal of the number entered. For example, $\boxed{2}\,\boxed{1/x}$ yields 0.5 on the display. Notice that 0.5 is the decimal equivalent of $\frac{1}{2}$. If you press $\boxed{1/x}$ again, then the display again shows 2. If you enter $\frac{1}{3}$ and press $\boxed{1/x}$, then $\frac{3}{1}$ is displayed. Notice that $\frac{3}{1}$ is equal to $1/\left(\dfrac{1}{3}\right)$.

integer division key

Another key available on many fraction calculators is the **integer division key,** $\boxed{\text{INT} \div}$ (or $\boxed{\div\,\text{R}}$). This key performs divisions and displays the quotient and the remainder. For example, $\boxed{1}\,\boxed{5}\,\boxed{4}\,\boxed{\text{INT} \div}\,\boxed{6}\,\boxed{=}$ displays $\underset{Q}{\rule{1em}{0pt}}25\rule{1em}{0pt}$ $\underset{R}{\rule{1em}{0pt}}4\rule{1em}{0pt}$, (or $25\,^R4$), which shows that the quotient is 25 and the remainder is 4.

Problem 9

Would you rather work for a month (31 days) and get $1,000,000 or be paid 1¢ the first day, 2¢ the second day, 4¢ the third day, and so on, but be allowed to keep only the amount that would be paid on the 31st day?

Understanding the Problem. Because we know that the wages are $1,000,000 for 31 days' work under the first option, we must compute the amount of pay under the second option. If 1¢ is paid for the first day, 2¢ for the second day, 4¢ for the third day, and so on, you need to find the amount paid on the 31st day. Then we can determine the better option.

■ ***Devising a Plan.*** One strategy is to *make a table* and look for a pattern for the amount of pay for each day. Table 1-15 shows a pattern for the second pay plan. From the table we can see that the pay for consecutive days generates a geometric sequence with ratio 2. The exponent in each case is one less than the number of the day. Thus the amount of money for the 31st day is 2^{30} cents. To see how great a number 2^{30} is, we could use a calculator. Then we could convert this number into dollars and compare it with $1,000,000 to determine which pay rate is greater.

Table 1-15

Day	Amount of Pay in Cents
1	1
2	$2 = 2^1$
3	$4 = 2^2$
4	$8 = 2^3$
5	$16 = 2^4$
6	$32 = 2^5$
.	.
.	.
.	.
31	?

Carrying Out the Plan. We can determine the value of 2^{30} in various ways on a calculator. If the calculator has a $\boxed{y^x}$ key, which allows the user to raise numbers to powers, then 2^{30} could be determined by pressing $\boxed{2}\,\boxed{y^x}\,\boxed{3}\,\boxed{0}\,\boxed{=}$. If the $\boxed{y^x}$ key is not present and the calculator has a constant feature, then that feature could be used. Another approach is to use the calculator to compute $2^{10} = 1024$, then compute $2^{30} = 2^{10} \cdot 2^{10} \cdot 2^{10} = 1024 \cdot 1024 \cdot 1024 = 1{,}073{,}741{,}824$. Depending on the calculator, this result may be displayed in scientific notation; for example, the calculator might read 1.0737 09, which means $1.0737 \cdot 10^9$, or 1,073,700,000. Notice that numbers in scientific notation are rounded. To convert this number of cents into dollars, we divide by 100. You can see that the rounded amount received on the 31st day is much greater than \$1,000,000. Hence, the second option is better.

On some calculators, you may see the word Error or E displayed when the number is too large for the display. Such calculators do not do exponential notation.

Looking Back. An alternative problem might be to consider which option is better if we keep only the money on the 25th day. How many days are needed before the second option is more attractive than the first? What if we were allowed to keep all the money from each day? How do the preceding answers change? Try to estimate which option is better without using a calculator.

• • •

Problem 10

Sara and David were reading the same novel. When Sara asked David what page he was reading, he replied that the product of the number of the page he was reading and the next page number was 98,282. What page was David reading?

Understanding the Problem. The product of the page number of the page David was reading and the next page number is 98,282. We are asked to find the number of the page David was reading.

Devising a Plan. Adjacent pages must have consecutive numbers. If we denote the page number David was on by x, then the next page number is $x + 1$. The product of these page numbers is 98,282, so we might *write the equation* as $x(x + 1) = 98{,}282$. To solve the equation, use the *guess and check* strategy. We can use a calculator to multiply various consecutive numbers, trying to obtain the product 98,282. Each new guess should be based on the information obtained from previous trials.

Carrying Out the Plan.   Table 1-16 shows a series of guesses. From the table we can see that the desired page number must be closer to 300 than to 400. Checking $x = 310$ yields $310 \cdot 311 = 96,410$, which shows that 310 is too small for the solution. Successive trials reveal that $313 \cdot 314 = 98,282$, so David was reading page 313.

Table 1-16

x	$x + 1$	$x(x + 1)$
100	101	$101 \cdot 101$, or 10,100
200	201	$200 \cdot 201$, or 40,200
300	301	$300 \cdot 301$, or 90,300
400	401	$400 \cdot 401$, or 160,400

Looking Back.   An alternative solution involves using the concept of square root. The desired page number is close to the number that when multiplied by itself yields the product 98,282. This number is called the *square root* of 98,282. Using a calculator, press the keys $\boxed{9}\,\boxed{8}\,\boxed{2}\,\boxed{8}\,\boxed{2}\,\boxed{\sqrt{}}$. This yields 313.4996. Thus a good guess for the desired page number is 313.

• • •

Ongoing Assessment 1-3

1. a. Place the digits 1, 2, 4, 5, and 7 in the following boxes so that in (i), the greatest product is obtained and in (ii), the greatest quotient is obtained:

(i) ☐ ☐ ☐
    × ☐ ☐

(ii) ☐ ☐ $\overline{)\ ☐\ ☐\ ☐}$

b. Use the same digits as in (a) to obtain (i) the least product and (ii) the least quotient.

2. Which of the following savings plans yields the greatest amount of money?
a. $10 a day for a year
b. $120 a week for a year
c. 25¢ an hour for a year
d. 1¢ a minute for a year

3. Vera spent $16.33 for three of the following items. Which three did she buy?
$5.77, $3.99, $4.33, $5.87, $6.47

4. Pick your favorite single-digit number greater than zero. Multiply it by 259. Now multiply your result by 429. What is your answer? Try it with other numbers. Why does it work?

5. Use your calculator's constant feature, if it has one, to count the number of terms in the following sequence:
1, 8, 15, 22, . . . , 113

6. If 0.2 oz of catsup is used on each of 22 billion hamburgers, how many 16-oz bottles of catsup are needed?

7. How many natural numbers that are evenly divisible by 5,230,010 can be displayed on your calculator without using scientific notation?

8. a. Suppose the $\boxed{7}$, $\boxed{8}$, $\boxed{9}$, and $\boxed{\div}$ keys on your calculator do not work. Devise ways to perform the following computations on your calculator without them:
(i) 756 + 183   (ii) 155 ÷ 31
b. Suppose your calculator's $\boxed{7}$, $\boxed{8}$, and $\boxed{+}$ keys are broken. How could you make your calculator display 73?

9. Determine the operation keys to make each of the following true. Assume the calculator is clear in each case.
a. $\boxed{6}$ ☐ $\boxed{7}$ ☐ $\boxed{8}$ $\boxed{=}$ ☐ 50
b. $\boxed{6}$ ☐ $\boxed{2}$ ☐ $\boxed{6}\boxed{0}$ ☐ $\boxed{3}$ $\boxed{=}$ ☐ 24

10. Billie has 1430 tennis balls to pack in boxes that hold 24 balls each. How many tennis balls will be left over after Billie has filled as many boxes as possible? (Use the integer division key if your calculator has one.)

11. Suppose you could spend $10 every minute, night and day. How much could you spend in a year? (Assume there are 365 days in a year.)

12. Using your calculator, determine what keys to press to generate each of the following sequences:
a. 5, 10, 15, 20, 25, . . .
b. 2, 4, 8, 16, 32, . . .

13. Suppose you enter a number on the calculator. Then you divide the number by 25, subtract 18 from it, and multiply it by 37. If the answer is 259, what is the original number?

14. The number 5! (read "five factorial") is defined to be $5 \cdot 4 \cdot 3 \cdot 2 \cdot 1$ and $4! = 4 \cdot 3 \cdot 2 \cdot 1$. Evaluate 10!. If your calculator has a factorial key, $\boxed{x!}$, work the exercise with and without using the key.

15. **a.** Multiply several two-digit numbers by 99 and study the products. What do you notice?
    b. Multiply several two-digit numbers by 999 and study the products. What do you notice?

16. If your calculator displays 0.3333333 when 1 is divided by 3, what other division could be performed to yield a display of 0.0333333?

17. Refer to the following pattern and answer questions (a) through (c):

$$1 = 2^1 - 1$$
$$1 + 2 = 2^2 - 1$$
$$1 + 2 + 2^2 = 2^3 - 1$$
$$1 + 2 + 2^2 + 2^3 = 2^4 - 1$$
$$1 + 2 + 2^2 + 2^3 + 2^4 = 2^5 - 1$$

   a. Write a simpler expression for $1 + 2 + 2^2 + 2^3 + 2^4 + 2^5$. Justify your answer.
   b. Write a simpler expression for the sum in the nth row in the above pattern.
   c. Use a calculator to check your answer in (b) for $n = 15$.

18. You may use your calculator to work at most two exercises in the following. You may not use a pencil or pen except to record your answers. For the parts that you did not need to use the calculator, explain why.
    a. $542 \cdot 618 = \underline{\hspace{1cm}}$.
    b. One times five thousand two hundred two is $\underline{\hspace{1cm}}$.
    c. 78 times 4297 is $\underline{\hspace{1cm}}$.
    d. 618 times 542 is $\underline{\hspace{1cm}}$.
    e. The product of 512 and zero is $\underline{\hspace{1cm}}$.
    f. Multiply 4297 by 78. $\underline{\hspace{1cm}}$
    g. $542 \cdot 600 + 542 \cdot 18 = \underline{\hspace{1cm}}$.

19. Answer as many of the following computations as possible without using a calculator or pencil and paper. Explain how you arrived at your answers. Let $A = 499$ and $B = 501$.
    a. $A + B = \underline{\hspace{1cm}}$. **e.** $100 \cdot A = \underline{\hspace{1cm}}$.
    b. $A \cdot B = \underline{\hspace{1cm}}$. **f.** $A \cdot 500 + A$.
    c. $B - A = \underline{\hspace{1cm}}$. **g.** Zero divided by A.
    d. $B \cdot A = \underline{\hspace{1cm}}$. **h.** 0 times A times B.

Communication

20. **a.** Work the following three computations using a calculator:
    (i) $37 \cdot 18 = \underline{\hspace{1cm}}$.
    (ii) $37 \cdot 21 = \underline{\hspace{1cm}}$.
    (iii) $37 \cdot 24 = \underline{\hspace{1cm}}$.

b. Predict $37 \cdot 27$. Explain how you arrived at your prediction and why your prediction did or did not work.

21. **a.** Find two positive integers whose product is 5459.
    b. Find the most efficient way to find the answer in (a) and explain your method.

Open-ended

22. How long would it take to tear paper into enough pieces so that everyone in the United States could have one piece of paper?

23. Suppose the letters of the alphabet had dollar values, as in $A = \$1$, $B = \$2$, $C = \$3$, and so on. Use these values to find words that are worth exactly \$100. For example, the value of *calculator* is $\$3 + 1 + 12 + 3 + 21 + 12 + 1 + 20 + 15 + 18 = \$106$.

Cooperative Learning

24. The distance around the world is approximately 40,000 km. Approximately how many people of average size in your group holding hands would it take to stretch around the world?

25. Work in pairs on the following version of a game called NIM. A calculator is needed for each pair.
    a. Player 1 presses $\boxed{1}$ and $\boxed{+}$ or $\boxed{2}$ and $\boxed{+}$. Player 2 does the same. The players take turns until the target number of 21 is reached. The first player to make the display read 21 is the winner. Determine a strategy for deciding who always wins.
    b. Try a game of NIM using the digits 1, 2, 3, and 4, with a target number of 104. The first player to reach 104 wins. What is the winning strategy?
    c. Try a game of NIM using the digits 3, 5, and 7, with a target number of 73. The first player to exceed 73 loses. What is the winning strategy?
    d. Now play Reverse NIM with the keys $\boxed{1}$ and $\boxed{2}$. Instead of $\boxed{+}$, use $\boxed{-}$. Put 21 on the display. Let the target number be 0. Determine a strategy for winning Reverse NIM.
    e. Try Reverse NIM using the digits 1, 2, and 3 and starting with 24 on the display. The target number is 0. What is the winning strategy?
    f. Try Reverse NIM using the digits 3, 5, and 7 and starting with 73 on the display. The first player to display a negative number loses. What is the winning strategy?

Review Problems

26. List the terms to continue a possible pattern in the following sequences:
    a. 7, 14, 21, 28, . . . **b.** 4, 1, 8, 1, 12, . . .

27. Find the nth term for the following sequence:
    12, 32, 52, 72, . . .

28. Find how many terms are in the following sequence:
    6, 10, 14, 18, . . . , 86

29. In how many ways can you make change for \$.21?

TECHNOLOGY CORNER

The following is a two-person game that involves a calculator and estimation skills. Pick two numbers from the clipboard, multiply these numbers, and mark their product on the gameboard that you are using with an 0 or an X as you play Tic-Tac-Toe. Three along any line wins.

Clipboard	
3	29
9	42
11	51
21	79
	91

Game 1		
3822	273	882
99	869	126
2291	63	1659

Game 2		
882	87	231
7189	378	4029
459	1911	1001

Game 3		
609	33	261
1479	3318	819
462	711	237

BRAIN TEASER   What holiday does the following array suggest?

A	B	C	D	E
F	G	H	I	J
K	M	N	O	P
Q	R	S	T	U
V	W	X	Y	Z

SOLUTION TO THE PRELIMINARY PROBLEM

Understanding the Problem.   Male bees have a mother but no father. Female bees have a mother and a father. We need to start with a particular male bee, go 10 generations back, and find the total number of bees.

Devising a Plan.   The strategy of *drawing a diagram* might help us to find the number of bees in different generations. If *m* represents a male and *f* a female, then the generations could be represented as shown in Figure 1-25.

Figure 1-25

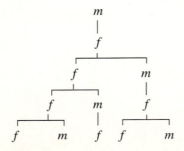

GENERATION	NUMBER IN GENERATION
Generation 0	1
Generation 1	1
Generation 2	2
Generation 3	3
Generation 4	5

Next, we could *make a table* to record the results and *look for a pattern*. Once we determined a pattern, we could find the total number of bees. The results from Figure 1-25 are recorded in Table 1-17.

Table 1-17

Number of Generations Back	Number in Generation
0	1
1	1
2	2
3	3
4	5
.	.
.	.
.	.
10	?

Carrying Out the Plan. A pattern appears from the sequence in Table 1-17. This sequence — 1, 1, 2, 3, 5, . . . — is the *Fibonacci* sequence in which each term starting with the third one is the sum of the two previous terms. If this pattern is correct, the sequence for the first 10 generations is

$$1, 1, 2, 3, 5, 8, 13, 21, 34, 55, 89.$$

Based on this pattern, you can calculate the total number of bees as the sum of these Fibonacci numbers: 232.

Note that this sequence of numbers has not been justified as really being a Fibonacci sequence, but that you did use inductive reasoning to arrive at this conclusion.

Looking Back. The problem can be generalized to any number of generations. Also, the technique of finding the sum of the first n Fibonacci numbers by taking the $(n + 2)$th term and subtracting 1 can be discovered. For example, the sum of the first six Fibonacci numbers $(1 + 1 + 2 + 3 + 5 + 8 = 20)$ can be obtained by taking the $(6 + 2)$th, or 8th, Fibonacci number, which is 21, and subtracting 1 to get the sum of 20. In this way, we could find the above sum of the 11 Fibonacci numbers by finding the 13th Fibonacci number and subtracting 1. We could then check that the result is 232. Other applications of Fibonacci numbers in nature could also be examined.

QUESTIONS FROM THE CLASSROOM

1. A student claims she checked that $n^{50} > 2^n$ (the symbol > designates "greater than") for $n = 1, 2, 3, . . . , 50$. Hence, she claims that $n^{50} > 2^n$ should be true for all values of n. How do you respond?

2. A student says she read that Thomas Robert Malthus (1766–1834), a renowned British economist and demographer, claimed that the increase of population will take place, if unchecked, in a geometric sequence, while the supply of food will increase in only an arithmetic sequence. This theory implies that population increases faster than food production. The student is wondering why. How do you respond?

3. A student notices that when she enters 0.3333333 × 3 on her calculator and then presses the ☐= key, the calculator displays 0.9999999. When she enters ☐1 ÷ ☐3 ☐= , the calculator displays 0.3333333. She then enters ☐× ☐3 and the

calculator displays 1 rather than 0.9999999 as before. She wonders where she made a mistake. How do you respond?

4. A student claims that since calculators are now used in schools, she shouldn't have to learn her basic facts such as $9 \times 6 = 54$. How do you respond?

5. A student claims that the sequence 6, 6, 6, 6, 6, . . . never

changes, so it is neither arithmetic nor geometric. How do you respond?

6. A student claims that two terms are enough to determine any sequence. For example, 3, 6, . . . means the sequence would be 3, 6, 9, 12, 15, ... What is your response?

CHAPTER OUTLINE

I. Mathematical patterns
   A. Patterns are an important part of problem solving.
   B. Patterns are used in **inductive reasoning** to form conjectures. Inductive reasoning is the method of making generalizations based on observations and patterns. A **conjecture** is a statement that is thought to be true but that has not yet been proved to be true or false.
   C. A **sequence** is a group of terms in a definite order.
      1. **Arithmetic sequence:** Each successive term is obtained from the previous one by the addition of a fixed number called the **difference.** The *n*th term is given by $a + (n - 1)d$, where *a* is the first term and *d* is the difference.
      2. **Geometric sequence:** Each successive term is obtained from its predecessor by multiplying it by a fixed number called the **ratio.** The *n*th term is given by ar^{n-1}, where *a* is the first term and *r* is the ratio.
      3. $a^n = \underbrace{a \cdot a \cdot a \cdot a \cdot a \cdot \ldots \cdot a}_{n \text{ terms}}$

      4. $a^\circ = 1$, where *a* is a natural number.
      5. Finding differences for a sequence is one technique for finding the next terms.
II. Problem solving
   A. Problem solving can be guided by the following four-step process:
      1. Understanding the problem
      2. Devising a plan
      3. Carrying out the plan
      4. Looking back
   B. Important problem-solving strategies include the following:

      1. Look for a pattern.
      2. Make a table.
      3. Examine a simpler or special case of the problem to gain insight into the solution of the original problem.
      4. Identify a subgoal.
      5. Examine related problems and determine if the same technique can be applied.
      6. Work backward.
      7. Write an equation.
      8. Make a diagram.
      9. Use guess and check.
      10. Use indirect reasoning.
   C. Beware of mind-sets!
III. Features of calculators
   A. Types of logic
      1. Without an algebraic operating system
      2. With an algebraic operating system
   B. Special features
      1. Constant feature
      2. Change-of-sign key
      3. Parentheses keys
      4. Percent key
      5. Power key
      6. Square-root key
      7. Memory keys
      8. Fraction-bar key
      9. Conversion from decimal to fraction and back key
      10. Reducing fractions key
      11. Division with quotient and remainder key
      12. Simplify key

CHAPTER REVIEW

1. List three more terms that complete a possible pattern in each of the following:
   a. 0, 1, 3, 6, 10,
   b. 52, 47, 42, 37,
   c. 6400, 3200, 1600, 800,
   d. 1, 2, 3, 5, 8, 13,
   e. 2, 5, 8, 11, 14,
   f. 1, 4, 16, 64,
   g. 0, 4, 8, 12,
   h. 1, 8, 27, 64,

2. Classify each sequence in Problem 1 as arithmetic, geometric, or neither.

3. Find a possible *n*th term in each of the following:
   a. 5, 8, 11, 14, . . .   **b.** 1, 8, 27, 64, . . .
   c. 3, 9, 27, 81, 243, . . .

4. Find the first five terms of the sequences whose *n*th term is given as follows:
   a. $3n + 2$ **b.** $n^2 + n$ **c.** $4n - 1$

5. Find the following sums:
   a. $2 + 4 + 6 + 8 + 10 + \ldots + 200$
   b. $51 + 52 + 53 + 54 + \ldots + 151$

6. a. Determine a possible pattern in the sequence
   1, 12, 123, 1234, 12,345, ...
   b. If the tenth term of the sequence in (a) is supposed to have 10 digits, what is the tenth term? Explain your reasoning.

7. Complete the following magic square; that is, complete the square so that the sum in each row, column, and diagonal is the same.

16	3	2	13
	10		
9		7	12
4		14	

8. How many years are there between the fifth day of the year 45 B.C. and the fifth day of the year A.D. 45?

9. A worm is at the bottom of a glass that is 20 cm deep. Each day the worm crawls up 3 cm and each night it slides back 1 cm. How long will it take the worm to climb out of the glass?

10. How many people can be seated at 12 square tables lined up end to end if each table individually holds four persons?

11. A shirt and a tie sell for $9.50. The shirt costs $5.50 more than the tie. What is the cost of the tie?

12. If fence posts are to be placed in a row 5 m apart, how many posts are needed for 100 m of fence?

13. A total of 129 players entered a single-elimination handball tournament. In the first round of play, the top-seeded player received a bye and the remaining 128 players played in 64 matches. Thus 65 players entered the second round of play. How many matches must be played to determine the tournament champion?

14. Given the six numbers 3, 5, 7, 9, 11, and 13, pick five of them that when multiplied together give 19,305.

15. If a complete turn of a car tire moves a car forward 6 ft, how many turns of the tire occur before the tire goes off its 50,000-mi warranty?

16. The members of Mrs. Grant's class are standing in a circle; they are evenly spaced and are numbered in order. The student with number 7 is standing directly across from the student with number 17. How many students are in the class?

17. A carpenter has three separate large boxes. Inside each large box are two medium-sized boxes. Inside each medium-sized box are five separate small boxes. How many boxes are there altogether?

18. How many different triangles are there in the following figure? Explain your reasoning.

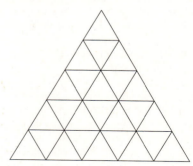

19. Mary left her home and averaged 16 km/hr riding her bicycle on an uphill trip to Larry's house. On the return trip over the same route, she averaged 20 km/hr. If it took 4 hr to make the return trip, how much cycling time did the entire trip take?

20. The perimeter of a rectangle is 68 ft. The length of the rectangle is 4 ft more than twice the width. Find the length and width of the rectangle. Explain your reasoning.

21. An ant farm can hold a total of 100,000 ants. If the farm held 1500 ants on the first day, 3000 ants on the second day, 6000 ants on the third day, and so on in this manner, in how many days will the farm be full?

22. Toma's team entered a mathematics contest where teams of students compete by answering questions that are worth either 3 points or 5 points. No partial credit is given. Toma's team scored 44 points on 12 questions. How many 5-point questions did the team answer correctly?

23. There are three baskets sitting next to each other on a high shelf so that you cannot see the contents of any basket. Under the first basket is a sign that says APPLES. Under the second basket is a sign that says ORANGES. And under the third basket is a sign that says APPLES AND ORANGES. Each basket is incorrectly labeled. One basket contains all apples, one all oranges, and one a combination of apples and oranges. Is it possible to reach up on the shelf and without looking into any of the baskets select one piece of fruit and on the basis of knowing what that piece of fruit is correctly label all three baskets? Explain your reasoning.

SELECTED BIBLIOGRAPHY

Bledsoe, G. "Hook Your Students on Problem Solving." *Arithmetic Teacher* 37 (December 1989): 16–20.

Brown, S., and M. Walter. *The Art of Problem Posing*. Philadelphia: Franklin Institute Press, 1991.

Campbell, P. "Implementing the Standards. The Vision of Problem Solving in the Standards." *Arithmetic Teacher* 37 (May 1990): 14–17.

Dick, T. "The Continuing Calculator Controversy." *Arithmetic Teacher* 35 (April 1988): 37–41.

Demana, F., and A. Osborne. "Chasing a Calculator: Four Function Foul-ups." *Arithmetic Teacher* 35 (March 1988): 2–3.

Gannon, G., and M. Martelli. "The Farmer and the Goose: A Generalization." *Mathematics Teacher* 86 (March 1993): 202–203.

Gill, A. "Multiple Strategies: Product of Reasoning and Communication." *Arithmetic Teacher* 40 (March 1993): 380–386.

Kersch, M., and J. McDonald. "How Do I Solve Thee? Let Me Count the Ways." *Arithmetic Teacher* 39 (October 1991): 38–41.

Krulik, S., and J. Rudnick. "For Better Problem Solving and Reasoning." *Teaching Children Mathematics* 1 (February 1994): 334–338.

Lambkin-Kroll, D., J. Masingila, and S. Mau. "Grading Cooperative Problem Solving." *Mathematics Teacher* 85 (November 1992): 619–627.

Mercer, J. "What Is Left to Teach If Students Can Use a Calculator." *Mathematics Teacher* 85 (September 1991): 415–417.

Moody, W. "A Program in Middle School Problem Solving." *Arithmetic Teacher* 38 (December 1990): 6–11.

Norman, F. "Figurate Numbers in the Classroom." *Arithmetic Teacher* 38 (March 1991): 42–45.

Polya, G. *How to Solve It*. Princeton, N.J.: Princeton University Press, 1957.

Scheibelhut, C. "I Do and I Understand, I Reflect and I Improve." *Teaching Children Mathematics* 1 (December 1994): 242–246.

Talton, C. "Let's Solve the Problem Before We Find the Answer." *Arithmetic Teacher* 36 (September 1988): 40–45.

Thompson, A. "On Patterns, Conjectures, and Proof: Developing Students." *Arithmetic Teacher* 33 (September 1985): 20–23.

Woodward, E. "Problem Solving in the Preservice Classroom." *Arithmetic Teacher* 39 (November 1991): 41–43.

2

SETS, FUNCTIONS, AND LOGIC

A reporter for a high school newspaper interviewed 15 seniors during lunch. He reported that 10 are taking mathematics and physics; 5 are taking physics and chemistry; 7 are taking chemistry and mathematics; and 3 are taking all three subjects. The editor chastised the reporter, claiming the poll was not accurate. Was the editor correct? Why or why not?

Georg Cantor, in the years 1871–1884, created *set theory,* a new area of mathematics. His theories had a profound effect on research and mathematics teaching.

H I S T O R I C A L   N O T E

Georg Cantor, 1845–1918, a German mathematician, was born of Danish parents in St. Petersburg, Russia. His family moved to Frankfurt when he was 11. Against his father's advice, Cantor pursued a career in mathematics and obtained his doctorate in Berlin at age 22. Most of his academic work was spent at the University of Halle. His hope of becoming a professor at the University of Berlin did not materialize, as his work gained little recognition during his lifetime.

Cantor suffered from nervous breakdowns and died in a mental hospital. His work was praised as an "astonishing product of mathematical thought, one of the most beautiful realizations of human activity . . . ."

The language of set theory was introduced into schools in the 1960s in the post-Sputnik era. However, numerous people came to believe that the new language and symbolism caused confusion for many children and some teachers. The following cartoon illustrates the feelings of many of these people.

PEANUTS reprinted by permission of UFS, Inc.

The basic set operations clarify and unify many mathematical ideas. These operations are useful for teachers in understanding the mathematics covered in elementary school from a more advanced standpoint. Many of the concepts in this chapter can be found in the elementary school curriculum but in a more informal setting, without the mathematical notation contained in this chapter. The *Teaching Standards* (p. 136) assert:

 Teachers need to experience the development of mathematical language and symbolism and how these have influenced the way we communicate mathematical ideas. In this chapter, we discuss set notation, relations between sets, and set operations and their properties. We also use the concept of a set to define relations and functions. In the last (optional) section, we introduce the fundamentals of logic.

Section 2-1   # Describing Sets

set • elements
members

A **set** is understood to be any collection of objects. Individual objects in a set are **elements,** or **members,** of the set. For example, each letter is an element of the set of letters in the English language.

We use braces to enclose the elements of a set and label the set with a capital letter. The set of letters of the English alphabet can be written as

$$A = \{a, b, c, d, e, f, g, h, i, j, k, l, m, n, o, p, q, r, s, t, u, v, w, x, y, z\}.$$

The order in which the elements are written makes no difference, and *each element is listed only once*. For example, the set of letters in the word *book* could be written as $\{b, o, k\}$, $\{o, b, k\}$, or $\{k, o, b\}$.

We symbolize an element belonging to a set by using the symbol $\in$. For example, $b \in A$. The fact that A does not contain the Greek letter α (alpha) is written as $\alpha \notin A$.

well defined   For a given set to be useful in mathematics, it must be **well defined.** If we are given a set and some particular object, the object does or does not belong to the set. For example, the set of all citizens of Pasadena, California, who ate rice on January 1, 1996, is well defined. We may not know if a particular resident of Pasadena ate rice or not, but we do know that that person either did or did not. On the other hand, the set of all tall people is not well defined because we do not know which particular people qualify as "tall" people.

natural numbers   We may use sets to define mathematical terms. For example, the set of **natural,** or
counting numbers   **counting, numbers** is defined by the following:

$$N = \{1, 2, 3, 4, \ldots\}.$$

Sometimes the individual elements of a set are not known or they are too numerous to
set-builder notation   list. In these cases, the elements are indicated by using **set-builder notation.** For example, the set of decimals between 0 and 1 can be written as

$$D = \{x \mid x \text{ is a decimal between 0 and 1}\}.$$

This is read "D is the set of all elements x such that x is a decimal between 0 and 1." The vertical line is read "such that."

• • •

Example 2-1   Write the following sets using set-builder notation:

a. $\{51, 52, 53, 54, \ldots, 498, 499\}$ **b.** $\{2, 4, 6, 8, 10, \ldots\}$
c. $\{1, 3, 5, 7, \ldots\}$ **d.** $\{1^2, 2^2, 3^2, 4^2, \ldots\}$

Solution   **a.** $\{x \mid x \text{ is a natural number greater than 50 and less than 500}\}$, or
$\{x \mid 50 < x < 500, x \in N\}$.

b. $\{x \mid x \text{ is an even natural number}\}$. Or because every even natural number can be written as 2 times some natural number, this set can be written as $\{x \mid x = 2n, n \in N\}$.

c. $\{x \mid x \text{ is an odd natural number}\}$. Or because every odd natural number can be written as some even number minus one, this set can be written as $\{x \mid x = 2n - 1, n \in N\}$.

d. $\{x \mid x \text{ is a square of a natural number}\}$ or $\{x \mid x = n^2, n \in N\}$.

• • •

Sets can have other sets as their members. For example, consider the set E of all countries in the European Economic Community. Denmark is an element of E, whereas a citizen of Denmark is not an element of E.

equal sets   Two sets are **equal** if, and only if, they contain exactly the same elements. The order in which the elements are listed does not matter. If A and B are equal, written $A = B$, then every element of A is an element of B, and every element of B is an element of A. If A does not equal B, we write $A \neq B$. Consider sets $D = \{1, 2, 3\}$, $E = \{2, 5, 1\}$, and $F = \{1, 2, 5\}$. Sets D and E are not equal; sets E and F are equal.

One-to-one Correspondence

one-to-one correspondence

Consider the set of people $P = \{$Tomas, Dick, Mari$\}$ and the set of swimming lanes $S = \{1, 2, 3\}$. Suppose each person in P is to swim in a lane numbered 1, 2, or 3 so that no two people swim in the same lane. Such a person-lane pairing is a **one-to-one correspondence.** One way to exhibit this one-to-one correspondence is Tomas $\leftrightarrow$ 1, Dick $\leftrightarrow$ 2, and Mari $\leftrightarrow$ 3, as shown in Figure 2-1.

Figure 2-1

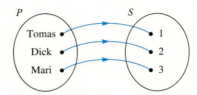

Other possible one-to-one correspondences exist between the sets P and S. There are several schemes for exhibiting them. For example, all six possible one-to-one correspondences between sets P and S can be listed as follows:

1. Tomas $\leftrightarrow$ 1	**2.** Tomas $\leftrightarrow$ 1	**3.** Tomas $\leftrightarrow$ 2
Dick $\leftrightarrow$ 2	Dick $\leftrightarrow$ 3	Dick $\leftrightarrow$ 1
Mari $\leftrightarrow$ 3	Mari $\leftrightarrow$ 2	Mari $\leftrightarrow$ 3
4. Tomas $\leftrightarrow$ 2	**5.** Tomas $\leftrightarrow$ 3	**6.** Tomas $\leftrightarrow$ 3
Dick $\leftrightarrow$ 3	Dick $\leftrightarrow$ 1	Dick $\leftrightarrow$ 2
Mari $\leftrightarrow$ 1	Mari $\leftrightarrow$ 2	Mari $\leftrightarrow$ 1

Notice that the diagram in (**1.**) as well as Figure 2-1 represent a single one-to-one correspondence between the sets P and S. The correspondence Tomas $\leftrightarrow$ 1 can also be a one-to-one correspondence but between two different sets, namely the sets $\{$Tomas$\}$ and $\{1\}$.

Definition of One-to-one Correspondence

If the elements of sets P and S can be paired so that for each element of P there is exactly one element of S and for each element of S there is exactly one element of P, then the two sets P and S are said to be in **one-to-one correspondence** (or matched).

I N V E S T I G A T I O N   2 - 1

● Consider a set of four people and a set of four swimming lanes.

   a. Exhibit all the one-to-one correspondences between the two sets.

   b. How many such one-to-one correspondences are there?

   c. Conjecture the number of one-to-one correspondences between two sets with five elements each and explain how you arrived at your conjecture. ●

Another method of demonstrating a one-to-one correspondence is to use a table, such as Table 2-1, where the lane numbers are listed across the top of the table and the possible pairings of swimmers to lanes are listed in the table.

Table 2-1

1	2	3
Tomas	Dick	Mari
Tomas	Mari	Dick
Dick	Tomas	Mari
Dick	Mari	Tomas
Mari	Tomas	Dick
Mari	Dick	Tomas

A tree diagram can also be used to list the possible one-to-one correspondences, as Figure 2-2 shows. To read the tree diagram and see the one-to-one correspondence, we follow each branch. The person occupying a specific lane in a correspondence is listed below the lane number. For example, the top branch gives the pairing (Tomas, 1), (Dick, 2), and (Mari, 3).

Figure 2-2

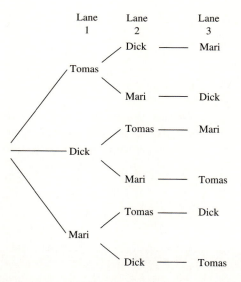

Observe that for lane 1, there are actually three choices at the start. Once that lane is filled, there are only two choices for lane 2 and finally only one choice for lane 3. Hence, there are $3 \cdot 2 \cdot 1$, or 6, possible one-to-one correspondences. The counting argument used to find the number of possible one-to-one correspondences is an example of the *Fundamental Counting Principle*.

Property

Fundamental Counting Principle   If event M can occur in m ways and, after it has occurred, event N can occur in n ways, then event M followed by event N can occur in $m \cdot n$ ways.

Equivalent Sets

Suppose a room contains 20 chairs and one student is sitting in each chair with no one standing. There is a one-to-one correspondence between the set of chairs and the set of students in the room. In this case, the set of chairs and the set of students are **equivalent sets.**

equivalent sets

Definition of Equivalent Sets

Two sets A and B are **equivalent,** written $A \sim B$, if and only if there exists a one-to-one correspondence between the sets.

The term *equivalent* should not be confused with *equal*. The difference should be made clear by the following example.

● ● ●

Example 2-2   Let

$$A = \{ p, q, r, s\}, B = \{a, b, c\}, C = \{x, y, z\}, D = \{b, a, c\}.$$

Compare the sets, using the terms *equal* and *equivalent*.

Solution   Sets A and B are not equivalent ($A \nsim B$) and not equal ($A \neq B$).
Sets A and C are not equivalent ($A \nsim C$) and not equal ($A \neq C$).
Sets A and D are not equivalent ($A \nsim D$) and not equal ($A \neq D$).
Sets B and C are equivalent ($B \sim C$) but not equal ($B \neq C$).
Sets B and D are equivalent ($B \sim D$) and equal ($B = D$).
Sets C and D are equivalent ($C \sim D$) but not equal ($C \neq D$).

● ● ●

Cardinal Numbers

The concept of one-to-one correspondence can be used to introduce children before they know how to count to the notion of two sets having the same number of elements. Suppose a child knows how to count only to three. The child might still tell that there are as many fingers on the left hand as on the right hand by matching the fingers on one hand with the ones on the other hand. Naturally placing the fingers so that the left thumb touches the right thumb, the left index finger touches the right index finger, and so on, exhibits a one-to-one correspondence between the fingers on the two hands. Similarly, without any counting, children realize that if every student in a class sits in a chair and no chairs are empty, there are as many chairs as students.

One-to-one correspondence between sets is often used to introduce the concept of a number as follows. (In elementary school, the approach is similar but without the abstract notation.) The five sets $\{a, b\}$, $\{p, q\}$, $\{x, y\}$, $\{b, a\}$, and $\{*, \#\}$ are equivalent to one another and share the property of "twoness." These sets have the same cardinal number, namely, 2. The **cardinal number** of a set X, denoted by $n(X)$, indicates the number of elements in the set X. If $D = \{a, b\}$, the cardinal number of D is 2, and we write $n(D) = 2$. If A is equivalent to B, then A and B have the same cardinal number; that is, $n(A) = n(B)$.

INVESTIGATION 2-4

● If $n(A) = n(B)$, sets A and B are equivalent, but not necessarily equal. Why? ●

---

finite set　　　A set is a **finite set** if the number of elements in the set is zero or a natural number. For example, the set of letters in the English alphabet is a finite set because it contains exactly 26 elements. Another way to think of this is that the set of letters in the English alphabet can be put into a one-to-one correspondence with the set $\{1, 2, 3, \ldots, 26\}$. The set of natural numbers N is an example of an **infinite set**, a set that is not finite.

infinite set

More about Sets

empty set • null set　　　A set that contains no elements has cardinal number 0 and is an **empty,** or **null, set.** The empty set is designated by the symbol $\varnothing$ or $\{\ \ \}$. Two examples of sets with no elements are the following:

$$C = \{x \mid x \text{ was a state of the United States before A.D. 1200}\}.$$
$$D = \{x \mid x \text{ is a natural number less than 1}\}.$$

REMARK　　The empty set is often incorrectly recorded as $\{\varnothing\}$. This set is not empty but contains one element. Likewise, $\{0\}$ does not represent the empty set.

---

universal set • universe　　　The **universal set,** or the **universe,** denoted by U, is the set that contains all elements being considered in a given discussion. For this reason, you should be aware of what the universal set is in any given problem. Suppose $U = \{x \mid x \text{ is a person living in California}\}$ and $F = \{x \mid x \text{ is a female living in California}\}$. The universal set and set F can be represented by a diagram, as in Figure 2-3(a) on the following page. The universal set is usually indicated by a large rectangle, and particular sets are indicated by geometric figures inside the rectangle, as shown in Figure 2-3(a). This figure is an example of a **Venn diagram,**

Venn diagram

named after the Englishman John Venn, who used such diagrams to illustrate ideas in logic. The set of elements in the universe that are not in *F* is the set of males living in California and is the **complement** of *F*. It is represented by the shaded region in Figure 2-3(b).

Figure 2-3

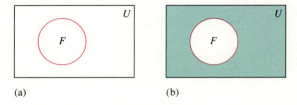

(a)   (b)

Definition of Set Complement

The **complement** of a set *F*, written $\overline{F}$, is the set of all elements in the universal set *U* that are not in *F*. that is $\overline{F} = \{x \mid x \in U \text{ and } x \notin F\}$.

REMARK   The key word in the definition of complement is *not*.

Example 2-3

a. If $U = \{a, b, c, d\}$ and $B = \{c, d\}$, find (i) $\overline{B}$; (ii) $\overline{U}$; (iii) $\overline{\varnothing}$.
b. If $U = \{x \mid x \text{ is an animal in the zoo}\}$ and $S = \{x \mid x \text{ is a snake in the zoo}\}$, describe $\overline{S}$.
c. If $U = N$, $E = \{2, 4, 6, 8, \ldots\}$, and $O = \{1, 3, 5, 7, \ldots\}$, find (i) $\overline{E}$; (ii) $\overline{O}$.

Solution   **a.** (i) $\overline{B} = \{a, b\}$; (ii) $\overline{U} = \varnothing$; (iii) $\overline{\varnothing} = U$.
b. Because the individual animals in the zoo are not known, $\overline{S}$ must be described using set-builder notation:

$$\overline{S} = \{x \mid x \text{ is an animal in the zoo that is not a snake}\}.$$

c. (i) $\overline{E} = O$; (ii) $\overline{O} = E$.

Subsets

Consider the sets $A = \{1, 2, 3, 4, 5, 6\}$ and $B = \{2, 4, 6\}$. All the elements of *B* are contained in *A* and *B* is a **subset** of *A*. We write $B \subseteq A$. In general, we have the following definition.

subset

Definition of Subset

B is a **subset** of *A*, written $B \subseteq A$, if and only if every element of *B* is an element of *A*.

This definition allows *B* to be equal to *A*. The definition is written with the phrase "if and only if," which means "if *B* is a subset of *A*, then every element of *B* is an element of *A*, and if every element of *B* is an element of *A*, then *B* is a subset of *A*." If both $A \subseteq B$ and $B \subseteq A$, then $A = B$.

proper subset   If *B* is a subset of *A* and *B* is not equal to *A*, then *B* is a **proper subset** of *A*, written $B \subset A$. This means that every element of *B* is contained in *A* and there is at least one element of *A* that is not in *B*.

To indicate this, sometimes a Venn Diagram like the one shown in Figure 2-4 is used.

Figure 2-4

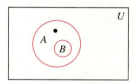

Example 2-4   Given $A = \{1, 2, 3, 4, 5\}$, $B = \{1, 3\}$, $P = \{x \mid x = 2^n - 1, n \in N\}$:

a. Which sets are subsets of each other?
b. Which sets are proper sets of each other?

Solution   **a.** Because $2^1 - 1 = 1$, $2^2 - 1 = 3$, $2^3 - 1 = 7$, $2^4 - 1 = 15$, and $2^5 - 1 = 31$, $P = \{1, 3, 7, 15, 31, \ldots\}$. Thus $B \subseteq P$. Also $B \subseteq A$, $A \subseteq A$, $B \subseteq B$, and $P \subseteq P$.
b. $B \subset A$ and $B \subset P$.

INVESTIGATION 2 - 5

a. Suppose $A \subset B$. Can we always conclude that $A \subseteq B$?

b. If $A \subseteq B$, does it follow that $A \subset B$?

When a set A is not a subset of another set B, we write $A \nsubseteq B$. To show that $A \nsubseteq B$, we must find at least one element of A that is not in B. If $A = \{1, 3, 5\}$ and $B = \{1, 2, 3\}$, then A is not a subset of B because 5 is an element of A but not of B. Likewise, $B \nsubseteq A$ because 2 belongs to B but not to A.

Figure 2-5 shows three different relations between two sets. Notice that in Figure 2-5(a), A and B have no elements in common, in (b) A and B have at least one element in common, and in (c) $B \subset A$.

Figure 2-5

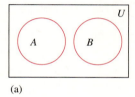

(a)

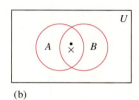

(b)

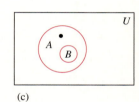

(c)

It is not obvious how the empty set fits the definition of a subset because no elements in the empty set are elements of another set. To investigate this problem, we use the strategies of *indirect reasoning* and *looking at a special case*.

For the set $\{1, 2\}$, either $\emptyset \subseteq \{1, 2\}$ or $\emptyset \not\subseteq \{1, 2\}$. Suppose $\emptyset \not\subseteq \{1, 2\}$. Then there must be some element in $\emptyset$ that is not in $\{1, 2\}$. Because the empty set has no elements, there cannot be an element in the empty set that is not in $\{1, 2\}$. Consequently, $\emptyset \not\subseteq \{1, 2\}$ is false. Therefore the only other possibility, $\emptyset \subseteq \{1, 2\}$, is true.

The same reasoning can be applied in the case of the empty set and any other set. In particular, note that the empty set is a subset of itself and a proper subset of any set other than itself.

Subsets and elements of sets are often confused. We say that $2 \in \{1, 2, 3\}$. But because 2 is not a set, we cannot substitute the symbol $\subseteq$ for $\in$. However, $\{2\} \subseteq \{1, 2, 3\}$ and $\{2\} \subset \{1, 2, 3\}$. Conversely, the symbol $\in$ should not be used between $\{2\}$ and $\{1, 2, 3\}$.

Inequalities: An Application of Set Concepts

The notion of a proper subset and the concept of one-to-one correspondence can be used to define the concept of "less than" among natural numbers. The set $\{a, b, c\}$ has fewer elements than the set $\{w, x, y, z\}$ because when we try to pair the elements of the two sets, as in

$$\{a, \quad b, \quad c\}$$
$$| \quad | \quad |$$
$$\{x, \quad y, \quad z \quad w\},$$

we see that there is an element of the second set that is not paired with any element of the first set. The set $\{a, b, c\}$ is equivalent to a proper subset of the set $\{x, y, z, w\}$.

In general, if A and B are finite sets, A has fewer elements than B (or $n(A) < n(B)$) if A is equivalent to a proper subset of B.

greater than We say that a is **greater than** b, written $a > b$, if and only if $b < a$. Defining the concept of "less than or equal to" in a similar way is explored in the Ongoing Assessment.

Problem 1

A committee of senators consists of Abel, Baro, Carni, and Davis. Suppose each member of the committee has one vote and a simple majority is needed either to pass or reject any measure. A measure that is neither passed nor rejected is considered to be blocked and will be voted on again. Determine the number of ways a measure could be passed or rejected and the number of ways a measure could be blocked.

Understanding the Problem.   A Senate committee consisting of four members — Abel, Baro, Carni, and Davis — requires a simple majority of votes either to pass or reject a measure. We are asked to determine how many ways the committee could pass or reject a proposal and how many ways the committee could block a proposal. To pass or reject a proposal requires a winning coalition, that is, a group of senators that can pass or reject the proposal, regardless of what the others do. To block a proposal, there must be a blocking coalition, that is, a group that can prevent any proposal from passing but that cannot reject the measure.

 Devising a Plan.   To solve the problem, we can *make a list* of subsets of the set of senators. Any subset of the set of senators with three or four members will form a winning coalition. Any subset of the set of senators with exactly two members will form a blocking coalition.

Carrying Out the Plan.   We list all subsets of the set $S = \{$ Abel, Baro, Carni, Davis $\}$ that have at least three elements and all subsets that have exactly two elements. For ease, we identify the members as follows: A — Abel, B — Baro, C — Carni, D — Davis. All the subsets are given next:

$\varnothing$	$\{A, B\}$	$\{A, B, C\}$	$\{A, B, C, D\}$
$\{A\}$	$\{A, C\}$	$\{A, B, D\}$	
$\{B\}$	$\{A, D\}$	$\{A, C, D\}$	
$\{C\}$	$\{B, C\}$	$\{B, C, D\}$	
$\{D\}$	$\{B, D\}$		
	$\{C, D\}$		

There are five subsets with at least three members that can form a winning coalition and pass or reject a measure and six subsets with exactly two members that can block a measure.

Looking Back.   Other questions that might be considered include the following:

1. How many minimal winning coalitions are there? In other words, how many subsets are there of which no proper subset could pass a measure?
2. Devise a method to solve this problem without listing all subsets.
3. In "Carrying Out the Plan," 16 subsets of $\{A, B, C, D\}$ are listed. Use that result to systematically list all the subsets of a committee of five senators. Can you find the number of subsets of the five-member committee without actually counting the subsets?

INVESTIGATION   2 - 6

● Suppose a committee of U.S. senators consists of five members.

a. How many winning coalitions are there now?
b. Compare the number of winning coalitions having exactly four members with the number of senators in the committee. What is the reason for the result?

c. Compare the number of winning coalitions having exactly three members with the number of subsets of the committee having exactly two members. What is the reason for the result? ●

Problem 1 suggests the general problem of finding the number of subsets that a set containing n elements has. To obtain a general formula, we use the strategy of *trying simpler cases* first.

1. If $B = \{a\}$, then B has two subsets, $\varnothing$ and $\{a\}$.
2. If $C = \{a, b\}$, then C has four subsets, $\varnothing$, $\{a\}$, $\{b\}$, and $\{a, b\}$.
3. If $D = \{a, b, c\}$, then D has eight subsets, $\varnothing$, $\{a\}$, $\{b\}$, $\{c\}$, $\{a, b\}$, $\{a, c\}$, $\{b, c\}$, and $\{a, b, c\}$.

Using the information from these cases, we *make a table and search for a pattern*, as seen in Table 2-2 on the following page.

Table 2-2

Number of Elements	Number of Subsets
1	2, or 2^1
2	4, or 2^2
3	8, or 2^3
.	.
.	.
.	.

Table 2-2 suggests that for 4 elements, there are 2^4, or 16, subsets. Is this guess correct? If $E = \{a, b, c, d\}$, then all the subsets of $D = \{a, b, c\}$ are also subsets of E. Eight new subsets are also formed by adjoining the element d to each of the eight subsets of D. The eight new subsets are $\{d\}$, $\{a, d\}$, $\{b, d\}$, $\{c, d\}$, $\{a, b, d\}$, $\{a, c, d\}$, $\{b, c, d\}$, and $\{a, b, c, d\}$. Thus there are twice as many subsets of set E (with four elements) as there are of set D (with three elements). Consequently, there are 16, or 2^4, subsets of a set with four elements. In a similar way, there are $2^4 + 2^4$ — that is, $2 \cdot 2^4$ or 2^5 — subsets of a set with five elements. In each case, the number of elements and the power of 2 used to obtain the number of subsets match exactly. In general it can be shown that *if there are n elements in a set, there are 2^n subsets that can be formed.* This result can also be justified by using the Fundamental Counting Principle.

The formula 2^n for the number of subsets of a set with n elements is based on the observation that adding one more element to a set doubles the number of possible subsets of the new set. If we apply this formula to the empty set — that is, when $n = 0$ — then we have $2^0 = 1$ because the empty set has only one subset — itself. The fact that $a^0 = 1$, where a is a natural number, is investigated in Chapter 6.

BRAIN TEASER   Bertrand Russell's antinomy, "Is the set of all sets that are not members of themselves a member of itself?" has become popularized in the following paradox: The town barber shaves all those males, and only those males, who do not shave themselves. Assuming the barber is a male who shaves, who shaves the barber?

Ongoing Assessment 2-1

1. Write the following sets by listing the members or using set-builder notation:
   a. The set of letters in the word *mathematics*
   b. The set of states in the continental United States
   c. The set of natural numbers greater than 20
   d. The set of states in the United States that border the Pacific Ocean

2. Rewrite the following statements using mathematical symbols:
   a. B is equal to the set whose elements are *x, y, z,* and *w.*
   b. The set consisting of the elements 1 and 2 is a proper subset of the set consisting of the elements 1, 2, 3, 4.

   c. 0 is not an element of the empty set.
   d. The set whose only element is 0 is not equal to the empty set.

3. Which of the following pairs of sets can be placed in one-to-one correspondence?
   a. $\{1, 2, 3, 4, 5\}$ and $\{m, n, o, p, q\}$
   b. $\{m, a, t, h\}$ and $\{f, u, n\}$
   c. $\{a, b, c, d, e, f, \ldots, m\}$ and $\{1, 2, 3, 4, 5, 6, \ldots, 13\}$
   d. $\{x \mid x$ is a letter in the word mathematics$\}$ and $\{1, 2, 3, 4, \ldots, 11\}$
   e. $\{\bigcirc, \triangle\}$ and $\{2\}$

4. How many different one-to-one correspondences are there between two sets with
   a. 5 elements each?
   b. 6 elements each?
   c. n elements each?

5. How many one-to-one correspondences are there between the sets $\{x, y, z, u, v\}$ and $\{1, 2, 3, 4, 5\}$ if in each correspondence
   a. x must correspond to 5?
   b. x must correspond to 5 and y to 1?
   c. x, y, and z must correspond to odd numbers?

6. Which of the following represent equal sets?
   $A = \{a, b, c, d\}$
   $B = \{x, y, z, w\}$
   $C = \{c, d, a, b\}$
   $D = \{x \mid x$ is one of the first four letters of the English alphabet$\}$
   $E = \varnothing$
   $F = \{\varnothing\}$
   $G = \{0\}$
   $H = \{\ \ \}$
   $J = \{x \mid x = 2n + 1, n \in N\}$
   $K = \{x \mid x = 2n - 1, n \in N\}$

7. Find the cardinal number of each of the following sets:
   a. $\{1, 3, 5, \ldots, 1001\}$
   b. $\{1, 2, 4, 8, 16, \ldots, 1024\}$
   c. $\{x \mid x = k^2, k = 1, 2, 3, \ldots, 100\}$
   d. $\{\{1, 2\}, \{3, 4\}, \{5, 6\}\}$
   e. $\{i + j \mid i \in \{1, 2, 3\}$ and $j \in \{1, 2, 3\}\}$

8. If U is the set of all college students and A is the set of all college students with a straight-A average, describe $\overline{A}$.

9. Suppose B is a proper subset of C.
   a. If $n(C) = 8$, what is the maximum number of elements in B?
   b. What is the least possible number of elements in B?

10. Suppose C is a subset of D and D is a subset of C.
   a. If $n(C) = 5$, find $n(D)$.
   b. What other relationship exists between sets C and D?

11. Indicate which symbol, $\in$ or $\notin$, makes each of the following statements true:
   a. $3 \underline{\hspace{1cm}} \{1, 2, 3\}$
   b. $0 \underline{\hspace{1cm}} \varnothing$
   c. $\{1\} \underline{\hspace{1cm}} \{1, 2\}$
   d. $\varnothing \underline{\hspace{1cm}} \varnothing$
   e. $\{1, 2\} \underline{\hspace{1cm}} \{1, 2\}$

12. Indicate which symbol, $\subseteq$ or $\nsubseteq$, makes each part of Problem 11 true.

13. If $A \nsubseteq B$ can we always conclude that $B \subset A$? Why?

14. Answer each of the following. If your answer is *no,* tell why.
   a. If $A = B$, can we always conclude that $A \subseteq B$?
   b. If $A \subseteq B$, can we always conclude that $A \subset B$?
   c. If $A \subset B$, can we always conclude that $A \subseteq B$?
   d. If $A \subseteq B$, can we always conclude that $A = B$?

15. Use the definition of *less than* to show each of the following:
   a. $2 < 4$ 　　 **b.** $3 < 100$ 　　 **c.** $0 < 3$

16. a. If $A = \{a, b, c, d, e, f\}$, how many proper subsets does A have?
   b. If a set B has n elements where n is some natural number, how many proper subsets does B have?

17. On a certain Senate committee there are seven senators: Abel, Brooke, Cox, Dean, Eggers, Funk, and Gage. Three of these members are to be appointed to a subcommittee. How many possible subcommittees are there?

Communication

18. Which of the following sets are well defined? Explain your answers.
   a. The set of wealthy school teachers
   b. The set of great books
   c. The set of natural numbers greater than 100
   d. The set of subsets of $\{1, 2, 3, 4, 5, 6\}$
   e. The set $\{x \mid x \neq x\}$

19. a. Describe three sets of which you are a member.
   b. Describe three sets that have no members.

20. Describe five subsets of a set of college professors.

21. Is $\varnothing$ a proper subset of every set? Why?

22. Define *less than or equal to* in a way similar to the definition of *less than.*

23. a. Give three examples of sets A and B and a universal set U such that $A \subset B$, find $\overline{A}$ and $\overline{B}$.
   b. Based on your observations, conjecture a relationship between $\overline{B}$ and $\overline{A}$.
   c. Justify your conjecture in (b) using a Venn diagram.

Open-ended

24. Find an infinite set A such that
   a. $\overline{A}$ is finite. 　　 **b.** $\overline{A}$ is infinite.

25. Give an example of an infinite set and describe infinitely many infinite subsets of the set.

26. Describe two sets from real-life situations such that it is clear from using one-to-one correspondence, and not from counting, that one set has fewer elements than the other.

Cooperative Learning

27. a. Using a calculator if necessary, estimate the time it would take a computer to list all the subsets of $\{1, 2, 3, \ldots, 64\}$. Assume the fastest computer can list one subset in approximately 1 microsecond (one millionth of a second).
   b. Estimate the time it would take the computer to exhibit all the one-to-one correspondences between the sets $\{1, 2, 3, \ldots, 64\}$ and $\{65, 66, 67, \ldots, 128\}$.

28. Examine different K–8 textbooks and report on which concepts from this section have been used and at what grade level. (Sometimes a concept may have been used informally and therefore may not appear in the index.)

Other Set Operations and Their Properties

Finding the complement of a set is an operation that acts on only one set at a time. In this section, we consider operations on two sets.

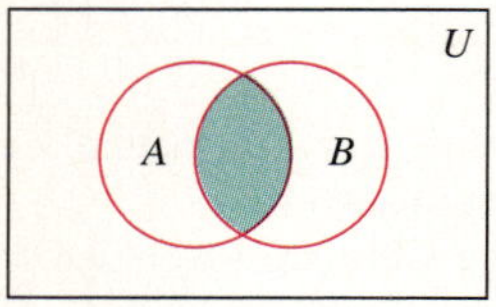

Set Intersection

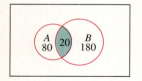

$A \cap B$

Figure 2-6

intersection

Suppose that during the fall quarter, a college wants to mail a survey to all its students who are enrolled in both art and biology classes. To do this, the school officials must identify those students who are taking both classes. If A and B are the sets of students taking art courses and the set of students taking biology courses during the fall quarter, respectively, then the derived set of students includes those common to A and B, or the **intersection** of A and B. The intersection of sets A and B is pictured in Figure 2-6.

Definition of Set Intersection

The **intersection** of two sets A and B, written $A \cap B$, is the set of all elements common to both A and B. $A \cap B = \{x \mid x \in A \text{ and } x \in B\}$.

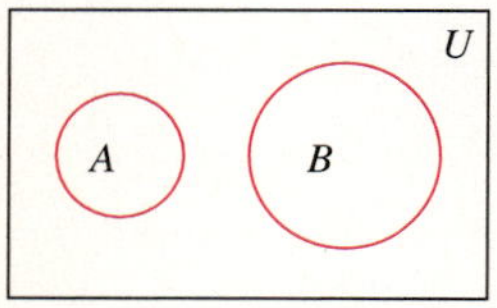

Figure 2-7

disjoint sets

The key word in the definition of intersection is *and*. In everyday language, as in mathematics, *and* implies that both conditions must be met. In the above example, the desired set is the set of those students enrolled in both art and biology.

If sets such as A and B have no elements in common, we call them **disjoint sets.** In other words, two sets A and B are disjoint if, and only if, $A \cap B = \varnothing$. For example, the set of males taking biology and the set of females taking biology are disjoint. The Venn diagram in Figure 2-7 implies that sets A and B are disjoint.

If A represents all students enrolled in art classes and B all students enrolled in biology classes, we may use a Venn diagram, taking into account that some students are enrolled in both subjects. If we know that 100 students are enrolled in art and 200 in biology and that 20 of these students are enrolled in both art and biology, we can record this information as in Figure 2-8. Notice that the total number of students in set A is 100 and the total in set B is 200.

Figure 2-8

Example 2-5

Find $A \cap B$ in each of the following:

a. $A = \{1, 2, 3, 4\}$, $B = \{3, 4, 5, 6\}$
b. $A = \{0, 2, 4, 6, \ldots\}$, $B = \{1, 3, 5, 7, \ldots\}$
c. $A = \{2, 4, 6, 8, \ldots\}$, $B = \{1, 2, 3, 4, \ldots\}$

Solution **a.** $A \cap B = \{3, 4\}$
b. $A \cap B = \varnothing$; therefore A and B are disjoint.
c. $A \cap B = A$ because all the elements of A are also in B.

Set Union

If A is the set of students taking art courses during the fall quarter and B is the set of students taking biology courses during the fall quarter, then the set of students taking art

union   or biology or both is the **union** of sets A and B. The union of sets A and B is pictured in Figure 2-9.

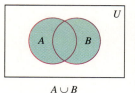

$A \cup B$

Figure 2-9

Definition of Set Union

The **union** of two sets A and B, written $A \cup B$, is the set of all elements in A or in B, $A \cup B = \{x \mid x \in A \text{ or } x \in B\}$.

The key word in the definition of union is *or*. In mathematics, *or* usually means "one or the other or both." This usage is known as the *inclusive or*.

• • •

Example 2-6   Find $A \cup B$ for each of the following:

a. $A = \{1, 2, 3, 4\}$, $B = \{3, 4, 5, 6\}$
b. $A = \{0, 2, 4, 6, \ldots\}$, $B = \{1, 3, 5, 7, \ldots\}$
c. $A = \{2, 4, 6, 8, \ldots\}$, $B = \{1, 2, 3, 4, \ldots\}$

Solution   **a.** $A \cup B = \{1, 2, 3, 4, 5, 6\}$
b. $A \cup B = \{0, 1, 2, 3, 4, \ldots\}$
c. $A \cup B = B$

• • •

I N V E S T I G A T I O N   2 - 7

• Notice that in Figure 2-8, $n(A \cup B) = 80 + 20 + 180 = 280$, but $n(A) + n(B) = 100 + 200 = 300$; hence in general $n(A \cup B) \neq n(A) + n(B)$. Use the concept of intersection of sets to write a formula for $n(A \cup B)$. •

Set Difference

If A is the set of students taking art classes during the fall quarter and B is the set of students taking biology classes, then the set of all students taking biology but not art is called the
complement of A relative   **complement of A relative to B**, or the **set difference** of B and A.
to B • **set difference**

Definition of Complement

The **complement of A relative to B**, written $B - A$, is the set of all elements in B that are not in A, $B - A = \{x \mid x \in B \text{ and } x \notin A\}$.

A Venn diagram representing $B - A$ is shown in Figure 2-10(a) on the following page. A Venn diagram for $B \cap \overline{A}$ is given in Figure 2-10(b).

Notice that $B \cap \overline{A} = B - A$ because $B \cap \overline{A}$ is, by definition of intersection and complement, the set of all elements in B and not in A.

Figure 2-10

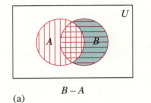

$B - A$

(a)

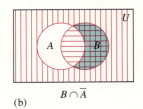

$B \cap \overline{A}$

(b)

• • •

Example 2-7   If $U = \{a, b, c, d, e, f, g\}$, $A = \{d, e, f\}$, $B = \{a, b, c, d, e, f\}$, and $C = \{a, b, c\}$, find each of the following:

a. $A - B$ **b.** $B - A$
c. $B - C$ **d.** $C - B$

Solution   **a.** $A - B = \varnothing$ **b.** $B - A = \{a, b, c\}$
               c. $B - C = \{d, e f\}$ **d.** $C - B = \varnothing$

• • •

Properties of Set Operations

Because the order of elements in a set is not important, $A \cup B$ is equal to $B \cup A$. This is the **commutative property of set union.** It does not matter in which order we write the sets when the union of two sets is involved. Similarly, $A \cap B = B \cap A$. This is the **commutative property of set intersection.**

commutative property of set union • commutative property of set intersection

---

I N V E S T I G A T I O N   2 - 8

● Use Venn diagrams and other means to find whether grouping is important when the same operation is involved. For example, is it always true that

$A \cap (B \cap C) = (A \cap B) \cap C$? Similar questions should be investigated involving union and set difference. ●

• • •

Example 2-8   Is grouping important when two different set operations are involved? For example, is it true that $A \cap (B \cup C) = (A \cap B) \cup C$?

Solution   To investigate this, we let $A = \{a, b, c, d\}$, $B = \{c, d, e\}$, and $C = \{d, e, f, g\}$. Then

$$A \cap (B \cup C) = \{a, b, c, d\} \cap (\{c, d, e\} \cup \{d, e, f, g\})$$
$$= \{a, b, c, d\} \cap \{c, d, e, f, g\}$$
$$= \{c, d\}$$

$$(A \cap B) \cup C = (\{a, b, c, d\} \cap \{c, d, e\}) \cup \{d, e, f, g\}$$
$$= \{c, d\} \cup \{d, e, f, g\}$$
$$= \{c, d, e, f, g\}.$$

In this case, $A \cap (B \cup C) \neq (A \cap B) \cup C$. So we have found a counterexample, that is, an example illustrating that the general statement is not always true.

• • •

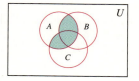

Figure 2-11

To discover an expression that is equal to $A \cap (B \cup C)$, consider the Venn diagram for $A \cap (B \cup C)$ shown by the shaded region in Figure 2-11. In the figure, $A \cap C$ and $A \cap B$ are subsets of the shaded region. The union of $A \cap C$ and $A \cap B$ is the entire shaded region. Thus $A \cap (B \cup C) = (A \cap B) \cup (A \cap C)$.

Property

Distributive Property of Set Intersection Over Union.

For all sets A, B, and C.

$$A \cap (B \cup C) = (A \cap B) \cup (A \cap C)$$

• • •

Example 2-9   Use set notation to describe the shaded portions of the Venn diagrams in Figure 2-12(a) and (b).

Figure 2-12

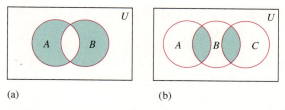

(a)   (b)

Solution   The solutions can be described in many different, but equivalent, forms. The following are possible answers:

a. $(A \cup B) \cap \overline{(A \cap B)}$, or $(A \cup B) - (A \cap B)$
b. $(A \cap B) \cup (B \cap C)$, or $B \cap (A \cup C)$

• • •

I N V E S T I G A T I O N   2 - 9

● If, on both sides of the equation in the *distributive property of set intersection over union,* the symbol ∩ is replaced by ∪ and the symbol ∪ is replaced by ∩, is the new property true? Explain why or why not. ●

Using Venn Diagrams as a Problem-solving Tool

Venn diagrams can be used as a problem-solving tool for modeling information, as shown in the following examples.

Example 2-10

Suppose *M* is the set of all students taking mathematics and *E* is the set of all students taking English. Identify the students described by each region in Figure 2-13.

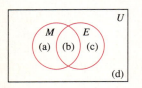

Figure 2-13

Solution

Region (a) contains all students taking mathematics but not English.
Region (b) contains all students taking both mathematics and English.
Region (c) contains all students taking English but not mathematics.
Region (d) contains all students taking neither mathematics nor English.

INVESTIGATION 2-10

● Draw a Venn diagram for 3 sets that create the maximum number of distinct regions. How many distinct regions are created? ●

Example 2-11

In a survey of 110 college freshmen investigating their high school backgrounds, the following information was gathered:

25 took physics
45 took biology
48 took mathematics
10 took physics and mathematics
8 took biology and mathematics
6 took physics and biology
5 took all 3 subjects

a. How many students took biology but neither physics nor mathematics?
b. How many took physics, biology, or mathematics?
c. How many did not take any of the 3 subjects?

Solution   **a.** To solve this problem, we *build a model using sets.* Because there are three distinct subjects, we should use three circles. The maximum number of regions of a Venn diagram determined by three circles is eight. In Figure 2-14, *P* is the set of students taking physics, *B* is the set taking biology, and *M* is the set taking mathematics. The shaded region represents the five students who took all three subjects. The lined region represents the students who took physics and mathematics, but who did not take biology.

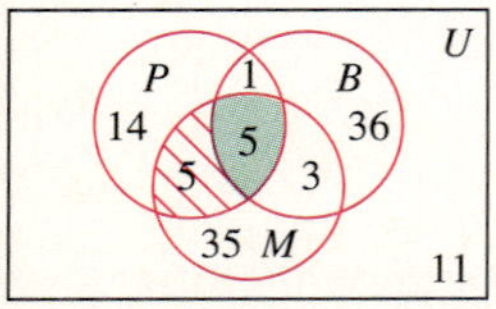

Figure 2-14

One mind-set to beware of in this problem is thinking that the 25 who took physics, for example, took only physics. That is not necessarily the case. If those students had been taking only physics, then we should have been told.

Because a total of 10 students took physics and mathematics and 5 of those also took biology, $10 - 5$, or 5, students took physics and math but not biology. Similarly, because 8 students took biology and mathematics and 5 took all 3 subjects, $8 - 5$, or 3, took biology and mathematics but not physics. Also $6 - 5$, or 1, student took physics and biology but not mathematics. To find the number of students who took biology but neither physics nor mathematics, we subtract from 45 (the total number that took biology) the number of those that are in the distinct regions that include biology and other subjects, that is, $1 + 5 + 3$, or 9. Because $45 - 9 = 36$, we know that 36 students took biology but not physics or mathematics.

b. To find the number of students in all the distinct regions in *P*, *M*, or *B*, we proceed as follows. The number of students who took physics but not mathematics or biology is $25 - (1 + 5 + 5)$, or 14. The number of students who took mathematics but neither physics nor biology is $48 - (5 + 5 + 3)$, or 35. Hence the number of students who took mathematics, physics, or biology is $35 + 14 + 36 + 3 + 5 + 5 + 1$, or 99.

c. Because the total number of students is 110, the number that did not take any of the three subjects is $110 - 99$, or 11.

• • •

Cartesian Products

Cartesian product   Another way to produce a set from two given sets is by forming the **Cartesian product.** This formation pairs the elements of one set with the elements of another set in a specific way. Suppose a person has three pairs of pants, $P = \{\text{blue, white, green}\}$, and two shirts, $S = \{\text{blue, red}\}$. According to the Fundamental Counting Principle, there are $3 \cdot 2$, or 6, possible different pant-and-shirt pairs as shown in Figure 2-15.

Figure 2-15

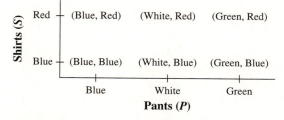

The pairs of pants and shirts form a set of all possible pairs in which the first member of the pair is an element of set *P* and the second member is an element of set *S*. The set of all possible pairs is given in Figure 2-15. Because the first component in each pair represents pants and the second component in each pair represents shirts, the order in which the components are written is important. Thus (green, blue) represents green pants and a blue shirt, whereas (blue, green) represents blue pants and a green shirt. Therefore the two pairs represent different outfits. Because the order in each pair is important, the pairs are called *ordered pairs*   **ordered pairs.** The positions that the ordered pairs occupy within the set of outfits is imma-
components   terial. Only the order of the **components** within each pair is significant.

The pant and shirt pairs suggest the following definition of equality for ordered pairs: $(x, y) = (m, n)$ *if, and only if, the first components are equal and the second components are equal.* A set consisting of ordered pairs such as the ones in the pants-and-shirt example is the Cartesian product of the set of pants and the set of shirts.

Definition of Cartesian Product

For any sets A and B, the **Cartesian product** of A and B, written $A \times B$ is the set of all ordered pairs such that the first element of each pair is an element of A and the second element of each pair is an element of B.

$$A \times B = \{(x, y) \mid x \in A \text{ and } y \in B\}$$

REMARK $A \times B$ is commonly read as "*A cross B.*"

Example 2-12   If $A = \{a, b, c\}$ and $B = \{1, 2, 3\}$, find each of the following:

a. $A \times B$ **b.** $B \times A$ **c.** $A \times A$

Solution   **a.** $A \times B = \{(a, 1), (a, 2), (a, 3), (b, 1), (b, 2), (b, 3), (c, 1), (c, 2), (c, 3)\}$
b. $B \times A = \{(1, a), (1, b), (1, c), (2, a), (2, b), (2, c), (3, a), (3, b), (3, c)\}$
c. $A \times A = \{(a, a), (a, b), (a, c), (b, a), (b, b), (b, c), (c, a), (c, b), (c, c)\}$

It is possible to form a Cartesian product involving the null set. Suppose $A = \{1, 2\}$. Because there are no elements in $\emptyset$, no ordered pairs (x, y) with $x \in A$ and $y \in \emptyset$ are possible, so $A \times \emptyset = \emptyset$. This is true for all sets A. Similarly, $\emptyset \times A = \emptyset$ for all sets A.

There is an analogy between the last equation and the multiplication fact that $0 \cdot a = 0$, where a is a natural number. In the next chapter, multiplication of natural numbers will be defined using the concept of Cartesian product.

Ongoing Assessment 2-2

1. Suppose $U = \{e, q, u, a, l, i, t, y\}$, $A = \{l, i, t, e\}$, $B = \{t, i, e\}$, and $C = \{q, u, e\}$. Decide whether the following pairs of sets are equal:
   a. $A \cap B$ and $B \cap A$
   b. $A \cup B$ and $B \cup A$
   c. $A \cup (B \cup C)$ and $(A \cup B) \cup C$
   d. $A \cup \emptyset$ and A
   e. $A \cup A$ and $A \cup \emptyset$
   f. $(A \cap A)$ and $(A \cap \emptyset)$

2. Tell whether each of the following is true or false for all sets A, B, or C. If false, give a counterexample.
   a. $A \cup \emptyset = A$
   b. $A - B = B - A$
   c. $A \cup A = A$
   d. $\overline{A \cap B} = \overline{A} \cap \overline{B}$
   e. $(A \cup B) \cup C = A \cup (B \cup C)$
   f. $(A \cup B) - A = B$
   g. $(A - B) \cup A = (A - B) \cup (B - A)$

3. If $B \subseteq A$, find a simpler expression for each of the following:
   a. $A \cap B$ **b.** $A \cup B$

4. For each of the following, shade the portion of the Venn diagram that illustrates the set:
   a. $A \cup B$ **b.** $A \cap \overline{B}$
   c. $\overline{A \cap B}$ **d.** $(A \cap B) \cup (A \cap C)$

e. $A \cap B$ **f.** $(A \cup B) \cap \overline{C}$

g. $(A \cap B) \cup C$ **h.** $(\overline{A} \cap B) \cup C$

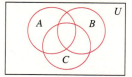

5. If S is a subset of universe U, find each of the following:

a. $S \cup \overline{S}$ **b.** $S \cup U$ **c.** $\varnothing \cup S$

d. $\overline{U}$ **e.** $S \cap U$ **f.** $\overline{\varnothing}$

g. $S \cap \overline{S}$ **h.** $S - \overline{S}$ **i.** $U \cap \overline{S}$

j. $\overline{\overline{S}}$ **k.** $\varnothing \cap S$ **l.** $U - \overline{S}$

6. For each of the following conditions, find $A - B$:

a. $A \cap B = \varnothing$

b. $B = U$

c. $A = B$

d. $A \subseteq B$

7. Use set notation to identify each of the following shaded regions:

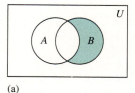

(a)

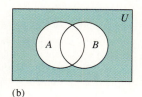

(b)

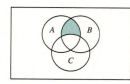

(c)

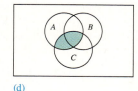

(d)

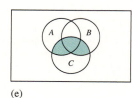

(e)

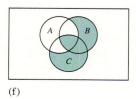

(f)

8. In the following, shade the portion of the diagram that represents the given sets:

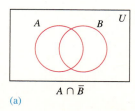

$A \cap \overline{B}$

(a)

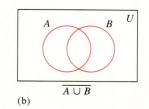

$\overline{A \cup B}$

(b)

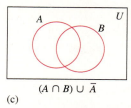

$(A \cap B) \cup \overline{A}$

(c)

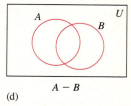

$A - B$

(d)

9. Use Venn diagrams to determine if each of the following is true:

a. $A \cup (B \cap C) = (A \cup B) \cap C$

b. $A \cap (B \cup C) = (A \cap B) \cup C$

c. $A - (B - C) = (A - B) - C$

10. For each of the following pairs of sets, explain which is a subset of the other. If neither is a subset of the other, explain why.

a. $A \cap B$ and $A \cap B \cap C$

b. $A \cup B$ and $A \cup B \cup C$

c. $A \cup B$ and $(A \cup B) \cap C$

d. $A - B$ and $B - A$

11. a. If A has three elements and B has two elements, what is the greatest number of elements possible in (i) $A \cup B$? (ii) $A \cap B$? (iii) $B - A$? (iv) $A - B$?

b. If A has n elements and B has m elements, what is the greatest number of elements possible in (i) $A \cup B$? (ii) $A \cap B$? (iii) $B - A$? (iv) $A - B$?

12. If $n(A) = 4$, $n(B) = 5$, and $n(C) = 6$, what is the greatest and least number of elements in

a. $A \cup B \cup C$?   **b.** $A \cap B \cap C$?

13. The equation $\overline{A \cup B} = \overline{A} \cap \overline{B}$ and a similar equation mentioned in part (b) are referred to as *DeMorgan's laws* in honor of the famous British mathematician who first discovered them.

a. Use Venn diagrams to show that $\overline{A \cup B} = \overline{A} \cap \overline{B}$.

b. Discover an equation similar to the one in part (a) involving $\overline{A \cap B}$, $\overline{A}$, and $\overline{B}$. Use Venn diagrams to show that the equation holds.

c. Verify the equations in (a) and (b) for specific sets.

14. If $A \cap B = A \cup B$, how are A and B related?

15. Given that the universe is the set of all humans, $B = \{x \mid x$ is a college basketball player$\}$, and $S = \{x \mid x$ is a college student more than 200 cm tall$\}$, describe each of the following in words:

a. $B \cap S$ **b.** $\overline{S}$ **c.** $B \cup S$

d. $B \cup S$ **e.** $\overline{B} \cap S$ **f.** $B \cap \overline{S}$

16. Suppose P is the set of all eighth-grade students at the Paxson school, with B the set of all students in the band and C the set of all students in the choir. Identify in words the students described by each region of the following figure:

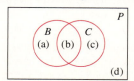

17. Of the eighth graders at the Paxson school, 7 played basketball, 9 played volleyball, 10 played soccer, 1 played basketball and volleyball only, 1 played basketball and soccer only, 2 played volleyball and soccer only, and 2 played volleyball, basketball, and soccer. How many played one or more of the three sports?

18. In a fraternity with 30 members, 18 take mathematics, 5 take both mathematics and biology, and 8 take neither mathematics nor biology. How many take biology but not mathematics?

19. Write the letters in the appropriate sections of the following Venn diagram using the following directions:

Set A contains the letters in the word *Iowa*.
Set B contains the letters in the word *Hawaii*.
Set C contains the letters in the word *Ohio*.

The universal set contains the letters in the word *Washington*.

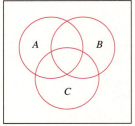

20. In Paul's bicycle shop, 40 bicycles are inspected. If 20 needed new tires and 30 needed gear repairs, answer the following:
  a. What is the greatest number of bikes that could have needed both?
  b. What is the least number of bikes that could have needed both?
  c. What is the greatest number of bikes that could have needed neither?

21. Classify the following as true or false. If false, give a counterexample. Assume that A and B are finite sets.
  a. If $n(A) = n(B)$, then $A = B$.
  b. If $A \sim B$, then $A \cup B$ is not equivalent to B.
  c. If $A - B = \varnothing$, then $A = B$.
  d. If $B - A = \varnothing$, then $B \subseteq A$.
  e. If $A \subset B$, then $n(A) < n(B)$.
  f. If $n(A) < n(B)$, then $A \subset B$.

22. Three announcers each tried to predict the winners of Sunday's professional football games. The only team not picked that is playing Sunday was the Giants. The choices for each person were as follows:

Phyllis: Cowboys, Steelers, Vikings, Bills
Paula: Steelers, Packers, Cowboys, Redskins
Rashid: Redskins, Vikings, Jets, Cowboys

If the only teams playing Sunday are those just mentioned, which teams will play which other teams?

23. Let $A = \{x, y\}$, $B = \{a, b, c\}$, and $C = \{0\}$. Find each of the following:

  a. $A \times B$ **b.** $B \times A$ **c.** $B \times \varnothing$
  d. $(A \cup B) \times C$ **e.** $A \cup (B \times C)$

24. For each of the following, the Cartesian product $C \times D$ is given by the following sets. Find C and D.
  a. $\{(a, b), (a, c), (a, d), (a, e)\}$
  b. $\{(1, 1), (1, 2), (1, 3), (2, 1), (2, 2), (2, 3)\}$
  c. $\{(0, 1), (0, 0), (1, 1), (1, 0)\}$

25. Answer each of the following:
  a. If A has five elements and B has four elements, how many elements are in $A \times B$?
  b. If A has m elements and B has n elements, how many elements are in $A \times B$?
  c. If A has m elements, B has n elements, and C has p elements, how many elements are in $(A \times B) \times C$?

26. If $A = \{1, 2, 3\}$, $B = \{0\}$, and $C = \varnothing$, find the number of elements in each of the following:
  a. $A \times C$ **b.** $B \times C$ **c.** $C \times C$

27. If the number of elements in set B is 3 and the number of elements in $(A \cup B) \times B$ is 24, what is the number of elements in A if $A \cap B = \varnothing$?

28. If A and B are nonempty sets such that $A \times B = B \times A$, does $A = B$?

29. Determine if each of the following is always, sometimes, or never true. In each case, explain your reasoning.
  a. If $A \subseteq B$, then $A \times A \subseteq B \times B$.
  b. If $A \subseteq B$ and $C \subseteq D$, then $A \times C \subseteq B \times D$.

30. If there are six teams in the Alpha league and five teams in the Beta league and if each team from one league plays each team from the other league exactly once, how many games are played?

31. José has four pairs of slacks, five shirts, and three sweaters. From how many different combinations can he choose if he chooses a pair of slacks, a shirt, and a sweater each day?

Communication

32. Answer each of the following and justify your answer:
  a. If $a \in A \cap B$, is it true that $a \in A \cup B$?
  b. If $a \in A \cup B$, is it true that $a \in A \cap B$?

33. The primary colors are red, blue, and yellow. If each is considered a set, write an explanation of what we would expect to get with the intersection of each of these sets from the regions pictured in the following figure:

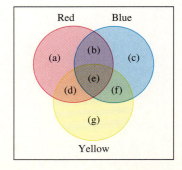

34. A pollster interviewed 500 university seniors who owned credit cards. She reported that 240 owned Goldcard, 290 had Supercard, and 270 had Thriftcard. Of those seniors, the report said that 80 owned only a Goldcard and a Supercard, 70 owned only a Goldcard and a Thriftcard, 60 owned only a Supercard and a Thriftcard, and 50 owned all 3 cards. When the report was submitted for publication in the local campus newspaper, the editor refused to publish it, claiming the poll was not accurate. Was the editor right? Why or why not?

35. a. Is the operation of forming Cartesian products commutative? Explain why or why not.
  b. Is the operation of forming Cartesian products associative? Explain why or why not.

36. The Red Cross looks for three types of antigens in blood tests: A, B, and Rh. When the antigen A or B is present, it is listed, but if both these antigens are absent, the blood is type O. If the Rh antigen is present, the blood is positive, otherwise, it is negative. If a laboratory technician reports the following results after testing the blood samples of 100 people, how many were classified as O negative? Explain your reasoning.

Number of Samples	Antigen in Blood
40	A
18	B
82	Rh
5	A and B
31	A and Rh
11	B and Rh
4	A, B, and Rh

Open-ended

37. Make up and solve a story problem concerning specific sets A, B, and C for which $n(A \cup B \cup C)$ is known and it is required to find $n(A)$, $n(B)$, and $n(C)$.

38. Describe a real-life situation that can be represented by each of the following:
  a. $A \cap \overline{B}$ **b.** $A \cap B \cap C$ **c.** $A - (B \cup C)$

Cooperative Learning

39. List as many sets and set operation properties as you can. They might include properties mentioned in the text or problems as well properties that your group discovers.

Compare your group's properties with those listed by others. Be prepared to show why your properties are true.

40. Use set operations like union, intersection, complement, and set difference to describe the shaded region in the following figure in as many ways as possible. Compare your expressions with those of other groups to see which has the most. What is the total number of different expressions found by all the groups? Which expressions appeared in all the groups?

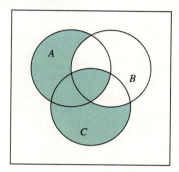

Review Problems

41. If $A = \{1, 2, 3, 4\}$ and $B = \{1, 2, 3, 4, 5\}$, answer the following questions:
  a. How many subsets of A do not contain the element 1?
  b. How many subsets of A contain the element 1?
  c. How many subsets of A contain either the element 1 or 2?
  d. How many subsets of A contain neither the element 1 nor 2?
  e. How many subsets of B contain the element 5 and how many do not?
  f. If all the subsets of A are known, how can all the subsets of B be systematically listed? How many subsets of B are there?

42. a. Which of the following sets are equal?
  b. Which sets are proper subsets of the other sets?

$$A = \{2, 4, 6, 8, 10, \ldots\}$$
$$B = \{x \mid x = 2n + 2, n = 0, 1, 2, 3, 4, \ldots\}$$
$$C = \{x \mid x = 4n, n \in N\}$$

43. Give examples from real life for each of the following:
  a. A one-to-one correspondence between two sets
  b. A correspondence between two sets that is not one-to-one

LABORATORY ACTIVITY

A set of attribute blocks consists of 32 blocks. Each block is identified by its own shape, size, and color. The 4 shapes in a set are square, triangle, rhombus, and circle; the 4 colors are red, yellow, blue, and green; the 2 sizes are large and small. In addition to the blocks, each set contains a group of 20 cards. Ten of the cards specify one of the attributes of the blocks (for example, red, large, square). The other 10 cards are negation cards and specify the lack of an attribute (for example, not green, not circle). Many set-type problems can be studied with these blocks. For example, let *A* be the set of all green blocks and *B* be the set of all large blocks. Using the set of all blocks as the universal set, describe elements in each set listed below to determine which are equal:

1. $A \cup B; B \cup A$
2. $\overline{A \cup B}; \overline{A} \cap \overline{B}$
3. $\overline{A \cap B}; \overline{A} \cup \overline{B}$
4. $A - B; A \cap \overline{B}$

Section 2-3   Functions

The following is an example of a game called "guess my rule," often used to introduce the concept of a function.

When Tom said 2, Noah said 5. When Dick said 4, Noah said 7. When Mary said 10, Noah said 13. When Liz said 6, what did Noah say? What is Noah's rule?

The answer to the first question may be 9, and the rule could be, "Take the original number and add 3"; that is, for any number *n*, Noah's answer is $n + 3$.

• • •

Example 2-13   Guess the teacher's rule for the following responses:

(a) You	Teacher	(b) You	Teacher	(c) You	Teacher
1	3	2	5	2	0
0	0	3	7	4	0
4	12	5	11	7	1
10	30	10	21	21	1

Solution   a. The teacher's rule could be, "Multiply the given number *n* by 3," that is, $3n$.
   b. The teacher's rule could be, "Double the original number *n* and add 1," that is, $2n + 1$.
   c. The teacher's rule could be, "If the number *n* is even, answer 0; if the number is odd, answer 1."

• • •

HISTORICAL   NOTE

The Babylonians (ca. 2000 B.C.) probably had a working idea of what a function was. To them, it was a table or a correspondence. René Descartes (1637), Gottfried Wilhelm von Leibnitz (1692), Johann Bernoulli (1718), Leonhard Euler (1750), Joseph Louis Lagrange (1800), and Jean Joseph Fourier (1822) were among the mathematicians contributing to the notion of a function. Leonhard Euler in 1734 first used the notation $f(x)$. In the late 1800s, Georg Cantor and others began to use the modern definition.

Another way to prepare students for the concept of a function is by using a "function machine." An example of a function machine is seen on the following student page from *Addison-Wesley Mathematics*, Grade 4, 1993. What goes in the machine is referred to as

Using Critical Thinking

LEARN ABOUT IT

"This is a great machine," said Carl. "You can put in a number and make it do any operation you want! It's easy to see that it is dividing by 4."

"It's not easy for me to see," said Lola. "I thought that the machine was subtracting!"

"You're both jumping to conclusions," said Ginger. "I just thought of a way that the machine could be subtracting *and* dividing!"

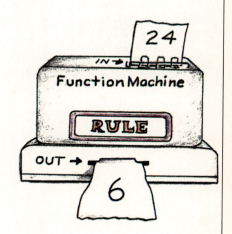

TALK ABOUT IT

1. What does a function machine do?

2. Why did Carl think that the machine was dividing by 4?

3. What do you think Lola meant? How could the machine produce 6 by subtracting?

4. Could Ginger be correct? Work together to figure out a rule that the machine could use to begin with 24 and produce 6 by subtracting and dividing.

5. What additional information might help you decide what rule the machine is actually using? Give examples.

6. Make up a rule for a function machine. Give some "in" and "out" numbers and ask a partner to discover the rule.

7. Can you think of any real-world machines that could be made to work like a function machine? Explain.

IN	OUT
24	6

input and what comes out as *output*. Thus, on the student page, if the input is 8, the output is 3. In later grades, a special notation for the output is used. For any input element x, the output is denoted by $f(x)$, read "f of x." For the function machine pictured on the student page, when the input is 24 the output would be written as $f(24)$. Because the output is 6, we have $f(24) = 6$. If the machine works according to the rule "divide by 2 and then subtract 6," we would have $f(24) = (24 \div 2) - 6 = 6$.

Example 2-14 Consider the function machine in Figure 2-16. What will happen if the numbers 0, 1, 3, and 6 are entered?

Solution If the numbers output are denoted by $f(x)$, the corresponding values can be described using Table 2-3.

Figure 2-16

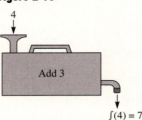

$f(4) = 7$

Table 2-3

x	$f(x)$
0	3
1	4
3	6
6	9

We can write an equation to depict the rule in Example 2-14 as follows. If the input is x, the output is $x + 3$; that is, $f(x) = x + 3$. The output values can be obtained by substituting the values 0, 1, 3, 4, and 6 for x in $f(x) = x + 3$, as shown:

$$f(0) = 0 + 3 = 3$$
$$f(1) = 1 + 3 = 4$$
$$f(3) = 3 + 3 = 6$$
$$f(4) = 4 + 3 = 7$$
$$f(6) = 6 + 3 = 9$$

In many applications, both the inputs and the outputs of a function machine are numbers. However, inputs and outputs may be any objects. For example, consider a particular candy machine that accepts only 25¢, 50¢, or 75¢ and outputs one of three types of candy. A function machine associates *exactly one output with each input*. If you enter some element x as input and obtain $f(x)$ as output, then every time you enter the same x as input, you will obtain the same $f(x)$ as output. The idea of a function machine associating exactly one output with each input according to some rule leads to the following definition.

Definition of Function

A **function** from set A to set B is a correspondence from A to B in which each element of A is paired with one, and only one, element of B.

domain   The set A in the previous definition is the set of all allowable inputs and is the **domain** of the function. The set B is any set that includes all the possible outputs. The set of all outrange   puts is the **range** of the function. Set B in the definition is any set that includes the range and can be the range itself. The distinction is made for convenience sake, since sometimes the range cannot be easily found. For example, consider corresponding to each student at a university the student's I.D. number. This is a function from the set of all students to the set S of natural numbers. The range in this case is all the I.D. numbers of students who are enrolled at the University. The range is a proper subset of the set S. Normally if no domain is given to describe a function, then the domain is assumed to have the most elements for which the rule is meaningful.

A calculator is a function machine. Suppose a student enters $\boxed{9}$ $\boxed{\times}$ $\boxed{K}$ on the calculator that has a constant key, $\boxed{K}$. The student then presses $\boxed{0}$ and hands the calculator to another student. The other student is to determine the rule by entering various numbers followed by the $\boxed{=}$ key. Machines with an automatic constant feature can also be used.

Other buttons on a calculator are function buttons. For example, the $\boxed{\pi}$ button always displays an approximation for π, such as 3.1415927; the $\boxed{+/-}$ button either displays a negative sign in front of a number or removes an existing negative sign; and the $\boxed{x^2}$ and $\boxed{\sqrt{}}$ buttons square numbers and take the square root of numbers, respectively.

Are all input-output machines function machines? Consider the machine in Figure 2-17. For any natural-number input x, the machine outputs a number that is less than x. If, for example, you input the number 10, the machine may output 9, since 9 is less than 10. If you input 10 again, the machine may output 3, since 3 is less than 10. Such a machine is not a function machine because the same input may give different outputs.

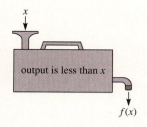

Figure 2-17

• • •

Example 2-15   Which, if any, of the parts of Figure 2-18 exhibits a function from A to B? If a correspondence is a function from A to B, find the range of the function.

Figure 2-18

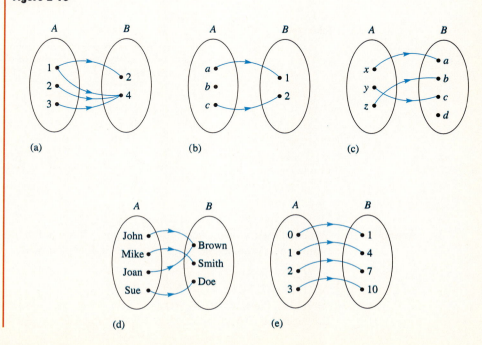

Solution   **a.** Figure 2-18(a) does not define a function from A to B, since the element 1 is paired with both 2 and 4.

   b. Figure 2-18(b) does not define a function from A to B, since the element b is not paired with any element of B. (It is a function from a subset of A to B.)

   c. Figure 2-18(c) does define a function from A to B, since there is one and only one arrow leaving each element of A. The fact that d, an element of B, is not paired with any element in the domain does not violate the definition. The range is $\{a, b, c\}$ and does not include d because d is not an output of this function, as no element of A is paired with d.

   d. Figure 2-18(d) illustrates a function, since there is only one arrow leaving each element in A. It does not matter that an element of set B, Brown, has two arrows pointing to it. The range is {Brown, Smith, Doe}.

   e. Figure 2-18(e) illustrates a function whose range is $\{1, 4, 7, 10\}$.

• • •

Figure 2-18(e) also illustrates a one-to-one correspondence between A and B. In fact, any one-to-one correspondence between A and B defines a function from A to B as well as a function from B to A.

A function can be represented in a variety of ways. A useful way to describe a function is in a table. Consider the information in Table 2-4 relating the amount spent on advertising and the resulting sales in a given month for a small business. If $A = \{0, 1, 2, 3, 4\}$ and $S = \{1, 3, 6, 8, 10\}$, the table describes a function from A to S.

The information in Table 2-4 can also be given using ordered pairs. The fact that when 0 is the input and 1 is the output is recorded as the ordered pair (0, 1). Similarly, the information in the second row is recorded as (1, 3) and the rest of the information as (2, 6), (3, 8), and (4, 10). The first component in the ordered pair is always an element in the domain and the second is the corresponding output.

Table 2-4

Amount of Advertising (In $1000s)	Amount of Sales (In $1000s)
0	1
1	3
2	6
3	8
4	10

• • •

Example 2-16   Which of the following sets of ordered pairs represent functions? If a set represents a function, give its domain and range. If it does not, explain why.

   a. $\{(1, 2), (1, 3), (2, 3), (3, 4)\}$
   b. $\{(1, 2), (2, 3), (3, 4), (4, 5)\}$
   c. $\{(1, 0), (2, 0), (3, 0), (4, 4)\}$
   d. $\{(a, b) \mid a \in N, b = 2a\}$

Solution   **a.** This is not a function because the input 1 has two different outputs.
   b. This is a function with domain {1, 2, 3, 4} and range {2, 3, 4, 5}.
   c. This is a function with domain {1, 2, 3, 4} and range {0, 4}. The output 0 appears more than once, but this does not contradict the definition of a function in that each input corresponds to only one output.
   d. This is a function with domain N and range E, the set of all even natural numbers.

• • •

Perhaps one of the most widely recognized representations of a function is a graph. Graphs are visual representations of functions and appear in newspapers and books and on television. To graph the function in Table 2-4, consider the set of ordered pairs {(0, 1), (1, 3), (2, 6), (4, 10)} and correspond to each ordered pair a point on the grid in Figure 2-19. We use the horizontal scale for the inputs and the vertical scale for the outputs and mark the point corresponding to (0, 1) by starting at 0 on the horizontal scale and going up 1 unit on the vertical scale. To mark the point that corresponds to (1, 3), we start at 0 and move 1 unit horizontally and then 3 units vertically. Marking the point that corresponds to

graphing   an ordered pair is referred to as **graphing** the ordered pair. The set of all points that correspond to all the ordered pairs is the graph of the function.

The scales on the horizontal and vertical axes in Figure 2-19 are the same; however, in applications of mathematics it is often convenient to have different scales. For example, on the following page look at the student page from *Addison-Wesley Mathematics,* Grade 7, 1993. On the horizontal axis, each year is represented by four units (each unit is one side of one small square), while on the vertical axis each unit represents $1000. The points on the graph have been connected. This implies that we could find the value of the car at any time between the purchase and the end of 5 years. For example, after 3 months the value is $13,000 and after 2 years the value is $8000. Try to answer the practice questions on the student page.

Figure 2-19

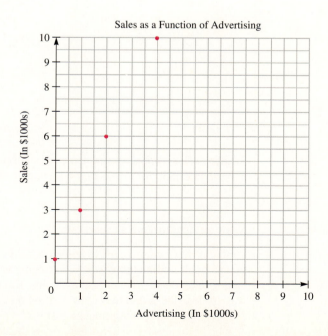

PRACTICE

The value of a car usually decreases or depreciates over time. Use the graph to decide if each statement is true or false.

1. A car's value drops fastest between the first and second years.

2. After two years, a car's value is about half its original value.

3. The depreciation rate stays the same after one year.

4. It is always better to buy a used car than a new car.

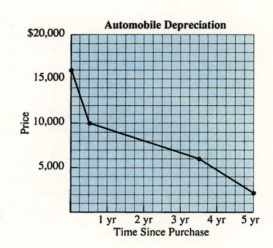

Example 2-17   Explain why a telephone company would not set rates for telephone calls as depicted on the graph in Figure 2-20.

Figure 2-20

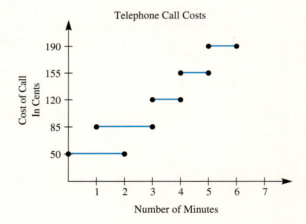

Solution   The graph does not depict a function. For example, a customer could be charged either 50¢ or 85¢ for the second minute of conversation.

More on Applications of Functions

Functions have many real-life applications. For example, on direct-dial long-distance calls you pay only for the minutes you talk. Suppose the weekday rate for a long-distance phone call from Madison, Wisconsin, to Urbana, Illinois, is 27¢ per minute. We have seen that one way to describe a function is by writing an equation. Based on the information in Table 2-5, the equation relating time to cost is $C = t \cdot 27$, where t is a natural number. This could also be written as $f(t) = 27t$, where $f(t)$ is the cost of the call in cents. If we restrict the time

Table 2-5

Number of Minutes Talked	Total Cost in Cents
1	$1 \cdot 27 = 27$
2	$2 \cdot 27 = 54$
3	$3 \cdot 27 = 81$
4	$4 \cdot 27 = 108$
5	$5 \cdot 27 = 135$
.	.
.	.
.	.
t	$t \cdot 27$

in minutes to the first 5 natural numbers, the function can be described as the set of ordered pairs {(1, 27), (2, 54), (3, 81), (4, 108), (5, 135)}. Figure 2-21(a) shows the graph of the function. The graph consists of 5 points that are not connected, since the phone company charges for any part of a minute t as if it were a full minute. The break in the vertical axis shown by ⌇ indicates that part of the vertical axis between 0 and 50 has been compressed and that the scale is not accurate between 0 and 50.

In graphing the function in Figure 2-21(a), we assumed the domain to be the set of natural numbers. Because the phone company charges for any part of a minute as if it were a full minute, the charge for any call that is 1 min long or less is 27¢. The charge for any call less than or equal to 2 min but longer than 1 min is 54¢. The cost is calculated similarly for calls between two consecutive minutes. The graph reflecting this information is shown in Figure 2-21(b). The filled dot at the right endpoint of each segment in the graph indicates that the point belongs to the graph, while the empty dot at the left endpoint of each segment indicates that the point does not belong to the graph. The domain of the function graphed in Figure 2-21(b) is the set of all positive numbers.

Figure 2-21

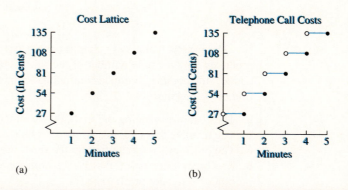

(a)   (b)

I N V E S T I G A T I O N   2 - 1 1

● Can the cost of 10.5 min of phone conversation from Madison, Wisconsin, to Urbana, Illinois, be found by substituting 10.5 into the formula $C = t \cdot 27$ developed above? Why or why not? ●

Functions and their graphs are frequently used in the business world, as the following example illustrates.

Example 2-18

In Figure 2-22, the blue graph shows the cost C in dollars of producing a given number of tee shirts. The red graph shows the revenue R in dollars from selling any number of tee shirts.

Figure 2-22

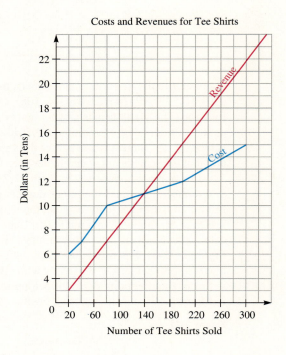

Costs and Revenues for Tee Shirts

The graphs technically should consist only of disconnected points because a factory produces only a whole number of tee shirts. However, for visual effect, it is customary to connect the points to produce continuous segments. Based on the information in the graphs, find the following:

a. The cost of producing the first 300 tee shirts
b. The revenue from the sale of the first 80 tee shirts
c. The profit or loss if the first 80 tee shirts are produced and sold
d. The break-even point, that is, the number of items that must be produced and sold in order for the net profit to be $0.

Solution   **a.** From the blue graph in Figure 2-22, we see that the cost corresponding to 300 tee shirts is $150.00.
b. From the red graph, we see that the revenue from the sale of the first 80 tee shirts is $70.00.
c. The cost of producing 80 tee shirts is $100. Because the profit is the difference between the cost and the revenue, the loss in this case is $100.00 − $70.00, or $30.00.

d. The break-even point is at point C, where the graphs intersect. At that point, the cost and the revenue are the same. The number of tee shirts corresponding to point C is 140.

• • •

Operations on Functions

Consider the function machines in Figure 2-23. If 2 is entered in the top machine, then $f(2) = 2 + 4 = 6$. Six is then entered in the second machine and $g(6) = 2 \cdot 6 = 12$. The functions in Figure 2-23 illustrate the **composition of two functions.** In the composition of two functions, the range of the first function becomes the domain of the second function.

composition of two functions

Figure 2-23

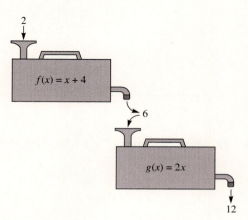

If the first function f is followed by a second function g, as in Figure 2-23, then we symbolize the composition of the functions as $g \circ f$. If we input 3 in the function machines of Figure 2-23, then the output is symbolized by $(g \circ f)(3)$. Because f acts first on 3, to compute $(g \circ f)(3)$ we find $f(3) = 3 + 4 = 7$ and then $g(7) = 2 \cdot 7 = 14$. Hence, $(g \circ f)(3) = 14$ and $(g \circ f)(3) = g(f(3))$. Also note that $(g \circ f)(x) = g(f(x)) = 2 \cdot f(x) = 2(x + 4)$ and hence $g(f(3)) = 2(3 + 4) = 14$.

• • •

Example 2-19   If $f(x) = 2x + 3$ and $g(x) = x - 3$, find the following:

a. $(f \circ g)(3)$ **b.** $(g \circ f)(3)$ **c.** $(f \circ g)(x)$ **d.** $(g \circ f)(x)$

Solution   **a.** $(f \circ g)(3) = f(0) = 2 \cdot 0 + 3 = 3$
b. $(g \circ f)(3) = g(9) = 9 - 3 = 6$
c. $(f \circ g)(x) = f(g(x)) = 2 \cdot g(x) + 3 = 2(x - 3) + 3 = 2x - 6 + 3 = 2x - 3$
d. $(g \circ f)(x) = g(f(x)) = f(x) - 3 = (2x + 3) - 3 = 2x$

• • •

REMARK   Example 2-19 shows that composition of functions is not commutative, since $(f \circ g)(3) \neq (g \circ f)(3)$.

Elementary school math texts introduce composition of two functions, as seen on the following student page from *Addison-Wesley Mathematics,* Grade 4, 1993. Complete the exercise on the student page.

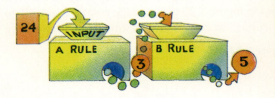

The output of function machine A is the input for function machine B. Study the example. Then figure out the two function rules and complete the table.

Input A	Output B
24	5
72	11
8	3
32	‖‖
40	‖‖
48	‖‖

Example 2-20   Find the range of $g \circ f$ for each of the following, where the domain of $g \circ f$ is the set $\{1, 2, 3\}$:

a. $f(x) = 2x$; $g(x) = 3x$
b. $f(x) = x + 2$; $g(x) = x - 2$

Solution   **a.** The composition follows in Figure 2-24 of the following page.

Figure 2-24

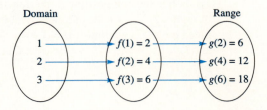

Thus the range of $g \circ f$ is the set $\{6, 12, 18\}$.
   b. The composition follows in Figure 2-25. Thus the range of $g \circ f$ is the set $\{1, 2, 3\}$.

Figure 2-25

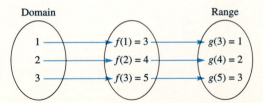

REMARK Under the function $g \circ f$ in Example 2-20(b), the image of every element in the domain is the element itself, that is, $(g \circ f)(1) = 1$, $(g \circ f)(2) = 2$, and $(g \circ f)(3) = 3$.

identity function Such a function is an **identity function.**

We have seen that a function can be represented in a variety of ways: a table, a function machine, pictures of sets and arrows, a set of ordered pairs, and a graph. Pictures of sets with arrows and function machines are mostly used as pedagogical devices in learning the concept of a function. The most common representations are a table, an equation, and a graph. Depending on the situation, one representation may be more useful than another. For example, if the domain of a function is a large set, a table is not a convenient representation. An equation is a compact way to represent a function, but if one is given a graph of a function, it is not always possible to find an equation that represents the function. In later chapters, we learn how to graph certain kinds of equations. Graphing calculators are capable of graphing most functions given by equations with specified domains.

TECHNOLOGY CORNER

A graphing calculator sketch of the function $y = 2x + 1$ for x between 0 and 5 is shown in Figure 2-26. Use a graphing calculator to sketch the graphs of $y = 2x + b$ for three different choices of b. What do the graphs seem to have in common? Why?

Figure 2-26

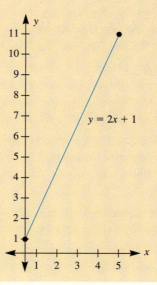

Ongoing Assessment 2-3

1. The following sets of ordered pairs are functions. Give a rule that describes each function.
   a. $\{(2, 4), (3, 6), (9, 18), (12, 24)\}$
   b. $\{(5, 3), (7, 5), (11, 9), (14, 12)\}$
   c. $\{(2, 8), (5, 11), (7, 13), (4, 10)\}$
   d. $\{(2, 5), (3, 10), (4, 17), (5, 26)\}$

2. Which of the following are functions from the set $\{1, 2, 3\}$ to the set $\{a, b, c, d\}$? If the set of ordered pairs is not a function, explain why not.

   a. $\{(1, a), (2, b), (3, c), (1, d)\}$ b. $\{(1, c), (3, d)\}$
   c. $\{(1, a), (2, b), (3, a)\}$ d. $\{(1, a), (1, b), (1, c)\}$

3. a. Draw a diagram of a function with domain $\{1, 2, 3, 4, 5\}$ and range $\{a, b\}$.
   b. How many possible functions are there in part (a)?
4. Suppose $f(x) = 2x + 1$ and the domain is $\{0, 1, 2, 3, 4\}$. Describe the function in the following ways:
   a. Draw an arrow diagram involving two sets.
   b. Use ordered pairs.
   c. Make a table.
   d. Draw a graph to depict the function.
5. Determine which of the following are functions from $W = \{0, 1, 2, 3, \ldots\}$ to W. If your answer is that it is not a function, explain why not.
   a. $f(x) = 2$, for all $x \in W$
   b. $f(x) = 0$ if $x \in \{0, 1, 2, 3\}$, and $f(x) = 3$ if $x \notin \{0, 1, 2, 3\}$
   c. $f(x) = x$
   d. $f(x) = 0$ for all $x \in W$ and $f(x) = 1$ if $x \in \{3, 4, 5, 6, \ldots\}$
   e. $f(x)$ is the sum of the digits in x and $x \in W$.
6. a. Write a rule for computing the cost of mailing a first-class letter based on its weight.
   b. Find the cost of mailing a 3-oz letter.
7. The dosage of a certain drug is related to the weight of a child as follows: 50 mg of the drug and an additional 15 mg for each 2 lb or fraction of 2 lb of body weight above 30 lb. Sketch the graph of the dosage as a function of the weight of a child for children weighing between 20 and 40 lb.
8. According to wildlife experts, the rate at which crickets chirp is a function of the temperature; that is, $C = T - 40$, where C is the number of chirps every 15 sec and T is the temperature in degrees Fahrenheit.
   a. How many chirps does the cricket make per second if the temperature is 70°F?
   b. What is the temperature if the cricket chirps 40 times in 1 min?
9. If taxi fares are $3.50 for the first half mile and $0.75 for each additional quarter mile, answer the following:
   a. What is the fare for a 2-mi trip?
   b. Write a rule for computing the fare for an n-mile trip by taxi.
10. For each of the following, guess Latifah's rule. In each case, if n is your input and $L(n)$ is Latifah's answer, express $L(n)$ in terms of n.

a.

You	Latifah
3	8
4	11
5	14
10	29

b.

You	Latifah
0	1
3	10
5	26
8	65

c.

You	Latifah
6	42
0	0
8	72
2	6

11. The following graph shows arithmetic achievement-test scores for students of a sixth-grade class. From the graph, estimate the following:
   a. The frequency of the score made most often
   b. The highest score obtained
   c. The number of boys who would have to score 54 on the test in order to match the number of girls scoring 54

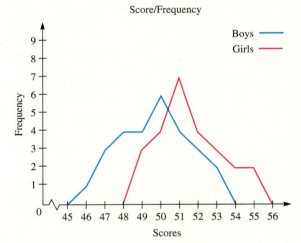

Score/Frequency

12. Find a rule for each of the following sequences, whose domains are the natural numbers:
   a. $3, 8, 13, 18, 23, \ldots$
   b. $3, 9, 27, 81, 243, \ldots$
   c. $2, 4, 6, 8, 10, \ldots$
13. Consider two function machines that are placed as shown. Find the final output for each of the following inputs:
   a. 0   **b.** 3   **c.** 10

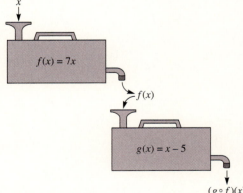

14. Let $t(n)$ represent the nth term of a sequence for $n \in N$. Answer the following:
   a. If $t(n) = 4n - 3$, which of the following are values of the function whose domain is N?
      (i) 1   (ii) 385   (iii) 389   (iv) 392
   b. If $t(n) = n^2$, which of the following are values of the function whose domain is N?
      (i) 1   (ii) 4   (iii) 9   (iv) 10   (v) 900

c. If $t(n) = n(n + 1)$ which are in the range of the function whose domain is N?
   (i) 2   (ii) 12
   (iii) 2550   (iv) 2600

15. Consider a function machine that accepts inputs as ordered pairs. Suppose the components of the ordered pairs are natural numbers and the first component is the length of the rectangle and the second is its width. The following machine computes the perimeter (the distance around a figure) of the rectangle. Thus for a rectangle whose length, l, is 3 and whose width, w, is 2, the input is (3, 2) and the output is $2 \cdot 3 + 2 \cdot 2$, or 10. Answer each of the following:
   a. For each of the following inputs, find the corresponding output: (1, 7), (2, 6), (6, 2), (5, 5).
   b. Find the set of all the inputs for which the output is 20.
   c. What is the domain and the range of the function?

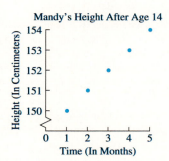

16. The following graph shows Mandy's height in centimeters measured every month starting 1 month after her fourteenth birthday. Answer the following:
   a. What was the change in Mandy's height from the first to the second month after her birthday?
   b. During which consecutive months was the change in Mandy's height the greatest?
   c. What missing information would enable you to find Mandy's change in height 1 month after her birthday?

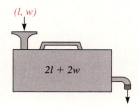

17. The following graph shows the relationship between the number of cars on a certain road at different times between 5 A.M. and 9 A.M.
   a. What was the increase in the number of cars on the road between 6:30 A.M. and 7:00 A.M.?
   b. During which half hour was the increase in the number of cars the greatest?

c. What was the increase in the number of cars between 8 A.M. and 8:30 A.M.?
d. During which half hour(s) did the number of cars decrease? By how much?

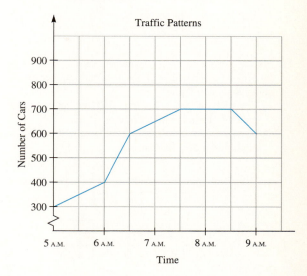

18. A health club charges a one-time initiation fee of $100 plus a membership fee of $40 per month.
   a. Write an expression for the cost function $C(x)$ that gives the total cost for membership at the health club for x months.
   b. Draw the graph of the function in (a).
   c. The health club decided to give its members an option of a higher initiation fee but a lower monthly membership charge. If the initiation fee is $300 and the monthly membership fee is $30, use a different color and draw on the same set of axes the cost graph under this plan.
   d. Determine from the graphs after how many months the second plan is less expensive for the member.

19. A particle is thrown straight up. We know its height H in feet after t seconds is given by the function $H(t) = 128t - 16t^2$.
   a. Find $H(2)$, $H(6)$, $H(3)$, and $H(5)$. Why are some of the outputs equal?
   b. Graph the function and from the graph find at what instant the ball is at its highest point. What is its height at that instant?
   c. How long will it take the particle to hit the ground?
   d. What is the domain of H?
   e. What is the range of H?

20. A rectangular plot is to be bounded on one side by a straight river and on the opposite side by a fence. Suppose 900 yd of fence are available and the length of the side of the rectangle parallel to the river is denoted by x.
   a. Find an expression for the area $A(x)$ in terms of x.
   b. Graph $A(x)$.

c. Use the graph in (b) or your calculator to estimate the length and width of the rectangle for which the area will be the largest.

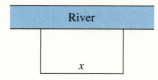

21. For each of the following sequences of matchstick figures, let $S(n)$ be the function giving the total number of matchsticks in the nth figure.
  a. For each of the following, find the total number of matchsticks in the first 4 figures.
  b. For each of the following, find as simple a formula as possible for $S(n)$ in terms of n.

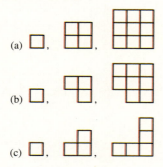

22. A function can be represented as a set of ordered pairs where the set of all the first components is the domain and the set of all the second components is the range. Is the converse also true? That is, is every set of ordered pairs a function whose domain is the set of first components and whose range is the second components? Justify your answer.

23. Suppose each point in the figure represents a child on a playground, the letters represent their names, and an arrow going from I to J means that I "is the sister of" J.

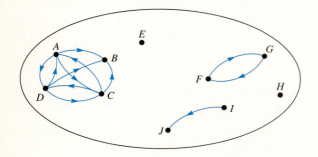

  a. Based on the information in the figure, who are definitely girls and who are definitely boys?
  b. Suppose we write "A is the sister of B" as an ordered pair (A, B). Based on the information in the diagram, write the set of all such ordered pairs.

c. Is the set of all ordered pairs in (b) a function with domain equal to the set of all first components of the ordered pairs and with range the set of all second components?

24. A generalization of the concept of a function is the concept of a **relation.** Given two sets A and B, a relation from A to B is any set of ordered pairs in which the first components are from A and the second are from B. Which of the following are functions and which are relations but not functions from the set of first components of the ordered pairs to the set of second components?
  a. {(Montana, Helena), (Oregon, Salem), (Illinois, Springfield), (Arkansas, Little Rock)}
  b. {(Pennsylvania, Philadelphia), (New York, New York), (New York, Niagara Falls), (Florida, Ft. Lauderdale)}
  c. {$(x, y) \mid x$ resides in Birmingham, Alabama, and x is the mother of y, where y is a U.S. resident}
  d. {(1, 1), (2, 4), (3, 9), (4, 16)}
  e. {$(x, y) \mid$ where x and y are natural numbers and $x + y$ is an even number}

25. a. Is the rule "has as mother" a function whose domain is the set of all people?
  b. Is the relation "has as brother" a function from the set of all boys to the set of all boys?

The following definitions are needed to answer problems 26 and 27.

A **relation on a set X.** This is any set of ordered pairs in which the first and second components are from X. A relation on X may have one or more of the following properties:

The Reflexive Property. A relation on a set X is reflexive if, and only if, for all a in X, a is related to a, that is (a, a) is in the set of ordered pairs.

The Symmetric Property. A relation on a set X is symmetric if, and only if, for all elements a and b in X, whenever a is related to b, then b is also related to a; that is, if (a, b) is in the set of ordered pairs, so is (b, a).

The Transitive Property. A relation on a set X is transitive if, and only if, for all elements a and b in X, whenever a is related to b and b is related to c, then a is related to c; that is, if (a, b) and (b, c) are in the set of ordered pairs, then (a, c) is also in the same set (a, b, and c do not have to be different).

An **equivalence relation** on a set X is any relation on X that satisfies the reflexive, symmetric, and transitive properties.

26. Tell whether each of the following is reflexive, symmetric, or transitive on the set of all people. Which are equivalence relations?
  a. "Is a parent of"
  b. "Is the same age as"
  c. "Has the same last name as"
  d. "Is the same height as"
  e. "Is married to"

f. "Lives within 10 mi of"

g. "Is older than"

27. Tell whether each of the following is reflexive, symmetric, or transitive on the set of subsets of a nonempty set. Which are equivalence relations?

a. "Is equal to"   **b.** "Is a proper subset of"

c. "Is not equal to"   **d.** "Has the same cardinal number as"

Communication

28. Does the diagram define a function from A to B? Why or why not?

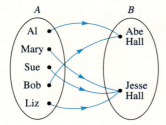

29. Is a one-to-one correspondence a function? Explain your answer and give an example.

30. Which of the following are functions from A to B. If your answer is "not a function," explain why not.

a. A is the set of mathematics faculty at the University. B is the set of all mathematics classes. To each mathematics faculty member, we associate the class that that person is teaching during a given term.

b. A is the set of mathematics classes at the University B is the set of mathematics faculty. To each mathematics class, we associate the teacher who is teaching the class.

c. A is the set of all U.S. senators and B is the set of all Senate committees. We associate each senator to the committee of which the senator is chairperson.

31. When a boat is put in the water, its hull is partially above and partially below the water. The part below the water is the "draft" and the part above the water is the "freeboard." The following table shows the relationship between the draft and freeboard for a 50-cm-deep boat:

Draft	Freeboard
5	45
10	40
15	35
20	30
30	20

a. Graph the freeboard as a function of the draft. Is it meaningful to connect the points graphed? Explain.

b. If d stands for the draft in centimeters and $f(d)$ for the freeboard, write an equation expressing $f(d)$ in terms of d.

Open-ended

32. Examine several newspapers and magazines and describe at least three examples of functions that appear. What is the domain and range of each function?

33. Give at least three examples of functions from A to B where neither A nor B are sets of numbers.

34. Draw a sequence of figures of matchsticks and describe the pattern in words. Find as simple an expression as possible for $S(n)$, the total number of matchsticks in the nth figure.

35. A function whose output is always the same regardless of the input is a **constant function.** Give several examples of constant functions from real life.

36. A function whose output is the same as its input is an **identity function.** Give several concrete examples of identity functions.

Cooperative Learning

37. Each person in a group picks a natural number and uses it as an input in the following function machine:

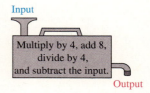

a. Compare your answers. Based on the answers, make a conjecture about the range of the function.

b. Based on your answer in (a), graph the function.

c. Write the function in the simplest possible way using $f(x)$ notation.

d. Justify your conjecture in (a).

e. Make up similar function machines and try different inputs in your group.

f. Devise a function machine in which the machine performs several operations, but the output is always the same as the input. Exchange your answer with someone in the group and check that the other person's function machine performs as required.

g. Write the functions the group came up with in the simplest way using $f(x)$ notation and graph them.

38. In the following two-person (or two-group) activity, one person presents the graphs of several arithmetic and several geometric sequences. The second person is required to find what kind of sequence corresponds to each graph and the simplest possible expression for $T(n)$, the nth term of the sequence. Compare your expressions for $T(n)$ and make a conjecture on how to tell from the graph if a sequence is arithmetic.

Review Problems

39. Determine whether the following sets are equivalent. Justify your answers.
  a. {2, 4, 6, 8, . . . , 1000} and {3, 6, 9, 12, 15, . . . , 1500}
  b. {1, 4, 7, 10, 13, . . . , 3001} and {1, 2, 3, 4, . . . , 1000}
  c. {0, 1, 2, 3, 4, . . .} and {1, 2, 3, 4, 5, . . .}
  d. $S = \{x \mid x = 2n, n \in N\}$ and $W = \{x \mid x = 4n, n \in N\}$

40. Decide which of the following are always true. If true, justify the statement and if false, provide a counterexample.
  a. $A - (B \cup C) = (A - B) \cap (A - C)$
  b. If $A \cup B = B$, then $A \subseteq B$.
  c. If $A \cap B = \varnothing$, then $\overline{A} \cup \overline{B} = U$.
  d. If $A \not\subseteq B$ and $B \not\subseteq C$, then $A \not\subseteq C$.

41. a. How many different one-to-one correspondences are possible between $A = \{a, b, c\}$ and $B = \{1, 2, 3\}$?
  b. How many elements are there in $A \times B$?

42. Classify each of the following as true or false. If true, justify the statement, and if false, provide a counterexample.
  a. If $A \cup B = A \cup C$, then $B = C$.
  b. If $A \cap B = A \cap C$, then $B = C$.
  c. If $A \cap B = \varnothing$ and $B \cap C = \varnothing$, then $A \cap C = \varnothing$.

  d. If $A \times \varnothing = B \times \varnothing$, then $A = B$.
  e. $\varnothing \times \varnothing = \varnothing$

43. A committee of senators has 6 members. A two-thirds vote is needed to carry any proposal. How many winning coalitions are there?

44. Oakridge has a population of 4800 and only one movie theater. One week the movie *The Lion King* was shown, and 3100 people went to see it. Next week, the movie *Apollo 13* was shown, and 2200 residents went to see it.
  a. What is the greatest number of town people that could have seen both movies? Justify your answer.
  b. What is the least number of people that could have seen both movies? Justify your answer.

45. Suppose U is the set of natural numbers {1, 2, 3, 4, . . .}. Write each of the following using set-builder notation:
  a. The set of even numbers greater than 12
  b. The set of numbers less than 14

46. If $U = \{a, b, c, d\}$, $A = \{a, b, c\}$, $B = \{b, c\}$, and $C = \{d\}$, find each of the following:
  a. $A \cup \overline{B}$ **b.** $\overline{A \cap B}$
  c. $A \cap \varnothing$ **d.** $B \cap C$
  e. $B - A$

BRAIN TEASER   Only 10 rooms were vacant in the Village Hotel. Eleven men went into the hotel at the same time, each wanting a separate room. The clerk, settling the argument, said, "I'll tell you what I'll do. I'll put two men in Room 1 with the understanding that I will come back and get one of them a few minutes later." The men agreed to this. The clerk continued, "I will put the rest of you men in rooms as follows: the third man in Room 2, the fourth man in Room 3, the fifth man in Room 4, the sixth man in Room 5, the seventh man in Room 6, the eighth man in Room 7, the ninth man in Room 8, and the tenth man in Room 9." Then the clerk went back and got the extra man he had left in Room 1 and put him in Room 10. Everybody was happy. What is wrong with this plan?

---

*Section 2-4   # Logic: An Introduction

statement   Logic is a tool used in mathematical thinking and problem solving. In logic, a **statement** *is a sentence that is either true or false, but not both.*

The following expressions are not statements because their truth values cannot be determined without more information.

  1. She has blue eyes.
  2. $x + 7 = 18$
  3. $2y + 7 > 1$
  4. $2 + 3$

Expressions (**1.**), (**2.**), and (**3.**) become statements if, for (**1.**), "she" is identified, and for (**2.**) and (**3.**), values are assigned to x and y, respectively. However, an expression involving he or she or x or y may already be a statement. For example, "If he is over 210 cm tall, then he is over 2 m tall," and "$2(x + y) = 2x + 2y$" are both statements because they are true no matter who he is or what the numerical values of x and y are.

negation

From a given statement, it is possible to create a new statement by forming a **negation.** The negation of a statement is a statement with the opposite truth value of the given statement. If a statement is true, its negation is false, and if a statement is false, its negation is true. Consider the statement "It is snowing." The negation of this statement may be stated simply as "It is not snowing."

• • •

Example 2-21

Negate each of the following statements:

a. $2 + 3 = 5$
b. A hexagon has 6 sides.
c. Today is not Monday.

Solution

a. $2 + 3 \neq 5$
b. A hexagon does not have 6 sides.
c. Today is Monday.

• • •

The statements "The shirt is blue" and "The shirt is green" are not negations of each other. A statement and its negation must have opposite truth values. If the shirt is actually red, then both of the above statements are false and, hence, cannot be negations of each other. However, the statements "The shirt is blue" and "The shirt is not blue" are negations of each other because they have opposite truth values no matter what color the shirt really is.

quantifiers

Some statements involve **quantifiers** and are more complicated to negate. Quantifiers include words such as *all, some, every,* and *there exists.*

• The quantifiers *all, every,* and *no* refer to each and every element in a set.
• The quantifiers *some* and *there exists at least one* refer to one or more, or possibly all, of the elements in a set.
• "All," "every," and "for each" are used synonymously. Similarly "some" and "there exists at least one" have the same meaning.

Consider the following statement involving the existential quantifier *some.* "Some professors at Paxson University have blue eyes." This means that at least one professor at Paxson University has blue eyes. It does not rule out the possibilities that all the Paxson professors have blue eyes or that some of the Paxson professors do not have blue eyes. Because the negation of a true statement is false, neither "Some professors at Paxson University do not have blue eyes" nor "All professors at Paxson have blue eyes" are negations of the original statement. One possible negation of the original statement is "No professors at Paxson University have blue eyes."

To discover if one statement is a negation of another, we use arguments similar to the preceding one to determine if they have opposite truth values in all possible cases.

General forms of qualified statements with their negations follow:

Statement	Negation
Some *a* are *b*.	No *a* is *b*.
Some *a* are not *b*.	All *a* are *b*.
All *a* are *b*.	Some *a* are not *b*.
No *a* is *b*.	Some *a* are *b*.

• • •

Example 2-22   Negate each of the following statements:

   a. All students like hamburgers.
   b. Some people like mathematics.
   c. There exists a counting number x such that $3x = 6$.
   d. For all counting numbers, $3x = 3x$.

Solution   **a.** Some students do not like hamburgers.
   b. No people like mathematics.
   c. For all counting numbers x, $3x \neq 6$.
   d. There exists a counting number x such that $3x \neq 3x$.

• • •

There is a symbolic system defined to help in the study of logic. If p represents a statement, the negation of the statement p is denoted by $\sim p$. **Truth tables** are often used to show all possible true-false patterns for statements. Table 2-6 summarizes the truth tables for p and $\sim p$.

truth table

Table 2-6

Statement p	Negation $\sim p$
T	F
F	T

Observe that p and $\sim p$ are analogous to sets P and $\overline{P}$. If x is an element of P, then x is not an element of $\overline{P}$.

Compound Statements

compound statement

From two given statements, it is possible to create a new, **compound statement** by using a connective such as *and*. For example, "It is snowing" and "The ski run is open" together with *and* give "It is snowing and the ski run is open." Other compound statements can be obtained by using the connective *or*. For example, "It is snowing or the ski run is open."

The symbols $\wedge$ and $\vee$ are used to represent the connectives *and* and *or*, respectively. For example, if p represents "It is snowing" and q represents "The ski run is open," then "It is snowing and the ski run is open" is denoted by $p \wedge q$. Similarly, "It is snowing or the ski run is open" is denoted by $p \vee q$.

The truth value of any compound statement, such as $p \wedge q$, is defined using the truth table of each of the simple statements. Because each of the statements p and q may be either true or false, there are four distinct possibilities for the truth of $p \wedge q$, as shown in Table 2-7. The compound statement $p \wedge q$ is the **conjunction** of p and q and is defined to be true if, and only if, both p and q are true. Otherwise, it is false.

conjunction

We can find similarities between conjunction and set intersection. Consider Table 2-8, which shows all possibilities of whether an element is a member of sets, P, Q, and $P \cap Q$. If we consider $\in$ analogous to T and $\notin$ analogous to F, we see that Tables 2-7 and 2-8 are equivalent. The language involving set intersection and the language involving *and* in logic are equivalent. Thus for every property involving set intersection, there should be an equivalent property involving *and*.

Table 2-7

p	q	Conjunction $p \wedge q$
T	T	T
T	F	F
F	T	F
F	F	F

Table 2-8

P	Q	$P \cap Q$
$\in$	$\in$	$\in$
$\in$	$\notin$	$\notin$
$\notin$	$\in$	$\notin$
$\notin$	$\notin$	$\notin$

disjunction   The compound statement $p \vee q$—that is, *p or q*—is a **disjunction.** In everyday language, *or* is not always interpreted in the same way. In logic, we use an *inclusive or*. The statement "I will go to a movie or I will read a book" means I will either go to a movie, or read a book, or do both. Hence, in logic, *p or q*, symbolized as $p \vee q$, is defined to be false if both *p* and *q* are false and true in all other cases. This is summarized in Table 2-9.

Like the analogy between *and* $\wedge$ and *intersection* $\cap$, we have a similar analogy between *or* $\vee$ and *union* $\cup$. Recall that $x \in P \cup Q$ if and only if $x \in P$ or $x \in Q$. As before, if $\in$ is analogous to *true* T and $\notin$ analogous to *false* F, we see that Tables 2-9 and 2-10 are equivalent.

Table 2-9

		Disjunction
p	*q*	$p \vee q$
T	T	T
T	F	T
F	T	T
F	F	F

Table 2-10

P	*Q*	$P \cup Q$
$\in$	$\in$	$\in$
$\in$	$\notin$	$\in$
$\notin$	$\in$	$\in$
$\notin$	$\notin$	$\notin$

• • •

Example 2-23   Given the following statements, classify each of the conjunctions and disjunctions as true or false:

$$p: \quad 2 + 3 = 5 \qquad q: \quad 2 \cdot 3 = 6 \qquad r: \quad 5 + 3 = 9 \qquad s: \quad 2 \cdot 4 = 9$$

a. $p \wedge q$ **b.** $p \wedge r$ **c.** $s \wedge q$ **d.** $r \wedge s$
e. $\sim p \wedge q$ **f.** $\sim(p \wedge q)$ **g.** $p \vee q$ **h.** $p \vee r$
i. $s \vee q$ **j.** $r \vee s$ **k.** $\sim p \vee q$ **l.** $\sim(p \vee q)$

Solution
    a. *p* is true and *q* is true, so $p \wedge q$ is true.
    b. *p* is true and *r* is false, so $p \wedge r$ is false.
    c. *s* is false and *q* is true, so $s \wedge q$ is false.
    d. *r* is false and *s* is false, so $r \wedge s$ is false.
    e. $\sim p$ is false and *q* is true, so $\sim p \wedge q$ is false.
    f. $p \wedge q$ is true [part (a)], so $\sim(p \wedge q)$ is false.
    g. *p* is true and *q* is true, so $p \vee q$ is true.
    h. *p* is true and *r* is false, so $p \vee r$ is true.
    i. *s* is false and *q* is true, so $s \vee q$ is true.
    j. *r* is false and *s* is false, so $r \vee s$ is false.
    k. $\sim p$ is false and *q* is true, so $\sim p \vee q$ is true.
    l. $p \vee q$ is true [part (g)], so $\sim(p \vee q)$ is false.

• • •

Not only are truth tables used to summarize the truth values of compound statements, they also are used to determine if two statements are logically equivalent. Two statements
logically equivalent   are **logically equivalent** if, and only if, they have the same truth values. If *p* and *q* are logically equivalent, we write $p \equiv q$.

I N V E S T I G A T I O N   2 - 1 2

● Recall the distributive property of set intersection over union: $A \cap (B \cup C) = (A \cap B) \cup (A \cap C)$. An analogous property for the statements *a, b,* and *c* is $a \wedge (b \vee c) \equiv (a \wedge b) \vee (a \wedge c)$. List as many prop-erties of set operations as you can, and possibly for each, state a corresponding property of statements. Be sure to include properties of complements of sets. ●

Conditionals and Biconditionals

conditionals • implications

hypothesis

conclusion

Statements expressed in the form "if *p*, then *q*" are called **conditionals,** or **implications,** and are denoted by $p \rightarrow q$. Such statements also can be read "*p* implies *q*." The "if" part of a conditional is called the **hypothesis** of the implication and the "then" part is called the **conclusion.**

Many types of statements can be put in "if-then" form. An example follows:

Statement: All first graders are 6 yr old.
If-then form: If a child is a first grader, then the child is 6 yr old.

An implication may also be thought of as a promise. Suppose Betty makes the promise, "If I get a raise, then I will take you to dinner." If Betty keeps her promise, the implication is true; if Betty breaks her promise, the implication is false. Consider the following four possibilities:

	p	*q*	
(1)	T	T	Betty gets the raise; she takes you to dinner.
(2)	T	F	Betty gets the raise; she does not take you to dinner.
(3)	F	T	Betty does not get the raise; she takes you to dinner.
(4)	F	F	Betty does not get the raise; she does not take you to dinner.

The only case in which Betty breaks her promise is when she gets her raise and fails to take you to dinner, case (2). If she does not get the raise, she can either take you to dinner or not without breaking her promise. The definition of implication is summarized in Table 2-11. Observe that the only case for which the implication is false is when *p* is true and *q* is false.

An implication may be worded in several equivalent ways, as follows:

Table 2-11

p	*q*	Implication $p \rightarrow q$
T	T	T
T	F	F
F	T	T
F	F	T

1. If the sun shines, then the swimming pool is open. (If *p*, then *q*.)
2. If the sun shines, the swimming pool is open. (If *p*, *q*.)
3. The swimming pool is open if the sun shines. (*q* if *p*.)
4. The sun is shining implies the swimming pool is open. (*p* implies *q*.)
5. The sun is shining only if the pool is open. (*p* only if *q*.)
6. The sun's shining is a sufficient condition for the swimming pool to be open. (*p* is a sufficient condition for *q*.)
7. The swimming pool's being open is a necessary condition for the sun to be shining. (*q* is a necessary condition for *p*.)

Any implication $p \rightarrow q$ has three related implication statements, as follows:

Statement:	If p, then q.	$p \rightarrow q$
Converse:	If q, then p.	$q \rightarrow p$
Inverse:	If not p, then not q.	$\sim p \rightarrow \sim q$
Contrapositive:	If not q, then not p.	$\sim q \rightarrow \sim p$

Example 2-24   Write the converse, the inverse, and the contrapositive for each of the following statements:

a. If $x \in A$, then $x \in A \cup B$.
b. If I am in San Francisco, then I am in California.

Solution   **a.** *Converse:*   If $x \in A \cup B$, then $x \in A$.
Inverse: If $x \notin A$, then $x \notin A \cup B$.
Contrapositive: If $x \notin A \cup B$, then $x \notin A$.
b. *Converse:*   If I am in California, then I am in San Francisco.
Inverse: If I am not in San Francisco, then I am not in California.
Contrapositive: If I am not in California, then I am not in San Francisco.

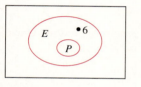

Figure 2-27

Example 2-24 shows that if an implication is true, its converse and inverse are not necessarily true. However, in each part of the example, the contrapositive is true. Let's check these observations on the statement: *If a number is of the form 2^n, where $n \in N$, the number is even.* This statement can be illustrated in a Venn diagram as in Figure 2-27. The set $P = \{x \mid x = 2^n, n \in N\}$ is a proper subset of the set E, the even natural numbers. (Why?) We check the truth of the converse, inverse, and contrapositive of the above statement.

Inverse: *If a number is not of the form 2^n where $n \in N$, then it is not even.* This is false, since 6 is not of the form 2^n, but it is even.

Converse: *If a number is even, then it is of the form 2^n, where $n \in N$.* This is false, since 6 is even but not a power of 2.

Contrapositive: *If a number is not even, then it is not of the form 2^n, where $n \in N$.* This is true, since in Figure 2-27, all numbers not in E are also not in P.

The contrapositive of the last statement is the original statement. Hence the above discussion suggests that if $p \rightarrow q$ is true, its contrapositive $\sim q \rightarrow \sim p$ is also true and if the contrapositive is true, the original statement must be true. It follows that a statement and its contrapositive cannot have opposite truth values. We summarize this in the following property.

Property

Equivalence of a statement and its contrapositive. The implication $p \rightarrow q$ and its contrapositive $\sim q \rightarrow \sim p$ are logically equivalent.

REMARK   The fact that a statement and its contrapositive are logically equivalent can also be established by showing that they have the same truth tables.

Connecting a statement and its converse with the connective *and* gives $(p \rightarrow q) \wedge$

if and only if $(q \rightarrow p)$. This compound statement can be written as $p \leftrightarrow q$ and usually is read **"p if and**
biconditional   **only if q."** The statement "p if and only if q" is a **biconditional.**

Earlier in this section, we discussed analogies between the conjunction $p \wedge q$ and set intersection and between the disjunction $p \vee q$ and set union. Similar analogies exist for implication. Consider the implication "If a flower is a violet, then it is blue." The set of violets is a subset of the set of blue objects. In general, the implication $p \rightarrow q$ is analogous to $P \subseteq Q$. In fact, the definition of $P \subseteq Q$ tells us that $x \in P$ implies $x \in Q$. Thus for every property involving set inclusion, we should have a corresponding property involving implications.

The following are some examples of true and false set properties and analogous properties of statements:

1. If $P \subseteq Q$, then $Q \subseteq P$. (False)
   If $p \rightarrow q$, then $\underline{q \rightarrow p}$. (False)
2. If $P \subseteq Q$, then $\overline{P} \subseteq \overline{Q}$. (False)
   If $p \rightarrow q$, then $\sim p \rightarrow \sim q$. (False)
3. If $P \subseteq Q$, then $\overline{Q} \subseteq \overline{P}$. (True)
   If $p \rightarrow q$, then $\sim q \rightarrow \sim p$. (True)

Valid Reasoning

valid reasoning   In problem solving, the reasoning used is said to be **valid** if the conclusion follows unavoidably from the hypotheses. Consider the following example:

Hypotheses: All roses are red.
              This flower is a rose.
Conclusion: Therefore this flower is red.

The statement "All roses are red" can be written as the implication "If a flower is a rose, then it is red" and pictured with the Venn diagram in Figure 2-28.

Figure 2-28

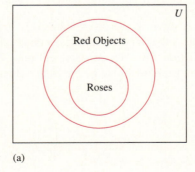
(a)

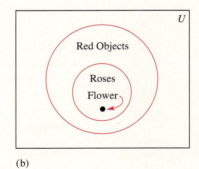
(b)

The information "This flower is a rose" implies that this flower must belong to the circle containing roses, as pictured in Figure 2-28(b). This flower also must belong to the circle containing red objects. Thus the reasoning is valid because it is impossible to draw a picture satisfying the hypotheses and contradicting the conclusion.

Consider the following argument:

Hypotheses: All elementary school teachers are mathematically literate.
               Some mathematically literate people are not children.
Conclusion: Therefore no elementary school teacher is a child.

Let *E* be the set of elementary school teachers, *M* be the set of mathematically literate people, and *C* be the set of children. Then the statement "All elementary school teachers are mathematically literate" can be pictured as in Figure 2-29(a). The statement "Some mathematically literate people are not children" can be pictured in several ways. Three of these are illustrated in Figure 2-29(b)–(d).

According to Figure 2-29(d), it is possible that some elementary school teachers are children, and yet the given statements are satisfied. Therefore the conclusion that "No elementary school teacher is a child" does not follow from the given hypotheses. Hence, the reasoning is not valid.

Figure 2-29

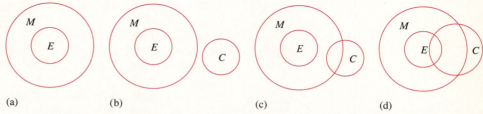

(a)   (b)   (c)   (d)

If only one picture can be drawn to satisfy the hypotheses of an argument and contradict the conclusion, the argument is not valid. However, to show that an argument is valid, *all* possible pictures must be considered to show that there are no contradictions. There must be no way to satisfy the hypotheses and contradict the conclusion if the argument is valid.

• • •

Example 2-25   Determine if the following argument is valid:

Hypotheses: In Washington, D.C., all lobbyists wear suits.
               No one in Washington, D.C., over 6 ft tall wears a suit.
Conclusion: Persons over 6 ft tall are not lobbyists in Washington, D.C.

Solution: If *L* represents the set of lobbyists and *P* the set of people who wear suits, the first hypothesis is pictured as shown in Figure 2-30(a). If *T* represents the set of people in Washington, D.C., over 6 ft tall, the second hypothesis is pictured in Figure 2-30(b). Because people over 6 ft tall are outside the circle representing suit wearers and lobbyists are in the circle *P*, the conclusion is valid and no person over 6 ft tall is a lobbyist in Washington, D.C.

Figure 2-30

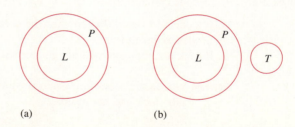

(a)   (b)

• • •

direct reasoning

Law of Detachment/
Modus Ponens

A different method for determining if an argument is valid uses **direct reasoning** and a form of argument called the **Law of Detachment** (or **Modus Ponens**). For example, consider the following true statements:

> If the sun is shining, then we shall take a trip.
> The sun is shining.

Using these two statements, we can conclude that we shall take a trip. In general, the Law of Detachment is stated as follows:

If the statement "if p, then q" is true, and p is true, then q must be true.

• • •

Example 2-26

Determine if each of the following arguments is valid:

a. Hypotheses: If you eat spinach, then you will be strong.
                You eat spinach.
    Conclusion: Therefore you will be strong.
b. Hypotheses: If Claude goes skiing, he will break the leg.
                If Claude breaks his leg, he cannot enter the dance contest.
                Claude goes skiing.
    Conclusion: Therefore Claude cannot enter the dance contest.

Solution
a. Using the Law of Detachment, we see that the conclusion is valid.
b. By using the Law of Detachment twice, we see that the conclusion is valid.

• • •

indirect reasoning

Modus Tollens

A different type of reasoning, **indirect reasoning,** uses a form of argument called **Modus Tollens.** For example, consider the following true statements:

> If Chicken Little had been hit by a jumping frog, he would have thought the earth was rising.
> Chicken Little did not think the earth was rising.

What is the conclusion? The conclusion is that Chicken Little did not get hit by a jumping frog. This leads us to the general form of Modus Tollens:

If we have a conditional accepted as true, and we know the conclusion is false, then the hypothesis must be false.

• • •

Example 2-27

Determine conclusions for each of the following true statements:

a. If a person lives in Boston, then the person lives in Massachusetts. Jessica does not live in Massachusetts.
b. If Jack is nimble, he will not get burned. Jack was burned.

Solution
a. Jessica does not live in Boston.
b. Jack was not nimble.

• • •

Chain Rule The final reasoning argument to be considered here involves the **Chain Rule.** Consider the following statements:

If I save, I will retire early.
If I retire early, I will become lazy.

What is the conclusion? The conclusion is that if I save, I will become lazy. In general, the Chain Rule can be stated as follows:

If "if p, then q" and "if q, then r" are true, then "if p, then r" is true.

Notice that the Chain Rule shows that implication has the transitive property.

People often make invalid conclusions based on advertising or other information. Consider, for example, the statement "Healthy people eat Super-Bran cereal." Are the following conclusions valid?

If a person eats Super-Bran cereal, then the person is healthy.
If a person is not healthy, the person does not eat Super-Bran cereal.

If the original statement is denoted by $p \rightarrow q$, where p is "a person is healthy" and q is "a person eats Super-Bran cereal," then the first conclusion is the converse of $p \rightarrow q$, that is, $q \rightarrow p$, and the second conclusion is the inverse if $p \rightarrow q$, that is, $\sim p \rightarrow \sim q$.

Example 2-28 Determine conclusions for each of the following sets of true statements:

a. If Alice follows the White Rabbit, she falls into a hole. If she falls into a hole, she goes to a tea party.
b. If Chicken Little is hit by an acorn, we think the sky is falling. If we think the sky is falling, we will go to the basement. If we go to the basement, we will stay there a month.

Solution **a.** If Alice follows the White Rabbit, she goes to a tea party.
b. If Chicken Little is hit by an acorn, we will stay in the basement for a month.

REMARK   Note that in Example 2-28(b), the Chain Rule can be extended to contain several implications.

Ongoing Assessment 2-4

1. Determine which of the following are statements and then classify each statement as true or false:
a. $2 + 4 = 8$ **b.** Shut the window.
c. Los Angeles is a state.   **d.** He is in town.
e. What time is it?   **f.** $5x = 15$
g. $3 \cdot 2 = 6$ **h.** $2x^2 > x$
i. This statement is false.   **j.** Stay put!

2. Use quantifiers to make each of the following true, where x is a natural number:
a. $x + 8 = 11$ **b.** $x + 0 = x$
c. $x^2 = 4$ **d.** $x + 1 = x + 2$
e. $x + 3 = 3 + x$ **f.** $3(x + 2) = 12$
g. $5x + 4x = 9x$.

3. Use quantifiers to make each equation in Problem 2 false.

4. Write the negation for each of the following statements:
  a. The book has 500 pages.
  b. Six is less than 8.
  c. $3 \cdot 5 = 15$
  d. Some people have blond hair.
  e. All dogs have 4 legs.
  f. Some cats do not have 9 lives.
  g. All squares are rectangles.
  h. Not all rectangles are squares.

5. Complete each of the following truth tables:

  a.

p	$\sim p$	$\sim(\sim p)$
T		
F		

  b.

p	$\sim p$	$p \vee \sim p$	$p \wedge \sim p$
T			
F			

  c. Based on part (a), is p logically equivalent to $\sim(\sim p)$?
  d. Based on part (b), is $p \vee \sim p$ logically equivalent to $p \wedge \sim p$?

6. If q stands for "This course is easy" and r stands for "Lazy students do not study," write each of the following in symbolic form:
  a. This course is easy, and lazy students do not study.
  b. Lazy students do not study, or this course is not easy.
  c. It is false that both this course is easy and lazy students do not study.
  d. This course is not easy.

7. If p is false and q is true, find the truth values for each of the following:
  a. $p \wedge q$ **b.** $p \vee q$
  c. $\sim p$ **d.** $\sim q$
  e. $\sim(\sim p)$ **f.** $\sim p \vee q$
  g. $p \wedge \sim q$ **h.** $\sim(p \vee q)$
  i. $\sim(\sim p \wedge q)$ **j.** $\sim q \wedge \sim p$

8. Find the truth value for each statement in Problem 7 if p is false and q is false.

9. For each of the following, is the pair of statements logically equivalent?
  a. $\sim(p \vee q)$ and $\sim p \vee \sim q$
  b. $\sim(p \vee q)$ and $\sim p \wedge \sim q$
  c. $\sim(p \wedge q)$ and $\sim p \wedge \sim q$
  d. $\sim(p \wedge q)$ and $\sim p \vee \sim q$

10. Complete the following truth table:

p	q	$\sim p$	$\sim q$	$\sim p \vee q$
T	T			
T	F			
F	T			
F	F			

11. Restate the following in a logically equivalent form:
  a. It is not true that both today is Wednesday and the month is June.
  b. It is not true that yesterday I both ate breakfast and watched television.
  c. It is not raining, or it is not July.

12. Write each of the following in symbolic form if p is the statement "It is raining" and q is the statement "The grass is wet."
  a. If it is raining, then the grass is wet.
  b. If it is not raining, then the grass is wet.
  c. If it is raining, then the grass is not wet.
  d. The grass is wet if it is raining.
  e. The grass is not wet implies that is not raining.
  f. The grass is wet if, and only if, it is raining.

13. For each of the following implications, state the converse, inverse, and contrapositive:
  a. If you eat Meaties, then you are good in sports.
  b. If you do not like this book, then you do not like mathematics.
  c. If you do not use Ultra Brush toothpaste, then you have cavities.
  d. If you are good at logic, then your grades are high.

14. Iris makes the true statement, "If it rains, then I am going to the movies." Does it follow logically that if it does not rain, then Iris does not go to the movies?

15. Consider the statement "If every digit of a number is 6, then the number is divisible by 3." Which of the following is logically equivalent to the statement?
  a. If every digit of a number is not 6, then the number is not divisible by 3.
  b. If a number is not divisible by 3, then some digit of the number is not 6.
  c. If a number is divisible by 3, then every digit of the number is 6.

16. Write a statement logically equivalent to the statement "If a number is a multiple of 8, then it is a multiple of 4."

17. Investigate the validity of each of the following arguments:
  a. All women are mortal.
     Hypatia was a woman.
     Therefore Hypatia was mortal.
  b. All squares are quadrilaterals.
     All quadrilaterals are polygons.
     Therefore all squares are polygons.
  c. All teachers are intelligent.
     Some teachers are rich.
     Therefore some intelligent people are rich.
  d. If a student is a freshman, then the student takes mathematics.
     Jane is a sophomore.
     Therefore Jane does not take mathematics.

18. For each of the following, form a conclusion that follows logically from the given statements:
    a. All college students are poor.
       Helen is a college student.
    b. Some freshmen like mathematics.
       All people who like mathematics are intelligent.
    c. If I study for the final, then I will pass the final.
       If I pass the final, then I will pass the course.
       If I pass the course, then I will look for a teaching job.
    d. Every equilateral triangle is isosceles.
       There exist triangles that are isosceles.

19. Write the following in if-then form:
    a. Every figure that is a square is a rectangle.
    b. All integers are rational numbers.
    c. Figures with exactly 3 sides may be triangles.
    d. It rains only if it is cloudy.

Communication

20. a. Write two logical equivalences discovered in problem 9(a)–(d). These equivalences are called DeMorgan's laws for *and* and *or*.
    b. Write an explanation of the analogy between DeMorgan's laws for sets and those found in part (a).

21. Translate each of the following statements into symbolic form. Give the meanings of the symbols that you use.
    a. If Mary's little lamb follows her to school, then its appearance there will break the rules and Mary will be sent home.
    b. If it is not the case that Jack is nimble and quick, then Jack will not make it over the candlestick.
    c. If the apple had not hit Isaac Newton on the head, then the laws of gravity would not have been discovered.

22. Determine the validity of the following conclusions. Explain your reasoning.
    a. If you study hard, you will get at least a B in this course.
       If you get at least a B in this course, you will graduate.
       Therefore if you study hard, you will graduate.
    b. All teachers are college graduates. Therefore if a person did not graduate from college, the person is not a teacher.
    c. All ducks have feathers. No mammals are ducks. Therefore no mammals have feathers.

23. Write a valid conclusion based on the following statements. Explain why the conclusion is valid.
    a. We go shopping if and only if I get a bonus. I got a bonus.
    b. All rectangles are parallelograms. This figure is not a parallelogram.
    c. If the day is sunny, we go hiking. If it is freezing, we don't go hiking.

Open-ended

24. Give two examples from mathematics for each of the following:
    a. A statement and its converse are true.
    b. A statement is true, but its converse is false.
    c. An "if and only if" true statement.
    d. An "if and only if" false statement.

Cooperative Learning

25. Each person in a group makes 5 statements similar to the ones in Examples 2-25 through 2-28 but concerning mathematical objects, each with a valid or invalid conclusion. The statements should be as varied as possible. Each group member exchanges his or her statements with another person—not revealing which are valid and which are not—and determines which of the other person's statements are valid and which are not. The two group members compare their answers and discuss any discrepancies.

26. Discuss the paradox arising from the following:
    a. This textbook is 1000 pages long.
    b. The author of this textbook is Dante.
    c. The statements (a), (b), and (c) are all false.

SOLUTION TO THE PRELIMINARY PROBLEM

Understanding the Problem.   A reporter interviewed 15 seniors and reported that 10 are taking mathematics and physics, 5 are taking physics and chemistry, 7 are taking chemistry and mathematics, and 3 are taking all three subjects. We are to determine whether the reported information is correct.

Devising a Plan.   We use the strategy of *drawing a picture,* with each group of students taking a particular subject as a circle as in Figure 2-31. The Venn diagram in Figure 2-31(a), shown on page 102 determines 8 distinct regions: *A, B, C, D, E, F,* and *G,* as well as *H,* the region outside the 3 circles. We are trying to find the number of students in each region and to check whether the sum of the numbers adds up to the total number of seniors the reporter claimed to interview, that is, 15.

Figure 2-31

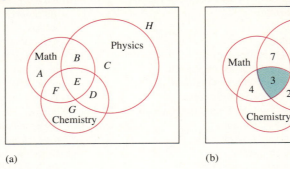

(a)   (b)

Carrying Out the Plan.   The fact that 3 students are taking all 3 subjects is indicated inside the region *E* in Figure 2-31(b). Because 10 students are taking mathematics and physics and 3 are taking all 3 subjects, the number of students taking mathematics and physics but not chemistry is 10 − 3, or 7, and is indicated inside the region *B* in Figure 2-31(a). Similarly, the number of students taking physics and chemistry but not math is 5 − 3, or 2, and the number taking mathematics and chemistry but not physics is 7 − 3, or 4. Because all seniors interviewed were taking one of the 3 subjects, the number of students outside the union of the 3 circles is 0. We have no information to enable us to find the number of students in other regions. However, the total number of students in the 4 regions *B, D, E,* and *F* is 7 + 2 + 4 + 3, or 16, which is impossible because the total number of students is only 15. Consequently the editor was right in claiming the report was incorrect.

Looking Back.   The problem can be altered by changing the numbers, giving more information, or even giving superfluous or contradictory information. For example, if the number of students taking physics and chemistry was 4 instead of 5, the total in the 4 regions would add up to 15. This would imply that no students took just 1 subject at the exclusion of the other 2. In such a case, if the reporter stated that some students took just mathematics but not physics or chemistry, the reporter would have been wrong. Similar problems can be devised using 4 subjects. What would be the maximum number of distinct regions then?

QUESTIONS FROM THE CLASSROOM

1. A student argues that {∅} is the proper notation for the empty set. What is your response?

2. A student asks, "If $A = \{a, b, c\}$ and $B = \{b, c, d\}$, why isn't it true that $A \cup B = \{a, b, c, b, c, d\}$?" What is your response?

3. A student says that she can show that if $A \cap B = A \cap C$, then it is not necessarily true that $B = C$; but she thinks that whenever $A \cap B = A \cap C$ and $A \cup B = A \cup C$, then $B = C$. What is your response?

4. A student claims that a finite set of numbers is any set that has a greatest element. Do you agree?

5. A student claims that the complement bar can be broken over the operation of intersections; that is, $\overline{A \cap B} = \overline{A} \cap \overline{B}$. What is your response?

6. A student claims that $\overline{A} \cap \overline{B}$ includes all elements that are not in *A*. What is your response?

7. A student asks whether a formula and a function are the same. What is your response?

8. A student states that either $A \subseteq B$ or $B \subseteq A$. Is the student correct?

9. A student is asked to find all one-to-one correspondences between 2 given sets. He finds the Cartesian product of the

sets and claims that his answer is correct because it includes all possible pairings between the elements of the sets. How do you respond?

10. A student argues that adding 2 sets A and B, or $A + B$, and taking the union of 2 sets, $A \cup B$, is the same thing. How do you respond?

11. A student asks whether a function from A to B is related to the cross product $A \times B$. How do you respond?

12. A student claims that the following machine does not represent a function machine because it accepts 2 inputs at once rather than a single input. How do you respond?

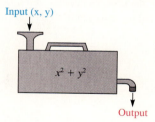

Input (x, y)

$x^2 + y^2$

Output

CHAPTER OUTLINE

I. Set definitions and notation
  A. A **set** can be described as any collection of objects.
  B. Sets should be **well defined** so that an object either does or does not belong to the set.
  C. An **element** is any **member** of a set.
  D. Sets can be specified by either listing all the elements or using **set-builder notation.**
  E. The **empty set,** written $\varnothing$, contains no elements.
  F. The **universal set** contains all the elements being discussed.

II. Relationships and operations on sets
  A. Two sets are **equal** if, and only if, they have exactly the same elements.
  B. Two sets A and B are in **one-to-one correspondence** if, and only if, each element of A can be paired with exactly one element of B and each element of B can be paired with exactly 1 element of A.
  C. Two sets A and B are **equivalent** if, and only if, their elements can be placed into one-to-one correspondence (written $A \sim B$).
  D. Set A is a **subset** of set B if, and only if, every element of A is an element of B (written $A \subseteq B$).
  E. Set A is a **proper subset** of set B if, and only if, every element of A is an element of B and there is at least one element of B that is not in A (written $A \subset B$).
  F. The **union** of two sets A and B is the set of all elements in A, in B, or in both A and B (written $A \cup B$).
  G. The **intersection** of two sets A and B is the set of all elements belonging to both A and B (written $A \cap B$).
  H. The **cardinal number** of a finite set S, $n(S)$ indicates the number of elements in the set.
  I. A set is **finite** if the number of elements in the set is zero or a natural number. Otherwise, the set is **infinite.**
  J. Two sets A and B are **disjoint** if they have no elements in common.
  K. The **complement** of a set A is the set consisting of the elements of the universal set not in A (written $\overline{A}$).

  L. The **complement of set A relative to set B** (set difference) is the set of all elements in B that are not in A (written $B - A$).
  M. The **Cartesian product** of sets A and B written $A \times B$ is the set of all ordered pairs such that the first element in each pair is from A and the second element of each pair is from B.

III. Functions
  A. A **function** from set A to B is a correspondence in which each element $a \in A$ is paired with one, and only one, element $b \in B$. If the function is denoted by f, we write $f(a) = b$. The element $a \in A$ is the input, and $f(a)$ is the output. A is the **domain** of the function. B is any set containing all the outputs. The set of all the outputs is the **range** of the function.
  B. A function can be represented by a table, an equation, a function machine, a set of ordered pairs, or a graph.

*IV. Logic
  A. A **statement** is a sentence that is either true or false but not both.
  B. The **negation** of a statement is a statement with the opposite truth value of the given statement. The negation of p is denoted by $\sim p$.
  C. The **compound statement** $p \wedge q$ is called the **conjunction** of p and q and is defined to be true if, and only if, both p and q are true.
  D. The compound statement $p \vee q$ is called the **disjunction** of p and q and is true if either p or q or both are true.
  E. Statements of the form "if p, then q" are called **conditionals** or **implications** and are false only if p is true and q is false.
  F. Given the conditional $p \rightarrow q$, the following can be found:
    1. Converse: $q \rightarrow p$
    2. Inverse: $\sim p \rightarrow \sim q$
    3. Contrapositive: $\sim q \rightarrow \sim p$

G. If $p \rightarrow q$ is true, the converse and the inverse are not necessarily true, but the contrapositive is true.

H. Two statements are **logically equivalent** if, and only if, they have the same truth value. An implication and its contrapositive are logically equivalent.

I. The statement "$p \rightarrow q$ and $q \rightarrow p$" is written $p \leftrightarrow q$ and referred to as "p if and only if q."

J. Laws to determine the validity of arguments include the **Law of Detachment, Modus Tollens,** and the **Chain Rule.**

CHAPTER 2 REVIEW

1. Write the set of letters of the Greek alphabet using set-builder notation.

2. List all the subsets of $\{m, a, t, h\}$.

3. Let

$U = \{x \mid x$ is a person living in Montana$\}$,
$A = \{x \mid x$ is a person 30 yr or older$\}$,
$B = \{x \mid x$ is a person less than 30 yr old$\}$, and
$C = \{x \mid x$ is a person who owns a pickup truck$\}$.

Describe in words a member of each of the following sets:

a. $\overline{A}$　　**b.** $A \cap C$　　**c.** $A \cup B$
d. $\overline{C}$　　**e.** $\overline{A \cap C}$　　**f.** $A - C$

4. Let

$U = \{u, n, i, v, e, r, s, a, l\}$,
$A = \{r, a, v, e\}$,　　$C = \{l, i, n, e\}$, and
$B = \{a, r, e\}$,　　$D = \{s, a, l, e\}$.

Find each of the following:

a. $A \cup B$　　　　　　**b.** $C \cap D$
c. $\overline{D}$　　　　　　**d.** $A \cap \overline{D}$
e. $\overline{B} \cup C$　　　　　**f.** $(B \cup C) \cap D$
g. $(\overline{A} \cup B) \cap (C \cap \overline{D})$　**h.** $(C \cap D) \cap A$
i. $n(\overline{C})$　　　　　**j.** $n(C \times D)$

5. Indicate the following sets by shading the figure:

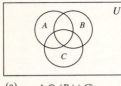
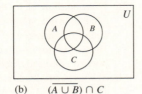

(a)　$A \cap (B \cup C)$　　　(b)　$\overline{(A \cup B)} \cap C$

6. Suppose you are playing a word game with seven letters. How many possible seven-letter words can there be?

7. a. Show one possible one-to-one correspondence between sets D and E if $D = \{t, h, e\}$ and $E = \{e, n, d\}$.
　　b. How many different one-to-one correspondences between sets D and E are possible?

8. Use a Venn diagram to determine whether $A \cap (B \cup C) = (A \cap B) \cup C$ for all sets A, B, and C.

9. Describe, using symbols, the shaded portion in each of the following figures:

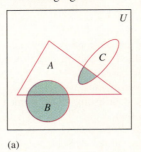

(a)　　　　　　　　　　(b)

10. Classify each of the following as true or false. If false, tell why.

a. For all sets A and B, either $A \subseteq B$ or $B \subseteq A$.
b. The empty set is a proper subset of every set.
c. For all sets A and B, if $A \sim B$, then $A = B$.
d. The set $\{5, 10, 15, 20, \ldots\}$ is a finite set.
e. No set is equivalent to a proper subset of itself.
f. If A is an infinite set and $B \subseteq A$, then B also is an infinite set.
g. For all finite sets A and B, if $A \cap B \neq \varnothing$, then $n(A \cup B) \neq n(A) + n(B)$.
h. If A and B are sets such that $A \cap B = \varnothing$, then $A = \varnothing$ or $B = \varnothing$.

11. Suppose P and Q are equivalent sets and $n(P) = 17$.
a. What is the minimum number of elements in $P \cup Q$?
b. What is the maximum number of elements in $P \cup Q$?
c. What is the minimum number of elements in $P \cap Q$?
d. What is the maximum number of elements in $P \cap Q$?

12. Case Eastern Junior College awarded 26 varsity letters in crew, 15 in swimming, and 16 in soccer. If awards went to 46 students and only 2 lettered in all sports, how many students lettered in two of the 3 sports?

13. Consider the set of northwestern states or provinces {Montana, Washington, Idaho, Oregon, Alaska, British Columbia, Alberta}. If a person chooses one element, show that in three yes or no questions, we can determine the element.

14. According to a student survey, 16 students liked history, 19 liked English, 18 liked mathematics, 8 like mathematics and English, 5 liked history and English, 7 liked history and mathematics, 3 liked all three subjects, and every student liked at least one of the subjects. Draw a Venn diagram describing this information and answer the following questions:

  a. How many students were in the survey?
  b. How many students liked only mathematics?
  c. How many students liked English and mathematics but not history?

15. Which of the following sets of ordered pairs are functions from the set of first components to the set of second components?

  a. $\{(a, b), (c, d), (e, a), (f, g)\}$
  b. $\{(a, b), (a, c), (b, b), (b, c)\}$
  c. $\{(a, b), (b, a)\}$

16. Consider the set of post offices, P, in the United States and the set of ZIP codes, Z, in the United States.

  a. Describe a function from P to Z.
  b. The first digit of a ZIP code divides the country into 10 sets of states. Each state is divided into an average of 10 smaller geographical areas, identified by the second and third digits of the code. The fourth and fifth digits identify a local delivery area. If I have the ZIP code 59801, describe a series of set operations the U.S. Postal Service might use to determine exactly where I live.

17. Given the following function rules and the domains, find the associated ranges:

  a. $f(x) = x + 3$ domain = $\{0, 1, 2, 3\}$
  b. $f(x) = 3x - 1$ domain = $\{5, 10, 15, 20\}$
  c. $f(x) = x^2$ domain = $\{0, 1, 2, 3, 4\}$
  d. $f(x) = x^2 + 3x + 5$ domain = $\{0, 1, 2\}$

18. Which of the following correspondences from A to B describe a function? If a correspondence is a function, find its range. Justify your answers.

  a. A is the set of college students, and B is the set of majors. To each college student corresponds his or her major.
  b. A is the set of books in the library, and B is the set N of natural numbers. To each book corresponds the number of pages in the book.
  c. $A = \{(a, b) \mid a \in N \text{ and } b \in N\}$, and $B = N$. To each element of A corresponds the number $4a + 2b$.
  d. $A = N$ and $B = N$. If x is even, then $f(x) = 0$ and if x is odd, then $f(x) = 1$.
  e. $A = N$ and $B = N$. To each natural number corresponds the sum of its digits.

19. A health club charges an initiation fee of $200 plus 1 mo of free membership and then $55 per month.

  a. If $C(x)$ is the total cost of membership in the club for x months, express $C(x)$ in terms of x.
  b. Graph $C(x)$ for the first 12 mo.
  c. Use the graph in (b) to find when the total cost of membership in the club will exceed $600.
  d. When will the total cost of membership exceed $6000?

20. Which of the following are statements?

  a. The moon is inhabited.
  b. $3 + 5 = 8$
  c. $x + 7 = 15$
  d. Some women have Ph.Ds in mathematics.

21. Negate each of the following:

  a. Some women smoke.
  b. $3 + 5 = 8$
  c. All heavy-metal rock is loud.
  d. Beethoven wrote only classical music.

22. Write the converse, inverse, and contrapositive of the following: If we have a rock concert, someone will faint.

23. Find valid conclusions for the following arguments:

  a. All Americans love Mom and apple pie.
  Joe Czernyu is an American.
  b. Steel eventually rusts.
  The Statue of Liberty has a steel structure.
  c. Albertina will pass Math 100 or be a dropout.
  Albertina is not a dropout.

24. Write the following argument symbolically and then determine its validity:

  If you are fair-skinned, you will sunburn.
  If you sunburn, you will not go to the dance.
  If you do not go to the dance, your parents will want to know why you didn't go to the dance.
  Your parents do not want to know why you didn't go to the dance.
  Therefore you are not fair-skinned.

SELECTED BIBLIOGRAPHY

Crouse, R. and A. Alison. "Tips for Beginners: The Human Coordinate System." *Mathematics Teacher* 84 (February 1991): 108–109.

Greenwood, J. "Name That Graph." *Mathematics Teacher* 88 (January 1995): 8–11.

Johnston, A. "Introducing Function and Its Notation." *Mathematics Teacher* 80 (October 1987): 558–560.

McGinty, R. and J. Van Beynen. "Deductive and Analytical Thinking." *Mathematics Teacher* 78 (March 1985): 188–194.

Mercer, J. "Teaching Graphing Concepts with Graphing Calculators." *Mathematics Teacher* 88 (April 1995): 268–273.

O'Daffer, P. "Inductive and Deductive Reasoning." *Mathematics Teacher* 83 (May 1990): 378–384.

O'Regan, P. "Intuition and Logic." *Mathematics Teacher* 81 (November 1988): 664–668.

Sanders, W. and R. Antes. "Teaching Logic with Logic Boxes." *Mathematics Teacher* 81 (November 1988): 643–647.

Schloemer, C. "Tips for Teaching Cartesian Graphing: Linking Concepts and Procedures." *Teaching Children Mathematics* (September 1994): 20–23.

Spence, L. "How Many Elements Are in a Union of Sets?" *Mathematics Teacher* 80 (November 1987): 666–670, 681.

3

NUMERATION SYSTEMS FOR THE AGES

In one week of tennis camp with 20 people in the mixed-doubles class, Gina was paired with seven male partners, Maria with eight, Tina with nine, and so on until Marva was paired with every male partner. How many males were there in the mixed-doubles class?

I n this chapter, you will need to develop number sense and operation sense for the set of whole numbers {0, 1, 2, 3, 4, 5, ...}. Having prospective teachers develop number sense and operations sense is in line with the *Teaching Standards* (p. 136): *Teachers of mathematics should have a well-defined number sense (including mental mathematics, estimation, and reasonableness of results) and an understanding of the use of number concepts, operations, and properties (including basic number theory), of the role of algorithms, and of place value.*

Hindu-Arabic system

Most number systems are based on the set of whole numbers. However, the symbols for those numbers vary from system to system. The **Hindu-Arabic system** of numbers in common use today relies on ten basic symbols: 0, 1, 2, 3, 4, 5, 6, 7, 8, and 9. These symbols represent single-digit numbers and are the cardinal numbers of all sets equivalent to those shown in Table 3-1.

Table 3-1

Symbol for Cardinal Number of Set	Set
0	$\varnothing$
1	{a}
2	{a, b}
3	{a, b, c}
4	{a, b, c, d}
5	{a, b, c, d, e}
6	{a, b, c, d, e, f}
7	{a, b, c, d, e, f, g}
8	{a, b, c, d, e, f, g, h}
9	{a, b, c, d, e, f, g, h, i}

Many people use the Hindu-Arabic system and take operations such as addition, subtraction, multiplication, and division for granted. As teachers, you will encounter students facing this mathematical number system for the first time. The Hindu-Arabic system is a very sophisticated system developed over a long period of time. It will be compared to other systems in this chapter. By comparing the Hindu-Arabic system with ancient systems using other bases, you may have a clearer picture of why we compute with whole numbers as we do.

Numeration Systems

In the Hindu-Arabic system, the symbols for single digits are also used to form other symbols, or **numerals,** to represent greater numbers. To represent numbers greater than 9, the Hindu-Arabic system relies on the following for development of the numerals.

numerals

1. All numerals are constructed from the ten basic digits.
2. Place value is based on repeated groupings of 10, the number base of the system.

place value

Because the Hindu-Arabic system is based on powers of 10, the system is sometimes called a base-ten, or a decimal, system. **Place value** is the concept that allows the value of a symbol to depend on its placement in a number. To find the value of a digit in a whole

face value

number, we multiply the place value of the digit times its **face value,** where the face value is a cardinal number, as shown in Table 3-1. For example, in the numeral 5984, the 5 has place value "thousands," the 9 has place value "hundreds," the 8 has place value "tens," and the 4 has place value "units," as seen in Figure 3-1. We could write 5984 in expanded form

expanded form

as $5 \cdot 1000 + 9 \cdot 100 + 8 \cdot 10 + 4 \cdot 1$, or $5 \cdot 10^3 + 9 \cdot 10^2 + 8 \cdot 10 + 4 \cdot 1$. The **expanded form** of a number represents the sum of the products of the face value of a digit times the place value of that digit. In the expanded form of 5984, exponents are frequently used. For exam-

factor

ple, 1000, or $10 \cdot 10 \cdot 10$, is written as 10^3. In this case, 10 is a **factor** of the product. The notion of exponents can be generalized in the following definition.

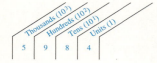

Figure 3-1

Definition of a^n

If a is any number and n is any natural number, then a^n is defined by the following equation:

$$a^n = \underbrace{a \cdot a \cdot a \cdots \cdot a}_{n \text{ factors}}.$$

Numbers have been recorded in many ways over the ages. The Babylonians used wedge-shaped marks pressed in wet clay. The Egyptians used papyrus and ink-filled brushes and based their system on tally marks. The Mayans introduced a symbol for zero. Perhaps the spook in the following cartoon felt that the college grad's new symbols were very sophisticated for that era. Table 3-2 shows some other ways that numbers have been recorded.

THE WIZARD OF ID   **Brant parker and Johnny hart**

YOU ◎✳✦!! COLLEGE GRADS THINK YOU'RE SO DANGED SMART!

©1992 by North America Syndicate, Inc. World rights reserved.

Table 3-2

Babylonian		▼	▼▼	▼▼▼	▼▼▼▼	▼▼▼ ▼▼	▼▼▼ ▼▼▼	▼▼▼▼ ▼▼▼	▼▼▼▼ ▼▼▼▼	▼▼▼▼▼ ▼▼▼▼	◁
Egyptian		I	II	III	IIII	III II	III III	IIII III	IIII IIII	III III III	∩
Mayan	👁	•	••	•••	••••	—	•̲	••̲	•••̲	••••̲	═
Greek		α	β	γ	δ	∈	φ	ζ	η	θ	ι
Roman		I	II	III	IV	V	VI	VII	VIII	IX	X
Hindu	0	I	7	3	8	4	6	ʌ	8	9	
Arabic	•	1	۲	۳	٤	۵	٦	۷	۸	۹	
Hindu-Arabic	0	1	2	3	4	5	6	7	8	9	10

Egyptian Numeration System

The Egyptian numeration system, which dates back to about 3400 B.C., used *tally marks.* Tally marks are scratches or marks like those in the cartoon that represent the items being counted. In a *tally numeration system,* there is a one-to-one correspondence between the marks and the items being counted. The first nine numerals in the Egyptian system in Table 3-2 show the use of tally marks. The Egyptians improved on the system based only on tally marks by developing a *grouping system* to represent certain sets of numbers. This makes the numbers easier to record. For example, the Egyptians used a heel bone symbol, ∩, to stand for a grouping of ten tally marks.

$$||||||||| \rightarrow \cap$$

Table 3-3 shows other numerals that the Egyptians used in their system.

Table 3-3

Egyptian Numeral	Description	Hindu-Arabic Equivalent
I	Vertical staff	1
∩	Heel bone	10
9	Scroll	100
⌡	Lotus flower	1,000
⌐	Pointing finger	10,000
⌒	Polliwog or burbot	100,000
⚱	Astonished man	1,000,000

additive property   The Egyptian system involved an **additive property;** that is, the value of a number was the sum of the face values of the numerals. The Egyptians customarily wrote the numerals in decreasing order from left to right. An example follows:

⌒	represents	100,000	
999	represents	300	$(100 + 100 + 100)$
∩∩	represents	20	$(10 + 10)$
II	represents	2	$(1 + 1)$
⌒999∩∩II	represents	100,322	

Babylonian Numeration System

The Babylonian numeration system was developed at about the same time as the Egyptian system. The symbols shown in Table 3-4 were made using a stylus either vertically or horizontally.

Table 3-4

Babylonian Numeral	Hindu-Arabic Equivalent
▼	1
<	10

The Babylonian numerals 1 through 59 were similar to the Egyptian numerals, but the staff and the heel bone were replaced by the symbols shown in Table 3-4. For example, ＜＜ ▼▼ represented 22.

Numbers greater than 59 were represented by repeated groupings of 60, much as we use groupings of 10 today. For example ▼▼ ＜＜ might represent $2 \cdot 60 + 20$, or 140. The space indicates that ▼▼ represents $2 \cdot 60$ rather than 2. The Babylonians chose to work with 60 because it can be evenly divided by many numbers. This simplifies division and operations with fractions.

The initial Babylonian system contained inadequacies. For example, the symbol ▼▼ could have represented 2 or $2 \cdot 60$ because the Babylonian system lacked a symbol for zero until after 300 B.C.

Numerals to the left of a second space have a value $60 \cdot 60$ times their face value, and so on.

＜＜ ▼	represents	$20 \cdot 60 + 1$, or 1201
＜▼ ＜▼ ▼	represents	$11 \cdot 60 \cdot 60 + 11 \cdot 60 + 1$, or $11 \cdot 60^2 + 11 \cdot 60 + 1$, or 40,261
▼ ＜▼ ＜▼ ▼	represents	$1 \cdot 60 \cdot 60 \cdot 60 + 11 \cdot 60 \cdot 60 + 11 \cdot 60 + 1$, or $1 \cdot 60^3 + 11 \cdot 60^2 + 11 \cdot 60 + 1$, or 256,261

Mayan and Chinese Numeration Systems

In numeration history, people frequently used parts of their bodies to count. Fingers could be matched to objects to stand for one, two, three, four, or five objects. Two hands could then stand for a set of ten objects. In warmer climates where people went barefoot, people may have used their toes as well as their fingers for counting.

R. Hemmings, in *Curriculum Opportunities in a Multi-Cultural Society,* identified an ancient Chinese culture that used parts of the fingers in a complicated counting system, as shown in Figure 3-2.

Figure 3-2

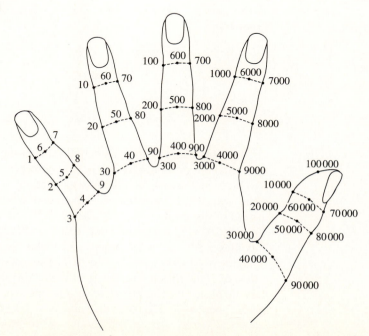

I N V E S T I G A T I O N   3 - 1

● In the Chinese counting system pictured in Figure 3-2, how are the parts of the fingers used to show place value? ●

The Mayans introduced a new attribute that was not present in the Egyptian or early Babylonian systems, namely, a symbol for zero. The Mayan system used only three symbols, which Table 3-5 shows.

Table 3-5

Mayan Numeral	Hindu-Arabic Equivalent
•	1
—	5
👁	0

The symbols for the first ten numerals are shown in Table 3-2. Notice the groupings of five, where each horizontal bar represents a group of five. Thus the symbol for 19 was ▬, or 3 fives and 4 ones. The symbol for 20 was 👁, which represents 1 group of twenty plus 0 ones. The Mayans wrote numbers vertically with the greatest value on top. In Figure 3-3(a), we have $2 \cdot 5 + 3 \cdot 1$, or 13 groups of twenty plus $2 \cdot 5 + 1 \cdot 1$, or 11 ones, for a total of 271. In Figure 3-3(b), we have $3 \cdot 5 + 1 \cdot 1$, or 16, groups of twenty and 0 ones, for a total of 320.

Figure 3-3

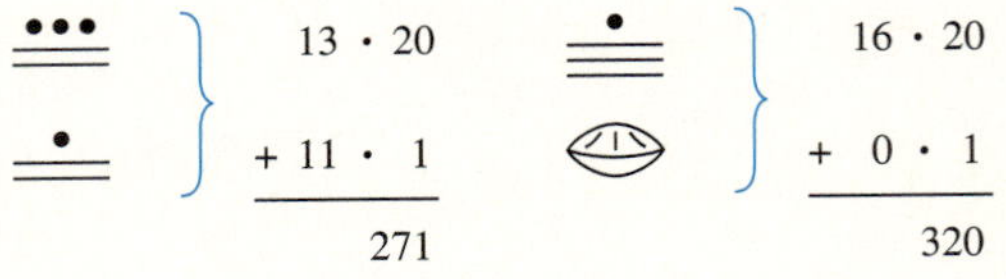

$$13 \cdot 20$$
$$+ 11 \cdot 1$$
$$271$$

$$16 \cdot 20$$
$$+ 0 \cdot 1$$
$$320$$

(a)   (b)

In a true base-twenty system, the value of the symbols in the third position vertically from the bottom should be 20^2, or 400. However, it is conjectured that the Mayans used $20 \cdot 18$, or 360, instead of 400. (The number 360 is an approximation of the length of a calendar year, which consisted of 18 months of 20 days each, plus 5 "unlucky" days.) Thus, instead of place values of 1, 20, 20^2, 20^3, 20^4, and so on, the Mayans used 1, 20, $20 \cdot 18$, $20^2 \cdot 18$, $20^3 \cdot 18$, and so on. For example, in Figure 3-4(a), we have $5 + 1$ (or 6) groups of 360, plus $5 + 5 + 2$ (or 12) groups of 20, plus $5 + 4$ (or 9) groups of 1, for a total of 2409. In Figure 3-4(b), we have $2 \cdot 5$ (or 10) groups of 360, plus 0 groups of 20, plus 2 ones, for a total of 3602. Spacing is important in the Mayan system. For example, if two horizontal bars are placed close together, as in ▬, the symbols represent $5 + 5 = 10$. If the bars are spaced apart, as in ▬, then the value is $5 \cdot 20 + 5 \cdot 1 = 105$.

Figure 3-4

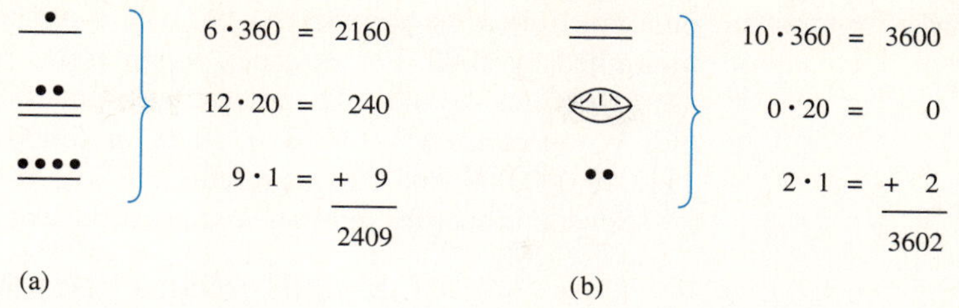

$$6 \cdot 360 = 2160$$
$$12 \cdot 20 = 240$$
$$9 \cdot 1 = + \ 9$$
$$\overline{2409}$$

(a)

$$10 \cdot 360 = 3600$$
$$0 \cdot 20 = 0$$
$$2 \cdot 1 = + \ 2$$
$$\overline{3602}$$

(b)

Roman Numeration System

The Roman numeration system remains in use today, as seen on cornerstones, on the opening pages of books, and on the faces of clocks. The basic Roman numerals are pictured in Table 3-6.

Table 3-6

Roman Numeral	Hindu-Arabic Equivalent
I	1
V	5
X	10
L	50
C	100
D	500
M	1000

Roman numerals can be combined by using an additive property. For example, MDCLXVI represents $1000 + 500 + 100 + 50 + 10 + 5 + 1 = 1666$, CCCXXVIII represents 328, and VI represents 6.

subtractive property   To avoid repeating a symbol more than three times, as in IIII, a **subtractive property** was introduced in the Middle Ages. For example, I is less than V, so if it is to the left of V, it is subtracted. Thus IV has a value of $5 - 1$, or 4, and XC represents $100 - 10$, or 90.

Some extensions of the subtractive property could lead to ambiguous results. For example, IXC could be 91 or 89. By custom, 91 is written XCI and 89 is written LXXXIX. In general, only one smaller number symbol can be to the left of a larger number symbol, and the pair must be one of those listed in Table 3-7.

Table 3-7

Roman Numeral	Hindu-Arabic Equivalent
IV	$5 - 1$, or 4
IX	$10 - 1$, or 9
XL	$50 - 10$, or 40
XC	$100 - 10$, or 90
CD	$500 - 100$, or 400
CM	$1000 - 100$, or 900

multiplicative property

The Romans adopted the use of bars to write large numbers. The use of bars is based on a **multiplicative property.** A bar over a symbol or symbols indicates that the value is multiplied by 1000. For example, $\overline{V}$ represents $5 \cdot 1000$, or 5000, and $\overline{CDX}$ represents $410 \cdot 1000$, or 410,000. To indicate even greater numbers, more bars appear. For example, $\overline{\overline{V}}$ represents $(5 \cdot 1000) \cdot 1000$, or 5,000,000; $\overline{\overline{CXI}}$, represents $111 \cdot 1000^3$, or 111,000,000,000; and $\overline{CXI}$ represents $110 \cdot 1000 + 1$, or 110,001.

Several properties might be used to represent some numbers, for example:

$$\overline{DCLIX} = \underbrace{(500 \cdot 1000)}_{\text{Multiplicative}} + \underbrace{(100 + 50)}_{\text{Additive}} + \underbrace{(10 - 1)}_{\text{Subtractive}} = 500,159.$$

Other Number Bases

The Luo peoples of Kenya used a *quinary,* or base five, system. (This system is described in the Ongoing Assessment 3-1.) A system of this type can be modeled by counting with only one hand. The digits available for counting are 0, 1, 2, 3, and 4.

In the "one-hand system," or base-five system, you count 1, 2, 3, 4, 10, where 10 represents one hand and no fingers. The one-hand system is a base-five system. Counting in base five proceeds as shown in Figure 3-5. We write the small "five" below the numeral as a reminder that the number is written in base five.

Figure 3-5

Base-five Symbol	Base-five Grouping	One-hand System
0_{five}		0 fingers
1_{five}	x	1 finger
2_{five}	xx	2 fingers
3_{five}	xxx	3 fingers
4_{five}	xxxx	4 fingers
10_{five}	(xxxxx)	1 hand and 0 fingers
11_{five}	(xxxxx) x	1 hand and 1 finger
12_{five}	(xxxxx) xx	1 hand and 2 fingers
13_{five}	(xxxxx) xxx	1 hand and 3 fingers
14_{five}	(xxxxx) xxxx	1 hand and 4 fingers
20_{five}	(xxxxx)(xxxxx)	2 hands and 0 fingers
21_{five}	(xxxxx)(xxxxx) x	2 hands and 1 finger

What number follows 44_{five}? There are no more two-digit numbers in the system after 44_{five}. In base ten, the same situation occurs at 99. We use 100 to represent 10 tens, or 1 hundred. In the base-five system, we need a symbol to represent 5 fives. To continue the analogy with base ten, we use 100_{five} to represent 1 group of 5 fives, 0 groups of five, and 0 units. To distinguish from "one hundred" in base ten, the name for 100_{five} is "one-zero-zero base five." The number 100 means $1 \cdot 10^2 + 0 \cdot 10^1 + 0$, whereas the number 100_{five} means $(1 \cdot 10^2 + 0 \cdot 10^1 + 0)_{\text{five}}$, or $(1 \cdot 5^2 + 0 \cdot 5^1 + 0)_{\text{ten}}$ or 25.

Example 3-1 | Convert 11244_{five} to base ten.

Solution $11244_{\text{five}} = 1 \cdot 5^4 + 1 \cdot 5^3 + 2 \cdot 5^2 + 4 \cdot 5 + 4 \cdot 1$

$= 1 \cdot 625 + 1 \cdot 125 + 2 \cdot 25 + 4 \cdot 5 + 4 \cdot 1$

$= 625 + 125 + 50 + 20 + 4$

$= 824$

Example 3-1 suggests a method for changing a base-ten number to a base-five number using powers of five. To convert 824 to base five, we divide by successive powers of five. A shorthand method for illustrating this conversion is in the following:

$$625\overline{)824} \quad 1 \qquad \text{How many groups of 625 in 824?}$$
$$-625$$

$$125\overline{)199} \quad 1 \qquad \text{How many groups of 125 in 199?}$$
$$-125$$

$$25\overline{)74} \quad 2 \qquad \text{How many groups of 25 in 74?}$$
$$-50$$

$$5\overline{)24} \quad 4 \qquad \text{How many groups of 5 in 24?}$$
$$-20$$

$$1\overline{)4} \quad 4 \qquad \text{How many 1s in 4?}$$
$$-4$$
$$0$$

Thus $824 = 11244_{\text{five}}$.

I N V E S T I G A T I O N   3 - 2

● A different method of converting 824 to base five is shown using successive divisions by 5. The quotient in each case is placed below the dividend and the remainder is placed on the right, on the same line with the quotient. The answer is read from bottom to top, that is, as 11244_{five}. Why does it work?

$$
\begin{array}{r|l}
5 & 824 \\
5 & \overline{164} \quad 4 \\
5 & \overline{32} \quad 4 \\
5 & \overline{6} \quad 2 \\
& 1 \quad\ 1
\end{array}
$$

Calculators with the integer division feature — $\boxed{\text{INT}\div}$ on a Texas Instrument calculator or $\boxed{\div R}$ on a Casio — can be used to change base-ten numbers to different number bases. For example, to convert 8 to base five, we enter $\boxed{8}\ \boxed{\text{INT}\div}\ \boxed{5}\ \boxed{=}$ and obtain $\underset{Q}{1}\ \underset{R}{3}$. This implies that $8 = 13_{\text{five}}$.

Historians tell of early tribes that used base two. Some Australian tribes still count "one, two, two and one, two twos, two twos and one, ..." Because base two has only two **binary system** digits, it is called the **binary system.** Base two is especially important because of its use in computers. One of the two digits is represented by the presence of an electrical signal and the other by the absence of an electrical signal. Although base two works well for computers, it is inefficient for everyday use because multidigit numbers are reached very rapidly in counting in this system.

Conversions from base two to base ten, and vice versa, may be accomplished in a manner similar to that used for base-five conversions.

Example 3-2   **a.** Convert 10111_{two} to base ten.
b. Convert 27 to base two.

Solution   **a.** $10111_{two} = 1 \cdot 2^4 + 0 \cdot 2^3 + 1 \cdot 2^2 + 1 \cdot 2^1 + 1$
$$= 16 + 0 + 4 + 2 + 1$$
$$= 23$$

Alternative Solution:

b.

16	27	1	How many groups of 16 in 27?
	− 16		
8	11	1	How many groups of 8 in 11?
	− 8		
4	3	0	How many groups of 4 in 3?
	− 0		
2	3	1	How many groups of 2 in 3?
	− 2		
1	1	1	How many 1s in 1?
	− 1		
	0		

Alternative Solution:

2	27	
2	13	1
2	6	1
2	3	0
	1	1

Thus 27 is equivalent to 11011_{two}.

Another commonly used number base system is the base-twelve, or duodecimal, system, known popularly as the "dozens" system. Eggs are bought by the dozen, and pencils are bought by the *gross* (a dozen dozens). In base twelve, there are twelve digits, just as there are ten digits in base ten, five digits in base five, and two digits in base two. In base twelve, new symbols are needed to represent the following groups of *x*'s:

$$\overbrace{x\,x\,x\,x\,x\,x\,x\,x\,x\,x}^{10\ x\text{'s}} \quad \text{and} \quad \overbrace{x\,x\,x\,x\,x\,x\,x\,x\,x\,x\,x}^{11\ x\text{'s}}$$

The new symbols chosen are *T* and *E*, respectively, so that the base-twelve digits are 0, 1, 2, 3, 4, 5, 6, 7, 8, 9, *T*, and *E*. Thus in base twelve we count "1, 2, 3, 4, 5, 6, 7, 8, 9, *T*, *E*, 10, 11, 12, . . . , 17, 18, 19, 1*T*, 1*E*, 20, 21, 22, . . . , 28, 29, 2*T*, 2*E*, 30, ..."

Example 3-3   **a.** Convert $E2T_{twelve}$ to base ten.   **b.** Convert 1277 to base twelve.

Solution

a. $E2T_{twelve} = 11 \cdot 12^2 + 2 \cdot 12^1 + 10$

$$= 11 \cdot 144 + 24 + 10$$

$$= 1584 + 24 + 10$$

$$= 1618$$

b.

$$144 \overline{\smash{)}1277} \quad 8 \qquad \text{How many groups of 144 in 1277?}$$
$$\underline{-1152}$$
$$12 \overline{\smash{)}125} \quad T \qquad \text{How many groups of 12 in 125}$$
$$\underline{-120}$$
$$1 \overline{\smash{)}5} \quad 5 \qquad \text{How many 1s in 5?}$$
$$\underline{-5}$$
$$0$$

Thus $1277 = 8T5_{\text{twelve}}$.

• • •

• • •

Example 3-4   A clerk in a store used shorthand to write the following:

$$g36_{\text{twelve}} = 1150_{\text{ten}}.$$

What is the value of g?

Solution   If the clerk was writing in base twelve on the left and base ten on the right, then the shorthand could represent the following in expanded form:

$$g \cdot 12^2 + 3 \times 12 + 6 = 1 \times 10^3 + 1 \times 10^2 + 5 \times 10 + 0$$
$$144g + 36 + 6 = 1150$$
$$144g + 42 = 1150$$
$$144g = 1008$$
$$g = 7$$

• • •

Ongoing Assessment 3-1

1. For each of the following, tell which numeral represents the greater number and why:
   a. $\overline{\text{MCDXXIV}}$ and $\overline{\overline{\text{MCDXXIV}}}$
   b. 4632 and 46,032
   c. $<\blacktriangledown\blacktriangledown$ and $<\ \blacktriangledown\blacktriangledown$
   d. $999\cap\cap||$ and $\mathbf{\mathit{g}}\cap|$
   e. ☷ and ☺

2. For each of the following, name both the succeeding and preceding numerals (one more and one less):
   a. MCMXLIX   **b.** $\overline{\text{MI}}$ **c.** CMXCIX
   d. $<<\ <\blacktriangledown$ **e.** $\mathbf{\mathit{g}}99$ **f.** ∴

3. The cornerstone on the building reads MCMXXII. When was this building built?

4. Write each of the following in Roman symbols:
   a. 121   **b.** 42   **c.** 89   **d.** 5282

5. Write each of the following in Egyptian symbols:
   a. 52   **b.** 103   **c.** 100,003   **d.** 38

6. Complete the following table, which compares symbols for numbers in different numeration systems:

	Hindu-Arabic	Babylonian	Egyptian	Roman	Mayan
a.	72				
b.		$<\ \blacktriangledown\blacktriangledown$			
c.			$\mathbf{\mathit{g}}99\cap\cap|||$		

7. For each of the following decimal numerals, give the place value of the underlined numeral:
   a. 827,3<u>6</u>7   **b.** 8,421,0<u>0</u>0
   c. 9<u>7</u>,998   **d.** <u>8</u>10,485

8. Rewrite each of the following as a base-ten numeral:
   a. $3 \cdot 10^6 + 4 \cdot 10^3 + 5$
   b. $2 \cdot 10^4 + 1$
   c. $3 \cdot 10^3 + 5 \cdot 10^2 + 6 \cdot 10$
   d. $9 \cdot 10^6 + 9 \cdot 10 + 9$

9. Study the following counting frame. In the frame, the value of each dot is represented by the number in the box below

the dot. For example, the following figure represents the number 154:

••	•••	••
64	8	1

What numbers are represented in the frames in (a) and (b)?

a.

• ••	••	•
25	5	1

b.

•		•	•
8	4	2	1

10. A certain 3-digit whole number has the following properties: The hundreds digit is greater than 7; the tens digit is an odd number; and the sum of the digits is 10. What is the number?

11. Write the first 15 counting numbers for each of the following bases:
   a. Base two **b.** Base three
   c. Base four **d.** Base eight

12. How many different digits are needed for base twenty?

13. Write 2032_{four} in expanded base-four notation.

14. Determine the greatest three-digit number in each of the following bases:
   a. Base two **b.** Base six
   c. Base ten **d.** Base twelve

15. Find the numbers preceding and succeeding each of the following:
   a. $EE0_{twelve}$ **b.** 100000_{two} **c.** 555_{six}
   d. 100_{seven} **e.** 1000_{five} **f.** 110_{two}

16. What, if anything, is wrong with the following numerals:
   a. 204_{four} **b.** 607_{five} **c.** $T12_{three}$

17. Convert each of the following base-ten numbers to numbers in the indicated bases:
   a. 432 to base five **b.** 1963 to base twelve
   c. 404 to base four **d.** 37 to base two
   e. $4 \cdot 10^4 + 3 \cdot 10^2$ to base twelve

18. Change 42_{eight} to base two.

19. Write each of the following numbers in base ten:
   a. 432_{five} **b.** 101101_{two} **c.** $92E_{twelve}$
   d. $T0E_{twelve}$ **e.** 111_{twelve} **f.** 346_{seven}

20. Suppose you have two quarters, four nickels, and two pennies. What is the value of your money in cents? Write a base-five representation to indicate the value of your fortune.

21. You are asked to distribute $900 in prize money. The dollar amounts for the prizes are $625, $125, $25, $5, and $1. How should this $900 be distributed in order to give the fewest number of prizes?

22. What is the minimum number of quarters, nickels, and pennies necessary to make 97¢?

23. Convert each of the following:
   a. 58 days to weeks and days
   b. 54 mo to years and months

24. **c.** 29 hr to days and hours
   d. 68 in. to feet and inches

24. A bookstore ordered 11 gross, 6 dozen, and 6 pencils. Express the number of pencils in base twelve and in base ten.

25. For each of the following, find *b*:
   a. $b2_{seven} = 44_{ten}$ **b.** $5b2_{twelve} = 734_{ten}$
   c. $23_{ten} = 25_b$

26. **a.** Anna's bank contains only pennies, nickels, and quarters. What is the minimum number of coins she could trade for 117 pennies?
   b. If she trades 2 quarters, 4 nickels, and 3 pennies for pennies, how many pennies will she have?

27. The Chinese abacus, depicted as follows, shows the number 5857:

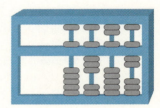

Discuss how the number 5857 is depicted and show how the number 4869 could be depicted.

28. Use the constant feature on a calculator to determine the value of $9 \cdot 9 \cdot 9 \cdot 9 \cdot 9 \cdot 9 \cdot 9$, or 9^7.

29. On a calculator, use only the keys $\boxed{1}$, $\boxed{2}$, $\boxed{3}$, $\boxed{4}$, $\boxed{5}$, $\boxed{6}$, $\boxed{7}$, $\boxed{8}$, and $\boxed{9}$, and fill the calculator's display to show each of the following:
   a. The greatest number possible if each key may be used only once
   b. The least number possible if each key may be used only once
   c. The greatest number possible if a key may be used more than once
   d. The least number possible if a key may be used more than once

30. In a game called WIPEOUT, we are to "wipe out" digits from a calculator's display without changing any of the other digits. "Wipeout" in this case means to replace the chosen digit(s) with a 0. For example, if the initial number is 54,321 and we are to wipe out the 4, we could subtract 4000 to obtain 50,321. Complete the following two problems and then try other numbers or challenge another person to wipe out a number from the number you have placed on the screen:
   a. Wipe out the 2s from 32,420.
   b. Wipe out the 5 from 67,357.

Communication

31. Describe situations where it is feasible to use the Roman numeral system today.

32. Ben claims that zero is the same as nothing. Explain how you as a teacher would respond to Ben's statement.

33. What are the major drawbacks to each of the following systems?
    a. Egyptian   **b.** Babylonian   **c.** Roman
34. Why are large numbers written with commas separating groups of three digits?
35. One reason listed for using base 60 in the Babylonian system is that 60 has a large number of factors. In the decimal system, the base 10 has fewer factors. Discuss advantages and disadvantages of the fewer number of factors.
36. For the last 600 yr, no significant changes have taken place in the Hindu-Arabic system. What suggestions for change might make the system better or easier to use?

Open-ended

37. George Gheverghese Joseph, in *The Crest of the Peacock: Non-European Roots of Mathematics,* London: Penguin Books (1991) (pp. 46–7), wrote that the Aztecs of Mexico developed a vigesimal (base-twenty) number system that used four different symbols. The unit symbol was a "blob" representing a maize seed-pod; the symbol for 20 was a flag, commonly used to mark land boundaries; 400 was represented by a schematic maize plant; and the symbol for 8000 is thought to be a "maize doll," similar to the decorative figures traditionally woven from straw in some European countries. Draw representations of the four basic symbols and depict the following numbers: 80, 100, 200, 300, and 10,000.

38. Claudia Zaslavsky describes in her book, *Africa Counts: Number Pattern in African Culture,* the quinary (base 5) counting system of the Luo peoples of Kenya as follows. The Luo system of finger gestures is a pure quinary one, and easy to describe. Again the symbols *T*, 1, 2, 3, and 4 are used to represent the thumb, forefinger, middle finger, ring finger, and little finger, respectively. The finger signs for the first five numbers are performed on the right hand. Describe how you could depict the numbers 1–19 in the Luo system.

Cooperative Learning

39. **a.** Create a numeration system with unique symbols and write a paragraph explaining the properties of the system.
    b. Complete the following table using the system:

Hindu-Arabic Numeral	Your System Numeral
1	
5	
10	
50	
100	
5,000	
10,000	
115,280	

40. An inspector of weights and measures uses a special set of weights to check the accuracy of scales. Various weights are placed on a scale to check accuracy of any amount from 1 oz through 15 oz. What is the least number of weights the inspector needs? What weights are needed to check the accuracy of scales from 1 oz through 15 oz? From 1 oz through 31 oz?

BRAIN TEASER   There are 3 nickels and 3 dimes concealed inside 3 boxes. Two coins are placed in each of the boxes, which are labeled 10¢, 15¢, and 20¢. The coins are placed in such a way that no box contains the amount of money shown on its label; for example, the box labeled 10¢ does not really have a total of 10¢ in it. What is the minimum number of coins that you would have to remove from a box, and from which box or boxes, to determine which coins are in which boxes?

Section 3-2   ## Addition and Subtraction of Whole Numbers

whole numbers

When zero is joined with the set of natural numbers, $N = \{1, 2, 3, 4, 5, \ldots\}$, we have the set of numbers called **whole numbers,** denoted by $W = \{0, 1, 2, 3, 4, 5, \ldots\}$.

    The K-4 *Standards* (p. 44) addresses the importance of teaching children a variety of ways to compute with whole numbers as well as the usefulness of calculators in solving problems. In addition, the *Teaching Standards* (p. 134) contains the following quote about teacher preparation:

    Central to the preparation for teaching mathematics is the development of a deep under-standing of the mathematics of the school curriculum and how it fits within the discipline

of mathematics. Too often, it is taken for granted that teachers' knowledge of the content of school mathematics is in place by the time they complete their own K–12 learning experiences. Teachers need opportunities to revisit school mathematics topics in ways that will allow them to develop deeper understandings of the subtle ideas and relationships that are involved between and among concepts.

In this section, we provide a variety of models for teaching computational skills and allow students to revisit mathematics at a level necessary to know in order to be a competent teacher.

Addition of Whole Numbers

Addition is a binary operation, a function that assigns an ordered pair of whole numbers to a single number. In the grid in Figure 3-6, each point on the lattice is assigned an ordered pair (a, b), where a is a length along the x-axis and b is a length on the y-axis.

Figure 3-6

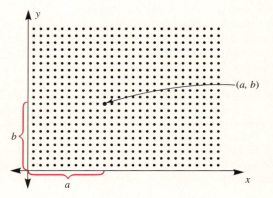

Addition takes each ordered pair in Figure 3-6 and assigns a single number to that pair. For example, in Figure 3-7, $(2, 3)$ is assigned to $2 + 3$, or 5; $(0, 0)$ is assigned to $0 + 0$, or 0; and so on.

Figure 3-7

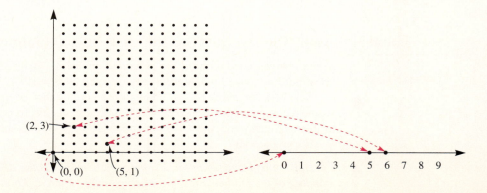

The addition of whole numbers can be modeled in other ways. We present next the set model and the number-line model.

Set Model

Suppose Jane has 4 pencils in one pile and 3 in another. If she combines the two groups of pencils, how many pencils are there in the combined group? Figure 3-8 shows the solution

Figure 3-8

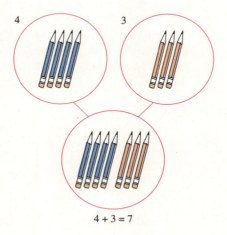

$$4 + 3 = 7$$

as it might appear in an elementary school text. The combined set of pencils is the union of the disjoint sets of 4 pencils and 3 pencils. After the sets have been combined, children count the pencils to determine that there are 7 pencils in all. Note the importance of the sets having no elements in common. If the sets have common elements, then an incorrect conclusion can be drawn.

Definition of Addition of Whole Numbers

Let A and B be two disjoint finite sets. If $n(A) = a$ and $n(B) = b$, then $a + b = n(A \cup B)$.

addends • sum   The numbers a and b in $a + b$ are the **addends** and $(a + b)$ is the **sum.**

I N V E S T I G A T I O N   3 - 3

● If the sets of elements in the preceding definition of addition of whole numbers have common elements, determine why the definition is incorrect. ●

HISTORICAL   NOTE

The symbol "+" first appeared in a 1417 manuscript and was a short way of writing the Latin word *et,* which means "and." However, Johann Widmann wrote a book in 1498 that made use of the + and − symbols for addition and subtraction. The word *minus* means "less" in Latin. First written as an *m,* it was later shortened to a horizontal bar.

Number-line Model

A number line may be used to model whole-number addition. Any line marked with two fundamental points, one representing 0 and the other representing 1, can be turned into a number line. The points representing 0 and 1 mark the ends of a *unit segment.* Other points may be marked and labeled as shown in Figure 3-9. Any two consecutive points in Figure 3-9 mark the ends of a segment that has the same length as the unit segment.

Figure 3-9

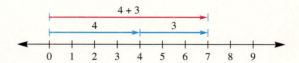

Addition problems can be modeled using directed arrows on the number line. For example, the sum of 4 + 3 is shown in Figure 3-9. Arrows representing the addends, 4 and 3, are combined into one arrow representing the sum. Figure 3-9 poses an inherent problem for students. If an arrow starting at 0 and ending at 3 represents 3, why should an arrow starting at 4 and ending at 7 represent 3? This question is given as an exercise in Ongoing Assessment 3-2.

Greater-than and Less-than Relations

greater than • less than

A number line can also be used to describe **greater-than** and **less-than** relations on the set of whole numbers. For example, in Figure 3-9, notice that 4 is to the left of 7 on the number line. We say, "four is less than seven," and we write $4 < 7$. We can also say "seven is greater than four" and write $7 > 4$. Since 4 is to the left of 7, there is a natural number that can be added to 4 to get 7, namely, 3. Thus $4 < 7$ because $4 + 3 = 7$. We can generalize this discussion to form the following definition of *less than.*

Definition of Less Than

For any whole numbers a and b, a is **less than** b, written $a < b$, if and only if there exists a natural number k such that $a + k = b$.

greater than or equal to •
less than or equal to

Sometimes equality is combined with the inequalities greater than and less than to give the relations **greater than or equal to** and **less than or equal to,** denoted by $\geq$ and $\leq$. The emphasis with respect to these symbols has to be on the *or.* Observe that "$3 < 5$ or $3 = 5$" is a true statement, so $3 \leq 5$ is true. Both $5 \geq 3$ and $3 \geq 3$ are true statements.

Whole-number Addition Properties

Because addition was defined as a binary operation, or a function that assigns an ordered pair to a single number, any time two whole numbers are added, you are guaranteed that a unique whole number will be obtained as an output. This property is sometimes referred to as the *closure property of addition of whole numbers.* We say that "the set of whole number is closed under addition." Figure 3-10(a) shows two additions. Pictured above the number line is $3 + 5$ and below the number line is $5 + 3$. The sums are exactly the same. Figure 3-10(b) shows the same sums obtained with colored rods with the result being the same. Both illustrations in Figure 3-10 demonstrate the idea that two whole numbers can be added in either order. This property is true in general and is the *commutative property of addition of whole numbers.* We say that "addition of whole numbers is commutative."

Figure 3-10

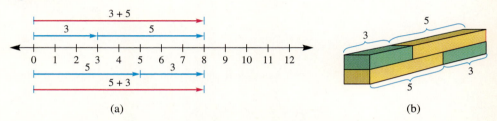

(a)　　　　　　　　　　　　　　　　　　　(b)

Property

Commutative Property of Addition of Whole Numbers　If a and b are any whole numbers, then $a + b = b + a$.

The commutative property of addition of whole numbers is not obvious to many young children. They may be able to find the sum $9 + 2$ and not be able to find the sum $2 + 9$. This is because one of the techniques used to teach addition is *counting on.* Using this technique, $9 + 2$ can be computed by starting at 9 and then counting on two more as "ten" and "eleven." To compute $2 + 9$, the *counting on* is more involved. Students need to understand that $2 + 9$ is another name for $9 + 2$.

Another property of addition is demonstrated when we select the order in which to add three or more numbers. For example, we could compute $24 + 8 + 2$ by grouping the 24 and the 8 together: $(24 + 8) + 2 = 32 + 2 = 34$. (The parentheses indicate that the first two numbers are grouped together.) We might also recognize that it is easy to add any number to 10 and compute it as $24 + (8 + 2) = 24 + 10 = 34$. This example illustrates the *associative property of addition of whole numbers.* In many elementary school texts in the lower grades, this property is referred to as the *grouping property for addition.*

Property

Associative Property of Addition of Whole Numbers　If a, b, and c are any whole numbers, then $(a + b) + c = a + (b + c)$.

When several numbers are being added, the parentheses are usually omitted, since the grouping does not alter the result.

Another property of addition of whole numbers is seen when one addend is 0. In Figure 3-11, set A has 5 blocks and set B has 0 blocks. The union of sets A and B has only 5 blocks.

Figure 3-11

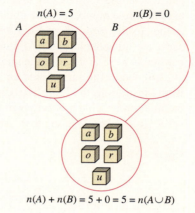

$$n(A) + n(B) = 5 + 0 = 5 = n(A \cup B)$$

This example illustrates the following property of whole numbers.

Property

Identity Property of Addition of Whole Numbers   There is a unique whole number 0, the **additive identity,** such that for any whole number a, $a + 0 = a = 0 + a$.

Example 3-5   Which properties justify each of the following?

a. $5 + 7 = 7 + 5$
b. $1001 + 733$ is a whole number.
c. $(3 + 5) + 7 = (5 + 3) + 7$
d. $(8 + 5) + 2 = 8 + (5 + 2)$
e. $(10 + 5) + (10 + 3) = (10 + 10) + (5 + 3)$

Solution   **a.** Commutative property of addition
b. Closure property of addition
c. Commutative property of addition
d. Associative property of addition
e. Commutative and associative properties of addition combined

Mastering Basic Addition Facts

Certain mathematical facts are *basic addition facts*. Basic addition facts are those involving a single digit plus a single digit. As the K-4 *Standards* (p. 19) point out: *Calculators do not replace the need to learn basic facts, to compute mentally, or to do reasonable paper-and-pencil computation.* One method of learning the basic facts is to organize them according to different strategies, listed as follows:

1. *Counting On.* The strategy of *counting on* from the *greater* of the addends is usually used when the other addend is 1, 2, or 3. For example, $5 + 3$ can be computed by starting at 5 and then counting on 6, 7, and 8. Likewise, $2 + 8$ would be computed by starting at 8 and then counting 9 and 10.
2. *Doubles.* The next strategy considered involves the use of *doubles.* Doubles such as $4 + 4$ and $6 + 6$ receive special attention with students. After doubles are mastered, *doubles + 1* and *doubles + 2* can be easily learned. For example, if a student knows $6 + 6 = 12$, then $6 + 7$ is $(6 + 6) + 1$, or one more than the double of 6, or 13. Likewise, $7 + 9$ is $(7 + 7) + 2$ or two more than the double of 7, or 16.
3. *Making 10.* Another strategy is that of *making 10* and then adding any leftover. For example, we could think of $8 + 5$ as shown in Figure 3-12. Notice that we are really using the associative property of addition.

Figure 3-12

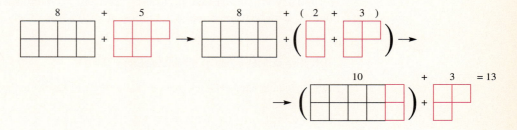

Many basic facts might be classified under more than one strategy. For example, we could find $9 + 8$ using *making 10* as $9 + (1 + 7) = (9 + 1) + 7 = 10 + 7 = 17$ or using a *double plus 1* as $(8 + 8) + 1$.

Subtraction of Whole Numbers

Subtraction of whole numbers can be modeled in several ways: the *set (take-away)* model, the *missing-addend* model, the *comparison* model, and the *number-line* model.

Take-away Model

One way to think about subtraction is this: Instead of imagining a second set of objects as being joined to a first set (as in addition), consider the second set as being *taken away* from a first set. For example, suppose we have 8 blocks and take away 3 of them, as shown in Figure 3-13. We record this process as $8 - 3 = 5$.

Figure 3-13

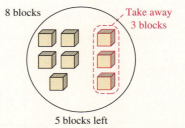

8 blocks

Take away 3 blocks

5 blocks left

Missing-addend Model

A second model for subtraction, the *missing-addend* model, relates subtraction and addition. Recall that in Figure 3-13, $8 - 3$ is pictured as 8 blocks "take away" 3 blocks. The number of blocks left is the number $8 - 3$, or 5. This can also be thought of as the number of blocks that could be added to 3 blocks in order to get 8 blocks, that is,

$$\boxed{8-3}+3=8.$$

missing addend   The number $8 - 3$, or 5, is the **missing addend** in the equation

$$\square + 3 = 8.$$

The missing addend model gives elementary students an opportunity to begin algebraic thinking. An unknown is a major part of the problem of trying to decide the difference of 8 minus 3.

Cashiers often use the missing-addend model. For example, if the bill for a movie is $8 and you pay $10, the cashier might say "8 and 2 is 10." This idea is generalized for all whole numbers a and b as seen in the definition of subtraction of whole numbers that follows.

Definition of Subtraction of Whole Numbers

For any whole numbers a and b, such that $a \geq b$, $a - b$ is the unique whole number c such that $a = b + c$.

Comparison Model

A third way to consider subtraction is by using a *comparison* model. Suppose we have 8 blocks and 3 balls and we want to know how many more blocks we have than balls. We can pair the blocks and balls, as shown in Figure 3-14, and determine that there are 5 more blocks than balls. We also write this as $8 - 3 = 5$.

Figure 3-14

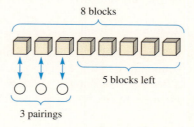

Number-line Model

Subtraction can also be modeled on a number line as suggested in Figure 3-15.

Figure 3-15

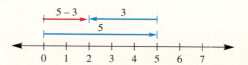

Properties of Subtraction

In an attempt to find $3 - 5$, we use the definition of subtraction: $3 - 5 = c$ if there is a solution to $c + 5 = 3$. Since there is no whole number c that satisfies the equation, $3 - 5$ is not meaningful in the set of whole numbers. For that reason, we discuss properties of subtraction in Chapter 4, where the set of integers is introduced and subtraction of any two integers is meaningful.

Ongoing Assessment 3-2

1. In the following, show that $5 < 7$ and $6 > 3$ by finding natural numbers k such that each is true:
   a. $5 + k = 7$ **b.** $6 = 3 + k$
2. In the definition of *less than,* can the natural number k be replaced by the whole number k? Why or why not?
3. Give an example to show why, in the definition of addition, sets A and B must be disjoint.
4. Explain whether the following given sets are closed under addition:
   a. $B = \{0\}$
   b. $T = \{0, 3, 6, 9, 12, \ldots\}$
   c. $N = \{1, 2, 3, 4, 5, \ldots\}$
   d. $V = \{3, 5, 7\}$
   e. $\{x \mid x \in W, x > 10\}$
5. Draw a picture of colored rods illustrating the commutative property of addition.
6. Rewrite each of the following subtraction problems as an equivalent addition problem:
   a. $x - 119 = 213$
   b. $213 - x = 119$
   c. $213 - 119 = x$
7. Each of the following is an example of one of the properties for addition of whole numbers. Identify the property illustrated.
   a. $6 + 3 = 3 + 6$
   b. $(6 + 3) + 5 = 6 + (3 + 5)$
   c. $(6 + 3) + 5 = (3 + 6) + 5$
8. Use the digits 2, 3, 8, and 0 to fill in the blanks in the following to make each statement true. Use each digit only once. List all possibilities for each case.
   a. $3280 < \underline{\quad\quad} < 8032$ **b.** $2803 < \underline{\quad\quad} < 3820$
9. Find the next three terms in each of the following sequences:
   a. 8, 13, 18, 23, 28, $\underline{\quad}$, $\underline{\quad}$, $\underline{\quad}$
   b. 98, 91, 84, 77, 70, 63, $\underline{\quad}$, $\underline{\quad}$, $\underline{\quad}$
10. If A, B, and C each stand for a different single digit from 1 to 9, answer the following if
$$A + B = C.$$
   a. What is the greatest digit that C could be? Why?
   b. What is the greatest digit that A could be? Why?
   c. What is the smallest digit that C could be? Why?

   d. If A, B, and C are even, what number(s) could C be? Why?
   e. If C is 5 more than A, what number(s) could B be? Why?
   f. If A is three times as great as B, then what number(s) could C be? Why?
   g. If A is odd and A is 5 more than B, what number(s) could C be? Why?
11. If A, B, C, and D each stand for a different single digit from 1 to 9, answer each of the following if

$$
\begin{array}{r}
A \\
+ B \\
\hline
CD
\end{array}
$$

   a. What is the value of C? Why?
   b. Can D be 1? Why?
   c. If D is 7, what values can A be?
   d. If A is 6 greater than B, then what is the value of D?
12. Find the total of the terms in the 50th row in the following figure:

1	1st row
$1 - 1$	2nd row
$1 - 1 + 1$	3rd row
$1 - 1 + 1 - 1$	4th row
$1 - 1 + 1 - 1 + 1$	5th row

13. Make each of the following a magic square:

   a.
	1	6
	5	7
4		2

   b.
17	10	
	14	
13	18	

14. **a.** Place whole numbers in the following four squares so that each pair has the sum shown. Note that one diagonal sum must be 20 and the other diagonal sum must be 7.

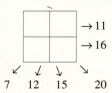

b. Will examples similar to the one in (a) always be possible with any numbers written for the sums as shown? Explain your answer.

15. a. Place the numbers 1, 2, 3, 4, 5, and 6 in the following boxes so that no square has a number greater than the one directly below it or directly to the right of it:

b. Can you find more than one way to place the numbers?

16. a. A domino set contains all number pairs from double-zero to double-six, with each number pair occurring only once; that is, the following domino counts as two-four and four-two. How many dominoes are in the set?

b. When considering the sum of all dots on a single domino in an ordinary set of dominoes, explain how the commutative property might be important.

17. Millie and Samantha began saving money at the same time. Millie plans to save $3 a month, and Samantha plans to save $5 a month. After how many months will Samantha have exactly $10 more than Millie?

18. String art is formed by connecting evenly spaced nails on the vertical and horizontal axes by line segments. Connect the nail farthest from the origin on the vertical axis with the nail closest to the origin on the horizontal axis. Continue until all nails are connected, as shown in the figure that follows. How many intersection points are created with 10 nails on each axis?

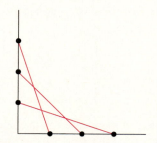

3 nails per axis
3 intersections

19. Make a calculator display numbers that have the following values:

a. Seven tens　　　　**b.** Nine thousands
c. Eleven hundreds　　**d.** Fifty-six tens
e. Three hundred forty-seven tens

20. Make a calculator count to 100 as follows (use a constant operation if available):

a. By ones　　**b.** By twos　　**c.** By fives

21. Make a calculator count backward from 27 to 0 as follows (use a constant operation if possible):

a. By ones　　**b.** By threes　　**c.** By nines

22. If a calculator is made to count by twos starting at 2, what is the thirteenth number in the sequence?

23. At a certain party, when the doorbell rang the first time, one guest arrived. On each successive ring, the number of arriving guests was 2 more than the number that had arrived on the previous ring. After 20 rings, how many guests had arrived?

24. a. At a volleyball game, the players stood in a row ordered by height. If Kent is shorter than Mischa, Sally is taller than Mischa, and Vera is taller than Sally, who is the tallest and who is the shortest?

b. Write possible heights for the players in (a).

Communication

25. In Figure 3-9, arrows were used to represent numbers in completing an addition. Explain whether you think an arrow starting at 0 and ending at 3 represents the same number as an arrow starting at 4 and ending at 7. How would you explain this to students?

26. The missing addend model was described as giving elementary students an opportunity to begin algebraic thinking. Describe in your words what algebraic thinking means.

27. Explain whether it is important for elementary students to learn various properties of addition of whole numbers.

28. Explain whether it is important for elementary students to learn more than one model for performing the operations of addition and subtraction.

29. Do elementary students still have to learn their basic facts when the calculator is a part of the curriculum? Why or why not?

30. How can the commutative property be used to help a child find the answer to $3 + 9$?

Open-ended

31. Describe any model not in this text that you might use to teach addition to students.

32. Investigate whether your calculator has constant addition and subtraction features. Write an example to show how each feature works.

33. Suppose $A \subseteq B$. If $n(A) = a$ and $n(B) = b$, then $b - a$ could be defined as $n(B - A)$. Choose two sets A and B and illustrate this definition.

Cooperative Learning

34. Draw pictures and write an explanation of how you might prove that subtraction is not a function on the set of ordered pairs of whole numbers.

35. Use groups of people to illustrate properties of addition.

36. Work with a group of other students in base five to determine what the addition facts might be. Use the addition models of this section to illustrate how addition facts in base five might be found.

a. CMLX   **b.** XXXIX

38. What are the advantages of the Babylonian system over the Egyptian system?

39. Write 5286 in expanded form.

Review Problems

37. Write the number that precedes each of the following:

BRAIN TEASER   Use Figure 3-16 to design an *unmagic square*. That is, use each of the digits 1, 2, 3, 4, 5, 6, 7, 8, and 9 exactly once so that every column, row, and diagonal adds to a different sum.

Figure 3-16

Section 3-3   # Multiplication and Division of Whole Numbers

Multiplication of Whole Numbers

In this section, we use three models to discuss multiplication: the *repeated-addition* model, the *array* model, and the *Cartesian-product* model.

Repeated-Addition Model

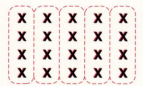

Figure 3-17

Suppose we have a classroom with 5 columns of 4 chairs each, as shown in Figure 3-17. How many chairs are there altogether? We can think of this as combining 5 sets of 4 objects into a single set.

The 5 columns of 4 suggest the following addition:

$$\underbrace{4 + 4 + 4 + 4 + 4}_{\text{five 4s}} = 20$$

HISTORICAL NOTE

William Oughtred (1575–1660), an English mathematician, placed emphasis on mathematical symbols. He first introduced the use of "St. Andrew's cross" (×) as the symbol for multiplication. This symbol was not readily adopted because, as Gottfried Wilhelm von Leibnitz (1646–1716) objected, it was too easily confused with the letter *x*. Leibnitz adopted the use of the dot (·) for multiplication, which then became commonly used.

The *repeated-addition* model can be illustrated in several ways, including the use of a number line and the use of arrays. For example, using colored rods of length 4, we could show that the combined length of five 4-rods has a combined length that can be found by joining the rods end-to-end, as in Figure 3-18(a). Figure 3-18(b) shows the process using arrows on a number line.

Figure 3-18

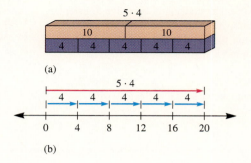

(a)

(b)

The Array Model

Another representation of repeated addition that is useful in exploring multiplication of whole numbers is an *array*. In Figure 3-19(a), we cross sticks to create intersection points thus forming an array of points. The number of points on a single vertical stick is 4 and there are five sticks forming a total of 5 · 4 points in the entire array. In Figure 3-19(b), the array is shown as a 4-by-5 grid. The number of squares required to fill in the grid is 20. These two illustrations are used to motivate the following definition of multiplication of whole numbers.

Figure 3-19

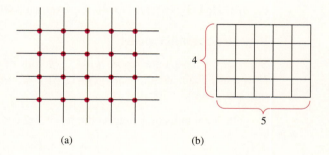

(a)   (b)

Definition of Multiplication of Whole Numbers

For any whole numbers a and $n \neq 0$,

$$n \cdot a = \underbrace{a + a + a + \cdots + a}_{n \text{ terms}}.$$

If $n = 0$, then $0 \cdot a = 0$.

Cartesian-Product Model

The *Cartesian-product* model offers a third way to discuss multiplication. Suppose you can order a soyburger on light or dark bread with one condiment: mustard, mayonnaise, or horseradish. To show the number of different soyburger orders that a waiter could write for the cook, we use a *tree diagram.* The ways of writing the order are listed in Figure 3-20, where the bread is chosen from the set $B = \{$ light, dark $\}$ and the condiment is chosen from the set $C = \{$ mustard, mayonnaise, horseradish $\}$.

Figure 3-20

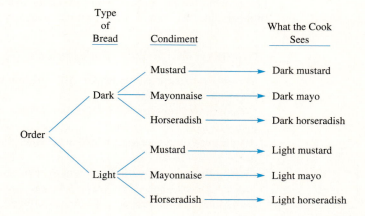

Each order can be written as an ordered pair, for example, (dark, mustard). The set of ordered pairs forms the Cartesian product $B \times C$. The Fundamental Counting Principle tells us that the number of ordered pairs in $B \times C$ is $2 \cdot 3$.

The preceding discussion demonstrates how multiplication can be defined in terms of Cartesian products. An alternative definition of multiplication of whole numbers follows.

Alternative Definition of Multiplication of Whole Numbers

For finite sets A and B, if $n(A) = a$ and $n(B) = b$, then $a \cdot b = n(A \times B)$.

product • factors

REMARK   In this definition, sets A and B do not have to be disjoint. The expression $a \cdot b$ is the **product** of a and b, and a and b are **factors.** Also, note that $A \times B$ indicates the Cartesian product, not multiplication. We multiply numbers, not sets.

I N V E S T I G A T I O N   3 - 4

● Can you define multiplication of whole numbers as a binary operation the way that addition was defined? If so, draw an illustration to show with what numbers on a number line such points as those with coordinates (2, 3), (0, 0) and (5, 1) are paired. ●

Properties of Whole-number Multiplication

As with addition, multiplication on the set of whole numbers is a binary function. Because of this, each ordered pair of whole numbers is paired with a unique whole number. As a result, the set of whole numbers is *closed* under multiplication. That is, if we multiply any two whole numbers, the result is a whole number. This property is referred to as the closure property of multiplication of whole numbers. In addition, multiplication on the set of whole numbers, like addition, has the commutative, associative, and identity properties.

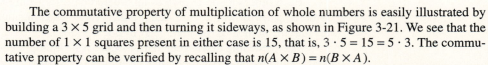

Properties of Multiplication of Whole Numbers

Closure Property of Multiplication of Whole Numbers For any whole numbers a and b, $a \cdot b$ is a unique whole number.

Commutative Property of Multiplication of Whole Numbers For any whole numbers a and b, $a \cdot b = b \cdot a$.

Associative Property of Multiplication of Whole Numbers For any whole numbers a, b, and c, $(a \cdot b) \cdot c = a \cdot (b \cdot c)$.

Identity Property of Multiplication of Whole Numbers There is a unique whole number 1 such that for any whole number a, $a \cdot 1 = a = 1 \cdot a$.

Zero Multiplication Property of Whole Numbers For any whole number a, $a \cdot 0 = 0 = 0 \cdot a$.

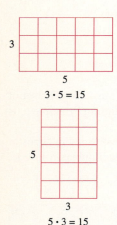

$3 \cdot 5 = 15$

$5 \cdot 3 = 15$

Figure 3-21

The commutative property of multiplication of whole numbers is easily illustrated by building a 3×5 grid and then turning it sideways, as shown in Figure 3-21. We see that the number of 1×1 squares present in either case is 15, that is, $3 \cdot 5 = 15 = 5 \cdot 3$. The commutative property can be verified by recalling that $n(A \times B) = n(B \times A)$.

The associative property of multiplication of whole numbers can be illustrated as follows. Suppose $a = 3$, $b = 5$, and $c = 4$. In Figure 3-22(a), we see a picture of $3 \cdot (5 \cdot 4)$ blocks. In Figure 3-22(b), we see the same blocks, this time arranged as $(3 \cdot 5) \cdot 4$. Because both sets of blocks in Figure 3-22(a) and (b) compress to the set shown in Figure 3-22(c), we see that $3 \cdot (5 \cdot 4) = (3 \cdot 5) \cdot 4$. The associative property is useful in computations such as the following:

$$3 \cdot 40 = 3 \cdot (4 \cdot 10) = (3 \cdot 4) \cdot 10 = 12 \cdot 10 = 120.$$

Figure 3-22

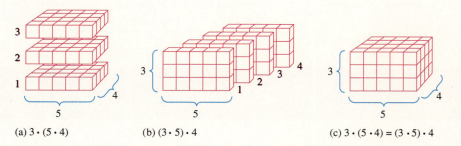

(a) $3 \cdot (5 \cdot 4)$ (b) $(3 \cdot 5) \cdot 4$ (c) $3 \cdot (5 \cdot 4) = (3 \cdot 5) \cdot 4$

The multiplicative identity for whole numbers is 1. For example, $3 \cdot 1 = 1 + 1 + 1 = 3$. In general, for any whole number a,

$$a \cdot 1 = \underbrace{1 + 1 + 1 + \cdots + 1}_{a \text{ terms}} = a.$$

Thus $a \cdot 1 = a$, which, along with the commutative property for multiplication, implies that $a \cdot 1 = a = 1 \cdot a$. Cartesian products can also be used to show that $a \cdot 1 = a = 1 \cdot a$.

Next, consider multiplication involving 0. For example, $6 \cdot 0 = 0 + 0 + 0 + 0 + 0 + 0 = 0$. Thus we see that multiplying 0 by 6 yields a product of 0 and, by commutativity, $0 \cdot 6 = 0$. This is an example of the zero multiplication property. This property can also be verified by using the definition of multiplication in terms of Cartesian products.

The Distributive Property of Multiplication over Addition

The next property we investigate is the basis for understanding multiplication algorithms. In Figure 3-23, $5 \cdot (3 + 4) = (5 \cdot 3) + (5 \cdot 4)$.

Figure 3-23

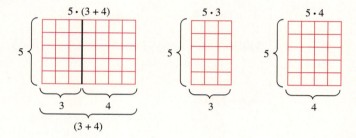

The properties of addition and multiplication also can be used to justify this result:

$$5 \cdot (3 + 4) = \underbrace{(3 + 4) + (3 + 4) + (3 + 4) + (3 + 4) + (3 + 4)}_{\text{5 terms}}$$

Definition of multiplication

$$= (3 + 3 + 3 + 3 + 3) + (4 + 4 + 4 + 4 + 4)$$

Commutative and associative properties of addition

$$= 5 \cdot 3 + 5 \cdot 4 \qquad \text{Definition of multiplication}$$

This example illustrates the *distributive property of multiplication over addition* for whole numbers, which is stated in general as follows.

Property

Distributive Property of Multiplication over Addition for Whole Numbers   For any whole numbers a, b, and c,

$$a \cdot (b + c) = a \cdot b + a \cdot c.$$

REMARK   Because the commutative property of multiplication of whole numbers holds, the distributive property of multiplication over addition can be rewritten as $(b + c) \cdot a = b \cdot a + c \cdot a$. The distributive property can be generalized to any finite number of terms. For example, $a \cdot (b + c + d) = a \cdot b + a \cdot c + a \cdot d$.

When multiplication is used and there is no confusion as in $a \cdot (b + c + d) = a \cdot b + a \cdot c + a \cdot d$, mathematical convention allows us to write $a(b + c + d) = ab + ac + ad$.

Students find the distributive property of multiplication over addition useful when doing *mental mathematics*. For example,

$$11 \cdot 17 = (10 + 1)17 = 10 \cdot 17 + 1 \cdot 17 = 170 + 17 = 187.$$

This property is used to combine like terms when we work with variables; for example, $3ab + 2ab = (3 + 2)ab = 5ab$.

Example 3-6

Use rectangles to model each of the following products:

a. $3(2x + y + 3)$ **b.** $(x + 2)5 + (x + 2)a$

Solution   **a.** $2x + y + 3$ can be modeled as a rectangular area in three parts as seen in Figure 3-24:

Figure 3-24

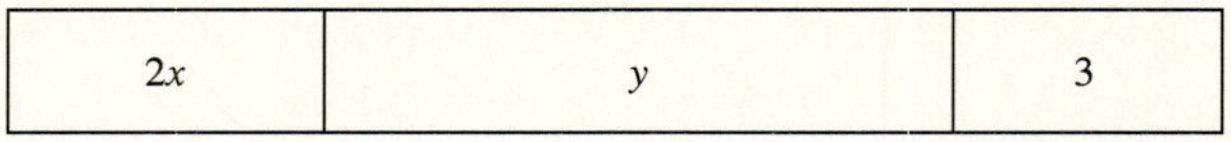

2x	y	3

Then the product of 3 times $2x + y + 3$ can be modeled as the total area, as in Figure 3-25:

Figure 3-25

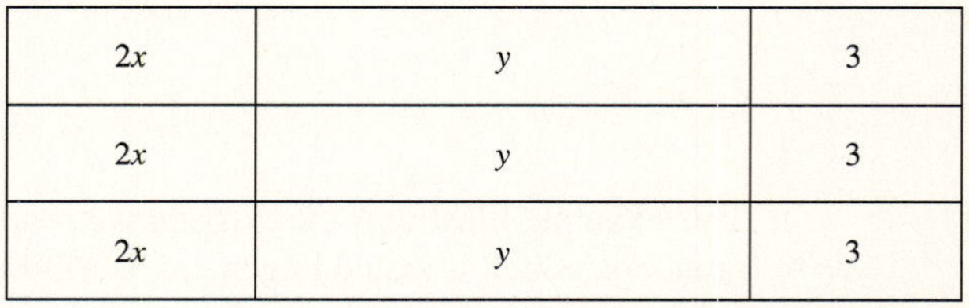

2x	y	3
2x	y	3
2x	y	3

Thus the product could be written as $3 \cdot 2x + 3y + 3 \cdot 3$, or $6x + 3y + 9$.

b. Because $x + 2$ is a factor of both addends, we could draw a rectangular area model, as in Figure 3-26:

Figure 3-26

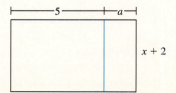

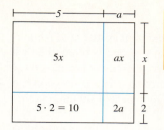

Figure 3-27

Because $x + 2$ is a sum, then it too could be modeled as a sum of two lengths with the combined areas pictured in Figure 3-27.

Thus the product might also be written as $5x + ax + 10 + 2a$.

• • •

Order of Operations

Difficulties involving the order of arithmetic operations sometimes arise. For example, many students will treat $2 + 3 \cdot 6$ as $(2 + 3)6$, while others will treat it as $2 + (3 \cdot 6)$. In the first case, the value is 30; in the second case, the value is 20. To avoid confusion, mathematicians agree that when no parentheses are present, multiplications are performed *before* additions. Thus, $2 + 3 \cdot 6 = 2 + 18 = 20$. This order of operations is not built into calculators that display an incorrect answer of 30.

Division of Whole Numbers

We discuss division using three models: the *set (partition)* model, the *missing-factor* model, and the *repeated-subtraction* model.

Set (Partition) Model

Suppose we have 18 cookies and want to give an equal number of cookies to each of 3 friends: Bob, Dean, and Charlie. How many should each person receive? If we draw a picture, we can see that we can divide (or partition) the 18 cookies into 3 *sets,* with an equal number of cookies in each set. Figure 3-28 shows that each friend received 6 cookies.

Figure 3-28

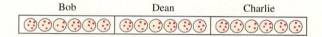

The answer may be symbolized as $18 \div 3 = 6$. Thus $18 \div 3$ is the number of cookies in each of 3 disjoint sets whose union has 18 cookies. In this approach to division, we partition a set into a number of equivalent subsets.

Missing-factor Model

Another strategy for dividing 18 cookies among 3 friends is to use the *missing-factor* model. If each friend receives c cookies, then the 3 friends receive $3c$, or 18, cookies. Hence, $3c = 18$. Since $3 \cdot 6 = 18$, then $c = 6$. We have answered the division computation by using multiplication. This leads us to the following definition of division of whole numbers.

Definition of Division of Whole Numbers

For any whole numbers a and b, with $b \neq 0$, $a \div b = c$ if, and only if, c is the unique whole number such that $b \cdot c = a$.

---

dividend • divisor • quotient

REMARK   The number a is the **dividend,** b is the **divisor,** and c is the **quotient.** Note that $a \div b$ can also be written as $\dfrac{a}{b}$ or $b\overline{)a}$.

Repeated-subtraction Model

Suppose we have 18 cookies and want to package them in cookie boxes that hold 6 cookies each. How many boxes are needed? We could reason that if one box is filled, then we would have $18 - 6$ (or 12) cookies left. If one more box is filled, then there are $12 - 6$ (or 6) cookies left. Finally, we could place the last 6 cookies in a third box. This discussion can be summarized by writing $18 - 6 - 6 - 6 = 0$. We have found by repeated subtraction that $18 \div 6 = 3$.

Calculators can be used to show that division of whole numbers can be thought of as repeated subtraction. For example, consider $135 \div 15$. If the calculator has a constant key, press $\boxed{1}\boxed{5}\boxed{-}\boxed{K}\boxed{1}\boxed{3}\boxed{5}\boxed{=}$ ... and then count how many times you must press the $\boxed{=}$ key in order to make the display read 0. Calculators with a different constant feature may require a different sequence of entries. For example, if the calculator has an automatic constant, we can press $\boxed{1}\boxed{3}\boxed{5}\boxed{-}\boxed{1}\boxed{5}\boxed{=}$ and then count the number of times we press the $\boxed{=}$ key to make the display read 0. Compare your answer with the one achieved by pressing this sequence of keys:

$$\boxed{1}\boxed{3}\boxed{5}\boxed{\div}\boxed{1}\boxed{5}\boxed{=}.$$

Division Algorithm

Just as subtraction of whole numbers is not always meaningful, division of whole numbers is not always meaningful. For example, to find $383 \div 57$ we look for a whole number c such that $57c = 383$.

Table 3-8 shows several products of whole numbers times 57. Since 383 is between 342 and 399, there is no whole number c such that $57c = 383$. Because no whole number c satisfies this equation, we see that $383 \div 57$ has no meaning in the set of whole numbers, and the set of whole numbers is not closed under division.

Table 3-8

$57 \cdot 1$	$57 \cdot 2$	$57 \cdot 3$	$57 \cdot 4$	$57 \cdot 5$	$57 \cdot 6$	$57 \cdot 7$
57	114	171	228	285	342	399

However, if 383 apples were to be divided among 57 students, each student would receive 6 apples and 41 apples would remain. The number 41 is the **remainder.** Thus 383 contains six 57s with a remainder of 41. Observe that the remainder is a whole number less than 57. The concept illustrated is the **division algorithm.**

> **Division Algorithm**
>
> Given any whole numbers a and b with $b \neq 0$, there exist unique whole numbers q (quotient) and r (remainder) such that
>
> $$a = bq + r \quad \text{with} \quad 0 \leq r < b.$$

Example 3-7 | If 123 is divided by a number and the remainder is 13, what are the possible divisors?

Solution   From the division algorithm, we have

$$123 = bq + 13 \quad \text{and} \quad b > 13.$$

Using the definition of subtraction, we have $bq = 123 - 13$, and hence $110 = bq$. Now we are looking for two numbers whose product is 110, where one number is greater than 13. Table 3-9 shows the pairs of factors of 110.

We see that 110, 55, and 22 are possible divisors because each is greater than 13. The numbers 1, 2, 5, 10, and 11 cannot be divisors.

• • •

Table 3-9

1	110
2	55
5	22
10	11

An alternative method of solving Example 3-7 is to use the integer division key on your calculator.

Division by 0 and 1

The whole numbers 0 and 1 deserve special attention with respect to division of whole numbers. Before reading on, try to find the values of the following three expressions:

$$\textbf{1. } 3 \div 0 \qquad \textbf{2. } 0 \div 3 \qquad \textbf{3. } 0 \div 0$$

Consider the following explanations:

1. By definition, $3 \div 0 = c$ if there is a unique number c such that $0 \cdot c = 3$. Since the zero property of multiplication states that $0 \cdot c = 0$ for any whole number c, there is no whole number c such that $0 \cdot c = 3$. Thus $3 \div 0$ is undefined because there is no answer to the equivalent multiplication problem.
2. By definition, $0 \div 3 = c$ if there exists a unique number c such that $3 \cdot c = 0$. The zero property of multiplication states that any number times 0 is 0. Since $3 \cdot 0 = 0$, then $c = 0$ and $0 \div 3 = 0$. Note that $c = 0$ is the only number that satisfies $3 \cdot c = 0$.
3. By definition, $0 \div 0 = c$ if there is a unique whole number c such that $0 \cdot c = 0$. Notice that for *any c*, $0 \cdot c = 0$. According to the definition of division, c must be unique. Since there is no *unique* number c such that $0 \cdot c = 0$, it follows that $0 \div 0$ is indeterminate, or undefined.

Division involving 0 may be summarized as follows. Let n be any natural number. Then

1. $n \div 0$ is undefined;
2. $0 \div n = 0$; and
3. $0 \div 0$ is indeterminate, or undefined.

Recall that $n \cdot 1 = n$ for any whole number n. Thus, by the definition of division, $n \div 1 = n$. For example, $3 \div 1 = 3$, $1 \div 1 = 1$, and $0 \div 1 = 0$.

Ongoing Assessment 3-3

1. Each ticket to the band concert costs $2.00. Each ticket to the football game costs $5.00. Jim bought 5 tickets to each event. What was his total bill?

2. For each of the following, find, if possible, the whole numbers that make the equations true:
   a. $3 \cdot \square = 15$ b. $18 = 6 + 3 \cdot \square$
   c. $\square \cdot (5 + 6) = \square \cdot 5 + \square \cdot 6$

3. In terms of set theory, the product na could be thought of as the number of elements in the union of n sets with a elements in each. If this were the case, what must be true about the sets?

4. In the Cartesian-product representation of multiplication, how would you model $2 \cdot 0$?

5. Determine if the following sets are closed under multiplication:
   a. $\{0, 1\}$ b. $\{0\}$
   c. $\{2, 4, 6, 8, 10, \ldots\}$ d. $\{1, 3, 5, 7, 9, \ldots\}$
   e. $\{1, 4, 7, 10, 13, \ldots\}$ f. $\{0, 1, 2\}$

6. a. If 5 is removed from the set of whole numbers, is the set closed with respect to addition?
   b. If 5 is removed from the set of whole numbers, is the set closed with respect to multiplication?
   c. Answer the same questions as (a) and (b) if 6 is removed from the set of whole numbers.

7. Rename each of the following using the distributive property for multiplication over addition so that there are no parentheses in the final answer:
   a. $(a + b)(c + d)$ b. $3(x + y + 5)$
   c. $\square(\triangle + \bigcirc)$ d. $(x + y)(x + y + z)$

8. Place parentheses, if needed, to make each of the following equations true:
   a. $4 + 3 \times 2 = 14$
   b. $9 \div 3 + 1 = 4$
   c. $5 + 4 + 9 \div 3 = 6$
   d. $3 + 6 - 2 \div 1 = 7$

9. The generalized distributive property for three terms states that for any whole numbers a, b, c, and d, $a(b + c + d) = ab + ac + ad$. Justify this property using the distributive property for two terms.

10. For each of the following, find whole numbers to make the statement true, if possible:
    a. $18 \div 3 = \square$
    b. $\square \div 76 = 0$
    c. $28 \div \square = 7$

11. Illustrate geometrically each of the following, using the concept of area:
    a. $a \cdot (b + c) = ab + ac$
    b. $(a + b) \cdot (c + d) = ac + ad + bc + bd$

12. Rewrite each of the following division problems as a multiplication problem:
    a. $40 \div 8 = 5$
    b. $326 \div 2 = x$
    c. $48 \div x = 16$
    d. $x \div 5 = 17$

13. Think of a number. Multiply it by 2. Add 2. Divide by 2. Subtract 1. How does the result compare with your original number? Will this work all the time? Explain your answer.

14. Show that, in general, each of the following is false if a, b, and c are whole numbers:
    a. $a \div b = b \div a$
    b. $(a \div b) \div c = a \div (b \div c)$

    c. $a \div (b + c) = (a \div b) + (a \div c)$
    d. $a \div b$ is a whole number.

15. Because the Jones's water meter was stuck, they were billed the same amount for water each month for 5 mo. If they paid $160, what was the monthly bill?

16. There were 17 sandwiches for 7 people on a picnic. How many whole sandwiches were there for each person if they were divided equally? How many were left over?

17. a. Find all pairs of whole numbers whose product is 36.
    b. Plot the points found in (a) on a grid.
    c. Compare the pattern shape formed by the points to the pattern shape that could be found by adding all pairs of whole numbers whose sum is 36.

18. A new model of car is available in 4 different exterior colors and 3 different interior colors. Use a tree diagram and specific colors to show how many different color schemes are possible for the car.

19. Tony has 5 ways to get from his home to the park. He has 6 ways to get from the park to school. How many ways can Tony get from his home to school by way of the park?

20. Students were divided into 8 teams with 9 on each team. Later the same students were divided into teams with 6 on each team. How many teams were there then?

21. To find $7 \div 5$ on the calculator, press $\boxed{7}\ \boxed{\div}\ \boxed{5}\ \boxed{=}$, which yields 1.4. To find the whole-number remainder, ignore the decimal portion of 1.4, multiply $5 \cdot 1$, and subtract this product from 7. The result is the remainder. Use a calculator to find the whole-number remainder for each of the following divisions:
    a. $28 \div 5$ b. $32 \div 10$
    c. $29 \div 3$ d. $41 \div 7$
    e. $49,382 \div 14$

22. In the following problems, use only the designated number keys on the calculator. You may use any function keys.
    a. Use the keys $\boxed{1}$, $\boxed{9}$, and $\boxed{7}$ exactly once each in any order and use any operations available to write as many of the whole numbers as possible from 1 to 20. For example, $9 - 7 - 1 = 1$ and $1 \cdot 9 - 7 = 2$.
    b. Use the $\boxed{4}$ key as many times as desired with any operations to display 13.
    c. Use the $\boxed{2}$ key three times with any operations to display 24.
    d. Use the $\boxed{1}$ key five times with any operations to display 100.

23. Pick one of the following statements that shows how the following could be accomplished: What is the cost for two adult and one student Joan Baez tickets?
    a. Multiply $17 by 2 and then add $15.
    b. Add $17 and $15 and then multiply by 2.

24. In each of the following, tell what computation must be done last:
    a. $5(16 - 7) - 18$ b. $54/(10 - 5 + 4)$
    c. $(14 - 3) + (24 \cdot 2)$ d. $21,045/345 + 8$

25. Is x/x always equal to 1? Explain your answer.
26. Is $x \cdot x$ ever equal to x? Explain your answer.
27. Describe all pairs of whole numbers whose sum and product are the same.
28. Write an algebraic expression for each of the following:
    a. Area, A, divided by π
    b. Feet, f, in yards
    c. Hours, h, in minutes
    d. Days, d, in weeks

Communication

29. Suppose a student argued that $0/0 = 0$ because "nothing divided by nothing" is "nothing." How would you help that person.
30. Sue claims the following is true by the distributive law, where a and b are whole numbers:

$$3(ab) = (3a)(3b).$$

How might you help her?
31. Can 0 be the identity for multiplication? Explain why or why not.
32. Write an explanation with an example showing when the use of an array for multiplication is not feasible.
33. Explain to a fellow student whether a set model can be used to show how multiplication by 0 yields 0.
34. Use any method to demonstrate why the quotient q in the division of a by b is the greatest whole number of b's in a.

Open-ended

35. Why do you think the use of a dot for multiplication is more popular in mathematics than the symbol $\times$?

36. Explain why you do or do not think division is a binary operation on the set of whole numbers.
37. Describe a real-life situation that could be represented by the expression $5 + 8 \cdot 6$.
★38. The binary operation $\odot$ is defined on the set $S = \{a, b, c\}$, as shown in the following table. For example, $a \odot b = b$ and $b \odot a = b$.

$\odot$	a	b	c
a	a	b	c
b	b	a	c
c	c	c	c

a. Is S closed with respect to $\odot$?
b. Is $\odot$ commutative on S?
c. Is there an identity for $\odot$ on S? If yes, what is it?
d. Is $\odot$ associative on S?

Review Problems

39. Write 75 in (a) Egyptian, (b) Roman, and (c) Babylonian numerals.
40. Graph the set of all ordered pairs of whole numbers whose sum is 36. What do you observe about the graph?
41. Count 5, 10, 15, 20, . . . , and explain both an addition and a multiplication pattern that could describe this counting.
42. Write 35,206 in expanded form.
43. Give a set that is not closed under addition.
44. Are the whole numbers commutative under subtraction? If not, give a counterexample.
45. Illustrate $11 - 3$ using a number-line model.

BRAIN TEASER Rosalie bought a bike for $50 and sold it for $60. Then she bought it back for $70 and sold it for $80. What is the financial outcome of these transactions?

LABORATORY ACTIVITY Enter a number less than 20 on the calculator. If the number is even, divide it by 2; if it is odd, multiply it by 3 and add 1. Next, use the number on the display. Follow the given directions. Repeat the process again.

1. Will the display eventually reach 1?
2. Which number less than 20 takes the most steps before reaching 1?
3. Do even or odd numbers reach 1 more quickly?
4. Investigate what happens with numbers greater than 20.

Algorithms, Mental Math, and Estimation for Whole-number Addition and Subtraction

In previous sections, the definitions of addition and subtraction were introduced. These definitions, along with a knowledge of basic facts and properties, are necessary to the performance of more complex additions and subtractions. More complex operations are commonly done by applying various algorithms. An **algorithm** (named for the ninth-century Arabian mathematician Mohammed al-Khowârizmî) is a step-by-step systematic procedure used to accomplish an operation. Every prospective elementary school teacher should know more than one algorithm for doing operations. Not all students learn in the same manner, and the shortest, most efficient algorithms may not be the best for every individual. In the *Standards* (p. 8), we find the following with regard to algorithms: *Similarly, the availability of calculators does not eliminate the need for students to learn algorithms. Some proficiency with paper-and-pencil computational algorithms is important, but such knowledge should grow out of problem situations that have given rise to the need for such algorithms.*

algorithm

Addition Algorithms

Paper-and-pencil algorithms need to be taught developmentally; that is, they must proceed from the concrete stage to the abstract stage at appropriate times. The use of concrete teaching aids — such as chips, bean sticks, an abacus, or base-ten blocks — helps provide insight into the creation of algorithms for addition. A set of base-ten blocks, shown in Figure 3-29, consists of *units, longs, flats,* and *blocks,* representing 1, 10, 100, and 1000, respectively.

Figure 3-29

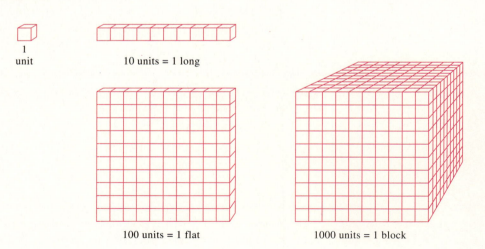

1 unit

10 units = 1 long

100 units = 1 flat

1000 units = 1 block

Students trade blocks by regrouping. That is, they take a set of base-ten blocks representing a number and trade them until they have the fewest possible pieces representing the same number. For example, suppose you have 58 units and want to trade them. What pieces do you have if you have the smallest number of pieces you can receive in a fair exchange? The units can be grouped into tens to form longs. Five sets of 10 units each can be traded for 5 longs. Thus, 58 units can be traded for 5 longs and 8 units. In terms of numbers, this is analogous to rewriting 58 as $5 \cdot 10 + 8$. In this case, you cannot receive flats or blocks.

Example 3-8

What is the fewest number of pieces you can receive in a fair exchange for 11 flats, 17 longs, and 16 units?

Solution   The 16 units can be traded for 1 long and 6 units.

11 flats	17 longs	16 units	(16 units = 1 long and 6 units)
	1 long	6 units	(Trade)
11 flats	18 longs	6 units	(After the first trade)

11 flats	18 longs	6 units	(18 longs = 1 flat and 8 longs)
1 flat	8 longs		(Trade)
12 flats	8 longs	6 units	(After the second trade)

	12 flats	8 longs	6 units	(12 flats = 1 block and 2 flats)
1 block	2 flats			(Trade)
1 block	2 flats	8 longs	6 units	(After the third trade)

In terms of numbers, this is analogous to rewriting $11 \cdot 10^2 + 17 \cdot 10 + 16$ as $1 \cdot 10^3 + 2 \cdot 10^2 + 8 \cdot 10 + 6$, which implies that there are 1286 units, the fewest number of pieces.

We now use base-ten blocks to help develop an algorithm for whole-number addition. Suppose we wish to add $14 + 23$. We show this computation with a concrete model in Figure 3-30(a), with an introductory algorithm in Figure 3-30(b) and the familiar algorithm in Figure 3-30(c).

Figure 3-30

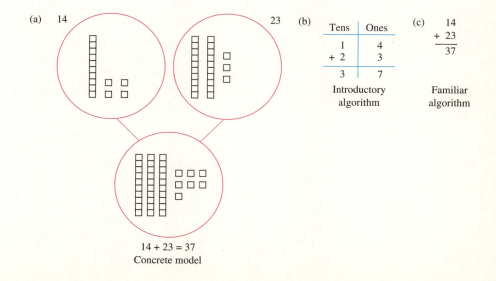

(a)   14   23   (b)

Tens	Ones
1	4
+ 2	3
3	7

Introductory
algorithm

(c)
```
   14
 + 23
 ----
   37
```
Familiar
algorithm

$14 + 23 = 37$
Concrete model

A formal justification for this addition is the following:

$14 + 23 = (1 \cdot 10 + 4) + (2 \cdot 10 + 3)$	Expanded form
$= (1 \cdot 10 + 2 \cdot 10) + (4 + 3)$	Commutative and associative properties of addition
$= (1 + 2) \cdot 10 + (4 + 3)$	Distributive property of multiplication over addition
$= 3 \cdot 10 + 7$	Single-digit addition facts
$= 37$	Place value

The mathematical justification of addition is not usually presented at the elementary school level. Some problems are more complicated than this one because they involve trading. This is described in terms of the base-ten blocks on the following student page from *Addison-Wesley Mathematics,* Grade 4, 1993.

After using concrete aids, children are ready to complete a computation such as 28 + 34. Figure 3-31(a) and (b) show introductory algorithms, whereas Figure 3-31(c) shows the traditional algorithm.

Figure 3-31

(a)

Tens	Ones	
2	8	
+3	4	
5	~~12~~	(Add)
+1	2	(Regroup)
6	2	

(b)

$$\begin{array}{rrl} & 2\ \ 8 & \\ + & 3\ \ 4 & \\ \hline & 1\ \ 2 & \text{(Sum of ones)} \\ + & 5\ \ 0 & \text{(Sum of tens)} \\ \hline & 6\ \ 2 & \end{array}$$

(c)

$$\begin{array}{r} {}^{1} \\ 28 \\ +\ 34 \\ \hline 62 \end{array}$$

Scratch Addition

scratch addition The **scratch addition** algorithm allows students to perform complicated additions by doing a series of additions involving only two single digits. An example follows:

1. $\begin{array}{r} 87 \\ 6\not{5}_2 \\ +\ 49 \\ \hline \end{array}$ Add the numbers in the units place starting at the top. When the sum is 10 or more, record this sum by scratching a line through the last digit added and writing the number of units next to the scratched digit. For example, since 7 + 5 = 12, the "scratch" represents 10 and the 2 represents the units.

2. $\begin{array}{r} 87 \\ 6\not{5}_2 \\ +\ 4\not{9}_1 \\ \hline \end{array}$ Continue adding the units, including any new digits written down. When the addition again results in a sum of 10 or more, as with 2 + 9 = 11, repeat the process described in (1).

3. $\begin{array}{r} {}^{2}87 \\ 6\not{5}_2 \\ +\ 4\not{9}_1 \\ \hline 1 \end{array}$ When the first column of additions is completed, write the number of units, 1, below the addition line. Count the number of scratches, 2, and add this number to the second column.

4. $\overset{2}{\cancel{8}}\overset{}{}_0 7$ Repeat the procedure for each successive column.
    $6 \overset{}{\cancel{5}}_2$
    $\underline{\overset{}{\cancel{4}}_0 \overset{}{\cancel{9}}_1}$
    $2\ 0\ 1$

What You Do	**What You Record**

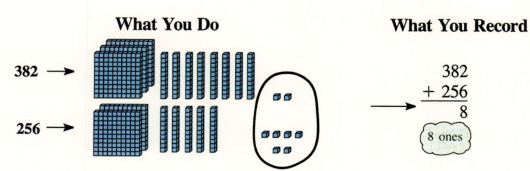

382 →
256 →

$$\begin{array}{r} 382 \\ +\ 256 \\ \hline 8 \end{array}$$

(8 ones)

1. Are there enough ones to make a trade?

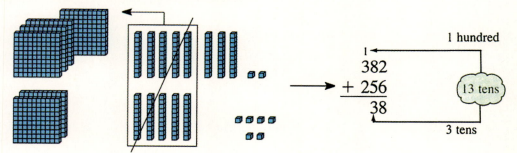

1 hundred

$$\begin{array}{r} \overset{1}{} 382 \\ +\ 256 \\ \hline 38 \end{array}$$

(13 tens)

3 tens

2. Are there enough tens to make a trade?

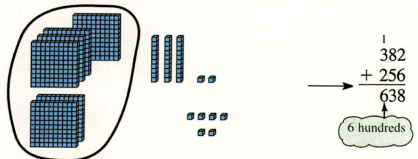

$$\begin{array}{r} \overset{1}{} 382 \\ +\ 256 \\ \hline 638 \end{array}$$

(6 hundreds)

3. How many hundreds are there after the trade?

4. What is the sum of 382 and 256?

Example 3-9 | Compute these additions using the scratch algorithm:

a. 296
840
+ 27

b. 1369
4813
5879
+ 6183

Solution **a.**

$$
\begin{array}{cccc}
^{1}2 & ^{1}\cancel{9}_{0} & 6 \\
 & \cancel{8}_{1} & 4 & 0 \\
+ & & 2 & \cancel{7}_{3} \\
\hline
1 & 1 & 6 & 3
\end{array}
$$

b.

$$
\begin{array}{cccc}
^{2}1 & ^{2}3 & ^{2}6 & 9 \\
4 & \cancel{8}_{3} & 1 & \cancel{3}_{2} \\
\cancel{5}_{2} & \cancel{8}_{1} & \cancel{7}_{6} & \cancel{9}_{1} \\
+ & 6 & 1 & \cancel{8}_{4} & 3 \\
\hline
1 & 8 & 2 & 4 & 4
\end{array}
$$

Mental Mathematics: Addition

Mental mathematics is an important tool in elementary schools. *Mental mathematics is the process of producing an exact answer to a computation without using external computational aids.* As stated in the *Standards* (p. 45): *Children need more time to explore and to invent alternative strategies for computing mentally. Both mental computation and estimation should be ongoing emphases that are integrated throughout all computational work.*

Several ways of performing mental addition follow:

1. *Adding from the left*

a. 67
+ 36

$60 + 30 = 90$ Add the tens.
$7 + 6 = 13$ Add the units.
$90 + 13 = 103$ Add the two sums.

b. 36
+ 36

$30 + 30 = 60$ Double 30.
$6 + 6 = 12$ Double 6.
$60 + 12 = 72$ Add the doubles.

2. *Breaking up and bridging*

67
+ 36

$67 + 30 = 97$ Add the first number to the tens in the second number.
$97 + 6 = 103$ Add this sum to the units in the second number.

3. *Trading off*

a. 67
+ 36

$67 + 3 = 70$ Add 3 to make a multiple of 10.
$36 - 3 = 33$ Subtract 3 to compensate for the 3 that was added.
$70 + 33 = 103$ Add the two numbers.

b. 67
+ 29

$67 + 30 = 97$ Add 30 (next multiple of 10 greater than 29).
$97 - 1 = 96$ Subtract 1 to compensate for the extra 1 that was added.

4. *Using compatible numbers*
Compatible numbers are numbers whose sums are easy to calculate mentally.

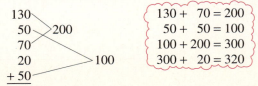

$130 + 70 = 200$
$50 + 50 = 100$
$100 + 200 = 300$
$300 + 20 = 320$

5. *Making compatible numbers*

$$
\begin{array}{r}
25 \\
+\,79 \\
\end{array}
\quad
\begin{array}{l}
25 + 75 = 100 \\
100 + 4 = 104 \\
\end{array}
\quad
\begin{array}{l}
25 + 75 \text{ adds to } 100. \\
\text{Add 4 more units.} \\
\end{array}
$$

TECHNOLOGY CORNER

The following map-coloring problem was used by Martha Hildebrandt, a past president of the National Council of Teachers of Mathematics, in a class at Emory University in the late 1960s, but it may be adapted for a spreadsheet.

Figure 3-32 contains a map of the western portion of the continental United States. Each state contains a number to indicate the approximate number of thousands of square miles in the state. For example, Montana contains approximately 147,000 mi^2. We are asked to color the map and are given four colors, numbered 1, 2, 3, and 4. The cost for coloring the map is $1, $2, $3, and $4, respectively, for each color per 1000 mi^2. For example, if Montana were colored with the number 2, the cost would be 2 · 147, or $294; if it were colored with the number 1, the cost would be 1 · 147, or $147. The goal is to color the map as cheaply as possible. There are only two rules to consider in coloring the map:

1. If two states have a common border, for example, Texas and Louisiana, they cannot be the same color.

2. When coloring Utah, Colorado, Arizona, and New Mexico, states that all touch each other at one point, you may color Colorado and Arizona, for example, the same color, but Utah and New Mexico must be colored differently. That is to say, at least three colors must be used in these four states.

Figure 3-32

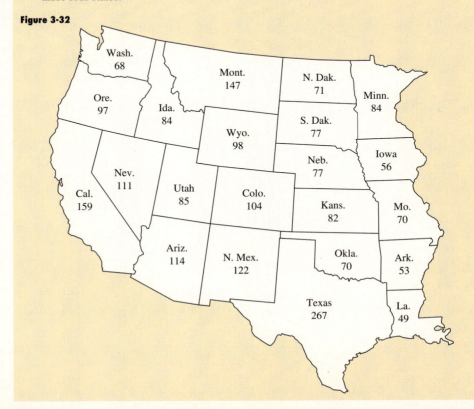

Use a spreadsheet with headings similar to those in Table 3-10 to record decisions and to update the computations as you try the problem.

Table 3-10

State	No. of Square Miles	Color Value	Cost = Product of Number of Square Miles × Color Value
Arizona	114		
Arkansas	53		
California	159		
⋮			
Wyoming	98		

Subtraction Algorithms

As with addition, base-ten blocks can provide a concrete model for subtraction. Consider 36 − 24. We do this computation in Figure 3-33(a) using base-ten blocks; in Figure 3-33(b) using an introductory algorithm based on the blocks; and finally in Figure 3-33(c) using the familiar algorithm. The slashes through the blocks show the ones taken away.

Notice that this subtraction problem can be checked by using the definition of subtraction: 36 − 24 = 12 because 12 + 24 = 36.

Subtractions become more involved when regrouping is necessary, as in 56 − 29. In the concrete model, 9 units cannot be taken from 6 units, so 1 long must be traded for 10 units, giving a total of 16. The three stages for working this problem are shown in Figure 3-34.

Figure 3-34

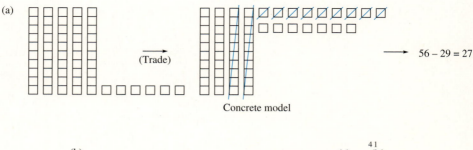

(a)

(Trade)

Concrete model

56 − 29 = 27

(b)

	Tens	Ones			Tens	Ones
	5	6			4	16
	− 2	9	→		− 2	9
					2	7

Introductory algorithm

(c)
$$\begin{array}{r} \overset{4\ 1}{5\!\!\!/6} \\ -\ 2\ 9 \\ \hline 2\ 7 \end{array}$$

Familiar algorithm

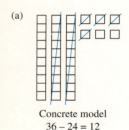

(a)

Concrete model
36 − 24 = 12

(b)

Tens	Ones
3	6
− 2	4
1	2

Introductory algorithm

(c)
$$\begin{array}{r} 36 \\ -\ 24 \\ \hline 12 \end{array}$$

Familiar algorithm

Figure 3-33

Mental Mathematics: Subtraction

1. *Subtracting in parts*

$$\begin{array}{r} 67 \\ -\,36 \\ \hline \end{array}$$

$67 - 30 = 37$
$37 - 6 = 31$

Subtract the tens in the second number from the first number.

Subtract the units in the second number from the difference.

2. *Making an easier problem*

$$\begin{array}{r} 71 \\ -\,39 \\ \hline \end{array}$$

$(71 + 1) = 72; (39 + 1) = 40$
$(72 - 40) = 32$

Add 1 to both numbers. Perform the subtraction, which is easier than the original problem.

(Notice that adding 1 to both numbers does not change the answer. Why?)

3. *Drop the zeros*

$$\begin{array}{r} 8700 \\ -\,500 \\ \hline \end{array}$$

$87 - 5 = 82$
$82 \rightarrow 8200$

Notice that there are two zeros in each number. Drop these zeros and perform the computation. Then replace the two zeros to obtain proper place value.

Another mental mathematics technique for subtraction is called "adding up." This method is based on the *missing addend* approach and is sometimes referred to as the "cashier's algorithm." An example of the cashier's algorithm follows.

Example 3-10

Noah owed $11 for his groceries. He used a $50 check to pay the bill. While handing Noah the change, the cashier said, "$11, $12, $13, $14, $15, $20, $30, $50." How much change did Noah receive?

Solution   Table 3-11 shows what the cashier said and how much money Noah received each time. Since $11 plus $1 is $12, Noah must have received $1 when the cashier said $12. The same reasoning follows for $13, $14, and so on. Thus the total amount of change that Noah received is given by $1 + $1 + $1 + $1 + $5 + $10 + $20 = $39. In other words, $50 − $11 = $39 because $39 + $11 = $50.

Table 3-11

What the Cashier Said	$11	$12	$13	$14	$15	$20	$30	$50
Amount of Money Noah Received Each Time	0	$1	$1	$1	$1	$5	$10	$20

Computational Estimation

Computational estimation is the process of forming an approximate answer to a numerical problem. Computational estimation is useful in determining whether an answer is reasonable when the computation is done on a calculator. As reflected in the *Standards* (p. 37): *Continual emphasis on computational estimation helps children develop creative and flexible thought processes and fosters in them a sense of mathematical power.*

The *front-end* computational estimation strategy is demonstrated in the following student page from *Addison-Wesley Mathematics,* Grade 5, 1993.

Front-End Estimation

LEARN ABOUT IT

You can use mental math to estimate sums.

Target 100

62	47	12	36
59	29	89	74
91	8	42	55

EXPLORE **Solve to Understand**

- How many pairs of numbers can you find on the bulletin board that have a sum within 10 of the target number 100?

- List the target pairs and tell whether each sum is more or less than 100.

TALK ABOUT IT

1. How would you find a number that forms a target pair with 32?

2. How can you see that 55 and 59 do not form a target pair?

3. Can you look only at the tens digits to find target pairs? Explain.

Front-end estimation is a method of estimation where we add the digits with the greatest place value (the front-end digits) to get a rough estimate. Then we use the rest of the digits to adjust the estimate.

Add the front-end digits. → Adjust using the other digits.

$$
\begin{array}{r}
3\,9\,6 \\
2\,6\,3 \\
+\ 5\,3\,7
\end{array}
$$

1,000 +

$$
\begin{array}{r}
3\,9\,6 \\
2\,6\,3 \\
+\ 5\,3\,7
\end{array}
$$

about 200 more

Estimate: 1,200

A summary of some of the common estimation strategies is given next with the example of the student page used as an illustration:

1. *Front-end strategy*
   From the student page, the following directions are followed:
   a. Find the total of the most important lead digits and use place value.
      The place value in the example gives 1000 as the sum.
   b. Adjust the estimate: 96 + 63 + 37 is about 200.
   Thus an estimate would be 1000 + 200, or 1200.

2. *Grouping to nice numbers strategy*
   The strategy used to obtain the adjustment in the preceding example is the *grouping to nice numbers* strategy, which means that numbers that "nicely" fit together are grouped. Another example is given here.

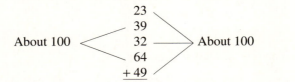

About 100 ⟨ 23 / 39 / 32 / 64 / + 49 ⟩ About 100   Therefore the sum is about 100 + 100, or 200.

3. *Clustering strategy*
   Clustering strategy is used when a group of numbers cluster around a common value. This strategy is limited to certain kinds of computations. In the next example, the numbers seem to cluster around 6000.

6200	1. Estimate the "average" — about 6000.
5842	2. Multiply the "average" by the number of values to obtain
6512	$5 \cdot 6000 = 30,000.$
5521	
+ 6319	

4. *Rounding strategy*
   Rounding is a way of cleaning up numbers so that they are easier to handle. Rounding enables us to find approximate answers to calculations, as follows:

4724	5000	Round 4724 to 5000.
+ 3192	+ 3000	Round 3192 to 3000.
	8000	Add the rounded numbers.
1267	1300	Round 1267 to 1300.
− 510	− 500	Round 510 to 500.
	800	Subtract the rounded numbers.

Performing estimations requires a knowledge of place value and rounding techniques. We illustrate a rounding procedure that can be generalized to all rounding situations. For example, suppose we wish to round 4724 to the nearest thousand. We may proceed in four steps (see also Figure 3-35).

a. Determine between which two consecutive thousands the number lies.
b. Determine the midpoint between the thousands.
c. Determine which thousand the number is closer to by observing whether it is greater than or less than the midpoint. (Not all texts use the same rule for rounding when a number falls at a midpoint.)

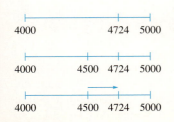

Figure 3-35

d. If the number to be rounded is greater than or equal to the midpoint, round the given number to the greater thousand; otherwise, round to the lesser thousand. In this case, we round 4724 to 5000.

5. *Range Strategy*

It is often useful to know into what *range* an answer falls. The range is determined by finding a low estimate and a high estimate and reporting that the answer falls in this interval. An example follows:

Problem	Low Estimate	High Estimate
378	300	400
+ 524	+ 500	+ 600
	800	1000

Thus a range for this problem is from 800 to 1000.

Addition in Bases Other Than Ten

A look at computation in other bases may provide insight into computation in base ten. Use of multibase blocks may be helpful in building an addition table for different bases and is highly recommended. A base five addition table is seen in Table 3-12.

Table 3-12   Addition Table (Base Five)

+	0	1	2	3	4
0	0	1	2	3	4
1	1	2	3	4	10
2	2	3	4	10	11
3	3	4	10	11	12
4	4	10	11	12	13

INVESTIGATION 3 - 5

● Determine how a number line might be used to model addition in base five. ●

Using the addition facts in Table 3-12, we develop algorithms for base-five addition similar to those for base-ten addition. Suppose we wish to add $12_{five} + 31_{five}$. We show the computation using a concrete model in Figure 3-36(a), an introductory algorithm in Figure 3-36(b), and the familiar algorithm in Figure 3-36(c). Additions in other number bases can be handled similarly.

Figure 3-36

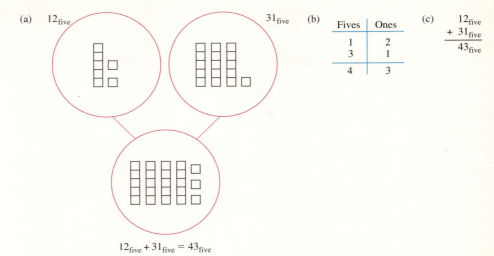

$12_{five} + 31_{five} = 43_{five}$

The subtraction facts for base five can also be derived from the addition-facts table by using the definition of subtraction. For example, to find $(12 - 4)_{five}$, recall that $(12 - 4)_{five} = c_{five}$ if, and only if, $(c + 4)_{five} = 12_{five}$. From Table 3-12, we see that $c = 3_{five}$. An example of subtraction involving regrouping, $32_{five} - 14_{five}$, is developed in Figure 3-37.

Figure 3-37

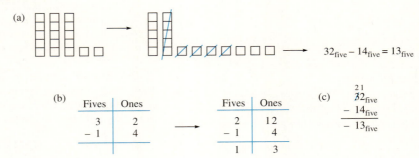

$32_{five} - 14_{five} = 13_{five}$

BRAIN TEASER The number on a license plate consists of five digits. When the license plate is looked at upside down, you can still read it, but the value of the upside-down number is 78,633 greater than the real license number. What is the license number?

Ongoing Assessment 3-4

1. Find the missing numbers in each of the following:

a.
```
     _ _ 1
  +   4 2 _
  _ _ 4 0 2
```

b.
```
    _ 0 2 5
    1 1 _ 6
  + 3 1 4 8
    6 _ 6 _
```

c.
```
    1 _ 6 9
    2 _ 9 4
    9 5 4 6
    9 _ _ 3
  + 7 _ 6 4
  2 8 7 7 6
```

d.
```
    2 _ 1
    4 5 _
  + _ 8 4
  1 3 2 6
```

2. Find the missing numbers in each of the following:

a.
```
   8 7 6 9 3
 - _ _ _ _ _
   4 1 2 7 9
```
b.
```
   8 1 3 5
 - 4 6 8 2
   _ _ _ _
```
c.
```
   3 _ _
 - 1 5 9
   _ 2 4
```
d.
```
   1 _ _ _ 6
 -   8 3 0 9
     4 9 8 7
```

3. Place the digits 7, 6, 8, 3, 5, and 2 in the boxes to obtain
    a. the greatest sum.   **b.** the least sum.

4. Place the digits 7, 6, 8, 3, 5, and 2 in the boxes to obtain
    a. the greatest difference.   **b.** the least difference.

5. At the beginning of the year, the library had 15,282 books. During fall quarter, 125 books were added; during winter quarter, 137 were added; and during spring quarter, 238 were added. How many books did the library have at the end of the school year?

6. Find the next three numbers in each of the following sequences:
    a. 9, 14, 19, 24, 29, _, _, _
    b. 97, 94, 91, 88, 85, _, _, _

7. Maria goes into a store with 87¢. If she buys a granola bar for 25¢, a balloon for 15¢, and a comb for 17¢, how much money does she have left?

8. Tom's diet allows only 1500 calories per day. For breakfast, Tom had skim milk (90 calories), a waffle with no syrup (120 calories), and a banana (119 calories). For lunch, he had $\frac{1}{2}$ cup of salad (185 calories) with mayonnaise (110 calories), and tea (0 calories). Then he "blew it" with pecan pie (570 calories). Can he have dinner consisting of steak (250 calories), a salad with no mayonnaise, and tea?

9. Wally kept track of last week's money transactions. His salary was $150 plus $54 in overtime and $260 in tips. His transportation expenses were $22, his food expenses were $60, his laundry costs were $15, his entertainment expenditures were $58, and his rent was $185. Did he save any money last week? If so, how much?

10. In the following problem, the sum is correct but the order of the numbers in each addend has been scrambled. Correct the addends to obtain the correct sum.

```
    2 8 3 4          □ □ □ □
 + 6 3 1 5       + □ □ □ □
    9 0 5 9          9 0 5 9
```

11. a. Would the clustering strategy of estimation be a good one to use in each of the following cases? Why or why not?

(i)	474		(ii)	483
	1467			475
	64			530
+	2445			503
			+	528

    b. Estimate each part of (a) using the following.
        (i) The front-end method
        (ii) Grouping to nice numbers
        (iii) Rounding

12. Dana obtained the following results for boxes of Girl Scout cookies sold for the week. She estimated total sales at 400 boxes. Do you think her estimate is too high or too low? Why?

Monday	38
Tuesday	92
Wednesday	74
Thursday	17
Friday	130

13. If 1 mo is approximately 4 wk and 1 yr is approximately 365 days or 52 wk, answer the following:
    a. Lewis and Clark spent approximately 2 yr, 4 mo, and 9 days exploring the territory in the Northwest. What is this time in weeks?
    b. It took Magellan 1126 days to circle the world. How many years is this?
    c. How many seconds old are you?
    d. Approximately how many times does your heart beat in 1 yr?

14. The Hawks played the Elks in a basketball game. Based on the information below, complete the scoreboard showing the number of points scored by each team during each quarter and the final score of the game.

TEAMS	QUARTERS				FINAL SCORE
	1	2	3	4	
Hawks					
Elks					

    a. The Hawks scored 15 points in the first quarter.
    b. The Hawks were behind by 5 points at the end of the first quarter.
    c. The Elks scored 5 more points in the second quarter than they did in the first quarter.
    d. The Hawks scored 7 more points than the Elks in the second quarter.
    e. The Elks outscored the Hawks by 6 points in the fourth quarter.
    f. The Hawks scored a total of 120 points in the game.
    g. The Hawks scored twice as many points in the third quarter as the Elks did in the first quarter.
    h. The Elks scored as many points in the third quarter as the Hawks did in the first two quarters combined.

15. Janet worked her addition problems by placing the partial sums as shown here:

$$
\begin{array}{r}
569 \\
+\,645 \\
\hline
14 \\
10 \\
11 \\
\hline
1214
\end{array}
$$

a. Use this method to work the following:

(i) $\begin{array}{r} 687 \\ +\,549 \\ \hline \end{array}$ (ii) $\begin{array}{r} +\,359 \\ +\,673 \\ \hline \end{array}$

b. Explain why this algorithm works.

16. Analyze the following computations. Explain what is wrong in each case.

a. $\begin{array}{r} 135 \\ +\,47 \\ \hline 172 \end{array}$ b. $\begin{array}{r} 87 \\ +\,25 \\ \hline 1012 \end{array}$ c. $\begin{array}{r} 57 \\ -\,38 \\ \hline 21 \end{array}$ d. $\begin{array}{r} 56 \\ -\,18 \\ \hline 48 \end{array}$

17. George is cooking an elaborate meal for Thanksgiving. He can cook only one thing at a time in his microwave oven. His turkey takes 75 min; the pumpkin pie takes 18 min; rolls take 45 sec; and a cup of coffee takes 30 sec to heat. How much time does he need to cook the meal?

18. Perform each of the following operations using the bases shown:

a. $43_{\text{five}} + 23_{\text{five}}$ b. $43_{\text{five}} - 23_{\text{five}}$
c. $432_{\text{five}} + 23_{\text{five}}$ d. $42_{\text{five}} - 23_{\text{five}}$
e. $110_{\text{two}} + 11_{\text{two}}$ f. $10001_{\text{two}} - 111_{\text{two}}$

19. Construct addition and multiplication tables for base eight.

20. Perform each of the following operations:

a.   3 hr 36 min 58 sec
    $+$ 5 hr 56 min 27 sec

b.   5 hr 36 min 38 sec
    $-$ 3 hr 56 min 58 sec

21. Perform each of the following operations (2 c = 1 pt, 2 pt = 1 qt, 4 qt = 1 gal):

a.   1 qt 1 pt 1 c
    $+$ 1 pt 1 c

b.   1 qt 1 c
    $-$ 1 pt 1 c

c.   1 gal 3 qt 1 c
    $-$ 4 qt 2 c

22. Mari is going to invite 20 friends to a party. She would like to have at least 2 c of cider for each guest. If cider is sold only by the gallon, how many gallons should she buy?

23. A palindrome is any number that reads the same backward as forward, for example, 121 and 2332. Try the following. Begin with any number. Is it a palindrome? If not, reverse the digits and add this reversed number to the original number. Is the result a palindrome? If not, repeat the above procedure until a palindrome is obtained. For example, start with 78. Because 78 is not a palindrome, we add: $78 + 87 = 165$. Because 165 is not a palindrome, we add: $165 + 561 = 726$. Again, 726 is not a palindrome, so we add $726 + 627$ to obtain 1353. Finally, 1353 + 3531 yields 4884, which is a palindrome.

a. Try this method with the following numbers:
(i) 93   (ii) 588   (iii) 2003
b. Find a number for which the procedure described takes more than five steps to form a palindrome.

24. Given the following addition problem, replace nine digits with 0s so that the sum of the numbers is 1111:

$$
\begin{array}{r}
999 \\
777 \\
555 \\
333 \\
111 \\
\hline
\end{array}
$$

25. Arrange eight 8s so that the sum is 1000.

26. a. Place the numbers 24 through 32 in the following circles so that the sums are the same in each direction:

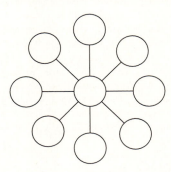

b. How many different numbers can be placed in the middle to obtain a solution?

27. Andrew's calculator was not functioning properly. When he pressed $\boxed{8}\,\boxed{+}\,\boxed{6}\,\boxed{=}$, the numeral 20 appeared on the display. When he pressed $\boxed{5}\,\boxed{+}\,\boxed{4}\,\boxed{=}$, 13 was displayed. When he pressed $\boxed{1}\,\boxed{5}\,\boxed{-}\,\boxed{3}\,\boxed{=}$, 9 was displayed. What do you think Andrew's calculator was doing?

28. The following is a supermagic square taken from an engraving called *Melancholia* by Dürer that includes the year (1514) it was constructed:

16	3	2	13
5	10	11	8
9	6	7	12
4	15	14	1

a. Find the sum of each row, the sum of each column, and the sum of each diagonal.
b. Find the sum of the four numbers in the center.
c. Find the sum of the four numbers in each corner.
d. Add 11 to each number in the square. Is the square still a magic square? Explain your answer.
e. Subtract 11 from each number in the square. Is the square still a magic square?

29. Use scratch addition to perform the following:

a.
$$432_{ten}$$
$$976_{ten}$$
$$+\ 1418_{ten}$$

b.
$$32_{five}$$
$$13_{five}$$
$$22_{five}$$
$$43_{five}$$
$$23_{five}$$
$$+\ 12_{five}$$

30. Perform each of the following operations:

a.
$$4\ gro\ 4\ dz\ 6\ ones$$
$$-\qquad 5\ dz\ 9\ ones$$

b.
$$2\ gro\ 9\ dz\ 7\ ones$$
$$+\ 3\ gro\ 5\ dz\ 9\ ones$$

31. In a small rural community, the elementary school has no refrigerators. Through a federally financed program, the school provides 1 c of milk per day for each student. Milk for the day is purchased at the local store each morning, and the school buys the exact amount necessary. The milk is available in gallons, half-gallons, quarts, pints, or cups, and the larger containers are better buys.

a. If 1 gal, 1 qt, and 1 pt of milk were purchased on Tuesday, how many students were at school that day?

b. On Wednesday, 31 students were at school. How much milk was purchased that day to make the best buy?

32. A *score* is equal to 20. Indicate each of the following as a base-ten number:

a. Three score and ten

b. Four score and seven

33. Determine what is wrong with the following:
$$22_{five}$$
$$+\ 33_{five}$$
$$55_{five}$$

34. Fill in the missing numbers in each of the following:

a.
$$2\ \_\ \_\ _{five}$$
$$-\qquad 2\ 2_{five}$$
$$\_\ 0\ 3_{five}$$

b.
$$2\ 0\ 0\ 1\ 0_{three}$$
$$-\quad 2\ \_\ 2\ \__{three}$$
$$1\ \_\ 2\ \_\ 1_{three}$$

Communication

35. Is the front-end estimate before the adjustment always less than the exact sum? Defend your answer.

36. Explain why the scratch addition algorithm works.

37. Explain why the following addition algorithm from an elementary school text works:

$$
\begin{array}{r|r}
2 & 7 \\
+\ 6 & 8 \\
\hline
1 & 5 \\
8 & \\
\hline
9 & 5 \\
\end{array}
$$

38. The diagram below, which is similar to one in the *Standards,* shows how decisions about which calculation procedure to use in numerical problems may be made. Use the diagram to discuss how calculators, pencil-and-paper computation, mental mathematics, and estimation are related.

39. Shakespeare, as one would expect, took numbers in stride in his writing. In one of his plays, the character Henry V reads the tale of the French slain at Agincourt:

This note doth tell me of ten thousand French
that in the field lie slain: of princes in this number,
And nobles bearing banners, there lie dead

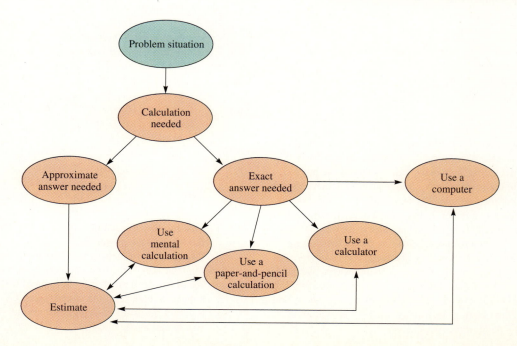

One hundred twenty-six; added to these
Of knights, esquires, and gallant gentlemen,
Eight thousand and four hundred; of the which
Five hundred were by yesterday dubb'd knights;
So that in these ten thousand they have lost
There are but sixteen hundred mercenaries.

Interpret the numbers in the quotation above. Is the quotation meaningful? Why?

Open-ended

40. Give several examples of real-world situations where an estimate, rather than an exact answer, is close enough.

41. Some texts show the partial sums in the computation as follows:

$$
\begin{array}{r}
14 \\
+\ 23 \\
\hline
7 \\
30 \\
\hline
37
\end{array}
$$

Develop at least one other algorithm for the addition of whole numbers.

42. Develop a rationale for why calculators either should or should not be used in school. Use mathematics education research in your development.

Cooperative Learning

43. Choose the money system of some country and investigate whether the system is a base-ten or some other base system. Decide whether values in the money system you chose can be easily added and subtracted.

Review Problems

44. Investigate the measuring of lengths in the metric system. Develop a plan for using place value with lengths to convert among different metric units.

45. Write 5280 in expanded form.

46. Give an example of the associative property of addition for whole numbers.

47. Illustrate $11 + 8$ using a number-line model.

48. What is the value of MCDX in Hindu-Arabic numerals?

49. Rename the following using the distributive property of multiplication over addition:
 a. $ax + a$ **b.** $3(x + y) + a(x + y)$

50. Jim has 5 new shirts and 3 new pairs of pants. How many combinations of new shirts and pants does he have?

**LABORATORY
ACTIVITY**

1. One type of Japanese abacus, *soroban,* is shown in Figure 3-38(a). In this abacus, a bar separates two sets of bead counters. Each counter above the bar represents five times the counter below the bar. Numbers are illustrated by moving the counter toward the bar. The number 7632 is pictured. Practice demonstrating and adding numbers on this abacus.

Figure 3-38

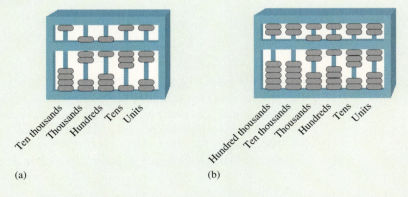

(a)   (b)

2. The Chinese abacus, *suan pan* (see Figure 3-38(b)), is still in use today. This abacus is similar to the Japanese abacus but has two counters above the bar. The number 7632 is also pictured on it. Practice demonstrating and adding numbers on this abacus. Compare the ease of using the two different versions.

Algorithms for Whole-number Multiplication and Division

Multiplication Algorithms

To develop algorithms for multiplying multidigit whole numbers, we use the strategy of *examining simpler computations first.* Consider $4 \cdot 12$. This computation could be pictured as in Figure 3-39 with 4 rows of 12 dots, or 48 dots. The dots in Figure 3-39 can also be partitioned to show that $4 \cdot 12 = 4 \cdot (10 + 2) = 4 \cdot 10 + 4 \cdot 2$. The numbers $4 \cdot 10$ and $4 \cdot 2$ are *partial products.*

Figure 3-39

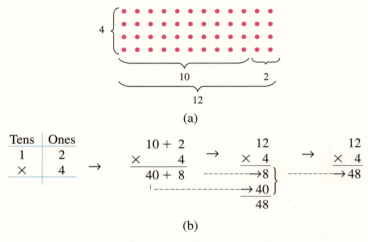

Figure 3-39(a) illustrates the distributive property of multiplication over addition on the set of whole numbers. The process leading to an algorithm for multiplying $4 \cdot 12$ is seen in Figure 3-39(b).

To compute products involving powers of 10, such as $3 \cdot 200$, we proceed as follows:

$$
\begin{aligned}
3 \cdot 200 &= 3 \cdot (2 \cdot 10^2) \\
&= (3 \cdot 2) \cdot 10^2 \\
&= 6 \cdot 10^2 \\
&= 6 \cdot 10^2 + 0 \cdot 10^1 + 0 \cdot 1 \\
&= 600
\end{aligned}
$$

We see that multiplying 6 by 10^2 results in annexing two zeros to 6. This idea can be generalized to the statement that *multiplication of any natural number by 10^n, where n is a natural number, results in annexing n zeros to the number.*

When multiplying powers of 10, an extension of the definition of exponents is used. For example, $10^2 \cdot 10^1 = (10 \cdot 10) \cdot 10 = 10^3$, or 10^{2+1}. In general, where a is a natural number and m and n are whole numbers, $a^m \cdot a^n$ is given by the following:

$$
a^m \cdot a^n = \underbrace{(a \cdot a \cdot a \cdot \ldots \cdot a)}_{m \text{ factors}} \cdot \underbrace{(a \cdot a \cdot a \cdot \ldots \cdot a)}_{n \text{ factors}}
$$

$$
= \underbrace{a \cdot a \cdot a \cdot \ldots \cdot a}_{m + n \text{ factors}} = a^{m+n}
$$

Consequently, $a^m \cdot a^n = a^{m+n}$.

Next we consider computations with 2-digit factors, such as $14 \cdot 23$. One possibility is to use the distributive property of multiplication over addition to write out all the partial products and add, as shown:

$$
\begin{array}{r}
14 \\
\times\, 23 \\
\hline
12 \\
30 \\
80 \\
+\, 200 \\
\hline
322
\end{array}
\quad
\begin{array}{l}
(3 \times 4) \\
(3 \times 10) \\
(20 \times 4) \\
(20 \times 10)
\end{array}
$$

Another approach is to write 14 as $10 + 4$ and use the distributive property of multiplication over addition, as follows:

$$
\begin{aligned}
14 \cdot 23 &= (10 + 4) \cdot 23 \\
&= 10 \cdot 23 + 4 \cdot 23 \\
&= 230 + 92 \\
&= 322
\end{aligned}
$$

This last approach leads to an algorithm for multiplication:

$$
\begin{array}{r}
23 \\
\times\, 14 \\
\hline
92 \\
230 \\
\hline
322
\end{array}
\quad
\begin{array}{l}
10 + 4 \\
(4 \cdot 23) \\
(10 \cdot 23)
\end{array}
\quad \text{or} \quad
\begin{array}{r}
23 \\
\times\, 14 \\
\hline
92 \\
23 \\
\hline
322
\end{array}
$$

We are accustomed to seeing the partial product 230 written without the zero, as 23. The placement of 23 with 3 in the tens column obviates having to write the 0 in the units column. When children first learn multiplication algorithms, they should be encouraged to include the zero in order to avoid errors and promote better understanding. Children should also be encouraged to *estimate* whether their answers are reasonable. In this exercise, we know that the answer must be between $10 \cdot 20 = 200$ and $20 \cdot 30 = 600$ because $10 < 14 < 20$ and $20 < 23 < 30$. Because 322 is between 200 and 600, the answer is reasonable.

Lattice Multiplication

lattice multiplication

The **lattice multiplication** algorithm for multiplying 14 and 23 follows. (Determining the reasons why lattice multiplication works is left as an exercise.)

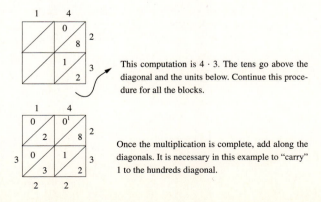

This computation is $4 \cdot 3$. The tens go above the diagonal and the units below. Continue this procedure for all the blocks.

Once the multiplication is complete, add along the diagonals. It is necessary in this example to "carry" 1 to the hundreds diagonal.

Mental Mathematics: Multiplication

As with addition and subtraction, mental mathematics is useful for multiplication. Several examples are given next:

1. *Front-end multiplying*

$$\begin{array}{r} 64 \\ \times\ 5 \\ \hline \end{array}$$

$60 \times 5 = 300$ Multiply the number of tens in the first number by 5.
$4 \times 5 = 20$ Multiply the number of units in the first number by 5.
$300 + 20 = 320$ Add the two products.

2. *Compatible number multiplication*

$2 \times 9 \times 5 \times 20 \times 5$ Rearrange as $9 \times (2 \times 5) \times (20 \times 5) =$
$9 \times 10 \times 100 = 9000$

3. *Thinking money*

a.
$$\begin{array}{r} 64 \\ \times\ 5 \\ \hline \end{array}$$
Think of the product as 64 nickels, which can be thought of as 32 dimes, which is $32 \times 10 = 320$ cents.

b.
$$\begin{array}{r} 64 \\ \times 50 \\ \hline \end{array}$$
Think of the product as 64 half-dollars, which is 32 dollars, or 3200 cents.

c.
$$\begin{array}{r} 64 \\ \times 25 \\ \hline \end{array}$$
Think of the product as 64 quarters, which is 32 half-dollars, or 16 dollars. Thus we have 1600 cents.

Division Algorithms

Algorithms for division can be developed by using repeated subtraction. Consider the following:

A shopkeeper is packaging juice in cartons that hold 6 bottles each. She has 726 bottles. How many cartons does she need?

We might reason that if 1 carton holds 6 bottles, then 10 cartons hold 60 bottles and 100 cartons hold 600 bottles. If 100 cartons are filled, there are $726 - 100 \cdot 6$, or 126, bottles remaining. If 10 more cartons are filled, then $126 - 10 \cdot 6$, or 66, bottles remain. Similarly, if 10 more cartons are filled, $66 - 10 \cdot 6$, or 6, bottles remain. Finally, 1 carton will hold the remaining 6 bottles. The total number of cartons necessary is $100 + 10 + 10 + 1$, or 121. This procedure is summarized in Figure 3-40(a). A more efficient method is shown in Figure 3-40(b).

Figure 3-40

(a)
$$\begin{array}{r} 6\overline{)726} \\ -600 \\ \hline 126 \\ -60 \\ \hline 66 \\ -60 \\ \hline 6 \\ -6 \\ \hline 0 \end{array}$$
100 sixes
10 sixes
10 sixes
1 six
121 sixes

(b)
$$\begin{array}{r} 6\overline{)726} \\ -600 \\ \hline 126 \\ -120 \\ \hline 6 \\ -6 \\ \hline 0 \end{array}$$
100 sixes
20 sixes
1 six
121 sixes

Divisions such as the one in Figure 3-40 are usually shown in elementary school texts in the most efficient form, as in Figure 3-41(b), in which the numbers in color in Figure 3-41(a) are omitted. The technique used in Figure 3-41(a) is often called "scaffolding" and may be used as a preliminary step to achieving Figure 3-41(b).

Figure 3-41

(a)
$$\begin{array}{r} 121 \\ \hline 1 \\ 20 \\ 100 \\ \hline 6)\,726 \\ -600 \\ \hline 126 \\ -120 \\ \hline 6 \\ -6 \\ \hline 0 \end{array}$$

(b)
$$\begin{array}{r} 121 \\ \hline 6)\,726 \\ -6 \\ \hline 12 \\ -12 \\ \hline 6 \\ -6 \\ \hline 0 \end{array}$$

Division in most elementary texts is taught using a four-step algorithm: *estimate, multiply, subtract,* and *compare.* This is demonstrated on the student page shown on the following page from *Addison-Wesley Mathematics,* Grade 3, 1993.

An example of division by a divisor of more than one digit is given next. Consider $32)\overline{2618}$.

1. Estimate the quotient in $32)\overline{2618}$. Because $1 \cdot 32 = 32$, $10 \cdot 32 = 320$, $100 \cdot 32 = 3200$, we see that the quotient is between 10 and 100.

2. Find the number of tens in the quotient. Because $26 \div 3$ is approximately 8, then 26 hundreds divided by 3 tens is approximately 8 tens. We then write the 8 in the tens place, as shown:

$$\begin{array}{r} 80 \\ \hline 32)\,2618 \\ -2560 \\ \hline 58 \end{array} \quad (32 \cdot 80)$$

3. Find the number of units in the quotient. Because $5 \div 3$ is approximately 1, then 5 tens divided by 3 tens is approximately 1. This is shown on the left in the following:

$$\begin{array}{r} 81 \\ \hline 1 \\ 80 \\ \hline 32)\,2618 \\ -2560 \\ \hline 58 \\ -32 \\ \hline 26 \end{array} \quad (32 \cdot 1)$$
$$\begin{array}{r} 81 \ \text{R26} \\ \hline 32)\,2618 \\ -256 \\ \hline 58 \\ -32 \\ \hline 26 \end{array}$$

4. Check: $32 \cdot 81 + 26 = 2618$.
   Normally in grade-school books, we see the format shown on the right, which places the remainder beside the quotient.

Because of the advent of calculators, many mathematics educators are suggesting that division by divisors of more than two digits should not be taught. What do you think?

Dividing
Finding Quotients and Remainders

EXPLORE Think About the Process

Amber took a roll of 32 pictures on her vacation. If she puts 6 pictures on each page of her photo book, how many pages can Amber fill? How many pictures will be left?

You divide because you are sharing equally.

Estimate the quotient.	Multiply.	Subtract.	Compare. Write the remainder beside the quotient.
$6\overline{)30}$ $6\overline{)32}$	5×6 $\begin{array}{r} 5 \\ 6\overline{)32} \\ 30 \end{array}$	$\begin{array}{r} 5 \\ 6\overline{)32} \\ -30 \\ \hline 2 \end{array}$	$\begin{array}{r} 5\ R\ 2 \\ 6\overline{)32} \\ -30 \\ \hline 2 \end{array}$ $2 < 6$

TALK ABOUT IT

1. Why is $30 \div 6$ a good way to estimate?

2. Is the remainder less than the divisor?

3. Use complete sentences to answer the problem.

The process just described is usually referred to as "long" division. Another technique, called "short" division, can be used when the divisor is a one-digit number and most of the work is done mentally. An example of short division is given next:

Decide where to start.	Divide the hundreds. Write the remainder by the tens.	Divide the tens. Write the remainder by the ones.	Divide the ones.

$$\begin{array}{r} 5 \\ 5\overline{)2\,8\,8\,0} \end{array} \qquad \begin{array}{r} 5 \\ 5\overline{)2\,8^3 8\,0} \end{array} \qquad \begin{array}{r} 5\,7 \\ 5\overline{)2\,8^3 8^3 0} \end{array} \qquad \begin{array}{r} 5\,7\,6 \\ 5\overline{)2\,8^3 8^3 0} \end{array}$$

Not enough thousands, $5 > 2$. $5 < 28$, so divide the hundreds.

$28 \div 5 = 5$ R3

$38 \div 5 = 7$ R3

$30 \div 5 = 6$ R0

Mental Mathematics: Division

1. *Breaking up the dividend*

$7\overline{)4256}$ $\qquad$ $7\overline{)42|56}$ $\qquad$ Break up the dividend into parts.

$$\begin{array}{r} 600 \;+\;\;\; 8 \\ 7\overline{)4200 \;+\; 56} \end{array}$$ Divide both parts by 7.

$600 + \;\;\;8 = 608$ $\qquad$ Add the answers together.

2. *Compatible numbers in division*

a. $3\overline{)105}$ $\qquad$ $105 = 90 + 15$ $\qquad$ Look for numbers that you recognize as divisible by 3 and having a sum of 105.

$$\begin{array}{r} 30 \;+\;\;\; 5 = 35 \\ 3\overline{)90 \;+\; 15} \end{array}$$ Divide both parts and add the answers.

b. $8\overline{)232}$ $\qquad$ $232 = 240 - 8$ $\qquad$ Look for numbers that are easily divisible by 8 and whose difference is 232.

$$\begin{array}{r} 30 \;-\; 1 = 29 \\ 8\overline{)240 \;-\; 8} \end{array}$$ Divide both parts and take the difference.

Estimation: Multiplication and Division

Examples of estimation strategies for multiplication and division are given next.

1. *Front-end multiplication*

$$\begin{array}{r} 524 \\ \times\,8 \\ \hline \end{array}$$

$500 \times 8 = 4000$ $\qquad$ Start multiplying at the front to obtain a first estimate.

$20 \times 8 = 160$ $\qquad$ Multiply the next important digit 8 times.

$4000 + 160 = 4160$ $\qquad$ Adjust the first estimate by adding the two numbers.

2. *Compatible numbers*

$5\overline{)4163}$ $5\overline{)4000}$ Change 4163 to a number close to it that you know is divisible by 5.

$\underline{800}$ Carry out the division and obtain the first estimate of 800.

$5\overline{)4000}$ Various techniques can be used to adjust the first estimate.

Multiplication and Division in Different Bases

As with addition and subtraction, we need to identify the basic facts of multiplication before we can use algorithms. The multiplication facts for base five are given in Table 3-13. These facts can be derived by using repeated addition.

Table 3-13   Multiplication Table (Base Five)

×	0	1	2	3	4
0	0	0	0	0	0
1	0	1	2	3	4
2	0	2	4	11	13
3	0	3	11	14	22
4	0	4	13	22	31

There are various ways to do the multiplication $21_{\text{five}} \cdot 3_{\text{five}}$.

Five	Ones
2	1
×	3

$\rightarrow$

$(20 + 1)_{\text{five}}$
$\times \qquad 3_{\text{five}}$
$\overline{(110 + 3)_{\text{five}}}$ $\text{-------}\rightarrow 3$
$\text{-------------}\rightarrow 110$

$\rightarrow$

21_{five}
$\times\ 3_{\text{five}}$
$\rightarrow 113_{\text{five}}$

$\rightarrow$

21_{five}
$\times\ 3_{\text{five}}$
$\overline{113_{\text{five}}}$

The multiplication of a two-digit number by a two-digit number is developed next:

23_{five}
$\times\ 14_{\text{five}}$
$\overline{22}$
130
30
$\underline{200}$
432_{five}

$(10 + 4)_{\text{five}}$
$(4 \cdot 3)_{\text{five}}$
$(4 \cdot 20)_{\text{five}}$
$(10 \cdot 3)_{\text{five}}$
$(10 \cdot 20)_{\text{five}}$

$\rightarrow 202$
$\rightarrow 230$
432_{five}

23_{five}
$\times\ 14_{\text{five}}$

Lattice multiplication can also be used to multiply numbers in various number bases. This is explored in Ongoing Assessment 3-5.

Division in different bases can be performed using the multiplication facts and the definition of division. For example, $22_{\text{five}} \div 3_{\text{five}} = c$ if, and only if, $c \cdot 3_{\text{five}} = 22_{\text{five}}$. From Table 3-13, we see that $c = 4_{\text{five}}$. As in base ten, computing multidigit divisions efficiently in different bases requires practice. The ideas behind the algorithms for division can be developed by using repeated subtraction, just as they were for base ten. For example, $3241_{\text{five}} \div 43_{\text{five}}$ is computed by means of the repeated-subtraction technique in Figure 3-42(a) and by means of the conventional algorithm in Figure 3-42(b). Thus $3241_{\text{five}} \div 43_{\text{five}} = 34_{\text{five}}$ with remainder 14_{five}.

Figure 3-42

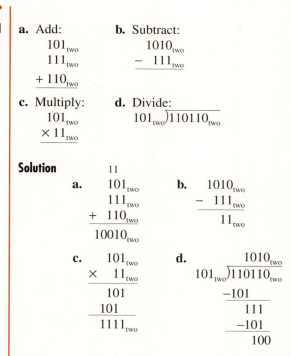

$$(a)\quad 43_{\text{five}}\overline{)\,3241_{\text{five}}}$$
$$\underline{-\ 430}\qquad (10\cdot43)_{\text{five}}$$
$$2311$$
$$\underline{-\ 430}\qquad (10\cdot43)_{\text{five}}$$
$$1331$$
$$\underline{-\ 430}\qquad (10\cdot43)_{\text{five}}$$
$$401$$
$$\underline{-\ 141}\qquad (2\cdot43)_{\text{five}}$$
$$210$$
$$\underline{-\ 141}\qquad (2\cdot43)_{\text{five}}$$
$$14\qquad (34\cdot43)_{\text{five}}$$

$$(b)\quad 43_{\text{five}}\overline{)\,3241_{\text{five}}}^{\,34_{\text{five}}}$$
$$\underline{-\ 234}$$
$$401$$
$$\underline{-\ 332}$$
$$14$$

Computations involving base two are demonstrated in Example 3-11.

● ● ●

Example 3-11

a. Add:
$$101_{\text{two}}$$
$$111_{\text{two}}$$
$$+\,110_{\text{two}}$$

b. Subtract:
$$1010_{\text{two}}$$
$$-\ 111_{\text{two}}$$

c. Multiply:
$$101_{\text{two}}$$
$$\times\,11_{\text{two}}$$

d. Divide:
$$101_{\text{two}}\overline{)\,110110_{\text{two}}}$$

Solution

a.
$$11$$
$$101_{\text{two}}$$
$$111_{\text{two}}$$
$$+\ 110_{\text{two}}$$
$$10010_{\text{two}}$$

b.
$$1010_{\text{two}}$$
$$-\ 111_{\text{two}}$$
$$11_{\text{two}}$$

c.
$$101_{\text{two}}$$
$$\times\ 11_{\text{two}}$$
$$101$$
$$101$$
$$1111_{\text{two}}$$

d.
$$101_{\text{two}}\overline{)\,110110_{\text{two}}}^{\,1010_{\text{two}}}$$
$$\underline{-101}$$
$$111$$
$$\underline{-101}$$
$$100$$

● ● ●

Problem 1

Pennies are placed in stacks on a checkerboard, with 1 penny on the first square, 2 on the second square, 4 on the third square, and 8 on the fourth square. The number of pennies in a stack doubles with each consecutive square. How high will the stack be on square number 64?

Understanding the Problem. There are to be 64 stacks of pennies placed on a checkerboard with the number of pennies in each stack determined by placing 1 penny on the first square of a checkerboard, 2 pennies on the second square, 4 pennies on the third square and so on, doubling the number of pennies on each consecutive square. We are to find the height of the stack of pennies on square number 64.

Devising a Plan.   Since the problem deals with the height of stacks of pennies, we must determine the number of pennies in a particular unit of length. Using a ruler, we see that it takes approximately 17 pennies to reach a 1-in. height. To determine the number of pennies in each stack, we use the strategy of *building a table,* as in Table 3-14.

Table 3-14

Number of Square	Number of Pennies
1	1
2	2
3	4
4	8
5	16
6	32
7	64
8	128

It would be cumbersome to carry the table out to 64 squares, so we must find a way to determine the number of pennies on a square without extending the table. The number of pennies form a geometric sequence. If we can find a formula for computing the nth term of this sequence, then we can find the number of pennies on the 64th square and, in turn, compute the height.

Carrying Out the Plan.   We see from Table 3-14 that the geometric sequence has first term 1 and fixed ratio 2, so the nth term is given by $1 \times 2^{n-1}$, or 2^{n-1}. Therefore the number of pennies on square 64 is 2^{63}. To find the height of the stacks of pennies in inches, we divide by 17 (17 pennies in 1 in.), then convert to feet by dividing by 12 (1 ft = 12 in.), and finally, convert to miles by dividing by 5280 (1 mi = 5280 ft).

Using a calculator with an $\boxed{y^x}$ key, we see that 2^{63} is approximately $9 \cdot 10^{18}$, which is a stack approximately 8×10^{12}, or 8 trillion mi, tall.

Looking Back.   The preceding answers for the 64th square are approximate and depend on the calculator being used and the rounding involved in the calculations. Related problems might include the following:

1. If a person could travel up the stack of pennies at 60 mph, how long would it take to reach the top of the stack on the 32nd and 64th squares?

2. What is the approximate value of the pennies on the 32nd square?

3. Could the stack of pennies on the 64th square reach the moon?

• • •

Ongoing Assessment 3-5

1. Perform the following multiplications using the lattice multiplication algorithm:

   a. 728
      × 94

   b. 306
      × 24

2. Explain why the lattice multiplication algorithm works.

3. Fill in the missing numbers in each of the following:

   a.
   ```
        4_6
      × 783
      1_78
      340 8
    - 982
    3335 _8
   ```

   b.
   ```
        327
      × 9_1
        327
      1_08
    - 9_3
    30__07
   ```

4. The following chart gives average water usage for 1 person for one day:

Use	Average Amount
Taking bath	110 L (liters)
Taking shower	75 L
Flushing toilet	22 L
Washing hands, face	7 L
Getting a drink	1 L
Brushing teeth	1 L
Doing dishes (one meal)	30 L
Cooking (one meal)	18 L

   a. Use the chart to calculate how much water you use each day.

   b. The average American uses approximately 200 L of water per day. Are you average?

   c. If there are 215,000,000 people in the United States, approximately how much water is used in the United States per day?

5. Simplify each of the following using properties of exponents. Leave answers as powers.

   a. $5^7 \cdot 5^{12}$
   b. $6^{10} \cdot 6^2 \cdot 6^3$
   c. $10^{296} \cdot 10^{17}$
   d. $2^7 \cdot 10^5 \cdot 5^7$

6. **a.** Which is greater, $2^{80} + 2^{80}$ or 2^{100}? Why?
   b. Which is greatest, 2^{101}, $3 \cdot 2^{100}$, or 2^{102}? Why?

7. The following model illustrates $14 \cdot 23$:

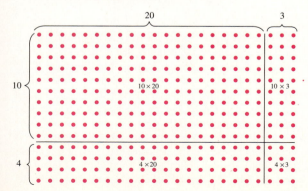

Draw similar models illustrating each of the following:

   a. $6 \cdot 23$
   b. $18 \cdot 25$

8. Consider the following:

   ```
        476
    × 293
        952    (2 · 476)
      4284    (9 · 476)
      1428    (3 · 476)
   139468
   ```

   a. Use the conventional algorithm to show that the answer is correct.

   b. Explain why the algorithm works.

   c. Try the method to multiply 84×363.

9. The Russian peasant algorithm for multiplying 27×68 follows. (Disregard remainders when halving.)

	Halves	Doubles	
→	27 ×	68	
Halve 27 →	13	136	Double 68.
Halve 13	6	272	Double 136.
Halve 6 →	3	544	Double 272.
Halve 3 →	1	1088	Double 544.

   In the "Halves" column, choose the odd numbers. In the "Doubles" column, circle the numbers paired with the odds from the "Halves" column. Add the circled numbers.

   ```
        68
      136
      544
    1088
    1836   This is the product of 27 · 68.
   ```

   Try this algorithm for $17 \cdot 63$ and other numbers.

10. Find the greatest possible whole-number value of n such that the following are true:

    a. $14n < 300$
    b. $21n \le 7459$
    c. $7n \le 2134$
    d. $483n < 79485$

11. Find the least possible whole-number value of n such that the following are true:

    a. $14n > 300$
    b. $23n \ge 4369$
    c. $123n > 782$
    d. $222n > 8654$

12. Use the distributive property of multiplication over addition or subtraction to compute mentally each of the following:

    a. $15 \cdot 12$
    b. $14 \cdot 102$
    c. $30 \cdot 99$.

13. Complete the following table:

a	b	$a \cdot b$	$a + b$
	56	3752	
32			110
		270	33

14. Answer the following questions based on the activity chart given next:

Activity	Calories Burned per Hour
Playing tennis	462
Snowshoeing	708
Cross-country skiing	444
Playing volleyball	198

   a. How many calories are burned during 3 hr of cross-country skiing?

   b. Jane played tennis for 2 hr while Carolyn played volleyball for 3 hr. Who burned more calories, and how many more?

   c. Lyle went snowshoeing for 3 hr and Maurice went cross-country skiing for 5 hr. Who burned more calories, and how many more?

15. On a 14-day vacation, Glenn increased his caloric intake by 1500 calories per day. He also worked out more than usual by swimming 2 hr a day. Swimming burns 666 calories per hour, and a net gain of 3500 calories adds 1 lb of weight. Did Glenn gain at least 1 lb during his vacation?

16. Sue purchased a $30,000 life-insurance policy at the price of $24 for each $1000 of coverage. If she pays the premium in 12 monthly installments, how much is each installment?

17. Perform each of the following divisions using both the repeated-subtraction and familiar algorithms:

   a. $8\overline{)623}$ **b.** $36\overline{)298}$ **c.** $391\overline{)4001}$

18. Place the digits 7, 6, 8, and 3 in the boxes $\square\overline{)\square\square\square}$ to obtain

   a. the greatest quotient.   **b.** the least quotient.

19. Rudy is buying a new car that costs $8600. The car salesman said Rudy could pay cash or pay $1500 down and $450 a month for 2 yr.

   a. Which option is more expensive?

   b. How much more expensive?

20. A 1K computer memory chip can store 1024 bits of information. How many bits of information can be stored in a 64K chip?

21. Using a calculator, Ralph multiplied by 10 when he should have divided by 10. The display read 300. What should the correct answer be?

22. Twenty members of the band plan to attend a festival. The band members washed 245 cars at $2 per car to help cover expenses. The school will match every dollar the band raises with a dollar from the school budget. The cost of renting the bus to take the band is 72¢ per mile and the round trip is 350 mi. The band members can stay in the dorm for 2 nights at $5 per person per night. Meals for the trip will cost $28 per person. Has the band raised enough money yet? If not, how many more cars do they have to wash?

23. The following figure shows four function machines. The output from one machine becomes the input for the one below it. Complete the accompanying chart.

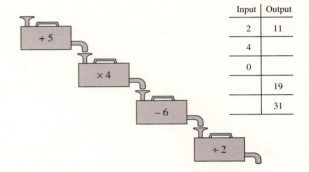

Input	Output
2	11
4	
0	
	19
	31

24. Choose three different digits.

   a. Form six different two-digit numbers from the numbers you chose. Each number can be used only once.

   b. Add the six numbers.

   c. Add the three digits you chose.

   d. Divide the answer in (b) by the answer in (c).

   e. Repeat (a)–(d) with three different numbers.

   f. Is the final result always the same? Why?

25. Consider the following multiplications. Notice that when the digits in the factors are reversed, the products are the same.

$$\begin{array}{r} 36 \\ \times\, 42 \\ \hline 1512 \end{array} \qquad \begin{array}{r} 63 \\ \times\, 24 \\ \hline 1512 \end{array}$$

   a. Find other multiplications where this procedure works.

   b. Find a pattern for the numbers that work in this way.

26. Molly read 160 pages in her book in 4 hr. Her sister Karly took 4 hr to read 100 pages in the same book. If the book is 200 pages long and if the two girls continued to read at these rates, how much longer would it take Karly to read the book than Molly?

27. Sami has a paper route with 38 customers. Each customer is charged $12 a month. She estimates that if she makes all her collections, she will collect about $600. Is her estimate low or high? Why? Discuss how she could get a closer estimate.

28. Discuss possible error patterns in each of the following:

    a.   34   **b.**   35   **c.**   34   **d.**   5 3

       $\times 8$ $\times 26$ $\times 6$ 5)2515

    2432   90   114 $-\ 25$

                                   15

                              $-\ 15$

                                     0

29. Mira is saving to buy a new computer. She has saved $356. The total cost of the machine is $980. Each week, she can save $30. How long will it take until she can purchase her computer?

30. To transport the complete student body of 1672 students to a talk given by the governor, the school plans to rent buses that can hold 29 students each. How many buses are needed? Will all the buses be full?

31. Larry's new car holds 40 L of gas. He drove 396 km and had 4 L left. How many kilometers does Larry's car get per liter?

32. What happens when you multiply any two-digit number by 101? Discuss why this happens.

33. Cynthia can buy skis, bindings, poles, and boots, or she can rent them each time she goes skiing. She can buy or rent individual items or she can buy or rent complete packages, as follows:

	Buy	*Rent*
Skis	$200	$25
Bindings	80	0
Poles	20	5
Boots	100	10
Complete ski package	330	30

    a. How much does she save on the complete ski package if she

       (i) buys?   (ii) rents?

    b. If she buys her own equipment, how many trips must she make so that buying the whole package costs less than renting?

34. Perform each of the following operations using the bases shown:

    a. $32_{five} \cdot 4_{five}$ **b.** $32_{five} \div 4_{five}$

    c. $43_{five} \cdot 23_{five}$ **d.** $143_{five} \div 3_{five}$

    e. $13_{eight} \cdot 5_{eight}$ **f.** $67_{eight} \div 4_{eight}$

    g. $10010_{two} \div 11_{two}$ **h.** $10110_{two} \cdot 101_{two}$

35. For what possible bases are each of the following computations correct:

    a.   213   **b.**   322

       $+\ 308$ $-\ 233$

       522   23

    c.   213   **d.**   101

       $\times 32$ 11)1111

       430          $-\ 11$

    1043   11

   11300 $-\ 11$

                         0

36. **a.** Use lattice multiplication to compute $(323_{five}) \cdot (42_{five})$.

    b. Find the smallest values of a and b so that $32_a = 23_b$.

37. Place the digits 7, 6, 8, and 3 in the boxes   □□□ to obtain $\times$ □

    a. the greatest product.   **b.** the least product.

38. Place the digits 7, 6, 8, 3, and 2 in the boxes   □□□ to obtain $\times$ □□

    a. the greatest product.   **b.** the least product.

39. If a cow produces 700 lb of hamburger and there are 4 Quarter Pounders to a pound, how many cows would it take to produce 21 billion Quarter Pounders?

40. Use a calculator to find the missing numbers in the following:

    a.   3 7   **b.**   __   **c.**   _)123

       $\times 43$ $\times 36$ $-\ 9$

     $----$ 558   33

             2790 $-\ 27$

   -591 $----$ 6

41. Find the products of the following and describe the pattern that emerges:

    a. 1×1 **b.** 99×99

       11×11 999×999

     111×111 9999×9999

   1111×1111

    c. Test the patterns discovered for 30 terms using a spreadsheet. If the patterns do not continue as expected, determine when the patterns stop.

42. Suppose a person can spend $1 per second. How much can that person spend in a minute? An hour? A day? A week? A month? A year? 20 years?

43. Suppose a friend chooses a number between 250,000 and 1,000,000. What is the least number of questions you must ask in order to guess the number if the friend answers only yes or no to the questions?

44. When $12 \times 483 = 5796$ is multiplied, every digit 1 through 9 is used either in one of the factors or in the product.

    a. Show that this also happens in the following:

       (i) 27×198 (ii) 48×159 (iii) 39×186

    b. Find other examples where all digits are used that have the following as factors:

       (i) 1963   (ii) 483   (iii) 297

    c. Which whole numbers 1 through 9, if any, cannot be the units digit of a factor when using every digit in multiplication as described above. Why?

Communication

45. Explain any connections you see between operations in base five and base ten.

46. Describe differences between the base-sixteen (hexadecimal) and base-ten systems.

47. If a student presented a new "algorithm" for computing with whole numbers, describe the process you would recommend to the student to determine if the algorithm would always work.

48. Pick a number. Double it. Multiply the result by 3. Add 24. Divide by 6. Subtract your original number. Is the result always the same? Write a convincing argument for your answer.

Open-ended

49. Choose what you consider to be the "best" algorithm studied in this section. Explain the reasoning behind your choice.

50. Lattice multiplication has been described as being most helpful to students who are having difficulty with traditional algorithms. Describe a process for testing this claim in a classroom action research project.

51. Long division has been recommended for reduced attention in elementary classrooms. Do you agree or disagree? Defend your answer.

Cooperative Learning

52. Just as an abacus was presented as a tool for computing, a slide rule was once very popular in this country for completing multiplications and divisions. A much simplified version of a slide rule consists of placing two rulers of the same length and using the same units one atop the other to make an adding ruler. Investigate how this might be done and prepare a presentation of how the adding rulers would work.

Review Problems

53. Write the number succeeding 673 in Egyptian numerals.

54. Write $3 \cdot 10^5 + 2 \cdot 10^2 + 6 \cdot 10$ as a Hindu-Arabic numeral.

55. Illustrate the identity property of addition for whole numbers.

56. Rename each of the following using the distributive property of multiplication over addition:
   a. $ax + bx + 2x$
   b. $3(a + b) + x(a + b)$

57. At the beginning of a trip, the odometer registered 52,281. At the end of the trip, the odometer registered 59,260. How many miles were traveled on this trip?

58. The registration for the computer conference was 192 people on Thursday, 215 on Friday, and 317 on Saturday. What was the total registration?

BRAIN TEASER   For each of the following, replace the letters with digits in such a way that the computation is correct. Each letter may represent only one digit.

a. LYNDON	**b.** MA
× B	MA
JOHNSON	+ MA
	EEL

LABORATORY ACTIVITY

1. Messages can be coded on paper tape in base two. A hole in the tape represents 1, whereas a space represents 0. The value of each hole depends on its position; from left to right, 16, 8, 4, 2, 1 (all powers of 2). Letters of the alphabet may be coded in base two according to their position in the alphabet. For example, G is the seventh letter. Since $7 = 1 \cdot 4 + 1 \cdot 2 + 1$, the holes appear as they do in Figure 3-43:

Figure 3-43

16 8 4 2 1

   a. Decode the following message:

b. Write your name on a tape using base two.

2. The following number game uses base-two arithmetic:

Card E		Card D		Card C		Card B		Card A	
16	24	8	24	4	20	2	18	1	17
17	25	9	25	5	21	3	19	3	19
18	26	10	26	6	22	6	22	5	21
19	27	11	27	7	23	7	23	7	23
20	28	12	28	12	28	10	26	9	25
21	29	13	29	13	29	11	27	11	27
22	30	14	30	14	30	14	30	13	29
23	31	15	31	15	31	15	31	15	31

a. Suppose a person's age appears on cards E, C, and B, and the person is 22. Can you discover how this works and why?

b. Design card F so that the numbers 1–63 can be used in the game. Note that cards A–E must also be changed.

SOLUTION TO THE PRELIMINARY PROBLEM

Understanding the Problem.   Twenty people were in a tennis camp in the mixed-doubles class. Gina was paired with seven male partners, Maria with eight, Tina with nine, and so on until Marva was paired with every male partner. The question is, how many males were there in the mixed-doubles class.

To solve this problem, we must know that a mixed-doubles pair consists of a male partner and a female partner. From the information given, we know that there was a total of 20 people, we know that there were at least four females, and we know that there were at least ten males. (Why?)

Devising a Plan.   There are two unknowns in the problem: the number of males and the number of females in the camp. If we knew either, we could find the other. One possible strategy is to make a table containing the number of known females, the number of partners they had, and a running total of people accounted. Table 3-15 provides an example.

Table 3-15

Females	Males	Total No. of People Accounted For
Gina	7	8
Maria	8	10
Tina	9	12
.		
.		
.		
Marva	?	20

By considering the patterns in Table 3-15, we should be able to determine the number of men and women in the camp.

The pattern in the middle column of Table 3-15 is that the number is increasing by one in each row. If we consider only that column, we do not know where to stop. If we consider the right-hand column, we see an arithmetic sequence starting at 8 and ending at 20 with a common difference of 2.

Carrying Out the Plan.   The number of terms in this sequence is the number of women. Subtracting that number from 20 gives the number of males. Because an arithmetic sequence's last term is the first term plus the common difference times 1 less than the number of terms, we should be able to find the number of terms in the sequence 8, 10, 12, . . . , 20 as follows:

$$20 = 8 + (\text{number of terms} - 1)2$$
$$12 = (\text{number of terms} - 1)2$$
$$6 = \text{number of terms} - 1$$
$$7 = \text{number of terms}$$

Hence, the number of males is $20 - 7 = 13$.

Looking Back.   The number of terms could have been found on a spreadsheet by using the fill-down feature on the right-hand column of Table 3-15. In this case, pencil and paper are sufficient.

QUESTIONS FROM THE CLASSROOM

1. A student asks "Does $2(3 \cdot 4)$ equal $(2 \cdot 3)(2 \cdot 4)$?" Is there a distributive property of multiplication over multiplication?

2. Since $39 + 41 = 40 + 40$, is it true that $39 \cdot 41 = 40 \cdot 40$?

3. The division algorithm, $a = bq + r$, holds for $a > b$; $a, b, q, r \in W$ and $b \neq 0$. Does the algorithm hold when $a < b$?

4. A student asks if 5 times 4 is the same as 5 multiplied by 4. How do you respond?

5. Can we define $0 \div 0$ as 1? Why or why not?

6. A student divides as follows. How do you help?

$$
\begin{array}{r}
15 \\
6\overline{)36} \\
\underline{6} \\
30 \\
\underline{30}
\end{array}
$$

7. When using Roman numerals, a student asks whether it is correct to write $\overline{\text{II}}$, as well as MI, for 1001. How do you respond?

8. A student claims that the expressions $(2^3)^2$ and $2^{(3^2)}$ are equal. How do you respond?

9. A student asks if division on the set of whole numbers is distributive over subtraction. How do you respond?

10. A student says that 0 is the identity for subtraction. How do you respond?

11. A student claims that on the following number line, the arrow doesn't really represent 3 because the end of the arrow does not start at 0. How do you respond?

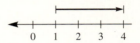

12. A student has read an article maligning the use of calculators in elementary school. How do you respond?

13. A parent complains about the use of manipulatives in the classroom and likens their use to the use of fingers to count. How do you respond?

14. A parent insists that his child should be writing in the mathematics classroom. How do you respond?

CHAPTER OUTLINE

I. Numeration systems

    A. Properties of numeration systems give basic structure to the systems.
        1. Additive property
        2. Place-value property
        3. Subtractive property
        4. Multiplicative property

II. Exponents

    A. For any whole number a and any natural number n,

$$a^n = \underbrace{a \cdot a \cdot a \cdot \ldots \cdot a}_{n \text{ factors}},$$

    where a is the **base** and n is the **exponent.**

    B. $a^0 = 1, a \in N$

    C. For any natural number a, with whole numbers m and n, $a^m \cdot a^n = a^{m+n}$.

III. Whole numbers

    A. The set of **whole numbers** W is $\{0, 1, 2, 3, \ldots\}$.

    B. The basic operations for whole numbers are addition, subtraction, multiplication, and division.
        1. Addition: If $n(A) = a$ and $n(B) = b$, where $A \cap B = \varnothing$, then $a + b = n(A \cup B)$. The numbers a and b are **addends** and $a + b$ is the **sum.**
        2. Subtraction: If a and b are any whole numbers, then $a - b$ is the unique whole number c such that $a = b + c$. The number a is the **minuend,** b is the **subtrahend,** and c is the **difference.**
        3. Multiplication: If a and b are any whole numbers, then

$$ab = \underbrace{b + b + b + \ldots + b}_{a \text{ terms}},$$

where a and b are **factors** and ab is the **product.**
        4. Multiplication: If A and B are sets such that $n(A) = a$ and $n(B) = b$, then $ab = n(A \times B)$.
        5. Division: If a and b are any whole numbers with $b \neq 0$, $a \div b$ is the unique whole number c such that $bc = a$. The number a is the **dividend,** b is the **divisor,** and c is the **quotient.**
        6. **Division algorithm:** Given any whole numbers a and b, with $b \neq 0$, there exist unique whole numbers q and r such that $a = bq + r$, with $0 \leq r < b$.

    C. Properties of addition and multiplication of whole numbers
        1. Closure: If $a, b \in W$, then $a + b \in W$ and $ab \in W$.
        2. Commutative: If $a, b \in W$, then $a + b = b + a$ and $ab = ba$.
        3. Associative: If $a, b, c \in W$, then $(a + b) + c = a + (b + c)$ and $a(bc) = (ab)c$.
        4. Identity: 0 is the unique identity element for addition of whole numbers; 1 is the unique identity element for multiplication.
        5. Distributive property of multiplication over addition: If $a, b, c \in W$, then $a(b + c) = ab + ac$.
        6. Zero multiplication property: For any whole number a, $a \cdot 0 = 0 = 0 \cdot a$.

    D. Relations on whole numbers
        1. $a < b$ if, and only if, there is a natural number c such that $a + c = b$.
        2. $a > b$ if, and only if, $b < a$.

CHAPTER REVIEW

1. Convert each of the following to base ten:
    a. $\overline{\text{CDXLIV}}$ b. 432_{five} c. $ET0_{\text{twelve}}$
    d. 1011_{two} e. 4136_{seven}

2. Convert each of the following numbers to numbers in the indicated system:
    a. 999 to Roman
    b. 86 to Egyptian
    c. 123 to Mayan
    d. 346_{ten} to base five
    e. 27_{ten} to base two

3. Simplify each of the following, if possible. Write your answers in exponential form, a^b.
    a. $3^4 \cdot 3^7 \cdot 3^6$ b. $2^{10} \cdot 2^{11}$
    c. $3^4 + 2 \cdot 3^4$ d. $2^{80} + 3 \cdot 2^{80}$

4. For each of the following, identify the properties of the operation(s) for whole numbers illustrated:
    a. $3 \cdot (a + b) = 3 \cdot a + 3 \cdot b$
    b. $2 + a = a + 2$
    c. $16 \cdot 1 = 1 \cdot 16 = 16$
    d. $6 \cdot (12 + 3) = 6 \cdot 12 + 6 \cdot 3$
    e. $3 \cdot (a \cdot 2) = 3 \cdot (2 \cdot a)$
    f. $3 \cdot (2 \cdot a) = (3 \cdot 2) \cdot a$

5. Using the definitions of less than or greater than, prove that each of the following inequalities is true:
    a. $3 < 13$ b. $12 > 9$

6. Explain why the product of $1000 \cdot 483$, namely, 483,000, has 0 for the hundreds, tens, and units digits.

7. Use both the scratch and the traditional algorithms to perform the following:

$$\begin{array}{r} 316 \\ 712 \\ + 91 \\ \hline \end{array}$$

8. Use both the traditional and the lattice multiplication algorithms to perform each of the following:

$$\begin{array}{r} 613 \\ \times\ 98 \end{array}$$

9. Use both the repeated-subtraction and the conventional algorithms to perform the following:
   a. $912\overline{)4803}$ b. $11\overline{)1011}$
   c. $23_{five}\overline{)3312}_{five}$ d. $11_{two}\overline{)1011}_{two}$

10. Use the division algorithm to check your answers in Problem 9.

11. For each of the following base-ten numbers, tell the place value for each of the circled digits:
    a. $4\textcircled{3}2$ b. $\textcircled{3}432$ c. $19\textcircled{3}24$

12. For each of the following, find all possible replacements to make the following statements true for whole numbers:
    a. $4 \cdot \square - 37 < 27$
    b. $398 = \square \cdot 37 + 28$
    c. $\square \cdot (3 + 4) = \square \cdot 3 + \square \cdot 4$
    d. $42 - \square \geq 16$

13. Use the distributive property of multiplication and addition facts, if possible, to rename each of the following:
    a. $3a + 7a + 5a$
    b. $3x^2 + 7x^2 - 5x^2$
    c. $x(a + b + y)$
    d. $(x + 5)3 + (x + 5)y$

14. If A, B, C, and D each stand for different single digits from 1 to 9, answer the following if

$$A + B + C = D.$$

   a. If $A = 2$, $B = 4$, and $D = 7$, then what is the value of C?
   b. What is the smallest number D could be?
   c. If B is 2 greater than A and 2 less than C, then what is the value of D?

15. You had a balance in your checking account of $720 before writing checks for $162, $158, and $33 and making a deposit of $28. What is your new balance?

16. Jim was paid $320 a month for 6 mo and $410 a month for 6 mo. What were his total earnings for the year?

17. A soft drink manufacturer produces 15,600 cans of his product each hour. Cans are packed 24 to a case. How many cases are produced in 4 hr?

18. A limited partnership of 120 investors sold a piece of land for $461,040. How much did each investor receive?

19. How many 12-oz cans of juice would it take to give 60 people one 8-oz serving each?

20. Heidi has a brown and a gray pair of slacks; a brown, a yellow, and a white blouse; and a blue and a white sweater. How many different outfits does she have if she wears slacks, a blouse, and a sweater?

21. I am thinking of a whole number. If I divide it by 13, then multiply the answer by 12, then subtract 20, and then add 89, I end up with 93. What was my original number?

22. Apples normally sell for 32¢ each. They go on sale for 3 for 69¢. How much money is saved if you purchase 2 dz apples?

23. A ski resort offers a weekend ski package for $80 per person or $6000 for a group of 80 people. Which would be the cheaper option for a group of 80?

24. The owner of a bicycle shop reported his inventory of bicycles and tricycles in an unusual way. He said he counted 126 wheels and 108 pedals. How many bikes and how many trikes did he have?

25. Josi has a job in which she works 30 hr/wk and gets paid $5/hr. If she works over 30 hr in a week, she receives $8/hr for each hour over 30 hr. If she worked 38 hr this week, how much did she earn?

26. In a television game show, there are five questions to answer. Each question is worth twice as much as the previous question. If the last question was worth $6400, what was the first question worth?

27. Explain which definition of multiplication of whole numbers you think will make the most sense to elementary students. Give a rationale for your answer.

28. Write an example of a base other than ten used in a real-life situation. How is it used?

29. Design with a fellow student a whole-number operation problem with at least three extensions beyond the original question.

30. Explain how you could use a calculator to help in adding two non-base ten whole numbers such as $27_{eight} + 65_{eight}$.

SELECTED BIBLIOGRAPHY

Bates, T., and L. Rousseau. "Will the Real Division Algorithm Please Stand Up?" *Arithmetic Teacher* 33 (March 1987): 42–46.

Bobis, J. "Using a Calculator to Develop Number Sense." *Arithmetic Teacher* 38 (January 1991): 42–45.

Bradbent, F. "Lattice Multiplication and Division." *Arithmetic Teacher* 34 (January 1987): 28–31.

Burns, M. "Introducing Division Through Problem-Solving Experiences." *Arithmetic Teacher* 38 (April 1991): 14–18.

Englert, G., and R. Sinicrope. "Making Connections with Two-Digit Multiplication." *Arithmetic Teacher* 41 (April 1994): 446–448.

Feinberg, M. "Using Patterns to Practice Basic Facts." *Arithmetic Teacher* 37 (April 1990): 38–41.

Gluck, D. "Helping Students Understand Place Value." *Arithmetic Teacher* 38 (March 1991): 10–13.

Guershon, H., and M. Behr. "Ed's Strategy for Solving Division Problems." *Arithmetic Teacher* 39 (November 1991): 38–40.

Hemmings, R. "Mathematics," in A. Craft and G. Bardell (eds.), *Curriculum Opportunities in a Multi-Cultural Society.* London: Harper and Row, 1984, pp. 113–32.

Hope, J. "Promoting Number Sense in School." *Arithmetic Teacher* 36 (February 1989): 12–16.

Hope, J., B. Reys, and R. Reys. *Mental Math in the Middle Grades.* Palo Alto: Dale Seymour Publishing, 1987.

Huinker, D. "Multiplication and Division Word Problems: Improving Students Understanding." *Arithmetic Teacher* 37 (October 1989): 8–12.

Kami, C., B. Lewis, and S. Livingston. "Primary Arithmetic: Children Inventing Their Own Procedures." *Arithmetic Teacher* 41 (December 1993): 200–203.

Kami, C., and L. Joseph. "Teaching Place Value and Double-Column Addition." *Arithmetic Teacher* 35 (February 1988): 48–52.

Moore, T. "More on Mental Computation." *Mathematics Teacher* 79 (March 1987): 168–169.

Nelson, D., G. Joseph, and J. Williams. *Multicultural Mathematics.* Oxford: Oxford University Press, 1993.

Reys, R. *Computational Estimation (Grades 6, 7, and 8).* Palo Alto: Dale Seymour Publishing, 1987.

Sowder, J. "Mental Computation and Number Sense." *Arithmetic Teacher* 37 (March 1990): 18–20.

Stanic, G., and W. McKillip. "Developmental Algorithms Have a Place in Elementary School Mathematics." *Arithmetic Teacher* 36 (January 1989): 14–16.

Sundar, V. "Thou Shalt Not Divide by Zero." *Arithmetic Teacher* 37 (March 1991): 50–51.

Thornton, C., and P. Smith. "Action Research: Strategies for Learning Subtraction Facts." *Arithmetic Teacher* 35 (April 1988): 8–12.

Trafton, P., and J. Zawojewski. "Meanings of Operations." *Arithmetic Teacher* 38 (November 1990): 18–22.

Vande Walle, J. "Redefining Computation." *Arithmetic Teacher* 38 (January 1991): 46–51.

Weare D., and J. Hiebert. "Place Value and Addition and Subtraction." *Arithmetic Teacher* 41 (January 1994): 272–274.

4

INTEGERS AND NUMBER THEORY

The teenaged members of the Central High Mathematics Club reported in the school newspaper that the product of their ages was 10,584,000. They challenged the readers to find the number of teenagers in the club and their ages. Solve the problem and explain your reasoning.

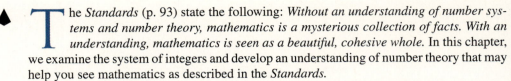

he *Standards* (p. 93) state the following: *Without an understanding of number systems and number theory, mathematics is a mysterious collection of facts. With an understanding, mathematics is seen as a beautiful, cohesive whole.* In this chapter, we examine the system of integers and develop an understanding of number theory that may help you see mathematics as described in the *Standards*.

Negative numbers are useful in everyday life. For example, Mount Everest (the highest point on Earth) is 29,028 ft above sea level, while the Dead Sea (the lowest point on Earth) is 1293 ft below sea level. We may symbolize these elevations as 29,028 and $^-$1293. In mathematics, the need for integers, including negative whole numbers, arises because subtractions cannot always be performed using only the set of whole numbers. To compute $4 - 6$ using the definition of subtraction for whole numbers, we must find a whole number n such that $6 + n = 4$. Because there is no such whole number n, the subtraction cannot be completed. To perform the computation, we must invent a new number. This new number is a *negative integer*. If we attempt to calculate $4 - 6$ on a number line, then we must, as with whole numbers, draw intervals to the left of 0. In Figure 4-1, $4 - 6$ is pictured as an arrow that starts at 0 and ends 2 units to the left of 0. The new number that corresponds to a point 2 units to the left of 0 is *negative two,* symbolized by $^-$2. Other numbers to the left of 0 are created similarly. The new set of numbers $\{^-1, ^-2, ^-3, ^-4, \ldots\}$ is the set of

negative integers   **negative integers.**

Figure 4-1

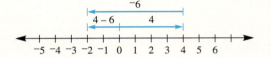

integers   The union of the set of negative integers and the set of whole numbers is the set of **integers.** The set of integers is denoted by I:

$$I = \{\ldots, ^-4, ^-3, ^-2, ^-1, 0, 1, 2, 3, 4, \ldots\}$$

Integers are an important part of the work with divisibility and in the study of modular arithmetic. Therefore it is natural that we examine the set of integers in close proximity to number theory. As a field of study, number theory started to flourish in the seventeenth century with the work of Pierre de Fermat (1605–1665). Topics in number theory that occur in the elementary school curriculum include factors, multiples, divisibility tests, prime numbers, prime factorizations, greatest common divisors, and least common multiples. The topic of congruences, introduced by Karl Gauss (1777–1855), is also incorporated into the elementary curriculum through clock arithmetic and modular arithmetic. This topic of congruences gives students a look at another mathematical system.

Section 4-1   Integers and the Operations of Addition and Subtraction

The importance of extending the number system beyond the whole numbers is recognized in the *Teaching Standards* (p. 136) as follows:

Teachers of mathematics should have a well-developed number sense (including mental mathematics, estimation, and reasonableness of results) and an understanding of the use of number concepts, operations, and properties (including basic number theory), of the role

of algorithms, and of place value. In setting the view of these ideas in the curriculum, teachers should be able to extend the number systems from the whole numbers to fractions and integers, then rationals and real numbers . . . .

In this section, we extend the number system to include integers.

Representations of Integers

In the set of integers, the symbol "−" is unfortunately used to indicate both a subtraction and a negative sign. To reduce confusion between the uses of this symbol in this text, a raised "⁻" sign is used for negative numbers, as in ⁻2, in contrast to the lower sign for subtraction. To emphasize that an integer is positive, some people use a raised plus sign, as in ⁺3. In this text, we use the plus sign for addition only and write ⁺3 simply as 3.

The negative integers are mirror images of the positive integers (Figure 4-1). For example, the mirror image of 5 is ⁻5 and the mirror image of 0 is 0. Similarly, the positive integers are mirror images of the negative integers. For example, 4 is the mirror image of ⁻4. Another term for "mirror image of" is "**opposite** of." Thus the opposite of 4 is denoted by ⁻4 and the opposite of ⁻4 can be denoted by ⁻(⁻4), or 4.

opposite

In the set of integers I, every element has an opposite that is also in I. This is not the case for the set W of whole numbers. If a is a nonzero element of W, its opposite ⁻a is not in the set W.

• • •

Example 4-1

For each of the following, find the opposite of x:

a. $x = 3$ **b.** $x = ⁻5$ **c.** $x = 0$

Solution   **a.** ⁻$x = ⁻3$ **b.** ⁻$x = ⁻(⁻5) = 5$ **c.** ⁻$x = ⁻0 = 0$

• • •

The value of ⁻x in Example 4-1(b) is 5. The *term* ⁻x *does not necessarily represent a negative integer.* In other words, x is a variable that can be replaced by some number, either positive, zero, or negative. For this reason, many teachers encourage students to refer to ⁻x as "the opposite of x" and not "minus x" or "negative x."

H I S T O R I C A L   N O T E

The dash has not always been used for both the subtraction operation and the negative sign. Other notations were developed but never adopted. One such notation was used by Mohammed al-Khowârizmî (ca. 825), who indicated a negative number by placing a small circle over it. For example, ⁻4 was recorded as 4̊. The Hindus denoted a negative number by enclosing it in a circle; for example, ⁻4 was recorded as ④. The symbols + and − first appeared in print in European mathematics in the late fifteenth century. The symbols referred not to addition or subtraction or to positive or negative numbers, but to surpluses and deficits in business problems.

Integer Addition

There are many ways to introduce operations on integers. Before formally defining the operations, we consider a more informal approach.

Figure 4-2

Chip Model

In the chip model, positive integers are represented by black chips and negative integers by red chips. One red chip neutralizes one black chip. Hence, the integer ⁻1 can be represented by 1 red chip, or 2 red and 1 black, or 3 red and 2 black, and so on. Similarly, every integer can be represented in many ways using chips. Figure 4-2 shows a chip model for the addition ⁻4 + 3. We put four red chips together with 3 black chips. Because 3 red chips neutralize 3 black ones, Figure 4-2 represents the equivalent of 1 red chip, or ⁻1.

The chip model is frequently used in elementary school, as seen in the following student page from *Addison-Wesley Mathematics,* Grade 7, 1993.

Adding Integers

LEARN ABOUT IT

EXPLORE Use Counting Chips

Each white chip represents ⁺1. Each red chip represents ⁻1. Since they are opposites, they have a sum of 0 and are said to "cancel each other." It's easy to see that the chips in box A represent ⁺2 if you first "cancel" the pairs of opposites.

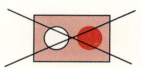

Work with a partner. One of you selects some white chips and records the integer the chips represent. The other selects some red chips and records the integer those chips represent. Combine both sets of chips and record the integer they represent. Repeat the activity several times using different numbers of red and white chips.

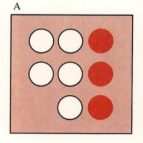

A

TALK ABOUT IT

1. When you and your partner combined chips, how did you decide what integer they represented?

2. What happens if you choose the same number of red and white counters?

You can use counting chips to model addition with integers.

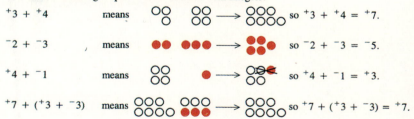

Charged-field Model

A model similar to the chip model uses positive and negative charges. A field has 0 charge if it has the same number of positive (+) and negative (−) charges. As in the chip model, a given integer can be represented in many ways using the *charged-field* model. Figure 4-3 uses the model for $3 + {}^-5$. Because 3 positive charges "neutralize" 3 negative charges, the net result is 2 negative ones. Hence, $3 + {}^-5 = {}^-2$.

Figure 4-3

Patterns

Addition of whole numbers was established in Chapter 3. Addition of integers can also be motivated by using patterns of addition of whole numbers. Notice that in the left-hand column, the first four facts are known from whole-number addition. Also notice that the 4 stays fixed and as the numbers added to 4 decrease by 1, the sum decreases by 1. Following this pattern, $4 + {}^-1 = 3$ and we can complete the remainder of the first column. Similar reasoning can be used to complete the computations in the right-hand column, where $^-2$ stays fixed and the other numbers decrease by 1 each time.

$$4 + 3 = 7 \qquad {}^-2 + 4 = 2$$
$$4 + 2 = 6 \qquad {}^-2 + 3 = 1$$
$$4 + 1 = 5 \qquad {}^-2 + 2 = 0$$
$$4 + 0 = 4 \qquad {}^-2 + 1 = {}^-1$$
$$4 + {}^-1 = 3 \qquad {}^-2 + 0 = {}^-2$$
$$4 + {}^-2 = 2 \qquad {}^-2 + {}^-1 = {}^-3$$
$$4 + {}^-3 = 1 \qquad {}^-2 + {}^-2 = {}^-4$$
$$4 + {}^-4 = 0 \qquad {}^-2 + {}^-3 = {}^-5$$
$$4 + {}^-5 = {}^-1 \qquad {}^-2 + {}^-4 = {}^-6$$
$$4 + {}^-6 = {}^-2 \qquad {}^-2 + {}^-5 = {}^-7$$

TECHNOLOGY CORNER

On a spreadsheet, in Column A enter 4 and fill down 20 rows. In Column B, enter 3 as the first entry and then write a formula to add $^-1$ to 3 for the second entry, add $^-1$ to the second entry to get the third entry, and fill down continuing the pattern. In Column C, find the sum of the respective entries in Columns A and B. What patterns do you observe? Repeat the problem by changing the entries in Column A to $^-4$ and repeating the process.

Number-line Model

Another model for addition of integers involves a number line used with a toy car. The car starts at 0, facing in a positive direction (to the right). To represent a positive integer, the car moves forward, and to represent a negative integer, it moves in reverse. For example, Figure 4-4(a)–(d) illustrates four different additions.

Figure 4-4

5 + 3 is seen as moving the car forward 5 units and then 3 more units forward for a net move of 8 units to the right from 0. Thus 5 + 3 = 8.

(a)
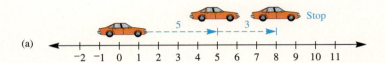

⁻5 + 3 is seen as moving the car 5 units in reverse and then moving it forward 3 units for a net move of 2 units to the left from 0. Thus ⁻5 + 3 = ⁻2.

(b)
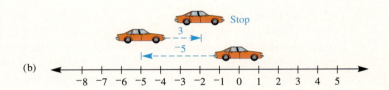

3 + ⁻5 is seen as moving the car 3 units forward and then 5 units in reverse for a net move of 2 units to the left from 0. Thus 3 + ⁻5 = ⁻2.

(c)
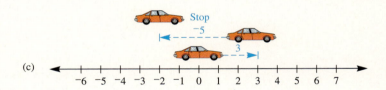

⁻3 + ⁻5 is seen as moving the car 3 units in reverse and then 5 more units in reverse for a net move of 8 units to the left from 0. Thus ⁻3 + ⁻5 = ⁻8.

(d)

Without the car, ⁻3 + ⁻5 can be pictured as in Figure 4-5.

Figure 4-5

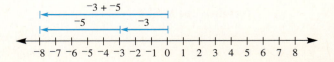

Figure 4-6 similarly depicts integer addition of $3 + {}^-5$.

Figure 4-6

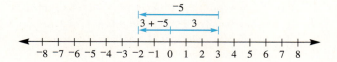

Example 4-2 involves a thermometer with a scale in the form of a vertical number line.

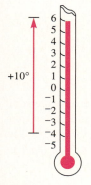

Figure 4-7

Example 4-2 | The temperature was $^-4°$C. In an hour, it rose $10°$C. What is the new temperature?

Solution   Figure 4-7 shows that the new temperature is $6°$C and that $^-4 + 10 = 6$.

Absolute Value

Because 4 and $^-4$ are opposites of each other, they are on opposite sides of 0 on the number line and are the same distance (4 units) from 0, as shown in Figure 4-8.

Figure 4-8

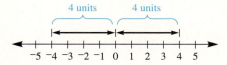

absolute value

Distance is always a positive number or zero. The distance between the points corresponding to an integer and 0 is called the **absolute value** of the integer. Thus the absolute value of both 4 and $^-4$ is 4, written as $|4| = 4$ and $|{}^-4| = 4$, respectively. (A more formal definition of absolute value as a function is given in Ongoing Assessment 4-1.)

Example 4-3 | Evaluate each of the following:

a. $|20|$ **b.** $|{}^-5|$ **c.** $|0|$ **d.** $^-|{}^-3|$ **e.** $|2 - 5|$

Solution   **a.** $|20| = 20$ **b.** $|{}^-5| = 5$ **c.** $|0| = 0$ **d.** $^-|{}^-3| = {}^-3$
e. $|2 - 5| = |{}^-3| = 3$

We can describe addition of integers as finding the difference or the sum of the absolute values of these integers and attaching an appropriate sign.

Properties of Integer Addition

Integer addition has all the properties of whole-number addition. These properties are summarized next.

> **Properties**
>
> Given integers a, b, and c:
> **Closure Property of Addition of Integers** $a + b$ is a unique integer.
> **Commutative Property of Addition of Integers** $a + b = b + a$
> **Associative Property of Addition of Integers** $(a + b) + c = a + (b + c)$
> **Identity Element of Addition of Integers** 0 is the unique integer such that, for all integers a,
> $0 + a = a = a + 0$.

additive inverse   We have seen that every integer has an opposite. This opposite is also called the **additive inverse.** The fact that each integer has a unique (one and only one) additive inverse is recorded below.

> **Uniqueness Property of Additive Inverse**
>
> For every integer a, there exists a unique integer ^-a, the additive inverse of a, such that $a + {}^-a = 0 = {}^-a + a$.

Observe that the additive inverse of ^-a can be written as $^-(^-a)$, or a. Because the additive inverse of ^-a must be unique, we have $^-(^-a) = a$. Other properties of addition of integers can be investigated by considering previously developed notions. For example, we saw that $^-2 + {}^-4 = {}^-6$, and we know that $^-6$ is the additive inverse of 6, or $2 + 4$. This leads us to the following:

$$^-2 + {}^-4 = {}^-(2 + 4).$$

This relationship is true in general and is stated next.

> **Properties of Additive Inverse**
>
> For any integers, a and b:
>
> 1. $^-(^-a) = a$
> 2. $^-a + {}^-b = {}^-(a + b)$

$\bullet \ \bullet \ \bullet$

Example 4-4 Find the additive inverse of each of the following:

a. $^-(3 + x)$ **b.** $(a + {}^-4)$ **c.** $^-3 + ({}^-x)$

Solution **a.** $3 + x$
b. $^-(a + {}^-4)$, which can be written as $^-(a) + {}^-({}^-4)$, or $^-a + 4$.
c. $^-[^-3 + ({}^-x)]$, which can be written as $^-({}^-3) + {}^-({}^-x)$, or $3 + x$.

$\bullet \ \bullet \ \bullet$

Integer Subtraction

As with integer addition, we explore several models for integer subtraction.

Chip Model

To find $3 - {}^-2$, we want to subtract –2 (or remove 2 red chips) from 3 black chips. We need to represent 3 so that at least 2 red chips are present. In Figure 4-9, 3 is represented using 2 red and 5 black chips. When the 2 red chips are removed, 5 black ones are left and, hence, $3 - {}^-2 = 5$.

Figure 4-9

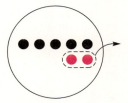

Charged-field Model

Integer subtraction can be modeled with a charged field. For example, consider ${}^-3 - {}^-5$. To subtract ${}^-5$ from ${}^-3$, we must represent ${}^-3$ so that at least 5 negative charges are present. An example is shown in Figure 4-10(a). To subtract ${}^-5$, remove the 5 negative charges, leaving 2 positive charges, as in Figure 4-10(b). Hence, ${}^-3 - {}^-5 = 2$.

Figure 4-10

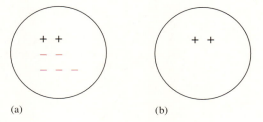

(a)   (b)

Patterns Model

We may find the difference of two integers by considering the following patterns, where we start with subtractions that we already know how to do. Both the pattern on the left and the pattern on the right start with $3 - 2 = 1$:

$$3 - 2 = 1 \qquad 3 - 2 = 1$$
$$3 - 3 = 0 \qquad 3 - 1 = 2$$
$$3 - 4 = ? \qquad 3 - 0 = 3$$
$$3 - 5 = ? \qquad 3 - {}^-1 = ?$$

In the pattern on the left, the difference decreases by 1. If we continue the pattern, we have $3 - 4 = {}^-1$ and $3 - 5 = {}^-2$. In the pattern on the right, the difference increases by 1. If we continue the pattern, we have $3 - {}^-1 = 4$ and $3 - {}^-2 = 5$.

Number-line Model

The number-line model used for integer addition may also be used to model integer subtraction. In Figure 4-11, the car starts at 0 and is pointed in a positive direction (to the right). In this model, the operation of subtraction corresponds to facing the car in a negative direction. We subtract a positive integer by moving the car forward and a negative integer by moving the car in reverse. Figure 4-11 shows some examples.

Figure 4-11

5 – 3 first tells you to move the car forward 5 units. The subtraction sign tells you to face the car in the negative direction. Finally, move forward 3 units for a net move of 2 units to the right from 0. Thus 5 – 3 = 2.

(a)
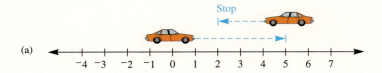

5 – ⁻3 first tells you to move the car forward 5 units. Then face it in a negative direction and move it in reverse 3 units. The net move is 8 units to the right of 0. Thus 5 – ⁻3 = 8.

(b)
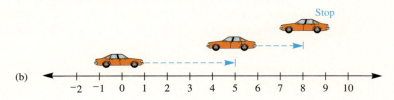

In ⁻5 – ⁻3, move the car 5 units in reverse. Then face it in a negative direction and move it in reverse 3 units. The net move is 2 units to the left of 0. Thus ⁻5 – ⁻3 = ⁻2.

(c)
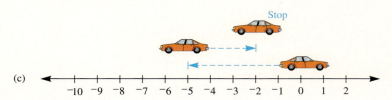

Subtraction as the Inverse of Addition

Subtraction of integers, like subtraction of whole numbers, can be defined in terms of addition. Recall that 5 − 3 can be computed by finding a whole number n as follows:

$$5 - 3 = n \quad \text{if, and only if,} \quad 5 = 3 + n.$$

Because 3 + 2 = 5, then $n = 2$.

Similarly, we compute 3 − 5 as follows:

$$3 - 5 = n \quad \text{if, and only if,} \quad 3 = 5 + n.$$

Because 5 + ⁻2 = 3, then $n = ⁻2$. In general, for integers a and b, we have the following definition of *subtraction*.

Definition of Subtraction

For integers a and b, $a - b$ is the unique integer n such that $a = b + n$.

From our previous work with addition of integers, we know that $3 - 5 = {}^{-}2$ and $3 + {}^{-}5 = {}^{-}2$. Hence, $3 - 5 = 3 + {}^{-}5$. In general, the following is true.

Property

For all integers a and b, $a - b = a + ({}^{-}b)$.

REMARK   The Closure Property of Subtraction of Integers holds, but the Commutative, Associative, and Identity properties do not hold for subtraction of integers.

Example 4-5   Use the definition of subtraction to compute the following:

a. $3 - 10$ **b.** ${}^{-}2 - 10$

Solution   **a.** Let $3 - 10 = n$. Then $10 + n = 3$, so $n = {}^{-}7$. Therefore $3 - 10 = {}^{-}7$.
   b. Let ${}^{-}2 - 10 = n$. Then $10 + n = {}^{-}2$, so $n = {}^{-}12$. Therefore ${}^{-}2 - 10 = {}^{-}12$.

Many calculators have a change-of-sign key, either $\boxed{\text{CHS}}$ or $\boxed{\text{+/-}}$, that allows computation with integers. For example, to compute $8 - ({}^{-}3)$, we would press $\boxed{8}\ \boxed{-}\ \boxed{3}\ \boxed{\text{+/-}}\ \boxed{=}$.

Example 4-6   Compute each of the following using the fact that $a - b = a + ({}^{-}b)$:

a. $2 - 8$ **b.** $2 - ({}^{-}8)$ **c.** ${}^{-}12 - ({}^{-}5)$ **d.** ${}^{-}12 - 5$

Solution   **a.** $2 - 8 = 2 + {}^{-}8 = {}^{-}6$
   b. $2 - ({}^{-}8) = 2 + {}^{-}({}^{-}8) = 2 + 8 = 10$
   c. ${}^{-}12 - ({}^{-}5) = {}^{-}12 + {}^{-}({}^{-}5) = {}^{-}12 + 5 = {}^{-}7$
   d. ${}^{-}12 - 5 = {}^{-}12 + {}^{-}5 = {}^{-}17$

Example 4-7   Write an expression equal to ${}^{-}(b + {}^{-}c)$ that contains no parentheses.

Solution ${}^{-}(b + {}^{-}c) = {}^{-}b + {}^{-}({}^{-}c) = {}^{-}b + c$

Example 4-8   Simplify each of the following:

a. $2 - (5 - x)$ **b.** $5 - (x - 3)$ **c.** ${}^{-}(x - y) - y$

Solution   **a.** $2 - (5 - x) = 2 + {}^-(5 + {}^-x)$
$$= 2 + {}^-5 + {}^-({}^-x)$$
$$= 2 + {}^-5 + x$$
$$= {}^-3 + x$$

b. $5 - (x - 3) = 5 + {}^-(x + {}^-3)$
$$= 5 + {}^-x + {}^-({}^-3)$$
$$= 5 + {}^-x + 3$$
$$= 8 + {}^-x$$
$$= 8 - x$$

c. ${}^-(x - y) - y = ({}^-x + y) - y$
$$= ({}^-x + y) + {}^-y$$
$$= {}^-x + (y + {}^-y)$$
$$= {}^-x + 0$$
$$= {}^-x$$

• • •

Order of Operations

Subtraction on the set of integers is neither commutative nor associative, as illustrated in these counterexamples:

$$5 - 3 \neq 3 - 5 \quad \text{because} \quad 2 \neq {}^-2$$
$$(3 - 15) - 8 \neq 3 - (15 - 8) \quad \text{because} \quad {}^-20 \neq {}^-4$$

Remember, any computations within parentheses must be completed before other computations.

An expression such as $3 - 15 - 8$ is ambiguous unless we know in which order to perform the subtractions. Mathematicians agree that $3 - 15 - 8$ means $(3 - 15) - 8$; that is, the subtractions in $3 - 15 - 8$ are performed in order from left to right. Similarly, $3 - 4 + 5$ means $(3 - 4) + 5$ and not $3 - (4 + 5)$. Thus $(a - b) - c$ may be written without parentheses as $a - b - c$.

• • •

Example 4-9   Compute each of the following:

a. $2 - 5 - 5$ **b.** $3 - 7 + 3$ **c.** $3 - (7 - 3)$

Solution   **a.** $2 - 5 - 5 = {}^-3 - 5 = {}^-8$
b. $3 - 7 + 3 = {}^-4 + 3 = {}^-1$
c. $3 - (7 - 3) = 3 - 4 = {}^-1$

• • •

TECHNOLOGY CORNER

a. On a graphing calculator, graph the function with equation $y = x - {}^-4$.
b. Using the graph in (a), describe what happens as x takes on values that are less than ${}^-4$, equal to ${}^-4$, and greater than ${}^-4$.

Ongoing Assessment 4-1

1. Find the opposite of each of the following integers. Write your answer in the simplest possible form.
   a. 2   **b.** ⁻5   **c.** *m*
   d. 0   **e.** ⁻*m*   **f.** *a* + *b*

2. Simplify each of the following:
   a. ⁻(⁻2)   **b.** ⁻(⁻*m*)   **c.** ⁻0

3. Evaluate each of the following:
   a. |⁻5| **b.** |10| **c.** ⁻|⁻5| **d.** |5|

4. Demonstrate each of the following additions using the charged-field model:
   a. 5 + ⁻3   **b.** ⁻2 + 3   **c.** ⁻3 + 2
   d. ⁻3 + ⁻2

5. Demonstrate each of the additions in Problem 4 using the colored-chips model.

6. Demonstrate each of the additions in Problem 4 using a number-line model.

7. Write an addition fact corresponding to each of the following sentences and then answer the question:
   a. A certain stock dropped 17 points and the following day gained 10 points. What was the net change in the stock's worth?
   b. The temperature was ⁻10°C and then it rose by 8°C. What is the new temperature?
   c. The plane was at 5000 ft and dropped 100 ft. What is the new altitude of the plane?
   d. A visitor in a Las Vegas casino lost $200, won $100, and then lost $50. What is the change in the gambler's net worth?
   e. In four downs, the football team lost 2 yd, gained 7 yd, gained 0 yd, and lost 8 yd. What is the total gain or loss?

8. On January 1, Jane's bank balance was $300. During the month, she wrote checks for $45, $55, $165, $35, and $100 and made deposits of $75, $25, and $400.
   a. If a check is represented by a negative integer and a deposit by a positive integer, express Jane's transactions as a sum of positive and negative integers.
   b. What was the balance in Jane's account at the end of the month?

9. Use the charged-field model to show each of the following:
   a. 3 − ⁻2 = 5   **b.** ⁻3 − 2 = ⁻5
   c. ⁻3 − ⁻2 = ⁻1

10. Use the car model to find the following:
   a. ⁻4 − ⁻1   **b.** ⁻4 − ⁻3

11. Use patterns to show the following:
   a. ⁻4 − ⁻1 = ⁻3   **b.** ⁻2 − 1 = ⁻3

12. Write the integer suggested by each of the following chip sequences:
   a. ●, ● ● ●, ● ● ● ● ●, ● ● ● ● ● ● ●, . . .
   b. ●, ● ● ●, ● ● ● ● ●, ● ● ● ● ● ● ●, . . .
   c. ● ● ●, ● ● ● ● ● ●, ● ● ● ● ● ● ● ● ●, ● ● ● ● ● ● ● ● ● ● ● ●, . . .

13. Perform each of the following:
   a. ⁻2 + (3 − 10)   **b.** [8 − (⁻5)] − 10
   c. (⁻2 − 7) + 10   **d.** ⁻2 − (7 + 10)
   e. 8 − 11 − 10   **f.** ⁻2 − 7 + 3

14. In each of the following, write a subtraction problem that corresponds to the question and an addition problem that corresponds to the question and then answer the question:
   a. The temperature is 55°F and is supposed to drop 60°F by midnight. What is the expected midnight temperature?
   b. Moses has overdraft privileges at his bank. If he had $200 in his checking account and he wrote a $220 check, what is his balance?

15. Donna picked the Knicks basketball team to win by 12 points. Instead, they lost by 21. By how many points did Donna misjudge the score?

16. Answer each of the following:
   a. In a game of Triominoes, Jack's scores in five successive turns are 17, ⁻8, ⁻9, 14, and 45. What is his total at the end of five turns?
   b. The largest bubble chamber in the world is 15 ft in diameter and contains 7259 gal of liquid hydrogen at a temperature of ⁻247°C. If the temperature is dropped by 11°C per hour for 2 consecutive hours, what is the new temperature?
   c. The greatest recorded temperature ranges in the world are around the "cold pole" in Siberia. Temperatures in Verkhoyansk have varied from ⁻94°F to 98°F. What is the difference between the high and low temperatures in Verkhoyansk?

17. The daily changes in Dolores's favorite stock were recorded as follows: 5, ⁻10, 8, ⁻2, 3, ⁻1, ⁻1. What was the change for the week?

18. Jim recorded his weight gains and losses during 8 wk as follows: ⁻2, ⁻4, 3, 0, ⁻2, ⁻3, 1, 3. How much did Jim gain or lose?

19. Motor oils protect car engines over a range of temperatures. These oils have names like 10W–40 or 5W–30. The following graph shows the temperatures, in degrees Fahrenheit, at which the engine is protected by a particular oil. Using the graph, find which oils can be used for the following temperatures:
   a. Between ⁻5° and 90°   **b.** Below ⁻20°
   c. Between ⁻10° and 50°   **d.** From ⁻20° to over 100°
   e. From ⁻8° to 90°

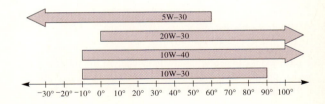

20. Simplify each of the following as much as possible:
    a. $3 - (2 - 4x)$
    b. $x - (^-x - y)$
    c. $4x - 2 - 3x$

21. Find all integers x such that the following are true:
    a. ^-x is positive.
    b. ^-x is negative.
    c. $^-x - 1$ is positive.
    d. $|x| = 2$
    e. $^-|x| = 2$
    f. $^-|x|$ is negative.
    g. $^-|x|$ is positive.

22. Columbus discovered America in 1492. Rome was founded 2275 yrs before that. When was Rome founded?

23. Let W stand for the set of whole numbers, I the set of integers, I^+ the set of positive integers, and I^- the set of negative integers. Find each of the following:
    a. $W \cup I$
    b. $W \cap I$
    c. $I^+ \cup I^-$
    d. $I^+ \cap I^-$
    e. $W - I$
    f. $I - W$
    g. $W - I^+$
    h. $W - I^-$
    i. $I \cap I$

24. Complete the magic square using the following integers: $^-13, ^-10, ^-7, ^-4, 2, 5, 8, 11$.

25. Place the integers 1 through 8 in the following boxes so that no two consecutive integers are in boxes that share a common side or vertex (corner):

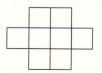

26. Let $f(x) = ^-x - 1$. Find the following:
    a. $f(^-1)$
    b. $f(100)$
    c. $f(^-2)$
    d. For which values of x will the output be 3?

27. Let $f(x) = |1 - x|$. Find the following:
    a. $f(10)$
    b. $f(^-1)$
    c. All the inputs for which the output is 1
    d. The range

28. The following is the definition for the absolute value function, where the domain is the set of integers:

    If x is a positive integer or 0, then $|x| = x$.
    If x is a negative integer, then $|x| = ^-x$.

    a. What is the range of this function?
    b. Use the definition to evaluate each of the following:
        i. $|5|$
        ii. $|^-5|$
        iii. $|0|$
        iv. $^-|^-7|$

29. Determine how many integers there are between the following given integers (not including the given integers):
    a. 10 and 100
    b. $^-30$ and $^-10$
    c. $^-10$ and 10
    d. x and y (if $x < y$)

30. Suppose $a = 6$, $b = 5$, $c = 4$, and $d = ^-3$. Insert parentheses in the expression $a - b - c - d$ to obtain the greatest possible and the least possible values. What are these values?

31. An arithmetic sequence may have a positive or negative difference. In each of the following arithmetic sequences, find the difference and write the next two terms:
    a. $0, ^-3, ^-6, ^-9$
    b. $7, 3, ^-1, ^-5$
    c. $x + y, x, x - y$
    d. $1 - 3x, 1 - x, 1 + x$

32. Find the sums of the following arithmetic sequences:
    a. $^-20 + ^-19 + ^-18 + \ldots + 18 + 19 + 20$
    b. $100 + 99 + 98 + \ldots + ^-50$
    c. $100 + 98 + 96 + \ldots + ^-6$

33. Explain why $b - a$ and $a - b$ are opposites of each other.

34. Classify each of the following as true or false. If false, give a counterexample.
    a. $|^-x| = |x|$
    b. $|x - y| = |y - x|$
    c. $|^-x + ^-y| = |x + y|$
    d. $|x^2| = x^2$
    e. $|x^3| = x^3$
    f. $|x^3| = x^2 |x|$

35. Assume the larger gear has 56 teeth and the smaller gear has 14 teeth. If the larger gear rotates 7 times per minute, how many times does the smaller gear rotate and in what direction in relation to the larger gear?

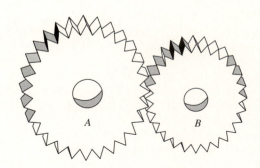

36. Find the opposites for each of the following, using the $\boxed{+/-}$ key on a calculator.
    a. 14
    b. 24
    c. $^-2$
    d. $^-5$

37. Complete each of the following integer arithmetic problems on the calculator, making use of the $\boxed{+/-}$ key. For example, to find $^-5 + ^-4$, press $\boxed{5}\ \boxed{+/-}\ \boxed{+}\ \boxed{4}\ \boxed{+/-}\ \boxed{=}$.
    a. $^-12 + ^-6$
    b. $^-7 + ^-99$
    c. $^-12 + 6$
    d. $27 + ^-5$
    e. $3 + ^-14$
    f. $^-7 - ^-9$
    g. $^-12 - 6$
    h. $16 - ^-7$

38. Estimate each of the following and then use a calculator to find the actual answer:
    a. $343 + ^-42 - 402$
    b. $^-1992 + 3005 - 497$
    c. $992 - ^-10003 - 101$
    d. $^-301 - ^-1303 + 4993$

Communication

39. Describe a realistic word problem that models $^-50 + (^-85) - (-30)$.

40. What real life applications of negative integers can you think of that were not mentioned in the text? Would any of these applications be useful in teaching about integers? Why?

41. A turnpike driver had car trouble. He knew that he had driven 12 mi from milepost 68 before the trouble started. Assuming he is confused and disoriented when he calls on his cellular phone for help, how can he determine his possible location? Explain.

42. a. Show that when $a + b$ is added to $^-a + ^-b$, the result is 0.
   b. Use part (a) and the definition of additive inverse to explain why $^-a + ^-b = ^-(a + b)$.

43. Addition of integers with like signs can be described using absolute values as follows:

   To add integers with like signs, add the absolute values of the integers. The sum has the same sign as the integers.

   Describe in a similar way how to add integers with unlike signs.

Open-ended

44. In the library at a well-known university, some floors are below ground level while others are above ground level. If the ground-level floor is designated the zero floor, design a system for using integers to number the floors and then design an operation system for the elevator to model addition and subtraction with integers.

45. Which model(s) would you use to teach addition and subtraction of integers? Explain why you chose the model you did.

46. Select a current middle-school text that introduces addition and subtraction of integers and discuss which models were used and how effective you think they would be with a group of students.

Cooperative Learning

47. Designate some class members as positive integers and some as negative integers. Design a method of illustrating with these classmates a method of modeling the addition and subtraction of integers.

BRAIN TEASER   If the digits 1 through 9 are written in order, it is possible to place plus and minus signs between the numbers or to use no operation symbol at all to obtain a total of 100. For example,

$$1 + 2 + 3 + ^-4 + 5 + 6 + 78 + 9 = 100.$$

Can you obtain a total of 100 using fewer plus or minus signs than in the given example? Notice that digits, such as 7 and 8, may be combined.

TECHNOLOGY CORNER   Type the following Logo (See Appendix I) programs on your computer:

```
TO ABS :X
   IF :X < 0 THEN OUTPUT (-:X)
   OUTPUT :X
END
```

(In LCSI replace IF :X < 0 THEN OUTPUT (− :X) with IF :X < 0 [OUTPUT — :X].)

Run this program and input the following values:

a. $^-7$ **b.** 0   **c.** 140   **d.** $^-21$

Multiplication and Division of Integers

We may approach multiplication of integers through a variety of models: *patterns, charged-field, chip,* and *number line.*

Patterns Model

First, we may approach multiplication of integers by using repeated addition. For example, if a running back lost 2 yd on each of three carries in a football game, then he had a net loss of $^-2 + {}^-2 + {}^-2$, or $^-6$, yards. Since $^-2 + {}^-2 + {}^-2$ can be written as $3 \cdot (^-2)$, using repeated addition, we have $3 \cdot (^-2) = {}^-6$.

Consider $(^-2) \cdot 3$. It is meaningless to say that there are $^-2$ threes in a sum. The following pattern can help develop a feeling for what $(^-2) \cdot 3$ should be:

$$4 \cdot 3 = 12$$
$$3 \cdot 3 = 9$$
$$2 \cdot 3 = 6$$
$$1 \cdot 3 = 3$$
$$0 \cdot 3 = 0$$
$$^-1 \cdot 3 = ?$$
$$^-2 \cdot 3 = ?$$

The first five products, 12, 9, 6, 3, and 0, are terms of an arithmetic sequence with fixed difference $^-3$. If the pattern continues, the next two terms in the sequence are $^-3$ and $^-6$. Thus it appears that $(^-2) \cdot 3 = {}^-6$. Also, $3 \cdot (^-2)$ equals $^-6$. If $(^-2) \cdot 3 = {}^-6$, we have $(^-2) \cdot 3 = 3 \cdot (^-2)$. This result is consistent with the commutative property of multiplication.

Next, consider $(^-2) \cdot (^-3)$. Using the previous results, we can develop this pattern:

$$(^-2) \cdot 3 = {}^-6$$
$$(^-2) \cdot 2 = {}^-4$$
$$(^-2) \cdot 1 = {}^-2$$
$$(^-2) \cdot 0 = 0$$
$$(^-2) \cdot (^-1) = ?$$
$$(^-2) \cdot (^-2) = ?$$
$$(^-2) \cdot (^-3) = ?$$

The first four products, $^-6$, $^-4$, $^-2$, and 0, are terms in an arithmetic sequence with fixed difference 2. If the pattern continues, the next 3 terms in the sequence are 2, 4, and 6. Thus it appears that $(^-2) \cdot (^-3) = 6$.

Charged-field Model and Chip Model

The *charged-field model* and *chip model* can be used to illustrate multiplication of integers, although an interpretation must be given to the signs. Consider Figure 4-12, where $3 \cdot (^-2)$ is pictured using a chip model.

To find $^-3(^-2)$ using the charged-field model, we interpret the signs as follows: $^-3$ is taken to mean "*remove 3 groups of*"; $^-2$ is taken to mean "*2 negative charges.*" To do this, we first start with a 0 charged field that includes at least 6 negative charges, as shown in Figure 4-13.

Figure 4-12

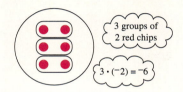

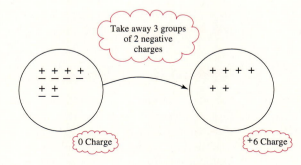

Figure 4-13

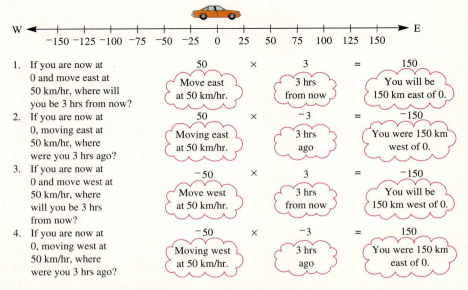

The result is a charge of positive 6, so $^-3? \cdot (^-2) = 6$.

Number-line Model

As for addition and subtraction, we demonstrate by using a car moving along a number line, according to the following rules:

1. Traveling to the left (west) means moving in the negative direction, and traveling to the right (east) means moving in the positive direction.
2. Time in the future is denoted by a positive value, and time in the past is denoted by a negative value.

Consider the number line shown in Figure 4-14. Various cases using this number line are given next.

Figure 4-14

W ←———————————————————→ E
$^-150$ $^-125$ $^-100$ $^-75$ $^-50$ $^-25$ 0 25 50 75 100 125 150

1. If you are now at 0 and move east at 50 km/hr, where will you be 3 hrs from now?

   50 (Move east at 50 km/hr.) × 3 (3 hrs from now) = 150 (You will be 150 km east of 0.)

2. If you are now at 0, moving east at 50 km/hr, where were you 3 hrs ago?

   50 (Moving east at 50 km/hr.) × $^-3$ (3 hrs ago) = $^-150$ (You were 150 km west of 0.)

3. If you are now at 0 and move west at 50 km/hr, where will you be 3 hrs from now?

   $^-50$ (Move west at 50 km/hr.) × 3 (3 hrs from now) = $^-150$ (You will be 150 km west of 0.)

4. If you are now at 0, moving west at 50 km/hr, where were you 3 hrs ago?

   $^-50$ (Moving west at 50 km/hr.) × $^-3$ (3 hrs ago) = 150 (You were 150 km east of 0.)

These models illustrate the following definition of *multiplication of integers*.

Definition of Multiplication of Integers

For any **whole numbers** a and b, the following holds:

1. $(\overline{\ }a)(\overline{\ }b) = ab$
2. $(\overline{\ }a)b = b(\overline{\ }a) = \overline{\ }(ab)$

Properties of Integer Multiplication

The set of integers has properties under multiplication analogous to those of the set of whole numbers under multiplication. These properties are summarized next.

Properties of Integer Multiplication

The set of integers I satisfies the following properties of multiplication for all integers $a, b, c \in I$:

Closure Property of Multiplication of Integers ab is a unique integer.

Commutative Property of Multiplication of Integers $ab = ba$.

Associative Property of Multiplication of Integers $(ab)c = a(bc)$

Multiplicative Identity Property   1 is the unique integer such that for all integers a, $1 \cdot a = a = a \cdot 1$.

Distributive Properties of Multiplication over Addition for Integers $a(b + c) = ab + ac$ and $(b + c)a = ba + ca$

Zero Multiplication Property of Integers   0 is the unique integer such that for all integers a, $a \cdot 0 = 0 = 0 \cdot a$

Another approach to showing that $(\overline{\ }2) \cdot 3 = \overline{\ }(2 \cdot 3)$ uses the uniqueness property of additive inverses. If we can show that $(\overline{\ }2) \cdot 3$ and $\overline{\ }(2 \cdot 3)$ are additive inverses of the same number, then they must be equal. By definition, the additive inverse of $(2 \cdot 3)$ is $\overline{\ }(2 \cdot 3)$. That $(\overline{\ }2) \cdot 3$ is also the additive inverse of $2 \cdot 3$ can be proved by showing that $(\overline{\ }2) \cdot 3 + 2 \cdot 3 = 0$. The proof follows.

$$(\overline{\ }2) \cdot 3 + 2 \cdot 3 = (\overline{\ }2 + 2) \cdot 3 \quad \text{Distributive property of multiplication over addition}$$
$$= 0 \cdot 3 \qquad\qquad \text{Additive inverse}$$
$$= 0 \qquad\qquad\quad \text{Zero multiplication}$$

Because $(\overline{\ }2) \cdot 3$ and $\overline{\ }(2 \cdot 3)$ are both additive inverses of $(2 \cdot 3)$ and because the additive inverse must be unique, $(\overline{\ }2) \cdot 3 = \overline{\ }(2 \cdot 3)$.

Using this approach, we could show the following general property.

> **Property**
>
> For any integers a and b, $(^-a)b = ^-(ab)$.

Similarly, we have the following property.

> **Property**
>
> For any integers a and b, $(^-a)(^-b) = ab$.

REMARK   It is important to note that in these properties, ^-a and ^-b are not necessarily negative and a and b are not necessarily positive.

Example 4-10

Find each of the following:

a. $(^-3) \cdot (^-15)$ **b.** $(^-5) \cdot 7$ **c.** $0 \cdot (^-3)$
d. $0 \cdot (^-n), n \in W$ **e.** $(^-5)^4$

Solution   **a.** $(^-3) \cdot (^-15) = 45$ **b.** $(^-5) \cdot 7 = ^-35$
c. $0 \cdot (^-3) = 0$ **d.** $0 \cdot (^-n) = 0$
e. $(^-5)^4 = (^-5) \cdot (^-5) \cdot (^-5) \cdot (^-5) = 625$

The distributive property of multiplication over subtraction follows from the distributive property of multiplication over addition:

$$a(b - c) = a(b + ^-c)$$
$$= ab + a(^-c)$$
$$= ab + ^-(ac)$$
$$= ab - ac$$

Consequently, $a(b - c) = ab - ac$. Similarly, we can show that $(b - c)a = ba - ca$.

> **Property**
>
> **Distributive Property of Multiplication over Subtraction for Integers**   For any integers a, b, and c.
>
> $$a(b - c) = ab - ac$$
> $$(b - c)a = ba - ca$$

Example 4-11

Simplify each of the following so that there are no parentheses in the final answer:
a. $(^-3)(x - 2)$ **b.** $(a + b)(a - b)$

Solution   **a.** $(^-3)(x-2) = (^-3)x - (^-3)(2) = ^-3x - (^-6) = ^-3x + 6$
b. $(a+b)(a-b) = (a+b)a - (a+b)b$
$$= (a^2 + ba) - (ab + b^2)$$
$$= a^2 + ab - ab - b^2$$
$$= a^2 - b^2$$
Thus $(a+b)(a-b) = a^2 - b^2$.

• • •

difference of squares   The result $(a+b)(a-b) = a^2 - b^2$ in Example 4-11(b) is commonly called the **difference-of-squares** formula.

• • •

Example 4-12   Use the difference-of-squares formula to aid in simplifying the following:

a. $(4+b)(4-b)$ **b.** $(^-4+b)(^-4-b)$

Solution   **a.** $(4+b)(4-b) = 4^2 - b^2 = 16 - b^2$
b. $(^-4+b)(^-4-b) = (^-4)^2 - b^2 = 16 - b^2$

• • •

I N V E S T I G A T I O N   4 - 1

● Determine how to use the difference of squares   **a.** $22 \cdot 18$ **b.** $24 \cdot 36$ **c.** $998 \cdot 1002$ ●
formula to compute the following mentally:

Both the difference-of-squares formula and the distributive properties of multiplication over addition and subtraction can be used for factoring.

• • •

Example 4-13   Factor each of the following completely:

a. $x^2 - 9$ **b.** $(x+y)^2 - z^2$ **c.** $^-3x + 5xy$ **d.** $3x - 6$

Solution   **a.** $x^2 - 9 = x^2 - 3^2 = (x+3)(x-3)$
b. $(x+y)^2 - z^2 = (x+y+z)(x+y-z)$
c. $^-3x + 5xy = x(^-3 + 5y)$
d. $3x - 6 = 3(x-2)$

• • •

Integer Division

In the set of whole numbers, $a \div b$, where $b \neq 0$, is the unique whole number c such that $a = bc$. If such a whole number c does not exist, then $a \div b$ is undefined. Division on the set of integers is defined analogously.

Definition of Integer Division

If a and b are any integers, with $b \neq 0$, then $a \div b$ is the unique integer c, if it exists, such that $a = bc$.

Example 4-14   Use the definition of division, if possible, to evaluate each of the following:

a. $12 \div (^-4)$ **b.** $^-12 \div 4$ **c.** $^-12 \div (^-4)$ **d.** $^-12 \div 5$

Solution   **a.** Let $12 \div (^-4) = c$. Then, $12 = ^-4c$, and consequently, $c = ^-3$. Thus $12 \div (^-4) = ^-3$.

b. Let $^-12 \div 4 = c$. Then, $^-12 = 4c$, and therefore $c = ^-3$. Thus $^-12 \div 4 = ^-3$.

c. Let $^-12 \div (^-4) = c$. Then, $^-12 = ^-4c$, and consequently, $c = 3$. Thus $^-12 \div (^-4) = 3$.

d. Let $^-12 \div 5 = c$. Then, $^-12 = 5c$. Because no integer c exists to satisfy this equation, $^-12 \div 5$ is undefined.

Example 4-14 suggests that *the quotient of two negative integers, if it exists, is a positive integer and the quotient of a positive and a negative integer, if it exists, or of a negative and a positive integer, if it exists, is negative.*

Order of Operations on Integers

The following rules apply to the order in which arithmetic operations are performed. Recall that when addition and multiplication appear in a problem without parentheses, multiplication is done first.

When addition, subtraction, multiplication, and division appear without parentheses, multiplications and divisions are done first in the order of their appearance from left to right, and then additions and subtractions are done in the order of their appearance from left to right. Any arithmetic operation appearing inside parentheses must be done first.

Example 4-15   Evaluate each of the following:

a. $2 - 5 \cdot 4 + 1$
b. $(2 - 5) \cdot 4 + 1$
c. $2 - 3 \cdot 4 + 5 \cdot 2 - 1 + 5$
d. $2 + 16 \div 4 \cdot 2 + 8$
e. $(^-3)^4$
f. $^-3^4$

Solution   **a.** $2 - 5 \cdot 4 + 1 = 2 - 20 + 1 = ^-18 + 1 = ^-17$

b. $(2 - 5) \cdot 4 + 1 = ^-3 \cdot 4 + 1 = ^-12 + 1 = ^-11$

c. $2 - 3 \cdot 4 + 5 \cdot 2 - 1 + 5 = 2 - 12 + 10 - 1 + 5 = 4$

d. $2 + 16 \div 4 \cdot 2 + 8 = 2 + 4 \cdot 2 + 8 = 2 + 8 + 8 = 10 + 8 = 18$

e. $(^-3)^4 = (^-3)(^-3)(^-3)(^-3) = 81$

f. $^-3^4 = ^-(3^4) = ^-(81) = ^-81$

REMARK   Notice that from Example 4-15(e) and (f), we have $(^-3)^4 \neq {}^-3^4$. By convention, $(^-3)^4$ means $(^-3)(^-3)(^-3)(^-3)$ and $^-3^4$ means $^-(3^4)$, or $^-(3 \cdot 3 \cdot 3 \cdot 3)$.

TECHNOLOGY CORNER

On a spreadsheet, in Column A enter 5 as the first entry and then write a formula to add $^-1$ to 5 for the second entry. Then add $^-1$ to the second entry and fill down continuing the pattern. In Column B, repeat the process. In Column C, find the product of the respective entries in Columns A and B. What patterns do you observe?

BRAIN TEASER   Express each of the numbers from 1 through 10 using 4 fours and any operations. For example,

$$1 = 44 \div 44, \text{ or}$$
$$1 = (4 \div 4)^{44}, \text{ or}$$
$$1 = {}^-4 + 4 + (4 \div 4).$$

Ongoing Assessment 4-2

1. Use patterns to show that $(^-1)(^-1) = 1$.
2. Use the charged-field model to show that $(^-4)(^-2) = 8$.
3. Use the number-line model to show that $(^-4)2 = {}^-8$.
4. The number of students eating in the school cafeteria has been decreasing at the rate of 20 per year. Assuming this trend continues, write a multiplication problem that describes the change in the number of students eating in the school cafeteria for each of the following:
   a. The change over the next 4 yr
   b. The situation 4 yr ago
   c. The change over the next n years
   d. The situation n years ago
5. Use the definition of division to find each quotient (if possible). If a quotient is not defined, explain why.
   a. $^-40 \div {}^-8$
   b. $143 \div (^-11)$
   c. $^-143 \div 13$
   d. $0 \div (^-5)$
   e. $^-5 \div 0$
   f. $0 \div 0$
6. Evaluate each of the following (if possible):
   a. $(^-10 \div {}^-2)(^-2)$
   b. $(^-40 \div 8)8$
   c. $(a \div b)b$
   d. $(^-10 \cdot 5) \div 5$
   e. $(ab) \div b$
   f. $(^-8 \div {}^-2)(^-8)$
   g. $(^-6 + {}^-14) \div 4$
   h. $(^-8 + 8) \div 8$
   i. $^-8 \div (^-8 + 8)$
   j. $(^-23 - {}^-7) \div 4$
   k. $(^-6 + 6) \div (^-2 + 2)$
   l. $^-13 \div (^-1)$
   m. $(^-36 \div 12) \div 3$
   n. $|^-24| \div (3 - 15)$
7. In a lab, the temperature of various chemical reactions was changing by a fixed number of degrees per minute. Write a multiplication problem that describes each of the following:

   a. The temperature at 8:00 P.M. was 32°C. If it dropped 3°C per minute, what is the temperature at 8:30 P.M.?
   b. The temperature at 8:20 P.M. was 0°C. If it dropped 4°C per minute, what is the temperature at 7:55 P.M.?
   c. The temperature at 8:00 P.M. was $^-20$°C. If it dropped 4°C per minute, what is the temperature at 7:30 P.M.?
   d. The temperature at 8:00 P.M. was 25°C. If it increased every minute by 3°C, what is the temperature at 7:40 P.M.?
   e. The temperature at 8:00 P.M. was 0°C. If it dropped d degrees per minute, what was the temperature m minutes before?
   f. The temperature at 8:00 P.M. was 20°C. If it increased every minute by d degrees, what was the temperature m minutes before?
8. a. On each of four consecutive plays in a football game, a team lost 11 yd. If lost yardage is interpreted as a negative integer, write the information as a product of integers and determine the total number of yards lost.
   b. If Jack Jones lost a total of 66 yd in 11 plays, how many yards, on the average, did he lose on each play?
9. In 1989, it was predicted that the farmland acreage lost to family dwellings over the next 9 yr would be 12,000 acres per year. If this prediction were true and if this pattern were to continue, how much acreage would be lost to homes by the end of 1996?

10. Show that the distributive property of multiplication over addition, $a(b + c) = ab + ac$ is true for each of the following values of a, b, and c:
    a. $a = {}^-1, b = {}^-5, c = {}^-2$
    b. $a = {}^-3, b = {}^-3, c = 2$
    c. $a = {}^-5, b = 2, c = {}^-6$

11. Compute each of the following:
    a. $({}^-2)^3$
    b. $({}^-2)^4$
    c. $({}^-10)^5 \div ({}^-10)^2$
    d. $({}^-3)^5 \div ({}^-3)$
    e. $({}^-1)^{10}$
    f. $({}^-1)^{15}$
    g. $({}^-1)^{50}$
    h. $({}^-1)^{151}$

12. Compute each of the following:
    a. ${}^-2 + 3 \cdot 5 - 1$
    b. $10 - 3 \cdot 7 - 4({}^-2) + 3$
    c. $10 - 3 - 12$
    d. $10 - (3 - 12)$
    e. $({}^-3)^2$
    f. ${}^-3^2$
    g. ${}^-5^2 + 3({}^-2)^2$
    h. ${}^-2^3$
    i. $({}^-2)^5$
    j. ${}^-2^4$

13. If x is an integer and $x \neq 0$, which of the following are always positive and which are always negative?
    a. ${}^-x^2$
    b. x^2
    c. $({}^-x)^2$
    d. ${}^-x^3$
    e. $({}^-x)^3$
    f. ${}^-x^4$
    g. $({}^-x)^4$
    h. x^4
    i. x
    j. ${}^-x$

14. Which of the expressions in Problem 13 are equal to each other for all values of x?

15. Identify the property of integers being illustrated in each of the following:
    a. $({}^-3) \cdot (4 + 5) = (4 + 5) \cdot ({}^-3)$
    b. ${}^-4 + {}^-7 \in I$
    c. $5 \cdot [4 \cdot ({}^-3)] = (5 \cdot 4) \cdot ({}^-3)$
    d. $({}^-9) \cdot [5 + ({}^-8)] = ({}^-9) \cdot 5 + ({}^-9) \cdot ({}^-8)$

16. Simplify each of the following:
    a. $({}^-x)({}^-y)$
    b. ${}^-2x({}^-y)$
    c. $({}^-x + y) + x + y$
    d. ${}^-1 \cdot x$
    e. $x - 2({}^-y)$
    f. $a - (a - b)$
    g. $y - (y - x)$
    h. ${}^-(x - y) + x$

17. Find all integers x (if possible) that make each of the following true:
    a. ${}^-3x = 6$
    b. ${}^-3x = {}^-6$
    c. ${}^-2x = 0$
    d. $5x = {}^-30$
    e. $x \div 3 = {}^-12$
    f. $x \div ({}^-3) = {}^-2$
    g. $x \div ({}^-x) = {}^-1$
    h. $0 \div x = 0$
    i. $x \div 0 = 1$
    j. $x^2 = 9$
    k. $x^2 = {}^-9$
    l. ${}^-x \div {}^-x = 1$
    m. ${}^-x^2$ is negative.
    n. ${}^-(1 - x) = x - 1$
    o. $x - 3x = {}^-2x$

18. Multiply each of the following and combine any possible terms:
    a. ${}^-2(x - 1)$
    b. ${}^-2(x - y)$
    c. $x(x - y)$
    d. ${}^-x(x - y)$
    e. ${}^-2(x + y - z)$
    f. ${}^-x(x - y - 3)$
    g. $({}^-5 - x)(5 + x)$
    h. $(x - y - 1)(x + y + 1)$
    i. $({}^-x^2 + 2)(x^2 - 1)$

19. Use the difference-of-squares formula to simplify each of the following, if possible:
    a. $52 \cdot 48$
    b. $(5 - 100)(5 + 100)$
    c. $({}^-x - y)({}^-x + y)$
    d. $(2 + 3x)(2 - 3x)$
    e. $(x - 1)(1 + x)$
    f. $213^2 - 13^2$

20. Factor each of the following expressions completely and then simplify, if possible:
    a. $3x + 5x$
    b. $ax + 2x$
    c. $xy + x$
    d. $ax - 2x$
    e. $x^2 + xy$
    f. $3x - 4x + 7x$
    g. $3xy + 2x - xz$
    h. $3x^2 + xy - x$
    i. $abc + ab - a$
    j. $(a + b)(c + 1) - (a + b)$
    k. $16 - a^2$
    l. $x^2 - 9y^2$
    m. $4x^2 - 25y^2$
    n. $(x^2 - y^2) + x + y$

21. a. Develop a formula for $(a - b)^2$.
    b. Use your results from (a) to compute each of the following in your head:
       (i) 98^2 (*Hint:* Write $98 = 100 - 2$.)
       (ii) 99^2
       (iii) 997^2

22. If x is positive and $y = {}^-x$, then determine which of the following statements is false?
    a. $x^2y > 0$
    b. $x + y = 0$
    c. xy is negative.
    d. xy^2 is positive.

23. a. Given a calendar for any month of the year, such as the one that follows, pick several 3×3 groups of numbers and find the sum of these numbers. How are the obtained sums related to the middle number?

JULY						
S	M	T	W	T	F	S
		1	2	3	4	5
6	7	8	9	10	11	12
13	14	15	16	17	18	19
20	21	22	23	24	25	26
27	28	29	30	31		

   ★b. Prove that the sum of any 9 digits in any 3×3 set of numbers selected from a monthly calendar will always be equal to 9 times the middle number.

24. In each of the following, find the next two terms. If a sequence is arithmetic or geometric, find its difference or ratio and the nth term.
    a. ${}^-10, {}^-7, {}^-4, {}^-1, 2, 5, \_\_, \_\_$
    b. $10, 7, 4, 1, {}^-2, {}^-5, \_\_, \_\_$
    c. ${}^-2, {}^-4, {}^-8, {}^-16, {}^-32, {}^-64 \_\_, \_\_$
    d. ${}^-2, 4, {}^-8, 16, {}^-32, 64, \_\_, \_\_$
    e. $2, {}^-2^2, 2^3, {}^-2^4, 2^5, {}^-2^6, \_\_, \_\_$

25. Find the sum of the first 100 terms in (a) and (b) of Problem 24.

26. Find the first five terms of the sequences whose nth term is as follows:
    a. $n^2 - 10$
    b. ${}^-5n + 3$
    c. $({}^-2)^n - 1$
    d. $({}^-2)^n + 2^n$
    e. $n^2({}^-1)^n$
    f. ${}^-n({}^-2)^n$
    g. $|10 - n|$
    h. $[1 + ({}^-1)^n] \cdot 2^n$

27. Find the first two terms of an arithmetic sequence in which the fourth term is $^-8$ and the 101st is $^-493$.

★**28.** Use the distributive property, the definition of additive inverse, and other properties of integers to justify each of the following:

    a. $(^-a)b = ^-(ab)$ (*Hint:* Show that $(^-ab) + ab = 0$.)

    b. $(^-a)(^-b) = ab$ (*Hint:* Use part (a) to show that $(^-a)(^-b) + ^-(ab) = 0$.)

29. Use the $\boxed{^+\!/\!_-}$ key on the calculator to compute each of the following:

    a. $^-27 \cdot 3$ **b.** $^-46 \cdot ^-4$

    c. $^-26 \div 13$ **d.** $^-26 \div ^-13$

Communication

30. Can $(^-x - y)(x + y)$ be multiplied by using the difference-of-squares formula? Explain why or why not.

31. Kahlil said that using the formula $(a + b)^2 = a^2 + 2ab + b^2$, he can find a similar formula for $(a - b)^2$. Examine his argument. If it is correct, supply any missing steps or justifications; if it is incorrect, point out why.

$$(a - b)^2 = [a + (^-b)]^2$$
$$= a^2 + 2a(^-b) + (^-b)^2$$
$$= a^2 - 2ab + b^2$$

32. Seventh-grader Nancy gave the following argument to show that $(^-a)b = ^-(ab)$ for all integers a and b: *I first show that $(^-1)a = ^-a$ by showing that $(^-1)a + a = 0$. Now*

$$(^-a)b = [(^-1)a] \cdot b$$
$$= (^-1) \cdot (ab)$$
$$= ^-(ab)$$

If the argument is valid, complete its details; if it is not valid, explain why not.

33. Hosni gave the following argument that $^-(a + b) = ^-a + ^-b$ for all integers a and b. If the argument is correct, supply the missing reasons. If it is incorrect, explain why not.

$$^-(a + b) = (^-1) \cdot (a + b)$$
$$= (^-1)a + (^-1)b$$
$$= ^-a + ^-b$$

34. The following graph shows the development of mathematics in different cultures. Explain the use of positive and negative numbers in the graph.

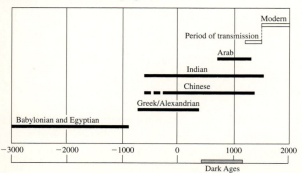

Open-ended

35. Give examples of situations that cannot be described using only the numbers in the set $\{1, 2, 3, 4, 5, \ldots\}$ and explain why.

36. On a national mathematics competition, scoring is accomplished using the formula 4 times the number done correctly minus the number done incorrectly. In this scheme, problems left blank are considered neither correct nor incorrect. Devise a scenario that would allow a student to have a negative score. Use a graph to illustrate different situations in which this could happen.

37. Which model would you use to teach multiplication of integers. Explain why you chose the model.

38. Select a current middle-school text that introduces multiplication and division of integers and discuss any models that were used and how effective you think they would be with a group of students.

Cooperative Learning

39. Devise a scheme for determining a grade-point average for a college student that allows negative quality points for a failing grade.

    a. Use your scheme to determine possible grades for a student with a positive, a zero, and a negative grade-point average.

    b. Compare your scheme with another class group and write a rationale for the use of the best scheme.

Review Problems

40. Illustrate $^-8 + ^-5$ on a number line.

41. Find the opposite of each of the following:

    a. $^-5$

    b. 7

    c. 0

42. Compute each of the following:

    a. $|^-14|$

    b. $|^-14| + 7$

    c. $8 - |^-12|$

    d. $|11| + |^-11|$

43. In the 1400s, European merchants used positive and negative numbers to label barrels of flour. For example, a barrel labeled $^+3$ meant the barrel was 3 lb overweight, whereas a barrel labeled $^-5$ meant the barrel was 5 lb underweight. If the following numbers were found on 100-lb barrels, what was the total weight of the barrels?

BRAIN TEASER   If $a, \ldots, z$ are integers, find the product

$$(x - a)(x - b)(x - c) \ldots (x - z).$$

Section 4-3   Divisibility

The concepts of *even* and *odd* are commonly used. For example, during water shortages in the summer in some parts of the country, houses with addresses ending with even numbers can water on even-numbered days of the month and houses with addresses ending with odd numbers can water on odd-numbered days. Some residents whose house numbers ended in zero did not know whether their addresses were considered odd or even. An even number is a number that is divisible by 2. An odd number is a number that is not divisible by 2. The fact that 12 is divisible by 2 can be stated in the following equivalent statements in the left-hand column:

Example	*General Statement*
12 is divisible by 2.	a is divisible by b.
2 is a divisor of 12.	b is a divisor of a.
12 is a multiple of 2.	a is a multiple of b.
2 is a factor of 12.	b is a factor of a.
2 divides 12.	b divides a.

divides   The statement that "2 divides 12" is written with a vertical segment as in $2|12$, where the vertical segment means *divides*. Likewise, **"b divides a"** can be written as $b|a$. Each statement in the previous right-hand column can be written as $b|a$. We write $5 \nmid 12$ to symbolize that 5 does not divide 12 or that 12 is not divisible by 5. The notation $5 \nmid 12$ also implies that 12 is not a multiple of 5 and 5 is not a factor of 12.

Definition

If a and b are any integers, then b divides a, written $b|a$, if, and only if, there is an integer c such that $a = bc$.

factor • divisor •
multiple

If $b|a$, then b is a **factor**, or a **divisor**, of a, and a is a **multiple** of b.
Do not confuse $b|a$ with b/a, which is interpreted as $b \div a$. The former, a relation, is either true or false. The latter, an operation, has a numerical value. To compare $0 \div 0$ and $0|0$, recall that $0 \div 0$ is undefined. However, $0|0$ is a true statement because $0 = 0 \cdot a$ for all integers a.

HISTORICAL   NOTE

Pierre de Fermat (1601–1665) was a lawyer and a magistrate who served in the provincial parliament in Toulouse, France. He devoted his leisure time to mathematics —a subject in which he had no formal training. After his death, his son decided to publish a new edition of Diophantus's *Arithmetica* with Fermat's notes. One of the notes in the margin of Fermat's copy asserted that the equation $x^n + y^n = z^n$ has no positive integer solutions if n is an integer greater than 2 and commented, "I have found an admirable proof of this, but the margin is too narrow to contain it." Many great mathematicians spent years trying to prove Fermat's assertion, now called "Fermat's Last Theorem." With the help of a computer, Fermat's Last Theorem was proved for all exponents up to 125,000. In 1983, a 29-year-old West German mathematician, Gerd Falting, made major progress toward the solution of the problem, for which he received the Field's Medal in Mathematics. In June 1993, Andrew Wiles, a Princeton University mathematician, announced that he had proved Fermat's Last Theorem. Wiles's proof, which was several hundred pages long, had strong support from the mathematics community. However, in December 1993 a gap in the proof was discovered. After 18 months of work and with the help of Richard Taylor of Cambridge University, Wiles filled the gap in the proof.

Example 4-16

Classify each of the following as true or false. Explain your answers.

a. $^-3|12$ **b.** $0|2$ **c.** 0 is even.   **d.** If $3|a$, then $3|na$, where n is any integer.
e. $8 \nmid 2$ **f.** For all integers, a, $1|a$.   **g.** For all integers a, $^-1|a$.

Solution   **a.** $^-3|12$ is true because $12 = {}^-4({}^-3)$.
b. $0|2$ is false because there is no integer c such that $2 = c \cdot 0$.
c. $2|0$ is true because $0 = 0 \cdot 2$; therefore 0 is even.
d. $3|na$ is true. If $3|a$, then there is an integer k so that $a = 3k$. Multiplying both sides of the equation by n, we have $an = (3k)n$. By the commutative, associative, and closure properties of multiplication of integers, we have $na = 3(nk)$, where nk is an integer, so $3|na$.
e. $8 \nmid 2$ is true because there is no integer c such that $2 = c \cdot 8$.
f. $1|a$ is true for all integers a because $a = a \cdot 1$.
g. $^-1|a$ is true for all integers a because $a = ({}^-a)({}^-1)$.

In Example 4-16(d), we see that if 3 divides a, 3 divides any integer multiple of a. This may be further generalized, as Theorem 4-1 shows.

Theorem 4-1

For any integers a and d, if $d|a$ and n is any integer, then $d|na$.

Figure 4-15

We can deduce other notions of divisibility from everyday models. Consider two packages of chewing gum each having five pieces, as in Figure 4-15. We can evenly divide each package of gum among five students. In addition, if we opened both packages and put all of the pieces in a bag, we could still evenly divide the pieces of gum among the five students. To generalize this notion, if we buy gum in larger packages with a pieces in one package and b pieces in a second package with both a and b divisible by 5, we can record the preceding discussion as follows:

$$\text{If } 5|a \text{ and } 5|b, \text{ then } 5|(a + b).$$

If the number, a, of pieces of gum in one package is divisible by five, but the number, b, of pieces in the other package is not, then the total, $a + b$, cannot be divided evenly among the five students. This can be recorded as follows:

$$\text{If } 5|a \text{ and } 5 \nmid b, \text{ then } 5 \nmid (a + b).$$

What, if anything, can you conclude if $5 \nmid a$ and $5 \nmid b$?

Since subtraction is defined in terms of addition, similar results hold for subtraction. These ideas may be generalized in Theorem 4-2.

Theorem 4-2

For any integers a, b, and d, the following holds:

a. If $d|a$ and $d|b$, then $d|(a + b)$.
b. If $d|a$ and $d \nmid b$, then $d \nmid (a + b)$.
c. If $d|a$ and $d|b$, then $d|(a - b)$.
d. If $d|a$ and $d \nmid b$, then $d \nmid (a - b)$.

The proofs of most theorems in this section are left as exercises, but the proof of Theorem 4-2(a) is given as an illustration.

Proof. Theorem 4-2(a) is equivalent to the following:

If a is a multiple of d and b is a multiple of d, then $a + b$ is a multiple of d.

Notice that "a is a multiple of d" means $a = m \cdot d$, for some integer m. Similarly "b is a multiple of d" means $b = n \cdot d$ for some integer n. To show that $a + b$ is a multiple of d, we add the above equations as follows:

$$a + b = md + nd.$$

Is $md + nd$ a multiple of d? Notice that $md + nd = (m + n)d$, so $a + b = (m + n)d$. Because $m + n$ is an integer, $a + b$ is a multiple of d.

Example 4-17

Classify each of the following as true or false, where x, y, and z are integers. If a statement is true, prove it. If a statement is false, provide a counterexample.

a. If $3|x$ and $3|y$, then $3|xy$.
b. If $3|(x + y)$, then $3|x$ and $3|y$.
c. If $9 \nmid a$, then $3 \nmid a$.

Solution
a. True. By Theorem 4-1, if $3|x$, then, for any integer k, $3|kx$. If $k = y$, then $3|yx$ or $3|xy$.
b. False. For example, $3|(7 + 2)$, but $3 \nmid 7$ and $3 \nmid 2$.
c. False. For example, $9 \nmid 21$, but $3|21$.

I N V E S T I G A T I O N   4 - 2

● In Example 4-17(a), is it true that $3|xy$ regardless of whether $3|y$ or $3 \nmid y$. Why? ●

• • •

Example 4-18 Five students found a padlocked money box, which had a deposit slip attached to it. The deposit slip was water-spotted, so the currency total appeared as shown in Figure 4-16. One student remarked that if the money listed on the deposit slip was in the box, it could easily be divided equally among the 5 students without using coins. How did the student know this?

Figure 4-16

Solution Because the units digit of the amount of the currency is 0, the solution to the problem is to determine whether any natural number whose units digit is 0 is divisible by 5. To attack this problem, *look for a pattern*. Natural numbers whose units digit is 0 form a pattern, that is, 10, 20, 30, 40, 50, ... These numbers are multiples of 10. We are to determine whether 5 divides all multiples of 10. Since 5|10, by Theorem 4-1, 5 divides any multiple of 10. Hence, 5 divides the amount of money in the box, and the student is correct.

• • •

Divisibility Rules

As shown in Example 4-18, sometimes it is handy to know if one number is divisible by another just by looking at it or by performing a simple test. We discovered that if a number ends in 0, then the number is divisible by 5. The same argument can be used to show that if a number ends in 5, it is divisible by 5. This is an example of a divisibility rule. Moreover, if the last digit of a number is neither 0 nor 5, then the number is not divisible by 5.

Elementary texts frequently state divisibility rules. However, such rules have limited use except for mental arithmetic. It is possible to determine whether 1734 is divisible by 17, either by using pencil and paper or a calculator. To check divisibility and avoid decimals, we can use a calculator with an integer division button, $\boxed{\text{INT}\div}$. On such a calculator, integer division may be performed using the following sequence of buttons:

$$\boxed{1}\boxed{7}\boxed{3}\boxed{4}\boxed{\text{INT}\div}\boxed{1}\boxed{7}\boxed{=}$$

to obtain the display $\underset{Q}{\boxed{\text{102}}}$ $\underset{Q}{\boxed{0}}$.

This implies $1734/17 = 102$ with a remainder of 0, which, in turn, implies 17|1734.

We could have determined this same result mentally by considering the following:

$$1734 = 1700 + 34.$$

Because 17|1700 and 17|34, by Theorem 4-2(a), we have 17|(1700 + 34), or 17|1734. Similarly, we could determine mentally that 17∤1735.

Divisibility Tests for 2, 5, and 10

To determine mentally whether a given integer n is divisible by another integer d, we think of n as the sum or difference of two integers where d divides at least one of these numbers. We try to choose numbers such that one of them is close to n and divisible by d, and the other number is relatively small. As an example, consider the divisibility of 358 by 2:

$$358 = 350 + 8$$
$$= 35(10) + 8$$

Now we know that 2|10, so that 2|35(10). We also know that 2|8, which tells us that 2|(35(10) + 8). Similarly, 2 divides any multiple of 10, so to determine the divisibility of any integer by 2, we consider only whether the units digit is divisible by 2. If it is, then by Theorem 4-2(a) the number is divisible by 2. If not, then by Theorem 4-2(b) the number is not divisible by 2.

We can develop a similar test for divisibility by 10. In general, we have the following divisibility rules.

Divisibility Test for 2

An integer is divisible by 2 if, and only if, its units digit is divisible by 2.

Divisibility Test for 5

An integer is divisible by 5 if, and only if, its units digit is divisible by 5, that is, if and only if, the units digit is 0 or 5.

Divisibility Test for 10

An integer is divisible by 10 if, and only if, its units digit is divisible by 10, that is, if, and only if, the units digit is 0.

Divisibility Tests for 4 and 8

When we consider divisibility rules for 4 and 8, we see that $4 \nmid 10$ and $8 \nmid 10$, so it is not a matter of checking the units digit for divisibility by 4 and 8. However, 4 (which is 2^2) divides 10^2, and 8 (which is 2^3) divides 10^3.

We first develop a divisibility rule for 4. Consider any four-digit number n such that $n = a \cdot 10^3 + b \cdot 10^2 + c \cdot 10 + d$. Our *subgoal* is to *write the given number as a sum of two numbers,* one of which is as great as possible and divisible by 4. We know that $4 | 10^2$ because $10^2 = 4 \cdot 25$ and, consequently, $4 | 10^3$. Because $4 | 10^2$, then $4 | b \cdot 10^2$ and $4 | a \cdot 10^3$. Finally, $4 | a \cdot 10^3$ and $4 | b \cdot 10^2$ imply $4 | (a \cdot 10^3 + b \cdot 10^2)$. Now the divisibility of $a \cdot 10^3 + b \cdot 10^2 + c \cdot 10 + d$ by 4 depends on the divisibility of $(c \cdot 10 + d)$ by 4. Notice that $c \cdot 10 + d$ is the number represented by the last two digits in the given number n. We summarize this in the following test.

Divisibility Test for 4

An integer is divisible by 4 if, and only if, the last two digits of the integer represent a number divisible by 4.

To investigate divisibility by 8, we note that the least positive power of 10 divisible by 8 is 10^3 since $10^3 = 8 \cdot 125$. Consequently, all integral powers of 10 greater than 10^3 also are divisible by 8. Hence, the following is a divisibility test for 8.

Divisibility Test for 8

An integer is divisible by 8 if, and only if, the last three digits of the integer represent a number divisible by 8.

Example 4-19   **a.** Determine whether 97,128 is divisible by 2, 4, and 8.
b. Determine whether 83,026 is divisible by 2, 4, and 8.

Solution   **a.** 2|97,128 because 2|8.   **b.** 2|83,026 because 2|6.
4|97,128 because 4|28.   4∤83,026 because 4∤26.
8|97,128 because 8|128.   8∤83,026 because 8∤026.

REMARK   In Example 4-19(a), it would have been sufficient to check that the given number is divisible by 8 because if $8|a$, then $2|a$ and $4|a$. (Why?) However, if $8 \nmid a$, we cannot conclude from this that $4 \nmid a$ or $2 \nmid a$. (Why?) This relationship is shown in Figure 4-17.

Figure 4-17

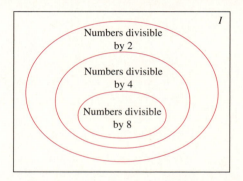

Divisibility Tests for 3 and 9

Next, we consider a divisibility test for 3. No power of 10 is divisible by 3, but the numbers 9, and 99, and 999, and others of this type are close to powers of 10 and are divisible by 3. For example, to determine whether 5721 is divisible by 3, we rewrite the number using 999, 99, and 9, as follows:

$$5721 = 5 \cdot 10^3 + 7 \cdot 10^2 + 2 \cdot 10 + 1$$
$$= 5(999 + 1) + 7(99 + 1) + 2(9 + 1) + 1$$
$$= 5 \cdot 999 + 5 \cdot 1 + 7 \cdot 99 + 7 \cdot 1 + 2 \cdot 9 + 2 + 1$$
$$= (5 \cdot 999 + 7 \cdot 99 + 2 \cdot 9) + (5 + 7 + 2 + 1)$$

The sum in the first set of parentheses is divisible by 3, so the divisibility of 5721 by 3 depends on the sum in the second set of parentheses. In this case, $5 + 7 + 2 + 1 = 15$ and $3|15$, so $3|5721$. Hence, to test 5721 for divisibility by 3, we test $5 + 7 + 2 + 1$ for divisibility by 3. Notice that $5 + 7 + 2 + 1$ is the sum of the digits of 5721. The example suggests the following test for divisibility by 3.

Divisibility Test for 3

An integer is divisible by 3 if, and only if, the sum of its digits is divisible by 3.

We can use an argument similar to the one used to demonstrate that $3|5721$ to prove the test for divisibility by 3 on any integer and in particular for any 4-digit number $n = a \cdot 10^3 + b \cdot 10^2 + c \cdot 10 + d$. Even though $a \cdot 10^3 + b \cdot 10^2 + c \cdot 10 + d$ is not necessarily divisible by 3, the number $a \cdot 999 + b \cdot 99 + c \cdot 9$ is close to n and *is* divisible by 3. We have the following:

$$
\begin{aligned}
a \cdot 10^3 + b \cdot 10^2 + c \cdot 10 + d &= a \cdot 1000 + b \cdot 100 + c \cdot 10 + d \\
&= a(999 + 1) + b(99 + 1) + c(9 + 1) + d \\
&= (a \cdot 999 + b \cdot 99 + c \cdot 9) + (a \cdot 1 + b \cdot 1 + c \cdot 1 + d) \\
&= (a \cdot 999 + b \cdot 99 + c \cdot 9) + (a + b + c + d)
\end{aligned}
$$

Because $3|9$, $3|99$, and $3|999$, it follows that $3|(a \cdot 999 + b \cdot 99 + c \cdot 9)$. If $3|(a + b + c + d)$, then $3|[(a \cdot 999 + b \cdot 99 + c \cdot 9) + (a + b + c + d)]$; that is, $3|n$. If, on the other hand, $3 \nmid (a + b + c + d)$, it follows from Theorem 4-2(b) that $3 \nmid n$.

Since $9|9$, $9|99$, $9|999$, and so on, a test similar to that for divisibility by 3 applies to divisibility by 9. (Why?)

Divisibility Test for 9

An integer is divisible by 9 if, and only if, the sum of the digits of the integer is divisible by 9.

Example 4-20

Use divisibility tests to determine whether each of the following numbers is divisible by 3 and divisible by 9:

a. 1002   **b.** 14,238

Solution   **a.** Because $1 + 0 + 0 + 2 = 3$ and $3|3$, it follows that $3|1002$. Because $9 \nmid 3$, it follows that $9 \nmid 1002$.

b. Because $1 + 4 + 2 + 3 + 8 = 18$ and $3|18$, it follows that $3|14{,}238$. Because $9|18$, it follows that $9|14{,}238$.

Example 4-21

The store manager has an invoice for 72 four-function calculators. The first and last digits on the receipt are illegible. The manager can read

$$\$\blacksquare 67.9\blacksquare.$$

What are the missing digits, and what is the cost of each calculator?

Solution   Let the missing digits be x and y so that the number is $x67.9y$ dollars, or $x679y$ cents. Because there were 72 calculators sold, the number on the invoice must be divisible by 72. Because the number is divisible by 72, it must be divisible by 8 and 9, which are factors of 72. For the number on the invoice to be divisible by 8, the three-digit number $79y$ must be divisible by 8. Because $79y$ must be divisible by 8, it is an even number. Therefore $79y$ must be either 790, 792, 794, 796, or 798. Only the number 792 is divisible by 8, so we know the last digit, y, on the invoice must be 2.

Because the number on the invoice must be divisible by 9, we know that 9 must divide $x + 6 + 7 + 9 + 2$, or $(x + 24)$. Since 3 is the only single digit that will make $(x + 24)$ divisible by 9, then x must be 3. Therefore the number on the invoice must be $367.92. The calculators must cost $367.92/72, or $5.11, each.

• • •

Divisibility Tests for 11 and 6

The divisibility test for 7 is usually harder to use than actually performing the division, so we omit the test. We state the divisibility test for 11 but omit the proof. Interested readers might try the proof.

Divisibility Test for 11

An integer is divisible by 11 if, and only if, the sum of the digits in the places that are even powers of 10 minus the sum of the digits in the places that are odd powers of 10 is divisible by 11.

For example, to test whether 8,471,986 is divisible by 11, we check whether 11 divides the difference $(6 + 9 + 7 + 8) - (8 + 1 + 4)$, or 17. Because $11 \nmid 17$, it follows from the divisibility test for 11 that $11 \nmid 8,471,986$. A number like 2772 is divisible by 11 because $(2 + 7) - (7 + 2) = 9 - 9 = 0$ and 0 is divisible by 11.

The divisibility test for 6 is related to the divisibility tests for 2 and 3. In Section 4-4, we show that if $2|n$ and $3|n$, then $2 \cdot 3|n$. Consequently, the following divisibility test is true.

Divisibility Test for 6

An integer is divisible by 6 if, and only if, the integer is divisible by both 2 and 3.

• • •

Example 4-22   The number 57,729,364,583 has too many digits for most calculator displays. Determine whether it is divisible by each of the following:

a. 2   **b.** 3   **c.** 5   **d.** 6
e. 8   **f.** 9   **g.** 10   **h.** 11

Solution   **a.** No, the last digit, 3, is not divisible by 2.
b. No, the sum of the digits is 59, which is not divisible by 3.
c. No, the last digit is neither 0 nor 5.
d. No, because the number is not divisible by 2 and by 3.
e. No, because the number formed by the last 3 digits, 583, is not divisible by 8.
f. No, because the sum of the digits is 59, which is not divisible by 9.
g. No, because the units digit is not 0.
h. Yes because $(3 + 5 + 6 + 9 + 7 + 5) - (8 + 4 + 3 + 2 + 7) = 35 - 24 = 11$ and 11 is divisible by 11.

• • •

I N V E S T I G A T I O N   4 - 3

● Fill in the blanks in the following so that the number is divisible by 9. List all possibilities. 12,506,5 __. ●

Problem 1

A class from Washington School visited a neighborhood cannery warehouse. The warehouse manager told the class that there were 11,368 cans of juice in the inventory and that the cans were packed in boxes of 6 or 24, depending on the size of the can. One of the students, Sam, thought for a moment and announced that there was a mistake in the inventory. Is Sam's statement correct? Why or why not?

Understanding the Problem. The problem is to determine if the manager's inventory of 11,368 cans was correct. To solve the problem, we must assume there are no partial boxes of cans; that is, a box must contain exactly 6 or exactly 24 cans of juice.

Devising a Plan. We know that the boxes contain either 6 cans or 24 cans, but we do not know how many boxes of each type there are. One strategy for solving this problem is to *find an equation* that involves the total number of cans in all the boxes.

The total number of cans, 11,368, equals the number of cans in all the 6-can boxes plus the number of cans in all the 24-can boxes. If there are n boxes containing 6 cans each, there are $6n$ cans altogether in those boxes. Similarly, if there are m boxes with 24 cans each, these boxes contain a total of $24m$ cans. Because the total was reported to be 11,368 cans, we have the equation $6n + 24m = 11,368$. Sam claimed that $6n + 24m \neq 11,368$.

One way to show that $6n + 24m \neq 11,368$ is to show that $6n + 24m$ and 11,368 do not have the same divisors. Both $6n$ and $24m$ are divisible by 6. This implies that $6n + 24m$ must be divisible by 6. If 11,368 is not divisible by 6, then Sam is correct.

Carrying Out the Plan. The divisibility test for 6 states that a number is divisible by 6 if, and only if, the number is divisible by both 2 and 3. Because 11,368 is an even number, it is divisible by 2. Is it divisible by 3?

The divisibility test for 3 states that a number is divisible by 3 if, and only if, the sum of the digits in the number is divisible by 3. We see that $1 + 1 + 3 + 6 + 8 = 19$, which is not divisible by 3, so 11,368 is not divisible by 3. Hence, Sam is correct.

Looking Back. Suppose 11,368 had been divisible by 6. Would that have implied that the manager was correct? The answer is no; it would have implied only that we would have to change our approach to the problem.

As a further Looking Back activity, suppose that, given different data, the manager is correct. Can we determine values for m and n? In fact, this can be done. If a computer is available, a program can be written to determine all possible natural-number values of m and n.

● ● ●

HISTORICAL   NOTE

A modern mathematician who worked in the area of number theory was American Julia Robinson (1919–1985). Robinson's work with the Russian mathematician Yuri Matijasevič on Diophantine equations led directly to the solution of the tenth of the famous set of 23 problems the German mathematician David Hilbert posed. Robinson was the first woman mathematician to be elected to the National Academy of Sciences and the first woman president of the American Mathematical Society. She died of leukemia at the age of sixty-five.

BRAIN TEASER   The following is an argument showing that an ant weighs as much as an elephant. What is wrong?

Let e be the weight of the elephant and a the weight of the ant. Let $e - a = d$. Consequently, $e = a + d$. Multiply each side of $e = a + d$ by $e - a$. Then simplify.

$$e(e - a) = (a + d)(e - a)$$
$$e^2 - ea = ae + de - a^2 - da$$
$$e^2 - ea - de = ae - a^2 - da$$
$$e(e - a - d) = a(e - a - d)$$
$$e = a$$

Thus the weight of the elephant equals the weight of the ant.

Ongoing Assessment 4-3

1. Classify each of the following as true or false. If false, tell why.
   a. 6 is a factor of 30.   b. 6 is a divisor of 30.
   c. 6|30.   d. 30 is divisible by 6.
   e. 30 is a multiple of 6.   f. 6 is a multiple of 30.

2. Using divisibility tests, answer each of the following:
   a. There are 1379 children signed up to play in a baseball league. If exactly 9 players are to be placed on each team, will any team be short of players?
   b. A forester has 43,682 seedlings to be planted. Can these be planted in an equal number of rows with 11 seedlings in each row?
   c. There are 261 students to be assigned to 9 teachers so that each teacher has the same number of students. Is this possible?
   d. Six friends win with a lottery ticket. The payoff is $242,800. Can the money be divided evenly?
   e. Jack owes $7812 on a new car. Can this amount be paid in 12 equal monthly installments?

3. Without using a calculator, test each of the following numbers for divisibility by 2, 3, 4, 5, 6, 8, 9, 10, and 11:
   a. 746,988   b. 81,342   c. 15,810
   d. 4,201,012   e. 1,001   f. 10,001

4. Determine each of the following without actually performing the division. Explain how you did it in each case.
   a. Is 34,015 divisible by 17?

   b. Is 34,051 divisible by 17?
   c. Is 19,031 divisible by 19?
   d. Is $2 \cdot 3 \cdot 5 \cdot 7$ divisible by 5?
   e. Is $(2 \cdot 3 \cdot 5 \cdot 7) + 1$ divisible by 5?

5. Justify each of the given statements, assuming that a, b, and c are integers. If a statement cannot be justified by one of the theorems in this section, answer "none."
   a. $4|20$ implies $4|113 \cdot 20$.
   b. $4|100$ and $4 \nmid 13$ imply $4 \nmid (100 + 13)$.
   c. $4|100$ and $4 \nmid 13$ imply $4 \nmid 1300$.
   d. $3|(a + b)$ and $3 \nmid c$ imply $3 \nmid (a + b + c)$.
   e. $3|a$ implies $3|a^2$.

6. Classify each of the following as true or false:
   a. If every digit of a number is divisible by 3, the number itself is divisible by 3.
   b. If a number is divisible by 3, then every digit of the number is divisible by 3.
   c. A number is divisible by 3 if, and only if, every digit of the number is divisible by 3.
   d. If a number is divisible by 6, then it is divisible by 2 and by 3.
   e. If a number is divisible by 2 and 3, then it is divisible by 6.
   f. If a number is divisible by 2 and 4, then it is divisible by 8.
   g. If a number is divisible by 8, then it is divisible by 2 and 4.

7. Classify each of the statements in Problem 6 as "sometimes," "always," or "never" true.

8. Devise a test for divisibility by each of the following numbers:

   a. 16   **b.** 25

9. When the two missing digits in the following number are replaced, the number is divisible by 99. What is the number?

$$85\_\_1$$

10. Fill each of the following blanks with the greatest digit that makes the statement true:

   a. $3|74\_$ **b.** $9|83\_45$ **c.** $11|6\_55$

11. Place a digit in the square, if possible, so that the number

$$527,4\,\square\,2$$

is divisible by

   a. 2   **b.** 3   **c.** 4   **d.** 9   **e.** 11

12. The bookstore marked some notepads down from $2.00 but still kept the price over $1.00. It sold all of them. The total amount of money from the sale of the pads was $31.45. How many notepads were sold?

13. A group of people ordered No-Cal candy bars. The bill was $2.09. If the original price of each was 12¢ but the price has been inflated, how much does each cost?

14. Leap years occur in years that are divisible by 4. However, if the year ends in two zeros, in order for the year to be a leap year, it must be divisible by 400. Determine which of the following are leap years:

   a. 1776   **b.** 1986   **c.** 2000   **d.** 2024

15. In a football game, a touchdown with an extra point is worth 7 points and a field goal is worth 3 points. Suppose that in a game the only scoring done by teams are touchdowns with extra points and field goals.

   a. Which of the scores 1 to 25 are impossible for a team to score?

   b. List all possible ways for a team to score 40 points.

   c. A team scored 57 points with 6 touchdowns and 6 extra points. How many field goals did the team score?

16. Complete the following table where n is the given integer.

	n	Remainder when n is divided by 9	Sum of the digits of n	Remainder when the sum of the digits of n is divided by 9
a.	31			
b.	143			
c.	345			
d.	2987			
e.	7652			

f. Make a conjecture about the remainder and the sum of the digits in an integer when it is divided by 9.

17. A test for checking computations is called *casting out nines*. Consider the sum $193 + 24 + 786 = 1003$. The remainders when 193, 24, and 786 are divided by 9 are 4, 6, and 3, respectively. The sum of the remainders, 13, has a remainder of 4 when divided by 9, as does 1003. Checking the remainders in this manner provided a quasi-check for the computation. Find the following sums and use casting out nines to check your sums:

   a. $12,343 + 4546 + 56$

   b. $987 + 456 + 8765$

   c. $10,034 + 3004 + 400 + 20$

   d. Will this check always work for addition? Give an example to illustrate your answer.

   e. Try the check on the subtraction, $1003 - 46$.

   f. Try the check on the multiplication, $345 \cdot 56$.

   g. Would it make sense to try the check on division? Why or why not?

18. Classify each of the following as true or false, assuming that a, b, c and d are integers. If a statement is false, give a counterexample.

   a. If $d|(a + b)$, then $d|a$ and $d|b$.

   b. If $d|(a + b)$, then $d|a$ or $d|b$.

   c. If $d|ab$, then $d|a$ or $d|b$.

   d. If $ab|c$, $a \neq 0$ and $b \neq 0$, then $a|c$ and $b|c$.

   e. $1|a$

   f. $d|0$

   g. If $a|b$ and $b|a$, then $a = b$.

   h. If $d|a$ and $d|b$, then $d|(ax + by)$ for any integers x and y.

   i. If $d \nmid a$ and $d \nmid b$, then $d \nmid (a + b)$.

   j. If $d|a^2$, then $d|a$.

   k. If $d \nmid a$, then $d \nmid a^2$.

   l. If $d \nmid a^2$, then $d \nmid a$.

★ **19.** Prove the following theorem: For any integers a, b, and c, if $a|b$ and $b|c$, then $a|c$.

★ **20.** Prove Theorem 4-2(b).

★ **21.** Prove the test for divisibility by 9 for any five-digit number.

22. **a.** Choose a two-digit number such that the number in the tens place is one greater than the number in the units place. Reverse the digits in your number, and subtract this number from your original number; for example, $87 - 78 = 9$. Make a conjecture concerning the results of performing these kinds of operations.

   b. Choose any two-digit number such that the number in the tens place is two greater than the number in the units place. Reverse the digits in your number, and subtract this number from your original number; for example, $31 - 13 = 18$. Make a conjecture concerning the results of performing these kinds of operations.

★**c.** Prove that for any two-digit number, if the digits are reversed and the numbers subtracted, the difference is a multiple of 9.

d. Investigate what happens whenever two-digit numbers with equal digit sums are subtracted; for example, $62 - 35 = 27$.

23. Using only divisibility tests, explain whether 6,868,395 is divisible by 15.

Communication

24. A customer wants to mail a package. The postal clerk determines the cost of the package to be $2.86, but only 6¢ and 15¢ stamps are available. Can the available stamps be used for the exact amount of postage for the package? Why or why not?

25. a. Jim uses his calculator to see if a number n is divisible by a number d. He finds that $n \div d$ has a display of 32. Does $d|n$? Why?

b. If $n \div d$ gives a display of 16.8, does $d|n$? Why?

26. Which divisibility tests are easiest to use? Why?

27. The numbers x and y are divisible by 5.

a. Is the sum of x and y divisible by 5? Why?

b. Is the difference of x and y divisible by 5? Why?

c. Is the product of x and y divisible by 5? Why?

d. Is the quotient of x and y divisible by 5? Why?

28. Why is it not always possible to test divisibility on a calculator?

29. Is the area of each of the following rectangles divisible by 4? Explain why or why not.

a.

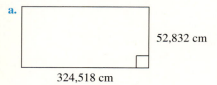

52,832 cm

324,518 cm

b.

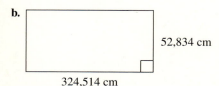

52,834 cm

324,514 cm

30. a. If 21 divides n, what other natural numbers divide n? Why?

b. If 16 divides n, what other natural numbers divide n? Why?

31. Can you find three consecutive natural numbers none of which is divisible by 3? Explain your answer.

32. Answer each of the following and justify your answers.

a. If a number is not divisible by 5, can it be divisible by 10?

b. If a number is not divisible by 10, can it be divisible by 5?

33. A number in which each digit except 0 appears exactly 3 times is divisible by 3. For example, 777,555,222 and 414,143,313 are divisible by 3. Explain why this statement is true.

34. A palindrome is a number that reads the same forward as backward.

a. Check the following four-digit palindromes for divisibility by 11:

i. 4554   ii. 9339   iii. 2002   iv. 2222

b. Are all four-digit palindromes divisible by 11? Why or why not?

c. Are all five-digit palindromes divisible by 11? Why or why not?

d. Are all six-digit palindromes divisible by 11? Why or why not?

35. The numbers 5872 and 2785 are a palindromic pair of numbers because reversing the order of the digits of one number gives the other number. Explain why in a palindromic pair, if one number is divisible by 3, then so is the other.

36. Enter any three-digit number on the calculator; for example, enter 243. Repeat it: 243,243. Divide by 7. Divide by 11. Divide by 13. What is the answer? Try it again with any other three-digit number. Will this always work? Why?

Open-ended

37. A breakfast food company had a contest in which numbers were placed in breakfast food boxes. A prize of $1000 was awarded to anyone who could collect numbers whose sum was 100. The company had thousands of cards made with the following numbers on them:

3   12   15   18   27   33   45   51   66   75   84   90

a. If the company did not make any more cards, is there a winning combination?

b. If the company is going to add one more number to the list and they want to make sure the contest has at most 1000 winners, suggest a strategy for them to use.

Cooperative Learning

38. If all the stamps in a stamp collection are placed in rows of 4, there are 2 stamps left. If they are placed in rows of 9, there are 7 stamps left. If placed in rows of 6, there are 4 left. What is the least number of stamps possible for this to occur?

TECHNOLOGY CORNER

The following Logo program will determine if a positive integer N is divisible by another integer X. Type it into your computer.

```
TO TESTDIV :N:X
   IF INTEGER (:N/:X) = :N/:X PRINT [OKAY] ELSE PRINT
      [NOT DIVISIBLE]
END
```

(In LCSI, replace PRINT [OKAY] *with* [PRINT [OKAY]] *and* PRINT [NOT DIVIS-IBLE] *with* [PRINT [NOT DIVISIBLE]].*)*

1. Run this program using various values for :N and :X.
2. How does the program compare to using the INT÷ button on a calculator?

BRAIN TEASER

Dee finds that she has an extraordinary social security number. Its nine digits contain all the numbers from 1 through 9. They also form a number with the following characteristics: when read from left to right, its first two digits form a number divisible by two, its first three digits form a number divisible by 3, its first four digits form a number divisible by 4, and so on, until the complete number is divisible by 9. What is Dee's social security number?

Section 4-4   Prime and Composite Numbers

When we write $a|b$, we say that a is a divisor of b. One method (sometimes called the "candy bar method") used in elementary schools to determine the divisors of a number is to use squares of paper and to represent the number as a rectangle. Such a rectangle resembles a candy bar formed with small squares. The dimensions of the rectangle are divisors of the number. For example, Figure 4-18 shows rectangles to represent 12.

Figure 4-18

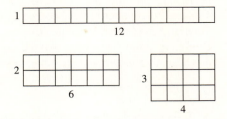

As the figure shows, the number 12 has six divisors: 1, 2, 3, 4, 6, and 12. If rectangles were used to find the divisors of 7, then we would find only a 1 × 7 rectangle, as Figure 4-19 shows. Thus 7 has exactly two divisors: 1 and 7.

To illustrate further the number of divisors of a number, we construct Table 4-1. Below each number listed across the top, we identify numbers less than or equal to 37 that have that number of positive divisors. For example, 12 is in the 6 column because it has six divisors, and 7 is in the 2 column because it has only two divisors.

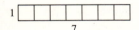

Figure 4-19

Table 4-1   Number of Factors

1	2	3	4	5	6	7	8	9
1	2	4	6	16	12		24	36
	3	9	8		18		30	
	5	25	10		20			
	7		14		28			
	11		15		32			
	13		21					
	17		22					
	19		26					
	23		27					
	29		33					
	31		34					
	37		35					

INVESTIGATION 4 - 4

a. What patterns do you see forming in Table 4-1?

b. Will there be other entries in the 1 column? Why?

c. What are the next three numbers in the 3 column?

d. Find an entry for the 7 column.

e. What kinds of numbers have an odd number of factors? Why?

The numbers in the 2 column are of particular importance. Notice that they have exactly two divisors, namely, 1 and themselves. Any positive integer with exactly two distinct, positive divisors is a *prime number,* or a **prime.** Any integer greater than 1 that has a positive factor other than 1 and itself is a *composite number,* or a **composite.** For example, 4, 6, and 16 are composites because they have positive factors other than 1 and themselves. The number 1 has only one positive factor, so it is neither prime nor composite. From the 2 column in Table 4-1, we see that the first 12 primes are 2, 3, 5, 7, 11, 13, 17, 19, 23, 29, 31, and 37. Other patterns in the table are explored in the problem set.

prime

composite

Example 4-23   Show that the following numbers are composite:

a. 1564   **b.** 2781   **c.** 1001

Solution   **a.** Since $2 | 4$, 1564 is divisible by 2 and is composite.

b. Since $3 | (2 + 7 + 8 + 1)$, 2781 is divisible by 3 and is composite.

c. Since $11 | [(1 + 0) - (0 + 1)]$, 1001 is divisible by 11 and is composite.

Prime Factorization

Composite numbers can be expressed as products of two or more whole numbers greater than 1. For example, $18 = 2 \cdot 9$, $18 = 3 \cdot 6$, or $18 = 2 \cdot 3 \cdot 3$. Each expression of 18 as a prod-

factorization   uct of factors is a **factorization.**

prime factorization   A factorization containing only prime numbers is a **prime factorization.** To find a prime factorization of a given composite number, first rewrite the number as a product of two smaller numbers. Continue the process, factoring the lesser numbers until all factors are primes. For example, consider 260:

$$260 = 26 \cdot 10 = 2 \cdot 13 \cdot 2 \cdot 5 = 2 \cdot 2 \cdot 5 \cdot 13 = 2^2 \cdot 5 \cdot 13.$$

factor tree   The procedure for finding a prime factorization of a number can be organized using a **factor tree,** as Figure 4-20(a) demonstrates. The last branches of the tree display the prime factors of 260.

A second way to factor 260 is shown in Figure 4-20(b). The two trees produce the same prime factorization, except for the order in which the primes appear in the products.

Figure 4-20

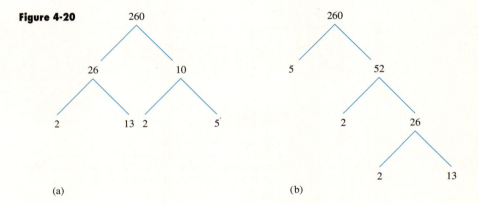

(a)   (b)

The *Fundamental Theorem of Arithmetic,* or the *Unique Factorization Theorem,* states that in general, if order is disregarded, the prime factorization of a number is unique.

Theorem 4-3

Fundamental Theorem of Arithmetic. Each composite number can be written as a product of primes in one, and only one, way, aside from variation in the order of the prime factors.

The Fundamental Theorem of Arithmetic is a basis for an algorithmic approach to finding the prime factorization of a number. For example, consider 260. We start with the smallest prime, 2, and see if it divides 260. If not, we try the next greater prime and check for divisibility by this prime. Once we find a prime that divides the number in question, we must find the quotient of the number divided by the prime. This step in the prime factorization of 260 is shown in Figure 4-21(a). Next we check whether the prime divides the quotient. If so, we repeat the process; if not, we try the next greater prime, 3, and check to see if it divides the quotient. We see that 260 divided by 2 yields 130, as shown in Figure 4-21(b). We continue the procedure, using greater primes, until a quotient of 1 is reached.

The original number is the product of all the prime divisors used. The complete procedure for 260 is shown in Figure 4-21(c). An alternative form is shown in Figure 4-21(d).

Figure 4-21

```
2 | 260        2 | 260        2 | 260              | 260
    130        2 | 130        2 | 130          2  | 130
                     65       5 |  65          2  |  65
   (a)               (b)     13 |  13          5  |  13
                                     1        13  |   1
                              (c)          (d) Alternative form
```

The primes in the prime factorization of a number are typically listed in increasing order from left to right and if a prime appears in a product more than once, exponential notation is used. Thus the factorization of 260 is written as $2^2 \cdot 5 \cdot 13$.

These two techniques are demonstrated in the following student page from *Addison-Wesley Mathematics,* Grade 8, 1993.

Prime Factorization

LEARN ABOUT IT

EXPLORE Study the Information
A standard concrete block measures 16 in. × 8 in. × 8 in. Half blocks measure 8 in. × 8 in. × 8 in. In a section of a masonry yard, there were 30 concrete half blocks.

$$2 \cdot 3 \cdot 5 = 30$$
One way to arrange 30 half blocks.

TALK ABOUT IT

1. How many different ways could you arrange the 30 half blocks into a rectangular prism?

Every composite number can be expressed as the product of prime numbers. You can construct a factor tree to find the **prime factors** of 84.

Start with any two factors of 84.

Continue to find factors until all factors are prime.

$2^2 \cdot 3 \cdot 7$ is the **prime factorization** of 84.

```
        84                                    84
       /  \                                  /  \
      6  •  14                              2  •  42
     / \    / \                                /  \
    2 • 3  2 • 7                              2  •  21
                                                  /  \
                                                 2 • 3 • 7
```

Examples Use repeated division by primes to find the prime factorization of each number.

A 60

```
2|60
2|30
3|15
```

B 231

```
3|231
7|77
  11
```

C 286

```
2|286
11|143
   13
```

INVESTIGATION 4 - 5

● Colored rods are used in the elementary-school classroom to teach many concepts. The rods vary in length from 1 cm to 10 cm. Various lengths have colors associated with them. For example, the 5 rod is yellow. Rods are shown in Figure 4-22 with their appropriate colors.

A row with all the same color rods is called a one-color train. For example, the following is a one-color train for 18:

a. What other rods can be used to form a one-color train for 18?

b. What one-color trains are possible for 24?

c. How many different one-color trains of 2 or more rods are possible for each prime number?

d. If a number can be represented by an all-red train, an all-green train, and an all-yellow train, what is the least number of factors it must have? What are they? ●

Figure 4-22

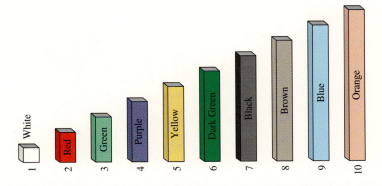

Problem 2

When his students asked Mr. Factor what his children's ages were, he answered, "I have three children. The product of their ages is 72 and the sum of their ages is the number of this room." The children asked for the door to be opened to verify the room number. Then, Sonja, the class math whiz, told the teacher that she needed more information to solve the problem. Mr. Factor said, "My oldest child is good at chess." Sonja then announced the correct ages for Mr. Factor's children. What are the ages of Mr. Factor's children?

Understanding the Problem. Mr. Factor has three children, and the product of their ages is 72. When Sonja was given the sum of the ages, she concluded that Mr. Factor did not provide enough information to determine the ages of the three children. After Mr. Factor announced that his oldest child is good at chess, Sonja was able to find the ages of the children. We are to determine the children's ages. From the given information, it seems that the fact that Mr. Factor has an oldest child is significant.

Devising a Plan. To find the possible ages, we need to find three positive integers whose product is 72. We can do this systematically by *listing* the possible ages if there is a 1-year-old child in the family and then listing all the possible ages; if there is a 2-year-old in the family; and so on. Because $1 \cdot 2 \cdot 36 = 72$, the combination (1, 2, 36) is a possibility. However, because it does not matter in what order we list the ages, the combination (2, 1, 36) is the same as (1, 2, 36). Knowing that $72 = 2^3 \cdot 3^2$ can help us to list all the possible combinations, along with the corresponding sums, in a *table*. After examining the table, we hope to be able to determine how the additional information can be used to solve the problem.

Carrying Out the Plan. Table 4-2 shows all the possible ages whose product is 72, along with the corresponding sums. Notice that all the sums other than 14 appear only once in Table 4-2. Sonja knew the sum of the ages but could not determine the ages. The only

Table 4-2

Age	Age	Age	Sum of the Ages
1	1	72	74
1	2	36	39
1	3	24	28
1	4	18	23
1	6	12	19
2	2	18	22
2	3	12	17
2	4	9	15
2	6	6	14
1	8	9	18
3	4	6	13
3	3	8	14

logical reason for this is that the classroom's number (the sum of the ages) must have been 14. There are two possible combinations that give the sum 14: (2, 6, 6) and (3, 3, 8). When Sonja was told that the oldest child was good at chess, she knew that (2, 6, 6) could not be a possible combination because if the children were 2, 6, and 6 years old, there would not be an oldest among them. Thus she concluded that the children's ages were 3, 3, and 8.

Looking Back. Is it possible to substitute another integer for 72 and solve the corresponding problem? If we choose the product of the ages to be 12, what similar problem can we pose? The possible triples are then (1, 1, 12), (1, 2, 6), (1, 3, 4), and (2, 2, 3), and the corresponding sums are 14, 9, 8, and 7. Given one of these numbers as a sum, we would be able to determine the triple, that is, the ages. But suppose Mr. Factor said, "The youngest does not like spinach." We would know then that the first and the last triple are not possible as they do not determine a youngest child. To determine which of the triples (1, 2, 6) and (1, 3, 4) represents the ages of his children, Mr. Factor could say, "The middle child is a year older than the youngest." We would know then that the ages of his children are 1, 2, and 6.

• • •

Number of Divisors

How many divisors does 24 have? Note that the question asks for the number of divisors, not just prime divisors. To aid in the listing, we group divisors as follows:

1, 2, 3, 4, 6, 8, 12, 24

The divisors of 24 occur in pairs, where the product of the divisors in each pair is 24. If 3 is a divisor of 24, then 24/3, or 8, is also a divisor of 24. In general, if a natural number k is a divisor of 24, then 24/k is also a divisor of 24.

Another way to think of the number of divisors of 24 is to consider the prime factorization $24 = 2^3 \cdot 3$. The divisors of 2^3 are 2^0, 2^1, 2^2, and 2^3. The divisors of 3 are 3^0 and 3^1. We know that 2^3 has $(3 + 1)$, or 4, divisors and 3^1 has $(1 + 1)$, or 2, divisors. Because each divisor of 24 is the product of a divisor of 2^3 and a divisor of 3^1, then we use the Fundamental Counting Principle (see Chapter 2) to conclude that 24 has $4 \cdot 2$, or 8, divisors. This is summarized in Table 4-3.

Table 4-3

Divisors of 2^3	$2^0 = 1$	$2^1 = 2$	$2^2 = 4$	$2^3 = 8$
Divisors of 3^1	$3^0 = 1$	$3^1 = 3$		
Divisors of $3^1 \cdot$ Divisors of 2^3 (Divisors of 24)	$3^0 \cdot 2^0 = 1$ $3^1 \cdot 2^0 = 3$	$3^0 \cdot 2^1 = 2$ $3^1 \cdot 2^1 = 6$	$3^0 \cdot 2^2 = 4$ $3^1 \cdot 2^2 = 12$	$3^0 \cdot 2^3 = 8$ $3^1 \cdot 2^3 = 24$

This discussion can be generalized as follows: If p is any prime raised to a natural number power, n, the divisors of p^n are $p^0, p^1, p^2, p^3, \ldots, p^n$. Therefore there are $(n + 1)$ divisors of p^n. Now, using the Fundamental Counting Principle, we can find the number of divisors of any number whose prime factorization is known. This is given as Theorem 4-4.

Theorem 4-4

If the prime factorization of a number, n, is $n = p_1^{q_1} \cdot p_2^{q_2} \cdot p_3^{q_3} \cdot \ldots \cdot p_m^{q_m}$, then the number of divisors of n is $(q_1 + 1)(q_2 + 1)(q_3 + 1) \cdot \ldots \cdot (q_m + 1)$.

• • •

Example 4-24   **a.** How many divisors does 2250 have?
b. Find all the divisors of 324.

Solution   **a.** The prime factorization of 2250 is $2 \cdot 3^2 \cdot 5^3$. By Theorem 4-4, there are $(1 + 1)(2 + 1)(3 + 1)$, or $2 \cdot 3 \cdot 4 = 24$, divisors of 2250.

b. The prime factorization of 324 is $2^2 \cdot 3^4$, so there are $3 \cdot 5$, or 15, divisors. The divisors of 2^2 are 1, 2, and 4; the divisors of 3^4 are 1, 3, 9, 27, and 81. Therefore the divisors of 324 are all the possible combinations of these 2 sets of divisors, as follows:

1, 3, 9, 27, 81, 2, 6, 18, 54, 162, 4, 12, 36, 108, and 324.

• • •

INVESTIGATION 4 - 6

● Is it necessary to divide 97 by 2, 3, 4, 5, 6, . . . , 96 to check if it is prime? Consider the following:

a. If 2 is not a divisor of 97, could any multiple of 2 be a divisor of 97? Why?

b. If 3 is not a divisor of 97, what other numbers could not be divisors of 97? Why?

c. If 5 is not a divisor of 97, what other numbers could not be divisors of 97? Why?

d. If 7 is not a divisor of 97, what other numbers could not be divisors of 97?

e. Conjecture what numbers we have to check for divisibility in order to determine if 97 is prime. ●

In Investigation 4-6, you might have found that to determine if a number is prime, you must check only divisibility by prime numbers less than the given number. (Why?) However, do we need to check all the primes less than the number? Suppose we want to check if 97 is prime and we find that 2, 3, 5, and 7 do not divide 97. Could a greater prime divide 97? If p is a prime greater than 7, then $p \geq 11$. If $p|97$, then $97/p$ divides 97. However, because $p \geq 11$ then $97/p$ must be less than 10 and hence cannot divide 97. (Why?) So we see that there is no need to check for divisibility by numbers other than 2, 3, 5, and 7. These ideas are generalized in the following theorems.

Theorem 4-5

If d is a factor of n, where $n \neq 0$, then $\dfrac{n}{d}$ is a divisor of n.

Suppose that p is the *least* prime factor of the number n. Then by Theorem 4-5, n/p is a factor of n, and because p is the least factor of n, then $p \leq n/p$. If $p \leq n/p$, then $p^2 \leq n$. This idea is summarized in the following theorem.

Theorem 4-6

If n is composite, then n has a prime factor p such that $p^2 \leq n$.

Theorem 4-6 can be used to help determine whether a given number is prime or composite. For example, consider the number 109. If 109 is composite, it must have a prime divisor p such that $p^2 \leq 109$. The primes whose squares do not exceed 109 are 2, 3, 5, and 7. Mentally, we can see that $2 \nmid 109$, $3 \nmid 109$, $5 \nmid 109$, and $7 \nmid 109$. Hence, 109 is prime. The argument used leads to the following theorem.

Theorem 4-7

If n is an integer greater than 1 and not divisible by any prime p, where $p^2 \leq n$, then n is prime.

REMARK   Because $p^2 \leq n$ implies that $p \leq \sqrt{n}$, Theorem 4-7 implies that to determine if a number n is prime, it is enough to check if any prime less than or equal to $\sqrt{n}$ is a divisor of n.

Example 4-25   **a.** Is 397 composite or prime?
b. Is 91 composite or prime?

Solution   **a.** The possible primes p such that $p^2 \leq 397$ are 2, 3, 5, 7, 11, 13, 17, and 19. Because $2 \nmid 397$, $3 \nmid 397$, $5 \nmid 397$, $7 \nmid 397$, $11 \nmid 397$, $13 \nmid 397$, $17 \nmid 397$, $19 \nmid 397$, the number 397 is prime.
b. The possible primes p such that $p^2 \leq 91$ are 2, 3, 5, and 7. Because 91 is divisible by 7, it is composite.

Problem 3

In an elaborate promotion for encouraging students to ride buses, Mountain Line Bus System (MLBS) took the first 1000 students to register at Kalispell College during fall quarter, wrote their names on pieces of paper numbered in sequence by ones from 1, and agreed to choose some pieces of paper for free passes. To choose the students Jacques, an employee of MLBS, first placed the pieces of paper in numerical order face-up. Next, he flipped over all the pieces of paper that were labeled with even numbers. Then he started again, this time changing every third piece of paper beginning with the third one. That is, he turned the face-down pieces face-up and turned the face-up pieces face-down. The process continued until Jacques completed his 1000th trip through the pieces of paper. How many free passes were awarded with this scheme?

Understanding the Problem.   The 1000 pieces of paper are numbered 1 through 1000. Jacques placed every piece of paper face-up and in numerical order, returned to the start and flipped over every even-numbered piece of paper, returned and changed the state of every third piece of paper starting with the paper numbered 3, and so on. We must determine the number of pieces of paper that are facing up when the entire process is completed and Jacques has made 1000 passes through the slips of paper.

Devising a Plan.   We use the strategy of *examining a simpler problem* in order to gain insight into the solution of the original problem. Suppose there were only 20 pieces of paper. If we denote a face-up piece of paper with a u and a face-down piece of paper with a t, we can record the state of each piece changed by Jacques, as shown in Table 4-4. For example, on his fourth pass, Jacques puts piece 4 face-up, piece 8 face-up, piece 12 face-down, piece 16 face-up, and piece 20 face-down.

Table 4-4

	Numbers of Pieces of Paper																			
	1	2	3	4	5	6	7	8	9	10	11	12	13	14	15	16	17	18	19	20
1	u	u	u	u	u	u	u	u	u	u	u	u	u	u	u	u	u	u	u	u
2		t		t		t		t		t		t		t		t		t		t
3			t			u			t			u			t			u		
4				u				u				t				u				u
5					t					u					u					t
6						t						u						t		
7							t							u						
8								t								t				
9									u									u		
10										t										u
11											t									
12												t								
13													t							
14														t						
15															t					
16																u				
17																	t			
18																		t		
19																			t	
20																				t

Order of Jacques's Pass

Table 4-4 shows that after 20 passes, the only face-up pieces are 1, 4, 9, and 16. Each of these numbers is a perfect square. We must determine if this pattern continues. If it does, we must find out the number of perfect squares less than 1000.

Carrying Out the Plan. To determine if the pattern continues, consider piece 25. This piece is face-up in Jacque's first pass, face-down on his fifth pass, and face-up on his 25th pass. This suggests that the pattern is correct. (Note that 1, 5, and 25 are the only positive divisors of 25.) What happens with a piece such as 26, which is not a perfect square? Piece 26 is face-up on the first pass, face-down on the second pass, face-up on the thirteenth pass, and face-down on the twenty-sixth pass, and remains in that position. In general, we see that a piece is changed only on the passes whose order divide the piece number.

For the piece to be face-up at the end, it must be face-up one more time than it is face-down; that is, the state must be changed an odd number of times. For this to happen, the number of the piece must have an odd number of divisors. We can show that the face-up pieces have numbers that are perfect squares by showing that only perfect squares have an odd number of divisors.

Recall that the divisors of a number appear in pairs. For example, the pairs of divisors of 80 and 81 are given by the following:

$$80 = 1 \cdot 80 = 2 \cdot 40 = 4 \cdot 20 = 5 \cdot 16 = 10 \cdot 8$$
$$81 = 1 \cdot 81 = 3 \cdot 27 = 9 \cdot 9$$

Thus 80 has ten distinct divisors, or five pairs. On the other hand, the perfect square 81 has five distinct divisors: the pairs 1 and 81 and 3 and 27, and a single divisor, 9, which is paired with itself. We know that if d is a divisor of n, then n/d is a divisor of n. Consequently, for all divisors d of n, if $d \neq n/d$, then each divisor can be paired with a different divisor, and n must have an even number of positive divisors. If for some divisor d, $d = n/d$, then $n = d^2$, and all the divisors of n, except d, are paired with a different divisor. Hence, the number of divisors of n is odd. Because $d = n/d$ occurs only when $n = d^2$, it follows that n has an odd number of divisors if and only if n is a perfect square. As a result, the face-up pieces contain numbers that are perfect squares less than 1000, namely, $1^2, 2^2, 3^2, \ldots, 31^2$. Therefore 31 passes were rewarded.

Looking Back.   This problem suggests the following questions:

1. On which turns will Jacques touch only one piece of paper?
2. How many times will a slip with a prime number on it be touched?
3. Determine a method to find the number of factors a number has without actually listing all the factors. (*Hint:* Consider prime factorizations.)

• • •

More about Primes

One way to find all the primes less than a given number is to use the Sieve of Eratosthenes, named after the Greek mathematician Eratosthenes (276–194 or 192 B.C.). If all the natural numbers greater than 1 are considered (or placed in the sieve), the numbers that are not prime are methodically crossed out (or drop through the holes of the sieve). The remaining numbers are prime. The following procedure illustrates this process:

1. In Table 4-5, we cross out 1 because 1 is not prime.
2. Circle 2 because 2 is prime.
3. Cross out other multiples of 2; they are not prime.
4. Circle 3 because 3 is prime.
5. Cross out other multiples of 3.
6. Circle 5 and 7 because they are primes; cross out their multiples.
7. In Table 4-5 on the following page we stop after step 6 because 7 is the greatest prime whose square, 49, is less than 100. All the numbers remaining in the list and not crossed out are prime.

Table 4-5

1	②	③	4	⑤	6	⑦	8	9	10
11	12	13	14	15	16	17	18	19	20
21	22	23	24	25	26	27	28	29	30
31	32	33	34	35	36	37	38	39	40
41	42	43	44	45	46	47	48	49	50
51	52	53	54	55	56	57	58	59	60
61	62	63	64	65	66	67	68	69	70
71	72	73	74	75	76	77	78	79	80
81	82	83	84	85	86	87	88	89	90
91	92	93	94	95	96	97	98	99	100

INVESTIGATION 4 - 7

● **a.** What patterns do you notice in Table 4-5?
b. What is the longest string of consecutive prime numbers in the table? Could there ever be a longer string if the table were larger?

c. What is the longest string of composite numbers listed in the original table? Could there be a longer string if the table were larger? ●

There are infinitely many whole numbers, infinitely many odd whole numbers, and infinitely many even whole numbers. Are there infinitely many primes? Because prime numbers do not appear in any known pattern, the answer to this question is not obvious. Euclid was the first to prove that there are infinitely many primes.

Mathematicians have long looked for a formula that produces only primes, but no one has ever found one. One result was the expression $n^2 - n + 41$, where n is a whole number. Substituting 0, 1, 2, 3, . . . , 40 for n in the expression always results in a prime number. However, substituting 41 for n gives $41^2 - 41 + 41$, or 41^2, a composite number.

In 1971, the largest known prime was $2^{19,937} - 1$, found by Bryant Tuckerman of IBM. In 1978, two high-school students (Laura Nickel and Curt Noll from Hayward, California) found a larger prime, $2^{23,209} - 1$, using 440 computer hours. Other larger primes have since been discovered, one of the latest being $2^{216,091} - 1$, which has 65,050 digits.

There are many interesting problems concerning primes. For example, Christian Goldbach (1690–1764) asserted in a letter to Euler that every even integer greater than 2 is **Goldbach's conjecture** the sum of two primes. This statement is known as **Goldbach's conjecture.** For example, $4 = 2 + 2$, $6 = 3 + 3$, $8 = 3 + 5$, $10 = 3 + 7$, $12 = 5 + 7$, and $14 = 3 + 11$. In spite of the simplicity of the statement, no one knows for sure whether the statement is true.

Problem 4

A woman with a basket of eggs finds that if she removes the eggs from the basket 2, 3, 4, 5, or 6 at a time, there is always 1 egg left. However, if she removes the eggs 7 at a time, there are no eggs left. If the basket holds up to 500 eggs, how many eggs does the woman have?

Understanding the Problem.   When a woman removes eggs from the basket 2, 3, 4, 5, or 6 at a time, there is always 1 egg left. That means that if the number of eggs is divided by 2, 3, 4, 5, or 6, the remainder is always 1. We also know that when she removes the eggs 7 at a time, there are no eggs left; that is, the number of eggs is a multiple of 7. Finally, we know that the basket holds up to 500 eggs. We have to find the number of eggs in the basket.

Devising a Plan.   One way to solve the problem is to *list* all the multiples of 7 between 7 and 500 and check which ones have a remainder of 1 when divided by 2, 3, 4, 5, and 6. Since this method is tedious, we look for a different approach. Let the number of eggs be n. Then, if n is divided by 2, the remainder is 1. Consequently, $n - 1$ will be divisible by 2. Similarly, 3, 4, 5, and 6 divide $n - 1$.

Since 2 and 3 divide $n - 1$, the primes 2 and 3 appear in the prime factorization of $n - 1$. Note that $4|(n - 1)$ implies that $2|(n - 1)$, and hence, from the information $2|(n - 1)$ and $4|(n - 1)$, we can conclude only that 2^2 appears in the prime factorization of $n - 1$. Since $5|(n - 1)$, 5 appears in the prime factorization of $n - 1$. The fact that $6|(n - 1)$ does not provide any new information, since it only implies that 2 and 3 are prime factors of $n - 1$, which we already know. Now, $n - 1$ may also have other prime factors. Denoting the product of these other prime factors by k, we have $n - 1 = 2^2 \cdot 3 \cdot 5 \cdot k = 60k$, where k is some natural number, and so $n = 60k + 1$. We now find all of the possible values for n in the form $60k + 1$ less than 500 and determine which ones are divisible by 7.

Carrying Out the Plan.   Because $n = 60k + 1$ and k is any natural number, we substitute $k = 1, 2, 3, \ldots$ to obtain the following possible values for n that are less than 500:

$$61, 121, 181, 241, 301, 361, 421, 481.$$

Among these values, only 301 is divisible by 7; hence, 301 is the only possible answer to the problem.

Looking Back.   In the preceding situation, we still had to test eight numbers for divisibility by 7. Is it possible to reduce the computations further? We know that $n = 60k + 1$ and that the possible values for k are $k = 1, 2, 3, 4, 5, 6, 7, 8$. We also know that $7|n$; that is, $7|(60k + 1)$. The problem is to find for which of the above values of k, $7|(60k + 1)$. The question would have been easier to answer if instead of $60k + 1$, we had a smaller number. We know that the least multiple of k closest to $60k$ that is divisible by 7 is $56k$. Since $7|(60k + 1)$ and $7|56k$, we conclude that $7|(60k + 1 - 56k)$; that is, $7|(4k + 1)$. We now see that $7|(60k + 1)$, if, and only if, $7|(4k + 1)$. The only value of k between 1 and 8 that makes $4k + 1$ divisible by 7 is 5. Consequently, $7|(60 \cdot 5 + 1)$, and 301 is the solution to the problem.

● ● ●

Ongoing Assessment 4-4

1. Determine which of the following numbers are primes:
   a. 149   b. 923   c. 433
   d. 101   e. 463   f. 897
2. What is the greatest prime you must consider to test whether 5669 is prime?
3. Use a factor tree to find the prime factorization for each of the following:
   a. 504   b. 2475   c. 11,250
4. a. Fill in the missing numbers in the following factor tree:

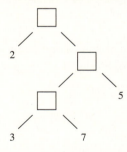

   b. How could you find the top number without finding the other two numbers?
5. Find the least positive number that is divisible by three different primes.
6. a. When the U.S. flag had 48 stars, the stars formed a 6×8 rectangular array. In what other rectangular arrays could they have been arranged?
   b. How many different rectangular arrays of stars could there be if there were only 47 states?
7. If the Spanish Armada had consisted of 177 galleons, could it have sailed in an equal number of small flotillas? If so, how many ships would have been in each?

8. Suppose the 435 members of the House of Representatives are placed on committees consisting of more than 2 members but less than 30 members. Each committee is to have an equal number of members and each member is to be on only one committee.
   a. What size committees are possible?
   b. How many committees are there of each size?
9. Mr. Arboreta wants to set out fruit trees in a rectangular array. For each of the following numbers of trees, find all possible numbers of rows if each row is to have the same number of trees:
   a. 36   b. 28   c. 17   d. 144
10. Find the least number divisible by each natural number less than or equal to 12.
11. The divisors of a locker number are 2, 5, and 9. If there are exactly nine additional divisors, what is the locker number?
12. a. Use the Fundamental Theorem of Arithmetic to justify that if $2|n$ and $3|n$, then $6|n$.
    b. Is it always true that if $a|n$ and $b|n$, then $ab|n^2$? Either prove the statement or give a counterexample.
13. Find the greatest 4-digit number that has exactly three factors.
14. Extend the Sieve of Eratosthenes to find all primes less than 200.
15. The prime numbers 11 and 13 are called **twin primes** because they differ by 2. Find all the twin primes less than 200. (The existence of infinitely many twin primes has not been proved.)
16. a. Find a composite number different from 41^2 that is of the form $n^2 - n + 41$.
    ★b. Prove that there are infinitely many composite numbers of the form $n^2 - n + 41$.

17. Show that if 1 were considered a prime, every number would have more than one prime factorization.
18. If $42 \mid n$, what other positive integers divide n?
19. Is it possible to find positive integers x, y, and z such that $2^x \cdot 3^y = 5^z$? Why or why not?
20. A prime such as 7331 is a superprime because any integers obtained by deleting digits from the right of 7331 are prime; for example, 733, 73, and 7.
    a. For a prime to be a superprime, what digits cannot appear in the number?
    b. Of the digits that can appear in a superprime, what digit cannot be the left-most digit of a superprime?
    c. Find all of the two-digit superprimes.
    d. Find a three-digit superprime.
21. It is not known whether there are infinitely many primes in the infinite sequence consisting only of ones: 1, 11, 111, 1111, ... Find infinitely many composite numbers in the sequence.
22. Find infinitely many composite numbers in the sequence whose nth term is $3n + 1$.
★23. Complete the details for the following proof, which shows that there are infinitely many prime numbers:

    If the number of primes is finite, then there is a greatest prime denoted by p. Consider the product of all the primes, $2 \cdot 3 \cdot 5 \ldots p$, and let $N = (2 \cdot 3 \cdot 5 \ldots p) + 1$. Because $N > p$, where p is the greatest prime, N is composite. Because N is composite, there is a prime q among the primes 2, 3, 5, . . . , p such that $q|N$. However, none of the primes 2, 3, 5, . . . , p divides N. (Why?)

    Consequently, $q \nmid N$, which is a contradiction. Thus the assumption that there are finitely many primes is false and the set of primes must be infinite.
24. If $2N = 2^6 \cdot 3^5 \cdot 5^4 \cdot 7^3 \cdot 11^7$, explain why $2 \cdot 3 \cdot 5 \cdot 7 \cdot 11$ is a factor of N.
25. Is $3^2 \cdot 2^4$ a factor of $3^4 \cdot 2^7$? Explain why or why not.
26. Explain why each of the following numbers is composite:
    a. $3 \cdot 5 \cdot 7 \cdot 11 \cdot 13$
    b. $(3 \cdot 4 \cdot 5 \cdot 6 \cdot 7 \cdot 8) + 2$
    c. $(3 \cdot 5 \cdot 7 \cdot 11 \cdot 13) + 5$
    d. $10! + 7$
    e. $10! + k$, where $k = 2, 3, 4, 5, 6, 7, 8, 9,$ or 10
27. Explain why $2^3 \cdot 3^2 \cdot 25^3$ is not a prime factorization and find the prime factorization of the number.

Communication

28. The number 173 is not divisible by 2, 3, 5, 7, 11, and 13. Explain why you can conclude that 173 is prime.
29. Explain why the product of two consecutive natural numbers greater than 1 must be composite.
30. Explain why a prime number must have an odd number of prime divisors.
31. Explain why the product of any three consecutive integers is divisible by 6.

32. Explain why the product of any four consecutive integers is divisible by 24.
33. In order to test for divisibility by 12, one student checked to determine divisibility by 3 and 4, while another checked for divisibility by 2 and 6. Are both students using a correct approach to divisibility by 12? Why or why not?
34. In the Sieve of Eratosthenes in Table 4-5, explain why, after we cross out all the multiples of 2, 3, 5, and 7, the remaining numbers are primes.

Open-ended

35. Describe how you could determine the prime factorization of a large number using a calculator. If your calculator has a ⃞ Simp ⃞ button, describe how it might be used to obtain the prime factorization.
36. a. In which of the following intervals do you think there are the most primes? Why? Check to see if you were correct.
    (i) 0–99 (ii) 100–199 (iii) 200–299
    b. What is the longest string of consecutive composite numbers in the intervals?
    c. How many twin primes (see Problem 15) are there in each interval?
    d. What patterns, if any, do you see for any of the questions above? Predict what might happen in other intervals.
37. It was reported that the greatest prime discovered so far has 65,050 digits. If you wrote this number out, how long a sheet of paper would you need?
38. A number is a **perfect number** if the sum of its factors (other than the number itself) is equal to the number. For example, 6 is a perfect number because its factors sum to 6, that is, $1 + 2 + 3 = 6$. An **abundant number** has factors whose sum is greater than the number itself. A **deficient number** is a number with factors whose sum is less than the number itself.
    a. Classify each of the following numbers as perfect, abundant, or deficient:
    (i) 12 (ii) 28 (iii) 35
    b. Find at least one more number that falls in each class.

Cooperative Learning

39. Ms. Tetley's class of 23 students was using square tiles to build rectangular shapes. Each student had more than 1 tile and each had a different number of tiles. Each student was able to build only one shape of rectangle. All tiles had to be used to build a rectangle and the rectangle could not have any holes. For example, a 2 × 6 rectangle uses 12 tiles and is considered the same as a 6 × 2 rectangle but is different from a 3 × 4 rectangle. The class did the activity using the least number of tiles. How many tiles did the class use? Divide the work among the members of your group to explore the various rectangles that could be made.

40. One year consists of 365 days, 5 hr, 48 min, and 45.5 sec. Some months have 28 days and others 30 or 31. We must consider leap years. Facts such as it takes 29.5 days for the moon to circle Earth are involved in designing a calendar. Throughout history, many other calendars have been suggested. With your group, design a new calendar. Explain why you made the choices you did.

Review Problems

41. Classify each of the following as true or false:
  a. 11 is a factor of 189.
  b. 1001 is a multiple of 13.
  c. $7 \mid 1001$ and $7 \nmid 12$ imply $7 \nmid (1001 - 12)$.
  d. If a number is divisible by both 7 and 11, then its prime factorization contains 7 and 11.

42. Test each of the following for divisibility by 2, 3, 4, 5, 6, 7, 8, 9, 10, and 11:
  a. 438,162   **b.** 2,345,678,910

43. Prove that if a number is divisible by 12, then it is divisible by 3.

44. Could $3376 be divided exactly among either 7 or 8 people?

LABORATORY ACTIVITY

In Figure 4-23, a spiral starts with 41 at its center and continues in a counterclockwise direction. Primes are written in and squares representing composites are shaded. Continue the spiral until you reach the prime 439. Check the primes along the diagonal. Can you find each of the primes from the formula $n^2 + n + 41$ by substituting appropriate values for *n*?

Figure 4-23

421		419										409								
	347								337							331		401
		281			277				271		269						
	349		223										211				
		283		173				167				163					
				131			127							263		397
					97											
	353		227			71			67		89					
						53										
		229			73		43				157				
431			179		101			41							
				137					47				257		
433			181		103			59		61				
	359		233		139			79			83				389
		293					107		109			113		199		317
											149		151			
								191		193			197		
				239		241							251		
439										307			311		313
		367					373						379		383

TECHNOLOGY CORNER

The following Logo programs will determine whether a number is prime. Type the programs into your computer and use them to do Problem 1 in Ongoing Assessment 4-4. To execute the program, type PRIME with the number you wish to check as input.

```
TO PRIME :N
   CHECK :N INTEGER (SQRT :N)
END
```

```
TO CHECK :N :D
  IF :N = 1 PRINT [NEITHER PRIME NOR COMPOSITE] STOP
  IF :D = 1 PRINT "PRIME STOP
  IF REMAINDER :N :D = 0 PRINT "COMPOSITE STOP
  CHECK :N :D- 1
END
```
(In LCSI, place brackets around PRINT [NEITHER PRIME NOR COMPOSITE] STOP,
PRINT "PRIME STOP, and PRINT "COMPOSITE STOP.)

Section 4-5   Greatest Common Divisor and Least Common Multiple

Consider the following situation:

 Two bands are to be combined to march in a parade. A 24-member band will march behind a 30-member band. The combined bands must have the same number of columns. What is the greatest number of columns in which they can march?

The bands could each march in two columns, and we would have the same number of columns, but this does not satisfy the condition of having the greatest number of columns. The number of columns must divide both 24 and 30. (Why?) Numbers that divide both 24 and 30 are 1, 2, 3, and 6. The greatest of these numbers is 6, so the bands should each march in columns of 6. The first band would have 6 columns with 4 members in each column, and the second band would have 6 columns with 5 members in each column.

In this problem, we have found the greatest number that divides both 24 and 30, that is, the **greatest common divisor (GCD).**

Definition

The **greatest common divisor (GCD)** of two integers a and b is the greatest integer that divides both a and b.

We can find the GCD in many ways. We show several ways next.

Colored Rods Model

We can build a model of two or more integers with colored rods to determine the GCD of two numbers. For example, consider finding the GCD of 6 and 8 using the 6 rod and the 8 rod, as in Figure 4-24.

Figure 4-24

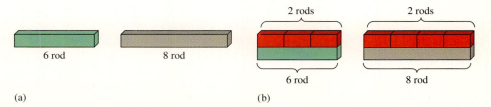

(a)   (b)

To find the GCD of 6 and 8, we must find the longest rod such that we can use multiples of that rod to build both the 6 rod and the 8 rod. The 1 rods and the 2 rods can be used to build both the 6 and 8 rods, as shown in Figure 4-24(b); the 3 rods can be used to build the 6 rod but not the 8 rod; the 4 rods can be used to build the 8 rod but not the 6 rod; the 5 rods can be used to build neither; and the 6 rods cannot be used to build the 8 rod. Therefore GCD(6, 8) = 2.

INVESTIGATION   4 - 8

● Explain how you could use colored rods to solve the marching band problem.   ●

The Intersection-of-Sets Method

In the *intersection-of-sets* method, we list all members of the set of positive divisors of the two numbers, then find the set of all *common divisors,* and, finally, pick the *greatest* element in that set. For example, to find the GCD of 20 and 32, denote the sets of divisors of 20 and 32 by D_{20} and D_{32}, respectively.

$$D_{20} = \{1, 2, 4, 5, 10, 20\}$$
$$D_{32} = \{1, 2, 4, 8, 16, 32\}$$

The set of all common positive divisors of 20 and 32 is

$$D_{20} \cap D_{32} = \{1, 2, 4\}.$$

Because the greatest number in the set of common positive divisors is 4, the GCD of 20 and 32 is 4, written GCD(20, 32) = 4.

The Prime Factorization Method

The intersection-of-sets method is rather time consuming and tedious if the numbers have many divisors. Another, more efficient, method is the *prime factorization method*. To find GCD(180, 168), first notice that

$$180 = 2 \cdot 2 \cdot 3 \cdot 3 \cdot 5$$
$$\text{and} \quad \Updownarrow \Updownarrow \searrow$$
$$168 = 2 \cdot 2 \cdot 2 \cdot 3 \cdot 7.$$

We see that 180 and 168 have two factors of 2 and one of 3 in common. These common primes divide both 180 and 168. In fact, the only numbers other than 1 that divide both 180 and 168 must have no more than two 2s and one 3 and no other prime factors in their prime factorizations. The possible common divisors are 1, 2, 2^2, 3, $2 \cdot 3$, and $2^2 \cdot 3$. Hence, the greatest common divisor of 180 and 168 is $2^2 \cdot 3$. The procedure for finding the GCD of two or more numbers by using the prime factorization method is summarized as follows:

To find the GCD of two or more integers, first find the prime factorizations of the given numbers and then take each common prime factor of the given numbers. The GCD is the prod-

uct of the common factors, each raised to the lowest power of that prime that occurs in either of the prime factorizations.

If we apply the prime factorization technique to finding GCD(4, 9), we see that 4 and 9 have no common prime factors. But that does not mean there is no GCD. We still have 1 as a common divisor, so GCD(4, 9) = 1. Numbers such as 4 and 9, whose GCD is 1, are **relatively prime** **relatively prime.** Both the intersection-of-sets method and the prime factorization method are found in *Addison-Wesley Mathematics, Grade 7,* 1993, as seen on the following student page.

Greatest Common Factor

EXPLORE **Analyze the Situation**

The 7th graders are going to divide a 36 ft by 44 ft field into equal squares. The sides of the squares will be whole number lengths. Each square will be sold for $5. A goat will wander in the field for 30 minutes. The last square the goat eats from will be the winning square. What sizes could the squares be? What is the largest size the squares could be?

TALK ABOUT IT

1. What picture could you draw to help solve the problem?

2. How do you know that the squares cannot be 5 ft by 5 ft?

3. Can the field be divided into 6 ft by 6 ft squares? Explain.

The largest factor that two or more numbers have in common is called their **greatest common factor (GCF).** If the GCF of two numbers is 1, the numbers are **relatively prime.**

Here are two methods for finding the GCF of 36 and 44.

Method 1 List the Factors	Method 2 Prime Factorization
Factors of 36: 1, 2, 3, 4, 6, 9, 12, 18, 36	$36 = 2 \cdot 2 \cdot 3 \cdot 3$
Factors of 44: 1, 2, 4, 11, 22, 44	$44 = 2 \cdot 2 \cdot 11$
Common factors: 1, 2, 4	$GCF = 2 \cdot 2 = 4$ The GCF is the
GCF = 4	product of all the prime factors 36 and 44 have in common.

Examples Find the GCF of each pair of numbers.

A 4, 5
   Factors of 4: 4, 2, 1
   Factors of 5: 5, 1
   GCF is 1; 4 and 5 are relatively prime.

B 45, 90
   $45 = 3 \cdot 3 \cdot 5$
   $90 = 2 \cdot 3 \cdot 3 \cdot 5$
   $GCF = 3 \cdot 3 \cdot 5 = 45$

• • •

Example 4-26   Find each of the following:

    a. GCD(108, 72)
    b. GCD(0, 13)
    c. GCD(x, y) if $x = 2^3 \cdot 7^2 \cdot 11 \cdot 13$ and $y = 2 \cdot 7^3 \cdot 13 \cdot 17$
    d. GCD(x, y, z) if $z = 2^2 \cdot 7$, using x and y from (b)

Solution   **a.** Since $108 = 2^2 \cdot 3^3$ and $72 = 2^3 \cdot 3^2$, it follows that GCD$(108, 72) = 2^2 \cdot 3^2 = 36$.
      b. Since $13 \cdot 0 = 0$ and $13 \cdot 1 = 13$, then GCD$(0, 13) = 13$.
      c. GCD$(x, y) = 2 \cdot 7^2 \cdot 13 = 1274$.
      d. Because $x = 2^3 \cdot 7^2 \cdot 11 \cdot 13$, $y = 2 \cdot 7^3 \cdot 13 \cdot 17$, and $z = 2^2 \cdot 7$, then GCD$(x, y, z) = 2 \cdot 7 = 14$. Notice that GCD$(x, y, z)$ can also be obtained by finding the GCD of z and 1274, the answer from (c).

• • •

Calculator Method

Calculators with a $\boxed{\text{Simp}}$ key can be used to find the GCD of two numbers. For example, to find the GCD(120, 180), use the following sequence of buttons to start: First, press $\boxed{1}\boxed{2}\boxed{0}\boxed{/}\boxed{1}\boxed{8}\boxed{0}\boxed{\text{Simp}}\boxed{=}$ to obtain the display $\boxed{\text{N/D} \rightarrow \text{n/d} \quad 60/90}$. By pressing the $\boxed{\text{x}\circ\text{y}}$ button, we see $\boxed{2}$ on the display as a common divisor of 120 and 180. By pressing the $\boxed{\text{x}\circ\text{y}}$ button again and pressing $\boxed{\text{Simp}}\boxed{=}\boxed{\text{x}\circ\text{y}}$, we see 2 again as a factor. The process is repeated to reveal 3 and 5 as other common factors. The GCD(120, 180) is the product of the common prime factors $2 \cdot 2 \cdot 3 \cdot 5$, or 60.

Euclidean Algorithm Method

Some numbers are hard to factor. For these numbers, another method is more efficient for finding the GCD. For example, suppose we want to find GCD(676, 221). If we could find two smaller numbers whose GCD is the same as GCD(676, 221), our task would be easier. From Theorem 4-2, every divisor of 676 and 221 is also a divisor of $676 - 221$ and 221. Conversely, every divisor of $676 - 221$ and 221 is also a divisor of 676 and 221. Thus the set of all the common divisors of 676 and 221 is the same as the set of all common divisors of $676 - 221$ and 221. Consequently, GCD (676, 221) = GCD$(676 - 221, 221)$. This process can be continued to subtract three 221s from 676 so that GCD$(676, 221) = $ GCD$(676 - 3 \cdot 221, 221) = $ GCD$(13, 221)$. To determine how many 221s can be subtracted from 676, we could have divided as follows:

$$
\begin{array}{r}
3 \\
221\overline{)676} \\
663 \\
\hline
13
\end{array}
$$

Continuing, we see that GCD$(13, 221) = $ GCD$(0, 13)$ from the following division:

$$
\begin{array}{r}
17 \\
13\overline{)221} \\
13 \\
\hline
91 \\
91 \\
\hline
0
\end{array}
$$

Because GCD(0, 13) = 13, the GCD(676, 221) = 13. Based on this illustration, we make the generalization outlined in the following theorem.

Theorem 4-8

If a and b are any whole numbers and $a \geq b$, then GCD (a, b) = GCD(r, b), where r is the remainder when a is divided by b.

Euclidean algorithm

Finding the GCD of two numbers by repeatedly using Theorem 4-8 until the remainder 0 is reached is referred to as the **Euclidean algorithm.**

● ● ●

Example 4-27

Use the Euclidean algorithm to find GCD(10,764, 2300).

Solution

$$\begin{array}{r} 4 \\ 2300)\overline{10764} \\ 9200 \\ \hline 1564 \end{array}$$ Thus GCD(10,764, 2300) = GCD(2300, 1564).

$$\begin{array}{r} 1 \\ 1564)\overline{2300} \\ 1564 \\ \hline 736 \end{array}$$ Thus GCD(2300, 1564) = GCD(1564, 736).

$$\begin{array}{r} 2 \\ 736)\overline{1564} \\ 1472 \\ \hline 92 \end{array}$$ Thus GCD(1564, 736) = GCD(736, 92).

$$\begin{array}{r} 8 \\ 92)\overline{736} \\ 736 \\ \hline 0 \end{array}$$ Thus GCD(736, 92) = GCD(92, 0).

Because GCD(92, 0) = 92, it follows that GCD(10,764, 2300) = 92.

● ● ●

REMARK   The procedure for finding the GCD by using the Euclidean algorithm can be stopped at any step at which the GCD is obvious.

A calculator with the integer division feature can also be used to perform the Euclidean algorithm. This feature yields the quotient and the remainder when doing a division. For example, if the integer division key looks like $\boxed{\text{INT}\div}$, then to find GCD(10,764, 2300) we proceed as follows:

$\boxed{1}\boxed{0}\boxed{7}\boxed{6}\boxed{4}\boxed{\text{INT}\div}\boxed{2}\boxed{3}\boxed{0}\boxed{0}\boxed{=}$ which displays $\underbrace{\qquad 4 \qquad}_{Q}$ $\underbrace{1564}_{R}$.

$\boxed{2}\boxed{3}\boxed{0}\boxed{0}\boxed{\text{INT}\div}\boxed{1}\boxed{5}\boxed{6}\boxed{4}\boxed{=}$ which displays $\underbrace{\qquad 1 \qquad}_{Q}$ $\underbrace{736}_{R}$.

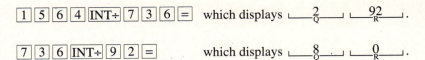

$\boxed{1}\boxed{5}\boxed{6}\boxed{4}\boxed{\text{INT}\div}\boxed{7}\boxed{3}\boxed{6}\boxed{=}$ which displays $\underset{Q}{\underline{\quad 2 \quad}}$ $\underset{R}{\underline{\quad 92 \quad}}$.

$\boxed{7}\boxed{3}\boxed{6}\boxed{\text{INT}\div}\boxed{9}\boxed{2}\boxed{=}$ which displays $\underset{Q}{\underline{\quad 8 \quad}}$ $\underset{R}{\underline{\quad 0 \quad}}$.

The last number we divided by before we obtained a 0 remainder is 92, so GCD (10764, 2300) = 92.

Least Common Multiple

Hot dogs are usually sold 10 to a package, while hot dog buns are usually sold 8 to a package. This mismatch causes troubles when one is trying to match hot dogs and buns. What is the least number of packages of each you could order so that there is an equal number of hot dogs and buns? The numbers of hot dogs that we could have are just the multiples of 10, that is, 10, 20, 30, 40, 50, ... Likewise the possible numbers of buns are 8, 16, 24, 32, 40, 48, ... We can see that the number of hot dogs matches the number of buns whenever 10 and 8 have multiples in common. This occurs at 40, 80, 120, ... In this problem, we are interested in the least of these multiples, 40. Therefore we could obtain the same number of hot dogs and buns in the least amount by buying 4 packages of hot dogs and 5 packages of buns. The answer 40 is the **least common multiple (LCM)** of 8 and 10.

least common multiple (LCM)

Definition

The **least common multiple (LCM)** of two positive integers is the least positive multiple that the two numbers have in common.

As with GCDs, there are several methods for finding least common multiples.

Colored Rods Method

We can use colored rods to determine the LCM of two numbers. For example, consider the 3 rod and the 4 rod in Figure 4-25(a). We build trains of 3 rods and 4 rods until they are the same length, as shown in Figure 4-25(b). The LCM is the common length of the train.

Figure 4-25

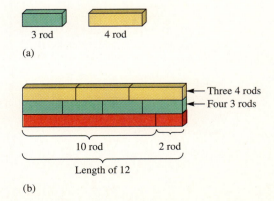

INVESTIGATION 4-9

● Explain how to use colored rods to solve the hot dog problem, that is, to find LCM(8, 10). ●

The Intersection-of-Sets Method

In the *intersection-of-sets* method, we first find the set of all positive *multiples* of both the first and second numbers, then find the set of all *common multiples* of both numbers, and finally pick the *least* element in that set. For example, to find the LCM of 8 and 12, denote the sets of positive multiples of 8 and 12 by M_8 and M_{12}, respectively.

$$M_8 = \{8, 16, 24, 32, 40, 48, 56, 64, 72, \ldots\}$$
$$M_{12} = \{12, 24, 36, 48, 60, 72, 84, 96, 108, \ldots\}$$

The set of common multiples is

$$M_8 \cap M_{12} = \{24, 48, 72, \ldots\}.$$

Because the least number in $M_8 \cap M_{12}$ is 24, the LCM of 8 and 12 is 24, written LCM(8, 12) = 24.

The Prime Factorization Method

The intersection-of-sets method for finding the LCM is often lengthy, especially when it is used to find the LCM of three or more natural numbers. Another, more efficient method for finding the LCM of several numbers is the *prime factorization method*. For example, to find LCM(40, 12), first find the prime factorizations of 40 and 12, namely, $2^3 \cdot 5$ and $2^2 \cdot 3$, respectively.

If $m = $ LCM(40, 12), then m is a multiple of 40 and must contain both 2^3 and 5 as factors. Also, m is a multiple of 12 and must contain 2^2 and 3 as factors. Since 2^3 is a multiple of 2^2, then $m = 2^3 \cdot 5 \cdot 3 = 120$. In general, we have the following:

To find the LCM of two natural numbers, first find the prime factorization of each number. Then take each of the primes that are factors of either of the given numbers. The LCM is the product of these primes, each raised to the greatest power of the prime that occurs in either of the prime factorizations.

Example 4-28 | Find the LCM of 2520 and 10,530.

Solution |
$$2520 = 2^3 \cdot 3^2 \cdot 5 \cdot 7$$
$$10{,}530 = 2 \cdot 3^4 \cdot 5 \cdot 13$$
$$\text{LCM}(2520, 10{,}530) = 2^3 \cdot 3^4 \cdot 5 \cdot 7 \cdot 13$$

The Euclidean Algorithm Method

To see the connection between the GCD and LCM, consider the GCD and LCM of 6 and 9. Because $6 = 2 \cdot 3$ and $9 = 3^2$, it follows that GCD(6, 9) = 3 and LCM(6, 9) = 18. Notice that GCD(6, 9) $\cdot$ LCM(6, 9) = $3 \cdot 18 = 54$, and 54 is the product of the original numbers 6 and 9. In general, for any two natural numbers a and b, the connection between their GCD and LCM is given by Theorem 4-9.

Theorem 4-9

For any two natural numbers a and b,

$$GCD(a, b) \cdot LCM(a, b) = ab.$$

This result is useful for finding the LCM of two numbers a and b when their prime factorizations are not easy to find. GCD (a, b) can be found by the Euclidean algorithm, the product ab can be found by simple multiplication, and LCM(a, b) can be found by division.

• • •

Example 4-29   Find LCM(731, 952).

Solution   By the Euclidean algorithm, GCD(731, 952) = 17. By Theorem 4-9, $17 \cdot$ LCM(731, 952) = $731 \cdot 952$. Consequently,

$$LCM(731, 952) = \frac{731 \cdot 952}{17} = 40{,}936.$$

• • •

Although Theorem 4-9 cannot be used to find the LCM of more than two numbers, it is possible to find the LCM for three or more numbers. For example, to find LCM(12, 108, 120), we can use the prime factorization method.

$$12 = 2^2 \cdot 3$$
$$108 = 2^2 \cdot 3^3$$
$$120 = 2^3 \cdot 3 \cdot 5$$

Then, LCM(12, 108, 120) = $2^3 \cdot 3^3 \cdot 5 = 1080$.

The Division-by-Primes Method

Another procedure for finding the LCM of several natural numbers involves *division by primes*. For example, to find LCM(12, 75, 120), we start with the least prime that divides at least one of the given numbers and divide as follows:

$$
\begin{array}{c|lcl}
2 & 12, & 75, & 120 \\
\hline
  & 6, & 75, & 60
\end{array}
$$

Because 2 does not divide 75, simply bring down the 75. To obtain the LCM using this procedure, continue the division process until the row of answers consists of relatively prime numbers.

$$
\begin{array}{r|rrr}
2 & 12, & 75, & 120 \\
2 & 6, & 75, & 60 \\
2 & 3, & 75, & 30 \\
3 & 3, & 75, & 15 \\
5 & 1, & 25, & 5 \\
\hline
& 1 & 5, & 1
\end{array}
$$

$\longrightarrow$ GCD is 3 (Why?)

Thus LCM(12, 75, 120) = $2 \cdot 2 \cdot 2 \cdot 3 \cdot 5 \cdot 1 \cdot 5 \cdot 1 = 2^3 \cdot 3 \cdot 5^2 = 600$.

Two methods of finding the LCM of two numbers are given on the following student page from *Addison-Wesley Mathematics,* Grade 7, 1993.

Least Common Multiple

LEARN ABOUT IT

EXPLORE Solve to Understand

Ralph picked two numbers, 6 and 8, out of a hat. Today every 6th customer will get a free sandwich and every 8th customer will get a free drink. Suppose 64 customers come into the store. Which ones will win both a free drink and a free sandwich?

TALK ABOUT IT

1. Which three customers were first to get free sandwiches? Free drinks?

2. Which customer was first to get both a free drink and a free sandwich?

To find the multiples of a number, multiply that number by 0, 1, 2, 3 and so on. The multiples of 12 are 0, 12, 24, 36, . . . The **least common multiple (LCM)** of two numbers is the smallest nonzero multiple which the numbers have in common.

Example Find the LCM of 12 and 18.

Method 1 List the nonzero multiples of each number until you reach a common multiple:

   multiples of 12: 12, 24, 36, . . .
   multiples of 18: 18, 36, . . .

The LCM of 12 and 18 is 36.

Method 2 List the prime factors of each number. Multiply the highest powers of each factor.

   $12 = 2 \cdot 2 \cdot 3 = 2^2 \cdot 3$
   $18 = 2 \cdot 3 \cdot 3 = 2 \cdot 3^2$

The LCM of 12 and 18 is $2^2 \cdot 3^2$ or 36.

Ongoing Assessment 4-5

1. Find the GCD and the LCM for each of the following using the intersection-of-sets method:
   a. 18 and 10   b. 24 and 36
   c. 8, 24, and 52

2. Find the GCD and the LCM for each of the following using the prime factorization method:
   a. 132 and 504   b. 65 and 1690
   c. 900, 96, and 630   d. 108 and 360
   e. 63 and 147   f. 625, 750, and 1000

3. Find the GCD for each of the following using the Euclidean algorithm:
   a. 220 and 2924   b. 14,595 and 10,856
   c. 122,368 and 123,152

4. Find the LCM for each of the following using any method:
   a. 24 and 36   b. 72 and 90 and 96
   c. 90 and 105 and 315

5. Find the LCM for each of the following pairs of numbers using Theorem 4-9 and the answers from Problem 3:
   a. 220 and 2924   b. 14,595 and 10,856
   c. 122,368 and 123,152

6. Use colored rods to find the GCD and the LCM of 6 and 10.

7. In Quinn's dormitory room, there are three snooze-alarm clocks, each of which is set at a different time. Clock A goes off every 15 min, clock B goes off every 40 min, and clock C goes off every 60 min. If all three clocks go off at 6:00 A.M., answer the following:
   a. How long will it be before the clocks go off together again after 6:00 A.M.?
   b. Would the answer to (a) be different if clock B went off every 15 min and clock A went off every 40 min?

8. If a number is greater than the GCD(9, 12), less than the LCM(2, 3), and the number is odd, what is it?

9. At the Senior All-night Party, a money chest contained enough money so that from 1 to 6 winners could share the money equally. The winners were to be chosen from those still in attendance at 4:00 A.M., and no one who had left early could win.
   a. What is the least amount of money that could be in the nonempty chest?
   b. If there were actually five winners, how much would each receive?
   c. If the prize money was to be given in $2 bills, how many bills were in the chest?

10. Midas has 120 gold coins and 144 silver coins. He wants to place his gold coins and his silver coins in stacks so that there are the same number of coins in each stack. What is the greatest number of coins that he can place in each stack?

11. Bill and Sue both work at night. Bill has every sixth night off and Sue has every eighth night off. If they are both off tonight, how many nights will it be before they are both off again?

12. By selling cookies at 24¢ each, José made enough money to buy several cans of pop costing 45¢ per can. If he had no money left over after buying the pop, what is the least number of cookies he could have sold?

13. Bijous I and II start their movies at 7:00 P.M. The movie at Bijou I takes 75 min, while the movie at Bijou II takes 90 min. If the shows run continuously, when will they start at the same time again?

14. Two bike riders ride around in a circular path. The first rider completes one round in 12 min and the second rider completes it in 18 min. If they both start at the same place and the same time and go in the same direction, after how many minutes will they meet again at the starting place?

15. Assume a and b are any natural numbers and answer the following:
   a. If GCD(a, b) = 1, find LCM(a, b).
   b. Find GCD(a, a) and LCM(a, a).
   c. Find GCD(a^2, a) and LCM(a^2, a).
   d. If $a|b$, find GCD(a, b) and LCM(a, b).
   e. If a and b are two different primes, find GCD(a, b) and LCM(a, b).
   f. What is the relationship between a and b if GCD(a, b) = a?
   g. What is the relationship between a and b if LCM(a, b) = a?

16. Classify each of the following as true or false. Justify your answers.
   a. If GCD(a, b) = 1, then a and b cannot both be even.
   b. If GCD(a, b) = 2, then both a and b are even.
   c. If a and b are even, then GCD(a, b) = 2.
   d. For all natural numbers a and b, LCM(a, b)|GCD(a, b).
   e. For all natural numbers a and b, LCM(a, b)|ab.
   f. GCD(a, b) ≤ a
   g. LCM(a, b) ≥ a

17. To find GCD(24, 20, 12), it is possible to find GCD(24, 20), which is 4, and then find GCD(4, 12), which is 4. Use this approach and the Euclidean algorithm to find GCD(120, 75, 105).

18. a. Show that 97,219,988,751 and 4 are relatively prime.
    b. Show that 181,345,913 and 11 are relatively prime.

19. The radio station gave away a discount coupon for every fifth and sixth caller. Every twentieth caller received free concert tickets. Which caller was first to get both a coupon and a concert ticket?

20. Jackie spent the same amount of money on cassette tapes that she did on compact discs. If tapes cost $12 and CDs $16, what is the least amount she could have spent on each?

21. Larry and Mary bought a special 360-day joint membership to a tennis club. Larry will use the club every other day, and Mary will use the club every third day. They both use the club on the first day. How many days will neither person use the club in the 360 days?

22. At the Party Store, paper plates come in packages of 30, paper cups in packages of 15, and napkins in packages of 20. What is the least number of plates, cups, and napkins that can be purchased so that there is an equal number of each?

23. Determine how many complete revolutions gear 2 in the following must make before the arrows are lined up again:

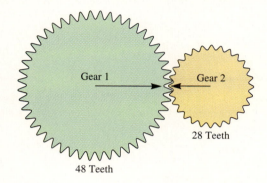

Gear 1
Gear 2
28 Teeth
48 Teeth

24. Determine how many complete revolutions each gear in the following must make before the arrows are lined up again:

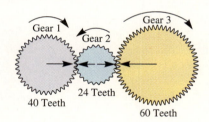

Gear 1
Gear 2
Gear 3
40 Teeth
24 Teeth
60 Teeth

25. Venn diagrams can be used to show factors of two or more numbers. Draw Venn diagrams to show the common factors for each of the following sets of three numbers:
   a. 10, 15, 60   **b.** 8, 16, 24
26. If p is a prime number, what are the factors of p^2?
27. Find all natural numbers x such that GCD(25, x) = 1 and $1 \leq x \leq 25$.

28. Given the set of numbers {61, 63, 65, 67, 70}, which one is a composite number between 62 and 72, has the sum of its digits as a prime number, and has more than 4 factors?

Communication

29. Can two numbers have a greatest common multiple? Explain your answer.
30. Describe to a sixth-grade student the difference between a divisor and a multiple.
31. Is it true that GCD (a, b, c) · LCM (a, b, c) = abc? Explain your answer.
32. a. You have seen many methods for finding the greatest common divisor. Which do you think is the best way to teach the concept to elementary students? Why?
   b. Answer the question in (a) for least common multiples.
33. Martha listed the prime numbers in order and then put them in groups of 5. She claimed she could find at least one pair of primes that are two units apart in each group of 5. For example, 2, 3, 5, 7, 11 has the primes 5 and 7 that are two units apart. Do you agree with Martha? Why or why not?

Open-ended

34. Is it possible for the GCD of two different numbers, each greater than 1, to be equal to the LCM of the two numbers? Explain your answer.

Review Problems

35. Find two whole numbers x and y such that $x \cdot y = 1,000,000$ and neither x nor y contains any zeros as digits.
36. Fill each blank space with a single digit that makes the corresponding statement true. Find all possible answers.
   a. 3 | 83 _ 51   **b.** 11 | 8 _ 691
   c. 23 | 103 _ 6
37. Is 3111 a prime? Prove your answer.
38. Find a number that has exactly six prime factors.
39. Produce the least positive number that is divisible by 2, 3, 4, 5, 6, 7, 8, 9, 10, and 11.
40. What is the greatest prime that must be used to determine if 2089 is prime?

TECHNOLOGY CORNER

1. Write a spreadsheet to generate the first 50 multiples of 3 and the first 50 multiples of 4. Describe the intersection of the 2 sets.
2. Use a spreadsheet to find the factors of 2486. How far down do you need to copy the formula to be sure you have found all the divisors?

	A	B
1	1	= 2486/A1
2	2	
3	3	

3. Make a spreadsheet with four columns:

Column A—the multiples of 6
Column B—the multiples of 9
Column C—the multiples of 12
Column D—the multiples of 15

a. What is the least number that appears in all four columns?
b. Explain how to find this number without using a spreadsheet.

BRAIN TEASER   For any $n \times m$ rectangle such that GCD(n, m) = 1, find a rule for determining the number of unit squares (1×1) that a diagonal passes through. For example, in the drawings in Figure 4-26 the diagonal passes through 8 and 6 squares, respectively.

Figure 4-26

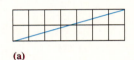

(a)   (b)

TECHNOLOGY CORNER

1. Type into your computer the following Logo procedure for finding the GCD of two positive integers and then use the procedure to find the GCD of the given numbers:

```
TO GCD :A :B
    IF :B = 0 OUTPUT :A
    OUTPUT GCD :B (REMAINDER :A :B)
END
```
(In LCSI, replace IF :B= 0 OUTPUT :A with IF :B= 0 [OUTPUT :A].)

a. GCD (676, 221)
b. GCD (10,764, 2300)

2. Use Theorem 4-9 and the preceding GCD procedure to write a procedure LCM for finding the LCM of any two positive integers, :*A* and :*B*.

---

*Section 4-6   Clock and Modular Arithmetic

In the *Teaching Standards* (p. 137), we find the following:

▲ *Investigations of selected algebraic structures should include examples such as clock arithmetic, modular systems, and matrices.*

In this section, we investigate clock arithmetic. Consider the following:

a. A doctor's prescription says to take a pill every 8 hr. If you take the first pill at 7:00 A.M., when should you take the next two pills?
b. Suppose you are following a bean soup recipe that calls for letting the beans soak for 12 hr. If you begin soaking them at 8:00 P.M., when should you take them out?

These situations involve being able to solve arithmetic problems using clocks. Most people can solve these problems without thinking much about what they are doing. It is possible to use the clock in Figure 4-27(a) to determine that 8 hr after 7:00 A.M. is 3:00 P.M., and 8 hr after that is 11:00 P.M. Also, 12 hr after 8:00 P.M. is 8:00 A.M. We could record these additions on the clock as

$$7 \oplus 8 = 3, \qquad 3 \oplus 8 = 11, \qquad 8 \oplus 12 = 8,$$

where $\oplus$ indicates addition on a 12-hr clock.

Figure 4-27   (a)   (b)

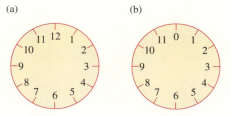

You probably noticed the special role of 12 when you found that $8 \oplus 12 = 8$. In 12-hr clock arithmetic, 12 acts like a 0 if you were adding in the set of whole numbers. For this reason, the 12 is often replaced by a 0, as in Figure 4-27(b). An addition table for the finite system based on the clock in Figure 4-27(b) is shown in Table 4-6.

Table 4-6

+	0	1	2	3	4	5	6	7	8	9	10	11
0	0	1	2	3	4	5	6	7	8	9	10	11
1	1	2	3	4	5	6	7	8	9	10	11	0
2	2	3	4	5	6	7	8	9	10	11	0	1
3	3	4	5	6	7	8	9	10	11	0	1	2
4	4	5	6	7	8	9	10	11	0	1	2	3
5	5	6	7	8	9	10	11	0	1	2	3	4
6	6	7	8	9	10	11	0	1	2	3	4	5
7	7	8	9	10	11	0	1	2	3	4	5	6
8	8	9	10	11	0	1	2	3	4	5	6	7
9	9	10	11	0	1	2	3	4	5	6	7	8
10	10	11	0	1	2	3	4	5	6	7	8	9
11	11	0	1	2	3	4	5	6	7	8	9	10

INVESTIGATION 4-10

● Examine Table 4-6 to determine if the following properties hold for $\oplus$ on the set of numbers in the table:

a. Commutative property of addition

b. Associative property of addition

c. Identity property of addition

d. Inverse property of addition ●

When we allow numbers other than those on the 12-hr clock to be added, such as $8 \oplus 24 = 8$, we find that numbers such as 24, 36, 48, . . . act like 0. Likewise, the numbers 13, 25, 37, . . . act like the number 1. Similarly, we can generate classes of numbers that act like each of the numbers on the 12-hr clock. The members of any one class differ by multiples of 12. Consequently, to perform additions on a 12-hr clock we perform regular addition, divide by 12, and record the remainder as the answer. For example, we can find $11 \oplus 8$ and $8 \oplus 12$ as follows:

$11 + 8 = 19$. Next divide $19 \div 12$. The quotient is 1 with a remainder of 7, which is the answer.

$8 + 12 = 20$. Next divide $20 \div 12$. The quotient is 1 with a remainder of 8, which is the answer.

Whenever the sum of digits on a 12-hr clock exceeds 12, add the numbers normally and then obtain the remainder when the sum is divided by 12.

To perform other operations on the clock, such as $2 \ominus 9$, where $\ominus$ denotes clock subtraction, we could interpret it as the time 9 hr before 2 o'clock. Counting backward (counterclockwise) 9 units from 2 reveals that $2 \ominus 9 = 5$. If subtraction on the clock is defined in terms of addition, we have $2 \ominus 9 = x$, if and only if $2 = 9 \oplus x$. Consequently, $x = 5$.

• • •

Example 4-30 | Perform each of the following computations on a 12-hr clock:

a. $8 \oplus 8$ **b.** $4 \ominus 12$ **c.** $4 \ominus 4$ **d.** $4 \ominus 8$

Solution   **a.** $(8 + 8) \div 12$ has remainder 4. Hence, $8 \oplus 8 = 4$.
b. $4 \ominus 12 = 4$, since, by counting forward or backward 12 hr, you arrive at the original position.
c. $4 \ominus 4 = 12$. This should be clear from looking at the clock, but it can also be found by using the definition of subtraction in terms of addition.
d. $4 \ominus 8 = 8$ because $8 \oplus 8 = 4$

• • •

Clock multiplication can be defined using repeated addition as with whole numbers. For example, $2 \otimes 8 = 8 \oplus 8 = 4$, where $\otimes$ denotes clock multiplication. Similarly, $3 \otimes 5 = (5 \oplus 5) \oplus 5 = 10 \oplus 5 = 3$.

Clock division can be defined in terms of multiplication. For example, $8 \oslash 5 = x$, where $\oslash$ denotes clock division, if, and only if, $8 = 5 \otimes x$ for a unique x in the set $\{1, 2, 3, . . . , 12\}$. Because $5 \otimes 4 = 8$, then $8 \oslash 5 = 4$.

• • •

Example 4-31 | Perform the following operations on a 12-hr clock, if possible:

a. $3 \otimes 11$ **b.** $2 \oslash 7$ **c.** $3 \oslash 2$ **d.** $5 \oslash 12$

Solution   **a.** $3 \otimes 11 = (11 \oplus 11) \oplus 11 = 10 \oplus 11 = 9$
b. $2 \oslash 7 = x$ if, and only if, $2 = 7 \otimes x$. Consequently, $x = 2$.
c. $3 \oslash 2 = x$ if, and only if, $3 = 2 \otimes x$. Multiplying each of the numbers 1, 2, 3, 4, . . . , 12 by 2 shows that none of the multiplications yields 3. Thus the equation $3 = 2 \otimes x$ has no solution, and consequently, $3 \oslash 2$ is undefined.

d. $5 \oplus 12 = x$ if, and only if, $5 = 12 \otimes x$. However, $12 \otimes x = 12$ for every x in the set $\{1, 3, 4, \ldots, 12\}$. Thus $5 = 12 \otimes x$ has no solution on the clock; and therefore $5 \oplus 12$ is undefined.

• • •

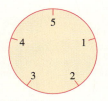

Figure 4-28

Adding or subtracting 12 on a 12-hr clock gives the same result. Thus 12 behaves as 0 does in a base-ten addition or subtraction and is the additive identity for addition on the 12-hr clock. Similarly, on a 5-hr clock 5 behaves as 0 does.

Addition, subtraction, and multiplication on a 12-hr clock can be performed for any two numbers, but as shown in Example 4-31(d) not all divisions can be performed. Division by 12, the additive identity, on a 12-hr clock either can never be performed or is not meaningful, since it does not yield a unique answer. However, there are clocks on which all divisions can be performed, except by the corresponding additive identities. One such clock is a 5-hr clock, shown in Figure 4-28.

Table 4-7

(a)

$\oplus$	1	2	3	4	5
1	2	3	4	5	1
2	3	4	5	1	2
3	4	5	1	2	3
4	5	1	2	3	4
5	1	2	3	4	5

(b)

$\otimes$	1	2	3	4	5
1	1	2	3	4	5
2	2	4	1	3	5
3	3	1	4	2	5
4	4	3	2	1	5
5	5	5	5	5	5

On this clock, $3 \oplus 4 = 2$, $2 \ominus 3 = 4$, $2 \otimes 4 = 3$, and $3 \oplus 4 = 2$. Since adding 5 to any number yields the original number, 5 is the additive identity for this 5-hr clock, as seen in Table 4-7(a). Consequently, you might suspect that division by 5 is not possible on a 5-hour clock. To determine which divisions are possible, consider Table 4-7(b), a multiplication table for 5-hr clock arithmetic. To find $1 \oplus 2$, we write $1 \oplus 2 = x$, which is equivalent to $1 = 2 \otimes x$. The second row of part (b) of the table shows that $2 \otimes 1 = 2$, $2 \otimes 2 = 4$, $2 \otimes 3 = 1$, $2 \otimes 4 = 3$, and $2 \otimes 5 = 5$. The solution of $1 = 2 \otimes x$ is $x = 3$, so $1 \oplus 2 = 3$. The information given in the second row of the table can be used to determine the following divisions:

$$2 \oplus 2 = 1 \text{ because } 2 = 2 \otimes 1$$
$$3 \oplus 2 = 4 \text{ because } 3 = 2 \otimes 4$$
$$4 \oplus 2 = 2 \text{ because } 4 = 2 \otimes 2$$
$$5 \oplus 2 = 5 \text{ because } 5 = 2 \otimes 5$$

Figure 4-29

Because every element occurs in the second row, division by 2 is always possible. Similarly, division by all other numbers, except 5, is always possible. In the problem set, you are asked to perform arithmetic on different clocks and to investigate for which clocks all computations, except division by the additive identity, can be performed.

Modular Arithmetic

Many of the concepts for clock arithmetic can be used to work problems involving a calendar. On the calendar in Figure 4-29, the five Sundays have dates 1, 8, 15, 22, and 29. Any two of these dates for Sunday differ by a multiple of 7. The same property is true for any other day of the week. For example, the second and thirtieth days fall on the same day, since $30 - 2 = 28$ and 28 is a multiple of 7. We say that 30 is congruent to 2, modulo 7, and we write $30 \equiv 2$ (mod 7). Similarly, because 18 and 6 differ by a multiple of 12, we write $18 \equiv 6$ (mod 12). This leads to the following definition.

Definition of Modular Congruence

For integers a and b, a **is congruent to** b **modulo** m, written $a \equiv b$ (mod m), if, and only, if $a - b$ is a multiple of m, where m is a positive integer greater than 1.

REMARK   This definition could be written as: $a \equiv b$ (mod m) if, and only if, $m|(a - b)$, where m is a positive whole number greater than 1.

Example 4-32   Tell why each of the following is true:

a. $23 \equiv 3$ (mod 10)
b. $23 \equiv 3$ (mod 4)
c. $23 \not\equiv 3$ (mod 7)
d. $10 \equiv {}^-1$ (mod 11)
e. $25 \equiv 5$ (mod 5)

Solution   **a.** $23 \equiv 3$ (mod 10) because $23 - 3$ is a multiple of 10.
b. $23 \equiv 3$ (mod 4) because $23 - 3$ is a multiple of 4.
c. $23 \not\equiv 3$ (mod 7) because $23 - 3$ is not a multiple of 7.
d. $10 \equiv {}^-1$ (mod 11) because $10 - ({}^-1) = 11$ is a multiple of 11.
e. $25 \equiv 5$ (mod 5) because $25 - 5 = 20$ is a multiple of 5.

Example 4-33   Find all integers x such that $x \equiv 1$ (mod 10).

Solution   The solution is $x \equiv 1$ (mod 10) if, and only if, $x - 1 = 10k$, where k is any integer. Consequently, $x = 10k + 1$. Letting $k = 0, 1, 2, 3, \ldots$ yields the sequence 1, 11, 21, 31, 41, ... Likewise, letting $k = {}^-1, {}^-2, {}^-3, {}^-4, \ldots$ yields the negative integers $^-9, ^-19, ^-29, ^-39, \ldots$. The two sequences can be combined to give the solution set

$$\{\ldots, {}^-39, {}^-29, {}^-19, {}^-9, 1, 11, 21, 31, 41, 51, \ldots\}.$$

In Example 4-33, the positive integers obtained, 1, 11, 21, 31, 41, 51, ..., differ from each other by a multiple of 10; hence, they are congruent to each other modulo 10. Notice that each of the numbers 1, 11, 21, 31, 41, 51, ... has a remainder of 1 when divided by 10. In general, *two whole numbers are congruent modulo m if, and only if, their remainders, on division by m, are the same.*

The $\boxed{\text{INT}\div}$ button on a calculator may be used to work with modular arithmetic. If we press the following sequence of buttons, we see that $4325 \equiv 5$ (mod 9) because the remainder when 4325 is divided by 9 is 5:

$$\boxed{4}\,\boxed{3}\,\boxed{2}\,\boxed{5}\,\boxed{\text{INT}\div}\,\boxed{9}\,\boxed{=}\,,$$

and the display shows a remainder of 5.

• • •

Example 4-34 Heidi signed a promissory note that will become due in 90 days. She is worried that it will become due on a weekend. She signed the note on a Monday. On what day of the week will it come due?

Solution Because $90 = 7 \cdot 12 + 6$, we know that $90 \equiv 6 \pmod 7$. On a fraction calculator, you could enter $\boxed{9}\,\boxed{0}\,\boxed{\text{INT}\div}\,\boxed{=}$, and a quotient of 12 with remainder 6 would be displayed. Therefore the note will come due 12 wk and 6 days after Monday, which is a Sunday.

• • •

Many properties of congruence are similar to properties for equality. Several of these are listed next.

Properties

For all integers a, b, and c:

1. $a \equiv a \pmod m$
2. If $a \equiv b \pmod m$, then $b \equiv a \pmod m$.
3. If $a \equiv b \pmod m$ and $b \equiv c \pmod m$, then $a \equiv c \pmod m$.
4. If $a \equiv b \pmod m$, then $a + c \equiv b + c \pmod m$.
5. If $a \equiv b \pmod m$, then $ac \equiv bc \pmod m$.
6. If $a \equiv b \pmod m$ and $c \equiv d \pmod m$, then $ac \equiv bd \pmod m$.
7. If $a \equiv b \pmod m$ and $c \equiv d \pmod m$, then $a + c \equiv b + d \pmod m$.
8. If $a \equiv b \pmod m$ and k is a natural number, then $a^k \equiv b^k \pmod m$.

With these properties, it is possible to solve a variety of problems, such as the following.

Problem 5

Find the remainder when 3^{100} is divided by 5.

Understanding the Problem. No calculator will accurately find 3^{100}, so we cannot actually divide 3^{100} by 5 to find the remainder. The remainder should be 0, 1, 2, 3, or 4 when a number is divided by 5.

Devising a Plan. Since a calculator will not solve the problem, we look for an alternative plan. The use of modular arithmetic will help if we can find small integers that are equivalent to powers of 3 and use the previously given properties 5 and 8 to build up 3^{100} and find its mod 5 equivalent.

Carrying Out the Plan. We know that $3^2 \equiv 4 \pmod 5$. Thus

$$3^3 \equiv 3 \cdot 4 \equiv 2 \pmod 5$$
$$3^4 \equiv 3 \cdot 2 \equiv 1 \pmod 5. \text{ (Multiply both sides by 3.)}$$

Using property 8, we see that $(3^4)^{25} \equiv 1^{25}$ (mod 5) or $3^{100} \equiv 1$ (mod 5). It follows that 3^{100} and 1 have the same remainder when divided by 5. Thus 3^{100} has remainder 1 when divided by 5.

Looking Back. This type of problem can be changed to find the remainders when dividing by different numbers or to find the units digit of numbers such as 2^{96}.

• • •

Example 4-35
a. If it is now Monday, October 14, on what day of the week will October 14 fall next year if next year is not a leap year?
b. If Christmas falls on Thursday this year, on what day of the week will Christmas fall next year if next year is a leap year?

Solution
a. Because next year is not a leap year, we have 365 days in the year. Because $365 = 52 \cdot 7 + 1$, we have $365 \equiv 1$ (mod 7). Thus 365 days after October 14 will be 52 wk and one day later. Thus October 14 will be on a Tuesday.
b. Because there are 366 days in a leap year, we have $366 \equiv 2$ (mod 7). Thus Christmas will be 2 days after Thursday, on Saturday.

• • •

Ongoing Assessment 4-6

1. Dr. Harper prescribed some medicine for Camile. She is supposed to take a dose every 6 hr. If she takes her first dose at 8:00 A.M., when should she take her next dose?
2. Sally is flying to North Carolina to see her mother. With all her transfers, the travel agent told her that it would take 7 hr to get there. If she leaves at 7:00 A.M. and stays in the same time zone, what time will she arrive?
3. Perform each of the following operations on a 12-hr clock, if possible:
   a. $7 \oplus 8$ **b.** $4 \oplus 10$ **c.** $3 \ominus 9$
   d. $4 \ominus 8$ **e.** $3 \otimes 9$ **f.** $4 \otimes 4$
   g. $1 \oslash 3$ **h.** $2 \oslash 5$
4. Perform each of the following operations on a 5-hr clock:
   a. $3 \oplus 4$ **b.** $3 \oplus 3$ **c.** $3 \otimes 4$
   d. $1 \otimes 4$ **e.** $3 \otimes 4$ **f.** $2 \otimes 3$
   g. $3 \oslash 4$ **h.** $1 \oslash 4$
5. **a.** Construct an addition table for a 7-hr clock.
   b. Using the addition table in (a), find $5 \ominus 6$ and $2 \ominus 5$.
   c. Using the addition table in (a), show that subtraction can always be performed on a 7-hr clock.
6. **a.** Construct a multiplication table for a 7-hr clock.
   b. Use the multiplication table in (a) to find $3 \oslash 5$ and $4 \oslash 6$.
   c. Use the multiplication table to find whether division by numbers different from 7 is always possible.
7. On a 12-hr clock, find each of the following:
   a. Additive inverse of 2   **b.** Additive inverse of 3
   c. $(^-2) \oplus (-3)$ **d.** $^-(2 \oplus 3)$
   e. $(^-2) \ominus (-3)$ **f.** $(^-2) \otimes (^-3)$
8. **a.** If April 23 falls on Tuesday, what are the dates of the other Tuesdays in April?
   b. If July 2 falls on Tuesday, list the dates of the Wednesdays in July.
   c. If September 3 falls on Monday, on what day of the week will it fall next year if next year is a leap year?
9. Fill in each of the following blanks so that the answer is nonnegative and the least possible number:
   a. $29 \equiv$ _____ (mod 5)
   b. $3498 \equiv$ _____ (mod 3)
   c. $3498 \equiv$ _____ (mod 11)
   d. $^-23 \equiv$ _____ (mod 10)
10. Show that each of the following statements is true:
   a. $81 \equiv 1$ (mod 8)
   b. $81 \equiv 1$ (mod 10)
   c. $1000 \equiv -1$ (mod 13)
   d. $10^{84} \equiv 1$ (mod 9)
   e. $10^{100} \equiv 1$ (mod 11)
   f. $937 \equiv 37$ (mod 100)
11. Show that $a \equiv 0$ (mod m) if, and only if, $m|a$.
12. Translate each of the following statements into the language of congruences:

a. 8|24   **b.** 3|⁻90
c. Any integer *n* divides itself.
13. **a.** Find all *x* such that $x \equiv 0 \pmod 2$.
    b. Find all *x* such that $x \equiv 1 \pmod 2$.
    c. Find all *x* such that $x \equiv 3 \pmod 5$.
14. Find the remainder for each of the following:
    a. 5^{100} is divided by 6.
    b. 5^{101} is divided by 6.
    c. 10^{99} is divided by 11.
    d. 10^{100} is divided by 11.
15. If Thanksgiving is November 29, on what day of the week is Christmas?
16. If July 4 is on a Tuesday, on what day is it next year if next year is not a leap year?
17. Use the fact that $100 \equiv 0 \pmod 4$ to find and prove a test for divisibility by 4.
18. Show that, in general, the cancellation property for multiplication does not hold for congruences; that is, show that $ac \equiv bc \pmod m$ does not always imply $a \equiv b \pmod m$.

Communication

19. Explain how the odometer on a car uses modular arithmetic. What is the mod?

Open-ended

20. A method of checking arithmetic computation called *casting out 9s* was introduced in Problem 17 in Ongoing Assessment 4-3.
    a. Review this technique and how it works.
    b. How is this technique related to the modular systems studied in this section?

Cooperative Learning

21. **a.** Construct the multiplication tables for 3-hr, 4-hr, 6-hr, and 11-hr clocks.
    b. On which of the clocks in (a) can divisions by numbers other than the additive identity always be performed? Explain your answer.
    c. How do the multiplication tables of clocks for which division can always be performed (except by an additive identity) differ from the multiplication tables of clocks for which division is not always meaningful?

LABORATORY ACTIVITY   Most publishers include an International Standard Book Number (ISBN) on their books. Suppose the ISBN for a book is 0-8053-0390-1. What do the numbers mean? Why are they used?

BRAIN TEASER   How many primes are in the following sequence?
9, 98, 987, 9876, ... , 987654321, 9876543219, 98765432198, ...

SOLUTION TO THE PRELIMINARY PROBLEM

Understanding the Problem.   The ages of some teenagers when multiplied together result in a product of 10,584,000. Using this information, we must find the number of teenagers in the Mathematics Club and their ages.

Devising a Plan.   One approach might be to use *guess and check* and try some ages 13–19 to see if a product of 10,584,000 could be obtained. Another approach is to find the *prime factorization* of 10,584,000 and see if these factors could lead to the ages of the Math Club members.

Carrying Out the Plan.   The prime factorization of 10,584,000 is

$$2 \cdot 2 \cdot 2 \cdot 2 \cdot 2 \cdot 2 \cdot 3 \cdot 3 \cdot 3 \cdot 3 \cdot 5 \cdot 5 \cdot 5 \cdot 7 \cdot 7.$$

The ages of the members must be combinations of these factors. If we choose a factor of 7, then the only other factor that can be paired with it and give a product in the range 13–19 is 2. This is true for each factor of 7, so there are two members who are 14 years old. A factor of 5 cannot be paired with 2 because this will give a product of 10 and 10 is not old enough for a teenager. Therefore the three 5s must be paired with the three 3s, giving us three members who are 15. This leaves only four factors of 2 that must all be grouped together in order to have a product in the range 13–19. This results in one student being 16. So we have two 14-year-olds, three 15-year-olds, and one 16-year-old.

Looking Back.   We should check that $14 \cdot 14 \cdot 15 \cdot 15 \cdot 15 \cdot 16$ yields a product of 10,584,000, which it does. The original problem can be changed by using differently aged teenagers or a different number of students.

QUESTIONS FROM THE CLASSROOM

1. A fourth-grade student devised the following subtraction algorithm for subtracting 84 − 27.

   Four minus seven equals negative three.

   $$\begin{array}{r} 84 \\ -\ 27 \\ \hline {}^{-}3 \end{array}$$

   Eighty minus twenty equals sixty.

   $$\begin{array}{r} 84 \\ -\ 27 \\ \hline {}^{-}3 \\ 60 \end{array}$$

   Sixty plus negative three equals fifty-seven.

   $$\begin{array}{r} 84 \\ -\ 27 \\ \hline {}^{-}3 \\ +\ 60 \\ \hline 57 \end{array}$$

   Thus the answer is 57. What is your response as a teacher?

2. A seventh-grade student does not believe that $^{-}5 < {}^{-}2$. The student argues that a debt of $5 is greater than a debt of $2. How do you respond?

3. An eighth-grade student claims she can prove that subtraction of integers is commutative. She points out that if a and b are integers, then $a - b = a + {}^{-}b$. Since addition is commutative, so is subtraction. What is your response?

4. A student computes $^{-}8 - 2(^{-}3)$ by writing $^{-}10(^{-}3) = 30$. How would you help this student?

5. A student says that his father showed him a very simple method for dealing with expressions like $^{-}(a - b + 1)$ and $x - (2x - 3)$. The rule is, if there is a negative sign before the parentheses, change the signs of the expressions inside the parentheses. Thus, $^{-}(a - b + 1) = {}^{-}a + b - 1$ and $x - (2x - 3) = x - 2x + 3$. What is your response?

6. A student shows you the following proof that $(^{-}1)(^{-}1) = 1$: There are two possibilities, either $(^{-}1)(^{-}1) = 1$ or $(^{-}1)(^{-}1) = {}^{-}1$. Suppose $(^{-}1)(^{-}1) = {}^{-}1$. Since $^{-}1 = (^{-}1) \cdot 1$, then $(^{-}1)(^{-}1) = {}^{-}1$ can be written as $(^{-}1)(^{-}1) = (^{-}1) \cdot 1$. By the cancellation property of multiplication, it follows that $^{-}1 = 1$, which is impossible. Hence, $(^{-}1)(^{-}1)$ cannot equal $^{-}1$ and must therefore equal 1. What is your reaction?

7. A student had the following picture of an integer and its opposite. Other students in the class objected, saying that ^{-}a should be to the left of 0. How do you respond?

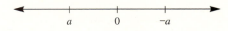

8. A student claims that $a|a$ and $a|a$ implies $a|(a - a)$, and hence, $a|0$. Is the student correct?

9. A student writes, "If $d \nmid a$ and $d \nmid b$, then $d \nmid (a + b)$." How do you respond?

10. Your seventh-grade class has just completed a unit on divisibility rules. One of the better students asks why divisibility by numbers other than 3 and 9 cannot be tested by dividing the sum of the digits by the tested number. How should you respond?

11. A student claims that a number with an even number of digits is divisible by 7 if, and only if, each of the numbers formed by pairing the digits into groups of two is divisible by 7. For example, 49,562,107 is divisible by 7, since each of the numbers 49, 56, 21, and 07 is divisible by 7. Is this true?

12. A sixth-grade student argues that there are infinitely many primes because "there is no end to numbers." How do you respond?

13. A student claims that a number is divisible by 21 if, and only if, it is divisible by 3 and by 7, and, in general, a num-

ber is divisible by $a \cdot b$ if, and only if, it is divisible by a and by b. What is your response?

14. A student claims that for any two integers a and b, GCD(a, b) divides LCM(a, b) and, hence, GCD(a, b) < LCM(a, b). Is the student correct? Why or why not?

15. A student claims that there are infinitely many triples of positive integers x and y, z that make the equation $x^2 + y^2 = z^2$ true. How do you respond?

16. A student argues that 1 should be a prime because it has 1 and itself as divisors. How do you respond?

17. A student asks about the relation between least common multiple and least common denominator. How do you respond?

CHAPTER OUTLINE

I. Basic concepts of integers

  A. The set of **integers,** I, is $\{\ldots, {}^{-}3, {}^{-}2, {}^{-}1, 0, 1, 2, 3, \ldots\}$.

  B. The distance from any integer to 0 is called the **absolute value** of the integer. The absolute value of an integer x is denoted $|x|$.

  C. Operations with integers

    1. Addition: For any integers a and b:

$$^{-}a + {}^{-}b = {}^{-}(a + b)$$

    2. Subtraction:

      a. If a and b are any integers, then $a - b = n$ if, and only if, $a = b + n$.

      b. For all integers a and b, $a - b = a + {}^{-}b$.

    3. Multiplication: For any integers a and b:

      a. $(^{-}a) \cdot (^{-}b) = ab$

      b. $(^{-}a) \cdot b = b \cdot (^{-}a) = {}^{-}(ab)$

    4. Division: If a and b are any integers with $b \neq 0$, then $a \div b$ is the unique integer c, if it exists, such that $a = bc$.

    5. Order of operations: When addition, subtraction, multiplication, and division appear without parentheses, multiplications and divisions are done first in the order of their appearance from left to right and then additions and subtractions are done in the order of their appearance from left to right. Any arithmetic in parentheses is done first.

II. The system of integers

  A. The set of integers, $I = \{\ldots, {}^{-}3, {}^{-}2, {}^{-}1, 0, 1, 2, 3, \ldots\}$, along with the operations of addition and multiplication, satisfy the following properties:

Property	+	×
Closure	Yes	Yes
Commutative	Yes	Yes
Associative	Yes	Yes
Identity	Yes, 0	Yes, 1
Inverse	Yes	No
Distributive property of multiplication over addition		

  B. Zero multiplication property of integers: $a \cdot 0 = 0 = 0 \cdot a$

  C. Addition property of equality: For any integers a, b, and c, if $a = b$, then $a + c = b + c$.

  D. Multiplication property of equality: For any integers a, b, and c, if $a = b$, then $ac = bc$.

  E. Substitution property: Any number may be substituted for its equal.

  F. Cancellation properties of equality:

    1. For any integers a, b, and c, if $a + c = b + c$, then $a = b$.

    2. For any integers a, b, and c, if $c \neq 0$ and $ac = bc$, then $a = b$.

  G. For all integers a, b, and c:

    1. $^{-}(^{-}a) = a$

    2. $a - (b - c) = a - b + c$

    3. $(a + b)(a - b) = a^2 - b^2$ **(difference-of-squares formula)**

III. Divisibility

  A. If a and b are any integers, then b **divides** a, denoted by $b|a$, if, and only if, there is an integer c such that $a = cb$.

  B. The following are basic divisibility theorems for integers a, b, and d:

    1. If $d|a$ and k is any integer, then $d|ka$.

    2. If $d|a$ and $d|b$, then $d|(a + b)$ and $d|(a - b)$.

    3. If $d|a$ and $d\nmid b$, then $d\nmid(a + b)$ and $d\nmid(a - b)$.

  C. Divisibility tests

    1. An integer is divisible by 2, 5, or 10 if, and only if, its units digit is divisible by 2, 5, or 10, respectively.

    2. An integer is divisible by 4 if, and only if, the last 2 digits of the integer represent a number divisible by 4.

    3. An integer is divisible by 8 if, and only if, the last 3 digits of the integer represent a number divisible by 8.

    4. An integer is divisible by 3 or by 9 if, and only if, the sum of its digits is divisible by 3 or 9, respectively.

    5. An integer is divisible by 11 if, and only if, the sum of the digits in the places that are even powers of 10 minus the sum of the digits in the places that are odd powers of 10 is divisible by 11.

6. An integer is divisible by 6 if, and only if, the integer is divisible by both 2 and 3.

IV. Prime and composite numbers

   A. Positive integers that have exactly two positive divisors are called **primes.** Integers greater than 1 and not primes are called **composites.**

   B. Fundamental Theorem of Arithmetic: Every composite number has one and only one prime factorization, aside from variation in the order of the prime factors.

   C. Criterion for determining if a given number n is prime: *If n is not divisible by any prime p such that $p^2 \leq n$, then n is prime.*

   D. If the prime factorization of a number, n, is $n = p_1{}^{q_1} \cdot p_2{}^{q_2} \cdot p_3{}^{q_3} \cdot \ldots \cdot p_m{}^{q_m}$, then the number of divisors of n is $(q_1 + 1)(q_2 + 1)(q_3 + 1) \cdot \ldots \cdot (q_m + 1)$.

V. Greatest common divisor and least common multiple

   A. The **greatest common divisor (GCD)** of two or more natural numbers is the greatest divisor, or factor, that the numbers have in common.

   B. Euclidean algorithm: If a and b are whole numbers and $a \geq b$, then $\mathrm{GCD}(a, b) = \mathrm{GCD}(b, r)$, where r is the remainder when a is divided by b. The procedure of finding the GCD of two numbers a and b by using the above result repeatedly is the *Euclidean algorithm.*

   C. The **least common multiple (LCM)** of two or more natural numbers is the least positive multiple that the numbers have in common.

   D. $\mathrm{GCD}(a, b) \cdot \mathrm{LCM}(a, b) = ab$.

   E. If $\mathrm{GCD}(a, b) = 1$, then a and b are **relatively prime.**

*VI. Modular arithmetic

   A. For any integers a and b, a **is congruent to** b **modulo** m if, and only if, $a - b$ is a multiple of m, where m is a positive integer greater than 1.

   B. Two integers are congruent modulo m if, and only if, their remainders upon division by m are the same.

CHAPTER REVIEW

1. Find the additive inverse of each of the following:
   a. 3   **b.** ^-a **c.** 0
   d. $x + y$ **e.** $^-x + y$ **f.** $(^-2)^5$ **g.** $^-2^5$

2. Perform each of the following operations:
   a. $(^-2 + {}^-8) + 3$ **b.** $^-2 - (^-5) + 5$
   c. $^-3(^-2) + 2$ **d.** $^-3(^-5 + 5)$
   e. $^-40 \div (^-5)$ **f.** $(^-25 \div 5)(^-3)$

3. For each of the following, find all integer values of x (if there are any) that make the given equation true:
   a. $^-x + 3 = 0$ **b.** $^-2x = 10$
   c. $0 \div (^-x) = 0$ **d.** $^-x \div 0 = {}^-1$
   e. $3x - 1 = {}^-124$ **f.** $^-2x + 3x = x$

4. Use a pattern approach to explain why $(^-2)(^-3) = 6$.

5. In each of the following chip models, the encircled chips are removed. Write the corresponding integer problem with its solution.

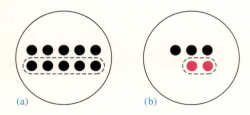

      (a)   (b)

6. a. Show that $(x - y)(x + y) = x^2 - y^2$.
   b. Use the result in (a) to compute $(^-2 - x)(^-2 + x)$.

7. Simplify each of the following expressions:
   a. ^-1x **b.** $(^-1)(x - y)$
   c. $2x - (1 - x)$ **d.** $(^-x)^2 + x^2$
   e. $(^-x)^3 + x^3$ **f.** $(^-3 - x)(3 + x)$

8. Factor each of the following expressions and then simplify, if possible:
   a. $x - 3x$
   b. $x^2 + x$
   c. $x^2 - 36$
   d. $81y^6 - 16x^4$
   e. $5 + 5x$
   f. $(x - y)(x + 1) - (x - y)$

9. Classify each of the following as true or false (all letters represent integers). Justify your answers.
   a. $|x|$ always is positive.
   b. For all x and y, $|x + y| = |x| + |y|$.
   c. If $a < {}^-b$, then $a < 0$.
   d. For all x and y, $(x - y)^2 = (y - x)^2$.
   e. $(^-a)(^-b)$ is the additive inverse of ab.

10. Find a counterexample to disprove each of the following properties on the set of integers:
   a. Commutative property of division
   b. Associative property of subtraction
   c. Closure property for division
   d. Distributive property of division over subtraction

11. If the temperature was $^-16°C$ and it rose by $9°C$, what is the new temperature?

12. A truck contains 150 small packages, some weighing 1 kg each and some weighing 2 kg each. How many packages of each weight are in the truck if the total weight of the packages is 265 kg?

13. Classify each of the following as true or false:
   a. $8|4$ **b.** $0|4$ **c.** $4|0$
   d. If a number is divisible by 4 and by 6, then it is divisible by 24.

   e. If a number is not divisible by 12, then it is not divisible by 3.

14. Classify each of the following as true or false. If false, show a counterexample.
   a. If $7|x$ and $7\nmid y$, then $7\nmid xy$.
   b. If $d\nmid(a+b)$, then $d\nmid a$ and $d\nmid b$.
   c. If $16|10^4$, then $16|10^6$.
   d. If $d|(a+b)$ and $d\nmid a$, then $d\nmid b$.
   e. If $d|(x+y)$ and $d|x$, then $d|y$.
   f. If $4\nmid x$ and $4\nmid y$, then $4\nmid xy$.

15. Test each of the following numbers for divisibility by 2, 3, 4, 5, 6, 8, 9, and 11:
   a. 83,160   **b.** 83,193

16. Assume that 10,007 is prime. Without actually dividing 10,024 by 17, prove that 10,024 is not divisible by 17.

17. Fill each blank with 1 digit to make each of the following true (find all the possible answers):
   a. $6|87\_4$
   b. $24|4\_856$
   c. $29|87\_\_4$

18. Determine whether each of the following numbers is prime or composite:
   a. 143   **b.** 223

19. How can you tell if a number is divisible by 24? Check 4152 for divisibility by 24.

20. Find the GCD for each of the following:
   a. 24 and 52
   b. 5767 and 4453

21. Find the LCM for each of the following:
   a. $2^3 \cdot 5^2 \cdot 7^3$, $2 \cdot 5^3 \cdot 7^2 \cdot 13$, and $2^4 \cdot 5 \cdot 7^4 \cdot 29$
   b. 278 and 279

22. Construct a number that has exactly five divisors. Explain your construction.

23. Find all divisors of 144.

24. Find the prime factorization of each of the following:
   a. 172   **b.** 288
   c. 260   **d.** 111

25. Jane and Ramon are running laps on a track. If they start at the same time and place and go in the same direction, with Jane running a lap in 5 min and Ramon running a lap in 3 min, how long will it take for them to be at the starting place at the same time if they continue to run at the same pace?

26. Candy bars priced at 50¢ each were not selling, so the price was reduced. Then they all sold in one day for a total of $31.93. What was the reduced price for each candy bar?

27. Two bells ring at 8:00 A.M. For the remainder of the day, one bell rings every half hour and the other bell rings every 45 min. What time will it be when the bells ring together again?

28. If the GCD of two positive whole numbers is 1, what can you say about the LCM of the two numbers? Explain your reasoning.

29. If we wanted each month of the year to have exactly the same number of days and there were exactly 365 days in a year, how many days are possible in each month?

30. If there were to be 9 boys and 6 girls at a party and the host wanted each to be given exactly the same number of candies that could be bought in packages containing 12 candies, what is the fewest number of packages that could be bought?

★**31.** Prove the test for divisibility by 9 using a 3-digit number n such that $n = a \cdot 10^2 + b \cdot 10 + c$.

∗**32.** Find the remainder of each of the following:
   a. 7^{100} is divided by 16.
   b. 7^{100} is divided by 17.
   c. 13^{1937} is divided by 10.

∗**33.** The length of a week was probably inspired by the need for market days and religious holidays. The Romans, for example, once used an 8-day week. Assuming April still had 30 days but was based on an 8-day week, if the first day of the month was on Sunday and the extra day after Saturday was called Venaday, on what day would the last day of the month fall?

∗**34.** In measuring angles of rotation that a light on a small island lighthouse sweeps, what mod system would be used and why?

SELECTED BIBLIOGRAPHY

Ballowe, J. "Teaching Difficult Problems Involving Absolute-value Signs." *Mathematics Teacher* 81 (May 1988): 373–374.

Battista, M. "A Complete Model for Operations on Integers." *Arithmetic Teacher* 30 (May 1983): 26–31.

Billstein, R. "Teach a Turtle to Add and Subtract." *The Computing Teacher* 14 (May 1987): 47–50.

Blocksma, M. *Reading the Numbers: A Survival Guide to the Measurements, Numbers, and Sizes Encountered in Everyday Life.* New York: Penguin Group, Viking Penguin, Inc., 1989.

Brumfiel, C. "Teaching the Absolute Value Function," *Mathematics Teacher* 73 (January 1980): 24–30.

Bunham, W. "Euclid and the Infinitude of Primes," *Mathematics Teacher* 80 (January 1987): 16–17.

Crowley, M. and K. Dunn. "On Multiplying Negative Numbers." *Mathematics Teacher* 78 (April 1985): 252–256.

Dearing, D. and B. Holtan. "Factors and Primes with a T Square." *Arithmetic Teacher* 34 (April 1987): 34.

Edwards, F. "Geometric Figures Make the LCM Obvious." *Arithmetic Teacher* 34 (March 1987): 17–18.

Ewbank, W. "LCM — Let's Put It in Its Place." *Arithmetic Teacher* 35 (November 1987): 45–47.

Hopkins, M. "Number Facts or Fantasy." *Arithmetic Teacher* 34 (March 1987): 38–42.

Kohn, J. "A Physical Model for Operations with Integers." *Mathematics Teacher* 71 (December 1978): 734–736.

Lott, J., Ed. "Menu Madness." *Student Math Notes.* Reston, VA: National Council of Teachers of Mathematics (May 1991).

Olson, M. "On the Ball." *Student Math Notes.* Reston, VA: National Council of Teachers of Mathematics (September 1990).

Peterson, I. *The Mathematical Tourist: Snapshots of Modern Mathematics.* New York: W. H. Freeman and Company, 1988.

Peterson, J. "Fourteen Different Strategies for Multiplication of Integers, or Why $(^-1)(^-1) = (^+1)$." *Arithmetic Teacher* 19 (May 1972): 396–403.

Sosenke, S. "Students as Textbook Authors." *Mathematics Teaching in the Middle School* 1 (September–October): 108–111.

Tirman, A. "Pythagorean Triples." *Mathematics Teacher* 79 (November 1986): 652–655.

Wyatt, C. "Clock Beaters." *Arithmetic Teacher* 34 (September 1986): 20.

5

RATIONAL NUMBERS AS FRACTIONS

A penny-mat is a mat that is typically handmade of small circular regions that have approximately the same area. One variation of such a mat has light-colored circles inside a border of dark-colored circles. Is it possible to make a mat with the same number of dark-colored and light-colored circles?

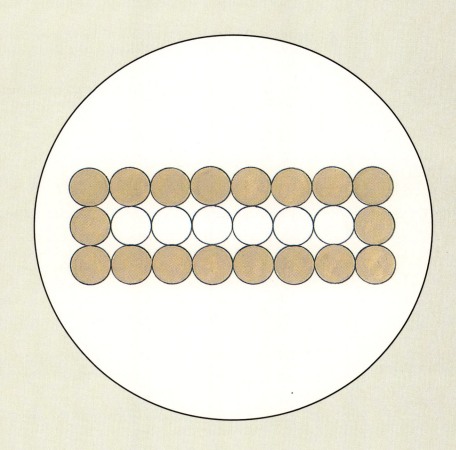

I n Chapter 4, we saw that because the equation $x + a = 0$ where $a \neq 0$ had no solution in the set of whole numbers, a new number, denoted by ^-a, was devised as the unique solution of the equation. Suppose a student wanted to know the solution to the problem of what number multiplied by 2 gives 3. The problem leads to the equation $2x = 3$, and the set of integers contains no solution to the equation. To solve the equation, a new number, $\frac{3}{2}$, was invented to solve the problem. In general, the unique solution for x in

fraction

the equation $bx = a$, where $b \neq 0$, is denoted by a/b. A **fraction** is a number of the form a/b, where a and b are any numbers ($b \neq 0$), not necessarily integers. In this chapter, we develop

rational numbers

a selected set of fractions known as **rational numbers.** The set of rational numbers is denoted by Q and is defined as follows:

$$Q = \{a/b \mid a \text{ and } b \text{ are integers and } b \neq 0\}.$$

In the *Teaching Standards* (p. 136), we find the following:

In setting the view of these ideas in the curriculum, teachers should be able to extend the number systems from the whole numbers to fractions and integers, then rationals and real numbers . . . .

In this chapter, we discuss addition, subtraction, multiplication, and division of rational numbers.

Section 5-1

The Set of Rational Numbers

Numbers such as $\frac{1}{3}, \frac{3}{5}$, and $\frac{2}{3}$ belong to the set of rational numbers. In the rational number

numerator   •   denominator

$\frac{a}{b}$, a is the **numerator** and b is the **denominator.** The rational number $\frac{a}{b}$ may also be represented as a/b or as $a \div b$. The word *fraction* is derived from the Latin word *fractus* meaning "to break." The word *numerator* comes from a Latin word meaning "numberer," and *denominator* comes from a Latin word meaning "namer." Hence, the numerator tells how many equal-sized parts there are, and the denominator tells what kind of parts there are.

The set of rational numbers is a subset of the set of fractions. Table 5-1 shows several different ways in which we use rational numbers.

Table 5-1   Uses of Rational Numbers

Use	Example
Division problem or solution to a multiplication problem	The solution to $2x = 3$ is $\frac{3}{2}$.
Partition, or part, of a whole	Joe received $\frac{1}{2}$ of Mary's salary each month for alimony.
Ratio	The ratio of Republicans to Democrats in the Senate is three to five.
Probability	When you toss a fair coin, the probability of getting heads is $\frac{1}{2}$.

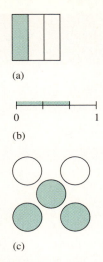

(a)

(b)

(c)

Figure 5-1

Figure 5-1 illustrates the use of rational numbers as part of a whole and as part of a given set. For example, in the area model in Figure 5-1(a), one part out of three congruent parts, or $\frac{1}{3}$ of the largest rectangle, is shaded. In Figure 5-1(b), two parts out of three parts, or $\frac{2}{3}$ of the unit segment, are shaded. In Figure 5-1(c), three circles out of five, or $\frac{3}{5}$ of the circles, are shaded.

H I S T O R I C A L   N O T E

The early Egyptian numeration system had symbols for fractions with numerators of 1. Most fractions with numerators other than 1 were expressed as a sum of different fractions with numerators of 1 $\left(\text{for example, } \frac{7}{12} = \frac{1}{3} + \frac{1}{4}\right)$.

Fractions with denominator 60 or powers of 60 were common in ancient Babylon about 2000 B.C., where 12,35 meant $12 + \frac{35}{60}$. The method was later adopted by the Greek astronomer Ptolemy (approximately A.D. 125). The same method was also used in Islamic and European countries and is presently used in the measurements of angles, where 13°19′ 47″ means $13 + \frac{19}{60} + \frac{47}{60^2}$.

The modern notation for fractions — a bar between numerator and denominator — is of Hindu origin. It came into general use in Europe in sixteenth-century books.

Our early exposure to fractions, or rational numbers, usually takes the form of oral descriptions rather than mathematical notations. We hear phrases such as "one half of a pizza," "one third of a cake," or "three fourths of a pie." The K–4 *Standards* (p. 58) contains the following with respect to introducing symbols for fractions:

▲ *Fraction symbols such as $\frac{1}{4}$ and $\frac{3}{2}$ should be introduced only after children have developed the concepts and oral language necessary for symbols to be meaningful and should be carefully connected to both the models and oral language necessary for symbols to be meaningful and should be carefully connected to both the models and oral language.*

We encounter such questions as "If three identical fruit bars are equally divided among four friends, how much does each get?" The answer is that each receives $\frac{3}{4}$ of a bar.

Rational numbers can be represented on a number line. Once the integers 0 and 1 are assigned to points on a line, every other rational number is assigned to a specific point. For example, to represent $\frac{3}{4}$ on the number line, we divide the segment from 0 to 1 into 4 segments of equal length. Then, starting from 0, we count 3 of these segments and stop at the mark corresponding to the right endpoint of the third segment of the rational number $\frac{3}{4}$. Figure 5-2 shows the points that correspond to $\frac{3}{4}, 1, \frac{5}{4}, 2, \frac{-3}{4}, ^-1, \frac{-5}{4},$ and $^-2$.

Figure 5-2

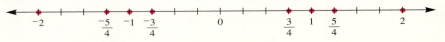

I N V E S T I G A T I O N   5 - 1

● **a.** Using the division representation of a rational number, show how every integer can be represented as a rational number.

b. Draw a Venn diagram showing the relationship among natural and whole numbers, integers, and rational numbers. ●

Equivalent Fractions

In the K–4 *Standards* (p. 32), we find the following:

 If conceptual understandings are linked to procedures, children will not perceive of mathematics as an arbitrary set of rules; will not need to learn or memorize as many procedures; and will have the foundation to apply, recreate, and invent new ones when needed.

equivalent fractions   An example of this is the use of paper folding to generate **equivalent fractions.** In Figure 5-3(a), one of three congruent parts, or $\frac{1}{3}$, is shaded. In Figure 5-3(b), each of the thirds has been folded in half so that now we have six sections, and two of six congruent parts, or $\frac{2}{6}$, are shaded. Thus both $\frac{1}{3}$ and $\frac{2}{6}$ represent exactly the same shaded portion. Although the symbols $\frac{1}{3}$ and $\frac{2}{6}$ do not look alike, they represent the same rational number and are equivalent fractions. However, because they represent equal amounts, we write $\frac{1}{3} = \frac{2}{6}$ and say that $\frac{1}{3}$ equals $\frac{2}{6}$.

Figure 5-3

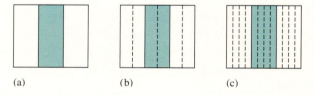

(a)   (b)   (c)

Figure 5-3(c) shows the rectangle with each of the original thirds folded into 4 equal parts with 4 of the 12 parts now shaded. Thus $\frac{1}{3}$ is equal to $\frac{4}{12}$ because the same portion of the model is shaded. Similarly, we could illustrate that $\frac{1}{3}, \frac{2}{6}, \frac{3}{9}, \frac{4}{12}, \frac{5}{15}, \ldots$ are equal. In other words, there are infinitely many ways of naming the rational number $\frac{1}{3}$. Similarly, there are infinitely many ways of naming any rational number.

This process of generating fractions equal to $\frac{1}{3}$ can be thought of as follows: If each of 3 equal-sized parts of a whole is halved, there must be twice as many of the smaller pieces. Hence, $\frac{1}{3} = \frac{2}{6}$. Similarly, $\frac{1}{3} = \frac{4}{12}$ because if each of 3 equal-sized parts of a whole is divided into 4 equal-sized parts, then there must be 4 times as many of the smaller pieces. In general, we have the *Fundamental Law of Fractions* for generating equivalent fractions.

Property

Fundamental Law of Fractions: For any fraction $\frac{a}{b}$ and any number $c \neq 0$, $\frac{a}{b} = \frac{ac}{bc}$.

The Fundamental Law of Fractions may be stated as follows: *The value of a fraction does not change if its numerator and denominator are multiplied by the same nonzero number.*

REMARK   The property is written in its most general form. At this stage, it is appropriate to say only that c is an integer. The property can later be generalized to be any number.

From the Fundamental Law of Fractions, $\frac{7}{-15} = \frac{-7}{15}$ because $\frac{7}{-15} = \frac{7 \cdot (-1)}{-15 \cdot (-1)} = \frac{-7}{15}$. Similarly, $\frac{a}{-b} = \frac{-a}{b}$. The form $\frac{-a}{b}$ is usually preferred.

• • •

Example 5-1   Find a value for x so that $\frac{12}{42} = \frac{x}{210}$.

Solution   By the Fundamental Law of Fractions, $\frac{12}{42} = \frac{12 \cdot 5}{42 \cdot 5} = \frac{60}{210}$. Hence, $\frac{x}{210} = \frac{60}{210}$, and $x = 60$.

• • •

Simplifying Fractions

simplifying fractions   The Fundamental Law of Fractions justifies a process called **simplifying fractions.** Consider the following:

$$\frac{60}{210} = \frac{6 \cdot 10}{21 \cdot 10} = \frac{6}{21}.$$

Also,

$$\frac{6}{21} = \frac{2 \cdot 3}{7 \cdot 3} = \frac{2}{7}.$$

We can simplify $\frac{60}{210}$ because the numerator and denominator have a common factor of 10.

Also, we can simplify $\frac{6}{21}$ because 6 and 21 have a common factor of 3. However, we can not simplify $\frac{2}{7}$ because 2 and 7 have no common factors other than 1. The fraction $\frac{2}{7}$ is

simplest (reduced) form   called the **simplest** (or **reduced**) **form** of $\frac{60}{210}$ because both 60 and 210 have been divided

by their greatest common divisor, 30. To write a fraction $\frac{a}{b}$ in simplest form, that is, its lowest terms, we divide both a and b by the GCD(a, b).

> ### Definition of Simplest Form
>
> A rational number $\dfrac{a}{b}$ is in simplest form if a and b have no common factor greater than 1, that is, if a and b are relatively prime.

An idea similar to the paper model in Figure 5-3 and that is used to find the lowest terms or simplest form of a fraction is illustrated on the following student page from *Addison-Wesley Mathematics,* Grade 6, 1993.

We can use scientific/fraction calculators to simplify fractions. For example, to simplify $\dfrac{6}{12}$, we enter $\boxed{6}\ \boxed{/}\ \boxed{1}\ \boxed{2}$ and press $\boxed{\text{SIMP}}\ \boxed{=}$, and 3/6 appears on the screen. At this point, an indicator tells us that this is not in simplest form, so we press $\boxed{\text{SIMP}}\ \boxed{=}$ again to obtain 1/2. At any time, we can view the factor that was removed by pressing the $\boxed{\text{x} \bigcirc \text{y}}$ key.

Another method for writing a fraction in simplest form is to find a factorization of the numerator and denominator and then divide both numerator and denominator by all the common factors. For example,

$$\frac{a^2b}{ab^2} = \frac{a(ab)}{b(ab)} = \frac{a}{b}.$$

Example 5-2   Write each of the following in simplest form:

a. $\dfrac{28ab^2}{42a^2b^2}$ b. $\dfrac{(a+b)^2}{3a+3b}$ c. $\dfrac{x^2+x}{x+1}$ d. $\dfrac{3+x^2}{3x^2}$ e. $\dfrac{3+3x^2}{3x^2}$

Solution   a. $\dfrac{28ab^2}{42a^2b^2} = \dfrac{2(14ab^2)}{3a(14ab^2)} = \dfrac{2}{3a}$

b. $\dfrac{(a+b)^2}{3a+3b} = \dfrac{(a+b)\cdot(a+b)}{3(a+b)} = \dfrac{a+b}{3}$

c. $\dfrac{x^2+x}{x+1} = \dfrac{x(x+1)}{x+1} = \dfrac{x(x+1)}{1(x+1)} = \dfrac{x}{1}$

d. $\dfrac{3+x^2}{3x^2}$ cannot be further reduced because $3+x^2$ and $3x^2$ have no factors in common except 1.

e. $\dfrac{3+3x^2}{3x^2} = \dfrac{3\cdot(1+x^2)}{3\cdot x^2} = \dfrac{1+x^2}{x^2}$

Equality of Fractions

We can use several methods to show that two fractions such as $\dfrac{12}{42}$ and $\dfrac{10}{35}$ are equal.

1. Reduce both fractions to the same simplest form:

$$\frac{12}{42} = \frac{2^2\cdot 3}{2\cdot 3\cdot 7} = \frac{2}{7} \text{ and } \frac{10}{35} = \frac{5\cdot 2}{5\cdot 7} = \frac{2}{7}.$$

Lowest Terms

LEARN ABOUT IT

EXPLORE   **Use Fraction Models**

Analyze the equivalent fraction strip that starts with $\frac{3}{4}$.

$\frac{3}{4}$	$\frac{6}{8}$	$\frac{9}{12}$	$\frac{12}{16}$	$\frac{15}{20}$	$\frac{18}{24}$	$\frac{21}{28}$	$\frac{24}{32}$	$\frac{27}{36}$	$\frac{30}{40}$

Below are three other fraction strips. Try to find the fraction that is first on each of these strips.

a. $\frac{5}{10}$ b. $\frac{4}{6}$ c. $\frac{3}{12}$

TALK ABOUT IT

1. What can you say about each fraction on the same strip?
2. Did you discover a method for finding the first fraction on the strip? Explain.

- A fraction is in **lowest terms** when the greatest common factor of the numerator and denominator is 1.

Here are two methods for finding the lowest-terms fractions.

■ To reduce a fraction to lowest terms: Divide the numerator and the denominator by any common factor and continue to divide until you find the lowest-terms fraction. $\frac{6 \div 2}{24 \div 2} = \frac{3}{12} \rightarrow \frac{3 \div 3}{12 \div 3} = \frac{1}{4}$	■ Divide the numerator and the denominator by the greatest common factor (GCF) to find the lowest-terms fraction. *6 is the GCF.* $\frac{6 \div 6}{24 \div 6} = \frac{1}{4}$ *1 is the only common factor of 1 and 4*

Thus

$$\frac{12}{42} = \frac{10}{35}.$$

2. Rewrite both fractions with the same least common denominator. Since LCM(42, 35) = 210, then

$$\frac{12}{42} = \frac{60}{210} \text{ and } \frac{10}{35} = \frac{60}{210}.$$

Thus

$$\frac{12}{42} = \frac{10}{35}.$$

3. Rewrite both fractions with a common denominator (not necessarily the least). A common multiple of 42 and 35 may be found by finding the product $42 \cdot 35$, or 1470. Now,

$$\frac{12}{42} = \frac{420}{1470} \text{ and } \frac{10}{35} = \frac{420}{1470}.$$

Hence,

$$\frac{12}{42} = \frac{10}{35}.$$

The third method suggests a general algorithm for determining if two fractions $\frac{a}{b}$ and $\frac{c}{d}$ are equal. Rewrite both fractions with common denominator bd. That is,

$$\frac{a}{b} = \frac{ad}{bd} \text{ and } \frac{c}{d} = \frac{bc}{bd}.$$

Because the denominators are the same, $\frac{ad}{bd} = \frac{bc}{bd}$ if, and only if, $ad = bc$. For example, $\frac{24}{36} = \frac{6}{9}$ because $24 \cdot 9 = 216 = 36 \cdot 6$. In general, the following property results.

Property

Two fractions $\frac{a}{b}$ and $\frac{c}{d}$ are **equal** if, and only if, $ad = bc$.

Using a calculator, we may determine if two fractions are equal by using the property that $\frac{a}{b} = \frac{c}{d}$ if, and only if, $ad = bc$. We see that $\frac{2}{4} = \frac{1098}{2196}$, since both $\boxed{2}\boxed{\times}\boxed{2}\boxed{1}\boxed{9}\boxed{6}\boxed{=}$ and $\boxed{4}\boxed{\times}\boxed{1}\boxed{0}\boxed{9}\boxed{8}\boxed{=}$ yield a display of 4392.

Ordering Rational Numbers

Children know that $\frac{7}{8} > \frac{5}{8}$ because if a pizza is divided into 8 parts, then 7 parts of a pizza is more than 5 parts. Similarly, $\frac{3}{7} < \frac{4}{7}$. Thus given two fractions with common positive denominators, the one with the greater numerator is the greater fraction. This can be written as follows.

Theorem 5-1

If a, b, and c are integers and $b > 0$, then $\frac{a}{b} > \frac{c}{b}$ if, and only if, $a > c$.

The condition $b > 0$ is essential in the property.

I N V E S T I G A T I O N   5 - 2

● Determine if Theorem 5-1 is true if $b < 0$. ●

The technique of comparing fractions with unlike denominators using a common denominator is demonstrated on the following portion of a student page from *Addison-Wesley Mathematics,* Grade 5, 1993.

Look at the denominators.	Write equivalent fractions with a common denominator.	Compare the numerators.	The fractions compare the same way the numerators compare.
$\frac{3}{8}$ Not the same $\frac{2}{3}$	$\frac{3}{8} = \frac{9}{24}$ The same $\frac{2}{3} = \frac{16}{24}$	$9 < 16$	$\frac{9}{24} < \frac{16}{24}$ so $\frac{3}{8} < \frac{2}{3}$

A general criterion for the greater-than relation on rational numbers can be developed for the case in which the denominators are positive. Using the common denominator bd, we can write the fractions $\frac{a}{b}$ and $\frac{c}{d}$ as $\frac{ad}{bd}$ and $\frac{bc}{bd}$. Because $b > 0$ and $d > 0$, $bd > 0$, we apply Theorem 5-1 to realize that $\frac{ad}{bd} > \frac{bc}{bd}$ if, and only if, $ad > bc$.

Denseness of Rational Numbers

The set of rational numbers has a very special property that is not present for the set of whole numbers or for the set of integers. Consider $\frac{1}{2}$ and $\frac{2}{3}$. To find a rational number between $\frac{1}{2}$ and $\frac{2}{3}$, we first rewrite the fractions with a common denominator, as $\frac{3}{6}$ and $\frac{4}{6}$. Because there is no whole number between the numerators 3 and 4, we next find two fractions equivalent to $\frac{1}{2}$ and $\frac{2}{3}$ with greater denominators. For example, $\frac{1}{2} = \frac{6}{12}$ and $\frac{2}{3} = \frac{8}{12}$, and $\frac{7}{12}$ is between the two fractions $\frac{6}{12}$ and $\frac{8}{12}$. So $\frac{7}{12}$ is between $\frac{1}{2}$ and $\frac{2}{3}$.

This property is generalized as follows.

Property

Given rational numbers $\frac{a}{b}$ and $\frac{c}{d}$, there is another rational number between these two numbers.

According to this property, there is another rational number between $\frac{a}{b}$ and the new rational number. Continuing this process, we see that between any two rational numbers $\frac{a}{b}$ and $\frac{c}{d}$, there are infinitely many rational numbers.

Example 5-3   Find two fractions between $\frac{1}{2}$ and $\frac{7}{18}$.

Solution   Because $\frac{1}{2} = \frac{1 \cdot 9}{2 \cdot 9} = \frac{9}{18}$, we see that $\frac{8}{18}$, or $\frac{4}{9}$, is between $\frac{7}{18}$ and $\frac{9}{18}$. To find another fraction between the given fractions, we find two fractions equivalent to $\frac{7}{18}$ and $\frac{9}{18}$ but with greater denominators. For example, $\frac{7}{18} = \frac{14}{36}$ and $\frac{9}{18} = \frac{18}{36}$.

We now see that $\frac{15}{36}, \frac{16}{36}$, and $\frac{17}{36}$ are all between $\frac{14}{36}$ and $\frac{18}{36}$.

Ongoing Assessment 5-1

1. Write a sentence illustrating the use of $\frac{7}{8}$ in each of the following ways:
   a. As a division problem
   b. As part of a whole
   c. As a ratio
2. For each of the following, write a fraction to represent the shaded portion:

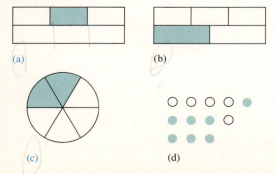

(a)   (b)

(c)   (d)

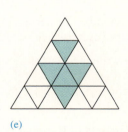

(e)   (f)

3. For each of the following four squares, write a fraction to represent the shaded portion. What property of fractions does the diagram illustrate?

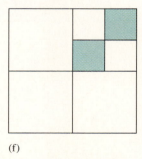

(a)   (b)   (c)   (d)

4. Complete each of the following figures so that it shows $\frac{3}{5}$:

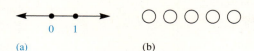

(a)   (b)

(c)

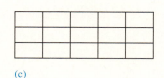

(d)

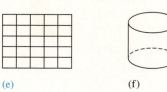

(e)   (f)

5. Refer to the following figure and represent each of the following as a fraction:
  a. The dots inside the circle as a part of all the dots
  b. The dots inside the rectangle as a part of all the dots
  c. The dots in the intersection of the rectangle and the circle as a part of all the dots
  d. The dots outside the circle but inside the rectangle as a part of all the dots

6. For each of the following, write three fractions equal to the given fraction:
  a. $\frac{2}{9}$ **b.** $\frac{-2}{5}$ **c.** $\frac{0}{3}$ **d.** $\frac{a}{2}$

7. Find the simplest form for each of the following fractions:
  a. $\frac{156}{93}$ **b.** $\frac{27}{45}$ **c.** $\frac{-65}{91}$
  d. $\frac{0}{68}$ **e.** $\frac{84^2}{91^2}$ **f.** $\frac{662}{703}$

8. Mr. Gonzales and Ms. Price gave the same test to their fifth-grade classes. In Mr. Gonzales's class, 20 out of 25 students passed the test, and in Ms. Price's class, 24 out of 30 students passed the test. One of Ms. Price's students heard about the results of the tests and claimed that the classes did equally well. Is the student right? Explain.

9. For the following, choose the expression in parentheses that equals or best describes the given fraction:
  a. $\frac{0}{0}$ (1, undefined, 0)   **b.** $\frac{5}{0}$ (undefined, 5, 0)
  c. $\frac{0}{5}$ (undefined, 5, 0)
  d. $\frac{2+a}{a}$ (2, 3, cannot be simplified)
  e. $\frac{15+x}{3x}$ $\left(\frac{5+x}{x}, 5, \text{cannot be simplified}\right)$
  f. $\frac{2^6+2^5}{2^4+2^7}$ $\left(1, \frac{2}{3}, \text{cannot be simplified}\right)$
  g. $\frac{2^{100}+2^{98}}{2^{100}-2^{98}}$ $\left(2^{196}, \frac{5}{3}, \text{too large to simplify}\right)$

10. Find the simplest form for each of the following fractions:
  a. $\frac{x}{x}$ **b.** $\frac{14x^2y}{63xy^2}$ **c.** $\frac{a^2+ab}{a+b}$
  d. $\frac{a^3+1}{a^3b}$ **e.** $\frac{a}{3a+ab}$ **f.** $\frac{a}{3a+b}$

11. Determine if the following pairs are equal:
  a. $\frac{3}{8}$ and $\frac{375}{1000}$ **b.** $\frac{18}{54}$ and $\frac{23}{69}$
  c. $\frac{6}{10}$ and $\frac{600}{1000}$ **d.** $\frac{17}{27}$ and $\frac{25}{45}$

12. Determine if the following pairs are equal by changing both to the same denominator:
  a. $\frac{10}{16}$ and $\frac{12}{18}$ **b.** $\frac{3}{12}$ and $\frac{41}{154}$
  c. $\frac{3}{-12}$ and $\frac{-36}{144}$ **d.** $\frac{-21}{86}$ and $\frac{-51}{215}$

13. A board is needed that is exactly $\frac{11}{32}$ in. wide to fill a hole. Can a board that is $\frac{3}{8}$ in. be shaved down to fit the hole? If so, how much must be shaved from the board?

14. Draw an area model to show that $\frac{3}{4}=\frac{6}{8}$.

15. If a fraction is equivalent to $\frac{3}{4}$ and the sum of the numerator and denominator is 84, what is the fraction?

16. The following two parking meters are next to each other with the times left as shown. Which meter has more time left on it? How much more?

Meter A

Meter B

17. Mr. Gomez filled his car's 16-gal gas tank. He took a short trip and used 6 gal of gas. Draw an arrow in the following figure to show what his gas gauge looked like after the trip:

18. Read each measurement as shown on the following ruler:

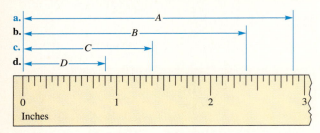

19. The numerator and denominator of a fraction are two-digit numbers, and the fraction is equivalent to $\frac{4}{7}$. The denominator is formed by reversing the order of the digits in the numerator $\left(\text{for example, } \frac{36}{63}\right)$. Find all other possible solutions.

20. Solve for x in each of the following:

    a. $\frac{2}{3} = \frac{x}{16}$ **b.** $\frac{3}{4} = \frac{-27}{x}$ **c.** $\frac{3}{x} = \frac{3x}{x^2}$

21. **a.** If $\frac{a}{c} = \frac{b}{c}$, what must be true?

    b. If $\frac{a}{b} = \frac{a}{c}$, what must be true?

22. Use a calculator to check whether each of the following pairs of fractions are equal:

    a. $\frac{24}{31}$ and $\frac{23}{30}$ **b.** $\frac{86}{75}$ and $\frac{85}{74}$

    c. $\frac{1513}{1691}$ and $\frac{1581}{1767}$

23. Let W be the set of whole numbers, I be the set of integers, and Q be the set of rational numbers. Classify each of the following as true or false:

    a. $W \subseteq Q$
    b. $(I \cup W) \subset Q$
    c. If Q is the universal set, $\bar{I} = W$.
    d. $Q \cap I = W$
    e. $Q \cap W = W$

24. In Amy's algebra class, 6 out of 31 students received A's on a test. The same test was given to Bren's class and 5 out of 23 students received A's. Which class had the higher rate of A's?

25. For each of the following pairs of fractions, replace the comma with the correct symbol (<, =, >) to make a true statement:

    a. $\frac{7}{8}, \frac{5}{6}$ **b.** $2\frac{4}{5}, 2\frac{3}{6}$ **c.** $\frac{-7}{8}, \frac{-4}{5}$

    d. $\frac{1}{-7}, \frac{1}{-8}$ **e.** $\frac{2}{5}, \frac{4}{10}$ **f.** $\frac{0}{7}, \frac{0}{17}$

26. Arrange each of the following in decreasing order:

    a. $\frac{11}{22}, \frac{11}{16}, \frac{11}{13}$

    b. $\frac{-1}{5}, \frac{-19}{36}, \frac{-17}{30}$

27. **a.** Choose several positive fractions less than 1. Square each of the fractions, and compare the size of the original fraction and its square. Make a conjecture concerning a fraction and its square.

    H **b.** Justify your conjecture in (a).

    c. If a fraction is greater than 1, make a conjecture concerning which is greater: the fraction or its square.

    H **d.** Justify your conjecture in (c).

28. If $\frac{a}{b} < 1$ and $\frac{c}{d} > 0$, compare the size of $\frac{c}{d}$ with $\frac{a}{b} \cdot \frac{c}{d}$.

29. If x and y are two rational numbers such that $x > 1$ and $y > 0$, which is greater: xy or y? Justify your answer.

30. Show that the sequence $\frac{1}{2}, \frac{2}{3}, \frac{3}{4}, \frac{4}{5}, \frac{5}{6}, \frac{6}{7}, \ldots$ is an increasing sequence; that is, show that each term in the sequence is greater than the preceding one.

31. **a.** Give an example to show that the system of whole numbers does not have the denseness property.

    b. Give an example to show that the system of integers does not have the denseness property.

32. For each of the following, find two rational numbers between the given fractions:

    a. $\frac{3}{7}$ and $\frac{4}{7}$ **b.** $\frac{-7}{9}$ and $\frac{-8}{9}$

    c. $\frac{5}{6}$ and $\frac{83}{100}$ **d.** $\frac{-1}{3}$ and $\frac{3}{4}$

33. Consider the following number grid. The circled numbers form a rhombus (that is, all sides are the same length).

1	2	3	4	5	6	7	8	9	10
11	12	13	14	15	16	17	18	19	20
21	22	23	24	25	26	27	28	29	30
31	32	33	34	35	36	37	38	39	40
41	42	43	44	45	46	47	48	49	50

    a. If A is the sum of the four circled numbers and B is the sum of the four interior numbers, find A/B.

    b. Form a rhombus by circling the numbers 6, 18, 25, and 37. Compute A and B as in (a) and then find A/B.

    c. How do the answers in (a) and (b) compare? Why does this happen?

34. A scale on a map is 12 mi to the inch. What is the airline mileage between two cities that are 38 in. apart on the map?

35. Six ounces is what part of a pound? A ton?

36. If a baseball player could run from home plate to first base in 4 sec and the distance between bases is 90 ft, estimate how long it would take the person to run the 100-yd dash?

Communication

37. When you multiply two positive fractions less than 1, how does the answer compare to the size of the fractions? Why?

38. Is there a whole number that does not have a reciprocal? Explain. (For example, 2 and $\frac{1}{2}$ are reciprocals.)

39. Should fractions always be reduced to their simplest form? Why or why not?

40. How would you respond to each of the following students?
   a. Iris claims that if we have two positive rational numbers, the one with the greatest numerator is the greatest.
   b. Shirley claims that if we have two positive rational numbers, the one with the greatest denominator is the least.

41. If we were to take the set of fractions equivalent to $\frac{1}{3}$ and graph them as points on a coordinate system so that the numerator becomes the *x*-coordinate and the denominator becomes the *y*-coordinate for that point, explain what type of graph we would get and why.

42. Write an explanation of how to convert inches to yards and vice versa.

Open-ended

43. List five types of measures that require rational numbers as the appropriate number of units in the measurements.

44. It has been argued by some that the system of integers is more understandable than the system of positive rational numbers. If you could decide which should be taught first in school, which would you choose and why?

Cooperative Learning

45. Assume the tallest person in the class is 1 unit tall and do the following:
   a. Find rational numbers to represent other members of the class.
   b. Order the class members according to height.
   c. Make a number line using the rational numbers for each person ordered according to the heights of class members.
   d. Use equivalent fractions to determine if the ordering is correct.

TECHNOLOGY CORNER

Let *a/b* be any rational number. To write *a/b* in simplest form, first determine which is greater, *a* or *b*. Suppose *a* is the lesser of *a* and *b*. Create a spreadsheet in which the first column contains the numbers 1 through *a*. Use the formula *a*/A1 to create the second column and the formula *b*/A1 to create the third column. Fill down *a* rows of columns 2 and 3. Now consider the numbers in the cells of these columns. If in both columns whole numbers with no decimal parts appear in the same row as the quotients, then *a/b* may be simplified to *c/d*, where *c* and *d* are the respective whole numbers. To determine if *a/b* may be further simplified, replace *a* with *c* and *b* with *d* and repeat the process as many times as is necessary to obtain the simplest form of *a/b*. You have obtained the simplest form when there are no whole numbers in the same row in the entire second and third columns.

Create a spreadsheet and try this method to write 60/210 in simplest form.

Section 5-2   Addition and Subtraction of Rational Numbers

To determine how to add two fractions in general, or two rational numbers in particular, we examine the addition of two particular fractions using Polya's four-step process.

Problem 1

Determine how to add the rational numbers 2/3 and 1/4.

Understanding the Problem.   We can model 2/3 and 1/4 as parts of a whole as seen in Figure 5-4, but we need a way to combine the two drawings to find the sum.

Figure 5-4

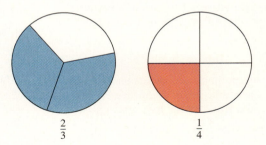

$$\frac{2}{3} \qquad\qquad \frac{1}{4}$$

■ ***Devising a Plan.***   We use the strategy of *solving a simpler problem* and consider adding rational numbers with the same denominators. To find the sum, 2/5 + 1/5, we use pictures as in Figure 5-5.

Figure 5-5

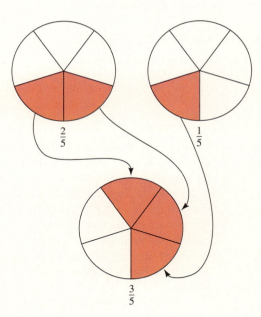

$$\frac{2}{5} \qquad\qquad \frac{1}{5}$$

$$\frac{3}{5}$$

Thus 2/5 + 1/5 = 3/5. We see that if the rational numbers have the same denominators, then the addition can be accomplished by adding the numerators and keeping the denominators the same. Now we consider the original problem: 2/3 + 1/4. We can find the sum by writing each with a common denominator and completing the computation as above.

Carrying Out the Plan.   From earlier work in the chapter, we know that 2/3 is equivalent to an infinite set of rational numbers, including 4/6, 6/9, 8/12, and so on. Also 1/4 is equivalent to an infinite set of rational numbers, including 2/8, 3/12, 4/16, and so on. By comparing the two sets of rational numbers, we see that 8/12 and 3/12 have the same denominator. One is 8 parts of 12 while the other is 3 parts of 12. Consequently, the sum is

2/3 + 1/4 = 8/12 + 3/12, or 11 parts of 12; that is, the sum is 11/12. Figure 5-6 illustrates the addition.

Figure 5-6

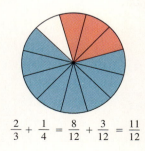

$$\frac{2}{3} + \frac{1}{4} = \frac{8}{12} + \frac{3}{12} = \frac{11}{12}$$

Looking Back. To add two rational numbers of unlike denominators, we considered equivalent rational numbers with like denominators. The common denominator for 2/3 and 1/4 was 12. This is also the least common denominator, or the LCM (3, 4). To add two fractions with unequal denominators such as 5/12 and 7/18, we could find equivalent fractions with the denominator as the LCM(12, 18), or 36. However, any common denominator will work as well, for example, 72 or even 12 · 18.

• • •

The generalization of Problem 1 leads us to the following definition for addition of rational numbers with like denominators.

Definition of Rational Number Addition

If $\dfrac{a}{b}$ and $\dfrac{c}{b}$ are rational numbers, then $\dfrac{a}{b} + \dfrac{c}{b} = \dfrac{a + c}{b}$.

By considering the sum $\dfrac{2}{3} + \dfrac{1}{4} = \dfrac{2 \cdot 4}{3 \cdot 4} + \dfrac{1 \cdot 3}{4 \cdot 3} = \dfrac{8}{12} + \dfrac{3}{12} = \dfrac{11}{12}$, we can generalize to the sum of two rational numbers with unlike denominators as in the following property.

Property

If $\dfrac{a}{b}$ and $\dfrac{c}{d}$ are any two rational numbers, then $\dfrac{a}{b} + \dfrac{c}{d} = \dfrac{ad + bc}{bd}$.

• • •

Example 5-4 Find each of the following sums:

a. $\dfrac{2}{15} + \dfrac{4}{21}$ **b.** $\dfrac{2}{-3} + \dfrac{1}{5}$ **c.** $\left(\dfrac{3}{4} + \dfrac{1}{5}\right) + \dfrac{1}{6}$ **d.** $\dfrac{3}{x} + \dfrac{4}{y}$

Solution **a.** $\dfrac{2}{15} + \dfrac{4}{21} = \dfrac{2 \cdot 7}{15 \cdot 7} + \dfrac{4 \cdot 5}{21 \cdot 5} = \dfrac{14}{105} + \dfrac{20}{105} = \dfrac{34}{105}$

b. $\dfrac{2}{-3} + \dfrac{1}{5} = \dfrac{(2)(5) + (-3)(1)}{(-3)(5)} = \dfrac{10 + {}^{-}3}{{}^{-}15} = \dfrac{7}{{}^{-}15} = \dfrac{7({}^{-}1)}{{}^{-}15({}^{-}1)} = \dfrac{{}^{-}7}{15}$

c. $\dfrac{3}{4} + \dfrac{1}{5} = \dfrac{3 \cdot 5 + 4 \cdot 1}{4 \cdot 5} = \dfrac{19}{20}$. Hence, $\left(\dfrac{3}{4} + \dfrac{1}{5}\right) + \dfrac{1}{6} = \dfrac{19}{20} + \dfrac{1}{6} = \dfrac{19 \cdot 6 + 20 \cdot 1}{20 \cdot 6}$

$= \dfrac{134}{120}$ or $\dfrac{67}{60}$.

d. $\dfrac{3}{x} + \dfrac{4}{y} = \dfrac{3y}{xy} + \dfrac{4x}{xy} = \dfrac{3y + 4x}{xy}$

• • •

I N V E S T I G A T I O N   5 - 3

● **a.** Complete the computation in Example 5-4(a) using the property $a/b + c/d = (ad + bc)/bd$.

b. Complete the computation in Example 5-4(c) using the LCM of all three denominators. ●

Mixed Numbers

mixed numbers   In everyday life, we often use **mixed numbers,** that is, numbers that are made up of an integer and a fractional part of an integer. For example, Figure 5-7 shows that the nail is $2\dfrac{3}{4}$ in. long. The mixed number $2\dfrac{3}{4}$ means $2 + \dfrac{3}{4}$. It is sometimes inferred that $2\dfrac{3}{4}$ means 2 times $\dfrac{3}{4}$, since xy means $x \cdot y$, but this is not correct. Also, the number $^-4\dfrac{3}{4}$ means $^-\left(4 + \dfrac{3}{4}\right)$, not $^-4 + \dfrac{3}{4}$.

Figure 5-7

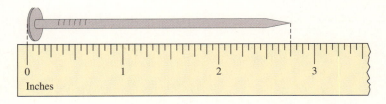

Inches

A mixed number is a rational number, and therefore it can always be written in the form $\dfrac{a}{b}$. For example,

$$2\dfrac{3}{4} = 2 + \dfrac{3}{4} = \dfrac{2}{1} + \dfrac{3}{4} = \dfrac{2 \cdot 4 + 1 \cdot 3}{1 \cdot 4} = \dfrac{8 + 3}{4} = \dfrac{11}{4}.$$

proper fraction   A fraction $\dfrac{a}{b}$, where $0 \le |a| < |b|$, is a **proper fraction.** For example, $\dfrac{4}{7}$ is a proper fraction, but $\dfrac{7}{4}, \dfrac{4}{4}$, and $\dfrac{-9}{7}$ are not.

· · ·

Example 5-5 Change each of the following mixed numbers to the form $\frac{a}{b}$, where a and b are integers:

a. $4\frac{1}{3}$ **b.** $^-3\frac{2}{5}$

Solution **a.** $4\frac{1}{3} = 4 + \frac{1}{3} = \frac{4}{1} + \frac{1}{3} = \frac{4 \cdot 3 + 1 \cdot 1}{1 \cdot 3} = \frac{12 + 1}{3} = \frac{13}{3}$

b. $^-3\frac{2}{5} = ^-\left(3 + \frac{2}{5}\right) = ^-\left(\frac{3}{1} + \frac{2}{5}\right) = ^-\left(\frac{3 \cdot 5 + 1 \cdot 2}{1 \cdot 5}\right) = \frac{^-17}{5}$

· · ·

· · ·

Example 5-6 Change $\frac{29}{5}$ to a mixed number.

Solution $\frac{29}{5} = \frac{5 \cdot 5 + 4}{5} = \frac{5 \cdot 5}{5} + \frac{4}{5} = 5 + \frac{4}{5} = 5\frac{4}{5}$

· · ·

REMARK   In elementary schools, problems like Example 5-6 are usually solved using division, as follows:

$$\begin{array}{r} 5 \\ 5\overline{)29} \\ \underline{25} \\ 4 \end{array}$$

Hence, $\frac{29}{5} = 5 + \frac{4}{5} = 5\frac{4}{5}$.

Scientific/fraction calculators can be used to change improper fractions to mixed numbers. For example, if we enter $\boxed{2}\boxed{9}\boxed{/}\boxed{5}$ and press $\boxed{Ab/c}$, then 5 ⊔ 4/5 appears, which means $5\frac{4}{5}$.

Because mixed numbers are rational numbers, the methods of adding rationals can be extended to include mixed numbers. The following page from *Addison-Wesley Mathematics,* Grade 8, 1993, shows methods of estimating sums of mixed numbers and adding mixed numbers.

We can also use scientific/fraction calculators to add mixed numbers. For example, to add $2\frac{4}{5} + 3\frac{5}{6}$, we enter $\boxed{2}\boxed{\text{Unit}}\boxed{4}\boxed{/}\boxed{5}\boxed{+}\boxed{3}\boxed{\text{Unit}}\boxed{5}\boxed{/}\boxed{6}\boxed{=}$, and the display reads 5 ⊔ 49/30. We then press $\boxed{Ab/c}$ to obtain 6 ⊔ 19/30, which means $6\frac{19}{30}$.

Adding and Subtracting Mixed Numbers

LEARN ABOUT IT

EXPLORE Study the Information

Designers and craftsmen often need to add and subtract mixed numbers to calculate lengths.

TALK ABOUT IT

1. Distance A is the sum of what two mixed numbers?

2. Estimate. Is length A less than 17 or greater than 17?

3. To find length B subtract $7\frac{5}{8}$ from what length?

To add or subtract mixed numbers with unlike denominators:

- Rename fractions with a common denominator.
- Add or subtract the fraction parts. Rename if necessary.
- Add or subtract the whole number parts.

Add, then rename

$$12\frac{3}{4} = 12\frac{6}{8}$$
$$+\ \ 4\frac{5}{8} = \ \ 4\frac{5}{8}$$
$$\overline{\qquad\qquad 16\frac{11}{8} = 17\frac{3}{8}}$$

Rename, then subtract

$$17\frac{3}{8} = 16\frac{11}{8}$$
$$-\ \ 7\frac{5}{8} = \ \ 7\frac{5}{8}$$
$$\overline{\qquad\qquad 9\frac{6}{8} = 9\frac{3}{4}}$$

Properties of Addition for Rational Numbers

Rational numbers have the following properties for addition: closure, commutative, associative, additive identity, and additive inverse. To emphasize the additive inverse property of rational numbers, we state it explicitly, as follows.

Property

Additive Inverse Property of Rational Numbers: For any rational number $\frac{a}{b}$, there exists a unique rational number $-\frac{a}{b}$, called the additive inverse of $\frac{a}{b}$, such that $\frac{a}{b} + \left(-\frac{a}{b}\right) = 0 = \left(-\frac{a}{b}\right) + \frac{a}{b}$.

Another form of $-\dfrac{a}{b}$ can be found by considering the sum $\dfrac{a}{b}+\dfrac{^-a}{b}$. Because

$$\frac{a}{b}+\frac{^-a}{b}=\frac{a+\,^-a}{b}=\frac{0}{b}=0,$$

it follows that $-\dfrac{a}{b}$ and $\dfrac{^-a}{b}$ are both additive inverses of $\dfrac{a}{b}$, so $-\dfrac{a}{b}=\dfrac{^-a}{b}$.

Example 5-7 | Find the additive inverses for each of the following:

a. $\dfrac{3}{5}$ **b.** $\dfrac{^-5}{11}$ **c.** $4\dfrac{1}{2}$

Solution **a.** $\dfrac{^-3}{5}$ or $-\dfrac{3}{5}$ **b.** $-\left(\dfrac{^-5}{11}\right)$ or $\dfrac{5}{11}$ **c.** $^-4\dfrac{1}{2}$

Properties of the additive inverse for rational numbers are analogous to those of the additive inverse for integers, as shown in Table 5-2. As with the set of integers, the set of rational numbers also has the addition property of equality.

Table 5-2

Integers	Rational Numbers
1. $^-(^-a)=a$	1. $-\left(-\dfrac{a}{b}\right)=\dfrac{a}{b}$
2. $^-(a+b)=\,^-a+\,^-b$	2. $-\left(\dfrac{a}{b}+\dfrac{c}{d}\right)=\dfrac{^-a}{b}+\dfrac{^-c}{d}$

Property

Addition Property of Equality: If $\dfrac{a}{b}$ and $\dfrac{c}{d}$ are any rational numbers such that $\dfrac{a}{b}=\dfrac{c}{d}$, and if $\dfrac{e}{f}$ is any rational number, then $\dfrac{a}{b}+\dfrac{e}{f}=\dfrac{c}{d}+\dfrac{e}{f}$.

Subtraction of Rational Numbers

In elementary school, subtraction of rational numbers is usually introduced by using a take-away model. If we have $\dfrac{6}{7}$ of a pizza and $\dfrac{2}{7}$ of the original pizza is taken away, $\dfrac{4}{7}$ of the pizza remains: that is, $\dfrac{6}{7}-\dfrac{2}{7}=\dfrac{6-2}{7}=\dfrac{4}{7}$. In general, subtraction of rational numbers with like denominators is determined as follows:

$$\frac{a}{b}-\frac{c}{b}=\frac{a-c}{b}.$$

In the following student page from *Addison-Wesley Mathematics,* Grade 4, 1993, we see that fraction pieces can be used for subtracting fractions.

Subtracting Fractions with Models
Unlike Denominators

Thirds   Sixths

LEARN ABOUT IT

<u>EXPLORE</u> **Use Fraction Pieces**

Use the thirds and sixths fraction pieces and these fraction cards. Follow the steps several times and record your results.

■ Choose a thirds and a sixths fraction card. The larger fraction is the *cover* fraction. The smaller is the *take away* fraction.

■ With fraction pieces, cover up the section of the whole shown on the *cover* fraction card, in this case, 5 sixths.

■ Trade the *take away* card for another card with an equivalent fraction that has the same denominator as the *cover* fraction.

■ Take away the part of the covered section shown on the new *take away* card.

■ Decide what part of the section is left. Complete an equation.

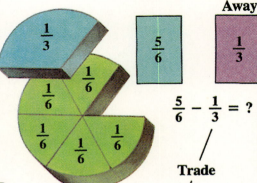

Cover   **Take Away**

$$\frac{5}{6} - \frac{1}{3} = ?$$

Trade

$$\frac{5}{6} - \frac{2}{6} = \frac{3}{6} \text{ or } \frac{1}{2}$$

Subtraction of rational numbers, like subtraction of integers, can be defined in terms of addition as follows.

Definition of Rational Number Subtraction

If $\frac{a}{b}$ and $\frac{c}{d}$ are any rational numbers, then $\frac{a}{b} - \frac{c}{d} = \frac{e}{f}$ if, and only if, $\frac{a}{b} = \frac{c}{d} + \frac{e}{f}$.

As with integers, we can see that subtraction of rational numbers can be performed by adding the additive inverses. The following theorem states this.

Now, using the definition of addition of rational numbers, we obtain the following:

$$\frac{a}{b} - \frac{c}{d} = \frac{a}{b} + \frac{-c}{d}$$

$$= \frac{ad + b(-c)}{bd}$$

$$= \frac{ad + {}^{-}(bc)}{bd}$$

$$= \frac{ad - bc}{bd}$$

We summarize this result in the following theorem.

Example 5-8 Find each difference in the following:

a. $\dfrac{5}{8} - \dfrac{1}{4}$ **b.** $5\dfrac{1}{3} - 2\dfrac{3}{4}$

Solution   **a.** One approach is to find the LCM for the fractions. Because LCM(8, 4) = 8, we have

$$\frac{5}{8} - \frac{1}{4} = \frac{5}{8} - \frac{2}{8} = \frac{3}{8}.$$

An alternative approach is as follows:

$$\frac{5}{8} - \frac{1}{4} = \frac{5 \cdot 4 - 8 \cdot 1}{8 \cdot 4} = \frac{5 \cdot 4 - 8 \cdot 1}{32} = \frac{12}{32} \text{ or } \frac{3}{8}.$$

b. Two methods of solution are given:

$$
\begin{array}{c|c}
\begin{aligned}
5\frac{1}{3} &= 5\frac{4}{12} = 4 + 1\frac{4}{12} = 4\frac{16}{12} \\
-2\frac{3}{4} &= -2\frac{9}{12} = -2\frac{9}{12} \quad\;\; = -2\frac{9}{12} \\
\hline
& \qquad\qquad\qquad\qquad\;\; 2\frac{7}{12}
\end{aligned}
&
\begin{aligned}
5\frac{1}{3} - 2\frac{3}{4} &= \frac{16}{3} - \frac{11}{4} \\
&= \frac{16 \cdot 4 - 3 \cdot 11}{3 \cdot 4} \\
&= \frac{64 - 33}{12} \\
&= \frac{31}{12} \text{ or } 2\frac{7}{12}
\end{aligned}
\end{array}
$$

Estimation with Rational Numbers

▲ In the 5–8 *Standards* (p. 97), we find: *Estimation is a powerful idea to be used both in solving problems and in checking the reasonableness of a result.* Consider, for example, a student who added $\frac{3}{4}$ and $\frac{1}{2}$ and obtained $\frac{4}{6}$ (most likely, the student confused this procedure with the procedure for multiplying fractions and added the numerators and then the denominators). An estimation of $\frac{3}{4} + \frac{1}{2}$ as a number greater than $\frac{1}{2} + \frac{1}{2}$ shows that the answer should be greater than 1 and that $\frac{4}{6}$ is unreasonable. Sometimes it is desirable to round fractions to a convenient fraction, such as $\frac{1}{2}, \frac{1}{3}, \frac{1}{4}, \frac{1}{5}, \frac{2}{3}, \frac{3}{4}$, or 1.

If a student had 59 correct answers out of 80 questions, the student answered $\frac{59}{80}$ of the questions correctly, which is approximately $\frac{60}{80}$, or $\frac{3}{4}$. Intuitively, we know $\frac{60}{80}$ is greater than $\frac{59}{80}$. On a number line, the greater fraction is to the right of the lesser. The estimate $\frac{3}{4}$ for $\frac{59}{80}$ is a high estimate. In a similar way, we can estimate $\frac{31}{90}$ by $\frac{30}{90}$, or $\frac{1}{3}$. In this case, the

▲ actual answer is greater than the estimate of $\frac{1}{3}$. As the K–4 *Standards* (p. 36) points out, *estimations enhance the abilities of children to deal with everyday quantitative situations.*

- - -

Example 5-9 | A sixth-grade class is collecting cans to take to the recycling center. Becky's group brought the following amounts (in pounds). About how many pounds does her group have all together?

$$1\frac{1}{8}, \, 3\frac{4}{10}, \, 5\frac{7}{8}, \, \frac{6}{10}$$

Solution   We can estimate the amount by using front-end estimation and then adjusting by using $0, \frac{1}{2}$, and 1 as reference points. The front-end estimate is $(1 + 3 + 5)$, or 9. The adjustment is $\left(0 + \frac{1}{2} + 1 + \frac{1}{2}\right)$, or 2. An adjusted estimate would be 11 lb.

- - -

Example 5-10 | Estimate each of the following:

a. $\frac{27}{13} + \frac{10}{9}$ **b.** $3\frac{9}{10} + 2\frac{7}{8} + \frac{11}{12}$

Solution   **a.** Because $\frac{27}{13}$ is more than 2 and $\frac{10}{9}$ is more than 1, an estimate is more than 3.

b. We first add the front-end parts to obtain $3 + 2$, or 5. Because each of the fractions, $\frac{9}{10}, \frac{7}{8}$, and $\frac{11}{12}$, is close to but less than 1, their sum is less than 3. The approximate answer is a number close to but less than 8.

• • •

Ongoing Assessment 5-2

1. Compute each of the following using any method:

   a. $\frac{1}{2} + \frac{2}{3}$ **b.** $\frac{3}{16} + \frac{7}{-8}$ **c.** $\frac{4}{12} - \frac{2}{3}$

   d. $\frac{5}{x} + \frac{-3}{y}$ **e.** $\frac{-3}{2x^2y} + \frac{5}{6xy^2} + \frac{7}{x^2}$ **f.** $\frac{-3}{2x} + \frac{3}{2y} + \frac{-1}{4xy}$

   g. $\frac{5}{6} + 2\frac{1}{8}$ **h.** $\frac{5}{2^4 \cdot 3^2} - \frac{1}{2^3 \cdot 3^4}$ **i.** $-4\frac{1}{2} - 3\frac{1}{6}$

2. Change each of the following fractions to mixed numbers:

   a. $\frac{56}{3}$ **b.** $\frac{14}{5}$ **c.** $-\frac{293}{100}$ **d.** $-\frac{47}{8}$

3. Change each of the following mixed numbers to fractions in the form $\frac{a}{b}$, where a and b are integers:

   a. $6\frac{3}{4}$ **b.** $7\frac{1}{2}$ **c.** $-3\frac{5}{8}$ **d.** $-4\frac{2}{3}$

4. Place the numbers 2, 5, 6, and 8 in the following boxes to make the equation true:

   $$\frac{\square}{\square} + \frac{\square}{\square} = \frac{23}{24}$$

5. Approximate each of the following situations with a convenient fraction. Explain your reasoning. Tell whether your estimate is high or low.

   a. Giorgio had 15 base hits out of 46 times at bat.
   b. Ruth made 7 goals out of 41 shots.
   c. Laura answered 62 problems correctly out of 80.
   d. Jonathan made 9 baskets out of 19.

6. Use the information in the following table to answer each of the following questions:

Team	Games Played	Games Won
Ducks	22	10
Beavers	19	10
Tigers	28	9
Bears	23	8
Lions	27	7
Wildcats	25	6
Badgers	21	5

   a. Which team won just over $\frac{1}{2}$ of its games?

   b. Which team won just under $\frac{1}{2}$ of its games?

   c. Which team won just over $\frac{1}{3}$ of its games?

   d. Which team won just under $\frac{1}{3}$ of its games?

   e. Which team won just over $\frac{1}{4}$ of its games?

   f. Which team won just under $\frac{1}{4}$ of its games?

7. Sort the following fraction cards into the ovals by estimating in which oval the fraction belongs:

   Sort these fraction cards   About 0   About $\frac{1}{2}$ About 1

$\frac{1}{10}$	$\frac{4}{7}$	$\frac{8}{12}$	$\frac{1}{3}$	$\frac{7}{8}$
$\frac{2}{5}$	$\frac{3}{10}$	$\frac{13}{10}$	$\frac{1}{100}$	$\frac{9}{18}$

8. Approximate each of the following fractions by $0, \frac{1}{4}, \frac{1}{2}, \frac{3}{4}$, or 1. Tell whether your estimate is high or low.

   a. $\frac{19}{39}$ **b.** $\frac{3}{197}$ **c.** $\frac{150}{201}$ **d.** $\frac{8}{9}$

   e. $\frac{113}{110}$ **f.** $\frac{-2}{117}$ **g.** $\frac{150}{198}$ **h.** $\frac{999}{2000}$

9. Without actually finding the exact answer, state which of the numbers given in parentheses in the following is the best approximation for the given sum or difference:

   a. $\frac{6}{13} + \frac{7}{15} + \frac{11}{23} + \frac{17}{35} \left(1, 2, 3, 3\frac{1}{2}\right)$

   b. $\frac{30}{41} + \frac{1}{1000} + \frac{3}{2000} \left(\frac{3}{8}, \frac{3}{4}, 1, 2\right)$

   c. $\frac{103}{300} + \frac{203}{601} - \frac{602}{897} \left(1, \frac{1}{3}, \frac{2}{3}, 0\right)$

   d. $\frac{1}{100} - \frac{1}{101} + \frac{1}{102} - \frac{1}{103} \left(\frac{1}{2}, 1, 0\right)$

10. Use estimation to answer each of the following:

    a. Juan needs to make $11\frac{1}{4}$ lb of breakfast cereal. He bought $4\frac{7}{8}$ lb of oats, $3\frac{1}{4}$ lb of cracked wheat, and $2\frac{15}{16}$ lb of triticale. Does Juan have enough grain?

b. Jill expected to drive from Eugene to Seattle in fewer than 5 hr. It took her $1\frac{3}{4}$ hr to get from Eugene to Portland and $3\frac{5}{12}$ hr to get from Portland to Seattle. Did Jill make the trip in fewer than 5 hr?

11. Compute each of the following mentally:

a. $1 - \frac{3}{4}$ 　　　　　**b.** $6 - \frac{7}{8}$

c. $3\frac{3}{8} + 2\frac{1}{4} - 5\frac{5}{8}$ 　　**d.** $2\frac{3}{5} + 4\frac{1}{10} + 3\frac{3}{10}$

12. The following ruler has regions marked M, A, T, H:

Use mental mathematics and estimation to determine which region each of the following falls into (for example, $\frac{12}{5}$ in. falls in region A).

a. $\frac{20}{8}$ in. 　**b.** $\frac{36}{8}$ in. 　**c.** $\frac{60}{16}$ in. 　**d.** $\frac{18}{4}$ in.

13. Determine what, if anything, is wrong with each of the following:

a. $2 = \frac{6}{3} = \frac{3+3}{3} = \frac{3}{3} + 3 = 1 + 3 = 4$

b. $1 = \frac{4}{2+2} = \frac{4}{2} + \frac{4}{2} = 2 + 2 = 4$

c. $\frac{ab+c}{a} = \frac{\cancel{a}b+c}{\cancel{a}} = b + c$

d. $\frac{a^2 - b^2}{a - b} = \frac{a \cdot \cancel{a} - b \cdot \cancel{b}}{\cancel{a} - \cancel{b}} = a - b$

e. $\frac{a+c}{b+c} = \frac{a+\cancel{c}}{b+\cancel{c}} = \frac{a}{b}$

14. A class consists of $\frac{2}{5}$ freshmen, $\frac{1}{4}$ sophomores, and $\frac{1}{10}$ juniors; the rest are seniors. What fraction of the class is seniors?

15. The Naturals Company sells its products in many countries. The following two circle graphs show the fractions of the company's earnings for 1980 and 1990.
Based on this information, answer the following questions:

a. In 1980, how much greater was the fraction of sales for Japan than for Canada?

b. In 1990, how much less was the fraction of sales for England than for the United States?

c. How much greater was the fraction of total sales for the United States in 1990 than in 1980?

d. Is it true that the amount of sales in dollars in Australia was less in 1980 than in 1990? Why?

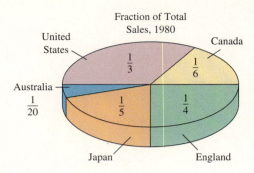

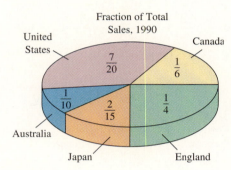

16. A clerk sold three pieces of ribbon. One piece was $\frac{1}{3}$ yd long, another was $2\frac{3}{4}$ yd long, and the third was $3\frac{1}{2}$ yd long. What was the total length of ribbon sold?

17. A recipe requires $3\frac{1}{2}$ c of milk. Ran put in $\frac{3}{4}$ c and then another cup. How much more milk does he need to put in?

18. Martine bought $8\frac{3}{4}$ yd of fabric. She wants to make a skirt using $1\frac{7}{8}$ yd, pants using $2\frac{3}{8}$ yd, and a vest using $1\frac{2}{3}$ yd. How much fabric will be left over?

19. A plywood board $15\frac{3}{4}$ in. long is cut from a $38\frac{1}{4}$-in. board. The saw cut takes $\frac{3}{8}$ in. How long is the piece of board left after cutting?

20. Students from Rattlesnake School formed four teams to collect cans for recycling during the months of April and May. The students received 10¢ for each 5 lb of cans. A record of their efforts follows:

Number of Pounds Collected

	Team 1	Team 2	Team 3	Team 4
April	$28\frac{3}{4}$	$32\frac{7}{8}$	$28\frac{1}{2}$	$35\frac{3}{16}$
May	$33\frac{1}{3}$	$28\frac{5}{12}$	$25\frac{3}{4}$	$41\frac{1}{2}$

a. Which team collected the most for the 2-mo period? How much did they collect?

b. What was the difference in the total amounts collected by the teams during the 2 mo?

21. Demonstrate by example that each of the following properties of rational numbers holds:

  a. Closure property of addition

  b. Commutative property of addition

  c. Associative property of addition

22. For each of the following sequences, discover a pattern and write three more terms of the sequence if the pattern continues. Which of the sequences are arithmetic, and which are not? Justify your answers.

  a. $\frac{1}{4}, \frac{1}{2}, \frac{3}{4}, 1, \frac{5}{4}, \ldots$ **b.** $\frac{1}{2}, \frac{2}{3}, \frac{3}{4}, \frac{4}{5}, \frac{5}{6}, \ldots$

  c. $\frac{2}{3}, \frac{5}{3}, \frac{8}{3}, \frac{11}{3}, \frac{14}{3}, \ldots$ **d.** $\frac{5}{4}, \frac{3}{4}, \frac{1}{4}, \frac{-1}{4}, \frac{-3}{4}, \ldots$

23. Find the nth term in each of the sequences in Problem 22.

24. Use the following diagram from a 1994 United Nations *Human Development Report* to answer the following questions:

  a. In 1991, of the countries pictured, what fraction of the world's water was used by Japan and the United States together?

  b. Similarly, what fraction of the world's pesticides was used by Japan and the United States together?

  c. What fraction more of the total amount of water used did France consume than India?

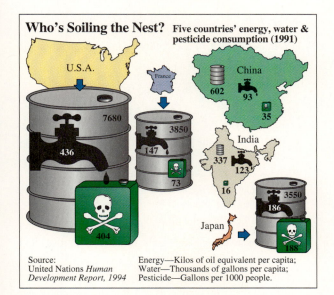

Who's Soiling the Nest? Five countries' energy, water & pesticide consumption (1991)

Source: United Nations *Human Development Report,* 1994

Energy—Kilos of oil equivalent per capita; Water—Thousands of gallons per capita; Pesticide—Gallons per 1000 people.

25. Use the following diagram from the same 1994 United Nations *Human Development Report* to answer the following questions:

a. What country had the greatest fraction of the total number of refugees?

b. What fraction less refugees depicted did Sri Lanka have than Afghanistan?

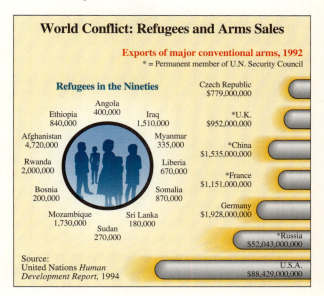

World Conflict: Refugees and Arms Sales

Source: United Nations *Human Development Report,* 1994

26. Insert five fractions between the numbers 1 and 2 so that the seven numbers (including 1 and 2) constitute an arithmetic sequence.

27. Let $f(x) = x + \frac{3}{4}$.

  a. Find the outputs if the inputs are the following:

    i. 0   ii. $\frac{4}{3}$ iii. $\frac{-3}{4}$

  b. For which inputs will the outputs be the following:

    i. 1   ii. $^-1$ iii. $\frac{1}{2}$

28. Let $f(x) = \frac{x+2}{x-1}$ and let the domain of the function be the set of all integers except 1. Find the following:

  a. $f(0)$ **b.** $f(^-2)$ **c.** $f(^-5)$ **d.** $f(5)$

29. a. Check that each of the following is true:

$$\frac{1}{3} = \frac{1}{4} + \frac{1}{3 \cdot 4} \qquad \frac{1}{4} = \frac{1}{5} + \frac{1}{4 \cdot 5}$$

$$\frac{1}{5} = \frac{1}{6} + \frac{1}{5 \cdot 6}$$

  b. Based on the examples in (a), write $\frac{1}{n}$ as a sum of two unit fractions, that is, as a sum of fractions with numerator 1.

  ★**c.** Prove your answer in (b).

Communication

30. Why should you consider the fractional parts of mixed numbers when you estimate?

31. Sally claims that it is easier to add two fractions if she adds the numerators and then adds the denominators. How can you help her?

32. Is any improper fraction equal to $\frac{4}{5}$? Why or why not?

33. Does each of the following properties hold for subtraction of rational numbers? Justify your answer.
 a. Closure   **b.** Commutative
 c. Associative   **d.** Identity
 e. Inverse

34. Explain an error pattern in each of the following. Describe how you would help a student making these errors.
 a. $\frac{13}{35}=\frac{1}{5}$, $\frac{27}{73}=\frac{2}{3}$, $\frac{16}{64}=\frac{1}{4}$

 b. $\frac{4}{5}+\frac{2}{3}=\frac{6}{8}$, $\frac{2}{5}+\frac{3}{4}=\frac{5}{9}$, $\frac{7}{8}+\frac{1}{3}=\frac{8}{11}$

 c. $8\frac{3}{4}-6\frac{1}{8}=2\frac{2}{4}$, $5\frac{3}{8}-2\frac{2}{3}=3\frac{1}{5}$, $2\frac{2}{7}-1\frac{1}{3}=1\frac{1}{4}$

 d. $\frac{2}{3}\cdot3=\frac{6}{9}$, $\frac{1}{4}\cdot6=\frac{6}{24}$, $\frac{4}{5}\cdot2=\frac{8}{10}$

Open-ended

35. Use the approximate population density (number of people per square mile) from the following table to answer the given questions:

Montana	Russia	United Kingdom	Nigeria	Bangladesh	United States
6	22	588	248	2028	68

 a. Explain why it is or is not feasible to add the numbers in the table for Montana and Russia to determine the population density of the combined country and state.
 b. Decide whether it is reasonable to decide that, based on the given data, the population of Bangladesh is approximately 355 times that of Montana.
 c. Using the data in the table, create and solve two questions that are reasonable for middle-school students to solve.

Cooperative Learning

36. Students should split up into small groups. Each group then decides on a menu for a dinner party. They choose the recipes that will be used to prepare the meal and combine the ingredients to determine how much of each is required for the total meal. For example, a bread recipe might call for 2 3/4 c flour and a dessert recipe might call for 1 1/3 c of flour. How much flour is needed for these two items?

37. Interview 10 people and ask them if and when they add and subtract fractions in their lives. Combine those responses with those of the rest of the class to get a view of how "ordinary" people must use computation of rational numbers in their daily lives.

Review Problems

38. Use the following graph and the marked points to answer the following:

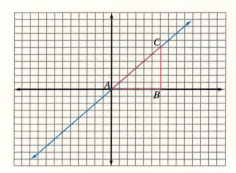

 a. Create a series of right triangles whose longest side (hypotenuse) lies along the slanted line. Use at least one marked point as a vertex of each triangle. Triangle *ABC* is given as an example.
 b. To get to point *C* from point *A* by traveling along the horizontal and vertical sides of the triangle, we must go down 6 units ($^-6$) and 6 units to the left ($^-6$). The ratio of directed segment lengths *CB* to *BA* is $^-6/(^-6)$, or 1. Find the ratio of directed segment lengths in the triangles created in (a).
 c. Make a conjecture about any triangles created in the manner described in (a).

39. Write each of the following fractions in simplest form:
 a. $\frac{14}{21}$ **b.** $\frac{117}{153}$ **c.** $\frac{5^2}{7^2}$ **d.** $\frac{a^2+a}{1+a}$ **e.** $\frac{a^2+1}{a+1}$

40. Determine if each of the following pairs of fractions is equal:
 a. $\frac{a^2}{b}$ and $\frac{a^2b^2}{b^3}$ **b.** $\frac{377}{400}$ and $\frac{378}{401}$
 c. $\frac{0}{10}$ and $\frac{0}{^-10}$ **d.** $\frac{a}{b}$ and $\frac{a+1}{b+1}$, where $a\neq b$

41. a. What month of the year has the smallest fraction of days of the year?
 b. What fraction of days of the year occur before July 4?
 c. How many days are actually in a year? Express this as a mixed number and as an improper fraction.

42. Show that the arithmetic mean of two rational numbers is between the two numbers; that is, for $0<\frac{a}{b}<\frac{c}{d}$, prove that
$$0<\frac{a}{b}<\frac{1}{2}\left(\frac{a}{b}+\frac{c}{d}\right)<\frac{c}{d}.$$

43. If the same positive number is added to the numerator and denominator of a positive proper fraction, is the new fraction greater than, less than, or equal to the original fraction? Justify your answer.

BRAIN TEASER When Professor Sum was asked by Mr. Little how many students were in his classes, he answered, "All of them study either languages, physics, or not at all. One half of them study languages only, one fourth of them study French, one seventh of them study physics only, and 20 do not study at all." How many students does Professor Sum have?

Section 5-3 Multiplication and Division of Rational Numbers

Multiplication of Rational Numbers

In the 5–8 *Standards* (p. 67), we find a call for the greater use of visual models as well as a greater emphasis on concepts. Researchers have shown that area as well as length models are effective in the teaching of fractions.

To motivate the definition of multiplication of rational numbers, we use the interpretation of multiplication as repeated addition. Using repeated addition, we can interpret $3 \cdot \left(\frac{3}{4}\right)$ as follows:

$$3 \cdot \left(\frac{3}{4}\right) = \frac{3}{4} + \frac{3}{4} + \frac{3}{4} = \frac{9}{4} = 2\frac{1}{4}.$$

The area model in Figure 5-8 shows this.

Figure 5-8

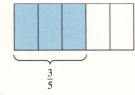

$$3 \quad \cdot \quad \frac{3}{4} \quad = \quad \frac{3}{4} \quad + \quad \frac{3}{4} \quad + \quad \frac{3}{4} \quad = \quad \frac{9}{4} \quad \text{or} \quad 2\frac{1}{4}$$

If the commutative property of multiplication of rational numbers is to be true, then $3 \cdot \left(\frac{3}{4}\right) = \left(\frac{3}{4}\right) \cdot 3 = \frac{9}{4}.$

Next, we consider what happens when both factors are fractions. If forests once covered about $\frac{3}{5}$ of Earth's land and only about $\frac{1}{2}$ of these forests remain, what fraction of Earth is covered with forests today? We can use an area model to find out.

Figure 5-9(a) shows a one-unit rectangle separated into fifths, with $\frac{3}{5}$ shaded. To find $\frac{1}{2}$ of $\frac{3}{5}$, we divide the shaded portion of the rectangle in Figure 5-9(a) into two equal parts and take one of those parts. The result would be the green portion of Figure 5-9(b). However, the green portion represents three parts out of 10, or $\frac{3}{10}$ of the one-unit rectangle.

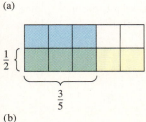

(a)

(b)

Figure 5-9

Thus

$$\frac{1}{2} \cdot \frac{3}{5} = \frac{3}{10} = \frac{1 \cdot 3}{2 \cdot 5}.$$

This discussion leads to the following definition of multiplication for rational numbers.

Definition of Rational Number Multiplication

If $\frac{a}{b}$ and $\frac{c}{d}$ are any rational numbers, then $\frac{a}{b} \cdot \frac{c}{d} = \frac{a \cdot c}{b \cdot d}.$

Example 5-11   Answer each of the following:

   a. If $\frac{5}{6}$ of the population of a certain city is considered to be middle class and $\frac{7}{11}$ of the city's population is female, what fraction of the population of that city is middle-class females?

   b. A builder wants to use $2\frac{1}{3}$ acres of land for each house lot in a tract. If 3 houses are built and $\frac{1}{5}$ of a house lot is used as a common park, how much land is required?

Solution   **a.** $\frac{5}{6} \cdot \frac{7}{11} = \frac{5 \cdot 7}{6 \cdot 11} = \frac{35}{66}$

   The fraction of the population that is middle-class females is $\frac{35}{66}$.

   b. $2\frac{1}{3} \cdot 3\frac{1}{5} = \frac{7}{3} \cdot \frac{16}{5} = \frac{7 \cdot 16}{3 \cdot 5} = \frac{112}{15} = 7\frac{7}{15}$

   The amount of land required for the houses and the park is $7\frac{7}{15}$ acres.

HISTORICAL NOTE

In the Middle Ages, mathematical skill was admired and supported by the monarchs. Leonardo of Pisa (1170–1230), known as Fibonacci, was the most prominent of the medieval mathematicians. In 1225, Fibonacci participated in a mathematical tournament before the Roman Emperor Frederic II, who came to Pisa with a group of mathematicians to test Fibonacci's immense reputation. One of the questions was to find a rational number that is a square, for example $\left(\frac{4}{9} = \left(\frac{2}{3}\right)^2\right)$, and that remains a square if it is decreased or increased by 5. Fibonacci found the number: $\frac{1681}{144}$, or $\left(\frac{41}{12}\right)^2$. When 5 is subtracted, it remains a square because $\frac{1681}{144} - 5 = \frac{961}{144} = \left(\frac{31}{12}\right)^2$, and when 5 is added, it remains a square because $\frac{1681}{144} + 5 = \frac{2401}{144} = \left(\frac{49}{12}\right)^2$.

Properties of Multiplication of Rational Numbers

Multiplication of rational numbers has properties analogous to the properties of addition of rational numbers. These include the following properties for multiplication: closure, commutative, associative, multiplicative identity, and multiplicative inverse. For emphasis, we give the last two properties.

Properties

Multiplicative Identity of Rational Numbers: The number 1 is the unique number such that for every rational number $\frac{a}{b}$,

$$1 \cdot \left(\frac{a}{b}\right) = \frac{a}{b} = \left(\frac{a}{b}\right) \cdot 1.$$

Multiplicative Inverse of Rational Numbers: For any nonzero rational number $\frac{a}{b}$, $\frac{b}{a}$ is the unique rational number such that $\frac{a}{b} \cdot \frac{b}{a} = 1 = \frac{b}{a} \cdot \frac{a}{b}$. The multiplicative inverse of $\frac{a}{b}$ is also called the **reciprocal** of $\frac{a}{b}$.

reciprocal

REMARK   The multiplicative inverse property is a property we obtain when we expand from the set of integers to the set of rational numbers.

Example 5-12

Find the multiplicative inverse of each of the following rational numbers:

a. $\frac{2}{3}$ **b.** $\frac{-2}{5}$ **c.** 4   **d.** 0   **e.** $6\frac{1}{2}$

Solution   **a.** $\frac{3}{2}$

b. $\frac{5}{-2}$, or $\frac{-5}{2}$

c. Because $4 = \frac{4}{1}$, the multiplicative inverse of 4 is $\frac{1}{4}$.

d. Even though $0 = \frac{0}{1}, \frac{1}{0}$ is undefined; there is no multiplicative inverse of 0.

e. Because $6\frac{1}{2} = \frac{13}{2}$, the multiplicative inverse of $6\frac{1}{2}$ is $\frac{2}{13}$.

Multiplication and addition are connected through the distributive property of multiplication over addition. Also there is a multiplication property of equality for rational numbers and a multiplication property of zero similar to those for whole numbers and integers.

Properties

Distributive Property of Multiplication over Addition for Rational Numbers: If $\frac{a}{b}, \frac{c}{d}$, and $\frac{e}{f}$ are any rational numbers, then

$$\frac{a}{b}\left(\frac{c}{d} + \frac{e}{f}\right) = \left(\frac{a}{b} \cdot \frac{c}{d}\right) + \left(\frac{a}{b} \cdot \frac{e}{f}\right).$$

Multiplication Property of Equality for Rational Numbers: If $\frac{a}{b}$ and $\frac{c}{d}$ are any rational numbers such that $\frac{a}{b} = \frac{c}{d}$, and $\frac{e}{f}$ is any rational number, then $\frac{a}{b} \cdot \frac{e}{f} = \frac{c}{d} \cdot \frac{e}{f}$.

Multiplication Property of Zero for Rational Numbers: If $\frac{a}{b}$ is any rational number, then $\frac{a}{b} \cdot 0 = 0 = 0 \cdot \frac{a}{b}$.

Example 5-13

A bicycle is on sale at $\frac{3}{4}$ of its original price. If the sale price is $330, what was the original price?

Solution   Let x be the original price. Then $\frac{3}{4}$ of the original price is $\frac{3}{4}x$. Because the sale price is $330, we have $\frac{3}{4}x = 330$. Solving for x gives

$$\frac{4}{3} \cdot \frac{3}{4}x = \frac{4}{3} \cdot 330$$

$$1 \cdot x = 440$$

$$x = 440.$$

Thus the original price was $440.

An alternative approach, which does not use algebra, follows. Because $\frac{3}{4}$ of the original price is $330, $\frac{1}{4}$ of the original price is $\frac{1}{3} \cdot 330$, or $110; thus $4 \cdot \frac{1}{4}$ of the original price is $4 \cdot 110$, or $440.

Problem 2

Sonja wants to build a square deck with the floor made out of 1-in. by 6-in. boards. She wants the deck to be 30 boards wide. Boards come in lengths of 6, 8, 10, 12, 14, 16, 18, and 20 ft and sell for 32¢ per ft. How many boards of what length must Sonja order to make the floor? What is the minimum cost of the floor if she orders only complete boards?

Understanding the Problem.   A square floor is to be made of 1-in. by 6-in. boards as described above. First we must understand that a 1-in. by 6-in. board is in reality $5\frac{1}{2}$ in. wide and $\frac{3}{4}$ in. thick. Only complete boards can be used. We need to find the minimum cost.

Devising a Plan. Because the deck is a square and the deck is 30 boards wide, the length of the deck must be $30 \cdot \left(5\frac{1}{2}\right) = 165$ in. From this information, we can find the length of the boards needed and the cost.

Carrying Out the Plan. Since the length is 165 in., we divide by 12 to convert to feet and obtain $13\frac{3}{4}$ ft. Hence, we need to order 30 of the 14-ft boards. This gives $30 \cdot 14$, or 420 ft at 32¢ per ft. Thus Sonja's bill would be 32¢ $\cdot$ 420 = \$134.40. This is the minimum cost because boards shorter than 14 ft will not work, boards longer than 14 ft cost more, and two lengths cannot be cut from any board.

Looking Back. We could vary this problem by changing the sizes of the deck or the boards. We could also work on related problems such as which size nail is needed to nail together three 1-in. by 6-in. boards so that the nail would go through two boards and go $\frac{1}{2}$ in. into the third board. (Nail sizes increase by $\frac{1}{4}$ in. For example, a 2-penny nail is 1 in. long; a 3-penny nail is $1\frac{1}{4}$ in. long; a 4-penny nail is $1\frac{1}{2}$ in. long, and so forth.) How many nails would be needed to nail down the deck?

● ● ●

Division of Rational Numbers

Recall that $6 \div 3$ means "How many 3s are there in 6?" We found that $6 \div 3 = 2$ because $3 \cdot 2 = 6$. Consider $3 \div \left(\frac{1}{2}\right)$, which is equivalent to finding how many halves there are in 3. We see from the area model in Figure 5-10 that there are 6 half pieces in the 3 whole pieces. We record this as $3 \div \left(\frac{1}{2}\right) = 6$. Also note that $\left(\frac{1}{2}\right) \cdot 6 = 3$.

Figure 5-10

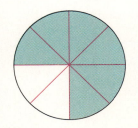

Figure 5-11

Next, consider $\left(\frac{3}{4}\right) \div \left(\frac{1}{8}\right)$. This means "how many $\frac{1}{8}$s are in $\frac{3}{4}$?" Figure 5-11 shows that there are six $\frac{1}{8}$s in the shaded portion, which represents $\frac{3}{4}$ of the whole. Therefore $\left(\frac{3}{4}\right) \div \left(\frac{1}{8}\right) = 6$. Also, note that $\left(\frac{1}{8}\right) \cdot 6 = \frac{3}{4}$.

In the previous examples, we saw a relationship between division and multiplication of rational numbers. We can define division for rational numbers formally in terms of multiplication in the same way that we define division for integers.

Definition of Rational Number Division

If $\frac{a}{b}$ and $\frac{c}{d}$ are any rational numbers and $\frac{c}{d}$ is not zero, then $\frac{a}{b} \div \frac{c}{d} = \frac{e}{f}$ if, and only if, $\frac{e}{f}$ is the unique

rational number such that $\frac{c}{d} \cdot \frac{e}{f} = \frac{a}{b}$.

REMARK   In the definition of division, $\frac{c}{d}$ is not zero because division by zero is impossi-

ble. Also, $\frac{c}{d} \neq 0$ implies that $c \neq 0$.

Algorithm for Division of Rational Numbers

The following student page from *Addison-Wesley Mathematics,* Grade 6, 1993, motivates a division algorithm for rational numbers. Note that the division sentence is associated with a multiplication sentence. The box on the right leads us to the familiar invert-and-multiply algorithm for division of rationals.

Dividing Fractions

LEARN ABOUT IT

EXPLORE **Analyze the Process**

A director has scheduled 15 minutes of a special animal program for a roving reporter's features about the zoo. How many $\frac{3}{4}$-minute zoo features can be shown?

Since we want to find the number of $\frac{3}{4}$-minute segments in 15 minutes, we divide 15 by $\frac{3}{4}$.

Here is **how** to divide by a fraction.	Here is **why** it works.
Multiply the dividend by the reciprocal of the divisor.	Multiply both numbers by $\frac{4}{3}$.
$15 \div \frac{3}{4} = 15 \times \frac{4}{3} = 20$	$15 \div \frac{3}{4} = (15 \times \frac{4}{3}) \div (\frac{3}{4} \times \frac{4}{3})$
reciprocals	$= (15 \times \frac{4}{3}) \div (\;1\;) = 15 \times \frac{4}{3}$

Using Figure 5-12, we can count 15 shaded 3/4s. There are also 15 unshaded 1/4s that need to be considered in trying to determine how many 3/4s fit in 15. Each three of the unshaded 1/4s is another 3/4, and there are five sets of the three 1/4s, thus making five 3/4s in the unshaded portion of 15. Thus we have a total of fifteen and five, or twenty, 3/4s in the 15 units.

Figure 5-12

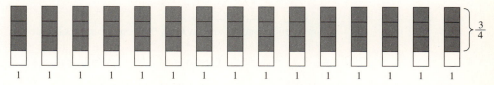

A slightly different way to consider the division, 15/(3/4), is to consider each 3/4 shaded portion as a unit and to ask how many 3/4 units there are in the 15 rectangles. Clearly there are 15 of the 3/4 units, but that does not take into account the unshaded portions. Each rectangle contains one 3/4 unit shaded and 1/3 of a 3/4 unit unshaded. There are 15 unshaded parts, each containing 1/3 of a 3/4 unit for a total of 15(1 + 1/3), or 15(4/3), or 20. Thus there are twenty 3/4s in 15.

INVESTIGATION 5 - 4

● Use the method of Figure 5-12 to determine how many 2/3s are in 6. ●

A modified method similar to this one could be used to find 5/(4/3) or to find how many 4/3s are in 5. Consider Figure 5-13(a), where 5 units are pictured.

Figure 5-13

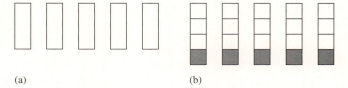

(a)   (b)

In Figure 5-13(b), we see that there are no complete 4/3s in any single one of the 5 units. If an entire rectangle (shaded and unshaded parts) is considered a unit, then each part is short 1/4 of a unit; that is, there are 5(1 − 1/4), or 5(3/4), or 15/4 of the 4/3 units in the 5 original rectangles.

A more traditional justification of the division algorithm follows. The algorithm for division of fractions is usually justified in the middle grades by using the Fundamental Law of Fractions, $\dfrac{a}{b} = \dfrac{ac}{bc}$, where a, b, and c are all fractions. For example,

$$\frac{2}{3} \div \frac{5}{7} = \frac{\dfrac{2}{3}}{\dfrac{5}{7}} = \frac{\dfrac{2}{3} \cdot \dfrac{7}{5}}{\dfrac{5}{7} \cdot \dfrac{7}{5}} = \frac{\dfrac{2}{3} \cdot \dfrac{7}{5}}{1} = \frac{2}{3} \cdot \frac{7}{5}.$$

Thus

$$\frac{2}{3} \div \frac{5}{7} = \frac{2}{3} \cdot \frac{7}{5}.$$

An alternative approach for developing an algorithm for division of fractions can be found by first dividing fractions that have equal denominators. For example, $\frac{9}{10} \div \frac{3}{10}$ $= 9 \div 3$ and $\frac{15}{23} \div \frac{5}{23} = 15 \div 5$. These examples suggest that when two fractions with the same denominators are divided, the result can be obtained by dividing the numerator of the first fraction by the numerator of the second. To divide fractions with different denominators, we rename the fractions so that the denominators are equal. Thus

$$\frac{a}{b} \div \frac{c}{d} = \frac{ad}{bd} \div \frac{bc}{bd} = ad \div bc = \frac{ad}{bc}.$$

Algorithm for Division of Fractions

$$\frac{a}{b} \div \frac{c}{d} = \frac{a}{b} \cdot \frac{d}{c}, \text{ where } \frac{c}{d} \neq 0.$$

Example 5-14 | A radio station provides 36 min for Public Service Announcements for every 24 hr of broadcasting.

a. What part of the broadcasting day is allotted to Public Service Announcements?
b. How many 3/4-min Public Service Announcements can be allowed in the 36 min?

Solution **a.** There are 60 min in an hour and 60 · 24 min in a day. Thus 36/(60 · 24), or 1/40, of the day is allotted for the announcements.
b. 36/(3/4) = 36(4/3), or 48, announcements are allowed.

Example 5-15 | We have $35\frac{1}{2}$ yd of material available to make shirts. Each shirt requires $\frac{3}{8}$ yd of material.

a. How many shirts can be made?
b. How much material will be left over?

Solution **a.** We need to find the integer part of the answer to $35\frac{1}{2} \div \frac{3}{8}$. The division follows:

$$35\frac{1}{2} \div \frac{3}{8} = \frac{71}{2} \cdot \frac{8}{3} = \frac{284}{3} = 94\frac{2}{3}$$

Thus we can make 94 shirts.

b. Because the division in (a) was by $\frac{3}{8}$, the amount of material left over is $\frac{2}{3}$ of $\frac{3}{8}$, or $\frac{2}{3} \cdot \frac{3}{8}$, or $\frac{1}{4}$ yd.

B R A I N   T E A S E R   A castle in the faraway land of Aluossim was surrounded by four moats. One day, the castle was attacked and captured by a fierce tribe from the north. Guards were stationed at each bridge. Juana was allowed to take a number of bags of gold from the castle as he went into exile. However, the guard at the first bridge demanded half the bags of gold plus one more bag. Juana met this demand and proceeded to the next bridge. The guards at the second, third, and fourth bridges made identical demands, all of which the prince met. When Juana finally crossed all the bridges, a single bag of gold was left. With how many bags did Juana start?

Ongoing Assessment 5-3

1. In the following figures, a unit rectangle is used to illustrate the product of two fractions. Name the fractions and their product.

 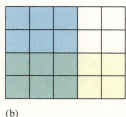

   (a)   (b)

2. Use a rectangular region to illustrate each of the following products:

   a. $\dfrac{3}{4} \cdot \dfrac{1}{3}$ **b.** $\dfrac{1}{5} \cdot \dfrac{2}{3}$ **c.** $\dfrac{2}{5} \cdot \dfrac{1}{3}$

3. Find each of the following products. Write your answers in simplest form.

   a. $\dfrac{49}{65} \cdot \dfrac{26}{98}$ **b.** $\dfrac{a}{b} \cdot \dfrac{b^2}{a^2}$ **c.** $\dfrac{xy}{z} \cdot \dfrac{z^2 a}{x^3 y^2}$

   d. $2\dfrac{1}{3} \cdot 3\dfrac{3}{4}$ **e.** $\dfrac{22}{7} \cdot 4\dfrac{2}{3}$ **f.** $\dfrac{-5}{2} \cdot 2\dfrac{1}{2}$

4. Use the distributive property to find each product.

   a. $4\dfrac{1}{2} \cdot 2\dfrac{1}{3}$ $\left[\text{\textit{Hint:}} \left(4 + \dfrac{1}{2}\right) \cdot \left(2 + \dfrac{1}{3}\right). \right]$

   b. $3\dfrac{1}{3} \cdot 2\dfrac{1}{2}$ **c.** $248\dfrac{2}{5} \cdot 100\dfrac{1}{8}$

5. Find the multiplicative inverse for each of the following:

   a. $\dfrac{-1}{3}$ **b.** $3\dfrac{1}{3}$

   c. $\dfrac{x}{y}$, if $x \neq 0$ and $y \neq 0$ **d.** $^{-}7$

6. Compute the following mentally. Find the exact answer.

   a. $3\dfrac{1}{4} \cdot 8$ **b.** $7\dfrac{1}{4} \cdot 4$ **c.** $9\dfrac{1}{5} \cdot 10$

   d. $8 \cdot 2\dfrac{1}{4}$ **e.** $3 \div \dfrac{1}{2}$ **f.** $3\dfrac{1}{2} \div \dfrac{1}{2}$

   g. $3 \div \dfrac{1}{3}$ **h.** $4\dfrac{1}{2} \div 2$

7. Choose the number from among the numbers in parentheses that best approximates each of the following:

   a. $3\dfrac{11}{12} \cdot 5\dfrac{3}{100}$ (8, 20, 15, 16)

   b. $2\dfrac{1}{10} \cdot 7\dfrac{7}{8}$ (16, 14, 4, 3)

   c. $20\dfrac{2}{3} \div 9\dfrac{7}{8}$ $\left(2, 180, \dfrac{1}{2}, 10\right)$

   d. $\dfrac{1}{101} \div \dfrac{1}{103}$ $\left(0, 1, \dfrac{1}{2}, \dfrac{1}{4}\right)$

8. Estimate the following:

   a. $5\dfrac{4}{5} \cdot 3\dfrac{1}{10}$ **b.** $4\dfrac{10}{11} \cdot 5\dfrac{1}{8}$

   c. $\dfrac{20\dfrac{8}{9}}{3\dfrac{1}{12}}$ **d.** $\dfrac{12\dfrac{1}{3}}{1\dfrac{7}{8}}$

9. Without actually doing the computations, in the following choose the number in parentheses that correctly describes each:

   a. $\dfrac{13}{14} \cdot \dfrac{17}{19}$ (greater than 1, less than 1)

   b. $3\dfrac{2}{7} \div 5\dfrac{1}{9}$ (greater than 1, less than 1)

   c. $4\dfrac{1}{3} \div 2\dfrac{3}{100}$ (greater than 2, less than 2)

   d. $16 \div 4\dfrac{3}{18}$ (greater than 4, less than 4)

   e. $16 \div 3\dfrac{8}{9}$ (greater than 4, less than 4)

10. A sewing project requires $6\dfrac{1}{8}$ yd of material that sells for 62¢ per yard and $3\dfrac{1}{4}$ yd that sells for 81¢ per yard. Choose from the following the best estimate for the cost of the project:

   a. Between $2 and $4   **b.** Between $4 and $6
   c. Between $6 and $8   **d.** Between $8 and $10

11. When you multiply a certain number by 3 and then subtract $\frac{7}{18}$, you get the same result as when you multiply the number by 2 and add $\frac{5}{12}$. What is the number?

12. Five eighths of the students at Salem State College live in dormitories. If 6000 students at the college live in dormitories, how many students are there in the college?

13. Di Paloma University had a faculty reduction and lost $\frac{1}{5}$ of its faculty. If 320 faculty members were left after the reduction, how many members were there originally?

14. Alberto owns $\frac{5}{9}$ of the stock in the North West Tofu Company. His sister, Renatta, owns half as much stock as Alberto. What part of the stock is owned by neither Alberto nor Renatta?

15. A person has $29\frac{1}{2}$ yd of material available to make doll uniforms. Each uniform requires $\frac{3}{4}$ yd of material.
    a. How many uniforms can be made?
    b. How much material will be left over?

16. A suit is on sale for $180. What was the original price of the suit if the discount was $\frac{1}{4}$ of the original price?

17. Every employee's salary at the Sunrise Software Company increases each year by $\frac{1}{10}$ of that person's salary the previous year.
    a. If Martha's present annual salary is $100,000, what will her salary be in 2 yr?
    b. If Aaron's present salary is $99,000, what was his salary 1 yr ago?
    c. If Juanita's present salary is $363,000, what was her salary 2 yr ago?

18. At a certain company, three times as many men as women apply for work. If $\frac{1}{10}$ of the applicants are hired and $\frac{1}{20}$ of the men who apply are hired, what fraction of the women who apply are hired?

19. Jasmine is reading a book. She has finished $\frac{3}{4}$ of the book and has 82 pages left to read. How many pages has she read?

20. John took out all his money from his bank savings account. He spent $50 on a radio and $\frac{3}{5}$ of what remained on presents. Half of what was left he put back in his checking account, and the remaining $35 he donated to charity. How much money did John originally have in his savings account?

21. Peter, Paul, and Mary start at the same time walking around a circular track in the same direction. Peter takes $\frac{1}{2}$ hr to walk around the track. Paul takes $\frac{5}{12}$ hr, and Mary takes $\frac{1}{3}$ hr.
    a. How many minutes does it take each person to walk around the track?
    b. How many times will each person go around the track before all three meet again at the starting line?

22. The formula for converting degrees Celsius (C) to degrees Fahrenheit (F) is $F = \left(\frac{9}{5}\right) \cdot C + 32$.
    a. If Samantha reads that the temperature is 32°C in Spain, what is the Fahrenheit temperature?
    b. If the temperature dropped to ⁻40°F in West Yellowstone, what is the temperature in degrees Celsius?

23. Glenn bought 175 shares of stock at $48\frac{1}{4}$ a share. A year later, he sold it at $35\frac{3}{8}$ a share. How much did Glenn lose on the transition?

24. Al gives $\frac{1}{2}$ of his marbles to Bev. Bev gives $\frac{1}{2}$ of these to Carl. Carl gives $\frac{1}{2}$ of these to Dani. If Dani has four marbles, how many did Al have originally?

25. Believe it or not! Graham Greater supposedly averaged a hit every 1 1/2 sec in trapshooting 2264 targets in 1 hr. Is the arithmetic true?

26. The fastest centipede can travel at a rate of 19 17/25 in. per second. How far can it travel in one hr if the rate remains constant?

27. The normal brain weight for an African bull elephant is 9 1/4 lb. Approximately how much would be the weight of 13 of the brains of these elephants?

28. Let $S = \frac{1}{2} + \frac{1}{2^2} + \frac{1}{2^3} + \ldots + \frac{1}{2^{64}}$.
    a. Use the distributive property of multiplication over addition to find an expression for $2S$.
    b. Show that $2S - S = S = 1 - \left(\frac{1}{2}\right)^{64}$.
    c. Find a simple expression for the sum
    $$\frac{1}{2} + \frac{1}{2^2} + \frac{1}{2^3} + \ldots + \frac{1}{2^n}.$$

29. In an arithmetic sequence, the first term is 1 and the hundredth term is 2. Find the following:
    a. The fiftieth term
    b. The sum of the first 50 terms

30. For each of the following sequences, (a) find a pattern and (b) write two more terms of the sequence, assuming the pattern continues. Which of the sequences are geometric?

Justify your answers.

i. $1, \dfrac{1}{2}, \dfrac{1}{4}, \dfrac{1}{8}, \dfrac{1}{16}, \ldots$ ii. $1, \dfrac{-1}{2}, \dfrac{1}{4}, \dfrac{-1}{8}, \dfrac{1}{16}, \ldots$

iii. $\dfrac{4}{3}, 1, \dfrac{3}{4}, \dfrac{9}{16}, \dfrac{27}{64}, \ldots$ iv. $\dfrac{1}{3}, \dfrac{2}{3^2}, \dfrac{3}{3^3}, \dfrac{4}{3^4}, \ldots$

31. There is a simple method for squaring any number that consists of a whole number and $\dfrac{1}{2}$. For example $\left(3\dfrac{1}{2}\right)^2 = 3 \cdot 4 + \left(\dfrac{1}{2}\right)^2 = 12\dfrac{1}{4}; \left(4\dfrac{1}{2}\right)^2 = 4 \cdot 5 + \left(\dfrac{1}{2}\right)^2 = 20\dfrac{1}{4}; \left(5\dfrac{1}{2}\right)^2 = 5 \cdot 6 + \left(\dfrac{1}{2}\right)^2 = 30\dfrac{1}{4}$.

a. Write a statement for $\left(n + \dfrac{1}{2}\right)^2$ that generalizes these examples, where n is a whole number.

★**b.** Justify this procedure.

32. Let $f(x) = \dfrac{3x + 4}{4x - 5}$, where the domain is all rational numbers for which the function has a value.

a. Find the outputs if the inputs are as follows:

i. 0 ii. $\dfrac{2}{5}$ iii. $\dfrac{-2}{5}$

b. For which inputs will the outputs be the following:

i. 0 ii. $\dfrac{2}{5}$ iii. $\dfrac{-1}{2}$

c. What value for x is not in the domain of the function?

33. Consider these products:

First product: $\left(1 + \dfrac{1}{1}\right)\left(1 + \dfrac{1}{2}\right)$

Second product: $\left(1 + \dfrac{1}{1}\right)\left(1 + \dfrac{1}{2}\right)\left(1 + \dfrac{1}{3}\right)$

Third product: $\left(1 + \dfrac{1}{1}\right)\left(1 + \dfrac{1}{2}\right)\left(1 + \dfrac{1}{3}\right)\left(1 + \dfrac{1}{4}\right)$

a. Calculate the value of each product. Based on the pattern in your answers, guess the value of the fourth product. Then check to determine if your guess is correct.

b. Guess the value of the hundredth product.

c. Find as simple an expression as possible for the nth product.

Communication

34. Suppose you divide a natural number, n, by a positive rational number less than 1. Will the answer always be less than n, sometimes less than n, or never less than n? Why?

35. If the fractions represented by points C and D on the following number line are multiplied, what point best represents the product? Explain why.

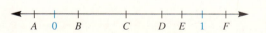

36. What are two reasonable estimates for $\dfrac{1}{7}$ of 39? Explain how you arrived at each estimate.

37. If the product of two numbers is 1 and one of the numbers is greater than 1, what do you know about the other number? Explain your answer.

38. A plumber needed five sections of $2\dfrac{1}{8}$-ft pipe. Can this pipe be cut from a 12-ft section? If so, how much pipe would be left over? If not, explain why.

39. Detect the error pattern in the following:

$$\left(\dfrac{5}{8}\right) \cdot \left(\dfrac{2}{3}\right) = \left(\dfrac{8}{5}\right) \cdot \left(\dfrac{2}{3}\right) = \dfrac{16}{15}$$

$$\left(\dfrac{1}{2}\right) \cdot \left(\dfrac{1}{4}\right) = \left(\dfrac{2}{1}\right) \cdot \left(\dfrac{1}{4}\right) = \dfrac{2}{4}$$

How might you work with the student who did this work?

40. Explain how you would work the following as a mental math problem rather than a pencil-and-paper activity:

$$\left(\dfrac{1}{4}\right) \cdot 15 \cdot 12$$

41. Show that the following properties do *not* hold for the division of rational numbers:

a. Commutative   **b.** Associative
c. Identity   **d.** Inverse

Open-ended

42. Would you use the problem in the following cartoon in your class? Why or why not? Solve the problem.

43. Most calculators give answers as decimals. What does research say about the use of decimals versus the use of fractions in middle school?

Cooperative Learning

44. Choose a brick building on your campus. Measure the height of one brick and the thickness of mortar between bricks. Estimate the height of the building and then calculate the height of the building. Were rational numbers used in your computations?

Review Problems

45. a. Maria noticed that every 30 sec, the temperature of a chemical reaction in her lab decreased by the same number of degrees. Initially, she measured the temperature as 28°C and 5 min later as ⁻12°C. In a second experiment, she noticed that the temperature of the chemical reaction was initially ⁻57°C and was decreasing by 3°C every minute. If she started the two experiments at the same time, when were the temperatures of the experiments the same? (*Hint:* A spreadsheet may be used to do the calculations.)

b. What was that temperature?

46. Perform each of the following computations. Leave your answers in simplest form.

a. $\dfrac{-3}{16} + \dfrac{7}{4}$

b. $\dfrac{1}{6} + \dfrac{-4}{9} + \dfrac{5}{3}$

c. $\dfrac{-5}{2^3 \cdot 3^2} - \dfrac{-5}{2 \cdot 3^3}$

d. $3\dfrac{4}{5} + 4\dfrac{5}{6}$

e. $5\dfrac{1}{6} - 3\dfrac{5}{8}$

f. $-4\dfrac{1}{3} - 5\dfrac{5}{12}$

47. Each student at Sussex Elementary School takes one foreign language. Two thirds of the students take Spanish, $\dfrac{1}{9}$ take French, $\dfrac{1}{18}$ take German, and the rest take some other foreign language. If there are 720 students in the school, how many do not take Spanish, French, or German?

B R A I N   T E A S E R

A woman's will decreed that her cats be shared among her three daughters as follows: $\dfrac{1}{2}$ of the cats to the eldest daughter, $\dfrac{1}{3}$ of the cats to the middle daughter, and $\dfrac{1}{9}$ of the cats to the youngest daughter. Since the woman had 17 cats, the daughters decided that they could not carry out their mother's wishes. The judge who held the will agreed to lend the daughters a cat so that they could share the cats as their mother wished. Now, $\dfrac{1}{2}$ of 18 is 9; $\dfrac{1}{3}$ of 18 is 6; and $\dfrac{1}{9}$ of 18 is 2. Since $9 + 6 + 2 = 17$, the daughters were able to divide the 17 cats and return the borrowed cat. They obviously did not need the extra cat to carry out their mother's bequest, but they could not divide 17 into halves, thirds, and ninths. Has the woman's will really been followed?

SOLUTION TO THE PRELIMINARY PROBLEM

Figure 5-14

Understanding the Problem.   We are to determine whether a penny-mat can be constructed using the same number of dark-colored and light-colored circular regions on the border and in the interior. An example mat is seen in Figure 5-14. The number of circles around the border should be one half of the total number of circles. Similarly, the number of circles in the interior is one half the total number of circles.

Devising a Plan.   To determine how many total circular regions there are in a penny-mat, we consider a method of developing the concept of multiplication of whole numbers and take the number of circles in each row and add this number for each of the columns of circles. In a similar manner, we can determine how many circles form the border. Because the number on the border is one half the total, we can develop an equation to solve the problem.

Carrying Out the Plan. As shown in Figure 5-15, suppose there are w white circles in each of r rows. Thus there are wr white circles.

Figure 5-15

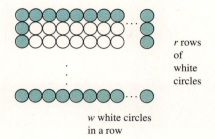

r rows
of
white
circles

w white circles
in a row

The number of dark circles can be counted as follows: On both the top and bottom rows are $w + 2$ dark circles. In addition, there are r dark circles on both the left and right, not counting the ones on the top row and the ones on the bottom row. Thus there are $2(w + 2) + 2r$ dark circles, and we have

$$wr = 2(w + 2) + 2r.$$

Using the distributive property of multiplication over addition, we have

$$wr = 2(w + 2 + r).$$

By the definition of division, we see that

$$\frac{wr}{2} = w + 2 + r.$$

Also, dividing by wr on both sides of the equation, we have

$$\frac{1}{2} = \frac{w + 2 + r}{wr}.$$

Using the definition of addition, we have

$$\frac{1}{2} = \frac{w}{wr} + \frac{2}{wr} + \frac{r}{wr}.$$

And reducing the fractions, we have

$$\frac{1}{2} = \frac{1}{r} + \frac{2}{wr} + \frac{1}{w}.$$

In making the mat, we know that $w \geq 3$ and $r \geq 3$. By trial and error and allowing w to be 3, we find that $r = 10$. With w and r having these values, we know that one size of mat that can be constructed is 5 circular regions by 12 circular regions.

Looking Back. We use the symmetry of the expression $\dfrac{1}{r} + \dfrac{2}{wr} + \dfrac{1}{w}$ to see that when w is 10 and r is 3, we get a solution. A different way to approach the problem is to consider the total number of circles to be $(w + 2)(r + 2)$. That number of circles is equal to $2wr$. This is equivalent to the following:

$$(w + 2)(r + 2) = 2wr$$

$$\left(\frac{w + 2}{w}\right)\left(\frac{r + 2}{r}\right) = 2$$

$$\left(1 + \frac{2}{w}\right)\left(1 + \frac{2}{r}\right) = 2$$

Again $w \neq 1, 2$, but when $w = 3$, $r = 10$, and the problem can be completed.

QUESTIONS FROM THE CLASSROOM

1. Is $\frac{0}{6}$ in simplest form? Why or why not?

2. A student says that taking one half of a number is the same as dividing the number by one half. Is this correct?

3. A student writes $\frac{15}{53} < \frac{1}{3}$ because $3 \cdot 15 < 53 \cdot 1$. Another student writes $\frac{1\cancel{5}}{\cancel{5}3} = \frac{1}{3}$. Where is the fallacy?

4. A student claims that the following is an arithmetic sequence. Is the student right?

$$\frac{1}{2}, \frac{2}{3}, \frac{3}{4}, \frac{4}{5}, \frac{5}{6}, \frac{6}{7}, \frac{7}{8}, \cdots$$

5. A student claims she found a new way to obtain a fraction between two positive fractions: If $\frac{a}{b}$ and $\frac{c}{d}$ are two positive fractions, then $\frac{a + c}{b + d}$ is between these fractions. Is she right?

6. A student claims that if $\frac{a}{b} = \frac{c}{d}$, then $\frac{a + c}{b + d} = \frac{a}{b} = \frac{c}{d}$. Is he right?

7. When working on the problem of simplifying

$$\frac{3}{4} \cdot \frac{1}{2} \cdot \frac{2}{3},$$

a student did the following:

$$\frac{3}{4} \cdot \frac{1}{2} \cdot \frac{2}{3} = \left(\frac{3 \cdot 1}{4 \cdot 2}\right)\left(\frac{3 \cdot 2}{4 \cdot 3}\right) = \frac{3}{8} \cdot \frac{6}{12} = \frac{19}{96}.$$

What was the error?

8. A student simplified the fraction $\frac{m + n}{p + n}$ to $\frac{m}{p}$. Is that student correct?

9. Without thinking, a student argued that a pizza cut into 12 pieces was more than a pizza cut into 6 pieces. How would you respond?

10. A student asks if adding the same very large number to both the numerator and the denominator of a fraction yields a quotient of 1. How do you respond?

CHAPTER OUTLINE

I. Fractions and rational numbers

   A. Numbers of the form $\frac{a}{b}$, where a and b are integers and $b \neq 0$, are called **rational numbers.**

   B. A rational number can be used as follows:

     1. A division problem or the solution to a multiplication problem

     2. A partition, or part, of a whole

     3. A ratio

     4. A probability

   C. Fundamental Law of Fractions: For any fraction $\frac{a}{b}$ and any number $c \neq 0$, $\frac{a}{b} = \frac{ac}{bc}$.

   D. Two fractions $\frac{a}{b}$ and $\frac{c}{d}$ are **equal** if, and only if, $ad = bc$.

   E. If GCD$(a, b) = 1$, then $\frac{a}{b}$ is said to be in **simplest form.**

   F. If $0 < |a| < |b|$, then $\frac{a}{b}$ is called a **proper fraction.**

II. Operations on rational numbers

   A. $\frac{a}{b} + \frac{c}{b} = \frac{a + c}{b}$

   B. $\frac{a}{b} + \frac{c}{d} = \frac{ad + bc}{bd}$

   C. $\frac{a}{b} - \frac{c}{d} = \frac{ad - bc}{bd}$

D. $\dfrac{a}{b} \cdot \dfrac{c}{d} = \dfrac{ac}{bd}$

E. $\dfrac{a}{b} \div \dfrac{c}{d} = \dfrac{a}{b} \cdot \dfrac{d}{c} = \dfrac{ad}{bc}$, where $c \neq 0$

III. Properties of rational numbers

A.

	Addition	Subtraction	Multiplication	Division
Closure	Yes	Yes	Yes	Yes, except for division by 0
Commutative	Yes	No	Yes	No
Associative	Yes	No	Yes	No
Identity	Yes	No	Yes	No
Inverse	Yes	No	Yes, except 0	No

B. Distributive property of multiplication over addition for rational numbers x, y, and z:

$$x(y + z) = xy + xz.$$

C. Denseness property: Between any two rational numbers, there is another rational number.

D. Multiplication Property of Equality: If $\dfrac{a}{b}$ and $\dfrac{c}{d}$ are any rational numbers such that $\dfrac{a}{b} = \dfrac{c}{d}$, and $\dfrac{e}{f}$ is any rational number, then $\dfrac{a}{b} \cdot \dfrac{e}{f} = \dfrac{c}{d} \cdot \dfrac{e}{f}$.

E. Multiplication Property of Zero for Rational Numbers: If $\dfrac{a}{b}$ is any rational number, then $\dfrac{a}{b} \cdot 0 = 0 = 0 \cdot \dfrac{a}{b}$.

CHAPTER REVIEW

1. For each of the following, draw a diagram illustrating the fraction:

   a. $\dfrac{3}{4}$ **b.** $\dfrac{2}{3}$ **c.** $\dfrac{3}{4} \cdot \dfrac{2}{3}$

2. Write three rational numbers equal to $\dfrac{5}{6}$.

3. Reduce each of the following rational numbers to simplest form:

   a. $\dfrac{24}{28}$ **b.** $\dfrac{ax^2}{bx}$ **c.** $\dfrac{0}{17}$

   d. $\dfrac{45}{81}$ **e.** $\dfrac{b^2 + bx}{b + x}$ **f.** $\dfrac{16}{216}$

4. Replace the comma with >, <, or = in each of the following pairs to make a true statement:

   a. $\dfrac{6}{10}, \dfrac{120}{200}$ **b.** $\dfrac{-3}{4}, \dfrac{-5}{6}$

   c. $\left(\dfrac{4}{5}\right)^{10}, \left(\dfrac{4}{5}\right)^{20}$ **d.** $\left(1 + \dfrac{1}{3}\right)^2, \left(1 + \dfrac{1}{3}\right)^3$

5. Find the additive and multiplicative inverses for each of the following:

   a. 3   **b.** $3\dfrac{1}{7}$ **c.** $\dfrac{5}{6}$ **d.** $-\dfrac{3}{4}$

6. Order the following numbers from least to greatest:

   $-1\dfrac{7}{8}, 0, -2\dfrac{1}{3}, \dfrac{69}{140}, \dfrac{71}{140}, \left(\dfrac{71}{140}\right)^{300}, \dfrac{1}{2}, \left(\dfrac{74}{73}\right)^{300}$

7. John has $54\dfrac{1}{4}$ yd of material. If he needs to cut the cloth into pieces that are $3\dfrac{1}{12}$ yd long, how many pieces can he cut? How much material will be left over?

8. Without actually performing the given operations, choose the most appropriate estimation (among the numbers in parentheses) for the following expressions:

   a. $\dfrac{30\frac{3}{8}}{4\frac{1}{9}} \cdot \dfrac{8\frac{1}{3}}{3\frac{8}{9}}$ (15, 20, 8)

   b. $\left(\dfrac{3}{800} + \dfrac{4}{5000} + \dfrac{15}{6}\right) \cdot 6$ (15, 0, 132)

   c. $\dfrac{1}{407} \cdot \dfrac{1}{1609}$ $\left(\dfrac{1}{4}, 4, 0\right)$

9. Justify the invert-and-multiply algorithm for division of rational numbers.

10. The ratio of boys to girls in Mr. Good's class is 3 to 5, the ratio of boys to girls in Ms. Garcia's is the same, and you know that there are 15 girls in Ms. Garcia's class. How many boys are in Ms. Garcia's class?

11. Find two rational numbers between $\dfrac{3}{4}$ and $\dfrac{4}{5}$.

12. Suppose the $\boxed{\div}$ button on your calculator is broken, but the $\boxed{1/x}$ button works. Explain how you could compute 504792/23.

13. Jim is starting a diet. When he arrived home, he ate $\dfrac{1}{3}$ of the half of pizza that was left from the previous night. The whole pizza contains approximately 2000 calories. How many calories did Jim consume?

14. If a person got heads on a flip of a fair coin one half the time and obtained 376 heads, how many times was the coin flipped?

15. If a person obtained 240 heads when flipping a coin 1000 times, what fraction of the time did the person obtain heads? Put the answer in simplest form.

16. If the University of New Mexico won 3/4 of its women's basketball games and 5/8 of its men's basketball games, explain whether it is reasonable to say that the University won 3/4 + 5/8 of its basketball games.

17. Explain why a negative rational number times a negative rational number is a positive rational number.

18. A student argues that the following fraction is not a rational number because it is not the quotient of two integers:

$$\frac{\frac{2}{3}}{\frac{3}{4}}$$

How would you respond?

19. If 2/3 of all students in the Academy are female and 2/5 of those are blondes, what fraction describes the number of blond females in the Academy?

20. What fraction of an hour is the minute hand of a clock not directly pointing at a numeral?

21. Explain which is greater: $^{-}11/9$ or $^{-}12/10$.

SELECTED BIBLIOGRAPHY

Bezuk, N. "Fractions in the Early Childhood Mathematics Curriculum." *Arithmetic Teacher* 35 (February 1988):56–60.

Blocksma, M. *Reading the Numbers: A Survival Guide to the Measurements, Numbers and Sizes Encountered in Everyday Life.* New York: Penguin Books, Ltd., 1989.

Collyer, S. "Adding Fractions." *Mathematics Teaching* 116 (September 1986):9.

Conaway, B., and R. Midkiff. "Connecting Literature, Language, and Fractions." *Arithmetic Teacher* 41 (April 1994): 430–434.

Cramer, K., and N. Bezuk. "Multiplication of Fractions: Teaching for Understanding." *Arithmetic Teacher* 39 (November 1991):34–37.

Edge, D. "Fractions and Panes." *Arithmetic Teacher* 34 (April 1987):13–17.

Ettline, J. "A Uniform Approach to Fractions." *Arithmetic Teacher* 32 (March 1985):42–43.

Friel, J., and G. Gannon. " 'What If . . . ?' A Case in Point." *Mathematics Teacher* 88 (April 1995):320–322.

Kalman, D. "Up Fractions! Up *n/m*!" *Arithmetic Teacher* 32 (April 1985):42–43.

Kennard, R. "Interpreting Fraction Form." *Mathematics Teaching* 112 (September 1985):46–47.

Lester, F. "Teacher Education: Preparing Teachers to Teach Rational Numbers." *Arithmetic Teacher* 31 (February 1984):54–56.

Mack, N. "Making Connections to Understand Fractions." *Arithmetic Teacher* 40 (February 1993):362–364.

Malcolm, P. S. "Understanding Rational Numbers." *Mathematics Teacher* 80 (October 1987):518–521.

Mathematical Association of America and National Council of Teachers of Mathematics. *A Sourcebook of Applications of School Mathematics.* Ed. by D. Bushaw et al. Reston: National Council of Teachers of Mathematics, 1980.

Nelson, D., et al. *Multicultural Mathematics: Teaching Mathematics from a Global Perspective.* Oxford: Oxford University Press, 1993.

Olson, A. *Mathematics through Paper Folding.* Reston: National Council of Teachers of Mathematics, 1975.

Ott, J. "A Unified Approach to Multiplying Fractions." *Arithmetic Teacher* 37 (March 1990):47–49.

Payne, J., and A. Towsley. "Implementing the Standards: Implications of NCTM's Standards for Teaching Fractions and Decimals." *Arithmetic Teacher* 37 (April 1990):23–26.

Post, T. "Fractions and Other Rational Numbers." *Arithmetic Teacher* 37 (September 1989):3, 28.

Post, T., and K. Cramer. "Research into Practice: Children's Strategies in Ordering Rational Numbers." *Arithmetic Teacher* 35 (October 1987):33–35.

Reys, B. "Promoting Number Sense in the Middle Grades." *Mathematics Teaching in the Middle School* 1 (September-October, 1994):114–120.

Steiner, E. "Division of Fractions: Developing Conceptual Sense with Dollars and Cents." *Arithmetic Teacher* 34 (May 1987):36–42.

Sweetland, R. "Understanding Multiplication of Fractions." *Arithmetic Teacher* 32 (September 1984):48–52.

Trafton, P., J. Zawojewski, R. Reys, and B. Reys. "Estimation with 'Nice' Fractions." *Mathematics Teacher* 79 (November 1986):629–630.

Van de Walle, J., and C. Thompson. "Fractions with Fraction Strips." *Arithmetic Teacher* 32 (December 1984):48–52.

Weygang, P. "Applications for the Classroom — Any Grade." *Applications in School Mathematics,* ed. by Sidney Sharron and Robert E. Reys. Reston: National Council of Teachers of Mathematics, 1979.

6

EXPONENTS AND DECIMALS

The dimensions of bacterial cells are measured in microns, where a micron is 0.001 mm. Under suitable conditions, bacterial cells divide in half every 20 to 30 min. If there are initially 100 bacteria that divide every 30 min and none of the bacteria die, approximately how many bacteria will there be after 10 days? If each bacterial cell is 4 microns long, what would be the total length of the bacteria in kilometers after 10 days if they were placed end to end?

A lthough the Hindu-Arabic numeration system discussed in Chapter 3 was perfected around the sixth century, the extension of the system to decimals by the Dutch scientist Simon Stevin did not take place until about a thousand years later. The only significant improvement in the system since Stevin's time has been in notation. Even today there is no universally accepted form of writing a decimal point. For example in the United States, we write 6.75; in England, this number is written as $6 \cdot 75$; and in Germany and France, it is written 6,75.

Decimals are a natural extension of our base-ten system. Arithmetic operations on decimals are often much easier than on rational numbers. We emphasize the appropriateness of a given representation depending on the situation, as recommended by the *Standards* (p. 88):

▲ *Discussing the appropriateness of certain representations in a given situation, such as the fact that it is better to write "68/100 dollars" on a check than reduce to "17/25 dollars," helps students recognize that there is no single, uniform way to represent a fraction but that the "best" way depends largely on the situation. Students learn, for example, that $\frac{15}{100}, \frac{3}{20},$ 0.15, and 15% are all representations of the same number, appropriate for a fraction of a dollar on a bank check, the probability of winning a game, the tax on a purchase of $2.98, and a discount, respectively. Similarly, they learn that +8, $\frac{8}{1}$, and 8.0 are all appropriate representations of the same number, depending on whether they are subtracting integers, adding fractions, or labeling a coordinate axis with rational numbers.*

To perform various operations with decimals, students must be familiar with exponents and their properties. Very large and very small numbers are commonly reported in scientific notation, which involves the use of positive and negative integer exponents, respectively. For this reason we start with a brief introduction to exponential notation and properties of integer exponents.

Section 6-1 | Integer Exponents and Decimals

Integer Exponents

Recall that a^m was defined for any number a and any natural number m as follows.

Definition of a to the mth Power

$a^m = \underbrace{a \cdot a \cdot a \ldots a}_{m\ factors}$, where a is any rational number and m is any natural number.

From the definition, $a^3 \cdot a^2 = (a \cdot a \cdot a) \cdot (a \cdot a) = a^{3+2}$. In a similar way, it follows that

(1) $$a^m \cdot a^n = a^{m+n},$$

where a is any number and m and n are natural numbers. The definition of a^m is valid if m is a whole number not 0. It is useful, however, to give meaning to a^0 when $a \neq 0$. How should it be defined? It would be convenient if all exponents satisfied the same properties, so we would like the exponent 0 to satisfy Eq. (1). If we substitute $m = 0$, Eq. (1) then becomes $a^0 \cdot a^n = a^{0+n} = a^n$. Because 1 is the only number that on multiplying by a^n gives a^n, we must have

(2) $$a^0 = 1, \text{ if } a \neq 0.$$

With the definition of a^0, Eq. (1) holds for any whole numbers m and n as long as 0^0 is not used.

These notions can be extended for rational number values of a. For example, consider the following:

$$\left(\frac{2}{3}\right)^4 = \frac{2}{3} \cdot \frac{2}{3} \cdot \frac{2}{3} \cdot \frac{2}{3}$$

$$\left(\frac{2}{3}\right)^2 \cdot \left(\frac{2}{3}\right)^3 = \left(\frac{2}{3} \cdot \frac{2}{3}\right) \cdot \left(\frac{2}{3} \cdot \frac{2}{3} \cdot \frac{2}{3}\right) = \left(\frac{2}{3}\right)^{2+3} = \left(\frac{2}{3}\right)^5$$

In general it can be shown that Eq. (1) holds when a is any rational number and consequently Eq. (2) remains true if a is a rational number and $a \neq 0$.

Exponents can also be extended to negative integers. Notice that as the exponents decrease by 1, the numbers on the right are divided by 10. Thus the pattern might be continued, as shown.

$$10^3 = 10 \cdot 10 \cdot 10$$
$$10^2 = 10 \cdot 10$$
$$10^1 = 10$$
$$10^0 = 1$$
$$10^{-1} = \frac{1}{10} = \frac{1}{10^1}$$
$$10^{-2} = \frac{1}{10} \cdot \frac{1}{10} = \frac{1}{10^2}$$
$$10^{-3} = \frac{1}{10^2} \cdot \frac{1}{10} = \frac{1}{10^3}$$

If the pattern is extended, then we would predict that $10^{-n} = \frac{1}{10^n}$. This is true, and in general, for any nonzero number a, $a^{-n} = \frac{1}{a^n}$.

REMARK   Another explanation for the definition of a^{-n} is as follows. If the property $a^m \cdot a^n = a^{m+n}$ is to hold for all integer exponents, then $a^{-n} \cdot a^n = a^{-n+n} = a^0 = 1$. Thus a^{-n} is the multiplicative inverse of a^n, and consequently, $a^{-n} = \frac{1}{a^n}$.

Consider whether the property $a^m \cdot a^n = a^{m+n}$ can be extended to include all powers of a, where the exponents are integers. For example, is it true that $2^4 \cdot 2^{-3} = 2^{4+-3} = 2^1$? The definitions of 2^{-3} and the properties of nonnegative exponents ensure this is true, as shown next:

$$2^4 \cdot 2^{-3} = 2^4 \cdot \frac{1}{2^3} = \frac{2^4}{2^3} = \frac{2^1 \cdot 2^3}{2^3} = 2^1$$

Also, $2^{-4} \cdot 2^{-3} = 2^{-4 + -3} = 2^{-7}$ is true because

$$2^{-4} \cdot 2^{-3} = \frac{1}{2^4} \cdot \frac{1}{2^3} = \frac{1 \cdot 1}{2^4 \cdot 2^3} = \frac{1}{2^{4+3}} = \frac{1}{2^7} = 2^{-7}.$$

In general, with integer exponents, the following property holds.

Property

For any nonzero rational number a and any integers m and n, $a^m \cdot a^n = a^{m+n}$.

Other properties of exponents can be developed by using the properties of rational numbers. For example,

$$\frac{2^5}{2^3} = \frac{2^3 \cdot 2^2}{2^3} = 2^2 = 2^{5-3} \qquad \frac{2^5}{2^8} = \frac{2^5}{2^5 \cdot 2^3} = \frac{1}{2^3} = 2^{-3} = 2^{5-8}.$$

With integer exponents, the following property holds.

Property

For any rational number a such that $a \neq 0$ and for any integers m and n, $\dfrac{a^m}{a^n} = a^{m-n}$.

At times, we may encounter an expression like $(2^4)^3$. This expression can be written as a single power of 2 as follows:

$$(2^4)^3 = 2^4 \cdot 2^4 \cdot 2^4 = 2^{4+4+4} = 2^{3 \cdot 4} = 2^{12}$$

In general, if a is a nonzero rational number and m and n are positive integers, then

$$(a^m)^n = \underbrace{a^m \cdot a^m \cdot a^m \cdot \ldots \cdot a^m}_{n \text{ factors}} = \overbrace{a^{m+m+\ldots+m}}^{n \text{ terms}} = a^{nm} = a^{mn}.$$

Does this property hold for negative-integer exponents? For example, does $(2^3)^{-4} = 2^{(3)(-4)} = 2^{-12}$? The answer is yes because $(2^3)^{-4} = \dfrac{1}{(2^3)^4} = \dfrac{1}{2^{12}} = 2^{-12}$. Also, $(2^{-3})^4 = \left(\dfrac{1}{2^3}\right)^4 = \dfrac{1}{2^3} \cdot \dfrac{1}{2^3} \cdot \dfrac{1}{2^3} \cdot \dfrac{1}{2^3} = \dfrac{1^4}{(2^3)^4} = \dfrac{1}{2^{12}} = 2^{-12}$.

Property

For any rational number $a \neq 0$ and any integers m and n,

$$(a^m)^n = a^{mn}.$$

Using the definitions and properties developed, we can derive additional properties. Notice, for example, that

$$\left(\frac{2}{3}\right)^4 = \frac{2}{3} \cdot \frac{2}{3} \cdot \frac{2}{3} \cdot \frac{2}{3} = \frac{2 \cdot 2 \cdot 2 \cdot 2}{3 \cdot 3 \cdot 3 \cdot 3} = \frac{2^4}{3^4}.$$

This property can be generalized as follows.

For any nonzero rational number $\dfrac{a}{b}$ and any integer m,

$$\left(\frac{a}{b}\right)^{m} = \frac{a^{m}}{b^{m}}.$$

From the definition of negative exponents, the above property, and division of fractions, we have

$$\left(\frac{a}{b}\right)^{-m} = \frac{1}{\left(\dfrac{a}{b}\right)^{m}} = \frac{1}{\dfrac{a^{m}}{b^{m}}} = \frac{b^{m}}{a^{m}} = \left(\frac{b}{a}\right)^{m}.$$

Consequently, $\left(\dfrac{a}{b}\right)^{-m} = \left(\dfrac{b}{a}\right)^{m}$.

A property similar to this holds for multiplication. For example,

$$(2 \cdot 3)^{-3} = \frac{1}{(2 \cdot 3)^{3}} = \frac{1}{2^{3} \cdot 3^{3}} = \left(\frac{1}{2^{3}}\right) \cdot \left(\frac{1}{3^{3}}\right) = 2^{-3} \cdot 3^{-3}$$

and in general, it is true that $(a \cdot b)^{m} = a^{m} \cdot b^{m}$ if a and b are rational numbers and m is an integer.

The definitions and properties of exponents are summarized in the following list. For any rational numbers a and b and integers m and n (as long as 0^{0} does not appear), we have the following:

1. $a^{m} = \underbrace{a \cdot a \cdot a \cdot \ldots \cdot a}$, where m is a positive integer

   $\qquad\qquad m$ factors

2. $a^{0} = 1$, where $a \neq 0$

3. $a^{-m} = \dfrac{1}{a^{m}}$, where $a \neq 0$

4. $a^{m} \cdot a^{n} = a^{m+n}$

5. $\dfrac{a^{m}}{a^{n}} = a^{m-n}$, where $a \neq 0$

6. $(a^{m})^{n} = a^{mn}$

7. $\left(\dfrac{a}{b}\right)^{m} = \dfrac{a^{m}}{b^{m}}$, where $b \neq 0$

8. $(ab)^{m} = a^{m} \cdot b^{m}$

9. $\left(\dfrac{a}{b}\right)^{-m} = \left(\dfrac{b}{a}\right)^{m}$

Observe that all the properties of exponents refer to powers with either the same base or the same exponent. To evaluate expressions using exponents where different bases or powers are used, perform all the computations or rewrite the expressions in either the same base or the same exponent if possible. For example, $\frac{27^4}{81^3}$ can be rewritten as $\frac{27^4}{81^3} = \frac{(3^3)^4}{(3^4)^3} = \frac{3^{12}}{3^{12}} = 1$.

• • •

Example 6-1 | Write each of the following in simplest form using positive exponents in the final answer:

a. $16^2 \cdot 8^{-3}$
b. $20^2 \div 2^4$
c. $(10^{-1} + 5 \cdot 10^{-2} + 3 \cdot 10^{-3}) \cdot 10^3$

Solution   **a.** $16^2 \cdot 8^{-3} = (2^4)^2 \cdot (2^3)^{-3} = 2^8 \cdot 2^{-9} = 2^{8+^-9} = 2^{-1} = \frac{1}{2}$

b. $\frac{20^2}{2^4} = \frac{(2^2 \cdot 5)^2}{2^4} = \frac{2^4 \cdot 5^2}{2^4} = 5^2$

c. $(10^{-1} + 5 \cdot 10^{-2} + 3 \cdot 10^{-3}) \cdot 10^3 = 10^{-1} \cdot 10^3 + 5 \cdot 10^{-2} \cdot 10^3 + 3 \cdot 10^{-3} \cdot 10^3$
$= 10^{-1+3} + 5 \cdot 10^{-2+3} + 3 \cdot 10^{-3+3}$
$= 10^2 + 5 \cdot 10^1 + 3 \cdot 10^0$
$= 153.$

• • •

Decimals

The word *decimal* comes from the Latin *decem,* meaning ten. Most people first see decimals when dealing with our notation for money. For example, a sign that says a bike costs $128.95 means the cost is one-hundred twenty-eight whole dollars and some part of a

decimal point   dollar. The dot in $128.95 is the **decimal point.** Because 95¢ is $\frac{95}{100}$ of a dollar, we have

$128.95 = 128 + \frac{95}{100}$ dollars. Because 95¢ is 9 dimes and 5 cents; one dime is $\frac{1}{10}$ of a dollar, and 1 cent is $\frac{1}{100}$ of a dollar, 95¢ is $9 \cdot \frac{1}{10} + 5 \cdot \frac{1}{100}$ of a dollar.

Consequently,

$$128.95 = 1 \cdot 10^2 + 2 \cdot 10 + 8 \cdot 1 + 9 \cdot \frac{1}{10} + 5 \cdot \frac{1}{10^2}.$$

The digits in 128.95 correspond to the place value groupings: 10^2, 10, 1, $\frac{1}{10}$, and $\frac{1}{10^2}$, respectively. Each group in the last sequence is $\frac{1}{10}$ of the group to the left. Thus, 12.61843 represents

$$12 + \frac{6}{10^1} + \frac{1}{10^2} + \frac{8}{10^3} + \frac{4}{10^4} + \frac{3}{10^5}, \quad \text{or} \quad 12\frac{61,843}{100,000}.$$

The decimal 12.61843 is read "twelve and sixty-one thousand eight hundred forty-three hundred-thousandths." (The decimal point is read as "and.") Each place to the right of a decimal point may be named by its power of 10. For example, the places of 12.61843 can be named as shown in Table 6-1.

Table 6-1

1	2	.	6	1	8	4	3
Tens	Units	And	Tenths	Hundredths	Thousandths	Ten-thousandths	Hundred-thousandths

Decimals can be introduced with concrete materials. We can use a set of base-ten blocks and decide that 1 flat represents 1 unit, 1 long represents $\frac{1}{10}$, and 1 cube represents $\frac{1}{100}$, as in Figure 6-1(a). In this model, Figure 6-1(b) represents 1.23.

Figure 6-1

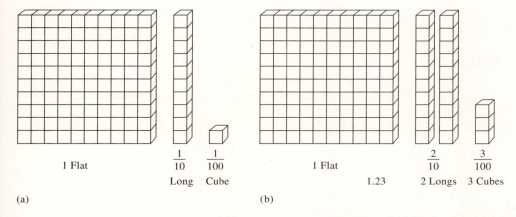

1 Flat $\frac{1}{10}$ $\frac{1}{100}$

Long   Cube

(a)

1 Flat   1.23 $\frac{2}{10}$ $\frac{3}{100}$

2 Longs   3 Cubes

(b)

To represent a decimal such as 2.235, we can think of the block shown in Figure 6-2(a) as a unit. Then a flat represents $\frac{1}{10}$ (one tenth of a block), a long represents $\frac{1}{100}$, and a cube represents $\frac{1}{1000}$. Using these objects, we show a representation of 2.235 in Figure 6-2(b).

Figure 6-2

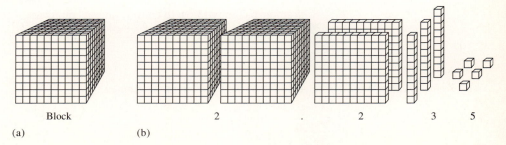

Block   2   .   2   3   5

(a)   (b)

THIENDE.   13

HET ANDER DEEL

DER THIENDE VANDE
WERCKINCHE.

I. VOORSTEL VANDE
VERGADERINGHE.

*Wefende ghegeven Thiendetalen te ver-
gaderen: hare Somme te vinden.*

TGHEGHEVEN. Het fijn drie oirdens van
Thiendetalen, welcker eerfte 27 ⓪ 8 ① 4 ②
7 ③, de tweede, 37 ⓪ 6 ① 7 ② 5 ③, de derde,
875 ⓪ 7 ① 8 ② 2 ③, TBEGHEERDE. Wy
moeten haer Somme vinden. WERCKING.
Men fal de ghegheven ghe-
talen in oirden ftellen als
hier neven, die vergaderen-
de naer de ghemeene manie
re der vergaderinghe van
heelegetalen aldus:

	⓪ ① ② ③
	2 7 8 4 7
	3 7 6 7 5
	8 7 5 7 8 2
	9 4 1 3 0 4

HISTORICAL NOTE

In 1584, Simon Stevin (1548–1620), a quartermaster general in the Dutch Army, wrote *La Thiende (The Tenth)*, a work that gave rules for computing with decimals. He not only stated rules for decimal computations but also suggested practical applications for decimals and recommended that his government adopt a system similar to the metric system. To show place value, Stevin used circled numerals between digits. For example, he wrote 0.4789 as 4①7②8③9④. Stevin also made contributions to military engineering and to physics in statics and hydrostatics. He also invented a sail-propelled carriage capable of carrying 28 people along the seashore.

Table 6-2 shows other examples of decimals, their fractional notations, and their common fractional forms.

Table 6-2

Decimal	Fractional Notation	Common Fraction
5.3	$5 + \dfrac{3}{10}$	$5\dfrac{3}{10}$, or $\dfrac{53}{10}$
0.02	$0 + \dfrac{0}{10} + \dfrac{2}{100}$	$\dfrac{2}{100}$
2.0103	$2 + \dfrac{0}{10} + \dfrac{1}{100} + \dfrac{0}{1000} + \dfrac{3}{10,000}$	$2\dfrac{103}{10,000}$, or $\dfrac{20,103}{10,000}$
$^-3.6$	$-\left(3 + \dfrac{6}{10}\right)$	$^-3\dfrac{6}{10}$, or $-\dfrac{36}{10}$

Decimals can be written in expanded form using place value and negative exponents. Thus

$$12.61843 = 1 \cdot 10^1 + 2 \cdot 10^0 + 6 \cdot 10^{-1} + 1 \cdot 10^{-2} + 8 \cdot 10^{-3} + 4 \cdot 10^{-4} + 3 \cdot 10^{-5}$$

Example 6-2 shows how to convert rational numbers, whose denominators are powers of 10, to decimals.

• • •

Example 6-2 | Convert each of the following to decimals:

a. $\dfrac{56}{100}$ **b.** $\dfrac{205}{10,000}$

Solution   a. $\dfrac{56}{100} = \dfrac{5 \cdot 10 + 6}{10^2} = \dfrac{5 \cdot 10}{10^2} + \dfrac{6}{10^2} = \dfrac{5}{10} + \dfrac{6}{10^2} = 0.56$

b. $\dfrac{205}{10,000} = \dfrac{2 \cdot 10^2 + 0 \cdot 10 + 5}{10^4} = \dfrac{2 \cdot 10^2}{10^4} + \dfrac{0 \cdot 10}{10^4} + \dfrac{5}{10^4}$

$= \dfrac{2}{10^2} + \dfrac{0}{10^3} + \dfrac{5}{10^4} = \dfrac{0}{10^1} + \dfrac{2}{10^2} + \dfrac{0}{10^3} + \dfrac{5}{10^4} = 0.0205$

• • •

We reinforce the ideas in Example 6-2 through the use of a calculator. In Example 6-2(a), press $\boxed{5}\,\boxed{6}\,\boxed{\div}\,\boxed{1}\,\boxed{0}\,\boxed{0}\,\boxed{=}$ and watch the display. Divide by 10 again and look at the new placement of the decimal point. Once more, divide by 10 (which amounts to dividing the original number, 56, by 10,000) and note the placement of the decimal point. This leads to the following general rule for dividing an integer by a power of 10:

To divide an integer by 10^n, count n digits from right to left, annexing zeros if necessary, and insert the decimal point to the left of the nth digit.

The fractions in Example 6-2 are easy to convert to decimals because the denominators are powers of 10. If the denominator of a fraction is not a power of 10, as in $\dfrac{3}{5}$, we use the problem-solving strategy of *converting the problem to one we already know how to do.* First, we change $\dfrac{3}{5}$ to a fraction in which the denominator is a power of 10, and then we convert the fraction to a decimal.

$$\frac{3}{5} = \frac{3 \cdot 2}{5 \cdot 2} = \frac{6}{10} = 0.6$$

The reason for multiplying the numerator and the denominator by 2 is apparent when we observe that $10 = 2 \cdot 5$. In general, because $10^n = (2 \cdot 5)^n = 2^n \cdot 5^n$, the prime factorization of the denominator must be $2^n \cdot 5^n$ in order for the denominator of a rational number to be 10^n. We use these ideas to write each fraction in Example 6-3 as a decimal.

• • •

Example 6-3   Express each of the following as decimals:

a. $\dfrac{7}{2^6}$ b. $\dfrac{1}{2^3 \cdot 5^4}$ c. $\dfrac{1}{125}$ d. $\dfrac{7}{250}$

Solution   a. $\dfrac{7}{2^6} = \dfrac{7 \cdot 5^6}{2^6 \cdot 5^6} = \dfrac{7 \cdot 15,625}{(2 \cdot 5)^6} = \dfrac{109,375}{10^6} = 0.109375$

b. $\dfrac{1}{2^3 \cdot 5^4} = \dfrac{1 \cdot 2^1}{2^3 \cdot 5^4 \cdot 2^1} = \dfrac{2}{2^4 \cdot 5^4} = \dfrac{2}{(2 \cdot 5)^4} = \dfrac{2}{10^4} = 0.0002$

c. $\dfrac{1}{125} = \dfrac{1}{5^3} = \dfrac{1 \cdot 2^3}{5^3 \cdot 2^3} = \dfrac{8}{(5 \cdot 2)^3} = \dfrac{8}{10^3} = 0.008$

d. $\dfrac{7}{250} = \dfrac{7}{2 \cdot 5^3} = \dfrac{7 \cdot 2^2}{(2 \cdot 5^3)2^2} = \dfrac{28}{(2 \cdot 5)^3} = \dfrac{28}{10^3} = 0.028$

• • •

A calculator can quickly convert fractions to decimals. For example, to find $\dfrac{7}{2^6}$, press $\boxed{7}\,\boxed{\div}\,\boxed{2}\,\boxed{y^x}\,\boxed{6}\,\boxed{=}$; to convert $\dfrac{1}{125}$ to a decimal, press $\boxed{1}\,\boxed{\div}\,\boxed{1}\,\boxed{2}\,\boxed{5}\,\boxed{=}$, or press

$\boxed{1}\,\boxed{2}\,\boxed{5}\,\boxed{1/x}\,\boxed{=}$. The display on some calculators may show $\boxed{8 \quad -03}$, which is the calculator's notation for $\dfrac{8}{10^3}$, or $8 \cdot 10^{-3}$. This notation, called *scientific notation,* is discussed in more detail later in this section.

terminating decimals   The answers in Example 6-3 are illustrations of **terminating decimals**—*decimals that can be written with only a finite number of places to the right of the decimal point.* If we attempt to rewrite $\dfrac{2}{11}$ as a terminating decimal using the method just developed, we first try to find a natural number b such that the following holds:

$$\frac{2}{11} = \frac{2b}{11b}, \qquad \text{where } 11b \text{ is a power of } 10.$$

By the Fundamental Theorem of Arithmetic (discussed in Chapter 4), the only prime factors of a power of 10 are 2 and 5. Because $11b$ has 11 as a factor, we cannot write $11b$ as a power of 10, and therefore $\dfrac{2}{11}$ cannot be written as a terminating decimal. A similar argument using the Fundamental Theorem of Arithmetic holds in general, so we have the following result.

Theorem 6-1

A rational number $\dfrac{a}{b}$ in simplest form can be written as a terminating decimal if, and only if, the prime factorization of the denominator contains no primes other than 2 or 5.

Example 6-4   Which of the following fractions can be written as terminating decimals?

a. $\dfrac{7}{8}$ **b.** $\dfrac{11}{250}$ **c.** $\dfrac{21}{28}$ **d.** $\dfrac{37}{768}$

Solution   **a.** $\dfrac{7}{8} = \dfrac{7}{2^3}$. Because the denominator is 2^3, $\dfrac{7}{8}$ can be written as a terminating decimal.

b. $\dfrac{11}{250} = \dfrac{11}{2 \cdot 5^3}$. The denominator is $2 \cdot 5^3$, so $\dfrac{11}{250}$ can be written as a terminating decimal.

c. $\dfrac{21}{28} = \dfrac{21}{2^2 \cdot 7} = \dfrac{3}{2^2}$. The denominator of the fraction in simplest form is 2^2, so $\dfrac{21}{28}$ can be written as a terminating decimal.

d. $\dfrac{37}{768} = \dfrac{37}{2^8 \cdot 3}$. This fraction is in simplest form and the denominator contains a factor of 3, so $\dfrac{37}{768}$ cannot be written as a terminating decimal.

REMARK   As Example 6-4(c) shows, to determine whether a rational number $\frac{a}{b}$ can be represented as a terminating decimal, we consider the prime factorization of the denominator *only* if the fraction is in simplest form.

Ordering Decimals

To find which of two given decimals is greater, we could convert each to rational numbers in the form $\frac{a}{b}$, where a and b are integers, and determine which is greater. For example, because $0.36 = \frac{36}{100}$ and $0.9 = 0.90 = \frac{90}{100}$ and $\frac{90}{100} > \frac{36}{100}$, it follows that $0.9 > 0.36$. One could also tell that $0.9 > 0.36$ because \$0.90 is 90¢ and \$0.36 is 36¢. This suggests how to order decimals without conversion to fractions. Another method is shown on the following student page from *Addison-Wesley Mathematics,* Grade 5, 1993. A similar procedure for repeating decimals is discussed in Section 6-3.

Scientific Notation

Decimals can be used to find which of two fractions is the greater. For example, to find which is greater, $\frac{3}{45,689}$ or $\frac{5}{76,146}$, we could convert each to a decimal. Many calculators will display the decimals for these fractions as $\boxed{6.5661319 \quad -05}$ and $\boxed{6.566333 \quad -05}$, respectively. The displays are in scientific notation. The first display is a notation for $6.5661319 \cdot 10^{-5}$ and the second for $6.566333 \cdot 10^{-5}$. Consequently, $\frac{3}{45,689} < \frac{5}{76,146}$.

Scientists introduced scientific notation to handle either very small or very large numbers. For example, "the sun is 93,000,000 mi from Earth" is expressed as "the sun is $9.3 \cdot 10^7$ mi from Earth." A micron, a metric unit of measure that is 0.000001 m, is written $1 \cdot 10^{-6}$ m.

Definition of Scientific Notation

In **scientific notation,** a positive number is written as the product of a number greater than or equal to 1 and less than 10 and an integer power of 10.

The following numbers are written in scientific notation:

$$8.3 \cdot 10^8, \ 1.2 \cdot 10^{10}, \text{ and } 7.84 \cdot 10^{-6}$$

The numbers $0.43 \cdot 10^9$ and $12.3 \cdot 10^{-6}$ are not in scientific notation because 0.43 and 12.3 are not greater than or equal to 1 and less than 10. To write a number like 934.5 in scientific notation, we divide by 10^2 to get 9.345 and then multiply by 10^2 to retain the value of the original number:

$$934.5 = (934.5/10^2) \cdot 10^2 = 9.345 \cdot 10^2.$$

Comparing and Ordering Decimals

EXPLORE   **Examine the Data**

Kerry found his state on a list of state populations per square mile. He looked at other states on the list and said, "It's easy to see that Nebraska has the fewest people per square mile."

State	Population per square mile
Colorado	29.2
Kansas	29.27
Nebraska	20.54
Oregon	27.31
Arizona	25.11

TALK ABOUT IT

1. At what place in the numbers did Kerry look to make the statement he made?

2. Which state on the list has the greatest number of people per square mile? How did you decide?

The steps you use to **compare** decimals are like those for whole numbers.

Compare 0.845 and 0.85.

- Line up the numbers by place value.

- Start at the left and find the first place where the digits are different.

- Compare those digits. The numbers compare the same way.

Example: 0.845
0.85

The digits in the hundredths place are different.

$4 < 5$ so $0.845 < 0.85$ or $0.85 > 0.845$

Here is one way to **order** decimals:

- Compare the numbers two at a time.

- List them from greatest to least or least to greatest.

Order 2.143, 0.214, and 2.14.
$2.143 > 2.14$ and $2.14 > 0.214$
In order: 2.143 ← greatest
2.14
0.214 ← least

This amounts to moving the decimal point two places to the left (dividing by 10^2) and then multiplying by 10^2. Similarly to write 0.000078 in scientific notation, we first multiply by 10^5 to obtain 7.8 and then divide by 10^5 or multiply by 10^{-5} to keep the original value:

$$0.000078 = (0.000078 \cdot 10^5) \cdot 10^{-5} = 7.8 \cdot 10^{-5}.$$

This amounts to moving the decimal point five places to the right and multiplying by 10^{-5}.

· · ·

Example 6-5 | Write each of the following in scientific notation:

a. 413,682,000
b. 0.0000231
c. 83.7
d. 10,000,000

Solution   **a.** $413{,}682{,}000 = (413{,}682{,}000/10^8) \cdot 10^8 = 4.13682 \cdot 10^8$
   b. $0.0000231 = (0.0000231 \cdot 10^5) \cdot 10^{-5} = 2.31 \cdot 10^{-5}$
   c. $83.7 = (83.7/10^1) \cdot 10^1 = 8.37 \cdot 10^1$
   d. $10{,}000{,}000 = (10{,}000{,}000/10^7) \cdot 10^7 = 1 \cdot 10^7$

· · ·

· · ·

Example 6-6 | Convert each of the following to standard numerals:

a. $6.84 \cdot 10^{-5}$ **b.** $3.12 \cdot 10^7$

Solution   **a.** $6.84 \cdot 10^{-5} = 6.84 \cdot \left(\dfrac{1}{10^5}\right) = 0.0000684$
   b. $3.12 \cdot 10^7 = 31{,}200{,}000$

· · ·

significant digits   In Example 6-6(a), the number $6.84 \cdot 10^{-5}$ is in scientific notation. The digits in 6.84 are called **significant digits.** Notice that if the number $6.84 \cdot 10^{-5}$ were written out in standard form, it would be 0.0000684. Even though there are eight digits in the number in standard form, only three are considered significant. Also consider the number 684,000. Written in scientific notation, this number is $6.84 \cdot 10^5$, and it too has only three significant digits. Because $604.3 = 6.043 \cdot 10^2$, it has four significant digits.

Numbers in scientific notation are easy to manipulate using the laws of exponents. For example, $(5.6 \cdot 10^5)(6 \cdot 10^4)$ can be rewritten as $(5.6 \cdot 6)(10^5 \cdot 10^4) = 33.6 \cdot 10^9$, which is $3.36 \cdot 10^{10}$ in scientific notation. Also,

$$(2.35 \cdot 10^{-15})(2 \cdot 10^8) = (2.35 \cdot 2)(10^{-15} \cdot 10^8) = 4.7 \cdot 10^{-7}.$$

Calculators with an $\boxed{\text{EE}}$ key can be used to represent numbers in scientific notation. For example, to find $5.2 \cdot 10^{16} \cdot 9.37 \cdot 10^4$, press

$$\boxed{5}\ \boxed{.}\ \boxed{2}\ \boxed{\text{EE}}\ \boxed{1}\ \boxed{6}\ \boxed{\times}\ \boxed{9}\ \boxed{.}\ \boxed{3}\ \boxed{7}\ \boxed{\text{EE}}\ \boxed{4}\ \boxed{=}\ .$$

Ongoing Assessment 6-1

1. Write each of the following in simplest form using positive exponents in the final answer:
   a. $3^{-7} \cdot 3^{-6}$ b. $3^7 \cdot 3^6$ c. $5^{15} \div 5^4$
   d. $5^{15} \div 5^{-4}$ e. $(-5)^{-2}$ f. $\dfrac{a^2}{a^{-3}}$, where $a \neq 0$
   g. $\dfrac{a}{a^{-1}}$, where $a \neq 0$ h. $\dfrac{a^{-3}}{a^{-2}}$, where $a \neq 0$

2. Write each of the following in simplest form using positive exponents in the final answer:
   a. $\left(\dfrac{1}{2}\right)^3 \cdot \left(\dfrac{1}{2}\right)^7$ b. $\left(\dfrac{1}{2}\right)^9 \div \left(\dfrac{1}{2}\right)^6$ c. $\left(\dfrac{2}{3}\right)^5 \cdot \left(\dfrac{4}{9}\right)^2$
   d. $\left(\dfrac{3}{5}\right)^7 \div \left(\dfrac{3}{5}\right)^7$ e. $\left(\dfrac{3}{5}\right)^{-7} \div \left(\dfrac{5}{3}\right)^4$ f. $\left[\left(\dfrac{5}{6}\right)^7\right]^3$

3. If a and b are rational numbers, with $a \neq 0$ and $b \neq 0$, and if m and n are integers, which of the following are true and which are false? Justify your answers.
   a. $a^m \cdot b^n = (ab)^{m+n}$ b. $a^m \cdot b^n = (ab)^{mn}$
   c. $a^m \cdot b^m = (ab)^{2m}$ d. $a^0 = 0$
   e. $(a+b)^m = a^m + b^m$ f. $(a+b)^{-m} = \dfrac{1}{a^m} + \dfrac{1}{b^m}$
   g. $a^{mn} = a^m \cdot a^n$ h. $\left(\dfrac{a}{b}\right)^{-1} = \dfrac{b}{a}$

4. Solve for the integer n in each of the following:
   a. $2^n = 32$ b. $n^2 = 36$
   c. $2^n \cdot 2^7 = 2^5$ d. $2^n \cdot 2^7 = 8$
   e. $(2+n)^2 = 2^2 + n^2$ f. $3^n = 27^5$

5. A human being has approximately 25 trillion ($25 \cdot 10^{12}$) red blood cells, each with an average radius of $4 \cdot 10^{-3}$ mm (millimeters).
   a. If these cells were placed end to end in a line, how long would the line be in millimeters?
   b. If 1 km is 10^6 mm, how long would the line be in kilometers?

6. Solve each of the following inequalities for x, where x is an integer:
   a. $3^x \leq 81$ b. $4^x < 8$
   c. $3^{2x} > 27$ d. $2^x > 1$

7. Determine which of the fractions in each of the following pairs is greater:
   a. $\left(\dfrac{1}{2}\right)^3$ or $\left(\dfrac{1}{2}\right)^4$ b. $\left(\dfrac{3}{4}\right)^{10}$ or $\left(\dfrac{3}{4}\right)^8$
   c. $\left(\dfrac{4}{3}\right)^{10}$ or $\left(\dfrac{4}{3}\right)^8$ d. $\left(\dfrac{3}{4}\right)^{10}$ or $\left(\dfrac{4}{5}\right)^{10}$
   e. $\left(\dfrac{4}{3}\right)^{10}$ or $\left(\dfrac{5}{4}\right)^{10}$ f. $\left(\dfrac{3}{4}\right)^{100}$ or $\left(\dfrac{3}{4} \cdot \dfrac{9}{10}\right)^{100}$

8. Suppose the amount of bacteria in a certain culture is given as a function of time by $Q(t) = 10^{10}(6/5)^t$, where t is the time in seconds and $Q(t)$ is the amount of bacteria after t seconds. Find the following:
   a. The initial number of bacteria (that is, the number of bacteria at $t = 0$)
   b. The number of bacteria after 2 sec

9. If $f(n) = \dfrac{3}{4} \cdot 2^n$, find the following:
   a. $f(0)$ b. $f(5)$ c. $f(-5)$
   d. The greatest integer value of n for which $f(n) < \dfrac{3}{400}$

10. If the nth term of a sequence is given by $a_n = 3 \cdot 2^{-n}$, answer the following:
    a. Find the first 5 terms.
    b. Show that the first 5 terms are in a geometric sequence.
    c. Find the first term that is less than $\dfrac{3}{1000}$.

11. In the following, determine which number is greater:
    a. 32^{50} or 4^{100} b. $(-27)^{-15}$ or $(-3)^{-75}$

12. Write each of the following in expanded form:
    a. 0.023   b. 206.06
    c. 312.0103   d. 0.000132

13. Rewrite each of the following as decimals:
    a. $4 \cdot 10^3 + 3 \cdot 10^2 + 5 \cdot 10 + 6 + 7 \cdot 10^{-1} + 8 \cdot 10^{-2}$
    b. $4 \cdot 10^3 + 6 \cdot 10^{-1} + 8 \cdot 10^{-3}$
    c. $4 \cdot 10^4 + 3 \cdot 10^{-2}$
    d. $2 \cdot 10^{-1} + 4 \cdot 10^{-4} + 7 \cdot 10^{-7}$

14. Write each of the following as numerals:
    a. Five hundred thirty-six and seventy-six ten-thousandths
    b. Three and eight thousandths
    c. Four hundred thirty-six millionths
    d. Five million and two tenths

15. Write each of the following terminating decimals as fractions:
    a. 0.436   b. 25.16   c. $^-316.027$
    d. 28.1902   e. $^-4.3$ f. $^-62.01$

16. Without performing the actual divisions, determine which of the following represent terminating decimals:
    a. $\dfrac{4}{5}$ b. $\dfrac{61}{2^2 \cdot 5}$ c. $\dfrac{3}{6}$ d. $\dfrac{1}{2^5}$ e. $\dfrac{36}{5^5}$
    f. $\dfrac{133}{625}$ g. $\dfrac{1}{3}$ h. $\dfrac{2}{25}$ i. $\dfrac{1}{13}$

17. Where possible, write each of the numbers in Problem 16 as terminating decimals.

18. Order each of the following decimals from greatest to least:
    a. 13.4919, 13.492, 13.49183, 13.49199
    b. $^-1.453, ^-1.45, ^-1.4053, ^-1.493$

19. Convert each of the following numbers to standard numerals:
    a. $3.2 \cdot 10^{-9}$
    b. $3.2 \cdot 10^9$
    c. $4.2 \cdot 10^{-1}$
    d. $6.2 \cdot 10^5$

20. Write the numerals in each of the following sentences in scientific notation:
    a. The diameter of Earth is about 12,700,000 m.
    b. The distance from Pluto to the sun is 5,797,000 km.
    c. Each year, about 50,000,000 cans are discarded in the United States.

21. Write the numerals in each of the following sentences in standard form:

    a. A computer requires $4.4 \cdot 10^{-6}$ sec to do an addition problem.

    b. There are about $1.99 \cdot 10^{4}$ km of coastline in the United States.

    c. Earth has existed for approximately $3 \cdot 10^{9}$ yr.

22. Write the results of each of the following in scientific notation:

    a. $(8 \cdot 10^{12}) \cdot (6 \cdot 10^{15})$

    b. $(16 \cdot 10^{12}) \div (4 \cdot 10^{5})$

    c. $(5 \cdot 10^{8}) \cdot (6 \cdot 10^{9}) \div (15 \cdot 10^{15})$

23. Given any reduced rational $\frac{a}{b}$ with $0 < a < b$, where b is of the form $2^{m} \cdot 5^{n}$ (m and n are whole numbers), determine a relationship between m and/or n and the number of digits in the terminating decimal. Justify your answer.

24. Which of the following numbers is the greatest: $100{,}000^{3}$, 1000^{5}, $100{,}000^{2}$? Justify your answer.

Communication

25. Explain why in the property $a^{m}/a^{n} = a^{m-n}$, we must have $a \neq 0$.

26. Explain how the property in problem 25 can be used to show why $a^{0} = 1$ for $a \neq 0$.

27. Explain how to determine when a negative number raised to a negative exponent results in a positive answer.

28. **a.** Which number is greater, 4^{300} or 3^{400}?

    b. Justify your answer to (a).

    c. What happens when you try to evaluate these numbers on a calculator using the $\boxed{y^{x}}$ key?

Open-ended

29. Use an encyclopedia or other sources to create a table for at least six large and six small quantities and their corresponding numerical values in scientific notation (for example, the nearest star, Alpha Centauri, is about 25 trillion, or $2.5 \cdot 10^{12}$, mi from Earth.)

30. Examine three elementary-school textbooks and report how the introductions of the topics of exponents, decimals, and scientific notation differ.

31. Invent games that would enhance students' understanding of each of the following (describe the rules of the games):

    a. Fractions representing terminating versus nonterminating decimals

    b. Order among decimals

    c. Scientific notation

Cooperative Learning

32. **a.** What is the greatest number that can be written using only three twos? How many digits does that number have?

    b. What is the greatest number that can be written with four twos? Estimate the number of digits this number has. (Proper use of a calculator is helpful.) Compare your group's answers with those of other groups.

33. Each member in a group should look up the size of some very small objects such as atoms, electrons, protons, and living organisms such as various bacteria and viruses.

    a. Order the objects in size from least to greatest.

    b. How many times greater is a bacterium than the smallest object you found?

    c. Compare your group's list with those of other groups in the class. What is the smallest object in all the lists?

TECHNOLOGY CORNER

The following Logo program will raise any number to a positive exponent:

```
TO POWER :BASE :EXP
  IF :EXP = 0 OUTPUT 1
  OUTPUT :BASE*(POWER :BASE :EXP -1)
END
```

    1. Run this program using various values for :BASE and :EXP.

    2. Execute PRINT POWER 2 (⁻3). What is the reason for the message displayed?

    3. Write a program for raising a nonzero number to any negative integer exponent.

Section 6-2   Operations on Decimals

To develop an algorithm for addition of terminating decimals, consider the sum $2.16 + 1.73$. In elementary school, base-ten blocks are recommended to demonstrate such an addition problem. Figure 6-3 shows how the addition can be performed.

Figure 6-3

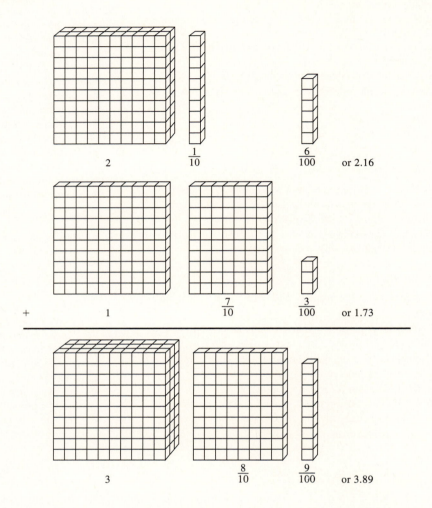

The computation in Figure 6-3 can also be approached by *changing it to a problem we already know how to solve,* that is, to a sum involving fractions. We then use the commutative and associative properties of addition to aid in the computation, as follows:

$$2.16 + 1.73 = \left(2 + \frac{1}{10} + \frac{6}{100}\right) + \left(1 + \frac{7}{10} + \frac{3}{100}\right)$$

$$= (2 + 1) + \left(\frac{1}{10} + \frac{7}{10}\right) + \left(\frac{6}{100} + \frac{3}{100}\right)$$

$$= 3 + \frac{8}{10} + \frac{9}{100}$$

$$= 3.89$$

Subtraction of terminating decimals also can be accomplished by lining up the decimal points and subtracting as with whole numbers. The following student page from *Addison-Wesley Mathematics,* Grade 5, 1993, shows this.

You have used blocks to find how many are left when you take away a decimal number. The example below shows that recording this is like recording what you do when subtracting whole numbers, except for lining up decimal points. Here is how you subtract 1.25 from 3.62.

What You Do	**What You Record**

1. Can you take away 5 hundredths without trading? How many tenths and hundredths are there after the trade?

Not enough hundredths to take away 5. Regroup.

Line up the decimal points to subtract.

$$\begin{array}{r} \overset{5\ 12}{3.\cancel{6}\cancel{2}} \\ -1.25 \\ \hline \end{array}$$

2. How many hundredths are left after you take away 5 hundredths?

$$\begin{array}{r} \overset{5\ 12}{3.\cancel{6}\cancel{2}} \\ -1.25 \\ \hline 7 \end{array}$$

3. How many tenths do you take away? how many ones?

Be sure to place the decimal point.

$$\begin{array}{r} \overset{5\ 12}{3.\cancel{6}\cancel{2}} \\ -1.25 \\ \hline 2.37 \end{array}$$

Multiplying Decimals

We can find algorithms for multiplication of terminating decimals by multiplying the corresponding fractions. Consider the product $(4.62)(2.4)$:

$$(4.62)(2.4) = \frac{462}{100} \cdot \frac{24}{10} = \frac{462}{10^2} \cdot \frac{24}{10^1} = \frac{462 \cdot 24}{10^2 \cdot 10^1} = \frac{11,088}{10^3} = 11.088$$

Notice that the answer to this computation was obtained by multiplying the whole numbers 462 and 24 and then dividing the result by 10^3.

The algorithm for multiplying decimals can be stated as follows:

If there are n digits to the right of the decimal point in one number and m digits to the right of the decimal point in a second number, multiply the two numbers, ignoring the decimals, and then place the decimal point so that there are n + m digits to the right of the decimal point in the product.

REMARK   There are $n + m$ digits to the right of the decimal point in the product because $10^n \cdot 10^m = 10^{n+m}$.

Example 6-7   Compute each of the following:

a. $(6.2)(1.43)$ **b.** $(0.02)(0.013)$ **c.** $(1000)(3.6)$

Solution   **a.**

$$
\begin{array}{r}
1.43 \\
\times\ 6.2 \\
\hline
286 \\
858 \\
\hline
8.866
\end{array}
$$

(2 digits after the decimal point)
(1 digit after the decimal point)

(3 digits after the decimal point)

b.
$$
\begin{array}{r}
0.013 \\
\times\quad 0.02 \\
\hline
0.00026
\end{array}
$$

c.
$$
\begin{array}{r}
3.6 \\
\times\quad 1000 \\
\hline
3600.0
\end{array}
$$

REMARK   Example 6-7(c) suggests that multiplication by 10^n, where n is a positive integer, results in moving the decimal point in the multiplicand n places to the right.

Dividing Decimals

Children can use play money to develop an algorithm for dividing terminating decimals, as shown in the following student page from *Addison-Wesley Mathematics,* Grade 5, 1993.

We can also approach this division by rewriting the decimal as a fraction and then using the procedure we learned to divide fractions.

$$9.42 \div 3 = \frac{942}{100} \div \frac{3}{1} = \frac{942}{100} \cdot \frac{1}{3} = \frac{314}{100} = 3.14$$

When the divisor is a whole number, we see that the division can be handled as with whole numbers and the decimal point can be placed directly over the decimal point in the dividend. When the divisor is not a whole number, as in $1.2032 \div 0.32$, we can obtain a whole-number divisor by expressing the quotient as a fraction and then multiplying the numerator and denominator of the fraction by 100.

$$\frac{1.2032}{0.32} = \frac{1.2032 \cdot 100}{0.32 \cdot 100} = \frac{120.32}{32}$$

You have divided play money into groups and recorded the amount in each group. You can use symbols to record the steps you followed. The steps are the same as when you divide with whole numbers. Here is how you divide $9.42 into 3 groups.

What You Do	**What You Record**

Show $9.42 as 9 ones, 4 dimes, 2 pennies.
Show 3 groups.

$$3\overline{)\$9.42}$$

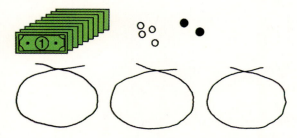

How many ones can be placed in each group?

$$3\overline{)\$9.42} \atop \quad 9 \atop \quad \overline{0}$$

⟵ 3 ones in each group

⟵ 9 ones shared in all

How many dimes can be placed in each group?

$$3\overline{)\$9.42} \atop \quad 9 \atop \quad \overline{04} \atop \quad \ \ 3 \atop \quad \ \ \overline{1}$$

⟵ 1 dime in each group

⟵ 3 dimes shared in all

⟵ 1 dime left over

Regroup 1 dime as 10 pennies.
How many pennies can be placed in each group?

$$3\overline{)\$9.42} \atop \quad 9 \atop \quad \overline{04} \atop \quad \ \ 3 \atop \quad \overline{12} \atop \quad 12 \atop \quad \ \overline{0}$$

⟵ 4 pennies in each group

⟵ 12 pennies shared in all

⟵ 0 pennies left over

This corresponds to rewriting the division problem in form (a) as an equivalent problem in form (b), as follows:

$$\textbf{a.}\ \ 0.32\overline{)1.2032} \quad \textbf{b.}\ \ 32\overline{)120.32}$$

In elementary-school texts, this process is usually described as "moving" the decimal point two places to the right in both the dividend and the divisor. This process is usually indicated with arrows, as shown next:

$$
\begin{array}{r}
3.7\,6 \\
0.3\,2\,\overline{)1.2\,0\,3\,2} \\
9\,6 \\
\hline
2\,4\,3 \\
2\,2\,4 \\
\hline
1\,9\,2 \\
1\,9\,2 \\
\hline
0
\end{array}
$$

Multiply divisor and dividend by 100.

• • •

Example 6-8 Compute each of the following:

a. $13.169 \div 0.13$ **b.** $9 \div 0.75$

Solution   **a.**
$$
\begin{array}{r}
1\,0\,1.3 \\
0.1\,3\,\overline{)1\,3.1\,6\,9} \\
1\,3 \\
\hline
1\,6 \\
1\,3 \\
\hline
3\,9 \\
3\,9 \\
\hline
0
\end{array}
$$

b.
$$
\begin{array}{r}
1\,2 \\
0.7\,5\,\overline{)9.0\,0} \\
7\,5 \\
\hline
1\,5\,0 \\
1\,5\,0 \\
\hline
0
\end{array}
$$

• • •

In Example 6-8(b), we annexed two zeros in the dividend because $\dfrac{9}{0.75} = \dfrac{9 \cdot 100}{0.75 \cdot 100} = \dfrac{900}{75}$.

• • •

Example 6-9 An owner of a gasoline station must collect a gasoline tax of $0.11 on each gallon of gasoline sold. One week, the owner paid $1595 in gasoline taxes. The pump price of a gallon of gas that week was $1.35.

   a. How many gallons of gas were sold during the week?
   b. What was the revenue after taxes for the week?

Solution   **a.** To find the number of gallons of gas sold during the week, we must divide the total gas tax bill by the amount of the tax per gallon.

$$\frac{1595}{0.11} = 14{,}500$$

Thus 14,500 gallons were sold.

b. To obtain the revenue after taxes, first determine the revenue before taxes. Then multiply the number of gallons sold by the cost per gallon.

$$(14{,}500)(\$1.35) = \$19{,}575$$

Next, subtract the cost remitted in gasoline taxes from the total revenue.

$$\$19{,}575 - \$1595 = \$17{,}980$$

Thus the revenue after gasoline taxes is $17,980.

• • •

Mental Computation

Some of the tools used for mental computations with whole numbers can be used to perform mental computations with decimals, as seen in the following:

1. *Breaking and bridging*

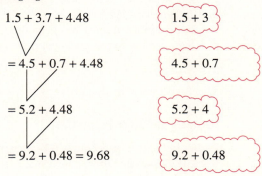

2. *Using compatible numbers*
(Decimal numbers are compatible when they add up to a whole number.)

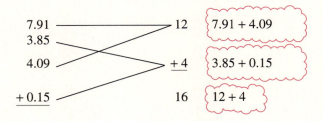

3. *Making compatible numbers*

$$
\begin{array}{rl}
9.27 = & 9.25 + 0.02 \\
+\,3.79 = & 3.75 + 0.04 \\
\hline
& 13.00 + 0.06 = 13.06
\end{array}
$$

4. *Balancing with decimals in subtraction*

$$
\begin{array}{rll}
4.63 = & 4.63 + 0.03 & = 4.66 \\
-\,1.97 = & -(1.97 + 0.03) & = -2.00 \\
\hline
& & 2.66
\end{array}
$$

5. *Balancing with decimals in division*

$$0.25\overline{)8}$$

×4   ×4

$$\frac{32}{1\overline{)32}}$$

REMARK   Balancing with decimals in division uses the property $\dfrac{a}{b} = \dfrac{a \cdot c}{b \cdot c}$.

Calculator Computations

The *Standards* (p. 94) recommends that students *select and use the most appropriate tool,* and should be prepared to *select and use appropriate mental, paper-and-pencil, calculator, and computer methods.*

For example, if a car has been driven 462.8 mi and in the process it used 11.7 gal of gas, then the number of miles per gallon is

$$11.7\overline{)462.8}.$$

This division can be done faster with a calculator than with pencil and paper.

Decimals and Their Properties

Earlier in the text, procedures for converting any rational number to a decimal were developed. For example, 7/8 can be written as a terminating decimal as follows:

$$\frac{7}{8} = \frac{7}{2^3} = \frac{7 \cdot 5^3}{2^3 \cdot 5^3} = \frac{875}{1000} = 0.875.$$

The decimal for 7/8 can also be found by division, as follows:

$$
\begin{array}{r}
0.875 \\
8\,\overline{)7.000} \\
\underline{6\ 4} \\
60 \\
\underline{56} \\
40 \\
\underline{40}
\end{array}
$$

Nonterminating Decimals

If we use a calculator to find a decimal representation for 2/11, the calculator will display 0.1818181. It seems that the block of digits 18 repeats itself. To examine what digits, if any, the calculator did not display, consider the following division:

$$
\begin{array}{r}
0.18 \\
11\,\overline{)2.00} \\
\underline{1\ 1} \\
90 \\
\underline{88} \\
2
\end{array}
$$

At this point, if the division is continued, the division pattern repeats, since the remainder 2 is the same as the original dividend. Thus the quotient is 0.181818 . . . . A decimal of this type is a **repeating decimal,** and the repeating block of digits is the **repetend.** The repeating decimal is written as $0.\overline{18}$, where the bar indicates that the block of digits underneath is repeated infinitely.

repeating decimal
repetend

Example 6-10

Convert the following to decimals:

a. $\dfrac{1}{7}$ b. $\dfrac{2}{13}$

Solution If we use a calculator to divide 1 by 7 and 2 by 13, the display will show 0.1428571 and 0.1538461, respectively. It seems that the division pattern repeats. Thus $\dfrac{1}{7} = 0.\overline{142857}$ and $\dfrac{2}{13} = 0.\overline{153846}$.

To see why in Example 6-10 the division pattern repeated as predicted, consider the following divisions:

a.

```
      0.142857
   7)1.000000
      7
      30
      28
      20
      14
       60
       56
       40
       35
        50
        49
         1
```

b.

```
       0.153846
   13)2.000000
      1 3
      70
      65
       50
       39
       110
       104
        60
        52
        80
        78
         2
```

In $\dfrac{1}{7}$, the remainders obtained in the division are 3, 2, 6, 4, 5, and 1. These are all the possible nonzero remainders that can be obtained when dividing by 7. If we had obtained a remainder of 0, the decimal would terminate. Consequently, the seventh division cannot produce a new remainder. Whenever a remainder recurs, the process repeats itself. Using similar reasoning, we could predict that the repetend for $\dfrac{2}{13}$ could not be longer than 12, as there are only 12 possible nonzero remainders. However, one of the remainders could repeat sooner than that, which is actually the case. In general, if $\dfrac{a}{b}$ is any rational number in simplest form with $b > a$ and it does not represent a terminating decimal, the repetend has at most $b - 1$ digits. Therefore *a rational number may always be represented either as a terminating decimal or as a repeating decimal.*

Example 6-11   Use a calculator to convert $\dfrac{1}{17}$ to a repeating decimal.

Solution   In using a calculator, if we press $\boxed{1}\ \boxed{\div}\ \boxed{1}\ \boxed{7}\ \boxed{=}$, we obtain the following, shown as part of a division problem:

$$\begin{array}{r} 0.0588235 \\ 17\overline{)1.} \end{array}$$

Without our knowing whether the calculator has an internal round-off feature and with the calculator's having an 8-digit display, we find the greatest number of digits to be trusted in the quotient is 6 following the decimal. (Why?) If we use those 6 places and multiply 0.058823 times 17, we may continue the operation as follows:

$$\boxed{\cdot}\ \boxed{0}\ \boxed{5}\ \boxed{8}\ \boxed{8}\ \boxed{2}\ \boxed{3}\ \boxed{\times}\ \boxed{1}\ \boxed{7}\ \boxed{=}$$

We then obtain 0.999991, which we may place in the preceding division:

$$\begin{array}{r} 0.058823 \\ 17\overline{)1.000000} \\ \underline{999991} \\ 9 \end{array}$$

Next, we divide 9 by 17 to obtain 0.5294118. Again ignoring the rightmost digit, we continue as before, completing the division as follows, where the repeating pattern is apparent:

$$\begin{array}{r} 0.0588235294117647\overline{0588235} \\ 17\overline{)1.00000000000000000000000} \\ \underline{999991} \\ 9000000 \\ \underline{8999987} \\ 13000000 \\ \underline{12999985} \\ 15 \end{array}$$

Thus $\dfrac{1}{17} = 0.\overline{0588235294117647}$, and the repetend is 16 digits long.

I N V E S T I G A T I O N   6 - 1

● In the Fibonacci sequence 1, 1, 2, 3, 5, 8, 13, 21, 34, . . . , each term starting from the third is the sum of the previous two terms. Use a calculator to investigate the behavior of the sequence by calculating the sequence of the ratios obtained by dividing each term (starting from the second) by the preceding term. The first few ratios are $\dfrac{1}{1}, \dfrac{2}{1}, \dfrac{3}{2}, \dfrac{5}{3}$, and $\dfrac{8}{5}$. In decimal form, these ratios are 1, 2, 1.5, 1.666, . . . , and 1.6.

a. Find the decimal representation of the next five ratios. What do you notice about the ratios?

b. Based on your observation in (a), determine whether the terms of the Fibonacci sequence from some term on can be approximated by a geometric sequence. Explain.

c. Using your answer to (b), approximate the fiftieth term in the Fibonacci sequence.

The following is an example in which a combination of the use of a calculator and reasoning is useful.

Example 6-12

In February 1992, the largest known prime number was discovered to be $2^{756,839} - 1$.

a. Approximately how many digits does the above prime number have?

b. Suppose all the digits of the prime number were written out next to each other. How far would the number reach if there were 5 digits per inch?

Solution **a.** If we try to compute the number on a calculator, we get an error because most calculators do not handle such large numbers. Notice, however, that $2^{10} = 1024$. Hence 2^{10} is approximately 10^3. For this reason, we proceed as follows:

$$2^{756,839} = 2^{75,683 \cdot 10 + 9} = 2^{75,683 \cdot 10} \cdot 2^9$$
$$= (2^{10})^{75,683} \cdot 2^9$$
$$= 512 \cdot (2^{10})^{75,683}$$

This last number is approximately $512 \cdot (10^3)^{75,683}$, or $512 \cdot 10^{3 \cdot 75,683}$, or $512 \cdot 10^{227,049}$. It has $227,049 + 3$, or $227,052$ digits. (Why?) Consequently $2^{756,839}$ has at least $227,052$ digits.

b. If we assume 5 digits per inch, $227,052$ digits, when written out, will be $227052/5$, or 45410.4, in. long. We calculate the length of all the digits in miles. Because 1 mi is 5280 ft and 1 ft = 12 in., 1 mi = $5280 \cdot 12$, or $63,360$ in. Hence, the length of all $227,052$ digits will be $45,410.4/63,360$, or approximately 0.7167, mi. Consequently, the prime number would reach about 0.7 mi when all its digits are written out.

Writing a Repeating Decimal in the Form $\frac{a}{b}$ Where $a, b \in I$

We have already considered how to write terminating decimals in the form $\frac{a}{b}$, where $a, b \in I$, $b \neq 0$. For example,

$$0.55 = \frac{55}{10^2} = \frac{55}{100}.$$

To write $0.\overline{5}$ in a similar way, we see that because the repeating decimal has infinitely many digits, there is no single power of 10 that can be placed in the denominator. To overcome this difficulty, we must somehow eliminate the infinitely repeating part of the decimal. Our *subgoal* is to write an equation for n without the repeating part. Suppose $n = 0.\overline{5}$. It can be shown that $10(0.555 \ldots) = 5.555 \ldots = 5.\overline{5}$. Hence, $10n = 5.\overline{5}$. Using this information, we subtract to obtain an equation whose solution can be written as a rational number in the form a/b, where a and b are integers and $b \neq 0$.

$$\begin{aligned} 10n &= 5.\overline{5} \\ -n &= -0.\overline{5} \\ \hline 9n &= 5 \end{aligned}$$

$$n = \frac{5}{9}$$

Thus $0.\overline{5} = \dfrac{5}{9}$. This result can be checked by performing the division $5 \div 9$. Performing the subtraction gives an equation containing only integers. The repeating blocks "cancel" each other.

Suppose a decimal has a repetend of more than one digit, such as $0.\overline{235}$. To write it in the form $\dfrac{a}{b}$, we can reasonably multiply by 10^3, since there is a three-digit repetend. Let $n = 0.\overline{235}$. Our *subgoal* is again to write an equation for n without the repeating part of the decimal:

$$1000n = 235.\overline{235}$$
$$-n = -0.\overline{235}$$
$$999n = 235$$
$$n = \frac{235}{999}$$

Hence, $0.\overline{235} = \dfrac{235}{999}$.

Notice that $0.\overline{5}$ repeats in one-digit blocks. Therefore, to write it in the form $\dfrac{a}{b}$, we first multiply by 10^1; $0.\overline{235}$ repeats in three-digit blocks, so we first multiply by 10^3. In general, *if the repetend is immediately to the right of the decimal point, first multiply by 10^n, where n is the number of digits in the repetend, and then continue as in the preceding cases.*

Now, suppose the repeating block does *not* occur immediately after the decimal point. For example, let $n = 2.3\overline{45}$. A strategy for solving this problem is to *change it to a related problem* we already know how to do; that is, change it to a problem where the repeating block immediately follows the decimal point. This is our new *subgoal*. To accomplish this, we multiply both sides by 10.

$$n = 2.3\overline{45}$$
$$10n = 23.\overline{45}$$

We now proceed as with previous problems. Because $10n = 23.\overline{45}$ and the number of digits in the repetend is 2, we multiply by 10^2 as follows:

$$100(10n) = 2345.\overline{45}$$

Thus

$$1000n = 2345.\overline{45}$$
$$-10n = -23.\overline{45}$$
$$990n = 2322$$
$$n = \frac{2322}{990}, \text{ or } \frac{129}{55}.$$

Hence, $2.3\overline{45} = \dfrac{2322}{990}$, or $\dfrac{129}{55}$.

To find the $\dfrac{a}{b}$ form of $0.\overline{9}$, we proceed as follows:

1. $n = 0.\overline{9}$
2. $10n = 9.\overline{9}$ (Multiply both sides of Eq. (1) by 10.)
3. $9n = 9$ (Subtract Eq. (1) from Eq. (2).)
     $n = 9/9$, or 1   (Solve Eq. (3) for *n*.)

Hence, $0.\overline{9} = 1$. This approach to the problem may not be convincing. Another approach to show that $0.\overline{9}$ is really another name for 1 is shown next:

(1) $$\frac{1}{3} = 0.33333333\ldots$$

(2) $$\frac{2}{3} = 0.66666666\ldots$$

Adding Eqs. (1) and (2), we have $1 = 0.99999999\ldots$, or $0.\overline{9}$. Can you show that $4.\overline{9} = 5$? Deciding whether $0.\overline{9} = 1$ hinges on understanding the meaning of the decimal $0.\overline{9}$. This decimal represents the infinite sum $\frac{9}{10} + \frac{9}{10^2} + \frac{9}{10^3} + \ldots$. In more advanced mathematics courses, such sums are defined as the limits of finite sums.

I N V E S T I G A T I O N   6 - 2

● Consider the following alternative approach to converting a repeating decimal to a fraction in the form $\frac{a}{b}$, where $a, b \in I$, and answer the questions that follow. If we try to convert $\frac{1}{3}$ to a decimal, we see

that $\frac{1}{3} = 0.3333\ldots$. Hence,

$$0.\overline{9} = 0.9999\ldots = 3 \cdot 0.3333\ldots = 3 \cdot \frac{1}{3} = 1.$$

Consequently,

$$0.\overline{1} = 0.1111\ldots = \frac{0.3333\ldots}{3} = \frac{1}{3} \div 3 = \frac{1}{9}.$$

Using a calculator or long division, we see that

$$\frac{1}{99} = 0.010101\ldots = 0.\overline{01}.$$

We also notice that

$$34 \cdot 0.010101\ldots = 0.343434\ldots = 0.\overline{34}.$$

Thus

$$0.\overline{34} = 34 \cdot 0.\overline{01} = 34 \cdot \frac{1}{99} = \frac{34}{99}.$$

Find a fraction in the form $\frac{a}{b}$, where $a, b \in I$, for each of the following using an approach similar to the one described previously:

a. $0.\overline{7}$ **b.** $0.\overline{07}$ **c.** $0.\overline{49}$ **d.** $0.\overline{345}$ ●

Ordering Repeating Decimals

We saw in Section 6-1 how to compare terminating decimals. To compare repeating decimals, such as $1.\overline{3478}$ and $1.34\overline{7821}$, we use a similar procedure. We write the decimals one under the other, in their equivalent forms without the bars, and line up the decimal points, as follows:

$$1.34783478\ldots$$
$$1.34782178\ldots$$

The digits to the left of the decimal points and the first four digits after the decimal points are the same in each of the numbers. However, since the digit in the hundred-thousandths place of the top number, which is 3, is greater than the digit 2 in the hundred-thousandths place of the bottom number, $1.\overline{3478}$ is greater than $1.34\overline{7821}$.

It is easy to compare two fractions, such as $\frac{21}{43}$ and $\frac{37}{75}$, using a calculator. We convert each to a decimal and then compare the decimals.

$$\boxed{2}\boxed{1}\boxed{\div}\boxed{4}\boxed{3}\boxed{=} \rightarrow 0.4883721$$
$$\boxed{3}\boxed{7}\boxed{\div}\boxed{7}\boxed{5}\boxed{=} \rightarrow 0.4933333$$

Examining the digits in the hundredths place, we see that

$$\frac{37}{75} > \frac{21}{43}.$$

Example 6-13 Find a rational number in decimal form between $0.\overline{35}$ and $0.\overline{351}$.

Solution First, line up the decimals.

$$0.353535\ldots$$
$$0.351351\ldots$$

Then, to find a decimal between these two, observe that starting from the left, the first place at which the two numbers differ is the thousandths place. Clearly, one decimal between these two is 0.352. Others include 0.3514, 0.351$\overline{5}$, and 0.35136. In fact, there are infinitely many others.

Rounding Decimals

Frequently, it is not necessary to know the exact numerical answer to a question. For example, if we want to know the distance to the moon or the population of New York City, the approximate answers of 239,000 mi and 7,800,000 people, respectively, may be adequate.

Often a situation determines how you should round. For example, suppose a purchase came to $38.65 and the cashier used a calculator to figure out the sales tax by multiplying $0.06 \cdot 38.65$. The display showed 2.319. Because the display is between 2.31 and 2.32 and it is closer to 2.32, the cashier rounds up the sales tax to 2.32. Suppose a display of 8.7345649 needs to be reported to the nearest hundredth. The display is between 8.73 and 8.74 but is closer to 8.73, so we round it down to 8.73. Next suppose the number 6.8675 needs to be rounded to the nearest thousandth. Notice that 6.8675 is exactly halfway between 6.87 and 6.868. In such cases, it is common practice to round up and therefore the answer to the nearest thousandth is 6.868.

Example 6-14 Round each of the following numbers:

a. 7.456 to the nearest hundredth
b. 7.456 to the nearest tenth
c. 7.456 to the nearest unit
d. 7456 to the nearest thousand
e. 745 to the nearest ten
f. 74.56 to the nearest ten

Solution
a. $7.456 \doteq 7.46$	**b.** $7.456 \doteq 7.5$
c. $7.456 \doteq 7$	**d.** $7456 \doteq 7000$
e. $745 \doteq 750$	**f.** $74.56 \doteq 70$

Rounding can also be done on some calculators using the $\boxed{\text{FIX}}$ key. If you want the number 2.3669 to be rounded to thousandths, you enter $\boxed{\text{FIX}}$ $\boxed{3}$. The display will show 0.000. If you then enter 2.3669 and press the $\boxed{=}$ key, the display will show 2.367.

Estimating in Decimal Computations

Rounded numbers can be useful for estimating answers to computations. For example, consider each of the following:

1. Karly goes to the grocery store to buy items that cost the following amounts. She estimates the total cost by rounding each amount to the nearest dollar and adding the rounded numbers.

$$
\begin{array}{rcr}
\$2.39 & \rightarrow & \$2 \\
0.89 & \rightarrow & 1 \\
6.13 & \rightarrow & 6 \\
4.75 & \rightarrow & 5 \\
+\,5.05 & \rightarrow & 5 \\
\hline
& & \$19
\end{array}
$$

Thus Karly's estimate for her grocery bill is \$19.

2. Karly's bill for car repairs was \$72.80, and she has a coupon for \$17.50 off. She can estimate her total cost by rounding each amount to the nearest ten dollars and subtracting.

$$
\begin{array}{rr}
\$72.80 & \$70 \\
-\,17.50 & -\,20 \\
\hline
& \$50
\end{array}
$$

Thus an estimate for the repair bill is \$50.

3. Karly sees a flash of lightning and hears the thunder 3.2 sec later. She knows that sound travels at 0.33 km/sec. She may estimate the distance she is from the lightning by rounding the time to the nearest unit and the speed to the nearest tenth and multiplying.

$$
\begin{array}{rcr}
0.33 & \rightarrow & 0.3 \\
\times\,3.2 & \rightarrow & \times\,3 \\
\hline
& & 0.9
\end{array}
$$

Thus Karly estimates that she is approximately 0.9 km from the lightning.

An alternative approach is to recognize that $0.33 \doteq \dfrac{1}{3}$ and 3.2 is close to 3.3, so an approximation using compatible numbers is $\left(\dfrac{1}{3}\right) \cdot 3.3$, or 1.1 km.

4. Karly wants to estimate the cost per kilogram of a frozen turkey that sells for \$17.94 and weighs 6.42 kg. She rounds and divides as follows:

$$
6.42\overline{)17.94} \;\rightarrow\; 6\overline{)18.00}^{\,3.00}
$$

Thus the turkey sells for approximately \$3.00/km.

When computations are performed with rounded numbers, the results may be significantly different from the original results. For example, suppose the distance, rounded to a tenth of a mile, along I-5 from Eugene to the first Albany exit is 42.6 mi, whereas the distance, rounded to the nearest tenth of a mile, from that exit to the first Salem exit is 22.4 mi. How far is it from Eugene to the first Salem exit? It seems that the answer is 42.6 + 22.4, or 65, mi. But how accurate is this answer? The distances might have been more accurately recorded as 42.55 and 22.35, when the sum would have been 64.9, or they may have been recorded as 42.64 and 22.44, when the sum would be 65.08, or 65.1 rounded to the nearest tenth. Thus the calculated sum of 65 mi could actually be 0.1 mi off in either direction. Similar errors may arise in other arithmetic operations.

Ongoing Assessment 6-2

1. If Maura went to the store and bought a chair for $17.95, a lawn rake for $13.59, a spade for $14.86, a lawn mower for $179.98, and two six-packs of mineral water for $2.43 each, what was the bill?
2. At 60°F, 1 qt of water weighs 2.082 lb. One cubic foot of water is 29.922 qt. What is the weight of a cubic foot of water to the nearest thousandth of a pound?
3. Complete the following magic square; that is, make the sum of every row, column, and diagonal the same:

8.2		
3.7	5.5	
	9.1	2.8

4. Keith bought 30 lb of nuts at $3.00/lb. and 20 lb of nuts at $5.00/lb. If he wanted to buy 10 more pounds of a different kind of nut to make the average price per pound equal to $4.50, what price should he pay for the additional 10 lb?
5. A kilowatt hour means 1000 watts of electricity are being used continuously for 1 hr. The electric utility company in Laura's town charges $0.03715 for each kilowatt hour used. Laura heats her house with three electric wall heaters that use 1200 watts per hour each.
   a. How much does it cost to heat her house for one day?
   b. How many hours would a 75-watt light bulb have to stay on to equal $1 in electricity charges?
6. Automobile engines used to be measured in cubic inches but are now usually measured in cubic centimeters. If 2.54 cm is equivalent to 1 in., answer the following:
   a. Susan's 1963 Thunderbird has a 390 in.^{3} engine. Approximately how many cubic centimeters is this?
   b. Dan's 1991 Taurus has a 3000 cm^3 engine. Approximately how many cubic inches is this?
7. Florence Griffith-Joyner set a world record for the women's 100-m dash at the 1988 Summer Olympics in Seoul, South Korea. She covered the distance in 10.49 sec. If 1 m is equivalent to 39.37 in., express Griffith-Joyner's speed in terms of miles per hour.
8. Continue the following decimal patterns (assume each sequence is either arithmetic or geometric):

a. 0.9, 1.8, 2.7, 3.6, 4.5
b. 0.3, 0.5, 0.7, 0.9, 1.1
c. 1, 0.5, 0.25, 0.125
d. 0.2, 1.5, 2.8, 4.1, 5.4
9. Find the decimal representation for each of the following:
   a. $\frac{4}{9}$ b. $\frac{2}{7}$ c. $\frac{3}{11}$
   d. $\frac{1}{15}$ e. $\frac{2}{75}$ f. $\frac{1}{99}$
   g. $\frac{5}{6}$ h. $\frac{1}{13}$
10. Describe how the following might be computed on a calculator: If a satellite flies at the rate of 1565 mph, how long would it take to reach the surface of the sun, which is 93,000,000 mi away?
11. A bank statement from a local bank shows that a checking account has a balance of $83.62. The balance recorded in the checkbook shows only $21.69. After checking the canceled checks against the record of these checks, the customer finds that the bank has not yet recorded six checks in the amounts of $3.21, $14.56, $12.44, $6.98, $9.51, and $7.49. Is the bank record correct? (Assume the person's checkbook records *are* correct.)
12. Find repeating decimals for each of the following:
    a. $\frac{1}{13}$ b. $\frac{1}{21}$ c. $\frac{3}{19}$
13. Round each of the following numbers as specified:
    a. 203.651 to the nearest hundred
    b. 203.651 to the nearest ten
    c. 203.651 to the nearest unit
    d. 203.651 to the nearest tenth
    e. 203.651 to the nearest hundredth
14. Jane's car travels 224 mi on 12 gal of gas. How many miles to the gallon does her car get, rounded to the nearest mile?
15. Convert each of the following repeating decimals to fractions:
    a. $0.\overline{4}$ b. $0.\overline{6}$ c. $1.\overline{39}$
    d. $0.5\overline{5}$ e. $^-2.3\overline{4}$ f. $^-0.\overline{02}$
16. Order each of the following decimals from greatest to least:

$$^-1.45\overline{4}, \ ^-1.\overline{454}, \ ^-1.4\overline{5}, \ ^-1.454\overline{4}, \ ^-1.454$$

17. Find three decimals between each of the two following pairs of decimals:

a. 3.2 and 3.22   **b.** 462.24 and 462.243

18. Find the decimal halfway between the two following decimals:

a. 0.4 and 0.5   **b.** 0.9 and 1.1

19. Audrey wants to buy some camera equipment to take pictures on her daughter's birthday. To estimate the total cost, she rounds each price to the nearest dollar and adds the rounded prices. What is her estimate for the items listed?

Camera	$54.56
Film	$ 4.50
Case	$17.85

20. Estimate the sum or difference in each of the following by using (i) rounding and (ii) front-end estimation. Then perform the computations to see how close your estimates are to the actual answers.

a.
```
  65.84
  24.29
  12.18
+ 19.75
```
b.
```
  89.47
- 32.16
```
c.
```
   5.85
   6.13
   9.10
+  4.32
```
d.
```
 223.75
- 87.60
```

21. The speed of light is approximately 186,000 mi/sec. It takes light from the nearest star, Alpha Centauri, approximately 4 yr to reach Earth. How many miles away is Alpha Centauri from Earth? Express the answer in scientific notation.

22. Continue the following decimal patterns:

a. $0, 0.\overline{3}, 0.\overline{6}, 1, 1.\overline{3}$

b. $0, 0.5, 0.\overline{6}, 0.75, 0.8, 0.8\overline{3}$

23. Suppose $a = 0.\overline{32}$ and $b = 0.\overline{123}$.

a. Find $a + b$ by adding from left to right. How many digits are in the repetend of the sum?

b. Find $a + b$ if $a = 1.2\overline{34}$ and $b = 0.\overline{1234}$. Is the answer a rational number? How many digits are in the repetend?

24. In each of the following geometric sequences, find the value of the indicated term. Write your answers in scientific notation.

a. $0.9, (0.9)^2, (0.9)^3, \ldots$ Find the 100th term.

b. $0.99, (0.99)^2, (0.99)^3, \ldots$ Find the 1,000th term.

c. $1.01, (1.01)^2, (1.01)^3, \ldots$ Find the 10,000th term.

d. $1.001, (1.001)^2, (1.001)^3, \ldots$ Find the 10^6th term.

e. Based on your answers in (a) through (d), state a conjecture.

25. Mary Kim invested $964 in 18 shares of stock. A month later, she sold the 18 shares at $61.48 per share. She also invested in 350 shares of stock for a total of $27,422.50. She sold this stock for $85.35 a share and paid $495 in total commissions. What was Mary Kim's profit or loss on the transactions to the nearest dollar? Explain your solution.

26. Luisa is traveling in Switzerland where the exchange rate is U.S. $1 = 1.19 Swiss francs for cash and U.S. $1 = 1.20 Swiss francs for traveler's checks.

a. Luisa is exchanging $235 in cash. How many Swiss francs will she get?

b. Luisa wants to buy a watch that costs 452.85 Swiss francs and hiking boots that cost 284.65 Swiss francs. What is the minimum number of dollars in traveler's checks that Luisa needs to exchange to purchase both?

c. Luisa wants to buy a suit that costs 687.75 Swiss francs. She has traveler's checks in U.S. dollars in denominations of $100 and $20. What is the least amount of dollars in traveler's checks she needs to exchange? Explain your solution.

Communication

27. The TGTBT Bank (Too Good To Be True) announced the following investment option. If at the end of the year the bank makes a specified profit, then it will pay investors $1.01 for each dollar for each day that dollar remains on deposit. If an investor puts $2647 in the bank on the morning of January 1 and the profit is calculated each day and reinvested, what is the maximum account balance she could have after (a) one day. (b) 2 days. (c) 365 days. Explain your solutions.

28. Explain why subtraction of terminating decimals can be accomplished by lining up the decimal points, subtracting as if the numbers were whole numbers, and then placing the decimal point in the difference.

29. Find the product of 0.22 and 0.35 on a calculator. How does the placement of the decimal point in the answer on the calculator compare with the placement of the decimal point using the rule in this chapter? Explain.

30. Investigate placement of the decimal point in the quotient obtained by performing the division $0.2436 \div 0.0006$. Explain your solution.

31. Use a calculator to find $\dfrac{26}{99}$ and $\dfrac{78}{99}$. Can you predict a decimal value for $\dfrac{51}{99}$? Will the technique used in your prediction always work? Explain why or why not?

32. The winner of the big sweepstakes has 15 min to decide whether to receive $1,000,000 cash immediately or to receive 1¢ on the first day of the month, 2¢ on the second day, 4¢ on the third, and so on, each day receiving double the previous day's amount, until the end of a 30-day month. However, only the amount received on that last day may be kept and all the rest of the month's "allowance" must be returned. Use a calculator to find which of these two options is more profitable and determine how much more profitable one way is than the other. Explain your solution.

33. A friend claims that every finite decimal is equal to some infinite decimal with all zeros from some place on. Is the claim true? Explain why or why not.

Open-ended

34. Notice that $\frac{1}{7} = 0.\overline{142857}$, 2/7= $0.\overline{285714}$, 3/7 = $0.\overline{428571}$, 4/7 = $0.\overline{571428}$, 5/7 = $0.\overline{714285}$, and 6/7 = $0.\overline{857142}$.

a. Describe a common property that all of these repeating decimals share.

b. Supposed you memorized the decimal form for $\frac{1}{7}$. How could you quickly find the answers for the decimal expansion of the rest of the above fractions? Describe as many ways as you can.

c. Find the other fractions that behave like $\frac{1}{7}$. In what way is the behavior similar?

d. Based on your answer in (a), describe shortcuts for writing $\frac{k}{14}$ as a repeating decimal for $k = 1, 2, 3, \ldots 11$.

Cooperative Learning

35. If the following pattern is continued indefinitely, the resulting figure is a *Sierpinski triangle:*

a. How many black triangles are in the tenth figure?

b. How many black triangles are in the *n*th figure?

c. Assuming the fastest computer in the world can draw 10^{12} triangles per second, estimate the amount of time it would take that computer to draw (i) the hundredth figure and (ii) the thousandth figure.

d. If the area of the first triangle is one unit, what is the area of the black region and the area of the white region in the fourth figure?

e. Work cooperatively to determine the area of the black region and the white region in the Sierpinski triangle. Discuss in your group a plan for solving the problem.

36. Choose a partner and play the <u>following</u> game. Write a repeating decimal of the form 0.*abcdef* . Tell your partner that the decimal is of that form but do not reveal the specific values for the digits. Your partner's objective is to find your repeating decimal. Your partner is allowed to ask you for the values of 6 digits that are at the 100th or larger place after the decimal point but not the digits in consecutive places. For example, your opponent may ask for the 100th, 200th, 300th, . . . digits but may not ask for the 100th and 101th digit. Switch roles at least once and see who was able to get the most digits of the partner's repetend. After playing the game, discuss in your group a strategy for asking your partner the least number of questions that will allow one to find the partner's repetend.

Review Problems

37. Which of the following are true? If a statement is true, justify it by referring to the properties of exponents. If it is false, explain why.

a. $x^{-n}/y^{-n} = (y/x)^n$ **b.** $xy^{-n} = 1/x^n y^n$

c. $(x + y)^0 = 2$ **d.** $(x^{-1} + y^{-1})^{-1} = x + y$

e. $x^m y^n = (xy)^{m+n}$ **f.** $0^{-3} = 0$

38. In the following, it is possible to find the greatest or the least integer *x* that satisfies the given condition. In each case, find such an *x* and indicate whether it is the greatest or the least.

a. $2^x \leq 1000$ **b.** $2^{-x} \geq 1000$

c. $3^{2x} > 81$ **d.** $10^x \leq 1/34,789$

39. a. Explain why $(a^4)^5 = a^{4 \cdot 5}$ without referring to the property $(a^m)^n = a^{mn}$.

b. Use the result of (a) to show that $(a^{-4})^{-5} = a^{(-4)\,(-5)}$.

40. Some digits in the following number have been covered by squares:

4 ☐☐ 3 ☐ . ☐☐ 8 ☐

If each of the digits 1 through 9 is used exactly once in the number, determine the number in each of the following cases:

a. The number is as great as possible.

b. The number is the least possible.

41. John is a payroll clerk for a small company. Last month, the employees' gross earnings (earnings before deductions) totaled $27,849.50. John deducted $1520.63 for social security, $723.30 for unemployment insurance, and $2843.62 for federal income tax. What was the employees' net pay (their earnings after deductions)?

TECHNOLOGY CORNER

The following REPETEND Logo procedure displays the repetend when a fraction is represented by a nonterminating decimal. (To find a repetend in the decimal expansion of 1/17, type REPETEND 1 17.)

```
TO REPETEND :A :B           TO REPETEND1:A :B :N
  REPETEND1 :A :B 1           PRINT QUOTIENT :A :B
END                          IF :N = :B + 1 [STOP]
                             REPETEND1 (REMAINDER :A :B)* 10 :B :N + 1
                            END
```

Run REPETEND to find the decimal expansions of 1/11, 1/17, and 1/29.

Section 6-3 Real Numbers

Every rational number can be expressed either as a repeating decimal or as a terminating decimal. The ancient Greeks discovered numbers that are not rational. Such numbers must have a decimal representation that neither terminates nor repeats. To find such decimals, we focus on the characteristics they must have:

1. There must be an infinite number of nonzero digits to the right of the decimal point.
2. There cannot be a repeating block of digits (a repetend).

One way to construct a nonterminating, nonrepeating decimal is to devise a pattern of infinite digits in such a way that there will definitely be no repeated block. Consider the number 0.1010010001 . . . . If the pattern shown continues, the next groups of digits are four zeros followed by 1, five zeros followed by 1, and so on. It is possible to describe a pattern for this decimal, but there is no repeating block of digits. Because this decimal is nonterminating and nonrepeating, it cannot represent a rational number. Numbers that are not **irrational numbers**   rational numbers are **irrational numbers.**

In the mid-eighteenth century, it was proved that the ratio of the circumference of a

π (pi)   circle to its diameter, symbolized by π **(pi)**, is an irrational number. The numbers $\frac{22}{7}$, 3.14,

or 3.14159 are rational-number approximations of π. The value of π has been computed to thousands of decimal places with no apparent pattern.

Square Roots

Irrational numbers occur in the study of area. For example, to find the area of a square, we use the formula $A = s^2$, where A is the area and s is the length of a side of the square. If a side of a square is 3 cm long, then the area of the square is 9 cm^2 (square centimeters). Conversely, we can use the formula to find the length of a side of a square, given its area. If the area of a square is 25 cm^2, then $s^2 = 25$, so $s = 5$ or $^-5$. Each of these solutions is a

square root   **square root** of 25. However, because lengths are always nonnegative, 5 is the only possible solution. The positive solution of $s^2 = 25$ (namely, 5) is the **principal square root** of 25

principal square root   and is denoted by $\sqrt{25}$. Similarly, the principal square root of 2 is denoted by $\sqrt{2}$. Note that $\sqrt{16} \neq {}^-4$ because $^-4$ is not the principal square root of 16. Can you find $\sqrt{0}$?

> **Definition of the Principal Square Root**
>
> If a is any whole number, the **principal square root** of a is the nonnegative number b such that $b^2 = a$.

HISTORICAL NOTE

The discovery of irrational numbers by members of the Pythagorean Society (founded by Pythagoras) is one of the greatest events in the history of mathematics. This discovery was very disturbing to the Pythagoreans, who believed that everything depended on whole numbers, so they decided to keep the matter secret. One legend has it that Hippasus, a society member, was drowned because he relayed the secret to persons outside the society.

In 1525, Christoff Rudolff, a German mathematician, became the first to use the symbol $\sqrt{}$, for a radical or a root.

Example 6-15

Find the following:

a. The square roots of 144
b. The principal square root of 144
c. $\sqrt{\dfrac{4}{9}}$

Solution

a. The square roots of 144 are 12 and $^{-}$12.
b. The principal square root of 144 is 12.
c. $\sqrt{\dfrac{4}{9}} = \dfrac{2}{3}$

Other Roots

We have seen that the positive solution to $x^2 = 25$ is denoted by $\sqrt{25}$. Similarly, the positive solution to $x^4 = 25$ is denoted $\sqrt[4]{25}$.

nth root
index

In general, the positive solution to $x^n = 25$ is $\sqrt[n]{25}$ and is the ***nth root*** of 25. The number n is the ***index***. Note that in the expression $\sqrt{25}$, the index 2 is understood and not expressed. In general, the positive solution to $x^n = b$, *where b is nonnegative*, is $\sqrt[n]{b}$. Substituting $\sqrt[n]{b}$ for x in the equation $x^n = b$ gives the following:

$$(\sqrt[n]{b})^n = b.$$

If b is negative, $\sqrt[n]{b}$ cannot always be defined. For example, consider $\sqrt[4]{^{-}16}$. If $\sqrt[4]{^{-}16} = x$, then $x^4 = ^{-}16$. Because any nonzero real number raised to the fourth power is positive, there is no real-number solution to $x^4 = ^{-}16$ and therefore $\sqrt[4]{^{-}16}$ is not a real number. Similarly, it is not possible to find *any* even root of a negative number. However, the value $^{-}2$ satisfies the equation $x^3 = ^{-}8$. Hence, $\sqrt[3]{^{-}8} = ^{-}2$. *In general, the odd root of a negative number is a negative number.*

Because $\sqrt{a}$, if it exists, is positive by definition, $\sqrt{(^{-}3)^2} = \sqrt{9} = 3$ and not $^{-}3$. Many students think that $\sqrt{a^2}$ always equals a. This is true if $a \geq 0$, but false if $a < 0$. *In general,* $\sqrt{a^2} = |a|$. Similarly, $\sqrt[4]{a^4} = |a|$ and $\sqrt[6]{a^6} = |a|$, but $\sqrt[3]{a^3} = a$ (why?). From this discussion, determine whether $\sqrt[^{-}4]{16}$ makes sense. Why or why not?

REMARK Notice that when n is even and $b > 0$, the equation $x^n = b$ has two solutions, $\sqrt[n]{b}$ and $^{-}\sqrt[n]{b}$. If n is odd, the equation has only one solution, $\sqrt[n]{b}$ for any real number b.

Irrationality of Square Roots and Other Roots

Some square roots are rational numbers. Others, like $\sqrt{2}$, are irrational numbers. To see this, note that $1^2 = 1$ and $2^2 = 4$ and that there is no whole number s such that $s^2 = 2$. Is there a rational number $\dfrac{a}{b}$ such that $\left(\dfrac{a}{b}\right)^2 = 2$? We use the strategy of *indirect reasoning*. If we assume there is such a rational number, then the following must be true:

$$\left(\frac{a}{b}\right)^2 = 2$$

$$\frac{a^2}{b^2} = 2$$

$$a^2 = 2b^2$$

If $a^2 = 2b^2$, then by the Fundamental Theorem of Arithmetic, the prime factorizations of a^2 and $2b^2$ are the same. In particular, the prime 2 appears the same number of times in the prime factorization of a^2 as it does in the factorization of $2b^2$. Because $b^2 = b \cdot b$, then no matter how many times 2 appears in the prime factorization of b, it appears twice as many times in $b \cdot b$. Also, a^2 has an even number of 2s for the same reason b^2 does. In $2b^2$, another factor of 2 is introduced, resulting in an odd number of twos in the prime factorization of $2b^2$ and, hence, of a^2. But 2 cannot appear both an odd number of times and an even number of times in the same prime factorization of a^2. We have a contradiction. This contradiction could have been caused only by the assumption that $\sqrt{2}$ is a rational number. Consequently, $\sqrt{2}$ must be an irrational number. We can use a similar argument to show that $\sqrt{3}$ is irrational or $\sqrt{n}$ is irrational, where n is a whole number but not the square of another whole number.

Pythagorean Theorem   Many irrational numbers can be interpreted geometrically. For example, we can find a point on a number line to represent $\sqrt{2}$ by using the **Pythagorean Theorem.** That is, if a and b are the lengths of the shorter sides (legs) of a right triangle and c is the length of the longer side (hypotenuse), then $a^2 + b^2 = c^2$, as shown in Figure 6-4.

Figure 6-4

Figure 6-5 shows a segment one unit long constructed perpendicular to a number line at point P. Thus two sides of the triangle shown are each one unit long. If $a = b = 1$, then $c^2 = 2$ and $c = \sqrt{2}$. To find a point on the number line that corresponds to $\sqrt{2}$, we need to find a point Q on the number line such that the distance from 0 to Q is $\sqrt{2}$. Because $\sqrt{2}$ is the length of the hypotenuse, the point Q can be found by marking an arc with center 0 and radius c. The intersection of the positive number line with the arc is Q.

Figure 6-5

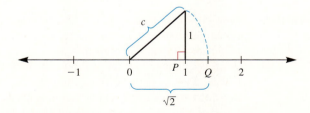

Similarly, other square roots can be constructed, as shown in Figure 6-6.

Figure 6-6

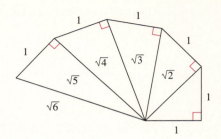

Estimating a Square Root

From Figure 6-5, we see that $\sqrt{2}$ must have a value between 1 and 2; that is, $1 < \sqrt{2} < 2$. To obtain a closer approximation of $\sqrt{2}$, we attempt to "squeeze" $\sqrt{2}$ between two numbers that are between 1 and 2. Because $(1.5)^2 = 2.25$ and $(1.4)^2 = 1.96$, it follows that $1.4 < \sqrt{2} < 1.5$. Because a^2 can be interpreted as the area of a square with side of length a, this discussion can be pictured geometrically, as in Figure 6-7.

Figure 6-7

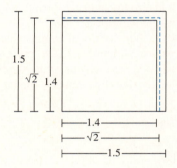

If we desire a more accurate approximation for $\sqrt{2}$, we can continue this squeezing process. We see that $(1.4)^2$, or 1.96, is closer to 2 than is $(1.5)^2$, or 2.25, so we choose numbers closer to 1.4 in order to find the next approximation. We find the following:

$$(1.42)^2 = 2.0164$$
$$(1.41)^2 = 1.9981$$

Thus $1.41 < \sqrt{2} < 1.42$. We can continue this process until we obtain the desired approximation. Note that if the calculator has a square-root key, we can obtain the approximation directly.

The System of Real Numbers

real numbers   The set of **real numbers** R is the union of the set of rational numbers and the set of irrational numbers. Real numbers represented as decimals can be terminating, repeating, or nonterminating and nonrepeating.

Every integer is a rational number as well as a real number. Every rational number is a real number, but not every real number is rational, as has been shown with $\sqrt{2}$. The relationships among these sets of numbers are summarized in the Venn diagram in Figure 6-8, where the universe is the set of real numbers and the complement of the set of rationals is the set of irrational numbers. The concept of fractions can now be extended to include all numbers of the form $\frac{a}{b}$, where a and b are real numbers with $b \neq 0$, such as $\frac{\sqrt{3}}{5}$.

Addition, subtraction, multiplication, and division are defined on the set of real numbers in such a way that all the properties of these operations on rationals still hold. The properties are summarized next.

Figure 6-8

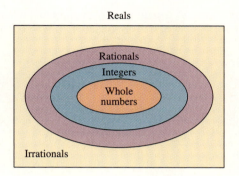

Properties

Closure Properties: For real numbers a and b, $a + b$ and ab are unique real numbers.

Commutative Properties: For real numbers a and b, $a + b = b + a$ and $ab = ba$.

Associative Properties: For real numbers a, b, and c, $a + (b + c) = (a + b) + c$ and $a(bc) = (ab)c$.

Identity Properties: The number 0 is the unique additive identity and 1 is the unique multiplicative identity such that, for any real number a, $0 + a = a = a + 0$ and $1 \cdot a = a = a \cdot 1$.

Inverse Properties: (1) For every real number a, ^-a is its unique additive inverse; that is, $a + {}^-a = 0 = {}^-a + a$. (2) For every nonzero real number a, $\frac{1}{a}$ is its unique multiplicative inverse; that is, $a\left(\frac{1}{a}\right) = 1 = \left(\frac{1}{a}\right)a$.

Distributive Property of Multiplication over Addition: For real numbers a, b, and c, $a(b + c) = ab + ac$.

Denseness Property: For real numbers a and b, there exists a real number c such that $a < c < b$.

Radicals and Rational Exponents

Scientific calculators have a $\boxed{y^x}$ key with which we can find the values of expressions like $3.41^{2/3}$ and $4^{1/2}$. What does $4^{1/2}$ mean? By extending the properties of exponents previously developed for integer exponents, we have $4^{1/2} \cdot 4^{1/2} = 4^{1/2 + 1/2} = 4^1$. This implies that $(4^{1/2})^2 = 4$, or $4^{1/2}$, is a square root of 4. The number $4^{1/2}$ is assumed to be the principal square root of 4, that is, $4^{1/2} = \sqrt{4}$. In general, if x is a nonnegative real number, then $x^{1/2} = \sqrt{x}$. Similarly, $(x^{1/3})^3 = x^{(1/3) \cdot 3} = x^1$, and $x^{1/3} = \sqrt[3]{x}$. This discussion leads to the following:

1. $x^{1/n} = \sqrt[n]{x}$, where $\sqrt[n]{x}$ is meaningful.
2. $(x^m)^{1/n} = \sqrt[n]{x^m}$
3. $x^{m/n} = \sqrt[n]{x^m}$

Example 6-16

Simplify each of the following if possible:

a. $16^{1/4}$ **b.** $32^{1/5}$ **c.** $(^-8)^{1/3}$ **d.** $(^-16)^{1/4}$

Solution   **a.** $16^{1/4} = \sqrt[4]{16} = 2$ **b.** $32^{1/5} = \sqrt[5]{32} = 2$ **c.** $(^-8)^{1/3} = \sqrt[3]{^-8} = ^-2$

d. Because every real number raised to the fourth power is positive, $\sqrt[4]{^-16}$ is not a real number. Consequently, $(^-16)^{1/4}$ is not a real number.

The properties of integer exponents also hold for rational exponents. These properties are equivalent to the corresponding properties of radicals if the expressions involving radicals are meaningful.

More Exponent Properties

Let r and s be any rational numbers, x and y be any real numbers, and n be any nonzero integer.

a. $x^{-r} = 1/x^r$

b. $(xy)^r = x^r y^r$ implies $(xy)^{1/n} = x^{1/n} y^{1/n}$ and $\sqrt[n]{xy} = \sqrt[n]{x}\,\sqrt[n]{y}$.

c. $\left(\dfrac{x}{y}\right)^r = \dfrac{x^r}{y^r}$ implies $\left(\dfrac{x}{y}\right)^{1/n} = \dfrac{x^{1/n}}{y^{1/n}}$ and $\sqrt[n]{\dfrac{x}{y}} = \dfrac{\sqrt[n]{x}}{\sqrt[n]{y}}$.

d. $(x^r)^s = x^{rs}$ implies $(x^{1/n})^s = x^{s/n}$ and hence, $(\sqrt[n]{x})^s = \sqrt[n]{x^s}$.

Property (d) could have been used to evaluate some of the expressions in Example 6-16. For example, $32^{1/5} = (2^5)^{1/5} = 2^{5 \cdot 1/5} = 2^1 = 2$.

The preceding properties can be used to write equivalent expressions for the roots of many numbers. For example, $\sqrt{96} = \sqrt{16 \cdot 6} = \sqrt{16} \cdot \sqrt{6} = 4 \cdot \sqrt{6}$. Similarly $\sqrt[3]{54} = \sqrt[3]{27 \cdot 2} = \sqrt[3]{27} \cdot \sqrt[3]{2} = 3 \cdot \sqrt[3]{2}$.

INVESTIGATION 6 - 3

● Compute $\sqrt[8]{10}$ on a calculator using the following sequence of keys:

$\boxed{10}\ \boxed{\sqrt{}}\ \boxed{\sqrt{}}\ \boxed{\sqrt{}}$

a. Explain why this approach works.

b. For what values of n can $\sqrt[n]{10}$ be compacted using only the $\boxed{\sqrt{}}$ key? Why? ●

Ongoing Assessment 6-3

1. Without using a radical sign, write an irrational number whose digits are twos and threes.

2. Arrange the following real numbers in order from least to greatest:

0.78, 0.7̄, 0.7̄8̄, 0.788, 0.78̄, 0.788̄,
0.77, 0.787787778 . . .

3. Arrange the following real numbers in order from greatest to least:

$$0.9, 0\overline{9}, 0\overline{98}, 0.\overline{98}, 0.9\overline{98}, 0\overline{898}$$

4. Determine which of the following represent irrational numbers:

   a. $\sqrt{51}$ **b.** $\sqrt{64}$ **c.** $\sqrt{324}$
   d. $\sqrt{325}$ **e.** $2 + 3\sqrt{2}$ **f.** $\sqrt{2} \div 5$

5. If possible find the square roots, correct to tenths, for each of the following and without using a calculator:

   a. 225   **b.** 251   **c.** 169
   d. 512   **e.** $^{-}81$ **f.** 625

6. Find the approximate square roots for each of the following, rounded to hundredths, by using the squeezing method:

   a. 17   **b.** 7   **c.** 21
   d. 0.0120   **e.** 20.3   **f.** 1.64

7. Classify each of the following as true or false. If false, give a counterexample.

   a. The sum of any rational number and any irrational number is a rational number.
   b. The sum of any two irrational numbers is an irrational number.
   c. The product of any two irrational numbers is an irrational number.
   d. The difference of any two irrational numbers is an irrational number.

8. Find three irrational numbers between 1 and 3.

9. Find an irrational number between $0.\overline{53}$ and $0.\overline{54}$.

10. If R is the set of real numbers, Q is the set of rational numbers, I is the set of integers, W is the set of whole numbers, and S is the set of irrational numbers, find each of the following:

    a. $Q \cup S$ **b.** $Q \cap S$ **c.** $Q \cap R$
    d. $S \cap W$ **e.** $W \cup R$ **f.** $Q \cup R$

11. If the following letters correspond to the sets listed in Problem 10, put a check mark under each set of numbers for which a solution to the problem exists (N is the set of natural numbers):

	N	I	Q	R	S
a. $x^2 + 1 = 5$					
b. $2x - 1 = 32$					
c. $x^2 = 3$					
d. $x^2 = 4$					
e. $\sqrt{x} = ^{-}1$					
f. $\frac{3}{4}x = 4$					

12. Determine for what real values of x, if any, each of the following statements is true:

    a. $\sqrt{x} = 8$ **b.** $\sqrt{x} = ^{-}8$ **c.** $\sqrt{-x} = 8$
    d. $\sqrt{-x} = ^{-}8$ **e.** $\sqrt{x} > 0$ **f.** $\sqrt{x} < 0$

13. A diagonal brace is placed in a 4 ft $\times$ 5 ft rectangular gate. What is the length of the brace to the nearest tenth of a foot? (*Hint:* Use the Pythagorean Theorem.)

14. For a simple pendulum of length l, given in centimeters, the time of the period T in seconds is given by $T = 2\pi\sqrt{\dfrac{l}{g}}$, where $g = 980$ cm/sec^2. Find the time T rounded to hundredths if

    a. $l = 20$ cm.   **b.** $l = 100$ cm.

15. The sequence $0.13, 0.1313, 0.131313, 0.13131313, \ldots$ is an increasing sequence, that is, each term is greater than the preceding one. Find the smallest possible rational number $\dfrac{a}{b}$, where a and b are integers, such that all terms of the above sequence are less than $\dfrac{a}{b}$. Justify your answer.

16. Write each of the following square roots in the form $a\sqrt{b}$, where a and b are integers and b has the least value possible:

    a. $\sqrt{180}$ **b.** $\sqrt{363}$ **c.** $\sqrt{252}$

17. Write each of the following in the simplest form $a\sqrt[n]{b}$, where a and b are integers, $b > 0$, and b has the least value possible:

    a. $\sqrt[3]{^{-}54}$ **b.** $\sqrt[5]{96}$ **c.** $\sqrt[3]{250}$ **d.** $\sqrt[5]{^{-}243}$

18. In each of the following geometric sequences, find the missing terms:

    a. $5, \_, \_, 10$ **b.** $2, \_, \_, \_, 1$ **c.** $\_, \sqrt{2}, \_, \_, \sqrt{5}$

19. The following exponential function approximates the number of bacteria after t hours: $E(t) = 2^{10} \cdot 16^t$.

    a. What is the initial number of bacteria, that is, the number when $t = 0$?
    b. After $\dfrac{1}{4}$ hr, how many bacteria are there?
    c. After $\dfrac{1}{2}$ hr, how many bacteria are there?

20. Without using a calculator, determine which is greater in each of the following. Explain your reasoning.

    a. $\sqrt{3}$ or $\sqrt[3]{4}$
    b. $\sqrt[3]{3}$ or $\sqrt{2}$
    c. $\sqrt{12} + \sqrt{14}$ or $\sqrt{11} + \sqrt{15}$

21. Write $\sqrt{2\sqrt{2\sqrt{2}}}$ in the form $\sqrt[n]{2^m}$, where n and m are positive integers.

22. Solve for x in the following, where x is a rational number:

    a. $3^x = 81$ **b.** $4^x = 8$
    c. $128^{-x} = 16$ **d.** $\left(\dfrac{4}{9}\right)^{3x} = \dfrac{32}{243}$

23. What is the value of $\sqrt[3]{(x - 2)^{-2}}$ when $x = 6$?

24. **a.** For what values of n is $\sqrt[n]{a}$ meaningful when $a < 0$?
    b. For what values of m and n is $\sqrt[n]{a^m}$ meaningful when $a < 0$?

25. Classify each of the following numbers as rational or irrational:

    a. $\sqrt{2} - \dfrac{2}{\sqrt{2}}$ **b.** $(\sqrt{2})^{-4}$

    c. $\dfrac{1}{1 + \sqrt{2}}$ **d.** $\dfrac{1}{1 + \sqrt{2}} + 1 - \sqrt{2}$

26. Graph each of the following functions for all real numbers in the indicated intervals:
    a. $f(x) = x^2,\ ^{-}5 \le x \le 5$
    b. $f(x) = \sqrt{x},\ 0 \le x \le 16$
    c. $f(x) = \sqrt{-x}$, (Choose an interval.)

★27. Prove that $\sqrt{3}$ is irrational.

★28. Prove that if p is a prime number, then $\sqrt{p}$ is an irrational number.

29. **a.** For what whole numbers m is $\sqrt{m}$ a rational number?
    ★**b.** Prove your answer in (a).

30. **a.** Show that $0.5 + \dfrac{1}{0.5} \ge 2$.

    ★**b.** Prove that any positive real number x plus its reciprocal $\dfrac{1}{x}$ is greater than or equal to 2.

Communication

31. Is it true that $\sqrt{a + b} = \sqrt{a} + \sqrt{b}$? Explain.

32. Pi (π) is an irrational number. Could $\pi = \dfrac{22}{7}$? Why or why not?

33. Without using a calculator or doing any computation, determine if $\sqrt{13} = 3.60\overline{5}$. Explain why or why not.

34. Is $\sqrt{x^2 + y^2} = x + y$ for all values of x and y? Explain your reasoning.

35. Answer the following as being true sometimes, always, or never. Justify your answers.
    a. $\sqrt{a^2} = a$ **b.** $\sqrt{(^{-}x)^2} = {^-}x$
    c. $\sqrt{(^{-}x)^2} = |x|$ **d.** $\sqrt{(a + b)^2} = a + b$
    e. $\sqrt[4]{a^2} = \sqrt{a}$

36. Without using a calculator, arrange the following in increasing order. Explain your reasoning.
    $(4/25)^{-1/3},\ (25/4)^{1/3},\ (4/25)^{-1/4}$

37. Using the $\boxed{\sqrt{}}$ key on a calculator, we find that $\sqrt{2} \doteq 1.41421356$, which is a rational number. However, $\sqrt{2}$ was proved to be an irrational number. Explain the discrepancy.

38. Consider the equation $\sqrt{x} + \sqrt{y} = \sqrt{z}$.
    a. Given any positive real-number values for x and y, is it always possible to find a positive real number for z so that the equation is true? Explain why or why not?
    b. Given positive real-number values for y and z, is it always possible to find x so that the equation is always true? Explain why or why not.

Open-ended

39. The sequence 1, 1.01, 1.001, 1.0001, . . . is an infinite sequence of rational numbers.

    a. Write several other infinite sequences of rational numbers.
    b. Write several infinite sequences of irrational numbers.

40. **a.** Place five irrational numbers between 1/2 and 3/4.
    b. Write an infinite sequence of irrational numbers all of whose terms are between 1/2 and 3/4.

Cooperative Learning

41. Let each member of a group choose a number between 0 and 1 on a calculator and check what happens when the $\boxed{x^2}$ key is pressed in succession until it is clear that there is no reason to go on.
    a. Compare your answers and write a conjecture based on what you observe.
    b. Use other keys on the calculator in a similar way. Describe the process and state a corresponding conjecture.
    c. Why do you get the result you do?

42. A calculator displays the following: $(3.7)^{2.4} = 23.103838$. In your group, discuss the meaning of the expression $(3.7)^{2.4}$ in view of what you know about exponents. Compare your findings with those of other groups.

Review Problems

43. **a.** Human bones make up 0.18 of a person's total body weight. How much do the bones of a 120-lb person weigh?
    b. Muscles make up about 0.4 of a person's body weight. How much do the muscles of a 120-lb person weigh?

44. John is a payroll clerk for a small company. Last month, the employees' gross earnings (earnings before deductions) totaled $27,849.50. John deducted $1520.63 for social security, $723.30 for unemployment insurance, and $2843.62 for federal income tax. What was the employees' net pay (their earnings after deductions)?

45. Write each of the following decimals as rational numbers:
    a. 16.72   **b.** 0.003   **c.** $^{-}5.07$ **d.** 0.123

46. Write a repeating decimal equal to each of the following without using more than one zero.

    a. 5   **b.** 5.1   **c.** $\dfrac{1}{2}$

47. Write 0.00024 as a fraction in simplest form.

48. Arrange the following from least to greatest:

$$4.09,\ 4.099,\ 4.0\overline{9},\ 4.09\overline{1}$$

49. Write $0.2\overline{4}$ as a fraction in simplest form.

50. Write each of the following as a standard numeral:
    a. $2.08 \cdot 10^5$ **b.** $3.8 \cdot 10^{-4}$

51. **a.** Show that $2^n + 2^{n+1} = 3 \cdot 2^n$.
    b. Find a result similar to the one in (a) for $3^n + 3^{n+1}$. Explain your reasoning.

52. Which of the following are true? If a statement is false, explain why.
    a. $2^n + 2^m = 2^{m+n}$ **b.** $a^n \cdot b^m = (a \cdot b)^{n+m}$
    c. $0^{-13} = 0$ **d.** $(a^{-m})^{-n} = 1/a^{-mn}$

53. Lake Ontario's salt content doubles every five years. If the present level is 25 parts per million answer the following.
  a. What will be the salt concentration of Lake Ontario after 25 years?
  b. Write an expression for the salt concentration after n years.

★**c.** If the Dead Sea has a salt concentration of 10,000 parts per million in how many years will the salt concentration of Lake Ontario be greater than that of the Dead Sea?

SOLUTION TO THE PRELIMINARY PROBLEM

Understanding the Problem. There are initially 100 bacteria, which double every 30 min. We need to find the number of bacteria after 10 days and the length of the bacteria if placed end to end. Each bacterium is 4 microns long and 1 micron = 0.001 mm.

Devising a Plan. The number of bacteria after the first 30 min is $100 \cdot 2$, and after the second 30-min, $(100 \cdot 2) \cdot 2$, or $100 \cdot 2^2$. After the third 30-min period, the number of bacteria is $(100 \cdot 2^2) \cdot 2$ or $100 \cdot 2^3$. Because after each 30 min we need to multiply the previous number of bacteria by 2, the number of bacteria after n 30-min periods will be $100 \cdot 2^n$. To find the number of bacteria after 10 days, we need to know how many 30-min periods there are in 10 days. In 10 days there are $10 \cdot 24 \cdot 60$ min and hence $\dfrac{10 \cdot 24 \cdot 60}{30}$, or 480, 30-min periods. Consequently, we need to calculate $100 \cdot 2^{480}$.

Carrying Out the Plan. The number of bacteria after 10 days is $100 \cdot 2^{480}$. To find the total length of the bacteria in kilometers, we first find the length in microns by multiplying the number of bacteria by 4 and then dividing the number of microns in 1 km. We know that $1 \text{ km} = 10^6 \text{ mm} = 10^6 \cdot 1000$, or 10^9 microns. (Because 1 micron = 0.001 mm, 1000 microns = 1 mm.) Thus the total length of the bacteria would be:

$$\frac{100 \cdot 2^{480} \cdot 4}{10^9} = \frac{2^{482}}{10^7} \text{ km}$$

If we try to use a calculator to compute $\dfrac{2^{482}}{10^7}$ an error message appears because the exponent is too large for the usual calculator. However, a calculator can compute a smaller power like 2^{48}. Consequently, we use the properties of exponents to write $2^{480} = (2^{10})^{48}$ and proceed as follows:

$$\text{Because } 2^{10} \doteq 1000,$$
$$2^{482} = (2^{10})^{48} \cdot 2^2$$
$$\doteq (10^3)^{48} \cdot 2^2$$
$$\doteq 4 \cdot 10^{144}.$$

Hence the total length of the bacteria is approximately $\dfrac{4 \cdot 10^{144}}{10^7}$ km or $4 \cdot 10^{137}$ km.

Looking Back. If we compare the total length of the bacteria to the distance from Earth to the sun, which is $1.5 \cdot 10^8$ km, we see that the total length of the bacteria is much larger than the distance to the sun.

We could check what would happen if a certain population grew at a slower pace such as by a factor 1.5 or even 1.01 every 30 min. We have also seen how by the use of the properties of exponents we could overcome the limiting power of a calculator.

QUESTIONS FROM THE CLASSROOM

1. A student claims that each of the following is an arithmetic sequence. Is the student right?
   a. 1.1, 1.01, 1.001, 1.0001, . . .
   b. $\frac{1}{2}, \left(\frac{1}{2}\right)^{-2}, \left(\frac{1}{2}\right)^{-5}, \left(\frac{1}{2}\right)^{-8}, \left(\frac{1}{2}\right)^{-11}, \ldots$

2. Why is $\sqrt{25} \neq {}^-5$?

3. A student claims that $\sqrt{(-5)^2} = {}^-5$ because $\sqrt{a^2} = a$. Is this correct?

4. Another student says that $\sqrt{(-5)^2} = [(^-5)^2]^{1/2} = (^-5)^{2/2} = (^-5)^1 = {}^-5$. Is this correct?

5. A student claims that the equation $\sqrt{-x} = 3$ has no solution, since the square root of a negative number does not exist. Why is this argument wrong?

6. A student reports that $^-438{,}340{,}000$ cannot be written in scientific notation. How do you respond?

7. A student multiplies $(6.5)(8.5)$ to obtain the following:

$$
\begin{array}{r}
8.5 \\
\times\ 6.5 \\
\hline
4\ 2\ 5 \\
5\ 1\ 0 \\
\hline
5\ 5.2\ 5
\end{array}
$$

However, when the student multiplies $8\frac{1}{2} \cdot 6\frac{1}{2}$, she obtains the following :

$$
\begin{array}{r}
8\frac{1}{2} \\
\times\ 6\frac{1}{2} \\
\hline
4\frac{1}{4} \qquad \left(\frac{1}{2}\cdot 8\frac{1}{2}\right)\\
48 \qquad (6\cdot 8)\\
\hline
52\frac{1}{4}
\end{array}
$$

How is this possible?

8. A student claims that 0.36 is greater than 0.9 because 36 is greater than 9. How do you respond?

9. A student says that the solution of $x^2 = 5$ is written as $x = \pm\sqrt{5}$ and therefore $\sqrt{5}$ has two values, one positive and one negative. How do you respond?

10. A student tries to calculate $0.999^{10{,}000}$ on a calculator and finds the answer to be $4.65173346 \cdot 10^{-5}$. The student wonders how it could be that a number like 0.999 so close to 1 when raised to some power could result in a number close to 0. How do you respond?

11. Explain how you would respond to the following:
    a. A student claims that $\frac{9443}{9444}$ and $\frac{9444}{9445}$ are equal because both display 0.9998941 on his scientific calculator when the divisions are performed.
    b. Another student claims that the fractions are not equal and wants to know if there is any way the same calculator can determine which is greater.

CHAPTER REVIEW

1. Write each of the following in simplest form with nonnegative exponents in the final answer:
   a. $\left(\frac{1}{2}\right)^4\left(\frac{1}{2}\right)^7$ b. $5^{-16} \div 5^4$
   c. $\left[\left(\frac{2}{3}\right)^7\right]^{-4}$ d. $3^{16} \cdot 3^2$

2. Write each of the following in expanded form:
   a. 32.012   b. 0.00103

3. Give a test to determine if a fraction can be written as a terminating decimal without one's actually performing the division. Explain why this test is valid.

4. A board is 442.4 cm long. How many shelves can be cut from it if each shelf is 55.3 cm long? (Disregard the width of the cuts.)

5. Write each of the following as a decimal:
   a. $\frac{4}{7}$ b. $\frac{1}{8}$
   c. $\frac{2}{3}$ d. $\frac{5}{8}$

6. Write each of the following as a fraction in simplest form:
   a. 0.28   b. $^-5.07$ c. $0.\overline{3}$ d. $2.0\overline{8}$

7. Round each of the following numbers as specified:
   a. 307.625 to the nearest hundredth
   b. 307.625 to the nearest tenth

c. 307.625 to the nearest unit

d. 307.625 to the nearest hundred

8. Answer each of the following and explain your answers:

   a. Is the set of irrational numbers closed under addition?

   b. Is the set of irrational numbers closed under subtraction?

   c. Is the set of irrational numbers closed under multiplication?

   d. Is the set of irrational numbers closed under division?

9. Find an approximation for $\sqrt{23}$ correct to three decimal places without using the $\boxed{y^x}$ or the $\boxed{\sqrt{}}$ keys.

10. Rewrite each of the following in scientific notation:

   a. 426.000

   b. $324 \cdot 10^{-6}$

   c. 0.00000237

   d. 0.325

11. What is the number of significant digits in each of the numbers in Problem 10?

12. Classify each of the following as rational or irrational (assume the patterns shown continue):

   a. 2.191199119991199991119 . . .

   b. $\dfrac{1}{\sqrt{2}}$ **c.** $\dfrac{4}{9}$

   d. 0.0011001100110011 . . .

   e. 0.001100011000011 . . .

13. Find in the following the form $a\sqrt{b}$ or $a\sqrt[n]{b}$, where a and b are integers and b has the least value possible:

   a. $\sqrt{242}$ **b.** $\sqrt{288}$

   c. $\sqrt{360}$ **d.** $\sqrt[3]{162}$

14. Suppose the amount of bacteria in a certain culture is diminishing and is given as a function of time by $Q(t) = 10^{14}(5/6)^t$, where t is time in seconds and $Q(t)$ is the amount of bacteria after t seconds. Find the following:

   a. The initial number of bacteria (that is the number of bacteria at $t = 0$)

   b. The number of bacteria after 10 sec

   c. How long it will take for all the bacteria to die?

15. Find the greatest or the least integer value of x (indicate which one) in the following:

   a. $3^x \le 1000$ **b.** $3^{-x} \le 1000$

   c. $2^x \ge 900$ **d.** $2^x \le 900$

16. Order each of the following decimals from greatest to least: 1.4519, 1.451$\overline{9}$, 1.45$\overline{19}$, 1.4$\overline{519}$, $^-$0.134, $^-$0.13401, $^-$0.134$\overline{01}$

17. Each of the following is a geometrical sequence. Find the missing terms.

   a. 5, __, 10   **b.** 1, __, __, __, 1/4

   c. $^-$0.4, __, __, 0.4   **d.** 10, __, __, __, __, 100

18. Write each of the following in scientific notation without using a calculator:

   a. 1783411.56   **b.** $347/10^8$ **c.** $49.3 \cdot 10^8$

   d. $29.4 \cdot 10^{12}/10^{-4}$ **e.** $0.47 \cdot 1000^{12}$ **f.** $3/5^9$

19. a. Find five decimals between 0.1 and 0.11 and order them from greatest to least.

   b. Find four decimals between 0 and 0.1 listed from least to greatest so that each decimal starting from the second is twice as large as the preceding one.

   c. Find four decimals between 0.1 and 0.2 and list them in increasing order so that the first one is halfway between 0.1 and 0.2, the second halfway between the first and 0.2, the third halfway between the second and 0.2, and similarly for the fourth one.

20. a. On the number line, find the decimals that correspond to points A, B, and C.

   b. Indicate by D the point that corresponds to 0.09 and by E the point that corresponds to 0.15.

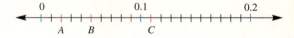

CHAPTER OUTLINE

I. Exponents

A. $a^m = \underbrace{a \cdot a \cdot a \cdot \ldots \cdot a}_{m \text{ factors}}$, where m is a positive integer and a is a rational number

B. Properties of exponents involving rational numbers

   1. $a^0 = 1$, where $a \ne 0$

   2. $a^{-m} = \dfrac{1}{a^m}$, where $a \ne 0$

   3. $a^m \cdot a^n = a^{m+n}$

   4. $\dfrac{a^m}{a^n} = a^{m-n}$, where $a \ne 0$

   5. $(a^m)^n = a^{mn}$

   6. $\left(\dfrac{a}{b}\right)^m = \dfrac{a^m}{b^m}$, where $b \ne 0$

   7. $(ab)^m = a^m \cdot b^m$

   8. $\left(\dfrac{a}{b}\right)^{-m} = \left(\dfrac{b}{a}\right)^m$

II. Decimals

A. Every rational number can be represented as a terminating or repeating decimal.

B. A rational number $\dfrac{a}{b}$, whose denominator is of the form $2^m \cdot 5^n$, where m and n are whole numbers, can be expressed as a **terminating decimal.**

C. A **repeating decimal** is a decimal with a block of digits, called the **repetend,** that repeat infinitely many times.

D. A number is in **scientific notation** if it is written as the product of a number n that is greater than or equal to 1 and an integral power of 10. The number of digits in n is called the number of **significant digits** of n.

E. An **irrational number** is represented by a nonterminating, nonrepeating decimal.

III. Real numbers

A. The set of **real numbers** is the set of all decimals, namely, the union of the set of rational numbers and the set of irrational numbers.

B. If a is any whole number, then the **principal square root** of a, denoted by $\sqrt{a}$, is the nonnegative number b such that $b \cdot b = b^2 = a$.

C. Square roots and nth roots can be found by using the **squeezing method.**

IV. Radicals and rational exponents

A. $\sqrt[n]{x}$, or $x^{1/n}$, is the **n th root** of x and n is the **index.**

B. The following properties hold for radicals if the expressions involving radicals are meaningful:

a. $\sqrt[n]{xy} = \sqrt[n]{x} \cdot \sqrt[n]{y}$

b. $\sqrt[n]{\dfrac{x}{y}} = \dfrac{\sqrt[n]{x}}{\sqrt[n]{y}}$

c. $(\sqrt[n]{x})^m = \sqrt[n]{x^m}$

SELECTED BIBLIOGRAPHY

Barson, A. and L. Barson. "Ideas." *Arithmetic Teacher* 35 (January 1988): 19–24.

Chow, P. and T. Lin. "Extracting Square Roots Made Easy." *Arithmetic Teacher* 29 (November 1981): 48–50.

Gluck, D. "Helping Students Understand Place Value." *Arithmetic Teacher* 38 (March 1991): 10–13.

Hooven, B. "Place Value Wheels." *Arithmetic Teacher* 39 (May 1992): 50.

Lester, F. "Teacher Education: Preparing Teachers to Teach Rational Numbers." *Arithmetic Teacher* 31 (February 1984): 54–56.

Malcom, P. S. "Understanding Rational Numbers." *Mathematics Teacher* 80 (October 1987): 518–521.

Payne, J. "Curricular Issues: Teaching Rational Numbers." *Arithmetic Teacher* 31 (February 1984): 14–17.

Prevost, F. "Teaching Rational Numbers—Junior High School." *Arithmetic Teacher* 31 (February 1984): 43–46.

Quintero, A. "Helping Children Understand Ratios." *Arithmetic Teacher* 34 (April 1987): 17–21.

Williams, S. E. and J. V. Copely, "Promoting Classroom Dialogue: Using Calculators to Discover Patterns in Dividing Decimals." *Mathematics Teaching in the Middle School* 1 (April 1994): 72–75.

7

APPLICATIONS OF MATHEMATICS

Some paper manufacturers have standardized the size and shape of sheets of paper. The ratio of the length-to-width of a rectangular piece of paper is such that cutting it in half, as shown, results in a rectangular piece of paper with the length-to-width ratio the same as the original piece. What is the length-to-width ratio of such a rectangular sheet of paper? Will that ratio remain the same after repeatedly cutting the paper in half, as shown in this drawing?

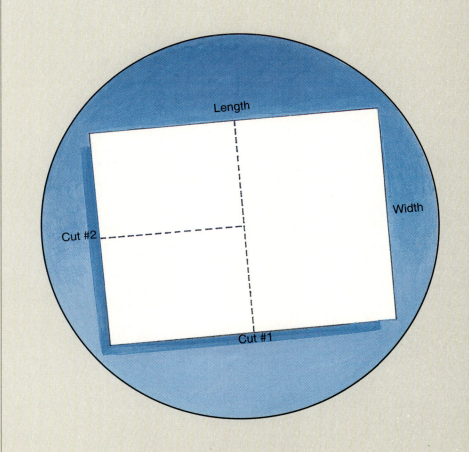

T he focus of this chapter is on applications of mathematics. A very useful tool for solving applied problems is *algebra*. In this chapter, we investigate algebraic thinking and how to solve equations and inequalities, use algebraic skills to solve word problems, graph and find equations of straight lines, and solve systems of equations. In addition, we discuss ratio and proportion and introduce the concepts of percent and interest. Throughout this chapter, the strategy of *writing an equation* is utilized.

Section 7-1 Algebraic Thinking

In each of the previous chapters, we encountered problems involving algebraic thinking. Generalizing a pattern, writing an expression for a function rule, and defining subtraction in terms of addition or division in terms of multiplication are examples of activities involving algebraic thinking. The *Standards* (p. 102) encourage teachers to engage children in a variety of activities that ease the transition from arithmetic to algebra:

It is essential that in grades 5–8 students explore algebraic concepts in an informal way to build a foundation for the subsequent formal study of algebra. Such informal explorations should emphasize physical models, data graphs, and other mathematical representations . . . .

The problem on the following student page from *Addison-Wesley Mathematics*, Grade 5, 1993 is an example of early algebraic thinking.

Working the problem on the student page, you will likely conjecture that the perimeter P of a figure is always 2 units greater than the number of triangles N in the figure, that is, $P = N + 2$. Such a rule relating two variables is an efficient and useful way to describe how two quantities are related.

Example 7-1 Table 7-1 relates the weight on the moon and the weight on Earth measured in the same units.

Table 7-1

Weight on Earth (lb)	1	2	3	4	5	100
Weight on Moon (lb)	0.16	0.32	0.48	0.64	0.80	16

Find the following:

a. Jody's weight on the moon if her weight on Earth is 120 lb.
b. A relationship between the weight of an object on the moon and its weight on Earth.
c. The weight on Earth of an object that weighs 100 lb on the moon.

Solution

a. Table 7-1 suggests that the weight on the moon is 0.16 times the weight of the same object on Earth. Hence Jody's weight of 120 lb on Earth is 0.16 · 120, or 19.2, lb on the moon.
b. If M is the weight on the moon and E the weight of the same object on Earth, we have

$$M = 0.16E.$$

c. Because the weight on the moon is 100, we substitute 100 into the formula in (b) as shown.

$$100 = 0.16E.$$

Exploring Algebra
More About Variables

You have learned that a **variable** can
stand for a single unknown number. A
variable can also be used to stand for a
range of numbers.

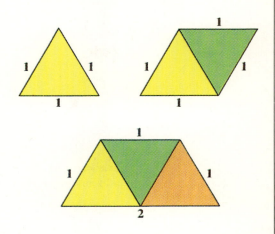

LEARN ABOUT IT

Work in groups.
Copy and complete the table at the right.
Make or draw triangles if you find that
helpful. Look for patterns.

Number of triangles	1	2	3	4	5	6	7	8	9	10
Perimeter	3	4	5							

TALK ABOUT IT

1. What is the perimeter when there are 6 triangles?

2. What is the perimeter when there are 10 triangles?

3. If you know the number of triangles, how can you find
   the perimeter?

In the table above, the number of triangles varies from 1 to
10. The perimeter varies from 3 to 12. Suppose N stands
for the number of triangles and P stands for the perimeter.
N and P are variables.

Using the definition of division, we obtain

$$\frac{100}{0.16} = E \quad \text{or} \quad E = 625 \text{ lb.}$$

Thus an object weighing 100 lb on the moon will weigh 625 lb on Earth.

• • •

Example 7-2   The owner of a storage company is planning to build square-type units arranged in 2 rows
and sharing walls as shown in Figure 7-1. Because the walls are readily available, the
designer wants to find a formula that will give the number of walls necessary for a given

number of storage units. If the number of storage units is *n* where *n* is even and the number of walls is *w*, find *w* in terms of *n*.

Figure 7-1

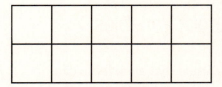

Solution One way to approach the problem is to start with the two leftmost walls and then add modular pieces made of 5 walls each, as shown in Figure 7-2. Each modular piece determines 2 storage units. Thus to obtain *n* units we need $\frac{n}{2}$ modular pieces. Because each modular piece consists of 5 walls, the total number of walls is $2 + 5 \cdot \frac{n}{2}$. Thus $w = 2 + \frac{5n}{2}$.

Figure 7-2

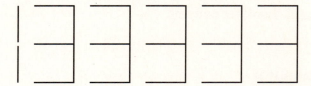

● ● ●

Developing Algebra Skills

To apply algebra in solving problems, you frequently need to translate given information into a symbolic expression involving quantities designated by letters. In all such examples, you may name the variables by letters of your choice. Frequently, the letters are chosen to make it easy to remember what quantities the variables represent.

• • •

Example 7-3

In each of the following, translate the given information into a symbolic expression involving quantities designated by letters:

a. One weekend, a music store sold twice as many CDs as cassettes and 25 fewer records than CDs. If the music store sold c cassettes, how many records and CDs did it sell?

b. French fries have about 12 calories apiece. A hamburger has about 600 calories. Akiva is on a diet of 2000 calories per day. If he ate f french fries and one hamburger, how many more calories can he consume that day?

c. First class postage in 1995 is 32¢ for the first ounce and 23¢ for each additional ounce. At this rate, what is the cost of mailing a letter that weighs z oz?

Solution **a.** Because c cassettes were sold, twice as many CDs as cassettes implies $2c$ CDs. Thus 25 fewer records than CDs implies $2c - 25$ records.

b. First, find how many calories Akiva consumed eating f french fries and one hamburger. Then, to find how many more calories he can consume, subtract this expression from 2000.

| 1 french fry | 12 calories |
| f french fries | $12f$ calories |

Therefore the number of calories in f french fries and one hamburger is

$$600 + 12f.$$

The number of calories left for the day is $2000 - (600 + 12f)$, or $2000 - 600 - 12f$, or $1400 - 12f$.

c. If a letter weighs z ounces, the first ounce costs 32¢ and the remaining $(z - 1)$ oz cost 23¢ each. The cost of the $(z - 1)$ oz therefore is $23(z - 1)$ cents. We have the following:

Cost of mailing a z-ounce letter = cost of first ounce + cost of next $(z - 1)$ oz

$$= 32 + 23(z - 1) \text{ cents}$$

• • •

Example 7-4

A teacher instructed her class as follows:

Take any number and add 15 to it. Now multiply that sum by 4. Next subtract 8 and divide the difference by 4. If you now subtract 12 from the quotient and tell me the number, I will tell you the number you started with.

Analyze the instructions to see how the teacher was able to determine the original number.

Solution Translate the information into an algebraic form.

Instructions	Discussion	Symbols
Take any number.	Since any number is used, you need a variable to represent the number. Let n be that variable.	n
Add 15 to it.	You are told to add 15 to "it." "It" refers to the variable n.	$n + 15$
Multiply that sum by 4.	You are told to multiply "that sum" by 4. "That sum" is $n + 15$.	$4(n + 15)$
Subtract 8.	You are told to subtract 8 from the product.	$4(n + 15) - 8$
Divide the difference by 4.	The difference is $4(n + 15) - 8$. Divide it by 4.	$\dfrac{4(n + 15) - 8}{4}$
Subtract 12 from the quotient and tell me the answer.	You are told to subtract 12 from the quotient.	$\dfrac{4(n + 15) - 8}{4} - 12$

Simplify the last expression as follows to see how the teacher could give the answer quickly:

$$\frac{4(n + 15) - 8}{4} - 12 = \frac{4n + 60 - 8 - 4 \cdot 12}{4}$$

$$= \frac{4n + 4}{4}$$

$$= \frac{4(n + 1)}{4}$$

$$= n + 1$$

The answer the student gives the teacher is 1 greater than the student's original number. To tell the student's number, the teacher merely subtracts 1 from the student's answer.

• • •

HISTORICAL NOTE

The word *algebra* comes from the Arabic book *Al-jabr wa'l muqabalah* written by Mohammed al-Khowârizmî (ca. 825). Algebra was introduced in Europe in the thirteenth and fourteenth centuries by Leonardo of Pisa (also called Fibonacci). Algebra was occasionally referred to as *Ars Magna,* or "the great art." Both Diophantus (ca. A.D. 250) and Francois Viète (1540–1603) have been called "fathers of algebra." Little is known about Diophantus, a Greek, except that he is supposed to have lived to be 84 years old and that he wrote *Arithmetica,* a treatise originally in 13 books. Viète was a French lawyer who devoted his leisure time to mathematics. Not liking the word *algebra,* he referred to the subject as "the analytic art."

The solutions of many applied problems involve the strategy of *writing an equation* and in some cases *writing an inequality.* Thus we first need to learn how to solve equations and inequalities.

Properties of Equations

To solve equations, we need several properties of equality. Children can discover many of these by using a balance scale. For example, consider two weights of amounts a and b on the balances, as in Figure 7-3(a). If the balance is level, then $a = b$. When we add an equal amount of weight c to both sides, the balance is still level, as in Figure 7-3(b).

Figure 7-3

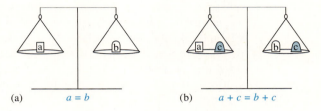

(a) $a = b$ (b) $a + c = b + c$

This demonstrates that if $a = b$, then $a + c = b + c$.

Similarly, if the scale is balanced with amounts a and b, as in Figure 7-4(a), and we put additional a's on one side and an equal number of b's on the other side, the scale remains level, as in Figure 7-4(b).

Figure 7-4

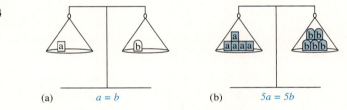

(a) $a = b$ (b) $5a = 5b$

Figure 7-4 suggests that if c is any real number and $a = b$, then $ac = bc$. These properties are summarized next.

Properties

The Addition Property of Equality   For any real numbers a, b, and c, if $a = b$, then $a + c = b + c$.
The Multiplication Property of Equality   For any real numbers a, b, and c, if $a = b$, then $ac = bc$.

The properties imply that we may add the same real number to both sides of an equation or multiply both sides of the equation by the same real number without affecting the equality. A new statement results from reversing the order of the *if* and *then* parts of the addition property of equality. The new statement is the *converse* of the original statement. In the case of the addition property, the converse is a true statement. The converse of the multiplication property of equality is also true when $c \neq 0$. These properties are summarized next.

Cancellation Properties of Equality

1. For any real numbers a, b, and c, if $a + c = b + c$, then $a = b$.
2. For any real numbers a, b, and c, with $c \neq 0$ if $ac = bc$, then $a = b$.

substitution property   Equality is not affected if we substitute a number for its equal. This property is referred to as the **substitution property.** Examples of substitution follow:

1. If $a + b = c + d$ and $d = 5$, then $a + b = c + 5$.
2. If $a + b = c + d$, if $b = e$, and if $d = f$, then $a + e = c + f$.

Properties of Inequalities

Before we consider solving equations and inequalities, we develop additional properties of inequalities for real numbers. Recall that for whole numbers, $5 > 3$ because 5 is to the right of 3 on the number line. Similarly, $^-3 > ^-5$ because $^-3$ is to the right of $^-5$.

Because 5 is to the right of 3 on a number line, there is a positive number that can be added to 3 to obtain 5, namely 2. Similarly, because $^-3$ is to the right of $^-5$, there is a positive number that can be added to $^-5$ to obtain $^-3$. In general we have the following definition.

Definition of Greater Than and Less Than

For any real numbers a and b, a is **greater than** b, written $a > b$, if, and only if, there exists a positive real number k such that $a = b + k$. Also, b is **less than** a, written $b < a$, if, and only if, $a > b$.

REMARK   If $a > b$, the definition of subtraction tells us that $a = b + k$ if, and only if, $a - b = k$. Hence $a > b$ if and only if $a - b$ is a positive number.

Many properties of inequalities are analogous to properties of equality. Table 7-2 summarizes properties of greater than and compares them to properties of the equality relation. Remember that if you multiply both sides of an inequality by a negative number, the inequality sign is reversed.

The following properties hold for real numbers a, b, and c.

Table 7-2

Property	Equality	Inequality (>)
Transitive	$a = b$ and $b = c$ implies $a = c$	$a > b$ and $b > c$ implies $a > c$
Addition	$a = b$ implies $a + c = b + c$	$a > b$ implies $a + c > b + c$
Multiplication	$a = b$ implies $ac = bc$	$a > b$ and $c > 0$ implies $ac > bc$ $a > b$ and $c < 0$ implies $ac < bc$
Cancellation for Addition	$a + c = b + c$ implies $a = b$	$a + c > b + c$ implies $a > b$
Cancellation for Multiplication	$ac = bc$ implies $a = b$, if $c \neq 0$	$ac > bc$ and $c < 0$ implies $a < b$ $ac > bc$ and $c > 0$ implies $a > b$

Analogous properties to those in Table 7-2 hold for the less than relation.

All of these properties can be proved using the definitions of > and < or using the property that $a > b$ if, and only if, $a - b$ is a positive real number. It is possible to combine properties of equality and inequality by using ≥ (greater than or equal to) or ≤ (less than or equal to).

Examples of the addition property of greater than follow:

$$5 > 2 \quad \text{implies} \quad 5 + 10 > 2 + 10$$
$$^-2 > {}^-5 \quad \text{implies} \quad {}^-2 + 2 > {}^-5 + 2$$
$$x > 3 \quad \text{implies} \quad x + 2 > 3 + 2$$

The following are examples of the multiplication property:

$$10 > 4 \text{ implies } 10 \cdot 0.2 > 4 \cdot 0.2, \text{ but } 10 \cdot (^-0.2) < 4 \cdot (^-0.2)$$
$$^-3 > {}^-5 \text{ implies } (^-3)2 > (^-5)2, \text{ but } (^-3)(^-2) < (^-5)(^-2)$$

REMARK   Because subtraction can be written in terms of addition and division can be written in terms of multiplication, whenever one wants to subtract from both sides or divide both sides of an equation or inequality a number different from 0, it is always possible to use the addition and multiplication properties of equal to or greater than in Table 7-2.

INVESTIGATION 7-1

• Construct a table analogous to Table 7-2 for properties of subtraction and division. •

Solving Equations and Inequalities

Part of the study of algebra involves operations on numbers and other elements represented by symbols. Finding solutions to equations and inequalities is one part of algebra.

To solve equations, we may use the properties of equality developed earlier. A balance scale can be used to demonstrate solving equations. Consider $3x - 14 = 1$. Put the equal expressions on the opposite pans of the balance scale. Since the expressions are equal, the pans should be level, as in Figure 7-5.

Figure 7-5

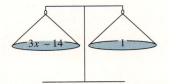

To solve for x, we use the properties of equality to manipulate the expressions on the scale so that after each step, the scale remains level and, at the final step, only an x remains on one side of the scale. The number on the other side of the scale represents the solution to the original equation. To find x in the equation of Figure 7-5, consider the scales pictured in successive steps in Figure 7-6. In Figure 7-6, each successive scale represents an equation that is equivalent to the original equation; that is, each has the same solution as the original. The last scale shows $x = 5$. To check that 5 is the correct solution, we substitute 5 into the original equation for x. Because $3 \cdot 5 - 14 = 1$ is a true statement, 5 is the solution to the original equation.

Figure 7-6

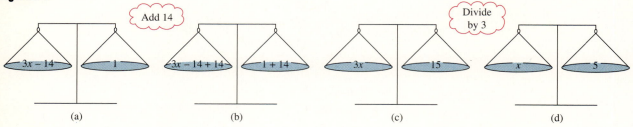

(a)   (b)   (c)   (d)

• • •

Example 7-5   Solve each of the following for x:

a. $x + 4 = {}^-6$ **b.** $x + 4 > {}^-6$

c. ${}^-x - 5 = 8$ **d.** ${}^-x - 5 \geq 8$

e. $\dfrac{1}{4}x + \dfrac{1}{5} = \dfrac{3}{8}x - \dfrac{1}{10}$

Solution   The solutions that follow show all the steps in the process:

a.
$$x + 4 = {}^-6$$
$$(x + 4) + {}^-4 = {}^-6 + {}^-4$$
$$x + (4 + {}^-4) = {}^-6 + {}^-4$$
$$x + 0 = {}^-10$$
$$x = {}^-10$$

b.
$$x + 4 > {}^-6$$
$$(x + 4) + {}^-4 > {}^-6 + {}^-4$$
$$x + (4 + {}^-4) > {}^-6 + {}^-4$$
$$x + 0 > {}^-10$$
$$x > {}^-10, x \in R$$

c.
$${}^-x - 5 = 8$$
$$({}^-x + {}^-5) + 5 = 8 + 5$$
$${}^-x + ({}^-5 + 5) = 13$$
$${}^-x + 0 = 13$$
$${}^-x = 13$$
$$({}^-x)({}^-1) = 13({}^-1)$$
$$x = {}^-13$$

d.
$${}^-x - 5 \geq 8$$
$$({}^-x + {}^-5) + 5 \geq 8 + 5$$
$${}^-x + ({}^-5 + 5) \geq 13$$
$${}^-x + 0 \geq 13$$
$${}^-x \geq 13$$
$$({}^-x)({}^-1) \leq 13({}^-1)$$
$$x \leq {}^-13, \ x \in R$$

e.
$$\frac{1}{4}x + \frac{1}{5} = \frac{3}{8}x - \frac{1}{10}$$

$$\frac{1}{4}x + \frac{1}{5} + \frac{{}^-1}{5} = \frac{3}{8}x + \left(-\frac{1}{10}\right) + \frac{{}^-1}{5}$$

$$\frac{1}{4}x + 0 = \frac{3}{8}x + \frac{{}^-3}{10}$$

$$\frac{{}^-3}{8}x + \frac{1}{4}x = \frac{{}^-3}{8}x + \frac{3}{8}x + \frac{{}^-3}{10}$$

$$\left(\frac{{}^-3}{8} + \frac{1}{4}\right)x = 0 + \frac{{}^-3}{10}$$

$$\frac{{}^-1}{8}x = -\frac{3}{10}$$

$$-8\left(\frac{-1}{8}x\right) = -8\left(\frac{-3}{10}\right)$$

$$x = \frac{24}{10} \text{ or } 2.4$$

• • •

Often there is more than one way to solve an equation or an inequality. Several methods for solving Example 7-5(e) follow:

1. First, add the fractions on each side of the inequality. Then, solve the resulting inequality.

$$\frac{1}{4}x + \frac{1}{5} = \frac{3}{8}x - \frac{1}{10}$$

$$\frac{(5x + 4)}{20} = \frac{(15x - 4)}{40}$$

One way to proceed is to obtain a common denominator on both sides of the inequality:

$$\frac{2(5x + 4)}{2 \cdot 20} = \frac{(15x - 4)}{40}$$

We multiply both sides by 40 and obtain the following:

$$2(5x + 4) = (15x - 4)$$

$$10x + 8 = 15x - 4$$

$$^{-}10x + 10x + 8 = {}^{-}10x + 15x - 4$$

$$8 = 5x - 4$$

$$8 + 4 = 5x - 4 + 4$$

$$12 = 5x$$

$$x = \frac{12}{5} \quad \text{or} \quad x = 2.4$$

2. First, multiply both sides of the inequality by the least common multiple (LCM) of all the denominators. (This gives an inequality that does not involve fractions.) Then, solve the resulting inequality.

$$\frac{1}{4}x + \frac{1}{5} = \frac{3}{8}x - \frac{1}{10}$$

Since LCM(4, 5, 8, 10) = 40,

$$40\left(\frac{1}{4}x + \frac{1}{5}\right) = 40\left(\frac{3}{8}x - \frac{1}{10}\right)$$

$$10x + 8 = 15x - 4.$$

Then we complete the solution as shown in Example 7-5.

Sometimes an exact solution to an equation or inequality involving radicals is desirable. In such a case, we leave a solution in radical form as shown in the following example.

Example 7-6

Solve each of the following and show the solution on a number line:

a. $x - 3 \leq \sqrt{2} + {}^{-}2$ **b.** $\dfrac{3x^2}{2} - 4 = 5$ **c.** $|x| \geq \sqrt{3}$

Solution   **a.** $x - 3 \leq \sqrt{2} + {}^{-}2$

$$x \leq \sqrt{2} + 1$$

Thus the solution is $x \leq \sqrt{2} + 1$, where x is a real number, is shown in Figure 7-7.

Figure 7-7

b. $\dfrac{3x^2}{2} - 4 = 5$

$$\dfrac{3x^2}{2} = 9$$

$$3x^2 = 18$$

$$x^2 = 6$$

$$x = \sqrt{6}, \text{ or } x = {}^{-}\sqrt{6}$$

The solution is shown on the number line in Figure 7-8.

Figure 7-8

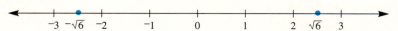

c. To solve $|x| \geq \sqrt{3}$, look for all the points on the number line whose distance from the origin is greater than or equal to $\sqrt{3}$. All such points are shown on the number line in Figure 7-9. The answer can be written as $x \leq {}^{-}\sqrt{3}$ or $x \geq \sqrt{3}$. Note that the answer could not be written as $\sqrt{3} \leq x \leq {}^{-}\sqrt{3}$ because this statement means that $\sqrt{3} \leq x$ and $x \leq {}^{-}\sqrt{3}$. By the transitive property of less than or equal to, the statement would imply that $\sqrt{3} \leq {}^{-}\sqrt{3}$, which is false.

Figure 7-9

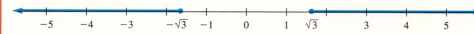

REMARK   If the inequality in Example 7-6(a) had been $x - 3 < \sqrt{2} + {}^{-}2$, then the solution would be $x < \sqrt{2} + 1$, as seen in Figure 7-10, with a hollow dot to indicate that $\sqrt{2} + 1$ is not included.

Figure 7-10

Ongoing Assessment 7-1

1. In the following, write an expression in terms of the given variable that represents the indicated quantity (that is, write the quantity as a function of the given variable).
   a. The distance traveled at a constant speed of 60 mph during t hours
   b. The cost of having a plumber spend x hours at your house if the plumber charges $20 for coming to the house and $25 per hour for labor
   c. The amount of money in cents in a jar containing d dimes and some nickels and quarters, if there are 3 times as many nickels as dimes and twice as many quarters as nickels
   d. The sum of three consecutive integers if the least integer is x
   e. The amount of bacteria after n minutes if the initial amount of bacteria is q and the amount of bacteria doubles every minute. (*Hint:* The answer should contain q as well as n.)
   f. The temperature after t hours if the initial temperature is 40°F and each hour it drops by 3°F
   g. Pawel's salary after 3 yr if the first year his salary was s dollars, the second year it was $5000 higher, and the third year it was twice as much as the second year
   h. The sum of three consecutive odd integers if the least integer is x
   i. The sum of three consecutive integers if the middle integer is m
   j. The product of three consecutive integers if the middle integer is m
2. Pluto, the farthest planet from the sun in our solar system, is also the smallest. The following table gives the weight P on Pluto for a given weight E on Earth measured in the same units.

Weight on Earth (E)	1	2	3	4	5	10	100
Weight on Pluto (P)	0.04	0.08	0.12	0.16	0.2	0.4	4

Based on the information given in the table, answer each of the following:
   a. Find a formula for P in terms of E.
   b. Express E in terms P.
   c. What is Debbie's weight on Pluto if her weight on Earth is 135 lb?
   d. Find the weight on Earth of an object that weighs 100 lb on Pluto.
3. a. If 1 U.S. dollar is worth 1.35 Swiss francs and 1 Swiss franc is worth 1.22 Dutch gilders, find a formula that will give a U.S. tourist the amount of Dutch gilders g for U.S. dollars d.
   b. Find a formula that will be useful for a Dutch tourist to convert gilders (g) to U.S. dollars (d).

4. Joel is designing squares made of match sticks. The following are 1×1, 2×2, and 3×3 such squares. How many match sticks will he need for
   a. a 10×10 square?
   b. an $n \times n$ square?

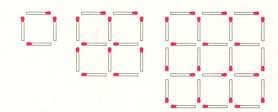

5. The formula for converting degrees Celsius (C) to degrees Fahrenheit (F) is $F = \left(\dfrac{9}{5}\right) \cdot C + 32$.
   a. Samantha reads that the temperature is 32°C in Spain. What is the Fahrenheit temperature?
   b. The temperature drops to ⁻40°F in West Yellowstone. What is the temperature in degrees Celsius?
6. To convert a temperature in degrees Fahrenheit (F) to a temperature in degrees Celsius (C), you need to subtract 32 from the temperature in degrees Fahrenheit and multiply the result by 5/9. Write a formula for C in terms of F.
7. To convert a temperature on the Celsius (C) scale to Kelvin (K) scale, you need to add 273.15 to the Celsius temperature.
   a. Write a formula for K in terms of C.
   b. Write a formula for converting from the Kelvin scale to the Celsius scale.
   c. Based on the information in (a) and (b), write formulas for converting from the Kelvin scale to the Fahrenheit scale and vice versa.
8. Write an equation relating the variables described in each of the following situations:
   a. The pay P for t hours if you are paid $8 an hour
   b. The pay P for t hours if you are paid $15 for the first hour and $10 for each additional hour
   c. The total pay P for a visit and t hours of gardening if you are paid $20 for the visit and $10 for each hour of gardening
   d. The total cost C of membership in a health club that charges a $300 initiation fee and $4 for each of n days attended
   e. The cost C of renting a midsized car for 1 day of driving m miles if the rent is $30 per day plus 35¢ per mile.
In the following problems, all of the variables are real numbers unless otherwise noted.
9. Solve each of the following:
   a. $3 - x = {}^-15$ b. $^-x + 3 > {}^-15$
   c. $^-x - 3 = 15$ d. $^-x - 3 \geq 15$

e. $^-3x + 5 = 11$

f. $^-3x + 5 \leq 11$

g. $^-5\,(x + 3) > 0$

h. $^-3(x + 5) = ^-4(x + 5) + 21$

i. $2.04 - 2.24x = ^-10.3$

j. $^-0.02 + 3.14x = ^-0.05$

k. $^-\sqrt{3}x \leq ^-\sqrt{3}$

l. $^-10^{-3}x \geq ^-0.001$

10. Solve each of the following:

a. $4 + 3x \geq \sqrt{5} - 7x$

b. $(2x - 1)^2 = 2$

c. $|x| \geq \sqrt{7}$

d. $|x| \leq \sqrt{2}$

e. $\dfrac{\left(\dfrac{1}{x} + \dfrac{1}{2}\right)}{0.875} = 1$

f. $\dfrac{2(x - 3)}{3(x - 2)} = 4$

11. Solve each of the following and if possible write your answers in the form a/b, where a and b are integers, $b \neq 0$, and $\dfrac{a}{b}$ is in simplest form. Check your answers by substituting them into the original equations.

a. $\dfrac{^-2}{x} + 3 = \dfrac{2}{3}$

b. $\dfrac{1}{5} = \dfrac{7}{3}x$

c. $\dfrac{1}{2}x - 7 = \dfrac{3}{4}x$

d. $\dfrac{2}{3}\left(\dfrac{1}{2}x - 7\right) = \dfrac{3}{4}x$

e. $\dfrac{^-2}{x - 3} + 1 = \dfrac{4}{5}$

f. $x \div \dfrac{3}{4} = \dfrac{5}{8}$

g. $\dfrac{2}{3 - x} - \dfrac{4}{5} = ^-1$

h. $\dfrac{^-2}{5}(10x + 1) = 1 - x$

12. Suppose $w = (xy)/z$, where x, y, and z are positive real numbers. If z is multiplied by 8 and y is divided by 2, how many times lesser or greater will the new value of w be in relation to its original value? Explain your answer.

13. A teacher instructed her class as follows: *Take any number, multiply it by 3, add 49, and divide the result by 7. Subtract 7 from the quotient, divide the new result by 3, and tell me your answer. I will tell you the original number.* To determine each student's original number, the teacher multiplied each answer by 7. Explain how the teacher was able to tell each student's original number.

14. A teacher instructed her class to use a calculator and proceed as follows: *Take any number, multiply it by 0.3, and then subtract 0.6. Next divide the result by 10^2, divide by 3,*

and subtract 0.55. Now multiply your result by 1000 and tell me the number you obtained. I will tell you your original number. The teacher was able to give each student's original number by adding 552 to each answer. Explain why this scheme always works.

15. Determine which of the following are true for all possible real-number values of x:

a. $3(x + 1) = 3x + 3$ **b.** $x - 3 = 3 - x$

c. $x + 3 = 3 + x$ **d.** $2(x - 1) + 2 = 3x - x$

e. $x^2 + 1 > 0$ **f.** $3x > 4x - x$

g. $|x| \geq ^-\sqrt{2}$

Communication

16. Students were asked to write an algebraic expression for the sum of three consecutive integers. One student wrote $x + (x + 1) + (x + 2) = 3x + 3$. Another wrote $(x - 1) + x + (x + 1) = 3x$. Explain who is correct and why.

17. A rod of length l was cut into two pieces of equal length. Then one of the pieces was halved again (and so on.) Find the length of the smallest piece after n cuts in terms of l and n. Explain your reasoning.

Open-ended

18. In Example 7-4, a teacher instructed her class to take any number and perform a series of computations using that number. The teacher was able to tell each student's original number by subtracting 1 from the student's answer. Create similar instructions for students so that the teacher needs only to do the following to obtain the student's original number:

a. Add 1 to the answer.

b. Multiply the answer by 2.

c. Square the answer.

d. Take the square root of the answer.

19. The inequality $|x| > ^-2$ is true for all real values of x. Write three different inequalities without using absolute values, each of which is true for all real values of x.

20. For each of the following, write an equation that satisfies the condition:

a. The equation is true for all real values of x.

b. The equation is not satisfied by any real number x.

c. The equation is true for all real values of $x \neq 0$ and false for $x = 0$.

d. The equation is true for all real values of x and y.

Cooperative Learning

21. Suppose $a > b + c$ and $c > d + e$. A student concludes that $a > b + d + e$ and justifies her answer by saying, "I substituted $d + e$ for c in the first inequality." Discuss in your group whether the student's conclusion and justification are correct.

22. Examine several elementary school textbooks for grades 1 through 4 and report on which algebraic concepts are introduced in each and how they are introduced.

TECHNOLOGY CORNER

The following Logo program finds the sum of the first `:N` terms of an arithmetic sequence whose first term is `:TERM` and whose difference is `:DIFF`.

```
TO SUMASEQ :TERM :DIFF :N
 SUMASEQ1 :TERM :DIFF 0 :N
END

TO SUMASEQ1 :TERM :DIFF :SUM :N
 IF :N = 0 PRINT :SUM STOP
 SUMASEQ :TERM + :DIFF :DIFF :SUM + :TERM :N-1
END
```

(In `LCSI` Logo, replace `PRINT :SUM STOP` with `[PRINT :SUM STOP]`.)

a. Use the SUMASEQ procedure to find the sum of an arithmetic sequence of positive integers.
b. Write a similar Logo program for the sum of the squares of the terms of the Fibonacci sequence 1, 1, 2, 3, 5, 8, 13, 21, . . . in which the first two terms are 1, 1 and each term starting from the third is the sum of its two preceding terms.
c. If F_n denotes the nth term of the Fibonacci sequence starting with 1, 1, check each of the following and write the next two rows to continue the pattern:

$$1^2 + 1^2 = 2 = F_2 \cdot F_3$$
$$1^2 + 1^2 + 2^2 = 6 = 2 \cdot 3 = F_3 \cdot F_4$$
$$1^2 + 1^2 + 2^2 + 3^2 = 15 = 3 \cdot 5 = F_4 \cdot F_5$$

d. Use (c) to conjecture a simple expression for $F_1^2 + F_2^2 + F_3^2 + \ldots + F_N^2$.
e. Use the Logo program from (a) to check your conjecture in (b) for :N = 9 and for :N = 10.

Section 7-2 Word Problems

We can use algebra to solve many types of problems. The following simple model demonstrates a method for solving word problems. Formulate the word problem as a mathematical problem, solve the mathematical problem, and then interpret the solution in terms of the original word problem.

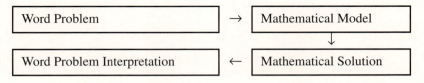

At the third-grade level, an example of this model appears as follows:

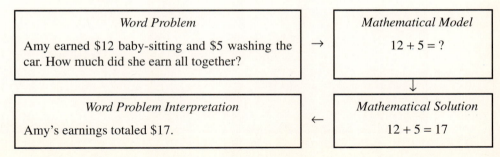

We can apply Polya's four-step problem-solving process to solving word problems in which the use of algebra is appropriate.

In *Understanding the Problem,* we identify what is given and what is to be found. In *Devising a Plan,* we assign letters to the unknown quantities and translate the information in the problem into a model involving equations or inequalities. In *Carrying Out the Plan,* we solve the equations or inequalities. In *Looking Back,* we interpret and check the solution in terms of the original problem. This process is demonstrated on the following student page from *Addison-Wesley Mathematics,* Grade 8, 1993.

Problem Solving
Using the Strategies

UNDERSTAND
ANALYZE DATA
PLAN
ESTIMATE
SOLVE
EXAMINE

LEARN ABOUT IT

Sometimes translating a verbal statement to an equation is the key to solving a problem. Read the verbal statement carefully, thinking about the meaning of each phrase.

> Sarah's paycheck from Water World for $48 is $4 more than twice what she earned last week. How much did she earn last week?

Rosanna used the strategy **Write an Equation** to solve this problem.

First Rosanna wrote the data from the problem in simpler terms.

> *4 more than twice last week's is 48*

She then represented the missing information with a variable.

> *x = amount earned last week*

Using the variable, she translated the simplified verbal statement into an equation.

> $2x$ $+$ 4 $=$ 48
> *twice last week   four more than   is   48*

Finally, she solved the equation, and checked her answer.

$$2x + 4 = 48$$
$$2x + 4 - 4 = 48 - 4$$
$$2x = 44$$
$$\frac{2x}{2} = \frac{44}{2}$$
$$x = 22$$

Check
$$2(22) + 4 \stackrel{?}{=} 48$$
$$44 + 4 = 48 \checkmark$$

Sometimes a translation of the information in a given problem is a straightforward process that leads to an equation and to the solution of the problem, as shown in the following examples.

Example 7-7 A bicycle is on sale at $\frac{3}{4}$ of its original price. If the sale price is $330, what was the original price?

Solution Let x be the original price. Then $\frac{3}{4}$ of the original price is $\frac{3}{4}x$. Because the sale price is $330, we have $\frac{3}{4}x = 330$. Solving for x gives the following:

$$\frac{4}{3} \cdot \frac{3}{4}x = \frac{4}{3} \cdot 330$$
$$1 \cdot x = 440$$
$$x = 440$$

Thus the original price was $440.

An alternative approach, which does not use algebra, follows. Because $\frac{3}{4}$ of the original price is $330, $\frac{1}{4}$ of the original price is $\frac{1}{3} \cdot 330$, or $110. Thus $4 \cdot \frac{1}{4}$ of the original price is $4 \cdot 110$, or $440.

Example 7-8 At the end of the month, Debbie was paid for her paper route. She spent $50 on records and then $\frac{2}{5}$ of the remaining money on books. After that, with $\frac{1}{3}$ of the remaining amount she bought presents; she was left with $48. How much was she paid at the end of the month?

Solution Let x denote Debbie's earnings in dollars from her paper route. After spending $50, she had $x - 50$ dollars left. She spent $\frac{2}{5}$ of that on books, so she was left with $\frac{3}{5}$ of $x - 50$, that is, $\frac{3}{5}(x - 50)$. Because she spent $\frac{1}{3}$ of this amount on presents, she was left with $\frac{2}{3}$ of the last amount; that is, $\frac{2}{3} \cdot \frac{3}{5}(x - 50)$. She was finally left with $48, so we have the following:

$$\frac{2}{3} \cdot \frac{3}{5}(x - 50) = 48$$

$$\frac{2}{5}(x - 50) = 48$$

$$\frac{5}{2} \cdot \frac{2}{5}(x - 50) = \frac{5}{2} \cdot 48$$

$$x - 50 = 120$$

$$x = 170$$

Consequently, Debbie earned $170 from her paper route.

• • •

I N V E S T I G A T I O N   7 - 2

Solve Example 7-8 by an alternative approach that uses the strategy of *working backwards* and that does not use algebra. ●

In the following problems, we demonstrate Polya's four-step problem-solving process in solving word problems.

Problem 1

Bruno has 5 books overdue at the library. The fine for overdue books is 10¢ a day per book. He remembers that he checked out an astronomy book a week earlier than four novels. If his total fine was $8.70, how long was each book overdue?

Understanding the Problem.   Bruno has five books overdue. He checked out an astronomy book seven days earlier than the four novels, so the astronomy book is overdue seven days more than the novels. The fine per day for each book is 10¢, and the total fine was $8.70. We need to find out how many days each book is overdue.

Devising a Plan.   Let x be the number of days that each of the four novels is overdue. The astronomy book is overdue seven days longer, that is, $x + 7$ days. To *write an equation* for x, we express the total fine in two different ways. The total fine is $8.70. This fine equals the fine for the astronomy book plus the fine for the four novels.

Fine for each of the novels = fine per day times the number of overdue days
$$\underbrace{}_{10} \cdot \underbrace{}_{x}$$

Fine for the four novels = 1 day's fine for four novels times number of overdue days

$$4 \cdot 10 \qquad \cdot \qquad x$$

$$= (4 \cdot 10)x$$
$$= 40x$$

Fine for the astronomy book = fine per day times the number of overdue days

$$10 \qquad \cdot \qquad (x+7)$$
$$= 10 \cdot (x+7) \quad \text{(in cents)}$$

Because each of the above expressions is in cents, we need to write the total fine of $8.70 as 870¢ to produce the following:

Fine for the four novels + fine for the astronomy book = total fine

$$40x \qquad + \qquad 10(x+7) \qquad = 870$$

Carrying Out the Plan. Solve the equation for x.

$$40x + 10(x+7) = 870$$
$$40x + 10x + 70 = 870$$
$$50x = 870 - 70$$
$$50x = 800$$
$$x = 16$$

Thus each of the four novels was 16 days overdue, and the astronomy book was overdue $x + 7$, or 23, days.

Looking Back. To check the answer, follow the original information. Each of the four novels was 16 days overdue, and the astronomy book was 23 days overdue. Because the fine was 10¢ per day per book, the fine for each of the novels was $16 \cdot 10$¢, or 160¢. Hence, the fine for all four novels was $4 \cdot 160$¢, or 640¢. The fine for the astronomy book was $23 \cdot 10$¢, or 230¢. Consequently, the total fine was 640¢ + 230¢, or 870¢, which agrees with the given information of $8.70 as the total fine.

Rather than letting x be the number of days that each of the four novels was overdue, we could designate the number of days the astronomy book was overdue by x. Then the number of days that each of the novels was overdue would be seven days less, that is, $x - 7$. Then, the total fine would be $10x + 40(x - 7) = 870$. Hence, $x = 23$ and $x - 7 = 16$, that is, 23 overdue days for the astronomy book and 16 days for each of the four novels.

• • •

Problem 2

In a small town, three children deliver all the newspapers. Abby delivers three times as many papers as Bob, and Connie delivers 13 more than Abby. If the three children delivered a total of 496 papers, how many papers does each deliver?

Understanding the Problem. The problem asks for the number of papers that each child delivers. It gives information that compares the number of papers that each child delivers as well as the total number of papers delivered in the town.

■ ***Devising a Plan.*** Let *a, b,* and *c* be the number of papers delivered by Abby, Bob, and Connie, respectively. We translate the given information into *equations* as follows:

Abby delivers three times as many papers as Bob: $a = 3b$
Connie delivers 13 more papers than Abby: $c = a + 13$
Total delivery is 496: $a + b + c = 496$

To reduce the number of variables, substitute $3b$ for a in the second and third equations:

$c = a + 13$ becomes $c = 3b + 13$

$a + b + c = 496$ becomes $3b + b + c = 496$

Next, make an equation in one variable, *b*, by substituting $3b + 13$ for *c* in the equation $3b + b + c = 496$, solve for *b*, and then find *a* and *c*.

Carrying Out the Plan.

$$3b + b + 3b + 13 = 496$$
$$7b + 13 = 496$$
$$7b = 483$$
$$b = 69$$

Thus $a = 3b = 3 \cdot 69 = 207$. Also, $c = a + 13 = 207 + 13 = 220$. So, Abby delivers 207 papers, Bob delivers 69 papers, and Connie delivers 220 papers.

Looking Back. To check the answers, follow the original information, using $a = 207$, $b = 69$, and $c = 220$. The information in the first sentence, "Abby delivers three times as many papers as Bob" checks, since $207 = 3 \cdot 69$. The second sentence, "Connie delivers 13 more papers than Abby" is true because $220 = 207 + 13$. The information on the total delivery checks, since $207 + 69 + 220 = 496$.

An alternative solution involves expressing all quantities in terms of a single variable. Let *x* be the number of papers Bob delivers and then express the number of papers Abby and Connie deliver in terms of *x*.

Information	*Mathematical Translation*
The number of papers Bob delivers.	x
Abby delivers three times as many as Bob.	$3x$
Connie delivers 13 more papers than Abby.	$3x + 13$
The total delivery is 496.	$x + 3x + (3x + 13) = 496$
Solve the equation.	$x + 3x + (3x + 13) = 496$
	$7x + 13 = 496$
	$7x = 483$
	$x = 69$

Hence, Bob delivers 69 papers. Because $3x = 3 \cdot 69 = 207$, Abby delivers 207 papers; $3x + 13 = 207 + 13 = 220$, so Connie delivers 220 papers.

If we had let *x* be the number of papers that Abby delivers, the problem would have been more complicated to solve because, according to that scenario, Bob delivers $x \div 3$ papers. If we had let *x* be the number of papers that Connie delivers, how would the numbers of Abby's and Bob's delivered papers have been expressed?

• • •

BRAIN TEASER The following is an argument showing that an ant weighs as much as an elephant. What is wrong?

Let *e* be the weight of the elephant and *a* the weight of the ant. Let $e - a = d$. Consequently, $e = a + d$. Multiply each side of $e = a + d$ by $e - a$. Then simplify.

$$e(e - a) = (a + d)(e - a)$$
$$e^2 - ea = ae + de - a^2 - da$$
$$e^2 - ea - de = ae - a^2 - da$$
$$e(e - a - d) = a(e - a - d)$$
$$e = a$$

Thus the weight of the elephant equals the weight of the ant.

Ongoing Assessment 7-2

1. If you multiply a number by ⁻6 and then add 20 to the product, the result is 50. What is the number?

2. David has three times as much money as Rick. Together, they have $400. How much does each have?

3. Factory A produces twice as many cars per day as factory B. Factory C produces 300 cars more per day than factory A. If the total production in the three factories is 7300 cars per day, determine how many cars per day are produced in each factory.

4. For a certain event, 812 tickets were sold for a total of $1912. If students paid $2 per ticket and nonstudents paid $3 per ticket, how many student tickets were sold?

5. The sum of three consecutive integers is 237. Find the three integers.

6. The sum of three consecutive even integers is 240. Find the three integers.

7. The sum of two integers is 21. The first number is twice the second number. Find the integers.

8. A man left an estate of $64,000 to three children. The eldest child received three times as much as the youngest. The middle child received $14,000 more than the youngest. How much did each child receive?

9. There are three consecutive even integers. Seven times the least equals five times the greatest. What are the three integers?

10. Di Paloma University had a faculty reduction and lost $\frac{1}{5}$ of its faculty. If 320 faculty members were left after the reduction, how many members were there originally?

11. When you multiply a certain number by 3 and then subtract $\frac{7}{18}$, you get the same result as when you multiply the number by 2 and add $\frac{5}{12}$. What is the number?

12. At Salem State College, $\frac{5}{8}$ of the students live in dormitories. If 6000 students at the college live in the dormitories, how many students attend the college?

13. A suit is on sale for $180. Determine the original price of the suit if the discount was $\frac{1}{4}$ of the original price.

14. If every employee's salary at the Sunrise Software Company increases each year by $\frac{1}{10}$ of that person's salary of the previous year, answer the following:
   a. Martha's present annual salary is $100,000. What will her salary be in 2 yr?
   b. Aaron's present salary is $99,000. What was his salary 1 yr ago?
   c. Juanita's present salary is $363,000. What was her salary 2 yr ago?

15. At a certain company, three times as many men as women apply for work. If $\frac{1}{10}$ of the applicants are hired and $\frac{1}{20}$ of the men who apply are hired, determine what fraction of the women who apply are hired.

16. Jasmine is reading a book. She has finished $\frac{3}{4}$ of the book and has 82 pages left to read. Determine how many pages she has read.

17. John took out all his money from his bank savings account. He spent $50 on a radio and $\frac{3}{5}$ of what remained on presents. Half of what was left he put back in his checking account, and the remaining $35 he donated to charity. How much money did John originally have in his savings account?

18. Of the students in Highland Junior High, $\frac{1}{5}$ graduated with an A in mathematics. Of the rest, $\frac{1}{4}$ graduated with a B and the remaining 600 with a C. How many students were in the school? Explain your reasoning.

19. Tira noticed that every 30 sec, the temperature of a chemical reaction in her lab was decreasing by the same number of degrees. Initially, the temperature was 28°C and 5 min later, $^{-}12$°C. In a second experiment, Tira noticed that the temperature of the chemical reaction was initially $^{-}57$°C and was decreasing by 3°C every minute. If she started the two experiments at the same time, when were the temperatures of the reactions the same? What was that temperature?

Communication

20. Explain why the following equation has no solution: $2\left(x - \frac{1}{2}\right) = {}^{-}4\left(3 - \frac{x}{2}\right).$

21. If each side of the equation $3x = 4x$ is divided by x, we get $3 = 4$. Does this imply that the equation has no solution? Explain why or why not.

Open-ended

22. Write a word problem whose solution involves solving an inequality and show how the inequality will solve the problem.

23. Suppose you teach seventh graders algebra as well as geography and you want to create a word problem that will reinforce the learning of both subjects. Make up at least one such problem and show how to solve it.

Cooperative Learning

24. Ask a partner to choose a number and not tell you what it is. Then instruct your partner to perform several operations of your choosing on the given number and ask your partner to report the final result. Based on the reported result, write an equation, solve it, and tell the number your partner chose. Exchange roles after completing the exercise.

25. Consider two salary options, one that pays a dollars initial salary with d dollars monthly raises and the other with b dollars initial salary and c dollars monthly raises.
    a. Choose numerical values for a, b, c, and d such that $a > b$ and $c > d$ and ask your partner to guess which system is better, assuming employment for a number of months specified by you.
    b. Analyze which option is better by setting up and solving the appropriate algebraic equation or inequality.

Review Problems

26. In the following, write an expression in terms of the given variable that represents the indicated quantity.
    a. The sum of three consecutive even integers if the middle integer is $2x$.
    b. The temperature after t hours if the temperature after the first hour is 10°C and each hour it increases by 2°C.

27. Solve each of the following:
    a. $\frac{^{-}1}{x} + 3.5 = \frac{2.5}{x}$ b. $^{-}3x < \frac{^{-}1}{2}$ c. $(x + 1)^2 > {}^{-}3$

Section 7-3   Lines in a Cartesian Coordinate System

The Cartesian coordinate system (named for René Descartes) enables us to study geometry using algebra and to interpret algebraic phenomena geometrically. A Cartesian coordinate system is constructed by placing two number lines perpendicular to each other, as shown in Figure 7-11. The intersection point of the two lines is the **origin,** the horizontal line is the **x-axis,** and the vertical line is the **y-axis.** The location of any point P can be described by an ordered pair of numbers.

origin

x-axis   •   y-axis

     If a perpendicular from P to the x-axis intersects at a point with coordinate a and a perpendicular from P to the y-axis intersects at a point with coordinate b, point P has coordinates (a, b). The first component in the ordered pair (a, b) is the **abscissa, or x-coordinate,** of P. The second component is the **ordinate, or y-coordinate,** of P. To each point in the plane, there corresponds an ordered pair (a, b) and vice versa. Hence, there is a one-to-one

abscissa   •   x-coordinate

ordinate   •   y-coordinate

Figure 7-11

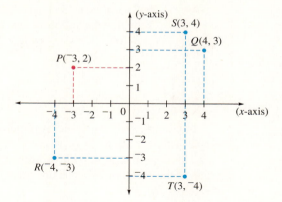

correspondence between all the points in the plane and all the ordered pairs of real numbers.

For example, in Figure 7-11, the x-coordinate of P is $^-3$ and the y-coordinate of P is 2, so P has coordinate ($^-3$, 2). Similarly, R has a coordinate ($^-4$, $^-3$), written as $R($ $^-4$, $^-3$).

Equations of Vertical and Horizontal Lines

Every point on the x-axis has a y-coordinate of zero. Thus the x-axis can be described as the set of all points (x, y) such that $y = 0$. This set of points on the x-axis has equation $y = 0$. Similarly, the y-axis can be described as the set of all points (x, y) such that $x = 0$ and y is an arbitrary real number. Thus $x = 0$ is the equation of the y-axis. If we plot the set of all points that satisfy a given condition, the resulting picture on the Cartesian coordinate **graph** system is called the **graph** of the set.

Example 7-9   Sketch the graph for each of the following:

a. $x = 2$ **b.** $y = 3$ **c.** $x < 2$ and $y = 3$

Solution   **a.** The equation $x = 2$ represents the set of all points (x, y) for which $x = 2$ and y is any real number. This set is the line perpendicular to the x-axis at $(2, 0)$, as in Figure 7-12.

     b. The equation $y = 3$ represents the set of all points (x, y) for which $y = 3$ and x is any real number. This set is the line perpendicular to the y-axis at $(0, 3)$, as in Figure 7-13.

Figure 7-12   **Figure 7-13**

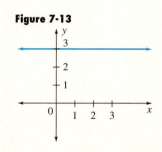

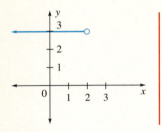

Figure 7-14

c. Together, the statements represent the set of all points (x, y) for which $x < 2$, but y is always 3. The set describes part of a line, as shown in Figure 7-14. Note that the hollow dot at $(2, 3)$ indicates that this point is not included in the solution.

• • •

In Example 7-9, we found the graphs of the equations $x = 2$ and $y = 3$. In general, the graph of the equation $x = a$, where a is some real number, is a line perpendicular to the x-axis through the point with coordinates $(a, 0)$, as shown in Figure 7-15. Similarly, the graph of the equation $y = b$ is a line perpendicular to the y-axis through the point with coordinates $(0, b)$.

Figure 7-15

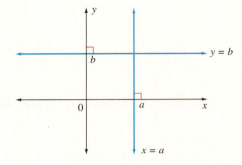

Equations of Other Lines

Table 7-3

Number of Term	Term
1	4
2	7
3	10
4	13
.	.
.	.
.	.
x	$3x + 1$

Consider the arithmetic sequence 4, 7, 10, 13, . . . in Table 7-3 whose xth term is $3x + 1$. If the number of the term is the x-coordinate and the corresponding term the y-coordinate, the set of points appear to lie on a line that is parallel to neither the x- nor y-axes, as in Figure 7-16.

Figure 7-16

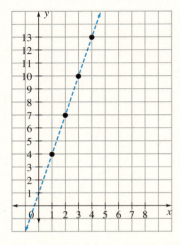

Do all points corresponding to arithmetic sequences lie along lines? To help answer this question, we consider the following sequences, the multiples of counting numbers in Table 7-4.

Table 7-4

Number of Term x	$1 \cdot x$	$2 \cdot x$	$\frac{1}{2} \cdot x$	$(^-1) \cdot x$	$(^-2) \cdot x$
1	1	2	$\frac{1}{2}$	$^-1$	$^-2$
2	2	4	1	$^-2$	$^-4$
3	3	6	$\frac{3}{2}$	$^-3$	$^-6$
4	4	8	2	$^-4$	$^-8$
5	5	10	$\frac{5}{2}$	$^-5$	$^-10$
6	6	12	3	$^-6$	$^-12$
.	.	.	.		
.	.	.	.		
.	.	.	.		
x	x	$2x$	$\frac{1}{2}x$	^-x	^-2x

If the sets of ordered pairs in the tables are plotted on a graph as in Figure 7-17, then the pairs of each table appear to determine lines. Those lines and their corresponding equations are given in Figure 7-17.

All five lines in Figure 7-17 have equations of the form $y = mx$, where m takes the values 2, 1, $\frac{1}{2}$, $^-1$, and $^-2$. If all points along a given dashed line are connected, then all the points on that line satisfy the corresponding equation. The number m is a measure of steepness and is called the **slope** of the line whose equation is $y = mx$. The graph goes up from left to right (increases) if m is positive, and it goes down from left to right (decreases) if m is negative.

slope

Figure 7-17

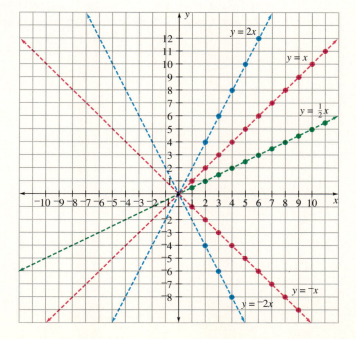

● In the equation $y = mx$, if m is 0, what happens to the line? What happens as m continues to increase? ●

All lines in Figure 7-17 pass through the origin. This is true for any line whose equation is $y = mx$. If $x = 0$, then $y = m \cdot 0 = 0$ and $(0, 0)$ is a point on the graph of $y = mx$. Conversely, it is possible to show that any nonvertical line passing through the origin has an equation of the form $y = mx$ for some value of m.

• • •

Example 7-10   Find the equation of the line that contains $(0, 0)$ and $(2, 3)$.

Solution   The line goes through the origin; therefore its equation has the form $y = mx$. To find the equation of the line, we must find the value of m. The line contains $(2, 3)$, so we substitute 2 for x and 3 for y in the equation $y = mx$ to obtain $3 = m \cdot 2$, and thus $m = \frac{3}{2}$. Hence, the required equation is $y = \frac{3}{2}x$.

• • •

Next, we consider equations of the form $y = mx + b$, where b is a real number. To do this, we examine the graphs of $y = x + 2$ and $y = x$. Given the graph of $y = x$, we can obtain the graph of $y = x + 2$ by "raising" each point on the first graph by 2 units. This is because for a certain value of x, the corresponding y value is 2 units greater. This is shown in Figure 7-18(a). Similarly, to sketch the graph of $y = x - 2$, we first draw the graph of $y = x$ and then lower each point vertically by 2 units, as shown in Figure 7-18(b).

Figure 7-18

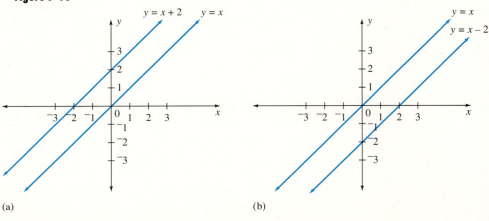

(a)   (b)

The graphs of $y = x + 2$ and $y = x - 2$ are straight lines. Moreover, the lines whose equations are $y = x$, $y = x + 2$, and $y = x - 2$ are parallel. In general, for a given value of m, the graph of $y = mx + b$ is a straight line through $(0, b)$ and parallel to the line whose equation is $y = mx$.

Further, the graph of the line $y = mx + b$, where $b > 0$, can be obtained from the graph of $y = mx$ by sliding $y = mx$ up b units, as shown in Figure 7-19. If $b < 0$, $y = mx$ must be slid down $|b|$ units.

The graph of $y = mx + b$ in Figure 7-19 crosses the y-axis at point $P(0, b)$. The value of

y-intercept y at the point of intersection of any line with the y-axis is the **y-intercept.** Thus b is the

slope-intercept form y-intercept of $y = mx + b$, and this form of the equation of a straight line is the **slope-intercept form.** Similarly, the value of x at the point of intersection of a line with the x-axis

x-intercept is the **x-intercept.**

Figure 7-19

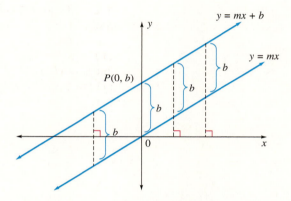

• • •

Example 7-11   Given the equation $y - 3x = {}^-6$, do the following:

a. Find the slope of the line.
b. Find the y-intercept.
c. Find the x-intercept.
d. Sketch the graph of the equation.

Solution   **a.** To write the equation in the form $y = mx + b$, we add $3x$ to both sides of the given equation to obtain $y = 3x + ({}^-6)$. Hence, the slope is 3.

b. The form $y = 3x + ({}^-6)$ shows that $b = {}^-6$, which is the y-intercept. (The y-intercept can also be found directly by substituting $x = 0$ in the equation and finding the corresponding value of y.)

c. The x-intercept is the x-coordinate of the point where the graph intersects the x-axis. At that point, $y = 0$. Substituting 0 for y in $y = 3x - 6$ gives 2 as the x-intercept.

d. The y-intercept and the x-intercept are located at $(0, {}^-6)$ and $(2, 0)$, respectively, on the line. We plot these points and draw the line through them to obtain the desired graph in Figure 7-20. Note that any two points of the line can be used to sketch the graph because any two points determine a line.

Figure 7-20

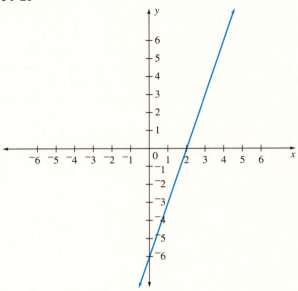

The equation $y = b$ can be written in slope-intercept form as $y = 0 \cdot x + b$. Consequently, its slope is 0 and its y-intercept is b. This should not be surprising. Because the line is parallel to the x-axis, its steepness, or slope, should be 0. Any vertical line has equation $x = a$ for some real number a. This equation cannot be written in slope-intercept form. The slope of a vertical line is undefined and will be discussed later in the chapter. In general, *every straight line has an equation of either the form $y = mx + b$ or $x = a$.* Any equation that can

linear equation   be put in one of these forms is a **linear equation.**

Equation of a Line

Every line has an equation of either the form $y = mx + b$ or $x = a$, where m is the slope and b is the y-intercept.

Systems of Linear Equations

The mathematical descriptions of many problems involve more than one equation, each having more than one unknown. To solve such problems, we must find a common solution to the equations, if it exists. An example is given on the following student page from *Addison-Wesley Mathematics,* Grade 8, 1993.

Exploring Algebra
Graphing Two Linear Equations

EXPLORE Study the Graph

Jack graphed the equation $y = x$, but was out of paper and had to use the same axis for $C = \frac{5}{9}(F - 32)$. Examine the outcome shown here. How many ordered pairs (x, y) will satisfy both equations?

TALK ABOUT IT

1. What is true about each ordered pair (x, y) on the line $y = x$?

2. Is the pair $(-40, -40)$ on the line $C = \frac{5}{9}(F - 32)$?

3. What is true for the Celsius and Fahrenheit readings at the point $(-40, -40)$?

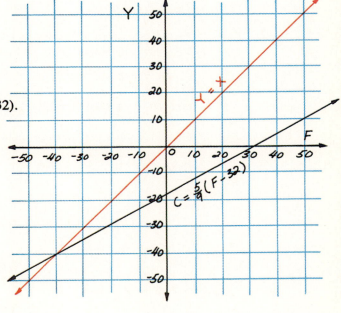

If two linear equations cross each other when graphed, that point is a solution to both equations. The two lines to the right appear to intersect at the point $(-1, 1)$. To check, substitute $(^-1, 1)$ in each equation.

$y = x + 2$	$y = -2x - 1$
$1 = -1 + 2$	$1 = -2 \cdot -1 - 1$
$1 = 1$	$1 = 2 - 1$
True.	True.

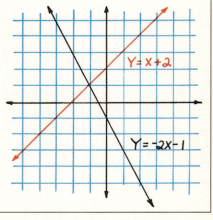

Any solution to a system of linear equations is an ordered pair (x, y) that satisfies both equations. Systems of linear equations arise in many story problems. Consider the following.

• • •

Example 7-12   May Chin ordered lunch for herself and several friends by phone without checking prices. Once, she paid $7.00 for five soyburgers and four orders of fries, and another time she paid $6.00 for four of each. Set up a system of equations with two unknowns representing the prices of a soyburger and an order of fries, respectively.

Solution   Let x be the price in dollars of a soyburger and y be the price of an order of fries. Five soyburgers cost $5x$ dollars, and four orders of fries cost $4y$ dollars. Because May paid $7.00 for the order, we have $5x + 4y = 7$. Similarly, $4x + 4y = 6$, or $2x + 2y = 3$.

• • •

An ordered pair satisfying both equations is a point that belongs to each of the lines. Figure 7-21 shows the graphs of $5x + 2y = 6$ and $x - 4y = {}^-1$. The two lines appear to intersect at $\left(1, \dfrac{1}{2}\right)$. Thus $\left(1, \dfrac{1}{2}\right)$ appears to be the solution of the given system of equations. This solution can be checked by substituting 1 for x and $\dfrac{1}{2}$ for y in each equation. Because two distinct lines intersect in only one point, $\left(1, \dfrac{1}{2}\right)$ is the only solution to the system.

Figure 7-21

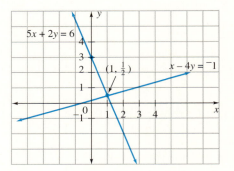

Substitution Method

Drawbacks to estimating a solution to a system of equations graphically include an inability to read noninteger real-number coordinates of points. However, there are algebraic methods for solving systems of linear equations. Consider, for example, the system $y = x + 3$ and $y = 2x - 1$. By substitution, $x + 3 = 2x - 1$, an equation with one unknown. Solving for x gives $3 + 1 = 2x - x$, and, hence, $4 = x$. Substituting 4 for x in either equation gives $y = 7$. Thus $(4, 7)$ is the solution to the given system. As before, this solution can be checked by substituting the obtained values for x and y in the original equation. This method for **substitution method**   solving a system of linear equations is called the **substitution method.**

• • •

Example 7-13   Solve the following system:

$$3x - 4y = 5$$
$$2x + 5y = 1$$

Solution   First, rewrite each equation, expressing y in terms of x.

$$y = \frac{3x - 5}{4} \text{ and } y = \frac{1 - 2x}{5}$$

Then equate the expressions for y and solve the resulting equation for x.

$$\frac{3x - 5}{4} = \frac{1 - 2x}{5}$$

$$5(3x - 5) = 4(1 - 2x)$$

$$15x - 25 = 4 - 8x$$

$$23x = 29$$

$$x = \frac{29}{23}$$

Substituting $\frac{29}{23}$ for x in $y = \frac{3x - 5}{4}$ gives $y = \frac{-7}{23}$. Hence, $x = \frac{29}{23}$ and $y = \frac{-7}{23}$. This can be checked by substituting the values for x and y in the original equations.

• • •

REMARK   Sometimes it is more convenient to solve a system of equations by expressing x in terms of y in one of the equations and substituting the obtained expression for x in the other equation.

Elimination Method

elimination method   The **elimination method** for solving two equations with two unknowns is based on eliminating one of the variables by adding or subtracting the original or equivalent equations. For example, consider the following system:

$$x - y = {}^-3$$
$$x + y = 7$$

By adding the two equations, we can eliminate the variable y. The resulting equation can then be solved for x.

$$\begin{aligned} x - y &= {}^-3 \\ \underline{x + y} &= \underline{\;7} \\ 2x\;\;\;\; &= 4 \\ x\;\;\;\; &= 2 \end{aligned}$$

Substituting 2 for x in the first equation (either equation may be used) gives $y = 5$. Checking this result shows that $x = 2$ and $y = 5$, or $(2, 5)$, is the solution to the system.

Often, another operation is required before equations are added so that an unknown can be eliminated. For example, consider the following system:

$$3x + 2y = 5$$
$$5x - 4y = 3$$

Adding the equations does not eliminate either unknown. However, if the first equation contained $4y$ rather than $2y$, the variable y could be eliminated by adding. To obtain $4y$ in the first equation, we multiply both sides of the equation by 2 to obtain the equivalent equation $6x + 4y = 10$. Adding the equations in the equivalent system gives the following:

$$6x + 4y = 10$$
$$5x - 4y = 3$$
$$\overline{11x = 13}$$
$$x = \frac{13}{11}$$

To find the corresponding value of y, we substitute $\frac{13}{11}$ for x in either of the original equations and solve for y, or we use the elimination method again and solve for y.

An alternative method is to eliminate the x-values from the original system by multiplying the first equation by 5 and the second by $^-3$ (or the first by $^-5$ and the second by 3). Then we add the two equations and solve for y.

$$15x + 10y = 25$$
$$^-15x + 12y = {}^-9$$
$$\overline{22y = 16}$$
$$y = \frac{16}{22}, \quad \text{or} \quad \frac{8}{11}$$

Consequently, $\left(\frac{13}{11}, \frac{8}{11}\right)$ is the solution of the original system. This solution, as always, should be checked by substitution in the *original* equations.

Solutions to Other Systems

All examples thus far have had unique solutions. However, other situations may arise. Geometrically, a system of two linear equations can be characterized as follows:

1. *The system has a unique solution if, and only if, the graphs of the equations intersect in a single point.*
2. *The system has no solution if, and only if, the equations represent parallel lines.*
3. *The system has infinitely many solutions if, and only if, the equations represent the same line.*

Finding the Equation of a Line Through Two Points

Because a line is determined by any two of its points, it is possible, given the coordinates of two points on a line, to find the equation of the line. For example, given $A(4, 2)$ and $B(1, 6)$, it is possible to find the equation of $\overleftrightarrow{AB}$. Because the line is not perpendicular to the x-axis (why?), it must be of the form $y = mx + b$. Substituting the coordinates of A and B in $y = mx + b$ results in the following equations:

$$2 = m \cdot 4 + b \quad \text{or} \quad 2 = 4m + b$$
$$6 = m \cdot 1 + b \quad \text{or} \quad 6 = m + b$$

To find the equation of the line, we must find the values of m and b. Solving for b in each of these equations gives $b = 2 - 4m$ and $b = 6 - m$, respectively. Consequently, $2 - 4m = 6 - m$, so $m = \frac{-4}{3}$. Substituting this value of m in either of the equations gives $b = \frac{22}{3}$. Hence, the equation of the line through A and B is $y = \dfrac{-4}{3}x + \dfrac{22}{3}$. The correctness of this equation can be checked by substituting the coordinates of the two given points, $A(4, 2)$ and $B(1, 6)$, in the equation.

Fitting a Line to Data

best-fitting line

In many practical situations, a relationship between two variables comes from collected data such as from population or business surveys. When the data is graphed, there may not be a single line that goes through all of the points, but the points may appear to approximate, or "follow," a straight line. In such cases, it is useful to find the equation of what seems to be the **best-fitting line.** Knowing the equation of such a line enables us to predict an outcome without actually performing the experiment.

REMARK   Some data may be scattered in a way that does not approximate a straight line and hence it may be impossible to find the best-fitting line for the data.

There are several different approaches to define, and hence find, the best-fitting line. We take a graphical approach as follows:

1. Choose a line that seems to follow the given points so that there are about an equal number of points below the line as above the line.
2. Determine two convenient points on the line and approximate the x- and y-coordinates of these points.
3. Use the points in (2) to determine the equation of the line.

Example 7-14

A shirt manufacturer noticed that the number of units sold depends on the price charged. The data in Table 7-5 shows the number of units sold for a given price per unit.

a. Find the equation of a line that seems to best fit the data.
b. Use the equation in (a) to predict the number of units that will be sold if the price per unit is $60.

Table 7-5

Price per Unit (In dollars)	Number of Units Sold (Thousands)
50	200
44	250
41	300
33	380
31	400
24.5	450
20	500
14.5	550

Solution   **a.** Figure 7-22(a) shows the graph of the data displayed in Table 7-5. Figure 7-22(b) shows a line that seems to fit the data so that approximately the same number of points are below the line as above the line. We choose the points (50, 200) and (20, 500), which are on the line in Figure 7-22(b).

Figure 7-22

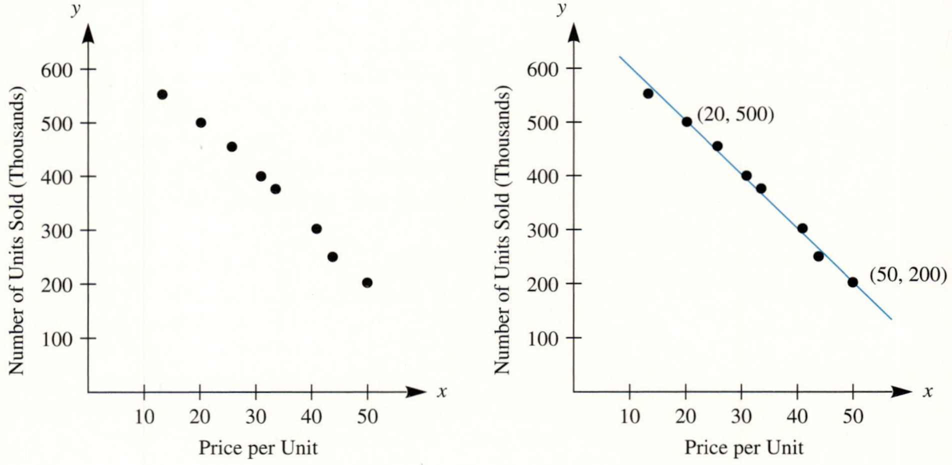

(a)

(b)

To find the equation of the line, we need to find m and b in the equation $y = mx + b$. Substituting the points (50, 200) and (20, 500) into this equation, we obtain the following:

$$200 = 50m + b$$
$$500 = 20m + b$$

One way to solve the equations is to express b in terms of m for each equation:

$$b = 200 - 50m$$
$$b = 500 - 20m$$

We equate the expressions for b and solve for m:

$$200 - 50m = 500 - 20m$$
$$200 - 500 = 50m - 20m$$
$$^-300 = 30m$$
$$m = {}^-10$$

Substituting this value for m, we obtain

$$b = 200 - 50(^-10) = 700.$$

Consequently, the equation of the fitted line is $y = {}^-10x + 700$.

b. Using the equation in (a), substitute $x = 60$ to obtain $y = {}^-10(60) + 700$, or $y = 100$. Thus we predict that 100,000 units will be sold if the price per unit is $60.

Ongoing Assessment 7-3

1. Sketch the graphs of the equations $y = {}^-x$ and $y = {}^-x + 3$ on the same coordinate system. How are the graphs related?

2. The graph of $y = mx$ is given in the following figure. Sketch the graphs for each of the following on the same figure. Explain your answers.
   a. $y = mx + 3$ b. $y = mx - 3$

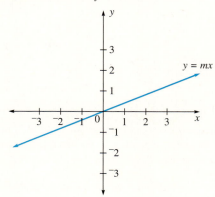

3. Sketch the graphs for each of the following equations:
   a. $y = \dfrac{-3}{4}x + 3$ b. $y = {}^-3$ c. $y = 15x - 30$

   d. $x = {}^-2$ e. $y = 3x - 1$ f. $y = \dfrac{1}{20}x$

4. Find the x-intercept and y-intercept for the equations in Problem 3, if they exist.

5. In the following, figure (a) below shows a dual scale thermometer and figure (b) at the top of the next column shows the corresponding points plotted on a graph.

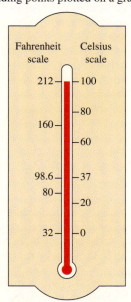

(a)

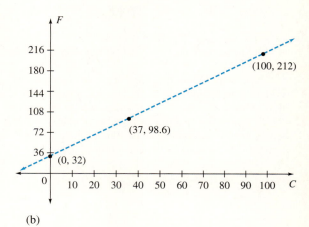

(b)

a. Use two of the points on the graph on the graph to develop a formula for conversion from degrees Celsius (C) to degrees Fahrenheit (F).

b. Use your answer in (a) to find a formula for converting from degrees F to degrees C.

6. Write each of the following equations in slope-intercept form and identify the slope and y-intercept:
   a. $3y - x = 0$
   b. $x + y = 3$
   c. $\dfrac{x}{3} + \dfrac{y}{4} = 1$
   d. $3x - 4y + 7 = 0$
   e. $x = 3y$
   f. $x - y = 4(x - y)$

7. For each of the following, write the equation of the line determined by the given pair of points in slope-intercept form or in the form $x = a$:
   a. $({}^-4, 3)$ and $(1, {}^-2)$
   b. $(0, 0)$ and $(2, 1)$
   c. $(0, 1)$ and $(2, 1)$
   d. $(2, 1)$ and $(2, {}^-1)$
   e. $\left(0, \dfrac{-1}{2}\right)$ and $\left(\dfrac{1}{2}, 0\right)$
   f. $({}^-a, 0)$ and $(a, 0)$, $a \neq 0$

8. Find the coordinates of two other points collinear (on the same line) with each of the following pairs of given points:
   a. $P(2, 2)$, $Q(4, 2)$ b. $P({}^-1, 0)$, $Q({}^-1, 2)$
   c. $P(0, 0)$, $Q(0, 1)$ d. $P(0, 0)$, $Q(1, 1)$

9. For each of the following, give as much information as possible about x and y:
   a. The ordered pairs $({}^-2, 0)$, $({}^-2, 1)$, and (x, y) represent collinear points.
   b. The ordered pairs $({}^-2, 1)$, $(0, 1)$, and (x, y) represent collinear points.
   c. The ordered pair (x, y) is in the fourth quadrant.

10. Consider the lines through $P(2, 4)$ and perpendicular to the x- and y-axes, respectively. Find both the area and the perimeter of the rectangle formed by these lines and the axes.

11. Find the equations for each of the following:
    a. The line containing $P(3, 0)$ and perpendicular to the x-axis
    b. The line containing $P(0, {}^-2)$ and parallel to the x-axis
    c. The line containing $P({}^-4, 5)$ and parallel to the x-axis
    d. The line containing $P({}^-4, 5)$ and parallel to the y-axis

12. Wildlife experts found that the number of chirps a cricket makes in 15-sec intervals is related to the temperature T in degrees Fahrenheit as shown in the following graph:

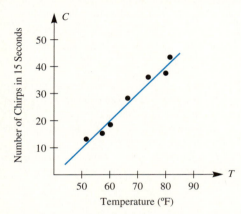

a. If C is the number of chirps in 15 sec, write a formula for C in terms of T (temperature in degrees Fahrenheit) that seems to best fit the data.
b. Use the equation in (a) to predict the number of chirps in 15 sec when the temperature is $90°$.
c. If N is the number of chirps per minute, write a formula for N in terms of T.

13. **a.** Graph the following data and find the equation of best-fitting line.
    b. Use your answer in (a) to predict the value of y when $x = 100$.

x	y
1	8.1
2	9.9
3	12
4	14.1
5	15.9
6	18
7	19.9

14. Use the equation $2x - 3y = 5$ for each of the following:
    a. Find four solutions of the equation.

b. Graph all the solutions for which ${}^-2 \le x \le 2$.
c. Graph all the solutions for which $0 \le y \le 2$.

15. Solve each of the following systems, if possible. Indicate whether the system has a unique solution, infinitely many solutions, or no solution.
    a. $y = 3x - 1$
    $\quad\;\; y = x + 3$
    b. $2x - 6y = 7$
    $\quad\;\; 3x - 9y = 10$
    c. $3x + 4y = {}^-17$
    $\quad\;\; 2x + 3y = {}^-13$
    d. $8y - 6x = 78$
    $\quad\;\; 9x - 12y = 12$
    e. $5x - 18y = 0$
    $\quad\;\; x - 24y = 0$
    f. $2x + 3y = 1$
    $\quad\;\; 3x - y = 1$

16. The vertices of a triangle are given by $(0, 0)$, $(10, 0)$, and $(6, 8)$. Show that the segments connecting $(5, 0)$ and $(6, 8)$, $(10, 0)$ and $(3, 4)$, and $(0, 0)$ and $(8, 4)$ intersect at a common point.

17. The owner of a 5000-gal oil truck loads the truck with gasoline and kerosene. The profit on each gallon of gasoline is 13¢ and on each gallon of kerosene is 12¢. How many gallons of each fuel did the owner load if the profit was $640.

18. At the end of 10 mo, the balance of an account earning simple interest is $2100.
    a. If, at the end of 18 mo, the balance is $2180, how much money was originally in the account?
    b. What is the rate of interest?

19. Josephine's bank contains 27 coins. If all the coins are either dimes or quarters and the value of the coins is $5.25, how many of each kind of coin are there?

20. **a.** Solve each of the following systems of equations. What do you notice about the answers?
    i. $\quad x + 2y = 3$
    $\quad\;\; 4x + 5y = 6$
    ii. $\quad 2x + 3y = 4$
    $\quad\;\;\; 5x + 6y = 7$
    iii. $\;31x + 32y = 33$
    $\quad\; 34x + 35y = 36$
    b. Write another system similar to those in (a). What solution did you expect? Check your guess.
    c. Write a general system similar to those in (a). What solution does this system have? Why?

Communication

21. Dahlia wanted to find what temperature has the same measure when measured in degrees Fahrenheit or degrees Celsius. To do that, she graphed the equation of the conversion formula $C = 5/9(F - 32)$. On the same coordinate system, she also graphed the equation $C = F$ and found the intersection point as $({}^-40, {}^-40)$. Explain why this procedure answers the question Dahlia asked.

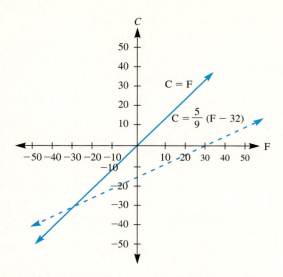

22. Explain in more than one way why two lines with the same slope are parallel.

23. Jonah tried to solve the equation $^{-}5x + y = 20$ by adding 5 to both sides. He wrote $5 - 5x + y = 5 + 20$ or $0 \cdot x + y = 25$ and finally $y = 25$. How would you help Jonah?

24. Fumio would like to know why two lines with an undefined slope are parallel. How would you respond?

Open-ended

25. Look for data in newspapers, magazines, or books whose graphs appear to be close to linear and find the equations of the lines that you think best fit the data.

26. Describe a real-life situation that can be modeled by a system of two equations with two unknowns. Solve your system and interpret your solutions in terms of your original real-life situation.

27. a. Write equations of two lines that intersect but when graphed look parallel.

b. At what point do those two lines intersect?

28. a. Write and graph a system of equations to model the distance from the starting line of two runners who run at the same speed and start at the same time.

b. Write and graph a system of equations to model the distance from the starting line of two runners who run at the same speed but start running from different points.

Cooperative Learning

29. Play the following game between your group and another group. Each group makes up four linear equations that have a common property and presents the equations to the other group. For example, one group could present the equations $2x - y = 0$, $4x - 2y = 3$, $y - 2x = 3$, and $3y - 6x = 5$. If the second group discovers a common property that the equations share, such as the graphs of the equations are four parallel lines, they get one point. Each group takes a specified number of turns.

Review Problems

30. A city with 120,000 people has been growing by 1800 people per year. At this rate, when will the population of the city exceed 165,000 people?

31. The sum of four consecutive odd numbers is 1014. What are the four numbers?

32. A farmer wants to use a fence to enclose a rectangular piece of land that lies alongside a barn. She wants the side parallel to the wall of the barn to be three times as long as the other two sides. She wants to use a total of 550 ft of fence. What should the dimensions of the rectangle be?

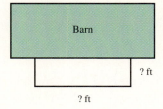

TECHNOLOGY CORNER

The following Logo procedure draws a line segment connecting two points (:X1, :Y1) and (:X2, :Y2):

```
TO SEGMENT :X1 :Y1 :X2 :Y2
  PENUP
  SETXY :X1 :Y1
  PENDOWN
  SETXY :X2 :Y2
END
```

(In LCSI, replace SETXY with SETPOS LIST.)

Use the SEGMENT procedure to write a procedure to draw a triangle given the coordinates of its three vertices.

Section 7-4   # Ratio and Proportion

Ratios are commonly encountered in everyday life. For example, there may be a 2-to-3 ratio of Democrats to Republicans on a certain legislative committee, a friend may be given a speeding ticket for driving 63 miles per hour, or eggs may cost 98¢ a dozen. Each of these

ratio   illustrates a **ratio.** A 1-to-2 ratio of males to females means that the number of males is $\frac{1}{2}$ the number of females, that is, there is one male for every two females. The ratio 1 to 2 can be written as $\frac{1}{2}$ or 1:2. In general, a ratio is denoted by $\frac{a}{b}$ or $a{:}b$, where $b \neq 0$.

In the 5-8 *Standards* (p. 89), we find the following concerning ratios and proportion:

▲   *Ratios should be introduced gradually through discussing the many situations in which they occur naturally. It takes little effort to relate these situations to students' interests: "If 245 of a company's 398 employees are women, how many of its 26 executives would you expect to be women?"*

Through these practical exercises, students should come to recognize that ratios are not directly measurable but they contain two units and that the order of the items in the ratio pair in a proportion is critical. Thus, 23 persons per square mile is very different from 23 square miles per person.

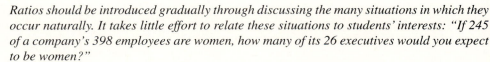

I N V E S T I G A T I O N   7 - 4

● Discuss the difference between *23 persons per square mile* and *23 square miles per person.* ●

• • •

Example 7-15   There were 7 males and 12 females in the Dew Drop Inn on Monday evening. In the Game Room next door were 14 males and 24 females.

a. Express the number of males to females at the Inn as a ratio.
b. Express the number of males to females at the Game Room as a ratio.

Solution   **a.** The ratio is $\frac{7}{12}$.   **b.** The ratio is $\frac{14}{24}$.

• • •

In Example 7-15, the ratios $\frac{7}{12}$ and $\frac{14}{24}$ are equal and proportional to each other. In general,

proportional   two ratios are **proportional** if, and only if, the fractions representing them are equal. Two
proportion   equal ratios form a **proportion.**

For example, $\frac{2}{3}$ and $\frac{8}{12}$ form a proportion because $\frac{2}{3} = \frac{8}{12}$, since $2 \cdot 12 = 8 \cdot 3$. Also $\frac{3}{4} \neq \frac{4}{5}$ because $3 \cdot 5 \neq 4 \cdot 4$. In general, we have the following property previously justified for rational numbers in Chapter 5.

Property

If a, b, c, and d are all real numbers and $b \neq 0$ and $d \neq 0$, then

$$\frac{a}{b} = \frac{c}{d} \text{ if, and only if, } ad = bc.$$

This property can be justified by multiplying each side of the proportion by bd.

Frequently, one term in a proportion is missing, as in

$$\frac{3}{8} = \frac{x}{16}.$$

This equation is a proportion if, and only if,

$$3 \cdot 16 = 8 \cdot x$$
$$48 = 8 \cdot x$$
$$6 = x$$

Another way to solve the equation is to multiply both sides by 16, as follows:

$$\frac{3}{8} \cdot 16 = \frac{x}{16} \cdot 16$$
$$3 \cdot 2 = x$$
$$x = 6$$

It is important to remember that in the ratio $a \div b$, a and b do not have to be integers. For example, if in Eugene, Oregon, $\frac{7}{10}$ of the population exercises regularly, then $\frac{3}{10}$ of the population does not exercise regularly, and the ratio of those who do to those who do not is $\frac{7}{10} : \frac{3}{10}$. However, since ratios are usually simplified, the last ratio can be written as $7 : 3$.

The following are examples of problems utilizing ratio and proportion.

Example 7-16   If there should be 3 tractors for every 4 farmers on a collective farm, how many tractors are needed for 44 farmers?

 Solution   We use the strategy of *setting up a table,* as shown in Table 7-6.

Table 7-6

Number of Farmers	3	x
Number of Tractors	4	44

The ratio of tractors to farmers should always be the same.

$$\begin{array}{l} \text{Tractors} \rightarrow \\ \text{Farmers} \rightarrow \end{array} \frac{3}{4} = \frac{x}{44}$$
$$3 \cdot 44 = 4 \cdot x$$
$$132 = 4x$$
$$33 = x$$

Thus 33 tractors are needed.

It is important to notice units of measure when we work with proportions. For example, if a turtle travels 5 in. every 10 sec, how many feet does it travel in 50 sec? If units of measure are ignored, we might set up the following proportion:

$$\frac{5 \text{ in.}}{10 \text{ sec}} = \frac{x \text{ ft}}{50 \text{ sec}}$$

This statement is incorrect. A correct statement must involve the same units in each ratio. We may write the following:

$$\frac{5 \text{ in.}}{10 \text{ sec}} = \frac{x \text{ in.}}{50 \text{ sec}}$$

This implies that $x = 25$. Consequently, since 12 in. $= 1$ ft, the turtle travels $\frac{25}{12}$ ft, or $2\frac{1}{12}$ ft.

• • •

Example 7-17   Kai, Paulus, and Judy made $2520 for painting a house. Kai worked 30 hr, Paulus worked 50 hr, and Judy worked 60 hr. They divided the money in proportion to the number of hours worked. How much did each earn?

Solution   If we denote the amount of money that Kai received by $30x$, then the amount of money Paulus received must be $50x$ because then, and only then, will the ratios of the amounts be the same as 30:50 as required. Similarly, Judy received $60x$. Because the total amount of money received is $30x + 50x + 60x$, we have

$$30x + 50x + 60x = 2520$$
$$140x = 2520$$
$$x = 18.$$

Hence,

$$\text{Kai received } 30x = 30 \cdot 18, \text{ or } \$540$$
$$\text{Paulus received } 50x = 50 \cdot 18, \text{ or } \$900$$
$$\text{Judy received } 60x = 60 \cdot 18, \text{ or } \$1080.$$

Dividing each of the amounts by 18 shows that the proportion is as required.

• • •

Consider the proportion $\frac{15}{30} = \frac{3}{6}$. Because the ratios in the proportion are equal fractions and because equal nonzero fractions have equal reciprocals, it follows that $\frac{30}{15} = \frac{6}{3}$. Also notice that the proportions are true because each results in $15 \cdot 6 = 30 \cdot 3$. In general, we have the following property:

Property

For any rational numbers $\frac{a}{b}$ and $\frac{c}{d}$, with $a \neq 0$ and $c \neq 0$, $\frac{a}{b} = \frac{c}{d}$ if, and only if, $\frac{b}{a} = \frac{d}{c}$.

Consider $\frac{15}{30} = \frac{3}{6}$ again. Notice that $\frac{15}{3} = \frac{30}{6}$; that is, the ratio of the numerators is proportional to the ratio of the corresponding denominators. In general we have the following property.

Property

For any rational numbers $\dfrac{a}{b}$ and $\dfrac{c}{d}$, with $c \neq 0$, $\dfrac{a}{b} = \dfrac{c}{d}$ if, and only if, $\dfrac{a}{c} = \dfrac{b}{d}$.

This property is true because each equation results in $ad = bc$.

Problem 3

In the Klysler car factory, robots assemble cars. If 3 robots can assemble 17 cars in 10 min, how many cars can 14 robots assemble in 45 min if all robots work at the same rate all the time?

Understanding the Problem.   We are to determine the number of cars that 14 robots can assemble in 45 min given that 3 robots can assemble 17 cars in 10 min. If we knew how many cars 1 robot could assemble in 45 min or how many cars 1 robot could assemble in 1 min, we could solve the problem.

Devising a Plan.   Let x be the number of cars that 14 robots assemble in 45 min. Because the robots work at the same rate, we can express this rate by taking the information that 3 robots assemble 17 cars in 10 min and equating it with the information that 14 robots assemble x cars in 45 min. The rate would be the number of cars (or parts of a car) that 1 robot can assemble in 1 min. We first need to find the number of cars that 1 robot can assemble in 1 min. Then, we need to write and solve the desired equation to solve the problem.

Carrying Out the Plan.   If 3 robots assemble 17 cars in 10 min, then the 3 robots assemble $\dfrac{17}{10}$ cars in 1 min. Consequently, 1 robot assembles $\dfrac{1}{3} \cdot \dfrac{17}{10}$, or $\dfrac{17}{30}$, of a car in 1 min.

Similarly, if 14 robots assemble x cars in 45 min, then the 14 robots assemble $\dfrac{x}{45}$ cars in 1 min. Thus 1 robot assembles $\dfrac{1}{14} \cdot \dfrac{x}{45}$, or $\dfrac{x}{14 \cdot 45}$, of a car in 1 min. Because the rates are equal, we have the proportion $\dfrac{x}{14 \cdot 45} = \dfrac{17}{30}$. Solving this equation, we obtain $x = 357$.

Therefore 357 cars are assembled.

Looking Back.   Another approach is to set up a table like Table 7-7, where x designates the number of cars that 14 robots assemble in 45 min.

Table 7-7

Number of Robots	Number of Cars	Time (Minutes)
3	17	10
14	x	45

We set up a proportion for the ratios between the number of robots and the number of cars if the time in each case is the same. Because LCM $(10, 45) = 90$, 3 robots produce $17 \cdot 9$ cars in 90 min. Looking at the second row of Table 7-8, we find that in 90 min, 14 robots will produce $2x$ cars.

Table 7-8

Number of Robots	Number of Cars	Time (Minutes)
3	$17 \cdot 9$	90
14	$2x$	90

Because in each case the time to produce the cars is the same, the ratios between the number of cars and the number of robots are proportional. Hence,

$$\frac{2x}{14} = \frac{17 \cdot 9}{3}$$

$$\frac{x}{7} = 17 \cdot 3$$

$$x = 17 \cdot 3 \cdot 7 = 357.$$

The problem can be solved without writing any equations, as follows. Because 1 robot assembles $\frac{17}{30}$ of a car in 1 min, 14 robots assemble $14 \cdot \frac{17}{30}$ cars in 1 min. Thus in 45 min, 14 robots assemble $45 \cdot 14 \cdot \frac{17}{30}$, or 357, cars.

The problem can be varied by changing the data or by considering two kinds of robots, each kind working at a different rate. Similar problems can be constructed concerning other jobs such as painting houses or washing cars.

• • •

Scale Drawings

scale Ratio and proportions are used in scale drawings. For example, if the scale is $1:300$ then the length of 1 cm in such a drawing represents 300 cm, or 3 m in true size. The **scale** is the ratio of the size of the drawing to the actual size of the object if measured in the same units. The following examples show the use of scale drawings.

• • •

Example 7-18 The following floor plan of the main floor of the house in Figure 7-23 is drawn in the scale of $1:300$. Find the dimensions in meters of the living room.

Figure 7-23

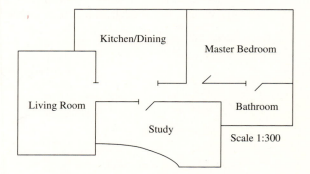

Solution In Figure 7-23, the dimensions of the living room measured with a centimeter ruler are approximately 3.7 cm by 2.5 cm. Because the scale is $1:300$, 1 cm in the drawing represents 300 cm, or 3 m in true size. Hence, 3.7 cm represents 3.7 · 3, or 11.1 m and 2.5 cm represents 2.5 · 3, or 7.5 m. Hence the dimensions of the living room are approximately 11.1 m by 7.5 m.

• • •

Direct Variation

directly proportional

direct variation

Many ratio and proportion problems can be viewed as rate problems. For example, if a phone company charges 10 cents for each minute of long distance conversation, then the cost C, for t minutes of call, is $C = 10t$ cents. We say that the cost is **directly proportional** to the time t. Because $C = 10t$ implies $\dfrac{C}{t} = 10$, the ratio between the total cost of the conversation and the time it takes is always 10. In general, two variables that are in the same ratio regardless of their values are in **direct variation.**

Behaviors of many natural phenomena can be modeled by direct variation. For example, consider the experiment of dropping a rubber ball from a given height and recording how high it bounces off a concrete floor. Table 7-9 shows the approximate bouncing heights B for several corresponding drop heights D and the measured values in inches of the corresponding ratios B/D.

Table 7-9

Drop Heights (D)	Bounce Heights (B)	B/D
15	11	$11/15 = 0.73$
25	18	$18/25 = 0.72$
30	21	$21/30 = 0.7$
40	28	$28/40 = 0.7$
50	35	$35/50 = 0.7$
60	42.5	$42.5/60 = 0.71$

Table 7-9 suggests that the ratio B/D is approximately 0.7. Although the ratio is not exactly 0.7 all the time, direct variation seems to be a good model for the bouncing ball. The equation $B/D = 0.7$ implies $B = 0.7\,D$. If the drop height is 100 in., we can expect the height of the bouncing ball to be about 0.7 · 100, or 70 in.

Figure 7-24 shows the graph of the equation $B = 0.7\,D$. The graph is a line through the origin with a slope of 0.7. In general, the graph of a direct variation is a line through the origin. (Why?)

Figure 7-24

Bouncing Ball Graph

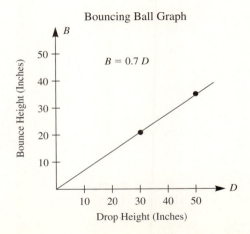

REMARK   The graph in Figure 7-24 is a graph of the equation $B = 0.7\,D$ and not of the data in Table 7-9. The graph only approximates the data in Table 7-9. Some of the ordered pairs in Table 7-9, such as (30, 21), are on the graph because 21/30 = 0.7. Other ordered pairs, such as (42.5, 60), are close to the line because 42.5/60 = 0.71 is close to 0.7.

Inverse Variation

Sometimes rather than the ratio between two variables, the product of the variables remains constant. Table 7-10 shows the relationship between the depth of water and the temperature at that depth off the coast of Hawaii.

Table 7-10

Depth (Meters)	Temperature (°C)	DT
1000	5	5000
1500	3.3	4950
2000	2.5	5000
2500	2	5000
3000	1.7	5100
4000	1.24	4960
5000	1	5000

Notice that when the depth D is 1000 m or greater, the product of the depth and the corresponding temperature T is always close to 5000. Thus the relationship between the two variables in this particular spot in the Pacific Ocean can be modeled by the equation $DT = 5000$. From this equation, we can express one variable in terms of the other. Because $T = 5000/D$, we say that the variables **vary inversely** or that T is **inversely proportional** to D. In general, *two variables x and y vary inversely if xy = c, where c is a constant;* that is, *c* remains the same for all allowed values of *x* and *y*. Figure 7-25 shows the graph of the equation $T = 5000/D$ for $D > 1000$ m. The graph is part of a curve called a **hyperbola.**

vary inversely •
inversely proportional

hyperbola

Figure 7-25

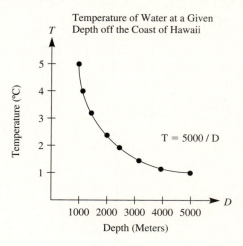

Temperature of Water at a Given Depth off the Coast of Hawaii

$T = 5000 / D$

• • •

Example 7-19   In each of the following, find whether the described variables are in direct variation, inverse variation, or neither.

a. The time t it takes to wait in line for tickets to a concert is related to the number of people p in line by the equation $t = cp$, where c is a constant.

b. The volume V of a gas (in cubic meters) at a constant temperature and the pressure P (in kilograms per cubic meter) are related by the equation $PV = 1.30$.

c. The fee d (in dollars) and the number of months m a member stays in the club is related by the equation $d = 300 + 50m$.

Solution   **a.** Because $t/p = c$ and c is constant, this is a direct variation.

b. This is an inverse variation.

c. Neither a direct nor inverse relation exists.

• • •

Levers

lever • fulcrum

A **lever** is a rigid bar placed over a support, the **fulcrum.** Levers have been used since antiquity to move heavy objects. Levers are involved in the design of various tools such as can openers, wrenches, and so on. Figure 7-26(a) shows a person pushing down at point A on a bar that pivots at point O and lifts a heavy weight at point B. Figure 7-26(b) shows a child and an adult on a balance in equilibrium.

Figure 7-26

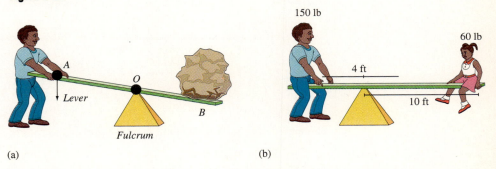

(a)   (b)

The child who weighs less than the adult in Figure 7-26(b) keeps the bar level by sitting further from the fulcrum than the adult. Notice that $60 \cdot 10 = 150 \cdot 4$; that is, the weight times the distance to the fulcrum has the same value for each person. If the child sat further from the fulcrum, say 11 ft, the balance would shift and so the adult would be lifted. In such a case, $60 \cdot 11 > 150 \cdot 4$. Archimedes (287–212 B.C.) formulated the law on which the above experiments are based.

Property: Law of the Lever

Two weights (or forces) on a lever balance if, and only if, the products of their weights (or forces) and the corresponding distances to the fulcrum are equal. If the products are not equal, the lever will tilt (downwards) in the direction of the weight that corresponds to the greater product.

A child weighing 30 lb at a distance of 20 ft will also balance the adult in Figure 7-26(b) because $150 \cdot 4 = 20 \cdot 30$. Similarly, a weight of 15 lb at a distance of 40 ft will also balance the adult. Any weight w will balance the adult if it is at a distance d such that $wd = 600$. Consequently, the variables w and d vary inversely.

Figure 7-27 shows a lever in equilibrium. If the weights w_1 and w_2 are at distance d_1 and d_2 from the fulcrum respectively, then

$$w_1 d_1 = w_2 d_2.$$

This equation implies the following proportion:

$$\frac{w_1}{w_2} = \frac{d_2}{d_1}$$

Figure 7-27

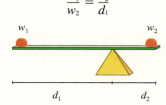

Because $\dfrac{d_2}{d_1} = \left(\dfrac{d_1}{d_2}\right)^{-1}$, at balance the ratio between the weights is inversely proportional to the ratio between the corresponding distances.

• • •

Example 7-20   For each of the levers in Figure 7-28(a) and (b), find x.

Figure 7-28

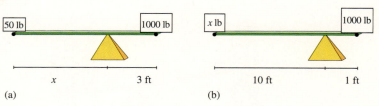

(a)   (b)

Solution   Using the Law of the Lever, we proceed as follows:

a. $50x = 3 \cdot 1000$

$x = 60$

Hence, $x = 60$ ft.

b. $x \cdot 10 = 1000 \cdot 1$

$x = 100$

Hence, $x = 100$ lb.

• • •

Example 7-21   Figure 7-29 shows that a weight of w lb at a distance x ft from a fulcrum balances a weight of 1000 lb at a distance 2 ft from the fulcrum. For different values of x, w takes on different values.

a. Write w as a function of x.
b. Graph the function in (a) using the fact that 2000 lb = 1 t (ton).
c. Interpret the behavior of the function in (b) for small and large values of x.

Figure 7-29

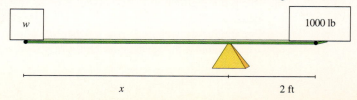

Solution   **a.** Using the Law of the Lever, we have

$$wx = 2 \cdot 1000,$$

$$w = 2000/x.$$

b. The values of w obtained from the function in (a) are in pounds (why?). Because 2000 lb = 1 t, $w = 1/x$, where x is measured in feet and the corresponding value of w is measured in tons.

Table 7-11 shows the values of x ranging from small positive values to large values. The values are graphed and connected in Figure 7-30.

Table 7-11

Balancing Weight w	Distance to Fulcrum x
100	$\dfrac{1}{100}$
10	$\dfrac{1}{10}$
1	1
$\dfrac{1}{2}$	2
$\dfrac{1}{3}$	3
$\dfrac{1}{4}$	4

Figure 7-30

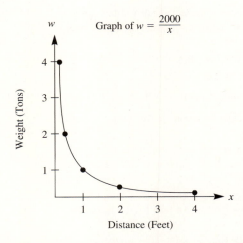

Graph of $w = \dfrac{2000}{x}$

c. For large values of x, the graph gets closer and closer to the x-axis and hence w gets smaller and smaller. This is consistent with the fact that when the distance to the fulcrum increases, a smaller weight is needed to balance the lever. When x gets smaller, w increases. This is consistent with the fact that if the distance to the fulcrum decreases, a larger weight is needed to balance the lever.

HISTORICAL NOTE

Archimedes (287–212 B.C.E.), a famous scientist of antiquity and one of the greatest mathematicians of all times, is credited with numerous scientific inventions. His design of various mechanical devices enabled Syracuse to delay for years the Roman siege of the city. Based on the Law of the Lever, Archimedes is reported to have boasted, "Give me a place to stand and I will move the earth." Apparently when working on his inventions, Archimedes was unaware of his surroundings. For example, once when in his bathtub, he discovered the principle of buoyancy. In the excitement of his discovery, he got out of the tub and ran through the streets stark naked shouting, "Eureka! Eureka!" translated as "I have found it! I have found it!" It has been reported that he died while preoccupied with solving a geometrical problem on a sand tray. Archimedes told a Roman soldier not to disturb him, whereupon the soldier, enraged, killed him.

Ongoing Assessment 7-4

1. Answer the following regarding the English alphabet:
   a. Determine the ratio of vowels to consonants.
   b. Write a word that has a ratio of 2:3 of vowels to consonants.

2. Solve for x in each of the following proportions:
   a. $\dfrac{12}{x} = \dfrac{18}{45}$ b. $\dfrac{x}{7} = \dfrac{-10}{21}$
   c. $\dfrac{5}{7} = \dfrac{3x}{98}$ d. $3\dfrac{1}{2}$ is to 5 as x is to 15.

3. There are approximately 2 lb of muscle for every 5 lb of body weight. For a 90-lb child, how much of the weight is muscle?

4. There are 5 adult drivers to each teenage driver in Aluossim. If there are 12,345 adult drivers in Aluossim, how many teenage drivers are there?

5. If 4 grapefruits sell for 79¢, how much do 6 grapefruits cost?

6. On a map, $\dfrac{1}{3}$ in. represents 5 mi. If New York and Aluossim are 18 in. apart on the map, what is the actual distance between them?

7. David read 40 pages of a book in 50 min. How many pages should he be able to read in 80 min if he reads at a constant rate?

8. A candle is 30 in. long. After burning for 12 min, the candle is 25 in. long. How long will it take for the whole candle to burn at the same rate?

9. Two numbers are in the ratio 3:4. Find the numbers if
   a. their sum is 98.
   b. their product is 768.

10. A rectangular yard has a width-to-length ratio of 5:9. If the distance around the yard is 2800 ft, what are the dimensions of the yard?

11. Gary, Bill, and Carmella invested in a corporation in the ratio of 2:4:5, respectively. If they divide the profit of $82,000 proportionally to their investment, how much will each receive?

12. Sheila and Dora worked $3\dfrac{1}{2}$ hr and $4\dfrac{1}{2}$ hr, respectively, on a programming project. They were paid $176 for the project. How much did each earn?

13. Vonna scored 75 goals in her soccer practice. If her success-to-failure rate is 5:4, how many times did she attempt a goal?

14. The rise and span for a house roof are identified as follows. The pitch of a roof is the ratio of the rise to the half-span.
   a. If the rise is 10 ft and the span is 28 ft, what is the pitch?
   b. If the span is 16 ft and the pitch is $\dfrac{3}{4}$, what is the rise?

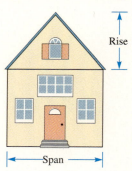

15. A grasshopper can jump 20 times its length. If jumping ability in humans were proportional to a grasshopper's, how far could a 6-ft-tall person jump?

16. Jim found out that after working for 9 mo he had earned 6 days of vacation time. How many days per year does he earn at this rate?

17. Gear ratios are used in industry. A gear ratio is the comparison of the number of teeth on two gears. When two gears are meshed, the revolutions per minute (rpm) are inversely proportional to the number of teeth; that is,

$$\frac{\text{rpm of large gear}}{\text{rpm of small gear}} = \frac{\text{number of teeth on small gear}}{\text{number of teeth on large gear}}$$

   a. The rpm ratio of the large gear to the small gear is 4:6. If the small gear has 18 teeth, how many teeth does the large gear have?
   b. The large gear revolves at 200 rpm and has 60 teeth. How many teeth are there on the small gear that has an rpm of 600?

18. A Boeing 747 jet is approximately 230 ft long and has a wingspan of 195 ft. If a scale model of the plane is about 40 cm long, what is the model's wingspan?

19. Jennifer weighs 160 lb on Earth and 416 lb on Jupiter. Find Amy's weight on Jupiter if she weighs 120 lb on Earth.

20. **a.** If the ratio of boys to girls in a class is 2:3, what is the ratio of boys to all the students in the class? Why?
   b. If the ratio of boys to girls in a class is *m:n*, what is the ratio of boys to all the students in the class?

21. A recipe calls for 1 tsp of mustard seeds, 3 c of tomato sauce, 1 1/2 c of chopped scallions, and 3 1/4 c of beans. If one ingredient is altered as specified, how must the other ingredients be changed to keep the proportions the same? Explain your reasoning.
   a. 2 c of tomato sauce
   b. 1 c of chopped scallions
   c. 1 3/4 c of beans

22. The electrical resistance of a wire, measured in ohms (Ω), is directly proportional to the length of the wire. If the electrical resistance of a 5 ft wire is 4.2 Ω, what is the resistance of 18 ft of the same wire?

23. The following lever is in equilibrium. The two weights are *A* (lb) and *B* (lb) and their respective distance from the fulcrum are *x* (in.) and *y* (in.).

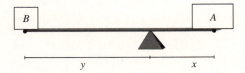

   a. If *A* is 3 times as heavy as *B*, find the ratio *x/y*.
   b. If *y/x* = 10 and *A* = 100 lb, what is *B*?
   c. If the distance from *B* to the fulcrum is 3 times the distance of *A* to the fulcrum and *A* + *B* = 10 lb, find *A* and *B*.

24. At a particular time, the ratio of the height of an object that is perpendicular to the ground to the length of its shadow is the same for all objects. If a 30-ft tree casts a shadow of 12 ft, how tall is a tree that cast a shadow of 14 ft?

25. In a photograph of a father and his daughter, the daughter's height is 2.3 cm and the father's height is 5.8 cm. If the father is actually 188 cm tall, how tall is the daughter?

26. On the following balance beam, the weights *x* and *y* are in balance.

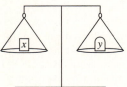

   Answer the following:
   a. Write an equation relating *x* and *y*.
   b. Express *y* as a function of *x*.
   c. Graph the function in (b).
   d. If *x* = 6 lb, find *y*.

27. In the following figure, a long beam is being used to lift a heavy object. A force equivalent to a weight of 50 lb is applied at the end of the beam 6 ft from the fulcrum. How far from the fulcrum should a force of 100 lb be applied to lift the same object?

28. The following table shows several possible widths *W* and corresponding lengths *L* of a rectangle whose area is 10 ft².

Width (*W*) (Feet)	Length (*L*) (Feet)	Area (Square Feet)
0.5	20	0.5 · 20 = 10
1	10	1 · 10 = 10
2	5	2 · 5 = 10
2.5	4	2.5 · 4 = 10
4	2.5	4 · 2.5 = 10
5	2	5 · 2 = 10
10	1	10 · 1 = 10
20	0.5	20 · 0.5 = 10

   a. Use the values in the table and some additional values to graph the length *L* on the vertical axis versus the width *W* of the horizontal axis.
   b. What is the algebraic relationship between *L* and *W*?
   c. Is the relationship in (b) a direct variation, inverse variation, or neither?
   d. Write *W* as a function of *L;* that is, express *W* in terms of *L*.
   e. Write *L* as a function of *W;* that is, express *L* in terms of *W*.

29. In each of the following (a)–(e) situations, do the following:

i. Find an equation that relates the given variables.

ii. Tell whether the given variable is in direct variation, inverse variation, or neither.

iii. Graph the equation in (i), placing the variable mentioned first on the vertical axis.

a. Debbie is riding her bike on a country road at a speed of 15 mph. Let d be the number of miles she rides in t hours.

b. Joshua is practicing typing and his typing speed varies. Let W be the number of words per minute and t the number of minutes it takes him to type a 4000-word assignment.

c. Anona is making a scale drawing of her garden using the scale $1:25$. Let L be the length between two points in her garden and S the distance between the corresponding points on the scale drawing.

d. A rectangle has width W, length L, and perimeter that is always 200 in.

e. The weight J of an object on Jupiter is 2.64 times the corresponding weight E of the same object on Earth.

30. Determine whether the following variables vary directly, inversely, or neither directly nor inversely:

a. $\dfrac{x}{y} = 2$ b. $yx^{-1} = 10$ c. $yx = 15$

d. $y = x^{-1}$ e. $x^{-1} + y^{-1} = 2$ f. $y = x + 1$

31. a. In Room A of the University Center are one man and two women; in Room B are two men and four women; and in Room C are five men and ten women. If all the people in Rooms B and C go to Room A, what will be the ratio of men to women in Room A?

★b. Prove the following generalization of the proportions used in (a):

$$\text{If } \frac{a}{b} = \frac{c}{d} = \frac{e}{f}, \text{ then } \frac{a}{b} = \frac{c}{d} = \frac{e}{f} = \frac{a + c + e}{b + d + f}.$$

★**32.** Prove that if $\dfrac{a}{b} = \dfrac{c}{d}$, then the following are true:

a. $\dfrac{a + b}{b} = \dfrac{c + d}{d}$ $\left(\text{Hint: } \dfrac{a}{b} + 1 = \dfrac{c}{d} + 1\right)$

b. $\dfrac{a}{a + b} = \dfrac{c}{c + d}$

c. $\dfrac{a - b}{a + b} = \dfrac{c - d}{c + d}$

Communication

33. Iris has found some dinosaur bones and a fossil footprint. The length of the footprint is 40 cm, the length of the thigh bone is 100 cm, and the length of the body is 700 cm.

a. What is the ratio of the footprint's length to the dinosaur's length?

b. Iris found a new track that she believes was made by the same species of dinosaur. If the footprint was 30 cm long and if the same ratio of foot length to body length holds, how long is the dinosaur?

c. In the same area, Iris also found a 50-cm thigh bone. Do you think this thigh bone belonged to the same dinosaur that made the 30-cm footprint that Iris found? Why or why not?

34. Suppose a 10-in. pizza costs \$4. For you to find the price x of a 14-in. pizza, is it correct to set up the proportion $\dfrac{x}{4} = \dfrac{14}{10}$? Why or why not?

35. The amount of gold in jewelry and other products is measured in karats (K), where 24K represents pure gold. The mark 14K on a chain indicates that the ratio between the mass of the gold in the chain and the mass of the chain is $14:24$. If a gold ring is marked 18K and it weighs 0.4 oz, what is the value of the gold in the ring if pure gold is valued at \$300 per oz? Explain your reasoning.

36. The approximate mass of the sun is $2.9 \cdot 10^{32}$ kg (kilograms) and the approximate mass of the hydrogen atom is $1.7 \cdot 10^{-29}$ kg. Is the mass of the hydrogen atom to your mass approximately the same as the ratio of your mass to the mass of the sun. Explain why or why not.

37. In a lightning storm, the time t between the flash of lightning and the bang of thunder is directly proportional to the distance d between the observer and the location of the lightning. Consequently, $t = cd$ for some constant c.

a. Discuss how the constant c could be computed the next time you experience a lightning storm.

b. Is the distance d directly proportional to the time t? Explain why or why not.

c. Let t_1, t_2 and d_1, d_2 be the times and corresponding distances for two different lightning strikes. Express the relationship among these quantities as a ratio and proportion and discuss how the ratio follows from the formula $t = cd$.

Open-ended

38. List three real-world situations that involve ratio and proportion and explain whether the ratios are proportional.

39. The mass of a person in kilograms is directly proportional to the person's weight in pounds. If x is the mass in kilograms and y the mass of the same object in pounds, then $y = cx$, where $c = 2.2$, a constant of proportionality. Find two other pairs of quantities where one quantity is directly proportional to the other and their relation is given by the equation $y = cx$. In each case, specify what x and y are and give the value of c.

40. Boyle's law states that at a given temperature, the product of the volume V of a gas and the pressure P is a constant c as follows:

$$PV = c$$

a. If at a given temperature, a pressure of 48 lb/in^2 compresses a certain gas to a volume of 960 in^3, what pressure would be necessary to compress the gas to a volume of 800 in^3 at the same temperature?

b. Explain why Boyle's law is mathematically similar to the Law of the Lever.

c. Find three other real-world situations in which the variables are related mathematically like the variables in Boyle's law. In each case, describe how the variables are related using ratio and proportion.

Cooperative Learning

41. Look up in different elementary-school textbooks how direct and inverse variations are introduced and report on your findings. Are these concepts related to ratio and proportion in these texts?

42. Archimedes's Law of the Lever can be extended to include a level with more than two weights like the one shown next. Formulate an extension of the Law of the Lever for any number of weights. Compare your statements and as a group come up with the clearest formulation of the extended law.

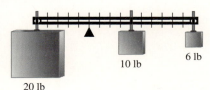

10 lb

6 lb

20 lb

Review Problems

43. A teacher asked her students to add three consecutive odd numbers and tell her the sum. The teacher was able to find each student's numbers by subtracting 6 from the sum and dividing the difference by 3. Use the strategy of *writing an equation* to explain how the teacher knew to perform the above procedure.

44. Find all real numbers x that satisfy each of the following:

a. $\dfrac{1}{3}x = \dfrac{3}{4}x$

b. $\dfrac{1}{2}x - 7 = \dfrac{3}{4}$

c. $^{-}0.01 + 3.14x = {}^{-}0.07$

d. $\dfrac{5}{x} - 0.34 = 0.91$

e. $\dfrac{^{-}1}{2}x + 3 > 2x$

f. $|x| \geq \sqrt{2}$

Section 7-5   # Percents

Percents are very useful in conveying information. People hear that there is a 60 percent chance of rain or that their savings accounts are drawing 6 percent interest. The word **percent** comes from the Latin phrase *per centum,* which means *per hundred.* For example, a bank that pays 6 percent simple interest on a savings account pays $6 for each $100 in the account for 1 yr; that is, it pays $\dfrac{6}{100}$ of whatever amount is in the account for 1 yr. The symbol, %, indicates percent. For example, we write 6% for $\dfrac{6}{100}$.

percent

In general, we have the following definition.

> **Definition of Percent**
>
> $$n\% = \dfrac{n}{100}$$

Thus $n\%$ of a quantity is $\dfrac{n}{100}$ of the quantity. Therefore 1% is one hundredth of a whole and 100% represents the entire quantity, whereas 200% represents $\dfrac{200}{100}$, or 2 times, the given quantity. Percents can be illustrated by using a hundreds grid. For example, what

Figure 7-31

percent of the grid is shaded in Figure 7-31. Because 30 out of the 100, or $\frac{30}{100}$, of the squaresare shaded, we say that 30% of the grid is shaded.

Because $n\% = \frac{n}{100}$, to convert a number to a percent we write it as a fraction with denominator 100; the numerator gives the amount of the percent. For example, $\frac{3}{4} = \frac{3 \cdot 25}{4 \cdot 25} = \frac{75}{100}$.

Hence, $\frac{3}{4} = 75\%$. Notice that to convert $\frac{75}{100}$ to a percent, we could have multiplied the fraction by 100. Thus $0.0002 = 100 \cdot 0.0002 = 0.02\%$. In general, to convert a number to a percent we multiply it by 100 and attach the % symbol.

Example 7-22

Write each of the following as a percent:

a. 0.03   **b.** $0.\overline{3}$

c. 1.2   **d.** 0.00042

e. 1   **f.** $\frac{3}{5}$

g. $\frac{2}{3}$ **h.** $2\frac{1}{7}$

Solution   **a.** $0.03 = 100 \cdot 0.03\% = 3\%$

b. $0.\overline{3} = 100 \cdot 0.\overline{3}\% = 33.\overline{3}\%$

c. $1.2 = 100 \cdot 1.2\% = 120\%$

d. $0.00042 = 100 \cdot 0.00042\% = 0.042\%$

e. $1 = 100 \cdot 1\% = 100\%$

f. $\frac{3}{5} = 100 \cdot \frac{3}{5}\% = \frac{300}{5}\% = 60\%$

g. $\frac{2}{3} = 100 \cdot \frac{2}{3}\% = \frac{200}{3}\% = 66.\overline{6}\%$

h. $2\frac{1}{7} = 100 \cdot 2\frac{1}{7}\% = \frac{1500}{7}\% = 214\frac{2}{7}\%$

A number can also be converted to a percent by using a *proportion*. For example, to write $\frac{3}{5}$ as a percent, find the value of n in the following proportion:

$$\frac{3}{5} = \frac{n}{100}$$

Solving the proportion, we obtain $\left(\frac{3}{5}\right) \cdot 100 = n$, or $n = 60$. Therefore $\frac{3}{5} = 60\%$.

Still another way to convert a number to a percent is to recall that $1 = 100\%$. Thus for example, $\frac{3}{4} = \frac{3}{4}$ of $1 = \frac{3}{4} \cdot 1 = \frac{3}{4} \cdot 100\% = 75\%$.

REMARK   The % symbol is crucial in identifying the meaning of a number. For example, $\frac{1}{2}$ and $\frac{1}{2}\%$ are different numbers: $\frac{1}{2} = 50\%$, which is not equal to $\frac{1}{2}\%$. Similarly, 0.01 is different from 0.01%, which is 0.0001.

In our computations, it is sometimes useful to convert percents to decimals. This can be done by writing the percent as a fraction and then converting the fraction to a decimal.

Example 7-23 Write each of the following percents as a decimal:

a. 5% **b.** 6.3% **c.** 100%

d. 250% **e.** $\frac{1}{3}$% **f.** $33\frac{1}{3}$%

Solution **a.** $5\% = \frac{5}{100} = 0.05$

b. $6.3\% = \frac{6.3}{100} = 0.063$

c. $100\% = \frac{100}{100} = 1$

d. $250\% = \frac{250}{100} = 2.50$

e. $\frac{1}{3}\% = \frac{\frac{1}{3}}{100} = \frac{0.\overline{3}}{100} = 0.00\overline{3}$

f. $33\frac{1}{3}\% = \frac{33\frac{1}{3}}{100} = \frac{33.\overline{3}}{100} = 0.\overline{3}$

Another approach to writing a percent as a decimal is first to convert 1% to a decimal. Because $1\% = \frac{1}{100} = 0.01$, we can conclude that $5\% = 5 \cdot 0.01 = 0.05$ and $6.3\% = 6.3 \cdot 0.01 = 0.063$. Calculators have a percent key. For example, if the keys $\boxed{3}\boxed{4}\boxed{.}\boxed{5}\boxed{\%}$ are pressed in the order given, many calculators will display 0.345. You should investigate how your calculator handles percents.

Application problems involving percents usually take one of the following forms:

1. Finding a percent of a number
2. Finding what percent one number is of another
3. Finding a number when a percent of that number is known

Before we consider examples illustrating these forms, recall what it means to find a fraction "of" a number. For example, $\frac{2}{3}$ of 70 means $\frac{2}{3} \cdot 70$. Similarly, to find 40% of 70, we have $\frac{40}{100}$ of 70, which means $\frac{40}{100} \cdot 70$, or $0.40 \cdot 70 = 28$.

Example 7-24 A house that sells for $92,000 requires a 20% down payment. What is the amount of the down payment?

Solution The down payment is 20% of $92,000, or $0.20 \cdot \$92,000 = \$18,400$. Hence, the amount of the down payment is $18,400.

• • •

Example 7-25   If Alberto has 45 correct answers on an 80-question test, what percent of his answers are correct?

Solution   Alberto has $\dfrac{45}{80}$ of the answers correct. To find the percent of correct answers, we need to convert $\dfrac{45}{80}$ to a percent. We can do this by multiplying the fraction by 100 and attaching the % symbol as follows:

$$\frac{45}{80} = 100 \cdot \frac{45}{80}\%$$
$$= 56.25\%$$

Thus 56.25% of the answers are correct.

An alternative solution uses proportion. Let n be the percent of correct answers and proceed as follows:

$$\frac{45}{80} = \frac{n}{100}$$
$$\frac{45}{80} \cdot 100 = n$$
$$n = \frac{4500}{80} = 56.25$$

• • •

Example 7-26   Forty-two percent of the parents of the school children in the Paxson School District are employed at Di Paloma University. If the number of parents employed by the University is 168, how many parents are in the school district?

Solution   Let n be the number of parents in the school district. Then 42% of n is 168. We *translate this information into an equation* and solve for n.

$$42\% \text{ of } n = 168$$
$$\frac{42}{100} \cdot n = 168$$
$$0.42 \cdot n = 168$$
$$n = \frac{168}{0.42} = 400$$

There are 400 parents in the school district.

The problem can be solved using a proportion. Forty-two percent, or $\dfrac{42}{100}$, of the parents are employed at the University. If n is the total number of parents, then $168/n$ also represents the fraction of parents employed there. Thus

$$\frac{42}{100} = \frac{168}{n}$$
$$42n = 100 \cdot 168$$
$$n = \frac{16{,}800}{42} = 400.$$

We can also solve the problem as follows:

$$42\% \text{ of } n \text{ is } 168.$$

$$1\% \text{ of } n \text{ is } \frac{168}{42}.$$

$$100\% \text{ of } n \text{ is } 100\left(\frac{168}{42}\right).$$

$$\text{Therefore } n \text{ is } 100\left(\frac{168}{42}\right), \text{ or } 400.$$

Example 7-27

Kelly bought a bicycle and a year later sold it for 20% less than what she paid for it. If she sold the bike for $144, what did she pay for it?

Solution We are looking for the original price P that Kelly paid for the bike. We know that she sold the bike for $144 and that this included a 20% loss. Thus we can *write the following equation:*

$$\$144 = P - \text{Kelly's loss}$$

Because Kelly's loss is 20% of P, we proceed as follows:

$$144 = P - 20\% \cdot P$$
$$144 = P - 0.20 \cdot P$$
$$144 = (1 - 0.20)P$$
$$144 = 0.80\,P$$
$$\frac{144}{0.80} = P$$
$$180 = P$$

Another approach is as follows. For each dollar Kelly invested in the bike, she is getting only $0.80 (why?). For the original price of P dollars, she is getting $144. Hence, we can set up the following proportion:

$$\frac{P}{1} = \frac{144}{0.80}, \quad \text{or} \quad P = 180.$$

Example 7-28

Westerner's Clothing Store advertised a suit for 10% off, for a savings of $15. Later, the manager marked the suit at 30% off the original price. What is the amount of the current discount?

Solution A 10% discount amounts to a $15 savings. We could find the amount of the current discount if we knew the original price. Thus finding the original price becomes our *subgoal.* Because 10% of P is $15, we have the following:

$$10\% \cdot P = \$15$$
$$0.10 \cdot P = \$15$$
$$P = \$150$$

To find the current discount, we calculate 30% of $150. Because $0.30 \cdot \$150 = \$45$, the amount of the 30% discount is $45.

In the *Looking Back* stage of problem solving, we check the answer and look for other ways to solve the problem. A different approach leads to a more efficient solution and confirms the answer. If 10% of the price is $15, then 30% of the price is 3 times $15, or $45.

• • •

Information in the form of a percent is frequently given in a table or a graph. The following example shows when conclusions can be made from such information.

• • •

Example 7-29

Suppose the gum-chewing habits of several professional groups was found to be as shown in Table 7-12.

Table 7-12

Chewing Habits	School Employees Teachers	Staff	Chemists	Scientists Physicists	Computer Scientists
Nonchewers	70%	60%	80%	90%	100%
Light Chewers	25%	30%	20%	5%	0%
Heavy Chewers	5%	10%	0%	5%	0%

In each of the following parts, there is additional information given followed by a conclusion. In each part, you need to determine which of the following is true:

1. The conclusion follows only from the table.
2. The conclusion follows either from the table alone or from the additional information alone.
3. The conclusion follows from the table and the additional information but not from each by itself.
4. It is impossible to deduce the conclusion from the table or from the additional information or both.
   a. *Additional information:* There are more nonchewing computer scientists than nonchewing chemists.
      Conclusion: There are more computer scientists than chemists.
   b. *Additional information:* The number of chemists is twice the number of computer scientists.
      Conclusion: There are more chewers among chemists than among computer scientists.
   c. *Additional information:* There are fewer nonchewing computer scientists than nonchewing physicists.
      Conclusion: There are fewer computer scientists than physicists.

Solution   a. Because the table gives percents and not the actual numbers, it's impossible to obtain from the table alone any information about the numbers in the various groups. The conclusion does not follow from the table alone. To determine if the conclusion follows from the table and the additional information, we proceed as follows. Let S denote the number of computer scientists and C the number of chemists. From Table 7-12, we know that 100% of the computer scientists are nonchewers. The number of nonchewing computer scientists is 100% of S, or S. The number of nonchewers among chemists is 80% of C, or $0.80\ C$. Thus the question is equivalent to checking whether the following is always true: If $S > 0.8\ C$, then $S > C$; if $S > 0.8\ C$, then S could be between $0.8\ C$ and C. Because there is no way to tell, the statement is not always true. (An actual counterexample can be given: If $C = 100$ and $S = 90$, then $S > 0.8\ C$, but $S < C$.) Consequently, the answer is (4).

b. From the table, we know that 0% of computer scientists chew. Thus there are no chewers among computer scientists. Because 20% of chemists chew, there are more chewers among chemists than among computer scientists. Consequently the answer is (1). (The additional information is irrelevant.)

c. If S denotes the number of computer scientists and P the number of physicists, then from the table we have $S < 0.9\ P$. We need to check whether this always implies that $S < P$. Because $S < 0.9\ P < 1 \cdot P$, by the transitive property of the less than relation, $S < P$. Consequently, the only correct answer is (3).

• • •

Mental Math with Percents

Mental math may be helpful when working with percents. Several techniques follow:

1. *Using fraction equivalents*
   Knowing fraction equivalents for some percents can make some computations easier. Table 7-13 gives several fraction equivalents.

Table 7-13

Percent	25%	50%	75%	$33\frac{1}{3}\%$	$66\frac{2}{3}\%$	10%	1%
Fraction Equivalent	$\frac{1}{4}$	$\frac{1}{2}$	$\frac{3}{4}$	$\frac{1}{3}$	$\frac{2}{3}$	$\frac{1}{10}$	$\frac{1}{100}$

These equivalents can be used in such computations as the following:

$$50\% \text{ of } \$80 = \left(\frac{1}{2}\right)80 = \$40$$

$$66\frac{2}{3}\% \text{ of } 90 = \left(\frac{2}{3}\right)90 = 60$$

2. *Using a known percent*
   Frequently, we may not know a percent of something, but we know a close percent of it. For example, to find 55% of 62, we might do the following:

$$50\% \text{ of } 62 = \left(\frac{1}{2}\right)(62) = 31$$

$$5\% \text{ of } 62 = \left(\frac{1}{2}\right)(10\%)(62) = \left(\frac{1}{2}\right)(6.2) = 3.1$$

Adding, we see that 55% of 62 is $31 + 3.1 = 34.1$.

Estimations with Percents

Estimations with percents can be used to determine whether answers are reasonable. Following are some examples:

1. To estimate 27% of 598, note that 27% of 598 is a little more than 25% of 598, but 25% of 598 is approximately the same as 25% of 600, or $\frac{1}{4}$ of 600, or 150. Here, we have adjusted 27% downward and 598 upward, so 150 should be a reasonable estimate. A better estimate might be obtained by estimating 30% of 600 and then subtracting 3% of 600 to obtain 27% of 600, giving 180 − 18, or 162.

2. To estimate 148% of 500, note that 148% of 500 should be slightly less than 150% of 500. 150% of 500 is 1.5(500) = 750. Thus 148% of 500 should be a little less than 750.

• • •

Example 7-30   Laura wants to buy a blouse originally priced at $26.50 but now on sale at 40% off. She has $17 in her wallet and wonders if she has enough cash. How can she mentally find out?

Solution   It is easier to find 40% of $25 (versus $26.50) mentally. One way is to find 10% of $25, which is $2.50. Now, 40% is 4 times that much, that is, 4 · $2.50, or $10. Thus Laura estimates that the blouse will cost $26.50 − $10, or $16.50. Since the actual discount is greater than $10 (40% of 26.50 is greater than 40% of 25), Laura will have to pay less than $16.50 for the blouse and, hence, she has enough cash.

• • •

Estimation is also used to check if an answer to a problem is reasonable, as seen on the following student page from *Addison-Wesley Mathematics,* Grade 8, 1993.

Sometimes it may not be clear which operations to perform with percent. The following example investigates this.

• • •

Example 7-31   Which of the following statements are true and which are false? Explain your answers.

a. Leonardo got a 10% raise at the end of his first year on the job and a 10% raise after another year. His total raise was 20% of his original salary.

b. Jung and Dina paid 45% of their first department store bill of $620 and 48% of the second department store bill of $380. They paid 45% + 48% = 93% of the total bill of $1000.

c. Bill spent 25% of his salary on food and 40% on housing. Bill spent 25% + 40% = 65% of his salary on food and housing.

d. In Bordertown, 65% of the adult population works in town, 25% works across the border, and 15% is unemployed.

e. In Clean City, the fine for various polluting activities is a certain percent of one's monthly income. The fine for smoking in public places is 40%, for driving a polluting car is 50%, and for littering is 30%. Mr. Schmutzig committed all three polluting crimes in one day and paid a fine of 120% of his monthly salary.

Solution   **a.** In applications, percent only has meaning when it represents part of a quantity. For example, 10% of a quantity and another 10% of the same quantity is 20% of that quantity. In Leonardo's case, the first 10% raise was calculated based on his original salary and the second 10% raise was calculated on his new salary. Consequently, the percentages cannot be added, and the statement is false.

Problem Solving
Determining Reasonable Answers

UNDERSTAND
ANALYZE DATA
PLAN
ESTIMATE
SOLVE
EXAMINE

LEARN ABOUT IT

An important part of evaluating an answer to a problem is to check your work. This chart shows some ways you can do this.

Check Your Work

- Is the arithmetic correct?
- Did you use the strategies correctly?
- Is the answer reasonable?

Example

Do not solve the problem. Decide if the answer given is reasonable. If it is not reasonable, explain why.

Problem: The graph shows the percentage increase in house prices from 1987 to 1988 in 7 states. Kaki paid $209,500 for a home in Hawaii in 1987. By how much had the price increased in 1988?

Answer: The price had increased by $3,016.80.

To check if the answer is reasonable, round 14.4% down to 14%. Then round $209,500 down to $200,000.

Multiply 200,000 by 14%.

The correct answer should be a little more than $28,000 because the numbers were rounded down.

$3,016.80 is not a reasonable answer.

Increase in Home Prices from 1987 to 1988.

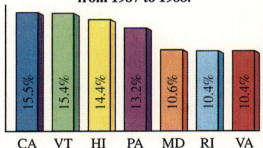

CA 15.5% VT 15.4% HI 14.4% PA 13.2% MD 10.6% RI 10.4% VA 10.4%

14.4% ⟶ 14%
$209,500 → $200,000

$200,000 · 0.14 = $28,000

b. The answer does not make sense. Jung and Dina paid less than $\frac{1}{2}$ of each bill, so they could not have paid 93% (almost all) of the total. In fact, $\frac{1}{2}$ of one bill plus $\frac{1}{2}$ of the other bill is not $\frac{1}{2} + \frac{1}{2}$ or 1, the full amount of the total bill, because the bills are different.

c. Because the percentages are of the same quantity, the statement is true.

d. Because the percentages are of the same quantity, that is, the number of adults, we can add them: 65% + 25% + 15% = 105%. But 105% of the population accounts for more (5% more) than the town's population, which is impossible. Hence, the statement is false.

e. Again, the percentages are of the same quantity, that is, the individual's monthly income. Hence, we can add them: 120% of one's monthly income is a stiff fine, but possible.

• • •

Ongoing Assessment 7-5

1. Express each of the following as percents:
   a. 7.89   **b.** 0.032   **c.** 193.1   **d.** 0.2
   e. $\frac{5}{6}$ **f.** $\frac{3}{20}$ **g.** $\frac{1}{8}$ **h.** $\frac{3}{8}$
   i. $\frac{5}{8}$ **j.** $\frac{1}{6}$ **k.** $\frac{4}{5}$ **l.** $\frac{1}{40}$

2. Convert each of the following percents to decimals:
   a. 16%   **b.** $4\frac{1}{2}\%$ **c.** $\frac{1}{5}\%$ **d.** $\frac{2}{7}\%$
   e. $13\frac{2}{3}\%$ **f.** 125%   **g.** $\frac{1}{3}\%$ **h.** $\frac{1}{4}\%$

3. Fill in the following blanks to find other expressions for 4%:
   a. _____ for every 100   **b.** _____ for every 50
   c. 1 for every _____   **d.** 8 for every _____
   e. 0.5 for every _____

4. Different calculators compute percents in various ways. To investigate this, consider 5 · 6%.
   a. If the following sequence of keys is pressed, is the correct answer of 0.3 displayed on your calculator?
   [5] [×] [6] [%] [=]
   b. Press [6] [%] [×] [5] [=]. Is the answer 0.3?

5. Answer each of the following:
   a. What is 6% of 34?
   b. 17 is what percent of 34?
   c. 18 is 30% of what number?
   d. What is 7% of 49?
   e. 61.5 is what percent of 20.5?
   f. 16 is 40% of what number?

6. Marc had 84 boxes of candy to sell. He sold 75% of the boxes. How many did he sell?

7. Gail made $16,000 last year and received a 6% raise. How much does she make now?

8. Gail received a 7% raise last year. If her salary is now $15,515, what was her salary last year?

9. Joe sold 180 newspapers out of 200. Bill sold 85% of his 260 newspapers. Ron sold 212 newspapers, 80% of those he had.

   a. Who sold the most newspapers? How many?
   b. Who sold the greatest percent of his newspapers? What percent?
   c. Who started with the greatest number of newspapers? How many?

10. If a dress that normally sells for $35 is on sale for $28, what is the "percent off"? (This could be called a *percent of decrease,* or a *discount.*)

11. A car originally cost $1700. One year later, it was worth $1400. What is the percent of depreciation?

12. On a certain day in Glacier Park, 728 eagles were counted. Five years later, 594 were counted. What was the percent of decrease in the number of eagles counted?

13. Mort bought his house in 1975 for $59,000. It was recently appraised at $95,000. What is the *percent of increase* in value?

14. Xuan weighed 9 lb when he was born. At 6 mo, he weighed 18 lb. What was the percent of increase in Xuan's weight? Explain your solution.

15. Sally bought a dress marked 20% off. If the regular price was $28.00, what was the sale price?

16. What is the sale price of a softball if the regular price is $6.80 and there is a 25% discount?

17. If a $\frac{1}{4}$-c serving of Crunchies breakfast food has 0.5% of the minimum daily requirement of Vitamin C, how many cups would you have to eat to obtain the minimum daily requirement of Vitamin C?

18. An airline ticket costs $320 without the tax. If the tax rate is 5%, what is the total bill for the airline ticket?

19. Bill got 52 correct answers on an 80-question test. What percent of the questions did he not answer correctly?

20. A real estate broker receives 4% of an $80,000 sale. How much does the broker receive?

21. A survey reported that $66\frac{2}{3}\%$ of 1800 employees favored a new insurance program. How many employees favored the new program?

22. A family has a monthly income of $3400 and makes a monthly house payment of $800. What percent of the income is the house payment?

23. A plumber's wage this year is $19.80 per hour. This is a 110% increase over last year's hourly wage. What is the dollar increase in the hourly wage over last year?

24. Soda is advertised at 45¢ a can or $2.40 a six-pack. If 6 cans are to be purchased, what percent is saved by purchasing the six-pack?

25. John paid $330 for a new mountain bicycle to sell in his shop. He wants to price it so that he can offer a 10% discount and still make 20% of the price he paid for it. At what price should the bike be marked?

26. The price of a suit that sold for $200 was reduced by 25%. By what percent must the price of the suit be increased to bring the price back to $200?

27. The car Elsie bought 1 yr ago has depreciated by $1116.88, which is 12.13% of the price she paid for it. How much did she pay for the car, to the nearest cent?

28. Solve each of the following using mental mathematics:
   a. 15% of $22   **b.** 20% of $120
   c. 5% of $38   **d.** 25% of $98

29. If we build a 10 × 10 model with blocks, as shown in the following figure, and paint the entire model, what percent of the cubes will have each of the following?
   a. Four faces painted
   b. Three faces painted
   c. Two faces painted

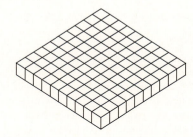

30. Answer the questions in Problem 29 for models of the following sizes:
   a. 9 × 9   **b.** 8 × 8
   c. 7 × 7   **d.** 12 × 12

31. For people to be safe but still achieve a cardiovascular training effect, they should monitor their heart rates while exercising. The maximum heart rate can be approximated by subtracting your age from 220. You can safely achieve a training effect if you maintain your heart rate between 60% and 80% of that number for at least 20 min three times a week.
   a. Determine the range for your age.
   b. At the top of a long hill, Jeannie slows her bike and takes her pulse. She counts 41 beats in 15 sec.
      i. Express in decimal form the amount of time in seconds between successive beats.
      ii. Express the amount in terms of minutes.

32. **a.** By what percent is 50 greater than 40?
   b. By what percent is 40 less than 50?

33. If you get a 20% raise but the cost of living remains steady, by what percent does your purchasing power increase?

34. If your income stays the same but the cost of living drops by 20%, by what percent does your purchasing power increase? Justify your answer.

35. A crew consists of 1 apprentice, 1 journeyman, and 1 master carpenter. The crew receives a check for $4200 for a job they just finished. A journeyman makes 200% of what an apprentice makes, and a master makes 150% of what a journeyman makes. How much does each person in the crew earn?

36. **a.** In an incoming freshman class of 500 students, only 20 claimed to be math majors. What percent of the freshman class is this?
   b. When the survey was repeated the next year, 5% of nonmath majors had decided to switch and become math majors.
      i. How many math majors are there now?
      ii. What percent of the freshman class do they represent?

37. Ms. Price has received a 10% raise in salary in each of the last 2 yrs. If her annual salary this year is $100,000, what was her salary 2 yrs ago, rounded to the nearest penny? (Why? Explain your reasoning.)

38. Use the pie charts from an information page from a state income tax instruction booklet to answer the following questions:

WHERE YOUR TAX DOLLAR GOES
Source of General Fund Revenues

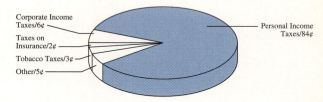

Expenditure of General Fund Revenues

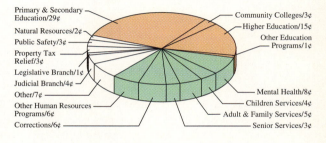

a. What percent of revenue comes from personal and corporate income taxes?

b. What percent of revenue from income taxes comes from corporate income taxes?

c. What percent of revenue is spent on education?

d. What percent of the education budget is devoted to primary and secondary education?

e. Find a combination of programs that spends exactly 50% of the human resources budget.

f. Many of the percents may have been rounded in the preparation of the pie charts. Does each pie chart total 100%?

39. A store is rented at $550 a month plus 8% of any gross annual income in excess of $250,000. If rent for 1 yr was $18,550, what was the gross income?

Communication

40. Harold and Maude are seated in a restaurant that does not accept credit cards when they discover they have only $40 in cash. They want to leave a 15% tip. Use mental math to determine how much they can spend on dinner and still have enough for the tip. Explain your solution.

41. Two equal amounts of money were invested in two different stocks. The value of the first stock increased by 15% the first year and then decreased by 15% the second year. The second stock decreased by 15% the first year and increased by 15% the second year. Was one investment better than the other? Explain your reasoning.

Open-ended

42. Write and solve a word problem whose solution involves the following. If one of these tasks is impossible, explain why.

a. Addition of percent

b. Subtraction of percent

c. Multiplication of percent

d. Division of percent

e. A percent whose decimal representation is raised to the second power

f. A percent greater than 100

43. Look at newspapers and magazines for information given in percents.

a. Based on your findings, write a problem that involves social science as well as mathematics.

b. Write a clear solution to your problem in (a).

44. a. Collect information involving percents that you think will be of interest to middle-school students in three different areas.

b. For each of the three areas in (a), write a question involving percent and solve it. The first question should be fairly easy, the second more difficult, and the third challenging.

Cooperative Learning

45. Find the percent of students in your class that engage in each of the following activities:

a. Studying and doing homework   b. Watching TV

Number of Hours per Week (h)	Percent
$h < 1$	
$1 \leq h < 3$	
$3 \leq h < 5$	
$5 \leq h < 10$	
$h \geq 10$	
Total	

Number of Hours per Week (h)	Percent
$h < 1$	
$1 \leq h < 5$	
$5 \leq h < 10$	
$h \geq 10$	
$h \geq 10$	
Total	

c. Did your totals add up to 100%? Why or why not?

Review Problems

46. The floor area of a rectangular apartment building is 1872 ft^2. On a scale drawing, it is shown as 14.5 in. × 5.5 in. What is the area represented by 4.25 in. × 8.75 in.?

47. The same item is manufactured in two different plants. In plant A, 30 people produce 30 items in 30 hr. In Plant B, 60 people produce 60 items in 60 hr. Which plant is more productive? Explain your reasoning.

48. Suppose the ratio of boys to girls in a class is 3:4. Find the percent of boys in the class and the percent of girls in the class. Does the total add up to 100%? Why or why not?

TECHNOLOGY CORNER

Spreadsheets can be used to solve mixture problems. For example, consider the problem of finding out how many liters of water need to be added to 5 L of pure lemon juice to change its concentration from 100% to less than 30% lemon juice.

Six lemonade mixtures were prepared starting from 5 L of pure lemon juice and adding water in 2 L increments. At each step, the percent of lemon juice in the mixture was calculated. The results of the process are summarized in the following spreadsheet. The formulas used to obtain the results in a particular column are given in row 12.

a. Explain how this spreadsheet can be used to help students solve the problem.

b. Explain the formulas in row 12.

	A	B	C	D
1	**Liters of**	**Liters of**	**Total Liters**	**% Lemon Juice**
2	**Lemon Juice**	**Water Added**	**in Mixture**	**in Mixture**
3	**(L)**	**(L)**	**(L)**	
4	5	0	5	100.00
5	5	2	7	71.43
6	5	4	9	55.56
7	5	6	11	45.45
8	5	8	13	38.46
9	5	10	15	33.33
10	5	12	17	29.41
11				
12	5	x	$5 + x$	$5/(5 + x)*100$
13	(where x is a multiple of 2)			

BRAIN TEASER The crust of a certain pumpkin pie is 25% of the pie. By what percent should the amount of crust be reduced in order to make it constitute 20% of the pie?

---

*Section 7-6 Computing Interest

interest When a bank advertises a $5\frac{1}{2}\%$ interest rate on a savings account, the **interest** is the amount of money the bank will pay for using that money. The original amount deposited or bor-
principal • interest rate rowed is the **principal.** The percent used to determine the interest is the **interest rate.** Interest rates are given for specific periods of time, such as years, months, or days. Interest
simple interest computed on the original principal is **simple interest.** For example, suppose we borrow $5000 from a company at a simple interest rate of 9% for 1 yr. The interest we owe on the loan for 1 yr is 9% of $5000, or $5000 · 0.09. In general, if a principal P is invested at an annual interest rate of r, then the simple interest after 1 yr is $Pr \cdot 1$; after t years, it is Prt. Thus if I represents simple interest, we have

$$I = Prt.$$

The amount needed to pay off a $5000 loan at 9% simple interest is the $5000 borrowed plus the interest on the $5000, that is, $5000 + 5000 \cdot 0.09$, or $5450. In general, *an*

amount/balance   **amount** (*or* **balance**) *A is equal to the principal P plus the interest I,* that is,

$$A = P + I = P + Prt = P(1 + rt).$$

Example 7-32   Vera opened a savings account that pays simple interest at the rate of $5\frac{1}{4}\%$ per year. If she deposits $2000 and makes no other deposits, find the interest and the final amount for the following time periods:

a. 1 yr   **b.** 90 days

Solution   **a.** To find the interest for 1 yr, we proceed as follows:

$$I = \$2000 \cdot 5\frac{1}{4}\% \cdot 1 = \$2000 \cdot 0.0525 = \$105$$

Her final amount at the end of 1 yr is

$$\$2000 + \$105 = \$2105.$$

b. When the interest rate is annual and the interest period is given in days, we represent the time as a fractional part of a year by dividing the number of days by 365. Thus

$$I = \$2000 \cdot 5\frac{1}{4}\% \cdot \frac{90}{365}$$

$$= \$2000 \cdot 0.0525 \cdot \frac{90}{365} \doteq \$25.89.$$

Hence,

$$A \doteq \$2000 + \$25.89$$

$$A \doteq \$2025.89.$$

Thus Vera's amount after 90 days is approximately $2025.89.

Example 7-33   Find the annual interest rate if a principal of $10,000 increased to $10,900 at the end of 1 yr.

Solution   Let the annual interest be $x\%$. We know that $x\%$ of $10,000 is the increase. Because the increase is $\$10,900 - \$10,000 = \$900$, we use the strategy of *writing an equation* for x as follows:

$$x\% \text{ of } 10,000 = 900$$

$$\frac{x}{100} \cdot 10,000 = 900$$

$$x = 9$$

Thus the interest is 9%. We can solve this problem mentally by asking, "What percent of 10,000 is 900?" Because 1% of 10,000 is 100, to obtain 900, we take 9% of 10,000.

Compound Interest

In business transactions, interest is usually calculated daily (365 times a year). In the case of savings, the earned interest is added daily to the principal, and each day the interest is earned on a different amount; that is, it is earned on the previous interest as well as the prin-

compound interest

cipal. When interest is computed in this way, it is called **compound interest.** Compounding usually is done annually (once a year), semiannually (twice a year), quarterly (4 times a year), or monthly (12 times a year). However, even when the interest is compounded, it is given as an annual rate. For example, if the annual rate is 6% compounded monthly, the interest per month is $\frac{6}{12}$%, or 0.5%. If it is compounded daily, the interest per day is $\frac{6}{365}$%. In general, *the interest rate per period is the annual interest rate divided by the number of periods in a year.*

Example 7-34

If you invest \$100 at 8% compounded quarterly, how much will you have in the account after 1 yr?

Solution   The quarterly interest rate is $\frac{1}{4} \cdot 8\%$, or 2%. It seems that we would have to calculate the interest four times. But we can also reason as follows. If at the beginning of any of the four periods there are x dollars in the account, at the end of that period there will be

$$x + 2\% \text{ of } x = x + 0.02x$$
$$= x(1 + 0.02)$$
$$= x \cdot 1.02 \text{ dollars.}$$

Hence, to find the amount at the end of any period, we need only multiply the amount at the beginning of the period by 1.02. From Table 7-14, we see that the amount at the end of the fourth period is $\$100 \cdot 1.02^4$. On a scientific calculator, we can find the amount using $\boxed{1}\,\boxed{0}\,\boxed{0}\,\boxed{\times}\,\boxed{1}\,\boxed{.}\,\boxed{0}\,\boxed{2}\,\boxed{y^x}\,\boxed{4}\,\boxed{=}$. The calculator displays 108.24322. Thus the amount at the end of 1 yr is approximately \$108.24.

Table 7-14

Period	Initial Amount	Final Amount
1	100	$100 \cdot 1.02$
2	$100 \cdot 1.02$	$(100 \cdot 1.02) \cdot 1.02$ or $100 \cdot 1.02^2$
3	$100 \cdot 1.02^2$	$(100 \cdot 1.02)^2 \cdot 1.02$ or $100 \cdot 1.02^3$
4	$100 \cdot 1.02^3$	$(100 \cdot 1.02^3) \cdot 1.02$ or $100 \cdot 1.02^4$

REMARK   Because the amount at the beginning of any period in Example 7-34 is r multiplied by the fixed number 1.02 to obtain the amount at the end of this period, the final amounts at the end of the periods form a geometric sequence. Hence, finding the final amount at the end of the nth period amounts to finding the nth term of a geometric sequence whose first term is $100 \cdot 1.02$ (amount at the end of the first period) and whose ratio is 1.02.

We can generalize the discussion in Example 7-34. If the interest rate per period is r (a fraction or a decimal) and the principal is P, then the amount A after n periods can be found as follows. If, at the beginning of any period, there are x dollars in the account, at the end of that period there will be x plus the interest I for that period. That is, $x + I = x + x \cdot r = x(1 + r)$. Hence, to find the amount at the end of any period, we need only to multiply the amount at the beginning of the period by $1 + r$. This is shown in Table 7-15. Therefore the amount at the end of the nth period is $P(1 + r)^n$, and we have the formula $A = P(1 + r)^n$.

Table 7-15

Period	Initial Amount	Final Amount
1	P	$P(1 + r)$
2	$P(1 + r)$	$[P(1 + r)](1 + r)$, or $P(1 + r)^2$
3	$P(1 + r)^2$	$[P(1 + r)^2](1 + r)$, or $P(1 + r)^3$
4	$P(1 + r)^3$	$[P(1 + r)^3](1 + r)$, or $P(1 + r)^4$
.	.	.
.	.	.
.	.	.
n	$P(1 + r)^{n-1}$	$[P(1 + r)^{n-1}](1 + r)$, or $P(1 + r)^n$

Because the amount at the end of each period is $(1 + r)$ times the amount at the beginning of that period, the amounts at the end of each period form a geometric sequence. So the answer $P(1 + r)^n$ is consistent with the nth term of a geometric sequence whose first term is $P(1 + r)$ and whose ratio is $1 + r$.

• • •

Example 7-35   Suppose you deposit $1000 in a savings account that pays 6% interest compounded quarterly.

a. What is the balance at the end of 1 yr?
b. What is the *effective annual yield* on this investment; that is, what is the rate that would have been paid if the amount had been invested using simple interest?

Solution   **a.** An annual interest rate of 6% earns $\frac{1}{4}$ of 6%, or an interest rate of $\frac{0.06}{4}$, in 1 quarter. Because there are 4 periods, we have the following:

$$A = 1000 \left(1 + \frac{0.06}{4}\right)^4 \doteq \$1061.36$$

The balance at the end of 1 yr is approximately $1061.36.

b. Because the interest earned is $1061.36 − $1000.00 = $61.36, the effective annual yield can be computed by using the simple interest formula, $I = Prt$.

$$61.36 = 1000 \cdot r \cdot 1$$

$$\frac{61.36}{1000} = r$$

$$0.06136 = r$$

$$6.136\% = r$$

The effective annual yield is 6.136%.

• • •

Example 7-36   To save for their child's college education, a couple deposits $3000 into an account that pays 7% annual interest compounded daily. Find the amount in this account after 8 yr.

Solution   The principal in the problem is $3000, the daily rate i is 0.07/365, and the number of compounding periods is 8 · 365, or 2920. Thus we have

$$A = \$3000\left(1 + \frac{0.07}{365}\right)^{2920} \doteq \$5251.7352.$$

Thus the amount in the account is approximately $5251.74.

• • •

Earnings using compound interest are compared to earnings using simple interest on the following student page from *Addison-Wesley Mathematics,* Grade 8, 1993. Use the graph in the student page to estimate the difference in earnings when $500 is invested for 25 yr using compound interest and simple interest.

ENRICHMENT
Compound Interest

If you had $500 in a savings account and earned 6% interest per year you could use the **simple interest** formula to find the interest you would earn in 2 years.

$I = Prt$ $P = \$500,$ $r = 0.06, t = 2.$
$I = \$500 \cdot 0.06 \cdot 2 = \$60.00$

Most banks and other financial institutions use **compound interest** instead of simple interest. The interest earned for each period is added on to the principal and interest is then calculated on the new amount. Money grows much more rapidly using compound interest.

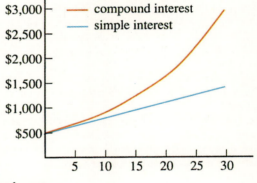

The formula for computing the amount using compound interest is.

$A = P(1 + r)^n$
A = amount, P = principal, r = interest rate per period
n = number of periods.

Example: What would principal of $500 amount to in 2 years at an interest rate of 6% per year compounded 4 times a year?

Solution: $P = 500, n = 8$ (4 · 2 year), $r = 0.015$ (0.06 ÷ 4)

Use a calculator to find A.

Display

1 [+] 0.015 [=] [yˣ] [8] [=] [×] 500 [=] 563.24629
$A = \$563.25.$

Ongoing Assessment 7-6

You will need a calculator for most of the following problems.

1. Complete the following compound-interest chart.

Compounding Period	Principal	Annual Rate	Length of Time (Years)	Interest Rate per Period	Number of Periods	Amount of Interest Paid
a. Semiannual	$1000	6%	2			
b. Quarterly	$1000	8%	3			
c. Monthly	$1000	10%	5			
d. Daily	$1000	12%	4			

2. Ms. Jackson borrowed $42,000 at 13% annual simple interest to buy her house. If she won the Irish Sweepstakes exactly 1 yr later and was able to repay the loan without penalty, how much interest would she owe?

3. Carolyn went on a shopping spree with her Bankamount card and made purchases totaling $125. If the interest rate is 1.5% per month on the unpaid balance and she does not pay this debt for 1 yr, how much interest will she owe at the end of the year?

4. A man collected $28,500 on a loan of $25,000 he made 4 yrs ago. If he charged simple interest, what was the rate he charged?

5. Burger Queen will need $50,000 in 5 yr for a new addition. To meet this goal, the company deposits money in an account today that pays 9% annual interest compounded quarterly. Find the amount that should be invested to total $50,000 in 5 yr.

6. A company is expanding its line to include more products. To do so, it borrows $320,000 at 13.5% annual simple interest for a period of 18 mo. How much interest must the company pay?

7. To save for their retirement, a couple deposits $4000 in an account that pays 9% interest compounded quarterly. What will be the value of their investment after 20 yr?

8. A car company is offering car loans at a simple-interest rate of 9%. Find the interest charged to a customer who finances a car loan of $7200 for 3 yr.

9. Johnny and Carolyn have three different savings plans, which accumulated the following amounts of interest for 1 yr.
   a. A passbook savings account that accumulated $53.90 on a principal of $980
   b. A certificate of deposit that accumulated $55.20 on a principal of $600
   c. A money-market certificate that accumulated $158.40 on a principal of $1200
   Which of these accounts paid the best interest rate for the year?

10. A hamburger costs $1.35 and the price continues to rise at a rate of 11% a year for the next 6 yr. What will the price of a hamburger be at the end of 6 yr?

11. If college tuition is $10,000 this year, what will it be 10 yr from now, assuming a constant inflation rate of 9% a year?

12. Sara invested money at a bank that paid 6.5% compounded quarterly. If she had $4650 at the end of 4 yr, what was her initial investment?

13. Adrien and Jarrell deposit $300 on January 1 in a holiday savings account that pays 1.1% per month interest and they withdraw the money on December 1 of the same year. What is the effective annual yield?

14. The number of trees in a rain forest decreases each month by 0.5%. If the forest has approximately $2.34 \cdot 10^9$ trees, how many trees will be left after 20 yr?

15. An amount of $3000 was deposited in a bank at a rate of 5% compounded quarterly for 3 yr. The rate then increased to 8% and was compounded quarterly for the next 3 yr. If no money was withdrawn, what was the balance at the end of this time? Explain your reasoning.

16. A money-market fund pays 14% annual interest compounded daily. What is the value of $10,000 invested in this fund after 15 yr? Explain your solution.

17. The New Age Savings Bank advertises 9% interest rates compounded daily, while the Pay More Bank pays 10.5% interest compounded annually. Which bank offers a better rate for a customer who plans to leave her money in for exactly 1 yr? Justify your answer.

18. A car is purchased for $15,000. If each year the car depreciates by 10% of its value the preceding year, what will its value be at the end of 3 yr? Explain your reasoning.

Communication

19. Because of a recession, the value of a new house depreciated 10% each year for 3 yr in a row. Then, for the next 3 yr, the value of the house increased 10% each year. Did the value of the house increase or decrease after 6 yr? Explain.

20. Determine the number of years (to the nearest tenth) it would take for any amount of money to double if it were deposited at a 10% interest rate compounded annually. Explain your reasoning.

21. An car parts manufacturer advertised three devices that could be installed in a car to save gas. The first could save 15% on fuel, the second 35% and the third 50%. Explain whether you could conclude that when all three devices were installed, the savings on fuel would be 100%?

Open-ended

22. The effect of depreciation can be computed using a formula similar to the formula for compound interest.
  a. Assume depreciation is the same each month. Write a problem involving depreciation and solve it.
  b. Develop a general formula for depreciation defining what each variable in the formula stands for.

23. Find four large cities around the world and an approximate percentage rate of population growth for the countries in which the cities are located. Estimate the population in each of the four cities in 25 yr.

24. State different situations that do not involve money in which a formula like the one for compound interest is used. In each case, state a related problem and write its solution.

Cooperative Learning

25. The federal *Truth in Lending Act* was passed in 1969 requiring lending institutions to quote an annual percentage rate (APR) that helps consumers compare the true cost of loans regardless of how each lending institution computes the interest and adds on costs.
  a. Call different banks and ask for their APR on some loans and the meaning of APR.
  b. Based on your findings in (a), write a clear definition of APR.
  c. Use the information given by your credit card (you may need to call the bank) and compute the APR on cash advances. Is your answer the same as that given by the bank? Compare the APR for different credit cards.

SOLUTION TO THE PRELIMINARY PROBLEM

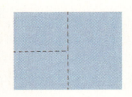

Understanding the Problem. The ratio of the length to the width of a piece of paper is such that cutting it as shown in Figure 7-32(a) results in a rectangular piece of paper with side lengths in the same ratio as the original piece. We need to find the length-to-width ratio of such a rectangular piece of paper and determine if that ratio stays the same after repeated cuttings.

Figure 7-32

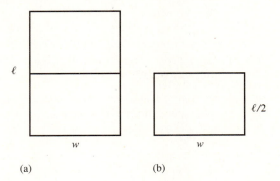

(a)   (b)

Devising a Plan. Figure 7-32(a) shows a piece of paper with length ℓ and width w. Figure 7-32(b) shows half of the original piece. It is required that $\dfrac{\ell}{w}$ will be the same as the ratio of the lengths of the piece in Figure 7-32(b). That ratio is either $\dfrac{\ell/2}{w}$ or $\dfrac{w}{\ell/2}$. Because the first ratio equals $\frac{1}{2} \cdot \frac{\ell}{w}$, it cannot be equal to $\frac{\ell}{w}$. Consequently, we must have

$$\frac{\ell}{w} = \frac{w}{\ell/2}.$$

We need to find the ratio $\frac{\ell}{w}$ for which the above proportion is true.

Carrying Out the Plan. There are various ways to find the value of $\frac{\ell}{w}$ from the proportion. One way is as follows. Because $\frac{w}{\ell/2} = w \cdot \frac{2}{\ell} = \frac{2w}{\ell}$, we have the following:

$$\frac{\ell}{w} = \frac{w}{\ell/2}$$

$$\frac{\ell}{w} = \frac{2w}{\ell}$$

$$\ell^2 = 2w^2$$

$$\frac{\ell^2}{w^2} = 2$$

$$\left(\frac{\ell}{w}\right)^2 = 2$$

$$\frac{\ell}{w} = \sqrt{2}$$

Consequently, the ratio between the length and the width of the original sheet of paper is $\sqrt{2}$ or approximately $1.414:1$.

Because the ratio of length to width of a halved sheet of paper is $\sqrt{2}$, this reasoning assures that after the half sheet is cut in half, the ratio of length to width of the resulting new pieces will remain $\sqrt{2}$. Subsequent cuts will result in pieces with the same ratio of length to width.

Looking Back. More than 2000 yr ago, Euclid posed the following question related to this problem:

"What is the ratio of length to width of a rectangle with the property that if a square is cut out of the rectangle, the remaining rectangle has the same length to width ratio as the original rectangle?"

In Figure 7-33, the width of a rectangle is designated by 1 unit. (This is possible no matter what the width.) (Why?) The length is designated by x (in the same units).

Figure 7-33

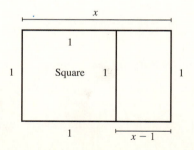

Euclid's condition will be satisfied if

$$\frac{x}{1} = \frac{1}{x-1}$$
$$x(x-1) = 1$$
$$x^2 - x - 1 = 0.$$

The solution of this equation, which can be approximated by using a graphing calculator as being 2.736, is called the *golden ratio*. The golden ratio occurs in nature and mathematics. The Greeks felt that rectangles whose sides are in the golden ratio are aesthetically most pleasing, a fact that has recently been substantiated by psychological studies.

CHAPTER OUTLINE

I. Equations and Inequalities
    A. Solutions of equations and inequalities are based on the following properties involving real numbers *a, b* and *c*.

Property	Equality	Inequality (>)
Transitive	$a = b$ and $b = c$ implies $a = c$	$a > b$ and $b > c$ implies $a > c$
Addition	$a = b$ implies $a + c = b + c$	$a > b$ implies $a + c > b + c$
Multiplication	$a = b$ implies $ac = bc$	$a > b$ and $c > 0$ implies $ac > bc$ $a > b$ and $c < 0$ implies $ac < bc$
Cancellation for Addition	$a + c = b + c$ implies $a = b$	$a + c > b + c$ implies $a > b$
Cancellation for Multiplication	$ac = bc$ implies $a = b$, if $c \neq 0$	$ac > bc$ and $c < 0$ implies $a < c$ $ac > bc$ and $c > 0$ implies $a > c$

    Analogous properties hold for the less than relation.
    B. Word problems can be solved by using the following model:

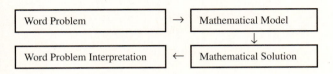

II. Linear Equations
    A. The equation of any nonvertical line can be written in the form $y = mx + b$, where m is the slope and b the y-intercept.
    B. The equation of any vertical line can be written in the form $x = a$.
    C. A system of **linear equations** can be solved graphically by drawing the graphs of the equations.

    D. A system of linear equations can be solved algbraically by either the **substitution method** or the **elimination method.**
    E. The **best-fitting line** is an equation of a straight line that approximates data that seem to follow a straight line.
III. Ratio and Proportion
    A. A fraction a/b is a **ratio.**
    B. A **proportion** is an equation of two ratios.
    C. Properties of proportions
        1. If $\dfrac{a}{b} = \dfrac{c}{d}$, then $\dfrac{b}{a} = \dfrac{d}{c}$, where $a \neq 0$ and $c \neq 0$.
        2. If $\dfrac{a}{b} = \dfrac{c}{d}$, then $\dfrac{a}{c} = \dfrac{b}{d}$, where $c \neq 0$.
    D. Two variables that are in the same ratio regardless of their values are in **direct variation.** If the product of two variables is the same regardless of their values, the variables **vary inversely.**

IV. Percent and Interest
   A. Percent means *per hundred.* Percent is written using the % symbol: $x\% = \dfrac{x}{100}$.

   B. Simple interest is computed using the formula $I = Prt$, where I is the interest, P is the principal, r is the annual interest rate, and t is the time in years.

   ***C.** When **compound interest** is involved, we use the formula $A = P(1 + i)^n$, where A is the balance, P is the principal, i is the interest rate per period, and n is the number of periods.

QUESTIONS FROM THE CLASSROOM

1. The teacher asked the class to solve the equation
$\dfrac{1}{4} + \dfrac{7}{4}\left(x + \dfrac{1}{5}\right) = x + \dfrac{6}{5}$. Nat wrote $\left(\dfrac{1}{4} + \dfrac{7}{4}\right)\left(x + \dfrac{1}{5}\right) = x + \dfrac{6}{5}$,
solved the equation, and got the answer $x = \dfrac{4}{5}$, which
is correct. The teacher told Nat he had obtained the correct answer by using an incorrect method. Nat in turn responded that his method will also work for the equation
$\dfrac{3}{8} + \dfrac{1}{4}(x - 1) = x - \dfrac{11}{8}$ and for the equation $1 + \dfrac{1}{2}\left(x - \dfrac{1}{4}\right) = x + \dfrac{1}{4}$. How would you respond?

2. A student claims that if $\dfrac{a}{b} = \dfrac{c}{d}$, then $\dfrac{a + c}{b + d} = \dfrac{a}{b} = \dfrac{c}{d}$. Is the student correct?

3. A student reported that she had the following rule for solving equations or inequalities: "Whenever an expression on one side of the equation or inequality is transferred to the other side with the opposite sign, an equivalent equation or inequality is obtained." Under what conditions is this rule true?

4. A student solving word problems always checks her solutions by substituting in equations rather than by following the written information. Is this an accurate check for the word problem?

5. A student says that $3\dfrac{1}{4}\% = 0.03 + 0.25 = 0.28$. Is this correct? Why?

6. A student reports that it is impossible to mark a product up 150% because 100% of something is all there is. What is your response?

7. A student argues that a $p\%$ increase in salary followed by a $q\%$ decrease is equivalent to a $q\%$ decrease followed by a $p\%$ increase because of the commutative property of multiplication. How do you respond?

8. A student argues that $0.01\% = 0.01$ because in 0.01%, the percent is already written as a decimal. How do you respond?

9. **a.** A student noticed that if y is directly proportional to x and x is directly proportional to z, then y is directly proportional to z. She would like to know if this is always true and why. How do you respond?

   b. What would your response be if y were inversely proportional to x and x inversely proportional to z?

CHAPTER REVIEW

1. Write an expression for each of the following quantities as a function of the given variable:
   a. The time t it takes to travel a distance of d miles at a constant speed of 65 mph
   b. The cost C of a telephone conversation for t minutes if the charge is 15 cents for the first minute and 8 cents for each additional minute
   c. The actual cost C of a telephone conversation for t minutes if the charge for each minute is 14 cents but the company gives a 40% discount on all calls
   d. The sum S of 100 consecutive integers if the greatest integer is x
   e. The weight V on Venus of an object that weighs m pound on Earth if a 100-lb object on Earth weighs 88 lb on Venus
   f. Ewa's salary E in dollars after 3 yr if her original salary S is increased by 5% the first year, 10% the second year, and 15% the third year.

2. Solve each of the following for x, where x is a number:
   a. $\dfrac{1}{4}x - \dfrac{3}{5} \leq \dfrac{1}{2}(3 - 2x)$ **b.** $\dfrac{x}{3} - \dfrac{x}{2} \geq \dfrac{-1}{4}$
   c. $\dfrac{2}{3}\left(\dfrac{3}{4}x - 1\right) = \dfrac{2}{3} - x$ **d.** $\dfrac{5}{6} = \dfrac{4 - x}{3}$

3. A truck contains 150 small packages, some weighing 1 kg and some weighing 2 kg. How many packages of each weight are in the truck if the total weight of the packages is 265 kg?

4. John has a collection of nickels and dimes. He has three more dimes than twice the number of nickels. If he has $2.05, how many of each type of coin does he have?

5. A certain college has 5715 undergraduates. There are 115 more seniors than juniors. The number of sophomores is twice the number of seniors, and the number of freshmen is twice the number of juniors. How many freshmen, sophomores, juniors, and seniors attend the college?

6. Two kegs contain equal quantities of beer. From one keg, 37 gal are drawn, and from the other, 7 gal are drawn. The quantity remaining in one keg is seven times that remaining in the other. How much did each keg contain at first?

7. In water (H_2O), the ratio of the weight of oxygen to the weight of hydrogen is approximately $8:1$. How many ounces of hydrogen is in 1 lb of water?

8. Use the following scale drawing and a marked ruler to approximate each of the following:
   a. The widest distance across Crater Lake
   b. The aerial distance from Wizard Island to the closest point of Mount Scott

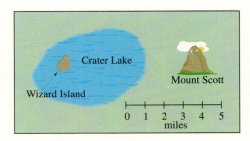

9. To estimate the number of fish in a lake, scientists use a tagging and recapturing technique. A number of fish are captured, tagged, and then released back into the lake. After a while, some fish are captured and the number of tagged fish is counted.

   Let T be the total number of fish captured, tagged, and released into the lake, n the number of fish in a recaptured sample, and t the number of fish found tagged in that sample. Finally let x be the number of fish in the lake. The assumption is that the ratio between tagged fish and the total number of fish in any sample is approximately the same and hence scientists assume $t/n = T/x$. Suppose 173 fish were captured, tagged, and released. Then 68 fish were recaptured and among them 21 were found to be tagged. Estimate the number of fish in the lake.

10. A manufacturer produces the same kind of computer chip in two different plants. In the first plant, the ratio of defective chips to good chips is $15:100$, and in the second plant, that ratio is $12:100$. A buyer of a large number of chips is aware that some come from the first plant and some from the second. However, she is not aware of how many come from each. The buyer would like to know the ratio of defective chips to good chips in any given order. Can she determine that ratio? If so, explain how. If not, explain why not.

11. Sketch the graphs for each of the following:
    a. $3x - y = 1$ b. $2x + 3y + 1 = 0$

12. In the presidential election of 1932, Franklin D. Roosevelt received 6,563,988 more votes than Herbert Hoover. If one fifth of Roosevelt's votes had been won by Herbert Hoover, then Hoover would have won the election by 2,444,622 votes. How many votes did each receive?

13. For each of the following, write the equation of the line determined by the given pair of points:
    a. $(2, {}^-3)$ and $({}^-1, 1)$
    b. $({}^-3, 0)$ and $({}^-3, 2)$
    c. $({}^-2, 3)$ and $(2, 3)$

14. Solve each of the following systems, if possible. If the system does not have a unique solution, explain why not.
    a. $x + 2y = 3$
       $2x - y = 9$
    b. $\dfrac{x}{2} + \dfrac{y}{3} = 1$
       $4y - 3x = 2$
    c. $x - 2y = 1$
       $4y - 2x = 0$

15. Answer each of the following:
    a. 6 is what percent of 24?
    b. What is 320% of 60?
    c. 17 is 30% of what number?
    d. 0.2 is what percent of 1?

16. Change each of the following to percents:
    a. $\dfrac{1}{8}$ b. $\dfrac{3}{40}$ c. 6.27
    d. 0.0123   e. $\dfrac{3}{2}$

17. Change each of the following percents to decimals:
    a. 60%   b. $\dfrac{2}{3}\%$ c. 100%

18. Sandy received a dividend that equals 11% of the value of her investment. If her dividend was $1020.80, how much was her investment?

19. Five computers in a shipment of 150 were found to be defective. What percent of the computers were defective?

20. On a mathematics examination, a student missed 8 of 70 questions. What percent of the questions, rounded to the nearest tenth, did the student do correctly?

21. A microcomputer system costs $3450 at present. This is 60% of the cost 4 yr ago. What was the cost of the system 4 yr ago? Explain your reasoning.

22. If, on a purchase of one new suit, you are offered successive discounts of 5%, 10%, or 20% in any order you wish, what order should you choose?

23. Jane bought a bicycle and sold it for 30% more than she paid for it. She sold it for $104. How much did she pay for it?

24. A company was offered a $30,000 loan at a 12.5% annual interest rate for 4 yr. Find the simple interest due on the loan at the end of 4 yr.

*25. A money-market fund pays 14% annual interest compounded quarterly. What is the value of a $10,000 investment after 3 yr?

SELECTED BIBLIOGRAPHY

Cave, R. "Graphing Bit by Bit." *Mathematics Teacher* 88 (May 1995): 372–374.

Charles, R. "Get the Most Out of Word Problems." *Arithmetic Teacher* 29 (November 1981): 39–40.

Coburn, T. "Percentage and the Hand Calculator." *Mathematics Teacher* 79 (May 1986): 361–367.

Curcio, F., and N. Bezuk. "Understanding Rational Numbers and Proportions." *Curriculum and Evaluation Standards for School Mathematics Addenda Series Grades 5–8* (National Council of Teachers of Mathematics) 1994.

Kieren, T.E., and A.T. Olson. "Imagination, Intuition, and Computing in School Algebra." *Mathematics Teacher* 82 (January 1982): 14–17.

Nord, G., and J. Nord. "An Example of Algebra in Lake Roosevelt." *Mathematics Teacher* 88 (February 1995): 116–120.

O'Daffer, P. G. "Strategy Spotlight—Write an Equation." *Arithmetic Teacher* 32 (May 1985): 14–15.

Quintero, A. "Helping Children Understand Ratios." *Arithmetic Teacher* 34 (April 1987): 17–21.

Rossini, B. "Using Percent Problems to Promote Critical Thinking." *Mathematics Teacher* 81 (January 1988): 31–34.

Schoenfeld, A., and A. Arcavi. "On the Meaning of Variable." *Mathematics Teacher* 81 (September 1988): 420–427.

Smith, L. "Mathematics on the Balance Beam." *School Science and Mathematics* 85 (October 1985): 494–497.

Soler, F., and R. Schuster. "Compound Growth and Related Situations: A Problem-Solving Approach." *Mathematics Teacher* 75 (November 1982): 640–643.

Usiskin, Z. "Why Elementary Algebra Can, Should, and Must Be an Eighth-Grade Course for Average Students." *Mathematics Teacher* 80 (September 1987): 428–438.

Wiebe, J. "Manipulating Percentages." *Mathematics Teacher* 79 (January 1986): 21, 23–26.

8

PROBABILITY

A Stanford University statistician, Bradley Efron, designed a set of nonstandard dice whose faces are numbered as shown in the accompanying figure. The dice are to be used in a game in which each player chooses a die and then rolls it. Whoever rolls the greatest number is the winner. What strategy should you use so that you have the best chance of winning this game?

Probability, with its roots in gambling, is useful in such areas as predicting sales, planning political campaigns, and determining insurance premiums. Some examples of uses of probability in everyday conversations include the following:

What is the probability that the Braves will win the World Series?

The odds are 2 to 1 that Millie will win the dog show.

There is no chance you will get a raise.

There is a 50% chance of rain today.

Probability plays an important role in both the K–4 and the 5–8 *Standards,* as shown in the following quote from the 5–8 *Standards* (p. 110):

▲ *To see how the predictions we hear and see every day are based on probability, students must use their knowledge of probability to solve problems. In modeling problems, conducting simulations, and collecting, graphing, and studying data, students will come to understand how predictions can be based on data. Mathematically derived probabilities can be determined by building a table or tree diagram, creating an area model, making a list, or using simple counting procedures. Students develop an appreciation of the power of simulation and experimentation by comparing experimental results to the mathematically derived probabilities.*

And in the *Teaching Standards* (p. 136), we find the following:

▲ *Students should have opportunities to explore empirical probability from simulations and from data they have collected and to analyze theoretical probability on the basis of a description of the underlying sample space. Probability trees and simulations using objects such as spinners, dice, slips of paper, and so on should be used to solve problems.*

In this chapter, we use tree diagrams and geometric probabilities (area models) to solve problems and to analyze games involving spinners, cards, and dice. Counting techniques are introduced and the role of simulations in probability is discussed.

HISTORICAL NOTE

The originator of probability theory is not known. However, Blaise Pascal (1623–1662), the French philosopher and mathematician, solved two gambling problems posed by the Chevalier de Meré, a professional gambler. Pascal and Pierre de Fermat (1601–1665) are considered the founders of probability theory. One of de Meré's questions to Pascal was how to divide the stakes if two players start, but fail to complete, a game in which the winner is the one who wins three matches out of five. A Dutch mathematician, Christian Huygens (1629–1695) also worked on the de Meré problem and as a result wrote *De ratiociniis in ludo alea,* the first treatise on probability.

Section 8-1 | # How Probabilities Are Determined

Probabilities are ratios, expressed as fractions, decimals, or percents, determined by considering results or outcomes of experiments. An **experiment** is an activity where the results can be observed and recorded. Each of the possible results of an experiment is an **outcome.** If we toss a coin that cannot land on its edge, there are two distinct possible outcomes: heads (*H*) and tails (*T*).

experiment
outcome

sample space

Outcomes

A set of all possible outcomes for an experiment is a **sample space.** In a single coin toss, the sample space S is given by $S = \{H, T\}$. The sample space can be modeled by a tree diagram, as shown in Figure 8-1. Each outcome of the experiment is designated by a separate branch in the tree diagram. The sample space S for rolling the standard die in Figure 8-2(a) is $S = \{1, 2, 3, 4, 5, 6\}$. A tree diagram for the sample space is given in Figure 8-2(b).

Figure 8-1

Figure 8-2

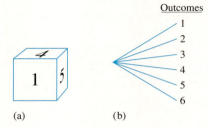

(a)   (b)

event

Any subset of a sample space is an **event.** For example, the set of all even-numbered rolls $\{2, 4, 6\}$ is a subset of all possible rolls of a die $\{1, 2, 3, 4, 5, 6\}$ and is an event.

● ● ●

Example 8-1

Suppose an experiment consists of drawing one slip of paper from a jar containing 12 slips of paper, each with a different month of the year written on it. Find each of the following:

a. The sample space S for the experiment
b. The event A consisting of outcomes having a month beginning with J
c. The event B consisting of outcomes having the name of a month that has exactly 4 letters
d. The event C consisting of outcomes having a month that begins with M or N

Solution

a. $S = \{$January, February, March, April, May, June, July, August, September, October, November, December$\}$
b. $A = \{$January, June, July$\}$
c. $B = \{$June, July$\}$
d. $C = \{$March, May, November$\}$

● ● ●

Determining Probabilities

Around 1900, the English statistician Karl Pearson tossed a coin 24,000 times and recorded 12,012 heads. During World War II, the Dane, John Kerrich, a prisoner of war, tossed a coin 10,000 times. A subset of his results is given in Table 8-1. The *relative frequency* column on the right is obtained by dividing the number of heads by the number of tosses of the coin.

Table 8-1

Number of Tosses	Number of Heads	Relative Frequency
10	4	0.400
50	25	0.500
100	44	0.440
500	255	0.510
1,000	502	0.502
5,000	2,533	0.507
8,000	4,034	0.504
10,000	5,067	0.507

After 10 tosses, the data in Table 8-1 suggest that heads might occur 4/10 of the time. After 50 tosses, the data in Table 8-1 suggest that we could expect heads about 25/50 of the time. As the number of Kerrich's tosses increased, he obtained heads close to half the time. The relative frequency for Pearson's 24,000 tosses gives a similar result of 12,012/24,000, or 0.5005.

experimentally • empirically

When a probability is determined by observing outcomes of experiments, it is said to be determined **experimentally,** or **empirically.** The exact number of heads that occurs when a fair coin is tossed a few times cannot be accurately predicted. A *fair coin* is a coin that is just as likely to land "heads" as it is to land "tails." Probabilities only suggest what will happen in the "long run." When a fair coin is tossed many times and the fraction (or proportion) of heads is near $\frac{1}{2}$, we say that the probability of heads occurring is $\frac{1}{2}$ and write $P(H) = \frac{1}{2}$.

theoretical probabilities

We assign **theoretical probabilities** to the outcomes under ideal conditions. For example, we could argue that since an ideal coin is symmetric and has two sides, then each side should appear about the same number of times if the coin is tossed many times. Again we would conclude that

$$P(H) = P(T) = 1/2.$$

equally likely

When one outcome is just as likely to occur as another, as in coin tossing, the outcomes are **equally likely.** In this text, by "probability" we mean *theoretical probability.* If an experiment is repeated many times, the experimental probability of the event's occurring should approach the theoretical probability of the event's occurring.

A *fair* die is a die that is just as likely to land showing any of the numerals 1 through 6. Its sample space S is given by $S = \{1, 2, 3, 4, 5, 6\}$, and $P(1) = P(2) = P(3) = P(4) = P(5) = P(6) = 1/6$. The probability of rolling an even number, that is, the probability of the event $E = \{2, 4, 6\}$, is 3/6, or 1/2. For a sample space with equally likely outcomes, the probability of an event A can be defined as follows.

Definition of Probability of an Event with Equally Likely Outcomes

For an experiment with sample space S and equally likely outcomes, the **probability of an event A** is given by

$$P(A) = \frac{\text{Number of elements of } A}{\text{Number of elements of } S} = \frac{n(A)}{n(S)}.$$

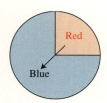

Figure 8-3

This definition applies only to a sample space that has equally likely outcomes. Applying the definition to a space with outcomes that are not equally likely leads to incorrect conclusions. For example, the sample space for spinning the spinner in Figure 8-3 is given by $S = \{\text{Red, Blue}\}$, but the outcome Blue is more likely to occur than is the outcome Red, so $P(\text{Red})$ is not equal to $\frac{1}{2}$ but to $\frac{90}{360}$, or $\frac{1}{4}$ (why?). If the spinner were spun 100 times, we could reasonably expect that about $\frac{1}{4}$, or 25, of the outcomes would be Red, whereas about $\frac{3}{4}$, or 75, of the outcomes would be Blue.

I N V E S T I G A T I O N   8 - 1

a. In an experiment of tossing a fair coin once, what is the sum of the probabilities of all the distinct outcomes in the sample space?

b. In an experiment of tossing a fair die once, what is the sum of the probabilities of all the distinct outcomes in the sample space?

c. Does the sum of the probabilities of all the distinct outcomes of any sample space always result in the same number? Why?

Example 8-2

at random

Let $S = \{1, 2, 3, 4, 5, \ldots, 25\}$. If a number is chosen **at random,** that is, with an equal chance of being drawn, calculate each of the following probabilities:

a. The event A that an even number is drawn
b. The event B that a number less than 10 and greater than 20 is drawn
c. The event C that a number less than 26 is drawn
d. The event D that a prime number is drawn
e. The event E that a number both even and prime is drawn

Solution   Each of the 25 numbers in set S has an equal chance of being drawn.

a. $A = \{2, 4, 6, 8, 10, 12, 14, 16, 18, 20, 22, 24\}$, so $n(A) = 12$. Thus

$$P(A) = \frac{n(A)}{n(S)} = \frac{12}{25}.$$

b. $B = \varnothing$, so $n(B) = 0$. Thus $P(B) = \frac{0}{25} = 0.$

c. $C = S$ and $n(C) = 25$. Thus $P(C) = \frac{25}{25} = 1.$

d. $D = \{2, 3, 5, 7, 11, 13, 17, 19, 23\}$, so $n(D) = 9$. Thus

$$P(D) = \frac{n(D)}{n(S)} = \frac{9}{25}.$$

e. $E = \{2\}$, so $n(E) = 1$. Thus $P(E) = \frac{1}{25}.$

impossible event

certain event

In Example 8-2(b), event B is the empty set. An event such as B that has no outcomes in it is an **impossible event** *and has probability* 0. If the word *and* were replaced by *or* in Example 8-2(b), then event B would no longer be the empty set. In Example 8-2(c), event C consists of drawing a number less than 26 on a single draw. Because every number in S is less than 26, $P(C) = \frac{25}{25} = 1$. An event that has probability 1 is a **certain event.**

Because an event is a subset of a sample space, an event can have no more outcomes than in the sample space. In addition, an event can have no fewer than 0 outcomes. Thus, if A is any event, it occurs between 0% and 100% of the time, and we have the following:

$$0\% \leq P(A) \leq 100\% \quad \text{or} \quad 0 \leq P(A) \leq 1$$

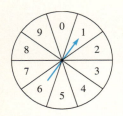

Figure 8-4

Consider one spin of the wheel shown in Figure 8-4. For this experiment, $S = \{0, 1, 2, 3, 4, 5, 6, 7, 8, 9\}$. If A is the event of spinning a number in the set $\{0, 1, 2, 3, 4\}$ and B is the event of spinning a number in the set $\{5, 7\}$, then using the definition of probability for equally likely events, $P(A) = n(A)/n(S) = 5/10$ and $P(B) = n(B)/n(S) = 2/10$. The probability of an event can be found by adding the probabilities of the various outcomes in the set. For example, event $B = \{5, 7\}$ can be represented as the union of two disjoint outcomes, that is, spinning a 5 or spinning a 7. Then $P(B)$ can be found by adding the probabilities of each outcome:

$$P(B) = P(5) + P(7) = 1/10 + 1/10 = 2/10$$

Likewise,

$$P(A) = 1/10 + 1/10 + 1/10 + 1/10 + 1/10 = 5/10.$$

These are special cases of the following property, which holds for all probabilities.

Property of Probability of an Event

The **probability of an event** is equal to the sum of the probabilities of all the outcomes in the event.

Example 8-3   If we draw a card at random from an ordinary deck of playing cards, what is the probability that the card is an ace?

Solution   There are 52 cards in a deck, and 4 are aces. If event A is drawing an ace, then $A = \left\{ \boxed{\spadesuit}, \boxed{\clubsuit}, \boxed{\diamondsuit}, \boxed{\heartsuit} \right\}$. We use the definition of probability for equally likely outcomes to compute the following:

$$P(A) = \frac{n(A)}{n(S)} = \frac{4}{52}$$

An alternative approach is to find the sum of each of the probabilities of the outcomes in the event, where the probability of drawing any single ace from the deck is $\frac{1}{52}$:

$$P(A) = \frac{1}{52} + \frac{1}{52} + \frac{1}{52} + \frac{1}{52} = \frac{4}{52}$$

Mutually Exclusive Events

Consider one spin of the wheel in Figure 8-4. For this experiment, we have $S = \{0, 1, 2, 3, 4, 5, 6, 7, 8, 9\}$. If $A = \{0, 1, 2, 3, 4\}$ and $B = \{5, 7\}$, then $A \cap B = \emptyset$. Two such events are **mutually exclusive** events. If event A occurs, then event B cannot occur, and we have the following definition.

Definition of Mutually Exclusive Events

Events A and B are **mutually exclusive** if $A \cap B = \emptyset$.

Each outcome in the preceding sample space S is equally likely, with probability $\frac{1}{10}$. Thus, if we write the probability of A or B as $P(A \cup B)$, we have the following:

$$P(A \cup B) = \frac{n(A \cup B)}{n(S)} = \frac{7}{10} = \frac{5+2}{10} = \frac{5}{10} + \frac{2}{10}$$

$$= \frac{n(A)}{n(S)} + \frac{n(B)}{n(S)} = P(A) + P(B)$$

The result developed in this example is true for any mutually exclusive events. In general, we have the following property.

Property

If events A and B are mutually exclusive, then $P(A \cup B) = P(A) + P(B)$.

For a sample space with equally likely outcomes, this property follows immediately from the fact that if $A \cap B = \emptyset$, then $n(A \cup B) = n(A) + n(B)$.

Complementary Events

complements

If the weather forecaster tells us that the probability of rain is 25%, what is the probability that it will not rain? These two events—rain and not rain—are **complements** of each other. Therefore if the probability of rain is 25%, or 1/4, the probability it will not rain is 100% − 25% = 75%, or 1 − 1/4 = 3/4. Notice that $P(\text{no rain}) = 1 − P(\text{rain})$. The two events rain and no rain are mutually exclusive because if one happens, the other cannot. Two mutually **complementary events** exclusive events whose union is the sample space are **complementary events.** If A is an event, the complement of A, written $\overline{A}$, is also an event. For example, consider the event $A = \{2, 4\}$ of tossing a 2 or a 4 using a standard die. The complement of A is the set $\overline{A} = \{1, 3, 5, 6\}$. Because the sample space is $S = \{1, 2, 3, 4, 5, 6\}$, we have $P(A) = 2/6$ and $P(\overline{A}) = 4/6$. Notice that $P(\overline{A}) = 1 − P(A)$. This is true in general for any set A and its complement, $\overline{A}$.

Property

If A is a set and $\overline{A}$ is the complement, then

$$P(A) + P(\overline{A}) = 1,$$

$$P(\overline{A}) = 1 − P(A), \text{ or } P(A) = 1 − P(\overline{A}).$$

Non-Mutually Exclusive Events

Consider the spinner in Figure 8-5. Let E be the event of spinning an even number and T the event of spinning a number divisible by 3, as follows:

$$E = \{0, 2, 4, 6, 8\}$$

$$T = \{0, 3, 6, 9\}$$

The event of spinning an even number and a number divisible by 3, denoted by $E \cap T$, is $\{0, 6\}$. Because $E \cap T = \{0, 6\}$, E and T are not mutually exclusive and $P(E \cup T) \neq P(E) + P(T)$. However, because each outcome is equally likely we can still use the definition of the probability of an event to compute the probability of E or T as follows:

$$P(E \cup T) = \frac{n(E \cup T)}{n(S)}$$

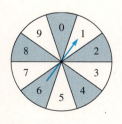

Figure 8-5

Because $E \cup T = \{0, 2, 4, 6, 8, 3, 9\}$, $n(E \cup T) = 7$. Also, $n(S) = 10$, and the $P(E \cup T) = \dfrac{7}{10}$.

In general, we can also compute the probability of E or T by using notions of sets from Chapter 2. We know

$$n(E \cup T) = n(E) + n(T) - n(E \cap T).$$

Therefore, for a sample space with equally likely outcomes:

$$P(E \cup T) = \frac{n(E \cup T)}{n(S)}$$

$$= \frac{n(E) + n(T) - n(E \cap T)}{n(S)}$$

$$= \frac{n(E)}{n(S)} + \frac{n(T)}{n(S)} - \frac{n(E \cap T)}{n(S)}$$

$$= P(E) + P(T) - P(E \cap T).$$

This result, although proved for events in a sample space with equally likely outcomes, is true in general, and the properties of probability are summarized next.

Properties of Probability

1. $P(\emptyset) = 0$ (impossible event).
2. $P(S) = 1$, where S is the sample space (certain event).
3. For any event A, $0 \le P(A) \le 1$.
4. If A and B are events and $A \cap B = \emptyset$, then $P(A \cup B) = P(A) + P(B)$.
5. If A and B are events, then $P(A \cup B) = P(A) + P(B) - P(A \cap B)$.
6. If A is an event, then $P(\overline{A}) = 1 - P(A)$.

• • •

Example 8-4   A golf bag contains 2 red tees, 4 blue tees, and 5 white tees.

  a. What is the probability of the event R that a tee drawn at random is red?
  b. What is the probability of the event "not R," that is, that a tee drawn at random is not red?
  c. What is the probability of the event that a tee drawn at random is either red (R) or blue (B), that is, $P(R \cup B)$.

Solution   **a.** Because the bag contains a total of $2 + 4 + 5$, or 11, tees and 2 tees are red,
$$P(R) = \frac{2}{11}.$$

  b. The bag contains 11 tees and 9 are not red, so the probability of "not R" is $\dfrac{9}{11}$. Also, notice that $P(\overline{R}) = 1 - P(R) = 1 - \dfrac{2}{11} = \dfrac{9}{11}$.

  c. The bag contains 2 red tees and 4 blue tees and $R \cap B = \emptyset$, so $P(R \cup B) = \dfrac{2}{11} + \dfrac{4}{11}$, or $\dfrac{6}{11}$.

• • •

Example 8-5 Find the probability of rolling a sum of 7 or 11 when rolling a fair pair of dice.

 Solution To solve this problem, we use the strategy of *making a table,* as in Figure 8-6(a), to show all possible outcomes of tossing the dice. We know that there are 6 possible results from tossing the first die and 6 from tossing the second die, so by the Fundamental Counting Principle, there are 6 · 6, or 36, entries in the table. It may be easier to read the results when they are recorded as ordered pairs, as in Figure 8-6(b), where the first component represents the number on the first die and the second component represents the number on the second die. To find the sample space for the event, we find the possible sums in rolling the pair of dice {2, 3, 4, 5, 6, 7, 8, 9, 10, 11, 12} by adding the components of the ordered pairs, as shown in Figure 8-6(c).

Figure 8-6

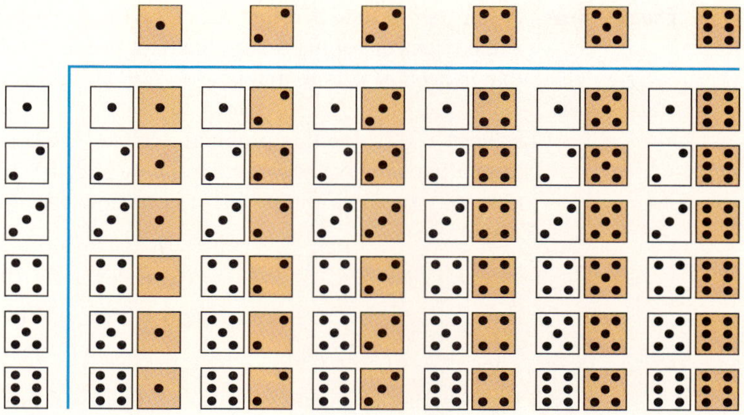

(a)

Number on Second Die (b)

	1	2	3	4	5	6
1	(1,1)	(1, 2)	(1, 3)	(1, 4)	(1, 5)	(1, 6)
2	(2, 1)	(2, 2)	(2, 3)	(2, 4)	(2, 5)	(2, 6)
3	(3, 1)	(3, 2)	(3, 3)	(3, 4)	(3, 5)	(3, 6)
4	(4, 1)	(4, 2)	(4, 3)	(4, 4)	(4, 5)	(4, 6)
5	(5, 1)	(5, 2)	(5, 3)	(5, 4)	(5, 5)	(5, 6)
6	(6, 1)	(6, 2)	(6, 3)	(6, 4)	(6, 5)	(6, 6)

Number on First Die

Number on Second Die (c)

	1	2	3	4	5	6
1	2	3	4	5	6	7
2	3	4	5	6	7	8
3	4	5	6	7	8	9
4	5	6	7	8	9	10
5	6	7	8	9	10	11
6	7	8	9	10	11	12

Number on First Die

Possible Sums

The event "a sum of 7" is derived from the set of ordered pairs in Figure 8-6(b), as follows:

$$\{(6, 1), (5, 2), (4, 3), (3, 4), (2, 5), (1, 6)\}$$

Each element in this set is equally likely and has probability 1/36 of happening when two dice are rolled. Therefore $P(7) = 6(1/36) = 6/36$. Similarly, $P(11) = 2(1/36) = 2/36$. The probabilities of each of the elements in the sample space can be calculated in the same way and are displayed in Table 8-2.

Table 8-2

Outcome	2	3	4	5	6	7	8	9	10	11	12
Probability	1/36	2/36	3/36	4/36	5/36	6/36	5/36	4/36	3/36	2/36	1/36

The probability of rolling a sum of 7 or 11 is given by $P(7 \text{ or } 11) = P(7) + P(11) = 6/36 + 2/36 = 8/36$.

• • •

• • •

Example 8-6   A fair pair of dice is rolled. Let E be the event of rolling a sum that is an even number and P the event of rolling a sum that is a prime number. Find the probability of rolling a sum that is even *or* prime, that is, $P(E \cup P)$.

Solution   To solve this problem, we use Table 8-2. We know that events E and P are not mutually exclusive because $E = \{2, 4, 6, 8, 10, 12\}$, $P = \{2, 3, 5, 7, 11\}$, and $E \cap P = \{2\}$. One way to solve the problem is to note that $E \cup P = \{2, 4, 6, 8, 10, 12, 3, 5, 7, 11\}$. Therefore

$$P(E \cup P) = P(2) + P(4) + P(6) + P(8) + P(10) + P(12) + P(3) + P(5) + P(7) + P(11)$$
$$= 1/36 + 3/36 + 5/36 + 5/36 + 3/36 + 1/36 + 2/36 + 4/36 + 6/36 + 2/36$$
$$= 32/36.$$

Another approach is to use a property of probabilities (Property 5) established earlier:

$$P(E \cup P) = P(E) + P(P) - P(E \cap P)$$
$$= 18/36 + 15/36 - 1/36$$
$$= 32/36$$

A third approach to finding $P(E \cup P)$ is to find $P(\overline{E \cup P})$ and subtract this probability from 1. Because $E \cup P = \{2, 3, 4, 5, 6, 7, 8, 10, 11, 12\}$, then $\overline{E \cup P} = \{9\}$ and $P(\overline{E \cup P}) = 4/36$. Hence, $P(E \cup P) = 1 - P(\overline{E \cup P}) = 1 - 4/36 = 32/36$.

• • •

Ongoing Assessment 8-1

1. When a thumbtack is dropped, it will land point up (⊥) or point down (∧). This experiment was repeated 80 times with the following results:

   Point up: 56 times   Point down: 24 times

   a. What is the experimental probability that the thumbtack will land point up?
   b. What is the experimental probability that the thumbtack will land point down?

c. If you were to try this experiment another 80 times, would you get the same results? Why?
d. Would you expect to get nearly the same results on a second trial? Why?

2. An experiment consists of selecting the last digit of a telephone number. Assume that each of the 10 digits is equally likely to appear as a last digit. List each of the following:
   a. The sample space
   b. The event consisting of outcomes that the digit is less than 5

c. The event consisting of outcomes that the digit is odd
d. The event consisting of outcomes that the digit is not 2
e. Find the probability of each of the events in (b)–(d).

3. The following spinner is spun:

Find the probabilities of obtaining each of the following:
a. *P*(factor of 35)
b. *P*(multiple of 3)
c. *P*(even number)
d. *P*(6 or 2)
e. *P*(11)
f. *P*(composite number)
g. *P*(neither a prime nor a composite)

4. A card is selected from an ordinary bridge deck consisting of 52 cards. Find the probabilities for each of the following:
a. A red card   b. A face card
c. A red card or a 10   d. A queen
e. Not a queen   f. A face card or a club
g. A face card and a club
h. Not a face card and not a club

5. A drawer contains 6 black socks, 4 brown socks, and 2 green socks. Suppose one sock is drawn from the drawer and that it is equally likely that any one of the socks is drawn. Find the probabilities for each of the following:
a. The sock is brown.
b. The sock is either black or green.
c. The sock is red.
d. The sock is not black.

6. Each letter of the alphabet is written on a separate piece of paper and placed in a box and then one piece is drawn at random.
a. What is the probability that the piece of paper has a vowel written on it?
b. What is the probability that it has a consonant written on it?

7. If the probability of being able to board a connecting flight to Boston is 0.2, what is the probability of missing the connecting flight?

8. Riena has six unmarked computer disks in a box, where each is dedicated to exactly one of English, mathematics, French, American history, chemistry, and computer science. Answer the following questions:
a. If she chooses a computer disk at random, what is the probability she chooses the English disk?
b. What is the probability that she chooses a disk that is neither math nor chemistry?

9. The following questions refer to a very popular dice game, craps, in which a player rolls two dice:
a. Rolling a sum of 7 or 11 on the first roll of the dice is a win. What is the probability of winning on the first roll?
b. Rolling a sum of 2, 3, or 12 on the first roll of the dice is a loss. What is the probability of losing on the first roll?
c. Rolling a sum of 4, 5, 6, 8, 9, or 10 on the first roll is neither a win nor a loss. What is the probability of neither winning nor losing on the first roll?
d. After rolling a sum of 4, 5, 6, 8, 9, or 10, a player must roll the same sum again before rolling a sum of 7. Which sum, 4, 5, 6, 8, 9, or 10, has the highest probability of occurring again?
e. What is the probability of rolling a sum of 1 on any roll of the dice?
f. What is the probability of rolling a sum less than 13 on any roll of the dice?
g. If the two dice are rolled 60 times, predict about how many times a sum of 7 will be rolled.

10. According to a weather report, there is a 30% chance it will rain tomorrow. What is the probability it will not rain tomorrow? Explain your answer.

11. A roulette wheel has 38 slots around the rim. The first 36 slots are numbered from 1 to 36. Half of these 36 slots are red, and the other half are black. The remaining 2 slots are numbered 0 and 00 and are green. As the roulette wheel is spun in one direction, a small ivory ball is rolled along the rim in the opposite direction. The ball has an equally likely chance of falling into any one of the 38 slots. Find each of the following:
a. The probability that the ball lands in a black slot
b. The probability that the ball lands on 0 or 00
c. The probability that the ball does not land on a number from 1 through 12
d. The probability that the ball lands on an odd number or on a green slot

12. If the roulette wheel in problem 11 is spun 190 times, predict about how many times the ball will land on 0 or 00.

13. Determine if each player has an equal probability of winning each of the following games:
a. Toss a fair coin. If heads appears, I win; if tails appears, you lose.
b. Toss a fair coin. If heads appears, I win; otherwise, you win.
c. Toss a fair die numbered 1 through 6. If 1 appears, I win; if 6 appears, you win.
d. Toss a fair die numbered 1 through 6. If an even number appears, I win; if an odd number appears, you win.
e. Toss a fair die numbered 1 through 6. If a number greater than or equal to 3 appears, I win; otherwise, you win.
f. Toss two fair dice numbered 1 through 6. If a 1 appears on each die, I win; if a 6 appears on each die, you win.
g. Toss two fair dice numbered 1 through 6. If the sum is 3, I win; if the sum is 2, you win.

h. Toss two dice numbered 1 through 6; one die is red and one is white. If the number on the red die is greater than the number on the white die, I win; otherwise, you win.

14. A bowler has made 45 strikes in the last 150 frames she has bowled. What is the estimated probability that she will get a strike in the next frame she bowls?

15. Suppose a fair coin is tossed twice. Find the probability for each of the following:
a. Exactly one head
b. At least one head
c. At most one head

16. In Sentinel High School, there are 350 freshmen, 320 sophomores, 310 juniors, and 400 seniors. If a student is chosen at random from the student body to represent the school, what is the probability that the chosen student is a freshman?

17. In each of the following, sketch a single spinner with the following characteristics:
a. The outcomes are *M, A, T,* and *H,* each with equally likely probability.
b. The outcomes are *R, A,* and *T* with $P(R) = 3/4$, $P(A) = 1/8$, and $P(T) = 1/8$.

18. In the game of "Between," two cards are dealt. You then pick a third card from the deck. To win, you must pick a card that has a value between the other two cards. The order of values is 2, 3, 4, 5, 6, 7, 8, 9, 10, J, Q, K, A, where the letters represent a jack, queen, king, and ace, respectively. Determine the probability of your winning if the first two cards dealt are the following:
a. A 5 and a jack
b. A 2 and a king
c. A 5 and a 6

19. Calculators, watches, scoreboards, and many other devices display numbers using arrays like the following. The device lights up different parts of the array (any segment lettered *a–g*), to display any single digit 0–9. Suppose a digit is chosen at random. Determine the probability for each of the following. (*Hint:* Use a digital watch to see which segments are lit up for the different numbers.)

a. Segment *a* will be lit.
b. Segment *b* will be lit.
c. Segments *e* and *b* will be lit.
d. Segments *e* or *b* will be lit.

20. If *A* is the set of students taking algebra and *C* is the set of students taking chemistry at Central High School,

describe in words what is meant by each of the following probabilities:
a. $P(A \cup C)$ **b.** $P(A \cap C)$ **c.** $1 - P(C)$

21. If *A* and *B* are mutually exclusive and if $P(A) = 0.3$ and $P(B) = 0.4$, what is $P(A \cup B)$?

22. A calculus class is composed of 35 men and 45 women. There are 20 business majors, 30 biology majors, 10 computer science majors, and 20 mathematics majors. No person has a double major. If a single student is chosen from the class, what is the probability that the student is the following:
a. Female
b. A computer science major
c. Not a mathematics major
d. A computer science major or a mathematics major

Communication

23. Explain whether events *A* and *B* can be mutually exclusive if $P(A) = 0.8$ and $P(B) = 0.9$.

24. Bobbie says that when she shoots a free throw in basketball, she will either make it or miss it. Because there are only two outcomes and one of them is making a basket, Bobbie claims the probability of her making a free throw is 1/2. Explain whether Bobbie's reasoning is correct.

25. If the following spinner is spun 100 times, Joe claims that the number 4 will occur most often because the greatest area of the spinner is covered by the number 4. What would you tell Joe about his conjecture? What is the probability that a 4 will occur on any spin?

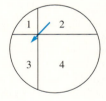

Open-ended

26. Suppose you toss a die once. Name two events that could result that are mutually exclusive.

27. Select any book, go to the first complete paragraph in it, and count the number of words the paragraph has. Now count the number of words that start with a vowel. If the paragraph has fewer than 100 words, continue to count words until there are more than 100 words from where you started. What is the experimental probability that a word chosen at random from the book starts with a vowel? Open the book to any page, choose a paragraph with more than 100 words, and count the number of words in it. Predict how many words will start with a vowel, and then count them to see how close you were.

28. List three real-world situations that do not involve weather or gambling where probability might be used.

29. For each of the following letters, describe an event, if possible, that has the approximate probability marked on the probability line:

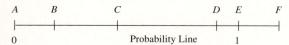

Cooperative Learning

30. Prepare a bag containing eight cubes of three different colors. Exchange bags with another group so that your group will not know the colors of the cubes. Without looking in the bag, draw a cube, record its color, and have a member of your group replace it. Repeat 50 times. Using experimental probability, guess the number of each color of cube in that bag. Explain how you arrived at your guess.

31. Form groups of three or four students. Each group has a pair of dice. Each player needs 18 markers and a sheet of paper with a gameboard drawn on it similar to the following:

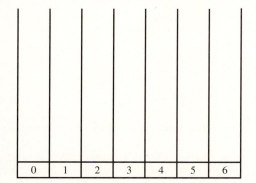

At the beginning of each game, each player places his/her markers on the boards in any arrangement above the numbers. Two players (or teams) then take turns rolling the dice. The result of each roll is the difference between the greater and the smaller of the two numbers. For example, if a 6 and a 4 were rolled, the difference would be $6 - 4$, or 2. All players who have a marker on the number that represents the difference can remove one marker. Only one marker can be removed each roll. The first player to remove all of his/her markers is the winner. The game may be stopped if it is clear that there can be no winner.

a. Play the game twice. What differences seem to occur most often? Least often?

b. Roll the dice 20 times and record how often the various differences occur. Using this information, explain how you would distribute your 18 markers to win.

c. Compute the theoretical probabilities for each possible difference. (Figure 8-6(a) might be useful.)

d. Use your answers to (d) to explain how you would arrange the markers in order to win the game.

32. The following game is played with two players and a single fair die numbered 1–6. The die is rolled and one person receives a score that is the square of the number appearing on the die. The other person will receive a score of four times the value showing on the die. The person with the greatest score wins.

a. Play the game several times to see if it appears to be a *fair game,* that is, a game that each player can have the same chance of winning.

b. Determine if this is a fair game. If it is not fair, who has the advantage? Explain how you arrived at your answer.

LABORATORY ACTIVITY

1. Suppose a paper cup is tossed in the air. The different ways it can land are shown here:

Top   Bottom   Side

Toss a cup 100 times and record each result. From this information, calculate the experimental probability of each outcome. Do the outcomes appear to be equally likely? Using experimental probabilities, predict how many times the cup will land on its side if tossed 100 times.

2. Toss a fair coin 100 times and record the results. From this information, calculate the experimental probability of getting heads on a particular toss. Does the experimental result agree with the expected theoretical probability of $\frac{1}{2}$?

3. Hold a coin upright on its edge under your forefinger on a hard surface and then spin it with your other finger so that it spins before landing. Repeat this experiment 100 times and calculate the experimental probability of the coin's landing on heads on a particular spin. Compare your experimental probabilities with those in activity 2.

TECHNOLOGY CORNER

The following Logo procedures simulate flipping a coin and output the result:

```
TO TOSS
  OUTPUT PICK.ONE [HEADS TAILS]
END
TO PICK.ONE :FLIP
  OUTPUT ITEM (1 + RANDOM COUNT :FLIP) :FLIP
END
```

Enter the procedures in your computer and then complete the following:

1. Execute PRINT TOSS.
2. To simulate tossing a coin 25 times, execute the following:
   REPEAT 25 [PRINT TOSS]
3. Using the results in Number 2, determine the experimental probability for obtaining HEADS. For obtaining TAILS.
4. Edit the Logo procedure TOSS to make the list be [HEADS HEADS TAILS TAILS TAILS]. Now execute the following: REPEAT 25 [PRINT TOSS]

What is the experimental probability for obtaining HEADS now? For obtaining TAILS now?

Section 8-2

Multistage Experiments with Tree Diagrams and Geometric Probabilities

In Section 8-1, we considered one-stage experiments, that is, experiments that were over after one step. For example, drawing one ball at random from the box containing a red, white, and green ball in Figure 8-7(a) is a one-stage experiment. A tree diagram for this experiment is shown in Figure 8-7(b).

Figure 8-7

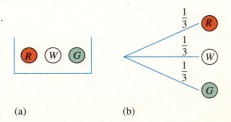

(a)   (b)

Next we consider a two-stage experiment. For example, a ball is drawn from the box in Figure 8-7(a) and its color is recorded. Then the ball is *replaced,* and a second ball is drawn and its color is recorded. A sample space for this experiment may be written as {*RR, RW, RG, WR, WW, WG, GR, GW, GG*}. A tree diagram for this experiment is given in Figure 8-8.

Figure 8-8

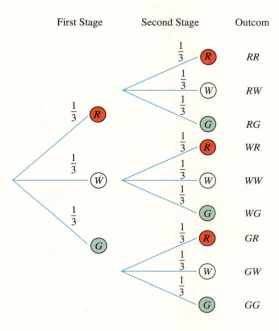

Each of the outcomes in the sample space is equally likely and there are nine total outcomes, so the probability of each outcome is 1/9.

The box in Figure 8-9(a) contains one colored ball and two white balls. If a ball is drawn at random and the color recorded, a tree diagram for the experiment might look like the one in Figure 8-9(b). Because each ball has the same chance of being drawn, we may combine the branches and obtain the tree diagram shown in Figure 8-9(c). Combining branches in this way is a common practice because it simplifies tree diagrams.

Figure 8-9

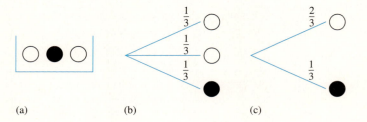

(a)   (b)   (c)

Suppose a ball is drawn at random from the box in Figure 8-9(a) and its color recorded. The ball is then *replaced,* and a second ball is drawn and its color recorded. The sample space for this two-stage experiment may be recorded using ordered pairs as {(●, ●),

($\bullet$, $\bigcirc$), ($\bigcirc$, $\bullet$), ($\bigcirc$, $\bigcirc$)} or, more commonly, as {$\bullet$ $\bullet$, $\bullet$ $\bigcirc$, $\bigcirc$ $\bullet$, $\bigcirc$ $\bigcirc$}, as shown in the tree diagram in Figure 8-10.

Figure 8-10

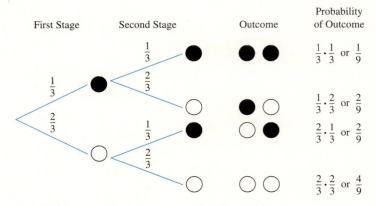

First Stage	Second Stage	Outcome	Probability of Outcome
	$\frac{1}{3}$ $\bullet$	$\bullet$ $\bullet$	$\frac{1}{3} \cdot \frac{1}{3}$ or $\frac{1}{9}$
$\frac{1}{3}$ $\bullet$ $\frac{2}{3}$	$\bigcirc$	$\bullet$ $\bigcirc$	$\frac{1}{3} \cdot \frac{2}{3}$ or $\frac{2}{9}$
$\frac{2}{3}$ $\frac{1}{3}$	$\bullet$	$\bigcirc$ $\bullet$	$\frac{2}{3} \cdot \frac{1}{3}$ or $\frac{2}{9}$
$\bigcirc$ $\frac{2}{3}$	$\bigcirc$	$\bigcirc$ $\bigcirc$	$\frac{2}{3} \cdot \frac{2}{3}$ or $\frac{4}{9}$

To assign the probability of the outcomes in this experiment, consider, for example, the path for the outcome $\bullet$ $\bigcirc$. In the first stage, the probability of obtaining a colored ball is $\frac{1}{3}$. Then, the probability of obtaining a white ball in the second stage (second draw) is $\frac{2}{3}$. Thus we expect to obtain a colored ball on the first draw $\frac{1}{3}$ of the time and then on the second draw, to obtain a white ball $\frac{2}{3}$ of those times that we obtained a colored ball on the first draw, that is, $\frac{2}{3}$ of $\frac{1}{3}$, or $\frac{2}{3} \cdot \frac{1}{3}$. Observe that this product may be obtained by multiplying the probabilities along the branches used for the path leading to $\bullet$ $\bigcirc$, that is, $\frac{1}{3} \cdot \frac{2}{3}$, or $\frac{2}{9}$. The probabilities shown in Figure 8-10 are obtained by following the paths leading to each of the four outcomes and multiplying the probabilities along the paths. This discussion yields the following property for tree diagrams.

Property: Multiplication Rule for Probabilities

For all multistage experiments, the probability of the outcome along any path is equal to the product of all the probabilities along the path.

REMARK   The sum of the probabilities on all the branches from any point always equals 1, and the sum of the probabilities for the possible outcomes must also be 1.

Look again at the box pictured in Figure 8-9. This time, suppose two balls are drawn one by one *without replacement*. A tree diagram for this experiment, along with the set of possible outcomes, is shown in Figure 8-11.

Figure 8-11

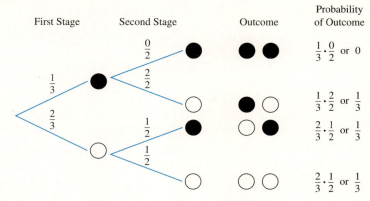

The denominators of the fractions along the second stage are all 2. Because the draws are made without replacement, there are only two balls remaining for the second draw.

Consider event A, consisting of the outcomes for drawing exactly one colored ball in the two draws without replacement. This event is given by $A = \{\bullet \bigcirc, \bigcirc \bullet\}$. Since the outcome $\bullet \bigcirc$ appears $\frac{1}{3}$ of the time, and the outcome $\bigcirc \bullet$ appears $\frac{1}{3}$ of the time, then either $\bullet \bigcirc$ or $\bigcirc \bullet$ will appear $\frac{2}{3}$ of the time. Thus $P(A) = \frac{1}{3} + \frac{1}{3} = \frac{2}{3}$.

Event B, consisting of outcomes for drawing *at least* one colored ball, could be recorded as $B = \{\bullet \bigcirc, \bigcirc \bullet, \bullet \bullet\}$. Because $P(\bullet \bigcirc) = \frac{1}{3}$, $P(\bigcirc \bullet) = \frac{1}{3}$, and $P(\bullet \bullet) = 0$, then $P(B) = \frac{1}{3} + \frac{1}{3} + 0 = \frac{2}{3}$. Because $\overline{B} = \{\bigcirc \bigcirc\}$ and $P(\overline{B}) = \frac{1}{3}$, the probability of B could have been computed as follows: $P(B) = 1 - P(\overline{B}) = 1 - \frac{1}{3} = \frac{2}{3}$.

• • •

Example 8-7

Figure 8-12 shows a box with eleven letters. Some letters are repeated. Suppose four letters are drawn at random from the box one by one without replacement. What is the probability of the outcome BABY, with the letters chosen in exactly the order given?

Figure 8-12

PROBABILITY

Solution   We do not need the entire tree diagram to find this probability because we are interested in only the branch leading to the outcome BABY. The portion needed is shown in Figure 8-13.

Figure 8-13

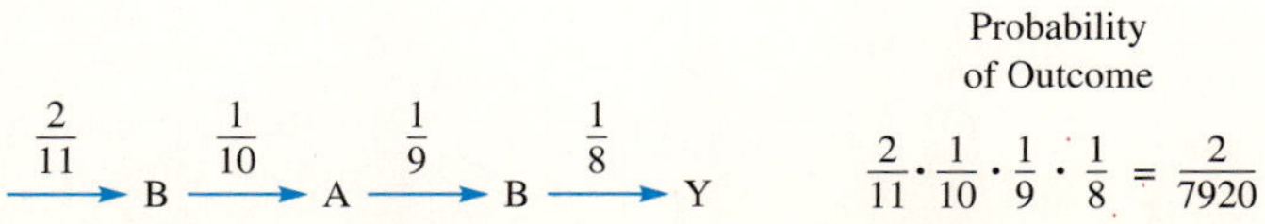

Probability
of Outcome

$$\frac{2}{11} \quad \frac{1}{10} \quad \frac{1}{9} \quad \frac{1}{8}$$
$$\longrightarrow B \longrightarrow A \longrightarrow B \longrightarrow Y \qquad \frac{2}{11} \cdot \frac{1}{10} \cdot \frac{1}{9} \cdot \frac{1}{8} = \frac{2}{7920}$$

The probability of the first B is $\frac{2}{11}$ because there are two B's out of eleven letters. The probability of the second B is $\frac{1}{9}$ because there are nine letters left after one B and one A have been chosen. Then, P(BABY) is $\frac{2}{7920}$, as shown.

• • •

In Example 8-7, suppose four letters are drawn one by one from the box and the letters are replaced after each drawing. In this case, the branch needed to find P(BABY) in the order drawn is pictured in Figure 8-14. Then, $P(\text{BABY}) = \left(\frac{2}{11}\right) \cdot \left(\frac{1}{11}\right) \cdot \left(\frac{2}{11}\right) \cdot \left(\frac{1}{11}\right)$, or $\frac{4}{14,641}$.

Figure 8-14

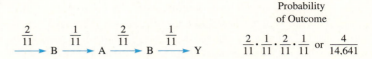

• • •

Example 8-8   Consider the three boxes in Figure 8-15. A letter is drawn from box 1 and placed in box 2. Then, a letter is drawn from box 2 and placed in box 3. Finally, a letter is drawn from box 3. What is the probability that the letter drawn from box 3 is *B*?

Figure 8-15

AAB	AB	ABBB
1	2	3

Solution   A tree diagram for this experiment is given in Figure 8-16. Notice that the denominators in the second stage are 3 rather than 2 because in this stage, there are now three letters in box 2. The denominators in the third stage are 5 because in this stage, there are five letters in box 3. To find the probability that a *B* is drawn from box 3, add the probabilities for the outcomes *AAB*, *ABB*, *BAB*, and *BBB* that make up this event.

Figure 8-16

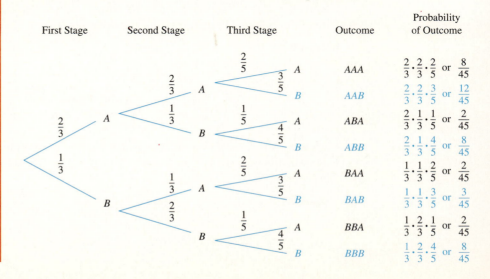

Thus the probability of obtaining a *B* on the draw from box 3 in this experiment is $\frac{12}{45}$ + $\frac{8}{45} + \frac{3}{45} + \frac{8}{45} = \frac{31}{45}$.

• • •

I N V E S T I G A T I O N   8 - 2

● Suppose that in Example 8-8, it is known that the letter *A* was drawn on the first draw. What is the probability that

a. the last letter drawn is a *B*?

b. the last letter drawn is an *A*?

c. the last 2 letters drawn will match, that is, 2 *A*'s or 2 *B*'s? ●

Modeling Games

The *Teaching Standards* contain statements that teachers need common experiences to build and extend their knowledge of mathematics. These standards also state (p. 135):

▲ *In the process of constructing and developing these experiences, appropriate attention to, and use of, mathematical modeling and technology should be included to enhance the teaching and learning of the mathematical ideas.*

We can use models to analyze games involving probability. Consider the following game, which Arthur and Guinevere play.

There are two colored marbles and one white marble in a box. Guinevere mixes the marbles, and Arthur draws two marbles at random without replacement. If the two marbles match, Arthur wins; otherwise, Guinevere wins. Is the game fair? We *develop a model* for analyzing the game. One possible model is a tree diagram, as shown in Figure 8-17.

Figure 8-17

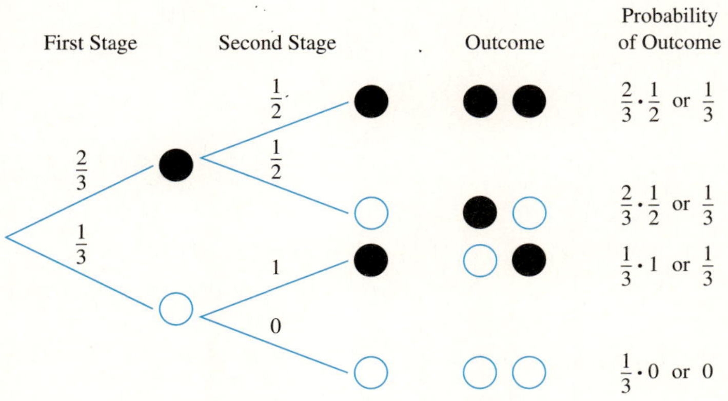

First Stage	Second Stage	Outcome	Probability of Outcome

The probability that the marbles are the same color is $\frac{1}{3} + 0$, or $\frac{1}{3}$, and the probability that they are not the same color is $\frac{1}{3} + \frac{1}{3}$, or $\frac{2}{3}$. Because $\frac{1}{3} \neq \frac{2}{3}$, the players do not have the same chance of winning.

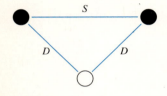

Figure 8-18

An alternative model for analyzing this game is given in Figure 8-18, where the colored and white marbles are shown along with the possible ways of drawing two marbles. Each line segment in the diagram represents one pair of marbles that could be drawn. S indicates that the marbles in the pair are the same color, and D indicates that the marbles are different colors. Because there are two D's in Figure 8-18, we see that the probability of drawing two different-colored marbles is $\frac{2}{3}$. Likewise, the probability of drawing two marbles of the same color is $\frac{1}{3}$. Because $\frac{2}{3} \neq \frac{1}{3}$, the players do not have an equal chance of winning. Will adding another white marble give each player an equal chance of winning? With two white and two colored marbles, we have the model in Figure 8-19. Therefore $P(D) = \frac{4}{6}$, or $\frac{2}{3}$, and $P(S) = \frac{2}{6}$, or $\frac{1}{3}$. We see that adding another white marble does not change the probabilities.

Figure 8-19

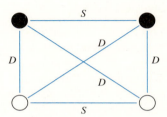

Next, consider a game with the same rules but using three colored marbles and one white marble. A model for this situation is shown in Figure 8-20.

Figure 8-20

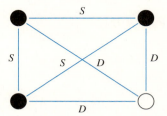

Thus the probability of drawing two marbles of the same color is $\frac{3}{6}$, and the probability of drawing two marbles of different colors is $\frac{3}{6}$. Finally, we have a game in which each player has an equal chance of winning.

Does each player have an equal chance of winning if only one white marble and one colored marble are used and the ball is replaced after the first draw? Can you find additional fair games involving different numbers of marbles? Can you find a pattern for the numbers of colored and white marbles that allow each player to have an equal chance of winning?

Problem 1

In a party game, a child is handed six strings, as shown in Figure 8-21(a). Another child ties the top ends two at a time, forming three separate knots, and the bottom ends, forming three separate knots, as in Figure 8-21(b). If the strings form one closed ring, as in Figure 8-21(c), the child wins a prize. What is the probability that the child wins a prize on the first try?

Figure 8-21

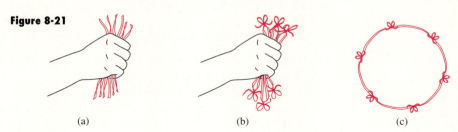

(a)   (b)   (c)

Understanding the Problem. The problem is to determine the probability that one closed ring will be formed. One closed ring means that all six pieces are joined end to end to form one, and only one, ring, as shown in Figure 8-21(c).

Devising a Plan. Figure 8-22(a) shows what happens when the ends of the strings of one set are tied in pairs at the top. Notice that no matter in what order those ends are tied, the result appears as in Figure 8-22(a).

Figure 8-22

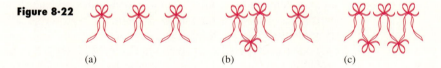

(a)   (b)   (c)

Then, the other ends are tied in a three-stage experiment. If we pick any string in the first stage, then there are five choices for its mate. Four of these choices are favorable choices for forming a ring. Thus the probability of forming a favorable first tie is $\frac{4}{5}$. Figure 8-22(b) shows a favorable tie at the first stage.

For any one of the remaining four strings, there are three choices for its mate. Two of these choices are favorable ones. Thus the probability of forming a favorable second tie is $\frac{2}{3}$. Figure 8-22(c) shows a favorable tie at the second stage.

Now, two ends remain. Since nothing can go wrong at the third stage, the probability of making a favorable tie is 1. If we use the probabilities completed at each stage and a single branch of a tree diagram, we can calculate the probability of performing three successful ties in a row and hence the probability of forming one closed ring.

Carrying Out the Plan. If we let *S* represent a successful tie at each stage, then the branch of the tree with which we are concerned is the one shown in Figure 8-23.

Figure 8-23

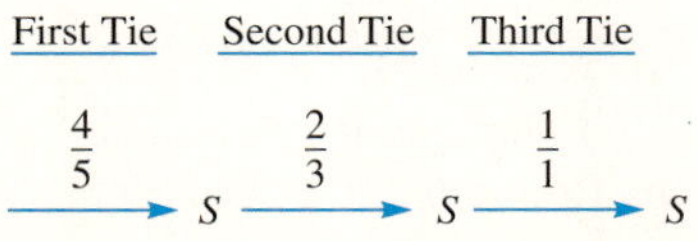

First Tie	Second Tie	Third Tie
$\frac{4}{5}$	$\frac{2}{3}$	$\frac{1}{1}$

$$\xrightarrow{} S \xrightarrow{} S \xrightarrow{} S$$

Thus the probability of forming one ring is $P(\text{ring}) = \frac{4}{5} \cdot \frac{2}{3} \cdot \frac{1}{1} = \frac{8}{15} = 0.5\bar{3}$.

Looking Back.   The probability that a child will form a ring on the first try is $\frac{8}{15}$. A class might simulate this problem several times with strings to see how the fraction of successes compares with the theoretical probability of $\frac{8}{15}$.

Related problems that could be posed for solution include the following:

1. If a child fails to get a ring ten times in a row, the child may not play again. What is the probability of such a streak of bad luck?
2. If the number of strings is reduced to three and the rule is that an upper end must be tied to a lower end, what is the probability of a single ring?
3. If the number of strings is three, but an upper end can be tied to either an upper or a lower end, what is the probability of a single ring?
4. What is the probability of forming three rings in the original problem?
5. What is the probability of forming two rings in the original problem?

• • •

Geometric Probability

A probability model using geometric shapes is called an *area model* in the *Standards*. When area models are used to determine probabilities geometrically, outcomes are associated with points chosen at random in a geometric region representing the sample space. For example, suppose we throw darts at a square target 2 units long on a side and divided into four congruent triangles, as shown in Figure 8-24. If the dart must hit the target somewhere and if all spots can be hit with equal probability, what is the probability that the dart will land in the shaded region? The entire target, which has an area of 4 square units, represents the sample space. The shaded area is the event of a successful toss. The area of the shaded part is $\frac{1}{4}$ of the sample space. Thus the probability of the dart's landing in the shaded region is the ratio of the area of the event to the area of the sample space, or $\frac{1}{4}$.

Figure 8-24

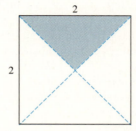

Other geometric probability problems are investigated in the problem set. The following Problem 2 is solved by using both tree diagrams and a geometric approach.

Problem 2

On a quiz show, a contestant stands at the entrance to a maze that opens into two rooms, as shown in Figure 8-25. The master of ceremonies' assistant is to place a new car in one room and a donkey in the other. The contestant must walk through the maze into one of the rooms and will win whatever is in that room. If the contestant makes each decision in the maze at random, in which room should the assistant place the car to give the contestant the best chance to win?

Figure 8-25

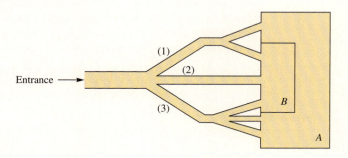

Understanding the Problem.   The contestant must first choose one of the paths marked 1, 2, or 3 and then choose other paths as she proceeds through the maze. To determine the room most likely to be chosen by the contestant, the assistant must be able to determine the probability of the contestant's reaching each room. To compute that probability, the assistant must understand what it means for something to be chosen at random and how to compute multistage probabilities.

Devising a Plan.   One way to determine where the car should be placed is to *model the choices* with a tree diagram and to compute the probabilities along the branches of the tree.

Carrying Out the Plan.   A tree diagram for the maze is shown in Figure 8-26, along with the possible outcomes and the probabilities of each branch. Thus room *B* has the greater probability of being chosen. This is where the car should be placed for the contestant to have the best chance of winning it.

Figure 8-26

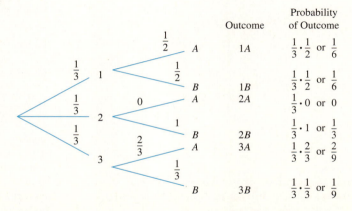

Looking Back.   An alternative model for this problem and for many probability problems is an area model. The rectangle in Figure 8-27(a) represents the first three choices that the contestant can make. Because each choice is equally likely, each is represented by an equal area. If the upper path is chosen, then rooms A and B have an equal chance of being chosen. If the middle path is chosen, then only room B can be entered. If the lower path is chosen, then room A is entered $\frac{2}{3}$ of the time. This can be expressed in terms of the area model shown in Figure 8-27(b). Dividing the rectangle into pieces of equal area, we obtain the model in Figure 8-27(c), in which the area representing room B is shaded. Because the area representing room B is greater than the area representing room A, room B has the greater probability of being chosen. If we want, Figure 8-27(c) can enable us to find the probability of choosing room B. Because the shaded area consists of 11 rectangles out of a total of 18 rectangles, the probability of choosing room B is $\frac{11}{18}$. We can vary the problem by changing the maze or by changing the locations of the rooms.

Figure 8-27

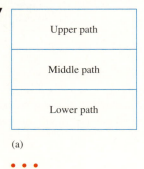

(a)

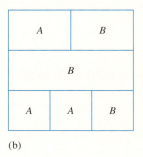

(b)

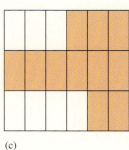

(c)

• • •

Ongoing Assessment 8-2

1. a. Use a tree diagram to develop the sample space for tossing a fair coin twice.
   b. Use a tree diagram to develop the sample space for an experiment consisting of tossing a fair coin and then rolling a die.
2. Suppose an experiment consists of spinning X and then spinning Y, as follows:

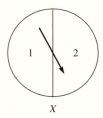

X

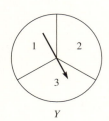

Y

Find the following:
a. The sample space S for the experiment
b. The event A consisting of outcomes from spinning an even number followed by an even number

   c. The event B consisting of outcomes from spinning at least one 2
   d. The event C consisting of outcomes from spinning exactly one 2
3. A box contains six letters, shown as follows. What is the probability of the outcome DAN in that order if three letters are drawn one by one (a) with replacement? (b) without replacement?

| RANDOM |

4. Following are three boxes containing letters:

MATH		AND		HISTORY
1		2		3

   a. From box 1, three letters are drawn one by one without replacement and recorded in order. What is the probability that the outcome is HAT?
   b. From box 1, three letters are drawn one by one with replacement and recorded in order. What is the probability that the outcome is HAT?

c. One letter is drawn at random from box 1, then another from box 2, and then another from box 3, with the results recorded in order. What is the probability that the outcome is HAT?

d. If a box is chosen at random and then a letter is drawn at random from the box, what is the probability that the outcome is A?

5. An executive committee consisted of ten members: four women and six men. Three members were selected at random to be sent to a meeting in Hawaii. A blindfolded woman drew three of the ten names from a hat. All three names drawn were women's. What was the probability of such luck?

6. Two boxes with letters follow. You are to choose a box and draw three letters at random, one by one, without replacement. If the outcome is SOS, you win a prize.

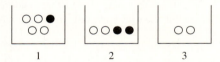

a. Which box should you choose?

b. Which box would you choose if the letters are to be drawn with replacement?

7. Following are three boxes containing balls. Draw a ball from box 1 and place it in box 2. Then draw a ball from box 2 and place it in box 3. Finally, draw a ball from box 3.

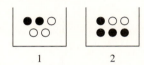

a. What is the probability that the last ball, drawn from box 3, is white?

b. What is the probability that the last ball drawn is colored?

8. An assembly line has two inspectors. The probability that the first inspector will miss a defective item is 0.05. If the defective item passes the first inspector, the probability that the second inspector will miss it is 0.01. What is the probability that a defective item will pass by both inspectors?

9. Following are two boxes containing colored and white balls. A ball is drawn at random from box 1. Then a ball is drawn at random from box 2, and the colors of balls from both boxes are recorded in order.

Find each of the following:

a. The probability of two white balls

b. The probability of at least one colored ball

c. The probability of at most one colored ball

d. The probability of ● ○ or ○ ●

10. A penny, a nickel, a dime, and a quarter are tossed. What is the probability of at least obtaining three heads?

11. Assume the probability is $\frac{1}{2}$ that a child born is a boy. What is the probability that if a family is going to have four children, they will all be boys?

12. Brittany is going to ascend a four-step staircase. At any time, she is just as likely to stride up one step or two steps. Find the probability that she will ascend the four steps in **a.** two strides. **b.** three strides. **c.** four strides.

13. A box contains five slips of paper. Each slip has one of the numbers 4, 6, 7, 8, or 9 written on it. A player reaches into the box and draws two slips and adds the two numbers. If the sum is even, the player wins. If the sum is odd, the player loses.

a. What is the probability that a player wins?

b. Does the probability change if the two numbers are multiplied? Explain.

14. Suppose we spin the following spinner with the first spin giving the numerator and the second spin giving the denominator of a fraction. What is the probability that the fraction will be greater than 1 1/2?

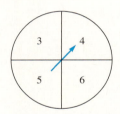

15. The following shows the numbers of symbols on each of the three dials of a standard slot machine:

Symbol	Dial 1	Dial 2	Dial 3
Bar	1	3	1
Bell	1	3	3
Plum	5	1	5
Orange	3	6	7
Cherry	7	7	0
Lemon	3	0	4
Total	20	20	20

Find the probability for each of the following:

a. three plums

b. three oranges

c. three lemons

d. No plums

16. If a person takes a five-question true-false test, what is the probability that the score is 100% correct if the person guesses on every question?

17. Rattlesnake and Paxson Colleges play four games against each other in a chess tournament. Rob Fisher, the chess whiz from Paxson, withdrew from the tournament, so the probabilities that Rattlesnake and Paxson will win each game are $\frac{2}{3}$ and $\frac{1}{3}$, respectively. Determine the following probabilities:

a. Paxson loses all four games.

b. The match is a draw with each school winning two games.

18. The combinations on the lockers at the high school consist of three numbers, each ranging from 0 to 39. If a combination is chosen at random, what is the probability that the first two numbers are multiples of 9 and the third number is a multiple of 4?

19. The following box contains the 11 letters shown. The letters are drawn one by one without replacement, and the results are recorded in order. Find the probability of the outcome MISSISSIPPI.

> MIIIIPPSSSS

20. Consider the following dart board: (Assume that all quadrilaterals are squares and that the *x*'s represent equal measures.)

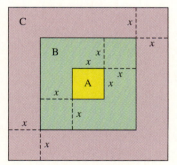

If a dart may hit any point on the board with equal probability, what is the probability that it will land in

a. Section A?   **b.** Section B?   **c.** Section C?

21. In the following square dart board, suppose a dart is equally likely to land in any region of the board.

Points are given as follows:

Region	Points
A	10
B	8
C	6
D	4
E	2

a. What is the total area of the board?

b. What is the probability of a dart's landing in each region of the board?

c. If two darts are tossed, what is the probability of scoring 20 points?

d. What is the probability that the dart will land in neither *D* nor *E*?

22. The land area of Earth is approximately 57,500,000 mi². The water area of Earth is approximately 139,600,000 mi². If a meteor lands at random on the planet, what is the probability, to the nearest tenth, that it will hit water?

23. An electric clock is stopped by a power failure. What is the probability that the second hand is stopped between the 3 and the 4?

24. A husband and wife discover that there is a 10% probability of their passing on a hereditary disease to any one of their children. If they plan to have three children, what is the probability that at least one child will inherit the disease?

25. Let $A = \{x|\ ^-1 < x < 1\}$ and $B = \{x|\ ^-3 < x < 2\}$. If a real number is picked at random from set *B*, what is the probability it will be in set *A*?

26. At a certain hospital, 40 patients have lung cancer, 30 patients smoke, and 25 have lung cancer and smoke. Suppose the hospital contains 200 patients. If a patient chosen at random is known to smoke, what is the probability that the patient has lung cancer?

27. There are 40 employees in a certain firm. We know that 28 of these employees are males, 2 of these males are secretaries, and 10 secretaries are employed by the firm. What is the probability that an employee chosen at random is a secretary, given that the person is a male?

28. In a certain population of caribou, the probability of an animal's being sickly is $\frac{1}{20}$. If a caribou is sickly, the probability of its being eaten by wolves is $\frac{1}{3}$. If a caribou is not sickly, the probability of its being eaten by wolves is $\frac{1}{150}$. If a caribou is chosen at random from the herd, what is the probability that it will be eaten by wolves?

★29. Carolyn will win a large prize if she wins two tennis games in a row out of three games. She is to play alternately against Billie and Bobby. She may choose to play Billie-Bobby-Billie or Bobby-Billie-Bobby. She wins against

Billie 50% of the time and against Bobby 80% of the time. Which alternative should she choose, and why?

★ **30.** Jane has two tennis serves, a hard serve and a soft serve. Her hard serve is in (a good serve) 50% of the time, and her soft serve is in (good) 75% of the time. If her hard serve is in, she wins 75% of her points. If her soft serve is in, she wins 50% of her points. Since she is allowed to re-serve one time if her first serve is out, what should her serving strategy be? That is, should she serve hard followed by soft; both hard; soft followed by hard; or both soft?

Communication

31. Jim rolled a fair die three times and obtained a 3 every time. He concluded that on the next roll, a 3 is more likely to occur than the other numbers. Explain whether this is true.

32. A witness to a crime observed that the criminal had blond hair and blue eyes and drove a red car. When the police look for a suspect, is the probability greater that they will find someone with blond hair and blue eyes or that they will find someone with blond hair and blue eyes who drives a red car? Explain your answer.

33. On August 18, 1913, the roulette wheel at a casino in Monte Carlo came up black 26 times in a row. Many people in the crowd during the streak placed large bets on the red because they were convinced that the "law of averages" would catch up with the wheel. If the wheel was fair, explain how you think the wheel would have shown on the 27th spin and why.

Open-ended

34. Explain how probability might be used by insurance companies.

35. Make up a fair game that involves rolling two regular dice. Explain why it is fair.

36. How can the faces of two cubes be numbered so that when they are rolled, the resulting sum is a number 1 to 12 inclusive and each sum has the same probability?

37. Use graph paper to design a dart board such that the probability of hitting a certain part of the board is $\frac{3}{5}$. Explain your reasoning.

Cooperative Learning

38. Play the following game in groups of two. One player chooses one of four equally likely outcomes from the sample space {*HH, HT, TH, TT*}, obtained by tossing a fair coin twice. The other player then chooses one of the other outcomes. A coin is flipped until either player's choice appears. For example, the first player chooses *TT* and the second player chooses *HT*. If the first two flips yield *TH*, then no one wins and the game continues. If, after five flips, the string *THHHT* appears, the second player is the winner because the sequence *HT* finally appeared. Play the game ten times and see if the game appears to be fair, that is, does each person have the same chance of winning? Analyze the game and explain whether the game is really fair.

39. Consider the three spinners *A*, *B*, and *C* shown in the following figure:

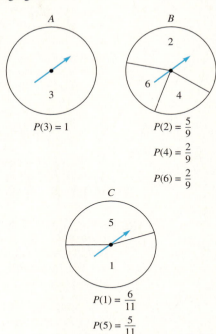

$$P(3) = 1$$

$$P(2) = \frac{5}{9}$$

$$P(4) = \frac{2}{9}$$

$$P(6) = \frac{2}{9}$$

$$P(1) = \frac{6}{11}$$

$$P(5) = \frac{5}{11}$$

a. Suppose there are only two players and that the first player chooses a spinner and then the second player chooses a different spinner and each person spins his/her spinner with the highest number winning. Play the game several times to get a feeling for it. Determine if this is a fair game. If it is not, which spinner should you choose in order to win?

b. This time play the same game with three players. If each player chooses a different spinner, is the game fair? Is the winning strategy the same as it was in (a)? Why or why not?

Review Problems

40. Match the following phrase to the probability that describes it:

a. A certain event   **(i)** $\frac{1}{1000}$

b. An impossible event   **(ii)** $\frac{999}{1000}$

c. A very likely event   **(iii)** 0

d. An unlikely event   **(iv)** $\frac{1}{2}$

e. A 50% chance   **(v)** 1

41. A date in the month of April is chosen at random. Find the probability of the date's being each of the following:

a. April 7

b. April 31

c. Before April 20

BRAIN TEASER Suppose that *n* people are in a room. Two people bet on whether at least two of the people in the room have a birthday on the same date during the year (for example, October 14). Assume that a person is as likely to be born on one day as another and ignore leap years. How many people must be in the room before the bet is even? (If *n* = 366, it is a sure bet.) Poll your class to see if two people have the same birthday. Use this information to find an experimental answer. Then find a theoretical solution. A calculator is very helpful for the computations.

Section 8-3 Using Simulations in Probability

Students can use simulations to study phenomena too complex to analyze by other means. Using simulations, students can estimate probabilities rather than determine probabilities analytically. The *Teaching Standards* (p. 136) assert

Students should have opportunities to explore empirical probability from simulations and from data they have collected and to analyze theoretical probability on the basis of a description of the underlying sample space. . . . The power of simulation as a problem-solving technique for making decisions under uncertainty should be a prominent experience.

Suppose we want to simulate the results of tossing a coin 100 times. We could do this using random digits, as in Table 8-3. Random-digit tables are lists of digits selected at random, often by a computer or calculator. To simulate the coin toss, pick a number at random to start and then read across the table, letting an even digit represent heads and an odd digit represent tails. Continue this process for 100 digits. The simulated probability of heads is the ratio of the number of even digits found (heads) to 100.

For example, if we choose the top two rows in Table 8-3 and use the first 100 numbers, we find that there are 44 even numbers. Because even numbers represent heads, the simulated probability of tossing a head is $P(H) = 44/100$. Notice that we did not obtain the theoretical probability of 1/2. However, if the number of random digits chosen was much greater, then the simulated probability should approach the theoretical probability.

Similarly, to simulate the probability of a couple's having two girls (GG) in an expected family, we could use the random-digit table with an even digit representing a girl and an odd digit representing a boy. Because there are two children, we need to consider pairs of digits. If we examine 100 pairs, then the simulated probability of GG will be the number of pairs of even digits divided by 100, the total number of pairs considered.

INVESTIGATION 8-3

a. Use the random-digit table to estimate the probability that in a family of three, there are two girls and one boy.

b. Determine the theoretical probability of the family's having two girls and one boy and

compare the answer to the simulated probability in (a).

c. Should the answers in (a) and (b) always be exactly the same? Why? How can you make sure that the answers are approximately the same?

Table 8-3 Random Digits

36422	93239	76046	81114	77412	86557	19549	98473	15221	87856
78496	47197	37961	67568	14861	61077	85210	51264	49975	71785
95384	59596	05081	39968	80495	00192	94679	18307	16265	48888
37957	89199	10816	24260	52302	69592	55019	94127	71721	70673
31422	27529	95051	83157	96377	33723	52902	51302	86370	50452
07443	15346	40653	84238	24430	88834	77318	07486	33950	61598
41348	86255	92715	96656	49693	99286	83447	20215	16040	41085
12398	95111	45663	55020	57159	58010	43162	98878	73337	35571
77229	92095	44305	09285	73256	02968	31129	66588	48126	52700
61175	53014	60304	13976	96312	42442	96713	43940	92516	81421
16825	27482	97858	05642	88047	68960	52991	67703	29805	42701
84656	03089	05166	67571	25545	26603	40243	55482	38341	97782
03872	31767	23729	89523	73654	24626	78393	77172	41328	95633
40488	70426	04034	46618	55102	93408	10965	69744	80766	14889
98322	25528	43808	05935	78338	77881	90139	72375	50624	91385
13366	52764	02407	14202	74172	58770	65348	24115	44277	96735
86711	27764	86789	43800	87582	09298	17880	75507	35217	08352
53886	50358	62738	91783	71944	90221	79403	75139	09102	77826
99348	21186	42266	01531	44325	61042	13453	61917	90426	12437
49985	08787	59448	82680	52929	19077	98518	06251	58451	91140
49807	32863	69984	20102	09523	47827	08374	79849	19352	62726
46569	00365	23591	44317	55054	99835	20633	66215	46668	53587
09988	44203	43532	54538	16619	45444	11957	69184	98398	96508
32916	00567	82881	59753	54761	39404	90756	91760	18698	42852
93285	32297	27254	27198	99093	97821	46277	10439	30389	45372
03222	39951	12738	50303	25017	84207	52123	88637	19369	58289
87002	61789	96250	99337	14144	00027	43542	87030	14773	73087
68840	94259	01961	42552	91843	33855	00824	48733	81297	80411
88323	28828	64765	08244	53077	50897	91937	08871	91517	19668
55170	71062	64159	79364	53088	21536	39451	95649	65256	23950

The following page from *Addison-Wesley Mathematics,* Grade 7, 1993, shows how middle-school students learn to use simulations to solve probability problems. Work the problems on the bottom of the student page using the random-digit table for the random-digit generator.

Example 8-9   A baseball player, Reggie, has a batting average of 0.400; that is, his probability of getting a hit on any particular time at bat is 0.400. Estimate the probability that he will get at least one hit in his next three times at bat.

Solution   We use a random-digit table to simulate this example. We choose a starting point and place the random digits in groups of three. Because Reggie's probability of getting a hit on any particular time at bat is 0.400, we could use the occurrence of four particular numbers from 0 through 9 to represent a hit. Suppose a hit is represented by the digits 0, 1,

ENRICHMENT
Simulating a Probability Problem

Robin Hood is returning from Nottingham to Sherwood Forest. The map shows the different routes he can take. The Sheriff of Nottingham is trying to catch Robin at one of the 4 bridges. The probability that Robin will find an open bridge is $\frac{1}{2}$. What is the probability that Robin will find an open route to Sherwood?

You can **simulate** or **model** the problem this way.

- Use a **random digit generator** to get a list of digits 0 to 9. Let even digits = open bridge and odd digits = closed bridge.
- Keep a record of open and closed bridges. Then after each trial use the map to decide if there is an open route for Robin Hood.

Trial 1: 2, 5, 1, 3
Trial 2: 7, 4, 4, 6

Trial	Bridge 1	Bridge 2	Bridge 3	Bridge 4	Open Route?
1	Open	Blocked	Blocked	Blocked	No
2	Blocked	Open	Open	Open	Yes

1. Try the simulation of the problem for 20 trials. How many times was there an open route?

2. What is the experimental probability of an open route?

   $$\text{Exp. P(Open)} = \frac{\text{No. of open routes}}{\text{No. of trials}}$$

3. Combine your results for 20 trials with those of your classmates. What is the probability of an open route using the combined trials?

4. Is Robin Hood more likely to find an open route to Sherwood Forest or is he more likely to find a blocked route?

2, and 3. At least one hit is obtained in three times at bat if, in any sequence of three digits, a 0, 1, 2, or 3 appears. Data for 50 trials are given next:

780	862	760	580	783	720	590	506	021	366
848	118	073	077	042	254	063	667	374	153
377	883	573	683	780	115	662	591	685	274
279	652	754	909	754	892	310	673	964	351
803	034	799	915	059	006	774	640	298	961

We see that a 0, 1, 2, or 3 appears in 42 out of the 50 trials. Thus an estimate for the probability of at least one hit on Reggie's next three times at bat is $\frac{42}{50}$. Try to determine the theoretical probability for this experiment.

• • •

From a random sample, we can deduce information about the population from which the sample was taken. To see how this can be done, consider Example 8-10.

• • •

Example 8-10   To determine the number of fish in a certain pond, suppose we capture 300 fish, mark them, and throw them back into the pond. Suppose that the next day, 200 fish are caught and 20 of these are already marked. These 200 fish are then thrown back into the pond. Estimate how many fish are in the pond.

Solution   Because 20 of the 200 fish are marked, we assume that $\frac{20}{200}$, or $\frac{1}{10}$, of the fish are marked. Thus $\frac{1}{10}$ of the population is marked. If n represents the population, then $\frac{1}{10}n = 300$ and $n = 300 \cdot 10 = 3000$. Hence, an estimate for the fish population of the pond is 3000 fish.

• • •

The following Peanuts cartoon also suggests a simulation problem concerning chocolate chip cookies.

• • •

Example 8-11   Suppose Lucy makes enough batter for exactly 100 chocolate chip cookies and mixes 100 chocolate chips into the batter. If the chips are distributed at random and Charlie chooses a cookie at random from the 100 cookies, estimate the probability that it will contain exactly one chocolate chip.

Solution   A simulation can be used to estimate the probability of choosing a cookie with exactly one chocolate chip. We construct a 10×10 grid, as shown in Figure 8-28(a), to represent the 100 cookies Lucy made. Each square (cookie) can be associated with some ordered pair, where the first component is for the horizontal scale and the second is for the vertical scale. For example, the squares (0, 2) and (5, 3) are pictured in Figure 8-28(a). Using the random-digit table, close your eyes and then take a pencil and point to one number to start. Look at the number and the number immediately following it. Consider these numbers as an ordered pair and continue on until 100 ordered pairs are obtained to represent the 100 cookies. For example, suppose we start at a 3 and the numbers following 3 are as follows:

$$39968 \qquad 80495 \qquad 00192 \ldots$$

Then the ordered pairs would be given as (3, 9), (9, 6), (8, 8), (0, 4), and so on. Use each pair of numbers as the coordinates for the square (cookie) and place a tally on the grid to represent each chip, as shown in Figure 8-28(b). We estimate the probability that a cookie has exactly one chip by counting the number of squares with exactly one tally and dividing by 100.

Figure 8-28

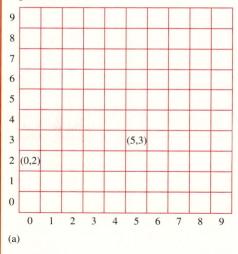

(a)

(b)

Table 8-4 shows the results of one simulation. Thus the estimate for the probability of Charlie's receiving a cookie with exactly one chip is $\dfrac{34}{100}$.

Table 8-4

Number of Chips	Number of Cookies
0	38
1	34
2	20
3	6
≥ 4	2

Try a simulation on your own and compare your results with the preceding ones and with the results given in Table 8-5, obtained by theoretical methods.

Table 8-5

Number of Chips	Number of Cookies
0	36.8
1	36.8
2	18.4
3	6.1
≥ 4	1.9

• • •

Problem 3

Assume Carmen Smith, a basketball player, makes free throws with 80% probability of success and is placed in a one-and-one situation where she is given a second foul shot only if the first shot goes through the basket. How can we simulate 25 attempts from the foul line in one-and-one situations to determine how many times we would expect Carmen to score 0 points, 1 point, and 2 points?

Understanding the Problem.   The probability that Carmen makes any given free throw is 80%. She is shooting in a one-and-one situation: If she misses the first shot, she receives 0 points; if she makes the first shot, she receives 1 point and is allowed to shoot *one* more time. Each basket made counts as 1 point. Thus Carmen has the opportunity to score 0, 1, or 2 points. We are to determine by simulation how many times Carmen can be expected to score 0 points, 1 point, and 2 points in 25 attempts at one-and-one situations.

Devising a Plan.   One way to simulate the problem is to use a random-digit table. Because Carmen's probability of making any basket is 80%, we could use the occurrence of a 0, 1, 2, 3, 4, 5, 6, or 7 to simulate making the basket and the occurrence of an 8 or a 9 to simulate missing the basket. Another way to simulate the problem is to construct a spinner with 80% of the spinner devoted to making a basket and 20% of the spinner devoted to missing the basket. This could be done by constructing the spinner with 80% of the 360 degrees (that is, 288 degrees) devoted to making the basket and 72 degrees devoted to missing the basket. A spinner for this simulation is shown in Figure 8-29.

Figure 8-29

Carrying Out the Plan.   We spin the spinner in Figure 8-29 to simulate 25 sets of one-and-one situations. If the spinner lands on "Miss," 0 points are recorded for the set. If the spinner lands on "Make," a second spin is taken. If the spinner shows another "Make," then 2 points are recorded; otherwise, 1 point is recorded. This is repeated for 25 sets and the results are recorded. Four simulations of 25 sets are given in Table 8-6. We used four trials to obtain a better estimate than we would get from only a single trial.

Table 8-6

Number of Points	Trial 1	Trial 2	Trial 3	Trial 4	Total	Estimated Probability
0	4	6	5	5	20	$\dfrac{20}{100}$
1	2	4	5	4	15	$\dfrac{15}{100}$
2	19	15	15	16	65	$\dfrac{65}{100}$

To solve the problem, we use the estimated probability and multiply by 25 to obtain the results in Table 8-7.

Table 8-7

Number of Points	Expected Number of Times Points Are Scored in 25 Attempts
0	5
1	3.75
2	16.25

Looking Back. We can compute the theoretical probability for this experiment by using a *tree diagram,* as shown in Figure 8-30. Thus theoretical estimates for the number of points scored in 25 attempts can be computed. These estimates are given in Table 8-8. Compare these results with the experimental probability obtained previously.

Figure 8-30

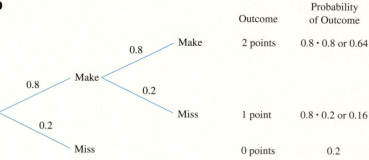

	Outcome	Probability of Outcome
Make — 0.8 — Make	2 points	0.8 · 0.8 or 0.64
Make — 0.2 — Miss	1 point	0.8 · 0.2 or 0.16
0.2 — Miss	0 points	0.2

Table 8-8

Number of Points	Expected Number of Times Points Are Scored in 25 Attempts
0	5
1	4
2	16

Geometric probability could also be used to solve this problem. We represent the sample space with the 10 × 10 grid shown in Figure 8-31(a) and separate it into two parts, with a vertical line to represent the dividing line between making 80% on the first shot and missing 20% on it. That is, 80 of the 100 squares are devoted to making the first shot, and 20 of the 100 squares are devoted to missing the first shot. If the first shot is made, a second shot is taken with an 80% probability of success. Therefore we subdivide the "Make" area from the first shot into 2 parts of 80% and 20%. This is done by marking off eight of the ten rows in the "Make" area. We then assign the appropriate number of points to each of the 13 areas, as shown in Figure 8-31(b). Now we see that 64 of the 100 squares (or 64% of the sample space) are devoted to scoring 2 points, 16 of the 100 squares (or 16%) are devoted to scoring 1 point, and 20 of the 100 squares (20%) are devoted to scoring 0 points. These results are consistent with the results obtained by using the tree diagram.

Figure 8-31

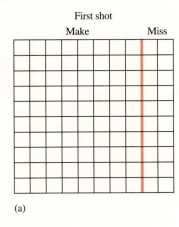

(a)

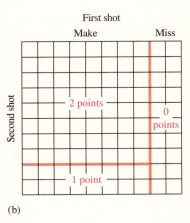

(b)

• • •

Ongoing Assessment 8-3

1. How might you use a deck of cards to simulate the birth of boys and girls?
2. The weather forecast for Pelican, Alaska, is for a 90% chance of rain on any given day.
   a. How might you simulate the probability of rain in Pelican on any given day?
   b. Use your simulation from (a) to estimate the probability of rain in Pelican for seven days in a row.
   c. What is the theoretical probability of not having rain for seven days in a row in Pelican?
3. Try the simulation of the problem on the student page of this section for 20 trials. How many times was there an open route?
4. How might you use a random-digit table to simulate each of the following?
   a. Tossing a single die
   b. Choosing three people at random from a group of 20 people
   c. Spinning the spinner, where the probability of each color is as shown in the following figure:

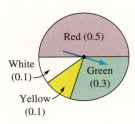

5. A school has 500 students. The principal is to pick 30 students at random from the school to go to the Rose Bowl. How can this be done by using a random-digit table?
6. In a certain city, the probability that it will rain on a certain day is 0.8 if it rained the day before. The probability that it will be dry on a certain day is 0.3 if it was dry the day before. It is now Sunday, and it is raining. Use the random-digit table to simulate the weather for the rest of the week.
7. It is reported that 15% of people who came into contact with a person infected with strep throat contracted the disease.

How might you use the random-digit table to simulate the probability that at least one child in a three-child family will catch the disease, given that each child has come into contact with the infected person?

8. Pick a block of two digits from the random-digit table. What is the probability that the block picked is less than 30?

9. An estimate of the fish population of a certain pond was found by catching 200 fish and marking and returning them to the pond. The next day, 300 fish were caught, of which 50 had been marked the previous day. Estimate the fish population of the pond.

10. Suppose that in the World Series, the two teams are evenly matched. The two teams play until one team wins four games, and no ties are possible.
    a. What is the maximum number of games that could be played?
    b. Use simulation to approximate the probabilities that the series will end in (i) four games and in (ii) seven games.

Communication

11. Write a paragraph to a middle-school student explaining why simulated probabilities that use only a few cases may not be very accurate.

12. The following plan was designed to boost the number of women in a certain country: If a woman gives birth to a boy, she could have no more children; if she gives birth to a girl, she can have another child. The country's leaders reasoned that in this way no family could have more than one boy, but many families would have more than one girl. Do you think this plan will result in boosting the number of women? Explain why or why not.

Open-ended

13. a. Suppose a baseball player has a batting average of 0.300. How might you simulate the probability that the player will get at least three hits if the player is at bat four times in the next game?
    b. Determine the probability of at least three hits at bat.

14. What is the probability that in a group of five people chosen at random, at least two will have birthdays in the same month? Design a simulation for this problem and try your simulation 10 times.

15. The probability of the home team's winning a basketball game is 80%. Describe a simulation of the probability that the home team will win three home games in a row.

16. Montana duck hunters are all perfect shots. Ten Montana hunters are in a duck blind when 10 ducks fly over. All 10 hunters pick a duck at random to shoot at, and all 10 hunters fire at the same time. How many ducks could be expected to escape, on the average, if this experiment were repeated a large number of times? How could this problem be simulated?

Cooperative Learning

17. The sixth-grade class decided that the ideal number of children in a family is four: two boys and two girls.
    a. As a group, design a simulation to determine the probability of two boys and two girls in a family of four.
    b. Have each person in your group try the simulation 25 times and compare the probabilities.
    c. Combine the results of all the members of your group and use this information to find a simulated probability.
    d. Compute the theoretical probability of having two boys and two girls in a family of four and compare your answer to the simulated probability.

18. Have you ever wondered how you would score on a 10-item true-false test if you guessed at every answer?
    a. Simulate your score by tossing a coin 10 times with heads representing true and tails representing false. Check your answers by using the following key and score yourself:

1	2	3	4	5	6	7	8	9	10
F	T	F	F	T	F	T	T	T	F

    b. Combine your results with those of others in your group to find the average (mean) number of correct answers for your group.
    c. How many items would you expect to get correct if the number of items was 30 instead of 10?
    d. What is the theoretical probability of your getting all the answers correct on a 10-item true-false test if all answers were chosen by flipping a coin?

19. a. Estimate how many cards you would expect to have to turn over on the average in an ordinary playing deck before an ace appeared.
    b. Have each person in your group either try the actual experiment or simulate it for 10 trials and find the average number of aces.
    c. Combine the results of all the members of your group and find the average number of cards that need to be drawn. How does this average compare to your individual estimate?

20. A cereal company places a coupon bearing a number from 1 to 9 in each box of cereal. If the numbers are distributed at random in the boxes, estimate the number of boxes, on the average, you would have to purchase in order to obtain all nine numbers. Explain how the random-digit table could be used to estimate the number of coupons. Each person in the group should simulate ten trials, and the results in the group should be combined to find the estimate.

Review Problems

21. Four coins are tossed. If exactly two heads are tossed, you win. If anything else is tossed, you lose. Is this a fair game? Explain why or why not.

22. A single card is drawn from an ordinary bridge deck. What is the probability of obtaining each of the following?

   a. A club   **e.** A spade or a heart

   b. A queen and a spade   **f.** The 6 of diamonds

   c. Not a queen   **g.** A queen or a spade

   d. Not a heart   **h.** Either red or black

23. From a sack containing seven red marbles, eight blue marbles, and four white marbles, marbles are drawn at random for several experiments. Determine the probability of each of the following events:

   a. One marble drawn at random is either red or blue.

   b. The first draw is red and the second is blue, where one marble is drawn at random, its color is recorded, the marble is replaced, and another marble is drawn.

   c. The event in (b) where the first marble is not replaced.

TECHNOLOGY CORNER

Enter the following Logo procedure into the computer to simulate the rolling of a die:

```
TO ROLL
   OUTPUT (1 + RANDOM 6)
END
```

Execute the procedure with the following line:

```
REPEAT 100 [PRINT ROLL]
```

Count the number of times each digit is printed to estimate the probabilities of obtaining a 1, 2, 3, 4, 5, or 6 when a die is tossed. (a) How close is this approximation to the theoretical probability for each of those events? (b) How would you change the procedure to simulate tossing two dice?

TECHNOLOGY CORNER

RANDINT(

RAND

Int

1. On some graphing calculators, if we choose the MATH menu and then select PRB, which stands for PROBABILITY, we find **RANDINT(**, the random integer feature. RANDINT(generates a random integer within a specified range. It requires two inputs that are the upper and lower boundries for the integers. For example, RANDINT(1, 10) generates a random integer from 1 through 10.

   a. How could you use RANDINT(to simulate tossing a single die?

   b. How could you use RANDINT(to simulate the sum of the numbers when tossing 2 dice?

2. Some graphing calculators have a **RAND** function, a random-digit generator. RAND generates and returns a random number greater than 0 and less than 1. For example, RAND might produce the numbers .5956605, .049599836, or .876572691. To have RAND produce random numbers from 1 to 10 as in (1), we enter int (10 *RAND) + 1. The **int** (greatest integer) feature is found in the MATH menu under NUM. The feature int returns the greatest integer less than or equal to a number.

   a. How could you use RAND to simulate tossing a single die?

   b. How could you use RAND to simulate tossing the sum of the numbers when tossing two dice?

3. Use one of these random features to simulate tossing two dice 30 times. Based on your simulation, what is the probability that a sum of 7 will occur?

Odds and Expected Value

Computing Odds

odds in favor People talk about the *odds in favor of* and the *odds against* a particular event's happening. When the **odds in favor** of the president's being reelected are 4 to 1, this refers to how likely the president is to win the election relative to how likely the president is to lose. The probability of the president's winning is four times the probability of losing. If W represents the event the president wins the election and L represents the event the president loses, then $P(W) = 4P(L)$ or as a proportion, we have

$$\frac{P(W)}{P(L)} = \frac{4}{1}, \text{ or } 4:1.$$

Because W and L are complements of each other, $L = \overline{W}$, we have

$$\frac{P(W)}{P(\overline{W})} = \frac{P(W)}{1 - P(W)} = \frac{4}{1}, \text{ or } 4:1.$$

The **odds against** the president's winning are how likely the president is to lose relative to how likely the president is to win. Using the information above, we have

$$\frac{P(L)}{P(W)} = \frac{1}{4}, \text{ or } 1:4.$$

Because $L = \overline{W}$, we have

$$\frac{P(\overline{W})}{P(W)} = \frac{1 - P(W)}{P(W)} = \frac{1}{4}, \text{ or } 1:4.$$

Formally, odds are defined as follows.

Definition of Odds

Let $P(A)$ be the probability that A occurs and $P(\overline{A})$ be the probability that A does not occur. Then the **odds in favor** of an event A are

$$\frac{P(A)}{P(\overline{A})}, \quad \text{or} \quad \frac{P(A)}{1 - P(A)},$$

and the **odds against** an event A are

$$\frac{P(\overline{A})}{P(A)}, \quad \text{or} \quad \frac{1 - P(A)}{P(A)}.$$

When odds are calculated for equally likely outcomes, the denominators of the probabilities divide out. Thus alternative definitions for odds in case of *equally likely* outcomes are as follows:

$$\text{Odds in favor} = \frac{\text{Number of favorable outcomes}}{\text{Number of unfavorable outcomes}}$$

$$\text{Odds against} = \frac{\text{Number of unfavorable outcomes}}{\text{Number of favorable outcomes}}$$

When you roll a die, the number of favorable ways of rolling a 4 in one throw of a die is 1, and the number of unfavorable ways is 5. Thus the odds in favor of rolling a 4 are 1 to 5.

Example 8-12 For each of the following, find the odds in favor of the events occurring:

a. Rolling a number less than 5 on a die
b. Tossing heads on a fair coin
c. Drawing an ace from an ordinary 52-card deck
d. Drawing a heart from an ordinary 52-card deck

Solution **a.** The probability of rolling a number less than 5 is $\frac{4}{6}$; the probability of rolling a number not less than 5 is $\frac{2}{6}$. The odds in favor of rolling a number less than 5 are $\left(\frac{4}{6}\right) \div \left(\frac{2}{6}\right)$, or $4:2$, or $2:1$.

b. $P(H) = \frac{1}{2}$ and $P(\overline{H}) = \frac{1}{2}$. The odds in favor of getting heads are $\left(\frac{1}{2}\right) \div \left(\frac{1}{2}\right)$, or $1:1$.

c. The probability of drawing an ace is $\frac{4}{52}$, and the probability of not drawing an ace is $\frac{48}{52}$. The odds in favor of drawing an ace are $\left(\frac{4}{52}\right) \div \left(\frac{48}{52}\right)$, or $4:48$, or $1:12$.

d. The probability of drawing a heart is $\frac{13}{52}$, or $\frac{1}{4}$, and the probability of not drawing a heart is $\frac{39}{52}$, or $\frac{3}{4}$. The odds in favor of drawing a heart are $\left(\frac{13}{52}\right) \div \left(\frac{39}{52}\right) = \frac{13}{39}$, or $13:39$, or $1:3$.

I N V E S T I G A T I O N 8 - 4

● In Example 8-12(a), there are four ways to roll a number less than 5 on a die (favorable outcomes) and two ways of not rolling a number less than 5 (unfavorable outcomes), so the odds in favor of rolling a number less than 5 are $4:2$, or $2:1$. Work the other three parts of Example 8-12 using this approach. ●

Given the probability of an event, it is possible to find the odds in favor of (or against) the event and vice versa. For example, if the odds in favor of an event A are $5:1$, then the following proportion holds:

$$\frac{P(A)}{1 - P(A)} = \frac{5}{1}$$

$$P(A) = 5[1 - P(A)]$$

$$6P(A) = 5$$

$$P(A) = \frac{5}{6}$$

The probability $\frac{5}{6}$ is a ratio. The exact number of favorable outcomes and the exact total of all outcomes are not necessarily known.

• • •

Example 8-13   In the following cartoon, find the probability of making totally black copies if the odds are 3 to 1 against making totally black copies:

TODAY'S ODDS	
Makes totally black copies	3-1
Makes copies with wavy black lines	4-1
Misfeeds	2-1
Gives no change	3-1
Gives double change	8-1
Mystery light appears and 2 or more of the above occur	5-1

COPIES 20¢

Cable

Solution   If the odds against making totally black copies are 3 to 1, B represents the event of making a totally black copy and $\overline{B}$ represents not making a totally black copy. We have

$$\frac{P(\overline{B})}{1 - P(\overline{B})} = \frac{3}{1}$$

$$P(\overline{B}) = 3(1 - P(\overline{B}))$$

$$P(\overline{B}) = \frac{3}{4}$$

$$P(B) = 1 - P(\overline{B}), \text{ or } 1 - \frac{3}{4}$$

$$P(B) = \frac{1}{4}.$$

• • •

Expected Value

Racetracks use odds for betting purposes. If the odds against Fast Jack are 3:1, this means the track will pay $3 for every $1 you bet. If Fast Jack wins, then for a $5 bet, the track will return your $5 plus $15 more, or $20. The 3:1 odds means the track expects Fast Jack to lose 3 out of 4 times in this situation. If the odds at racetracks were accurate, bettors would receive an even return for their money, that is, bettors would not expect to win or lose money in the long run. For example, if the stated odds of 3:1 against Fast Jack were accurate, then the probability of Fast Jack's losing the race would be 3/4 and for Fast Jack's winning 1/4. If we compute the expected average winnings (expected value) over the long run, the gain is $3 for every $1 bet for a win and a loss of $1 otherwise. The expected value, E, is computed as follows:

$$E = 3(1/4) + {}^-1(3/4) = 0$$

Therefore the expected value is $0. If the racetrack gave accurate odds, it could not stay in business because it could not cover its expenses and make a profit. This is why the track overestimates the horses' chances of winning by about 20%.

Consider the spinner in Figure 8-32, with the payoff in each sector of the circle. Using area models, we can assign the following probabilities to each region:

$$P(\$1.00) = \frac{1}{2} \qquad P(\$2.00) = \frac{1}{4} \qquad P(\$3.00) = \frac{1}{8} \qquad P(\$4.00) = \frac{1}{8}$$

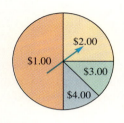

Figure 8-32

Should the owner of this spinner expect to make money over an extended period of time if the charge is $2.00 per spin?

To determine the average payoff over the long run, we find the product of the probability of landing on the payoff and the payoff itself and then find the sum of the products. This computation is given by

$$E = (1/2)1 + (1/4)2 + (1/8)3 + (1/8)4 = 1.875.$$

The owner can expect to pay out about $1.88 per spin. This is less than the $2.00 charge, so the owner should make a profit if the spinner is used many times. The sum of the products in this example, $1.875, is the **expected value,** *or mathematical expectation,* of the experiment of spinning the wheel in Figure 8-32 once. The owner's expected average earnings are $2.00 − $1.875 = $0.125 per spin and the player's expected average earnings (loss) are ⁻$.125.

The expected value is an average of winnings over the long run. Expected value can be used to predict the average result of an experiment when it is repeated many times. But *an expected value cannot be used to determine the outcome of any single experiment.*

Definition of Expected Value

If, in an experiment, the possible outcomes are numbers $a_1, a_2, \ldots, a_n$, occurring with probabilities $p_1, p_2, \ldots, p_n$, respectively, then the **expected value** (mathematical expectation) E is given by the equation

$$E = a_1 \cdot p_1 + a_2 \cdot p_2 + a_3 \cdot p_3 + \ldots + a_n \cdot p_n.$$

Example 8-14   Suppose you pay $5.00 to play the following game. Two coins are tossed. You receive $10 if two heads occur, $5 if exactly one head occurs, and nothing if no heads appear. Is this a fair game, that is, are the net winnings $0? (Note that this definition is consistent with the previous definition that a game is fair if each player has the same chance of winning.)

Solution   Before we determine the average payoff, recall that $P(HH) = \frac{1}{4}$, $P(HT \text{ or } TH) = \frac{1}{2}$, and $P(TT) = \frac{1}{4}$. To find the expected value, we perform the following computation:

$$E = \left(\frac{1}{4}\right) \cdot (\$10) + \left(\frac{1}{2}\right) \cdot (\$5) + \left(\frac{1}{4}\right) \cdot (0) = \$5$$

Because the price of playing is equal to the average payoff, the net winnings are $0. This is a fair game.

Problem 4

Al and Betsy played a coin-tossing game in which a fair coin was tossed until a total of either three heads or three tails occurred. Al was to win when a total of three heads were tossed, and Betsy was to win when a total of three tails were tossed. Each bet $50 on the game. If the coin was lost when Al had two heads and Betsy had one tail, how should the stakes be fairly split if the game is not continued?

Understanding the Problem.   Al and Betsy each bet $50 on a coin-tossing game in which a fair coin was to be tossed five times. Al was to win when a total of three heads was obtained; Betsy was to win when a total of three tails was obtained. When Al had two heads and Betsy had one tail, the coin was lost. The problem is how to split the stakes fairly.

If the stakes of the game are to be split fairly, then there could be many interpretations. Possibly, though, the best is to split the pot in proportion to the probabilities of each player's winning the game when play was halted. We must calculate the expected value for each player and split the pot accordingly.

Devising a Plan.   A third head would make Al the winner, whereas Betsy needs two more tails to win. A *tree diagram* that simulates the completion of the game allows us to find the probability of each player's winning the game. Once the probabilities are found, all we need do is multiply the probabilities by the amount of the pot, $100, to determine each player's fair share.

Carrying Out the Plan.   The tree diagram in Figure 8-33 shows the possibilities for game winners if the game is completed. We can find the probabilities of each player's winning as follows:

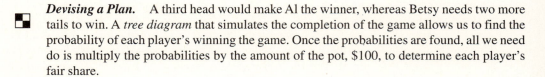

$$P(\text{Betsy wins}) = \frac{1}{2} \cdot \frac{1}{2} = \frac{1}{4}$$

$$P(\text{Al wins}) = 1 - \frac{1}{4} = \frac{3}{4}$$

Figure 8-33

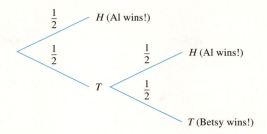

Hence, the fair way to split the stakes is for Al to receive $\frac{3}{4}$ of $100, or $75, whereas Betsy should receive $\frac{1}{4}$ of $100, or $25.

Looking Back. The problem could be made even more interesting by assuming that the coin is not fair so that the probability is not $\frac{1}{2}$ for each branch in the tree diagram. Other possibilities arise if the players have unequal amounts of money in the pot or if more tosses are required in order to win.

• • •

Ongoing Assessment 8-4

1. **a.** What are the odds in favor of drawing a face card from an ordinary deck of playing cards?
   b. What are the odds against drawing a face card?
2. On a single roll of a pair of dice, what are the odds against rolling a sum of 7?
3. If the probability of a boy's being born is $\frac{1}{2}$, and a family plans to have four children, what are the odds against having all boys?
4. Diane tossed a coin nine times and got nine tails. Assume that Diane's coin is fair and answer each of the following questions:
   a. What is the probability of tossing a tail on the tenth toss?
   b. What is the probability of tossing ten more tails in a row?
   c. What are the odds against tossing ten more tails in a row?
5. If the odds against Sam's winning his first prize fight are 3 to 5, then what is the probability that he will win the fight?
6. What are the odds in favor of tossing at least two heads if a fair coin is tossed three times?
7. If the probability of rain for the day is 60%, what are the odds against its raining?
8. On an American roulette wheel, half of the slots numbered 1–36 are red and half are black. Two slots, numbered 0 and 00, are green. What are the odds against a red slot's coming up on any spin of the wheel?
9. On a tote board at a race track, the odds for Gameylegs are listed as 26:1. Tote boards list the odds that the horse will lose the race. If this is the case, what is the probability of Gameylegs's winning the race?
10. The following chart shows the probabilities assigned by Stu to the number of hours spent on homework on a given night:

Hours	Probability
1	0.15
2	0.20
3	0.40
4	0.10
5	0.05
6	0.10

If Stu's friend Stella calls and asks how long his homework will take, what would you expect his answer to be, based on this table?

11. You pay $2.00 to play a game in which two dice are rolled. If a sum of 7 appears, you win $10; otherwise, you lose $2.00. If you intend to play this game for a long time, should you expect to make money, lose money, or come out about even? Explain.

12. On a roulette wheel are 36 slots numbered 1–36 and 2 slots numbered 0 and 00. You can bet on a single number. If the ball lands on your number, you receive 35 chips plus the chip you played.
    a. What is the probability that you will land on 17?
    b. What are the odds against landing on 17?
    c. If each chip is worth $1, what is the expected payoff for a player who plays the number 17 for a long time?

13. Suppose five quarters, five dimes, five nickels, and ten pennies are in a box. One coin is selected at random. What is the expected value of this experiment?

14. If the odds in favor of Fast Leg's winning a horse race are 5 to 2 and the first prize is $14,000, what is the expected value of Fast Leg's winning?

15. Al and Betsy are playing a coin-tossing game in which a fair coin is tossed. Al wins when a total of ten heads are tossed, and Betsy wins when a total of ten tails are tossed.
    a. If nine heads and eight tails have been tossed and the game is stopped, how should a pot of $100 be fairly divided?
    b. What are the odds against Betsy's winning at the time the game was stopped in (a)?
    c. Suppose eight heads and five tails have been tossed when the game is stopped. How should a pot of $100 be fairly divided?
    d. What are the odds in favor of Al's winning at the time the game was stopped in (c)?

16. Suppose you pay $5.00 to play a game in which two coins are tossed. You receive $10 if two heads occur, $5 if exactly one head occurs, and $0 if no heads appear. Is this a fair game?

17. Lori spends $1.00 for one ticket in a raffle with a $100 prize. If 200 tickets are sold, is $1.00 a fair price to pay for the ticket?

Communication

18. Explain the difference between odds and probability.

19. A prominent newspaper reported that the odds of getting AIDS in June 1991 were 68,000 to 1. Explain why you believe or disbelieve this report.

20. A game involves tossing two coins. A player wins $1.00 if both tosses result in heads. What should you pay to play this game in order to make it a fair game? Explain your answer.

Open-ended

21. An insurance company sells a policy that pays $50,000 in case of accidental death. According to company figures, the rate of accidental death is 47 per 100,000 population. What annual premium should the company charge for this coverage? Explain how much profit the company will make under your plan, how you determined the amount of profit needed for the company, and how the annual premium was computed.

Cooperative Learning

22. As a group, design a game that involves either cards, dice, or spinners.
    a. Write the rules so that any person who wants to play can understand the game.
    b. Write a description explaining whether the game is fair and how you arrived at your conclusion.
    c. Calculate the odds of each player's winning.
    d. If betting is involved, discuss expected values.
    e. Exchange a game with another group and compare your analysis of their game with the one they did of your group's game.

Review Problems

23. Refer to the following spinners and write the sample space for each of the following experiments:
    a. Spin spinner 1 once.
    b. Spin spinner 2 once.
    c. Spin spinner 1 once and then spin spinner 2 once.
    d. Spin spinner 2 once and then roll a die.
    e. Spin spinner 1 twice.
    f. Spin spinner 2 twice.

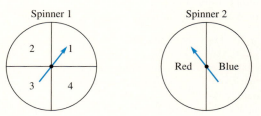

24. Draw a spinner with two sections, red and blue, such that the probability of getting (Blue, Blue) on two spins is $\frac{25}{36}$.

25. When drawing two letters from the alphabet with replacement, find the probability of getting two vowels.

Section 8-5   ## Methods of Counting

Permutations of Unlike Objects

permutation   An arrangement of things in a definite order with no repetitions is a **permutation.** For example, RAT, RTA, ART, ATR, TRA, and TAR are all different arrangements of the three letters R, A, and T. Notice that order is important and there are no repetitions. Determining the number of possible arrangements of the three letters without making a list can be done using the *Fundamental Counting Principle.* Because there are three ways to choose the first letter, two ways to choose the second letter, and one way to choose the third letter, there are $3 \cdot 2 \cdot 1$ or six ways of arranging the letters. It is common to record the number of permutations of three objects taken three at a time as $_3P_3$. Therefore, $_3P_3 = 6$.

Consider how many ways the owner of an ice cream parlor can display ten ice cream flavors in a row along the front of the display case. The first position can be filled in ten ways, the second position in nine ways, the third position in eight ways, and so on. By the Fundamental Counting Principle, there are $10 \cdot 9 \cdot 8 \cdot 7 \cdot 6 \cdot 5 \cdot 4 \cdot 3 \cdot 2 \cdot 1$, or 3,628,800, ways to display the flavors. If there were 16 flavors, there would be $16 \cdot 15 \cdot 14 \cdot 13 \cdot \ldots \cdot 3 \cdot 2 \cdot 1$ ways to arrange them. In general, *if there are n objects, then the number of possible ways to arrange the objects in a row is the product of all the natural numbers from n to*

n **factorial (n!)**   *1, inclusive.* This expression is called **n factorial** and is denoted by **n!,** as shown next.

$$n! = n \cdot (n-1) \cdot (n-2) \cdot \ldots \cdot 3 \cdot 2 \cdot 1$$

For example, $5! = 5 \cdot 4 \cdot 3 \cdot 2 \cdot 1$, $3! = 3 \cdot 2 \cdot 1$, and $1! = 1$. Using factorial notation is helpful in counting and probability problems.

Many calculators have a factorial key such as $\boxed{x!}$. To use this key, enter a whole number and then press the factorial key. For example, to compute 5!, press $\boxed{5}$ $\boxed{x!}$ and 120 will appear on the display.

Consider the set of people in a small club, {Al, Betty, Carl, Dan}. For them to elect a president and a secretary, order is important and no repetitions are possible. Counting the number of possibilities is a permutation problem. Since there are four ways of choosing a president and then three ways of choosing a secretary, by the Fundamental Counting Principle, there are $4 \cdot 3$, or 12, ways of choosing a president and a secretary. Choosing two officers from a club of four is a permutation of four people chosen two at a time. The number of possible permutations of four objects taken two at a time, denoted by $_4P_2$, may be counted using the Fundamental Counting Principle, as seen in Figure 8-34. Therefore we have $_4P_2 = 4 \cdot 3$, or 12.

Figure 8-34

In general, *if n objects are chosen r at a time, then the number of possible permutations, denoted by $_nP_r$, is*

$$_nP_r = n \cdot (n-1) \cdot (n-2) \cdot \ldots \cdot [n-(r-1)]$$

or

$$_nP_r = n \cdot (n-1) \cdot (n-2) \cdot \ldots \cdot (n-r+1).$$

The formula for the number of permutations can be written in terms of factorials. Consider the number of permutations of 20 objects three at a time:

$$_{20}P_3 = 20 \cdot 19 \cdot 18$$
$$= \frac{20 \cdot 19 \cdot 18 \, (17 \cdot \ldots \cdot 3 \cdot 2 \cdot 1)}{(17 \cdot \ldots \cdot 3 \cdot 2 \cdot 1)}$$
$$= \frac{20!}{17!}$$
$$= \frac{20!}{(20-3)!}.$$

This can be generalized as follows:

$$_nP_r = \frac{n!}{(n-r)!}.$$

$_nP_n$ is the number of permutations of n objects chosen n at a time — that is, the number of ways of rearranging n objects in a row. We have seen that this number is $n!$. If we use the formula for $_nP_r$ to compute $_nP_n$, we obtain

$$_nP_r = \frac{n!}{(n-n)!} = \frac{n!}{0!}.$$

Consequently, $n! = n!/0!$. To make this equation true, we define $0!$ to be 1.

Many calculators, especially graphing calculators, can calculate the number of permutations of n objects taken r at a time. This feature or key is usually denoted by $\boxed{_nP_r}$. To use this key, enter the value of n, then press $\boxed{_nP_r}$, followed by the value of r. If you then press $\boxed{=}$ or $\boxed{\text{ENTER}}$, the number of permutations is displayed.

I N V E S T I G A T I O N   8 - 5

● Assume a permutation key is not available on your calculator but a factorial key, $\boxed{x!}$, is. Explain   how to use this key to compute permutations. ●

Example 8-15

a. A baseball team has nine players. Find the number of ways the manager can arrange the batting order.

b. Find the number of ways of choosing three initials from the alphabet if none of the letters can be repeated.

Solution

a. Because there are nine ways to choose the first batter, eight ways to choose the second batter, and so on, there are $9 \cdot 8 \cdot 7 \cdot \ldots \cdot 2 \cdot 1 = 9!$, or 362,880, ways of arranging the batting order. Using the formula for permutations, we have $_9P_9 = 9!/0! = 362,880$.

b. There are 26 ways of choosing the first letter, 25 ways of choosing the second letter, and 24 ways of choosing the third letter. Hence, there are $26 \cdot 25 \cdot 24$, or 15,600, ways of choosing the 3 letters. Using the formula for permutations, we have $_{26}P_3 = \dfrac{26!}{23!} = 26 \cdot 25 \cdot 24 = 15,600$.

Permutations Involving Like Objects

In the previous counting examples, each individual object to be counted was distinct. Suppose we wanted to rearrange the letters in the word ZOO. How many choices would we have? A tree diagram, as in Figure 8-35, suggests that there might be $3 \cdot 2 \cdot 1 = 3!$, or 6, possibilities. However, looking at the list of possibilities shows that ZOO, OZO, and OOZ each appears twice because the O's are not different. We need to determine how to remove the duplication in arrangements such as this where some objects are the same. To eliminate the duplication, we divide the number of arrangements shown by the number of ways the two O's can be rearranged, which is 2!. Consequently, there are $\frac{3!}{2!}$, or 3, ways of arranging the letters in ZOO. The arrangements are ZOO, OZO, and OOZ.

Figure 8-35

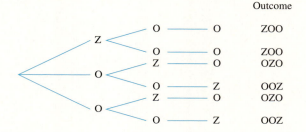

Permutations of Like Objects

If a set contains n elements, of which r_1 are of one kind, r_2 are of another kind, and so on through r_k, then the number of different arrangements of all n elements is equal to

$$\frac{n!}{r_1! \cdot r_2! \cdot r_3! \cdot \ldots \cdot r_k!}.$$

Example 8-16 | Find the number of rearrangements of the letters in each of the following words:

a. bubble   **b.** statistics

Solution   **a.** There are six letters with *b* repeated three times. Hence, the number of arrangements is

$$\frac{6!}{3!} = 6 \cdot 5 \cdot 4 = 120.$$

b. There are ten letters in the word *statistics,* with three *s*'s, three *t*'s, and two *i*'s duplicated in the word. Hence, the number of arrangements is

$$\frac{10!}{3! \cdot 3! \cdot 2!} = \frac{10 \cdot 9 \cdot 8 \cdot 7 \cdot 6 \cdot 5 \cdot 4 \cdot 3 \cdot 2 \cdot 1}{3 \cdot 2 \cdot 1 \cdot 3 \cdot 2 \cdot 1 \cdot 2 \cdot 1} = 50,400.$$

Combinations

Reconsider the club {Al, Betty, Carl, Dan}. Suppose a two-person committee is selected with no chair. In this case, order is not important, and an Al-Betty choice is the same as a

combination

Betty-Al choice. An arrangement of objects in which the order does not make any difference is called a **combination.** A comparison of the results of electing a president and secretary for the club and the results of simply selecting a two-person committee are shown in Figure 8-36. We see that the number of combinations is the number of permutations divided by 2, or

$$\frac{4 \cdot 3}{2} = 6.$$

Because each two-person choice can be arranged in 2!, or 2, ways, we divide the number of permutations by 2.

Figure 8-36

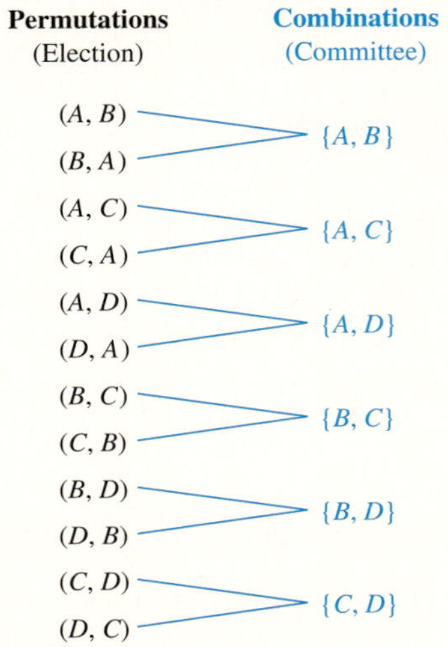

Permutations
(Election)

Combinations
(Committee)

Permutations (Election)	Combinations (Committee)
(A, B) (B, A)	$\{A, B\}$
(A, C) (C, A)	$\{A, C\}$
(A, D) (D, A)	$\{A, D\}$
(B, C) (C, B)	$\{B, C\}$
(B, D) (D, B)	$\{B, D\}$
(C, D) (D, C)	$\{C, D\}$

In how many ways can a committee of three people be selected from the club {Al, Betty, Carl, Dan}? To solve this problem, we proceed as we did above and find the number of ways to select three people from a group of four for three offices, say president, vice president, and secretary (a permutation problem) and then use this result to see how many different combinations of people are possible for the committee. A partial list for both problems is shown in Figure 8-37.

Figure 8-37

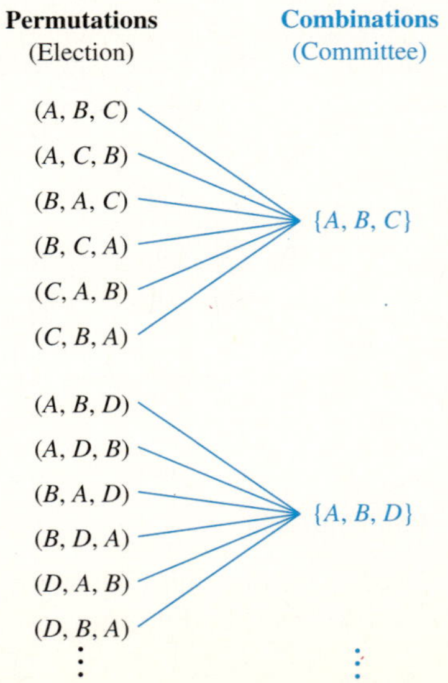

Permutations
(Election)

Combinations
(Committee)

Permutations (Election)	Combinations (Committee)
(A, B, C) (A, C, B) (B, A, C) (B, C, A) (C, A, B) (C, B, A)	$\{A, B, C\}$
(A, B, D) (A, D, B) (B, A, D) (B, D, A) (D, A, B) (D, B, A)	$\{A, B, D\}$
⋮	⋮

By the Fundamental Counting Principle, if order is important the number of ways to choose three people from the list of four is $4 \cdot 3 \cdot 2$, or 24. However, with each triple chosen, there are 3!, or 6, ways to rearrange the triple, as seen in Figure 8-37. Therefore there are 3! times as many permutations as combinations. To find the number of combinations, we divide the number of permutations, 24, by 3!, or 6, to obtain 4. The four committees are $\{A, B, C\}$, $\{A, B, D\}$, $\{B, C, D\}$, and $\{A, C, D\}$.

In general, we use the following rule to count combinations: *To find the number of combinations possible in a counting problem, first use the Fundamental Counting Principle to find the number of permutations and then divide by the number of ways in which each choice can be arranged.*

Symbolically, the number of combinations of n objects taken r at a time is denoted by $_nC_r$. From the preceding rule, we develop the following formula:

$$_nC_r = \frac{_nP_r}{_rP_r} = \frac{\dfrac{n!}{(n-r)!}}{r!} = \frac{n!}{r!(n-r)!}$$

It is not necessary to memorize this formula, since we can always find the number of combinations by using the reasoning developed in the committee example. Such reasoning is used on the following student page from *Addison-Wesley Mathematics,* Grade 8, 1993.

• • •

Example 8-17

The Library of Science Book Club offers three free books from a list of 42. If you circle three choices from a list of 42 numbers on a postcard, how many possible choices are there?

Solution   By the Fundamental Counting Principle, there are $42 \cdot 41 \cdot 40$ ways to choose the three free books. Because each set of three circled numbers could be rearranged $3 \cdot 2 \cdot 1$ different ways, there is an extra factor of 3! in the original $42 \cdot 41 \cdot 40$ ways. Therefore the number of combinations possible for three books is

$$\frac{42 \cdot 41 \cdot 40}{3!} = 11{,}480.$$

• • •

• • •

Example 8-18

At the beginning of the second quarter of a mathematics class for elementary-school teachers, each of the class's 25 students shook hands with each of the other students exactly once. How many handshakes took place?

Solution   Since the handshake between persons A and B is the same as that between persons B and A, this is a problem of choosing combinations of 25 people two at a time. There are

$$\frac{25 \cdot 24}{2!} = 300$$

different handshakes.

• • •

Combinations

LEARN ABOUT IT

EXPLORE Fill in the Table

Work in groups. Tonya, Cathy, Dave, and Kuey are on the ballot for the student council. The election judge reports the first and second place winners.

- Make a list of all the possible outcomes of the election.
- Make a list of all the pairs who could be selected to the student council.

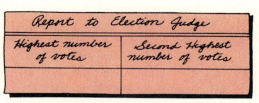

Report to Election Judge	
Highest number of votes	*Second highest number of votes*

TALK ABOUT IT

1. Would (Tonya, Dave) and (Dave, Tonya) be counted as different on the report?

2. Would the listings (Tonya, Dave) and (Dave, Tonya) be considered the same in the school paper?

The election judge distinguishes between the order of the two candidates; he is concerned with **permutations.** The students, on the other hand are concerned only with which two students are selected. They are not concerned with order.

List of Permutations					
C, D	C, J	C, T	D, J	D, T	J, T
D, C	J, C	T, C	J, D	T, D	T, J

A selection of a number of objects from a set of objects, without regard to order, is called a **combination** of the objects.

Selections		
C and D	C and J	C and T
D and J	D and T	J and T

Number of Combinations of 2 selected from 4. $= \dfrac{4 \cdot 3}{2 \cdot 1}$ $\dfrac{\text{permutations of 2 students from 4 students}}{\text{permutation of 2 students from 2 students}}$

Examples Find the number of combinations.

A Choose 3 candidates from 7.

$$\frac{7 \times 6 \times 5}{3 \times 2 \times 1} = 35$$

B Choose 4 candidates from 6.

$$\frac{6 \times 5 \times 4 \times 3}{4 \times 3 \times 2 \times 1} = 15$$

TRY IT OUT

Find the number of combinations.

1. 2 letters from E, L, and K

2. 3 people from a group of 6

Problem 5

In the following cartoon, suppose Peppermint Patty took a six-question true-false test. If she answered each question true or false at random, what is the probability that she answered 50% of the questions correctly?

Understanding the Problem. A score of 50% indicates that Peppermint Patty answered $\frac{1}{2}$ of the six questions, or three questions, correctly. She answered the questions true or false at random, so the probability that she answered a given question correctly is $\frac{1}{2}$. We are asked to determine the probability that Patty answered exactly three of the questions correctly.

Devising a Plan. We do not know which three questions Patty missed. She could have missed any three out of six on the test. Suppose she answered questions 2, 4, and 5 incorrectly. In this case, she would have answered questions 1, 3, and 6 correctly. We can compute the probability of this set of answers by *using the branch of a tree diagram,* as in Figure 8-38, where C represents a correct answer and I represents an incorrect answer.

Figure 8-38

Multiplying the probabilities along the branches, we obtain $\left(\frac{1}{2}\right)^6$ as the probability of answering questions 1–6 in the following way: $C\,I\,C\,I\,I\,C$. There are other ways to answer exactly three questions correctly: for example, $C\,C\,C\,I\,I\,I$. The probability of answering questions 1–6 in this way is also $\left(\frac{1}{2}\right)^6$. The number of ways to answer the questions is simply the number of ways of arranging three C's and three I's in a row, which is also the number of ways of choosing three correct questions out of six, that is, $_6C_3$. Because all these arrangements give Patty a score of 50%, the desired probability is the sum of the probabilities for each arrangement.

Carrying Out the Plan. There are $_6C_3$, or 20, sets of answers similar to the one in Figure 8-38, with three correct and three incorrect answers. The product of the probabilities for each of these sets of answers is $\left(\frac{1}{2}\right)^6$, so the sum of the probabilities for all 20 sets is $20 \cdot \left(\frac{1}{2}\right)^6$, or approximately 0.3125. Thus Peppermint Patty has a probability of 0.3125 of obtaining a score of exactly 50% on the test.

Looking Back.   It seems paradoxical to learn that the probability of obtaining a score of 50% on a six-question true-false test is not close to $\frac{1}{2}$. As an extension of the problem, suppose a passing score is a score of at least 70%. Now what is the probability that Peppermint Patty will pass? What is the probability of her obtaining a score of at least 50% on the test? If the test is a six-question multiple-choice test with five alternative answers for each question, what is the probability of obtaining a score of at least 50% by random guessing?

• • •

Problem 6

Stephen placed three letters in envelopes while he was having a telephone conversation. He addressed the envelopes and sealed them without checking if each letter was in the correct envelope. What is the probability that each of the letters was inserted correctly?

Understanding the Problem.   Stephen sealed three letters in addressed envelopes without checking to see if each was in the correct envelope. We are to determine the probability that each of the three letters was placed correctly. This probability could be found if we knew the sample space, or at least how many elements are in the sample space.

Devising a Plan.   To aid in solving the problem, we represent the respective letters as *a*, *b*, and *c* and the respective envelopes as *A, B,* and *C*. For example, a correctly placed letter *a* would be in envelope *A*. To construct the sample space, we use the strategy of *making a table.* The table should show all the possible permutations of letters in envelopes. Once the table is completed, we can determine the probability that each letter is correctly placed.

Carrying Out the Plan.   Table 8-9 is constructed by using the envelope labels *A, B,* and *C* as headings and listing all possibilities of letters *a, b,* and *c* below the headings. Case 1 is the only case out of 6 in which each of the envelopes is labeled correctly, so the probability that each envelope is labeled correctly is $\frac{1}{6}$.

Table 8-9

Addresses

Letters		A	B	C
	1	a	b	c
	2	a	c	b
	3	b	a	c
	4	b	c	a
	5	c	a	b
	6	c	b	a

Looking Back.   Is the probability of having each letter placed incorrectly the same as the probability of having each letter placed correctly? A first guess might be that the probabilities are the same, but that is not true. Why?

We also could have used a counting argument to solve the problem. Given an envelope, there is only one correct letter to place in the envelope. Thus there is one correct way to place the letters in the envelopes. By the Fundamental Counting Principle, there are $3 \cdot 2 \cdot 1$ ways of choosing the letters to place in the envelopes, so the probability of having the letters correctly placed is $\frac{1}{6}$.

• • •

Ongoing Assessment 8-5

1. In a car race, there are six Chevrolets, four Fords, and two Pontiacs. In how many ways can the twelve cars finish if we consider only the makes of the cars?

2. The eighth-grade class at a grade school has 16 girls and 14 boys. How many different possible boy-girl dates can be arranged?

3. If a coin is tossed five times, in how many different ways can the sequence of heads and tails appear?

4. The telephone prefix for a university is 243. The prefix is followed by four digits. How many telephones are possible before a new prefix is needed?

5. Radio stations in the United States have call letters that begin with either K or W. Some have a total of three letters, whereas others have four letters. How many sets of three-letter call letters are possible? How many sets of four-letter call letters are possible?

6. Carlin's Pizza House offers three kinds of salads, 15 kinds of pizza, and four kinds of desserts. How many different three-course meals can be ordered?

7. Decide whether each of the following is true or false:
   a. $6! = 6 \cdot 5!$ b. $3! + 3! = 6!$
   c. $\frac{6!}{3!} = 2!$ d. $\frac{6!}{3} = 2!$
   e. $\frac{6!}{5!} = 6$ f. $\frac{6!}{4!2!} = 15$
   g. $n!(n + 1) = (n + 1)!$

8. In how many ways can the letters in the word SCRAMBLE be rearranged?

9. How many two-person committees can be formed from a group of six people?

10. Find the number of ways to rearrange the letters in the following words:
    a. OHIO
    b. ALABAMA
    c. ILLINOIS
    d. MISSISSIPPI
    e. TENNESSEE

11. Assume a class has 30 members.
    a. In how many ways can a president, vice president, and secretary be selected?
    b. How many committees of three people can be chosen?

12. A basketball coach was criticized in the newspaper for not trying out every combination of players. If the team roster has 12 players, how many five-player combinations are possible?

13. A five-volume numbered set of books is placed randomly on a shelf. What is the probability that the books will be numbered in the correct order from left to right?

14. Take 10 points in a plane, no three of them on a line. How many straight lines can be drawn if each line is drawn through a pair of points?

15. Sally has four red flags, three green flags, and two white flags. How many nine-flag signals can she run up a flagpole?

16. Find the number of shortest paths from point A to point B along the edges of the cubes in each of the following. (For example, in (a) one shortest path is A-C-D-B.)

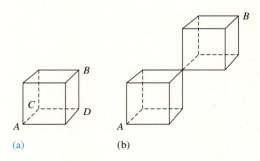

(a)   (b)

17. At a party, 28 handshakes took place. Each person shook hands exactly once with each of the others present. How many people were at the party?

18. A committee of three people is selected at random from a set consisting of seven Americans, five French people, and three English people.
    a. What is the probability that the committee consists of all Americans?
    b. What is the probability that the committee has no Americans?

19. How many different five-card hands can be dealt from a standard deck of 52 playing cards?

20. License plates in a certain state have three letters followed by three digits. How many different plates are possible if no repetitions of letters or numbers are allowed?

21. In a certain lottery game, 54 numbers are randomly mixed and six are selected. A person must pick all six numbers to win. Order is not important. What is the probability of winning?

22. Social Security numbers are in the form ### - ## - ####, where each symbol represents any number 0–9. How many Social Security numbers are possible using this format?

23. The probability of a basketball player's making a free throw successfully at any time in a game is $\frac{2}{3}$. If the player attempts ten free throws in a game, what is the probability that exactly six are made?

★24. In how many ways can five couples be seated in a row of ten chairs if no couple is separated?

Communication

25. The terms *Fundamental Counting Principle, permutations,* and *combinations* are all used to work with counting problems. In your own words, explain how all these terms are related and how they are used.

26. Explain why $0! = 1$.

27. a. A bicycle lock has three reels, each of which contains the numbers 0–9. To open the lock, you must enter the numbers in the correct order, such as 369 or 455, where one number is chosen from each reel. How many different possibilities are there for the numbers to open the lock? Explain how you arrived at your answer.
b. These kinds of locks are called *combination* locks. Explain why this is probably not a good name for these locks for someone who has studied counting problems.

Open-ended

28. Suppose the Department of Motor Vehicles uses only six spaces and the numbers 0–9 to create its license plates.
a. How many license plates are possible?
b. Based on the 1990 census, determine whether there are any states in which the answer in (a) might provide enough license plates?

c. If you were in charge of making license plates for the state of California, describe the method you would use to ensure you would have enough license plates available.

Cooperative Learning

29. The following triangular array of numbers is a part of **Pascal's triangle:**

```
                            1              (0)
                         1     1           (1)
                      1     2     1        (2)
                   1     3     3     1     (3)
                1     4     6     4     1  (4)
             1     5    10    10    5    1 (5)
          1     6    15    20    15    6   1 (6)
```

Row

a. In your group, decide how the triangle was constructed and complete the next two rows.
b. Describe at least three number patterns that are present in Pascal's triangle.
c. Find the sum of the numbers in each row. Predict the sum of the numbers in row ten.
d. The entries in row two are just $_2C_0$, $_2C_1$, and $_2C_2$. Have different members of your group investigate whether a similar pattern holds for other rows in Pascal's triangle.
e. Describe how you could use combinations to find any entry in Pascal's triangle or vice versa.

Review Problems

30. Two cards are drawn at random without replacement from a deck of 52 cards. What is the probability that
a. at least one card is an ace?
b. exactly one card is red?

31. If two regular dice are tossed, what is the probability of tossing a sum greater than 10?

32. Two coins are tossed. You win $5.00 if both coins are heads and $3.00 if both coins are tails and lose $4.00 if the coins do not match. What is the expected value of this game. Is this a fair game?

BRAIN TEASER An airplane can complete its flight if at least $\frac{1}{2}$ of its engines are working. If the probability that an engine fails is 0.01 and all engine failures do not depend on each other, what is the probability of a successful flight if the plane has

a. two engines?   **b.** four engines?

SOLUTION TO THE PRELIMINARY PROBLEM

Understanding the Problem. Four special dice have been designed as shown in Figure 8-39. One has two 0's and four 4's, one has all three's, one has four 2's and two 6's, and the last has three 1's and three 5's. Each of two players chooses a die. Both dice are rolled and the greatest value rolled is the winner. If we play the game, we must decide how to choose a die to have the best chance of winning.

Figure 8-39

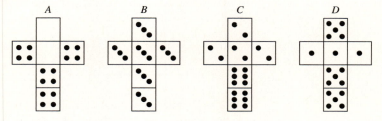

Devising a Plan. Because no one die stands out as being clearly better than the others, one strategy might be to *examine specific cases and look for a pattern.* Suppose the other player chooses die *B*, which rolls a 3 all the time. If we then choose die *C*, a 2 is rolled 4/6, or 2/3, of the time. Therefore die *B* beats die *C* 2/3 of the time. If we choose die *D*, we would roll a 5 half the time and a 1 half the time. This is a fair game because each player has the same probability of winning. If we choose die *A*, then a 4 is rolled 4/6, or 2/3, of the time and die *A* beats die *B* 2/3 of the time. Therefore if the other player chooses die *B*, we should choose die *A* and we will win about 2/3 of the time. If we consider the other choices in a similar way, then we might be able to come up with a winning strategy.

Carrying Out the Plan. Suppose the other player chooses die *A*. Then if we choose die *B*, we lose 2/3 of the time (why?) and hence this would not be a good choice. This leaves the choices of die *C* or *D*. These are a little more complicated to analyze. We construct Tables 8-10 and 8-11, which show all possibilities for these die tosses. The winning die in each case is labeled with the appropriate letter in the table.

Table 8-10

		Die *C*					
		2	2	2	2	6	6
	0	*C*	*C*	*C*	*C*	*C*	*C*
	0	*C*	*C*	*C*	*C*	*C*	*C*
Die *A*	4	*A*	*A*	*A*	*A*	*C*	*C*
	4	*A*	*A*	*A*	*A*	*C*	*C*
	4	*A*	*A*	*A*	*A*	*C*	*C*
	4	*A*	*A*	*A*	*A*	*C*	*C*

Table 8-11

		Die *D*					
		5	1	5	5	1	1
	0	*D*	*D*	*D*	*D*	*D*	*D*
	0	*D*	*D*	*D*	*D*	*D*	*D*
Die *A*	4	*D*	*A*	*D*	*D*	*A*	*A*
	4	*D*	*A*	*D*	*D*	*A*	*A*
	4	*D*	*A*	*D*	*D*	*A*	*A*
	4	*D*	*A*	*D*	*D*	*A*	*A*

From Table 8-10, we see that the probability of die *C* beating die *A* is 16/36, or 4/9, and from Table 8-11, we see the probability of die *D* beating die *A* is 24/36, or 2/3. Therefore if the other person chooses die *A*, we should choose die *D* and we will win about 2/3 of the time. Similar analysis can be done if the other person chooses die *C* or *D*. The results of this analysis and the best choices are given in Table 8-12.

Table 8-12

First Person's Choice	Second Person's Choice	Probability of Second Choice Winning
A	*D*	2/3
B	*A*	2/3
C	*B*	2/3
D	*C*	2/3

Table 8-12 shows that these dice are truly remarkable in that no matter which die the other player chooses, you can always choose one that will beat it 2/3 of the time. Therefore the strategy for playing this game is to go second and make your choice of die based on the information in Table 8-12.

Looking Back.   The game can be played many times to see how close the experimental probabilities match the theoretical probabilities. Is it possible to design a fifth die that will fit with these four such that the same idea holds?

QUESTIONS FROM THE CLASSROOM

1. A student claims that if a fair coin is tossed and comes up heads five times in a row, then, according to the law of averages, the probability of tails on the next toss is greater than the probability of heads. What is your reply?

2. A student observes the following spinner and claims that the color red has the highest probability of appearing, since there are two red areas on the spinner. What is your reply?

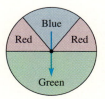

3. A student tosses a coin three times, and tails appears each time. The student concludes that the coin is not fair. What is your response?

4. An experiment consists of tossing a coin twice. The student reasons that there are three possible outcomes: two heads, one head and one tail, or two tails. Thus $P(HH) = \frac{1}{3}$. What is your reply?

5. In response to the question, "If a fair die is rolled twice, what is the probability of rolling a pair of fives?" a student replies, "One third, because $\frac{1}{6} + \frac{1}{6} = \frac{1}{3}$." How do you respond?

6. A student wonders why probabilities cannot be negative. What is your response?

7. A student claims that "if the probability of an event is $\frac{3}{5}$, then there are three ways the event can occur and only five elements in the sample space." How do you respond?

8. A student does not understand the meaning of $_4P_0$. The student wants to know how we can consider permutations of four objects chosen zero at a time. How do you respond?

9. A student wants to know why, if we can define 0! as 1, we cannot define $\frac{1}{0}$ as 1. How do you respond?

10. A student is not sure when to add and when to multiply probabilities. How do you respond?

CHAPTER OUTLINE

I. Probability

   A. Probabilities can be determined **experimentally (empirically)** or **theoretically.**

   B. A **sample space** is the set of all possible outcomes of an **experiment.**

   C. An **event** is a subset of a sample space.

   D. Outcomes are **equally likely** if each outcome is as likely to occur as another.

   E. If all outcomes of an experiment are *equally likely,* the **probability of an event** A from sample space S is given by

$$P(A) = \frac{n(A)}{n(S)}.$$

   F. An **impossible event** is an event with a probability of zero. An impossible event can never occur.

   G. A **certain event** is an event with a probability of 1. A certain event is sure to happen.

   H. Two events are **mutually exclusive** if, and only if, exactly one of the events can occur at any given time — that is, if, and only if, the events are disjoint.

   I. The probability of the **complement of an event** is given by $P(\overline{A}) = 1 - P(A)$, where A is the event and $\overline{A}$ is its complement.

   J. **Multiplication Rule for Probabilities** For all **multistage experiments,** the probability of the outcome along any path of a tree diagram is equal to the product of all the probabilities along the path.

   K. **Simulations** can play an important part in probability. Fair coins, dice, spinners, and random-digit tables are useful in performing simulations.

II. Odds and expected value

   A. The **odds in favor** of an event A are given by

$$\frac{P(A)}{P(\overline{A})} = \frac{P(A)}{1 - P(A)}.$$

   B. The **odds against** an event A are given by

$$\frac{P(\overline{A})}{P(A)} = \frac{1 - P(A)}{P(A)}.$$

   C. If, in an experiment, the possible outcomes are numbers $a_1, a_2, \ldots, a_n$, occurring with probabilities $p_1, p_2, \ldots, p_n$, respectively, then the **expected value** E is defined as

$$E = a_1 \cdot p_1 + a_2 \cdot p_2 + a_3 \cdot p_3 + \ldots + a_n \cdot p_n.$$

   D. A **fair game** is a game in which each player has an equal chance of winning. If money is involved, the net winnings or expected value is $0.

III. Counting principles

   A. **Fundamental Counting Principle** If an event M can occur in m ways and, after it has occurred, event N can occur in n ways, then event M followed by event N can occur in $m \cdot n$ ways.

   B. **Permutations** are arrangements in which order is important:

$$_nP_r = \frac{n!}{(n-r)!}$$

   C. The expression $n!$, called n **factorial,** represents the product of all the natural numbers less than or equal to n. $0!$ is defined as 1.

   D. **Permutations of like objects** If a set contains n elements, of which r_1 are of one kind, r_2 are of another kind, and so on through r_k, then the number of different arrangements of all n elements is equal to

$$\frac{n!}{r_1! \cdot r_2! \cdot r_3! \cdot \ldots \cdot r_k!}.$$

   E. **Combinations** are arrangements in which order is *not* important. To find the number of combinations possible, first use the Fundamental Counting Principle to find the number of permutations and then divide by the number of ways in which each choice can be arranged:

$$_nC_r = \frac{_nP_r}{_rP_r}$$

CHAPTER REVIEW

1. Suppose the names of the days of the week are placed in a box and one name is drawn at random.

   a. List the sample space for this experiment.

   b. List the event consisting of outcomes that the day drawn starts with the letter T.

   c. What is the probability of drawing a day that starts with T?

2. If you have a jar of 1000 jelly beans and you know that $P(\text{Blue}) = \frac{4}{5}$ and $P(\text{Red}) = \frac{1}{8}$, list several things you can say about the beans in the jar.

3. In the 1960 presidential election, John F. Kennedy received 34,226,731 votes and Richard M. Nixon received

34,108,157. If a voter is chosen at random, answer the following:

a. What is the probability that the person voted for Kennedy?

b. What is the probability that the person voted for Nixon?

c. What are the odds that a person chosen at random did not vote for Nixon?

4. A box contains three red balls, five black balls, and four white balls. Suppose one ball is drawn at random. Find the probability of each of the following events:

a. A black ball is drawn.

b. A black or a white ball is drawn.

c. Neither a red nor a white ball is drawn.

d. A red ball is not drawn.

e. A black ball and a white ball are drawn.

f. A black or white or red ball is drawn.

5. One card is selected at random from an ordinary set of 52 cards. Find the probability of each of the following events:

a. A club is drawn.

b. A spade and a 5 are drawn.

c. A heart or a face card is drawn.

d. A jack is not drawn.

6. A box contains five colored balls and four white balls. If three balls are drawn one by one, find the probability that they are all white if the draws are made as follows:

a. With replacement

b. Without replacement

7. Consider the following two boxes. If a letter is drawn from box 1 and placed into box 2 and then a letter is drawn from box 2, what is the probability that the letter is an L?

| LINUS | LUCY |
| 1 | 2 |

8. Use the following boxes for a two-stage experiment. First select a box at random and then select a letter at random from the box. What is the probability of drawing an A?

| MY | DEAR | AUNT | SALLY |
| 1 | 2 | 3 | 4 |

9. Consider the following boxes. Draw a ball from box 1 and put it into box 2. Then draw a ball from box 2 and put it into box 3. Finally, draw a ball from box 3. Construct a tree diagram for this experiment and calculate the probability that the last ball chosen is colored.

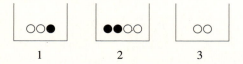

1   2   3

10. What are the odds in favor of drawing a jack when one card is drawn from an ordinary deck of playing cards?

11. A die is rolled once. What are the odds against rolling a prime number?

12. If the odds in favor of a certain event are 3 to 5, what is the probability that the event will occur?

13. A game consists of rolling two dice. Rolling double ones pays $7.20. Rolling double sixes pays $3.60. Any other roll pays nothing. What is the expected value for this game?

14. A total of 3000 tickets have been sold for a drawing. If one ticket is drawn for a single prize of $1000, what is a fair price for a ticket?

15. How many four-digit numbers can be formed if the first digit cannot be zero and the last digit must be 2?

16. A club consists of ten members. In how many different ways can a group of three people be selected to go on a European trip?

17. Find the number of different ways that four flags can be displayed on a flagpole, one above the other, if ten different flags are available.

18. Five women live together in an apartment. Two have blue eyes. If two of the women are chosen at random, what is the probability that they both have blue eyes?

19. Five horses (Applefarm, Bandy, Cash, Deadbeat, and Egglegs) run in a race.

a. In how many ways can the first-, second-, and third-place horses be determined?

b. Find the probability that Deadbeat finishes first and Bandy finishes second in the race.

c. Find the probability that the first-, second-, and third-place horses are Deadbeat, Egglegs, and Cash, in that order.

20. Al and Ruby each roll an ordinary die once. What is the probability that the number of Ruby's roll is greater than the number of Al's roll?

21. Amy has a quiz on which she is to answer any three of the five questions. If she is equally well versed on all questions and chooses three questions at random, what is the probability that question 1 is not chosen?

22. On a certain street are three traffic lights. At any given time, the probability that a light is green is 0.3. What is the probability that a person will hit all three lights when they are green?

23. A three-stage rocket has the following probabilities for failure. The probability for failure at stage one is $\frac{1}{6}$; at stage two, $\frac{1}{8}$; and at stage three, $\frac{1}{10}$. What is the probability of a successful flight, given that the first stage was successful?

24. How could each of the following be simulated by using a random-digit table?

a. Tossing a fair die

b. Picking three months at random from the 12 months of the year

c. Spinning the spinner shown

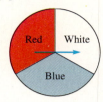

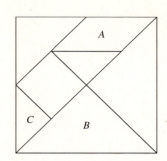

25. If a dart is thrown at the following tangram dart board and we assume the dart lands at random on the board, what is the probability of its landing in each of the following areas?
a. Area *A*
b. Area *B*
c. Area *C*

26. The points *M, N, O, P,* and *Q* in the following figure represent exits on a highway. An accident occurs at random between points *M* and *Q*. What is the probability that it has occurred between *N* and *O*?

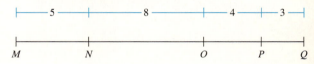

SELECTED BIBLIOGRAPHY

Bright, G. "Teaching Mathematics with Technology: Probability Simulations." *Arithmetic Teacher* 36 (May 1989): 16–18.

Brulag, D. "Choice and Chance in Life: The Game of 'Skunk.'" *Mathematics Teaching in the Middle School* 1 (April 1994): 28–33.

English, L. "Problem Solving with Combinations." *Arithmetic Teacher* 40 (October 1992): 72–77.

Erickson, D., M. Frank, and R. Kelley. "WITPO (What Is the Probability Of)." *Mathematics Teacher* 84 (April 1991): 258–264.

Fennell, F. "Implementing the *Standards:* Probability." *Arithmetic Teacher* 38 (December 1990): 18–22.

Hatfield, L. "Explorations with Chance." *Mathematics Teacher* 85 (April 1992): 280–282.

Kanold, C. "Teaching Probability Theory Modeling Real Problems." *Mathematics Teacher* 85 (April 1994): 232–235.

Lappan, G., et al. "Area Models for Probability." *Mathematics Teacher* 80 (November 1987): 650–654.

Lappan, G., and M. Winter. "Probability Simulation in Middle School." *Mathematics Teacher* 73 (September 1980): 446–449.

Litwiller, B., and D. Duncan. "Combinatorics Connections: Playoff Series and Pascal's Triangle." *Mathematics Teacher* 85 (October 1992): 532–535.

Litwiller, B., and D. Duncan. "Matching Garage Door Openers." *Mathematics Teacher* 85 (March 1992): 217–219.

Martin, H., and J. Zawojewski. "Dealing with Data and Chance: An Illustration from the Middle School Addendum to the Standards." *Arithmetic Teacher* 41 (December 1993): 220–223.

May, E. "Are Seven-Game Baseball Playoffs Fairer?" *Mathematics Teacher* 85 (October 1992): 528–531.

National Council of Teachers of Mathematics. *Dealing with Data and Chance. Grades 5–8 Addenda Book* (Reston, VA: NCTM) 1994.

Shaughnessy, M. "Probability and Statistics." *Mathematics Teacher* 86 (March 1993): 244–248.

Shaughnessy, J., and T. Dick. "Monty's Dilemma: Should You Stick or Switch?" *Mathematics Teacher* 84 (April 1991): 252–256.

Shulte, A. "Learning Probability Concepts in Elementary School Mathematics." *Arithmetic Teacher* 34 (January 1987): 32–33.

Shultz, H., and B. Leonard. "Probability and Intuition." *Mathematics Teacher* 82 (January 1989): 52–53.

Walton, K. "Probability, Computer Simulation, and Mathematics." *Mathematics Teacher* 83 (January 1990): 22–25.

Woodword, E., and M. Woodword. "Expected Value and the Wheel of Fortune Game." *Mathematics Teacher* 87 (January 1994): 13–17.

9

STATISTICS: AN INTRODUCTION

In a teachers' retirement system, a teacher's retirement income is based on the average of the teacher's salaries over the previous five years of employment. One teacher is going to retire in five years and is on the bargaining team to negotiate the teachers' contract for those five years. The bargaining team has several options, including (1) taking a fixed dollar amount as a salary increase for each person for each of the next five years, (2) taking a 4% increase in salary each year of the next five years, or (3) receiving no salary increases in each of the first three years but receiving a 10% salary increase in each of the last two years. Which salary scheme and which average would be most beneficial to the negotiator who is planning to retire at the end of the five-year period?

For a long time, the word *statistics* referred to numerical information about state or political territories. The word itself comes from the Latin *statisticus,* meaning "of the state." The study of statistics has taken several centuries to develop.

Statistics are both used and abused. Sometimes the abuse is of little consequence and entirely unintentional. This may or may not be true in Shoe's case in the following cartoon. Here, one question to ask is how the poll was taken. Do you think the same type of persons are willing to take the time to answer a survey poll, or are most surveys answered by a cross-section of the populace?

SHOE

Statistics plays an important role in the *Standards* at both the K–4 level and the 5–8 level. Following is an excerpt from the 5–8 *Standards* (p. 105):

▲ *In grades K–4, students begin to explore basic ideas of statistics by gathering data appropriate to their grade level, organizing them in charts or graphs, and reading information from displays of data. These concepts should be expanded in the middle grades. . . . Students need to be actively involved in each of the steps that comprise statistics, from gathering information to communicating results.*

And in the *Teaching Standards* (p. 136), we find the following concerning what all teachers of grades K–12 should know:

▲ *Teachers should have a variety of experiences in the collection, organization, representation, analysis, and interpretation of data. Key statistical concepts for all teachers include measures of central tendency, measures of variation (range, standard deviation, interquartile range, and outliers), and general distributions. Representations of data should include various types of graphs, including bar, line, circle, and pictographs as well as line plots, stem-and-leaf plots, box plots, histograms, and scatter plots.*

Additional statistical topics, including misuses of statistics, are listed for teachers of grades 5–8. In this chapter, we cover the statistics topics listed in the *Teaching Standards.*

HISTORICAL NOTE

The seventeenth-century work of John Graunt (1620–1674) and the eighteenth-century work of Adolph Quetelet (1796–1874) both involved making predictions on the collection of data. Graunt dealt with birth and death records, while Quetelet dealt with crime and mortality rates. Florence Nightingale (1820–1910) worked with mortality tables during the Crimean War to get British hospitals changed to improve care. Other notables who worked with data collection and analysis include Sir Francis Galton (1822–1911) and Gregor Mendel (1822–1884). In the twentieth century, work continued by Ronald Fisher (1890–1962) in genetics and Andrei Nikolaevich Kolmogorov (1903–1987), who also was chairman of the Commission for Mathematical Education under the Presidium of the Academy of Sciences of the U.S.S.R. Also working in this century have been John Tukey (1915–), who developed many of the current graphical representations used to depict statistics, including stem-and-leaf plots, and Gertrude Mary Cox (1900–1978), who wrote *Experimental Designs* in 1950, a classic textbook on design and analysis of replicated experiments.

Section 9-1 Statistical Graphs

Visual illustrations are an important part of statistics. Such illustrations or graphs take many forms: pictographs, circle graphs, pie charts, line plots, stem-and-leaf plots, frequency tables, histograms, bar graphs, and frequency polygons or line graphs. A *graph* is a picture

data that displays **data.** Data can be presented in various forms once they are collected. The K–4 *Standards* point out (p. 55) that

Children should learn that data can be displayed in different ways and that depending on the question being asked, one type of display might be more appropriate than another. A variety of experiences helps children build a foundation for creating conventional graphs.

In elementary school, graphs may be constructed with real objects, as shown in the following primary text page from *Mathematics Their Way,* 1976.

Pictographs

pictograph Another type of graph that children often construct and that we see in newspapers and magazines is a **pictograph.** In a pictograph, a symbol or an icon is used to represent a quantity of items. A *key* is usually presented, which tells what the symbol represents. Pictographs are frequently used to show comparisons of outputs as in Figure 9-1. A major disadvantage of pictographs is evident in Figure 9-1(a). The month of September contains a partial bundle of newspapers. It is impossible to tell from the graph the weight of that bundle with any accuracy.

Figure 9-1

Recycled Newspapers

Each ▱ represents 10 kg.

Months	Weights of Newspapers
July	▱ ▱ ▱ ▱
Aug.	▱ ▱ ▱ ▱ ▱
Sept.	▱ ▱ ▱ ▱ ▱ ▱ ▱
Oct.	▱ ▱ ▱ ▱ ▱ ▱ ▱
Nov.	▱ ▱ ▱ ▱
Dec.	▱ ▱ ▱

Weights of Newspapers

(a)

Hillview Fifth-grade
Student Distribution

Each ☂ represents 5 students.

Teacher	Students per Class
Ames	☂ ☂ ☂ ☂
Ball	☂ ☂ ☂ ☂
Cox	☂ ☂ ☂
Day	☂ ☂ ☂ ☂ ☂
Eves	☂ ☂ ☂
Fagin	☂ ☂

Students per Class

(b)

6
GRAPHING

Real Graphs Comparing Two Groups

"Are you wearing a scary or a friendly mask on Halloween?"

"Do you want to use white or wheat bread for your cinnamon toast?"

"Are you wearing boots or shoes?"

"Do you choose a chocolate or vanilla cookie for a treat?"

"Which paste jars need filling?"

"Are the soles of your shoes smooth or bumpy?"

Line Plots

line plot

Next we examine a **line plot.** A line plot is somewhat like a pictograph, but no numerical values are lost in the graph. Line plots provide a quick, simple way of organizing data. Typically, we use them when there is only one group of data with fewer than 50 values.

Suppose the 30 students in Abel's class received the following test scores:

| 82 | 97 | 70 | 72 | 83 | 75 | 76 | 84 | 76 | 88 | 80 | 81 | 81 | 52 | 82 |
| 82 | 73 | 98 | 83 | 72 | 84 | 84 | 76 | 85 | 86 | 78 | 97 | 97 | 82 | 77 |

A line plot for this class consists of a horizontal number line on which each score is denoted by an x above the corresponding number line value, as shown in Figure 9-2. The number of x's above each score indicates how many times each score occurred.

Figure 9-2

Scores on Abel's Class Test

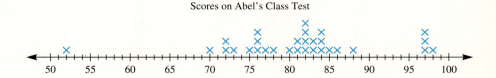

Figure 9-2 yields information about Abel's exam. For example, 3 students scored 76 and 4 scored greater than 90. We also see that the low score was 52, the high score was 98, and the most frequent score was 82. Several features of the data become more obvious when

outlier

line plots are used. For example, outliers, clusters, and gaps are apparent. An **outlier** is a data point whose value is significantly larger or smaller than other values, such as the score

cluster

of 52 in Figure 9-2. (Outliers are discussed in greater detail in the next section.) A **cluster**

gap

is an isolated group of points, such as the one located at the scores 97 and 98. A **gap** is a large space between points, such as the one between 88 and 97.

If a line plot is constructed on grid paper, then shading in the squares with x's and adding a vertical axis depicting the scale allows the formation of a *bar graph,* as in Figure 9-3. (Bar graphs are discussed in more detail later in this section.)

Figure 9-3

Scores on Abel's Class Test

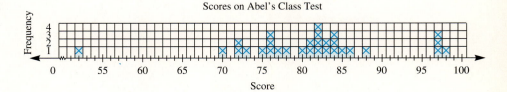

Stem-and-Leaf Plots

stem-and-leaf plot

The **stem-and-leaf plot** is closely related to the line plot except that the number line is usually vertical and digits are used rather than x's. A stem-and-leaf plot of test scores for Abel's class is shown in Figure 9-4.

Figure 9-4

Scores on Abel's Class Test

```
5 | 2
6 |
7 | 0223566678
8 | 0112222334444568       9 | 7 represents 97
9 | 7778
```

stems

leaves

The numbers on the left side of the vertical line are the **stems,** and the numbers on the right side are the **leaves.** In Figure 9-4, the stems are the tens digits of the scores on the test and the leaves are the units digits. In this case, the legend "9|7 represents 97" shows how to read the plot. We now construct a stem-and-leaf plot using the data in Table 9-1, which lists the presidents of the United States and their ages at death.

Table 9-1

President	Age at Death	President	Age at Death	President	Age at Death
George Washington	67	Millard Fillmore	74	Theodore Roosevelt	60
John Adams	90	Franklin Pierce	64	William Taft	72
Thomas Jefferson	83	James Buchanan	77	Woodrow Wilson	67
James Madison	85	Abraham Lincoln	56	Warren Harding	57
James Monroe	73	Andrew Johnson	66	Calvin Coolidge	60
John Q. Adams	80	Ulysses Grant	63	Herbert Hoover	90
Andrew Jackson	78	Rutherford Hayes	70	Franklin Roosevelt	63
Martin Van Buren	79	James Garfield	49	Harry Truman	88
William H. Harrison	68	Chester Arthur	57	Dwight Eisenhower	78
John Tyler	71	Grover Cleveland	71	John Kennedy	46
James K. Polk	53	Benjamin Harrison	67	Lyndon Johnson	64
Zachary Taylor	65	William McKinley	58	Richard Nixon	81

The presidents died in their 40s, 50s, 60s, 70s, 80s, or 90s. Thus we concentrate on numbers from 40 to 99. We choose the tens digits of the numbers as the stems. The leaves are the units digits. The plot is formed by placing the stem digits in a column from least to greatest on the left side of a vertical line, as shown in Figure 9-5(a). The leaves (which represent the units digits of the ages) are given on the right side of the vertical line, in whichever row contains their stem, as shown in Figure 9-5(b).

Figure 9-5

Stem	Leaf
4	
5	
6	
7	
8	
9	

(a)

Ages of Presidents at Death

4	96
5	36787
6	785463707034
7	3891470128
8	35081
9	00

4 | 9 represents 49 years old

(b)

In Figure 9-5(b), the top row has 4 as a stem and 9 and 6 as leaves. These numbers represent the ages 49 and 46, the ages at death of James Garfield and John Kennedy, respectively. The graph should be titled and accompanied by a legend telling how to interpret the symbols used in it.

ordered stem-and-leaf plot

In some sense, the data in Figure 9-5(b) are still not orderly because the numbers within each leaf are not in order from least to greatest on a given row. To make an **ordered stem-and-leaf plot,** we arrange the leaves on their given rows from least to greatest, starting at the left, as in Figure 9-6.

Figure 9-6

Ages of Presidents at Death

```
4 | 69
5 | 36778
6 | 003344567778
7 | 0112347889        4 | 9 represents 49
8 | 01358                 years old
9 | 00
```

There is no unique way to construct stem-and-leaf plots. Smaller numbers are usually placed at the top so that when the plot is turned counterclockwise 90°, it resembles a bar-graph or a histogram (discussed later in this section). Important advantages of stem-and-leaf plots are that they can be created by hand rather easily and that they do not become unmanageable when the number of values becomes large. Moreover, no original values are lost in a stem-and-leaf plot. For example, we can still tell that the youngest age at death was 46 and that exactly two presidents died when they were 90. A disadvantage of stem-and-leaf plots is that we do lose some information; for example, we know from the plot that a president died at age 88, but we do not know which one.

Following is a summary of how to construct a stem-and-leaf plot.

1. Find the high and low values of the data.
2. Decide on the stems.
3. List the stems in a column from least to greatest.
4. Use each piece of data to create leaves to the right of the stems on the appropriate rows.
5. If the plot is to be ordered, list the leaves in order from least to greatest.
6. Add a legend identifying the values represented by the stems and leaves. For example, 5 | 6 represents 56.
7. Add a title explaining what the graph is about.

The following student page, from *Addison-Wesley Mathematics,* Grade 7, 1993, shows another example of the construction of a stem-and-leaf plot. This plot uses hundreds as the stems and the tenths and hundredths digits as the leaves. An alternative way to do this is to use stems such as 37 with a leaf of 5 to represent 375 cents. Advantages and disadvantages of doing this are discussed in the Ongoing Assessment 9-1.

If two sets of related data with a similar number of data values are to be compared, a *back-to-back stem-and-leaf plot* can be used. In this case, two plots are made: one with leaves to the right, and one with leaves to the left. For example, if Abel gave the same test to two classes, he might prepare a back-to-back stem-and-leaf plot, as shown in Figure 9-7.

Figure 9-7

Abel's Test Class Scores

Second-period Class		Fifth-period Class
20	5	2
531	6	24
99987542	7	1257
875420	8	4456999
1	9	2457
	10	0

0 | 5 | represents a score of 50

| 5 | 2 represents a score of 52

I N V E S T I G A T I O N   9 - 1

● In the stem-and-leaf plots in Figure 9-7, which class do you think did better on the test? Why? ●

Stem and Leaf Plots

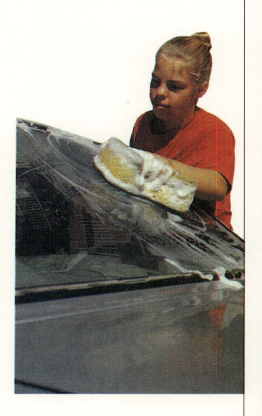

LEARN ABOUT IT

Data can often be organized in ways to make easy comparisons. One way to organize data is with a **stem and leaf plot.**

EXPLORE **Analyze the Data**

Twenty students with summer jobs were surveyed concerning how much they earned per hour. The data are: $3.75, $4.25, $3.90, $4.50, $4.50, $5.25, $4.75, $5.75, $6.10, $4.60, $4.85, $5.10, $5.15, $4.80, $4.70, $4.80, $5.10, $6.05, $4.25, $4.90

TALK ABOUT IT

1. Did any student earn less than $3 an hour?

2. What is the greatest salary?

3. Were most salaries in the $3, $4, $5, or $6 range?

Here's how to organize the data above using a stem and leaf plot.

	stem	leaf
Step 1: Set up the table.	3	75, 90
Step 2: Choose the stems.	4	25, 50, 50, 75, 60, 85, 80, 70, 80, 25, 90
Enter them in the table.	5	25, 75, 10, 15, 10
Step 3: Enter the leaves.	6	10, 5

SECTION 9-1 *Statistical Graphs* **479**

Example 9-1

Group the presidents in Table 9-1 into two groups, the first consisting of George Washington to Ulysses Grant and the second consisting of Rutherford Hayes to Richard Nixon.

a. Create back-to-back stem-and-leaf plots of the two groups and see if there appears to be a difference in ages at death between the two groups.
b. Which group of presidents seems to have lived longer?

Solution **a.** Because the ages at death vary from 46 to 90, the stems vary from 4 to 9. In Figure 9-8, the first 18 presidents are listed on the left and the remaining 18 on the right.

Figure 9-8

Ages of Presidents at Death

Early Presidents		Later Presidents

	4	96	
63	5	787	
364587	6	707034	
741983	7	0128	
053	8	18	
0	9	0	

3 | 8 | represents
83 years old

| 6 | 7 represents
67 years old

b. The early presidents seem, on average, to have lived longer because the ages at the high end, especially in the 70s and 80s, come more often from the early presidents. The ages at the lower end come more often from the later presidents. For the stems in the 50s and 60s, the numbers of leaves are about equal.

A stem-and-leaf plot shows how wide a range of values the data cover, where the values are concentrated, whether the data has any symmetry, where gaps in the data are, and whether any data points are decidedly different from the rest of the data.

Frequency Tables

frequency table

A slightly different way to display data is to use a frequency table. A **frequency table** shows how many times a certain piece of data occurs. For example, suppose Dan offers the following deal. He rolls a die. If any number other than 6 appears, he pays $5. If a 6 appears, you pay him $5. With a fair die, the probability of Dan's winning is $\frac{1}{6}$. Thus Dan will not win unless 6 appears considerably more often than could normally be expected. The data in Table 9-2 show the results of 60 rolls with Dan's die.

Table 9-2

Results of Dan's Die Tosses									
1	6	6	2	6	3	6	6	4	6
6	2	6	6	4	5	6	6	2	6
3	6	6	5	6	6	4	6	5	6
6	5	6	2	4	2	5	6	3	4
3	6	4	6	3	6	6	5	6	6
6	4	6	3	6	3	6	4	6	5

The results of Dan's die tosses may be summarized as shown in the frequency table in Table 9-3.

Table 9-3

Number	Tally	Frequency
1	I	1
2	ӀӀӀӀӀ	5
3	ӀӀӀӀӀ II	7
4	ӀӀӀӀӀ III	8
5	ӀӀӀӀӀ II	7
6	ӀӀӀӀӀ ӀӀӀӀӀ ӀӀӀӀӀ ӀӀӀӀӀ ӀӀӀӀӀ ӀӀӀӀӀ II	32
	Total	60

According to the frequency table, 6 appears many more times than could be expected from a fair die. (If the die were fair, the number of sixes should be closer to $\frac{1}{6} \cdot 60$, or 10.)

Histograms and Bar Graphs

histogram The data from Table 9-3 may be pictured graphically using a **histogram,** a graph that is closely related to a stem-and-leaf plot. Figure 9-9 shows a histogram of the frequencies in Table 9-3.

Figure 9-9

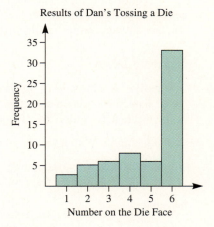

A histogram is made up of adjoining vertical rectangles, or bars. In this case, the numbers on the die are shown on the horizontal axis. The numbers along the vertical axis give the scale for the frequency. The frequencies of the numbers on the die are shown by the bars, which are all the same width. The higher the bar, the greater the frequency. The scale on the vertical axis must also be of uniform interval size. In addition, all histograms should have the axes labeled and should include a title identifying the graph's content.

Histograms can easily be made from single-sided stem-and-leaf plots. For example, if we take the stem-and-leaf plot in Figure 9-5(b) and enclose each row (set of leaves) in a bar, as in Figure 9-10, we have what looks like a histogram. We can make Figure 9-10 resemble Figure 9-9 by rotating the graph 90° counterclockwise. Histograms show gaps and clusters just as stem-and-leaf plots do. However, with a histogram we cannot retrieve data as we can in a stem-and-leaf plot. Another disadvantage of a histogram is that it is often necessary to estimate the heights of the bars.

Figure 9-10

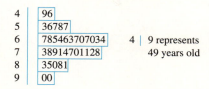

Ages of Presidents at Death

```
4 | 96
5 | 36787
6 | 785463707034          4 | 9 represents
7 | 38914701128               49 years old
8 | 35081
9 | 00
```

bar graph

A **bar graph** is like a histogram except that a bar graph has spaces between the bars. A typical bar graph showing the heights in centimeters of five students is given in Figure 9-11.

Figure 9-11

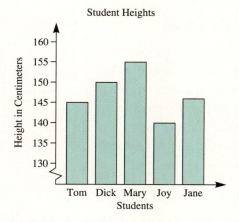

Student Heights

The break in the vertical axis, denoted by a squiggle, indicates that part of the scale has been omitted; therefore the scale is not accurate from 0 to 130. The height of each bar represents the height in centimeters of each student named on the horizontal axis. Each space between bars is usually one half the width of the bars.

double-bar graph

Double-bar graphs can be used to make comparisons in data. For example, the data in the back-to-back stem-and-leaf plot of Figure 9-8 can be pictured as shown in Figure 9-12. The dark-colored bars represent the later presidents, while the light-colored bars represent the earlier presidents.

Figure 9-12

Ages of Presidents at Death

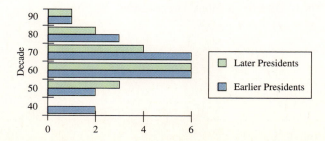

The following student page from *Addison-Wesley Mathematics,* Grade 6, 1993, shows a double-bar graph. Note that bar graphs can be drawn either vertically or horizontally.

Reading Graphs

LEARN ABOUT IT

EXPLORE Study the Data

Every week, Jose tries to improve his swimming times. This **double bar graph** shows his best times for two different weeks and three different events. The numbers along the bottom of the graph are called the **scale** of the graph.

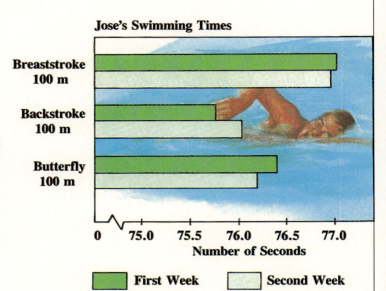

TALK ABOUT IT

1. Why do you think the graph above is called a double bar graph?
2. What numbers are missing along the scale? Why do you think they were left out?
3. What do the two bars for each event compare?

- A squiggle at the beginning of a scale means that part of the scale has been omitted.
- On most graphs you must estimate to find the approximate number represented by the bar or point on a graph.

The bar represents about 76.2 on the scale.

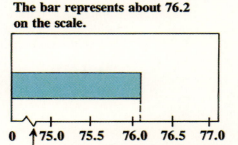

The graph in Figure 9-12 was constructed using a spreadsheet. For this particular graph, the data in Table 9-4 was defined based on the back-to-back stem-and-leaf plot and entered in the spreadsheet as in Figure 9-13.

Table 9-4

Decade of Death	Later Presidents	Earlier Presidents
40	2	0
50	2	3
60	6	6
70	6	4
80	3	2
90	1	1

Figure 9-13

	A	B	C
1	40	2	0
2	50	2	3
3	60	6	6
4	70	6	4
5	80	3	2
6	90	1	1

With some spreadsheets, like that used to construct Figure 9-13, we can alternatively use column A for one axis and plot the double-bar graph using columns B and C.

Use the data in Table 9-5 to construct two separate single-bar graphs of the number of live births in the mountain states for 1990 and 1991. Then construct a double-bar graph using a spreadsheet. Can you see any noticeable changes in the registered live births for the 2 yr?

Table 9-5 Live Births (Thousands) in the Mountain States in 1990 and 1991

State	1990	1991
Montana	11.6	10.0
Idaho	16.4	16.0
Wyoming	7.0	6.6
Colorado	53.5	49.0
New Mexico	27.4	22.6
Arizona	69.0	59.2
Utah	36.3	34.4
Nevada	21.6	18.6

Data was taken from *Statistical Abstract of the United States: 1994.* Washington, DC: U.S. Bureau of the Census, 1994, page 77.

Line Graphs and Frequency Polygons

line graph   Another graphical form used in presenting the data is a line graph. A **line graph** typically shows the trend of a variable over time. Time is usually marked on the horizontal axis with the variable being considered marked on the vertical axis. An example is seen in Figure 9-14, where Sanna's weight over 10 yr is depicted. Observe that consecutive data points are connected by line segments.

Figure 9-14

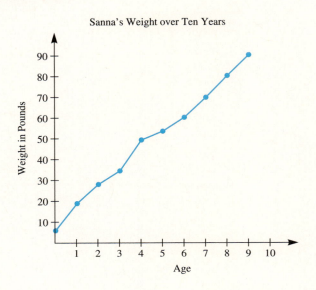

Line graphs are sometimes used to depict data from frequency tables, but such data may or may not involve time. A more appropriate type of graph for data from frequency tables is a frequency polygon that combines some aspects of line graphs with data that may

frequency polygon   or may not be depicted over time. A **frequency polygon** is formed by the line graph that connects the set of data points (x, y), where x is the midpoint of an interval and y is the frequency of the interval. The base of the frequency polygon is a portion of the horizontal axis. A frequency polygon is often constructed from a histogram. For example, in Figure 9-15 the results of Dan's tossing a die are depicted in a frequency polygon.

Figure 9-15

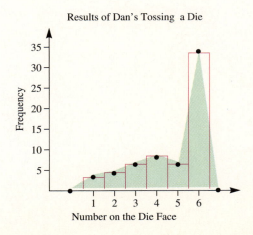

Frequency polygons are sometimes used for illustrative purposes without a histogram so as to make a graph seem less cluttered. A danger in doing this can be that the data are interpreted as continuous. For example, from Figure 9-15 we could assume there is a die face with a value of 1.5 when on a standard die this is untrue.

A frequency polygon is often used when geometric probability is used to compare an outcome to the entire set of outcomes. For example, the probability that Dan tosses a 3 or a 4 can be computed from the frequency table or estimated from the frequency polygon. That probability is approximately 15/60, or 25% of the time. (Geometric probabilities using frequency polygons are more typically used when data are continuous, not discrete, and when frequency tables may not be used to tabulate an entire set of data. The use of areas as percent of the whole is seen in Section 9.3 where we discuss normal curves.)

Grouped Data

The greater the amount of data, the more difficult it becomes to construct a frequency table for individual items. In such cases, the data may be grouped. For example, consider the scores in Table 9-6. A stem-and-leaf plot for this data is shown in Figure 9-16.

Table 9-6

50 Students' Scores									
52	56	25	56	68	73	66	64	56	100
20	39	9	50	98	54	54	40	50	96
36	44	18	97	109	65	21	60	44	54
92	49	37	94	72	88	89	35	59	34
48	32	15	53	84	72	88	16	52	60

Figure 9-16

```
Student Scores
 0 | 9
 1 | 856
 2 | 051
 3 | 692754
 4 | 84904
 5 | 266034460924
 6 | 856400
 7 | 232
 8 | 4898
 9 | 27486              10 | 9 represents
10 | 09                 a score of 109
```

The construction of the stem-and-leaf plot leads to a grouping of scores in intervals, or **classes**. For the data in Figure 9-16, the following classes are used: 0–9, 10–19, 20–29, 30–39, 40–49, 50–59, 60–69, 70–79, 80–89, 90–99, and 100–109. Each class has an interval size of 10; that is, 10 different scores can fall within the interval 0 through 9. (Students often incorrectly report the interval size as 9 because $9 - 0 = 9$.)

The **grouped frequency table** for the data in Table 9-16 with intervals of length 10 is given in Table 9-7. Figure 9-16 contains more information than does Table 9-7 because the raw scores themselves are not available in the table. Although Table 9-7 shows that 12 scores fall in the interval 50–59, it does not show the particular scores in the interval. The greater the size of the interval, the greater the amount of information lost. The choice of interval size may vary. Classes should be chosen to accommodate *all* the data, and each item should fit into only one class; that is, the classes should not overlap.

A bar graph or histogram can be used to display the data from a grouped frequency table. A bar graph of the data in Table 9-7 is shown in Figure 9-17(a). Rather than placing the intervals below the bars as in Figure 9-17, we could represent each interval by a single **class mark**   score known as a **class mark.** To find the class mark, we find the midpoint of each class; for example, $(0+9)/2 = 4.5$, $(10+19)/2 = 14.5$, and so on. Class marks are used in the graph in Figure 9-17(b).

Table 9-7

Classes	Tally	Frequency
0–9	I	1
10–19	III	3
20–29	III	3
30–39	JHT I	6
40–49	JHT	5
50–59	JHT JHT II	12
60–69	JHT I	6
70–79	III	3
80–89	IIII	4
90–99	JHT	5
100–109	II	2
	Total	50

Figure 9-17

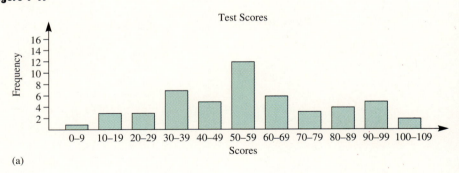

(a)

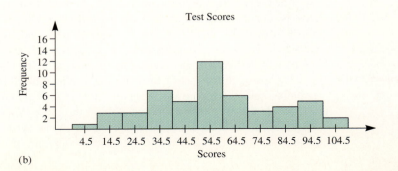

(b)

Circle Graphs (Pie Charts)

circle graph • pie chart

Another type of graph used to represent data is the circle graph. A **circle graph,** or **pie chart,** consists of a circular region partitioned into disjoint sections, with each section representing a part or percentage of the whole. A circle graph shows how parts are related to the whole. An example of a circle graph is given in Figure 9-18.

Figure 9-18

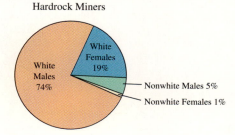

Hardrock Miners

White Females 19%
White Males 74%
Nonwhite Males 5%
Nonwhite Females 1%

Example 9-2 shows how a circle graph can be constructed from given data.

• • •

Example 9-2

Construct a circle graph for the information in Table 9-8, which is based on information taken from a U.S. Bureau of the Census Report, 1994.

Table 9-8

Age	Number of U.S. People (Nearest Million)
Under 5	20
5–19	54
20–29	39
30–44	62
45–65	48
Over 65	32
Total	255

Solution   The entire circle of 360° represents the total 255 million people. The area of each sector of the graph is proportional to the fraction or percent of the population the section represents. For example, the sector for the under-5 group is 20/255, or approximately 8% of the circle. Because the whole circle is 360°, then 8% of 360, which is approximately 29°, should be devoted to the under-5 group. Similarly, we can compute the number of degrees for each age group, as shown in Table 9-9. (What formulas could be used in a spreadsheet to create columns 3 and 4?)

Table 9-9

Age	Ratio	Approximate Percent	Approximate Degrees
Under 5	20/255	8	29
5–19	54/255	21	76
20–29	39/255	15	54
30–44	62/255	24	86
45–65	48/255	19	68
Over 65	32/255	13	47
Total	255/255	100	360

The percents and degrees in Table 9-9 are only approximate. A compass can be used to draw a circle and a protractor can be used to draw the sectors in the circle graph, as shown in Figure 9-19.

Figure 9-19

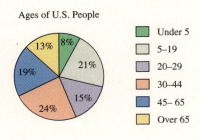

Ages of U.S. People

- Under 5
- 5–19
- 20–29
- 30–44
- 45–65
- Over 65

• • •

Ongoing Assessment 9-1

1. Make a pictograph to represent the data in the following table. Use ▯ to represent 10 glasses of lemonade sold.

Glasses of Lemonade Sold

Day	Tally	Frequency
Monday	ЖЖЖ	15
Tuesday	ЖЖЖЖ	20
Wednesday	ЖЖЖЖЖЖ	30
Thursday	Ж	5
Friday	ЖЖ	10

2. The following pictograph shows the approximate number of people who speak the six most common languages on Earth.
   a. About how many people speak Spanish?
   b. About how many people speak English?
   c. About how many more people speak Mandarin than Arabic?

Number of People Speaking the Six
Most Common Languages

Arabic	● ◗
English	● ● ● ◖
Hindi	● ● ◗
Mandarin	● ● ● ● ● ◖
Russian	● ● ◖
Spanish	● ● ◗

Each ● represents 100 million people.

3. Following are the ages of the 30 students from Washington School who participated in the city track meet. Draw a line plot to represent these data.

10	10	11	10	13	8	10	13	14	9
14	13	10	14	11	9	13	10	11	12
11	12	14	13	12	8	13	14	9	14

4. The following stem-and-leaf plot gives the weight in pounds of all 15 students in the Algebra 1 class at East Junior High:
   a. Write the weights of the 15 students.
   b. What is the weight of the lightest student in the class?
   c. What is the weight of the heaviest student in the class?

**Weights of Students in East Junior
High Algebra 1 Class**

```
 7 | 24
 8 | 112578
 9 | 2478
10 | 3          10 | 3 represents
11 |               103 lb
12 | 35
```

5. Draw a histogram based on the stem-and-leaf plot in Problem 4.
6. Toss a coin 30 times.
   a. Construct a line plot for the data.
   b. Draw a histogram for the data.
7. The following figure shows a bar graph of the rainfall in centimeters during the last school year.

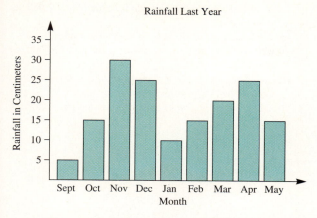

Rainfall Last Year

a. Which month had the most rainfall, and how much did it have?

b. How much total rain fell in October, December, and January?

8. HKM Company employs 40 people of the following ages:

34	58	21	63	48	52	24	52	37	23
23	34	45	46	23	26	21	18	41	27
23	45	32	63	20	19	21	23	54	62
41	32	26	41	25	18	23	34	29	26

a. Draw a stem-and-leaf plot for the data.

b. Are more employees in their 40s or in their 50s?

c. How many employees are less than 30 years old?

d. What percent of the people are 50 years or older?

9. Given the following bar graph, estimate the length of the following rivers:

a. Mississippi

b. Columbia

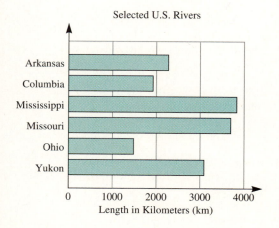

Selected U.S. Rivers

10. Draw a bar graph to represent the data in the following table:

Distances from the Sun

Planet	Distance (Millions of Miles)
Earth	93
Mars	142
Mercury	36
Venus	67

11. The following table shows the total car sales for Johnson's car lot from January through June. Draw a bar graph for the data.

Month	Jan.	Feb.	Mar.	Apr.	May	June
Number of Cars Sold	90	86	92	96	90	100

12. Five coins are tossed 64 times. A distribution for the number of heads obtained is shown in the following table. Draw a histogram for the data.

Number of Heads	0	1	2	3	4	5
Frequency	2	10	20	20	10	2

13. The following table shows the grade distribution for the final examination in the mathematics course for elementary teachers:

Grade	Frequency
A	4
B	10
C	37
D	8
F	1

a. Draw a bar graph of the data.

b. Draw a circle graph of the data.

14. The following are the amounts (to the nearest dollar) paid by 25 students for textbooks during the fall term:

35	42	37	60	50
42	50	16	58	39
33	39	23	53	51
48	41	49	62	40
45	37	62	30	23

a. Draw an ordered stem-and-leaf plot to illustrate the data.

b. Construct a grouped frequency table for the data, starting the first class at $15.00 with intervals of $5.00 each.

c. Draw a histogram of the data.

d. Draw a frequency polygon of the data.

e. Explain whether a frequency polygon is an appropriate graph to use here.

15. The following horizontal bar graph gives the top speeds of several animals:

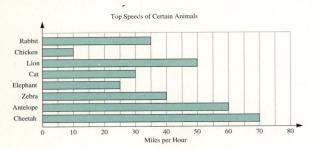

Top Speeds of Certain Animals

a. Which is the slowest animal shown?

b. How fast can a chicken run?

c. Which animal can run twice as fast as a rabbit?

d. Can a lion outrun a zebra?

16. The following bar graph shows the life expectancies for men and women:

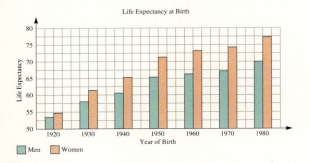

Life Expectancy at Birth

a. Whose life expectancy has changed the most since 1920?

b. In 1920, about how much longer was a woman expected to live than a man?

c. In 1980, about how much longer was a woman expected to live than a man?

17. The following graph shows how the value of a car depreciates each year. This graph allows us to find the trade-in value of a car for each of 5 yr. The percents given in the graph are based on the selling price of the new car.

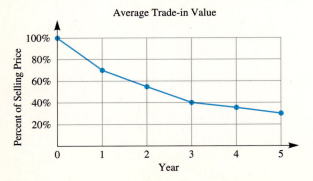

Average Trade-in Value

a. What is the approximate trade-in value of a $12,000 car after 1 yr?

b. How much has a $20,000 car depreciated after 5 yr?

c. What is the approximate trade-in value of a $20,000 car after 4 yr?

d. Dani wants to trade in her car before it loses half its value. When should she do this?

18. Use the following circle graph to answer the following questions:

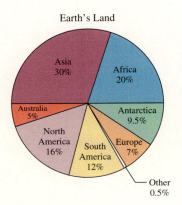

Earth's Land

a. Which is the largest continent?

b. Which continent is about twice the size of Antarctica?

c. How does Africa compare in size to Asia?

d. Which two continents make up about half of Earth's surface?

e. What is the ratio of the size of Australia to North America?

f. If Europe has approximately 4.1 million mi^2 of land, what is the total area of the land on Earth?

19. A list of presidents, with the number of children for each, follows:

1. Washington, 0	**2.** J. Adams, 5
3. Jefferson, 6	**4.** Madison, 0
5. Monroe, 2	**6.** J. Q. Adams, 4
7. Jackson, 0	**8.** Van Buren, 4
9. W. H. Harrison, 10	**10.** Tyler, 14
11. Polk, 0	**12.** Taylor, 6
13. Fillmore, 2	**14.** Pierce, 3
15. Buchanan, 0	**16.** Lincoln, 4
17. A. Johnson, 5	**18.** Grant, 4
19. Hayes, 8	**20.** Garfield, 7
21. Arthur, 3	**22.** Cleveland, 5
23. B. Harrison, 3	**24.** McKinley, 2
25. T. Roosevelt, 6	**26.** Taft, 3
27. Wilson, 3	**28.** Harding, 0
29. Coolidge, 2	**30.** Hoover, 2
31. F. D. Roosevelt, 6	**32.** Truman, 1
33. Eisenhower, 2	**34.** Kennedy, 3
35. L. B. Johnson, 2	**36.** Nixon, 2

37. Ford, 4   **38.** Carter, 3
39. Reagan, 4   **40.** Bush, 5
41. Clinton, 1

   a. Construct a line plot for these data.
   b. Make a frequency table for these data.
   c. What is the most frequent number of children?
20. The following table depicts the number of deaths from Acquired Immunodeficiency Syndrome (AIDS) by age in 1985 and 1992:

Age	1985	1992
Under 5	96	192
5–12	10	36
13–29	1329	3809
30–39	3013	10265
40–49	1396	5855
50–59	590	1760
60 and over	248	758

   a. Are the data appropriate for constructing a back-to-back stem-and-leaf plot for display?
   b. Are any patterns of difference evident in the comparison of the two groups of data?

Communication

21. Discuss an example of when a circle graph would be preferable to a bar graph or a line graph.
22. Discuss an example of when a line graph would be preferable to a bar graph.
23. Discuss an example of a set of data for which a stem-and-leaf plot is more informative than a histogram.
24. The following graphs give the temperatures for a certain day. Which graph is more helpful for guessing the actual temperature at 10:00 A.M.? Why?

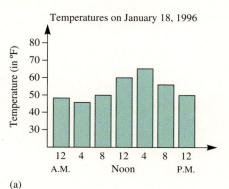

(a)

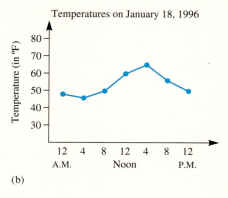

(b)

Open-ended

25. Find six recent examples of uses of different types of visual representations of data in your newspaper. Explain whether you think the representations are appropriate.
26. The federal budget is typically depicted with one type of visual representation. Which one is used and why?
27. Tell whether it would be more appropriate to use a bar graph or a line graph for each of the following. Then draw the appropriate graph in each case.

   a. U.S. Population   **b.** Continents of the World

Year	Population
1920	105,710,620
1930	122,775,046
1940	131,669,275
1950	150,697,361
1960	179,323,175
1970	203,302,031
1980	226,545,805

Continent	Area in Square Miles (mi²)
Africa	11,694,000
Antarctica	5,100,000
Asia	16,968,000
Australia	2,966,000
Europe	4,066,000
North America	9,363,000
South America	6,886,000

Cooperative Learning

28. For each of the following topics, collect information to be shared with the class on availability, cost, appropriateness for what grade levels, and so on.
   a. Computer statistical packages on campus
   b. Computer statistical packages in local stores
29. In groups, collect data on head circumference of class members in centimeters. Make a frequency table of all class data, choose an appropriate graph, and display the data. If you were a seller of hats, what is the most common size head for which you would purchase hats?

Many spreadsheets, statistical packages, and graphing calculators will produce a variety of graphs from 1 set of data. Examine any available technology you have and use the data in Example 9-2 to see what graphs you can construct. Figure 9-20 is a three-dimensional bar graph representation of the data in Table 9-9 constructed using a computer spreadsheet.

Figure 9-20

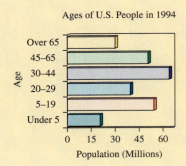

Ages of U.S. People in 1994

Section 9-2 Measures of Central Tendency and Variation

The media present us with a variety of data and statistics. For example, we find in the *World Almanac* that the average person's lifetime includes 6 yr of eating, 4 yr of cleaning, 2 yr of trying to return telephone calls to people who never seem to be in, 6 mo waiting at stop lights, 1 yr looking for misplaced objects, and 8 mo opening junk mail. In the previous section, we examined data by looking at graphs to display the overall distribution of values. In this section, we describe specific aspects of data by using a few carefully chosen numbers. Two important aspects of data are its *center* and its *spread*. The mean, median, and mode are **measures of central tendency** that describe where data are centered. Each of these measures is a single number that describes the data. However, each does it slightly differently. The *range, variance,* and *standard deviation* introduced later in this section describe the spread of data.

measures of central tendency

A word that is often used in statistics is *average*. Most of the time, average means *typical*. To explore more about averages, examine the following set of data for three teachers, each of whom claims that his or her class scored better *on the average* than the other two classes did:

Mr. Smith: 62, 94, 95, 98, 98

Mr. Jones: 62, 62, 98, 99, 100

Ms. Rivera: 40, 62, 85, 99, 99

All of these teachers are correct in their assertions because each has used a different number to characterize the scores in his or her class. In the following, we examine how each teacher can justify the claim.

Computing Means

arithmetic mean
average • mean

The number commonly used to characterize a set of data is the **arithmetic mean,** frequently called the **average,** or the **mean.** To find the mean of scores for each of the teachers given previously, we find the sum of the scores in each case and divide by 5, the number of scores.

$$\text{Mean (Smith):} \quad \frac{62 + 94 + 95 + 98 + 98}{5} = \frac{447}{5} = 89.4$$

$$\text{Mean (Jones):} \quad \frac{62 + 62 + 98 + 99 + 100}{5} = \frac{421}{5} = 84.2$$

$$\text{Mean (Rivera):} \quad \frac{40 + 62 + 85 + 99 + 99}{5} = \frac{385}{5} = 77$$

In terms of the mean, Mr. Smith's class scored better than the others. In general, we define the *arithmetic mean* as follows.

Definition of Mean

The **arithmetic mean** of the numbers $x_1, x_2, \ldots, x_n$, denoted by $\bar{x}$ and read "x bar," is given by

$$\bar{x} = \frac{x_1 + x_2 + x_3 + \cdots + x_n}{n}.$$

Understanding the Mean as a Balance Point

Because the mean is the most widely used measure of central tendency, we provide a model for thinking about it. Suppose a student at a rural school reports that the mean number of pets for the six students in a group is 5. Do we know anything about the distribution of these pets? One way to have a mean of 5 is that all six students have exactly five pets, as shown in the line plot in Figure 9-21(a). In this graph, all the pets are centered at the mean of 5.

Figure 9-21

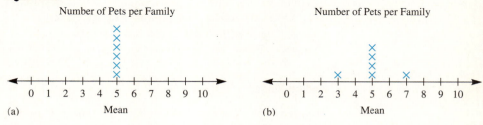

(a)   Mean   (b)   Mean

If we change the line plot as shown in Figure 9-21(b), the mean is still 5. Notice that the new line plot could be obtained by moving one value from Figure 9-21(a) 2 units to the right and then balancing this by moving one value 2 units to the left. We can think of the mean as a *balance point,* where the total distance on one side of the mean (fulcrum) is the same as the total distance on the other side.

Consider Figure 9-22, which shows the number of children for each family in a group. The mean of 5 is the balance point where the sum of the total distances above the mean equals the sum of the total distances below the mean. The sum of the distances below the mean is $1 + 2 + 2 + 3$, or 8. The sum of the distances above the mean is $3 + 5$, or 8. In this case, we see that the data are centered about the mean, but the mean does not belong to the set of data.

Figure 9-22

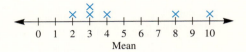

Number of Children per Family

Mean

Computing Medians

median   The value exactly in the middle of an ordered set of numbers is the **median.** To find the median for the teachers' scores, we arrange each of their scores in increasing order and pick the middle score. Intuitively, we know that half the scores are greater than the median and half are less.

Median (Smith) :   62, 94, (95,) 98, 98   median = 95

Median (Jones) :   62, 62, (98,) 99, 100   median = 98

Median (Rivera):   40, 62, (85,) 99, 99   median = 85

In terms of the median, Mr. Jones's class scored better than the others.

With an odd number of scores, as in the present example, the median is the middle score. With an even number of scores, however, the median is defined as the mean of the middle two scores. Thus to find the median, we add the middle two scores and divide by 2. For example, the median of the scores

64, 68, $\boxed{70, 74}$ 82, 90

is given by

$$\frac{70 + 74}{2}, \text{ or } 72.$$

In general, to find the median for a set of n numbers, proceed as follows.

> **1.** Arrange the numbers in order from least to greatest.
> **2. a.** If n is odd, the median is the middle number.
>   **b.** If n is even, the median is the mean of the two middle numbers.

Finding Modes

mode   The **mode** of a set of data is the number that appears most frequently, if there is one. In some distributions, no number appears more than once. In other distributions, there may be more than one mode. For example, the set of scores 64, 79, 80, 82, 90 has no mode. (Some would say that this set of data has five modes, but because no one score appears more than another, we prefer to say there is no mode.)

bimodal   The set of scores 64, 75, 75, 82, 90, 90, 98 is **bimodal** (two modes) because both 75 and 90 are modes. It is possible for a set of data to have too many modes for this type of number to be useful in describing the data.

For the three classes listed previously, if the mode is used as the criterion, Ms. Rivera's class scored better than the others.

Mode (Smith): 62, 94, 95, 98, 98   mode = 98
Mode (Jones): 62, 62, 98, 99, 100   mode = 62
Mode (Rivera): 40, 62, 85, 99, 99   mode = 99

Example 9-3 Find (a) the mean, (b) the median, and (c) the mode for the following collection of data:

$$60 \quad 60 \quad 70 \quad 95 \quad 95 \quad 100$$

Solution a. $\bar{x} = \dfrac{60 + 60 + 70 + 95 + 95 + 100}{6} = \dfrac{480}{6} = 80$

b. The median is $\dfrac{70 + 95}{2}$, or 82.5.

c. The set of data is bimodal and has both 60 and 95 as modes.

Example 9-4 When the data values are all the same, the mean, median, and mode are all the same. Describe a situation in which not all the data points are the same and the mean, median, and mode are still the same.

Solution Answers may vary. For example, one set of data is 92, 94, 94, 94, 96, in which the mean, median, and mode are all 94.

Choosing the Most Appropriate Average

Although the *mean* is the number most commonly used to describe a set of data, it may not always be the most appropriate choice.

Example 9-5 Suppose a company employs 20 people. The president of the company earns $200,000, the vice president earns $75,000, and 18 employees earn $10,000 each. Is the mean the best number to choose to represent the "average" salary for the company?

Solution The mean salary for this company is

$$\frac{\$200{,}000 + \$75{,}000 + 18(\$10{,}000)}{20} = \frac{\$455{,}000}{20} = \$22{,}750.$$

In this case, the mean salary of $22,750 is not representative. Either the median or mode, both of which are $10,000, would better describe the typical salary. Notice that *the mean is affected by extreme values.*

In most cases, the *median* is not affected by extreme values. The median, however, can also be misleading, as shown in the following example.

Example 9-6 Suppose nine students make the following scores on a test:

$$30, 35, 40, 40, 92, 92, 93, 98, 99$$

Is the median the best "average" to represent the set of scores?

Solution   The median score is 92. From that score, one might infer that the individuals all scored very well, yet 92 is certainly not a typical score. In this case, the mean of approximately 69 might be more appropriate than the mode. However, with the spread of the scores, neither is very appropriate for this distribution.

• • •

The *mode,* too, can be misleading in describing a set of data with very few items for many frequently occurring items, as shown in the following example.

• • •

Example 9-7   Is the mode an appropriate "average" for the following test scores?

$$40, 42, 50, 62, 63, 65, 98, 98$$

Solution   The mode of the set of scores is 98 because this score occurs most frequently. The score of 98 is not representative of the set of data because of the large spread of scores.

• • •

The choice of which number to use to represent a particular set of data is not always easy. In the example involving the three teachers, each teacher chose the number that best suited his or her claim. The type of number used should always be specified.

Problem 1

Students of Dr. Van Horn were asked to keep track of their own grades. One day, Dr. Van Horn asked the students to report their grades. One student had lost the papers but claims to remember the grades on four of six assignments: 100, 82, 74, and 60. In addition, the student remembered that the mean of all six papers was 69, and the other two papers had identical grades. What were the grades on the other two homework papers?

Understanding the Problem.   The student had scores of 100, 82, 74, and 60 on four of six papers. The mean of all six papers was 69, and two identical scores were missing. The missing scores must be less than 60; otherwise, from observation, the mean could not be less than three of the four known scores and greater than the fourth one given.

 Devising a Plan.   To find the missing grades, we use the strategy of *writing an equation* for x. The mean is obtained by finding the sum of the scores and then dividing by the number of scores, which is 6. So if we let x stand for each of the two missing grades, we have

$$69 = \frac{100 + 82 + 74 + 60 + x + x}{6}.$$

Carrying Out the Plan.   We now solve the equation as follows:

$$69 = \frac{100 + 82 + 74 + 60 + x + x}{6}$$

$$69 = \frac{316 + 2x}{6}$$

$$49 = x$$

Since the solution to the equation is $x = 49$, each of the two missing scores was 49.

Looking Back. The answer of 49 seems reasonable, since the mean of 69 is less than three of the four given scores. We can check this by computing the mean of the scores 100, 82, 74, 60, 49, 49 and showing that it is 69.

• • •

Measures of Dispersion

The mean, median, and mode provide information about where the central portion of a distribution is located, but they provide limited information about the whole distribution. If you sit in the sauna for 30 min and then in a freezer for 30 min, the average temperature of your surroundings for this hour might sound comfortable. In this case, we need at least one more statistic to better understand the data. We need a *measure of dispersion* or *spread* to tell how much the data are "scattered." The need for a measure of spread is shown in the following discussion.

Suppose Professors Abel and Babel each taught a section of a graduate statistics course and each had six students. Both professors gave the same final exam. The results, along with the means for each group of scores, are given in Table 9-10, with stem-and-leaf plots in Figure 9-23(a) and (b), respectively. As the stem-and-leaf plots show, the sets of data are very different. The first is more spread out, or varies more, than the second. However, each set has 60 as the mean. Each median also equals 60. Although the mean and the median for these two groups are the same, the two distributions of scores are very different.

Table 9-10

Abel's Class Scores	Babel's Class Scores
100	70
80	70
70	60
50	60
50	60
10	40
$\bar{x} = \dfrac{360}{6} = 60$	$\bar{x} = \dfrac{360}{6} = 60$

Figure 9-23

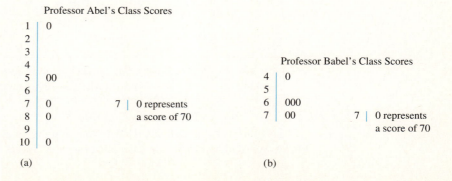

Professor Abel's Class Scores

```
 1 | 0
 2 |
 3 |
 4 |
 5 | 00
 6 |
 7 | 0            7 |  0 represents
 8 | 0                  a score of 70
 9 |
10 | 0
```

(a)

Professor Babel's Class Scores

```
4 | 0
5 |
6 | 000
7 | 00              7 |  0 represents
                         a score of 70
```

(b)

range

There are several ways to measure the spread of data. The simplest way is to subtract the least data value from the greatest data value. This difference is the **range.** The range for Professor Abel's class is 100 − 10, or 90. The range for Professor Babel's class is 70 − 40, or 30. Although the range is easy to calculate, it has the disadvantage of being determined by two scores. For example, the sets of scores 10, 20, 25, 30, 100 and 10, 80, 85, 90, 90, 100 both have a range of 90.

Variance and Standard Deviation

variance
standard deviation

The two most commonly used measures of dispersion are the **variance** and the **standard deviation.** These measures are based on how far the scores are from the mean. To find out how far each value differs from the mean, we subtract each value in the data from the mean to obtain the deviation. Some of these deviations may be positive, and others may be negative. Because the mean is the balance point, the total of the deviations above the mean equals the total of the deviations below the mean. (The mean of the deviations is 0 because the sum of the deviations is 0.) Squaring the deviations makes them all positive. The mean of the squared deviations is the *variance.* Because the variance involves squaring the deviations, it does not have the same units of measurement as the original observations. For example, lengths measured in feet have a variance measured in square feet. To obtain the same units as the original observations, we take the square root of the variance and obtain the *standard deviation.*

The steps involved in calculating the variance v and standard deviation s of n numbers are as follows.

1. Find the mean of the numbers.
2. Subtract the mean from each number.
3. Square each difference found in step 2.
4. Find the sum of the squares in step 3.
5. Divide by n to obtain the variance, v.
6. Find the square root of v to obtain the standard deviation, s.

These six steps can be summarized for the numbers $x_1, x_2, x_3, \ldots, x_n$ as follows, where $\bar{x}$ is the mean of these numbers:

$$s = \sqrt{v} = \sqrt{\frac{(x_1 - \bar{x})^2 + (x_2 - \bar{x})^2 + (x_3 - \bar{x})^2 + \cdots + (x_n - \bar{x})^2}{n}}$$

REMARK In some textbooks, this formula involves division by $n - 1$ instead of by n. Division by $n - 1$ is more useful for advanced work in statistics.

The variances and standard deviations for the final exam data from the classes of Professors Abel and Babel are calculated by using Tables 9-11 and 9-12, respectively.

Table 9-11 Abel's Scores

x	$x - \bar{x}$	$(x - \bar{x})^2$
100	40	1600
80	20	400
70	10	100
50	⁻10	100
50	⁻10	100
10	⁻50	2500
Totals 360	0	4800

$$\bar{x} = \frac{360}{6} = 60$$

$$v = \frac{4800}{6} = 800$$

$$s = \sqrt{800} \doteq 28.3$$

Table 9-12 Babel's Scores

x	$x - \bar{x}$	$(x - \bar{x})^2$
70	10	100
70	10	100
60	0	0
60	0	0
60	0	0
40	-20	400
Totals 360	0	600

$$\bar{x} = \frac{360}{6} = 60$$

$$v = \frac{600}{6} = 100$$

$$s = \sqrt{100} = 10$$

Values far from the mean on either side will have larger positive squared deviations, whereas values close to the mean will have smaller positive squared deviations. Therefore the standard deviation is a larger number when the values from a set of data are widely spread and a smaller number (close to 0) when the data values are close together. This is further illustrated in Example 9-8.

• • •

Example 9-8

Professor Boone gave two group exams. Exam A had grades of 0, 0, 0, 100, 100, 100, and exam B had grades of 50, 50, 50, 50, 50, 50. Find the following for each exam:

a. Mean   **b.** Median   **c.** Standard deviation

Solution   **a.** The means for exams A and B are each 50.
   b. The medians for the exams are each 50.
   c. The standard deviations for exams A and B are as follows:

$$s_A = \sqrt{\frac{3(0 - 50)^2 + 3(100 - 50)^2}{6}} = 50$$

$$s_B = \sqrt{\frac{6(50 - 50)^2}{6}} = 0$$

• • •

Box Plots

box plot

Line plots or stem-and-leaf plots become unwieldy when a large amount of data is involved. A **box plot,** or a *box-and-whisker plot,* is a display that is especially useful for handling many data values. When there is only one variable, box plots make it easy to see patterns of the data. When two or more variables are present, box plots allow us to explore the data and draw informal conclusions. Box plots show only certain statistics rather than all the data. A box plot is a visual representation of what is called the *five-number summary.* This summary consists of the median, the quartiles, and the least and greatest values in the distribution. The center, the spread, and the overall range of distribution are immediately evident by looking at a box plot.

To construct a box plot, we must find the *lower quartile* and the *upper quartile* of a given set of data. If scores are arranged from least to greatest, the lower quartile, the median, and the upper quartile divide the data into four groups that are approximately the same size. Consider the following set of test scores:

$$20 \quad 25 \quad 40 \quad 50 \quad 50 \quad 60 \quad 70 \quad 75 \quad 80 \quad 80 \quad 90 \quad 100 \quad 100$$

We first find the median, which is 70, and draw a line segment through it:

$$20 \quad 25 \quad 40 \quad 50 \quad 50 \quad 60 \quad 7|0 \quad 75 \quad 80 \quad 80 \quad 90 \quad 100 \quad 100$$

Next, we consider only the data values to the left of the segment and draw a line segment where the median of those values is located:

$$20 \quad 25 \quad 40 \quad | \quad 50 \quad 50 \quad 60$$

lower quartile
first quartile (Q_1)
upper quartile (Q_3)

The score of $45 = (40 + 50)/2$ is the median of the scores less than the median of all scores and therefore is the **lower quartile.** The lower quartile is often called the **first quartile** and is denoted by Q_1. Similarly, we can find the upper (or third) quartile (Q_3), which is $(80 + 90)/2$, or 85. The **upper quartile (Q_3)** is the median of the scores greater than the median of all scores. Thus we have divided the scores into four groups of three scores each:

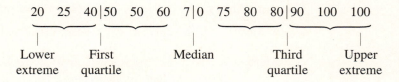

interquartile range (IQR)

The **interquartile range (IQR)** is the difference between the upper quartile and the lower quartile. In this case, IQR $= 85 - 45 = 40$. The IQR is itself another useful measure of variation because it is less influenced by extreme values. The IQR contains the middle 50% of the values.

Next we draw short horizontal segments at the median and the two quartiles, and we connect them to form a *box.* We then draw segments from each end of the box to the extreme values. These segments are *whiskers.* The result is the upright box plot shown on the right-hand side of Figure 9-24. Similarly, a box plot can be drawn lengthwise by using a horizontal scale.

Figure 9-24

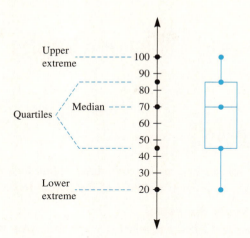

The box plot gives a fairly clear picture of the spread of the data. If we look at the graph in Figure 9-24, we can see that the median is 70, the maximum value is 100, the minimum value is 20, and the upper and lower quartiles are 45 and 85.

In the box plot in Figure 9-24, the median is above the center of the box and so there are more scores above than below it. Another example of the construction of a box plot is given on the following student page from *Addison-Wesley Mathematics,* Grade 8, 1993.

Example 9-9   What are the minimum and maximum values, the median, and the lower and upper quartiles of the box plot shown in Figure 9-25?

Figure 9-25

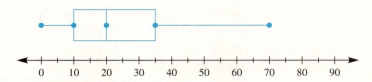

Solution   The minimum value is 0, the maximum value is 70, the median is 20, the lower quartile is 10, and the upper quartile is 35.

Outliers

An *outlier* is a value that is widely separated from the rest of a group of data. For example, in a set of scores such as

$$91 \quad 92 \quad 92 \quad 93 \quad 93 \quad 93 \quad 94$$

Box and Whisker Graphs

LEARN ABOUT IT

Graphic images help us interpret data. A **box and whisker graph** is one way to provide a picture of the central tendency of data.

EXPLORE Study the Table

You can draw a box and whisker graph to display the data given in the stem and leaf plot at the right.

TALK ABOUT IT

1. How many items of data are listed in the stem and leaf plot?

2. List the data in order. Which item has the highest value? Which item has the lowest value?

3. What is the median of the data?

stem	leaf
18	5
16	8
12	8, 3
8	7, 3, 1
6	4, 4
4	8
3	6, 3

To complete a box and whisker graph of the above data follow the steps below.

- Find the median of the upper half of the data and label it Q_U to represent the **upper quartile.**
- Find the median of the lower half of the data and label it Q_L to represent the **lower quartile.**
- Mark an appropriate vertical scale and draw a box that connects the upper quartile to the lower quartile. A line across the box indicates the median. Label the median "MD." For this data, MD = 82.
- Draw lines, "whiskers," from the box to the **highest** (H) and **lowest** (L) data items.

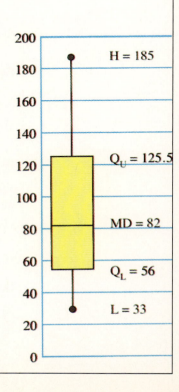

TRY IT OUT

Draw a box and whisker graph for each of these sets of data.

1. 12, 23, 24, 24, 28, 37, 49, 51, 53, 54, 54, 63, 65, 67, 92, 98

2. 23, 45, 46, 46, 49, 25, 72, 48, 63, 18, 29, 53

all data are grouped close together and no values are widely separated. However, in a set of scores such as

$$21 \quad 92 \quad 92 \quad 93 \quad 93 \quad 93 \quad 95 \quad 150$$

both 21 and 150 are widely separated from the rest of the data. These values are potential outliers. The upper and lower extreme values are not necessarily outliers. In data such as

$$75 \quad 90 \quad 91 \quad 92 \quad 92 \quad 93 \quad 93$$

outlier
    it is not easy to decide, so we develop a convention for determining outliers. *An **outlier** is any value that is more than 1.5 times the interquartile range above the upper quartile or below the lower quartile.* Statisticians sometimes use values different from 1.5 to determine outliers.

    It is common practice to indicate outliers with asterisks. Whiskers are then drawn to the extreme points that are not *outliers.* To investigate how this works, consider Example 9-10.

Example 9-10

Draw a box plot of the data in Table 9-13 and show any outliers.

Table 9-13   Final Medal Standings for Top 20 Countries — 1992 Olympics

Unified Team	112
United States	108
Germany	82
China	54
Cuba	31
Hungary	30
South Korea	29
France	29
Australia	27
Spain	22
Japan	22
Britain	20
Italy	19
Poland	19
Canada	18
Romania	18
Bulgaria	16
Netherlands	15
Sweden	12
New Zealand	10

$Q_3 = 30.5$ (between Cuba 31 and Hungary 30)

Median $(Q_2) = 22$ (between Spain 22 and Japan 22)

$Q_1 = 18$ (between Canada 18 and Romania 18)

Solution   The extreme scores are 112 and 10, the median is 22, and the quartiles are 18 and 30.5, with IQR = 12.5. Outliers are scores that are greater than 30.5 + 1.5(12.5), or 49.25, or less than 18 − 1.5(12.5), or ⁻0.75. Therefore, in this data set there are four outliers: 54, 82, 108, and 112. A box plot is given in Figure 9-26. Notice that the whisker stops at the extreme point, 10, on the lower end and at 31 on the upper end. The score of 31 is the greatest score that is not an outlier. The outliers are indicated by asterisks.

Figure 9-26

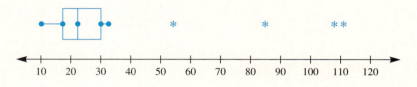

Comparing Sets of Data

Box plots are used primarily for large sets of data or for comparing several distributions. The stem-and-leaf plot is usually a much clearer display for a single distribution. Several box plots drawn below the same number line give us the easiest comparison of medians, extreme scores, and the quartiles for the sets of data. As an example, we construct box plots comparing the data in Table 9-14.

Table 9-14   Median Earnings of Males and Females, 1960–1992
(Full-time Workers Age 15 and Over)

Year	Women	Men
1960	$ 3,257	$ 5,368
1970	5,323	8,966
1980	11,197	18,612
1983	13,915	21,881
1984	14,780	23,218
1985	15,624	24,195
1986	16,232	25,256
1987	16,911	25,946
1988	17,606	26,656
1989	18,769	27,331
1990	19,822	27,678
1991	20,553	29,421
1992	21,440	30,358

Data taken from *Information Please Almanac Atlas and Yearbook 1995*, 48th Edition. Boston: Houghton Mifflin Company, 1995.

Before constructing horizontal box plots, we find the five important values for each group of data. These values are given in Table 9-15.

Table 9-15

Value	Women	Men
Maximum	$21,440.00	$30,358.00
Upper quartile	19,295.50	27,504.50
Median	16,232.00	25,256.00
Lower quartile	12,556.00	20,246.50
Minimum	3,257.00	5,368.00

In this example, the IQR for men is $7,258.00. The lower cutoff point for outliers is $20,246.50 − 1.5(7,258.00)$, or $9,359.50. There are two salaries, $5,368.00 and $8,966.00, less than the cutoff point and thus are outliers. Checking reveals there are no outliers in the women's salaries.

Next we draw the horizontal scale and construct the box plots for the women and men using the data in Table 9-15 as shown in Figure 9-27.

Figure 9-27

Salary (Thousands)

From Figure 9-27, we can see that the length of the box (IQR) for men is longer than the box (IQR) for women. This implies that the salaries for men have varied more over time than have those of women. The salaries for men have been higher than those for women, since the extreme values, median, and quartiles for the men are greater than those for women. Also, approximately 60% of the median salaries for men are greater than those for the median of all women over the time period.

INVESTIGATION   9 - 2

● Using only the data from 1983–1992 in Table 9-14, decide whether there are any outliers. How do you think the two box plots would compare for this data versus the comparison made in Figure 9-27? ●

Using Box Plots

Although we cannot spot clusters or gaps in box plots as we can with stem-and-leaf or line plots, we can more easily compare data from different sets. With box plots, we do not need to have sets of data that are approximately the same size, as we did for stem-and-leaf plots. To compare data from two or more sets using their box plots, we first study the boxes to see if they are located in approximately the same places. Next, we consider the lengths of the boxes to see if the variability of the data is about the same. We also check whether the median, the quartiles, and the extreme values in one set are greater than those in another set. If they are, the data in the first set are greater than those of the other set, no matter how we compare them. If they are not, we can continue to study the data for other similarities and differences.

BRAIN TEASER The speeds of racing cars were timed after 3 mi, $4\frac{1}{2}$ mi, and 6 mi. One driver averaged 140 mph for the first 3 mi, 168 mph for the next $1\frac{1}{2}$ mi, and 210 mph for the last $1\frac{1}{2}$ mi. What was the driver's mean speed for the total 6-mi run?

Ongoing Assessment 9-2

1. Calculate the mean, the median, and the mode for each of the following data sets:
   a. 2, 8, 7, 8, 5, 8, 10, 5
   b. 10, 12, 12, 14, 20, 16, 12, 14, 11
   c. 18, 22, 22, 17, 30, 18, 12
   d. 82, 80, 63, 75, 92, 80, 92, 90, 80, 80
   e. 5, 5, 5, 5, 5, 10

2. a. If each of six students scored 80 on a test, find each of the following for the set of six scores:
   i. Mean
   ii. Median
   iii. Mode
   b. Make up another set of six scores that are not all the same but in which the mean, median, and mode are all 80.

3. The mean score on a set of 20 tests is 75. What is the sum of the 20 test scores?

4. The tram at a ski area has a capacity of 50 people with a load limit of 7500 lb. What is the mean weight of the passengers if the tram is loaded to capacity?

5. The mean for a set of 28 scores is 80. Suppose two more students take the test and score 60 and 50. What is the new mean?

6. The names and ages for each person in a family of five follow:

Name	Dick	Jane	Kirk	Jean	Scott
Age	40	36	8	6	2

   a. What is the mean age?
   b. Find the mean of the ages 5 yr from now.
   c. Find the mean 10 yr from now.
   d. Describe the relationships among the means found in (a), (b), and (c).

7. Suppose you own a hat shop and decide to order hats in only *one* size for the coming season. To decide which size to order, you look at last year's sales figures, which are itemized according to size. Should you find the mean, median, or mode for the data? Why?

8. A table showing Jon's fall quarter grades follows. Find his grade point average for the term (A = 4, B = 3, C = 2, D = 1, F = 0).

Course	Credits	Grade
Math	5	B
English	3	A
Physics	5	C
German	3	D
Handball	1	A

9. If the mean weight of seven tackles on a team is 230 lb and the mean weight of the four backfield members is 190 lb, what is the mean weight of the 11-person team?

10. If 99 people had a mean income of $12,000, how much is the mean income increased by the addition of a single income of $200,000?

11. The following table gives the annual salaries of the 40 dancers of a certain troupe.
    a. Find the mean annual salary for the troupe.
    b. Find the median annual salary.
    c. Find the mode.

Salary	Number of Dancers
$ 18,000	2
22,000	4
26,000	4
35,000	3
38,000	12
44,000	8
50,000	4
80,000	2
150,000	1

12. Refer to the following chart. In a gymnastics competition, each competitor receives six scores. The highest and lowest scores are eliminated, and the official score is the mean of the four remaining scores.

Gymnast	Scores					
Balance Beam						
Meta	9.2	9.2	9.1	9.3	9.8	9.6
Lisa	9.3	9.1	9.4	9.6	9.9	9.4
Olga	9.4	9.5	9.6	9.6	9.9	9.6
Uneven Bars						
Meta	9.2	9.1	9.3	9.2	9.4	9.5
Lisa	10.0	9.8	9.9	9.7	9.9	9.8
Olga	9.4	9.6	9.5	9.4	9.4	9.4
Floor Exercises						
Meta	9.7	9.8	9.4	9.8	9.8	9.7
Lisa	10.0	9.9	9.8	10.0	9.7	10.0
Olga	9.4	9.3	9.6	9.4	9.5	9.4

   a. If the only events in the competition are the balance beam, the uneven bars, and the floor exercise, find the winner of each event.
   b. Find the overall winner of the competition if the overall winner is the person with the highest combined official scores.

13. Maria needed 8 gal of gas to fill her car's gas tank. The mileage odometer read 42,800 mi. When the odometer read 43,030, Maria filled the tank with 12 gal. At the end of the trip, she filled the tank with 18 gal and the odometer read 43,390 mi. How many miles per gallon did she get for the entire trip?

14. If Janet traveled 45 mi in 90 min, what was her mean speed?

15. Emily worked the following hours for the week. How many hours did she average (mean) per day for the week?

Monday: $5\frac{1}{2}$ hr   Tuesday: $3\frac{1}{2}$ hr   Wednesday: $5\frac{1}{4}$ hr

Thursday: $6\frac{3}{4}$ hr   Friday: 8 hr

16. The youngest person in the company is 24 years old. The range of ages is 34 yr. How old is the oldest person in the company?

17. Choose the set(s) of numbers that fits the descriptions given in each of the following:
    a. The mean is 6.
       The range is 6.
       Set *A*:   3,   5,   7,   9
       Set *B*:   2,   4,   6,   8
       Set *C*:   2,   3,   4,   15
    b. The mean is 11.
       The median is 11.
       The mode is 11.
       Set *A*:   9,   10,   10,   11,   12,   12,   13
       Set *B*:   11,   11,   11,   11,   11,   11,   11
       Set *C*:   9,   11,   11,   11,   11,   12,   12
    c. The mean is 3.
       The median is 3.
       It has no mode.
       Set *A*:   0, $2\frac{1}{2}$, $6\frac{1}{2}$
       Set *B*:   3,   3,   3,   3
       Set *C*:   1,   2,   4,   5

18. What is the standard deviation of the heights of seven trapeze artists if their heights are 175 cm, 182 cm, 190 cm, 180 cm, 192 cm, 172 cm, and 190 cm?

19. a. If all the numbers in a set are equal, what is the standard deviation?
    b. If the standard deviation of a set of numbers is zero, must all the numbers in the set be equal?

20. In a Math 131 class at DiPaloma University, the grades on the first exam were as follows:

    96 71 43 77 75 76 61
    83 71 58 97 76 74 91
    74 71 77 83 87 93 79

    a. Find the mean.
    b. Find the median.
    c. Find the mode.
    d. Find the variance of the scores.
    e. Find the standard deviation of the scores.

21. To receive an A in a class, Willie needs at least a mean of 90 on five exams. Willie's grades on the first four exams were 84, 95, 86, and 94. What minimum score does he need on the fifth exam to receive an A in the class?

22. Ginny's median score on three tests was 90. Her mean score was 92 and her range was 6. What were her three test scores?

23. The mean of five numbers is 6. If one of the five numbers is removed, the mean becomes 7. What is the value of the number that was removed?

24. Construct a box plot for the following gas mileages per gallon of various company cars:

$$22 \quad 18 \quad 14 \quad 28 \quad 30 \quad 12 \quad 38 \quad 22$$
$$30 \quad 39 \quad 20 \quad 18 \quad 14 \quad 16 \quad 10$$

25. Following are box plots comparing the ticket prices of two performing arts theaters:
   a. What is the median ticket price for each theater?
   b. Which theater has the greatest range of prices?
   c. What is the highest ticket price at either theater?
   d. Make some statements comparing the ticket prices at the two theaters.

Box Office Ticket Prices

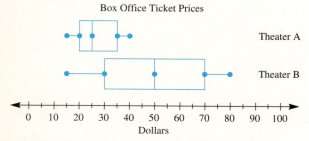

26. Construct a box plot for the following set of test scores. Indicate outliers, if any, with asterisks.

$$20 \quad 95 \quad 40 \quad 70 \quad 90 \quad 70 \quad 80 \quad 80 \quad 90 \quad 95$$

27. The following table shows the heights in feet of the tallest ten buildings in Los Angeles and in Minneapolis:

Los Angeles	Minneapolis
858	950
750	775
735	668
699	579
625	561
620	447
578	440
571	416
534	403
516	366

   a. Draw horizontal box plots to compare the data.
   b. Are there any outliers in this data? If so, which values are they?

28. In a school system, teachers start at a salary of $15,200 and have a top salary of $31,800. The teachers' union is bargaining with the school district for next year's salary increment.
   a. If every teacher is given a $1000 raise, what happens to each of the following?
      i. Mean   ii. Median   iii. Extremes
      iv. Quartiles   v. Standard deviation
   b. If every teacher received a 5% raise, what does this do to the following?
      i. Mean   ii. Standard deviation

29. a. Find the mean and the median of the following arithmetic sequences:
      i. 1, 3, 5, 7, 9
      ii. 1, 3, 5, 7, 9, . . . , 199
      iii. 7, 10, 13, 16, . . . , 607
   b. Based on your answers in (a), make a conjecture about the mean and the median of any arithmetic sequence.

30. If you were considering ages and wanted one number to represent the age at which a person can get a driver's license, which "average" would you use and why?

31. A movie chain conducts a popcorn poll in which each person entering a theater and buying a box of popcorn is asked a yes-no question. Which "average" do you think is used to report the result and why?

32. When a government agency reports the rainfall for a state for a year, which "average" do you think they use and why?

Communication

33. Carl had scores of 90, 95, 85, and 90 on his first four tests.
   a. Find the median, mean, and mode.
   b. Carl scored a 20 on his fifth exam. Which of the three averages would Carl want the instructor to use to compute his grade? Why?
   c. Which measure is affected the most by an extreme score?

34. The mean of the five numbers given below is 50:

$$20 \quad 35 \quad 50 \quad 60 \quad 85$$

   a. Add four numbers to the list so that the mean of the nine numbers is still 50.
   b. Explain how you could choose the four numbers to add to the list so that the mean did not change.
   c. How does the mean of the four numbers you added to the list compare to the original mean of 50? Why?

35. Sue drives 5 mi at 30 mph and then 5 mi at 50 mph. Is the mean speed for the trip 40 mph? Why or why not?

36. What happens to the mean and to the standard deviation of a set of data when the same number is added to each value in the data? Why?

★37. Show that the following formula for variance is equivalent to the one given in the text:

$$v = \frac{x_1^2 + x_2^2 + \cdots + x_n^2}{n} - \bar{x}^2$$

Open-ended

38. Use the data in the following table to compare the number of persons (in thousands) below the poverty level in the periods 1973–1982 and 1983–1992. Use any form of graphical representation to make the comparison and explain why you chose the representation that you did.

Year	Number (Thousands)	Year	Number (Thousands)
1973	22,973	1983	35,303
1974	23,370	1984	33,700
1975	25,877	1985	33,064
1976	24,975	1986	32,370
1977	24,720	1987	32,221
1978	24,497	1988	31,745
1979	26,072	1989	31,528
1980	29,272	1990	33,585
1981	31,822	1991	35,708
1982	34,398	1992	36,880

Data taken from *Information Please Almanac Atlas and Yearbook 1995*, 48th Edition. Boston: Houghton Mifflin Company, 1995.

Cooperative Learning

39. In your class, form groups of first-year, second-year, third-year, fourth-year, and other students. Draw box plots to analyze the ages of the different groups. Examine the five box plots together and as a class, predict the composition according to the age of the next term's class.

40. In small groups, determine a method of finding the number and types of graphs and statistical representations used in at least two newspapers in your campus library. Based on your findings, write a report defending which type(s) of representation should be emphasized in a journalistic statistics class.

Review Problems

41. If you were opening a sporting goods store and were relying on the data in the following graph, what type of equipment would you stock the most of and why?

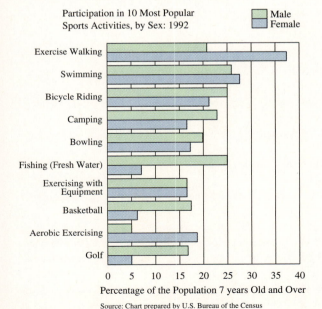

Participation in 10 Most Popular Sports Activities, by Sex: 1992

Source: Chart prepared by U.S. Bureau of the Census

Data taken from *Information Please Atlas and Yearbook 1995*, 48th Edition.

42. Consider the following graph depicting the percent distribution of a state's lottery proceeds in 1993:

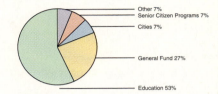

Percent Distribution of 1993 State Lottery Proceeds ($9 Billion)

Source: Chart prepared by U.S. Bureau of the Census.

a. What is the number of degrees in each sector of the pie chart?
b. Explain whether you believe the information in the graph.

43. Given the following bar graph, answer the following:
a. Which mountain is the highest? Approximately how high is it?
b. Which mountains are higher than 6000 m?

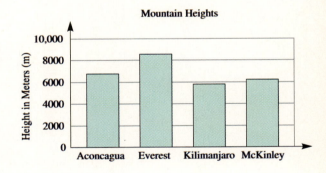

44. Following are raw test scores from a history test:

86	85	87	96	55
90	94	82	68	77
88	89	85	74	90
72	80	76	88	73
64	79	73	85	93

a. Construct an ordered stem-and-leaf plot for the given data.
b. Construct a grouped frequency table for these scores with intervals of 5, starting the first class at 55.
c. Draw a histogram of the data.
d. Draw a frequency polygon of the data.
e. If a circle graph of the grouped data in (b) were drawn, how many degrees would be in the section representing the 85–89 interval?

BRAIN TEASER The mean age of the first seven people to arrive at Grandpa Elmer's birthday party was 21. When Jeff, who is 29, arrived at the party, the mean age increased to 22. Mary, who is also 29, arrived next. Did the mean age increase to 23 with Mary's arrival? The tenth and last person to arrive was Grandpa Elmer, and the mean age increased to 30 yr. How old is Grandpa Elmer on this birthday?

**LABORATORY
ACTIVITY**

We can model the mean as a measure of central tendency using a strip of cardboard that is 1 in. wide and 1 ft long with holes 1 in. apart and $\frac{1}{8}$ in. from the edge, as in Figure 9-28.

Figure 9-28

Use string and tape to suspend the strip from a desk with the string tied through a hole punched between 56 and 57. Paper clips of equal size are then used to investigate means as in Figure 9-29.

Figure 9-29

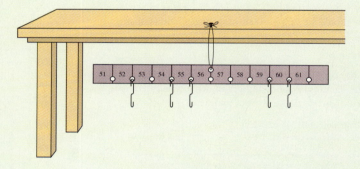

1. **a.** If paper clips are hung in the holes at 51, 53, and 60, where should an additional clip be hung in order to achieve a balance?
   b. If paper clips are hung at 51, 54, and 60, where should two additional paper clips be hung to achieve a balance?
   c. If paper clips are hung at 51, 53, 54, and 55, where should four additional clips be hung to achieve a balance?
2. Find the mean of the data of all the numbers in each part in (1) and compare this answer with the number in the center of the strip.
3. Would any of the means in (2) change if we hung an additional paper clip in the center of the strip?
4. Find the median and mode for 51, 53, 54, 56, 58, 58, and 59.
5. Hang paper clips in each hole in (4). If a number appears more than once, hang that number of paper clips in the hole. Is there a balance around the median? Is there a balance around the mode?
6. Under what conditions do you think there would be a balance around the (a) mean, (b) median, and (c) mode? Test your conjecture using the cardboard strip.

TECHNOLOGY CORNER

Use a graphing calculator or create a spreadsheet to find the variance and standard deviation of the set of scores 32, 41, 47, 53, and 57. If you use a spreadsheet, make column A be the set of scores, column B the score minus the mean, and column C the square of the difference of the score and the mean. Compute the variance and the standard deviation.

*Section 9-3

Normal Distributions

To understand how standard deviations are used as measures of dispersion, we consider normal distributions. The graphs of normal distributions are bell-shaped normal curves. These curves often describe large distributions such as IQ scores for the population of the United States.

normal curve   A **normal curve** is a smooth, bell-shaped curve that depicts values distributed symmetrically about the mean. (The mean, median, and mode all have the same value.) The normal curve is a theoretical distribution that extends infinitely in both directions. It gets closer and closer to the *x*-axis but never reaches it. On a normal curve, about 68% of the values lie within one standard deviation of the mean, about 95% lie within two standard deviations, and about 99.8% are within three standard deviations. The percents represent approximations of the total percent of area under the curve. The curve and the percent are illustrated in Figure 9-30.

Figure 9-30

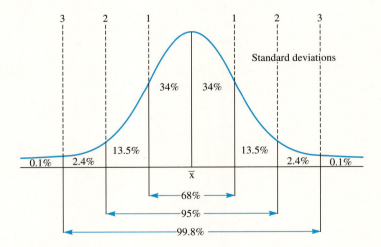

Suppose the area under the curve represents the population of the United States. Psychologists claim that the mean IQ is 100 and the standard deviation is 15. They also claim that an IQ score of over 130 represents a superior score. Because 130 is equal to the mean plus two standard deviations, we see from Figure 9-30 that only 2.5% of the population falls into this category.

• • •

Example 9-11   A standardized test had a mean of 500 and a standard deviation of 100. Suppose 10,000 students took the test and their scores had a bell-shaped distribution, thereby making it possible to use a normal curve to approximate the distribution.

a. How many scored between 400 and 600?
b. How many scored between 300 and 700?
c. How many scored between 200 and 800?

Solution   **a.** Since one standard deviation on either side of the mean is from 400 to 600, about 68% of the scores fall in this interval. Thus 0.68(10,000), or 6800, students scored between 400 and 600.

b. About 95% of 10,000, or 9500, students scored between 300 and 700.

c. About 99.8% of 10,000, or 9980, students scored between 200 and 800.

• • •

REMARK   About 0.2%, or 20, students' scores in Example 9-11 fall outside three standard deviations. About ten of these students did very well on the test, and about ten did very poorly.

H I S T O R I C A L   N O T E

Abraham De Moivre (1667–1754), a French Huguenot, was the first to develop and study the normal curve. He was one of the first to study actuarial information, in his book *Annuities upon Lives.* He also worked in trigonometry and complex numbers. De Moivre's work with the normal curve went essentially unnoticed. Later, the normal curve was developed independently by Pierre Laplace (1749–1827) and Karl Friedrich Gauss (1777–1855). Gauss found so many applications for the normal curve that it is sometimes referred to as the *Gaussian curve.*

In the following cartoon, two people are talking about grading "on a curve." What exactly does that mean?

"No, I don't grade on a curve...it's too complicated."

Typically, when students are discussing "grading on a curve," they are discussing methods of raising test scores to give themselves better grades. Consider the following to discover what "grading on a normal curve" might mean.

Suppose a group of students asked their teacher to grade "on a curve." If the teacher gave a test to 200 students and the mean on the test was 71, with a standard deviation of 7, the graph in Figure 9-31 shows how the grades could be assigned. In Figure 9-31, the teacher has used the normal curve in grading. The use of the normal curve presupposes that the teacher had a mound-shaped distribution of scores and also that the teacher arbitrarily decided to use the lines marking standard deviations to determine the boundaries of the A's, B's, C's, D's, and F's. Thus, based on the normal curve in Figure 9-31, Table 9-16 shows the range of grades that the teacher might assign if the grades are rounded. Students who ask their teachers to grade on the curve may wish to reconsider if the normal curve is to be used.

Figure 9-31

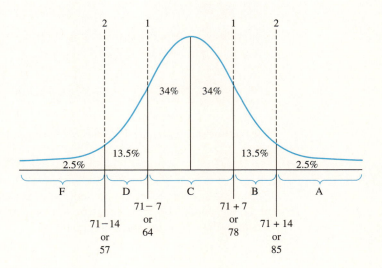

Table 9-16

Test Score	Grade	Number of People per Grade	Percentage Receiving Grade
85 and above	A	5	2.5%
78–84	B	27	13.5%
64–77	C	136	68%
57–63	D	27	13.5%
Below 57	F	5	2.5%

percentiles   When students take a standardized test such as the ACT or SAT, their scores are often reported in **percentiles.** A percentile shows a person's score relative to other scores. For example, if a student's score is at the 82nd percentile, this means that approximately 82% of those taking the test scored lower than the student and approximately 18% scored higher.

Comparing Scores from Different Tests

Scores by themselves may have very little meaning. For example, a student's score of 20 on a math quiz does not mean much unless we know more about the possible set of points on the test and how the other students scored. However, if we knew that the quiz on which a student received a score of 20 had a mean of 16 and a standard deviation of 2.2, we would have enough information to determine the relation of the score to the rest of the class scores.

Now suppose the student received a score of 52 on a second quiz, where the mean was 48 and the standard deviation was 3.1. Did the student do better on the first quiz or on the second quiz? We need a way to compare the scores in these two cases.

One way to deal with this problem is to translate all scores into *standard scores*. One such standard score is the *z*-score. A *z*-score is the number of standard deviations a score is from the mean. A positive *z*-score indicates that the score is greater than the mean; a negative *z*-score indicates that the score is less than the mean.

> ### Definition of *z*-Score
>
> The *z*-**score** of any number *x* in a normal distribution is given by
>
> $$z = \frac{x - \bar{x}}{s},$$
>
> where *x* is the score, $\bar{x}$ is the mean, and *s* is the standard deviation.

For the student's two quizzes, we have the following:

$$z = \frac{20 - 16}{2.2} \doteq 1.81 \quad \text{and} \quad z = \frac{52 - 48}{3.1} \doteq 1.29$$

Because the *z*-score related to the score of 20 is greater than the *z*-score related to the score of 52, the student did better in relation to the rest of the class on the first quiz. To see why we make this claim, we solve the equation

$$z = \frac{x - \bar{x}}{s}$$

for *x* to obtain $x = \bar{x} + sz$. Therefore the raw score on the first quiz was $\bar{x} + 1.81s$; that is, 1.81 standard deviations above the mean. On the second quiz, the score was $\bar{x} + 1.29s$, or 1.29 standard deviations above the mean.

Consider three student scores on a test with a mean of 71 and a standard deviation of 7. If the student scores are 71, 64, and 85, then the respective *z*-scores are as follows:

$$z = \frac{71 - 71}{7} = 0 \qquad \text{(Student 1)}$$

$$z = \frac{64 - 71}{7} = {}^-1 \qquad \text{(Student 2)}$$

$$z = \frac{85 - 71}{7} = 2 \qquad \text{(Student 3)}$$

Figure 9-32 can be used to interpret the *z*-scores *if the scores in the class have a bell-shaped distribution*. A *z*-score of 0 indicates that the score of 71 is the mean. A *z*-score of

⁻1 indicates that the score of 64 is one standard deviation below the mean. Similarly, a z-score of 2 indicates that the score of 85 is two standard deviations above the mean. Using Figure 9-32, we can see that 97.5% of the students taking the test scored lower than the third student.

Figure 9-32

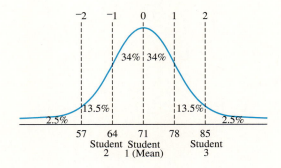

In comparisons of results from various tests taken by the same reference group, z-scores are useful. Suppose a group of students took both an English test and a mathematics test. Then a comparison of the z-scores would be reasonable. If a college class and a fourth-grade class took a mathematics test, a comparison of z-scores would not be reasonable because the reference groups are different.

Example 9-12

For a certain group of people, the mean height is 182 cm, with a standard deviation of 11 cm. Juanita's height has a z-score of 1.4. What is her height?

Solution   We use the formula for z-scores, $z = \dfrac{x - \bar{x}}{s}$. We know that $z = 1.4$, $\bar{x} = 182$, and $s = 11$.

$$1.4 = \frac{x - 182}{11}$$

$$15.4 = x - 182$$

$$x = 197.4$$

Therefore Juanita's height is 197.4 cm.

In a large group of scores, such as may be obtained on various standardized tests, we generally expect the scores to approximate a normal curve. If all scores are translated to z-scores, then with any given z-score we should be able to determine the approximate percent of people who scored either above or below this z-score. For example, suppose a z-score on a test is 1.5. In determining the percent of people who scored below this, we know from the graph in Figure 9-32 that the percent is more than 84% and less than 97.5%. Table 9-17 can be used to find that percent.

Table 9-17

z-score	Percentage Below	z-score	Percentage Below	z-score	Percentage Below
⁻3.0	0.13	⁻1.0	15.87	1.0	84.13
⁻2.9	0.19	⁻0.9	18.41	1.1	86.43
⁻2.8	0.26	⁻0.8	21.19	1.2	88.49
⁻2.7	0.35	⁻0.7	24.20	1.3	90.32
⁻2.6	0.47	⁻0.6	27.42	1.4	91.92
⁻2.5	0.62	⁻0.5	30.85	1.5	93.32
⁻2.4	0.82	⁻0.4	34.46	1.6	94.52
⁻2.3	1.07	⁻0.3	38.21	1.7	95.54
⁻2.2	1.39	⁻0.2	42.07	1.8	96.41
⁻2.1	1.79	⁻0.1	46.02	1.9	97.13
⁻2.0	2.27	0.0	50.00	2.0	97.73
⁻1.9	2.87	0.1	53.98	2.1	98.21
⁻1.8	3.59	0.2	57.93	2.2	98.61
⁻1.7	4.46	0.3	61.79	2.3	98.93
⁻1.6	5.48	0.4	65.54	2.4	99.18
⁻1.5	6.68	0.5	69.15	2.5	99.38
⁻1.4	8.08	0.6	72.58	2.6	99.53
⁻1.3	9.68	0.7	75.80	2.7	99.65
⁻1.2	11.51	0.8	78.81	2.8	99.74
⁻1.1	13.57	0.9	81.59	2.9	99.81
				3.0	99.87

Table 9-17 gives the percent of scores falling below a given z-score for normal distributions. The percent corresponding to any observation from a normal distribution can be found by converting the observation to a corresponding z-score and then looking in the table. In our example, approximately 93.32% of the population had z-scores below 1.5. More detailed tables show z-scores carried out to more decimal places. Figure 9-33 provides a graphical representation of the type of information given in Table 9-17.

Figure 9-33

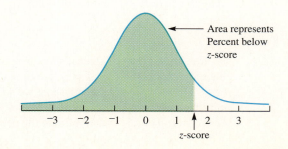

Area represents Percent below z-score

z-score

Example 9-13

Suppose the grades on a certain test are normally distributed and we want to grade an exam so that a grade of C is given to all students scoring within 1.2 standard deviations of the mean. What percent of the students should receive C's?

Solution Table 9-17 shows that 88.49% of the population scored fewer than 1.2 standard deviations above the mean. We know that 50% of the population scored below the mean. Therefore 88.49% − 50% = 38.49% of the population lies between the mean and 1.2 standard deviations. Because the normal curve is symmetric, we have the same percent on the other side of the mean, for a total of 2 · (38.49%) = 76.98%. Therefore approximately 77% of the students should receive C's.

Example 9-14

The heights of young U.S. women are approximately normally distributed with a mean of 65.5 in. and a standard deviation of 2.5 in.

a. What is the *z*-score for a woman who is 69 in. tall?
b. What is the *z*-score for a woman who is 60 in. tall?
c. What percent of the population of young U.S. women fall below each of these heights?

Solution **a.** A woman 69 in. tall has a *z*-score of

$$\frac{69 - 65.5}{2.5} = 1.4.$$

b. A woman 60 in. tall has a *z*-score of

$$\frac{60 - 65.5}{2.5} = {}^-2.2.$$

c. If $z = 1.4$, then from Table 9-17 the percent of the population below this height is 91.92%. If $z = {}^-2.2$, the percent of the population below this height is 1.39%.

Scattergrams

We often wonder if there is a relationship between two sets of data. For example, at the college level, mathematics placement exams are given to determine readiness for calculus. If students who score better on the exam do better in calculus than students who do poorly, we say that there is a positive correlation between the placement scores and achievement in the course. We can analyze relationships between two sets of data by using a **scattergram,** such as the one in Figure 9-34(a). In this figure, the points are not connected like those in a line graph, and there may be more than one point for a given number on either scale. Figure 9-34(a) shows that the highest score was 10 and the lowest was 1. We see that three students studied 4 hr for the test and that the mode was 5 hr.

scattergram

All of the points on a scattergram usually do not fall on a particular line, but on some scattergrams the points fall near the **trend line.** The trend line is used to make predictions. If the trend line slopes up from left to right as in Figure 9-34(b), then we say there is a *positive correlation*. From the trend line in Figure 9-34(b), we see that students who studied 7 hr typically scored six correct answers.

trend line

Figure 9-34

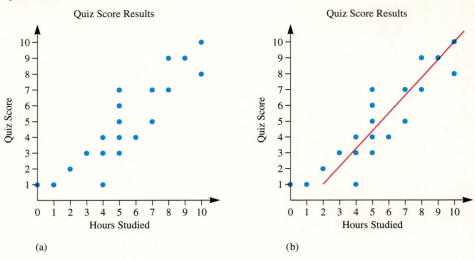

(a)

(b)

In Figure 9-34, note that a student who studied 4 hr did no better than one who did not study at all. Although there is a possible correlation between studying and scoring well on a quiz, the example illustrates that studying for a long time does not guarantee a good quiz score. We can use scattergrams and trend lines to make predictions but cannot deduce cause and effect based on them.

If the trend line slopes downward to the right, we can also make predictions; we say there is a *negative correlation*. If the points do not approximately fall on any line, we say there is *no correlation*. Scattergrams also show clusters of points and outliers. Examples of various correlations are given in Figure 9-35.

Figure 9-35

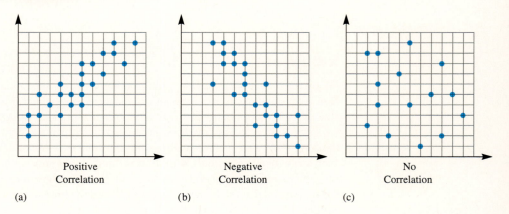

Positive Correlation

Negative Correlation

No Correlation

(a)

(b)

(c)

The following student page from *Addison-Wesley Mathematics,* Grade 7, 1993, gives an example of a scattergram.

Scattergrams

EXPLORE **Examine the graph**

Ordered pairs of data called **data points** can be shown in a **scattergram.** Here, each data point stands for the cost and rating of one brand of windsurfer board.

Brands	
A Freestyle Surfer	E Wild Board
B Tahiti Board	F Shark Board
C Caribbi 270	G XJ300 Wind
D Surfer Mate	H Sleek Surf
	J Breeze Board

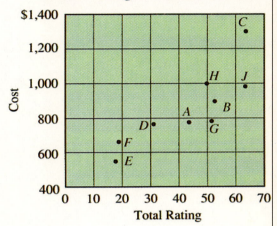

Consumer Ratings: Windsurfer Boards

TALK ABOUT IT

1. Which board is the most expensive? the least expensive?

2. Which board has the highest rating? the lowest rating?

3. Which boards would you consider to be good buys? Why?

One relationship between measured quantities is the **correlation.**

Positive Correlation
Both sets of data increase together.

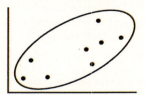

Negative Correlation
One set of data increases as the other decreases.

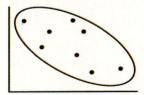

If data points are scattered over the graph, we say there is **no correlation.**

TECHNOLOGY CORNER

Many spreadsheets and graphing calculators allow the creation of scattergrams, or *scatterplots*. Figure 9-36 shows a scattergram of the data in Table 9-18 created with a spreadsheet.

Table 9-18

Years of School Completed	Median Income for Women	Median Income for Men
Fewer than 9	$ 7,942	$12,206
12 no diploma	9,784	15,928
12 diploma	13,266	22,765
> 12 but < 16	16,611	26,873
16	24,126	36,691

Figure 9-36

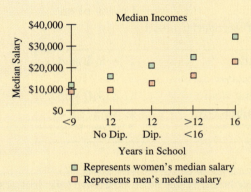

□ Represents women's median salary
□ Represents men's median salary

Investigate the possibility of creating a scattergram using the data in Table 9-18 on your spreadsheet.

Ongoing Assessment 9-3

1. The mean IQ score for 1500 students is 100, with a standard deviation of 15. Assuming the scores have a normal curve, determine the following:
   a. How many have an IQ between 85 and 115?
   b. How many have an IQ between 70 and 130?
   c. How many have an IQ over 145?
2. Sugar Plops boxes say they hold 16 oz. To make sure they do, the manufacturer fills the box to a mean weight of 16.1 oz, with a standard deviation of 0.05 oz. If the weights have a normal curve, what percent of the boxes actually contain 16 oz or more?
3. For certain workers, the mean wage is $5.00/hr, with a standard deviation of $0.50. If a worker is chosen at random, what is the probability that the worker's wage is between $4.50 and $5.50? Assume a normal distribution of wages.

4. A job-applicant test consisted of three parts: verbal, quantitative, and logical reasoning. The mean and standard deviation for each part are as follows:

	Verbal	Quantitative	Logical Reasoning
$\bar{x}$	84	118	14
s	10	18	4

   a. Holly's scores were 90 on verbal, 133 on quantitative, and 18 on logical reasoning. Determine her z-score for each part.
   b. Use the answers in (a) to determine each of the following:
      i. On which part did she perform relatively the highest?

ii. On which part did she perform relatively the lowest?

iii. To determine an overall composite score, we find the mean of the *z*-scores. What is Holly's composite score?

5. The average phone call in a certain town lasts 4 min with a standard deviation of 2 min. What percent of the calls lasts fewer than 2 min? Assume a normal distribution.

6. According to psychologists, IQs are normally distributed with a mean of 100 and a standard deviation of 15.
   a. What percent of the population have IQs between 100 and 130?
   b. What percent of the population have IQs lower than 85?

7. Use Table 9-17 to find the percents of scores below each of the following *z*-scores:
   a. ⁻2.3   b. 1.7   c. ⁻2.0

8. Use Table 9-17 to find the percent of scores between *z*-scores of 1.4 and 1.5.

9. The weights of newborn babies are distributed normally with a mean of approximately 105 oz and a standard deviation of 20 oz. If a newborn is selected at random, what is the probability that the baby weighs less than 125 oz?

10. If the mean is 63 and a score of 53 corresponds to a *z*-score of ⁻1.25, what is the standard deviation?

11. On a certain exam, the mean is 72 and the standard deviation is 9. If a grade of A is given to any student who scores at least two standard deviations above the mean, what is the lowest score that a person could receive and still get an A?

12. Assume the heights of U.S. women are approximately normally distributed, with a mean of 65.5 in. and a standard deviation of 2.5 in. Within what range are the heights of 95% of U.S. women?

13. A tire company tested a particular model of tire and found the tires to be normally distributed with respect to wear. The mean was 28,000 mi, and the standard deviation was 2500 mi. If 2000 tires are tested, about how many are likely to wear out before 23,000 mi?

14. A standardized mathematics test was given to 10,000 students, and the scores were normally distributed. The mean was 500, and the standard deviation was 60. If a student scored below 440 points, the student was considered deficient in mathematics. About how many students were rated deficient?

15. Coach Lewis kept track of the basketball team's high-jump records for a 10-yr period, as follows:

Year	1987	1988	1989	1990	1991	1992
Record (Nearest In.)	65	67	67	68	70	74

Year	1993	1994	1995	1996
Record (Nearest In.)	77	78	80	81

a. Draw a scattergram for the data.
b. What kind of correlation is there for these data?

16. Refer to the following scattergram regarding movie attendance:

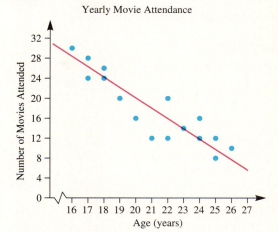

Yearly Movie Attendance

a. What type of correlation exists for these data?
b. About how many movies does an average 25-year-old attend?
c. From the data in the scattergram, conjecture how old you think a person is who attends 16 movies a year.

Communication

17. In a normal distribution, how are the mean and the median related? Why?

18. In the normal curve of Figure 9-32, the graph is drawn as a smooth curve. If the curve depicts a number of students taking a standardized test, explain whether the curve in reality would be smooth.

19. A normal curve is sometimes used in the discussion of a statistics principle known as the Central Limit Theorem. Look in textbooks or encyclopedias to investigate the meaning of this theorem. Then explain in your own words what it says.

Open-ended

20. a. Draw two different normal curves that depict scores on a nationally standardized test that have the same mean but one has twice as many students taking it as the other.
    b. How do you think the two curves are related?
    c. Will the percents marking standard deviations be the same as those given in Figure 9-32?

21. Write a set of test scores that do not fit a normal distribution and explain how you might "use a curve" to assign grades with your distribution.

Cooperative Learning

22. a. Predict the mean number of letters in the last names of people in your town.
    b. To test the prediction, let each group of students take a page from a telephone directory and make a frequency count of the number of letters in the last names of the people listed.

c. Combine the totals from all the groups and plot the data on a graph with the x-axis showing the number of letters in the last name and the y-axis showing the frequencies obtained.

d. Describe the type of graph that results.

Review Problems

23. On the English 100 exam, the scores were as follows:

$$
\begin{array}{cccc}
43 & 91 & 73 & 65 \\
56 & 77 & 84 & 91 \\
82 & 65 & 98 & 65 \\
\end{array}
$$

a. Find the mean. **b.** Find the median.
c. Find the mode. **d.** Find the variance.
e. Find the standard deviation.

24. If the mean of a set of 36 scores is 27 and two more scores of 40 and 42 are added, what is the new mean?

25. On a certain exam, Tony corrected 10 papers and found the mean for his group to be 70. Alice corrected the remaining 20 papers and found that the mean for her group was 80. What is the mean of the combined group of 30 students?

26. Following are the men's gold-medal times for the 100-m run in the Olympic games from 1896 to 1964. Construct an ordered stem-and-leaf plot for the data.

Year	Time (Seconds)
1896	12.0
1900	11.0
1904	11.0
1908	10.8
1912	10.8
1920	10.8
1924	10.6
1928	10.8
1932	10.3
1936	10.3
1948	10.3
1952	10.4
1956	10.5
1960	10.2
1964	10.0

27. Following are the record swimming times of the women's 100-m freestyle and 100-m butterfly in the Olympics from 1960 to 1992. Draw box plots of the two sets of data using the same number line to compare them.

Year	Time — 100-m Freestyle (Seconds)	Time — 100-m Butterfly (Seconds)
1960	61.20	69.50
1964	59.50	64.70
1968	60.00	65.50
1972	58.59	63.34
1976	55.65	60.13
1980	54.79	60.42
1984	55.92	59.26
1988	54.93	59.00
1992	54.64	58.62

Section 9-4   Abuses of Statistics

Statistics are frequently used and abused. Benjamin Disraeli (1804–1881), an English prime minister, once remarked, "There are three kinds of lies: lies, damned lies, and statistics." People sometimes deliberately use statistics to mislead others. In the past, this has been seen in advertising. More often, the misuse of statistics is the result of misinterpreting what the statistics actually mean. For example, if we were told that the "average" depth of water in a lily pond was 2 ft, most of us would presume that a heron could stand up in any part of the pond. That this is not necessarily the case is seen in the following cartoon.

Consider an advertisement reporting that of the people responding to a recent survey, 98% said that Buffepain is the most effective pain reliever of headaches and arthritis of all those tested. To certify that the statistics are not being misused, the following information should have been reported:

1. The number of people surveyed
2. The number of people responding
3. How the people participating in the survey were chosen
4. The number and type of pain relievers tested

Without the information listed, the following situations are possible, all of which could cause the advertisement to be misleading:

1. Suppose 1,000,000 people nationwide were sent the survey, and only 50 responded. This would mean that there was only a 0.005% response, which would certainly cause us to mistrust the ad.
2. Of the 50 responding in (1), suppose 49 responses were affirmative. The 98% claim is true, but 999,950 people did not respond at all.
3. Suppose all the people sent the survey were chosen from a town in which the major industry was the manufacture of Buffepain. It is very doubtful that the survey would represent an unbiased sample.
4. Suppose only two "pain relievers" were tested: Buffepain, whose active ingredient is 100% aspirin, and a placebo containing only powdered sugar.

This is not to say that advertisements of this type are all misleading or dishonest but simply that statistics are only as honest as their users. The next time you hear an advertisement such as "After using Ultraguard toothpaste, Joseph has 40% fewer cavities," you might ask whether Joseph has 40% fewer teeth than an average person.

Another example of the misuse of statistics is a headline from a student newspaper in Texas that claimed that "$33\frac{1}{3}$% of the Female Mathematics Faculty Marry Their Students."

The headline was in fact true, since there were three female mathematics faculty members and one of them *did* marry one of her students. As we can see, statistics can be used to distort facts without really lying.

A different type of misuse of statistics involves graphs. Among the things to look for in a graph are the following. If they are not there, then the graph may be misleading.

1. Title
2. Labels on both axes of a line or bar chart and on all sections of a pie chart
3. Source of the data
4. Key in a pictograph
5. Uniform size of symbols in a pictograph
6. Scale: Does it start with zero? If not, is there a break shown?
7. Scale: Are the numbers equally spaced?

To see how this is an example of a misleading use of graphs, consider how graphs can be used to distort data or exaggerate certain pieces of information. Graphs using a break in the vertical axis can be used to create different visual impressions, which are sometimes misleading. For example, consider the two graphs in Figure 9-37, which represent the number of girls trying out for basketball at each of three middle schools. As we can see, the graph in Figure 9-37(a) portrays a different picture than the one in Figure 9-37(b).

Figure 9-37

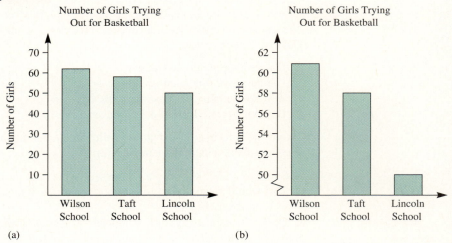

(a)   (b)

A frequency polygon, histogram, or bar graph can be altered by changing the scale of the graph. For example, consider the data in Table 9-19 for the number of graduates from a community college for the years 1992 to 1996.

Table 9-19

Year	1992	1993	1994	1995	1996
Number of Graduates	140	180	200	210	160

The graphs in Figure 9-38(a) and (b) represent the same data, but different scales are used in each. The statistics presented are the same, but these graphs do not convey the same psychological message. In Figure 9-38(b), the spacing of the years on the horizontal axis of the graph is more spread out and that for the numbers on the vertical axis is more condensed than in Fig. 9-38(a). Both of these changes minimize the variability of the data. A college administrator might use the graph in Figure 9-38(b) to convince people that the college was not in serious enrollment trouble.

Figure 9-38

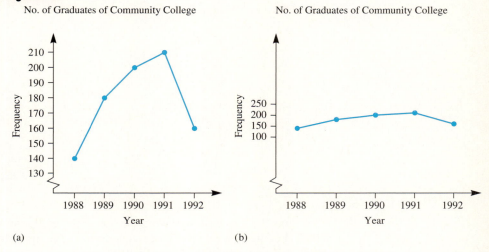

(a)

(b)

Another error that frequently occurs in all arenas is the use of continuous curve graphs, as in Figure 9-38, to depict data that are discrete (a finite number of data values). In Figure 9-38, it may or may not make sense to discuss the enrollment at 1992.5, yet the way in which the graph is constructed leads us to believe that such a value exists. In some schools, there are no summer classes and having enrollment as depicted is meaningless.

Other ways to distort bar graphs include omitting a scale, as in Figure 9-39(a). The scale is given in Figure 9-39(b).

Figure 9-39

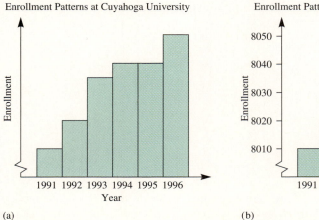
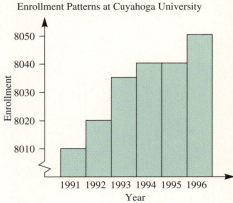

(a)

(b)

Other graphs can also be misleading. Suppose, for example, that the number of boxes of cereal sold by Sugar Plops last year was 2 million and the number of boxes of cereal sold by Korn Krisps was 8 million. The Korn Krisps executives prepared the graph in Figure 9-40 to demonstrate the data. The Sugar Plops people objected. Do you see why?

The graph in Figure 9-40 clearly distorts the data, since the figure for Korn Krisps is both four times as high and four times as wide as the bar for Sugar Plops. Thus the area of the box face representing Korn Krisps is 16 times the comparable area representing Sugar Plops, rather than four times the area, as would be justified by the original data.

Figure 9-40

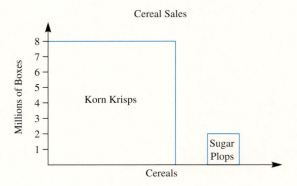

Figure 9-41 shows how the comparison of Sugar Plops and Korn Krisps cereals might look if the figures were made three-dimensional. The figure for Korn Krisps has a volume 64 times the volume of the Sugar Plops figure.

Figure 9-41

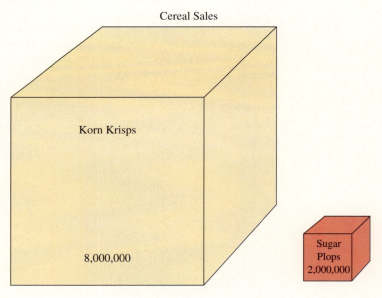

Circle graphs easily become distorted when attempts are made to depict them as three-dimensional. Many graphs of this type do not acknowledge either the variable thickness of the depiction or the distortion due to perspective. Observe that the 27% sector pictured in

Figure 9-42 looks far greater than the 23% sector, although they should be very nearly the same size.

Figure 9-42

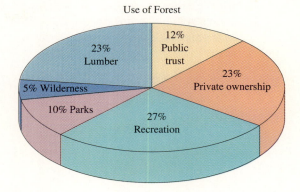

Use of Forest

The final examples of the misuses of statistics involve misleading uses of mean, median, and mode. All these are "averages" and may be used to suit a person's purposes. As discussed in Section 9-2 in the example involving the teachers Smith, Jones, and Rivera, each teacher had reported that his or her class had done better than the other two. Each of the teachers was using a different number to represent the test scores.

The use of statistics in this way is often misleading. For example, company administrators wishing to portray to prospective employees a rosy salary picture may find a mean salary of $38,000 for line workers as well as upper management in the schedule of salaries. At the same time, a union that is bargaining for salaries may include part-time employees as well as line workers and will exclude all management personnel in order to present a mean salary of $29,000 at the bargaining table. The important thing to watch for when a mean is reported is disparate cases in the reference group. If the sample is small, then a few extremely high or low scores can have a great influence on the mean.

Suppose Figure 9-43 shows the salaries of both management and line workers of the company. If the median is being used as the average, then the median might be $33,500, which is representative of neither major group of employees. The bimodal distribution allows the median to be nonrepresentative of the distribution.

Figure 9-43

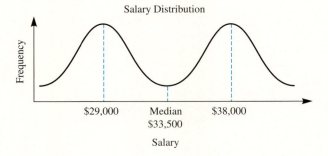

Salary Distribution

To conclude the comments on the misuse of statistics, consider a quote from Darrell Huff's book *How to Lie with Statistics* (p. 8):

So it is with much that you read and hear. Averages and relationships and trends and graphs are not always what they seem. There may be more in them than meets the eye, and there may be a great deal less.

> *The secret language of statistics, so appealing in a fact-minded culture, is employed to sensationalize, inflate, confuse, and oversimplify. Statistical methods and statistical terms are necessary in reporting the mass data of social and economic trends, business conditions, "opinion" polls, census. But without writers who use the words with honesty and understanding and readers who know what they mean, the result can be semantic "nonsense."*

Ongoing Assessment 9-4

This entire set of assessment items are appropriate for communication and cooperative learning. Many are open ended and several lend themselves to further investigation. Because the questions involve concepts from throughout the chapter, no review items are included.

1. Discuss whether the following claims could be misleading. Explain why and how.
   a. A car manufacturer claims its car is quieter than a glider.
   b. A motorcycle manufacturer claims that more than 95% of its cycles sold in the United States in the last 15 yr are still on the road.
   c. A company claims its fruit juice has 10% more fruit solids than is required by U.S. government standards. (The government requires 10% fruit solids.)
   d. A brand of bread claims to be 40% fresher.
   e. A used-car dealer claims that a car he is trying to sell will get up to 30 mpg.
   f. Sudso claims that its detergent will leave your clothes brighter.
   g. A sugarless gum company claims that eight of every ten dentists responding to the survey recommend sugarless gum.
   h. Most accidents occur in the home. Therefore, to be safer, you should stay out of your house as much as possible.
   i. Over 95% of the people who fly to a certain city do so on Airline A. Therefore most people prefer Airline A to other airlines.

2. The city of Podunk advertised that its temperature was the ideal temperature in the country because its mean temperature was 25°C. What possible misconceptions could people draw from this advertisement?

3. Jenny averaged 70 on her quizzes during the first part of the quarter and 80 on her quizzes during the second part of the quarter. When she found out that her final average for the quarter was not 75, she went to argue with her teacher. Give a possible explanation for Jenny's misunderstanding.

4. Suppose the following circle graphs are used to illustrate the fact that the number of elementary teaching majors at teachers' colleges has doubled between 1980 and 1990,

while the percent of male elementary teaching majors has stayed the same. What is misleading about the way the graphs are constructed?

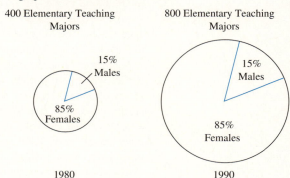

5. What is wrong with the following line graph?

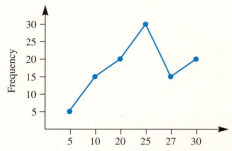

6. Can you draw any valid conclusions about a set of data in which the mean is less than the median?

7. A student read that nine out of ten pickup trucks sold in the last 10 yr are still on the road. She concluded that the average life of a pickup is around 10 yr. Is she correct?

8. General Cooster once asked a person by the side of a river if the river was too deep to ride his horse across. The person responded that the average depth was 2 ft. If General Cooster rode out across the river, what assumptions did he make on the basis of the person's information?

9. Doug's Dog Food Company wanted to impress the public with the magnitude of the company's growth. Sales of Doug's Dog Food had doubled from 1995 to 1996, so the company displayed the following graph, in which the radius of the base and the height of the 1996 can are double those of the 1995 can. What does the graph really show with respect to the growth of the company? (*Hint:* The volume of a cylinder is given by $V = \pi r^2 h$, where r is the radius of the base and h is the height.)

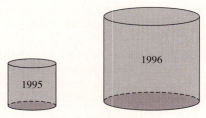

Doug's Dog Food Sales

10. Explain what is wrong with the following graph:

Sales of Brands

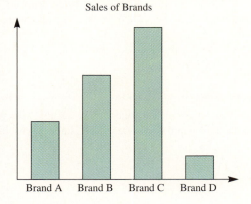

11. Refer to the following pictograph:

Drivers in Fatal Accidents

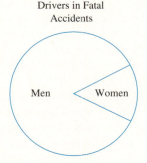

Ms. McNulty claims that on the basis of this information, we can conclude that men are worse drivers than women. Discuss whether you can reach that conclusion from the pictograph or you need more information. If more information is needed, what would you like to know?

12. The following graph was prepared to compare prices of camcorders at three different stores:

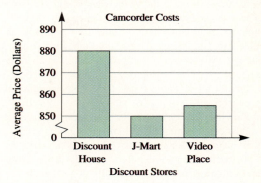

Which of the following statements is true? Explain why or why not.
- **a.** Prices vary widely at the three stores.
- **b.** The price at Discount House is four times as great as that at J-Mart.
- **c.** The prices at J-Mart and Video Place differ by less than $10.

13. The following table gives the number of accidents per year on a certain highway for a 5-yr period:

Year	1992	1993	1994	1995	1996
Number of Accidents	24	26	30	32	38

- **a.** Draw a bar graph to convince people that the number of accidents is on the rise and that something should be done about it.
- **b.** Draw a bar graph to show that the rate of accidents is constant, and that nothing needs to be done.

14. Write a list of scores for which the mean and median are not representative of the list.

15. The following graph depicts the mean center of population of the United States and shows how the center has shifted from 1790 to 1990. Based solely on this graph, could you conclude that the population of the coastal west has increased since 1790?

Source: U.S. Bureau of the Census, *1990 Census of Population and Housing, Population and Housing Unit Counts, United States* (1990 CPH-2-1).

16. The data in the graph of Problem 15 roughly follows a line. If the mean center of the population continues to move westward in the next 200 years, where would you expect it to be at the end of that period? At the end of 400 years?

17. Problem 26 in Ongoing Assessment 9-3 shows a table of values for the times of the gold-medalists from 1896 through 1964. Assume that pattern continues and answer (a)–(c).

   a. Predict the winning time of the gold medalist in this event in 1992.

   b. Find the winning time in 1992 and test your prediction.

   c. Predict the winning time in the year 2996.

   d. Explain whether you think the pattern can continue.

18. A prospective homeowner considered the dropping interest rates for house loans in the early 1990s and decided to wait until the year 2000 to buy. Explain what type of statistics might be used in making this decision and whether you consider the prospective homeowner's decision to be wise.

19. A student made 99 on a quiz and was ecstatic over the grade. What other information might you need in order to decide if the student was justified in being happy?

20. A school administrator reports to you, a school board member, that the "average" number of students in a class in a school is 32. What other information might you need in order to predict whether any single classroom was overcrowded?

21. Consider a state such as Montana that has both mountains and prairies. What numbers might you report to depict the "average" height above sea level of such a state? Why?

22. Is it possible for a state or country to have a mean sea level height that is negative? If so, what might such a region look like?

23. Describe how you might pick a random sample of adults that is representative of the members of your town.

24. A very large and successful manufacturer of computer chips released data in the early 1990s stating that approximately 65% of its chips were defective when they came off the assembly line. Give some reasons why this statistic could be accurate and yet the company could still be successful.

25. The *Standards* (p. 105) contains the following quote: *Students in grades 5–8 have a keen interest in trends in music, movies, fashion, and sports.* What types of data would you expect the NCTM to have to substantiate that claim?

BRAIN TEASER   A racetrack measures 1 mi around. If you drive around the track once and average 30 mph, what speed must you average on your second trip around the track in order to average 60 mph for the two laps?

SOLUTION TO THE PRELIMINARY PROBLEM

Understanding the Problem.   The problem is for a negotiator for a new contract to determine the most beneficial salary scheme and average to use in a retirement plan. The options are (1) taking a fixed dollar amount as a salary increase for every person for each of the next 5 yr, (2) taking a 4% increase in salary each year of the next 5 yr, and (3) receiving no salary increases in each of the first 3 yr but receiving a 10% salary increase in each of the last 2 yr of the 5-year plan. The retirement income is based on the average of the salaries of the last 5 yr of employment, and the negotiator plans to retire in 5 yr.

In this problem, we do not know the salary of the negotiator and we do not know the amount of the fixed increase to be added to the salary in option (1). Because we do not know these numbers, it may be impossible to find a definitive answer to the question for all people. However, we should be able to determine a condition that each person could use to find the answer individually.

Devising a Plan.   We use the mean, median, and mode as the three averages in answering the problem. It should be noted that the following are true:

   1. Under option (1), the salaries for successive years form an arithmetic sequence.

   2. Under option (2), the salaries for successive years form a geometric sequence.

To consider the problem carefully, we need to find the mean, median, and mode for each option. In both option (1) and option (2), the salaries are increasing each year and thus there is no mode. In option (3), the salary is fixed in the first 3 yr and increases in each of the last two. Thus the mode is the first year's salary in option (3) and is the lowest of all the salaries. The negotiator should not choose the mode in any case.

Carrying Out the Plan. We consider the mean and median for each option in turn.

Option (1): If the current year's salary is s and the fixed increase is f, then the salaries in the progressive years under consideration are $s + f$, $s + 2f$, $s + 3f$, $s + 4f$, and $s + 5f$. In this set of salaries, both the mean and the median are $s + 3f$. (Why?)

Option (2): Using s as the current year's salary, we find the salaries in progressive years are as follows:

$$s + 0.04s = 1.04s$$
$$1.04s + 0.04(1.04s) = (1.04^2)s$$
$$(1.04^2)s + 0.04(1.04^2)s = (1.04^3)s$$
$$(1.04^3)s + 0.04(1.04^3)s = (1.04^4)s$$
$$(1.04^4)s + 0.04(1.04^4)s = (1.04^5)s$$

The median is $(1.04^3)s$, or approximately $1.1249s$. The mean is $[1.04s + (1.04^2)s + (1.04^3)s + (1.04^4)s + (1.04^5)s]/5$, or approximately $1.1266s$. In this case, the mean is greater than the median, so the mean is the best choice.

Option (3): Using reasoning comparable to that used in option (2), we find the set of salaries for the 5-yr period is s, s, s, $1.10s$, and 1.10^2s. The median is s and should be rejected in any event because it is the lowest of all the salaries listed. The mean for option 3 is $(s + s + s + 1.10s + 1.10^2s)/5$, or approximately $1.062s$.

All the possible retirement salaries are $s + 3f$, $1.1249s$, $1.1266s$, s, and $1.062s$. Certainly $s < s + 3f$ and $1.062s < 1.1249s < 1.1266s$. (Why?) The only necessary question to answer is which of $s + 3f$ and $1.1266s$ is greater? The following are all equivalent:

$$s + 3f > 1.1266s$$
$$3f > 0.1266s$$
$$f > 0.0422s$$

To determine the best option, the negotiator has only to multiply the current salary by 0.0422 and compare the product to the amount of the fixed salary increase. If f is greater, as in the inequality, then that is the option to choose. If not, the negotiator needs to use the mean with the 4% salary increase in each of the 5-yr periods.

Looking Back. An extension of the problem is to restrict the average to the best 3 yr of salary in each case. Does your answer change? Another option is to change the percents of increase for the period in option (2) or to change option (3) in some way.

QUESTIONS FROM THE CLASSROOM

1. A student asks, "If the average income of each of ten people is $10,000 and one person gets a raise of $10,000, is the median, the mean, or the mode changed and, if so, by how much?"

2. A student asks for an example of when the mode is the be average. What is your response?

3. A student says that a stem-and-leaf plot is always the be way to present data. How do you respond?

4. Suppose the class takes a test and the following averages are obtained: mean, 80; median, 90; mode, 70. Tom, who scored 80, would like to know if he did better than half the class. What is your response?

5. A student wants to know the advantages of presenting data in graphical form rather than in tabular form. What is your response? What are the disadvantages?

6. A student asks if it is possible to find the mode for data in a grouped frequency table. What is your response?

7. A student asks if she can draw any conclusions about a set of data if she knows that the mean for the data is less than the median. How do you answer?

8. A student asks if it is possible to have a standard deviation of ‾5. How do you respond?

9. Mel's mean on ten tests for the quarter was 89. She complained to the teacher that she should be given an A because she missed the cutoff of 90 by only a single point. Did she really miss an A by only a single point?

10. A student claims that bar graphs can be used to give the same information as line graphs, so no one should have to learn how to do line graphs. What is your response?

11. A student asks, "Is it always true that in any set of data, there must be at least one data point in the data that is less than or equal to the mean and at least one data point greater than or equal to the mean?"

12. A student asks if the precision with which manufacturers must calibrate their tools is at all related to statistics. How do you respond?

13. A student wants to know if there is such a thing as average deviation and if anyone ever uses it. How do you relate average deviation to standard deviation and its use?

CHAPTER OUTLINE

I. Descriptive statistics
Information can be summarized in each of the following forms:
1. **Pictographs**
2. **Line plots**
3. **Stem-and-leaf plots**
4. **Frequency tables**
5. **Histograms**
6. **Bar graphs**
7. **Frequency polygons** or **line graphs**
8. **Circle graphs** or **pie charts**
9. **Box plots**

II. Measures of central tendency
  A. The **mean** of n given numbers is the sum of the numbers divided by n.
  B. The **median** of a set of numbers is the middle number if the numbers are arranged in numerical order; if there is no middle number, the median is the mean of the two middle numbers.
  C. The **mode** of a set of numbers is the number or numbers that occur most frequently in the set.

III. Measures of variation
  A. The **range** is the difference between the greatest and least numbers in the set.
  B. The **variance** is found by subtracting the mean from each value, squaring each of these differences, finding the sum of these squares, and dividing by n, where n is the number of observations.

  C. The **standard deviation** is equal to the square root of the variance.
  D. **Box plots** focus attention on the median, the quartiles, and the extremes and invite comparisons among them.
    1. The **lower quartile** is the median of the subset of data less than the median of all the values in the data set.
    2. The **upper quartile** is the median of the subset of data greater than the median of all the values in the data set.
    3. The **interquartile range (IQR)** is calculated as the difference between the upper quartile and the lower quartile.
    4. An **outlier** is any value more than 1.5 IQR above the upper quartile or more than 1.5 IQR below the lower quartile.
  *E. In a **normal curve,** approximately 68% of the values are within one standard deviation of the mean, 95% are within two standard deviations of the mean, and 99.8% are within three standard deviations of the mean.
  *F. A **z-score** gives the position of a score in relation to the remainder of the distribution, using the standard deviation as the unit of measure.

$$z = \frac{x - \bar{x}}{s}$$

  *G. **Scattergrams** or **scatterplots** are graphs of ordered pairs that allow us to examine the relationship (correlation) between two sets of data.

CHAPTER REVIEW

1. Suppose you read that "the average family in Rattlesnake Gulch has 2.41 children." What average is being used to describe the data? Explain your answer. Suppose the sentence had said 2.5? Then what are the possibilities?

2. At Bug's Bar-B-Q restaurant, the average weekly wage for full-time workers is $150. There are ten part-time employees whose average weekly salary is $50 and the total weekly payroll is $3950. How many full-time employees are there?

3. Find the mean, the median, and the mode for each of the following groups of data:
   a. 10, 50, 30, 40, 10, 60, 10
   b. 5, 8, 6, 3, 5, 4, 3, 6, 1, 9

4. Find the range, variance, and standard deviation for each set of scores in Problem 3.

5. The mass, in kilograms, of each child in Ms. Rider's class follows:

   40 49 43 48 46 42 49 39 47 49
   42 41 42 39 41 40 45 43 44 42

   a. Make a line plot for the data.
   b. Make an ordered stem-and-leaf plot for the data.
   c. Make a frequency table for the data.
   d. Make a bar graph of the data.

6. The grades on a test for 30 students follow:

   96 73 61   76   77 84
   78 98 98   80   67 82
   61 75 79   90   73 80
   85 63 86 100   94 77
   86 84 91   62   77 64

   a. Make a grouped frequency table for these scores, using four classes and starting the first class at 61.
   b. Draw a histogram of the grouped data.
   c. Draw a frequency polygon of the data. Is it appropriate?

7. The budget for the Wegetem Crime Co. is $2,000,000. Draw a circle graph to indicate how the company spends its money where $600,000 is spent on bribes, $400,000 for legal fees, $300,000 for bail money, $300,000 for contracts, and $400,000 for public relations.

8. What, if anything, is wrong with the following bar graph?

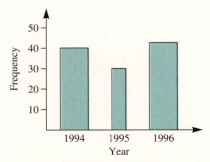

Results of Dan's Tossing a Die

Number on the Die Face

9. The mean salary of 24 people is $9000. How much will one additional salary of $80,000 increase the mean salary?

10. A cheetah can run 70 mph, a lion can run 50 mph, and a human can run 28 mph. Draw a bar graph to represent these data.

11. The life expectancies at birth for males and females are given in the following table:

Year	Male	Female
1970	67.1	74.7
1971	67.4	75.0
1972	67.4	75.1
1973	67.6	75.3
1974	68.2	75.9
1975	68.8	76.6
1976	69.1	76.8
1977	69.5	77.2
1978	69.6	77.3
1979	70.0	77.8
1980	70.0	77.5
1981	70.4	77.8
1982	70.9	78.1
1983	71.0	78.1
1984	71.2	78.2
1985	71.2	78.2
1986	71.3	78.3
1987	71.5	78.4
1988	71.4	78.3
1989	71.8	78.5

   a. Draw back-to-back ordered stem-and-leaf plots to compare the data.
   b. Draw box plots to compare the data.

12. Larry and Marc took the same courses last quarter. Each bet that he would receive the better grades. Their courses and grades are as follows:

Course	Larry's Grades	Marc's Grades
Math (4 credits)	A	C
Chemistry (4 credits)	A	C
English (3 credits)	B	B
Psychology (3 credits)	C	A
Tennis (1 credit)	C	A

Marc claimed that the results constituted a tie, since both received 2 A's, 1 B, and 2 C's. Larry said that he won the bet because he had the higher grade-point average for the quarter. Who is correct? (Allow 4 points for an A, 3 points for a B, 2 points for a C, 1 point for a D, and 0 points for an F.)

13. Following are the lengths in yards of the nine holes of the University Golf Course:

160	360	330
350	180	460
480	450	380

Find each of the following measures with respect to the lengths of the holes:

a. Median

b. Mode

c. Mean

d. Standard deviation

14. The speeds in miles per hour of 30 cars were checked by radar. The data are as follows:

62	67	69	72	75	60	58	86	74	68
56	67	82	88	90	54	67	65	64	68
74	65	58	75	67	65	66	64	45	64

a. Find the median.

b. Find the upper and lower quartiles.

c. Draw a box plot for the data and indicate outliers (if any) with asterisks.

d. What percent of the scores is in the interquartile range?

e. If every person driving faster than 70 mph received a ticket, what percent of the drivers received speeding tickets?

f. Is the median in the center of the box? Why or why not?

15. The heights of 1000 girls at East High School were measured, and the mean was found to be 64 in., with a standard deviation of 2 in. If the heights are approximately normally distributed, about how many of the girls are

a. over 68 in. tall?

b. between 60 and 64 in. tall?

c. If a girl is selected at random at East High School, what is the probability that she will be over 66 in. tall?

*16. A standardized test has a mean of 600 and a standard deviation of 75. If 1000 students took the test and their scores approximated a normal curve, how many scored between 600 and 750?

*17. If a student scored 725 on the test in Problem 16, what is his or her z-score?

*18. Two companies tested their products to determine the average (mean) life of their products. Company A had an average life of 150 hr with a standard deviation of 10 hr. Company B had an average life of 145 with a standard deviation of 2 hr. Which company would you rather buy from? Explain why.

*19. The following scattergram was obtained from the girls trying out for the high-school basketball team:

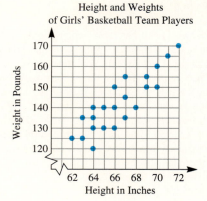

Height and Weights of Girls' Basketball Team Players

a. What kind of correlation exists between the heights and weights that are listed?

b. What is the weight of the girl who is 72 in. tall?

c. How tall is the girl who weighs 145 lb?

d. What is the mode of the heights?

e. What is the range of the weights?

20. The Nielsen Television Index rating of 30 means that an estimated 30% of American televisions are tuned to the show with that rating. The ratings are based on the preferences of a scientifically selected sample of 1200 homes.

a. Discuss possible ways in which viewers could bias this sample.

b. How could networks attempt to bias the results?

21. List and give examples of several ways to misuse statistics graphically.

22. Discuss the value of a graphical representation such as the following. If you were attempting to lure workers to your state, should you use this type of representation or another in order to put your state in a good light? Explain why.

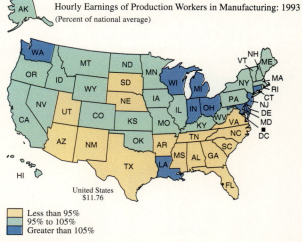

Hourly Earnings of Production Workers in Manufacturing: 1993
(Percent of national average)

United States
$11.76

Less than 95%
95% to 105%
Greater than 105%

Note: 1992 data for Maine.
Source: Chart prepared by U.S. Bureau of the Census.

23. The following graph shows three line graphs. Write an explanation of how the line labeled "Total" may have been obtained from the other two lines.

Fishery Products—Domestic Catch and Imports: 1970 to 1992

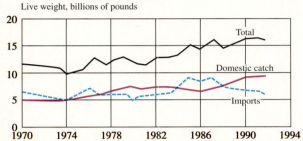

Source: Chart prepared by U.S. Bureau of the Census.

24. Explain whether you think it is reasonable for a ski resort to advertise excellent skiing because the runs have 64 in. of snow at the top of the hill and 23 in. at the bottom.

SELECTED BIBLIOGRAPHY

Barbella, P. "Realistic Examples in Elementary Statistics." *Mathematics Teacher* 80 (December 1987): 740–743.

Barnes, S., K. D. Michalowicz, and D. Lee. "Now & Then: Some Moments in the History of Statistics: The Measurement of Uncertainty." *Mathematics Teaching in the Middle School* 1 (November-December 1994): 211–217.

Bloom, S. "Data Buddies: Primary-Grade Mathematicians Explore Data." *Teaching Children Mathematics* 1 (October 1994): 80–86.

Browning, C., D. E. Channell, and R. A. Meyer. "Preparing Teachers to Present Techniques of Exploratory Data Analysis." *Mathematics Teaching in the Middle School* 1 (September-October 1994): 166–172.

Bryan, E. "Exploring Data with Box Plots." *Mathematics Teacher* 81 (November 1988): 658–663.

Burrill, G. "Statistics and Probability." *Mathematics Teacher* 83 (February 1990): 113–118.

Corwin, R., and S. Friel. *Statistics: Prediction and Sampling.* Palo Alto, Calif: Dale Seymour Publishing, 1990.

Davis, G. "Using Data Analysis to Explore Class Enrollment." *Mathematics Teacher* 83 (February 1990): 104–106.

Fennell, F. "Ya Gotta Play to Win: A Probability and Statistics Unit for the Middle Grades." *Arithmetic Teacher* 31 (March 1983): 26–30.

Friel, S., and R. Corwin. "The Statistics Standards in K–8 Mathematics." *Arithmetic Teacher* 38 (October 1990): 35–39.

Goldman, P. "Teaching Arithmetic Averaging: An Activity Approach." *Arithmetic Teacher* 37 (March 1990): 38–43.

Grummer, D. "Plotting Margo's Party." *Teaching Children Mathematics* 2 (November 1995): 176–179.

Hitch, C., and G. Armstrong. "Daily Activities for Data Analysis." *Arithmetic Teacher* 41 (January 1994): 242–245.

Huff, D. *How to Lie with Statistics.* New York: Norton, 1954.

Kader, G., and M. Perry. "Learning Statistics with Technology." *Mathematics Teaching in the Middle School* 1 (September–October 1994): 130–136.

Karp, K. "Telling Tales: Creating Graphs Using Multicultural Literature." *Teaching Children Mathematics* 1 (October 1994): 87–91.

Kelly, I., and J. Beamer. "Central Tendency and Dispersion: The Essential Union." *Mathematics Teacher* 79 (January 1986): 59–65.

Kimberling, C. "Mean, Standard Deviation, and Stopping the Stars." *Mathematics Teacher* 77 (November 1984): 633–636.

Korithoski, T. P., and P. A. Korithoski. "Mean or Meaningless?" *Arithmetic Teacher* 41 (December 1993): 194–197.

Landwehr, J., and A. Watkins. *Exploring Data.* Palo Alto, Calif.: Dale Seymour Publishing, 1994.

Landwehr, J., and A. Watkins. "Stem-and-Leaf Plots." *Mathematics Teacher* 78 (October 1985): 528–532, 537–538.

Litton, N. "Graphing from A to Z." *Teaching Children Mathematics* 2 (December 1995): 220–223.

MacDonald, A. "A Stem-Leaf Plot: An Approach to Statistics." *Mathematics Teacher* 75 (January 1982): 25, 27, 28.

Mitchem, J. "Paradoxes in Averages." *Mathematics Teacher* 82 (April 1989): 250–253.

Rosenberg, M. "Learn about Statistics — Math League Baseball." *Arithmetic Teacher* 41 (April 1994): 459–461.

Taylor, L., and J. A. Nichols. "Graphing Calculators Aren't Just for High School Students." *Mathematics Teaching in the Middle School* 1 (November-December 1994): 190–196.

Wilson, M., and C. Krapfl. "Exploring Mean, Median, and Mode with a Spreadsheet." *Mathematics Teaching in the Middle School* 1 (September-October 1995): 490–495.

10

INTRODUCTORY GEOMETRY

The cover of a soccer ball consists of pentagons and regular hexagons as shown in the accompanying figure. Can a pattern similar to the one on the soccer ball be used to tile a floor? Why or why not?

T he word *geometry* comes from two Greek words, *ge* and *metria,* meaning "earth measuring." The approach to geometry developed by the ancient Greeks has been used for over 2000 yr as the basis of geometry.

H I S T O R I C A L   N O T E

Little is known of Euclid of Alexandria (ca. 300 B.C.), although legend has it that he studied geometry for its beauty and logic. Euclid is best known for *The Elements,* a work so systematic and encompassing that many earlier mathematical works were simply discarded and lost to all future generations. *The Elements,* composed of 13 books, included not only geometry but arithmetic and topics in algebra. Euclid set up a *deductive system* by starting with a set of statements that he assumed to be true and showing that geometric discoveries followed logically from these assumptions.

Research suggests that children may learn geometry along the lines of a structure for reasoning developed by Dina and Pierre van Hiele of the Netherlands in the 1950s. The following van Hiele levels were modified by Alan Hoffer in 1981:

Level 0: Students recognize figures by their global appearance. They say such words as *triangle* and *square* but do not recognize properties of these figures.

Level 1: Students analyze component parts of figures but do not interrelate figures and properties. They may know that all sides of a square are congruent and that the diagonals of a rhombus are perpendicular bisectors of each other.

Level 2: Students may relate figures and their properties, but they do not organize sequences of statements to justify their observations. They may know that all squares are rhombuses but may not be able to state why in an organized way. Students can reason informally.

Level 3: Students at this level can reason deductively within the mathematical system to justify their observations. They understand the need for a proof.

Level 4: Students at this level can compare different axiom systems with a high degree of rigor, even without concrete models.

Section 10-1   Basic Notions

 According to the 5–8 *Standards* (p. 113) *"Students should learn to use correct vocabulary, including such common terms as* and, or, all, some, always, never, *as well as such words as* parallel, *and* perpendicular." The *Standards* (p. 113) further suggests that such vocabulary should be learned in an investigative manner.

In this section, we discuss some basic notions of geometry. The fundamental building blocks of geometry—*points, lines,* and *planes*—are *undefined* terms (that is, they are left undefined) in order to avoid circular definitions. An example showing a circular definition and the frustration involved in starting out without some basic undefined notions is given in the following cartoon.

Because other geometric concepts are developed from such undefined terms, an intuitive description of points, lines, and planes is given next.

Points

point • space

Although we cannot give formal definitions for points and lines, we can describe them informally. A **point** represents a location in space where **space** is the set of all points. A point has no dimension. We use physical models such as those in Figure 10-1 to demonstrate points. Points are usually represented by dots and a capital letter, as in Figure 10-1(d).

Figure 10-1

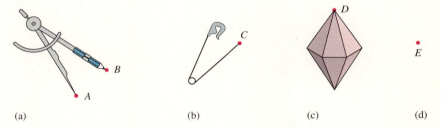

(a) (b) (c) (d)

Lines

line

A **line** has no thickness and extends forever in two directions. A "straight" highway centerline, as illustrated in Figure 10-2(a), might be considered a line in the everyday world. We represent a line as shown in Figure 10-2(b), where the arrowheads indicate the directions of the line. We name a line with either a single lowercase letter or by using 2 points on the line. The line in Figure 10-2(b) can be written as ℓ or $\overleftrightarrow{AB}$. In Figure 10-2(b), points A and B are on ℓ and there is no other line through A and B. We summarize this in the following property.

Figure 10-2

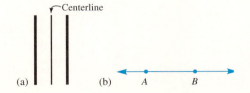

Centerline

(a) (b) A B

Property of a Line

Through two given points, exactly one line can be drawn.

REMARK   We have only *intuitively* described the terms *point* and *line; we have not actu-ally defined them.* "A location in space" and "has no dimensions" do not define a point, as the terms "space" and "dimension" have not been defined themselves. Also, we have not defined "straight" as used in describing a line.

---

collinear

between

When we discuss situations involving points and lines, we rely on such undefined rela-tions as "contains," "belongs to," "is on," and "is between." In Figure 10-3, for example, line ℓ contains points *A, B,* and *C* but does not contain point *D*. Also, points *A, B,* and *C* belong to line ℓ, but point *D* does not. Similarly, points *A, B,* and *C* are **collinear** because they lie on a single line, but points *B, C,* and *D* are noncollinear because there is no single line that contains them. If three collinear points *A, B,* and *C* are arranged as in Figure 10-3, *B* is **between** *A* and *C*. Point *D* is not between *B* and *C*.

Figure 10-3

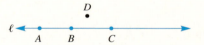

Using points, lines, and the *concept of betweenness,* we can define other geometric fig-ures. Commonly used subsets of a line are segments and rays. These are defined in Table 10-1.

Table 10-1

Definition	Illustration
A **line segment,** or **segment,** is a subset of a line that contains two points of the line and all points between those two points.	$\overline{AB}$ or $\overline{BA}$
A **ray** is a subset of a line that contains one point and all points on the line on one side of the point.	$\overrightarrow{AB}$

● Determine whether rays, segments, and lines in each of the following pairs are equal:

(i) $\overrightarrow{AB}$ and $\overrightarrow{BA}$

(ii) $\overline{AB}$ and $\overline{BA}$

(iii) $\overleftrightarrow{AB}$ and $\overleftrightarrow{BA}$.

Justify your answers. ●

Planes

plane

A tabletop, a floor, a ceiling, a wall, or any other smooth level surface is commonly thought of as a **plane.** However, a plane extends endlessly in two directions. A plane is usually represented by a four-sided figure, as pictured in Figure 10-4, and it is commonly denoted by a lowercase Greek letter, such as alpha (α), beta (β), or gamma (γ), or by capital letters representing three noncollinear points, such as *ABC*. Thus plane γ in Figure 10-4(c) can be referred to as plane *ABC*. If two points are in a plane, the line determined by these points is in the plane, as seen in Figure 10-4(c).

Figure 10-4

(a)

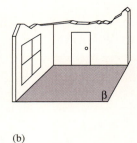

(b)

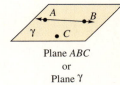

Plane *ABC*
or
Plane γ

(c)

● How many planes containing three collinear points are possible? What real-life object illustrates your answer? Draw a picture illustrating your answer. ●

coplanar points

In Figure 10-5, points such as *D, G,* and *E* that belong to the same plane are **coplanar points.** Figure 10-5 also shows noncoplanar points *D, G, E,* and *F*. These points are

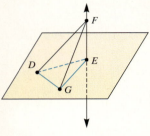

Figure 10-5   skew lines

noncoplanar because no single plane contains all four points. Points are *noncoplanar* if no one plane can contain them.

Similarly, we can define *coplanar* and *noncoplanar lines.* For example, in Figure 10-5 lines $\overleftrightarrow{DF}$ and $\overleftrightarrow{GF}$ are coplanar because they lie in the plane *DFG*. Are lines $\overleftrightarrow{GF}$ and $\overleftrightarrow{DE}$ coplanar? They seem to be. The following argument shows that they are not.

Suppose lines $\overleftrightarrow{DE}$ and $\overleftrightarrow{GF}$ are coplanar. Then points *D, E, F,* and *G* would be coplanar. Points *D, G,* and *E* are coplanar as they are in the same plane. Because these three non-collinear points determine a unique plane and the point *F* is not in that plane, no single plane can contain *D, E, G,* and *F.* Hence the four points are not coplanar and lines $\overleftrightarrow{GF}$ and $\overleftrightarrow{DE}$ are not coplanar. Two lines that cannot lie in the same plane are **skew lines.**

I N V E S T I G A T I O N   1 0 - 3

● How many planes are determined by four noncoplanar points *D, G, E,* and *F* in Figure 10-5? ●

Definitions and illustrations of various types of lines are given in Table 10-2. Exercises using these definitions are given in the Ongoing Assessment 10-1.

Table 10-2

Definition	Illustration
Two coplanar lines *m* and *n* are **intersecting lines** if, and only if, they have exactly one point in common.	*n* *P* *m*
Concurrent lines are lines that contain the same point. Concurrent lines may be either coplanar or noncoplanar.	*o* *q* *n* *P* *m*
Two distinct coplanar lines *m* and *n* that have no points in common are **parallel lines,** written $m \parallel n$.	*m* *n* $m \parallel n$
Two lines that cannot be contained in the same plane are **skew lines.** $\overleftrightarrow{AB}$ and $\overleftrightarrow{CD}$ are skew lines	*A* *C* *B* *D*

Two segments, two rays, or a ray and a segment are parallel if they lie on parallel lines. Although skew lines do not intersect, they are not parallel (why?).

Other examples of some of the basic geometric figures just discussed are given in the following student page from *Mathematics in Action,* Macmillan/McGraw-Hill, Grade 5, 1991.

DEVELOPING A CONCEPT

Geometry Around Us

Some basic geometric figures are suggested in this picture.

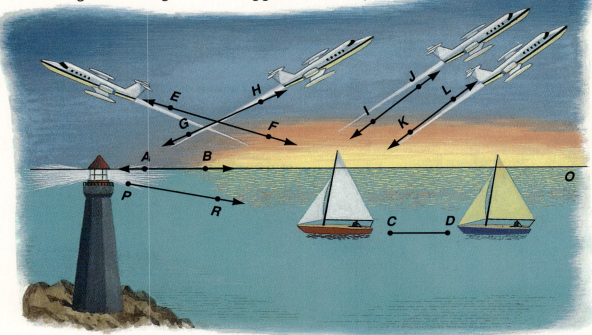

	Read	Symbol
The source of the light from the lighthouse suggests a point. A **point** is an exact location in space.	point *P*	*P*
A light beam coming from the lighthouse suggests a ray. A **ray** is part of a line.	ray *PR*	$\overrightarrow{PR}$
The horizon suggests a line. A **line** is made up of points and goes on and on in both directions.	line *AB* or line *BA*	$\overleftrightarrow{AB}$ or $\overleftrightarrow{BA}$
The distance between the ships suggests a line segment. A **line segment** is part of a line.	line segment *CD* or line segment *DC*	$\overline{CD}$ or $\overline{DC}$
The surface of the ocean suggests a plane. A **plane** is a flat surface that goes on and on in all directions.	plane *O*	plane *O*
The pair of jet trails at the top left suggest intersecting lines. **Intersecting lines** cross each other. The pair of jet trails at the top right suggest parallel lines. **Parallel lines** are lines in the same plane that never intersect.	$\overleftrightarrow{EF}$ intersects $\overleftrightarrow{GH}$ $\overleftrightarrow{IJ}$ is parallel to $\overleftrightarrow{KL}$ $\overleftrightarrow{IJ} \parallel \overleftrightarrow{KL}$	

Other Relations among Points, Lines, and Planes

A model of two walls intersecting in a segment suggests that if two distinct planes have any points in common, then that set of points is a line, as in Figure 10-6(a). If we consider the spine of a book to be a line and each page to be a plane, as in Figure 10-6(b), we see that infinitely many planes can contain a given line.

It is surprising to many students that three distinct planes may intersect in three ways: They may have a line in common, no common points, or just a single common point. In Figure 10-6(a), the walls and the floor (three distinct planes) intersect at a single point, the corner.

Figure 10-6

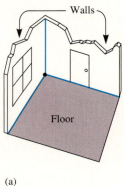

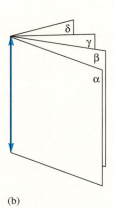

(a)   (b)

I N V E S T I G A T I O N   1 0 - 4

● We have seen that two distinct points determine a unique line. If lines were defined as "great circles" on a globe (circles resulting from the intersection of the globe and a plane through the center of the globe), would there be a unique line through two different points? Would it matter where the points were located? ●

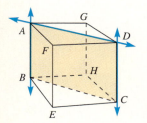

Figure 10-7

We have seen that three noncollinear points determine a unique plane. Implicit in this property are several other ways of determining a plane. Some of these are listed next and are illustrated in terms of the cube shown in Figure 10-7.

1. A line and a point not on the line determine a plane. (*Example:* $\overleftrightarrow{AB}$ and point C determine plane ABC.)
2. Two parallel lines determine a plane. (*Example:* $\overleftrightarrow{AB}$ and $\overleftrightarrow{CD}$ determine plane ABC.)
3. Two intersecting lines determine a plane. (*Example:* $\overleftrightarrow{AB}$ and $\overleftrightarrow{DA}$ determine plane ABD. Note that plane ABD and plane ABC are the same plane.)

We summarize the properties of points, lines, and planes next.

Properties of Points, Lines, and Planes

1. There is exactly one line that contains any two distinct points.
2. If two points lie in a plane, then the line containing the points lies in the plane.
3. If two distinct planes intersect, then their intersection is a line.
4. There is exactly one plane that contains any three distinct noncollinear points.
5. A line and a point not on the line determine a plane.
6. Two parallel lines determine a plane.
7. Two intersecting lines determine a plane.

Two distinct planes either intersect in a line or are parallel. In Figure 10-8(a), planes α and β are parallel; that is, they have no points in common. Figure 10-8(b) shows planes that intersect in $\overleftrightarrow{AB}$.

Figure 10-8

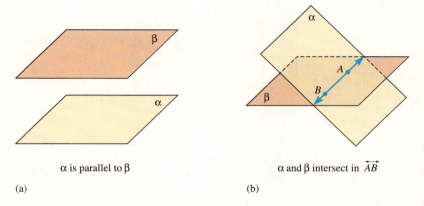

α is parallel to β α and β intersect in $\overleftrightarrow{AB}$

(a)   (b)

A line and a plane can be related in one of three possible ways. If a line and a plane have no points in common, the line is parallel to the plane, as in Figure 10-9(a). If two points of a line are in the plane, then the entire line containing the points is contained in the plane, as in Figure 10-9(b). If a line intersects a plane but is not contained in the plane, it intersects the plane at only one point, as in Figure 10-9(c).

Figure 10-9

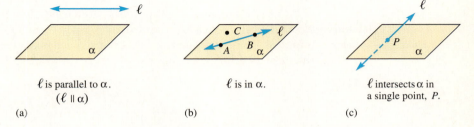

ℓ is parallel to α. ℓ is in α. ℓ intersects α in
($\ell \parallel \alpha$)   a single point, P.

(a)   (b)   (c)

A line in a plane separates the plane into two half-planes and the line itself. In Figure 10-9(b), line ℓ separates plane ABC into two half-planes. A half-plane may be specified by the line determining the half-plane and one point in the half-plane, such as the half-plane determined by $\overleftrightarrow{AB}$ and containing point C in Figure 10-9(b). A line and the two half-planes determined by the line are three disjoint subsets of a plane. Points, lines, and planes are all subsets of space. A plane separates space into two half-spaces. A plane and the two half-spaces determined by the plane are three disjoint subsets of space. The notion of a half-plane might be modeled by one side of a road on a plane. Can you think of a model for a half-space?

Angles

angle

side • vertex

When two rays share a common endpoint, an **angle** is formed, as shown in Figure 10-10(a). The rays of an angle are the **sides** of the angle, and the common endpoint is the **vertex** of the angle. An angle can be named by three different points: the vertex and a point on each ray, with the vertex always listed between the other two points. Thus the angle in Figure 10-10(a) may be named ∠CBA or ∠ABC. The latter is read "angle ABC." When there is no risk of confusion, it is customary simply to name an angle by its vertex, by a number, or by a lowercase Greek letter. The angle in Figure 10-10(a) also can therefore be named ∠B or ∠1. In Figure 10-10(b), however, more than one angle has vertex P, namely, ∠QPR, ∠RPS, and ∠QPS. Thus the notation ∠P is inadequate for naming any one of the angles α, β, or ∠QPS.

In Figure 10-10(c), ∠B separates the plane into three disjoint sets: the interior of the angle, the angle itself, and the exterior of the angle. Using the concept of the interior of an angle, we define adjacent angles, such as ∠QPR and ∠RPS in Figure 10-10(b), as follows:

adjacent angles

Adjacent angles are angles that share a common vertex and a common side and have nonoverlapping interiors.

Figure 10-10

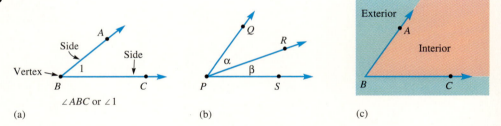

(a) ∠ABC or ∠1   (b)   (c)

Angle Measurement

degree

An angle is measured according to the amount of "opening" between its sides. A unit commonly used for measuring angles is the **degree.** A complete rotation about a point has a measure of 360°. One degree is then $\frac{1}{360}$ of a complete rotation. Figure 10-11 shows that ∠BAC has a measure of 30 degrees, written $m(\angle BAC) = 30°$. The measuring device pictured in the figure is a **protractor.** A degree is subdivided into 60 equal parts —

protractor

minutes • seconds

minutes — and each minute is further subdivided into 60 equal parts — **seconds.** The measurement 29 degrees, 47 minutes, 13 seconds is written 29°47′ 13″.

Figure 10-11

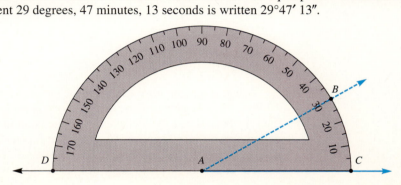

Example 10-1

a. In Figure 10-12, find the measure of $\angle BAC$ if $m(\angle 1) = 47°45'$ and $m(\angle 2) = 29°58'$.

b. Express $47°45'$ as a number of degrees.

Figure 10-12

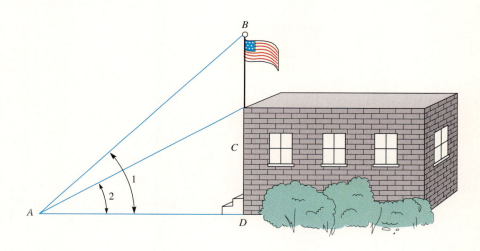

Solution   **a.** $m(\angle BAC) = 47°45' - 29°58'$
$$= 46°(60 + 45)' - 29°58'$$
$$= 46°105' - 29°58'$$
$$= (46 - 29)° + (105 - 58)'$$
$$= 17°47'$$

b. $47°45' = 47\dfrac{45°}{60} = 47.75°$

Types of Angles

We can create different types of angles by paper folding, especially with wax paper. Consider the folds shown in Figure 10-13(a) and (b). A piece of paper is folded in half and then reopened. If any point on the fold line labeled ℓ is chosen as the vertex, then the measure of the angle pictured is 180°. If the paper is refolded and folded once more, as shown in Figure 10-13(c), and then is reopened, as shown in Figure 10-13(d), four angles of the same size are created. Each angle has measure 90° and is a right angle.

Figure 10-13

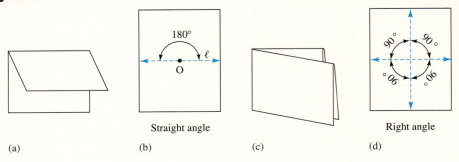

(a) (b) Straight angle (c) (d) Right angle

If the paper is folded as shown in Figure 10-14 and reopened, then angles α and β are formed, with measures that are less than 90° and greater than 90°, respectively. (Note that β has measure less than 180°.) Angle α is an *acute* angle while β is an *obtuse* angle.

Figure 10-14

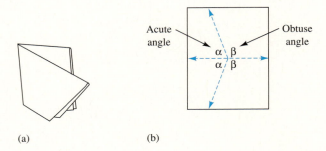

(a) (b)

The different types of planar angles just discovered are shown in Figure 10-15, along with their definitions.

Figure 10-15

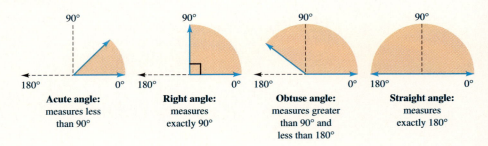

Acute angle: measures less than 90°

Right angle: measures exactly 90°

Obtuse angle: measures greater than 90° and less than 180°

Straight angle: measures exactly 180°

The symbol ⌐ denotes a right angle.

Perpendicular Lines

perpendicular lines

When two lines intersect so that the angles formed are right angles, as in Figure 10-16, the lines are **perpendicular lines.** In Figure 10-16, lines m and n are perpendicular, and we write $m \perp n$. Two intersecting segments, two intersecting rays, or one segment and one ray that intersect are perpendicular if they lie on perpendicular lines. For example, in Figure 10-16, $\overline{AB} \perp \overline{BC}$, $\overrightarrow{BA} \perp \overrightarrow{BC}$, and $\overleftrightarrow{AB} \perp \overleftrightarrow{BC}$.

Figure 10-16

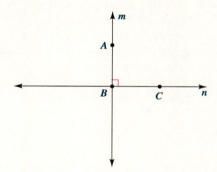

A Line Perpendicular to a Plane

If a line and a plane intersect, they can be perpendicular. For example, consider Figure 10-17, where planes β and γ represent two walls intersecting along $\overleftrightarrow{AB}$. The edge $\overleftrightarrow{AB}$ is perpendicular to the floor. Also, every line in the plane of the floor (plane α) passing through point A is perpendicular to $\overleftrightarrow{AB}$. This discussion should help you understand what is meant by a line perpendicular to a plane.

Figure 10-17

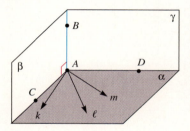

Dihedral Angles

The plane containing one wall and the plane containing the floor of a typical room such as α or β in Figure 10-17 are perpendicular planes. One way to determine whether two planes are perpendicular is to determine the measure of an angle formed by the intersecting planes. If the angle formed by the planes is a right angle, then the planes are perpendicular.

dihedral angle   A **dihedral angle** is the union of two half-planes and the common line defining the half-planes. The half-planes are usually referred to as the *faces* of the dihedral angle, and the common line is referred to as the *edge* of the dihedral angle. In Figure 10-18, dihedral angle *O-AC-D* is formed by the intersecting planes α and β. Note that point O is in plane α, $\overleftrightarrow{AC}$ is the edge of the dihedral angle, and point D is in plane β. In what other ways could the dihedral angle be named?

Figure 10-18

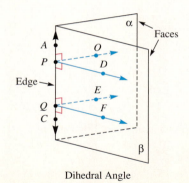

Dihedral Angle

With a given dihedral angle, we can associate a planar angle by choosing a point *P* on the edge of the dihedral angle and drawing two rays, one in each face, perpendicular to the edge. In Figure 10-18, ∠*OPD* and ∠*EQF* are planar angles associated with the dihedral angle. It can be shown that ∠*OPD* and ∠*EQF* are congruent and, in general, that all planar angles associated with a given dihedral angle are congruent. This property enables us to measure a dihedral angle. *We define the measure of a dihedral angle as the measure of any of the associated planar angles.*

Ongoing Assessment 10-1

1. Letters on a computer monitor are formed when a series of pixels (picture elements) are lighted. The more lights used, the more distinct the letter becomes. Consider the following magnified symbol for the number 1. Is the symbol a true geometric segment? Why or why not?

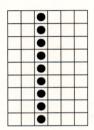

2. For the following figure, answer the following:
   a. Name two pairs of skew lines.
   b. Are $\overleftrightarrow{BD}$ and $\overleftrightarrow{FH}$ parallel, skew, or intersecting lines?
   c. Are $\overleftrightarrow{BD}$ and $\overleftrightarrow{GH}$ parallel?
   d. Find the intersection of $\overleftrightarrow{BD}$ and plane *EFG*.
   e. Find the intersection of $\overleftrightarrow{BH}$ and plane *DCG*.
   f. Name two pairs of perpendicular planes.
   g. Name two lines that are perpendicular to plane *EFH*.
   h. Name a planar angle that could be used to measure dihedral angle *E-FH-B*.
   i. What is the measure of dihedral angle *D-HG-F*?

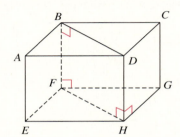

3. Use the following drawing of one of the Great Pyramids of Egypt to find the following:
   a. The intersection of $\overline{AD}$ and $\overline{CE}$

   b. The dihedral angle formed by planes *BDE* and *BDA*
   c. The intersection of planes *ABC*, *ACE*, and *BCE*
   d. The intersection of $\overleftrightarrow{AD}$ and $\overleftrightarrow{CA}$
   e. A pair of skew lines
   f. A pair of parallel lines
   g. A plane is not determined by one of the triangular faces or by the base

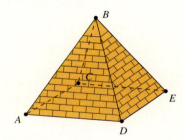

4. Determine how many pairs of adjacent angles are in the following figure:

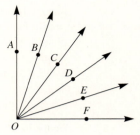

5. Identify a possible physical model for each of the following:
   a. Perpendicular lines
   b. An acute angle
   c. An obtuse angle
   d. An obtuse dihedral angle
   e. An acute dihedral angle
   f. A line containing two distinct points
   g. Four noncoplanar points

6. Find the measure of each of the following angles:
   a. ∠EAB
   b. ∠EAD
   c. ∠GAF
   d. ∠CAF

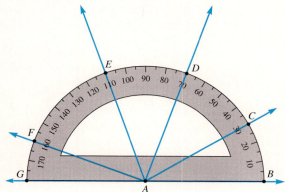

7. Use a protractor to find the measure of each of the following pictured angles:

Paper scissors

(a)

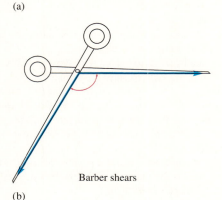

Barber shears

(b)

8. a. Perform each of the following operations. Leave your answers in simplest form.
   i. 18°35′ 29″ + 22°55′ 41″
   ii. 93°38′ 14″ − 13°49′ 27″
   b. Express each of the following in degrees, minutes, and seconds, without decimals:

   i. 0.9°
   ii. 15.13°

9. Consider a correctly set clock that starts ticking at noon and answer the following:
   a. Find the measure of the angle swept by the hour hand by the time it reaches
      i. 3 P.M.
      ii. 12:25 P.M.
      iii. 6:50 P.M.
   b. Find the exact angle between the minute and the hour hand at 1:15 P.M.
   c. At what time between 12 noon and 1 P.M. will the angle between the hands be 180°?

10. Mario was studying right angles and wondered if during his math class the minute and hour hands of the clock formed a right angle. If his class meets from 2:00 P.M. to 2:50 P.M., determine whether a right angle is formed. If it is, figure out to the nearest minute when the hands form the right angle.

11. Determine how many rays are determined by each of the following:
   a. Three collinear points
   b. Four collinear points
   c. Five collinear points
   d. *n* collinear points

12. Find out how many lines are determined by the following:
   a. Three noncollinear points
   b. Four points, no three of which are collinear
   c. Five points, no three of which are collinear
   d. *n* points, no three of which are collinear

13. Refer to the following table.
   a. Sketch the possible intersections of the given number of lines. (Using dry spaghetti may help.) Three sketches are given for you.

Number of Intersection Points

		0	1	2	3	4	5
	2		╳	Not possible	Not possible	Not possible	Not possible
	3					Not possible	Not possible
Number of Lines	4				⊕		⊕
	5						
	6						

   b. Given *n* lines, find a formula for determining the greatest possible number of intersection points.

14. Trace each of the following drawings. In your tracings, use dashed lines for segments that would not be seen and solid lines for segments that would be seen. (Different people may see different perspectives.)

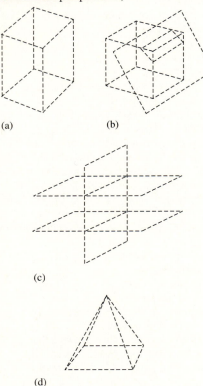

(a)   (b)

(c)

(d)

15. Into how many regions can a plane be separated by each of the following? (Do not count the lines.)
   a. Two parallel lines
   b. Two intersecting lines
   c. Three parallel lines
   d. Three lines that intersect in a single point
   e. n lines that intersect in a single point
16. Given the following three sets, list all regions that must be empty:

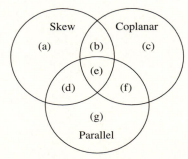

17. Prove that if two parallel planes are intersected by a third plane, the lines of intersection are parallel.

18. Write Logo procedures to draw each of the following:
   a. A procedure called ANGLE with input :SIZE to draw a variable-sized angle
   b. A procedure called SEGMENT with input :LENGTH to draw a variable-sized segment
   c. A procedure called PERPENDICULAR with inputs :LENGTH1 and :LENGTH2 to draw two variable-sized perpendicular segments
   d. A procedure called PARALLEL with inputs :LENGTH1 and :LENGTH2 to draw two variable-sized parallel segments

Communication

19. Forest rangers use degree measures to identify directions and locate critical spots such as fires. In the following drawing, a forest ranger at tower A observes smoke at a bearing of 149° (clockwise from the north), while another forest ranger at tower B observes the same source of smoke at a bearing of 250° (clockwise from the north).

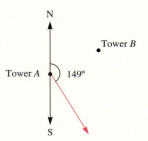

   a. Choose two locations for A and B and use a protractor and a straightedge to locate the source of the smoke.
   b. Explain how the forest rangers could find the location of the fire.
   c. Describe other situations in which location can be determined by using similar methods.
20. Explain mathematically why a three-legged stool is always stable and a four-legged stool sometimes rocks.
21. a. Is it possible for a line to be perpendicular to one line in a plane but not perpendicular to the plane? Explain.
   b. Is it possible for a line to be perpendicular to two distinct lines in a plane and yet not be perpendicular to the plane? Explain.
   c. If a line not in a given plane is perpendicular to two distinct lines in the plane, is the line necessarily perpendicular to the plane? Explain.
22. Is it possible to locate four points in a plane such that the number of lines determined by the points is not 1, 4, or 6? Explain.

Cooperative Learning

23. Each member of your group should use a protractor to make a triangle out of cardboard that has one angle measuring 30° and another 50°. Answer the following and compare your solutions with other members of your group:

a. Show how to use the triangle (without a protractor) to draw an angle with measure 40°.

b. Is there more than one way to draw an angle as in (a) using the triangle? Explain.

c. What other angles can be drawn with the triangle? Why?

24. Given *n* points in space, no 3 of which are collinear and no 4 of which are coplanar, find (i) the number of lines and (ii) the number of planes that can be determined for each of the following. (In (a), (b), and (c), work individually. Work on (d) as a group.)

    a. *n* = 3   **b.** *n* = 4   **c.** *n* = 5

    d. Any natural number, *n* (your answer should be in terms of *n*). Write a group solution so that a person who did not know how to answer the question could understand your solution.

Open-ended

The following activities involve Level 0 of the van Hiele structure for learning geometry:

25. Within the classroom, identify a physical object with the following shapes:

    a. Parallel lines   **b.** Parallel planes

    c. Skew lines   **d.** Dihedral angle

    e. Right angles

26. On a sheet of dot paper or on a geoboard, shown as follows, create the following shapes:

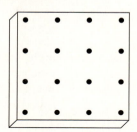

    a. Right angle   **b.** Acute angle

    c. Obtuse angle   **d.** Adjacent angles

    e. Parallel lines   **f.** Intersecting lines

TECHNOLOGY CORNER

Use Logo to predict the outcomes by sketching the corresponding figure when each of the following is executed. Check your predictions on the computer.

    a. RT 900 FD 50

    b. LT 900 FD 50

    c. REPEAT 4 [FD 50 RT 90]

    d. REPEAT 5 [FD 60 RT 72]

    e. REPEAT 5 [FD 60 RT 144]

LABORATORY ACTIVITY

Many geometric ideas can be experienced through paper folding. Consider the following construction of perpendicular lines and answer the questions that follow:

Fold one corner of a sheet of paper over and crease it along the fold.

Fold any part of the crease onto itself.

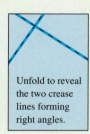

Unfold to reveal the two crease lines forming right angles.

a. Explain why the two crease lines are perpendicular.

b. Use a sheet of paper and follow the above instructions to create two pairs of perpendicular lines.

c. Use paper folding to create angles with the following measures:

    i. 45°   ii. 135°   iii. 22° 30′

(*Mathematics Through Paper Folding* by Olsen and *Geometric Exercises in Paper Foldings* by Row are listed in the bibliography as resource books.)

Section 10-2   Polygonal Curves

Suppose we were to take a pencil and draw a path on a piece of paper without lifting the pencil and without retracing any part of the path except for single points. The fact that we are drawing on a sheet of paper restricts us to a plane and the fact that we do not lift the pencil implies that we have no breaks in our drawing or that the curve is "connected."

closed curve   In Figure 10-19, each curve is in the plane and is connected, but there are some obvious differences between the curves. For example, the **closed curves** in (b), (c), (f), (g), (h), (i), (j), and (k) could be drawn by starting and stopping at the same point. The closed curves in (b) and (f) cross themselves, whereas those in (c), (g), (h), (i), (j), and (k) do not. A **simple curve**   **simple curve** does not cross itself. The curves in (c), (g), (h), (i), (j), and (k) are simple closed curves. The curves in (d), (e), (f), (g), (h), and (j) are made up entirely of line segments and are **polygonal curves. Polygons** are simple, closed polygonal curves, as in **polygonal curve** • **polygons**   Figure 10-19 (g), (h), and (j).

Figure 10-19

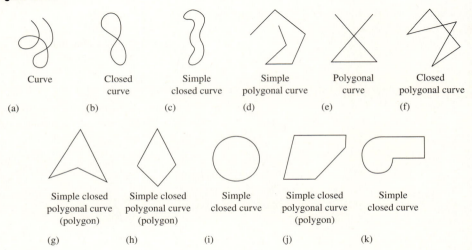

Curve	Closed curve	Simple closed curve	Simple polygonal curve	Polygonal curve	Closed polygonal curve
(a)	(b)	(c)	(d)	(e)	(f)

Simple closed polygonal curve (polygon)	Simple closed polygonal curve (polygon)	Simple closed curve	Simple closed polygonal curve (polygon)	Simple closed curve
(g)	(h)	(i)	(j)	(k)

The line segments forming a polygon are the *sides* of the polygon. A point where two sides meet is a *vertex* of the polygon. Every simple closed polygon separates the plane into three disjoint subsets: the interior of the polygon, the exterior of the polygon, and the polygon itself. This is illustrated in Figure 10-20(b). Together, a polygon and its interior form a **polygonal region**   **polygonal region.**

Figure 10-20

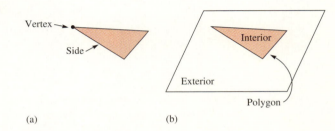

(a)   (b)

Whether a point is inside or outside a curve is not always obvious. This is explored in the next investigation.

INVESTIGATION ·1 0 - 5

● Determine whether point *X* is inside or outside the simple closed curve of Figure 10-21. Explain your reasoning so that it can be generalized to other simple closed curves. ●

Figure 10-21

More about Polygons

convex polygon

The polygon in Figure 10-22(a) has no indentations, while the one in Figure 10-22(b) is indented. Mathematically, if the segment connecting any two points of a polygonal region is a subset of the polygonal region, then the polygon is a **convex polygon.** For example, in Figure 10-22(a) no matter which two points of the hexagonal region are chosen as the endpoints of a segment, the entire segment lies in the hexagonal region. This is not the case in Figure 10-22(b), where it is possible to draw a segment between two points of the polygonal region such that part of the segment lies outside the region. Figure 10-22(b) shows a

concave polygon

concave polygon.

Polygons are classified according to the number of sides or vertices they have. For example, consider the polygons listed in Table 10-3.

Table 10-3

Convex polygon

(a)

Concave polygon

(b)

Figure 10-22

Polygon	Number of Sides or Vertices
Triangle	3
Quadrilateral	4
Pentagon	5
Hexagon	6
Heptagon	7
Octagon	8
Nonagon	9
Decagon	10
n-gon	n

interior angle, or angle, of a
polygon • exterior angle of
a polygon

A polygon is referred to by the capital letters that represent its consecutive vertices, such as shown in Figure 10-23: *ABCD* or *CDAB* (but not *BCAD*). Any two sides of a polygon having a common vertex determine an **interior angle,** or **angle, of the polygon,** such as ∠1 of polygon *ABCD* in Figure 10-23(a). An **exterior angle of a polygon** is determined by a side of the polygon and the extension of a contiguous side of the polygon. An example is ∠2 in Figure 10-23(b). Any line segment connecting nonconsecutive vertices of a polygon is a diagonal. In Figure 10-23(a), segment $\overline{AC}$ is a diagonal of polygon *ABCD*.

Figure 10-23

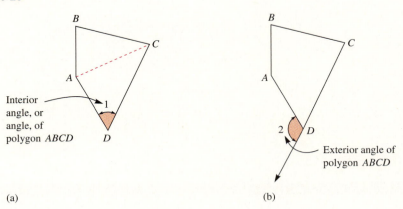

(a)   (b)

String art is often constructed on the basis of polygons and their diagonals. Problem 1 investigates the number of diagonals in such a polygon.

Problem 1

How many diagonals does the 24-gon pictured in Figure 10-24 have?

Figure 10-24

Understanding the Problem.   We have a polygon with 24 sides and are to determine how many different diagonals can be drawn.

■ *Devising a Plan.* We use the strategy of *examining related simpler cases* of the problem in order to develop a pattern for the original problem. Figure 10-25 shows that a triangle has no diagonals, a square has two diagonals, a pentagon has five, and a hexagon has nine.

Figure 10-25

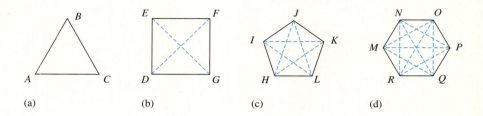

(a)   (b)   (c)   (d)

Examining Figure 10-25(d), we see that from any vertex, we can draw only three diagonals from that vertex. In general, we cannot draw a diagonal from a chosen vertex to itself or to either of the two adjacent vertices. In Figure 10-25(d), the number of diagonals that can be drawn from any one vertex is three less than the total number of vertices, that is, $6 - 3$, or 3. Similarly, in a polygon with 24 sides, the number of diagonals that can be drawn from any one vertex is three less than the number of vertices, that is, $24 - 3$, or 21. Because 21 diagonals emanate from each of the 24 vertices, we should be able to use this information to determine the total number of diagonals.

Carrying Out the Plan. It might appear that we have 24(21), or 504, diagonals in a 24-gon. However, based on this notion, we should also have $6(6 - 3)$, or 18, diagonals in a hexagon. This result does not agree with the actual number of nine. This is because each diagonal is determined by two vertices and when we counted the number of diagonals from each vertex, we counted each diagonal twice. Hence, in a 24-gon, there must be 24(21)/2, or 252, diagonals.

Looking Back. Using this reasoning, we conclude that the number of diagonals in an n-gon is $n(n-3)/2$. This formula gives results consistent with the number of diagonals pictured in Figure 10-25. An alternative solution to this problem uses the notion of combinations. The number of ways that all the vertices in an n-gon can be connected two at a time is the number of combinations of n vertices chosen two at a time, that is, $_nC_2$, or $\dfrac{n(n-1)}{2}$. This number of segments includes both the number of diagonals and the number of sides. If we subtract the number of sides n from $\dfrac{n(n-1)}{2}$, the number of diagonals is $\dfrac{n(n-1)}{2} - n$. This expression can be simplified to $\dfrac{n(n-3)}{2}$.

• • •

Congruent Segments and Angles

congruent parts   Most modern industries operate on the notion of creating **congruent parts,** parts that are of the same size and shape. For example, the specifications for all cars of a particular model are the same, and all parts produced for that model are basically the same. Most frequently, when we discuss congruent figures, we are discussing figures in a plane.

congruent segments   For example, two line **segments** are **congruent** ($\cong$) if a tracing of one line segment can be fitted exactly on top of the other. If $\overline{AB}$ is congruent to $\overline{CD}$, we write $\overline{AB} \cong \overline{CD}$. Two

congruent angles

angles are **congruent** if they have the same measure. Congruent segments and congruent angles are shown in Figure 10-26(a) and (b), respectively.

Figure 10-26

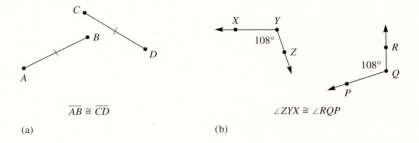

$$\overline{AB} \cong \overline{CD}$$

(a)

$$\angle ZYX \cong \angle RQP$$

(b)

Regular Polygons

regular polygons

Polygons in which all the angles are congruent and all the sides are congruent are **regular polygons.** A regular polygon is both *equiangular* and *equilateral.* A regular triangle is an equilateral triangle. A regular pentagon and a regular hexagon are illustrated in Figure 10-27. The congruent sides and congruent angles are marked.

Figure 10-27

Polygon	Example
Regular pentagon	Pentagon (world's largest office building)
Regular hexagon	Hexnut

Triangles and Quadrilaterals

Triangles may be classified according to their angle measures, as shown in Table 10-4. Triangles and quadrilaterals may also be classified as shown in Table 10-5.

Table 10-4

Definition	Illustration	Example
A triangle containing one right angle is a **right triangle.**		
A triangle in which all the angles are acute is an **acute triangle.**		YIELD
A triangle containing one obtuse angle is an **obtuse triangle.**		

Table 10-5

Definition	Illustration	Example
A triangle with no sides congruent is a **scalene triangle.**		
A triangle with at least two sides congruent is an **isosceles triangle.**		
A triangle with three sides congruent is an **equilateral triangle.**		
A **trapezoid** is a quadrilateral with at least one pair of parallel sides.		
A **kite** is a quadrilateral with at least two distinct pairs of consecutive sides congruent.		
An **isosceles trapezoid** is a trapezoid with one pair of base angles congruent. (Equivalently, an isosceles trapezoid is a trapezoid with two nonadjacent sides congruent.)		
A **parallelogram** is a quadrilateral in which each pair of opposite sides is parallel.		
A **rectangle** is a parallelogram with a right angle. (Equivalently, a rectangle is a quadrilateral with four right angles.)		
A **rhombus** is a parallelogram with all sides congruent. (Equivalently, a rhombus is a quadrilateral with all sides congruent.)		
A **square** is a rectangle with all sides congruent. (Equivalently, a square is a quadrilateral with four right angles and four congruent sides.)		

Some texts give different definitions for a trapezoid. Many elementary texts define a trapezoid as a quadrilateral with *exactly* one pair of parallel sides. Note the definition of a trapezoid on the following student page from *Addison-Wesley Mathematics*, Grade 4, 1993. An excellent teaching aid, a *tangram,* is used on this page.

Classifying Quadrilaterals

LEARN ABOUT IT

EXPLORE   Use a Tangram Puzzle

- How many quadrilaterals of different shapes can you make using any combination of pieces A and B? Draw each one.

- How many different quadrilaterals can you make with pieces C, D, and E? Draw each one.

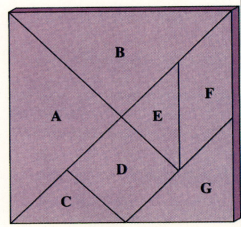

Tangram Puzzle

TALK ABOUT IT

1. Which of your quadrilaterals have at least one right angle?

2. Which have one pair of parallel sides?

3. Which have two pairs of sides that are the same length?

4. Which have all sides the same length?

Here are some types of quadrilaterals.

Square

All sides the same length
All angles right angles

Rectangle

Two pairs of same-length sides
All angles right angles

Trapezoid

Exactly one pair of parallel sides

Parallelogram

Two pairs of same-length sides
Two pairs of parallel sides

Hierarchy among Polygons

Every triangle is a polygon, and every equilateral triangle is also isosceles. However, not every isosceles triangle is equilateral. Using set concepts, we can say that the set of all triangles is a proper subset of the set of all polygons. Also, the set of all equilateral triangles is a proper subset of the set of all isosceles triangles. This hierarchy is shown in Figure 10-28, where more general terms appear above more specific ones.

Figure 10-28

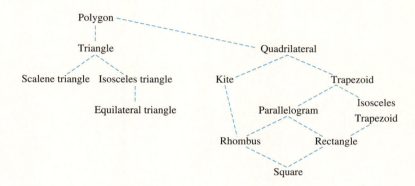

INVESTIGATION 10-6

● Use the definitions in Tables 10-4 and 10-5 to experiment with several drawings to decide which of the following are true:

1. An equilateral triangle is isosceles.
2. A square is a regular quadrilateral.
3. If one angle of a rhombus is a right angle, then all the angles of the rhombus are right angles.

4. A square is a rhombus with a right angle.
5. All the angles of a rectangle are right angles.
6. A rectangle is an isosceles trapezoid.
7. Some isosceles trapezoids are kites.
8. If a kite has a right angle, then it must be a square. ●

Ongoing Assessment 10-2

1. Determine for each of the following which of the figures labeled (1)–(10) can be classified under the given term:
   a. Polygonal curve
   b. Simple polygonal curve
   c. Closed polygonal curve
   d. Polygon
   e. Convex polygon
   f. Concave polygon

(1)   (2)   (3)   (4)   (5)   (6)   (7) (8)   (9)   (10)

2. Which of the printed capital letters of the English alphabet are simple, closed curves?
3. What is the maximum number of intersection points between a quadrilateral and a triangle (where no sides of the polygons are on the same line)?
4. What type of polygon must have a diagonal such that part of the diagonal falls outside of the polygon?
5. Which of the following figures are convex, and which are concave? Why?

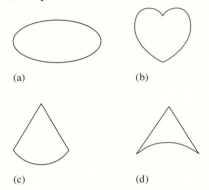

(a)   (b)

(c)   (d)

6. If possible, draw the following triangles. If it is not possible, state why.
   a. An obtuse scalene triangle
   b. An acute scalene triangle
   c. A right scalene triangle
   d. An obtuse equilateral triangle
   e. A right equilateral triangle
   f. An obtuse isosceles triangle
   g. An acute isosceles triangle
   h. A right isosceles triangle
7. Determine how many diagonals each of the following has:
   a. Decagon
   b. 20-gon
   c. 100-gon
8. Identify each of the following triangles as scalene, isosceles, or equilateral:

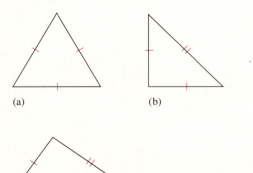

(a)   (b)

(c)

9. Describe regions (a) and (b) in the following Venn diagram:

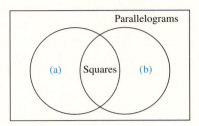

Parallelograms

(a)   Squares   (b)

10. Use the labeled points in the following drawing to answer the questions:

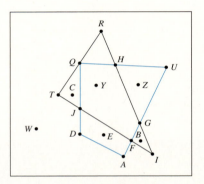

a. Which points belong to triangle *TRI*?
b. Which points belong to the interior of the quadrilateral *QUAD*?
c. Which points belong to the exterior of triangle *TRI*?
d. Which points belong to triangle *TRI* and quadrilateral *QUAD*?
e. Which points belong to the intersection of the interiors of triangle *TRI* and quadrilateral *QUAD*?
11. Write Logo procedures to draw each of the following:
   a. A simple polygonal curve
   b. A closed polygonal curve
   c. A nonsimple nonclosed polygonal curve
   d. A simple closed polygonal curve
12. Write a Logo program to draw each of the following:
   a. A square
   b. A rectangle

Communication

13. a. Fold a rectangular piece of paper to create a square. Describe your procedure in writing and orally with a classmate. Explain why your approach creates a square.
   b. Crease the square in (a) so that the two diagonals are shown. Use paper folding to show that the diagonals of a square are congruent and perpendicular and bisect each other. Describe your procedure and explain why it works.

Open-ended

14. On a geoboard, construct each of the following:

    a. A scalene triangle

    b. A square

    c. A trapezoid

    d. A convex hexagon

    e. A concave quadrilateral

    f. A parallelogram

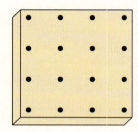

Cooperative Learning

15. Work with a partner. One of you should construct a figure on a geoboard or draw it on a piece of paper and name it. Do not show the figure to your partner but tell your partner the properties of the figure that you think are sufficient to identify it. Have your partner try to identify the figure you constructed. Your partner earns 1 point if the figure is correctly identified and 2 points if a figure is found that has all the required attributes but is different from the one you drew. Each of you should take the same number of turns. Try this with each of the following types of figures:

    a. Scalene triangle

    b. Isosceles triangle

    c. Square

    d. Parallelogram

    e. Trapezoid

    f. Rectangle

    g. Regular polygon

    h. Rhombus

    i. Isosceles trapezoid

    j. A kite that is not a rhombus

16. Car engines have fan belts, like the one shown in the following figure, to keep the engine cool. The large pulley is a **driver** and the smaller one is a **follower**.

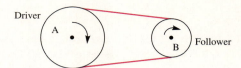

When the driver rotates by an angle whose measure is α, it causes the follower to rotate by an angle whose measure is β. The angles are related by the following formula:

$$\frac{\alpha}{\beta} = \frac{diameter\ of\ B}{diameter\ of\ A}$$

   a. With a partner, investigate how the chain and sprockets in a modern bicycle are related to the concept of a fan belt. Say the larger sprocket of the chain has 40 teeth and the smaller one 10 teeth. If the larger sprocket makes one full revolution, how many revolutions will the smaller sprocket make?

   b. Why do you think it is useful to create a fan belt by crossing the belt as shown in the following figure? Discuss the answer in your group and compare it with other groups' answers.

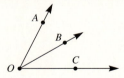

Review Problems

17. If three distinct rays with the same vertex are drawn as shown in the following figure, then three different angles are formed: $\angle AOB$, $\angle AOC$, and $\angle BOC$:

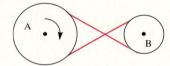

   a. How many different angles are formed by using 10 distinct noncollinear rays with the same vertex?

   b. How many different angles are formed by using n distinct noncollinear rays with the same vertex?

18. Determine the possible intersection sets of a line and an angle.

19. Classify the following as true or false. If false, tell why.

    a. A ray has two endpoints.

    b. For any points M and N, $\overleftrightarrow{MN} = \overleftrightarrow{NM}$.

    c. Skew lines are coplanar.

    d. $\overrightarrow{MN} = \overrightarrow{NM}$

    e. A line segment contains an infinite number of points.

    f. If two distinct planes intersect, their intersection is a line segment.

TECHNOLOGY CORNER

Use Logo to create each of the following figures. In each case, give the sequence of commands used to create the figure.

a. A figure similar to the following.

b. A figure that resembles the following but that is made of ten squares.

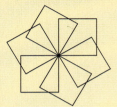

LABORATORY ACTIVITY

1. The following van Hiele Level 1 activity consists of using cutouts of different quadrilaterals. Sort the shapes according to the following attributes:

  a. Number of parallel sides

  b. Number of right angles

  c. Number of congruent sides

  d. Polygons with congruent diagonals

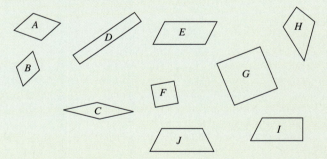

2. Use the cutouts to identify properties characteristic of different classes of figures. For example, "Congruent opposite sides describe a parallelogram."

BRAIN TEASER

Given three buildings *A, B,* and *C,* as shown in the following figure, and three utility centers for electricity (*E*), gas (*G*), and water (*W*), determine whether it is possible to connect each of the three buildings to each of the three utility centers without crossing lines.

Section 10-3 # Linear Measure

To measure a segment, we must decide on a unit of measure and find how many of these units fit into the segment. Early attempts at measurement lacked a standard unit object and so used hands, arms, and feet as units of measure. These early crude measurements were eventually refined and standardized by the English into a very complicated system.

The English System

Originally, in the English system, a yard was the distance from the tip of the nose to the end of an outstretched arm of an adult person and a foot was the length of a human foot. In 1893, the United States defined the yard and other units in terms of metric units. Some units of length in the English system and relationships among them are summarized in Table 10-6.

Table 10-6

Unit	Equivalent in Other Units
yard (yd)	3 ft
foot (ft)	12 in.
mile (mi)	1760 yd, or 5280 ft

Example 10-2 Convert each of the following:

a. 218 ft = _____ yd **b.** 8432 yd = _____ mi
c. 0.2 mi = _____ ft **d.** 64 in. = _____ yd

Solution **a.** Because 1 ft = $\frac{1}{3}$ yd, 218 ft = $218 \cdot \frac{1}{3}$ yd $\doteq$ 72.67 yd.

b. Because 1 yd = $\frac{1}{1760}$ mi, 8432 yd = $8432 \cdot \frac{1}{1760}$ mi $\doteq$ 4.79 mi.

c. 1 mi = 5280 ft. Hence, 0.2 mi = $0.2 \cdot 5280$ ft = 1056 ft.

d. We first find a connection between yards and inches. We have 1 yd = 3 ft and 1 ft = 12 in. Hence, 1 yd = 3 ft = $3 \cdot 12$ in. = 36 in. Hence, 1 in. = $\frac{1}{36}$ yd; therefore 64 in. = $64 \cdot \frac{1}{36}$ yd $\doteq$ 1.78 yd.

The Metric System

metric system

At this time, the United States is the only major industrial nation in the world that continues to use the English system. However, the use of the **metric system** in the United States has been increasing, particularly in the scientific community and in industry. *The 1995 World Almanac* points out: *"The Trade Act of 1988 and other legislation declare the metric system the preferred system of weights and measures of U.S. trade and commerce, call for the federal government to adopt metric specifications, and mandate the Commerce Dept. to oversee the program. The conversion process is currently under way; however, the metric system has not become the system of choice for most American's daily use."* In the *Teaching Standards* (p. 136), we find the following: *"Of particular importance should be an understanding of the Systeme Internationale d' Unites (the metric system.)"*

The metric system, a decimal system, was proposed in France in 1670 by Gabriel Mouton. However, not until the French Revolution in 1790 did the French Academy of Sciences bring various groups together to develop the system. The Academy recognized the need for a standard base unit of linear measurement. The members chose $\frac{1}{10,000,000}$ of the distance from the equator to the North Pole on a meridian through Paris as the base unit of length and called it the **meter (m).** In 1960, the meter was redefined in terms of krypton 86 wavelengths and still later as the distance traveled by light in a vacuum during $\frac{1}{299,792,458}$ sec. Since 1893, the yard in the United States has been defined as $\frac{3600}{3937}$ of a meter, whatever the definition of a meter.

The scientific definition of meter may not be very meaningful in everyday life. However, if you turn your head away from your outstretched arm, the distance from your nose to the fingertips of the outstretched hand is about 1 m (see Fig. 10-29). Also, 1 m is about the distance from a doorknob to the floor.

Different units of length in the metric system are obtained by multiplying a power of ten times the base unit. The prefixes for these units, the multiplication factors, and their symbols are given in Table 10-7.

Table 10-7

Prefix	Symbol	Factor	
kilo	k	1000	(one thousand)
*hecto	h	100	(one hundred)
*deka	da	10	(ten)
*deci	d	0.1	(one tenth)
centi	c	0.01	(one hundredth)
milli	m	0.001	(one thousandth)

*Not commonly used

The metric prefixes combined with the base unit meter name the different units of length. Table 10-8 gives these units, their relationship to the meter, and the symbol for each.

Table 10-8

Unit	Symbol	Relationship to Base Unit	
kilometer	km	1000	meters
*hectometer	hm	100	meters
*dekameter	dam	10	meters
meter	**m**	**base**	**unit**
*decimeter	dm	0.1	meter
centimeter	cm	0.01	meter
millimeter	mm	0.001	meter

*Not commonly used

REMARK   Two other prefixes, mega (1,000,000) and micro (0.000001), are used, respectively, for very large and very small units.

For easy references for metric measures of length, estimations for a meter, a decimeter, a centimeter, and a millimeter are shown in Figure 10-29. The kilometer is commonly used for measuring longer distances. Because "kilo" stands for 1000, 1 km = 1000 m. Nine football fields, including end zones, laid end to end are approximately 1 km long.

Figure 10-29

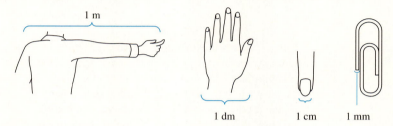

Conversions among metric lengths are accomplished by multiplying or dividing by powers of ten. As with money, we simply move the decimal point to the left or right, depending on the units. For example,

0.123 km = 1.23 hm = 12.3 dam = 123 m = 1230 dm = 12,300 cm = 123,000 mm.

It is possible to convert units by using the chart in Figure 10-30. We count the number of steps from one unit to the other and move the decimal point that many steps in the same direction.

Figure 10-30

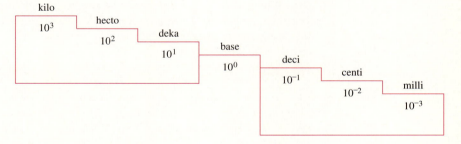

Example 10-3 | Convert each of the following:

a. 1.4 km = _____ m   **b.** 285 mm = _____ m   **c.** 0.03 km = _____ cm

Solution   **a.** To change kilometers to meters, we must either multiply by 1000, because 1 km = 1000 m, or move the decimal point three places to the right. Hence, 1.4 km = 1400 m.

b. To change from millimeters to meters, we must either multiply by 0.001, because 1 mm = 0.001 m, or move the decimal point three places to the left. Thus 285 mm = 0.285 m.

c. To change kilometers to centimeters, we must first multiply by 1000 to convert kilometers to meters and then multiply by 100 to convert meters to centimeters. Therefore we move the decimal five places to the right to obtain 0.03 km = 3000 cm.

Units of length are referred to as *linear measures* and are commonly measured with rulers. Figure 10-31 shows part of a centimeter ruler. Rulers can be used to measure distance.

Figure 10-31

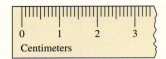

Measuring distances in the real world frequently results in errors. Because of this, many industrial plants using parts from a variety of sources rely on portable calibration units that are taken from plant to plant to test measuring instruments used in constructing the parts. This is done so that the final assembly plant can fit all the parts together to make the product. To calibrate the measuring instruments, technicians must establish the greatest possible error (GPE) allowable in order to obtain the final fit. The following student page from *Addison-Wesley Mathematics,* Grade 7, 1993, shows one approach to GPE for middle-school students.

When drawings are given, we assume that the measures listed are accurate. When actually measuring figures in the real world, we find that such accuracy is usually impossible.

Triangle Inequality

You may have heard the expression "The shortest distance between two points is a straight line." A person using the expression may have good intentions, but the statement is actually false. (Why?) The shortest among all the polygonal paths connecting two points A and B is along the segment $\overline{AB}$. This fact follows from the **Triangle Inequality,** which is one of the basic properties of distance listed next.

Properties

1. The distance between any two points A and B is greater than or equal to 0, written $AB \geq 0$. (Thus the length of $\overline{AB}$ is denoted by AB.)
2. The distance between any two points A and B is the same as the distance between B and A, written $AB = BA$.
3. *Triangle Inequality:* For any three points A, B, and C, the distance between A and B plus the distance between B and C is greater than or equal to the distance between A and C, written $AB + BC \geq AC$.

In the special case in which A, B, and C are collinear and B is between A and C, as in Figure 10-32(a), we have $AB + BC = AC$. Otherwise, if A, B, and C are not collinear, as in Figure 10-32(b), then $AB + BC > AC$.

Figure 10-32

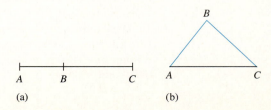

Precision in Measurement

LEARN ABOUT IT

EXPLORE Study the Chart

The chart shows the measurements of coins from five different countries. The coins were first measured using centimeters (A). They were measured again using millimeters (B). Place the coins in order from largest to smallest using each set of measurements.

Coin	A	B
	Diameter (nearest cm)	Diameter (nearest mm)
Haiti 10 centimes	2 cm	2.1 cm
Panama $\frac{1}{4}$ balboa	2 cm	2.4 cm
Peru 10 centavos	2 cm	2.1 cm
Greenland kroner	3 cm	3.3 cm
Liberia 50 cent	3 cm	2.9 cm

TALK ABOUT IT

1. Which coin has the largest diameter?

2. Why do you think the Panamanian and the Peruvian coins have the same A measurements, but different B measurements?

3. How could you make an even more precise measurement of the Haitian coin?

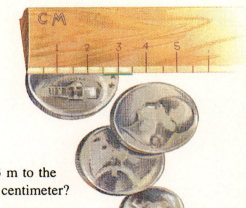

The **greatest possible error (GPE)** of a measurement is half (0.5) the measurement unit used. For example, if the diameter of a coin is measured at 3 cm to the nearest cm, the actual length of the diameter must be between 2.5 cm and 3.5 cm. In this case the GPE is 0.5 cm.

Example Which measurement is more precise, 23 m to the nearest meter or 23.40 m to the nearest centimeter?

The GPE of the first measurement is 0.5 m. The GPE of the second is 0.5 cm. This means 23.40 m to the nearest centimeter is a more precise measurement than 23 m to the nearest meter.

REMARK   Notice the difference between AB, $\overline{AB}$, and $\overleftrightarrow{AB}$. AB is the distance between two points A and B and therefore a nonnegative real number, $\overline{AB}$ is the segment connecting points A and B and therefore a set of points. $\overleftrightarrow{AB}$ is the line through points A and B.

Distance around a Plane Figure

perimeter   The **perimeter** of a simple closed curve is the length of the curve, that is, the distance around the figure. If a figure is a polygon, its perimeter is the sum of the lengths of the sides. A perimeter is always expressed in linear measure.

Example 10-4   Find the perimeter of each of the shapes in Figure 10-33.

Figure 10-33

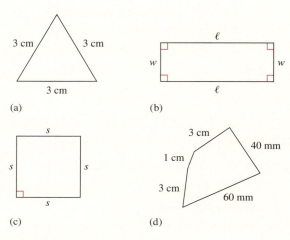

(e) a regular *n*-gon with side *s*.

Solution   **a.** The perimeter is $3(3) = 9$ cm.
b. The perimeter is $2w + 2l$.
c. The perimeter is $4s$.
d. Because 40 mm = 4 cm and 60 mm = 6 cm, the perimeter is $1 + 3 + 4 + 6 + 3 = 17$ cm.
e. Because all sides of a regular *n*-gon are congruent, the perimeter is *ns*.

Circles

In Figure 10-34, the regular 24-gon resembles a circle. The more sides a regular *n*-gon has, the closer it resembles a circle. (This type of thinking has led to a procedure in Logo for drawing a turtle-type circle as in the following Technology Corner.) A **circle** is defined by
circle
center   the set of all points in a plane that lie the same distance from a given point, the **center.**

Figure 10-34

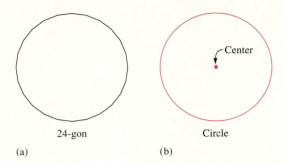

24-gon   Circle

(a)   (b)

To instruct the turtle to draw a figure that looks like a circle (*turtle-type circle*), we tell the turtle to move forward a little and turn a little and then repeat this sequence of motions until it comes back to its original position. The turtle is then told to go forward 1 unit and turn right 1°. This sequence of motions repeated 360 times yields a turtle-type circle, as shown in Figure 10-35.

Figure 10-35

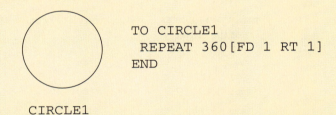

```
TO CIRCLE1
  REPEAT 360[FD 1 RT 1]
END
```

CIRCLE1

Figure 10-35 shows a Logo procedure CIRCLE and its output. Explore how to draw larger and smaller turtle-type circles using similar procedures.

Construction of Circles

Ancient Greek mathematicians constructed geometric figures with a straightedge (no markings on it) and a collapsible compass. Figure 10-36 shows a modern compass. It can be used to mark off and duplicate lengths and to construct circles or arcs with a radius of a given measure. To draw a circle when given the radius PQ of a circle, we follow the steps illustrated in the figure.

Figure 10-36

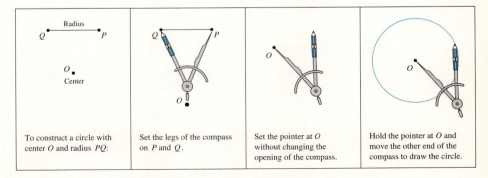

| To construct a circle with center O and radius PQ: | Set the legs of the compass on P and Q. | Set the pointer at O without changing the opening of the compass. | Hold the pointer at O and move the other end of the compass to draw the circle. |

Constructing a circle when given its radius

The figure formed in Figure 10-36 is a circle with center O and is called circle O. Any other circle is congruent to circle O if the radii of the two circles are congruent. In general, *two circles are congruent if their radii are congruent.*

Circumference of a Circle

circumference

The perimeter of a circle is its **circumference.** The ancient Greeks discovered that if they divided the circumference of any circle by the length of its diameter, they always obtained approximately the same number. The number is approximately 3.14 (see the Laboratory Activity at the end of this section). Today, the ratio of circumference C to diameter d is

pi

symbolized as π **(pi)**. *For most practical purposes, π is approximated by* $\frac{22}{7}$, $3\frac{1}{7}$, *or* 3.14.

These values are only approximations and are not exact values of π. For example, the "exact" circumference of a circle with diameter 6 cm is 6π cm.

A circumference is always expressed in linear measure. In the late eighteenth century, mathematicians proved that the ratio $\frac{C}{d}$, or π, is not a terminating or repeating decimal. Rather, it is an irrational number.

The relationship $\frac{C}{d} = \pi$ is a formula for finding the circumference of a circle and normally is written as $C = \pi d$ or $C = 2\pi r$ because the length of diameter d is twice the radius (r) of the circle.

HISTORICAL   NOTE

$\pi = 3.14159$
26535
89793
23846
26433
83279
50288
41971
69399
37510
58209
.
.
.

Archimedes (b. 287 B.C.) found an approximation for π given by the inequality $3\frac{10}{71} < \pi < 3\frac{10}{70}$. A Chinese astronomer thought that $\pi = \frac{355}{113}$. Ludolph van Ceulen (1540–1610), a German mathematician, calculated π to 35 decimal places. The approximation was engraved on his tombstone. Leonhard Euler adopted the symbol π in 1737 and caused its wide usage. In 1761, Johann Lambert, an Alsatian mathematician, proved that π is an irrational number. In 1989, Columbia University mathematicians and Soviet émigré brothers, David and Gregory Chudnovsky, used computers to establish 480 million digits of π. If these digits were printed along a line, the line would extend 600 mi.

Arc Length

The length of an arc depends on the radius of the circle and the central angle determining the arc. If the central angle has a measure of 180°, as in Figure 10-37(a), the arc is a

semicircle

semicircle. The length of a semicircle is $\frac{1}{2} \cdot 2\pi r$, or πr. The length of an arc whose central angle is $\theta°$ can be developed as in Figure 10-37(b) by using proportional reasoning. Since a circle has 360°, an angle of $\theta°$ determines $\theta/360$ of a circle. Because the circumference of a circle is $2\pi r$, an arc of $\theta°$ has length $\frac{\theta}{360} \cdot 2\pi r$, or $\frac{\pi r\theta}{180}$.

Figure 10-37

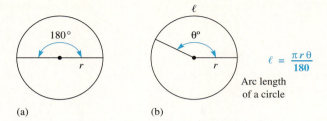

$$\ell = \frac{\pi r \theta}{180}$$

Arc length
of a circle

(a)   (b)

Example 10-5 | Find each of the following:

a. The circumference of a circle if the radius is 2 m
b. The radius of a circle if the circumference is 15π m
c. The length of a 25° arc of a circle of radius 10 cm
d. The radius of an arc whose central angle is 87° and whose length is 154 cm

Solution   **a.** $C = 2\pi(2) = 4\pi$; thus the circumference is 4π m.

b. $C = 2\pi r$ implies $15\pi = 2\pi r$. Hence, $r = \dfrac{15}{2}$ and the radius is $\dfrac{15}{2}$ m.

c. The arc length is $\dfrac{\pi r \theta}{180} = \dfrac{\pi \cdot 10 \cdot 25}{180}$ cm, or $\dfrac{25\pi}{18}$ cm, or approximately 4.36 cm.

d. The arc length ℓ is $\dfrac{\pi r \theta}{180}$, so that $154 = \dfrac{\pi r \cdot 87}{180} \doteq 101.4$

LABORATORY ACTIVITY

To approximate the value of π, you need string, a marked ruler, and several different-sized round tin cans or jars. Pick a can and wrap the string tightly around the can. Use a pen to mark a point on the string where the beginning of the string meets the string again. Unwrap the string and measure its length. Next, determine the diameter of the can by tracing the bottom of the can on a piece of paper. Fold the circle onto itself to find a line of symmetry. The chord determined by the line is a diameter of the circle. Measure the diameter and determine the ratio of the circumference to the diameter. (Use the same units in all of your measurements.) Repeat the experiment with at least three cans and find the average of the corresponding ratios.

Ongoing Assessment 10-3

1. Use the following picture of a ruler to find each of the following lengths in centimeters:

a. *AB*	**b.** *DE*	**c.** *CJ*	**d.** *EF*
e. *IJ*	**f.** *AF*	**g.** *IC*	**h.** *GB*

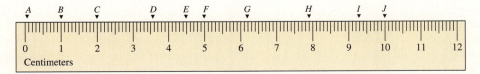

2. Convert each of the following:
   a. 100 in. = _____ yd
   b. 400 yd = _____ in.
   c. 300 ft = _____ yd
   d. 372 in. = _____ ft
3. Draw segments that you estimate to be of the following lengths. Use a metric ruler to check the estimates.
   a. 10 mm   **b.** 100 mm   **c.** 1 cm
   d. 10 cm   **e.** 0.01 m   **f.** 15 cm
   g. 0.1 m   **h.** 27 mm
4. Estimate the length of the following segment and then measure it:

   Express the measurement in each of the following units:
   a. Millimeters   **b.** Centimeters
5. Choose an appropriate metric unit and estimate each of the following measures:
   a. The length of a pencil
   b. The diameter of a nickel
   c. The width of the top of a desk
   d. The thickness of the top of a desk
   e. The length of this sheet of paper
   f. The height of a door
   g. Your height
   h. Your hand span
6. Redo Problem 5 using English measures.
7. Complete the following table:

Item	m	cm	mm
a. Length of a piece of paper		35	
b. Height of a woman	1.63		
c. Width of a filmstrip			35
d. Length of a cigarette			100
e. Length of two meter sticks laid end to end	2		

8. For each of the following, place a decimal point in the number to make the sentence reasonable:
   a. A stack of 10 dimes is 1000 mm high.
   b. The desk is 770 m high.
   c. The distance from one side of a street to the other is 100 m.
   d. A dollar bill is 155 cm long.
   e. The basketball player is 1950 cm tall.
   f. A new piece of chalk is about 8100 cm long.
   g. The speed limit in town is 400 km/hr.

9. List the following in decreasing order:
   8 cm, 5218 mm, 245 cm, 91 mm, 6 m, 700 mm.
10. Draw each of the following as accurately as possible:
    a. A regular polygon whose perimeter is 12 cm
    b. A circle whose circumference is 4 in.
    c. A triangle whose perimeter is 4 in.
    d. A nonconvex quadrilateral whose perimeter is 8 cm
11. Guess the perimeter of each of the following figures in centimeters and then check the estimates using a ruler:

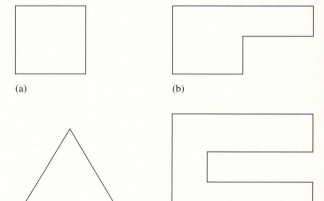

(a)   (b)

(c)   (d)

12. Complete each of the following:
    a. 10 mm = _____ cm
    b. 262 m = _____ km
    c. 3 km = _____ m
    d. 30 mm = _____ m
    e. 35 m = _____ cm
    f. 359 mm = _____ m
    g. 647 mm = _____ cm
    h. 0.1 cm = _____ mm
    i. 5 km = _____ m
    j. 51.3 m = _____ cm
13. Draw a triangle ABC. Measure the length of each of its sides in millimeters. For each of the following, tell which is greater and by how much:
    a. $AB + BC$ or AC
    b. $BC + CA$ or AB
    c. $AB + CA$ or BC
14. Determine whether the following can or cannot be the lengths of the sides of a triangle. Why?
    a. 23 cm, 50 cm, 60 cm
    b. 10 cm, 40 cm, 50 cm
    c. 410 mm, 260 mm, 14 cm
15. Do you think it is possible to draw a square whose perimeter is exactly equal to the sum of the length of its diagonals? Justify your answer.

16. Take an $8\frac{1}{2} \times 11$-in. piece of typing paper, fold it as shown in the following figure, and then cut the folded paper along the diagonal segment:

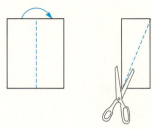

a. Rearrange the pieces to find a triangle with the minimum perimeter.
b. Arrange the pieces to form a triangle with the maximum perimeter.

17. The following figure made of 6 unit squares has a perimeter of 12 units. The figure is made in such a way that any two squares share a common side or a common vertex or have no points in common and each square shares an edge with another.

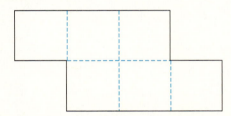

a. Add more squares to the figure so that the perimeter of the new figure is 18.
b. What is the minimum number of squares required to make a figure of perimeter 18?
c. What is the maximum number of squares that can be used to make a figure of perimeter 18?

18. Three toothpicks can be used to form an equilateral triangle (recorded as a 1-1-1 triangle). No triangle can be formed using 4 toothpicks. If 7 toothpicks are used, 2 isosceles triangles (shown as follows) can be formed. Complete the following table if toothpicks must be placed end to end in the same plane:

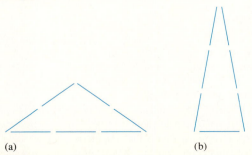

(a)   (b)

Number of Toothpicks	Possible Triangles	Type of Triangle
3	1-1-1	Equilateral
4	none	N.A.
5	2-2-1	Isosceles
6	2-2-2	Equilateral
7	3-2-2 or 3-3-1	Isosceles
8		
9		
10		
11		
12		

19. For each of the following circumferences, find the length of the radius of the circle:
a. 12π cm   **b.** 6 m   **c.** 0.67 m   **d.** 92π cm

20. For each of the following, if a circle has the dimensions given, determine its circumference:
a. 6 cm diameter   **b.** 3 cm radius
c. $\frac{2}{\pi}$ cm radius   **d.** 6π cm diameter

21. What happens to the circumference of a circle if the length of the radius is doubled?

22. The following figure is a circle whose radius is r units. The diameters of the two semicircular regions inside the large circle are both r units as well. Compute the length of the curve that separates the shaded and white regions.

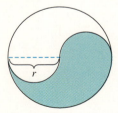

23. Astronomers use a light year to measure distance. A light year is the distance light travels in 1 yr. The speed of light is 300,000 km/sec.
a. How long is 1 light year in kilometers?
b. The nearest star (other than the sun) is Alpha Centauri. It is 4.34 light years from Earth. How far is that in kilometers?
c. How long will it take a rocket traveling 60,000 km/hr to reach Alpha Centauri?
d. How long will it take the rocket in (c) to travel to the sun if it takes approximately 8 min 19 sec for light from the sun to reach Earth?

B.C.   **by johnny hart**

24. Jet planes can exceed the speed of sound, so a new measurement called *Mach number* was invented to measure the speed of such planes. Mach 2 is twice the speed of sound. (Mach number is a number indicating the ratio of the speed of an object through a medium to the speed of sound in the medium.) The speed of sound in air is approximately 344 m/sec.
    a. Express Mach 2.5 in kilometers per hour.
    b. Express Mach 3 in meters per second.
    c. Express the speed of 5000 km/hr as a Mach number.
25. In the cartoon, Clumsy describes a foot-long hot dog as being 6 in. long. If that is the case, what would you expect the lengths of each of the following to be in "foot longs"?
    a. Yard   **b.** Mile
26. Refer to the following figure and determine the perimeter of the paint lane and the semicircle determined by the free-throw line on a basketball court:

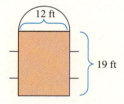

27. Regarding the polygons constructed as follows, what can you say about the numbers that can be the perimeters of the polygons constructed? Explain your answer.

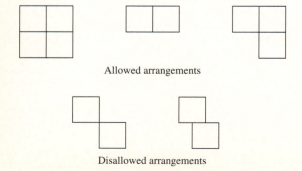

28. Use squares 1 unit on a side to form polygons as in Problem 27. Then complete the following table to try to determine a formula for the maximum and minimum areas of polygons with fixed perimeters. (*Hint:* Count the squares to determine the areas.)

Perimeter	Minimum Area	Maximum Area
4	1	1
6	2	2
8	3	4
10	4	
12		9
14		
16		
18		
20		
22		
24		
26		
$2n$		

Communication

29. A student has a tennis can containing three tennis balls. To the student's surprise, the perimeter of the top of the can is longer than the height of the can. The student wants to know if this fact can be explained without performing any measurements. Can you help?
30. In track, the second lane from the inside of the track is longer than the inside lane. Use this information to explain why, in running events that require a complete lap of the track, runners are lined up at the starting blocks as shown in the following figure:

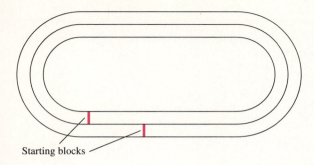

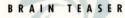
Starting blocks

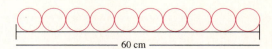
60 cm

a. Each member of the group should choose a specific number of circles and find the length of wire needed to make a 60-cm chain with the chosen number of circles.
b. Compare your results and make a conjecture based on the results.
c. Justify your conjecture.

Open-ended

31. Observe that it is possible to build a triangle with toothpicks having sides of 3, 4, and 5 toothpicks as shown and answer the questions that follow.

a. Find two other triples of toothpicks that can be used as sides of a triangle and two other triples that cannot be used to create a triangle.
b. Describe how to tell whether a given triple of numbers *a, b, c* can be used to construct a triangle with sides of *a, b,* and *c* toothpicks. Explain why your rule is valid.

32. Draw a circle of any size using an object such as a coin or a jar. Then make any measurements and calculations necessary to give precise directions to the Logo turtle to walk around the circle. (The turtle can walk only along straight segments of given length and turn in place by a specified angle.) Explain your reasoning.

Cooperative Learning

33. Jerry wants to design a gold chain 60-cm long made of thin gold wire circles, each of which is the same size. He wants to use the least amount of wire and wonders what the radius of each circle should be.

Review Problems

34. For the accompanying figure, answer each of the following and justify your answers:
a. Are points *B, C, E,* and *H* coplanar?
b. Are all three of the labeled points coplanar?
c. Are $\overleftrightarrow{EH}$ and $\overleftrightarrow{CG}$ parallel?

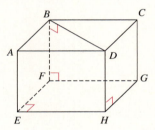

35. On a geoboard, construct each of the following:
a. A right isosceles triangle
b. An isosceles trapezoid
c. A convex kite
d. A rhombus
e. A concave kite

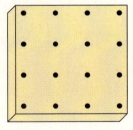

BRAIN TEASER Suppose a wire is stretched tightly around Earth. (The radius of Earth is approximately 6400 km.) Then suppose the wire is cut and its length is increased by 20 m. It is then placed back around the planet so that it is the same distance from Earth at every point. Could you walk under the wire?

LABORATORY ACTIVITY

1. As a van Hiele Level 1 activity, use a metric ruler to find the perimeter, in millimeters, of each of the following figures:

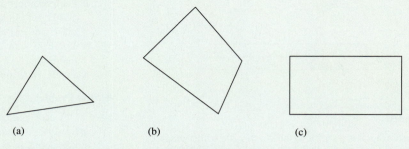

(a)   (b)   (c)

2. As a van Hiele Level 1 activity, use an English ruler to measure the indicated part of each of the following figures in inches:

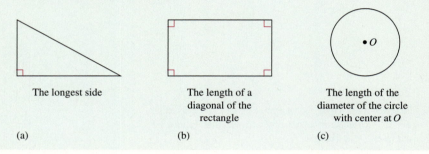

The longest side   The length of a   The length of the
                          diagonal of the   diameter of the circle
                          rectangle   with center at O

(a)   (b)   (c)

Section 10-4   More about Angles

In Figure 10-38, two sets of railroad tracks cross each other, thus forming the angles marked 1, 2, 3, and 4.

Figure 10-38

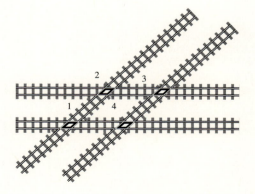

vertical angles   **Vertical angles** are pairs of angles such as ∠1 and ∠3 and appear any time two lines intersect. Another pair of vertical angles in Figure 10-38 is ∠2 and ∠4.

Other pairs of angles appear frequently enough that it is convenient to refer to them by specific names. Figure 10-38 also illustrates supplementary angles. Two angles are **supplementary angles** if the sum of their measures is 180°. For example, angles 1 and 2 form a pair of supplementary angles. Angles 1 and 2 are *supplements* of each other.

supplementary angles

complementary angles

Two angles are **complementary angles** if the sum of their measures is 90°. Each is a *complement* of the other. Figure 10-39 shows examples of supplementary and complementary angles.

Figure 10-39

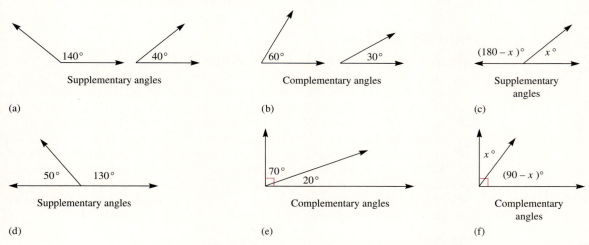

140°   40°
Supplementary angles
(a)

60°   30°
Complementary angles
(b)

$(180 - x)°$ $x°$
Supplementary
angles
(c)

50°   130°
Supplementary angles
(d)

70°   20°
Complementary angles
(e)

$x°$ $(90 - x)°$
Complementary
angles
(f)

Angles are also formed when a line intersects two distinct lines. Any line that intersects a pair of lines is a **transversal** of those lines. In Figure 10-40(a), line *p* is a transversal of lines *m* and *n*. Angles formed by these lines are named according to their placement in relation to the transversal and the two given lines. Various types of angles, together with examples of each in Figure 10-40, are listed next.

transversal

Figure 10-40

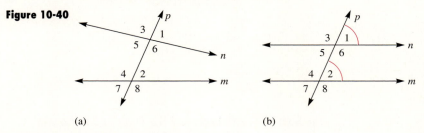

(a)   (b)

interior angles

exterior angles

alternate interior angles

alternate exterior angles

corresponding angles

Interior angles: ∠2, ∠4, ∠5, ∠6

Exterior angles: ∠3, ∠1, ∠7, ∠8

Alternate interior angles: ∠5 and ∠2, ∠4 and ∠6

Alternate exterior angles: ∠1 and ∠7, ∠3 and ∠8

Corresponding angles: ∠3 and ∠4, ∠5 and ∠7, ∠1 and ∠2, ∠6 and ∠8

Suppose corresponding angles such as ∠1 and ∠2 are congruent, as in Figure 10-40(b). With this assumption, and because ∠1 and ∠5 are congruent vertical angles, we know that the pair of alternate interior angles ∠2 and ∠5 are also congruent. Similarly, each pair of corresponding angles, alternate interior angles, and alternate exterior angles are congruent.

If we further examine Figure 10-40(b), we see that lines *m* and *n* appear to be parallel when ∠1 is congruent to ∠2. Conversely, if the lines are parallel, the sets of angles mentioned previously are congruent. This is true and is summarized in the following theorem, which we state without proof.

Theorem 10-1

If any two distinct lines are cut by a transversal, then a pair of corresponding angles, alternate interior angles, or alternate exterior angles are congruent if, and only if, the lines are parallel.

Constructing Parallel Lines

A method commonly used by architects to construct a line ℓ through a given point *P* parallel to a given line *m* is shown in Figure 10-41. Place the edge $\overline{AB}$ of triangle *ABC* on line *m*, as shown in Figure 10-41(a). Next, place a ruler on side $\overline{AC}$. Keeping the ruler stationary, slide triangle *ABC* along the ruler's edge until its side $\overline{AB}$ (marked $\overline{A'B'}$) contains point *P*, as in Figure 10-41(b). Use the side $\overline{A'B'}$ to draw the line ℓ through *P* parallel to *m*.

To show that the construction produces parallel lines, notice that when triangle *ABC* slides, the measures of its angles are unchanged. The angles of triangle *ABC* and triangle *A'B'C'* in Figure 10-41 are correspondingly congruent angles. ∠*A* and ∠*A'* are corresponding angles formed by *m* and ℓ and the transversal $\overline{EF}$. Because corresponding angles are congruent, Theorem 10-1 implies that ℓ ∥ *m*. In Chapter 11, we show how to construct parallel lines using only a compass and straightedge.

Figure 10-41

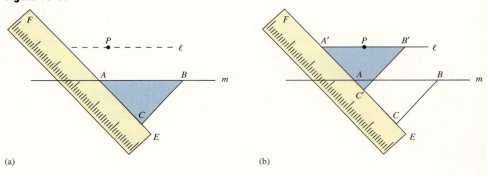

(a)   (b)

The Sum of the Measures of the Angles of a Triangle

The sum of the measures of the angles in a particular triangle can be shown intuitively to be 180°. We show this by using a torn triangle, as shown in Figure 10-42. Angles 1, 2, and 3 of triangle *ABC* in Figure 10-42(a) are torn as pictured and then replaced as shown in Figure 10-42(b). The three angles seem to form a single line ℓ.

Figure 10-42

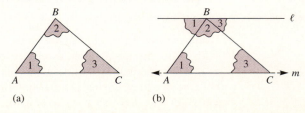

(a)   (b)

Repeat this experiment by drawing at least two other triangles, cutting them out, tearing off the angles, and fitting them as shown in Figure 10-42(b). The angle measures in each case seem to add up to a straight angle, which measures 180°. This conclusion, which is based on several observations, is an example of *inductive reasoning* discussed in Chapter 1. In contrast, *deductive reasoning* shows that a statement is true by using the given information, previously defined and undefined terms, theorems or statements assumed to be true, and logic. Unless we can examine all cases, a conclusion based on *inductive reasoning* may be only a conjecture that is probably, but not necessarily, true. A conclusion based on *deductive reasoning* must be true if the hypotheses is true.

Next, we use deductive reasoning to show that the sum of the measures of the interior angles in every triangle is 180°. In Figure 10-42(b), the line ℓ appears to be parallel to m. This suggests drawing a line ℓ parallel to $\overrightarrow{AC}$ through vertex B of triangle ABC, as in Figure 10-43(a), and showing that the angles formed are congruent to the interior angles of the triangle.

Figure 10-43

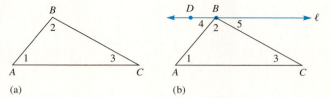

(a)   (b)

In Figure 10-43(b), ℓ and $\overleftrightarrow{AC}$ are parallel, with transversals $\overleftrightarrow{AB}$ and $\overleftrightarrow{BC}$, so it follows that alternate interior angles are congruent. Consequently, $m(\angle 1) = m(\angle 4)$ and $m(\angle 3) = m(\angle 5)$. Thus $m(\angle 1) + m(\angle 2) + m(\angle 3) = m(\angle 4) + m(\angle 2) + m(\angle 5) = 180°$. So, $m(\angle 1) + m(\angle 2) + m(\angle 3) = 180°$. From this, we obtain the following theorem.

Theorem 10-2

The sum of the measures of the interior angles of a triangle is 180°.

An alternative technique for showing that the sum of the measures of the angles in a triangle is 180° is shown in Figure 10-44. Suppose we start at vertex A in Figure 10-44(a) facing B, walk all the way around the triangle, and stop at the same position and pointed in the same direction as when we started. Then we turn 360°. Thus 360° is the sum of the shaded exterior angles of the triangle. Since an exterior angle and its adjacent interior angle are supplementary, the sum of all the interior and exterior angles is $3 \cdot 180°$, or 540°. By subtracting 360° — the sum of the measures of the exterior angles — we obtain $540° - 360°$, or 180°. Thus the sum of the measures of the interior angles of the triangle is 180°.

Figure 10-44

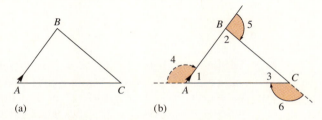

(a)   (b)

This discussion can be generalized to the following theorem concerning the sum of measures of the exterior angles of any convex polygon.

Theorem 10-3

The sum of the exterior angles of any convex polygon is 360°.

Example 10-6

In the framework for a bridge shown in Figure 10-45(a), *ABCD* is a parallelogram. If ∠*ADC* of the parallelogram measures 50°, what are the measures of the other angles of the parallelogram?

Figure 10-45

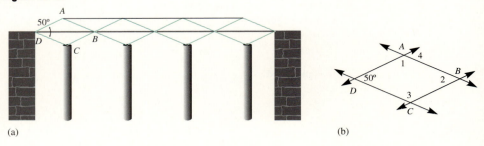

(a)   (b)

Solution   Refer to Figure 10-45(b). We draw the lines containing the sides of parallelogram *ABCD*. ∠*ADC* has a measure of 50°, and ∠4 and ∠*ADC* are corresponding angles formed by parallel lines $\overleftrightarrow{AB}$ and $\overleftrightarrow{CD}$ cut by transversal $\overleftrightarrow{AD}$. So it follows that $m(\angle 4) = 50°$. Because ∠1 and ∠4 are supplementary, $m(\angle 1) = 180° - 50° = 130°$. Using similar reasoning, we find that $m(\angle 2) = 50°$ and $m(\angle 3) = 130°$.

Example 10-7

A carpenter needs to cut an angle in a beam. The beam has parallel edges $\overline{AB}$ and $\overline{CD}$, as shown in Figure 10-46(a). Given the measures of the angles shown, find *x*.

Figure 10-46

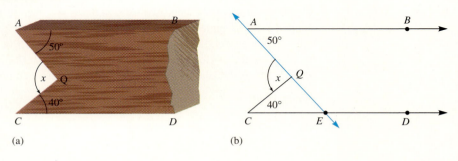

(a)   (b)

Solution   We know how to *solve a related problem* when angles are formed by parallel lines and a transversal. To obtain a transversal, we extend $\overrightarrow{AQ}$ as shown in Figure 10-46(b). Then we use alternate interior angles formed by transversal $\overleftrightarrow{AQ}$ cutting parallel rays $\overrightarrow{AB}$ and $\overrightarrow{CD}$ to see that $m(\angle AEC) = 50°$. Thus $m(\angle CQE) = 180 - (50 + 40) = 90°$. Because ∠*AQC* is supplementary to ∠*CQE*, $x = 180 - 90 = 90°$.

I N V E S T I G A T I O N   1 0 - 7

● An alternative solution to Example 10-7 involves drawing a line through Q parallel to $\overleftrightarrow{AB}$ in Figure 10-46(b). Then x is a sum of the measures of two angles whose measures can be found. Complete this solution. ●

● ● ●

Example 10-8   **a.** In Figure 10-47, $m \| n$ and k is a transversal. Explain why $m(\angle 1) + m(\angle 2) = 180°$.

Figure 10-47

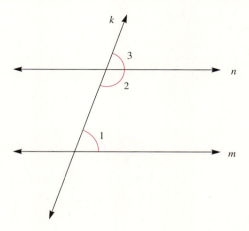

b. In Figure 10-48, $m \| n$ and k is a transversal. The angle measures marked by the same letters are equal. Show that for every choice of transversal k, $m(\angle ACB) = 90°$.

Figure 10-48

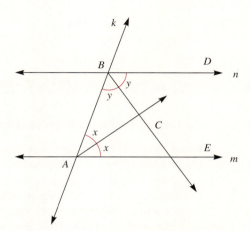

Solution   **a.** Because $\angle 1$ and $\angle 3$ are corresponding angles and $m \| n$, $m(\angle 1) = m(\angle 3)$. Also because $\angle 2$ and $\angle 3$ are supplementary angles, $m(\angle 2) + m(\angle 3) = 180°$. Substituting $m(\angle 1)$ for $m(\angle 3)$, we have $m(\angle 2) + m(\angle 1) = 180°$.

b. To show that $m(\angle ACB) = 90°$, we notice from (a) that $2x + 2y = 180°$, or $x + y = 90°$. In $\triangle ABC$, $m(\angle C) + x + y = 180°$. We substitute $x + y = 90°$ into this equation and obtain $m(\angle C) + 90° = 180°$, or $m(\angle C) = 90°$.

I N V E S T I G A T I O N   1 0 - 8

● When a plane flies directly from New York to London and then to Nairobi and back to New York, it flies along the sides of a spherical triangle, as shown in Figure 10-49(a), approximately following the surface of Earth. On a sphere, the shortest path between two points is along an arc of a great circle. A great circle is obtained when a plane through the center of the sphere intersects the sphere. (An example of a great circle is the equator.) To obtain a great circle through two given points on the sphere, we need consider only

a plane through the two points and the center of the sphere. A great circle through points *A* and *B* is shown in Figure 10-49(b). A spherical triangle consists of three points on the sphere and arcs of large circles (theshortest path) connecting the points. If the sphere is large like Earth, then in the vicinity of each vertex the arcs look like segments and the angles of a spherical triangle at each vertex can be thought of as the angle formed by the straight lines.

Figure 10-49

(a)

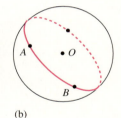

(b)

a. How many great circles go through the North Pole and the South Pole on the globe?

b. Describe a spherical triangle that has one vertex at the North Pole and the other two vertices on the equator.

c. Is there a spherical triangle with three right angles? If so, find one.

d. What can be said about the sum of the measures of the angles of a spherical triangle?   ●

The Sum of the Measures of the Interior Angles of a Convex Polygon with *n* Sides

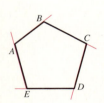

Figure 10-50

We can find the sum of the measures of all the interior angles in any convex *n*-gon. We first illustrate the approach for a convex pentagon. Extend each side of the pentagon as shown in Figure 10-50 so that at each vertex, an exterior angle is formed. Because at each vertex an interior angle and the corresponding exterior angle are supplementary, the sum of the measures of all the exterior and interior angles of the pentagon is $5 \cdot 180°$. By Theorem 10-3, the sum of the measures of the exterior angles is $360°$, so the sum of the measures of the interior angles is $5 \cdot 180° - 360°$, or $540°$. The same reasoning applies to any convex *n*-gon. The sum of the measures of an interior angle and the corresponding exterior angle at each vertex is 180°. Because there are n vertices, the sum of the measures of all the interior and exterior angles is $n \cdot 180°$. The sum of the measures of the exterior angles is 360°, so the sum of the measures of the interior angles is $n \cdot 180° - 360°$, or $(n - 2)180°$.

In a regular n-gon, all n interior angles are congruent and the sum of their measures is $180n - 360$, so the measure of a single angle is $\dfrac{180n - 360}{n}$, or $\dfrac{(n - 2)180°}{n}$.

The results from this discussion are summarized by the following theorem.

Theorem 10-4

a. The sum of the measures of the interior angles of any convex polygon with n sides is $180n - 360$, or $(n - 2)180°$.

b. The measure of a single interior angle of a regular n-gon is $\dfrac{180n - 360}{n}$, or $\dfrac{(n - 2)180°}{n}$.

I N V E S T I G A T I O N   1 0 - 9

● We can use the fact that the sum of the measures of a triangle's interior angles is 180° to find the sum of the measures of the interior angles of a quadrilateral by dividing the quadrilateral into two triangles. Because the sum of the measures of the interior angles in each triangle is 180°, the sum of the measures of the interior angles in the quadrilateral is $2 \cdot 180°$, or 360°. Use this approach to find the sum of the measures of the interior angles for any convex n-gon. Is your result the same as in Theorem 10-4? ●

Example 10-9

a. Find the measure of each angle of a regular decagon.

b. Find the number of sides of a regular polygon, each of whose angles has a measure of 175°.

Solution

a. Because a decagon has ten sides, the sum of the measures of the angles of a decagon is $10 \cdot 180 - 360$, or 1440°. A regular decagon has ten angles, all of which are congruent, so each one has a measure of $\dfrac{1440°}{10}$, or 144°. As an alternative solution, each exterior angle is $\dfrac{360°}{10}$, or 36°. Hence, each interior angle is $180 - 36$, or 144°.

b. Each interior angle of the regular polygon is 175°. Thus the measure of each exterior angle of the polygon is $180° - 175°$, or 5°. Because the sum of the measures of all exterior angles of a convex polygon is 360°, the number of exterior angles is $\dfrac{360}{5}$, or 72. Hence, the number of sides is 72.

BRAIN TEASER   Find the sum of the measures of ∠1, ∠2, ∠3, ∠4, and ∠5 in any five-pointed star like the one in the following figure:

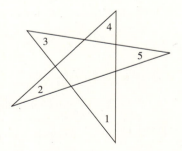

Ongoing Assessment 10-4

1. For each of the following, sketch a pair of angles whose intersection is given:
   a. The empty set
   b. Exactly two points
   c. Exactly three points
   d. Exactly four points
   e. More than four points

2. If five lines all meet in a single point, how many pairs of vertical angles are formed?

3. Find the measure of the third angle in each of the following triangles:

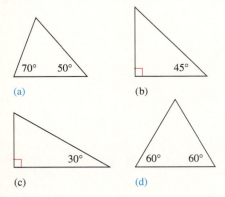

(a)   (b)

(c)   (d)

4. For each of the following figures, determine whether *m* and *n* are parallel lines. Justify your answers.

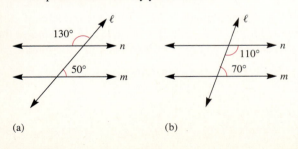

(a)   (b)

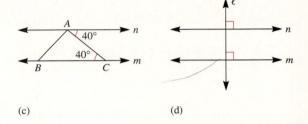

(c)   (d)

5. Two angles are complementary and the ratio of their measures is 7:2. What are the angle measures?

6. **a.** In a regular polygon, the measure of each angle is 162°. How many sides does the polygon have?
   b. Find the measure of each of the angles of a regular dodecagon.

7. In the following figure, $\overleftrightarrow{DE} \parallel \overleftrightarrow{BC}$, $\overleftrightarrow{EF} \parallel \overleftrightarrow{AB}$, and $\overleftrightarrow{DF} \parallel \overleftrightarrow{AC}$. Also, $m(\angle 1) = 45°$ and $m(\angle 2) = 65°$. Find each of the following values:
   a. $m(\angle 3)$
   b. $m(\angle D)$
   c. $m(\angle E)$
   d. $m(\angle F)$

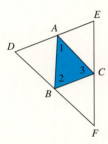

8. In the following figures, find the measures of the angles marked *x* and *y*:

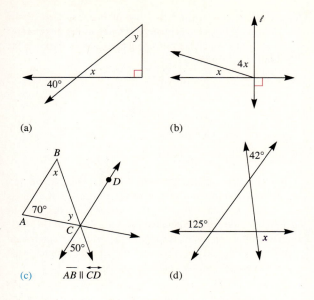

(a)

(b)

(c) $\overline{AB} \parallel \overleftrightarrow{CD}$

(d)

9. a. Determine the measure of an angle whose measure is twice that of its complement.

  b. If two angles of a triangle are complementary, what is the measure of the third angle?

10. Find the sum of the measures of the marked angles in each of the following figures:

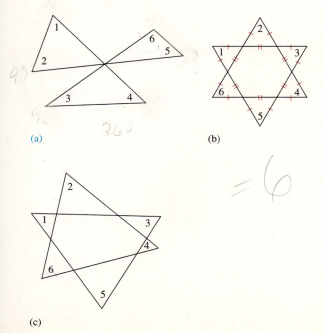

(a)

(b)

(c)

11. Find the measures of the angles marked *a* and *b* in the following figure:

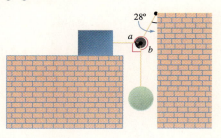

12. Calculate the measure of each angle of a pentagon, where the measures of the angles form an arithmetic sequence and the least measure is 60°.

13. Two sides of a regular octagon are extended as shown in the following figure. Find the measure of ∠1.

14. Find the measure of angle *x* in the following figure:

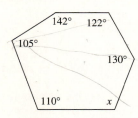

15. Find the measures of angles 1, 2, and 3 given that *TRAP* is a trapezoid with $\overline{TR} \parallel \overline{PA}$.

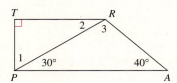

16. Home plate on a baseball field has three right angles and two congruent angles. Refer to the following figure and find the measures of each of these two congruent angles:

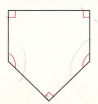

17. Using any tools, construct each of the following:
    a. A convex nonregular equiangular hexagon
    b. A regular pentagon
    c. A regular hexagon
    d. A regular octagon

18. Refer to the following figure and answer (a) and (b):

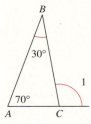

a. Find $m(\angle 1)$.
b. $\angle 1$ is an exterior angle of $\triangle ABC$. Use your answer in (a) to make a conjecture concerning the measure of an exterior angle of a triangle. Justify your conjecture.
Refer to the following figure and answer (c) and (d):

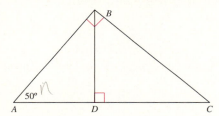

c. If $m(\angle ABC) = 90°$ and $\overline{BD} \perp \overline{AC}$ and $m(\angle A) = 50°$, find the measure of all the angles of $\triangle ABC$, $\triangle ADB$, and $\triangle CDB$.
d. If $m(\angle A) = \alpha$ in (c), find the measures of all the angles of $\triangle ABC$, $\triangle ADB$, and $\triangle CDB$ in terms of α.

Communication

19. Explain how you might find a measure of an angle of a staircase that will describe the staircase's steepness.
20. **a.** If one angle of a triangle is obtuse, can another also be obtuse? Why or why not?
    b. If one angle in a triangle is acute, can the other two angles also be acute? Why or why not?
    c. Can a triangle have two right angles? Why or why not?
    d. If a triangle has one acute angle, is the triangle necessarily acute? Why or why not?
21. In the following figure, A is a point not on line ℓ. Discuss whether it is possible to have two distinct perpendicular segments from A to ℓ in a plane.

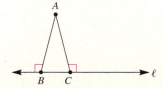

22. **a.** Explain how to find the sum of the measures of the angles of any convex pentagon by choosing any point P in the interior and constructing triangles, as shown in the following figure:

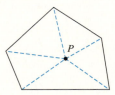

b. Using the method suggested by the diagram in (a), explain how to find the sum of the measures of the angles of any convex n-gon. Is your answer in (b) the same as the one already obtained in this section, $n \cdot 180 - 360$?

23. In the following figure, the legs of the ladder are congruent. If the ladder makes an angle of 120° with the ground, what is x? Explain your reasoning.

24. Explain how, through paper folding, you would show each of the following:
    a. In an equilateral triangle, all the interior angles are congruent.
    b. An isosceles trapezoid has two pairs of congruent angles.
25. **a.** Explain how to find the sum of the measures of the interior angles of a quadrilateral like the following:

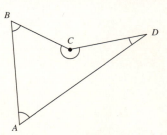

b. Conjecture whether the formula for the sum of the measures of the angles of a convex polygon is true for nonconvex polygons.
c. Justify your conjecture in (b) for pentagons and hexagons and explain why you think your conjecture is true in general.

26. Regular hexagons have been used to tile floors. Can a floor be tiled using only regular pentagons? Why or why not?

27. The following Logo procedure POLY will draw polygons and stars for different inputs of N and ANGLE:

```
TO POLY :N :ANGLE
  REPEAT :N[FD 60 RT :ANGLE]
END
```

Try different values for :N and :ANGLE to produce several drawings. Conjecture when POLY will draw a polygon and when it will draw a figure that is not a polygon.

28. Study the following figure. Notice that you can determine a parallelogram if you know the length of two sides, :L and :W, and the measure of one angle, :A.

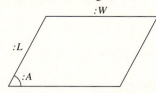

a. Write a procedure called PARALLELOGRAM with inputs :L, :A, and :W that draws such a parallelogram.

b. Write a procedure called RECTANGLE that calls the PARALLELOGRAM procedure to draw a rectangle.

c. Write a procedure called RHOMBUS that calls the PARALLELOGRAM procedure to draw a rhombus.

d. How could a square of size 50 be generated by the PARALLELOGRAM procedure?

e. How could a square of size 50 be generated by the RHOMBUS procedure?

Open-ended

29. When you walk around a polygonal figure, at each vertex you need to turn either right (clockwise) or left (counterclockwise). If a turn to the left is measured by a positive number of degrees and a turn to the right by a negative number of degrees, draw three different nonconvex polygons. In each case, find the sum of the measures of the turn angles, assuming you start at a vertex facing in the direction of a side, walk around the polygon, and end up at the same vertex facing in the same direction as when you started.

30. In Investigation 10-9, you may have found that on a sphere a triangle with three right angles is possible. List other geometric properties of figures on a sphere that are different from corresponding properties in the plane.

Cooperative Learning

31. In $\triangle ABC$, $\overrightarrow{AD}$ and $\overrightarrow{BD}$ are *angle bisectors,* that is, they divide the angles at A and B into congruent angles.

a. If the measures of $\angle A$ and $\angle B$ are known, then $m(\angle D)$ can be found. Why?

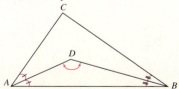

b. Suppose the measures of $\angle A$ and $\angle B$ are not known but that of $\angle C$ is. Can $m(\angle D)$ still be found? To answer this question, assign each member of your group a triangle with different angles but with the same measure for $\angle C$. Each person should compute $m(\angle D)$ for his or her triangle. Use the results to make a conjecture related to the previous question.

c. Discuss a strategy for answering the question in (b) and write a solution to be distributed to the entire class.

32. Each person in your group is to draw a large triangle like $\triangle ABC$ in the following figure and cut it out. Obtain the crease $\overline{BB'}$ by folding the triangle at B so that A falls on some point A' on $\overline{AC}$. Next, unfold and fold the top B along $\overline{BB'}$ so that B falls on B'. Then fold vertices A and C to match point B', as shown in the following figures:

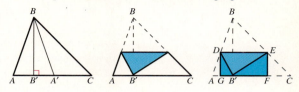

a. Why is $\overline{BB'}$ perpendicular to $\overline{AC}$?

b. What theorem does the folded figure illustrate? Why?

c. The folded figure seems to be a rectangle. Explain why.

d. What is the length of the base of the rectangle in terms of the base $\overline{AC}$ of $\triangle ABC$? Why?

Review Problems

33. Complete each of the following:

a. 100 mm = _____ cm   **b.** 10.4 cm = _____ mm

c. 350 mm = _____ m   **d.** 0.04 m = _____ mm

e. 8 km = _____ m   **f.** 6504 m = _____ km

34. Find the perimeters for each of the following if all arcs shown are semicircles:

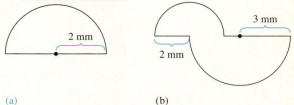

(a)   (b)

35. On the following geoboard, the distance between two adjacent nails in a row or column is 1 unit. Draw all possible polygons whose perimeters are 10 units.

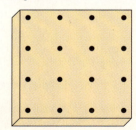

36. In each of the following, find the required properties. If this is not possible, explain why.

a. Two properties that hold true for all rectangles but not for all rhombuses

b. Two properties that hold true for all squares but not for all isosceles trapezoids

c. Two properties that hold true for all parallelograms but not for all squares

---

TECHNOLOGY CORNER

1. In the following figure, $a \parallel b$ and $\overrightarrow{PQ}$ is a transversal. The angles at P and Q have been trisected (divided into three congruent angles). The trisecting rays form the quadrilateral *ABCD*.

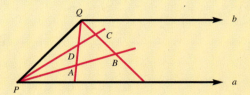

Use geometry utility software to draw several figures like the one shown. In each case, measure the angles of the quadrilateral *ABCD*. In the quadrilateral *ABCD*, make a conjecture about $m(\angle D)$ and $m(\angle B)$.

2. Refer to the following figure:

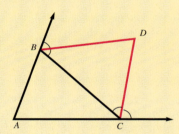

Use geometry utility software to draw $\angle A$ and choose points B and C on the sides of the angle. Draw $\triangle ABC$ and construct the angle bisectors of the exterior angles of $\triangle ABC$ at B and C. Mark as D the point of intersection of the angle bisectors. Measure $\angle D$ a few times for the same $\angle A$ but different choices for B and C. Make a conjecture based on your results and justify your conjecture.

LABORATORY ACTIVITY

As a van Hiele Level 2 activity, prepare a set of cards labeled with the following names of quadrilaterals: rectangle, parallelogram, square, trapezoid, rhombus, and quadrilateral. Use colored strings and develop a Venn diagram, arranging the cards in their proper places as subsets of the Venn diagram, if possible.

Section 10-5   Geometry in Three Dimensions

Simple Closed Surfaces

A visit to the grocery store exposes us to many three-dimensional objects that have simple closed surfaces. Examples are shown in Figure 10-51.

Figure 10-51

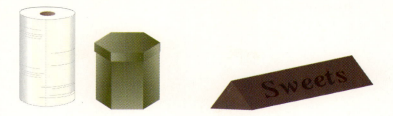

simple closed surface

sphere

center

A **simple closed surface** has exactly one interior, has no holes, and is hollow. An example is a sphere. A **sphere** is defined as the set of all points at a given distance from a given point, the **center.** As with the relation of a polygon to the plane containing it, a simple closed surface partitions space into three disjoint sets: points outside the surface, points belonging to the surface, and points inside the surface. The union of all points on a simple closed surface and all interior points is referred to as a **solid.**

solid

Figure 10-52

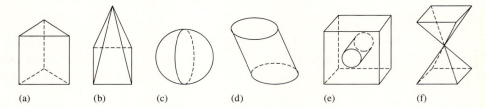

| (a) | (b) | (c) | (d) | (e) | (f) |

polyhedron

face

vertices

edges

Figures 10-52(a), (b), (c), and (d) are examples of simple closed surfaces; (e) and (f) are not. A **polyhedron** (polyhedra is the plural) is a simple closed surface made up of polygonal regions, or **faces.** (Recall that a polygonal region is formed by a polygon and its interior.) The word *polyhedron* is self-explanatory: *poly* means "many" and *hedron* means "flat surfaces." The vertices of the polygonal regions are the **vertices** of the polyhedron, and the sides of each polygonal region are the **edges** of the polyhedron. Figures 10-52(a) and (b) are examples of polyhedra, but (c), (d), (e), and (f) are not.

prism

bases

A **prism** is a polyhedron in which two congruent polygonal faces lie in parallel planes and the other faces are bounded by parallelograms. Figure 10-53 shows four different prisms. The upper and lower parallel faces of a prism are the **bases** of the prism. See the faces *ABC* and *DEF* at the bottom and top of the prism in Figure 10-53(a). A prism usually is named after its bases, as the figure suggests.

Figure 10-53

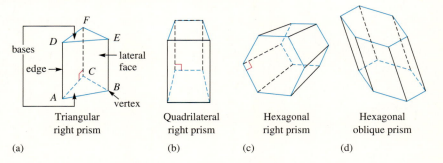

| Triangular right prism | Quadrilateral right prism | Hexagonal right prism | Hexagonal oblique prism |
| (a) | (b) | (c) | (d) |

lateral face

right prism

oblique prism

The faces other than the bases are the **lateral faces** of a prism. They are bounded by parallelograms. If the lateral faces of a prism are all bounded by rectangles, the prism is a **right prism.** The first three prisms in Figure 10-53 are right prisms. Figure 10-53(d) is an **oblique prism** because some of its faces are *not* bounded by rectangles.

Students often have trouble drawing three-dimensional figures. Figure 10-54 gives an example of how to draw a pentagonal prism.

Figure 10-54

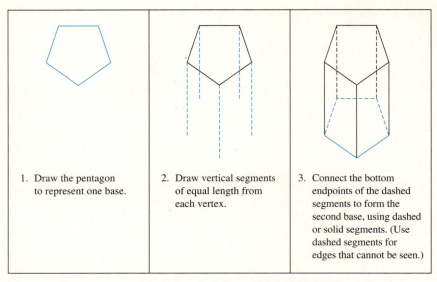

1. Draw the pentagon to represent one base.

2. Draw vertical segments of equal length from each vertex.

3. Connect the bottom endpoints of the dashed segments to form the second base, using dashed or solid segments. (Use dashed segments for edges that cannot be seen.)

An example of students working with spatial visualization and drawing three-dimensional figures is given on the following student page from *Heath Mathematics Connections,* Grade 6, 1992.

base

apex

A **pyramid** is a polyhedron determined by a simple closed polygonal region, a point not in the plane of the region, and triangular regions determined by the point and each pair of consecutive vertices of the polygonal region. The polygonal region is the **base** of the pyramid, and the point is the **apex.** As with a prism, the faces other than the base are **lateral faces.** Pyramids are classified according to their bases, as shown in Figure 10-55.

Figure 10-55

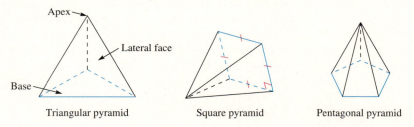

Triangular pyramid   Square pyramid   Pentagonal pyramid

To draw a pyramid, follow the steps in Figure 10-56.

Figure 10-56

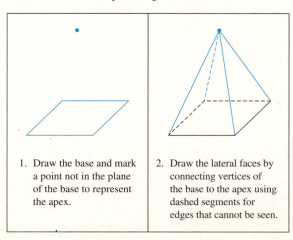

1. Draw the base and mark a point not in the plane of the base to represent the apex.

2. Draw the lateral faces by connecting vertices of the base to the apex using dashed segments for edges that cannot be seen.

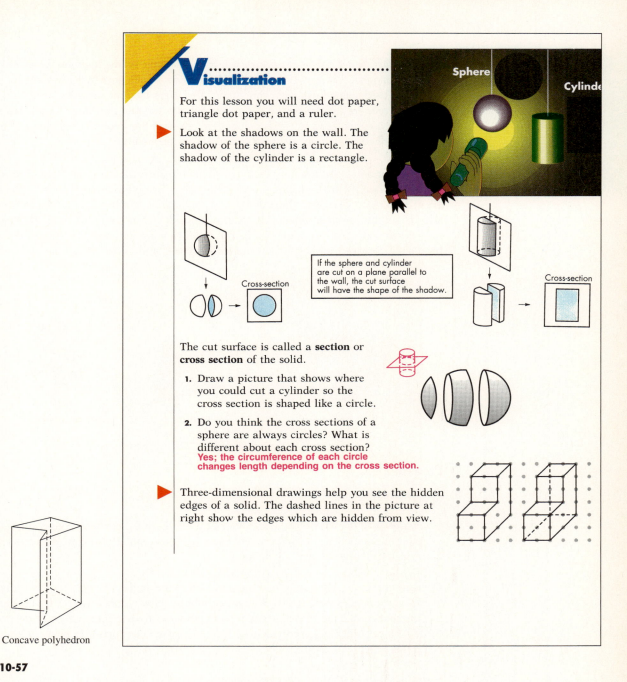

Visualization

For this lesson you will need dot paper, triangle dot paper, and a ruler.

▶ Look at the shadows on the wall. The shadow of the sphere is a circle. The shadow of the cylinder is a rectangle.

If the sphere and cylinder are cut on a plane parallel to the wall, the cut surface will have the shape of the shadow.

Cross-section

Cross-section

The cut surface is called a **section** or **cross section** of the solid.

1. Draw a picture that shows where you could cut a cylinder so the cross section is shaped like a circle.

2. Do you think the cross sections of a sphere are always circles? What is different about each cross section?
Yes; the circumference of each circle changes length depending on the cross section.

▶ Three-dimensional drawings help you see the hidden edges of a solid. The dashed lines in the picture at right show the edges which are hidden from view.

Concave polyhedron

Figure 10-57

Regular Polyhedra

convex polyhedron

A polyhedron is a **convex polyhedron** if, and only if, the segment connecting any two points in the interior of the polyhedron is itself in the interior. Figure 10-57 shows a concave polyhedron (that is, one that is caved in).

regular polyhedron

A **regular polyhedron** is a convex polyhedron whose faces are congruent regular polygonal regions such that the number of edges that meet at each vertex is the same for all the vertices of the polyhedron.

H I S T O R I C A L   N O T E

The regular solid polyhedra are known as the **Platonic solids,** after the Greek philoso-pher Plato (ca. 350 B.C.). Plato attached a mystical significance to the five regular poly-hedra, associating them with what he believed were the four elements (earth, air, fire, water) and the universe. Plato suggested that the smallest particles of earth have the form of a cube, those of air an octahedron, those of fire a tetrahedral, those of water an icosahedron, and those of the universe a dodecahedron.

Regular polyhedra have fascinated mathematicians for centuries. At least three of them were identified by the Pythagoreans (ca. 500 B.C.). Two others were known to the follow-ers of Plato (ca. 350 B.C.). Three of the five polyhedra occur in nature in the form of crys-tals of sodium sulphantimoniate, sodium chloride (common salt), and chrome alum, respectively, as seen in Figure 10-58. The other two do not occur in crystalline form but have been observed as skeletons of microscopic sea animals called radiolaria.

Figure 10-58

Cube   Tetrahedron   Octahedron

Problem 2

How many regular polyhedra are there?

Understanding the Problem.   Each face of a regular polyhedron is congruent to each of the other faces of that polyhedron, and each face is a regular polygon. We are to find the number of different regular polyhedra.

Devising a Plan.   The sum of the measures of all the angles at a vertex of a regular poly-hedron must be less than 360°. (Do you see intuitively why this is true?) We next examine the measures of the interior angles of regular polygons to determine which of the polygons could be faces of a regular polyhedron. Then we try to determine how many types of poly-hedra there are.

Carrying Out the Plan.   We determine the size of an angle of some regular polygons as shown in Table 10-9. Could a regular heptagon be a face of a regular polyhedron? At least three figures must fit together at a vertex to make a polyhedron. (Why?) If three angles of a regular heptagon were together at one vertex, then the sum of the measures of these angles would be $\dfrac{3 \cdot 900°}{7}$, or $\dfrac{2700°}{7}$, which is greater than 360°. Similarly, more than three angles cannot be used at a vertex. Thus a heptagon cannot be used to make a regular polyhedron.

Table 10-9

Polygon	Measure of an Interior Angle
Triangle	60°
Square	90°
Pentagon	108°
Hexagon	120°
Heptagon	$\left(\dfrac{900}{7}\right)°$

The measure of an interior angle of a regular polygon increases as the number of sides of the polygon increases (why?). Thus any polygon with more than six sides will have an interior angle greater than 120°. So if three angles were to fit together at a vertex, the sum of the measures of the angles would be greater than 360°. This means the only polygons that might be used to make regular polyhedra are equilateral triangles, squares, regular pentagons, and regular hexagons. Consider the possibilities given in Table 10-10.

Notice that we were not able to use six equilateral triangles to make a polyhedron because 6(60°) = 360° and the triangles would lie in a plane. Similarly, we could not use four squares or any hexagons. We also could not use more than three pentagons because if we did, the sum of the measures of the angles would be more than 360°.

Table 10-10

Polygon	Measure of an Interior Angle	Number of Polygons at a Vertex	Sum of the Angles at the Vertex	Polyhedron Formed	Model
Triangle	60°	3	180°	**Tetrahedron**	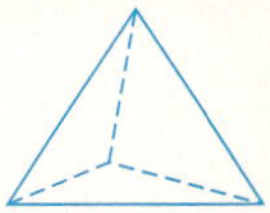
Triangle	60°	4	240°	**Octahedron**	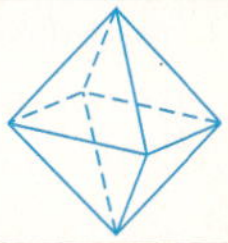
Triangle	60°	5	300°	**Icosahedron**	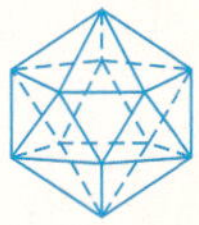
Square	90°	3	270°	**Cube**	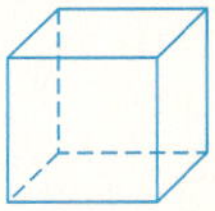
Pentagon	108°	3	324°	**Dodecahedron**	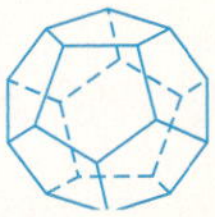

semiregular polyhedra   ***Looking Back.*** Interested readers may want to investigate **semiregular polyhedra.** These are also formed by using regular polygons as faces, but the regular polygons used need not have the same number of sides. For example, a semiregular polyhedron might have squares and regular octagons as its faces.

• • •

The patterns in Figure 10-59, called *nets,* may be used to construct the five regular polyhedra. It is left as an exercise to determine other patterns for constructing the regular polyhedra.

Figure 10-59

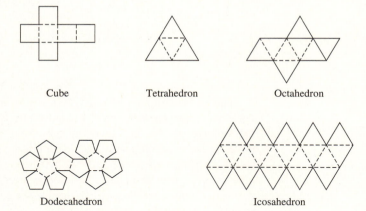

Cube   Tetrahedron   Octahedron

Dodecahedron   Icosahedron

INVESTIGATION 10-10

● A simple relationship among the number of faces, the number of edges, and the number of vertices of any polyhedron was discovered by the French mathematician and philosopher René Descartes (1596–1650) and rediscovered by the Swiss mathematician Leonhard Euler (1707–1783). Table 10-11 suggests a relationship among the numbers of vertices (V), edges (E), and faces (F). This relationship is known as **Euler's formula.**

a. State a relationship suggested by the table.
b. Try your relationship on other polyhedra such as the ones in Figure 10-53 and Figure 10-55. ●

Table 10-11

Name	V	F	E
Tetrahedron	4	4	6
Cube	8	6	12
Octahedron	6	8	12
Dodecahedron	20	12	30
Icosahedron	12	20	30

HISTORICAL NOTE

Leonhard Euler went blind in 1766 and for the remaining 17 years of his life continued to do mathematics by dictating to a secretary and by writing formulas in chalk on a slate for his secretary to copy down. He published 530 papers in his lifetime and left enough work to supply the *Proceedings of the St. Petersburg Academy* for the next 47 years.

Cylinders and Cones

A cylinder is an example of a simple closed surface that is not a polyhedron. Consider line segment $\overline{AB}$ and a line ℓ as shown in Figure 10-60. When $\overline{AB}$ moves so that it always remains parallel to a given line ℓ and points A and B trace simple closed planar curves other than polygons, the surface generated by $\overline{AB}$, along with the simple closed curves and their interiors, forms a **cylinder.** The simple closed curves traced by A and B, along with their interiors, are the **bases** of the cylinder and the remaining points constitute the *lateral surface of the cylinder.* Three different cylinders are pictured in Figure 10-60.

cylinder
bases

Figure 10-60

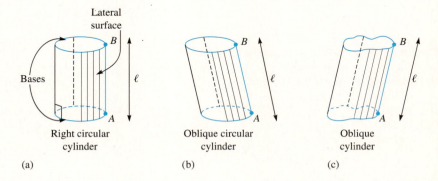

Right circular cylinder
(a)

Oblique circular cylinder
(b)

Oblique cylinder
(c)

circular cylinder
right cylinder
oblique cylinder

If a base of a cylinder is a circular region, the cylinder is a **circular cylinder.** If the line segment forming a cylinder is perpendicular to a base, the cylinder is a **right cylinder.** Cylinders that are not right cylinders are **oblique cylinders.** The cylinder in Figure 10-60(a) is a right cylinder; those in Figures 10-60(b) and (c) are oblique cylinders.

cone
vertex

Suppose we have a simple closed curve, other than a polygon, in a plane and a point P not in the plane of the curve. The union of line segments connecting point P to each point of a simple closed curve and the simple closed curve and the interior of the curve is a **cone.** Cones are pictured in Figure 10-61. Point P is the **vertex** of the cone. The points of the cone not in the base constitute the *lateral surface of the cone.* A line segment from vertex P perpendicular to the plane of the base is the **altitude.** A **right circular cone,** such as the one in Figure 10-61(a), is a cone whose altitude intersects the base (a circular region) at the center of the circle. Figure 10-61(b) illustrates an oblique cone, and Figure 10-61(c) illustrates an **oblique circular cone.**

altitude • right circular cone

oblique circular cone

Figure 10-61

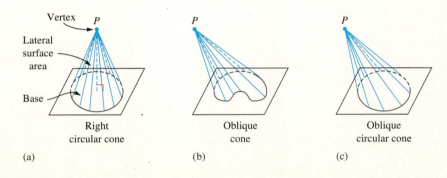

Right circular cone
(a)

Oblique cone
(b)

Oblique circular cone
(c)

Ongoing Assessment 10-5

1. Identify each of the following polyhedra. If a polyhedron can be described in more than one way, give as many names as possible.

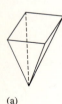 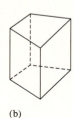 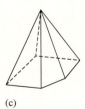

(a)   (b)   (c)

2. Given the following tetrahedron, name the following:
   a. Vertices   **b.** Edges   **c.** Faces
   d. Intersection of face *DRW* and edge $\overline{RA}$

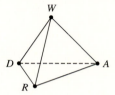

3. Identify five different shapes of containers that can be found in a grocery store.

4. Determine for each of the following the minimum number of faces possible:
   a. Prism   **b.** Pyramid   **c.** Polyhedron

5. Classify each of the following as true or false:
   a. If the lateral faces of a prism are rectangles, it is a right prism.
   b. Every pyramid is a prism.
   c. Every pyramid is a polyhedron.
   d. The bases of a prism lie in perpendicular planes.
   e. The bases of all cones are circles.
   f. A cylinder has only 1 base.
   g. All lateral faces of an oblique prism are rectangular regions.
   h. All regular polyhedra are convex.

6. If possible, sketch each of the following:
   a. An oblique square prism
   b. An oblique square pyramid
   c. A noncircular right cone
   d. A noncircular cone that is not right

7. For each of the following, draw a prism and a pyramid that have the given region as a base:
   a. Triangle   **b.** Pentagon
   c. Regular hexagon

8. Two prisms are sketched on the following dot paper. Complete the drawings by using dashed segments for the hidden edges.

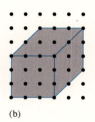

(a)   (b)

9. Name each polyhedron that can be constructed using the following nets:

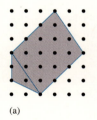

(a)   (b)   (c)

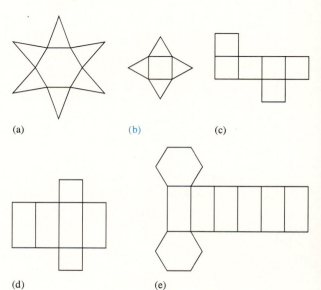

(d)   (e)

10. The figure on the left in each of the following represents a card attached to a wire as shown. Match each figure on the left with what it would look like if you were to revolve it by spinning the wire between your fingers.

(a)

   (see figures)

(i)   (ii)   (iii)   (iv)

(b)

(i)   (ii)   (iii)   (iv)

11. Which of the following three-dimensional figures could be used to make the shadow shown in (a)? in (b)?

(a)

(i)

(ii)

(iii)

(iv)

(b)

(i)

(ii)

(iii)

(iv)

12. A diagonal of a prism is any segment determined by 2 vertices that do not lie in the same face, as shown in the following figure.

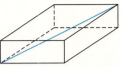

Complete the following table showing the total number of diagonals for various prisms:

Prism	Vertices per Base	Diagonals per Vertex	Total Number of Diagonals
Quadrilateral	4	1	4
Pentagonal	5		
Hexagonal			
Heptagonal			
Octagonal			
.			
.			
.			
n-gonal			

13. Consider a jar with a lid, as illustrated in the following figure. The jar is half filled with water. In each of the marked drawings, sketch the water.

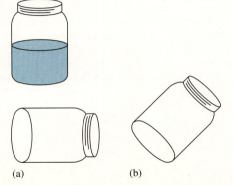
(a)   (b)

14. On the left of each of the following figures is a net for a three-dimensional object. On the right are several objects. Which object will the net fold to make?

(a)

(1)   (2)   (3)   (4)

(b)

(1)   (2)   (3)   (4)

15. Sketch the intersection of each of the following with the plane shown:

Cube

Remainder of unseen figure completes the cube

(a)   (b)

Sphere

Right pentagonal prism

(c)   (d)

Right circular cone (plane parallel to base)

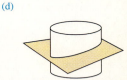
Right circular cylinder (plane not parallel to base)

(e)   (f)

16. For each of the following three-dimensional figures, draw all possible cross-sections when the three-dimensional figure is sliced by a plane.
  a. Cube   **b.** Cylinder

17. For each of the following figures, find $V + F - E$, where V, E, and F stand, respectively, for the number of vertices, edges, and faces:

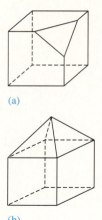

(a)

(b)

18. Complete the following table for each of the polyhedra described in the table:

Polyhedron	Vertices	Faces	Edges
a.		8	12
b.	20	30	
c.	6		15

State the relationship suggested by the table.

19. Answer each of the following questions about a pyramid and a prism, each having an *n*-gon as a base:
 a. How many faces does each have?
 b. How many vertices does each have?
 c. How many edges does each have?
 d. Use your answers to (a), (b), and (c) to verify Euler's formula for all pyramids and all prisms.

Communication

20. a. Can a prism have exactly 33 edges? Explain why or why not.
 b. Can a pyramid have exactly 33 edges? Explain why or why not.

21. How many possible pairs of bases does a rectangular prism have? Explain.

22. A circle may be considered a "many-sided" polygon. Use this notion to describe the relationship between each of the following:
 a. A pyramid and a cone
 b. A prism and a cylinder

23. Can either or both of the following be drawings of a quadrilateral pyramid? If yes, where would you be standing in each case? Explain why.

(a)

(b)

Open-ended

24. Make a three-dimensional drawing of a house and a two-dimensional net for the house. Include tabs for folding. Cut out and fold the net.

25. When a box in the shape of a right prism, like the one in the following figure, is cut by a plane halfway between the opposite sides and parallel to these sides, that plane is a *plane of symmetry*. If a mirror is placed at the plane of symmetry, the reflection of the front part of the box will look just like the back part. Draw several space figures and find the number of planes of symmetry for each. Summarize your results in a table. Can you identify any figures with infinitely many planes of symmetry?

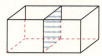

Cooperative Learning

26. In a 2-person game, draw a three-dimensional figure without showing it to your partner. Tell your partner the shape of all possible cross-sections of your figure with a plane that you think are sufficient to identify your figure. If your partner can identify your figure, 1 point is earned by your partner. If a figure is identified that has all the cross-sections listed but that figure is not your figure, 2 points are earned by your partner. Each of you should take an equal number of turns.

27. Some of the following nets can be folded into a cube. Have each person in your group draw all the nets that can be folded into a cube. Share your findings with the group and decide how many such different nets there are. Discuss what "different" means in this case. Finally, compare your group's answers with those of other groups.

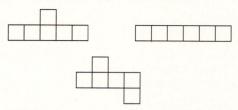

28. Choose different triples of points on the edges of each of the following figures. Then find the cross-section of where a plane through each triple of points intersects the figure. (The following figures show only a few examples. What are the possible figures that can be obtained in this manner?)

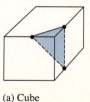
(a) Cube

(b) Tetrahedron

Review Problems

29. If two angles of 1 triangle are congruent to two angles of another triangle, must the third angles of both be congruent? Why or why not?

30. Triangles *ABC* and *CDE* are equilateral triangles (see the following figure). Find the measure of ∠*BCD*.

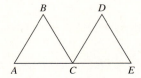

31. What is the measure of each angle in a regular nonagon?

32. Classify the following as true or false. If false, tell why.
  a. Every rhombus is a parallelogram.
  b. Every polygon has at least three sides.

  c. Triangles can have at most two acute angles.

33. Assume that lines ℓ, *m*, and *n* are in the same plane and state a theorem based on the following figure. Justify your answer.

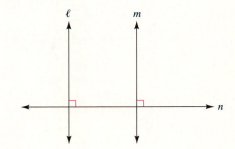

Use technology to draw a staircase similar to that shown in the following figure:

A rectangular region can be rolled to form the lateral surface of a right circular cylinder. What shape of paper is needed to make an oblique circular cylinder? (See "Making a Better Beer Glass" by A. Hoffer.)

As a van Hiele Level 2 activity, consider for a structure made of cubes the front view, the side view looking from the right, and the top view. Build the structure.

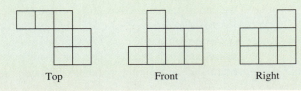

Top   Front   Right

Networks

In the 1700s, the people of Königsberg, Germany, used to enjoy walking over the bridges of the Pregel River. There were two islands in the river and seven bridges over it, as shown in Figure 10-62. These walks eventually led to the following problem.

Königsberg Bridge Problem

Is it possible to walk across all the bridges so that each bridge is crossed exactly once on the same walk?

Figure 10-62

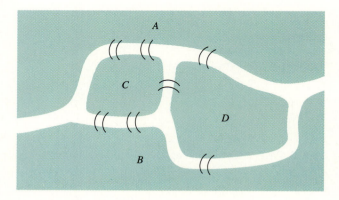

There is no restriction on where to start the walk or where to finish. Leonhard Euler became interested in this problem and solved it in 1736. He made the problem much simpler by representing the land masses, islands, and bridges in a **network,** as shown in the colored portion of Figure 10-63.

network

Figure 10-63

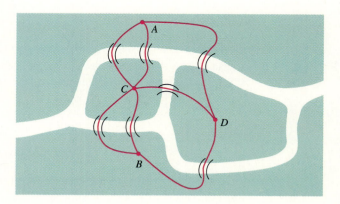

vertices • arcs   The points in a network are **vertices,** and the curves are **arcs.** Using a network diagram, we can restate the Königsberg bridge problem as follows: *Is there a path through the network beginning at some vertex and ending at the same or another vertex such that each arc is traversed exactly once?* A network having such a path is **traversable;** that is, each arc is passed through exactly once. A network that is traversable in such a way that the starting point and the stopping point are the same as an **Euler circuit.**

traversable

Euler circuit

We can walk around an ordinary city block, as illustrated in Figure 10-64(a), and because the starting point is the same as the stopping point, the network is an Euler circuit. We need not start at any particular point, and, in general, we can traverse any simple closed curve. Now consider walking around two city blocks and down the street that runs between them (see Figure 10-64b). To traverse this network, it is necessary to start at vertex B or C. Starting at points other than B or C might suggest that the figure is not traversable, but this is not the case, as shown in Figure 10-64(b). If we start at B, we end at C and vice versa. Note that it is permissible to pass through a vertex more than once, but an arc may be traversed only once. Vertices B and C are endpoints of three line segments, and each of the other vertices are endpoints of two segments.

Figure 10-64

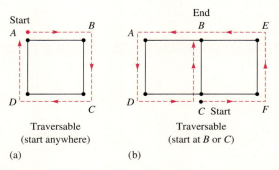

Traversable   Traversable
(start anywhere)   (start at B or C)

(a)   (b)

A traversable network is the type of network, or route, that a highway inspector would like to have if given the responsibility of checking out all the roads in a highway system. The inspector needs to traverse each road (arc) in the system but would save time by not having to make any repeat journeys during any inspection tour. It would be feasible for the inspector to go through any town (vertex) more than once on the route. Consider the networks in Figure 10-65. Is it possible for the highway inspector to do the job with these networks without traversing any road twice?

Figure 10-65

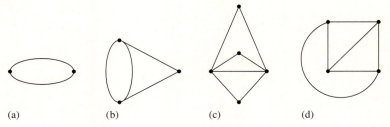

(a)   (b)   (c)   (d)

The first three networks in Figure 10-65 are traversable; the fourth network, (d), is not. Notice that the number of arcs meeting at each vertex in networks (a) and (c) is even. Any such vertex is an **even vertex.** If the number of arcs meeting at a vertex is odd, it is an **odd vertex.** In network (b), only the odd vertices will work as starting or stopping points. In network (d), which is not traversable, all the vertices are odd. If a network is traversable, each arrival at a vertex other than a starting or a stopping point requires a departure. Thus each vertex that is not a starting or stopping point must be even. The starting and stopping vertices in a traversable network may be even or odd, as seen in Figure 10-65(a) and (b), respectively.

even vertex

odd vertex

In general, networks have the following properties:

1. *If a network has all even vertices, it is traversable. Any vertex can be a starting point, and the same vertex must be the stopping point. Thus the network is an Euler circuit.*
2. *If a network has two odd vertices, it is traversable. One odd vertex must be the starting point, and the other odd vertex must be the stopping point.*

I N V E S T I G A T I O N   1 0 - 1 1

● **a.** Is there a traversable network with more than two odd vertices? Why or why not?

b. Is there a network with exactly one odd vertex? ●

Example 10-10   Which of the networks in Figure 10-66 are traversable?

Figure 10-66

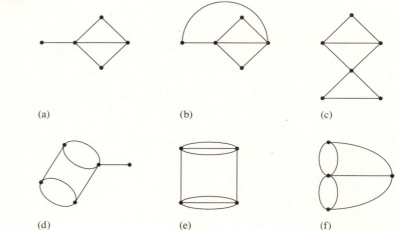

(a)   (b)   (c)

(d)   (e)   (f)

Solution • Networks in (b) and (e) have all even vertices and therefore are traversable.
  • Networks in (a) and (c) have exactly two odd vertices and are traversable.
  • Networks in (d) and (f) have four odd vertices and are not traversable.

The network in Figure 10-66(f) represents the Königsberg bridge problem. It has four odd vertices and consequently is not traversable. Hence, no walk configuration is possible to solve the problem.

A problem similar to the highway inspector problem involves a traveling salesperson. Such a person might have to travel networks comparable to those of the highway inspector. However, the salesperson is interested only in visiting each town (vertex) once, not necessarily in following each road. It is not known for which networks this can be accomplished. Can you find a route for the traveling salesperson for each network in Figure 10-66?

A different type of application of network problems is discussed in Example 10-11.

Example 10-11

Look at the floor plan of the house shown in Figure 10-67. Is it possible for a security guard to go through all the rooms of the house and pass through each door exactly once?

Figure 10-67

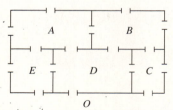

Solution   Represent the floor plan as a network, as in Figure 10-68. Designate the rooms and the outside as vertices and the paths through the doors as arcs. The network has more than two odd vertices, namely, *A, B, D,* and *O.* Thus the network is not traversable, and it is impossible to go through all the rooms and pass through each door exactly once.

Figure 10-68

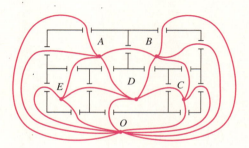

Ongoing Assessment 10-6

1. Which of the following networks are traversable? If the network is traversable, draw an appropriate path through it, labeling the starting and stopping vertices. Indicate which networks are Euler circuits.

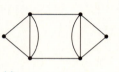

(a)

(b)

(c)

(d)

(e)

(f)

(g)

(h)

(i)

(j)

2. Which of the networks in Problem 1 can be efficiently traveled by a traveling salesperson, with no vertex visited more than once?

3. A city contains one river, three islands, and ten bridges, as shown in the following figure. Is it possible to take a walk around the city by starting at any land area, returning after visiting every part of the city, and crossing each bridge exactly once? If so, show such a path both on the original figure and on the corresponding network.

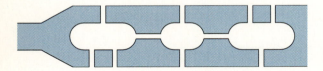

4. Refer to the following floor plans:

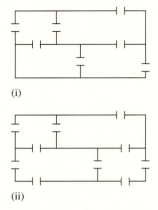

(i)

(ii)

a. Draw a network that corresponds to each floor plan.
b. Determine whether a person could pass through each room of each house by passing through each door exactly once. If it is possible, draw the path such a trip would involve.

5. Refer to the following floor plans:

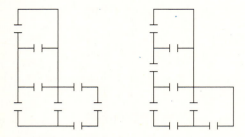

Can a person walk through each door once and only once and also go through both of the following houses in a single path? If it is possible, draw the path such a trip would involve.

6. The following drawing represents the floor plan of an art museum. All tours begin and end at the entry. If possible, design a tour route that will allow a person to see every room but not go through any room twice.

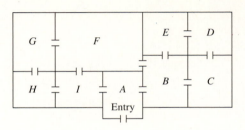

7. Each network in Problem 1 separates the plane into several subsets. If R is the number of interior and exterior regions of the plane, V is the number of vertices, and A is the number of arcs, complete the following chart using each of the networks. (The first one is done for you.)

Network	R	V	A	$R + V - A$
(a)	6	6	10	2

8. Molly is making her first trip to the United States and would like to tour the eight states pictured in the following figure. She would like to plan her trip so that she can cross each border between neighboring states exactly once — that is, the Washington-Oregon border, the Washington-Idaho border, and so on.

Is such a trip possible? If so, does it make any difference in which state she starts her trip?

Communication

9. The following network is not an Euler circuit:

a. Add two arcs to the network so that the resulting network will be an Euler circuit.
b. Add exactly one arc so that the resulting network will be an Euler circuit.
c. Explain a real-life application in which the answer in (b) is useful.

10. If you were commissioned to build an eighth bridge to make the Königsberg bridge problem traversable, where would you build your bridge? Is there more than one location where you could build it? Explain why.

Open-ended

11. Draw a network that is not traversable using as few vertices and arcs as possible.

12. Draw a network that is not an Euler circuit and then add the least number of edges possible so that the new network will be an Euler circuit.

13. One application of Euler circuits is the checking of parking meters. List other real-life applications that could involve the use of Euler circuits. In each case, give a concrete example and describe the corresponding Euler circuit.

Cooperative Learning

14. *Traveler's Dodecahedron* is a puzzle invented in 1857 by the Irish mathematician William Rowen Hamilton. It consists of a wooden dodecahedron (a polyhedron with 12 regular pentagons as faces) with a peg at each vertex of the dodecahedron. The 20 vertices are labeled with the names of different cities around the world. The solver of the puzzle is to find a path that starts at some city, travels along the

edges, goes through each of the remaining cities exactly once, and returns to the starting city. The path traveled is to be marked by a string connecting the pegs.

a. Find a solution to the puzzle, first on the following network and then on the following dodecahedron. Compare your answer with those of other members of your group.

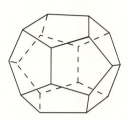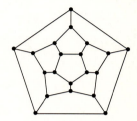

b. Play the following game with a partner. Draw a polyhedron that can be traversed in the way described earlier in this problem. Also draw a two-dimensional network for the polyhedron similar to the one shown in (a). Ask your partner to answer the question posed in (a) for the new polyhedron and the accompanying network. Then switch roles. The person who draws the polyhedron with the greatest number of vertices wins.

LABORATORY ACTIVITY

1. Take a strip of paper like the one shown in the following figure. Give 1 end a half-twist and join the ends by taping them. The surface obtained is called a Möbius strip.

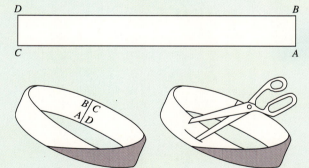

a. Use a pencil to shade one side of a Möbius strip. What do you discover?

b. Imagine cutting a Möbius strip all around midway between the edges. What do you predict will happen? Now do the cutting. What is the result?

c. Imagine cutting a Möbius strip one third of the way from an edge and parallel to the edge all the way through until you return to the starting point. Predict the result. Then do the cutting. Was your prediction correct?

d. Imagine cutting around a Möbius strip one fourth of the way from an edge. Predict the result. Then do the cutting. How does the result compare with the result of the experiment in (c)?

2. **a.** Take a strip of paper and give it two half-twists (one full twist). Then join the ends together. Answer the questions in part 1.
   b. Repeat the experiment in (a), using three half-twists.
   c. Repeat the experiment in (a), using four half-twists. What do you find for odd-numbered twists? Even-numbered twists?
3. Take two strips of paper and tape each of them in a circular shape. Join them as shown next.

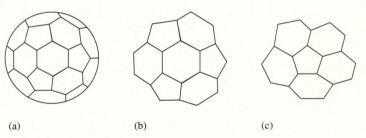

   a. What happens if you cut completely around the middle of each strip as shown?
   b. Repeat part (a) if both strips are Möbius strips. Does it make any difference if the half-twists are in opposite directions?

SOLUTION TO THE PRELIMINARY PROBLEM

Understanding the Problem.   The cover of a soccer ball consists of regular pentagons and regular hexagons as shown in Figure 10-69(a). We must determine whether a similar pattern as shown in Figure 10-69(b) but using regular polygons can be used to tile a floor.

Figure 10-69

(a)   (b)   (c)

Devising a Plan.   We must see whether it is possible to fit, without gaps, a pattern like that in Figure 10-69(b) or Figure 10-69(c) but made with regular polygons. This will be possible if, and only if, the sum of the measures of the angles around any vertex of every polygon is 360°. If the hexagons as well as the pentagons are to be regular, we could compute the interior angles of each and check if the sum of the measures of the three angles around any vertex is 360°.

Carrying Out the Plan.   For a pattern resembling that in Figure 10-69(b) but made of regular polygons, the sum of the measures of all the interior angles of a regular hexagon is 180° · 4. Hence each interior angle measures (180° · 4)/6, or 120°. Similarly, each interior angle of a regular pentagon has measure (180° · 3)/5, or 108°. Consequently, the sum of the measures of the 3 angles around each vertex of the hexagon is 120° + 120° + 108°, or 348°. Because the sum is not 360°, a tiling with regular hexagons and regular pentagons like in Figure 10-69(b) is not possible on a plane. A tiling resembling Figure 10-69(c) is also impossible on the plane because the sum of the measures of the 3 angles around a vertex of the pentagon is 120° + 120° + 108°, which is not 360°.

Looking Back.   Is the tiling of a floor possible with some other pair of different regular polygons?

QUESTIONS FROM THE CLASSROOM

1. Henry claims that a line segment has a finite number of points because it has two endpoints. How do you respond?

2. A student claims that if any two planes that do not intersect are parallel, then any two lines that do not intersect should also be parallel. How do you respond?

3. A student says that it is actually impossible to measure an angle, since each angle is the union of two rays that extend infinitely and therefore continue forever. What is your response?

4. Maggie claims that to make the measure of an angle greater, you just extend the rays further. How do you respond?

5. A student asks whether a polygon whose sides are congruent is necessarily a regular polygon and whether a polygon with all angles congruent is necessarily a regular polygon. How do you answer?

6. A student thinks that a square is the only regular polygon with all right angles. The student asks if this is true and if so, why. How do you answer?

7. A student says that a line is parallel to itself. How do you reply?

8. A student claims that if line segments $\overline{AB}$ and $\overline{CD}$ are in the same plane and do not intersect, then they are parallel. How do you respond?

9. A student claims that angles 1 and 2, as shown in the following figure, are congruent because they are vertical angles. How do you respond?

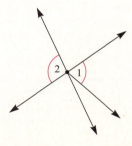

10. A student asks how to find the shortest path between two points A and B on a right circular cylinder. How do you respond?

11. One student says, "My sister's high-school geometry book talked about equal angles. Why don't we use the term 'equal angles' instead of 'congruent angles'?" How do you reply?

12. A student says there can be only 360 different rays emanating from a point, since there are only 360° in a circle. How do you respond?

13. Jodi identifies the following figure in (a) as a rectangle and the figure in (b) as a square. She claims that the figure in (b) is not a rectangle because it is a square. How do you respond?

(a)   (b)

14. Millie claims that a rhombus is regular because all of its sides are congruent. How do you respond?

I. Basic geometric notions

  A. Points, lines, and planes

    1. Points, lines, and **planes** are basic, but undefined, terms.

    2. Collinear points are points that belong to the same line.

    3. Important subsets of lines are **segments** and **rays.**

    4. Coplanar points are points that lie in the same plane. **Coplanar lines** are defined similarly.

    5. Two lines with exactly one point in common are **intersecting lines.**

    6. Concurrent lines are lines that contain a common point.

    7. Two distinct coplanar lines with no points in common are **parallel.**

    8. Skew lines are lines that cannot be contained in the same plane.

    9. Parallel planes are planes with no points in common.

    10. Space is the set of all points.

    11. An **angle** is the union of two rays with a common endpoint.

    12. Angles are classified according to size as **acute, obtuse, right,** or **straight.**

    13. Two lines that meet to form a right angle are **perpendicular.**

    14. A **dihedral angle** is the union of two half-planes and the common line defining the half-planes.

  B. Plane figures

    1. A **closed curve** is a curve that, when traced, has the same starting and stopping points and may cross itself at individual points.

    2. A **simple curve** is a curve that does not cross itself when traced, although the starting and stopping points may be the same.

    3. A **polygonal curve** is a curve made up of line segments.

    4. A **polygon** is a simple closed polygonal curve.

      a. A **diagonal** is any line segment connecting two nonconsecutive vertices of a polygon.

      b. A **convex polygon** is one such that if any two points of the polygonal region are connected by a segment, the segment is a subset of the polygonal region.

      c. A **concave polygon** is a nonconvex polygon.

      d. A **regular polygon** is a polygon in which all the angles are congruent and all the sides are congruent.

    5. A **polygonal region** is the union of a polygon and its interior.

    6. Triangles are classified according to the lengths of their sides as **scalene, isosceles,** or **equilateral** and

according to the measures of their angles as **acute, obtuse,** or **right.**

    7. Quadrilaterals with special properties are **trapezoids, parallelograms, rectangles, kites, isosceles trapezoids, rhombuses,** and **squares.**

    8. A **circle** is a set of points in a plane each of which lies at the same distance from a given point, called the **center.**

II. Linear Measure

  A. The English system

    Linear measure

    1 ft = 12 in.

    1 yd = 3 ft

    1 mi = 5280 ft = 1760 yd

  B. The metric system

    A summary of relationships among prefixes and the base unit of linear measure follows:

Prefix	Unit	Relationship to Base Unit	Symbol
kilo	kilometer	1000 meters	km
*hecto	hectometer	100 meters	hm
*deka	dekameter	10 meters	dam
	meter	**1 meter**	**m**
*deci	decimeter	0.1 meter	dm
centi	centimeter	0.01 meter	cm
milli	millimeter	0.001 meter	mm

*Not commonly used.

  C. Distance

    1. Distance properties. Given points *A, B,* and *C*:

      a. $AB \geq O$

      b. $AB = BA$

      c. $AB + BC \geq AC$

    2. The distance around a two-dimensional figure is the **perimeter.** The distance *C* around a circle is the **circumference.** $C = 2\pi r = \pi d$, where *r* is the **radius** of the circle and *d* is the **diameter.**

III. Theorems involving angles

  A. Supplements of the same angle, or of congruent angles, are congruent.

  B. Complements of the same angle, or of congruent angles, are congruent.

  C. Vertical angles formed by intersecting lines are congruent.

  D. If any two distinct lines are cut by a transversal, then a pair of **corresponding angles, alternate interior angles,** *or* **alternate exterior angles** are congruent if, and only if, the lines are parallel.

  E. The sum of the measures of the angles of a triangle is 180°.

F. The sum of the measures of the interior angles of any convex polygon with *n* sides is $180n - 360$, or $180(n - 2)$. One angle of the polygon measures $\dfrac{180n - 360}{n}$, or $\dfrac{180(n-2)}{n}$.

G. The sum of the measures of the exterior angles of any convex polygon is 360°.

IV. Three-dimensional figures

  A. A **polyhedron** is a simple closed surface formed by polygonal regions.

  B. Three-dimensional figures with special properties are **prisms, pyramids, regular polyhedra, cylinders, cones,** and **spheres.**

*V. Networks

  A. A **network** is a collection of points or **vertices** and a collection of curves or **arcs.**

  B. A vertex of a network is called an **even vertex** if the number of arcs meeting at the vertex is even. A vertex is an **odd vertex** if the number of arcs meeting at a vertex is odd.

  C. A network is called **traversable** if there is a path through the network such that each arc is passed through exactly once.

    1. If all the vertices of a network are even, then the network is traversable. Any vertex can be a starting point, and the same vertex must be the stopping point.

    2. If a network has two odd vertices, it is traversable. One odd vertex must be the starting point, and the other must be the stopping point.

    3. If a network has more than two odd vertices, it is not traversable.

    4. No network has exactly one odd vertex.

  D. A network that is traversable by starting and ending at the same point is an **Euler circuit.**

CHAPTER REVIEW

1. Sketch diagrams such that each of the following is true:
  a. The intersection of two segments is a segment.
  b. The intersection of two rays is a ray.
  c. The intersection of two rays is a segment.
  d. The intersection of two angles is an angle.
  e. The intersection of two angles is a segment.

2. Refer to the following line *m*:

  a. List three different names for the line.
  b. Name two different rays on *m* that have endpoint *B*.
  c. Find a simpler name for $\overrightarrow{AB} \cap \overrightarrow{BA}$.
  d. Find a simpler name for $\overrightarrow{BA} \cap \overrightarrow{AC}$.

3. In the following figure, $\overleftrightarrow{PQ}$ is perpendicular to α:

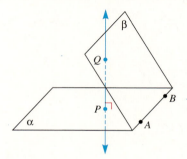

  a. Name a pair of skew lines.
  b. Using only the letters in the figure, name as many planes as possible that are each perpendicular to α.

  c. What is the intersection of planes *APQ* and β?
  d. Is there a single plane containing *A, B, P,* and *Q*? Explain your answer.

4. Draw each of the following curves:
  a. A simple closed curve
  b. A closed curve that is not simple
  c. A concave hexagon
  d. A convex decagon

5. a. Can a triangle have two obtuse angles? Justify your answer.
  b. Can a parallelogram have four acute angles? Justify your answer.

6. In a certain triangle, the measure of one angle is twice the measure of the smallest angle. The measure of the third angle is seven times greater than the measure of the smallest angle. Find the measures of each of the angles in the triangle.

7. a. Explain how to derive an expression for the sum of the measures of the angles in a convex *n*-gon.
  b. In a certain regular polygon, the measure of each angle is 176°. How many sides does the polygon have?

8. Sketch each of the following:
  a. Three planes that intersect in a point
  b. A plane and a cone that intersect in a circle
  c. A plane and a cylinder that intersect in a segment
  d. Two pyramids that intersect in a triangle

9. Sketch drawings to illustrate different possible intersections of a square pyramid and a plane.

10. In a periscope, a pair of mirrors are placed parallel to each other. If the dotted line in the following figure represents a path of light and $m(\angle 1) = m(\angle 2) = 45°$, find $m(\angle 3)$ and $m(\angle 4)$:

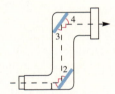

11. Find $6°48'\,59'' + 28°19'\,36''$. Write your answer in simplest terms.

12. In the figure, ℓ is parallel to m, and $m(\angle 1) = 60°$. Find each of the following:
  a. $m(\angle 3)$ **b.** $m(\angle 6)$ **c.** $m(\angle 8)$

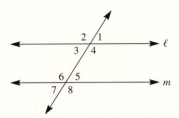

13. a. Draw a large triangle ABC and tear off two of its angles ($\angle B$ and $\angle C$). Fit the angles on the exterior of the third angle, as shown in the following figure. What theorems does the experiment illustrate?

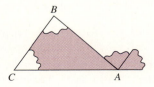

  ★b. The experiment in (a) suggests an approach to a proof of the theorem that it illustrates. Write the proof.

14. Given three segments of length p, q, and r, where $p > q$, determine if it is possible to construct a triangle with sides of length p, q, and r in each of the following cases. Justify your answers.
  a. $p - q > r$
  b. $p - q = r$

15. Complete the following. (Use a calculator when convenient.)
  a. 50 ft = _____ yd
  b. 947 yd = _____ mi
  c. 0.75 mi = _____ ft
  d. 349 in. = _____ yd

16. The vertices of a regular hexagon $ABCDEF$ are on a circle with center O and radius r (see the following figure).

Assume that all the marked angles with vertex O have the same measure. Also assume that in a triangle, two sides are congruent if, and only if, the angles opposite these sides are congruent.

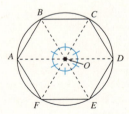

  a. Show that the length of each side of the hexagon is r.
  b. The Babylonians and ancient Hebrews calculated the circumference of a circle by finding the perimeter of a regular hexagon whose vertices are on the circle. By doing so, they made an error. Calculate by what percent of the actual circumference of the circle the error was.

17. If a cube, as pictured next, intersects a plane, what possible figures can be obtained by the intersection. Sketch the planes and figures obtained in each case.

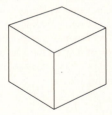

18. If a pyramid has an octagon for a base, how many lateral faces does it have?

19. If ABC is a right triangle and $m(\angle A) = 42°$, what is the measure of the other acute angle?

★20. a. Which of the following networks are traversable?
  b. Find a corresponding path for the networks that are traversable.

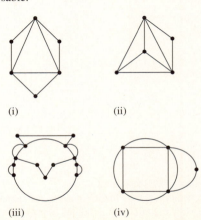

SELECTED BIBLIOGRAPHY

Adele, G. "When Did Euclid Live? An Answer Plus a Short History of Geometry." *Mathematics Teacher* 82 (September 1989): 460–463.

Bledsoe, G. "Guessing Geometric Shapes." *Mathematics Teacher* 80 (March 1987): 178–180.

Bright, G., and J. Harvey. "Games, Geometry, and Teaching." *Mathematics Teacher* 81 (April 1988): 250–259.

Bright, G., and J. Harvey. "Learning and Fun with Geometry Games." *Arithmetic Teacher* 35 (April 1988): 22–26.

Carroll, W. "Cross Sections of Clay Solids." *Arithmetic Teacher* 35 (March 1988): 6–11.

Dutch, S. "Folding *n*-pointed Stars and Snowflakes." *Mathematics Teacher* 87 (November 1994): 630–637.

Famighetti, R. "Weights and Measures." *The World Almanac and Book of Facts 1995.* Funk and Wagnalls Corporation (1994): 557.

Fuys, D., D. Geddes, and R. Tischler. *The van Hiele Model of Thinking in Geometry among Adolescents.* Reston, Va.: National Council of Teachers of Mathematics (1988).

Hoffer, A. "Making a Better Beer Glass." *Mathematics Teacher* 75 (May 1982): 378–379.

Hoffer, A. *Van Hiele-based Research.* In R. Lesh and M. Landau, *Acquisition of Mathematics Concepts and Processes.* New York: Academic Press (1983).

Irard, J. "Developing Spatial Skills with Three-Dimensional Puzzles." *Arithmetic Teacher* 37 (January 1994): 44–47.

Kriegler, S. "The Tangram — It's More Than an Ancient Puzzle." *Arithmetic Teacher* 38 (May 1991): 38–43.

Morrow, L. "Geometry through the Standards." *Arithmetic Teacher* 38 (April 1991): 21–25.

Olson, A. T. *Mathematics through Paper Folding.* Washington, D.C.: NCTM (1975).

Posamentier, A. "Geometry: A Remedy for the Malaise of Middle School Mathematics." *Mathematics Teacher* 82 (December 1989): 678–680.

Row, T. S. *Geometric Exercises in Paper Folding.* Dover Publications, Inc. (1966).

Souza, R. "Golfing with a Protractor." *Arithmetic Teacher* 35 (April 1988): 52–56.

Teppo, A. "Van Hiele Levels of Geometric Thought Revisited." *Mathematics Teacher* 84 (March 1991): 210–221.

Thiessen, D., and M. Matthias. "Selected Children's Books for Geometry." *Arithmetic Teacher* 37 (December 1989): 47–51.

Van Hiele. *Structure and Insight.* New York: Academic Press (1986).

Wilson, M. "Measuring a van Hiele Geometry Sequence: A Reanalysis." *Journal for Research in Mathematics Education* 21 (May 1990): 230–237.

Winter, M., et al. *Middle Grades Mathematics* Project Spatial Visualization. Menlo Park, Calif.: Addison-Wesley (1986).

Woodward, E., and Brown, R. "Polydrons and Three-Dimensional Geometry." *Arithmetic Teacher* 41 (April 1994): 451–458.

11

CONSTRUCTIONS AND SIMILARITY

A particular kaleidoscope is a right prism with an equilateral triangle as a base. A beam of light is reflected at a 60° angle from a point P on a side of the triangular base, as shown in the accompanying figure. The beam is reflected in the plane of the base to the different mirrored surfaces and continues bouncing at 60° angles. Find the length of the path of the reflected light when it reaches the point at which it originated.

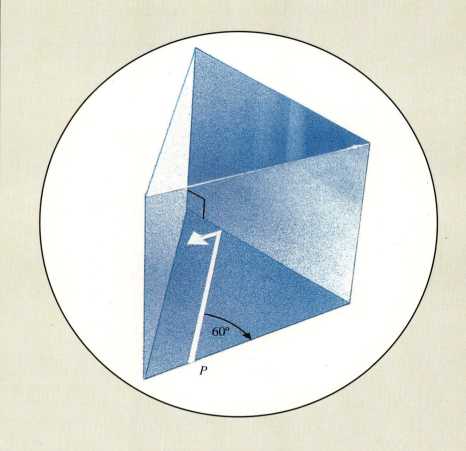

The *Standards* (p. 112) recommends that students in grades 5–8 *examine and discover relationships and develop spatial sense by constructing, drawing, measuring, visualizing, comparing, transforming, and classifying geometric figures.* Similarly the *Teaching Standards* (p. 137) notes that . . . *symmetry, congruence, similarity, measurement, trigonometry, and other notions can be investigated through two- and three-dimensional physical models, drawings, and computer graphics, emphasizing visualization.*

In this chapter we introduce, through constructions and visualization, the concepts of similarity and congruence. The last section is optional and develops right triangle trigonometry using ratios and a calculator.

Section 11-1 Congruence through Constructions

similar
congruent

In mathematics, the word **similar** (~) describes objects that have the same shape but not necessarily the same size, while the word **congruent** (≅) describes objects that have the same size as well as the same shape. Whenever two figures are congruent, they are also similar. However, the converse is not true (why?). Examples of similar and congruent objects are seen in Figure 11-1.

Figure 11-1

Symmetry Work 22

(a)

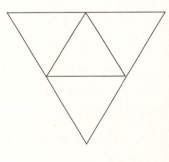

(b)

Figure 11-1(a) shows sets of congruent fish (and birds) in an Escher print. Figure 11-1(b) contains both congruent and similar equilateral triangles. The smaller triangles are congruent. They also are similar to the large one that contains them. In addition, Figure 11-1(b) depicts an example of a **rep-tile,** a figure that is used to construct a larger similar figure. In Figure 11-1(b), one of the smaller equilateral triangles is a rep-tile.

rep-tile

Before studying congruent and similar figures, we first consider some notation and review definitions from Chapter 10. For example, *any two line segments are congruent if they have the same length, while 2 angles are congruent if they have the same measure.* The length of line segment $\overline{AB}$ is denoted by AB. Symbolically, we may write the following about congruent segments and angles:

$$\overline{AB} \cong \overline{CD} \text{ if, and only if, } AB = CD$$

$$\angle ABC \cong \angle DEF \text{ if, and only if, } m(\angle ABC) = m(\angle DEF)$$

I N V E S T I G A T I O N   1 1 - 1

● Are any two segments similar? Are any two angles with the same measure similar? ●

H I S T O R I C A L   N O T E

The straight line and circle were considered the basic geometric figures by the Greeks and the straightedge and compass are their physical analogs. It is believed that the Greek philosopher Plato (ca. 427–347 B.C.) rejected the use of mechanical devices other than the straightedge and compass for geometric constructions because use of other tools emphasized practicality rather than "ideas," which he regarded as more important.

Geometric Constructions

A *geometric construction* is a task in which we are given some geometric elements such as points, segments, angles, or circles and we derive other elements by using certain well-defined instruments.

Ancient Greek mathematicians constructed geometric figures with a straightedge (no markings on it) and a collapsible compass. Figure 11-2 shows a modern compass. It can be used to mark off and duplicate lengths and to construct circles or arcs with a radius of a given measure. To draw a circle when given the radius PQ of a circle, we follow the steps illustrated in Figure 11-2.

Figure 11-2 *Constructing a circle given its radius*

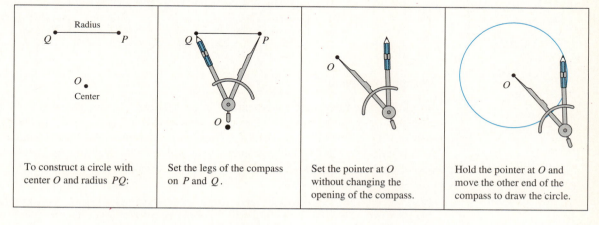

| To construct a circle with center O and radius PQ: | Set the legs of the compass on P and Q. | Set the pointer at O without changing the opening of the compass. | Hold the pointer at O and move the other end of the compass to draw the circle. |

The figure formed in Figure 11-2 is a circle with center O and is referred to as circle O. Any circle is similar to any other circle because they have the same shape. However, *any circle is congruent to another circle if, and only if, the radii of the two circles are congruent.*

arc   An **arc** of a circle is any part of the circle that can be drawn without lifting a pencil.
center of arc (The entire circle could be considered as an arc.) The **center of an arc** is the center of the

circle containing the arc. If there is no danger of ambiguity in a discussion, the endpoints of the arc are used to name the arc, otherwise three points are used in the naming. In Figure 11-3, $\overset{\frown}{AB}$ is a **minor arc** and $\overset{\frown}{ADB}$ is a **major arc.** If the major arc and the minor arc of a circle are the same size, each is a **semicircle.**

minor arc • major arc

semicircle

Figure 11-3

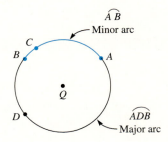

Minor arc $\overset{\frown}{AB}$

Major arc $\overset{\frown}{ADB}$

Constructing Segments

There are many ways to construct a segment congruent to a given segment $\overline{AB}$. A natural approach is to use a ruler, measure $\overline{AB}$, and then draw a congruent segment. A different way is to trace $\overline{AB}$ onto a piece of paper. A third method is to use a straightedge and a compass as in Figure 11-4.

Figure 11-4   Constructing a line segment congruent to a given segment

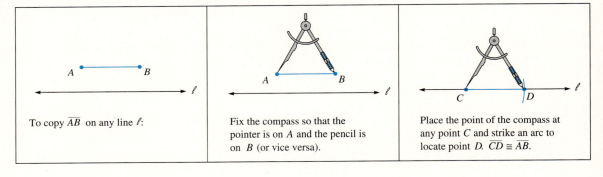

To copy $\overline{AB}$ on any line ℓ:

Fix the compass so that the pointer is on A and the pencil is on B (or vice versa).

Place the point of the compass at any point C and strike an arc to locate point D. $\overline{CD} \cong \overline{AB}$.

Triangle Congruence

Informally, two figures are congruent if it is possible to fit one figure onto the other so that all matching parts coincide. If we were to trace $\triangle ABC$ in Figure 11-5 and put the tracing over $\triangle A'B'C'$ so that the tracing of A is over A', the tracing of B is over B', and the tracing of C is over C', $\triangle ABC$ would coincide with $\triangle A'B'C'$. This suggests the following definition of congruent triangles.

Definition of Congruent Triangles

$\triangle ABC$ is congruent to $\triangle A'B'C'$, written $\triangle ABC \cong \triangle A'B'C'$, if $\angle A \cong \angle A'$, $\angle B \cong \angle B'$, $\angle C \cong \angle C'$, $\overline{AB} \cong \overline{A'B'}$, $\overline{BC} \cong \overline{B'C'}$, and $\overline{AC} \cong \overline{A'C'}$.

To use the above definition to show that two triangles are congruent, we need to find a one-to-one correspondence between the vertices of one triangle and the vertices of the other triangle such that each pair of corresponding angles and each pair of corresponding sides are congruent. Figure 11-5 shows such a one-to-one correspondence and $\triangle ABC \cong \triangle A'B'C'$.

Figure 11-5

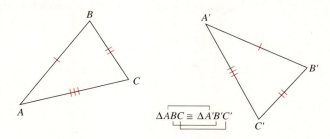

$\triangle ABC \cong \triangle A'B'C'$

REMARK   The statement "Corresponding parts of congruent triangles are congruent" is sometimes abbreviated as CPCTC.

I N V E S T I G A T I O N   1 1 - 2

● In Figure 11-5, if $\triangle ABC \cong \triangle A'B'C'$, list all possible ways that the congruence can be symbolized.   ●

• • •

Example 11-1   Assume that each of the pairs of triangles in Figure 11-6 is congruent and write an appropriate symbolic congruence for each.

Figure 11-6

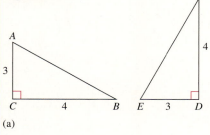
(a)

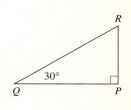
(b)

Solution   a. Vertex C corresponds to D because the angles at C and D are right angles. Also, because $\overline{CB} \cong \overline{DF}$ and C corresponds to D, B corresponds to F. Consequently, A corresponds to E. Thus $\triangle ABC \cong \triangle EFD$.

   b. Vertex C corresponds to P because the angles at C and P are both right angles. To establish the other correspondences, we first find the missing angles in the triangles. We see that $m(\angle B) = 90° - 60° = 30°$ and $m(\angle R) = 90° - 30° = 60°$. Consequently, A corresponds to R because $m(\angle A) = m(\angle R) = 60°$, and B corresponds to Q because $m(\angle B) = m(\angle Q) = 30°$. Thus $\triangle ABC \cong \triangle RQP$.

• • •

Side, Side, Side Property (SSS)

In an automotive assembly line, the entire production process is designed in such a way that the same bodies of the same model cars are congruent to each other. (Outside paint and different colors of upholstery fabric and interiors provide individual differences.) Calibration experts work to ensure that car parts are interchangeable so that the same part fits on all basic models of the same car. For the cars to be congruent, the parts must be congruent. In the assembly line of automotive production, decisions have to be made about the minimal set of items to consider for eventual congruency. In considering congruence of figures in geometry, we apply the same process.

If three sides and three angles of one triangle are congruent to the corresponding three sides and three angles of another triangle, then we can conclude from the definition of congruent triangles that the triangles are congruent. However, do we need to know that all six parts of one triangle are congruent to the corresponding parts of the second triangle in order to conclude that the triangles are congruent?

Consider the triangle formed by attaching three segments, as in Figure 11-7. Such a triangle is *rigid;* that is, its size and shape cannot be changed. Because of this property, a manufacturer can make duplicates if the lengths of the sides are known. Many bridges or other structures that have exposed frameworks demonstrate the practical use of the rigidity of triangles, as seen in Figure 11-8.

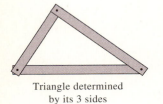

Triangle determined
by its 3 sides

Figure 11-7

Figure 11-8

Because a triangle is completely determined by its three sides, we have the following property.

Property

Side, Side, Side (SSS)   If the three sides of one triangle are congruent, respectively, to the three sides of a second triangle, then the triangles are congruent.

Example 11-2   For each part in Figure 11-9, use SSS to explain why the given triangles are congruent:

Figure 11-9

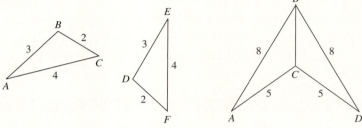

Solution   **a.** $\triangle ABC \cong \triangle EDF$ by SSS because $\overline{AB} \cong \overline{ED}$, $\overline{BC} \cong \overline{DF}$, and $\overline{AC} \cong \overline{EF}$.
b. $\triangle ABC \cong \triangle DBC$ by SSS because $\overline{AB} \cong \overline{DB}$, $\overline{AC} \cong \overline{DC}$, and $\overline{BC} \cong \overline{BC}$.

Constructing a Triangle Given Three Sides

Using the SSS property, we can construct a triangle $A'B'C'$ congruent to a given triangle ABC if we know the lengths of the three sides. We can do this on a geometry drawing utility or with a compass and straightedge, as in Figure 11-10.

Figure 11-10

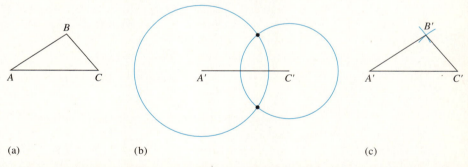

(a)   (b)   (c)

First, we construct a segment congruent to one of the three segments. For example, we may construct $\overline{A'C'}$ so that it is congruent to $\overline{AC}$. To complete the triangle construction, we must locate the other vertex, B'. The distance from A' to B' is AB. All points at a distance AB from A' are on a circle with center at A' and radius of length AB. Similarly, B' must be on a circle with center C' and radius of length BC. The only possible locations for B' are at the points where the two circles intersect. Either point is acceptable. Usually, a picture of the construction shows only one possibility and the construction uses only arcs, as pictured in Figure 11-10(c).

REMARK   Starting the construction with a segment $\overline{A'B'}$ congruent to $\overline{AB}$ or with $\overline{B'C'}$ congruent to $\overline{BC}$ would also result in triangles congruent to $\triangle ABC$.

INVESTIGATION 11-3

● From using the SSS construction as in Figure 11-10, we could think that given any three segments, we could construct a triangle whose sides are congruent to the given segments. To determine if this is true, cut at least ten pieces of straws of different lengths. Make all the possible triangles and answer the following questions:

a. Could a triangle be constructed from each of the three pieces of straws?

b. If three pieces were exactly the same length, what type of triangle could be constructed?

c. If the length of one piece of straw is the exact sum of the lengths of the other two pieces, can a triangle be constructed from the three pieces? Why or why not?

d. If one piece of straw is longer than the two other pieces put together, can a triangle be constructed from the three pieces? Why or why not? ●

TECHNOLOGY CORNER

Use the *Geometer's Sketchpad* or another geometry drawing utility to do the following:

a. Construct any triangle *ABC*.
b. Measure each of its sides.
c. Draw a segment $\overline{A'B'}$ congruent to $\overline{AB}$.
d. Draw a circle with center *A'* and radius of length *AC*.
e. Draw a circle with center *B'* and radius *BC*.
f. Label a point of intersection of the two circles as *C'*.
g. Measure $\overline{B'C'}$ and $\overline{A'C'}$. Compare these lengths to *BC* and *AC*.
h. Measure and compare the following pairs of angles: $\angle ABC$ and $\angle A'B'C'$, $\angle BCA$ and $\angle B'C'A'$, and $\angle CAB$ and $\angle C'A'B'$.
i. What can you say about the two triangles?

The previous Technology Corner and Investigation both lend credence to the following property.

Property

Triangle Inequality   The sum of the measures of any two sides of a triangle must be greater than the measure of the third side.

Constructing Congruent Angles

We use the SSS notion of congruent triangles to construct an angle congruent to a given angle $\angle B$ by making $\angle B$ a part of an isosceles triangle and then reproducing this triangle, as in Figure 11-11.

Figure 11-11 shows how to construct an angle congruent to a given angle. However, with the compass and straightedge alone, it is impossible in general to construct an angle

Figure 11-11   Copying an angle

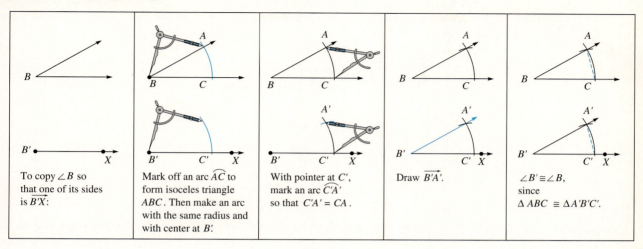

| To copy ∠B so that one of its sides is B'X: | Mark off an arc AC to form isoceles triangle ABC. Then make an arc with the same radius and with center at B'. | With pointer at C', mark an arc C'A' so that C'A' = CA. | Draw B'A'. | ∠B'≅∠B, since △ ABC ≅ △A'B'C'. |

with a particular given measure. For example, an angle of measure 20° cannot be constructed with a compass and a straightedge only, as these are inappropriate tools for such constructions. Instead, a protractor or some other measuring tool must be used. A geometry drawing utility can also be used to construct angles of particular measure. However, such constructions are, of necessity, approximations (why?).

Side, Angle, Side Property (SAS)

We have seen that, given three segments, no more than one triangle can be constructed. Could more than one triangle be constructed from only two segments? Consider Figure 11-12(b), which shows three different triangles with sides congruent to the segments given in Figure 11-12(a). The length of the third side depends on the measure of the angle **included angle**   between the other two sides. This angle is the **included angle.**

Figure 11-12

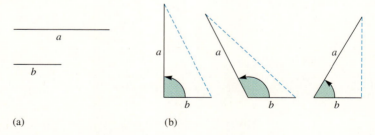

(a)   (b)

It appears that if we knew the lengths of two sides and the measure of the angle included between them, we could construct a unique triangle. This is true, and we can **Side, Angle, Side (SAS)**   express the rule as the **Side, Angle, Side (SAS)** property.

> **Property**
>
> **Side, Angle, Side (SAS)**   If two sides and the included angle of one triangle are congruent to two sides and the included angle of another triangle, respectively, then the two triangles are congruent.

Example 11-3

For each part of Figure 11-13, use SAS to show that the given pair of triangles are congruent.

Figure 11-13

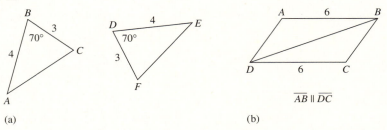

(a)   (b)

$\overline{AB} \parallel \overline{DC}$

Solution   a. $\triangle ABC \cong \triangle EDF$ by SAS because $\overline{AB} \cong \overline{ED}$, $\angle B \cong \angle D$, and $\overline{BC} \cong \overline{DF}$.
   b. Because $\overline{AB} \cong \overline{CD}$ and $\overline{DB} \cong \overline{BD}$, we need either another side or another angle to show that the triangles are congruent. We know nothing about the sides except that $\overline{AB} \parallel \overline{DC}$. Since parallel segments $\overline{AB}$ and $\overline{DC}$ are cut by transversal $\overline{BD}$, we have alternate interior angles $\angle ABD$ and $\angle BDC$ congruent. Now $\triangle ABD \cong \triangle CDB$ by SAS.

The SAS property of triangle congruence allows us to investigate a number of properties of triangles. For example, in Figure 11-14, consider isosceles triangle ABC with $\overline{AB} \cong \overline{AC}$. We fold a crease through vertex A to fold vertex B onto vertex C. If point D is the intersection of the crease and $\overline{BC}$, then $\angle BAD \cong \angle CAD$ and $\angle ABD \cong \angle ACD$ and $\overline{AD}$ is the perpendicular bisector of $\overline{BC}$.

Figure 11-14

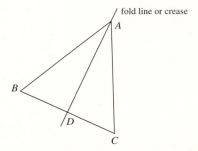

fold line or crease

The properties discovered are true in general and are summarized in Theorem 11-1.

Theorem 11-1

The following holds for every isosceles triangle:
a. The angles opposite the congruent sides are congruent. (Base angles of an isosceles triangle are congruent.)
b. The altitude of an isosceles triangle that contains the point of intersection of the congruent sides bisects the angle formed by those sides and is the perpendicular bisector of the third side of the triangle.

In Figure 11-14, notice that if point A is equidistant from the endpoints B and C, then A is on the perpendicular bisector of $\overline{BC}$. The converse of this statement is also true and is stated next.

Theorem 11-2

Any point on the perpendicular bisector of a segment is equidistant from the endpoints of the segment.

Constructions Involving Two Sides and an Angle of a Triangle

Figure 11-15 shows how to construct a triangle congruent to $\triangle ABC$ by using two sides $\overline{AB}$ and $\overline{AC}$ and the included angle, $\angle A$, formed by these sides. First, a ray with an arbitrary endpoint A' is drawn, and $\overline{A'C'}$ is constructed congruent to $\overline{AC}$. Then, $\angle A'$ is constructed so that $\angle A' \cong \angle A$ and B' is marked on the side of $\angle A'$ not containing C' so that $\overline{A'B'} \cong \overline{AB}$. Connecting B' and C' completes $\triangle A'B'C'$ so that $\triangle A'B'C' \cong \triangle ABC$.

Figure 11-15

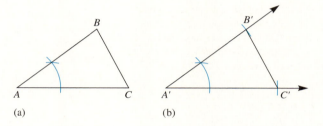

(a)   (b)

INVESTIGATION 11-4

● If, in two triangles, two sides and an angle not included between these sides are congruent, respectively, determine whether the triangles must be congruent.

a. If they are congruent, explain why you believe this is true.

b. If they are not congruent, state as few additional conditions as possible that can be placed on the sides or angles making the triangles congruent. ●

Ongoing Assessment 11-1

1. **a.** Use any tool to draw triangle ABC in which BC is greater than AC. Measure the angles opposite $\overline{BC}$ and $\overline{AC}$. Compare the angle measures. What did you find?
   b. Based on your finding in (a), make a conjecture concerning the lengths of sides and the measures of angles of a triangle.
2. Use any tools to construct each of the following, if possible:
   a. A segment congruent to $\overline{AB}$ and an angle congruent to $\angle CAB$.

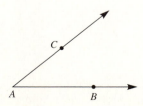

   b. A triangle with sides of lengths 2 cm, 3 cm, and 4 cm

c. A triangle with sides of lengths 4 cm, 3 cm, and 5 cm (what kind of triangle is it)

d. A triangle with sides 4 cm, 5 cm, and 10 cm

e. An equilateral triangle with sides 5 cm

f. A triangle with sides 6 cm and 7 cm and an included angle of measure 75°

g. A triangle with sides 6 cm and 7 cm and a nonincluded angle of measure 40°

h. A triangle with sides 6 cm and 6 cm and a nonincluded angle of measure 40°

i. A right triangle with legs 4 cm and 8 cm (the legs include the right angle)

3. For each of the conditions in Problem 2(b)–(i), does the given information determine a unique triangle? Explain why or why not.

4. How many different triangles can be constructed with toothpicks by connecting the toothpicks only at their ends if each triangle can contain at most five toothpicks per side?

5. For each of the following, determine whether the given conditions are sufficient to prove that $\triangle PQR \cong \triangle MNO$. Justify your answers.

a. $\overline{PQ} \cong \overline{MN}, \overline{PR} \cong \overline{MO}, \angle P \cong \angle M$
b. $\overline{PQ} \cong \overline{MN}, \overline{PR} \cong \overline{MO}, \overline{QR} \cong \overline{NO}$
c. $\overline{PQ} \cong \overline{MN}, \overline{PR} \cong \overline{MO}, \angle Q \cong \angle N$

6. A rancher designed a wooden gate as illustrated in the following figure. Explain the purpose of the diagonal boards on the gate.

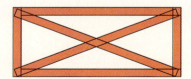

7. A rural homeowner had his television antenna held in place by three guy wires, as shown in the following figure. If the distances to each of the stakes from the base of the antenna are the same, what is true about the lengths of the wires? Why?

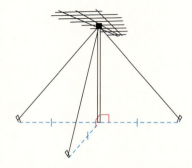

8. A group of students on a hiking trip wants to find the distance AB across a pond (see the following figure). One student suggests choosing any point C, connecting it with

B, and then finding point D such that $\angle DCB \cong \angle ACB$ and $\overline{DC} \cong \overline{AC}$. How and why does this help in finding the distance AB?

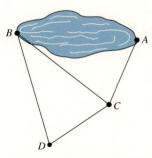

9. Using only a compass and a straightedge, perform each of the following:

a. Reproduce $\angle A$ shown in the following figure:

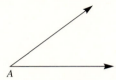

b. Construct an equilateral triangle with the following side $\overline{AB}$.

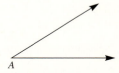

c. Construct a 60° angle.

d. Construct an isosceles triangle with $\angle A$ (see the following figure) as the angle included between the two congruent sides:

10. Refer to the following figure and, using only a compass and a straightedge, perform each of the following:

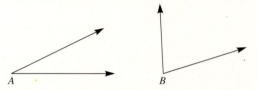

a. Construct $\angle C$ so that $m(\angle C) = m(\angle A) + m(\angle B)$.

b. Using the angles in (a), construct $\angle C$ so that $m(\angle C) = m(\angle B) - m(\angle A)$.

11. An equilateral triangle ABC is congruent to itself.

a. Write all possible true correspondences between the triangle and itself.

b. Use one of your answers in (a) to show that an equilateral triangular is also equiangular.

12. a. Find at least five examples of congruent objects.
  b. Find at least five examples of similar objects that are not congruent.

13. a. Draw a circle and use any method to mark off six points that are equally spaced on the circumference of the circle, as shown in the following figure:

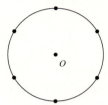

  b. Connect each of the points to point O and connect the points in order around the circle to form a regular hexagon.
  c. Explain why all of the triangles are congruent.
  d. Use the methods of this problem to construct a regular hexagon on a geometric drawing utility.

14. Suppose polygon $ABCD$ is any square with diagonals $\overline{AC}$ and $\overline{BD}$ intersecting in point F, as shown in the following figure:

  a. What is the relationship between point F and the diagonals $\overline{BD}$ and $\overline{AC}$? Why?
  b. What are the measures of angles BFA and AFD? Why?

15. a. If the diagonals of a quadrilateral bisect each other, what kind of quadrilateral must it be? Why?
  b. If the diagonals of a quadrilateral bisect each other and are congruent to each other, what type of quadrilateral can it be?
  c. If the diagonals of a quadrilateral are perpendicular bisectors of each other, what type of quadrilateral can it be?

16. Construct several noncongruent rhombuses and several noncongruent parallelograms that are not rhombuses. In each case, construct the diagonals.
  a. Based on your observations, what is true about the angles formed by the diagonals of a rhombus that is not necessarily true about the angles formed by the diagonals of a parallelogram that is not a rhombus?
  b. Justify your conjecture in (a).

17. What kind of figure is a quadrilateral in which both pairs of opposite sides are congruent? Why?

18. Write a definition for congruent arcs.

19. What minimum amount of information must you know in order to be sure that two cubes are congruent?

20. What is the least number of congruent parts that one must know in order to be sure that square pyramids are congruent?

21. How many different one-to-one correspondences could be listed between the following:
  a. Vertices of two triangles
  b. Vertices of two quadrilaterals
  c. Vertices of two n-gons

22. In a pair of right triangles, suppose two legs of one are congruent respectively to two legs of the other. Explain whether the triangles are congruent and why.

23. If two triangles are congruent, what can be said about their perimeters? Why?

24. Write a Logo procedure to draw a variable-sized equilateral triangle.

25. Logo programs can be used to construct triangles based on parts of a triangle. Type the following program into your computer and then run the following:
  a. SAS 50 75 83
  b. SAS 60 120 60

```
TO SAS  :SIDE1  :ANGLE  :SIDE2
    DRAW
    FORWARD :SIDE1
    RIGHT 180 - :ANGLE
    FORWARD :SIDE2
    HOME
END
```
(In LCSI, replace DRAW with CLEARSCREEN (CS).)

26. Following is a different procedure for constructing a triangle when two sides and an included angle are given. Compare this procedure to the one in Problem 25.

```
TO SAS1  :SIDE1  :ANGLE  :SIDE2
   DRAW
   BACK :SIDE1
   RIGHT :ANGLE
   FORWARD :SIDE2
   HOME
END
```
(In LCSI, replace DRAW with CLEARSCREEN (CS).)

  a. If SAS1 50 190 60 were executed, what would be the result?
  b. Is it possible in reality to draw a triangle with sides of 50 and 60 units and an included angle of 190°? Why?
  c. What line could be added to the procedure to correct the "bug" you encountered in (b)?

Communication

27. Explain whether you think the SSS and SAS properties can be used to determine if two triangles are similar. Use drawings constructed using a geometry utility or other tools to make your argument.

28. Write arguments to convince the class that Theorems 11-1 and 11-2 are true.

29. Explain whether a brick wall of a building is a rep-tile. Use drawings to explain your answer.
30. Why do you think most quilts contain congruent pieces?

Open-ended

31. Design a quilt pattern that involves rep-tiles or find a pattern and describe the rep-tiles involved.
32. Describe a minimal set of conditions that can be used to argue that two quadrilaterals are congruent.

Cooperative Learning

33. Make a set of drawings of congruent figures and write a journal article to convince a group of fellow students that the correspondence among vertices is necessary for determining that two triangles are congruent.

LABORATORY ACTIVITY

In this van Hiele Level 3 activity, you are given the names of shapes as follows:

　　a. Parallelogram
　　b. Rectangle
　　c. Kite
　　d. Rhombus
　　e. Square

　i. For each shape, list sufficient properties to define that shape. For example, if given the words *isosceles triangle,* you might say that it is a triangle with at least two sides congruent.
　ii. Now by using your answer in (i) for each shape, derive other properties of the shape. For example, you could show that the base angles are congruent in the isosceles triangle.

Section 11-2　## Other Congruence Properties

Angle, Side, Angle (ASA)

Triangles can be determined to be congruent by SSS and SAS. Can a triangle be constructed congruent to a given triangle by using two angles and a side? Figure 11-16 shows the construction of a triangle $A'B'C'$ such that $\overline{A'C'} \cong \overline{AC}$, $\angle A' \cong \angle A$, and $\angle C' \cong \angle C$. It seems that $\triangle A'B'C' \cong \triangle ABC$. This construction illustrates the **Angle, Side, Angle (ASA)** property of congruence.

Angle, Side, Angle (ASA)

Figure 11–16

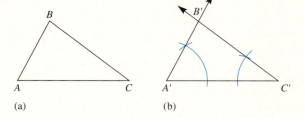

(a)　　　　　(b)

REMARK　Tick marks are used to show congruent segments or angles.

Property

Angle, Side, Angle (ASA)　If two angles and the included side of one triangle are congruent to two angles and the included side of another triangle, respectively, then the triangles are congruent.

In Figure 11-17, $\triangle ABC$ and $\triangle DEF$ have two pairs of angles congruent and a pair of sides congruent. If $\angle A \cong \angle D$ and $\angle B \cong \angle E$, we can deduce that $\angle C \cong \angle F$ because both are equal to $180° - (70 + 40)°$. Then, since $\overline{AC} \cong \overline{DF}$, we have $\triangle ABC \cong \triangle DEF$ by ASA.

Figure 11-17

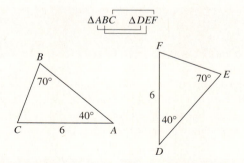

In general, by using the ASA property, we can justify the following property.

Property

Angle, Angle, Side (AAS)   If two angles and a corresponding side of one triangle are congruent to two angles and a corresponding side of another triangle, respectively, then the two triangles are congruent.

Example 11-4   Show that each of the pairs of triangles in Figure 11-18 is congruent.

Figure 11-18

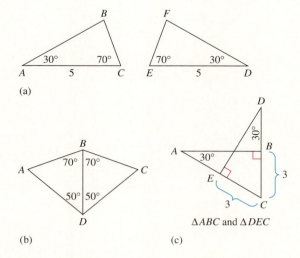

Solution   **a.** $\angle A \cong \angle D$, $\overline{AC} \cong \overline{DE}$, and $\angle C \cong \angle E$. Consequently, by ASA, $\triangle ABC \cong \triangle DFE$.
b. $\angle ABD \cong \angle CBD$, $\overline{BD} \cong \overline{BD}$, and $\angle ADB \cong \angle CDB$. Consequently, by ASA, $\triangle ABD \cong \triangle CBD$.
c. $\angle A \cong \angle D$, $\angle ABC \cong \angle DEC$, and $\overline{BC} \cong \overline{EC}$. Consequently, by AAS, $\triangle ABC \cong \triangle DEC$.

Is it possible to have two angles and a side of one triangle congruent to two angles and a side of another triangle and yet not have two congruent triangles? This question is explored in Ongoing Assessment 11-2.

INVESTIGATION 11-5

● Use a geometry drawing utility or any other tools to construct another triangle with angles congruent to corresponding angles in the original triangle but such that no corresponding segments are congruent.

Determine if knowing that the corresponding angles in two triangles are congruent is enough to decide that the two triangles are congruent. ●

Using properties of congruent triangles, we can deduce various properties of quadrilaterals. Table 11-1 summarizes the definitions and lists some properties of six quadrilaterals. These and other properties of quadrilaterals are further investigated in Ongoing Assessment 11-2.

Table 11-1

Quadrilateral and Its Definition	Properties of the Quadrilateral
Trapezoid: A quadrilateral with at least one pair of parallel sides	Consecutive angles between parallel sides are supplementary.
Parallelogram: A quadrilateral in which each pair of opposite sides is parallel	**a.** Opposite sides are congruent. **b.** Opposite angles are congruent. **c.** Diagonals bisect each other. **d.** A parallelogram has all the properties of a trapezoid.
Rectangle: A parallelogram with a right angle	**a.** A rectangle has all the properties of a parallelogram. **b.** All the angles of a rectangle are right angles. **c.** A quadrilateral in which all the angles are right angles is a rectangle. **d.** A quadrilateral in which the diagonals are congruent and bisect each other is a rectangle.

Table 11-1 Continued

Quadrilateral and Its Definition	Properties of the Quadrilateral
Kite: A quadrilateral with two distinct pairs of consecutive sides congruent	**a.** Lines containing the diagonals are perpendicular to each other. **b.** A line containing 1 diagonal is a bisector of the other. **c.** A line containing one diagonal bisects nonconsecutive angles.
Rhombus: A parallelogram with all sides congruent	**a.** A rhombus has all the properties of a parallelogram. **b.** A quadrilateral in which all the sides are congruent is a rhombus. **c.** The diagonals of a rhombus are perpendicular to each other. **d.** Diagonals bisect opposite angles. **e.** A rhombus has all the properties of a kite.
Square: A rectangle with all sides congruent	A square has all the properties of a parallelogram, a rectangle, and a rhombus.

Ongoing Assessment 11-2

1. Use any tools to construct each of the following, if possible:
   a. A triangle with angles measuring 60° and 70° and an included side of 8 in.
   b. A triangle with angles measuring 60° and 70° and a non-included side of 8 cm on a side of the 60° angle
   c. A right triangle with one acute angle measuring 75° and a leg of 5 cm on a side of the 75° angle
   d. A triangle with angles measuring 30°, 70°, and 80°
2. For each of the conditions in Problem 1(a)–(d), is it possible to construct two noncongruent triangles? Explain why or why not.
3. For each of the following, determine whether the given conditions are sufficient to prove that $\triangle PQR \cong \triangle MNO$. Justify your answers.
   a. $\angle Q \cong \angle N, \angle P \cong \angle M, \overline{PQ} \cong \overline{MN}$
   b. $\angle R \cong \angle O, \angle P \cong \angle M, \overline{QR} \cong \overline{NO}$
   c. $\overline{PQ} \cong \overline{MN}, \overline{PR} \cong \overline{MO}, \angle N \cong \angle Q$
   d. $\angle P \cong \angle M, \angle Q \cong \angle N, \angle R \cong \angle O$
4. A parallel ruler, shown as follows, can be used to draw parallel lines. The distance between the parallel segments $\overline{AB}$ and $\overline{DC}$ can vary. The ruler is constructed so that the distance between A and B equals the distance between D and

C. The distance between A and C is the same as the distance between B and D. Explain why $\overline{AB}$ and $\overline{DC}$ are always parallel.

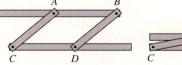 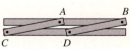

5. In each of the following, choose as many of the words *parallelogram, rectangle, rhombus, trapezoid, kite,* or *square* so that the resulting sentence is true. If none of the words makes the sentence true, answer "none" and justify your answer.
   a. A quadrilateral is a _____ if, and only if, its diagonals bisect each other.
   b. A quadrilateral is a _____ if, and only if, its diagonals are congruent.
   c. A quadrilateral is a _____ if, and only if, its diagonals are perpendicular to each other.
   d. A quadrilateral is a _____ if, and only if, its diagonals are congruent and bisect each other.

e. A quadrilateral is a _____ if, and only if, its diagonals are perpendicular to each other and bisect each other.

f. A quadrilateral is a _____ if, and only if, its diagonals are congruent and perpendicular to each other and they bisect each other.

g. A quadrilateral is a _____ if, and only if, a pair of opposite sides is parallel and congruent.

6. Create several trapezoids that have a pair of nonparallel sides congruent. Measure all angles and make a conjecture about the relationships among pairs of angles.

7. In both the ASA and the AAS properties of congruence, if two angles of one triangle were congruent respectively to two angles of another triangle, what must be true about the third angles of the triangles? Justify your answer.

8. a. For two right triangles, give a minimal set of conditions based on ASA and AAS to argue that the two triangles are congruent.

   b. Using your answer in (a), write two theorems that can be used to show that right triangles are congruent.

9. Classify each of the following statements as either true or false. If the statement is false, provide a counterexample.

   a. The diagonals of a square are perpendicular bisectors of each other.

   b. If all sides of a quadrilateral are congruent, the quadrilateral is a rhombus.

   c. If a rhombus is a square, it must also be a rectangle.

   d. An isosceles trapezoid can be a rectangle.

   e. A square is a trapezoid.

   f. A trapezoid is a parallelogram.

   g. A parallelogram is a trapezoid.

   h. No rectangle is a rhombus.

   i. No trapezoid is a square.

   j. Some squares are trapezoids.

10. a. Construct quadrilaterals having exactly one, two, and four right angles.

    b. Can a quadrilateral have exactly three right angles? Why?

    c. Can a parallelogram have exactly two right angles? Why?

11. Each fourth grader is given a protractor, two 30-cm sticks, and two 20-cm sticks and is asked to form a quadrilateral with a 75° angle. Sketch all possibilities.

12. The game of Triominoes has equilateral-triangular playing pieces with numbers at each vertex, shown as follows:

If two pieces are placed together as shown in the following figure, explain what type of quadrilateral is formed:

13. Describe a set of minimal conditions to determine if two regular polygons are congruent.

14. A **sector** of a circle is a pie-shaped section bounded by two radii and an arc. What is a minimal set of conditions for determining that two sectors of the same circle are congruent?

15. Draw two quadrilaterals such that two angles and an included side in one quadrilateral are congruent respectively to two angles and an included side in the other quadrilateral. However, the quadrilaterals are not congruent.

16. The following figure is a kite:

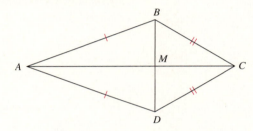

   a. Argue that $\overline{AC}$ bisects $\angle A$ and $\angle C$.

   b. Let M be the point on which the diagonals of kite $ABCD$ intersect. Measure $\angle AMD$ and make a conjecture concerning the angle between the diagonals of a kite. Justify your conjecture.

   c. Show that $\overline{BM} \cong \overline{MD}$.

17. a. In an isosceles trapezoid, make a conjecture concerning the lengths of the sides opposite the congruent angles.

    b. Make a conjecture concerning the diagonals of an isosceles trapezoid.

    c. Justify your conjectures in (a) and (b).

18. Using a straightedge and a compass, construct any convex kite. Then construct a second kite that is not congruent to the first but whose sides are congruent to the corresponding sides of the first kite.

19. a. What type of figure is formed by joining the midpoints of a rectangle (see the following figure)?

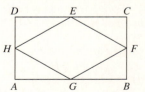

   ★ b. Prove your answer in (a).

   c. What type of figure is formed by joining the midpoints of the sides of a parallelogram?

★**d.** Prove your answer in (c).

e. Make a conjecture concerning the type of figure that is formed by joining the midpoints of any quadrilateral.

20. What information is needed to determine congruency for each of the following?

   a. Two squares

   b. Two rectangles

   c. Two parallelograms

21. Suppose polygon *ABCD* shown in the following figure is any parallelogram:

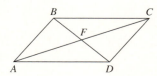

Use congruent triangles to justify each of the following:

   a. $\angle A \cong \angle C$ and $\angle B \cong \angle D$ (opposite angles are congruent).

   b. $\overline{BC} \cong \overline{AD}$ and $\overline{AB} \cong \overline{CD}$ (opposite sides are congruent).

   c. $\overline{BF} \cong \overline{DF}$ and $\overline{AF} \cong \overline{CF}$ (the diagonals bisect each other).

   d. $\angle DAB$ and $\angle ABC$ are supplementary.

22. a. Logo programs can be used to construct triangles using the ASA property. Type the given procedures into your computer and then run the following:

   i. ASA 60 50 70

   ii. ASA 80 50 60

   iii. AAS 60 50 70

   iv. AAS 130 20 50

```
TO ASA :ANGLE1 :SIDE :ANGLE2
   DRAW
   FORWARD 120
   BACK 120
   LEFT :ANGLE1
   FORWARD :SIDE
   RIGHT (180 − :ANGLE2)
   FORWARD 120
END
TO AAS :ANGLE1 :ANGLE2 :SIDE
   ASA :ANGLE1 :SIDE 180 −
   (:ANGLE1 + :ANGLE2)
END
```

   (In LCSI, replace DRAW with CLEARSCREEN (CS).)

   b. Predict the outcomes when the following are executed:
(i) AAS 130 50 100 (ii) AAS 90 45 120

   c. Add a line to the ASA procedure so that inputs for angles that are impossible in a triangle are not allowed.

23. a. Write a Logo procedure called RHOMBUS with inputs :SIDE and :ANGLE in which the first variable is the length of the side of the rhombus and the second is the measure of an interior angle of the rhombus.

   b. Execute RHOMBUS 80 50 and RHOMBUS 80 130. What is the relationship between the two figures? Why?

   c. Write a Logo procedure called SQ.RHOM with input :SIDE that will draw a square by calling on the RHOMBUS procedure.

24. Write a Logo procedure for starting at home and drawing an isosceles triangle given the length of two congruent sides and the measure of two congruent angles.

Communication

25. Explain whether mathematical congruence is the same as manufacturer's congruence.

26. Stan is standing on the bank of a river wearing a baseball cap. Standing erect and looking directly at the other bank, he pulls the bill of his cap down until it just obscures his vision of the opposite bank. He then turns around, being careful not to disturb the cap, and picks out a spot that is just obscured by the bill of his cap. He then paces off the distance to this spot and claims that the distance across the river is approximately equal to the distance he paced. Is Stan's claim true? Why?

27. Most ironing boards are collapsible for storage and can be adjusted to fit the height of the person using them. The surface of the board, though, remains parallel to the floor regardless of the height. Explain how to construct the legs of an ironing board to ensure the surface is always parallel to the floor.

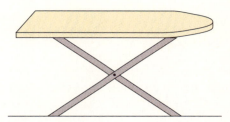

Open-ended

28. a. Go to a wallpaper store and examine the pattern books. Determine whether all rolls of a specific pattern of wallpaper are congruent.

   b. On an individual roll of wallpaper, determine the length of wallpaper before a pattern is repeated.

   c. If you were wallpapering a room, explain how congruence or noncongruence could save you money.

29. The United States Post Office tries to make all stamps of a particular variety congruent. For example, all Marilyn Monroe stamps are intended to be congruent. Find examples of stamps of a particular variety that were noncongruent. What was the result of the production of noncongruent stamps?

Cooperative Learning

30. a. Record the definitions of trapezoid and kite given in different grade 6–8 and secondary-school geometry textbooks.

b. Compare the definitions found with those in this text and with those other groups found.

c. Defend the use of one definition over another.

Review Problems

31. In the following regular pentagon, find all the triangles congruent to $\triangle ABC$ and that have only one point in common with $\triangle ABC$. Show that the triangles actually are congruent.

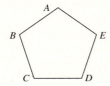

32. If possible, construct a triangle that has the following three segments *a, b,* and *c* as its sides:

33. Construct an equilateral triangle whose sides are congruent to the following segment:

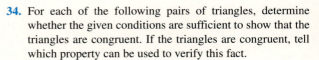

34. For each of the following pairs of triangles, determine whether the given conditions are sufficient to show that the triangles are congruent. If the triangles are congruent, tell which property can be used to verify this fact.

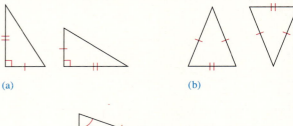

(a)   (b)

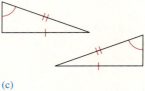

(c)

LABORATORY ACTIVITY

As a van Hiele Level 3 activity, consider the statements "If a quadrilateral has opposite sides congruent, then it is a parallelogram" and "If one pair of sides of a quadrilateral is congruent and parallel, then the quadrilateral is a parallelogram." Show that if one statement is true, then the other must also be true.

Section 11-3 Other Constructions

We use the definition of a rhombus and the following properties to accomplish basic compass-and-straightedge constructions:

1. A rhombus is a parallelogram in which all the sides are congruent.
2. The diagonals of a rhombus are perpendicular to each other.
3. The diagonals of a rhombus bisect the opposite angles.
4. The diagonals of a rhombus bisect each other.

Constructing Parallel Lines

To construct a line parallel to a given line ℓ through a point P not on ℓ, as in the leftmost panel of Figure 11-19, our strategy is to construct a rhombus with one of its vertices at P and one of its sides on line ℓ. Because the opposite sides of a rhombus are parallel, one of the sides through P will be parallel to ℓ. This construction is shown in Figure 11-19.

Figure 11-19 Constructing parallel lines (rhombus method)

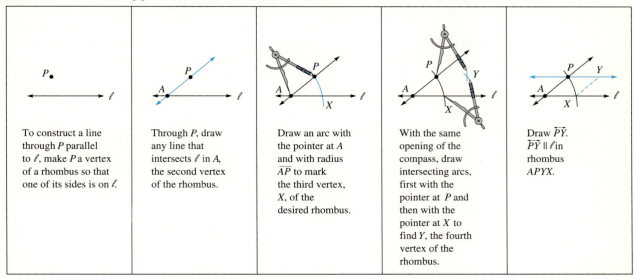

To construct a line through *P* parallel to *ℓ*, make *P* a vertex of a rhombus so that one of its sides is on *ℓ*.	Through *P*, draw any line that intersects *ℓ* in *A*, the second vertex of the rhombus.	Draw an arc with the pointer at *A* and with radius $\overline{AP}$ to mark the third vertex, *X*, of the desired rhombus.	With the same opening of the compass, draw intersecting arcs, first with the pointer at *P* and then with the pointer at *X* to find *Y*, the fourth vertex of the rhombus.	Draw $\overrightarrow{PY}$. $\overrightarrow{PY} \parallel \ell$ in rhombus *APYX*.

Figure 11-20 shows another way to do the construction. If congruent corresponding angles are formed by a transversal cutting two lines, then the lines are parallel. Thus the first step is to draw a transversal through *P* that intersects *ℓ*. The angle marked α is formed by

Figure 11-20 Constructing parallel lines (corresponding angle method)

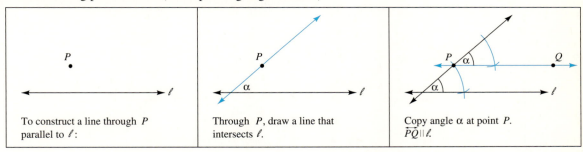

To construct a line through *P* parallel to *ℓ*:	Through *P*, draw a line that intersects *ℓ*.	Copy angle α at point *P*. $\overleftrightarrow{PQ} \parallel \ell$.

INVESTIGATION 11-6

● Parallel lines are frequently constructed either using a ruler and one triangle or using two triangles. If a ruler and a triangle are used, the ruler is left fixed and the triangle is slid so that one side of the triangle touches the ruler at all times. In Figure 11-21, the hypotenuses of the right triangles are all parallel (also the legs not on the ruler are all parallel). How can this method be used to accomplish the construction in Figure 11-20? ●

Figure 11-21

the transversal and line ℓ. By constructing an angle with a vertex at P congruent to α, we create congruent corresponding angles; therefore $\overrightarrow{PQ} \parallel \ell$.

Paperfolding can be used to construct parallel lines. For example, in Figure 11-22(a) if we wish to construct a line m parallel to line p through point Q, we can fold a perpendicular to line p so that the fold line does not contain point Q, as shown in Figure 11-22(b). Then by marking the image of point Q and connecting point Q and its image, Q', we have $\overline{QQ'}$ parallel to line p (why?).

Figure 11-22

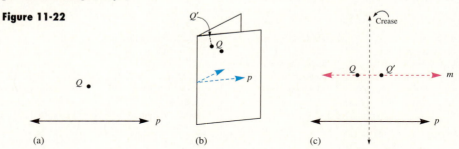

(a)   (b)   (c)

Constructing Angle Bisectors

angle bisector   Another construction based on a property of a rhombus is the construction of an **angle bisector,** a ray that separates an angle into two congruent angles. The diagonal of a rhombus with vertex A bisects $\angle A$, as shown in Figure 11-23.

Figure 11-23   Bisecting an angle

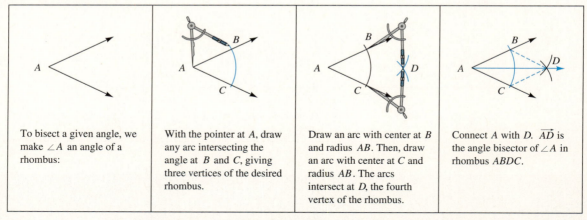

| To bisect a given angle, we make $\angle A$ an angle of a rhombus: | With the pointer at A, draw any arc intersecting the angle at B and C, giving three vertices of the desired rhombus. | Draw an arc with center at B and radius AB. Then, draw an arc with center at C and radius AB. The arcs intersect at D, the fourth vertex of the rhombus. | Connect A with D. $\overrightarrow{AD}$ is the angle bisector of $\angle A$ in rhombus $ABDC$. |

We can bisect an angle by folding a line through the vertex so that one side of the angle folds onto the other side. For example, in Figure 11-24 we bisect $\angle ABC$ by folding and creasing the paper through the vertex B so that $\overrightarrow{BA}$ coincides with $\overrightarrow{BC}$.

Figure 11-24

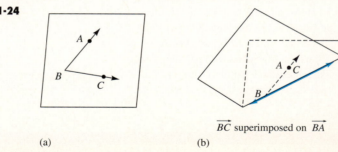

$\overrightarrow{BC}$ superimposed on $\overrightarrow{BA}$

(a)   (b)

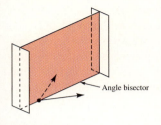

A Mira is a plastic device that acts as a reflector so that the image of an object can be seen behind the Mira. The drawing edge of the Mira acts as a folding line on paper. Any construction demonstrated in this text using paper folding can also be done with a Mira. To construct the bisector of an angle with a Mira, we place the drawing edge of the Mira on the vertex of the angle and reflect one side of the angle onto the other, as shown in Figure 11-25.

Figure 11-25

Angle bisector

Constructing Perpendicular Lines

To construct a line through P perpendicular to line ℓ, where P is not a point on ℓ, as in Figure 11-26, recall that the diagonals of a rhombus are perpendicular to each other. If we construct a rhombus with a vertex at P and two vertices A and B on ℓ, as in Figure 11-26, the segment connecting the fourth vertex Q to P is perpendicular to ℓ because $\overline{AB}$ and $\overline{PQ}$ are diagonals of the rhombus.

Figure 11-26   Constructing a perpendicular to a line from a point not on a line

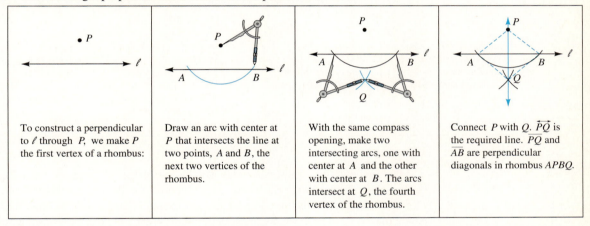

| To construct a perpendicular to ℓ through P, we make P the first vertex of a rhombus: | Draw an arc with center at P that intersects the line at two points, A and B, the next two vertices of the rhombus. | With the same compass opening, make two intersecting arcs, one with center at A and the other with center at B. The arcs intersect at Q, the fourth vertex of the rhombus. | Connect P with Q. $\overrightarrow{PQ}$ is the required line. PQ and $\overline{AB}$ are perpendicular diagonals in rhombus $APBQ$. |

perpendicular bisector   The line perpendicular to a segment at its midpoint is the **perpendicular bisector** of the segment. To construct the perpendicular bisector of a line segment, as in Figure 11-27, we use the fact that the diagonals of a rhombus are perpendicular bisectors of each other.

Figure 11-27   Bisecting a line segment

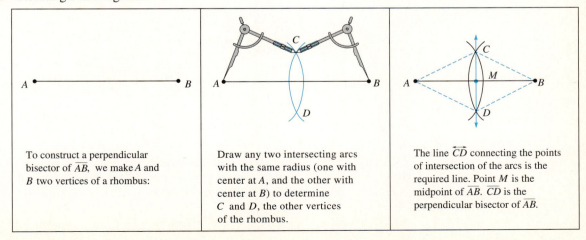

| To construct a perpendicular bisector of $\overline{AB}$, we make A and B two vertices of a rhombus: | Draw any two intersecting arcs with the same radius (one with center at A, and the other with center at B) to determine C and D, the other vertices of the rhombus. | The line $\overleftrightarrow{CD}$ connecting the points of intersection of the arcs is the required line. Point M is the midpoint of $\overline{AB}$. $\overline{CD}$ is the perpendicular bisector of $\overline{AB}$. |

The construction yields a rhombus such that the original segment is one of the diagonals of the rhombus and the other diagonal is the perpendicular bisector, as in Figure 11-27.

Constructing a perpendicular to a line ℓ at a point M on ℓ is based on the same property of a rhombus just used. That is, the diagonals of a rhombus are perpendicular bisectors of each other. Observe in Figure 11-27 that $\overline{CD}$ is a perpendicular to $\overline{AB}$ through M. Thus we construct a rhombus whose diagonals intersect at point M, as in Figure 11-28.

Figure 11-28   Constructing a perpendicular to a line from a point on the line

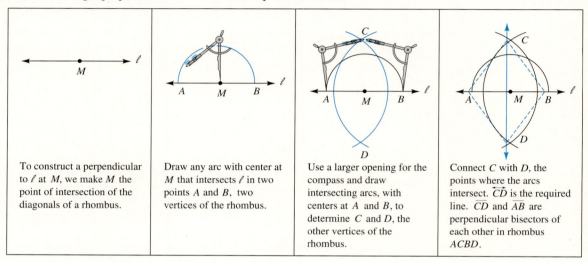

To construct a perpendicular to ℓ at M, we make M the point of intersection of the diagonals of a rhombus.	Draw any arc with center at M that intersects ℓ in two points A and B, two vertices of the rhombus.	Use a larger opening for the compass and draw intersecting arcs, with centers at A and B, to determine C and D, the other vertices of the rhombus.	Connect C with D, the points where the arcs intersect. $\overleftrightarrow{CD}$ is the required line. $\overleftrightarrow{CD}$ and $\overline{AB}$ are perpendicular bisectors of each other in rhombus $ACBD$.

Perpendicularity constructions can also be completed by means of paper folding or by using a Mira. To use paper folding to construct a perpendicular to a given line ℓ at a point P on the line, we fold the line onto itself, as shown in Figure 11-29(a). The fold line is perpendicular to ℓ. To perform the construction with a Mira, we place the Mira with the drawing edge on P, as shown in Figure 11-29(b), so that ℓ is reflected onto itself. The line along the drawing edge is the required perpendicular.

Figure 11-29

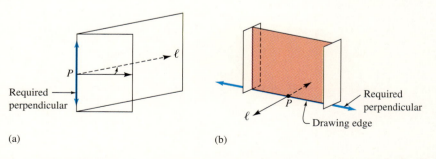

(a)   (b)

altitude   Constructing perpendiculars is useful in locating altitudes of a triangle. An **altitude** of a triangle is the perpendicular segment from a vertex of the triangle to the line containing the opposite side of the triangle. The construction of altitudes is described in Example 11-5.

Example 11-5 Given triangle *ABC*, construct an altitude from vertex *A* in each part of Figure 11-30.

Figure 11-30

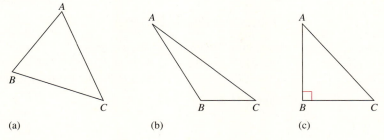

(a) (b) (c)

Solution **a.** An altitude is the perpendicular from a vertex to the line containing the opposite side of a triangle, so we need to construct a perpendicular from point *A* to the line containing $\overline{BC}$. Such a construction is shown in Figure 11-31. $\overline{AD}$ is the required altitude.

Figure 11-31

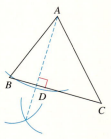

b. The construction of the altitude from vertex *A* is shown in Figure 11-32. Notice that the required altitude $\overline{AD}$ does not intersect the interior of $\triangle ABC$.

Figure 11-32

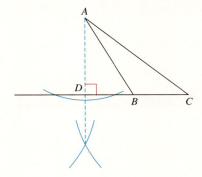

c. Triangle *ABC* is a right triangle. The altitude from vertex *A* is the side $\overline{AB}$. No construction is required.

TECHNOLOGY CORNER
Use a geometry drawing utility to draw all the altitudes of a triangle. Make conjectures about the altitudes of each of the following types of triangles: acute, right, and obtuse.

Properties of Angle Bisectors

Consider the angle bisector in Figure 11-33. It seems that any point P on the angle bisector is equidistant from the sides of the angle; that is, $PD = PE$. (The distance from a point to a line is the length of the perpendicular from the point to the line.)

Figure 11-33

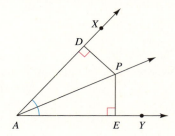

To justify this, we find two congruent triangles that have these segments as corresponding sides. The only triangles pictured are $\triangle ADP$ and $\triangle AEP$. Because $\overrightarrow{AP}$ is the angle bisector, $\angle DAP \cong \angle EAP$. Also, $\angle PDA$ and $\angle PEA$ are right angles and are thus congruent. $\overline{AP}$ is congruent to itself, so $\triangle PDA \cong \triangle PEA$ by AAS. Thus $\overline{PD} \cong \overline{PE}$ because they are corresponding parts of congruent triangles PDA and PEA. Consequently, we have the following theorem.

Theorem 11-3

Any point P on an angle bisector is equidistant from the sides of the angle.

INVESTIGATION 11-7

● Use a geometry drawing utility or any other tool to demonstrate that if a point is in the interior of an angle and is equidistant from the sides of the angle, the point must be on the angle bisector of that angle. ●

Ongoing Assessment 11-3

1. Refer to the following figure and use a compass and a straightedge to construct a line m through P parallel to ℓ, using each of the following:
a. Alternate interior angles

b. Alternate exterior angles

$P \bullet$

$\longleftrightarrow \ell$

2. For each of the following items compare these methods of constructions: paper folding, Mira, compass and straightedge, and geometric drawing utility (if available). Give advantages and disadvantages of each method.
  a. Bisector of ∠*A*
  b. Perpendicular bisector of $\overline{AB}$
  c. Perpendicular from point *P* to line *m*

3. Construction companies avoid vandalism at night typically by hanging expensive pieces of equipment from the boom of a crane, as shown in the following figure:

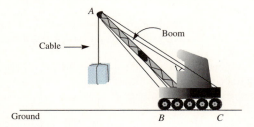

  a. If you consider a triangle with two vertices *A* and *B* as marked in the above figure and the intersection of a line through the cable holding the equipment and the ground as the third vertex, what type of triangle is formed?
  b. If you consider the triangle formed by points *A, B,* and *C,* describe where the altitude containing vertex *A* of the triangle is.

4. Construct the perpendicular bisectors of each of the following triangles. Use any desired method.

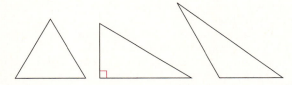

  a. Make a conjecture about the perpendicular bisectors of the sides of an acute triangle.
  b. Make a conjecture about the perpendicular bisectors of the sides of a right triangle.
  c. Make a conjecture about the perpendicular bisectors of the sides of an obtuse triangle.

5. a. Describe the relationship between any point on a perpendicular bisector of a segment and the endpoints of the segment it bisects.
  b. Given triangle *ABC,* as in the following figure, construct a point *P* that is equidistant from the three vertices of the triangle. Explain why your construction is correct.

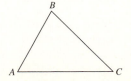

c. Repeat (b) for the following obtuse triangle:

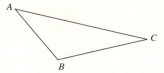

  d. Repeat (b) and (c) and construct a circle with center at *P* and radius *AP.* This circle **circumscribes the triangle** and the triangle is **circumscribed by the circle.**

6. A **median** of a triangle is a segment from a vertex of the triangle to the midpoint of the opposite side. Construct the three medians of each triangle in Problem 4. Their point of intersection is the **centroid,** the center of gravity of the triangle.

7. a. What is true about the perpendicular distance to each of the sides of an angle from any point on the angle bisector of the angle?
  b. Given the following triangle *ABC,* construct the point *P* that is common to all the angle bisectors of the interior angles of the triangle. The single point of intersection of the angle bisectors is the **incenter** of the triangle.

  c. In part (b), construct a perpendicular from point *P* to one side of the triangle. Let the perpendicular distance from *P* to the side of the triangle be *PX.*
  d. Construct a circle with center at *P* and radius *PX.* This circle **inscribes the triangle** or is the **inscribed circle** of the triangle.

8. A **chord** of a circle is a segment with endpoints on the circle.
  a. Construct a circle, several chords, and a perpendicular bisector of each chord. Make a conjecture concerning the perpendicular bisector of a chord and the center of the circle.
  b. Justify your conjecture in (a).
  c. Given a circle with an unmarked center, find the center of the circle.

9. Given $\overline{AB}$ in the following figure, construct a square with $\overline{AB}$ as a side:

10. Suppose you are "charged" 10¢ each time you use your straightedge to draw a line segment and 10¢ each time you use your compass to draw an arc. Using only a compass and a straightedge, determine the cheapest way to construct a square. Explain your reasoning.

11. Given *A, B,* and *C* as vertices, use a compass and a straight-edge to construct a parallelogram:

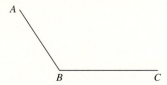

12. In the following concave quadrilateral *APBQ*, $\overline{PQ}$ and $\overline{AB}$ are the diagonals: $\overline{AP} \cong \overline{BP}$, $\overline{AQ} \cong \overline{BQ}$, and $\overline{PQ}$ has been extended until it intersects $\overline{AB}$ at *C*:

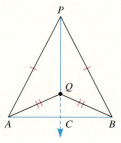

   a. Make a conjecture concerning $\overrightarrow{PQ}$ and $\overline{AB}$.
   b. Justify your conjecture in (a).
   c. Make conjectures concerning the relationships between $\overrightarrow{PQ}$ and $\angle APB$ and between $\overrightarrow{QC}$ and $\angle AQB$.
   d. Justify your conjectures in (c).

13. Use definitions of quadrilaterals to classify quadrilateral *APBQ* in Problem 12.

14. Using any tools, construct each of the following, if possible. If the construction is not possible, explain why.
   a. A square, given one side
   b. A square, given one diagonal
   c. A rectangle, given one diagonal
   d. A parallelogram, given two of its adjacent sides
   e. A rhombus, given two of its diagonals
   f. A triangle with two obtuse angles
   g. A parallelogram with exactly three right angles
   h. A kite with two right angles
   i. A kite with three right angles
  ★j. An isosceles triangle, given its base and the angle opposite the base.
  ★k. A trapezoid, given four of its sides

15. Using only a compass and a straightedge, construct angles with each of the following measures:
   a. 30°
   b. 15°
   c. 45°
   d. 75°
   e. 105°

16. Given $\overline{AB}$ in the following figure, use a compass and a straightedge to construct the perpendicular bisector of $\overline{AB}$.

You are not allowed to put any marks below $\overline{AB}$.

17. a. Explain why the hypotenuses in Figure 11-21 are all parallel.
   b. Use the "sliding triangle" method described in Figure 11-21 to construct a line through a point *P* parallel to a line ℓ.

18. Draw a line ℓ and a point *P* not on the line and use the sliding triangle method described in Figure 11-21 to construct a perpendicular to ℓ through *P* using a straightedge and a right triangle.

19. Use a compass to construct a circle. Without changing the setting of the compass, place the tip of the compass on the circumference of the circle and strike an arc that intersects the circle in two points. Use each of those points and continue the process until no new points are found. Connect the points on the circumference of the circle in order and describe the figure determined. Prove that the figure is a regular polygon.

20. Use the construction of Problem 19 to construct an equilateral triangle inscribed in a circle.

21. Describe how the constructions of a regular hexagon and an equilateral triangle could be accomplished by a Mira and by paper folding.

22. Describe how to inscribe a square in any circle. Explain why your construction produces a square.

23. Use Problem 22 to describe how to inscribe a regular octagon in a circle.

24. Write a Logo procedure to draw an equilateral triangle and three segments containing the altitudes of the triangle, as shown in the following figure:

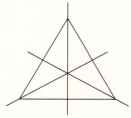

25. Use variables to write a Logo procedure to draw each of the following:
   a. The angle bisector of a variable-sized angle
   b. The perpendicular bisector of a variable-sized segment
   c. A set of two variable-sized parallel segments

Communication

26. Describe how you could use a Mira or paper folding to find the center of a circle.
27. Given an angle and a roll of tape, describe how you might construct the bisector of the angle.
28. Suppose you are standing on the center line of a flat, straight highway and looking along the center line. Describe the perceived relationship between the side lines of the highway and the center line you see in the distance.
29. Write a letter to a curriculum developer explaining whether or not the geometry curriculum in grades 5–8 should include construction problems using only a compass and straightedge.

Open-ended

30. Explain whether you think there is a single perpendicular from a point to a line on a sphere if a line is defined as a great circle of the sphere.
31. Explain whether you think there are parallel lines on a sphere.
32. Explain whether your geometry drawing utility allows the construction of regular polygons.

Cooperative Learning

33. Form small groups and have each write a description of the three famous geometry construction problems of antiquity. Discuss why these problems occupied the minds of geometers and decide as a class whether these problems are pertinent today.

Review Problems

34. Given that $\overleftrightarrow{AB} \parallel \overleftrightarrow{ED}$ and $\overline{BC} \cong \overline{CE}$ in the following figure, if $\overline{AB}$ cannot be measured explain why $\overline{AC} \cong \overline{CD}$.

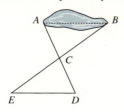

35. Draw $\triangle ABC$. Then construct $\triangle PQR$ congruent to $\triangle ABC$ using each of the following combinations:
    a. Two sides of $\triangle ABC$ and an angle included between these sides
    b. The three sides of $\triangle ABC$
    c. Two angles and a side included between these angles
36. a. *LUCY* is a trapezoid with diagonals intersecting at O. Is this enough information to conclude that *LUCY* contains one or more pairs of congruent triangles? Which ones are congruent, if any? Justify your answer.
    b. Suppose *LUCY* is an isosceles trapezoid, with $\overline{LY} \cong \overline{UC}$, as shown in the following figure. Answer the question in (a).

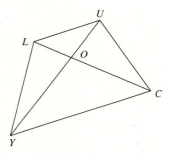

37. In $\triangle ABC$, name the *included side* between angles $\angle ABC$ and $\angle CAB$.
38. In $\triangle ABC$, name the *included angle* between sides $\overline{AB}$ and $\overline{BC}$.
39. In two right triangles, $\triangle ABC$ and $\triangle DEF$, if $\angle A$ and $\angle D$ are congruent and $\overline{AC}$ and $\overline{DF}$ are congruent, what do we know about the two triangles? Why?

LABORATORY ACTIVITY

As a van Hiele Level 0 activity on a geoboard, construct right triangles, squares, rectangles, and other polygons. Which of the following, if any, can you construct?

a. Pentagon
b. Hexagon
c. Equilateral triangle
d. Circle

TECHNOLOGY CORNER

Use a geometry drawing utility to do each of the following:

1. a. Draw a circle. Mark its center and draw any angle whose vertex is the center and whose sides intersect the circle, as in Figure 11-34. Such an angle is a **central angle** of the circle. The measure of a central angle and its intercepted arc are considered to be the same measure.

central angle

Figure 11-34

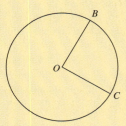

b. Choose any point *P* on the circumference of the circle that is not in the interior of ∠*BOC*. Draw ∠*BPC* and find its measure. ∠*BPC* is an **inscribed angle of the circle.**

inscribed angle

c. Make a conjecture about the measures of ∠*BOC* and ∠*BPC*.

2. Draw an inscribed triangle in a circle in such a way that one side of the triangle is a diameter of the circle. Find the measure of the angle that does not have the diameter as a side. Make a conjecture about the measure of any such angle.

Section 11-4   Similar Triangles and Similar Figures

When a germ is examined under a microscope or when a slide is projected on a screen, the shapes in each case remain the same, but the sizes are altered. *Two figures that have the same shape but not necessarily the same size are* **similar.** For example, on the following student page of Silver, Burdett, and Ginn, *Mathematics: Exploring Your World,* Grade 7, 1991, we see a photograph enlarged to poster size. The ratio of the corresponding sides, $\frac{24}{8}$, or 3, is the **scale factor.** Also, the ratio of the length of the larger picture to the length of the smaller picture is 3.

scale factor

It seems that in any enlargement such as that on the student page, the results will be similar. That is, the corresponding angle measures remain the same and the corresponding sides are proportional. In particular, the observations about similar figures (having corresponding angles congruent and corresponding sides being proportional) extend to triangles, as given in the following definition.

Definition of Similar Triangles

$\triangle ABC$ is similar to $\triangle DEF$, written $\triangle ABC \sim \triangle DEF$, if, and only if, $\angle A \cong \angle D$, $\angle B \cong \angle E$, $\angle C \cong \angle F$, and $\dfrac{AB}{DE} = \dfrac{AC}{DF} = \dfrac{BC}{EF}$.

Many copy machines reduce or enlarge pictures. How are the copy and the original alike? How are they different?

Similar Figures

The nature photographer often interprets nature's power and beauty. This dramatic photograph was enlarged to poster size. Find the length of the poster.

These rectangles are **similar** because they have the same shape.

10 in.

8 in.

▶ When two figures are similar, the ratios of the lengths of corresponding sides are equal. That is, the corresponding sides are in proportion.

$$\frac{\text{length} \longrightarrow 10}{\text{width} \longrightarrow 8} = \frac{n}{24}$$

$$10 \times 24 = 8 \times n$$

$$240 = 8n$$

$$30 = n$$

The length of the poster is 30 in.

24 in.

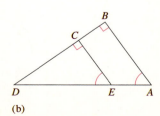

Example 11-6

Given the pairs of similar triangles in Figure 11-35, find a one-to-one correspondence among the vertices of the triangles such that the corresponding angles are congruent. Then write the proportion for the corresponding sides that follows from the definition.

Figure 11-35

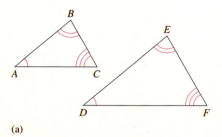

(a)

(b)

Solution   a.   △ABC ~ △DEF

$$\frac{AB}{DE} = \frac{BC}{EF} = \frac{AC}{DF}$$

b.   △ABD ~ △ECD

$$\frac{AB}{EC} = \frac{BD}{CD} = \frac{AD}{ED}$$

• • •

Angle, Angle, Angle Property (AAA)

As with congruent triangles, minimal conditions may be used to determine when two triangles are similar. For example, suppose two triangles each have angles with measures of 50°, 30°, and 100°, but the side opposite the 100° angle is 5 units long in one of the triangles and 1 unit long in the other.

    The triangles appear to have the same shape, as shown in Figure 11-36. The figure suggests that if the angles of the two triangles are congruent, then the sides are proportional **Angle, Angle, Angle (AAA)**   and the triangles are similar. This statement is true in general. It is the **Angle, Angle, Angle** property of similarity for triangles, abbreviated **AAA.**

Figure 11-36

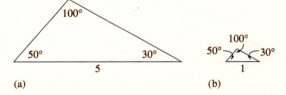

(a)   (b)

Property of Similar Triangles — Angle, Angle, Angle (AAA)

Angle, Angle, Angle (AAA)   If three angles of one triangle are congruent, respectively, to the three angles of a second triangle, then the triangles are similar.

    Given the measures of any two angles of a triangle, the measure of the third angle can be found. Hence, if two angles in one triangle are congruent to two angles in another triangle, then the third angles must also be congruent. Consequently, the AAA condition may be **Angle, Angle (AA)**   reduced to **Angle, Angle (AA).**

• • •

Example 11-7   For each part of Figure 11-37, find a pair of similar triangles.

Figure 11-37

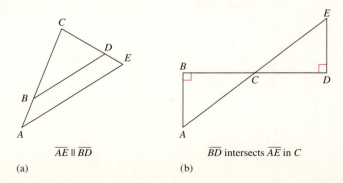

$\overline{AE} \parallel \overline{BD}$ $\overline{BD}$ intersects $\overline{AE}$ in C

(a)   (b)

Solution
 a. Because $\overline{AE} \parallel \overline{BD}$, congruent corresponding angles are formed by a transversal cutting the parallel segments. Thus $\angle CBD \cong \angle CAE$ and $\angle CDB \cong \angle CEA$. Also, $\angle C \cong \angle C$, so $\triangle CBD \sim \triangle CAE$ by AA.

 b. $\angle B \cong \angle D$ because both are right triangles. Also, $\angle ACB \cong \angle ECD$ because they are vertical angles. Thus $\triangle ACB \sim \triangle ECD$ by AA.

• • •

INVESTIGATION 11-8

● Congruency of corresponding angles is sufficient to prove that two triangles are similar. Is the same condition sufficient to prove other polygons are similar to each other? Explain your answer. ●

• • •

Example 11-8

In Figure 11-38, find x.

Figure 11-38

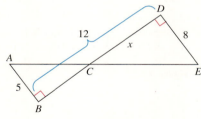

$$\triangle ABC \sim \triangle EDC$$

Solution $\triangle ABC \sim \triangle EDC$, so

$$\frac{AB}{ED} = \frac{AC}{EC} = \frac{BC}{DC}.$$

Now, $AB = 5$, $ED = 8$, and $CD = x$, so $BC = 12 - x$. Thus

$$\frac{5}{8} = \frac{12 - x}{x}$$

$$5x = 8(12 - x)$$

$$5x = 96 - 8x$$

$$13x = 96$$

$$x = \frac{96}{13}.$$

• • •

Problem 1

For her art project, Rosa needed a wooden triangle that had one 18 in. side. The angles of the triangle needed to have measures 36°, 84°, and 60°. Rosa had a carpenter make such a triangle. A few months later, she needed another triangle with the same specifications. The first carpenter was unavailable, so she contacted a different one. When the second triangle arrived, she was surprised that it was not congruent to the first one. Explain how this is possible.

Understanding the Problem.   We are to explain how two triangles with one 18 in. side and angles of measures 36°, 84°, and 60° could be different sizes. To explain how this is possible, we construct two noncongruent triangles with Rosa's specifications.

Devising a Plan.   First, we need to construct a triangle with the given side and angles. Then, because the second triangle has the same angles, it must be similar to the first by AAA. Consequently, we try to construct a triangle similar to the first but not congruent to it.

Carrying Out the Plan.   In Figure 11-39, $\overline{AB}$ represents the 18-in. side. We then use a protractor to construct $\angle A$ measuring 60° and $\angle B$ measuring 36°. Hence, $m(\angle C) = 84°$ (why?). Next, we are to construct a noncongruent triangle similar to $\triangle ABC$ with one side as long as $\overline{AB}$. Because this may seem difficult, we consider *a simpler but related problem.* We drop the condition that the triangle must have a side of length AB and consider constructing a triangle similar to $\triangle ABC$. This can be conveniently achieved by using one of the existing vertices of $\triangle ABC$ and drawing a side parallel to the opposite side. For example, in Figure 11-39 $\overline{C_1B_1} \parallel \overline{CB}$ and $\triangle ACB \sim \triangle AC_1B_1$ (why?). There are infinitely many such triangles AC_1B_1. We imagine sliding $\overrightarrow{BC}$ along $\overrightarrow{AB}$ and $\overrightarrow{AC}$ so that $\overline{B_1C_1} \parallel \overline{BC}$ and until $AC_1 = AB$. Consequently, $\triangle ACB$ and $\triangle AC_1B_1$ are two noncongruent similar triangles such that $AC_1 = AB$ and therefore there are two noncongruent triangles with Rosa's specifications.

Figure 11-39

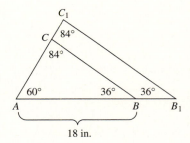

C_1

C 84°

84°

60°

A

36°   36°

B B_1

18 in.

Looking Back.   If Rosa gave each carpenter the measurements of two sides of the desired triangles and all the angles, could she then be sure to obtain a unique triangle? If she told the carpenter where the 18 in. side should be (for example, between the 36° and 60° angles), would that ensure her new triangle would be congruent to the old one?

• • •

Properties of Proportion

Similar triangles give rise to various properties involving proportions. For example, in Figure 11-40 if $\overline{BC} \parallel \overline{DE}$, then $\dfrac{AB}{BD} = \dfrac{AC}{CE}$. This can be justified as follows: $\overline{BC} \parallel \overline{DE}$, so

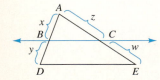

Figure 11-40

$\triangle ADE \sim \triangle ABC$ (why?). Consequently, $\dfrac{AD}{AB} = \dfrac{AE}{AC}$, which may be written as follows:

$$\frac{x+y}{x} = \frac{z+w}{z}$$

$$\frac{x}{x} + \frac{y}{x} = \frac{z}{z} + \frac{w}{z}$$

$$1 + \frac{y}{x} = 1 + \frac{w}{z}$$

$$\frac{y}{x} = \frac{w}{z}$$

$$\frac{x}{y} = \frac{z}{w}$$

This result is summarized in the following theorem.

Theorem 11-4

If a line parallel to one side of a triangle intersects the other sides, then it divides those sides into proportional segments.

The converse of Theorem 11-4 is also true. That is, if in Figure 11-40 we know that $\dfrac{AB}{BD} = \dfrac{AC}{CE}$, then we can conclude that $\overline{BC} \parallel \overline{DE}$. We summarize this result in the following theorem.

Theorem 11-5

If a line divides two sides of a triangle into proportional segments, then the line is parallel to the third side.

Similarly, if lines parallel to $\overline{DE}$ intersect $\triangle ADE$, as shown in Figure 11-41, so that $a = b = c = d$, it can be shown that $e = f = g = h$. This result is stated in the following theorem.

Figure 11-41

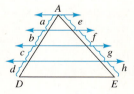

Theorem 11-6

If parallel lines cut off congruent segments on one transversal, then they cut off congruent segments on any transversal.

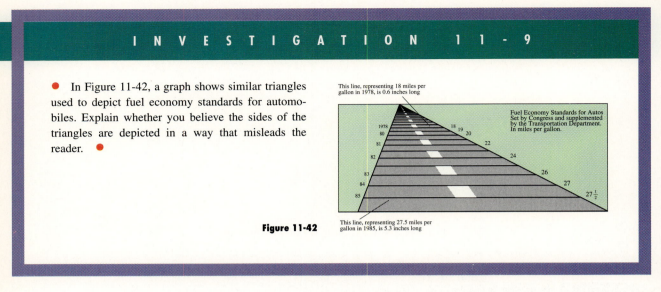

● In Figure 11-42, a graph shows similar triangles used to depict fuel economy standards for automobiles. Explain whether you believe the sides of the triangles are depicted in a way that misleads the reader. ●

This line, representing 18 miles per gallon in 1978, is 0.6 inches long

Fuel Economy Standards for Autos Set by Congress and supplemented by the Transportation Department. In miles per gallon.

Figure 11-42

This line, representing 27.5 miles per gallon in 1985, is 5.3 inches long

Theorem 11-6 can be used to divide a given segment into any number of congruent parts. For example, using only a compass and a straightedge, we can divide segment $\overline{AB}$ in Figure 11-43 into three congruent parts by making the construction resemble Figure 11-41.

Figure 11-43 Separating a segment into congruent parts

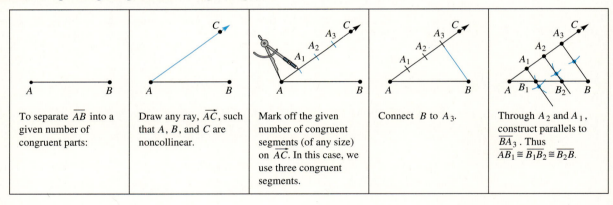

To separate $\overline{AB}$ into a given number of congruent parts:	Draw any ray, $\overrightarrow{AC}$, such that A, B, and C are noncollinear.	Mark off the given number of congruent segments (of any size) on $\overrightarrow{AC}$. In this case, we use three congruent segments.	Connect B to A_3.	Through A_2 and A_1, construct parallels to $\overline{BA_3}$. Thus $\overline{AB_1} \cong \overline{B_1B_2} \cong \overline{B_2B}$.

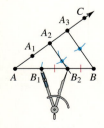

Figure 11-44

REMARK   It is necessary to construct only $\overline{A_2B_2}$. We can then use a compass to mark off point B_1, thus making $B_1B_2 = BB_2$, as in Figure 11-44.

Indirect Measurements

Similar triangles have long been used to make indirect measurements. Thales of Miletus (ca. 600 B.C.) is believed to have determined the height of the Great Pyramid of Egypt by using ratios involving shadows, similar to those pictured in Figure 11-45. The sun is so far away that it should make approximately congruent angles at B and B'. Because the angles at C and C' are right angles, $\triangle ABC \sim \triangle A'B'C'$. Hence,

$$\frac{AC}{A'C'} = \frac{BC}{B'C'}.$$

Figure 11-45

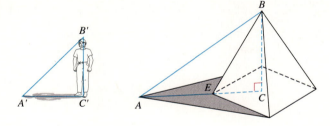

And because $AC = AE + EC$, the following proportion is obtained:

$$\frac{AE + EC}{A'C'} = \frac{BC}{B'C'}$$

The person's height and shadow can be measured. Also, the length AE of the shadow of the pyramid can be measured, and EC can be found because the base of the pyramid is a square. Each term of the proportion except the height of the pyramid is known. Thus the height BC of the pyramid can be found by solving the proportion.

• • •

Example 11-9

On a sunny day, a tall tree casts a 40-m shadow. At the same time, a meter stick held vertically casts a 2.5-m shadow. How tall is the tree?

Solution   In Figure 11-46, the triangles are similar by AA because the tree and the stick both meet the ground at right angles and the angles formed by the sun's rays are congruent (because the shadows are measured at the same time).

$$\frac{x}{40} = \frac{1}{2.5}$$
$$2.5x = 40$$
$$x = 16$$

The tree is 16 m tall.

Figure 11-46

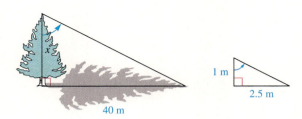

1 m

2.5 m

40 m

• • •

Using Similar Triangles to Determine Slope

In Chapter 7, we defined the slope of a line with equation $y = mx + b$ to be m. The slope is a measure of steepness of a line. A different way to discuss the steepness of a line is to consider how much the line "rises" in relation to how much it "runs." In Figure 11-47, line m is steeper than line n. In other words, line m rises higher than line n for the same horizontal run.

Figure 11-47

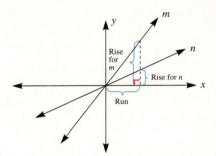

We express the steepness as the ratio $\dfrac{\text{rise}}{\text{run}}$. In Figure 11-48(a), right triangles have been constructed and shaded on several lines. In each triangle, the horizontal side is the run and the vertical side is the rise.

Figure 11-48

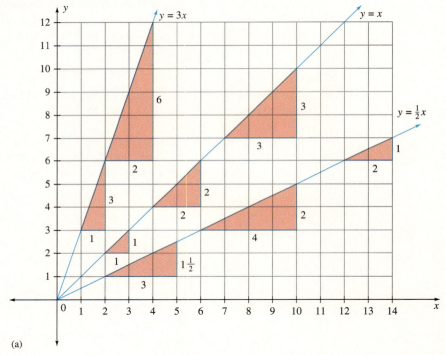

(a)

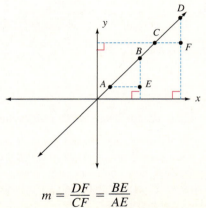

$$m = \frac{DF}{CF} = \frac{BE}{AE}$$

(b)

The slope of each line in Figure 11-48(a) can be calculated as the rise over the run in any of the shaded triangles, with hypotenuse (the side opposite the right angle) along the given line. To test this fact, notice that

$$\text{for } y = \frac{1}{2}x, \quad m = \frac{\text{rise}}{\text{run}} = \frac{1\frac{1}{2}}{3} = \frac{2}{4} = \frac{1}{2}$$

$$\text{for } y = x, \quad m = \frac{\text{rise}}{\text{run}} = \frac{1}{1} = \frac{2}{2} = \frac{3}{3}$$

$$\text{for } y = 3x, \quad m = \frac{3}{1} = \frac{6}{2}.$$

Figure 11-48(b) illustrates the situation generally when a line is inclined from the left upward to the right.

Using the previous notion, we find that the slope of a line $\overleftrightarrow{AB}$ is the change in y-coordinates divided by the corresponding change in x-coordinates of any two points on $\overleftrightarrow{AB}$. The difference $x_2 - x_1$ is the **run,** and the difference $y_2 - y_1$ is the **rise.** Thus the slope is often

run • rise

defined as "rise over run," or $\dfrac{\text{rise}}{\text{run}}$. The slope formula can be interpreted geometrically, as

shown in Figure 11-49. The ratio $\dfrac{y_2 - y_1}{x_2 - x_1}$ is always the same, regardless of which two points on a given nonvertical line are chosen.

Figure 11-49

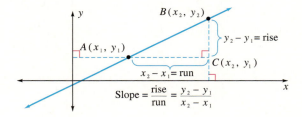

$$\text{Slope} = \frac{\text{rise}}{\text{run}} = \frac{y_2 - y_1}{x_2 - x_1}$$

The discussion of slope is summarized in the following formula.

Slope Formula

Given two points $A(x_1, y_1)$ and $B(x_2, y_2)$ with $x_1 \neq x_2$, the slope m of the line $\overleftrightarrow{AB}$ is

$$m = \frac{y_2 - y_1}{x_2 - x_1} = \frac{\text{rise}}{\text{run}}.$$

By multiplying both the numerator and the denominator on the right side of the slope formula by $^-1$, we obtain

$$m = \frac{y_2 - y_1}{x_2 - x_1} = \frac{(y_2 - y_1)(^-1)}{(x_2 - x_1)(^-1)} = \frac{y_1 - y_2}{x_1 - x_2}.$$

This shows that while it does not matter which point is named (x_1, y_1) and which is named (x_2, y_2), *the order of the coordinates in the subtraction must be consistent.*

When a line is inclined from the left downward to the right, the slope is negative. This is illustrated in Figure 11-50, where the graph of the line $y = {}^-2x$ is shown. The slope of line $y = {}^-2x$ can be calculated as $\dfrac{\text{rise}}{\text{run}} = \dfrac{{}^-4}{2} = \dfrac{{}^-2}{1}$.

Figure 11-50

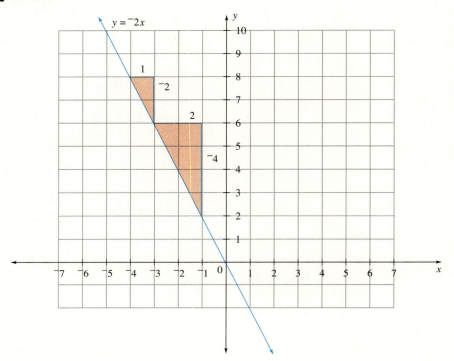

Example 11-10   **a.** Given $A(3, 1)$ and $B(5, 4)$, find the slope of $\overleftrightarrow{AB}$.
b. Find the slope of the line passing through the points $A({}^-3, 4)$ and $B({}^-1, 0)$.

Solution   **a.** $m = \dfrac{4 - 1}{5 - 3} = \dfrac{3}{2}$,   or $\dfrac{1 - 4}{3 - 5} = \dfrac{{}^-3}{{}^-2} = \dfrac{3}{2}$

b. $m = \dfrac{4 - 0}{{}^-3 - ({}^-1)} = \dfrac{4}{{}^-2} = {}^-2$,   or $\dfrac{0 - 4}{{}^-1 - ({}^-3)} = \dfrac{{}^-4}{2} = {}^-2$

Given any point on the line and the slope of the line, we use the slope formula to find the equation of a line. In Figure 11-51, line ℓ has slope m and contains a given point (x_1, y_1). Point (x, y) represents any other point on line ℓ if, and only if, the slope determined by points (x_1, y_1) and (x, y) is m. We use the slope formula and proceed as follows:

$$\frac{y - y_1}{x - x_1} = m$$

$$y - y_1 = m(x - x_1)$$

Figure 11-51

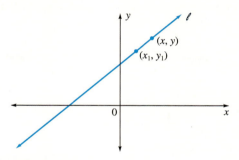

point-slope form   The result is the **point-slope form** of a line.

Point-Slope Form of a Line

The equation of a line with slope m through a given point (x_1, y_1) is $y - y_1 = m(x - x_1)$.

B R A I N   T E A S E R   Two neighbors, Smith and Wesson, plan to erect flagpoles in their yards. Smith wants a 10-ft pole, and Wesson wants a 15-ft pole. To keep the poles straight while the concrete bases harden, guy wires are to be tied from the tops of the flagpoles to a fence post on the property lines and to the bases of the flagpoles, as shown in Figure 11-52. How high should the fence post be and how far apart should they erect flagpoles for this scheme to work?

Figure 11-52

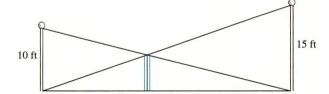

10 ft   15 ft

L A B O R A T O R Y
A C T I V I T Y   The device pictured in the following figure is called a pantograph. It is used to draw enlarged versions of figures. Well-made adjustable pantographs are available from drafting or art supply stores, but you can make a crude one from wooden lath or other material.

In Figure 11-53, the red dots represent either brads or nuts and bolts. The strips are made of lath or cardboard and are rigid. A pointer at D is used to trace along an original figure, which causes the pencil at F to draw an enlarged version of the figure. Make or obtain a pantograph and experiment with enlarging figures. Explain how and why this works.

Figure 11-53

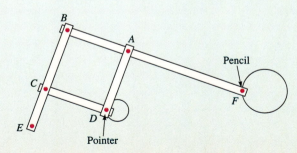

Ongoing Assessment 11-4

1. Which of the following are always similar? Why?
   a. Any two equilateral triangles
   b. Any two squares
   c. Any two rectangles
   d. Any two rhombuses
   e. Any two circles
   f. Any two regular polygons
   g. Any two regular polygons with the same number of sides

2. Use grid paper to draw figures that have sides three times as large as the given ones, as shown in the following figure:

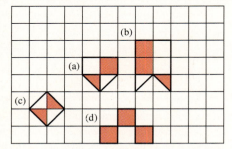

3. a. Construct a triangle with sides of lengths 4 cm, 6 cm, and 8 cm.
   b. Construct another triangle with sides of lengths 2 cm, 3 cm, and 4 cm.
   c. Make a conjecture about the similarity of triangles that have proportional sides only.

4. a. Construct a triangle with sides of lengths 4 cm and 6 cm and an included angle measuring 60°.
   b. Construct a triangle with sides of lengths 2 cm and 3 cm and an included angle measuring 60°.
   c. Make a conjecture about the similarity of triangles that have two sides proportional and congruent included angles.

5. a. Sketch two nonsimilar polygons for which corresponding angles are congruent.
   b. Sketch two nonsimilar polygons for which corresponding sides are proportional.

6. Examine several examples of similar polygons and make a conjecture concerning the ratio of their perimeters.

7. a. Which of the following pairs of triangles are similar? If they are similar, explain why.

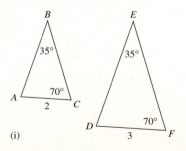

(i)

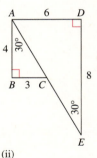

(ii)

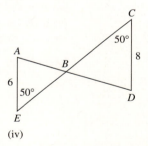

(iii)

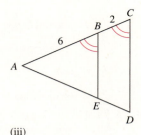

(iv)

   b. For each pair of similar triangles, find the scale factor of the sides of the triangles.

8. Assume that in the following figures the triangles in each part are similar and find the measures of the unknown sides:

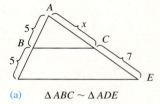

(a)   △ABC ~ △ADE

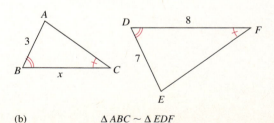

(b)   △ABC ~ △EDF

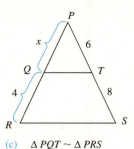

(c) △ *PQT* ~ △ *PRS*

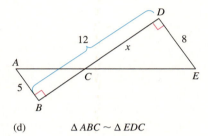

(d) △ *ABC* ~ △ *EDC*

9. Given the following figure, use a compass and a straight-edge to separate $\overline{AB}$ into five congruent pieces:

10. In the following right triangle *ABC*, $\overline{CD} \perp \overline{AB}$:

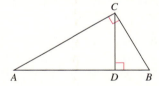

  a. Find three pairs of similar triangles. Justify your answers.

  b. Write the corresponding proportions for each set of similar triangles.

11. In the following cartoon, if a smaller map were obtained and its scale were half the size of the original scale, would the distance to be traveled be any different? Why?

12. In the following figure, find the distance *AB* across the pond using the similar triangles shown:

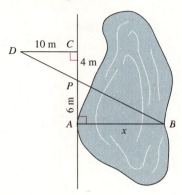

13. To find the height of a tree, a group of Girl Scouts devised the following method. A girl walks toward the tree along its shadow until the shadow of the top of her head coincides with the shadow of the top of the tree. If the girl is 150 cm tall, her distance to the foot of the tree is 15 m, and the length of her shadow is 3 m, how tall is the tree?

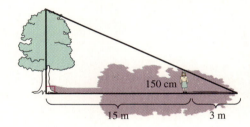

14. The angle bisector of one of the angles in an isosceles triangle is constructed. This angle bisector partitions the original triangle into two isosceles triangles.

  a. What are the angle measures of the original triangle? (There are two possibilities.)

  b. Which, if any, triangles are congruent? similar? Explain your answers.

15. Samantha wants to know how far above the ground the top of a leaning flagpole is. At high noon, when the sun is

directly overhead, the shadow cast by the pole is 7 ft long. Samantha holds a plumb bob with a string 3 ft long up to the flagpole and determines that the point of the plumb bob touches the ground 13 in. from the base of the flagpole. How far above the ground is the top of the pole?

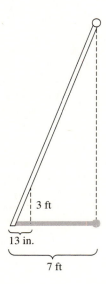

3 ft

13 in.

7 ft

16. Dian has prepared a report on the gorilla, an endangered species, for her Earth Week information booth. For her backdrop, she wants to project a life-sized image of a gorilla on a screen. She has a slide showing a gorilla standing erect. In the slide, the image of the gorilla is $\frac{3}{4}$ in. tall. Dian's research shows that adult gorillas often reach 6 ft in height. If the bulb in the slide projector is 3 in. from the slide, where should the projector be placed so that the gorilla appears life-size on the screen?

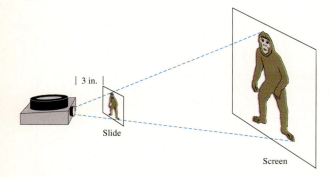

3 in.

Slide

Screen

17. For each of the following, find the slope, if it exists, of the line determined by the given pair of points:

a. (4, 3) and ($^-$5, 0)
b. ($^-$4, 1) and (5, 2)
c. ($\sqrt{5}$, 2) and (1, 2)
d. ($^-$3, 81) and ($^-$3, 198)
e. (1.0001, 12) and (1, 10)
f. (a, a) and (b, b)

18. Write the equation of each line in Problem 17.

19. Find the coordinates of two other points collinear (on the same line as) with each of the following pairs of given points:

a. $P(2, 2)$, $Q(4, 2)$
b. $P($^-$1, 0)$, $Q($^-$1, 2)$
c. $P($^-$3, 0)$, $Q(3, 0)$
d. $P(0, $^-$2)$, $Q(0, 3)$
e. $P(0, 0)$, $Q(1, 1)$

20. Explain why all pairs of regular octagons are similar.

21. If the ratio of corresponding sides of two similar triangles is $1/k$, what is the ratio of their perimeters? Why?

22. If you took cross-sections of a typical ice cream cone parallel to the circular opening where the ice cream is normally placed, explain whether the cross-sections would be similar.

23. Must all cross-sections of a circular cylinder be similar? Why? Draw a sketch to illustrate your answer.

24. a. Write a procedure called RECTANGLE that draws a rectangle of variable size with inputs :LEN and :WID. Then write a procedure called SIM.RECT that draws a rectangle whose sides measure twice as long as those of the rectangle drawn by RECTANGLE when the same inputs are used for :LEN and :WID.
    b. Write a procedure called SIM.RECTANGLE that draws a rectangle similar to the one drawn by RECTANGLE, with a scale factor called :SCALE that affects the size of the rectangle.
    c. Write a procedure called PARALLELOGRAM that draws a parallelogram of variable size with inputs :LEN, :WID, and :ANGLE. Then write a procedure called SIM.PAR that generates similar parallelograms.

25. a. Write a Logo procedure called TRISECT that draws a line segment of length determined by input :LEN and has the turtle divide it into three congruent parts.
    b. Write a procedure called PARTITION that draws a line segment of length determined by input :LEN and has the turtle divide it into :NUM parts, where :NUM is also an input.

Communication

26. Do you think any two cubes are similar? Why or why not?

27. Architects frequently use scale drawings to construct models of projects. Are the models similar to the finished product? Why or why not?

28. Assuming the lines on an ordinary piece of notebook paper are parallel and equidistant, describe a method for using the

paper to divide a piece of licorice evenly among 2, 3, 4, or 5 children. Explain why it works.

Open-ended

29. Build two similar towers out of blocks.
    a. Why are they similar?
    b. What is the ratio of the heights of the towers?
    c. What is the ratio of the perimeters of the bases of the towers?
    d. If one unit of paint would cover one face of a tower, what is the ratio between the number of units of paint required to paint the faces and the base of each tower?
    e. If one block represents one unit of volume for a tower, what is the ratio of the volumes of the two towers?
    f. Describe any relationships among the answers to (b)–(e).
30. In the past, artists painted babies as miniature adults. Explain whether you think babies and adults are mathematically similar.

Cooperative Learning

31. A building was to be built on a triangular piece of property. The architect was given the measurements of the angles of the triangular lot as approximately 54°, 39°, and 87° and the lengths of two of the sides as 100 m and 80 m. When the architect began the design on drafting paper, she drew a triangle to scale with the corresponding measures and found that the lot was considerably smaller than she had been led to believe. It appeared that the proposed building would not fit. The surveyor was called. He confirmed each of the measurements and could not see any problem with the size. Neither the architect nor surveyor could understand the reason for the other's opinion.
    a. Have one person in your group play the part of the architect and explain why she felt she was correct.

b. Have one person in the group explain the reason for the miscommunication.
c. Have the group suggest a way to provide an accurate description of the lot.

Review Problems

32. If a person holds a mirror at arm's length and looks into it, is the image seen congruent to the original? Why or why not?
33. Given the following base of an isosceles triangle and the altitude to that base, construct the triangle:

_____

Base

_____

Altitude

34. Given the following length of a side of the triangle, construct an altitude of an equilateral triangle.

_____

35. Write a paragraph describing how you could construct an isosceles right triangle when given the length of the hypotenuse of the 45°-45°-90° triangle.
36. Use a compass and a straightedge to draw a pair of obtuse vertical angles and the angle bisector of one of these angles. Extend the angle bisector. Does the extended angle bisector bisect the other vertical angle? Justify your answer.
37. Write a Logo procedure called TRI30 to draw a 30°-60°-90° triangle when given the length of the hypotenuse, :HYPOT.
38. Write a procedure called RTISOS to draw an isosceles right triangle when given the length of the hypotenuse, :HYPOT.

TECHNOLOGY CORNER

In 1975, Benoit Mandelbrot invented the word *fractal* to describe certain irregular and fragmented shapes. These shapes are such that if one looks at a small part of the shape, the small part resembles the larger shape. These shapes are somewhat like rep-tiles, although the smaller structures of fractals are not necessarily identical to the larger structure. (Recall that with rep-tiles, the smaller structures are similar and are identical in all aspects except size.) Fractal geometry was introduced for the purpose of modeling natural phenomena such as irregular coastlines, arteries and veins, the branching structure of plants, the thermal agitation of molecules in a fluid, and sponges.

Figure 11-54 shows an example of a fractal—a computer-generated picture of the Mandelbrot set known as the "Tail of the Seahorse."

Figure 11-54

Earlier, in 1906, Helge von Koch came up with a curve that has infinite perimeter. To visualize this curve, we construct in Figure 11-55 a sequence of polygons $S_1, S_2, S_3, \ldots$ as follows:

a. S_1 is an equilateral triangle.
b. S_2 has an equilateral triangle constructed on each side of S_1 but with the base removed.
c. S_3 is obtained from S_2 like S_2 was obtained from S_1.

We continue in a similar way to obtain the other polygons of the sequence in Figure 11-55(d) and (e). These polygons come closer and closer to a curve, called the *snowflake curve,* which is another example of a fractal. Type the following SNOWFLAKE procedure into your computer and display the polygons shown in Figure 11-55.

If S_1 has perimeter 3 units, what is the perimeter of S_2 and S_3? What do you think happens to the perimeter of the snowflakes as the number of sides of the polygons increases?

Figure 11-55

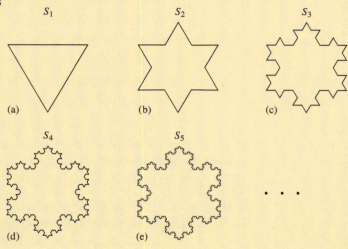

```
TO SNOWFLAKE :LEVEL
  CS PU SETXY 90 52
  MAKE "SIZE 180
  MAKE "N 5 - :LEVEL
  MAKE "LEVEL 1
  REPEAT :N[MAKE "LEVEL :LEVEL *3]
  REPEAT 3[DRAW.IT :SIZE :LEVEL RT 120]
END
```
(In LCSI replace SETXY 90 52 with SETPOS [90 52].)


```
TO DRAW.IT :SIZE :LEVEL
  IF :SIZE < :LEVEL THEN FD :SIZE STOP
  DRAW.IT :SIZE/3 :LEVEL LT 60
  DRAW.IT :SIZE/3 :LEVEL RT 120
  DRAW.IT :SIZE/3 :LEVEL LT 60
  DRAW.IT :SIZE/3 :LEVEL
END
```
(In LCSI replace IF :SIZE < :LEVEL THEN FD :SIZE STOP with IF :SIZE < :LEVEL [FD :SIZE STOP].)

BRAIN TEASER A toy maker wants to cut the plastic rectangle *EFGH* in Figure 11-56 into 4 right triangles and a rectangle. Given the measurements shown, determine how long $\overline{CE}$ is.

Figure 11-56

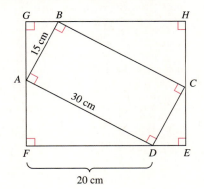

20 cm

*Section 11-5 Trigonometry Ratios via Similarity

Measurements of buildings, structures, and some other objects are frequently required in many occupations. For example, in a tourist brochure advertising California, one region boasts a sequoia tree of great height, such as the one pictured in Figure 11-57.

From the previous section, we know how to find the height of the tree by using shadows and similar triangles. The mathematical notion of trigonometry might also be used to find the required height of the tree.

Trigonometry developed from a need to compute distances and angle measures, especially in map making, surveying, and range finding for artillery use. Today, trigonometry is an indispensable tool in many applied problems in both science and technology. The word

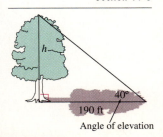

Angle of elevation

Figure 11-57

trigonometry **trigonometry** is derived from the Greek words *trigonom,* which means triangle, and *metron,* which means measurement. In this section, we study the basics of right triangle trigonometry, which has applications to measuring distances and angles.

The definition of trigonometric functions in a right triangle is based on properties of similar triangles. Earlier in this chapter, we saw that corresponding sides of similar triangles are proportional. Consequently, in two similar triangles the ratio of one side to another in one triangle will be the same as the ratio of the corresponding sides in the second triangle. Consider the two similar triangles in Figure 11-58. Both are right triangles, and each has an angle with measure 30°.

Figure 11-58

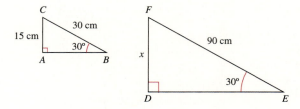

We could find x using the following proportion:

$$\frac{x}{90} = \frac{15}{30},$$

which implies that $x = 45$ cm. If we use this property, it follows that in any right triangle the ratio between the side opposite the angle with measure 30° and the side opposite the right **hypotenuse** angle, the **hypotenuse,** will be the same as that ratio in the smaller triangle in Figure 11-58; that is, $\frac{15}{30}$, or $\frac{1}{2}$.

Suppose we use a protractor to construct a right triangle with an angle measuring 37° and measure both the hypotenuse and the side opposite this angle, as shown in Figure 11-59. The ratio between the side opposite the angle with measure 37° and the hypotenuse is $\frac{60}{100}$, or 0.6. Since measurements are approximate, the ratio also is only an approximation. This ratio is the "sine of 37°," or the *sin* 37. Thus, in a right triangle having an angle with measure 37°,

$$sin\ 37 = \frac{\text{length of side opposite the 37° angle}}{\text{length of hypotenuse}}.$$

Figure 11-59

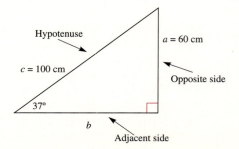

cosine (cos) • **tangent (tan)**   Other ratios such as the **cosine (cos)** and **tangent (tan)** between lengths of sides in a right triangle are also useful and are defined in reference to Figure 11-60 as follows:

Figure 11-60

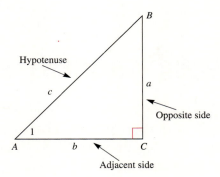

$$sin(\angle 1) = \frac{a}{c} = \frac{\text{length of opposite side}}{\text{length of hypotenuse}}$$

$$cos(\angle 1) = \frac{b}{c} = \frac{\text{length of adjacent side}}{\text{length of hypotenuse}}$$

$$tan(\angle 1) = \frac{a}{b} = \frac{\text{length of opposite side}}{\text{length of adjacent side}}$$

T E C H N O L O G Y C O R N E R

Using a geometry drawing utility, draw a right triangle *ABC* with right angle at *C*. Measure each side of the triangle and find the measures of ∠*ABC* and ∠*BAC*. Determine whether your geometry utility has built-in functions for sine, cosine, and tangent. If so, these functions are usually constructed in such a way that you may enter an angle measure by entering the *sin* (measure of the angle) and pressing Return or Enter for the computer to find the ratio automatically. Cosine and tangents are found similarly. Build a table with headings similar to Table 11-2 that contains the following information.

Table 11-2

Angle	Angle Meas.	Opp. Side Meas.	Adj. Side Meas.	Hyp. Meas.	Opp. Hypot.	Sine of Angle	Adj. Hypot.	Cosine of Angle	Opp. Adj.	Tangent of Angle

1. What is true about the ratios you found using measurements and the sines, cosines, and tangents found automatically?
2. Explain whether you think it is necessary to find the measures of the sides of a triangle to determine the sine, cosine, and tangent ratios.

Students in upper middle grades use trigonometric ratios to find measurements, as seen on the following student page from *Houghton Mifflin Mathematics,* Grade 8, 1991.

TANGENT RATIOS

Triangle *MNP* is a right triangle. The **hypotenuse** is the side opposite the right angle. The **legs** are the other two sides. The leg next to $\angle M$ is the **adjacent** side. The leg opposite $\angle M$ is the **opposite** side.

In a right triangle, the ratio of the length of the side opposite an angle to the length of the side adjacent to the angle is called the **tangent** of the angle.

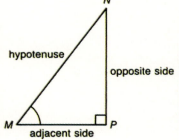

Tangent of *M*: $\tan M = \dfrac{\text{length of opposite side}}{\text{length of adjacent side}} = \dfrac{NP}{PM}$

The tangents of congruent angles are equal. Tangent values for angles from 0° to 90° are listed in the table on page 441. Part of the table is shown here.

In triangle *RST*, $\angle R = 40°$. Write an equation and then substitute a value from the table to find *ST*.

$$\tan 40° = \frac{\text{opposite side}}{\text{adjacent side}} = \frac{ST}{RT}$$

ANGLE	TANGENT
0°	0.0000
5°	0.0875
10°	0.1763
15°	0.2679
20°	0.3640
25°	0.4663
30°	0.5774
35°	0.7002
40°	0.8391
45°	1.0000

Substitute the value of tan 40° from the table.

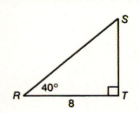

$$0.8391 = \frac{ST}{8}$$
$$8 \times 0.8391 = ST$$
$$6.7128 = ST$$

Using Trigonometry Tables

In the seventeenth century, John Napier devised trigonometric tables to 14 decimal places. Today, with the help of a computer, we can find the values of the trigonometric functions to any desired degree of accuracy. Table 11-3 gives rounded trigonometric values for some angle measures.

Table 11-3

Degrees	sin	cos	tan
5	0.0872	0.9962	0.0875
10	0.1736	0.9848	0.1763
15	0.2588	0.9659	0.2679
20	0.3420	0.9397	0.3640
25	0.4226	0.9036	0.4663
30	0.5000	0.8660	0.5774
35	0.5736	0.8192	0.7002
40	0.6428	0.7660	0.8391
45	0.7071	0.7071	1.0000

Example 11-11

Find the height of the sequoia tree pictured in Figure 11-61.

Figure 11-61

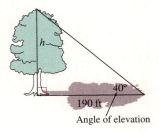

190 ft

40°

Angle of elevation

Solution To find the height of the tree, we use the following trigonometric ratio and Table 11-3:

$$tan\ 40° = \frac{h}{190}$$

$$190(tan\ 40°) = h$$

$$190(0.8391) \doteq h$$

$$159.4 \doteq h$$

Thus the height of the tree is approximately 159.4 ft.

Using Trigonometric Ratios on a Calculator

Tables of trigonometric ratios were essential in all parts of the world until calculators became readily available. Trigonometry in right triangles as we use it today is primarily done using a scientific calculator, graphing calculator, or computer. For example, in a given right triangle with an acute angle of 40°, we can use the $\boxed{\text{SIN}}$, $\boxed{\text{COS}}$, and $\boxed{\text{TAN}}$ buttons to find the respective values of 0.643, 0.766, and 0.839 assigned to a 40° angle.

Each of the trigonometry buttons is a function button that requires an angle measure input either in degrees or radians. Because we use degrees in this text, make sure your calculator is set to use degrees and not radians. One method for telling whether your calculator is in the degree mode is to press $\boxed{3}\boxed{0}\boxed{\text{SIN}}$ to find the sine of 30°. If your answer is 0.5, or .5, then the calculator is in the proper mode. If not, consult a manual to see what you must do to put your calculator in degree mode.

• • •

Example 11-12 | Use a calculator to find x in Figure 11-62:

Figure 11-62

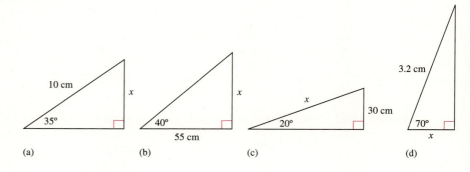

    (a)   (b)   (c)   (d)

Solution   **a.** $\dfrac{x}{10} = sin\ 35$

$x = 10\ sin\ 35$

To find the answer on your calculator, press the following keys:

$$\boxed{1}\boxed{0}\boxed{\times}\boxed{3}\boxed{5}\boxed{\text{SIN}}$$

The resulting display is 5.7357644, or approximately 5.7, cm.

b. $\dfrac{x}{55} = tan\ 40$

$x = 55\ tan\ 40$

$x = 46.1505$, or approximately 46.2, cm

c. $\dfrac{30}{x} = sin\ 20$

$x = \dfrac{30}{sin\ 20}$

$x = 87.719$, or approximately 87.7, cm

d. $\dfrac{x}{3.2} = cos\ 70$

$x = 3.2\ cos\ 70$

$x = 1.094$, or approximately 1.1, cm

• • •

INVESTIGATION 11-10

● In Example 11-12, use Figure 11-62(a) to find x using the cosine function instead of the sine function.   ●

Sometimes the lengths of the sides of a right triangle are given and we need to find the measures of the angles of the triangle. If, for example, a triangle has sides measuring 3 m, 4 m, and 5 m, as shown in Figure 11-63, we can find the measure of angle A by first finding the $sin\ (\angle A)$. We have $sin(\angle A) = 4/5$. The $\boxed{INV}$ (or possibly the $\boxed{SIN^{-1}}$) key on your calculator can be used in conjunction with the $\boxed{SIN}$ key to find the measure of the angle as follows:

$$\boxed{4}\ \boxed{\div}\ \boxed{5}\ \boxed{=}\ \boxed{INV}\ \boxed{SIN}\ .$$

Figure 11-63

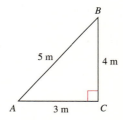

Thus, the angle has measure approximately 53.1°.

● ● ●

Example 11-13   Find x in each part of Figure 11-64:

Figure 11-64

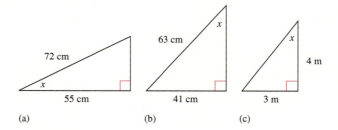

(a)   (b)   (c)

Solution   **a.** $cos\ x = \dfrac{55}{72}$

We press

$$\boxed{5}\ \boxed{5}\ \boxed{\div}\ \boxed{7}\ \boxed{2}\ \boxed{=}\ \boxed{INV}\ \boxed{COS}$$

to obtain 40.191756, so x is approximately 40.2°.

b. $sin\ x = \dfrac{41}{63}$

We press

$$\boxed{4}\,\boxed{1}\,\boxed{\div}\,\boxed{6}\,\boxed{3}\,\boxed{=}\,\boxed{\text{INV}}\,\boxed{\text{SIN}}$$

to obtain 40.601466, or approximately 40.6°.

c. $\tan x = \dfrac{3}{4}$

We press

$$\boxed{3}\,\boxed{\div}\,\boxed{4}\,\boxed{\text{INV}}\,\boxed{\text{TAN}}$$

to obtain 36.869898, or approximately 36.9°.

• • •

Finding Measurements Using Trigonometric Ratios

Just as the angle of elevation was used to find the height of the sequoia tree, we can use an *angle of depression* to find measures, as demonstrated in Example 11-14.

• • •

Example 11-14   From the top of Mount Sentinel, the measure of the angle of depression of the Administration Building is 18°, as illustrated in Figure 11-65. If the top of Mount Sentinel is 1575 ft, how far through the air is the top of the mountain from the base of the building?

Figure 11-65

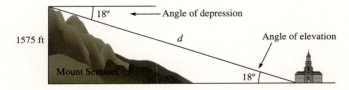

Solution   In Figure 11-65, the measure of the angle of elevation must equal the measure of the angle of depression (why?). Using trigonometric ratios, we have the following:

$$\sin 18° = \frac{1575}{d}$$

$$d = \frac{1575}{\sin 18°}$$

$$d \approx \frac{1575}{0.31}, \text{ or approximately 5081, ft}$$

Thus the air distance is approximately 5081 ft.

• • •

• • •

Example 11-15   To measure the height of a flagpole on top of a building, a surveyor measures the distance to the building and the two angles from point *B*, as shown in Figure 11-66. Find the height of the flagpole.

Figure 11-66

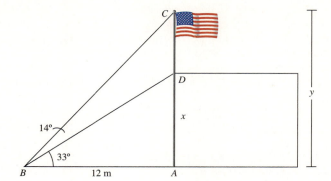

Solution   We need to find *CD* in Figure 11-66. Because *CD* is not a length of a side of a right triangle, but *y* and *x* whose difference is *CD* are, we must find *x* and *y* first. The solution then is $CD = y - x$. In triangle *BDA*, we have the following:

$$tan\ 33 = \frac{x}{12}$$

$$x = 12\ tan\ 33$$

In triangle *BCA*, we have the following:

$$tan(14 + 33) = \frac{y}{12}$$

$$y = 12\ tan\ (14 + 33)$$

Therefore $CD = 12\ tan\ (14 + 33) - 12\ tan\ 33$. Using the calculator we find 5.075 on the display. Thus the height of the pole atop the building is about 5.1 m.

• • •

I N V E S T I G A T I O N   1 1 - 1 1

● **a.** Find a relationship among the $sin(\angle A)$, $cos(\angle A)$, and $tan(\angle A)$.
b. Calculate $(sin(\angle A))^2 + (cos(\angle A))^2$ for different

measures of $\angle A$. Conjecture the value of the expression in general. ●

Ongoing Assessment 11-5

1. For each of the following figures, solve for *x* and express each *x* length to the nearest hundredth:

(a)

(b)

(c)

(d)

2. The angle of elevation of a 15-ft ladder is 70°. Find out how far the base is from the wall.

3. A diagonal is drawn in a 12-in. square floor tile. Find the sine, cosine, and tangent of the angle formed by the diagonal and a side.

4. Determine the height of a tree if it casts a shadow 7 m long on level ground when the angle of elevation of the sun is 50°.

5. Vectors are used in science to depict forces with both magnitudes and directions. If a force of 14 lb is directed at an angle measuring 38° from the horizontal as depicted in the following figure, determine the vertical and horizontal components as pictured:

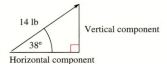

6. To find the length of a lake, a person set stakes at point *A* and made the following measurements:

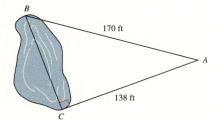

   a. What is the measure of angle *BAC*? (*Hint:* Use estimation skills and your calculator to find out.)
   b. What is the length of the lake?
7. How many feet of cable will it take to anchor a guy wire to a 30-ft pole if the angle of elevation is 28°?
8. As a plane takes off, it flies 1500 ft along a straight path and rises at an angle measuring 22°.
   a. What is its vertical rise when it has flown 1500 ft?
   b. After it has flown 1500 ft, how far has it moved horizontally?
9. A gutter cleaner wants to reach a gutter 40 ft above the ground. Find the length of the shortest ladder that can be used if the steepest angle at which it can be leaned against the house has measure 75°.
10. A jet plane cruising at 450 mph climbs at an angle measuring 13°. Determine how much altitude the jet gains in 5 min.
11. a. Complete the following chart.

Angle Measure	Sine	Cosine	Square of Sine	Square of Cosine	Sum of Columns 4 and 5
10°					
20°					
30°					
40°					
50°					
60°					
70°					
80°					

   b. Make a conjecture about the sum of the squares of the sines and cosines of various angles.
12. Find the height of a tree whose horizontal shadow is 120 ft when the angle of elevation of the sun from the tip of the shadow measures 68°.
13. A highway that has a 6% grade rises 6 ft vertically for every 100 ft horizontally. Which trigonometric ratio is being used in reporting the 6% grade? Explain why.
14. The slope of a line in coordinate geometry is described as the rise divided by the run. Which trigonometric ratio does the slope represent? Explain your answer.
15. In navigational terms, a bearing is defined as the number of degrees a direction is from due north. If a plane flying 120 mph has flown 1 hr at a bearing of 32°, how far has it flown in a horizontal direction? In a vertical direction?
16. Find *x* in each of the following:

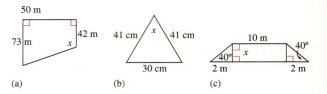

(a)   (b)   (c)

17. Explore how Logo treats trigonometric ratios by evaluating each of the following on your computer:
   a. *sin* 42°   b. *cos* 42°   c. *tan* 42°
18. Use Logo and play turtle to predict what the following procedure will construct. Then execute the program to evaluate what the procedure does.

```
TO MYSTERY :S
   FD :S RT 90 FD :S
   RT 135 FD :S/SIN 45 LT 135
   REPEAT 4 [FD :S LT 90]
END
```

SOLUTION TO THE PRELIMINARY PROBLEM

Understanding the Problem.   A kaleidoscope is in the shape of a prism with an equilateral triangle as a base. A beam of light is reflected at a 60° angle from point *P* on a side of the triangular base, as shown in Figure 11-67. The beam is reflected in the plane of the base to the different mirrored surfaces and continues bouncing at 60° angles. We are to find the length of the path of the reflected light. In Figure 11-67, the length of a side of the triangular base is *a*. We try to write the length of the path in terms of *a*.

Figure 11-67

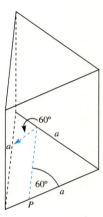

Because angles formed by the reflecting light and the mirrors continue to have measures of 60°, the paths followed by the light are parallel to the various sides of the triangular base (why?). Consequently, similar triangles are formed. We do not know where point *P* is located. A question to ask is, does the length of the path change if the location of *P* changes?

Devising a Plan.   We use the strategy of *looking at simpler cases*. For example, if *P* is located at one of the vertices, then the path of light would follow only the sides of the triangular base, thus resulting in a length of the light's path that is exactly equal to the length of the perimeter of the triangular base. For example, if the length of a side of the base is *a* units the path of light formed when *P* is at a vertex is 3*a* units, the perimeter of the base.

Another simpler case is when *P* is located at the midpoint of a side of the base of the kaleidoscope, as in Figure 11-68. In this case, $PQ = (1/2)AC = (1/2)a$, $QR = (1/2)AB = (1/2)a$, and $RP = (1/2)BC = (1/2)a$ (why?). Now

$$PQ + QR + RP = (1/2)a + (1/2)a + (1/2)a = (1/2)(a + a + a) = (1/2)(3a).$$

Thus the length of the path is one half the perimeter of the triangular base.

Figure 11-68

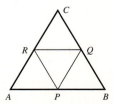

In the previous simpler cases, we have two different answers. The question remains as to whether we can choose P as any point on side $\overline{AB}$ and generalize some solution.

Carrying Out the Plan. To generalize and solve the problem, we locate a general point P on one side of the equilateral triangular base, as in Figure 11-69. In Figure 11-69, the path P-Q-R-S-T-U-P is made of three congruent parts: P-Q-R, R-S-T, and T-U-P (why?). Thus if we find the length of one of these pieces and multiply that result by 3, we will have the length of the path. Now, $PQ + QR = AR + QR = AR + RC = AC = a$. Thus the length of the path of light is $3a$, or the perimeter of the base.

Figure 11-69

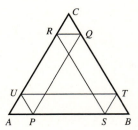

Although it may seem odd, in a general case where P is not one of the vertices or the midpoint of a side, the length of the path of light is exactly the same as the perimeter of the triangle.

Looking Back. An interesting exercise is to determine if there are other polygonal bases of kaleidoscopes such that the reflection of a path of light is the same as the perimeter of the figure. What happens if the polygonal base is not regular?

QUESTIONS FROM THE CLASSROOM

1. On a test, a student wrote $AB \cong CD$ instead of $\overline{AB} \cong \overline{CD}$. Is this answer correct? Why?
2. A student asks if there are any constructions that cannot be done with a compass and a straightedge. How do you answer?
3. A student asks for a mathematical definition of congruence that holds for all figures. How do you respond? Is your response the same for similarity?
4. One student claims that by trisecting $\overline{AB}$ and drawing $\overrightarrow{CD}$ and $\overrightarrow{CE}$, as shown in the following figure, she has trisected $\angle ACB$:

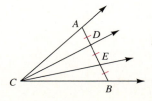

How do you convince her that her construction is wrong?
5. A student claims that polygon $ABCD$ in the following drawing is a parallelogram if $\angle 1 \cong \angle 2$. Is he correct? Why?

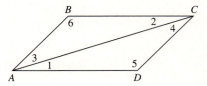

6. A student claims that when the midpoints of the sides of any polygon are connected, a polygon similar to the original results. Is this true? Why?
7. A student asks why $\cong$ rather than $=$ is used to discuss triangles that have the same size and shape. What do you say?
8. A student draws the following figure and claims that because every triangle is congruent to itself, we can

write $\triangle ABC \cong \triangle BCA$. What is your response?

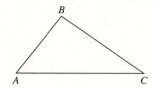

9. A student asks whether there is an AAAA similarity condition for quadrilaterals. How do you respond?
10. A student asks if, for the same n, all regular n-gons are similar. How do you respond?
11. A student says she thinks all circles are similar but would like to know why. How do you answer her?

CHAPTER OUTLINE

I. Similarity
  A. Two polygons are **similar** if, and only if, their corresponding angles are congruent and their corresponding sides are proportional.
  B. **AAA** (or **AA**): If three (two) angles of one triangle are congruent to three (two) angles of a second triangle, respectively, the triangles are similar.

II. Congruence
  A. Two geometric figures are **congruent** if, and only if, they have the same size and shape.
  B. Two triangles are congruent if they satisfy any of the following properties:
    1. **Side, Side, Side (SSS)**
    2. **Side, Angle, Side (SAS)**
    3. **Angle, Side, Angle (ASA)**
    4. **Angle, Angle, Side (AAS)**
  C. **Triangle Inequality:** The sum of the measures of any two sides of a triangle must be greater than the measure of the third side.
  D. Corresponding parts of congruent figures are congruent.
  E. A **rep-tile** is a figure that is used in the construction of a similar figure.

III. Circles
  A. An **arc** of a circle is any part of the circle that can be drawn without lifting a pencil. The **center of an arc** is the center of the circle containing the arc.
  B. A **chord** is a segment whose endpoints lie on a circle.

IV. Proportion
  A. If a line parallel to one side of a triangle intersects the other sides, it divides those sides into proportional segments.
  B. If parallel lines cut off congruent segments on one transversal, they cut off congruent segments on any transversal.

V. Constructions that can be accomplished using a compass and a straightedge
  A. Copy a line segment.
  B. Copy a circle.
  C. Copy an angle.
  D. Bisect a segment.
  E. Bisect an angle.
  F. Construct a perpendicular from a point to a line.
  G. Construct a perpendicular bisector of a segment.
  H. Construct a perpendicular to a line through a point on the line.
  I. Construct a parallel to a line through a point not on the line.
  J. Divide a segment into congruent parts.
  K. Inscribe some regular polygons in a circle.
  L. Circumscribe a circle about a triangle.
  M. Inscribe a circle in a triangle.

VI. Similar Triangles and Coordinates
  A. Slope formula: Given two points $A(x_1, y_1)$ and $B(x_2, y_2)$, the slope m of line AB is given by the following:
$$m = \frac{y_2 - y_1}{x_2 - x_1} = \frac{\text{rise}}{\text{run}}$$
  B. The equation of a line with slope m through a given point with coordinates (x_1, y_1) is $y - y_1 = m(x - x_1)$.

* VII. Trigonometric Functions
  In a right triangle, as follows, we have the following:

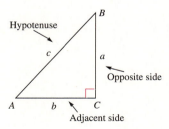

$$sin(\angle BAC) = \frac{a}{c} = \frac{\text{length of opposite side}}{\text{length of hypotenuse}}$$

$$cos(\angle BAC) = \frac{b}{c} = \frac{\text{length of adjacent side}}{\text{length of hypotenuse}}$$

$$tan(\angle BAC) = \frac{a}{b} = \frac{\text{length of opposite side}}{\text{length of adjacent side}}$$

CHAPTER REVIEW

1. Each of the following figures contains at least one pair of congruent triangles. Identify them and tell why they are congruent.

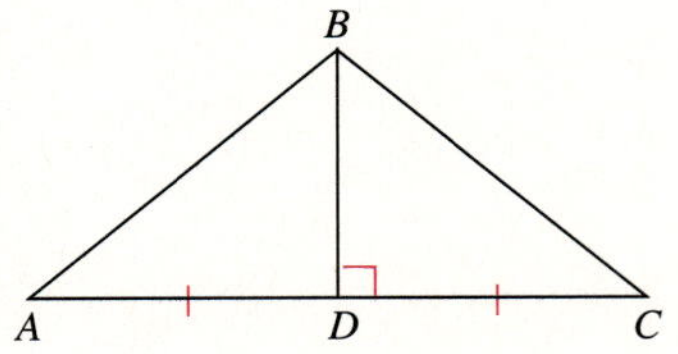

(a)

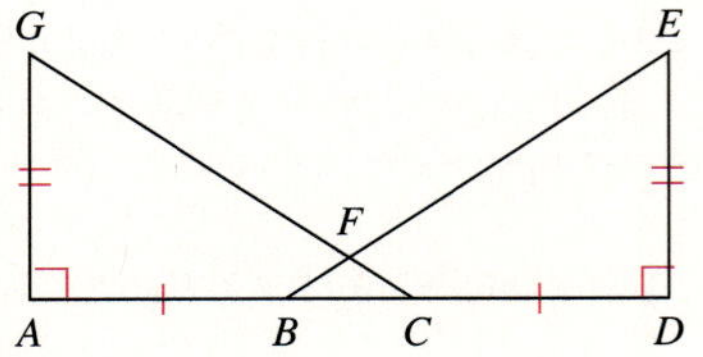

(b)

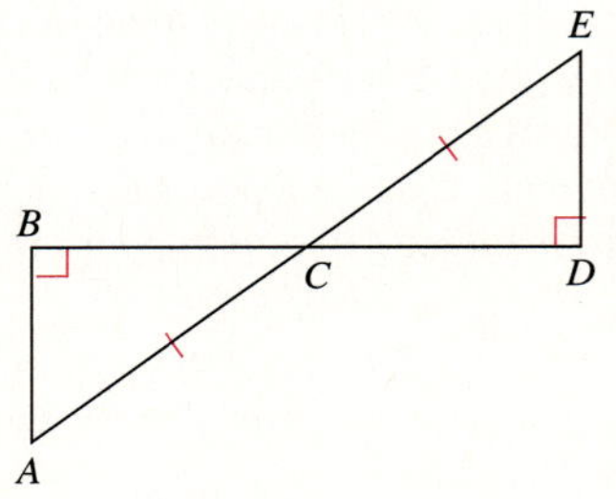

(c)

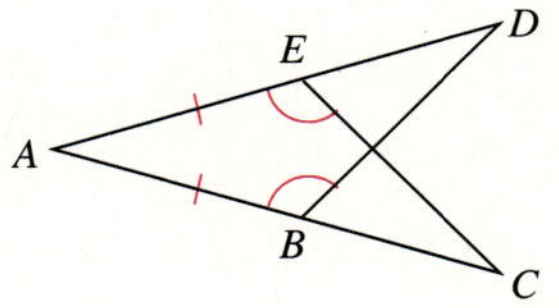

(d)

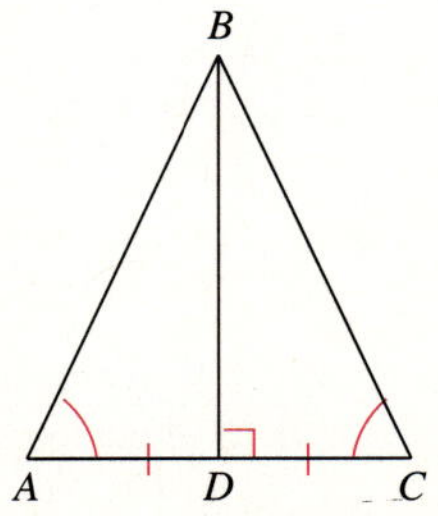

(e)

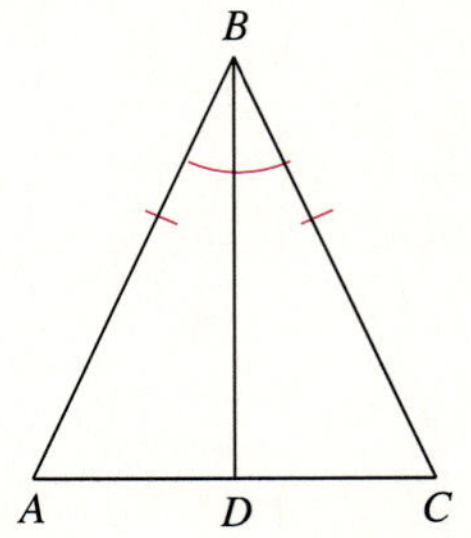

(f)

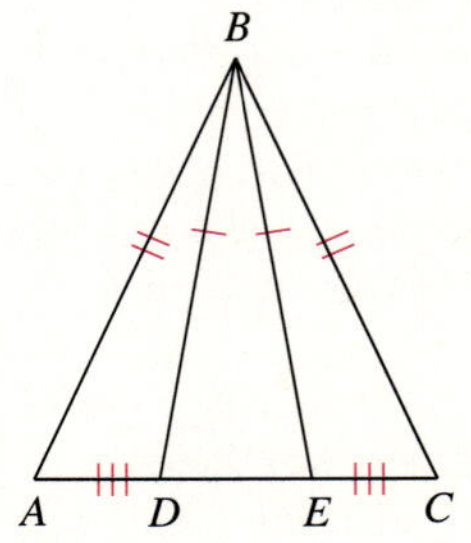

(g)

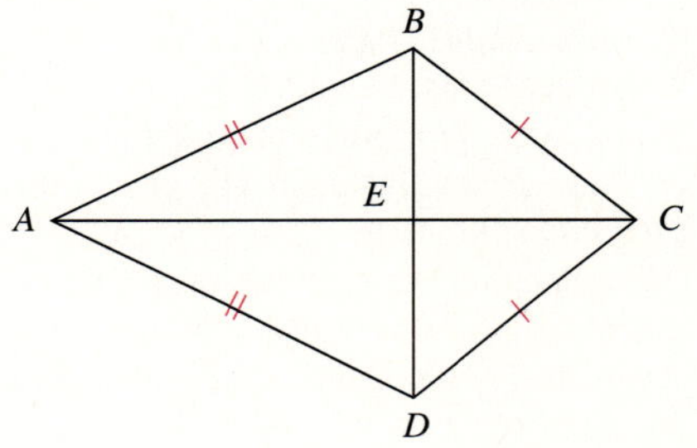

(h)

2. In the following figure, *ABCD* is a square and $\overline{DE} \cong \overline{BF}$. What kind of figure is *AECF*? Justify your answer.

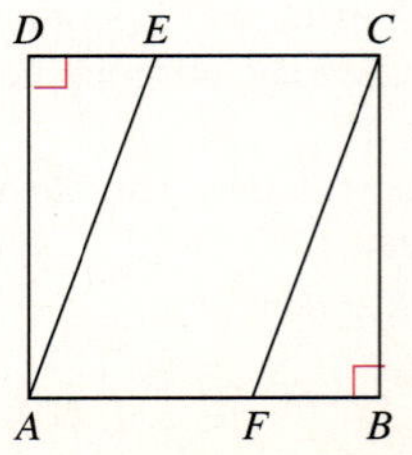

3. Construct each of the following by (1) using a compass and straightedge and (2) paperfolding:

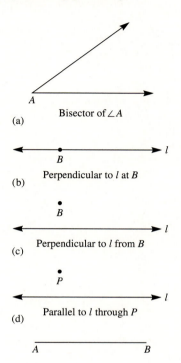

(a) Bisector of ∠A

(b) Perpendicular to *l* at *B*

(c) Perpendicular to *l* from *B*

(d) Parallel to *l* through *P*

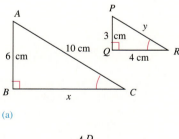

4. For each of the following pairs of similar triangles, find the missing measures:

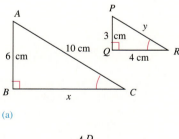

(a)

(b)

5. Divide the following segment into five congruent parts:

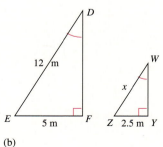

6. If *ABCD* is a trapezoid, $\overline{EF} \parallel \overline{AD}$ and $\overline{AC}$ is a diagonal. What is the relationship between $\frac{a}{b}$ and $\frac{c}{d}$? Why?

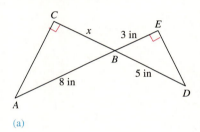

7. Given the following figure, construct a circle that contains *A* and *B* and has its center on *ℓ*:

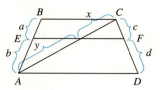

8. For each of the following figures, show that appropriate triangles are similar and find *x* and *y*:

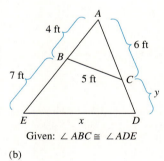

(a)

Given: ∠ *ABC* ≅ ∠*ADE*

(b)

9. Determine whether each of the following is true or false. If false, explain why.
   a. A radius of a circle is a chord of the circle.
   b. If a radius bisects a chord of a circle, then it is perpendicular to the chord.

10. A person 2 m tall casts a shadow 1 m long when a building has a 6-m shadow. How high is the building?

11. a. Which of the following polygons can be inscribed in a circle? Assume that all sides of each polygon are congruent and that all the angles of polygons (iii) and (iv) are congruent.

b. Based on your answer in (a), make a conjecture about what kinds of polygons can be inscribed in a circle.

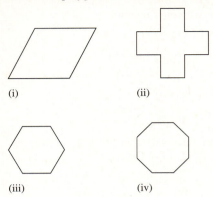

(i)   (ii)

(iii)   (iv)

12. Determine the vertical height of the playground slide shown in the following figure:

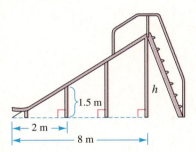

1.5 m

h

2 m

8 m

13. Find the distance *d* across the river sketched as follows:

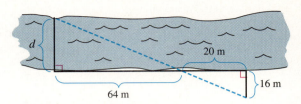

d

20 m

16 m

64 m

14. Is the following statement always true, always false, or true in some cases and false in others? Explain your answer.
    A quadrilateral whose diagonals are congruent and perpendicular is a square.

15. For each of the following, write the equation of the line determined by the given pair of points:
    a. $(2, {}^-3)$ and $({}^-1, 1)$ **b.** $({}^-3, 0)$ and $(3, 2)$

16. Use slope to determine if there is a single line through the points with coordinates $(4, 2)$, $(0, {}^-1)$, and $(7, {}^-5)$. Explain your reasoning.

*17. If the length of one side of an equilateral triangle is 6 cm, how long is its altitude?

*18. What is the measure of an angle whose sine and cosine are equal?

*19. If a triangle contains an angle of measure of 72°, explain how you might find *sin* 72.

*20. In a regular hexagon whose sides each have length 4 cm, find out the length of a segment from the center of the hexagon perpendicular to one of the sides.

*21. How are the angle of depression and the angle of elevation from an object on the ground to an object in the air related? Why?

SELECTED BIBLIOGRAPHY

Burger, W. "Geometry," *Arithmetic Teacher* 32 (February 1985): 52–56.

Cain, B. "The Basic Constructions." *Mathematics Teaching in the Middle School* 1 (September-October 1994): 137.

Eves, H. *An Introduction to the History of Mathematics with Cultural Connections.* Philadelphia: Saunders College Publishing (1990).

Friedlander, A., and G. Lappan. "Similarity: Investigations at the Middle Grade Level." In *Learning and Teaching Geometry, K–12.* Reston, Va.: National Council of Teachers of Mathematics (1987).

Hurd, S. "An Application of the Criteria ASASA for Quadrilaterals." *Mathematics Teacher* 81 (February 1988): 124–126.

Lappan, G., and R. Even. "Similarity in the Middle Grades." *Arithmetic Teacher* 35 (May 1988): 32–35.

Lappan, G., and E. Phillips. "Spatial Visualization." *Mathematics Teacher* 79 (November 1984): 618–623.

Lennie, J. "A Lab Approach for Teaching Basic Geometry." *Mathematics Teacher* 79 (October 1986): 523–524.

Mathematics Resource Project. *Geometry and Visualization.* Palo Alto, Calif.: Creative Publications (1985).

Newton, J. "From Pattern-Block Play to Logo Programming." *Arithmetic Teacher* 35 (May 1988): 6–9.

Robertson, J. "Geometric Constructions Using Hinged Mirrors." *Mathematics Teacher* 79 (May 1986): 380–386.

Senk, S. L., and D. B. Hirschorn. "Multiple Approaches to Geometry: Teaching Similarity." *Mathematics Teacher* 83 (April 1990): 274–280.

Tarte, L. "Dropping Perpendiculars the Easy Way." *Mathematics Teacher* 80 (January 1987): 30–31.

Taylor, L. "Exploring Geometry with the Geometer's Sketchpad." *Arithmetic Teacher* 40 (November 1992): 187–191.

Van de Walle, J., and C. Thompson. "Promoting Mathematical Thinking." *Arithmetic Teacher* 32 (February 1985): 7–13.

Walter, M. *Boxes, Squares, and Other Things.* Reston, Va.: National Council of Teachers of Mathematics (1970).

12

MORE CONCEPTS OF MEASUREMENT

A farmer has a plot of land in the shape of a square that is 100 m on a side. An irrigation system can be installed with the option of one large circular sprinkler or four small sprinklers, as shown in the accompanying figure. The farmer wants to know which plan will provide water to the greatest percent of land in the field if the cost and the watering pattern are not taken into account.

I n the Teaching *Standards* (p. 136), we find the following:

> *The attributes of what we measure include length, area, volume, capacity, time, temperature, angles, weight, and mass. Teachers should understand that the units to record measure are different from the process of measurement itself. These ideas should be reinforced through varied experiences, using both standard and nonstandard units where students learn to estimate lengths, areas, and so on. Of particular importance should be an understanding of the Systeme International d'Unites (the metric system).*

In this chapter, we use metric and English systems of measurement for length, area, volume, mass, and temperature with the philosophy that students should learn to think within a system. Consequently, conversions among units of measure in the metric and the English systems are not considered.

We develop formulas for the areas of plane figures and for surface areas and volumes of solids. We also use the concept of area in discussing the Pythagorean Theorem. The *Standards* (p. 116) for grades 5-8 states: *The curriculum should focus on the development of understanding, not the rote memorization of formulas.* In that regard, we attempt to show how area and volume formulas can be developed through exercises that show different developmental techniques, as well as applications of the formulas.

Section 12-1   Areas of Polygons and Circles

area   Using a square as the basic unit, the **area** of a region is the number of such squares required to tessellate the region, that is, cover the region completely with no overlaps and no gaps. *Area is always expressed in square units.* A square measuring 1 in. on a side has an area of one square inch, denoted by 1 in.^{2}. A square measuring 1 cm on a side has an area of one square centimeter, denoted by 1 cm^2. A square measuring 1 m on a side has an area of 1 m^2.

Areas on a Geoboard

In the teaching of the concept of area, intuitive activities should precede the development of formulas. Many such activities can be accomplished on a geoboard. A geoboard is shown on the following student page from *Addison-Wesley Mathematics,* Grade 7, 1993. Note that on the top of the student page, one square unit is shown and the distance between two adjacent dots is one unit. Note that figure *ABCDE* on the student page has area 5 1/2 square units. This area was obtained by using the *addition principle.* According to this principle, we find the area of a shape by adding the areas of the shapes that can be used to create the original shape without overlapping. Areas can also be determined using the *half-rectangle principle,* as shown on the student page. Work the problems on the bottom of the page to make sure you understand these two principles.

To find the area of quadrilateral *ABCD* in Figure 12-1, construct the rectangle *EFCG* around the quadrilateral and then subtract the areas of triangles *EAD, BFC,* and *DGC.* The area of the rectangle *EFCG* is 6 square units. The area of $\triangle EAD$ is $\frac{1}{2}$ square unit, and the area of $\triangle BFC$ is half the area of rectangle *BFCK,* or $\frac{1}{2}$ of 2, or 1, square unit. Similarly, the area of $\triangle DGC$ is half the area of rectangle *DHCG,* that is, $\frac{1}{2} \cdot 3$, or $\frac{3}{2}$, square units. Consequently, the area of *ABCD* is $6 - \left(\frac{1}{2} + 1 + \frac{3}{2}\right)$, or 3, square units.

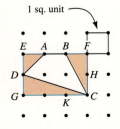

1 sq. unit

Figure 12-1

Exploring the Concept of Area

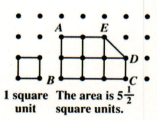

LEARN ABOUT IT

The **area** of a figure is the number of square units needed to cover the figure. Polygon *ABCDE* has an area of $5\frac{1}{2}$ square units.

1 square unit   The area is $5\frac{1}{2}$ square units.

EXPLORE   Study the Information

Figure F at the right has been divided into regions that are rectangles or triangles. Trace Figure F on dot paper. Divide Figure F into the least possible number of rectangular and triangular regions. How many regions did you make?

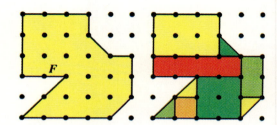

TALK ABOUT IT

1. Find the area of each rectangle that you indicated for Figure F.

2. Find the area of each triangle that you indicated for Figure F.

3. What is the total area of Figure F?

Here are two principles you can use to find the areas of some figures.

HALF-RECTANGLE PRINCIPLE The area of a triangle is half the area of a rectangle. Look at the area of the shaded triangles.

ADDITION PRINCIPLE If you divide an irregular figure into rectangles and triangles, you can find the area of the figure by adding the areas of the rectangles and triangles.

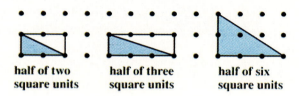

half of two square units : half of three square units : half of six square units

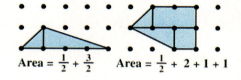

Area $= \frac{1}{2} + \frac{3}{2}$ Area $= \frac{1}{2} + 2 + 1 + 1$

Example 12-1 Using a geoboard, find the areas of each of the shaded figures in Figure 12-2.

Figure 12-2

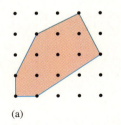

(a)

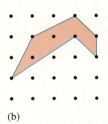

(b)

Solution a. We construct a square around the hexagon and then subtract the areas of regions (a), (b), (c), (d), and (e) from the area of this square, as shown in Figure 12-3. Therefore the area of the hexagon is $16 - (3 + 1 + 1 + 1 + 1)$, or 9, square units. The addition principle could also be used in this problem.

Figure 12-3

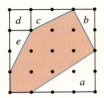

b. The area of the hexagon equals the area of the surrounding rectangle shown in Figure 12-4 minus the sum of the areas of figures (a), (b), (c), (d), (e), (f), and (g). Thus the area of the hexagon is $12 - (3 + 1 + \frac{1}{2} + \frac{1}{2} + 1 + 1 + 1)$, or 4, square units.

Figure 12-4

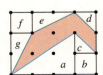

I N V E S T I G A T I O N   1 2 - 1

● Instead of using a square for the unit of area, find how many of each of the following shapes are contained in Figure 12-5:

Figure 12-5

a. Triangles

b. Rhombuses

c. Trapezoids

Converting Units of Area

The price of new carpet for a house is quoted in terms of square yards, for example, $12.50/yd^2. The basic units of area in the English system are the square inch (in.^{2}), the square foot (ft^2), the square yard (yd^2), the square mile (mi^2), and, for land measure, the acre (A). In the metric system, the basic units are the square millimeter (mm^2), the square centimeter (cm^2), the square meter (m^2), the square kilometer (km^2), and, for land measure, the hectare (ha). It is often necessary to convert from one area measure to another within a system.

To determine how many 1-cm squares are in a square meter, look at Figure 12-6(a). There are 100 cm in 1 m, so each side of the square meter has a measure of 100 cm. Thus it takes 100 rows of 100 1-cm squares each to fill a square meter, that is, $100 \cdot 100$, or 10,000 1-cm squares. Because the area of each centimeter square is 1 cm $\cdot$ 1 cm, or 1 cm^2, there are 10,000 cm^2 in 1 m^2. In general, the area A of a square that is s units on a side is s^2, as shown in Figure 12-6(b).

Figure 12-6

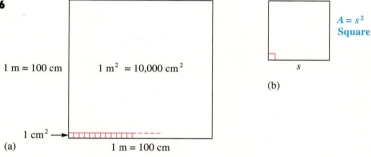

$1 \text{ m} = 100 \text{ cm}$ $1 \text{ m}^2 = 10,000 \text{ cm}^2$

$A = s^2$
Square

s

(b)

1 cm^2

(a) $1 \text{ m} = 100 \text{ cm}$

Other metric conversions of area measure can be developed similarly. For example, Figure 12-7(a) shows that $1 \text{ m}^2 = 10,000 \text{ cm}^2 = 1,000,000 \text{ mm}^2$. Likewise, Figure 13-7(b) shows that $1 \text{ m}^2 = 0.000001 \text{ km}^2$. Similarly, $1 \text{ cm}^2 = 100 \text{ mm}^2$ and $1 \text{ km}^2 = 1,000,000 \text{ m}^2$.

Figure 12-7

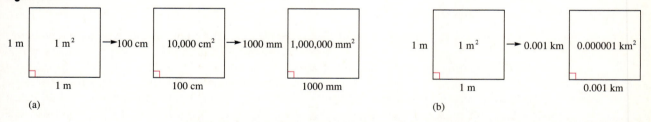

(a)   (b)

Table 12-1 shows the symbols for metric units of area and their relationship to the square meter.

Table 12-1

Unit	Symbol	Relationship to Square Meter
square kilometer	km^2	1,000,000 m^2
*square hectometer	hm^2	10,000 m^2
*square dekameter	dam^2	100 m^2
square meter	**m**^{2}	**1** m^2
*square decimeter	dm^2	0.01 m^2
square centimeter	cm^2	0.0001 m^2
square millimeter	mm^2	0.000001 m^2

*Not commonly used.

Example 12-2   Convert each of the following:

a. $5 \text{ cm}^2 = \underline{\hspace{1cm}} \text{ mm}^2$ **b.** $124,000,000 \text{ m}^2 = \underline{\hspace{1cm}} \text{ km}^2$

Solution   **a.** $1 \text{ cm}^2 = 100 \text{ mm}^2$ implies $5 \text{ cm}^2 = 5 \cdot 1 \text{ cm}^2 = 5 \cdot 100 \text{ mm}^2 = 500 \text{ mm}^2$.

b. $1 \text{ m}^2 = 0.000001 \text{ km}^2$ implies $124,000,000 \text{ m}^2 = 124,000,000 \cdot 1 \text{ m}^2 = 124,000,000 \cdot 0.000001 \text{ km}^2 = 124 \text{ km}^2$.

REMARK   Students sometimes confuse the area of 5 cm^2 with the area of a square 5 cm on each side. The area of a square 5 cm on each side is $(5 \text{ cm})^2$, or 25 cm^2. Five squares each 1 cm by 1 cm have the area of 5 cm^2. Thus $5 \text{ cm}^2 \neq (5 \text{ cm})^2$.

Based on the relationship among units of length in the English system, it is possible to convert among English units of area. For example, because 1 yd = 3 ft, it follows that $(1 \text{ yd})^2 = 1 \text{ yd} \cdot 1 \text{ yd} = 3 \text{ ft} \cdot 3 \text{ ft} = 9 \text{ ft}^2$. Similarly, because 1 ft = 12 in., $(1 \text{ ft})^2 = 1 \text{ ft} \cdot 1 \text{ ft} = 12 \text{ in.} \cdot 12 \text{ in.} = 144 \text{ in.}^2$ Table 12-2 summarizes various relationships among units of area in the English system.

Table 12-2

Unit of Area	Equivalent of Other Units
1 ft^2	$\frac{1}{9} \text{ yd}^2$, or 144 in.^2
1 yd^2	9 ft^2
1 mi^2	$3,097,600 \text{ yd}^2$, or $27,878,400 \text{ ft}^2$

Land Measure

One application of area today is in land measure. The common unit of land measure in the English system is the **acre.** There are 4840 yd^2 in 1 acre. For very large land measures in the English system, the **square mile** (mi^2), or 640 acres, is used.

In the metric system, small land areas are measured in terms of a square unit 10 m on a side, called an **are** (pronounced "air") and denoted by **a.** Thus $1 \text{ a} = 10 \text{ m} \cdot 10 \text{ m}$, or 100 m^2. Larger land areas are measured in **hectares.** A hectare is 100 a. A hectare, denoted by **ha,** is the amount of land whose area is $10,000 \text{ m}^2$. It follows that 1 ha is the area of a square that is 100 m on a side. For very large land measures, the **square kilometer,** denoted by km^2, is used. One square kilometer is the area of a square with a side 1 km, or 1000 m, long. Land area measures are summarized in Table 12-3.

acre

square mile

are (a)

hectare (ha)

square kilometer

Table 12-3

Unit of Area	Equivalent in Other Units
1 a	100 m^2
1 ha	100 a, or $10,000 \text{ m}^2$
1 km^2	$1,000,000 \text{ m}^2$
1 acre	4840 yd^2
1 mi^2	640 acres

Example 12-3
a. A square field has a side of 400 m. Find the area of the field in hectares.
b. A square field has a side of 400 yd. Find the area of the field in acres.

Solution
a. $A = (400 \text{ m})^2 = 160,000 \text{ m}^2 = \dfrac{160,000}{10,000} \text{ ha} = 16 \text{ ha}$

b. $A = (400 \text{ yd})^2 = 160,000 \text{ yd}^2 = \dfrac{160,000}{4840} \text{ acre} \doteq 33.1 \text{ acre}$

Area of a Rectangle

To measure area, we may count the number of units of area contained in any given region. For example, suppose the square in Figure 12-8(a) represents 1 square unit. Then, the rectangle *ABCD* in Figure 12-8(b) contains $3 \cdot 4$, or 12, square units.

Figure 12-8

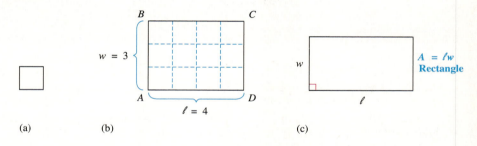

(a)   (b)   (c)

If the unit in Figure 12-8(a) is 1 cm^2, then the area of rectangle *ABCD* is 12 cm^2. In general, the area *A* of any rectangle may be found by multiplying the lengths of two adjacent sides ℓ and w, or $A = \ell w$, as given in Figure 12-8(c).

Example 12-4
Find the area of each rectangle in Figure 12-9.

Figure 12-9

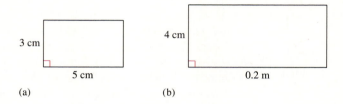

(a)   (b)

Solution
a. $A = (3 \text{ cm})(5 \text{ cm}) = 15 \text{ cm}^2$

b. First, write the lengths of the sides in the same unit of length. Because 0.2 m = 20 cm, $A = (4 \text{ cm})(20 \text{ cm}) = 80 \text{ cm}^2$. Alternatively, 4 cm = 0.04 m, so $A = (0.04 \text{ m})(0.2 \text{ m}) = 0.008 \text{ m}^2$.

INVESTIGATION 12-2

● Estimate, without looking, the area in square centimeters of a dollar bill. Measure and calculate how close your estimate is to the actual area.   ●

Area of a Parallelogram

■ The area of a parallelogram can be found by *reducing the problem to one that we already know how to solve,* in this case, finding the area of a rectangle. To develop the area formula for a parallelogram, complete the following investigation.

INVESTIGATION 12-3

● Cut out a parallelogram *ABCD* similar to the one in Figure 12-10(a). Now cut off a shaded triangle as shown and move it to the right to obtain a rectangle.

a. How do the areas of the parallelogram and the rectangle compare? Why?

b. How does this experiment lead to the formula for finding the area of a parallelogram?   ●

Figure 12-10

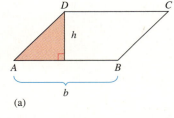

(a)

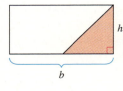

$A = bh$
Parallelogram

(b)

base
height

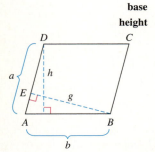

Figure 12-11

In general, any side of a parallelogram can be designated as a **base**. The **height** (*h*) is the distance between the bases and is always the length of a segment perpendicular to the lines containing the bases. Investigation 12-3 suggests that the area of parallelogram *ABCD* is given by $A = bh$, that is, the length of the base times the corresponding height. Similarly, in Figure 12-11, *EB*, or *g*, is the height that corresponds to the bases $\overline{AD}$ and $\overline{BC}$, each of which has measure *a*. Consequently, the area of the parallelogram *ABCD* is *ag*. Similarly, its area can be expressed as *bh*. Therefore $A = ag$ or *bh*.

Area of a Triangle

The formula for the area of a triangle can be derived from the formula for the area of a parallelogram. To explore this, work through Investigation 12-4.

INVESTIGATION 12 - 4

● Cut out a parallelogram and then cut it along one diagonal to form two triangles. Compare the areas of the two triangles. Repeat this with other parallelograms and form a conjecture involving the area of the parallelogram and the triangles. ●

Suppose $\triangle BAC$ in Figure 12-12(a) has base b and height h. Let $\triangle BAC'$ be the image of $\triangle BAC$ when $\triangle BAC$ is rotated 180° about M, the midpoint of $\overline{AB}$, as in Figure 12-12(b). Proving that quadrilateral $BCAC'$ is a parallelogram is left as an exercise. Parallelogram $BCAC'$ has area bh and is constructed of congruent triangles BAC and BAC'. So the area of $\triangle ABC$ is $\frac{1}{2}bh$. In general, the area of a triangle is equal to half the product of the length of a side and the altitude to that side.

Figure 12-12

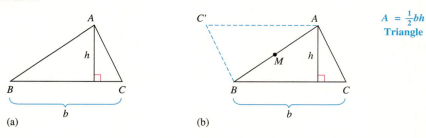

$A = \frac{1}{2}bh$
Triangle

(a)   (b)

In Figure 12-13, $\overline{BC}$ is a base of $\triangle ABC$, and the corresponding height h_1, or AE, is the distance from the opposite vertex A to the line containing $\overline{BC}$. Similarly, $\overline{AC}$ can be chosen as a base. Then h_2, or BG, the distance from the opposite vertex B to the line containing $\overline{AC}$, is the corresponding height. If $\overline{AB}$ is chosen as a base, then the corresponding height is h_3, or FC. Thus the area A of $\triangle ABC$ is

$$A = \frac{bh_1}{2} = \frac{ah_2}{2} = \frac{ch_3}{2}.$$

Figure 12-13

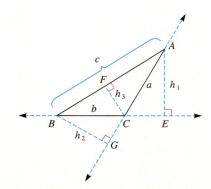

Example 12-5 Find the areas in Figure 12-14. Assume the quadrilaterals in (a) and (b) are parallelograms.

Figure 12-14

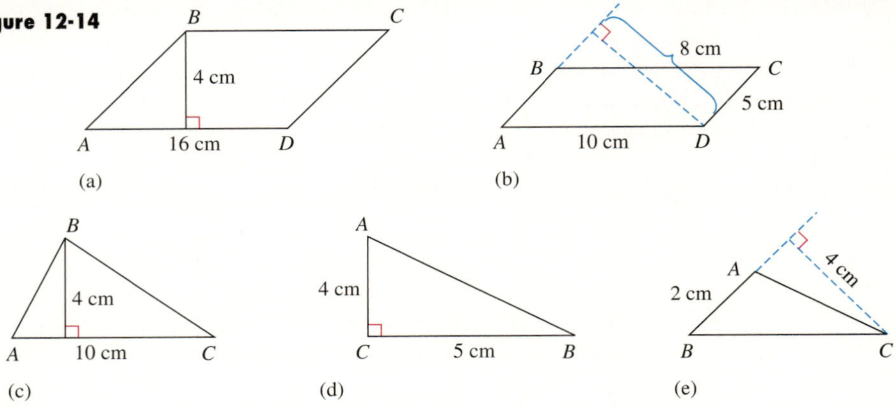

(a)

(b)

(c)

(d)

(e)

Solution

a. $A = bh = (16 \text{ cm})(4 \text{ cm}) = 64 \text{ cm}^2$

b. $A = bh = (5 \text{ cm})(8 \text{ cm}) = 40 \text{ cm}^2$

c. $A = \frac{1}{2}bh = \frac{1}{2}(10 \text{ cm})(4 \text{ cm}) = 20 \text{ cm}^2$

d. $A = \frac{1}{2}bh = \frac{1}{2}(5 \text{ cm})(4 \text{ cm}) = 10 \text{ cm}^2$

e. $A = \frac{1}{2}bh = \frac{1}{2}(2 \text{ cm})(4 \text{ cm}) = 4 \text{ cm}^2$

Area of a Trapezoid

The formula for the area of a trapezoid can also be developed informally, as shown in Investigation 12-5.

I N V E S T I G A T I O N   1 2 - 5

● Cut out a trapezoid *ABCD* as shown in Figure 12-15. Rotate the trapezoid 180° clockwise about the midpoint *M* of $\overline{BC}$. Use the figure obtained from the union of the original trapezoid and its image to derive the formula for the area of a trapezoid. ●

Figure 12-15

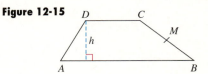

Areas of general polygons can also be found by partitioning the polygons into triangles, finding the areas of the triangles, and summing those areas. In Figure 12-16(a), trapezoid *ABCD* has bases b_1 and b_2 and height *h*. By connecting points *B* and *D*, as in Figure 12-16(b), we create two triangles: one with base $\overline{AB}$ and height *DE* and the other with base $\overline{CD}$ and height *BF*. Because $\overline{DE} \cong \overline{BF}$, each has length *h*. Thus the areas of triangles *ADB* and *DCB* are $\frac{1}{2}(b_1 h)$ and $\frac{1}{2}(b_2 h)$, respectively.

Hence, the area of trapezoid $ABCD$ is $\frac{1}{2}(b_1h) + \frac{1}{2}(b_2h)$, or $\frac{1}{2}h(b_1 + b_2)$. That is, the area of a trapezoid is equal to half the height times the sum of the lengths of the bases.

Figure 12-16

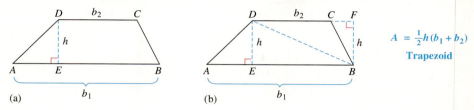

(a)

(b)

$$A = \tfrac{1}{2}h(b_1 + b_2)$$

Trapezoid

Example 12-6 Find the areas of the trapezoids in Figure 12-17.

Figure 12-17

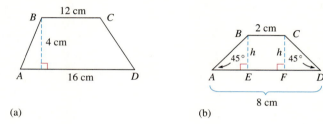

(a)

(b)

Solution **a.** $A = \frac{1}{2}h(b_1 + b_2) = \frac{1}{2}(4 \text{ cm})(12 \text{ cm} + 16 \text{ cm}) = 56 \text{ cm}^2$

 b. To find the area of trapezoid $ABCD$, we *use the strategy of determining a subgoal* of finding the height, h. In Figure 12-17(b), $BE = CF = h$. Also, $\overline{BE}$ is a side of $\triangle ABE$, which has angles with measures of 45° and 90°. Consequently, the third angle in triangle ABE is $180 - (45 + 90)$, or 45°. Therefore $\triangle ABE$ is isosceles and $AE = BE = h$. Similarly, it follows that $FD = h$. Because $AD = 8 \text{ cm} = h + EF + h$, we could find h if we knew the value of EF. From Figure 12-17(b), $EF = BC = 2$ cm because $BCFE$ is a rectangle (why?) and opposite sides of a rectangle are congruent. Now $h + EF + h = h + 2 + h = 8$ cm.

Thus $h = 3$ cm and the area of the trapezoid is $A = \frac{1}{2}(3 \text{ cm})(2 \text{ cm} + 8 \text{ cm})$, or 15 cm^2.

Problem 1

Larry purchased a plot of land surrounded by a fence. The former owner had subdivided the land into 13 equal-sized square plots, as shown in Figure 12-18. To reapportion the property into two plots of equal area, Larry wishes to build a single, straight fence beginning at the far left corner (point P on the drawing). Is such a fence possible? If so, where should the other end be?

Figure 12-18

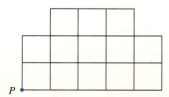

Understanding the Problem.   We want to divide the land in Figure 12-18 into two plots of equal area by means of a straight fence starting at point P. *A subgoal* is to find the other endpoint. Because the area of the entire plot is 13 square units, the area of each part formed by the fence must be $\frac{1}{2} \cdot 13$, or $6\frac{1}{2}$ square units.

Devising a Plan.   To find an approximate location for the fence, consider a fence connecting P with point A, as shown in Figure 12-19. The area of the land below fence $\overline{PA}$ is the sum of the areas of $\triangle APD$ and the rectangle $DAFE$. The area of $\triangle APD$ is 4 and the area of rectangle $DAFE$ is 2, so the area below the fence $\overline{PA}$ is $4 + 2$, or 6, square units. We want an area of $6\frac{1}{2}$ square units. Consequently, the other end of the fence should be above point A.

Figure 12-19

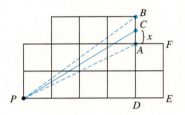

A similar argument shows that the area below $\overline{PB}$ is 8 square units and the end of the fence should be below B. Thus the other end of the fence should be at a point C between A and B. To find the exact location of point C, we designate CA by x. We then *write an equation* for x by finding the area below $\overline{PC}$ in terms of x, make the area equal to $6\frac{1}{2}$, and solve for x.

Carrying Out the Plan.   The area below $\overline{PC}$ equals the area of $\triangle PCD$ plus the area of the rectangle $DAFE$. The area of $\triangle PCD$ is

$$\frac{PD \cdot DC}{2} = \frac{4(2 + x)}{2} = 2(2 + x).$$

The area of rectangle $DAFE$ is 2, so $2(2 + x) + 2$ should equal half the area of the plot. Consequently, we have the following:

$$2(2 + x) + 2 = 6\frac{1}{2}$$

$$4 + 2x + 2 = \frac{13}{2}$$

$$2x = \frac{1}{2}$$

$$x = \frac{1}{4}$$

Therefore the fence should be built along the line connecting point P to the point C, which is $\frac{1}{4}$ unit directly above point A. Point C can be found by dividing $\overline{AB}$ into four congruent parts.

Looking Back.   We check that the solution is correct by finding the area above $\overline{PC}$. The problem can be varied by changing the shape of the plot. Another variation is to ask if Larry could divide the plot into thirds, fourths, and so on. We could also approach the problem as if Larry wanted to subdivide the land but wanted to use the existing lines that mark the squares.

• • •

Area of a Regular Polygon

The area of a triangle can be used to find the area of any regular polygon, as illustrated *using a simpler case* involving a regular hexagon (see Figure 12-20a). The hexagon can be separated into 6 congruent triangles, each with a vertex at the center, with side s and height a. (The height of such a triangle of a regular polygon is the *apothem* and is denoted by a.) The area of each triangle is $\frac{1}{2}as$. Because six triangles make up the hexagon, the area of the hexagon is $6(\frac{1}{2}as)$, or $\frac{1}{2}a(6s)$. However, $6s$ is the perimeter p of the hexagon, so the area of the hexagon is $\frac{1}{2}ap$. The same process can be used to develop the formula for the area of any regular polygon. That is, the area of any regular polygon is $\frac{1}{2}ap$, where a is the height of one of the triangles involved and p is the perimeter of the polygon, as shown in Figure 12-20(b).

Figure 12-20

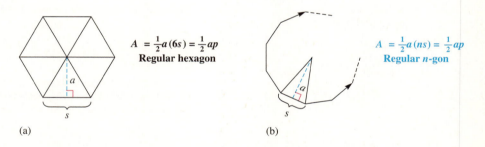

$$A = \tfrac{1}{2}a(6s) = \tfrac{1}{2}ap$$
Regular hexagon

$$A = \tfrac{1}{2}a(ns) = \tfrac{1}{2}ap$$
Regular n-gon

(a)   (b)

Area of a Circle

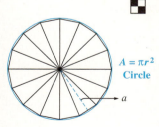

$A = \pi r^2$
Circle

Figure 12-21

We use the strategy of *examining a related problem* to find the area of a circle. The area of a regular polygon inscribed in a circle, as in Figure 12-21, approximates the area of the circle, and we know that the area of any regular n-gon is $\frac{1}{2}ap$, where a is the height of a triangle of the n-gon and p is the perimeter. If the number of sides n is made very large, then the perimeter and the area of the n-gon are close to those of the circle.

Also, the apothem a is approximately equal to the radius r of the circle, and the perimeter p approximates the circumference $2\pi r$. Because the area of the circle is approximately equal to the area of the n-gon, $\frac{1}{2}ap \doteq \frac{1}{2}r \cdot 2\pi r = \pi r^2$. In fact, the area of the circle is precisely πr^2.

A similar approach to the preceding derivation of the area of a circle was given in 1609 by the astronomer Johann Kepler (1571–1630). The approach shown on the following student page from *Addison-Wesley Mathematics,* Grade 8, 1993, is similar to Kepler's.

Area of Circles

kiva A
36 ft

ki
3

tower

LEARN ABOUT IT

EXPLORE Study the Situation

At Mesa Verde in Colorado, Pueblo Indians
built the Cliff Palace, a multi-storied building
with about 200 rooms. It includes a tower and circular
underground rooms called kivas. Could it be that the Pueblos
discussed that the ratio $\frac{C}{d}$ is constant? What is this numerical value?

TALK ABOUT IT

1. What are the radius and diameter of
   kiva A?

2. Use the formula $C = \pi d$ to find the
   circumference of kiva B. Use 3.14 for π.

Here is why $A = \pi r^2$ is a reasonable formula for the area of a circle.

A circle is divided
into equal parts.

r

The parts fit together to form a shape like a parallelogram.

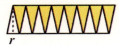
r

This figure has the same area as the circle.
The base is equal to half the circumference $\left(\frac{1}{2}\pi d = \pi r\right)$
and the height is equal to the radius (r).

The area of the figure above is approximately equal to the base
times the height. $A = \pi r \cdot r = \pi r^2$.

What are the areas of kiva A and kiva B?

Area of kiva A
$A = \pi \cdot 18^2 = \pi \cdot 324$
$\approx 3.14 \cdot 324 = 1{,}017.36$

Area of kiva B
$A = \pi \cdot 17^2 = \pi \cdot 289$
$\approx 3.14 \cdot 289 = 907.46$

The area of kiva A is about 1,017.36 ft^2 and of kiva B is about
907.46 ft^2.

Area of a Sector

sector   A **sector** of a circle is a pie-shaped region of the circle determined by an angle whose ver-
central angle   tex is the center of the circle. This angle is called a **central angle.** The area of a sector
depends on the radius of the circle and the measure of the central angle determining the sec-

tor. If the angle has a measure of 90°, as in Figure 12-22(a), the area of the sector is one fourth the area of the circle, or $\frac{90}{360}\pi r^2$. In any circle, there are 360°, so the area of a sector whose central angle has measure θ degrees is $\frac{\theta}{360}(\pi r^2)$, as shown in Figure 12-22(b).

Figure 12-22

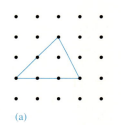

(a)

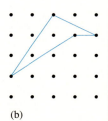

$A = \frac{\theta}{360}(\pi r^2)$
Sector of a circle

(b)

Ongoing Assessment 12-1

1. Choose the most appropriate metric units (cm^2, m^2, or km^2) and English units ($in.^2$, yd^2, mi^2) for measuring each of the following:
   a. Area of a sheet of notebook paper
   b. Area of a quarter
   c. Area of a desktop
   d. Area of a classroom floor
   e. Area of a parallel parking space
   f. Area of an airport runway
2. Estimate and then measure each of the following using cm^2, m^2, or km^2.
   a. Area of a door   b. Area of a chair seat
   c. Area of a desktop   d. Area of a chalkboard
3. Complete the following conversion table:

Item	m^2	cm^2	mm^2
a. Area of a sheet of paper		588	
b. Area of a cross-section of a crayon			192
c. Area of a desktop	1.5		
d. Area of a dollar bill		100	
e. Area of a postage stamp		5	

4. Complete the following conversions using a calculator:
   a. $4000\ ft^2 =$ _____ yd^2
   b. $10^6\ yd^2 =$ _____ mi^2
   c. $10\ mi^2 =$ _____ A
   d. $3\ A =$ _____ ft^2
5. Complete each of the following:
   a. A football field is about 49 m × 100 m or _____ m^2.
   b. About _____ a are in two football fields.

c. About _____ ha are in two football fields.
6. Find the areas of each of the following figures if the distance between two adjacent dots in a row or a column is one unit:

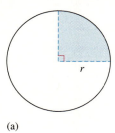

(a)

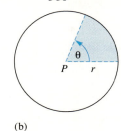

(b)

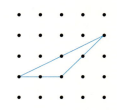

(c)

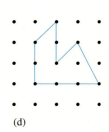

(d)

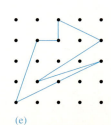

(e)

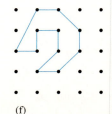

(f)

7. If all vertices of a polygon are points on square-dot paper, the polygon is called a **lattice polygon.** In 1899, G. Pick discovered a surprising theorem involving *I*, the number of dots *inside* the polygon, and *B*, the number of dots that lie *on* the polygon. The theorem states that the area of any lattice polygon is $I + \frac{1}{2}B - 1$. Check that this is true for the polygon in Problem 6.

8. Find the area of △*ABC* in each of the following triangles:

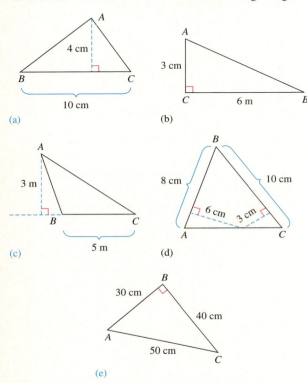

(a)   (b)

(c)   (d)

(e)

9. Find the area of each of the following quadrilaterals:

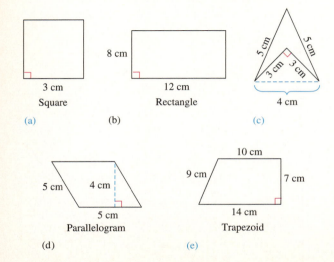

(a) Square   (b) Rectangle   (c)

(d) Parallelogram   (e) Trapezoid

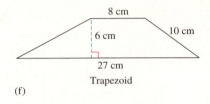

(f) Trapezoid

10. **a.** A rectangular piece of land is 1300 m × 1500 m.
   i. What is the area in square kilometers?
   ii. What is the area in hectares?
b. A rectangular piece of land is 1300 yd × 1500 yd.
   i. What is the area in square miles?
   ii. What is the area in acres?
c. Explain which measuring system you would rather use to solve (a) and (b).

11. For a parallelogram whose sides are 6 cm and 10 cm, which of the following is true?
a. The data are insufficient to enable us to determine the area.
b. The area equals 60 cm².
c. The area is greater than 60 cm².
d. The area is less than 60 cm².

12. If the diagonals of a rhombus are *a* and *b* units long, find the area of the rhombus in terms of *a* and *b*.

13. Find the cost of carpeting the following rectangular rooms:
a. Dimensions: 6.5 m × 4.5 m; cost = $13.85/m²
b. Dimensions: 15 ft × 11 ft; cost = $30/yd²

14. Find the area of each of the following. Leave your answers in terms of π.

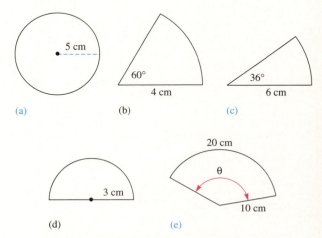

(a)   (b)   (c)

(d)   (e)

15. Joe uses stick-on square carpet tiles to cover his 3 m × 4 m bathroom. If each tile is 10 cm on a side, how many tiles does he need?

16. A rectangular plot of land is to be seeded with grass. If the plot is 22 m × 28 m and a 1-kg bag of seed is needed for 85 m² of land, how many bags of seed are needed?

17. Find the area of each of the following regular polygons:

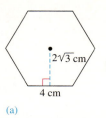

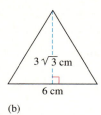

(a)   (b)

18. Suppose the largest square peg possible is placed in a circular hole as shown in the following figure and that the largest circular peg possible is placed in a square hole. In which case is there a smaller percent of space wasted?

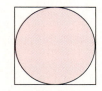

19. a. If a circle has a circumference of 8π cm, what is its area?
   b. If a circle of radius r and a square with a side of length s have equal areas, express r in terms of s.
20. Find the area of each of the following shaded parts. Assume all arcs are circular.

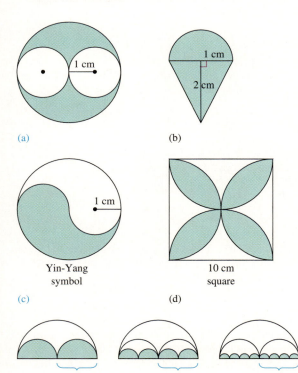

(a)   (b)

Yin-Yang
symbol

10 cm
square

(c)   (d)

(e)   (f)   (g)

21. A circular flower bed is 6 m in diameter and has a circular sidewalk around it 1 m wide. Find the area of the sidewalk in square meters.

22. a. If the area of a square is 144 cm^2, what is its perimeter?
   b. If the perimeter of a square is 32 cm, what is its area?
23. a. What happens to the area of a square when the length of each side is doubled?
   b. If the ratio of the sides of two squares is 1 to 5, what is the ratio of their areas?
24. a. What happens to the area of a circle if its diameter is doubled?
   b. What happens to the area of a circle if its radius is increased by 10%?
   c. What happens to the area of a circle if its circumference is tripled?
25. A rectangular field is 64 m × 25 m. Shawn wants to fence a square field that has the same area as the rectangular field. How long are the sides of the square field?
26. A store has wrapping paper on sale. One package is 3 rolls of $2\frac{1}{2}$ ft × 8 ft for $6.00. Another package is 5 rolls of $2\frac{1}{2}$ ft × 6 ft for $8.00. Which is the better buy?
27. Find the shaded area enclosed by two semicircles and two tangents to the semicircles as shown in the following figure:

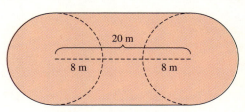

28. An aircraft company starts with a rectangular piece of metal measuring 10 in. × 10 in. and wants to remove a strip x in. wide from all sides to form another rectangle with an area of 64 in.^{2} Find x.
29. The following figure consists of five congruent squares. Find a line through point P that divides the figure into two parts of equal area.

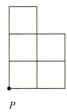

P

30. a. Sketch a graph showing the relationship between the length and width of all rectangles with perimeters of 12 cm.
   b. Sketch a graph showing the relationship between the length and width of all rectangles with areas of 12 cm^2.
31. For a dartboard (see the following figure), Joan is trying to determine how the area of the outside cross-hatched region compares with the area of the shaded region so that she can determine payoffs. How do they compare?

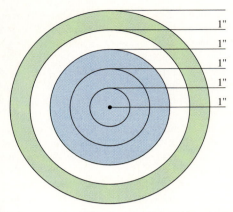

32. Complete and explain how to use geometric shapes to find an algebraic expression for each of the following:

a. $a(b + c)$

b. $(a + b)(c + d)$

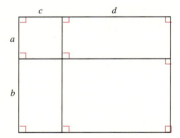

33. a. If the ratio of the sides of two squares is $2:3$, determine the ratio of the areas. Justify your answer.

b. If the ratio between the diagonals of two squares is $2:3$, determine the ratio of their areas. Justify your answer.

34. a. If, in two similar triangles, the ratio of the lengths of the corresponding sides is $2:1$, determine the ratio of their areas.

b. Make a conjecture about the relationship between the ratio of the areas of two similar triangles and the ratio of the corresponding sides.

c. Justify your conjecture in (b).

35. a. The screens of two television sets are similar rectangles. The 20-in. set (the length of the diagonal is 20 in.) costs $400, whereas the 27-in. set with similar features costs $600. If a customer is concerned about the size of the viewing area and is willing to pay the same amount per square foot, determine the better buy. Explain.

b. What should the length of the diagonal of a TV set be in order for the viewing area to be twice the viewing area of the 20-in. set?

★36. In the following figure, quadrilateral $ABCD$ is a parallelogram and P is any point on $\overline{AC}$. Prove that the area of $\triangle BCP$ is equal to the area of $\triangle DPC$.

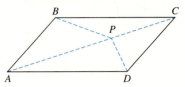

Communication

37. Describe two different methods for approximating the area of a circle.

38. a. If a 10-in. (diameter) pizza costs $10, how much should a 20-in. pizza cost? Explain the assumptions you made in your answer.

b. If the ratio between the diameters of two pizzas is $1:k$, what should the ratio be between the prices? Explain the assumptions you made in your answer.

39. In the following figure, $\ell \parallel \overleftrightarrow{AB}$. If the area of $\triangle ABP$ is 10 cm^2, what are the areas of $\triangle ABQ$, $\triangle ABR$, $\triangle ABS$, $\triangle ABT$, and $\triangle ABU$? Explain your answers.

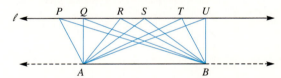

40. a. Explain how the following drawing can be used to determine a formula for the area of $\triangle ABC$:

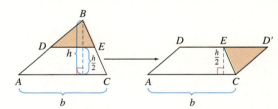

b. Use paper cutting to reassemble $\triangle ABC$ in (a) into parallelogram $ADD'C$.

41. The area of a parallelogram can be found by using the concept of a half-turn (a turn by 180°). Consider the parallelogram $ABCD$ and let M and N be the midpoints of $\overline{AB}$ and $\overline{CD}$, respectively. Rotate the shaded triangle with vertex M about M by 180° clockwise and rotate the shaded triangle with vertex N about N by 180° counterclockwise. What kind of figure do you obtain? Now complete the argument to find the area of the parallelogram.

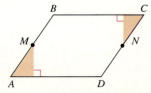

Open-ended

42. Draw 2 rectangles that have the same perimeter but different areas.

43. a. Estimate the area in square centimeters that your handprint will cover.
   b. Trace the outline of your hand on square centimeter grid paper and use the outline to obtain an estimate for the area. Explain how you arrived at your estimate.

Cooperative Learning

44. Use 5 squares to build the following shape and discuss the questions that follow:

   a. What is the area of this shape?
   b. What is the perimeter of this shape?
   c. Add squares to the shape such that each square added touches a complete edge with at least one other square.
   i. What is the minimum number of squares that can be added so that the shape has a perimeter of 18?
   ii. What is the maximum number?
   iii. What is the maximum area the new shape could have and still have a perimeter of 18?

   d. Using the five squares, have members of the group start with shapes different from the one above and answer the questions in (c). Discuss your results.
   e. Explore shapes that are made up of more than 5 squares.

45. Consider the following figures made of five congruent squares constructed in such a way that any two share a common side or a common vertex or have no points in common and each square shares an edge with another. Each square is considered a unit square.

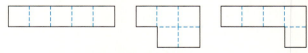

   As a group, investigate the following:
   a. What are the greatest and least perimeters possible of a figure made of unit squares whose area is
   i. 5?   **ii.** 6?   **iii.** 30?
   Draw the appropriate figures.
   b. What are the greatest and least possible areas of a figure made of unit squares whose perimeter is
   i. 12 units?
   ii. 26 units?
   Draw the appropriate figures.
   c. What is the greatest possible perimeter of a figure made of unit squares whose area is *n* square units?
   ★d. What is the least possible area of a figure made of unit squares whose perimeter is 2*n* units long?

**TECHNOLOGY
CORNER**

Use a geometry utility such as "Geometer's Sketchpad" to explore area concepts such as the following:

1. Complete each of the following:
   a. Construct a segment and label the endpoints *A* and *B*.
   b. Choose a point not on $\overline{AB}$ and label it *C*.
   c. Select $\overline{AB}$ and the point *C* and construct a line through *C* parallel to $\overline{AB}$.
   d. Choose a point on the new line and label it *D*.
   e. Select points *A* and *D* and construct a segment connecting points *A* and *D*.
   f. Select $\overline{AD}$ and point *B* and construct a line through *B* parallel to $\overline{AD}$.
   g. Select the two constructed lines. Construct the point at their intersection and label it *E*.
   h. Select the vertices (*E, D, A, B*) and construct the interior of the polygon.
   i. Measure the area of the polygon.
   j. Select ∠*DAB* and measure the angle.
   k. Move point *D* along $\overleftrightarrow{DC}$ and find the area of all the new parallelograms formed by *D, C, B,* and *A*. How are the areas related?
   l. How does this activity lead to the formula for finding the area of a parallelogram if you know how to find the area of a rectangle?

2. Complete each of the following:
   a. Repeat steps (a) through (d) from part 1.

b. Select points *A*, *B*, and *D* and construct segments connecting these points to form a triangle.

c. Select the vertices *A*, *D*, and *B* and construct the interior of the polygon.

d. Measure the area of △*ADB*.

e. Move point *D* along $\overrightarrow{DC}$ and find the area of all the triangles that are formed by *A*, *D*, and *B*.

f. How do these areas compare with the area of the original triangle?

g. How can this activity be used to motivate the formula for finding the area of a triangle?

3. Take your triangle and line in 2(b) and add a line through *B* parallel to $\overline{AD}$ to form a parallelogram. Find the area of the parallelogram and compare it to the area of the triangle. How can this activity be used to motivate the formula for finding the area of a triangle?

4. Devise a way to motivate the formula for finding the area of a trapezoid using the geometry utility.

LABORATORY ACTIVITY

As van Hiele Level 2 activities, answer the following without using any area formulas:

1. On a 5 × 5 geoboard, make △*DEF* as shown in Figure 12-23. Keep the rubber band around *D* and *E* fixed and move the vertex *F* to all the possible locations so that the triangles formed will have the same area as the area of △*DEF*. How do the locations for the third vertex relate to *D* and *E*?

Figure 12-23

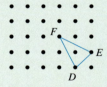

2. On a 5 × 5 geoboard, construct, if possible, squares of areas 1, 2, 3, 4, 5, 6, and 7 square units.

3. On a 5 × 5 geoboard, construct triangles that have areas $\frac{1}{2}$, 1, $1\frac{1}{2}$, 2, . . . , until the maximum-sized triangle is reached.

BRAIN TEASER

The rectangle in Figure 12-24(b) was apparently formed by cutting the square in Figure 12-24(a) along the dotted lines and reassembling the pieces as pictured.

1. What is the area of the square in (a)?

2. What is the area of the rectangle in (b)?

3. How do you explain the discrepancy between the areas?

Figure 12-24

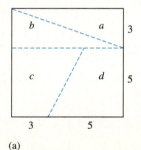

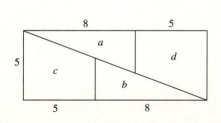

(a)   (b)

Section 12-2 The Pythagorean Theorem

Surveyors often have to calculate distances that cannot be measured directly such as horizontal distances on mountain sides or distances across water, as illustrated in Figure 12-25.

Figure 12-25

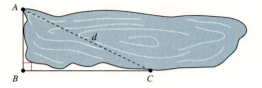

To accomplish these measurements, they use one of the most remarkable and useful theorems in geometry: the Pythagorean Theorem. This theorem was illustrated on a Greek stamp in 1955, as shown in Figure 12-26, to honor the 2500th anniversary of the founding of the Pythagorean School.

Figure 12-26

hypotenuse
legs

In the triangle on the stamp, the side opposite the right angle is the **hypotenuse.** The other two sides are **legs.** Interpreted in terms of area, the Pythagorean Theorem states that the area of a square with the hypotenuse of a right triangle as a side is equal to the sum of the areas of the squares with the legs as sides.

H I S T O R I C A L   N O T E

Pythagoras (ca. 582–507 B.C.), a Greek philosopher and mathematician, was head of a group known as the Pythagoreans. Members of the group regarded Pythagoras as a demigod and attributed all their discoveries to him. The Pythagoreans believed in the transmigration of the soul from one body to another. One of Pythagoras's most unusual discoveries was the dependence of the musical intervals on the ratio of the length of strings at the same tension, with the ratio 2:1 giving the octave, 3:2 the fifth, and 4:3 the fourth.

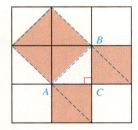

Figure 12-27

Because the Pythagoreans affirmed geometric results on the basis of special cases, mathematical historians believe it is possible they may have discovered the theorem by looking at a floor tiling like the one illustrated in Figure 12-27.

Each square can be divided by its diagonal into two congruent isosceles right triangles, so we see that the shaded square constructed with $\overline{AB}$ as a side consists of four triangles, each congruent to $\triangle ABC$. Similarly, each of the shaded squares with legs $\overline{BC}$ and $\overline{AC}$ as sides consists of two triangles congruent to $\triangle ABC$. Thus the area of the larger square is equal to the sum of the areas of the two smaller squares. The theorem is true in general and is stated as follows using Figure 12-28.

Figure 12-28

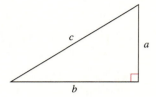

Theorem 12-1

Pythagorean Theorem: If a right triangle has legs of lengths a and b and hypotenuse of length c, then $c^2 = a^2 + b^2$.

There are hundreds of known proofs for the Pythagorean Theorem. The classic book *The Pythagorean Proposition,* by E. Loomis, contains many of these proofs. Some proofs involve the strategy of *drawing diagrams* with a square area c^2 equal to the sum of the areas a^2 and b^2 of two other squares. One such proof is given in Figure 12-29; others are discussed in Ongoing Assessment 12-2. In Figure 12-29(a), the measures of the legs of a right triangle *ABC* are a and b and the measure of the hypotenuse is c. We draw a square with sides of length $a + b$ and subdivide it, as shown in Figure 12-29(b). In Figure 12-29(c), another square with side of length $a + b$ is drawn and each of its sides is divided into two segments of length a and b, as shown.

Figure 12-29

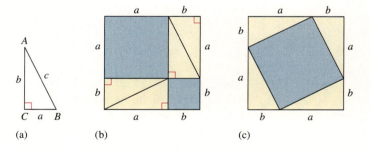

Each yellow triangle is congruent to $\triangle ABC$ (why?). Consequently, each triangle has hypotenuse c and the same area, $\frac{1}{2}ab$. Thus the length of each side of the inside gray quadrilateral in Figure 12-29(c) is c and so the figure is a rhombus. In fact, it is possible to show that the figure is a square whose area is c^2. To complete the proof, we consider the four triangles in Figure 12-29(b) and (c). Because the areas of the sets of four triangles in both Figure 12-29(b) and (c) are equal, the sum of the areas of the two shaded squares in Figure 12-29(b) equals the area of the shaded square in Figure 12-29(c), that is, $a^2 + b^2 = c^2$.

INVESTIGATION   12 - 6

● Henry Perigal, a London stockbroker, discovered what has been called the "paper and scissors" proof of the Pythagorean Theorem. It is illustrated in Figure 12-30. Explain how this figure could be used to justify the theorem.   ●

Figure 12-30

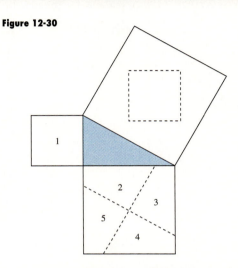

Example 12-7 | For each drawing in Figure 12-31, find the value of x.

Figure 12-31

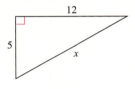

(a)   (b)

Rectangle

Solution   **a.** By the Pythagorean Theorem:

$$5^2 + 12^2 = x^2$$
$$25 + 144 = x^2$$
$$169 = x^2$$
$$13 = x$$

b. In the rectangle, the diagonal partitions the rectangle into two right triangles, each with lengths 5 units and width x units. Thus we have the following:

$$5^2 + x^2 = 7^2$$
$$25 + x^2 = 49$$
$$x^2 = 24$$
$$x = \sqrt{24}, \text{ or approximately 4.9 units.}$$

Example 12-8

The size of a rectangular television screen is given as the length of the diagonal of the screen. If the length of the screen is 24 cm and the width is 18 cm, as shown in Figure 12-32, what is the diagonal length?

Figure 12-32

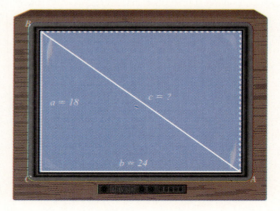

Solution   A right triangle is formed with the diagonal as the hypotenuse and the legs of measure 24 cm and 18 cm. The Pythagorean Theorem can be used to find the length of the diagonal.

$$c^2 = 18^2 + 24^2$$
$$c^2 = 324 + 576$$
$$c^2 = 900$$
$$c = 30$$

Because all the measurements are in centimeters, the diagonal has length 30 cm.

When using the Pythagorean Theorem, we must work with a right triangle. At times, though, the segment whose length we want to find may not be a side of any known right triangle. The following examples deal with such situations.

Example 12-9

A pole $\overline{BD}$, 28 ft high, is perpendicular to the ground. Two wires $\overline{BC}$ and $\overline{BA}$, each 35 ft long, are attached to the top of the pole and to stakes A and C on the ground, as shown in Figure 12-33. If points A, D, and C are collinear, how far are the stakes A and C from each other?

Figure 12-33

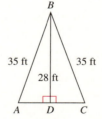

Solution $\overline{AC}$ is not a side in any known right triangle, but we want to find AC. Because a point equidistant from the endpoints of a segment must be on a perpendicular bisector of the segment, then $AD = DC$. Therefore AC is twice as long as DC. Now, we have a *subgoal* of finding DC. We may find DC by applying the Pythagorean Theorem in triangle BDC. This results in the following:

$$28^2 + (DC)^2 = 35^2$$
$$(DC)^2 = 35^2 - 28^2$$
$$DC = \sqrt{441}, \text{ or } 21 \text{ ft}$$
$$AC = 2 \cdot DC = 42 \text{ ft}$$

• • •

Example 12-10   How tall is the Great Pyramid of Cheops, a right regular square pyramid, if the base has a side 775 ft and the slant height is 608 ft?

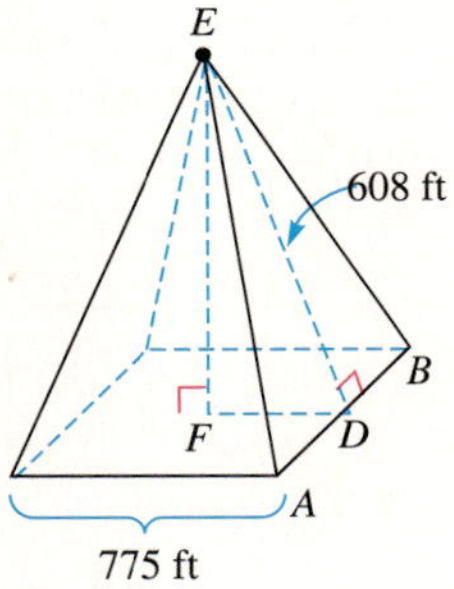

Solution   In Figure 12-34, $\overline{EF}$ is a leg of a right triangle formed by $\overline{FD}$, $\overline{EF}$, and $\overline{ED}$. Because the pyramid is a right regular pyramid, $\overline{EF}$ intersects the base at its center. Thus $DF = \left(\dfrac{1}{2}\right)AB$, or $\left(\dfrac{1}{2}\right)775$, or 387.5 ft. Now ED, the slant height, has length 608 ft, and we can apply the Pythagorean Theorem as follows:

$$(EF)^2 + (DF)^2 = (ED)^2$$
$$(EF)^2 + (387.5)^2 = (608)^2$$
$$(EF)^2 = 219{,}507.75$$
$$EF \doteq 468.5 \text{ ft}$$

Thus the Great Pyramid is 468.5 ft tall.

Figure 12-34

E

608 ft

B

F   D

A

775 ft

• • •

Special Right Triangles

An isosceles right triangle has two legs of equal length and two 45° angles. Any such triangle is a **45°-45°-90° right triangle.** Drawing a diagonal of a square forms two of these triangles, as shown in Figure 12-35.

45°-45°-90° right triangle

Figure 12-35

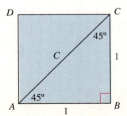

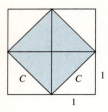

Figure 12-36

In Figure 12-36, we see several 45°-45°-90° triangles. Each side of the shaded square is a hypotenuse of a 45°-45°-90° triangle. The area of the shaded square is 2 square units (why?). Therefore $c^2 = 2$ and $c = \sqrt{2}$. Another way to see that $c = \sqrt{2}$ is to apply the Pythagoren Theorem on one of the nonshaded triangles. Because $c^2 = 1^2 + 1^2 = 2$, then $c = \sqrt{2}$.

In the isosceles right triangle pictured in Figure 12-35, each leg is 1 unit long and the hypotenuse is $\sqrt{2}$ units long. This property is generalized when the isosceles right triangle has a leg of length a, as follows.

Property

Property of 45°-45°-90° Triangle: In an isosceles right triangle, if the length of each leg is a, then the hypotenuse has length $a\sqrt{2}$.

Similarly, the following student page from *Addison-Wesley Mathematics,* Grade 8, 1993, shows that a 30°-60°-90° triangle is half of an equilateral triangle. When the equilateral triangle has side 2 units long, then in the 30°-60°-90° triangle, the leg opposite the 30° angle is 1 unit long and the leg opposite the 60° angle has a length of $\sqrt{3}$.

This example may also be generalized using the triangle in Figure 12-37. When the side of the equilateral triangle ABC is $2s$, then in triangle ABD, the side opposite the 30° angle, $\overline{BD}$, is s units long, and AD may be found using the Pythagorean Theorem to have a length of $s\sqrt{3}$ units. This discussion is generalized in the following property.

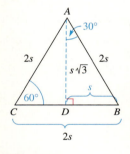

Figure 12-37

Property

Property of 30°-60°-90° Triangle: In a 30°-60°-90° triangle, the length of the hypotenuse is two times as long as the leg opposite the 30° angle and the leg opposite the 60° angle is $\sqrt{3}$ times the shorter leg.

Converse of the Pythagorean Theorem

The converse of the Pythagorean Theorem is also true. It provided a useful way for early surveyors, sometimes called Egyptian rope stretchers, to determine right angles. Figure 12-38(a) shows a knotted rope with 12 equally spaced knots. Figure 12-38(b) shows how the rope might be held to form a triangle with sides of lengths 3, 4, and 5. The triangle formed is a right triangle and contains a 90° angle.

Figure 12-38

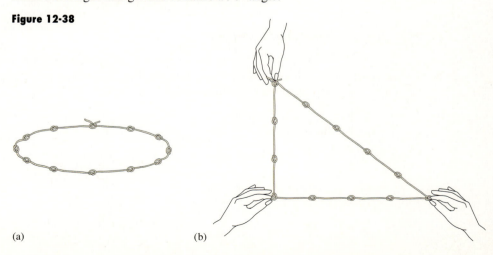

(a)   (b)

30°–60° Right Triangles

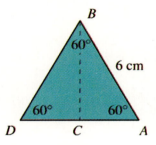

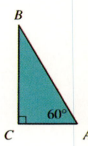

LEARN ABOUT IT

EXPLORE Copy the Triangle
Work in groups. Copy and cut out equilateral triangle *ABD*. Fold the triangle along its line of symmetry. $\overline{BC}$.

TALK ABOUT IT

1. How long is $\overline{AC}$ if the length of each side of △*ABD* is 6 cm?

2. How does m ∠*ABC* compare to m ∠*ABD*? Why is △*ABC* called a 30°–60° right triangle?

In any **30°–60° right triangle,** the length of the leg opposite the 30° angle is half the length of the hypotenuse.

Using this fact and applying the Pythagorean Relationship to the triangles below, we can make the following conclusion.

$$z^2 + 1^2 = 2^2$$
$$z^2 = 2^2 - 1^2 = 4 - 1 = 3$$
$$z = \sqrt{3}$$

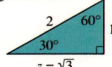

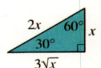

In any 30°–60° right triangle, the length of the leg opposite the 60° angle is $\sqrt{3}$ times the length of the leg opposite the 30° angle.

Example Find the lengths *x* and *y* of the legs of this triangle.

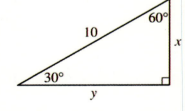

x is half the length of the hypotenuse, so $x = \frac{10}{2} = 5$.

y is $\sqrt{3}$ times *x*, so $y = 5 \cdot \sqrt{3}$.

Given a triangle with sides of lengths *a*, *b*, and *c* such that $a^2 + b^2 = c^2$, must the triangle be a right triangle? The answer is yes, and we state the following theorem without proof.

Theorem 12-2

Converse of the Pythagorean Theorem: If $\triangle ABC$ is a triangle with sides of lengths a, b, and c such that $a^2 + b^2 = c^2$, then $\triangle ABC$ is a right triangle with the right angle opposite the side of length c.

Example 12-11

Determine whether the following can be the lengths of the sides of a right triangle:

a. 51, 68, 85   **b.** 2, 3, $\sqrt{13}$ **c.** 3, 4, 7

Solution
a. $51^2 + 68^2 = 7225 = 85^2$, so 51, 68, and 85 can be the lengths of the sides of a right triangle.
b. $2^2 + 3^2 = 4 + 9 = 13 = (\sqrt{13})^2$, so 2, 3, and $\sqrt{13}$ can be the lengths of the sides of a right triangle.
c. $3^2 + 4^2 \neq 7^2$, so the measures cannot be the lengths of the sides of a right triangle. In fact, since $3 + 4 = 7$, these segments do not form a triangle.

INVESTIGATION 12-7

a. Draw three segments that could be used to form the sides of a right triangle and discuss how you would show that these three lengths determine a right triangle.
b. Multiply the lengths of the three segments in (a) by a fixed number and determine if the

resulting three lengths could be sides of a right triangle.
c. Repeat the experiment in (a) and (b) using three new numbers. Form a conjecture based on your experiments.

The Distance Formula

Given the coordinates of two points A and B, we can find the distance AB. We first consider the special case in which the 2 points are on one of the axes. For example, in Figure 12-39, $A(2, 0)$ and $B(5, 0)$ are on the x-axis. The distance between these two points is 3 units:

$$AB = OB - OA = 5 - 2 = 3$$

Figure 12-39

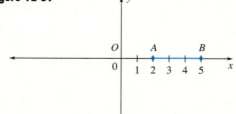

(a)   (b)

In general, if two points P and Q are on the x-axis, as in Figure 12-39(b), with x-coordinates x_1 and x_2, respectively, and $x_2 > x_1$, then $PQ = x_2 - x_1$. In fact, *the distance between two points on the x-axis is always the absolute value of the difference between the x-coordinates of the points* (why?). A similar result holds for any two points on the y-axis.

Figure 12-40 shows two points in the plane: $C(2, 5)$ and $D(6, 8)$. The distance between C and D can be found by using the strategy of *looking at a related problem.* We know how to find the length of a segment if the segment is a side or the hypotenuse of a right triangle. We obtain a right triangle by drawing perpendiculars from the points to the x-axis and to the y-axis, respectively, thus defining triangle CDE. The lengths of the legs of triangle CDE are found by using horizontal and vertical distances and properties of rectangles.

$$CE = |6 - 2| = 4$$
$$DE = |8 - 5| = 3$$

Figure 12-40

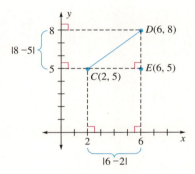

The distance between C and D can be found by applying the Pythagorean Theorem to the triangle.

$$CD^2 = DE^2 + CE^2$$
$$= 3^2 + 4^2$$
$$= 25$$
$$CD = \sqrt{25}, \text{ or } 5$$

The method can be generalized to find a formula for the distance between any two points $A(x_1, y_1)$ and $B(x_2, y_2)$. Construct a right triangle with $\overline{AB}$ as one of its sides by drawing a segment through A parallel to the x-axis and a segment through B parallel to the y-axis, as shown in Figure 12-41. The lines containing the segments intersect at point C, thus forming right triangle ABC. Now, apply the Pythagorean Theorem.

Figure 12-41

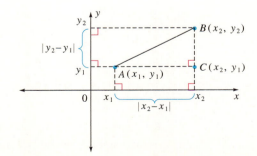

In Figure 12-41, we see that $AC = |x_2 - x_1|$ and $BC = |y_2 - y_1|$. By the Pythagorean Theorem, $(AB)^2 = |x_2 - x_1|^2 + |y_2 - y_1|^2$, and consequently $AB = \sqrt{|x_2 - x_1|^2 + |y_2 - y_1|^2}$. Because $|x_2 - x_1|^2 = (x_2 - x_1)^2$ and $|y_2 - y_1|^2 = (y_2 - y_1)^2$, $AB = \sqrt{(x_2 - x_1)^2 + (y_2 - y_1)^2}$.

distance formula   This result is known as the **distance formula.**

Distance Formula

The distance between the points $A(x_1, y_1)$ and $B(x_2, y_2)$ is given by

$$AB = \sqrt{(x_2 - x_1)^2 + (y_2 - y_1)^2}.$$

I N V E S T I G A T I O N   1 2 - 8

● Investigate whether it makes any difference in the distance formula if $(x_1 - x_2)$ and $(y_1 - y_2)$ are used instead of $(x_2 - x_1)$ and $(y_2 - y_1)$, respectively. ●

Example 12-12   For each of the following, determine the distance between P and Q:

a. $P(2, 7)$, $Q(3, 5)$
b. $P(0, 0)$, $Q(3, {}^{-}4)$

Solution   **a.** $PQ = \sqrt{(3 - 2)^2 + (5 - 7)^2} = \sqrt{1 + 4} = \sqrt{5}$

b. $PQ = \sqrt{(0 - 3)^2 + [0 - ({}^{-}4)]^2} = \sqrt{9 + 16} = \sqrt{25} = 5$

Example 12-13   **a.** Show that $A(7, 4)$, $B({}^{-}2, 1)$, and $C(10, {}^{-}5)$ are the vertices of an isosceles triangle.
b. Show that $\triangle ABC$ in (a) is a right triangle.

Solution   **a.** Using the distance formula, we find the lengths of the sides.

$$AB = \sqrt{({}^{-}2 - 7)^2 + (1 - 4)^2} = \sqrt{({}^{-}9)^2 + ({}^{-}3)^2} = \sqrt{90}$$

$$BC = \sqrt{[10 - ({}^{-}2)]^2 + ({}^{-}5 - 1)^2} = \sqrt{12^2 + ({}^{-}6)^2} = \sqrt{180}$$

$$AC = \sqrt{(10 - 7)^2 + ({}^{-}5 - 4)^2} = \sqrt{3^2 + ({}^{-}9)^2} = \sqrt{90}$$

Thus $AB = AC$, and so the triangle is isosceles.
b. Because $(\sqrt{90})^2 + (\sqrt{90})^2 = (\sqrt{180})^2$, $\triangle ABC$ is a right triangle with $\overline{BC}$ as hypotenuse and $\overline{AB}$ and $\overline{AC}$ as legs.

Ongoing Assessment 12-2

1. a. In the following cartoon, is Hobbes's square really a square? Why?

   b. If Hobbes's figure in the second panel is a rectangle that is 6 units by 3 units, how long is y?

   c. If Hobbes draws a rectangle with each dimension doubled, how does the length of the diagonal change?

2. Use the Pythagorean theorem to find x in each of the following:

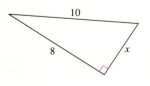

(a)

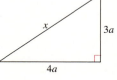

(b)

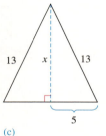

(c)

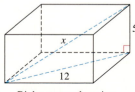

Equilateral triangle

(d)

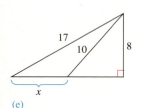

(e)

Right rectangular prism

(f)

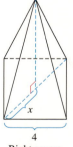

4

Right square pyramid

(g)

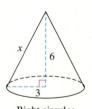

Right circular cone

(h)

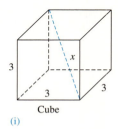

Cube

(i)

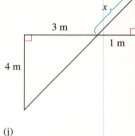

(j)

3. If the hypotenuse of a right triangle is 30 cm long and one leg is twice as long as the other, how long are the legs of the triangle?

4. For each of the following, determine whether the given numbers represent lengths of sides of a right triangle:

   a. 10, 24, 16

   b. 16, 34, 30

   c. $\sqrt{2}, \sqrt{2}, 2$

   d. 2, $\sqrt{3}$, 1

   e. $\sqrt{2}\sqrt{3}, \sqrt{5}$

   f. $\frac{3}{2}, \frac{4}{2}, \frac{5}{2}$

5. What is the longest line segment that can be drawn in a right rectangular prism that is 12 cm wide, 15 cm long, and 9 cm high?

6. Two airplanes depart from the same place at 2:00 P.M. One plane flies south at a speed of 376 km/hr, and the other flies west at a speed of 648 km/hr. How far apart are the airplanes at 5:30 P.M.?

7. Starting from point A, a boat sails due south for 6 mi, then due east for 5 mi, and then due south for 4 mi. How far is the boat from A?

8. A 15-ft ladder is leaning against a wall. The base of the ladder is 3 ft from the wall. How high above the ground is the top of the ladder?

9. In the following figure, two poles are 25 m and 15 m high. A cable 14 m long joins the tops of the poles. Find the distance between the poles.

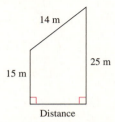

10. Find the area of each of the following:

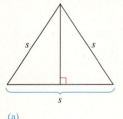

(a)   (b)

11. For each of the following, solve for the unknowns:

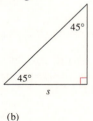

(a)   (b)

12. A builder needs to calculate the dimensions of a regular hexagonal window. Assuming the altitude CD of the window is 1.3 m, find the width AB (O is the midpoint of $\overline{AB}$) in the following figure:

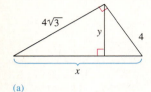

13. The length of the diagonal $\overline{AC}$ of a rhombus ABCD is 20 cm. The distance between $\overline{AB}$ and $\overline{DC}$ is 12 cm. Find the length of the sides of the rhombus and the length of the other diagonal.

14. If $\overline{AB}$, a diameter of circle O, has length 10 cm, point C is on circle O, and AC is 6 cm, how long is $\overline{BC}$?

15. Georgette wants to put a diagonal brace on a gate that is 3 ft wide and 5 ft high. If she uses a board that is 6 in. wide and 8 ft long, how much will she have left?

16. If a third baseman on the base throws to first base, how far is the ball thrown? (*Hint:* The distance from home plate to first base is 90 ft.)

17. What is the longest piece of straight spaghetti that will fit in a cylindrical can that has a radius of 2 in. and height of 10 in.?

18. If possible, draw a square with the given number of square units on a geoboard grid. (You will have to draw your own geoboard grid.)
    a. 5
    b. 7
    c. 8
    d. 14
    e. 15

19. Use the following drawing to prove the Pythagorean Theorem by using corresponding parts of similar triangles △ACD, △CBD, and △ABC. Lengths of sides are indicated by a, b, c, x, and y. (*Hint:* Show that $b^2 = cx$ and $a^2 = cy$.)

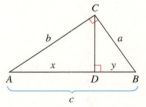

20. An access ramp enters a building 1 m above ground level and starts 3 m from the building. How long is the ramp?

21. To make a homeplate for a neighborhood baseball park, we can cut the plate from a square, as shown in the following figure. If A, B, and C are midpoints of the sides of the square, what are the dimensions of the square to the nearest tenth of an inch?

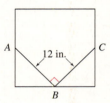

22. A company wants to lay cable across a lake. To find the length of the lake, they made the following measurements. What is the length of the lake?

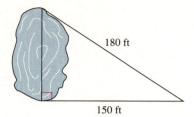

180 ft

150 ft

23. A CB radio station *C* is located 3 mi from the interstate highway *h*. The station has a range of 6.1 mi in all directions from the station. If the interstate is along a straight line, how many miles of highway are in the range of this station?

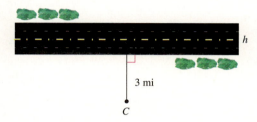

h

3 mi

C

24. Before James Garfield was elected president of the United States, he discovered a proof of the Pythagorean Theorem. He formed a trapezoid like the one that follows and found the area of the trapezoid in two different ways. Can you discover his proof?

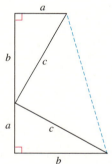

a

b

c

a

c

b

25. Use the following figure to prove the Pythagorean Theorem by first proving that the quadrilateral with side *c* is a square. Then, compute the area of the square with side $a + b$ in two different ways: (a) as $(a + b)^2$ and (b) as the sum of the areas of the 4 triangles and the square with side *c*.

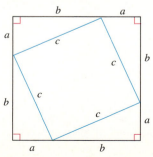

b *a*

a

c

c

b

c

b

c

a

a *b*

26. Construct semicircles on right triangle *ABC* with $\overline{AB}$, $\overline{BC}$, and $\overline{AC}$ as diameters. Is the area of the semicircle on the hypotenuse equal to the sum of the areas of the semicircles on the legs?

27. On each side of a right triangle, construct an equilateral triangle. Is the area of the triangle constructed on the hypotenuse always equal to the sum of the areas of the triangles constructed on the legs?

28. For each of the following, find the length of $\overline{AB}$:
   a. $A(0, 3)$, $B(0, 7)$
   b. $A(0, 3)$, $B(4, 0)$
   c. $A(^-1, 2)$, $B(3, ^-4)$
   d. $A(4, ^-5)$, $B\left(\dfrac{1}{2}, \dfrac{^-7}{4}\right)$
   e. $A(5, 3)$, $B(5, ^-2)$

29. Find the perimeter of the triangle with vertices at $A(0, 0)$, $B(^-4, ^-3)$, and $C(^-5, 0)$.

30. Show that $(0, 6)$, $(^-3, 0)$, and $(9, ^-6)$ are the vertices of a right triangle.

31. Show that the triangle whose vertices are $A(^-2, ^-5)$, $B(1, ^-1)$, and $C(5, 2)$ is isosceles.

32. Find *x* if the distance between $P(1, 3)$ and $Q(x, 9)$ is 10 units.

33. If the hypotenuse in a 30°-60°-90° triangle is $c/2$ units, what is the length of the side opposite the 60° angle? Explain your answer.

Communication

34. Given the following square, describe how to use a compass and a straightedge to construct a square whose area is as follows:
   a. Twice the area of the given square
   b. Half the area of the given square

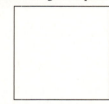

35. What does it mean if a sign marking an incline on a highway says 6% grade?

36. If the hypotenuse and a leg of one right triangle are congruent to the hypotenuse and a leg of another right triangle, respectively, must the triangles be congruent? Explain.

37. Gail tried the Egyptian method of using a knotted rope to determine a right angle so that she could build a shed. She placed her knots so that each was 1 ft from the next. She stretched out her rope in the form of a triangle whose sides were of lengths 5, 12, and 13 ft. Did she have a right angle? Explain why or why not.

Open-ended

38. Draw several different kinds of triangles including a right triangle. Draw a square on each of the sides of the triangles.

Compute the areas of the squares and use this information to investigate whether the Pythagorean Theorem works for only right triangles. Use a geometry utility if available.

39. Find an application from real life in which knowing the Pythagorean Theorem would be useful. Write a problem about the application to share with the class.

40. Pythagorean triples are three natural numbers *a, b,* and *c* that satisfy the relationship $a^2 + b^2 = c^2$. The least three numbers that are Pythagorean triples are 3-4-5. Another triple is 5-12-13 because $5^2 + 12^2 = 13^2$.

  a. Find two other Pythagorean triples.

  b. Does doubling each number in a Pythagorean triple result in a new Pythagorean triple? Why or why not?

  c. Does adding a fixed number to each number in a Pythagorean triple result in a new Pythagorean triple? Why or why not?

  d. Suppose $a = 2uv$, $b = u^2 - v^2$, and $c = u^2 + v^2$, where *u* and *v* are whole numbers. Determine whether *a-b-c* is a Pythagorean triple.

Cooperative Learning

41. There are over 300 different proofs of the Pythagorean Theorem. Have each person in the group find a proof not given in the text and present the proof to the group. Decide on your favorite proof and be prepared to present it to the class.

42. Have each person in the group use a 1-m string to make a different right triangle. Measure each side to the nearest centimeter. Use these measurements to see if the Pythagorean Theorem holds for your measurements. If not, explain why the results may not be exact.

Review Problems

43. Arrange the following in decreasing order: 3.2 m, 322 cm, 0.032 km, 3.020 mm.

44. Find the area of each of the following figures:

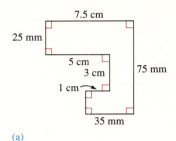

(a)

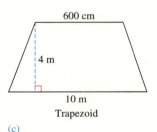

(b)

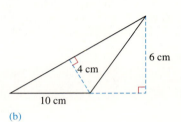

Trapezoid

(c)

45. Complete the following table, which concerns circles:

	Radius	Diameter	Circumference	Area
a.	5 cm			
b.		24 cm		
c.				17π m^2
d.			20π cm	

46. A 10-m wire is wrapped around a circular region. If the wire fits exactly, what is the area of the region?

BRAIN TEASER   A spider is sitting at *A*, the midpoint of the edge of the ceiling in the room shown in Figure 12-42. It spies a fly on the floor at *C*, the midpoint of the edge of the floor. If the spider must walk along the wall, ceiling, or floor, what is the length of the shortest path the spider can travel to reach the fly?

Figure 12-42

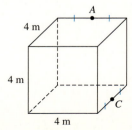

**LABORATORY
ACTIVITY**

As a van Hiele Level 1 activity, consider the drawings in Figure 12-43. Without using formulas, check whether the area of the square constructed on the hypotenuse of the shaded right triangle equals the sum of the areas of the squares constructed on the legs of the triangle.

Figure 12-43

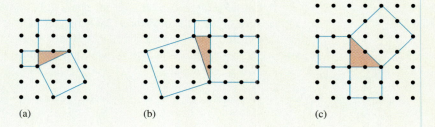

(a)   (b)   (c)

**TECHNOLOGY
CORNER**

Use a geometry utility to determine the relationship between the length of the hypotenuse of a 45°-45°-90° triangle and the length of a leg.

a. Construct a 45°-45°-90° triangle, label the vertices as in the following figure, and measure the lengths of the sides. Record the data for triangle 1 in the following table and compute the ratio.

	AC	CB	AB	AB/CB
Triangle 1				
Triangle 2				
Triangle 3				
Triangle 4				

b. Repeat (a) for three other triangles.
c. Make a conjecture about the relationship between the length of the hypotenuse and the length of a leg for these triangles.
d. Given a 30°-60°-90° triangle, determine the relationship between the lengths of the hypotenuse and the shorter leg and the relationships between the lengths of the longer and shorter legs.

Section 12-3   Surface Areas

Painting houses, buying roofing, seal-coating driveways, and buying carpet are among the common applications that involve computing areas. In many real-world problems, we must find the surface areas of such three-dimensional figures as prisms, cylinders, pyramids, cones, and spheres. Formulas for finding these areas are usually based on finding the area of two-dimensional pieces of the three-dimensional figures. In this section, we use the notion of a **net,** a two-dimensional pattern that can be used to construct three-dimensional figures, to aid in determining surface areas of the figures.

net

Surface Area of Right Prisms

Consider the cereal box from the following student page from *Addison-Wesley Mathematics*, Grade 8, 1993. To find the amount of cardboard necessary to make the box, we cut the box along the edges and make it lie flat. We obtain a net and see that the box is composed of a series of rectangles. We find the area of each rectangle and sum those areas to find the surface area of the box.

A similar process can be used for many three-dimensional figures. For example, the surface area of the cube in Figure 12-44(a) is the sum of the areas of the faces of the cube. Because each of the six faces is a square of area 16 cm^2, the surface area is $6 \cdot (16$ cm$^2)$, or 96 cm^2, or in general, for a cube whose edge is e units, the surface area is $6e^2$.

Figure 12-44

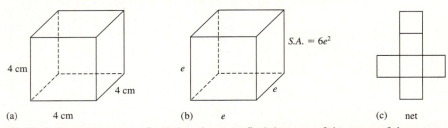

$S.A. = 6e^2$

(a)   4 cm   (b) e (c)   net

To find the surface area of a right prism, we find the sum of the areas of the rectangles that make up the lateral faces and the areas of the top and bottom. The sum of the areas of

lateral surface area • the lateral faces is the **lateral surface area.** The **surface area** (*S.A.*) is the sum of the lat-

surface area   eral surface area and the area of the bases.

I N V E S T I G A T I O N   1 2 - 9

● Figure 12-45 shows a right pentagonal prism with a net for the prism. If B stands for the area of each of the prism's bases, then show that the surface area of the prism could be computed as $S.A. = ph + 2B$, where p is the perimeter of the base of the prism and h is the height. Does this formula hold for all right prisms? Why or why not? ●

Figure 12-45

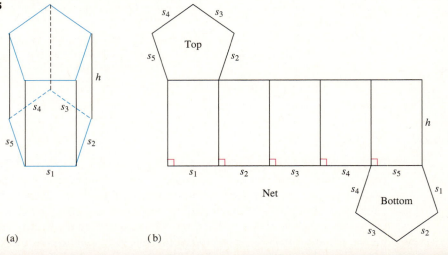

(a)   (b)

Surface Area

LEARN ABOUT IT

EXPLORE Analyze the Situation

Eileen Monaghan is a designer of cereal boxes which are made by folding a single piece of cardboard. She needs to decide what size rectangle is needed to make one box. What size piece would you order?

TALK ABOUT IT

1. What is the area of the front of the box?

2. Can the box be made from a 21 in. × 12 in. piece of cardboard?

3. What is the total area of all six pieces of the box?

The total area of the cut apart box is called the **surface area** of the box. In a similar way we define the surface area of any **space figure** or **solid** such as a prism, a cylinder and a pyramid. Imagine cutting each apart and laying it flat. This process is demonstrated for the cylinder.

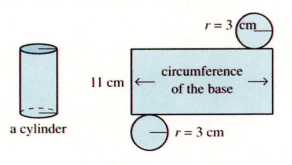

Area of each circle $= \pi \cdot 3^2 \approx 28.26$ cm^2
Area of the rectangle $= 2\pi \cdot 3 \cdot 11$
≈ 207.24 cm^2
Surface Area $\approx 2 \cdot 28.26 + 207.24$
$= 263.76$ cm^2

Example 12-14   Find the surface area of each of the right prisms in Figure 12-46.

Figure 12-46

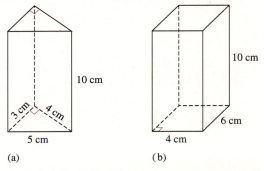

(a)   (b)

Solution   **a.** Each base is a right triangle. The area of the bases is $2(1/2 \cdot 3 \cdot 4)$, or 12 cm^2. The area of the three lateral faces is $4 \cdot 10 + 3 \cdot 10 + 5 \cdot 10$, or 120 cm^2. Thus the surface area is $12 \text{ cm}^2 + 120 \text{ cm}^2$, or 132 cm^2.

b. The area of the bases is $2(4 \cdot 6)$, or 48 cm^2. The lateral surface area is $2 \cdot (10 \cdot 6) + 2 \cdot (4 \cdot 10)$, or 200 cm^2. Thus the surface area is 248 cm^2.

Surface Area of a Cylinder

To find the surface area of the right circular cylinder shown in Figure 12-47, we cut off the bases and slice the lateral surface open by cutting along any line perpendicular to the bases. Such a slice is shown as a dotted segment in Figure 12-47(a). Then we unroll the cylinder to form a rectangle, as shown in Figure 12-47(b). To find the total surface area, we find the area of the rectangle and the areas of the top and bottom circles. The length of the rectangle is the circumference of the circular base $2\pi r$, and its width is the height of the cylinder h. Hence, the area of the rectangle is $2\pi rh$. The area of each base is πr^2. Because the surface area is the sum of the areas of the two circular bases and the lateral surface area, we have

$$S.A. = 2\pi r^2 + 2\pi rh.$$

Figure 12-47

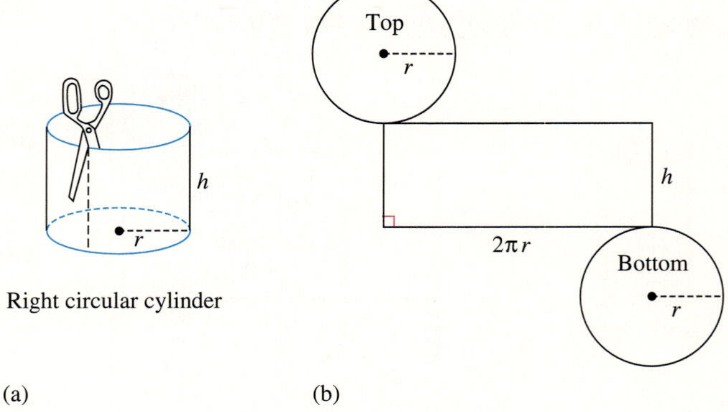

Right circular cylinder

(a)   (b)

Surface Area of a Pyramid

The surface area of a pyramid is the sum of the lateral surface area of the pyramid and the area of the base. A right regular pyramid is a pyramid such that the segments connecting the apex to each vertex of the base are congruent and the base is a regular polygon. The lateral faces of the right regular pyramid pictured in Figure 12-48 are congruent triangles. Each triangle has an altitude of length ℓ, called the *slant height*. Because the pyramid is right regular, each side of the base has the same length b. To find the lateral surface area of a right regular pyramid, we need to find the area of one face $\frac{1}{2}b\ell$ and multiply it by n, the number of faces. Adding the lateral surface area $n\left(\frac{1}{2}b\ell\right)$ to the area of the base B gives the surface area.

Figure 12-48

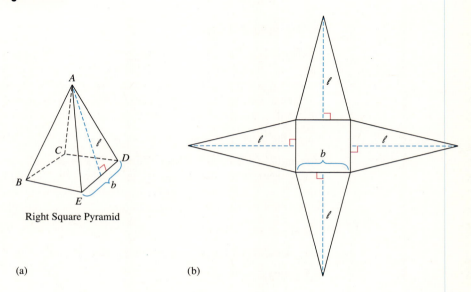

Right Square Pyramid

(a)   (b)

• • •

Example 12-15   Find the surface area of the right regular pyramid in Figure 12-49.

Solution   The surface area consists of the area of the square base plus the area of the four triangular faces. Hence, the surface area is

$$4 \text{ cm} \cdot 4 \text{ cm} + 4 \cdot \left(\frac{1}{2} \cdot 4 \text{ cm} \cdot 5 \text{ cm}\right) = 16 \text{ cm}^2 + 40 \text{ cm}^2$$
$$= 56 \text{ cm}^2.$$

• • •

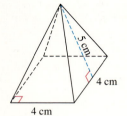

Figure 12-49

• • •

Example 12-16   The Great Pyramid of Egypt is a right square pyramid with a height of 148 m and a square base with perimeter of 930 m. The altitude of each triangular face is 188 m. The basic shape of the Transamerica Building in San Francisco is a right square pyramid that has a height of 260 m and a square base with a perimeter of 140 m. The altitude of each triangular face is 261 m. How do the lateral surface areas of the two structures compare?

Solution   The length of one side of the square base of the Great Pyramid is $\frac{930}{4}$, or 232.5, m. Likewise the length of one side of the square base of the Transamerica Building is 35 m. The lateral surface area (*L.S.A.*) of the two are computed below.

(Great Pyramid) $L.S.A. = 4 \cdot (1/2 \cdot 232.5 \cdot 188) = 87{,}420 \text{ m}^2$

(Transamerica) $L.S.A. = 4 \cdot (1/2 \cdot 35 \cdot 261) = 18{,}270 \text{ m}^2$

Therefore the lateral surface area of the Great Pyramid is approximately 4.8 times greater than that of the Transamerica Building.

• • •

Surface Area of a Cone

It is possible to find a formula for the surface area of a cone by approximating the cone with a pyramid. As shown in Figure 12-50, we inscribe in the circular base of the cone a regular polygon with many sides. The polygon can be used as the base of a regular right pyramid. The lateral surface area of the pyramid is close to the lateral surface area of the cone. The greater the number of faces of the pyramid, the closer the surface area of the pyramid is to that of the cone. The lateral surface of the pyramid is $\frac{1}{2}p \cdot h$, where p is the perimeter of the base and h is the height of each triangle. With many sides in the pyramid, the perimeter of its base is close to the perimeter of the circle, $2\pi r$. The height of each triangle of the pyramid is close to the slant height ℓ, a segment that connects the vertex of the cone with a point on the circular base, as shown in Figure 12-50(b). Consequently, it is reasonable that the lateral surface of the cone becomes $\frac{1}{2} \cdot 2\pi r \cdot \ell$, or $\pi r \ell$. To find the total surface area of the cone, we add πr^2, the area of the base. Thus $S.A. = \pi r^2 + \pi r \ell$.

Figure 12-50

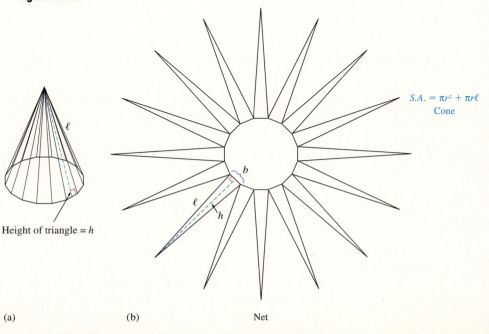

$S.A. = \pi r^2 + \pi r\ell$
Cone

Height of triangle = h

(a)   (b)   Net

• • •

Example 12-17   Given the cone in Figure 12-51, find the surface area of that cone.

5 cm

4 cm

3 cm

Right circular cone

Figure 12-51

Solution   The base of the cone is a circle with radius 3 cm and area $\pi(3 \text{ cm})^2$, or $9\pi \text{ cm}^2$. The lateral surface has area $\pi(3 \text{ cm})(5 \text{ cm})$, or $15\pi \text{ cm}^2$. Thus we have the following surface area:

$$S.A. = \pi(3 \text{ cm})^2 + \pi(3 \text{ cm})(5 \text{ cm})$$
$$= 9\pi \text{ cm}^2 + 15\pi \text{ cm}^2$$
$$= 24\pi \text{ cm}^2$$

• • •

Surface Area of a Sphere

Finding a formula for the surface area of a sphere is a simple task using calculus, but it is not easy in elementary mathematics. The surface area of a sphere is four times the area of a great circle of the sphere. Therefore the formula is $S.A. = 4\pi r^2$, as pictured in Figure 12-52.

Figure 12-52

$S.A. = 4\pi r^2$
Sphere

Create different cones from sectors of a circle. Use a compass to draw a sector of a circle whose diameter is almost as large as the width of a page of paper. Draw two such sectors that have the same radii but different central angles. In one sector, make the central angle have measure smaller than 180°, and in the other, make it have measure greater than 180°. Then make a cone from each sector by gluing the edges of each sector together. Can you predict which cone will be taller? Without performing the experiment, can you explain which cone will be taller?

Ongoing Assessment 12-3

1. Find the surface area of each of the following:

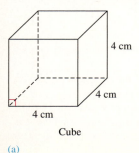

4 cm

4 cm

4 cm

Cube

(a)

6 cm

12 cm

Right circular cylinder

(b)

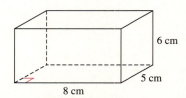

6 cm

5 cm

8 cm

Right rectangular prism

(c)

4 cm

Sphere

(d)

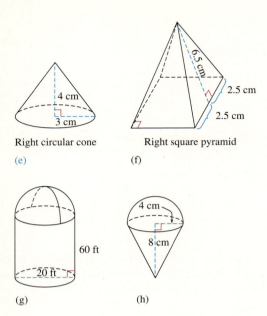

Right circular cone (e)

Right square pyramid (f)

60 ft

(g)

4 cm
8 cm

(h)

2. How many liters of paint are needed to paint the walls of a room that is 6 m × 4 m × 2.5 m if 1 L of paint covers 20 m²? (Assume there are no doors or windows.)

3. The napkin ring pictured in the following figure is to be resilvered. How many square millimeters must be covered?

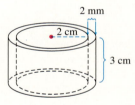

2 mm

2 cm

3 cm

4. Assume the radius of Earth is 6370 km and Earth is a sphere. What is its surface area?

5. Two cubes have sides of length 4 cm and 6 cm, respectively. What is the ratio of their surface areas?

6. Suppose one cylinder has radius 2 m and height 6 m and another has radius 6 m and height 2 m.
  a. Which cylinder has the greater lateral surface area?
  b. Which cylinder has the greater total surface area?

7. The base of a right pyramid is a regular hexagon with sides of length 12 m. The altitude of the pyramid is 9 m. Find the total surface area of the pyramid.

8. A soup can has a 2 5/8-in. diameter and is 4 in. tall. What is the area of the paper that will be used to make the label for the can if the paper covers the entire lateral surface area?

9. A square piece of paper 10 cm on a side is rolled to form the lateral surface area of a cylinder and then a top and bottom are added. What is the surface area of the cylinder?

10. Approximately how much material is needed to make the tent illustrated in the following figure (both ends and the bottom should be included):

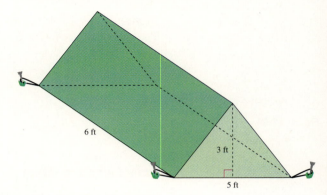

6 ft

3 ft

5 ft

11. The top of a rectangular box has an area of 88 cm². The sides have area 32 cm² and 44 cm². What are the dimensions of the box?

12. How does the surface area of a box (including top and bottom) change if
  a. each dimension is doubled?
  b. each dimension is tripled?
  c. each dimension is multiplied by a factor of k?

13. How does the lateral surface area of a cone change if
  a. the slant height is tripled but the radius of the base remains the same?
  b. the radius of the base is tripled but the slant height remains the same?
  c. the slant height and the radius of the base are tripled?

14. What happens to the surface area of a sphere if the radius is
  a. doubled?
  b. tripled?

15. Find the surface area of a square pyramid if the area of the base is 100 cm² and the height of the pyramid is 20 cm.

16. Suppose a structure is composed of cubes with at least one face of each cube connected to the face of another cube, as shown in the following figure:

  a. If one cube is added, what is the maximum surface area the structure can have?
  b. If one cube is added, what is the minimum surface area the structure can have?
  c. Is it possible to design a structure so that one can add a cube and yet add nothing to the surface area of the structure? (*Hint:* Cubes might have to be glued together.) Explain your answer.

17. The sector shown in the following figure is rolled into a cone so that the dotted edges just touch. Find the following:
    a. The lateral surface area of the cone
    b. The total surface area of the cone

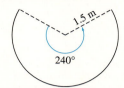

18. Each region in the following figure revolves about the indicated axis. For each case, sketch the three-dimensional figure obtained and find its surface area.

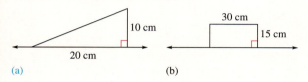

(a)   (b)

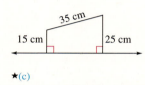

★(c)

19. The total surface area of a cube is 10,648 cm². What is the length of each of the following?
    a. One of the sides
    b. A diagonal that is not a diagonal of a face

★20. Find the total surface area of the following stand, which was cut from a right circular cone:

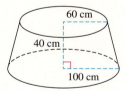

★21. A cylinder is inscribed in a cone, shown as follows. Find the lateral surface area of the cylinder if the height of the cone is 40 cm, the height of the cylinder 30 cm, and the radius of the base of the cone is 25 cm.

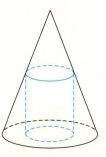

Communication

22. Which do you think would melt faster in an ice chest: a block of ice made from a gallon of water or ice cubes made from a gallon of water? Explain why.

23. A student wonders if she doubles each measurement of a cereal box, will she need twice as much cardboard to make the new box. How would you help her decide?

24. Explain why the opposite faces of a rectangular prism have equal areas but the faces of a right triangular prism do not have to have equal areas.

25. Tennis balls are packed tightly three to a can that is shaped like a cylinder.
    a. Estimate how the surface area of the balls compares to the lateral surface area of the can. Explain how you arrived at your estimate.
    b. See how close your estimate in (a) was by actually computing the surface area of the balls and the lateral surface area of the can.

Open-ended

26. One method of estimating body surface area in burn victims uses the fact that 100 handprints will approximately cover the whole body.
    a. What percent of the body surface area is the surface area of two handprints?
    b. Estimate the percent of the body surface area of one arm. Explain how you arrived at your estimate.
    c. Estimate your body surface area in square centimeters. Explain how you arrived at your estimate.
    d. Find the area of the flat part of your desk. How does the area of the desk compare with the surface area of your body?

27. Design a net for a polyhedron in such a way that the surface area of the polyhedron is 10 cm². Explain what polyhedron the net will form and why its surface area is 10 cm².

Cooperative Learning

28. **a.** Shawn used small cubes to build a bigger cube that was solid and was three cubes long on each side. He then painted all the sides of the new, large cube red. He dropped the newly painted cube and all the little cubes came apart. He noticed that some cubes had only one side painted, some had two sides painted, and so on. Describe the number of cubes with 0, 1, 2, 3, 4, 5, or 6 sides painted. Have each member of the group choose a different number of sides and then combine your data to see if it makes sense. Look for any patterns that occur.
    b. What would the answers be if the large cube was four small cubes long on a side?
    c. Make a conjecture about how to count the cubes if the large cube were *n* small cubes long on a side.

Review Problems

29. Complete each of the following:

a. $10 \text{ m}^2 =$ _____ cm^2 b. $13{,}680 \text{ cm}^2 =$ _____ m^2

c. $5 \text{ cm}^2 =$ _____ mm^2 d. $2 \text{ km}^2 =$ _____ m^2

e. $10^6 \text{ m}^2 =$ _____ km^2 f. $10^{12} \text{ mm}^2 =$ _____ m^2

30. The sides of a rectangle are 10 cm and 20 cm. Find the length of a diagonal of the rectangle.

31. The length of the side of a rhombus is 30 cm. If the length of one diagonal is 40 cm, find the length of the other diagonal.

32. Find the perimeters and the areas of the following figures:

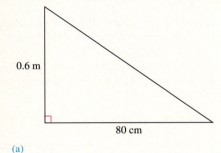

(a)

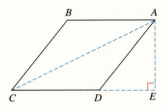

Trapezoid

(b)

33. In the following figure, the length of the longer diagonal $\overline{AC}$ of rhombus $ABCD$ is 40 cm; $AE = 24$ cm. Find the length of a side of the rhombus and the length of the other diagonal.

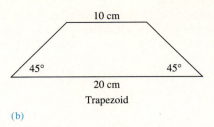

TECHNOLOGY CORNER

Find various-shaped cardboard containers and cut them apart to form nets. Make sure the nets are smaller in size than your computer screen.

a. Estimate the surface area of the nets.

b. Trace the perimeter of each net on a transparency sheet and hang the sheet on the monitor of your computer. Use a geometry utility to trace the outline from the transparency and compute the area.

c. Compare your estimate in (a) with the answer in (b).

BRAIN TEASER

A manufacturer of paper cups wants to produce paper cups in the form of truncated cones 16 cm high, with one circular base of radius 11 cm and the other of radius 7 cm, as shown in Figure 12-53. When the base of such a cup is removed and the cup is slit and flattened, the flattened region looks like a part of a circular ring. To design a pattern to make the cup, the manufacturer needs the data required to construct the flattened region. Find these data.

Figure 12-53

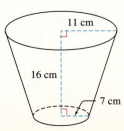

1. As a van Hiele Level 1 activity, use four cubes of the same size to build shapes such as the ones shown in Figure 12-54. In each case, find the surface area using a square face of the cube as a unit of area.

Figure 12-54

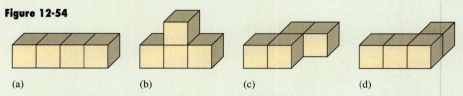

(a)   (b)   (c)   (d)

2. As a van Hiele Level 2 activity, consider the various figures that can be built by using four congruent cubes in such a way that any two cubes in your figure (a) have no points in common, (b) have an edge in common, or (c) have a whole face in common.
   i. What figure will have the greatest surface area?
   ii. What figure will have the least surface area?

Section 12-4 Volumes

In Section 12-3, we investigated surface areas of various-shaped containers. In this section, we explore how much the containers will hold. This distinction is sometimes confused by elementary-school students. Whereas the surface area is the number of square units covering a three-dimensional figure, volume describes how much space a three-dimensional figure will hold. The unit of measure for volume must be a shape that tessellates the space. Cubes tessellate space, that is, they can be stacked so that they leave no gaps and fill space. Standard units of volume are based on cubes and are *cubic units.* A cubic unit is the amount of space enclosed within a cube that measures 1 unit on a side. The distinction between surface area and volume is demonstrated in the following student page from *Addison-Wesley Mathematics,* Grade 8, 1993. Read through the student page and work the exercises on the bottom of the page.

Volume of Right Rectangular Prisms

The volume of a rectangular right prism can be measured by determining how many cubes are needed to build it. To find the volume, count how many cubes cover the base and then how many layers of these cubes are used to fill the prism. As shown in Figure 12-55(a), there are $8 \cdot 4$, or 32, cubes required to cover the base and there are five such layers. The volume of the rectangular prism is $8 \cdot 4 \cdot 5$, or 160 cubic units. For any rectangular right prism with dimensions ℓ, w, and h measured in the same linear units, the volume of the prism is given by the area of the base, ℓw, times the height, h, or $V = \ell w h$, as shown in Figure 12-55(b).

Figure 12-55

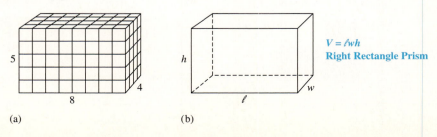

(a)   (b)

$V = \ell w h$
Right Rectangle Prism

Comparing Surface Area and Volume

EXPLORE Study the Information

Some questions about a container relate to the amount of surface on the container and other questions relate to the amount the container will hold. That's the distinction between **surface area** and **volume**.

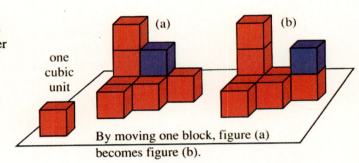

one cubic unit

By moving one block, figure (a) becomes figure (b).

TALK ABOUT IT

1. How does the volume of figure (a) compare with the volume of figure (b)?

2. Moving the shaded cube from one position to another changes the surface area by how many square units?

3. Estimate which building has the greater surface area.

The surface area is the number of square units on the surface of a solid. The volume of a solid is the number of cubic units needed to make the solid. A cubic unit is a cube with edges one unit in length. To find the volume of some solids, you can count the number of cubic units in the solid.

To find the volume, count

To find the surface area, count

The volume is 5 cubic units

The surface area is 22 square units

Find the volume and the surface area of each of these solids.

1.

2.

3.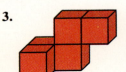

4.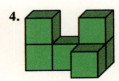

Converting Metric Measures of Volume

cubic centimeter

cubic meter

The most commonly used metric units of volume are the **cubic centimeter** and the **cubic meter.** A cubic centimeter is the volume of a cube whose length, width, and height are each 1 cm. One cubic centimeter is denoted by 1 cm^3. Similarly, a cubic meter is the volume of a cube whose length, width, and height are each 1 m. One cubic meter is denoted by 1 m^3. Other metric units of volume are symbolized similarly.

Figure 12-56 shows that since 1 dm = 10 cm, 1 dm^3 = (10 cm) · (10 cm) · (10 cm) = 1000 cm^3.

Figure 12-56

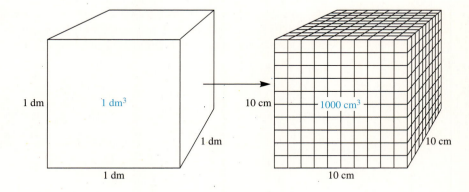

Figure 12-57 shows that 1 m^3 = 1,000,000 cm^3 and that 1 dm^3 = 0.001 m^3.

Figure 12-57

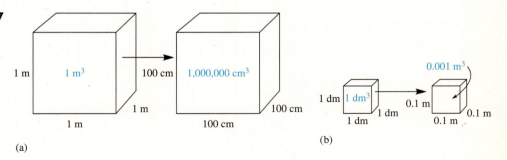

(a)

(b)

Each metric unit of length is 10 *times as great as the next smaller unit. Each metric unit of area is* 100 *times as great as the next smaller unit. Each metric unit of volume is* 1000 *times as great as the next smaller unit.* For example:

$$1 \text{ cm} = 10 \text{ mm}$$
$$1 \text{ cm}^2 = 100 \text{ mm}^2$$
$$1 \text{ cm}^3 = 1000 \text{ mm}^3$$

Because 1 cm = 0.01 m, then 1 cm^3 = (0.01 · 0.01 · 0.01) m^3, or 0.000001 m^3. Thus to convert from cubic centimeters to cubic meters, we need only move the decimal point six places to the left.

Example 12-18 | Convert each of the following:

a. 5 m^3 = _____ cm^3 **b.** 12,300 mm^3 = _____ cm^3

Solution   **a.** 1 m = 100 cm, so 1 m³ = (100 cm)(100 cm)(100 cm), or 1,000,000 cm³. Thus
5 m³ = (5)(1,000,000 cm³) = 5,000,000 cm³.

   b. 1 mm = 0.1 cm, so 1 mm³ = (0.1 cm)(0.1 cm)(0.1 cm), or 0.001 cm³. Thus
12,300 mm³ = 12,300(0.001 cm³) = 12.3 cm³.

• • •

In the metric system, cubic units may be used for either dry or liquid measure, although
liter   units such as liters and milliliters are usually used for liquid measures. By definition, a **liter,**
symbolized by L, equals, or is the capacity of, a cubic decimeter; that is, 1 L = 1 dm³. (In
the United States, L is the symbol for liter, but this is not universally accepted.)

Because 1 L = 1 dm³ and 1 dm³ = 1000 cm³, it follows that 1 L = 1000 cm³ and
1 cm³ = 0.001 L. Also, 0.001 L = 1 milliliter = 1 mL. Hence, 1 cm³ = 1 mL. These relationships are summarized in Figure 12-58 and Table 12-4.

Figure 12-58

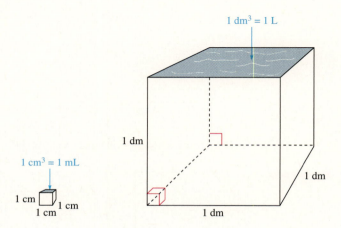

Table 12-4

Unit	Symbol	Relation to Liter
kiloliter	kL	1000 liters
*hectoliter	hL	100 liters
*dekaliter	daL	10 liters
liter	**L**	**1 liter**
*deciliter	dL	0.1 liter
centiliter	cL	0.01 liter
milliliter	mL	0.001 liter

*Not commonly used.

• • •

Example 12-19   Convert each of the following as indicated:

a. 27 L = _____ mL   **b.** 362 mL = _____ L

c. 3 mL = _____ cm³   **d.** 3 m³ = _____ L

Solution   **a.** 1 L = 1000 mL, so 27 L = 27 · 1000 mL = 27,000 mL.

   b. 1 mL = 0.001 L, so 362 mL = 362(0.001 L) = 0.362 L.

    c. 1 mL = 1 cm^3, so 3 mL = 3 cm^3.

    d. 1 m^3 = 1000 dm^3 and 1 dm^3 = 1 L, so 1 m^3 = 1000 L and 3 m^3 = 3000 L.

• • •

Converting English Measures of Volume

Basic units of volume in the English system are the cubic foot (1 ft^3), the cubic yard (1 yd^3), and the cubic inch (1 in.^{3}). In the United States, 1 gal = 231 in.^{3}, which is about 3.8 L, and 1 qt = $\frac{1}{4}$ gal, or about 58 in.^{3}

    Relationships among the one-dimensional units enable us to convert from one unit of volume to another, as shown in the following example.

• • •

Example 12-20

Convert each of the following, as indicated.

    a. 45 yd^3 = _____ ft^3

    b. 4320 in.^{3} = _____ yd^3

    c. 10 gal = _____ ft^3

    d. 3 ft^3 = _____ yd^3

Solution   **a.** Because 1 yd^3 = (3 ft)^3 = 27 ft^3, 45 yd^3 = 45 · 27 ft^3, or 1215 ft^3.

    b. Because 1 in. = $\frac{1}{36}$ yd, 1 in.^{3} = $\left(\frac{1}{36}\right)^3$ yd^3. Consequently, 4320 in.^{3} = 4320 · $\left(\frac{1}{36}\right)^3$ yd^3 $\doteq$ 0.0926 yd^3, or approximately 0.1 yd^3.

    c. Because 1 gal = 231 in.^{3} and 1 in.^{3} = $\left(\frac{1}{12}\right)^3$ ft^3, 10 gal = 2310 in.^{3} = 2310$\left(\frac{1}{12}\right)^3$ ft^3 $\doteq$ 1.337 ft^3, or approximately 1.3 ft^3.

    d. As seen in (a), 1 ft^3 = $\frac{1}{27}$ yd^3. Hence 3 ft^3 = 3 · $\frac{1}{27}$ yd^3 = $\frac{1}{9}$ yd^3.

• • •

Volumes of Prisms and Cylinders

We have shown that the volume of a right rectangular prism, as shown in Figure 12-59, involves multiplying the area of the base times the height. If we denote the area of the base by B and the height by h, then $V = Bh$.

Figure 12-59

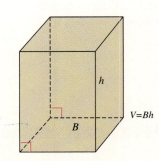

Formulas for the volumes of many three-dimensional figures can be derived using the volume of a right prism. In Figure 12-60(a), a rectangular solid box has been sliced into thin layers. If the layers are shifted to form the solids in Figure 12-60 (b) and (c), the volume of each of the three solids is the same as the volume of the original rectangular box. This idea is the basis for **Cavalieri's Principle.**

Cavalieri's Principle

Two solids with bases in the same plane have equal volumes if every plane parallel to the bases intersects the solids in cross-sections of equal area.

Figure 12-60

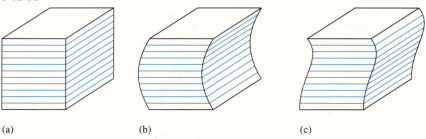

(a)   (b)   (c)

H I S T O R I C A L   N O T E

Bonaventura Cavalieri (1598–1647), an Italian mathematician and disciple of Galileo, contributed to the development of geometry, trigonometry, and algebra in the Renaissance. He became a Jesuit at an early age and later, after reading Euclid's *Elements,* was inspired to study mathematics. In 1629, Cavalieri became a professor at Bologna and held that post until his death. Cavalieri is best known for his principle concerning the volumes of solids.

I N V E S T I G A T I O N   1 2 - 1 0

● The two right prisms in Figure 12-61 have the same height. How do their volumes compare? Explain why. ●

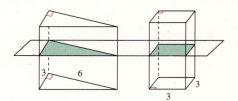

Figure 12-61

INVESTIGATION 12-11

● Consider the right prism and right cylinder in Figure 12-62(a) and (c) as stacks of papers. If the papers are shifted as shown in Figure 12-62(b) and (d), an oblique prism and an oblique cylinder, respectively, are formed.

a. Explain how the volume of the oblique prism is related to the volume of the right prism.

b. Explain how the volume of the oblique cylinder is related to the volume of the right cylinder. ●

Figure 12-62

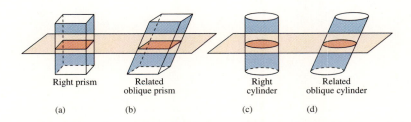

| Right prism | Related oblique prism | Right cylinder | Related oblique cylinder |
| (a) | (b) | (c) | (d) |

The volume of a cylinder can be approximated using prisms with increasing numbers of sides in their bases. The volume of each prism is the product of the area of the base and the height. Similarly, the volume V of a cylinder is the product of the area of the base B and the height h, that is, $V = Bh = \pi r^2 h$.

● ● ●

Example 12-21 Find the volume of each figure in Figure 12-63.

Figure 12-63

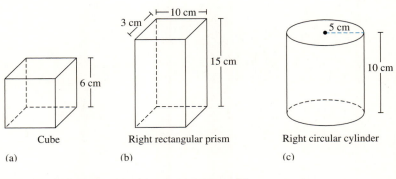

Cube	Right rectangular prism	Right circular cylinder
(a)	(b)	(c)

Solution **a.** $V = Bh = (6 \text{ cm} \cdot 6 \text{ cm}) \cdot 6 \text{ cm} = 216 \text{ cm}^3$
b. $V = Bh = (10 \text{ cm} \cdot 3 \text{ cm}) \cdot 15 \text{ cm} = 450 \text{ cm}^3$
c. $V = \pi r^2 h = \pi (5 \text{ cm})^2 \cdot 10 \text{ cm} = 250\pi \text{ cm}^3$

● ● ●

Volumes of Pyramids and Cones

Figure 12-64(a) and (b) show a right prism and a right pyramid with congruent bases and equal heights.

Figure 12-64

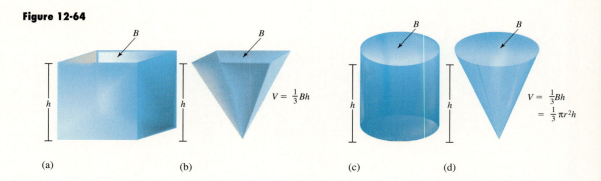

(a) (b) (c) (d)

How are the volumes of these containers related? Students may explore the relationship by filling the pyramid with water, sand, or rice and pouring the contents into the prism. They should find that it takes three full pyramids to fill the prism. Therefore the volume of the pyramid is equal to one third the volume of the prism. This relationship between prisms and pyramids with congruent bases and heights, respectively, is true in general, that is, for a pyramid $V = (1/3)Bh$, where B is the area of the base and h is the height. The same relationship holds between the volume of a cone and the volume of a cylinder, where they share congruent bases and equal heights, as shown in Figure 12-64(c) and (d). Therefore the volume of a cone is given by $V = (1/3)Bh$, or $V = (1/3)\pi r^2 h$.

Another way to determine the area of a pyramid in terms of a prism is to start with a cube and the four diagonals from one vertex drawn to the other vertices, as shown in Figure 12-65(a). We can see that there are three pyramids formed inside the cube as shown in Figure 12-65 (b), (c), and (d).

Figure 12-65

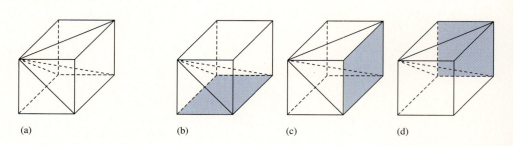

(a) (b) (c) (d)

The three pyramids are identical in size and shape, do not overlap, and their union is the whole cube. Therefore, each pyramid has volume one third that of the cube. This result is true in general, and once again we see that for a pyramid $V = (1/3)Bh$, where B is the area of the base and h is the height. This can be demonstrated by building three paper models of the pyramids and fitting them together into a prism. A net that can be enlarged and used for the construction is given in Figure 12-66.

Figure 12-66

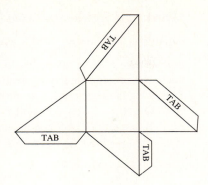

Example 12-22

Find the volume of each figure in Figure 12-67.

Figure 12-67

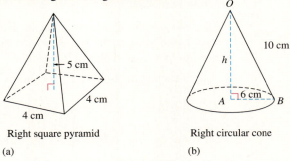

Right square pyramid

(a)

Right circular cone

(b)

Solution   **a.** The figure is a pyramid with a square base whose area is 4 cm · 4 cm and whose height is 5 cm. Hence, $V = \frac{1}{3}Bh = \frac{1}{3}(4 \text{ cm} \cdot 4 \text{ cm})(5 \text{ cm}) = \frac{80}{3} \text{ cm}^3$.

b. The base of the cone is a circle of radius 6 cm. Because the volume of the cone is given by $V = \frac{1}{3}\pi r^2 h$, we need to know the height. In the right triangle OAB, $OA = h$ and by the Pythagorean Theorem, $h^2 + 6^2 = 10^2$. Hence, $h^2 = 100 - 36$, or 64, and $h = 8$ cm. Thus $V = \frac{1}{3}\pi r^2 h = \frac{1}{3}\pi(6 \text{ cm})^2(8 \text{ cm}) = 98\pi \text{ cm}^3$.

Example 12-23

Figure 12-68 is a net for a pyramid. If each triangle is equilateral, find its volume.

Figure 12-68

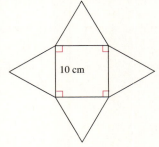

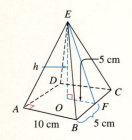

Figure 12-69

Solution The folded-up pyramid obtained is shown in Figure 12-69. The volume of the pyramid is $V = \frac{1}{3} Bh = \frac{1}{3} \cdot 10^2 h$. We must find h. Notice that h is a leg in the right triangle EOF, where F is the midpoint of $\overline{CB}$. We know that $OF = 5$ cm. If we knew EF, we could find h by applying the Pythagorean Theorem to $\triangle EOF$. To find the length of $\overline{EF}$, notice that $\overline{EF}$ is a leg in the right triangle EBF. ($\overline{EF}$ is the perpendicular bisector of $\overline{BC}$ in the equilateral triangle BEC.) In the right triangle EBF, we have $(EB)^2 = (BF)^2 + (EF)^2$. Because $EB = 10$ cm and $BF = 5$ cm, it follows that $10^2 = 5^2 + (EF)^2$, or $EF = \sqrt{75}$ cm $\doteq 8.66$ cm. In $\triangle EOF$, we have $h^2 + 5^2 = (EF)^2$, or $h^2 + 25 = 75$. Thus, $h = \sqrt{50}$ cm $\doteq 7.07$ cm, and $V \doteq \frac{1}{3} \cdot 10^2 \cdot 7.07 \doteq 235.7$ cm^3.

• • •

Volume of a Sphere

To find the volume of a sphere, imagine that a sphere is composed of a great number of congruent pyramids with apexes at the center of the sphere and that the vertices of the base touch the sphere, as shown in Figure 12-70. If the pyramids have very small bases, then the height of each pyramid is nearly the radius r. Hence, the volume of each pyramid is $\frac{1}{3} Bh$ or $\frac{1}{3} Br$, where B is the area of the base. If there are n pyramids each with base area B, then the total volume of the pyramids is $V = \frac{1}{3} nBr$. Because nB is the total surface area of all the bases of the pyramids and because the sum of the areas of all the bases of the pyramids is very close to the surface area of the sphere, $4\pi r^2$, the volume of the sphere is given by

$$V = \frac{1}{3} (4\pi r^2)r = \frac{4}{3} \pi r^3.$$

Figure 12-70

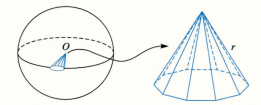

Example 12-24 | Find the volume of a sphere whose radius is 6 cm.

Solution $V = \frac{4}{3}\pi(6 \text{ cm})^3 = \frac{4}{3}\pi(216 \text{ cm}^3) = 288\pi \text{ cm}^3$

• • •

Problem 2

A manufacturer of metal cans has a large quantity of rectangular metal sheets 20 cm × 30 cm. Without cutting the sheets, the manufacturer wants to make cylindrical pipes with circular cross-sections from some of the sheets and box-shaped pipes with square cross-sections from the other sheets. The volume of the box-shaped pipes is to be greater than the volume of the cylindrical pipes. Is this possible? If so, how would the pipes be made and what are their volumes?

Understanding the Problem.   We are to use 20 cm $\times$ 30 cm rectangular sheets of metal to make some cylindrical pipes as well as some box-shaped pipes with square cross-sections that have a greater volume than do the cylindrical pipes. Is this possible, and if so, how should the pipes be designed and what are their volumes?

Figure 12-71 shows a sheet of metal and two sections of pipe made from it, one cylindrical and the other box-shaped. A model for such pipes can be designed from a piece of paper by bending it into a cylinder or by folding it into a right rectangular prism, as shown in the figure.

Figure 12-71

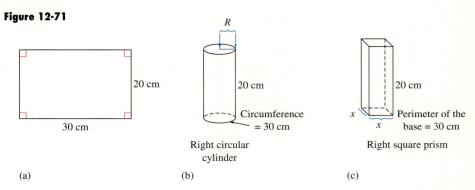

(a)   (b)   (c)

Devising a Plan.   If we compute the volume of the cylinder in Figure 12-71(b) and the volume of the prism in Figure 12-71(c), we can determine which is greater. If the prism has a greater volume, the solution of the problem will be complete. Otherwise, we look for other ways to design the pipes before concluding that a solution is impossible.

To compute the volume of the cylinder, we find the area of the base. The area of the circular base is πr^2. To find r, we note that the circumference of the circle $2\pi r$ is 30 cm. Thus $r = \dfrac{30}{2\pi} \doteq 4.77$ cm, and the area of the circle is $\pi r^2 \doteq \pi(4.77)^2 \doteq 71.48$ cm^2.

With the given information, we can also find the area of the base of the rectangular box. Because the perimeter of the base of the prism is $4x$, we have $4x = 30$, or $x = 7.5$ cm. Thus the area of the square base is $x^2 = (7.5)^2$, or 56.25 cm^2.

Carrying Out the Plan.   Denoting the volume of the cylindrical pipe by V_1 and the volume of the box-shaped pipe by V_2, we have $V_1 \doteq 71.48 \cdot 20$, or approximately 1429.6 cm^3. For the volume of the box-shaped pipe, we have $V_2 \doteq 56.25 \cdot 20$, or 1125 cm^3. We see that in the first design for the pipes, the volume of the cylindrical pipe is greater than the volume of the box-shaped pipe. This is not the required outcome.

Rather than bending the rectangular sheet of metal along the 30-cm side, we could bend it along the 20-cm side to obtain either pipe, as shown in Figure 12-72. Denoting the radius of the cylindrical pipe by r, the side of the box-shaped pipe by y, and their volumes by V_3 and V_4, respectively, we have $V_3 = \pi r^2 \cdot 30 = \pi(20/2\pi)^2 \cdot 30 = (10^2 \cdot 30)/\pi$, or approximately 954.9 cm^3. Also, $V_4 = y^2 \cdot 30 = \left(\dfrac{20}{4}\right)^2 \cdot 30 = 25 \cdot 30$, or 750 cm^3. Because $V_2 = 1125$ cm^3 and $V_3 = 945.9$ cm^3, we see that the volume of the box-shaped pipe with an altitude of 20 cm is greater than the volume of the cylindrical pipe with an altitude of 30 cm.

Figure 12-72

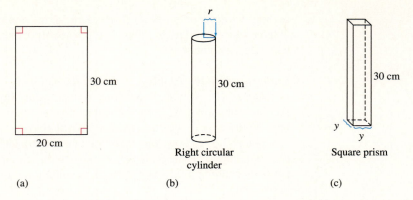

Right circular
cylinder

(a)   (b)   (c)

Looking Back.   We could ask for the volumes of other three-dimensional objects that can be obtained by bending the rectangular sheets of metal. Also, because the lateral surface areas of the four types of pipes were the same but their volumes were different, we might want to investigate whether there are other cylinders and prisms that have the same lateral surface area and the same volume. Is it possible to find a circular cylinder with lateral surface area of 600 cm^2 and smallest possible volume? Similarly, is there a circular cylinder with the given surface area and greatest possible volume?

• • •

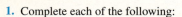

Ongoing Assessment 12-4

1. Complete each of the following:
   a. 8 m^3 = _____ dm^3
   b. 500 cm^3 = _____ m^3
   c. 675,000 m^3 = _____ km^3
   d. 3 m^3 = _____ cm^3
   e. 7000 mm^3 = _____ cm^3
   f. 0.002 m^3 = _____ cm^3
   g. 400 in.^{3} = _____ yd^3
   h. 25 yd^3 = _____ ft^3
   i. 0.2 ft^3 = _____ in.^{3}
   j. 1200 in.^{3} = _____ ft^3

2. If a faucet is dripping at the rate of 15 drops/min and there are 20 drops/mL, how many liters of water are wasted in a 30-day month?

3. Find the volume of each of the following:

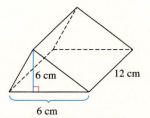

(c) Right triangular prism

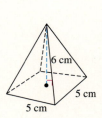

(d) Square pyramid

(e) Right circular cone

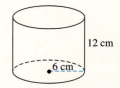

(f) Right circular cylinder

(g) Sphere

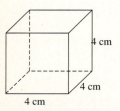

(a) Right rectangular prism

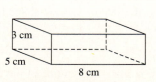

(b) Right rectangular prism

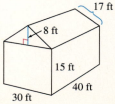

(h)

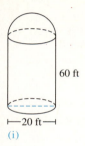

60 ft

20 ft

(i)

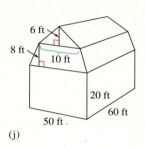

6 ft

8 ft

10 ft

20 ft

60 ft

50 ft

(j)

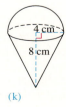

4 cm

8 cm

(k)

	a.	b.	c.	d.
Length	20 cm	10 cm	2 dm	15 cm
Width	10 cm	2 dm	1 dm	2 dm
Height	10 cm	3 dm		
Volume (cm³)				
Volume (dm³)				7.5 dm³
Volume (L)			4 L	

10. Determine how many liters a right cylindrical tank holds if it is 6 m long and 13 m in diameter.

11. Earth's diameter is approximately four times the moon's and both bodies are spheres. What is the ratio of their volumes?

12. A bread pan is 18 cm × 18 cm × 5 cm. How many liters does it hold?

13. An Olympic-sized pool in the shape of a right rectangular prism is 50 m × 25 m. If it is 2 m deep throughout, how many liters of water does it hold?

14. A standard straw is 25 cm long and 4 mm in diameter. How much liquid can be held in the straw at one time?

15. **a.** What happens to the volume of an aquarium that is in the shape of a rectangular prism if the length, width, and height are all doubled?

   b. From your answer to (a), conjecture what happens to the volume of the aquarium if all the measurements are tripled.

   c. When you multiply each linear dimension of an aquarium by a positive value *n*, what happens to the volume?

16. The Great Pyramid of Egypt is a right square pyramid with height of 148 m and a square base with a perimeter of 930 m. The Transamerica Building in San Francisco has the basic shape of a right square pyramid that has a square base with a perimeter of 140 m and a height of 260 m. Which one has the greater volume and by how many times greater?

17. The Great Pyramid of Egypt has a square base of 756 ft on a side and a height of 481 ft. How many apartments 35 ft × 20 ft × 8 ft would be needed to have a volume equivalent to that of the Great Pyramid's?

18. A rectangular-shaped swimming pool with dimensions 10 m × 25 m is being built. The pool has a shallow end that is uniform in depth and a deep end that drops off as shown in the following figure. What is the volume of this pool in cubic meters?

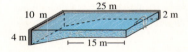

25 m

10 m

2 m

4 m

15 m

4. Complete the following chart:

	a.	b.	c.	d.	e.	f.
cm³		500			750	4800
dm³	2					
L			1.5			
mL				5000		

5. Place a decimal point in each of the following to make it an accurate sentence:

   a. A paper cup holds about 2000 mL.

   b. A regular soft drink bottle holds about 320 L.

   c. A quart milk container holds about 10 L.

   d. A teaspoonful of cough syrup is about 500 mL.

6. Determine the volume of silver needed to make the napkin ring in the following figure out of solid silver. Give your answer in cubic millimeters.

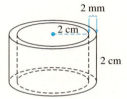

2 mm

2 cm

2 cm

7. Two cubes have sides of lengths 4 cm and 6 cm, respectively. What is the ratio of their volumes?

8. What happens to the volume of a sphere if the radius is doubled?

9. Complete the following chart for right rectangular prisms with the given dimensions:

19. How many liters of water can be held in a hose that has a 3-cm diameter and length 50 m?

20. If 50 steel marbles that are 1 cm in diameter are melted down, will enough steel result to build a marble that is 4 cm in diameter? Explain.

21. A cone-shaped paper water cup has a height of 8 cm and a radius of 4 cm. If the cup is filled with water to half its height, what portion of the volume of the cup is filled with water?

22. If each edge of a cube is increased by 30%, what happens to the cube's volume?

23. Earth's diameter is approximately 7927 mi. What is its approximate volume?

24. One freezer measures 1.5 ft × 1.5 ft × 5 ft and sells for $350. Another freezer measures 2 ft × 2 ft × 4 ft and sells for $400. Which freezer is the better buy in terms of cubic feet per dollar?

25. A tennis can in the shape of a cylinder holds three tennis balls snugly. If the radius of a tennis ball is 3.5 cm, what percent of the tennis ball can is occupied by air?

26. A box is packed with six soda cans, as in the following figure. What percent of the volume of the interior of the box is not occupied by the cans?

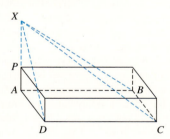

27. A regular square pyramid is 3 m high and the perimeter of its base is 16 m. Find the volume of the pyramid.

28. A right rectangular prism with base *ABCD* as the bottom is shown in the following figure.

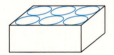

Suppose *X* is drawn so that $AX = 3 \cdot AP$, where *AP* is the height of the prism and *X* is connected to *A, B, C,* and *D* to form a pyramid. How do the volumes of the pyramid and the prism compare?

29. A right cylindrical can is to hold exactly 1 L of water. What should be the height of the can if the radius is 12 cm?

30. A theater decides to change the shape of its popcorn container from a regular box to a right regular pyramid and charge only half as much as shown in the following figure.

If the containers are the same height and the tops are the same size, is this a bargain for the customer? Explain.

31. Which is the better buy: a grapefruit 5 cm in radius that costs 22¢ or a grapefruit 6 cm in radius that costs 31¢? Explain.

32. Two spherical cantaloupes of the same kind are sold at a fruit and vegetable stand. The circumference of one is 60 cm and that of the other is 50 cm. The larger melon is $1\frac{1}{2}$ times as expensive as the smaller. Which melon is the better buy and why?

33. An engineer is to design a square-based pyramid whose volume is to be 100 m³.
    a. Find the dimensions (the length of a side of the square and the altitude) of one such pyramid.
    b. How many (noncongruent) such pyramids are possible? Why?

34. A square pyramid has a lateral surface area of 2 m². Its height equals the length of the side of the square base. Find the volume of the pyramid.

35. A square sheet of cardboard measuring *y* cm on a side is to be used to produce an open-top box when the maker cuts off a small square *x* cm by *x* cm from each corner and bends up the sides.
    a. Find the volume of the box if *y* = 200 cm and *x* = 20 cm.
    ★b. Assume *y* is known. Find the expression for the volume *V* as a function of *x*.

36. In the 1950s, 45 rpm records had 3.5-in. radii and a hole in the middle with a 1.5-in. diameter. If each record was $\frac{1}{16}$ in. thick, approximately what was the volume of a stack of 20 records?

37. A scoop of ice cream that is a perfect sphere with radius 5 cm fits exactly along one of its great circles in a sugar cone, as shown in the following figure.

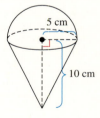

Suppose the ice cream melts and the cone does not absorb any of it. If the cone is 10 cm tall, will it hold the melted ice cream? If not, how tall would the cone have to be to hold the melted ice cream?

★38. Half of the air is let out of a spherical balloon. If the balloon remains in the shape of a sphere, how does the radius of the smaller balloon compare to the original radius?

Communication

39. a. Which will increase the volume of a circular cylinder more: doubling its height or doubling its radius? Explain.

b. Is your answer the same for a circular cone? Why?

40. Write a one-page paper to a sixth-grade student explaining the difference between surface area and volume.

41. Explain how the formula for the volume of a cone might be derived from the formula for the volume of a pyramid.

42. Explain how you would find the volume of an irregular shape.

Open-ended

43. A right circular cylinder has a 4-in. diameter, is 6 in. high, and is completely full of water. Design a right rectangular prism that will hold the water as exactly as possible.

44. Circular-shaped cookies are to be packaged 48 to a box. Each cookie is approximately 1 cm thick and has a diameter of 6 cm. Design a box that will hold this volume of cookies and has the least amount of surface area.

45. Design a cylinder that will hold 1 L of juice. Give the dimensions of your cylinder and tell why you designed the shape as you did.

Cooperative Learning

46. a. Find many different types of cans that are in the shape of a cylinder. Measure the height and diameter for each can.
 b. Find the surface area of each can.
 c. Find the volume of each can.
 d. Compute the ratio of surface area/volume for each can.
 e. Compare your results with those of other groups.
 f. Based on the information collected, write recommendations to the manufacturers of the cans about an ideal surface area/volume ratio.

Review Problems

47. Find the surface areas of the following figures:

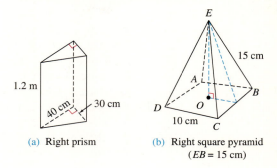

(a) Right prism   (b) Right square pyramid
                          (*EB* = 15 cm)

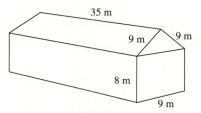

(c) Barn (include floor)

48. The diagonal of a rectangle has measure 1.3 m, and a side of the rectangle has measure 120 cm. Find the following:
 a. Perimeter of the rectangle
 b. Area of the rectangle

49. Find the area of a triangle that has sides of 3 m, 3 m, and 2 m.

50. A poster is to contain 0.25 m² of printed matter, with margins of 12 cm at top and bottom and 6 cm at each side. Find the width of the poster if its height is 74 cm.

LABORATORY ACTIVITY

1. As a van Hiele Level 1 activity, work with 30 congruent cubes. Build the cube with greatest volume possible by stacking the cubes. How many of the given cubes did you need to build your cube?

2. As a van Hiele Level 2 activity, use 24 congruent cubes to build solids that have the following characteristics:
 a. The greatest possible surface area
 b. The least possible surface area

---

*Section 12-5 ## Mass and Temperature

Three centuries ago, Isaac Newton pointed out that in everyday life, *weight* is used for what is really mass. *Mass* is a quantity of matter as opposed to *weight,* which is a force exerted by gravitational pull. When astronauts are in orbit above Earth, their weights have changed even though their masses remain the same. In common parlance on Earth, weight and mass are still used interchangeably. In the English system, weight is measured in avoirdupois units such as tons, pounds, and ounces. One pound (lb) equals 16 ounces (oz) and 2000 lb equals 1 English ton.

gram   In the metric system, the base unit for mass is the **gram,** denoted by g. An ordinary paper clip or a thumbtack each has a mass of about 1 g. As with other base metric units, prefixes are added to gram to obtain other units. For example, a kilogram (kg) is 1000 g. Two standard loaves of bread have a mass of about 1 kg. A person's mass also is measured in kilograms. A newborn baby has a mass of about 4 kg. Another unit of mass is the metric ton (t), which is equal to 1000 kg. The metric ton is used to record the masses of objects such as cars and trucks. A small foreign car has a mass of about 1 t. Mega (1,000,000) and micro (0.000001) are other prefixes used with the base unit.

Table 12-5 lists metric units of mass. Conversions involving metric units of mass are handled in the same way as conversions involving metric units of length.

Table 12-5

Unit	Symbol	Relationship to Gram
ton (metric)	t	1,000,000 grams
kilogram	kg	1000 grams
*hectogram	hg	100 grams
*dekagram	dag	0 grams
gram	**g**	**1 gram**
*decigram	dg	0.1 gram
*centigram	cg	0.01 gram
milligram	mg	0.001 gram

*Not commonly used.

Example 12-25   Complete each of the following:

a. 34 g = _____ kg   **b.** 6836 kg = _____ t

Solution   **a.** 34 g = 34(0.001 kg) = 0.034 kg
            b. 6836 kg = 6836(0.001 t) = 6.836 t

The relationship among the units of volume, capacity, and mass in the metric system is illustrated on the following student page from *Addison-Wesley Mathematics,* Grade 6, 1993, and in Figure 12-73.

Figure 12-73

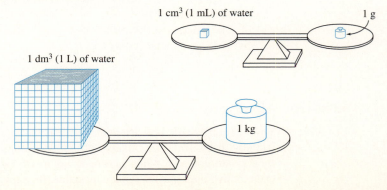

Volume, Capacity, and Mass
Metric Units

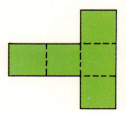

LEARN ABOUT IT

In the metric system, volume, capacity, and mass are all related to each other.

EXPLORE Use a Pattern

Work in groups to build an open-top box that is 10 cm on each edge. Imagine that your box can be filled with water.

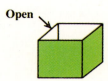

Open

TALK ABOUT IT

1. What in your room do you think would have about the same mass as your box of water?

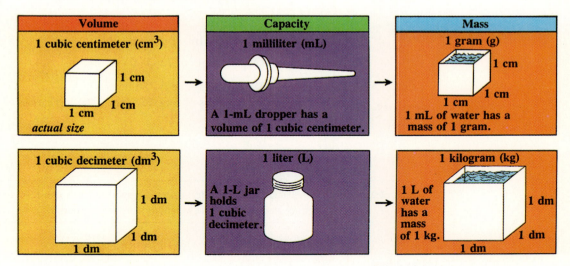

Volume	Capacity	Mass
1 cubic centimeter (cm³)	**1 milliliter (mL)**	**1 gram (g)**
actual size	A 1-mL dropper has a volume of 1 cubic centimeter.	1 mL of water has a mass of 1 gram.
1 cubic decimeter (dm³)	**1 liter (L)**	**1 kilogram (kg)**
	A 1-L jar holds 1 cubic decimeter.	1 L of water has a mass of 1 kg.

A **milligram (mg)** is a very small unit of mass. It is 1 thousandth of a gram (0.001 g).

A **kiloliter** is a very large unit of capacity. It is 1 thousand liters (1,000 L).

TRY IT OUT

Choose the best estimate.

1. can of juice
   825 mL   825 L   825 kL

2. bowling ball
   7 mg   7 g   7 kg

3. bathtub
   225 mL   225 L   225 kL

INVESTIGATION 12-12

● Investigate the following relationships:

a. 1 cm³ of water has a mass of 1 _____

b. 1 dm³ of water has a mass of 1 _____.

c. 1 L of water has a volume of 1 _____.

d. 1 cm³ of water has a capacity of 1 _____.

e. 1 mL of water has a mass of 1 _____.

f. 1 m³ of water has a capacity of 1 _____.

g. 1 m³ of water has a mass of 1 _____. ●

• • •

Example 12-26   A waterbed measures 180 cm × 210 cm × 20 cm.

a. How many liters of water can it hold?

b. What is its mass in kilograms when it is full of water?

Solution   **a.** The volume of the waterbed is found by multiplying the length ℓ times the width w times the height h.

$$V = \ell w h$$
$$= 180 \text{ cm} \cdot 210 \text{ cm} \cdot 20 \text{ cm}$$
$$= 756{,}000 \text{ cm}^3, \text{ or } 756{,}000 \text{ mL}$$

Because 1 mL = 0.001 L, the volume is 756 L.

b. Because 1 L of water has a mass of 1 kg, 756 L of water has a mass of 756 kg, which is 0.756 t.

• • •

REMARK   To see one advantage of the metric system, suppose the bed is 6 ft × 7 ft × 9 in. Try to find the volume in gallons and the weight of the water in pounds.

Temperature

degree Kelvin   The base unit of temperature for the metric system, the **degree Kelvin,** is used only for scientific measurements and is an absolute temperature. The freezing point of water is 273° on this scale. For normal temperature measurements in the metric system, the base unit is the

degree Celsius   **degree Celsius,** named for Anders Celsius, the Swedish scientist who invented the system. The Celsius scale has 100 equal divisions between 0 degrees Celsius (0°C), the freezing point of water, and 100 degrees Celsius (100°C), the boiling point of water, as seen in Figure 12-74. In the English system, the Fahrenheit scale has 180 equal divisions between 32°F, the freezing point of water, and 212°F, the boiling point of water.

Figure 12-74 gives other temperature comparisons of the two scales and further illustrates the relationship between them. Because the Celsius scale has 100 divisions between the freezing point and the boiling point of water, whereas the Fahrenheit scale has 180 divisions, the relationship between the two scales is 100 to 180, or 5 to 9. For every 5 degrees on the Celsius scale, there are 9 degrees on the Fahrenheit scale, and for each degree on the Fahrenheit scale, there is $\frac{5}{9}$ degree on the Celsius scale. Because the ratio between the number of degrees above freezing on the Celsius scale and the number of degrees above freezing on the Fahrenheit scale remains the same and equals $\frac{5}{9}$, we may convert temperature from one system to the other.

For example, suppose we want to convert 50° on the Fahrenheit scale to the corresponding number on the Celsius scale. On the Fahrenheit scale, 50° is 50 − 32, or 18°, above freezing, but on the Celsius scale, it is $\frac{5}{9} \cdot 18$, or 10°, above freezing. Because the freezing temperature on the Celsius scale is 0°, 10° above freezing is 10° Celsius. Thus 50°F = 10°C. In general, F degrees is $F - 32$ above freezing on the Fahrenheit scale, but only $\frac{5}{9}(F - 32)$ above freezing on the Celsius scale. Thus we have the relation $C = \frac{5}{9}(F - 32)$. If we solve the equation for F, we obtain $F = \frac{9}{5}C + 32$. Rather than your memorizing these formulas, we encourage you to reason as shown to convert from one scale to the other.

Figure 12-74

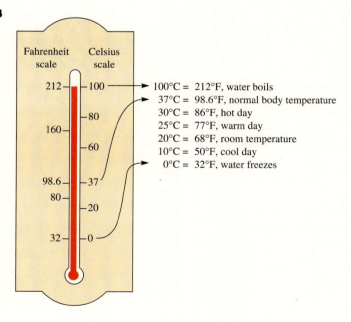

the following correspondences appear beside the thermometer:

100°C = 212°F, water boils
37°C = 98.6°F, normal body temperature
30°C = 86°F, hot day
25°C = 77°F, warm day
20°C = 68°F, room temperature
10°C = 50°F, cool day
0°C = 32°F, water freezes

Example 12-27   Convert 20°C to degrees Fahrenheit.

Solution   For 100 divisions on the Celsius scale, we have 212 − 32, or 180, divisions on the Fahrenheit scale. Hence, for every 1 degree on the Celsius scale, there are $\frac{180}{100}$, or $\frac{9}{5}$, degrees on the Fahrenheit scale. Because 20°C is 20° above freezing, on the Fahrenheit scale it would be $\frac{9}{5} \cdot 20$, or 36, degrees above freezing, or $32 + 36$, or 68 degrees. Thus $20°C = 68°F$.

• • •

HISTORICAL NOTE

Gabriel Daniel Fahrenheit (1686–1736) was a German physicist who contributed to the construction of improved thermometers and introduced the scale bearing his name. He lived most of his life in England and Holland and made a living manufacturing meteorological instruments.

Anders Celsius (1701–1744) was a Swedish astronomer. He was a professor at the University of Uppsala. In 1742, he described the centigrade scale in a paper before the Swedish Academy of Sciences.

Ongoing Assessment 12-5

1. For each of the following, select the appropriate metric unit of measure (gram, kilogram, or metric ton):
   a. Car
   b. Adult
   c. Can of frozen orange juice
   d. Elephant
   e. Jar of mustard
   f. Bag of peanuts
   g. Army tank
   h. Cat
   i. Dictionary

2. For each of the following, choose the correct unit (milligram, gram, or kilogram) to make each sentence reasonable:
   a. A staple has a mass of about 340 _____ .
   b. A professional football player has a mass of about 110 _____ .
   c. A vitamin tablet has a mass of about 1100 _____ .
   d. A dime has a mass of 2 _____ .
   e. The recipe said to add 4 _____ of salt.
   f. One strand of hair has a mass of 2 _____ .

3. Complete each of the following:
   a. 15,000 g = _____ kg
   b. 8000 kg = _____ t
   c. 0.036 kg = _____ g
   d. 72 g = _____ kg
   e. 4320 mg = _____ g
   f. 3 g 7 mg = _____ g
   g. 5 kg 750 g = _____ g
   h. 5 kg 750 g = _____ kg
   i. 0.03 t = _____ kg
   j. 2.6 lb = _____ oz
   k. 25 oz = _____ lb
   l. 50 oz = _____ lb
   m. 3.8 lb = _____ oz

4. A paper dollar has a mass of approximately 1 g. Is it possible to lift $1,000,000 in the following denominations:
   a. $1 bills
   b. $10 bills
   c. $100 bills
   d. $1000 bills
   e. $10,000 bills

5. A fish tank, which is a right rectangular prism, is 40 cm × 20 cm × 20 cm. If it is filled with water, what is the mass of the water?

6. In a grocery store, one kind of meat costs $5.80/kg. How much does 400 g of this meat cost?

7. If a certain spice costs $20/kg, how much does 1 g cost?

8. Abel bought a kilogram of Moxwill coffee for $9 and Babel bought 400 g of the same brand of coffee for $4.60. Who made the better buy? Why?

9. Convert each of the following from degrees Fahrenheit to the nearest integer degree Celsius:
   a. 10°F
   b. 0°F
   c. 30°F
   d. 100°F
   e. 212°F
   f. 40°F

10. Answer each of the following:
    a. The thermometer reads 20°C. Can you go snow skiing?
    b. The thermometer reads 26°C. Will the outdoor ice rink be open?
    c. Your temperature is 37°C. Do you have a fever?
    d. Your body temperature is 39°C. Are you ill?
    e. It is 40°C. Will you need a sweater at the outdoor concert?
    f. The temperature reads 35°C. Should you go water skiing?
    g. The temperature reads ⁻10°C. Is it appropriate to go ice fishing?
    h. Your bath water is 16°C. Will you have a hot, warm, or chilly bath?
    i. It's 30°C in the room. Are you comfortably hot or cold?

11. Convert each of the following from degrees Celsius to the nearest integer degree Fahrenheit:
    a. 10°C
    b. 0°C
    c. 30°C
    d. 100°C
    e. 212°C
    f. ⁻40°C

12. A heart pumps about 60 mL of blood in one heartbeat. Approximately how much blood does your heart pump in one week?

13. a. Rainfall is usually measured in linear measure. Suppose St. Louis received 2 cm of rain on a given day. If a certain lot in St. Louis has measure 1 ha, how many liters of rainfall fell on the lot?

   b. What is the mass of the water that fell on the lot?

14. An aquarium in the shape of a right rectangular prism measures 25 in. × 18 in. × 9 in. When it is filled with water, what is the weight of the water? (Assume 1 gal of water is 231 in.^{3} and weighs 8.3 lb.)

Communication

15. a. Can two empty boxes that have the same weight have different volumes? Explain.

   b. Can two empty boxes that have the same volume have different weights? Explain.

16. Read the following problems (i) and (ii):

   i. A tank in the shape of a cube 5 ft 3 in. on a side is filled with water. Find the volume in cubic feet, the capacity in gallons, and the weight of the water in pounds.

   ii. A tank in the shape of a cube 2 m on a side is filled with water. Find the volume in cubic meters, the capacity in liters, and the mass of the water in kilograms.

   Discuss which problem is easier to work and why the metric system has an advantage over the English system in this case.

17. Explain whether the air temperature increases a greater amount with a 10-degree increase on the Celsius or a 10-degree increase on the Fahrenheit scale.

Open-ended

18. Describe how time could be saved if only the metric system were taught in elementary school instead of both the English and metric systems.

19. If only the metric system were taught in elementary school, what implications would this have for the topics that are taught in mathematics?

Cooperative Learning

20. As a group, design a hands-on lesson for a sixth-grade class showing the relationship between volume, capacity, and mass in the metric system. Also design situations in which students have to estimate capacities and masses of several objects.

Review Problems

21. Find the perimeter and the area of the following figures:

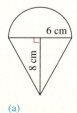

(a)

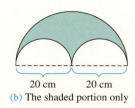

20 cm   20 cm
(b) The shaded portion only

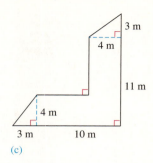

(c)

22. Complete the following:

   a. 350 mm = _____ cm

   b. 1600 cm^2 = _____ m^2

   c. 0.4 m^2 = _____ mm^2

   d. 5.2 m^3 = _____ cm^3

   e. 5.2 m^3 = _____ L

   f. 3500 cm^3 = _____ m^3

23. Determine whether each of the following is a right triangle:

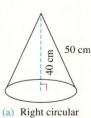

(a)   (b)

(c)   (d)

24. A person walks 5 km north, 3 km east, 1 km north, and then 2 km east. How far is the person from the starting point?

25. Find the volume and the surface area of each of the following solids:

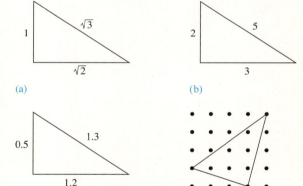

(a) Right circular cone

(b) Right prism in which the faces are either rectangles or right triangles

**LABORATORY
ACTIVITY**

1. Record the mass of each U.S. coin. Which coin has the greatest mass? Which of the following sets have the same mass?
   a. A half-dollar vs. two quarters
   b. A quarter vs. two dimes and a nickel
   c. A dime vs. two nickels
   d. A dime vs. ten pennies
   e. A nickel vs. five pennies
2. Record the temperature of the room on a Celsius thermometer. Pour 200 mL of water into a liter container. Record the temperature of the water. Add 100 mL of ice to the water. Wait 1 min. and record the temperature of the ice water.

SOLUTION TO THE PRELIMINARY PROBLEM

Understanding the Problem.   A square plot of land is 100 m on a side. One large circular sprinkler or four small circular sprinklers can be installed to irrigate in the patterns shown in Figure 12-75. We need to decide which option will provide water to the greatest percent of land. Intuition might tell us that the larger sprinkler waters the larger area.

Figure 12-75

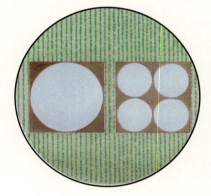

Devising a Plan.   The area of the square is 100 m × 100 m, or 10,000 m². We can compute the area of the large circular area and calculate the percent of the square covered by the larger sprinkler. Next, we can compute the area of one of the small circles, multiply this by four, and then compute the percent of the square covered by the four smaller sprinklers. We can then compare the percent and make a decision on the two systems.

Carrying Out the Plan.   The radius of the large circle is 50 m and the radius of a small circle is 25 m. The area of the large circle is given by $A = \pi r^2 = \pi(50 \text{ m})^2 = 2500\pi \text{ m}^2$. The fraction of the square covered by the large sprinkler is $2500\pi/10{,}000$, or about 78.5%.

The area of one small circle is $A = \pi(25 \text{ m})^2 = 625\pi \text{ m}^2$ and the area of four small circles is $4 \times 625\pi \text{ m}^2$, or $2500\pi \text{ m}^2$. The fraction of the square covered by the four small sprinklers is $2500\pi/10{,}000 \text{ m}^2$, or about 78.5%.

Therefore both sprinkler systems cover the same percent of the square field and it does not matter which system is used if the only selection criterion is the amount of land covered by the system.

Looking Back. The number of circles contained in the square or the size of the square can be changed. Will the percent always be the same? The problem can also be varied by changing the shape of the field into such different shapes as rectangles, parallelograms, or trapezoids. Related problems are given next.

1. To make lids, we cut congruent circles out of a rectangular piece of tin, as shown in Figure 12-76. Find what percent of the tin is wasted by our doing this.

Figure 12-76

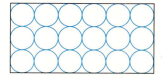

2. Suppose we have a rectangular piece of tin the same size as in (1), but we cut out smaller congruent circles. Also suppose that the circles are still tangent to each other and to the sides of the rectangle. What percent of the tin is wasted if the radius of each circle is as follows?
   a. Half the radius of the circles in (1)
   b. One third the radius of the circles in (1)

QUESTIONS FROM THE CLASSROOM

1. A student asks if the units of measure must be the same for each term in order to use the formulas for volumes. How do you respond?
2. As part of the discussion of the Pythagorean Theorem, squares were constructed on each side of a right triangle. A student asks, "If different similar figures are constructed on each side of the triangle, does the same type of relationship still hold?" How do you reply?
3. A student asks, "Can I find the area of an angle?" How do you respond?
4. A student argues that a square has no area because its interior can be thought of as the union of infinitely many points, each of which has no area. How do you react?
5. A student asks whether the volume of a prism can ever be the same number as its surface area. How do you answer?
6. A student asks, "Why should the United States switch to the metric system?" How do you reply?
7. A student claims that in a triangle with 20° and 40° angles, the side opposite the 40° angle is twice as long as the side opposite the 20° angle. How do you reply?

8. A student interpreted 5 cm^3 as shown in Figure 12-77. What is wrong with this interpretation?

Figure 12-77

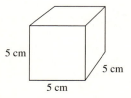

5 cm
5 cm
5 cm

9. A student claims that because are and hectare are measures of area, we should say "square are" and "square hectare." How do you respond?
10. A student claims that the area of his hand does not exist because it cannot be found by any formula. How do you respond?
11. A student claims that since a circular cylinder has a curved surface, its lateral surface area should not be expressed in square units. How do you respond?

CHAPTER OUTLINE

I. The English system
   A. Area measure
      1. Units commonly used are the **square inch** (in.^{2}), **square yard** (yd^2), and **square foot** (ft^2).
      2. Land can be measured in **acres.**
   B. Volume measure
      Units commonly used are the **cubic inch** (in.^{3}), **cubic foot** (ft^3), **cubic yard** (yd^3), and **gallon.**
   *C. Mass
      Units of mass commonly used are **pound** (lb), **ounce** (oz) (1 oz $= \frac{1}{16}$ lb), and **ton** (1 ton = 2000 lb).

II. The metric system
   A. Area measure
      1. Units commonly used are the **square kilometer** (km^2), **square meter** (m^2), **square centimeter** (cm^2), and **square millimeter** (mm^2).
      2. Land can be measured using the **are** (100 m^2) and the **hectare** (10,000 m^2).
   B. Volume measure
      1. Units commonly used are the **cubic meter** (m^3), **cubic decimeter** (dm^3), and **cubic centimeter** (cm^3).
      2. 1 dm^3 = 1 L and cm^3 = 1 mL.
   *C. Mass
      1. Units of mass commonly used are the **milligram** (mg), **gram** (g), **kilogram** (kg), and **metric ton** (t).
      2. 1 L and 1 mL of water have masses of approximately 1 kg and 1 g, respectively.
   *D. Temperature
      1. The official unit of metric temperature is the **degree Kelvin,** but the unit commonly used is the **degree Celsius.** (In the English system, the unit of temperature is the **degree Fahrenheit.**)
      2. Basic temperature reference points are the following:
         100°C — boiling point of water
         37°C — normal body temperature
         20°C — comfortable room temperature
         0°C — freezing point of water
      3. $C = \frac{5}{9}(F - 32)$ and $F = \frac{9}{5}C + 32$

III. Areas
   A. Formulas for areas
      1. **Square:** $A = s^2$, where s is a side.
      2. **Rectangle:** $A = \ell w$, where ℓ is the length and w is the width.
      3. **Parallelogram:** $A = bh$, where b is the base and h is the height.

   4. **Triangle:** $A = \frac{1}{2}bh$, where b is the base and h is the altitude to that base.
   5. **Trapezoid:** $A = \frac{1}{2}h(b_1 + b_2)$, where b_1 and b_2 are the bases and h is the height.
   6. **Regular polygon:** $A = \frac{1}{2}ap$, where a is the apothem and p is the perimeter.
   7. **Circle:** $A = \pi r^2$, where r is the radius.
   8. **Sector:** $A = \theta\,\pi r^2/360$, where θ is the measure of the central angle forming the sector and r is the radius of the circle containing the sector.

   B. **The Pythagorean Theorem:** In any right triangle, the square of the length of the hypotenuse is equal to the sum of the squares of the lengths of the legs.
   C. Triangle relations
      1. Property of 30°-60°-90° triangle: The length of the hypotenuse in a 30°-60°-90° triangle is two times the length of the leg opposite the 30° angle, and the length of the leg opposite the 60° angle is $\sqrt{3}$ times the length of the short leg.
      2. Property of 45°-45°-90° triangle: The length of the hypotenuse of a 45°-45°-90° triangle is $\sqrt{2}$ times the length of a leg.
   D. **Converse of the Pythagorean Theorem:** In any triangle ABC with sides of lengths a, b, and c such that $a^2 + b^2 = c^2$, $\triangle ABC$ is a right triangle with the right angle opposite the side of length c.

IV. Surface areas and volumes
   A. Formulas for areas
      1. **Right prism:** $S.A. = 2B + ph$, where B is the area of a base, p is the perimeter of the base, and h is the height of the prism.
      2. **Right circular cylinder:** $S.A. = 2\pi r^2 + 2\pi rh$, where r is the radius of the circular base and h is the height of the cylinder.
      3. **Right circular cone:** $S.A. = \pi r^2 + \pi r\ell$, where r is the radius of the circular base and ℓ is the slant height.
      4. **Right regular pyramid:** $S.A. = B + \frac{1}{2}p\ell$, where B is the area of the base, p is the perimeter of the base, and ℓ is the slant height.
      5. **Sphere:** $S.A. = 4\pi r^2$, where r is the radius of the sphere.
   B. Formulas for volumes
      1. **Right prism:** $V = Bh$, where B is the area of the base and h is the height.
         a. **Right rectangular prism:** $V = \ell wh$, where ℓ is the length, w is the width, and h is the height.
         b. **Cube:** $V = e^3$, where e is an edge.

2. Right circular cylinder: $V = \pi r^2 h$, where r is the radius of the base and h is the height of the cylinder.

3. Pyramid: $V = \frac{1}{3}Bh$, where B is the area of the base and h is the height of the pyramid.

4. Circular cone: $V = \frac{1}{3}\pi r^2 h$, where r is the radius of the circular base and h is the height.

5. Sphere: $V = \frac{4}{3}\pi r^3$, where r is the radius of the sphere.

CHAPTER REVIEW

1. Determine the area of the shaded region in the following figure:

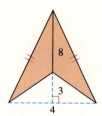

2. Determine the area of the shaded region on each of the following geoboards if the unit of measure is 1 cm^2:

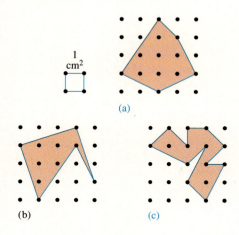

(a)

(b)   (c)

3. Find the area of the kite shown in the following figure:

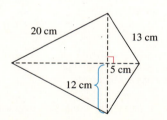

4. Explain how the formula for the area of a trapezoid can be found by using the following figures:

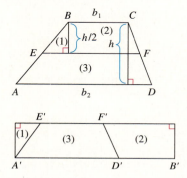

5. Use the following figure to find each of the following areas:
  a. The area of the hexagon
  b. The area of the circle

6. Find the area of each shaded region in the following figures:

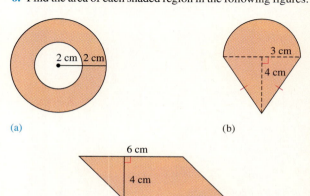

(a)   (b)

(c)

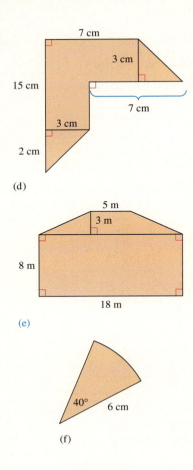

(d)

(e)

(f)

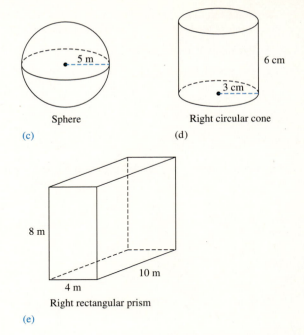

Sphere

(c)

Right circular cone

(d)

Right rectangular prism

(e)

9. Find the lateral surface area of the following right circular cone:

7. For each of the following, determine whether the measures represent sides of a right triangle. Explain your answers.
   a. 5 cm, 12 cm, 13 cm
   b. 40 cm, 60 cm, 104 cm

8. Find the surface area and volume of each of the following figures:

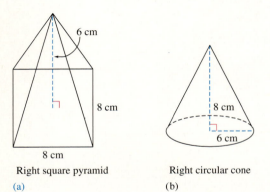

Right square pyramid

(a)

Right circular cone

(b)

10. Doug's Dog Food Company wants to impress the public with the magnitude of the company's growth. Sales of Doug's Dog Food doubled from 1994 to 1995, so the company is displaying the following graph, which shows the radius of the base and the height of the 1995 can to be double those of the 1994 dog food can. What does the graph really show with respect to the company's growth? Explain your answer.

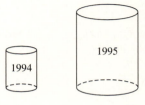

11. Complete each of the following:
   *a. A very heavy object has mass that is measured in _____ .
   b. A cube whose length, width, and height are each 1 cm has a volume of _____ .

*c. If the cube in (b) is filled with water, the mass of the water is _____ .

d. Which has a larger volume: 1 L or 1 dm^3?

e. If a car uses 1 L of gas to go 12 km, the amount of gas needed to go 300 km is _____ L.

f. 20 ha = _____ a

g. 51.8 L = _____ cm^3

h. 10 km^2 = _____ m^2

i. 50 L = _____ mL

j. 5830 mL = _____ L

k. 25 m^3 = _____ dm^3

l. 75 dm^3 = _____ mL

*m. 52,813 g = _____ kg

*n. 4800 kg = _____ t

12. Two cones are defined to be similar if the ratio between their heights equals the ratio between their radii. If two similar cones have heights h_1 and h_2, find the ratio between their volumes in terms of h_1 and h_2.

13. a. A tank that is a right rectangular prism is 1 m × 2 m × 3 m. If the tank is filled with water, what is the mass of the water?

b. Suppose the tank is exactly half full of water and then a heavy metal sphere of radius 30 cm is put into the tank. How high is the water now if the height of the tank is 3 m?

14. For each of the following, fill in the correct unit to make the sentence reasonable:

a. Anna filled the gas tank with 80 _____ .

*b. A man has a mass of about 82 _____ .

*c. The textbook has a mass of 978 _____ .

*d. A nickel has a mass of 5 _____ .

*e. A typical adult cat has a mass of about 4 _____ .

*f. A compact car has a mass of about 1.5 _____ .

g. The amount of coffee in the cup is 180 _____ .

15. For each of the following, decide if the situation is likely or unlikely:

a. Carrie's bath water has a temperature of 15°C.

b. Anne found 26°C too warm and so lowered the thermostat to 21°C.

c. Jim is drinking water that has a temperature of ⁻5°C.

d. The water in the teakettle has a temperature of 120°C.

e. The outside temperature dropped to 5°C, and ice appeared on the lake.

16. Complete each of the following:

*a. 2 dm^3 of water has a mass of _____ g.

*b. 1 L of water has a mass of _____ g.

*c. 3 cm^3 of water has a mass of _____ g.

*d. 4.2 mL of water has a mass of _____ kg.

e. 0.2 L of water has a volume of _____ m^3.

SELECTED BIBLIOGRAPHY

Binswanger, R. "Discovering Perimeter and Area with Logo." *Arithmetic Teacher* 36 (September 1988): 18–24.

Clopton, E. "Sharing Teaching Ideas: Area and Perimeter Are Independent." *Mathematics Teacher* 84 (January 1991): 33–35.

Cohen, D. "Estimating the Volumes of Solid Figures with Curved Surfaces." *Mathematics Teacher* 84 (May 1991): 392–395.

Kilmer, J. "Triangles of Equal Area and Perimeter and Inscribed Circles." *Mathematics Teacher* 81 (January 1988): 65–69.

Lamphere, P. "Geoboard Patterns and Figures." *Teaching Children Mathematics* 1 (January 1995): 282–287.

Miller, W., and L. Wagner. "Pythagorean Dissection Puzzles." *Mathematics Teacher* 86 (April 1993): 302–308, 313–314.

Naraine, B. "If Pythagoras Had a Geoboard." *Mathematics Teacher* 86 (February 1993): 137–140, 145–148.

Nowlin, D. "Practical Geometry Problems: The Case of the Ritzville Pyramids." *Mathematics Teacher* 86 (March 1993): 198–200.

Parker, J., and C. Widmer. "Patterns in Measurement." *Arithmetic Teacher* 40 (January 1993): 292–295.

Pudelka, P. "Sharing Teaching Ideas: Formulas and Sugar Cubes." *Mathematics Teacher* 83 (February 1990): 119–120.

Shultz, J. "Area Models — Spanning the Mathematics of Grades 1–9." *Arithmetic Teacher* 39 (October 1991): 42–46.

Smith, L. "Areas and Perimeters of Geoboard Polygons." *Mathematics Teacher* 83 (May 1990): 392–398.

Stone, M. "Teaching Relationships between Area and Perimeter with the Geometer's Sketchpad." *Mathematics Teacher* 87 (November 1994): 590–594.

Stover, D. "Sharing Teaching Ideas: Area of a Triangle," *Mathematics Teacher* 83 (February 1990): 120.

Taylor, L. "Exploring Geometry with the Geometer's Sketchpad." *Arithmetic Teacher* 40 (November 1992): 187–191.

Usnick, V., P. Lamphere, and G. Bright. "A Generalized Area Formula." *Mathematics Teacher* 85 (December 1992): 752–754.

13

MOTION GEOMETRY AND TESSELLATIONS

An architect designed a gable on a house as a triangular region. After the gable was built, the owner decided to install a square window in the gable so that the corners of the window are on the sides of the triangle as shown in the accompanying figure. The architect has a sketch of the gable and window but does not know what size the window should be. Show how to determine the length of a side of the square window.

Euclid envisioned moving one geometric figure in a plane and placing it on top of another to determine if the two figures were congruent. Intuitively, we know this can be done by making a tracing of one figure, then shifting, turning, or flipping the tracing, and finally placing it back down atop the other figure. Elementary school students seem to be able to identify congruences by this type of predeductive activity. The 5–8 *Standards* (p. 114) supports this approach: *Explorations of flips, slides, turns, stretchers, and shrinkers will illuminate the concepts of congruence and similarity.*

Motion geometry is introduced in this chapter, along with an optional section on *tessellations* of the plane, that is, the filling of a plane with repetitions of a figure in such a way that no figures overlap and there are no gaps.

H I S T O R I C A L   N O T E

In 1872, at age 23, Felix Klein (1849–1925) was appointed to a chair at the University of Erlangen, Germany. His inaugural address, referred to as the *Erlanger Programm,* described geometry as the study of properties of figures that do not change under a particular set of transformations. Specifically, Euclidean geometry was described as the study of such properties of figures as area and lengths, which remain unchanged under a set of transformations called *isometries.*

Section 13-1   ## Translations and Rotations

Translations

translation/slide

Figure 13-1 shows a child moving down a slide without any accompanying twisting or turning. This type of motion is a **translation,** or **slide.**

Figure 13-1

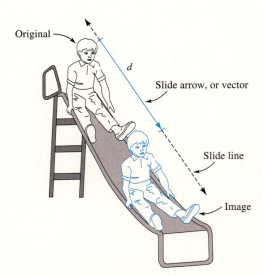

Original

d

Slide arrow, or vector

Slide line

Image

In the figure, the child has moved a certain distance in a certain direction along a line. The distance and direction the original figure is moved are marked with a **slide arrow,** or **vector,** along a **slide line** to obtain the **image.**

slide arrow/vector
slide line • image

Definition of a Translation

A **translation** is a motion of a plane that moves every point of the plane a specified distance in a specified direction along a straight line.

Figure 13-2 shows a translation that takes $\triangle ABC$ to $\triangle A'B'C'$. The translation is determined by the slide arrow, or vector from M to N. The vector determines the image of any point in the plane in the following way: The image of a point A in the plane is the point A' obtained by sliding A along a line parallel to $\overleftrightarrow{MN}$ in the direction from M to N by the distance MN. (MN is denoted by d in Figure 13-2.) Dashed segments have been used to connect the vertices of $\triangle ABC$ with their respective images under the translation. Notice that $AA' = BB' = CC' = d$ and $\overline{AA'} \parallel \overline{BB'} \parallel \overline{CC'}$. It appears that under the translation, figures do not change their shapes or sizes.

Figure 13-2

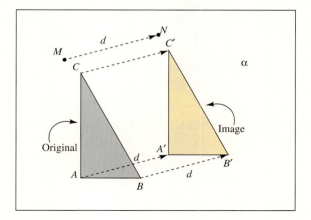

A translation preserves both length and angle size (and hence the congruence) of figures. Any motion that preserves distance is an **isometry** (derived from Greek and meaning "equal measure"), or **rigid motion.** Thus a translation is an isometry.

isometry
rigid motion

Constructions of Translations

The image of a figure under a translation can be constructed with tracing paper or by using only a compass and straightedge. To construct a translation image, we first need to know how to find the image of a given point. Suppose we have a translation determined by the slide arrow from M to N, as shown in Figure 13-3(a). A', the image of A under this translation, shown in Figure 13-3(b), must be such that $\overline{AA'}$ is parallel to $\overline{MN}$ and $AA' = MN$. This implies that $AA'NM$ is a parallelogram (why?). Hence, to find A' we construct parallelogram $AA'NM$, where A, N, and M are given.

To construct the parallelogram efficiently, first recall that a quadrilateral in which each pair of opposite sides is congruent is a parallelogram. Thus we construct vertex A' by making $AA' = MN$ and $NA' = MA$. This is shown in Figure 13-3(b).

Figure 13-3

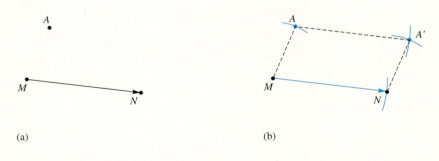

(a)   (b)

REMARK   There exist two parallelograms with vertices A, M, and N, but only one, as indicated in Figure 13-3(b), takes A to A' in the direction of the arrow $\overrightarrow{MN}$.

To find the image of a triangle under a translation, we find the images of the three vertices by using a process similar to that used in Figure 13-3 and connect these images with segments to form the triangle's image.

It also is often possible to use a geoboard or a grid to find an image of a segment, as the following example shows.

Example 13-1   Find the image of $\overline{AB}$ under the translation from X to X' pictured on the dot paper in Figure 13-4.

Figure 13-4

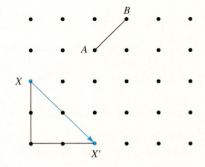

Solution X' is the image of X under the translation. So it could be obtained from X by shifting X two units vertically down and then two units horizontally to the right, as shown in Figure 13-5. This shifting determines the slide arrow from X to X'. The image of each point on the dot paper can be obtained by first shifting it two units down and then two units to the right. The image of $\overline{AB}$ is found in this way in Figure 13-5.

Figure 13-5

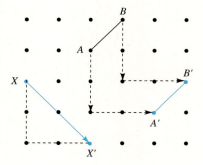

● ● ●

● Suppose the image of any point P is determined by shifting the point 2 units up and then 3 units to the left, as shown in Figure 13-6. Is this a translation? If so, draw the slide arrow and find its length. If not, explain why not. ●

Figure 13-6

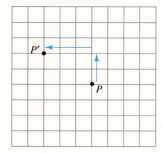

Coordinate Representation of Translations

In many applications of mathematics such as computer graphics, it is necessary to use translations in a coordinate system. In Figure 13-7, $\triangle A'B'C'$ is the image of $\triangle ABC$ under the translation defined by the slide arrow from O to P, where O is the origin and P has coordinates $(5, {}^-2)$. Point P is the image of point O under the given translation. The point $P(5, {}^-2)$ can be obtained by moving O horizontally to the right 5 units and then 2 units down. As each point in the triangle is translated in the direction from O to P by the same distance OP, we can obtain the image of any point by moving horizontally to the right 5 units and then vertically 2 units down (why?). This is shown in Figure 13-7 for points A, B, C and their corresponding images A', B', and C'.

Figure 13-7

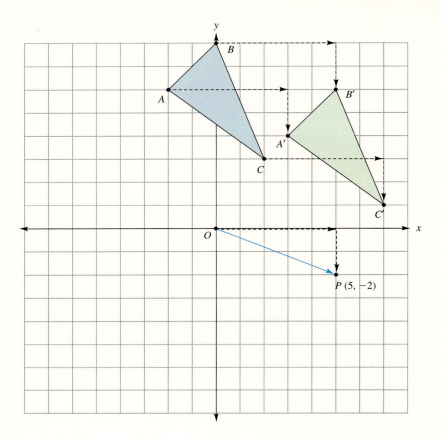

Table 13-1 shows how the coordinates of the image vertices A', B', and C' in Figure 13-7 are obtained from the coordinates of A, B, and C.

Table 13-1

Point (x, y)	Image Point $(x + 5, y - 2)$
$A\ (^-2, 6)$	$A'\ (3, 4)$
$B\ (0, 8)$	$B'\ (5, 6)$
$C\ (2, 3)$	$C'\ (7, 1)$

This discussion suggests that we could describe a translation by showing how the coordinates of any point (x, y) are changed. The translation described in Table 13-1 can be written symbolically as $(x, y) \rightarrow (x + 5, y - 2)$.

Definition of a Translation in a Coordinate System

A translation is a function from the plane to the plane such that to every point (x, y) corresponds the point $(x + a, y + b)$ for real numbers a and b.

In general, the point $(x + a, y + b)$ is the image of the point (x, y) and the translation is symbolized as $(x, y) \rightarrow (x + a, y + b)$.

Example 13-2

Find the coordinates of the images of $A(0, 0)$, $B(2, 2)$, $C(4, 0)$, and $D(2, {}^-2)$ under each of the following translations. In each case, draw the quadrilateral *ABCD* and its image.

a. $(x, y) \rightarrow (x - 2, y + 4)$
b. A translation determined by the slide arrow from $P(0, 0)$ to $Q({}^-2, 4)$
c. A translation determined by the slide arrow from $S(4, {}^-3)$ to $T(2, 1)$

Solution   **a.** Because $(x, y) \rightarrow (x - 2, y + 4)$, the images A', B', C', and D' of the corresponding points *A, B, C,* and *D* can be found as follows:

$$A(0, 0) \rightarrow A'(0 - 2, 0 + 4), \text{ or } A'({}^-2, 4)$$
$$B(2, 2) \rightarrow B'(2 - 2, 2 + 4), \text{ or } B'(0, 6)$$
$$C(4, 0) \rightarrow C'(4 - 2, 0 + 4), \text{ or } C'(2, 4)$$
$$D(2, {}^-2) \rightarrow D'(2 - 2, {}^-2 + 4), \text{ or } D'(0, 2)$$

The square *ABCD* and its image $A'B'C'D'$ are shown in Figure 13-8.

Figure 13-8

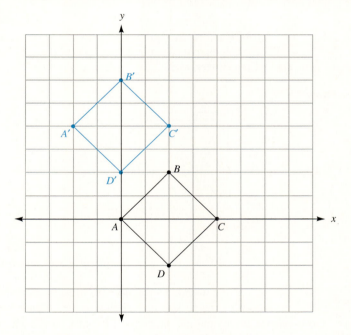

b. To obtain the image of any point in the plane under the translation from *P* to *Q*, we also move 2 units to the left and then 4 units up. Consequently, the image of any point (x, y) is $(x + ({}^-2), y + 4)$, or $(x - 2, y + 4)$. This is the same translation as in (a) and hence the graph is the same as that in (a).

c. We could move from $S(4, {}^-3)$ to $T(2, 1)$ by moving a certain number of units horizontally and then a certain number of units vertically. Because $4 + ({}^-2) = 2$ and ${}^-3 + 4 = 1$, moving 2 units to the left and then 4 units up will take us from *S* to *T*. The image of any point (x, y) under the translation from *S* to *T* can be obtained in the same way; that is, the image of any point (x, y) is $(x - 2, y + 4)$. Thus this graph also is the same as that obtained in (a).

Rotations

rotation/turn

A **rotation,** or **turn,** is another kind of isometry. Figure 13-9 illustrates congruent figures resulting from a rotation about point O.

Figure 13-9

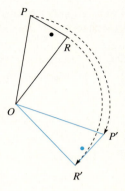

A rotation can be constructed by using tracing paper, as in Figure 13-10. In Figure 13-10(a), $\triangle ABC$ and point O are traced on tracing paper. Holding point O fixed, we turn the tracing paper to obtain the image, $\triangle A'B'C'$, as shown in Figure 13-10(b). Point O is the **turn center**, and $\angle COC'$ is the **turn angle.**

turn center • turn angle

Figure 13-10

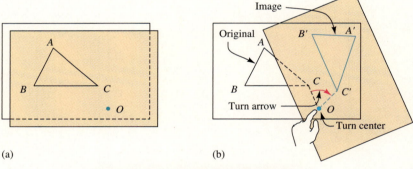

(a)   (b)

Construction of a Rotation Using Tracing Paper

To determine a rotation, we must know three pieces of data: the turn center; the direction of the turn, either clockwise or counterclockwise; and the amount of the turn. The amount and the direction of the turn can be illustrated by a **turn arrow,** or it can be specified as a number of degrees.

turn arrow

Figure 13-11 shows an example of a rotation about point O through 30° in a counterclockwise direction. The image of the letter **F** is shown in green.

Figure 13-11

This discussion leads to the following definition.

> **Definition of Rotation**
>
> A **rotation** is a motion of the plane determined by holding one point — the center — fixed and rotating the plane about this point by a certain amount in a certain direction.

Construction of a Rotation Using a Compass and Straightedge

Consider a rotation about O through a given angle and direction as in Figure 13-12(a). What must be done to find the image of any point P in the plane under the rotation? We draw a circle with center O and radius OP, as in Figure 13-12(b). Then, starting at P, we move along the circle — counterclockwise if $\alpha > 0$ and clockwise if $\alpha < 0$ — until we locate the point P' such that $m(\angle POP') = \alpha$. Using a compass and a straightedge, we can find the location of P' by constructing $\angle POP'$ congruent to the angle of rotation so that P' will be drawn in the desired direction indicated by the amount of the rotation, or the turn angle. This is illustrated in Figure 13-12(b).

Figure 13-12

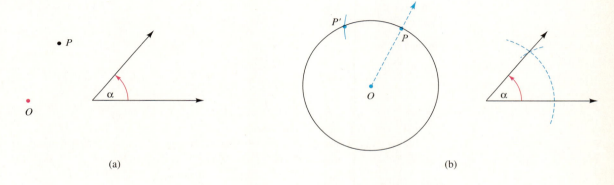

(a)   (b)

REMARK   Because a rotation is an isometry, the image of a figure under a rotation is congruent to the original figure. It can be shown that under any isometry, the image of a line is a line, the image of a circle is a circle, and the images of parallel lines are parallel lines.

For certain angles like 90°, rotations may be constructed on a geoboard or dot paper, as demonstrated in Example 13-3.

Example 13-3   Find the image of $\triangle ABC$ under the rotation with center O, as shown in Figure 13-13.

Figure 13-13

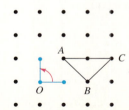

Solution $\triangle A'B'C'$, the image of $\triangle ABC$, is shown in Figure 13-14. The image of A is A' because $\angle A'OA$ is a right angle (why?) and $OA = OA'$. Similarly B' is the image of B. To find the location of C', we use the fact that $\triangle A'B'C' \cong \triangle ABC$ and hence $\angle B \cong \angle B'$. The location of point C' shown makes $\angle B \cong \angle B'$, $C'B' = CB$ (why?), and the direction of the rotation is counterclockwise as specified.

Figure 13-14

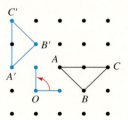

A rotation of 360° about a point will move any figure onto itself. A rotation of 180° **half-turn** about a point is also of particular interest. Such a rotation is a **half-turn.** Because a half-turn is a rotation, it has all the properties of rotations. Figure 13-15 shows some shapes and their images under a half-turn about point O.

Figure 13-15

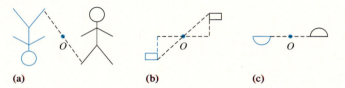

(a)   (b)   (c)

Figure 13-16 shows a point P and its image P' under a half-turn about O. Because $\angle POP'$ measures 180°, points P, O, and P' are collinear.

Figure 13-16

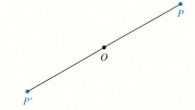

These observations make it easy to construct an image of a figure under a half-turn using a straightedge and a compass, as demonstrated in the following example.

Example 13-4   Use a compass and a straightedge to find the image of a line ℓ under a half-turn about point O (see Figure 13-17).

Figure 13-17

Solution   Because a line is determined by two points and the image of a line is a line, it is sufficient for us to pick any two points on ℓ and find the images of these points under the half-turn. In Figure 13-18, we pick two arbitrary points A and B on ℓ and find their images A' and B' by drawing $\overrightarrow{AO}$ and marking off $OA' = OA$ so that O is the midpoint of $\overline{AA'}$. We find B' similarly. The line connecting A' and B' is the image of ℓ. The result is illustrated in Figure 13-18.

Figure 13-18

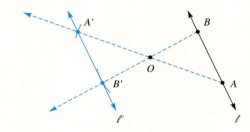

• • •

An Application of Rotations: Slopes of Perpendicular Lines

Transformations can be used to investigate various mathematical relationships. For example, consider the relationship between the slopes of two perpendicular lines, neither of which is vertical.

We first consider a special case in which the lines go through the origin. Suppose the slopes of the lines ℓ_1 and ℓ_2, shown in Figure 13-19, are m_1 and m_2, respectively. Because the slope of a line is equal to rise over run, the slope of ℓ_1 can also be determined from $\triangle OAB$, in which we choose $OA = 1$. We have $m_1 = \dfrac{\text{rise}}{\text{run}} = \dfrac{BA}{1} = BA$.

Figure 13-19

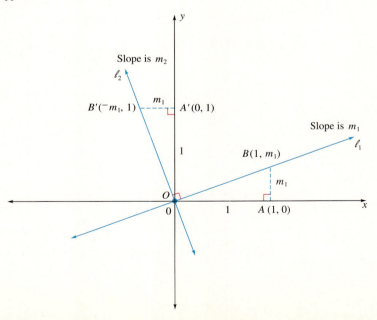

We then rotate the plane 90° counterclockwise about center O. The image of ℓ_1 is ℓ_2. To determine the image of $\triangle OBA$, we need only determine the images of each of the vertices of the triangle. The image of O is O itself. The image of A is A' on the y-axis (why?), and the image of B is B' on ℓ_2 (why?). Because rotation preserves congruence, $\triangle OB'A' \cong \triangle OBA$; consequently, $\angle B'A'O'$ is a right angle, $A'B' = m_1$, and $OA' = 1$. Thus as shown in Figure 13–19, point B' is at $(^-m_1, 1)$. We can use the slope formula to find the slope of ℓ_2 as follows:

$$m_2 = \frac{1 - 0}{-m_1 - 0} = \frac{1}{-m_1} = \frac{^-1}{m_1}.$$

Thus $m_2 = {}^-1/m_1$, or $m_1 m_2 = {}^-1$.

The relationship between the slopes m_1 and m_2 of two perpendicular lines (neither of which is vertical) that do not intersect at the origin can always be found using two lines parallel to the original lines but that pass through the origin. Because parallel lines have equal slopes the relationship between the slopes of the perpendicular lines is the same as the relationship between the slopes of the perpendicular lines through the origin, that is, $m_1 m_2 = {}^-1$.

It is also possible to prove the converse statement, that is, if the slopes of two lines satisfy the condition $m_1 m_2 = {}^-1$, then the lines are perpendicular. We summarize these results in the following property.

Property of Slopes of Perpendicular Lines

Two lines, neither of which is vertical, are perpendicular if, and only if, their slopes m_1 and m_2 satisfy the condition $m_1 m_2 = {}^-1$. Any vertical line is perpendicular to a line with slope 0.

Example 13-5 | Find the equation of line ℓ through point $(^-1, 2)$ and perpendicular to the line $y = 3x + 5$.

Solution   If m is the slope of ℓ as in Figure 13-20, then ℓ can be written as $y = mx + b$.

Figure 13-20

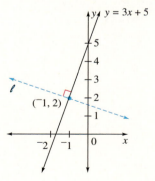

Because the line $y = 3x + 5$ has slope 3 and is perpendicular to ℓ, we have $m \cdot 3 = {}^-1$; therefore $m = -\frac{1}{3}$. Consequently, the equation of ℓ is

$$y = -\frac{1}{3}x + b.$$

Because the point $(^-1, 2)$ is on ℓ, we can substitute $x = {}^-1, y = 2$ in $y = -\dfrac{1}{3}x + b$ and solve for b as follows:

$$2 = -\frac{1}{3} \cdot ({}^-1) + b$$

$$\frac{5}{3} = b$$

Consequently, the equation of ℓ is

$$y = -\frac{1}{3}x + \frac{5}{3}.$$

• • •

Ongoing Assessment 13-1

1. For each of the following, find the image of the given quadrilateral under a translation from A to B:

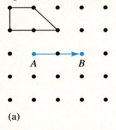

(a)

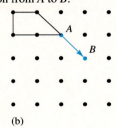

(b)

2. Find the figure whose image is given in each of the following under a translation from X to X':

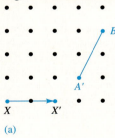

(a)

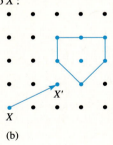

(b)

3. Construct the image of $\overline{BC}$ under the translation pictured in the following figure by using the following:
  a. Tracing paper
  b. Compass and straightedge

4. Find the coordinates of the image for each of the following points under the translation defined by $(x, y) \rightarrow (x + 3, y - 4)$:
  a. $(0, 0)$ **b.** $({}^-3, 4)$
  c. $({}^-6, {}^-9)$ **d.** $(7, 14)$

5. Find the coordinates of the points whose images under the translation $(x, y) \rightarrow (x - 3, y + 4)$ are the following:
  a. $(0, 0)$ **b.** $({}^-3, 4)$
  c. $({}^-6, {}^-9)$ **d.** $(7, 14)$

6. Consider the translation $(x, y) \rightarrow (x + 3, y - 4)$. In each of the following, draw the image of the figure under the translation and find the coordinates of the points of the image.

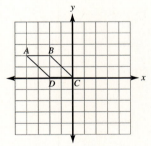

(a)

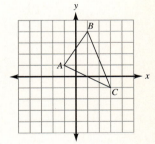

(b)

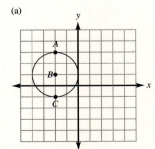

(c)

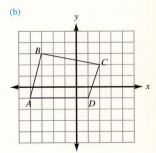

(d)

7. Consider the translation $(x, y) \rightarrow (x + 3, y - 4)$. In each of the following, draw the figure whose image is shown:

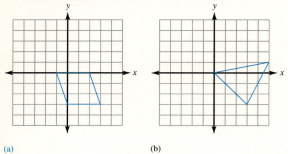

(a)   (b)

8. Find the image of the following quadrilateral in a 90° counterclockwise rotation about O:

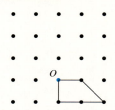

9. For each of the following, use only a compass and a straightedge to find the image of the figure under the rotation about point O by the given angle and direction. Check your answers using tracing paper.

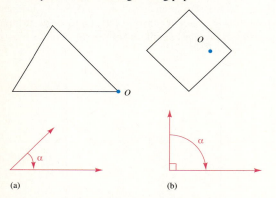

(a)   (b)

10. The images of $\overline{AB}$ under various rotations are given in the following figures. Find $\overline{AB}$ in each case.

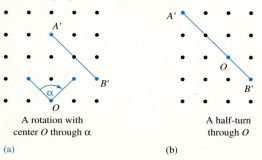

A rotation with   A half-turn
center O through α through O

(a)   (b)

11. a. The image of NOON is still NOON after a special half-turn. List some other words that have the same property. What letters can such words contain?

b. 1961 is the image of 1961 after a special half-turn. What other natural numbers less than 10,000 have this property?

12. a. Refer to the following figure and use paper folding or any other method to show that if P' is the image of P under rotation about point O by a given angle, then O is on the perpendicular bisector of $\overline{PP'}$.

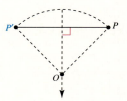

b. $\triangle A'B'C'$ shown in the following figure was obtained by rotating $\triangle ABC$ about a certain point O. Explain how to find the point O and the angle of rotation.

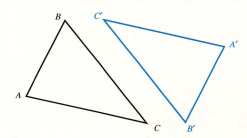

13. The images of any point under a rotation by certain angles can be found with only a compass and straightedge (without the use of a protractor). Construct the image of P when it is rotated about O, as shown in the following figure, for angles with the following measures and direction:

a. 90° counterclockwise   **b.** 90° clockwise
c. 45° counterclockwise   **d.** 60° clockwise
e. 30° counterclockwise

• P

• O

14. For each of the following points, find the coordinates of the image point under a half-turn about the origin:

a. $(4, 0)$ **b.** $(0, 3)$ **c.** $(2, 4)$
d. $(^-2, 5)$ **e.** $(^-2, ^-4)$ **f.** (a, b)

15. In each of the following figures, find the image of the figure under a half-turn about O:

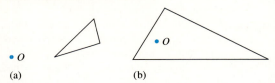

(a)   (b)

16. Draw any line and label it ℓ. Use tracing paper to find ℓ', the image of ℓ under each of the following rotations. In each case, describe in words how ℓ' is related to ℓ.
  a. Half-turn about point O on ℓ
  b. Half-turn about a point O, not on ℓ
  c. A 90° turn counterclockwise about point O, not on ℓ
  d. A 60° turn counterclockwise about point O, not on ℓ

17. a. For each of the following, find the coordinates of A', the image of A under rotation about the origin counterclockwise by a right angle.

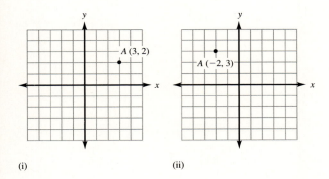

(i)   (ii)

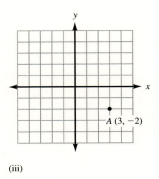

(iii)

  b. Based on your answers in (a), conjecture the coordinates of A', the image of A under the rotation about the origin counterclockwise by a right angle if the coordinates of A are (a, b).
  c. Justify your conjecture in (b).

18. a. Find the final image of $\triangle ABC$ by performing two rotations in succession each with center O, one by angle α and the other by angle β in directions as shown in the figure.

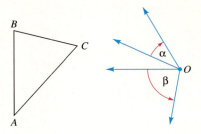

  b. Is the order of the rotations important?
  c. Could the result have been accomplished in one rotation?

19. In the following figure, construct through point P the segment $\overline{AB}$ that is bisected by point P, where A is on line ℓ and B is on line m:

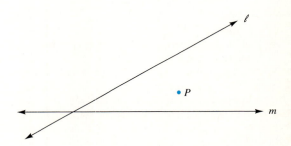

★ **20.** The people of Climate County want to build a road connecting Sunny Street and Shady Lane. They want the road to be parallel to and the same length as the west side of Rainbow Park. Show where the new road should be built and explain why you placed the road there.

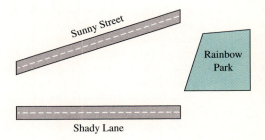

21. a. Translations may be explored in Logo by using a figure called an EE. Type the following programs into your computer and then run the following with the turtle starting at home with heading 0:
  (i) `SLIDE 40 45`
  (ii) `SLIDE 200 57`
  (iii) `SLIDE (-50) (-75)`

```
TO SLIDE :DIRECTION :DISTANCE
  EE
  PENUP
  SETHEADING :DIRECTION
  FORWARD :DISTANCE
  PENDOWN
  SETHEADING 0
  EE
END
TO EE
  FORWARD 50 RIGHT 90
  FORWARD 25 BACK 25
  LEFT 90 BACK 25
  RIGHT 90 FORWARD 10
  BACK 10 LEFT 90
  BACK 25 RIGHT 90
  FORWARD 25 BACK 25
  LEFT 90
END
```

b. Edit the SLIDE procedure in (a) so that it will slide an equilateral triangle.

22. Write a Logo procedure called ROTATE that will draw a square and produce the image of the square when the square is rotated by an arbitrary angle :A about one of its vertices.

23. Write a Logo procedure called TURN.CIRCLE that will draw a circle passing through the home of the turtle and produce the image of the circle under the following transformations:
  a. A half-turn about the turtle's home
  b. A 90° counterclockwise rotation about the turtle's home

Communication

24. If we are given two congruent nonparallel segments, is it always possible to find a rotation so that the image of one segment will be the other segment? Explain why or why not.

25. In each of the following, decide whether it is possible to find the image of every point in the plane under the transformation. Explain your reasoning.
  a. A translation if one point and its image are known
  b. A rotation if two points and their images are known
  c. A half-turn if one point and its image are known
  d. A rotation by 90° counterclockwise if one point and its image are known
  e. A rotation by 45° clockwise if one point is given and it is known that its image is the point itself

26. When $\triangle ABC$ in the following figure is rotated about a point O by 360°, each of the vertices traces a path.

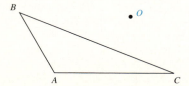

a. What geometric figure does each vertex trace?
b. Identify all points O for which two vertices trace an identical path. Justify your answer.
c. Given any $\triangle ABC$, is there a point O such that the three vertices trace an identical path? If so, describe how to find such a point. Justify your answer.

27. For each of the following figures, trace the figure on tracing paper, rotate the tracing by 180° about the given point O, sketch the image, and then make a conjecture about the kind of figure that is formed by the union of the original figure and its image. In each case, explain why you think your conjecture is true.

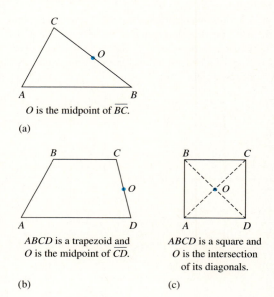

O is the midpoint of $\overline{BC}$.

(a)

ABCD is a trapezoid and O is the midpoint of $\overline{CD}$.

(b)

ABCD is a square and O is the intersection of its diagonals.

(c)

Open-ended

28. A drawing of a cube, shown in the following figure, can be created by drawing a square *ABCD*, finding its image under translation defined by the slide arrow from A to A' so that $AA' = AB$, and connecting the points A, B, C, and D with their corresponding images.

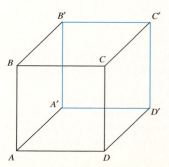

Draw several other perspective geometric figures using translations. In each case, name the figures and indicate the slide arrow that defines the translation.

29. Wall stenciling has been used to obtain an effect similar to that of wallpapering. The stencil pattern shown in the following figure can be used to create a border on a wall.

Measure the length of a wall of a room and design your own stencil pattern to create a border. Cut the pattern from a sheet of plastic or cardboard. Define the translation that will accomplish creating an appropriate border for the wall.

30. The following pattern can be created by rotating figure *A* about *O* by the indicated angle, then rotating the image *B* about *O* by the same angle, and then rotating the image *C* about *O* by the same angle, and so on until one of the images coincides with the original figure *A*.

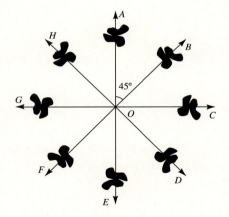

Make several designs with different numbers of congruent figures around a circle in which the image of each figure under the same rotation is the next figure and so that one of the images coincides with the original figure.

Cooperative Learning

31. Mark a point *A* on a sheet of paper and set a straightedge through *A* as shown in the following figure. Find a circular shape (a jar lid is a good choice) and mark point *P* on the edge of the shape. Place the shape on the straightedge so that *P* coincides with *A*. Consider the path traced by *P* as the circle rolls so that its edge stays in contact with the straightedge all the time and until *P* comes in contact with the straightedge again at point *B*.

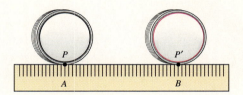

a. Have one member of your group roll the circular shape and another draw the path traced by *P* as accurately as possible.
b. Have each member of the group identify the transformations that are involved in the experiment. Compare your answers.
c. Discuss how to check if the path traced by point *P* is an arc of a circle.
d. Find the length of $\overline{AB}$.

32. In the following figure, *A'* is the image of *A* under the rotation about *O* by $\angle A'OA$ counterclockwise. *A'* is also the image of *A* under the reflection in line ℓ, which is the perpendicular bisector of $\overline{AA'}$.

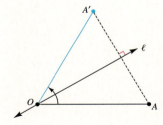

a. Write an explanation to convince your fellow students that what was just described does not imply that a rotation can be accomplished by a reflection. Explain why no rotation can be accomplished by a reflection.
b. Compare your individual written explanations and write a combined group explanation.

33. Suppose the square *ABCD* in the following figure rolls along a straight line.
a. Have one member of your group roll the square and another draw the path traced by *A* as the square rolls and comes in contact with the line again. What are the transformations involved in this experiment?
b. Discuss how to determine if the path traced by *A* is the arc of a circle.
c. Find the length of $\overline{AA'}$.

TECHNOLOGY CORNER

Use a geometry utility to draw an equilateral triangle and two altitudes of the triangle. Let O be the point at which the altitudes intersect. Rotate the triangle by 120° about O in any direction. Make a conjecture based on this experiment. Do you think your conjecture may be true for some triangles that are not equilateral? Why?

BRAIN TEASER

In the drawing below, a coin is shown above and touching another coin. Suppose the top coin is rotated around the circumference of the bottom coin until it rests directly below the bottom coin. Will the head be straight up or upside down? Explain why.

LABORATORY ACTIVITY

1. As a van Hiele Level 1 activity, look around your classroom and find and list the following:
   a. Congruent objects such that a translation will take one object to another
   b. Congruent objects such that a rotation will take one object to another
2. As a van Hiele Level 3 activity, use a compass and a straightedge to construct in the following drawing two perpendicular chords of equal length through points P and Q.

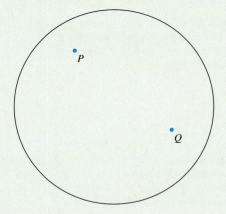

Section 13-2   Reflections and Glide Reflections

Reflections

reflection/flip

Another isometry is a **reflection,** or **flip.** One example of a reflection often encountered in our daily lives is a mirror image. Figure 13-21 shows a figure with its mirror image.

Figure 13-21

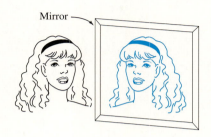

Mirror

Another reflection is shown in the following B.C. cartoon.

B.C.   **by johnny hart**

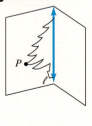

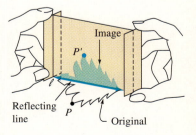

We can simulate reflections in a plane in various ways. Consider the half tree shown in Figure 13-22(a). Folding the paper along the **reflecting line** and drawing the image gives the **mirror image,** or *image,* of the half tree. In Figure 13-22(b), the paper is shown unfolded.

reflecting line
mirror image

Another way to simulate a reflection in a line involves using a Mira. This way is illustrated in Figure 13-22(c).

Figure 13-22

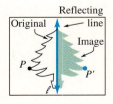

(a)   (b)   (c)

In Figure 13-23(a), the image of P under a reflection in line ℓ is P'. $\overline{PP'}$ is both perpendicular to and bisected by ℓ, or equivalently, ℓ is the perpendicular bisector of $\overline{PP'}$.

Figure 13-23

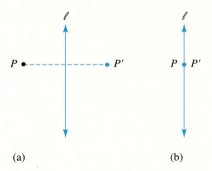

(a)   (b)

In Figure 13-23(b), P is its own image under the reflection in line ℓ. If ℓ were a mirror, then P' would be the mirror image of P. This leads us to the following definition of a reflection.

Definition of Reflection

A **reflection** in a line ℓ is a motion of a plane that pairs each point P of the plane with a point P' in such a way that ℓ is the perpendicular bisector of $\overline{PP'}$, as long as P is not on ℓ. If P is on ℓ, then $P = P'$.

In Figure 13-24, we see another property of a reflection. In the original triangle ABC, if we walk clockwise around the vertices, starting at vertex A, we see the vertices in the order A-B-C. However, in the reflection image of triangle ABC, if we start at A' (the image of A) and walk clockwise, we see the vertices in the following order: A'-C'-B'. Thus a reflection does something that neither a translation nor a rotation does; it reverses the orientation of the original figure.

Figure 13-24

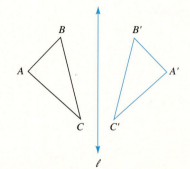

There are many methods of constructing a reflection image. We already illustrated such constructions with paper folding and tracing and a Mira. Next, we further illustrate the construction of the image of a figure under a reflection in a line with tracing paper and a compass and straightedge.

Constructing a Reflection by Using Tracing Paper

Figure 13-25(a) shows the use of tracing paper. We trace the original figure, the reflecting line, and a point on the reflecting line, which we use as a reference point. When we flip the tracing paper over to perform the reflection, we align the reflecting line and the reference point, as in Figure 13-25(b). Aligning the reference point ensures that no translating occurs along the reflecting line when the reflection is performed. If we wish the image to be on the paper with the original, we may indent the tracing paper or acetate sheet to mark the images of the original vertices.

Figure 13-25

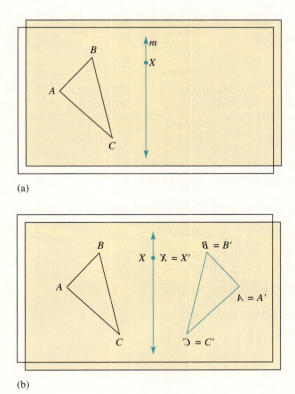

(a)

(b)

Constructing a Reflection by Paper Folding

Paper folding and mirrors are often used in elementary school to explore reflection in a line, as shown on the following student page from *Addison-Wesley Mathematics,* Grade 7, 1993.

Reflection in a Line

LEARN ABOUT IT

EXPLORE   Complete the Activity

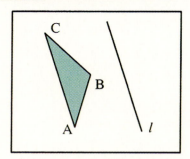

Draw △ABC and line *l*. Fold along *l* keeping △ABC on the outside of the paper.

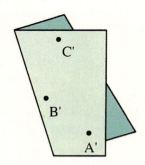

Mark points A', B', and C' that coincide with the vertices of △ABC.

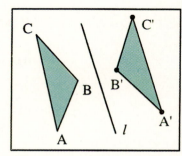

Unfold the paper and draw △A'B'C'.

TALK ABOUT IT

1. Set a mirror on line *l* perpendicular to the paper. What do you see?

2. How is the fold line *l* related to $\overline{BB'}$?

When you look at △ABC, in the mirror on the reflection line *l*, △ABC appears to be △A'B'C'. So, △A'B'C' is called the mirror or **reflection image** of △ABC in line *l*.

The reflection image of ABCD in *l* is EFGH.

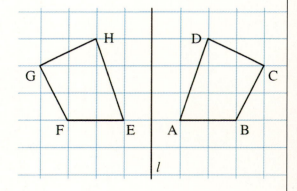

Constructing a Reflection Using a Compass and a Straightedge

The image of a point and the image of a line under a reflection are considered in the following investigation and example.

INVESTIGATION 13-2

● Use the definition of a reflection in a line and properties of a rhombus to construct the image P' of point P in Figure 13-26 under reflection in line m using only a compass and straightedge. ●

Figure 13-26

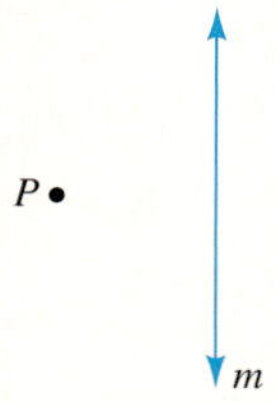

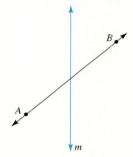

(a)

Example 13-6 Describe how to construct the image of $\overleftrightarrow{AB}$ under a reflection in line m in Figure 13-27.

Figure 13-27

Solution Under a reflection, the image of a line is a line. Thus, to find the image of $\overleftrightarrow{AB}$, it is sufficient to choose any two points on the line and find their images. The images determine the line that is the image of $\overleftrightarrow{AB}$. We choose two points whose images are easy to find. Point X, the intersection of $\overleftrightarrow{AB}$ and m, is its own image. If we choose point A and use a compass and straightedge, we produce the construction shown in Figure 13-28.

Figure 13-28

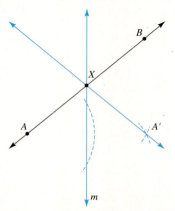

Constructing a Reflection on Dot Paper or a Geoboard

On dot paper or a geoboard, the images of figures under a reflection can sometimes be found by inspection, as seen in Example 13-7.

Example 13-7

Find the image of △*ABC* under a reflection in line *m*, as in Figure 13-29.

Figure 13-29

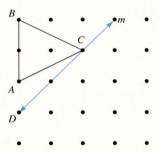

Solution The image of *A'B'C'* is given in Figure 13-30. Note that *C* is the image of itself and the images of the vertices *A* and *B* are *A'* and *B'* such that *m* is the perpendicular bisector of $\overline{AA'}$ and $\overline{BB'}$.

Figure 13-30

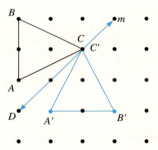

It is possible to find the reflecting line, if we are given an original figure and its reflection image. An example of this is provided in Example 13-8.

Example 13-8

Given △*ABC* and its reflection image △*A'B'C'*, as shown in Figure 13-31, find the line of reflection.

Figure 13-31

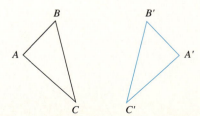

Solution   The reflecting line *m* is the perpendicular bisector of the connecting points and their images of all the segments. Thus it is sufficient to find the perpendicular bisector of $\overline{AA'}$. This is shown in Figure 13-32. Any vertex other than *A* could also have been used.

Figure 13-32

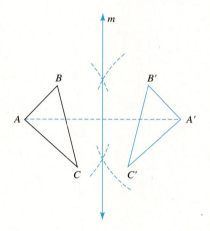

• • •

I N V E S T I G A T I O N   1 3 - 3

● Describe how to find the line of reflection in Example 13-8 using paper folding.   ●

Problem 1

Two farm houses are located away from a road, as shown in Figure 13-33. A telephone company wants to construct a telephone pole at the edge of the road so that the total length of the telephone cable is as short as possible. Where should the pole be located?

Figure 13-33

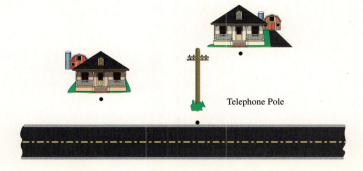

Telephone Pole

Understanding the Problem.   To understand the problem better, we first *draw a diagram,* as seen in Figure 13-34. We label the houses H and T and the road r. We need to find the point P to represent the telephone pole on the road so that the distance $HP + PT$ is as short as possible.

Figure 13-34

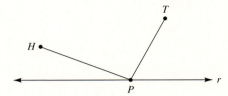

Devising a Plan.   From the properties of reflections, we know that if T' is the reflection of point T in line r, then r is the perpendicular bisector of $\overline{TT'}$ as shown in Figure 13-35(a). Hence, any point on r is equidistant from T and T' and $PT = PT'$. Therefore we may solve the problem by *solving a related problem.* We find a point P on r such that the path from H to P and then to T' is as short as possible. The shortest path connecting H and T' is a segment. The intersection of $\overline{HT'}$, and r determines the point on the road at which the pole should be placed.

Figure 13-35

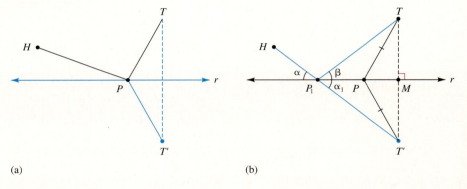

(a)   (b)

Carrying Out the Plan.   Connect H and T' as shown in Figure 13-35(b). The point of intersection P_1 is the required point. The pole should be located at P_1.

Looking Back.   To prove that the path from H to P_1 to T is the shortest possible, we need to prove that $HP_1 + P_1T < HP + PT$, where P is any point on r different from P_1. Because $HP_1 + P_1T = HP_1 + P_1T' = HT'$ (why?) and $HP + PT = HP + PT'$ (why?), the inequality that we need to prove is equivalent to $HT' < HP + PT'$. This last inequality follows from the Triangle Inequality.

• • •

REMARK   In Figure 13-35, notice the relationships among angles whose measures are marked α, α_1, and β. Because α and α_1 are measures of vertical angles, $\alpha = \alpha_1$ Because the image of $\angle TP_1P$ under reflection in r is $\angle T'P_1P$ the measures of these angles are equal, that is, $\alpha_1 = \beta$. Consequently, $\alpha = \beta$. This implies that if the path from H to P_1 to T is the shortest possible, then the acute angle formed by $\overline{HP_1}$ and r is congruent to the acute angle formed by $\overline{TP_1}$ and r. The converse of this statement is also true; that is, if the angles are congruent, the path is the shortest possible.

Reflections in a Coordinate System

For some reflection lines like the x-axis and y-axis and the line $y = x$, it is quite easy to find the coordinates of the image, given the coordinates of the point. In Figure 13-36, the line $y = x$ bisects the angle between the x-axis and y-axis. The image of $A(1, 4)$ is the point $A'(4, 1)$. Also the image of $B(^-3, 0)$ is $B'(0, ^-3)$. It is left as an exercise to show that in general the image of $P(a, b)$ is the point $P'(b, a)$. Consequently, the reflection in the line $y = x$ exchanges the coordinates of the point. Is this still true if the point is not above line $y = x$?

Figure 13-36

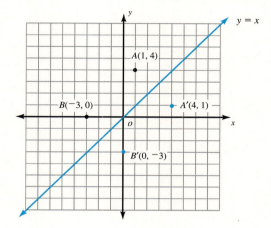

Glide Reflections

glide reflection   Another basic isometry is a **glide reflection.** An example of a glide reflection is shown in the footprints of Figure 13-37. We consider the footprint labeled F_1 to have been translated to footprint F_2 and then reflected over line m to yield F_3, the image of F_1.

Figure 13-37

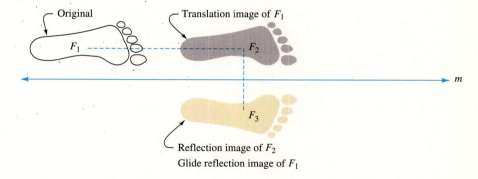

The illustration in Figure 13-37 leads us to the following definition.

Definition of Glide Reflection

A **glide reflection** is a motion consisting of a translation followed by a reflection in a line parallel to the slide arrow.

Another illustration of a glide reflection is shown in Figure 13-38. In that figure, $\triangle A_1B_1C_1$ is the image of $\triangle ABC$ under a translation taking M to N, and $\triangle A'B'C'$ is the image of $\triangle A_1B_1C_1$ under a reflection in m, where m is parallel to $\overrightarrow{MN}$. Hence, the glide reflection takes $\triangle ABC$ to $\triangle A'B'C'$.

Figure 13-38

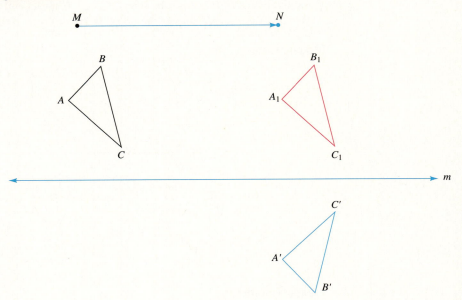

Because constructing a glide reflection involves constructing a translation and a reflection, which we have already seen how to perform, the task of constructing a glide reflection is not a new problem. Exercises involving the construction of images of figures under glide reflections are given in Ongoing Assessment 13-2.

We have seen that under an isometry, the image of a figure is a congruent figure. Also, given two congruent figures, it is possible to show that one can be transformed to the other by isometries.

The following example shows one illustration of such a transformation.

Example 13-9

ABCD in Figure 13-39 is a rectangle. Describe a sequence of isometries to show (a) $\triangle ADC \cong \triangle CBA$; (b) $\triangle ADC \cong \triangle BCD$; and (c) $\triangle ADC \cong \triangle DAB$.

Figure 13-39

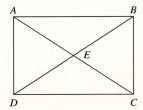

Solution **a.** A half-turn with center *E* is one such transformation.

     b. A reflection in a line passing through *E* and parallel to $\overline{AD}$ is one such transformation.

     c. A reflection in a line passing through *E* and parallel to $\overline{DC}$ is one such transformation.

• • •

Light Reflecting from a Surface

When a ray of light bounces off a mirror or when a billiard ball bounces off the rail of a billiards table, the **angle of incidence,** the angle formed by the incoming ray in Figure 13-40 and a line perpendicular to the mirror, is congruent to the **angle of reflection,** the angle between the reflected ray and the line perpendicular to the mirror.

Figure 13-40

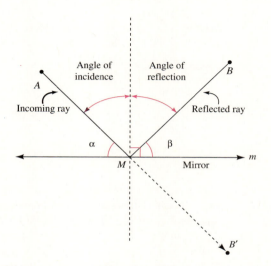

As suggested in the Remark following Problem 1, the path *A-M-B* is the shortest path connecting *A* with *B* through a point on the mirror *m*. Thus light travels through the shortest path possible. As a result, if we are given two points *A* and *B* and a mirror, we can find how a beam of light should be directed from source *A* towards the mirror by finding *B′*, the reflection of *B* in *m*. The point *M* at which the beam should be aimed is obtained by intersecting $\overleftrightarrow{AB'}$ with *m*.

INVESTIGATION 13-4

● In Figure 13-40, the measure of the angle of incidence equals the measure of the angle of reflection. Use this fact to show that $\alpha = \beta$, that is, the measure of the angle between the mirror and the incoming ray equals the measure of the angle between the mirror and the reflected ray. ●

• • •

Example 13-10

It is sometimes desirable to shine a beam of light so that it will reflect parallel to a given surface. In Figure 13-41, a mirror *m* is placed in such a way that it makes an angle of measure 35° with the surface *s*. A beam of light originating from point *A* on *s* is sent towards the mirror so that it is reflected parallel to *s*. What angle does the beam of light make with the surface *s*?

Figure 13-41

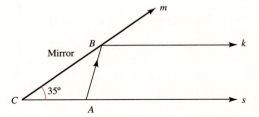

Solution   In Figure 13-42, we designate the measure of the desired angle between the beam from *A* and the surface *s* by *x*.

Figure 13-42

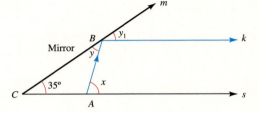

Because the light is reflected from the mirror, the measures of the angles *y* and y_1 marked at *B* are equal. Because $k \parallel s$ and *m* is a transversal, we have $y_1 = 35°$. The fact that $y = y_1$ implies that $y = 35°$. Because *x* is the measure of an exterior angle in $\triangle ABC$, we have

$$x = 35° + y = 35° + 35° = 70°.$$

Thus the beam of light is aimed at an angle that makes a 70° angle with the surface if *k* is parallel to *s*.

• • •

Ongoing Assessment 13-2

1. For each of the following figures, find the image of the given quadrilateral under a reflection in ℓ.

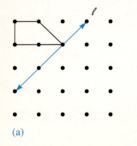

(a)

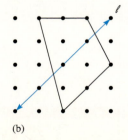

(b)

2. In the following figure, find the image of $\triangle ABC$ under a reflection in line ℓ.

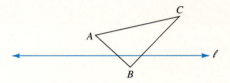

3. Draw a line and then draw a circle whose center is not on the line. Find the image of the circle under a reflection in the line.

4. Determine which of the following figures have a reflecting line such that the image of the figure under the reflecting line is the figure itself. In each case, find as many such reflecting lines as possible, sketching appropriate drawings.
   a. Circle
   b. Segment
   c. Ray
   d. Square
   e. Rectangle
   f. Scalene triangle
   g. Isosceles triangle
   h. Equilateral triangle
   i. Trapezoid whose base angles are not congruent
   j. Isosceles trapezoid
   k. Arc
   l. Kite
   m. Rhombus
   n. Regular hexagon
   o. Regular *n*-gon

5. Determine the final result when △ABC is reflected in line ℓ and then its image is reflected again in ℓ (see the following figure).

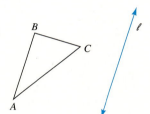

6. a. Refer to the following figure and suppose line ℓ and *m* are parallel and △ABC is reflected in ℓ to obtain △A'B'C' and then △A'B'C' is reflected in *m* to obtain △A''B''C''. Determine whether the same final image is obtained if △ABC is reflected first in *m* and then its image is reflected in ℓ.

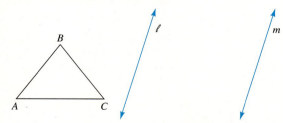

   b. Conjecture what single transformation will take △ABC directly to △A''B''C''. Check your conjecture using tracing paper.

7. a. For the following figure, use any construction method to find the image of △ABC if △ABC is reflected in ℓ to obtain △A'B'C' and then △A'B'C' is reflected in *m* to obtain △A''B''C'' (ℓ and *m* intersect at *O*).

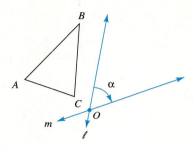

   b. Conjecture what single transformation will take △ABC directly to △A''B''C''. Check your conjecture using tracing paper.
   c. Answer the question in (a) for the case in which ℓ and *m* are perpendicular.

8. Use a Mira if available to investigate Problems 6 and 7.

9. a. The word TOT is its own image when it is reflected through a vertical line through O, as shown in the following figure. List some other words that are their own images when reflected similarly.

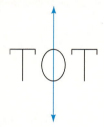

   b. The image of BOOK is still BOOK when it is reflected through a horizontal line. List some other words that have the same property. Which uppercase letters can you use?

   c. The image of 1881 is 1881 after reflection in either a horizontal or vertical line, as shown in the following figure. What other natural numbers less than 2000 have this property?

10. A glide reflection was defined as a translation followed by a reflection in appropriate lines.

a. Determine whether the same final image is obtained if the reflection is followed by the translation.

b. Use your answer in (a) to determine whether the reflection and translation involved in the glide reflection are commutative.

11. For the following figure numbered 1, decide whether a reflection, a translation, a rotation, or a glide reflection will transform the figure into each of the other numbered figures. (There may be more than one possible answer.)

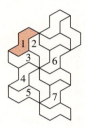

12. Two cities, represented by points A and B in the following figure, are located near two perpendicular roads as shown.

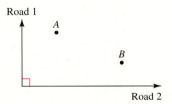

The cities' mayors want to build another road connecting A with a point P on road 1, then connecting P with a point Q on road 2, and finally connecting Q with B. How should the road $APQB$ be constructed so that it is as short as possible? Copy the figure and use a straightedge and a compass, a Mira, or paper folding to construct the shortest possible path. Explain why the path you found is the shortest.

13. Determine the length of the shortest path connecting A to B through a point C on the x-axis for each of the following figures.

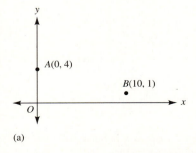

(a)

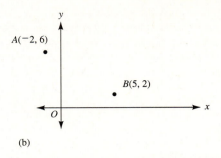

(b)

14. Given points $A(3, 4)$, $B(2, {}^-6)$, and $C({}^-2, 5)$, find the coordinates of the images of these points under each of the following transformations.

a. Reflection in the x-axis

b. Reflection in the y-axis

c. Reflection in the line $y = x$

d. Reflection in the line $y = {}^-x$

15. a. Conjecture what the image of a point with coordinates (x, y) will be under each of the transformations in Problem 14.

b. Suppose a point with coordinates (x, y) is reflected in the x-axis and then its image P' is reflected in the y-axis to obtain P''. What are the coordinates of P'' in terms of x and y? Justify your answer.

Communication

16. When a billiard ball bounces off a side of a pool table, the angle of incidence is usually congruent to the angle of reflection. In the following figure showing a scale drawing of a pool table, a cue ball is at point A. Show how a player should aim to hit two sides of the table and then the ball at B. Justify your solution.

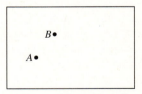

17. In the following figure representing a miniature golf course, explain and justify the procedure showing how to aim the ball so that it gets in the hole if it is to bounce off

a. one wall only.   **b.** two walls.

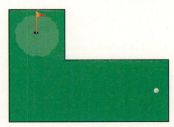

18. **a.** Draw an isosceles triangle *ABC* and then construct a line such that the image of △*ABC* when reflected in the line is △*ABC*. Explain why the line you constructed has the required property.
    b. For what kind of triangles is it possible to find more than one line with the property in (a)? Justify your answer.
    c. Given a scalene triangle *ABC*, is it possible to find a line ℓ such that when △*ABC* is reflected in ℓ, its image is △*ABC*? Explain your answer.
    d. Draw a circle with center *O* and a line with the property that the image of the circle, when reflected in the line, is the original circle. Identify all such lines. Justify your answer.

19. Use the following drawing to explain how a periscope works.

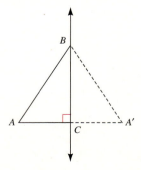

Open-ended

20. Design several different wall stencil patterns using a reflection (see Problem 29 in Ongoing Assessment 13-1). In each case, explain how you would use the stencil in practice.
21. Design wall stencil patterns using a glide reflection.
22. If a right triangle △*ABC* is reflected in one of its legs as shown in the following triangle, the triangle and its image form an isosceles triangle △*ABA'*.

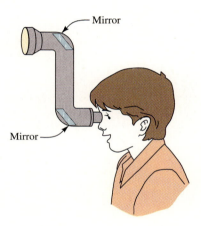

From the properties of reflection, we can deduce that the base angles in an isosceles triangle are congruent and that the altitude to the base bisects ∠*ABA'* as well as $\overline{AA'}$.

Apply the concept of reflection to deduce properties of other geometric figures by reflecting a scalene triangle in one of its sides, a right angle trapezoid in one of its sides, and other figures. In each case, define the reflection, list the geometric properties of the figure obtained from the union of your original figure and its image, and justify the properties.

Cooperative Learning

23. A ray of light bounces off two perpendicular mirrors as shown in the following figure.

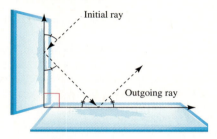

   a. Have each member of your group construct two perpendicular rays and then choose an initial ray and construct the corresponding outgoing ray. (This can also be done with two mirrors placed perpendicular to each other.)
   b. Compare your results with those of the rest of the group and together state a conjecture concerning the relationship between the initial ray and the outgoing ray.
   c. As a group, devise a justification of your conjecture in (b).

24. In the following figure representing a pool table, ball *B* is sent on a path that makes a 45° angle with the table wall, as shown. It bounces off the wall five times and returns to its original position.

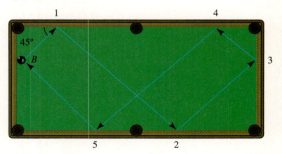

   a. Have each member of your group use graph paper to construct rectangular models of different-sized pool tables. Simulate the experiment using any tools (such as a straightedge, compass, and protractor) by choosing different positions for ball *B*.

b. Share the results of your experiments with the rest of the group and together conjecture for which dimensions of the pool table and for what positions of *B* the experiment described in the problem will work.

Review Exercises

25. Which capital printed letters of the English alphabet are their own images under a rotation?

26. Which capital letters of the English alphabet are their own images under a half-turn?

27. MOW is an example of a word that could be transformed into itself by which isometry?

28. a. Find all possible rotations that transform a circle into itself.

  b. By what other kinds of transformations can a circle be transformed onto itself?

29. Cut a scalene triangle *ABC* out of cardboard. Mark *N* and *M* as the midpoints of sides $\overline{AB}$ and $\overline{AC}$, respectively. Construct $\overline{MP}$ and $\overline{NQ}$ perpendicular to the base $\overline{BC}$. Cut out $\triangle CMP$ and $\triangle BNQ$ and rotate them about *M* and *N* respectively by 180°. By taping the parts, you should obtain a figure like *PP'Q'Q* in the following figure.

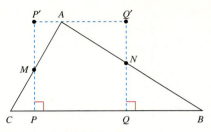

a. What kind of figure is this?

b. How is its area related to the area of $\triangle ABC$?

c. Justify your answers to (a) and (b).

30. Explain how a translation can be used to construct a rectangle whose area is equal to that of the parallelogram *ABCD* in the following figure.

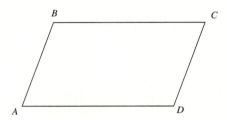

TECHNOLOGY CORNER

Enter the following Logo procedures into your computer:

```
TO SQ
  REPEAT 4 [FD 40 RT 90]
END
TO FSQ
  REPEAT 4 [FD 40 LT 90]
END
```

Describe the transformations illustrated in each of the following:

```
(a) TO MOVE1
      SQ
      RT 150
      SQ
    END
(b) TO MOVE2
      SQ
      FSQ
    END
(c) TO MOVE3
      SQ
      PU RT 45 FD 60 PD
      SQ
    END
```

BRAIN TEASER Two cities are on opposite sides of a river, as shown in the following figure.

$A \bullet$

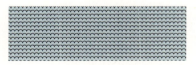

$B \bullet$

The cities' engineers want to build a bridge across the river that is perpendicular to the banks of the river and access roads to the bridge so that the total distance between the cities is as short as possible. Where should the bridge and the roads be built?

LABORATORY ACTIVITY As a van Hiele Level 1 activity, take a 1 × 1 ft square of linoleum tile and carve a pattern in the tile comparable to the one shown in the following figure:

Next, spread ink over the uncarved surface and press a piece of paper onto the ink, being careful not to let the paper slide across the tile. Next, remove the paper and consider the printed impression made on it. How are the images on the printed paper and the original carved tile related to one another?

Section 13-3 Size Transformations

The transformations we have investigated so far preserved distance. Consequently, the image of a figure under one of these transformations was a figure congruent to the original. A different type of transformation happens when a slide is projected on a screen. All objects on the slide are enlarged on the screen by the same factor. Figure 13-43 is another example of such a transformation.

The point O is the *center* of the *size transformation* and 2 is the *scale factor*. Points O, A, and A' are collinear and $OA' = 2 \cdot OA$; also, O, C, and C' are collinear and $OC' = 2 \cdot OC$. Similarly, O, B, and B' are collinear and $OB' = 2 \cdot OB$. It can be shown that each side of $\triangle A'B'C'$ is twice as long as the corresponding side of $\triangle ABC$.

Figure 13-43

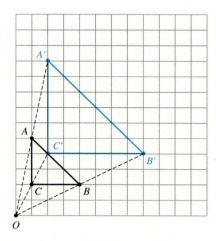

In general, we have the following definition.

Definition of Size Transformation

A size transformation from the plane to the plane with center O and scale factor r ($r > 0$) is a transformation that assigns to each point A in the plane a point A', such that O, A, and A' are collinear and $OA' = r \cdot OA$ and so that O is not between A and A'.

Figure 13-44 shows the image of a point A under a size transformation with scale factor $r > 1$.

Figure 13-44

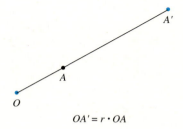

$$OA' = r \cdot OA$$

• • •

Example 13-11   **a.** In Figure 13-45(a), find the image of point P under a size transformation with center O and scale factor $\dfrac{2}{3}$.

Figure 13-45

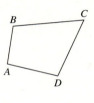

O

(a)

O

(b)

b. Find the image of the quadrilateral $ABCD$ in Figure 13-45(b) under the size transformation with center O and scale factor $\frac{2}{3}$.

Solution **a.** In Figure 13-46(a), we connect O with P and divide $\overline{OP}$ into three equal parts. The point P' is the image of P because $OP' = \frac{2}{3}OP$.

b. We find the image of each of the vertices and connect the images to obtain the quadrilateral $A'B'C'D'$ shown in Figure 13-46(b).

Figure 13-46

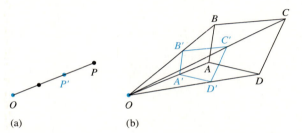

O

(a)

O

(b)

In Figure 13-46(b), the sides of the quadrilateral $A'B'C'D'$ are all parallel to the corresponding sides of the original quadrilateral and the angles of the quadrilateral $A'B'C'D'$ are congruent to the corresponding angles of quadrilateral $ABCD$. Also, each side in the quadrilateral $A'B'C'D'$ is $\frac{2}{3}$ as long as the corresponding side of quadrilateral $ABCD$. These properties are true for any size transformation and are summarized in the following theorem.

Theorem 13-1

A size transformation with center O and scale factor r $(r > 0)$ has the following properties:
  1. The image of a line segment is a line segment parallel to the original segment and r times as long.
  2. The image of an angle is an angle congruent to the original angle.

From Theorem 13-1, it follows that the image of a polygon under a size transformation is a similar polygon (why?). However, for any two similar polygons it is not always possible to find a size transformation so that the image of one polygon under the transformation is the other polygon. But, given two similar polygons, we can "move" one polygon to a place so that it will be the image of the other under a size transformation. The following examples show such instances.

• • •

Example 13-12   Show that △*ABC* in Figure 13-47 is the image of △*ADE* under a size transformation. Identify the center of the size transformation and the scale factor.

Figure 13-47

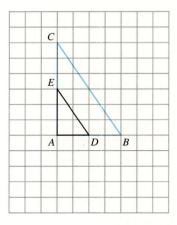

Solution   Because $\dfrac{AB}{AD} = \dfrac{AC}{AE} = 2$, we choose *A* as the center of the size transformation and 2 as the scale factor. Notice that under this transformation, the image of *A* is *A* itself. The image of *D* is *B*, and the image of *E* is *C*.

• • •

• • •

Example 13-13   Show that △*ABC* in Figure 13-48 is the image of △*APQ* under a succession of isometries with a size transformation.

Figure 13-48

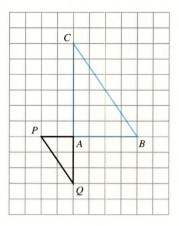

Solution   We use the strategy of *looking at a related problem*. In Example 13-12, the common vertex served as the center of the size transformation. This was possible because the corresponding sides of the triangles were parallel. To achieve a similar situation, we first transform △*APQ* by a half-turn in *A* and obtain △*AP'Q'*, as shown in Figure 13-49.

Figure 13-49

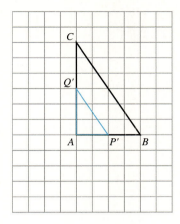

Now C is the image of Q' under a size transformation with center at A and scale factor 2. B is the image of P', and A is the image of itself under this transformation. Thus $\triangle ABC$ can be obtained from $\triangle APQ$ by first finding the image of $\triangle APQ$ under a half-turn in A and then applying a size transformation with center A and a scale factor 2 to that image.

• • •

Examples 13-12 and 13-13 are a basis for an alternative definition of similar figures.

Definition of Similar Figures

Two figures are similar if it is possible to transform one onto the other by a sequence of isometries followed by a size transformation.

Applications of Size Transformations

perspective drawing One way to make an object appear three-dimensional is to use a **perspective drawing.** For example, to make a letter appear three-dimensional we can use a size transformation with an appropriate center O and a scale factor, as shown in Figure 13-50, for the letter L.

Figure 13-50

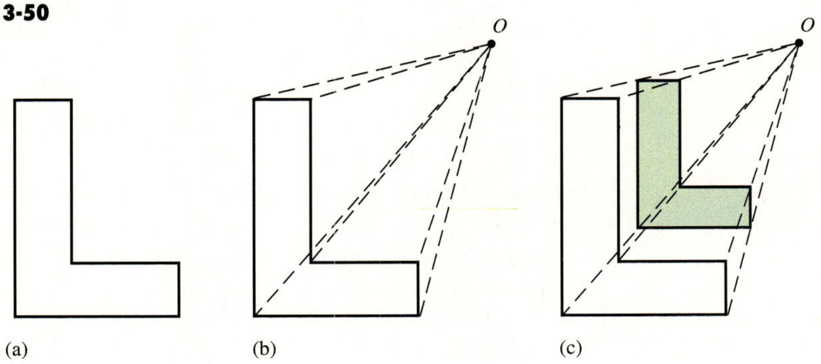

(a)	(b)	(c)

When a picture of an object is taken, the object appears upside down on the negative. The picture of the object on the negative can be interpreted as an image under composition of a half-turn and a size transformation. Figure 13-51(a) illustrates the image of an arrow from A to B under a composition of a half-turn followed by a size transformation with scale factor $\frac{1}{2}$.

Figure 13-51

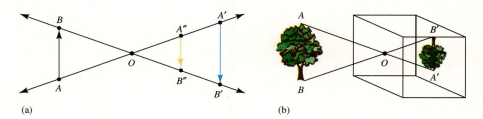

(a)   (b)

The image A' of A under the half-turn with center O is found on the ray opposite $\overrightarrow{OA}$ so that $OA' = OA$. The point B', the image of B under the half-turn, is found similarly on the ray opposite $\overrightarrow{OB}$. The images of A' and B' under the size transformation are A'' and B'', respectively. Consequently, the image of the arrow from A to B under the composition of the half-turn followed by the size transformation is the arrow from A'' to B''. Figure 13-51(b) illustrates another composition of a half-turn and a size transformation in a simple box camera.

• • •

Example 13-14   In Figure 13-52(a), $\overline{A''B''}$ is the image of a candle $\overline{BA}$ produced by a box camera. Given the measurement of the figure, find the height of the candle.

Figure 13-52

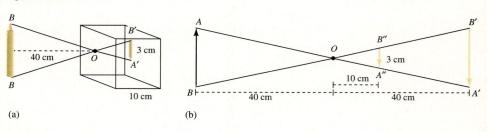

(a)   (b)

Solution   Figure 13-52(b) shows $\overline{A''B''}$ as the image of $\overline{BA}$ under the composition of a half-turn about O followed by a size transformation with center O. The image of the candle under a half-turn about point O is $\overline{B'A'}$ and $B'A' = BA$. The image of $\overline{B'A'}$ under an appropriate size transformation with center O is $\overline{A''B''}$. The scale factor of the size transformation is $\frac{10}{40}$, or $\frac{1}{4}$ (why?). Consequently, $A''B'' = \frac{1}{4} \cdot A'B'$. Substituting $A''B'' = 3$ cm, we get

$3 = \frac{1}{4} \cdot A'B'$ and hence $A'B' = 12$ cm. Thus $AB = A'B' = 12$ cm and the candle is 12 cm tall.

• • •

Ongoing Assessment 13-3

1. In the following figures, describe a sequence of isometries followed by a size transformation so that the larger triangle is the final image of the smaller one.

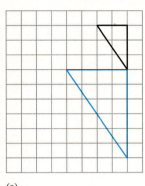
(a)

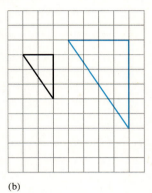
(b)

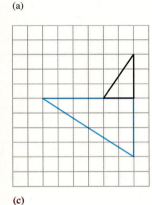
(c)

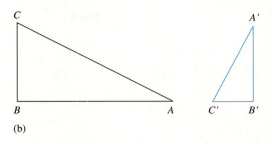
(b)

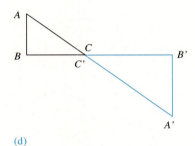
(c)

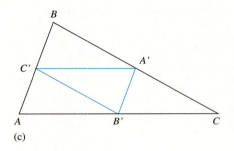
(d)

2. In the following drawing, find the image of $\triangle ABC$ under the size transformation with center O and scale factor $\frac{1}{2}$:

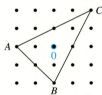

3. In each of the following drawings, find transformations that will take $\triangle ABC$ to its image, $\triangle A'B'C'$, which is similar:

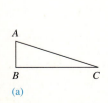
(a)

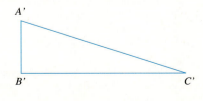
(a)

4. In each of the following figures, the smaller one is the image of the larger under a size transformation. In each case, find the scale factor and the length of x and y as pictured.

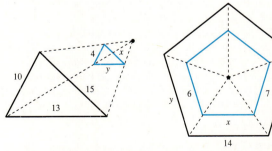

5. The following figure shows a camera lens where $A'B'$ is the width of a 35 mm film and $\overline{AB}$ is the object being photographed. The distance from the film to the lens (known as the focal length) is 60 mm, and the distance from the lens to the object being photographed is 7 m. Assume that the photograph of the object fills up the entire 35 mm film.

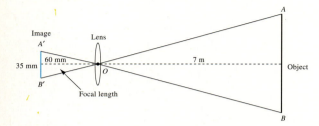

a. What can be said about the relationship between $\triangle AOB$ and $\triangle A'OB'$?

b. What is the length of the object?

c. What focal length would be necessary if the object were 14 m long and still 7 m from the lens?

6. Each of the following figures describes a size transformation with center O. Find the scale factor and the lengths designated by x and y.

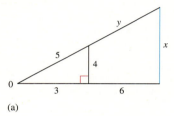

(a)

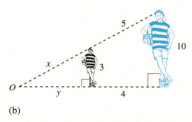

(b)

7. a. Find the coordinates of the images of A (2, 3), B (3, 4) and C ($^-2$, 3) under a size transformation with the center at the origin and a scale factor of 3.

  b. From on your answer to (a), conjecture the coordinates of the image of the point (x, y) under a size transformation with the center at the origin and a scale factor r.

8. If a size transformation with center O and scale factor r takes a quadrilateral $ABCD$ to $A'B'C'D'$, what size transformation will take $A'B'C'D'$ back to $ABCD$?

Communication

9. Which of the following properties do not change under a size transformation? Explain how you can be sure of your answers.

  a. Distance between points

  b. Angle measure

  c. Parallelism; that is, if two lines are parallel to each other, then their images are parallel to each other.

10. Given two similar figures, explain how to tell if there is a size transformation that transforms one of the figures onto the other.

11. a. Consider two consecutive size transformations, each with center O and corresponding scale factors $\frac{1}{2}$ and $\frac{1}{3}$, respectively. Suppose the image of figure F under the first transformation is F' and the image of F' under the second transformation is F''. What single transformation will map F directly onto F''? Explain why.

  b. What would be the answer to (a) if the scale factors were r_1 and r_2?

12. Copy the following figure onto grid paper and determine the center and the scale factor of the size transformation. Explain why there is only one possibility for the center.

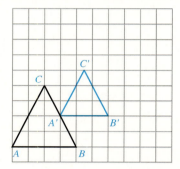

13. Is the image of a circle with center O under a size transformation with center O always a circle? Explain why or why not.

Open-ended

14. Describe several real-life situations other than the ones discussed in this section in which size transformations occur.

Cooperative Learning

15. Have different members of your group draw several figures and find their images under a size transformation with a scale factor of 3.

  a. How does the perimeter of each image compare to the perimeter of the original figure? Compare your answers.

  b. How does the area of each image compare to the area of the original figure? Compare your answers.

  c. Make a conjecture concerning the relationship between the perimeter of each image and the perimeter of the original figure under a size transformation with a scale factor r.

  d. Repeat (c) for the area of each figure.

  e. Discuss your findings and come up with a group conjecture.

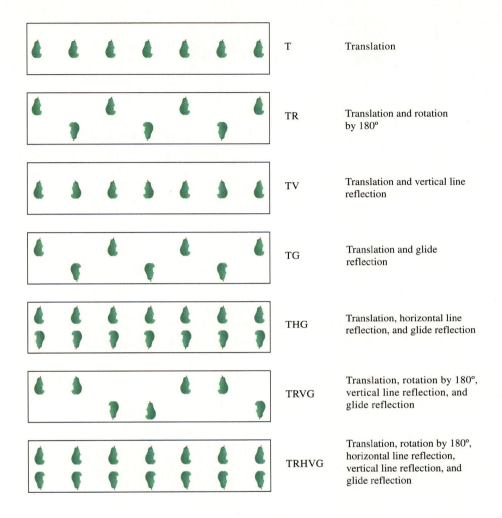

T	Translation
TR	Translation and rotation by 180°
TV	Translation and vertical line reflection
TG	Translation and glide reflection
THG	Translation, horizontal line reflection, and glide reflection
TRVG	Translation, rotation by 180°, vertical line reflection, and glide reflection
TRHVG	Translation, rotation by 180°, horizontal line reflection, vertical line reflection, and glide reflection

16. A *frieze pattern* is a pattern that extends indefinitely in both directions and the image of the pattern under a translation is the original pattern. Above are seven different frieze patterns, each of which is the image of itself under a translation and also by the other isometries indicated. Every frieze pattern can be classified into one of these seven categories.

a. Have each member of your group draw one or two of the patterns (depending on the size of the group) on tracing paper or a transparency with a corresponding label using the letters *T, R, H, V,* or *G,* as in the figure. Exchange the drawings so that each member of your group checks how each of the patterns can be transformed onto itself by each of the isometries. Compare your answers with those of your group members.

b. Create other more elaborate patterns for each of the seven categories and present each pattern to a partner for identification. (Label the patterns with numbers 1 through 7, keeping to yourself the corresponding *T, R, H, V, G* labeling.) Compare your partner's answers with yours.

Review Problems

17. Describe a transformation that would "undo" each of the following:
  a. A translation determined by slide arrow from *M* to *N*.
  b. A rotation of 75° with center *O* in a clockwise direction
  c. A rotation of 45° with center *A* in a counterclockwise direction

d. A glide reflection that is the composition of a reflection in line *m* and a translation that takes *A* to *B*

e. A reflection in line *n*.

18. In the following coordinate plane, find the images of each of the given points in the transformation that is the composition of a reflection in line *m* followed by a reflection in line *n*.

a. (4, 3)   **b.** (0, 1)

c. (⁻1, 0)   **d.** (0, 0)

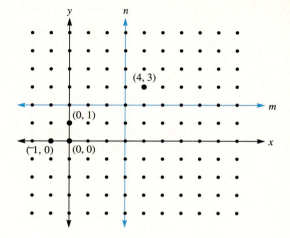

LABORATORY ACTIVITY

As a van Hiele Level 3 activity, consider △*ABC* and its image after it is reflected in lines *m*, *n*, and *p* in order in the following figure:

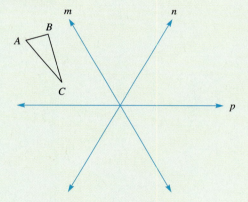

Find a single line *q* that could be used to reflect the original △*ABC* onto the final image. Explain why it is always possible to find such a line.

Section 13-4   ## Symmetries

Line Symmetries

The concept of a reflection can be used to identify line symmetries of a figure. All the drawings in Figure 13-53 have symmetries about the dashed lines.

Figure 13-53

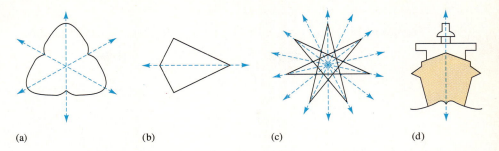

(a) (b) (c) (d)

line of symmetry   Mathematically, a geometric figure has a **line of symmetry** ℓ if it is its own image under a reflection in ℓ. A method of creating a symmetrical figure is seen in Example 13-15.

• • •

Example 13-15 In Figure 13-54, we are given a figure and a line m. Do the minimum amount of drawing to create a figure from the given figure so that the result is symmetric about line m.

Figure 13-54

Solution   For the resulting figure both to be symmetric about line m and to incorporate the existing figure, we need to reflect the existing figure about line m. The desired result of doing that is the combination of the original figure and the image. The resulting figure is shown in Figure 13-55.

Figure 13-55

• • •

794   CHAPTER 13   *Motion Geometry and Tessellations*

• • •

Example 13-16

How many lines of symmetry does each drawing in Figure 13-56 have?

Figure 13-56

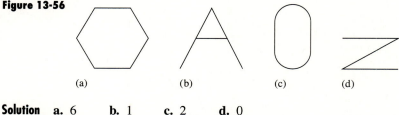

(a)   (b)   (c)   (d)

Solution   **a.** 6   **b.** 1   **c.** 2   **d.** 0

• • •

Problem 2

At the site of an ancient settlement, archaeologists found a fragment of a saucer as shown in Figure 13-57. To restore the saucer, the archaeologists need to determine the radius of the original saucer. How can they do this?

Figure 13-57

Understanding the Problem.   The border of the shard shown in Figure 13-57 was part of a circle. To reconstruct the saucer, we are to determine the radius of the circle of which the shard is a part.

   Devising a Plan.   A *model* can be used to determine the radius. We trace an outline of the circular edge of the three-dimensional shard on a piece of paper. The result is an arc of a circle, as shown in Figure 13-58. To determine the radius, we find the center *O*. A circle has infinitely many lines of symmetry and each line passes through the center of the circle, where all the lines of symmetry intersect.

Figure 13-58

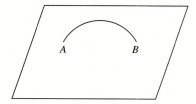

Carrying Out the Plan.   To find a line of symmetry, fold the paper containing $\overarc{AB}$ so that a portion of the arc is folded onto itself. Then unfold the paper and draw the line of symmetry on the fold mark, as shown in Figure 13-59(a). By refolding the paper in Figure 13-59(a) so that a different portion of the arc $\widehat{AB}$ is folded onto itself, we can determine a second line of symmetry, as shown in Figure 13-59(b). The two dotted lines of symmetry intersect at O, the center of the circle of which $\widehat{AB}$ is an arc. To complete the problem, measure the length of either $\overline{OB}$ or $\overline{OA}$. (They should be the same.)

Figure 13-59

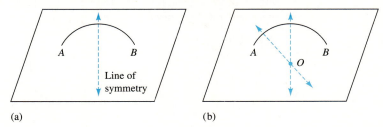

(a)   (b)

Looking Back. In the first fold, endpoint B of the arc was folded onto another point of the arc. Label this other point X. The result is shown in Figure 13-60. Because the center of the circle lies on the perpendicular bisector of a chord (why?) and the fold line ℓ is a line of symmetry of the circle containing $\widehat{AB}$, the fold line must be the perpendicular bisector of $\overline{XB}$ and it must contain the center of the circle. We could have used this property to determine the center of the circle by choosing two chords on the arc and finding the point on which the perpendicular bisectors of the chords intersect. Alternatively, we could have used a compass and a straightedge.

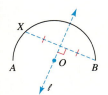

Figure 13-60

A related problem is: What would happen if the piece of pottery had been part of a sphere? Would the same ideas still work?

• • •

Rotational (Turn) Symmetries

rotational symmetry/
turn symmetry

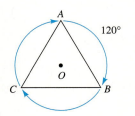

Figure 13-61

A figure has **rotational symmetry,** or **turn symmetry,** when the traced figure can be rotated less than 360° about some point so that it matches the original figure. Note that the condition "less than 360°" is necessary because any figure will coincide with itself if it is rotated 360°. In Figure 13-61, the equilateral triangle coincides with itself after a rotation of 120° about point O. Hence, we say that the triangle has 120° rotational symmetry. Also in Figure 13-61, if we were to rotate the triangle another 120°, we would find again that it matches the original. So we can say that the triangle also has 240° rotational symmetry.

In general, if a figure has $\alpha°$ rotational symmetry, it also will coincide with itself when rotated by $n\alpha°$ for any positive integer n. For this reason, in rotational symmetry the smallest possible angle measure that turns the figure onto itself is reported if possible. Notice that a circle has a rotational symmetry by any turn around its center.

Other examples of figures that have rotational symmetry are shown in Figure 13-62. Figures 13-62(a), (b), (c), and (d) have 72°, 90°, 180°, and 180° rotational symmetries, respectively [(a) and (b) also have other rotational symmetries].

Figure 13-62

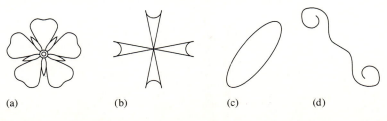

(a)   (b)   (c)   (d)

In general, we can determine whether a figure has rotational symmetry by tracing it and turning the tracing about a point (the center of the figure) to see if it aligns on the figure before the tracing has turned in a complete circle, or 360°. The amount of the rotation can be determined by measuring the angle $\angle POP'$ through which a point P is rotated around a point O to match another point P' when the figures align. Such an angle, $\angle POP'$, is labeled with points P, O, and P' in Figure 13-63 and has measure 120°. Point O, the point held fixed when the tracing is turned, is the turn center.

Figure 13-63

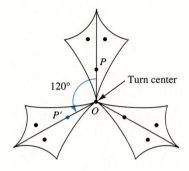

Example 13-17   Determine the amount of the turn for the rotational symmetries of each part of Figure 13-64.

Figure 13-64

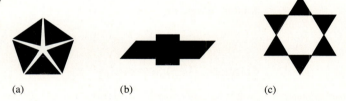

(a) (b) (c)

Solution   **a.** The amounts of the turns are $\frac{360°}{5}$ or 72°, 144°, 216°, and 288°.

b. The amount of the turn is 180°.

c. The amounts of the turns are 60°, 120°, 180°, 240°, and 300°.

The rotation in Figure 13-64(b) exemplifies yet another type of symmetry, namely, point symmetry.

Point Symmetry

point symmetry   Any figure that has 180° rotational symmetry is said to have **point symmetry** about the turn center. Figures with point symmetry are shown in Figure 13-65.

Figure 13-65

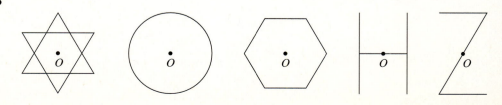

Suppose P is any point of a figure with point symmetry, such as in Figure 13-66(a). If the figure is rotated 180° about its center, point O, there is a corresponding point P', as shown in part (b) of the figure. Points P, O, and P' are on the same line, and O divides the segment connecting points P and P' into two parts of equal length, that is, O is the midpoint of $\overline{PP'}$.

Figure 13-66

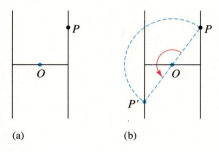

(a)   (b)

Plane Symmetry

plane of symmetry   A three-dimensional figure has a **plane of symmetry** when every point of the figure on one side of the plane has a mirror image on the other side of the plane. Examples of figures with plane symmetry are shown in Figure 13-67. Solids can also have point symmetry, line symmetry, and turn symmetry. These symmetries are analogous to the two-dimensional symmetries and are investigated in Ongoing Assessment 13-4.

Figure 13-67

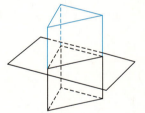

Geometric figures in a plane can be classified according to the number of symmetries they have. Consider a triangle described as having exactly one line of symmetry and no turn symmetries. What could the triangle look like? The only possibility is a triangle in which two sides are congruent, that is, an isosceles triangle. The line of symmetry passes through a vertex, as shown in Figure 13-68.

Figure 13-68

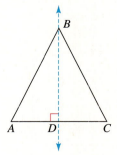

Just as we used the number of lines of symmetry to describe an isosceles triangle, we can describe equilateral and scalene triangles in terms of the number of lines of symmetry they have. This is left as an exercise.

A square, as in Figure 13-69, can be defined as a four-sided figure with four lines of symmetry—d_1, d_2, h, and v—and three turn symmetries about point O. In fact, we can use lines of symmetry and turn symmetries to define various types of quadrilaterals normally used in geometry. It is left as an exercise to see how these definitions differ from those in Chapter 10.

Figure 13-69

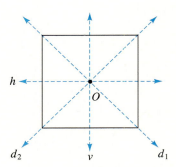

Ongoing Assessment 13-4

1. Various international signs have symmetries. Determine which of the following have (i) line symmetry, (ii) rotational symmetry, and/or (iii) point symmetry.

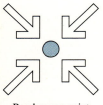

Rendezvous point

(a)

Light switch

(b)

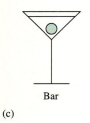

Bar

(c)

Observation deck

(d)

2. Design symbols that have each of the following symmetries, if possible.
   a. Line symmetry but not rotational symmetry
   b. Rotational symmetry but not point symmetry
   c. Rotational symmetry but not line symmetry
3. In each of the following figures, complete the sketches so that they have line symmetry about ℓ.

Line symmetry about ℓ

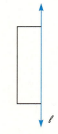

Line symmetry about ℓ

4. a. Determine the number of lines of symmetry in each of the following flags.
   b. Sketch the lines of symmetry for each.

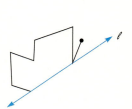

Switzerland

(i)

South Korea

(ii)

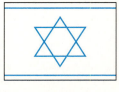

Israel

(iii)

Barbados

(iv)

5. a. Determine how many lines of symmetry the following figure has.

b. Does the figure have rotational symmetry?

6. Find the lines of symmetry, if any, for each of the following trademarks.

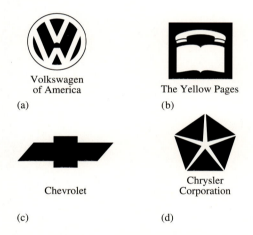

Volkswagen of America
(a)

The Yellow Pages
(b)

Chevrolet
(c)

Chrysler Corporation
(d)

7. In each of the following figures, complete the sketches so that they have the indicated symmetry.

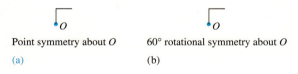

Point symmetry about *O*
(a)

60° rotational symmetry about *O*
(b)

8. Determine how many planes of symmetry, if any, each of the following three-dimensional vehicle controls has.

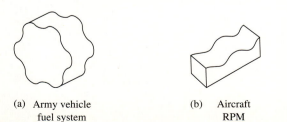

(a) Army vehicle fuel system

(b) Aircraft RPM

(c) Army vehicle special-purpose equipment

(d) Automotive finger-operated continuous multiturn

9. Write a Logo procedure that draws a square and produces a figure with rotational symmetry of (a) 60°; (b) 120°; (c) 180°; (d) 240°; (e) 300°.

10. Write a Logo procedure that draws an equilateral triangle and produces a figure with rotational symmetry of (a) 60°; (b) 120°; (c) 240°; (d) 300°.

Communication

11. Answer each of the following. If your answer is no, provide a counterexample.
  a. If a figure has point symmetry, must it have rotational symmetry? Why?
  b. If a figure has rotational symmetry, must it have point symmetry? Why?
  c. Can a figure have point, line, and rotational symmetry? If so, sketch a figure that has these properties.
  d. If a figure has point symmetry, must it have line symmetry? Is the converse true? Why?
  e. If a figure has both point and line symmetry, must it have rotational symmetry? Why?

Open-ended

12. If possible, sketch a triangle that satisfies each of the following:
  a. It has no lines of symmetry.
  b. It has exactly one line of symmetry.
  c. It has exactly two lines of symmetry.
  d. It has exactly three lines of symmetry.

13. Sketch a figure that has point symmetry but no line symmetry.

14. a. In the following figure, *ABCD* is a rectangular sheet of paper. Fold the paper so that the opposite edges $\overline{AB}$ and $\overline{CD}$ coincide (the crease $\overline{EF}$ is created). Then fold the resulting rectangle *ABEF* so that $\overline{BE}$ and $\overline{AF}$ coincide (the crease $\overline{HG}$ is created). The rectangle *AFGH* is obtained. Now cut a curved piece of paper out of the corner *G* as shown and unfold the paper. Describe all the symmetries that the unfolded figure has.

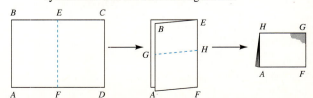

b. Repeat the experiment in (a) by successively folding a new sheet of paper three times and cutting out a curved piece containing a corner that resulted from the three folds. Predict all the symmetries of the unfolded figure. Check your answer by unfolding the paper.

15. For each of the following, use paper folding or any other method to create, if possible, two nonsimilar finite figures that have the specified symmetries:

a. Point symmetry but no other symmetries
b. Exactly one line of symmetry
c. Exactly two lines of symmetry but no rotational symmetry
d. 45° rotational symmetry

Cooperative Learning

16. With a partner, design a three-mirror kaleidoscope by fastening three mirrors together, each perpendicular to a flat surface so that they form an equilateral triangle prism as shown in the following figure. Place colored paper with a pattern (or design your own pattern) in the base of the kaleidoscope. Peer over the edge of the kaleidoscope to view the generated figure. Repeat the experiment for different patterns.

17. With another person or group, play the following game several times. First, draw a polygon that has different kinds of symmetries. Without revealing your polygon to your partner, tell your partner all you know about the symmetries of the figure. Next, from this information, your opponent attempts to draw the type of figure you drew. If your opponent produces a figure of the type you drew, he or she earns two points. If your opponent produces a different figure having the symmetries that you reported or if you failed to reveal some of the symmetries of your polygon, your opponent gets three points. Alternate roles several times.

Review Problems

18. For each of the following cases, find the image of the given figure using paper folding:

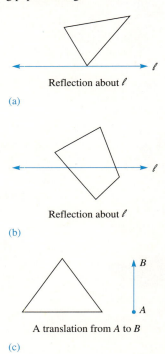

Reflection about ℓ

(a)

Reflection about ℓ

(b)

A translation from *A* to *B*

(c)

19. Construct each image in Problem 18 using a compass and a straightedge.

The following INSPI procedure produces drawings that have various symmetries, depending on the inputs for :ANGLE:

```
TO INSPI :SIDE :ANGLE
  FD :SIDE RT :ANGLE
  INSPI :SIDE :ANGLE + 5
END
```

Some of these drawings are shown in the following figure:

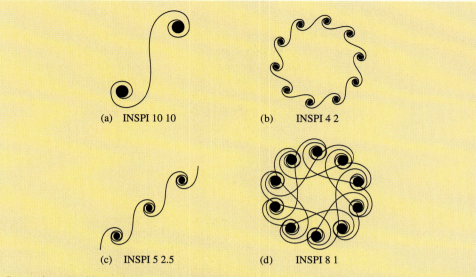

(a)   INSPI 10 10

(b)   INSPI 4 2

(c)   INSPI 5 2.5

(d)   INSPI 8 1

Determine what kinds of symmetries each figure has. Try some of your own inputs and see what drawings they produce and what kinds of symmetries the resulting figures have.

LABORATORY ACTIVITY

As a van Hiele Level 1 activity, consider the following figure:

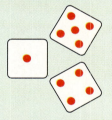

If this figure is reflected and then rotated, which of the following is a possible result?

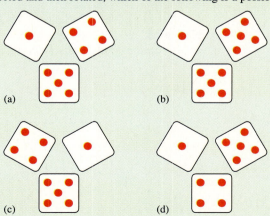

(a)

(b)

(c)

(d)

tessellation

*Section 13-5   Tessellations of the Plane

In this section we use concepts from motion geometry to study *tessellations* of the plane. A **tessellation** of a plane is the filling of the plane with repetitions of figures in such a way that no figures overlap and there are no gaps. (Similarly, one can tessellate space.) The tiling of a floor and various mosaics are examples of tessellations. Maurits C. Escher, born in the Netherlands in 1902, was a master of tessellations. Many of his drawings have fascinated mathematicians for decades. An example of his work, *Study of Regular Division of the Plane with Reptiles* (pen, ink, and watercolor), 1939, contains an exhibit of a tessellation of the plane by a lizardlike shape, as shown in Figure 13-70.

Figure 13-70

At the heart of the tessellation in the figure, we see a regular hexagon. But perhaps the simplest tessellation of the plane can be achieved with squares. Figure 13-71 shows two different tessellations of the plane with squares.

Figure 13-71

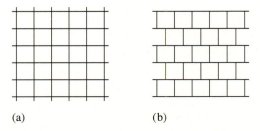

(a)   (b)

Tessellations are commonly studied in elementary school, as shown on the following student page from *Addison-Wesley Mathematics,* Grade 8, 1993.

Tessellations

LEARN ABOUT IT

A collection of polygons form a **tessellation** if they cover the entire plane with no overlapping. The tessellation at right is based on a sketch from one of Leonardo da Vinci's notebooks. It shows ways in which both squares and triangles can tessellate the plane. Would any quadrilateral or triangle tessellate the plane?

EXPLORE Use Dot Paper

Work in groups. Arrange about 12 of each polygon on dot paper to form a tessellation of that polygon.

TALK ABOUT IT

1. In your tessellation of triangles do your vertices of the triangles touch other triangles only at vertices? How many triangles surround each vertex?

2. In your tessellation of quadrilaterals how many of them surround each vertex?

Did your tessellations look something like these? How are we using the relationships about the sum of the measures of a polygon?

$$m\angle 1 + m\angle 2 + m\angle 3 = 180°$$

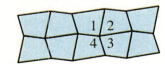

$$m\angle 1 + m\angle 2 + m\angle 3 + m\angle 4 = 360°$$

All triangles tessellate the plane. All quadrilaterals tessellate the plane.

Regular Tessellations

Tessellations with regular polygons are appealing and interesting because of their simplicity. Figure 13-72 shows portions of tessellations with equilateral triangles (a) and with regular hexagons (b).

Figure 13-72

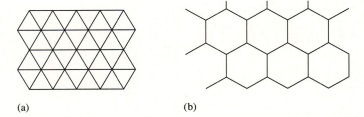

(a)   (b)

To determine other regular polygons that tessellate the plane, we investigate the possible size of the interior angle of a tessellating polygon. If n is the number of sides of a regular polygon, then because the sum of the measures of the exterior angles is 360°, the measure of an exterior angle is $360°/n$. Hence, the measure of an interior angle is $180° - 360°/n$. Table 13-2 gives some values of n, the type of regular polygon related to each, and the angle measure of an interior angle found by using the expression $180° - 360°/n$.

Table 13-2

Number of Sides (n)	Regular Polygon	Measure of Interior Angle
3	Triangle	60°
4	Square	90°
5	Pentagon	108°
6	Hexagon	120°
7	Heptagon	900/7°
8	Octagon	135°
9	Nonagon	140°
10	Decagon	144°

If a regular polygon tessellates the plane, the sum of the congruent angles of the polygons around every vertex must be 360°. Thus 360 divided by the angle measure gives the number of angles around a vertex and hence must be an integer. If we divide 360° by each of the angle measures in the table, we find that of these measures only 60°, 90°, and 120° divide 360°; hence, only an equilateral triangle, a square, and a regular hexagon can tessellate the plane.

Can other regular polygons tessellate the plane? Notice that $\frac{360}{120} = 3$. Hence, 360 divided by a number greater than 120 also is smaller than 3. However, the number of sides of a polygon cannot be less than 3. Because a polygon with more than six sides has an interior angle greater than 120°, it actually is not necessary to consider polygons with more than six sides.

Next, we consider tessellating the plane with arbitrary convex quadrilaterals. Before reading on, you may wish to investigate the problem yourself, with the help of cardboard quadrilaterals. Figure 13-73 shows an arbitrary convex quadrilateral and a way to tessellate the plane with the quadrilateral. Successive 180° turns of the quadrilateral about the midpoints P, Q, R, and S of its sides will produce four congruent quadrilaterals around a common vertex. Notice that the sum of the measures of the angles around vertex A is $a + b + c + d$. This is the sum of the measures of the interior angles of the quadrilateral, or 360°.

Figure 13-73

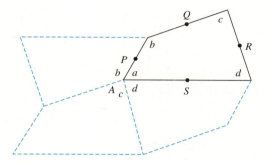

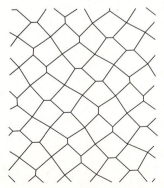

Figure 13-74

As we saw earlier in this section, a regular pentagon does not tessellate the plane. However, some nonregular pentagons do. One is shown in Figure 13-74, along with a tessellation of the plane by the pentagon.

HISTORICAL NOTE

Determining which irregular pentagons tessellate is a surprisingly rich problem. Mathematicians thought they had solved it when they had classified eight types of pentagons that would tessellate. They believed they had all of them. But then in 1975, Marjorie Rice, a woman with no formal training in mathematics, discovered a ninth type of tessellating pentagon. She went on to discover four more by 1977. Her interest was piqued by reading an article in *Scientific American* by Martin Gardner. Two of the pentagons she found are shown in Figure 13-75. The problem of how many different types of pentagons tessellate remains unsolved.

Figure 13-75

Type 9 discovered in February 1976   Type 13 discovered in December 1977

Ongoing Assessment 13-5

1. On dot paper, draw a tessellation of the plane using the following figures.

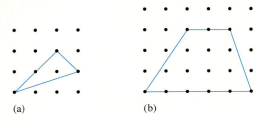

   (a)   (b)

2. a. Tessellate the plane with the following quadrilateral.

  b. Is it possible to tessellate the plane with any quadrilateral? Why or why not?

3. On square-dot paper, use each of the following four pentominoes, one at a time, to make a tessellation of the plane, if possible. (A pentomino is a polygon composed of five congruent, nonoverlapping squares.) Which of the pentominoes tessellate the plane?

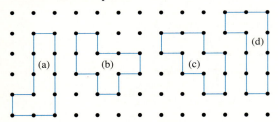

4. We have seen that equilateral triangles, squares, and regular hexagons are the only regular polygons that will tessellate the plane by themselves. However, there are many ways to tessellate the plane by using combinations of these and other regular polygons, as shown in the following figure.

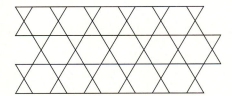

Try to produce other such tessellations by using the following.

  a. Only equilateral triangles, squares, and regular hexagons

  b. Regular octagons (8-gons) and squares

5. The **dual of a tessellation** is the tessellation obtained by connecting the centers of the polygons in the original tessellation that share a common side. The dual of the tessellation of equilateral triangles is the tessellation of regular hexagons, shown in color in the following figure.

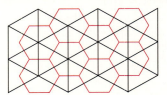

Describe and show the dual of each of the following:

  a. The regular tessellation of squares shown in Figure 13-71(a)

  b. The tessellation of squares in Figure 13-71(b)

  c. A tessellation of regular hexagons

6. Write Logo procedures to draw tessellations with the following figures. Have each tessellation appear on the screen in the form of two vertical strips.

  a. Squares   **b.** Equilateral triangles

  c. Regular hexagons

7. A sidewalk is made of tiles of the type shown in the following figure:

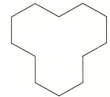

Each tile is made of three regular hexagons from which three sides have been removed. Write a Logo procedure to draw a tessellation composed of four such figures.

Communication

8. The following figure is a partial tessellation of the plane with the trapezoid *ABCD*:

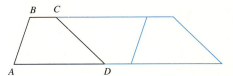

  a. Explain how the tessellation can be used to find a formula for the area of the trapezoid.

  b. Tessellate the plane with a triangle and show how the tessellation can be used to find the relationship between the length of the segment connecting the midpoints of the two sides of a triangle and the length of the third side.

9. Explain in your own words why only three types of regular polygons tessellate the plane.

Open-ended

10. There are endless numbers of figures that tessellate a plane. In the following drawing, the shaded figure is shown to tessellate the plane.

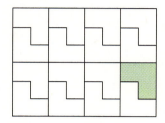

Design several different polygons and show how each can tessellate the plane. What transformations are used in each of your designs? Explain how they are used to tessellate the plane.

11. Examine different quilt patterns or floor coverings and make a sketch of those you found that tessellate a plane.

12. A cube will tessellate space but a sphere will not. List several other solids that will tessellate the space and several that will not.

Cooperative Learning

13. Each member of a small group is to find a drawing by M. C. Escher that does not appear in this text and in which the concept of tessellation is used. Each then shows the other members of the group, in detail, how he or she thinks Escher created the tessellation in his or her drawing.

14. **a.** Convince the members of your group that the following figure containing six equilateral triangles tessellates the plane:

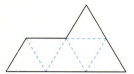

  b. As a group, find different figures that contain six equilateral triangles. How many such figures can you find? Discuss the meaning of "different."

  c. Find some of the figures in (b) that are *rep-tiles* (recall from Section 11.1 that a rep-tile is a figure whose copies can be used to form a larger figure similar to itself). Convince other members of your group that your figures are rep-tiles and that they tessellate the plane.

LABORATORY ACTIVITY

As a van Hiele Level 0 activity, use pattern blocks to construct tessellations using each of the following types of pieces:

1. Squares
2. Equilateral triangles
3. Octagons and squares
4. Rhombuses

SOLUTION TO THE PRELIMINARY PROBLEM

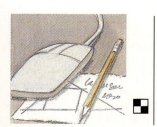

Understanding the Problem. $\triangle ABC$ in Figure 13-76 is a scale drawing of a triangular gable. We need to inscribe a square window *DEFG* in the gable so that the vertices of the square are on the sides of the triangle, as shown in Figure 13-76. Then we could measure the side of the square and multiply its length by the scale factor to obtain the actual length of each beam.

Devising a Plan.   We use the strategy of first *solving a simpler problem*. We could easily draw a square $D'E'F'G'$ with only three vertices on the sides of the triangle (how?) as shown

Figure 13-76

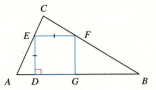

in Figure 13-77(a). If we construct several such squares like the ones in Figure 13-77(b), we notice that the vertices marked F', F'', F''', and A are collinear (on the same line). This is because each square in Figure 13-77(b) can be created with a size transformation with center A (why?). Thus, to find the point F on $\overline{CB}$, we may connect A with F' and the place at which $\overrightarrow{AF'}$ intersects $\overline{CB}$ is the vertex F.

Figure 13-77

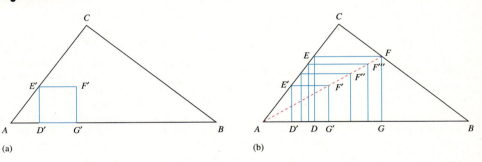

(a)   (b)

Carrying Out the Plan. To construct a square with one vertex on $\overline{AC}$ and two on $\overline{AB}$, choose an arbitrary point E' on $\overline{AC}$, as shown in Figure 13-78. Then drop a perpendicular from E' to $\overline{AB}$. The foot of the perpendicular is D'. Next, find G' so that $D'G' = D'E'$. The line parallel to $\overline{AB}$ through E' and the line perpendicular to $\overline{AB}$ through G' intersect at F'. The vertex F of the required square $DEFG$ and the points F' and A are collinear.

Thus, to find F, we connect A and F' and find the point F where $\overrightarrow{AF'}$ intersects $\overline{BC}$. Through F we draw lines parallel and perpendicular to $\overline{AB}$ and label the corresponding points of intersection with the sides $\overline{AC}$ and $\overline{AB}$ of the triangle as E and G. The perpendicular from E to $\overline{AB}$ determines the vertex D. The quadrilateral $DEFG$ is the required square.

Figure 13-78

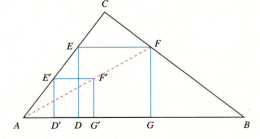

Looking Back. The square $D'E'F'G'$ can be chosen so that E' is any point on $\overline{AC}$ or even on the extension of $\overline{AC}$. Try the construction with E' at C.

A geometry utility software can be used to construct a square like $E'D'G'F'$. The vertex F' can then be "dragged" so that the remaining vertices stay on the sides of the triangle and the figure remains a square until vertex F' touches side $\overline{CB}$. This approach amounts to "eye-balling" the point on which F' touches $\overline{CB}$. The exact location of F' can be found as described in *Carrying Out the Plan* by drawing the line through *A* and *F'* and finding where the line intersects $\overline{CB}$.

A related question is how to find the length of the side of the square if all the measurements of the triangle are known (e.g., sides, angles, altitudes). This can be done using properties of similar triangles. We could generalize the problem by inscribing a square in other figures. A similar approach will work if we try to inscribe a square in a semicircle.

QUESTIONS FROM THE CLASSROOM

1. A student asks, "If I have a point and its image, is that enough to determine whether the image was found using a translation, reflection, rotation, or glide reflection?" How do you respond?

2. Another student asks a question similar to Question 1 but is concerned about a segment and its image. How do you respond to this student?

3. A student claims that a kite has no lines of symmetry. How do you respond?

4. A student says that every three-dimensional figure that has plane symmetry automatically has line symmetry. Do you agree?

5. A student says that in a size transformation with the scale factor 0, we do not have a transformation. Is that true?

6. A student asks if every translation on a grid can be accomplished by a translation along a vertical direction followed by a translation along a horizontal direction. How do you respond?

7. A student asks why the images of two perpendicular lines will also be perpendicular under a size transformation. How do you respond?

CHAPTER OUTLINE

I. Motions of the Plane
   A. **Isometries** are transformations that preserve distance.
      1. A **translation** is a motion of the plane that moves every point a specified distance in a specified direction along a straight line.
      2. A **rotation** is a motion of the plane determined by holding one point (the center) fixed and rotating the plane about this point by a certain amount in a certain direction.
      3. A **half-turn** is a rotation of 180°.
      4. Properties of a rotation can be used to show that two lines, neither of which is vertical, are perpendicular if, and only if, their slopes m_1 and m_2 satisfy the condition $m_1m_2 = {}^-1$.
      5. A **reflection** in a line *m* is a motion among points of the plane that pairs each point *P* of the plane with a point *P'* in such a way that *m* is the perpendicular bisector of $\overline{PP'}$, as long as *P* is not on *m*. If *P* is on *m*, then *P = P'*.
      6. A **glide reflection** is the composition of a translation and a reflection in a line parallel to the slide arrow of the translation.
   B. A **size transformation** *S* from the plane to the plane has the following properties: Some point *O*, the center of the size transformation, is its own image. For any other point *Q* of the plane, its image *Q'* is such that $OQ'/OQ = r$, where *r* is a positive real number and *O*, *Q*, and *Q'* are collinear.
   C. Two figures are **similar** if it is possible to transform one onto the other by a sequence of isometries followed by a size transformation.

II. Symmetries
   A. A figure has a **line symmetry** if it is its own image under a reflection.
   B. A figure has **rotational symmetry** if it is its own image under a rotation of less than 360° about its center.
   C. A figure has **point symmetry** if it has 180° rotational symmetry.
   D. A three-dimensional figure has a **plane of symmetry** when every point of the figure on one side of the plane has a mirror image on the other side of the plane.

*III. Tessellations
   A **tessellation** of a plane is the filling of the plane with repetitions of figures in such a way that no figures overlap and there are no gaps.

CHAPTER REVIEW

1. Complete each of the following motions.

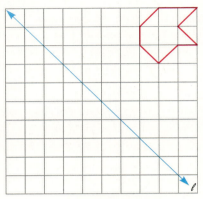

A reflection in ℓ

(a)

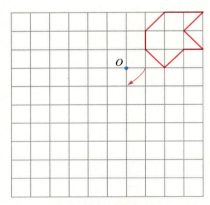

A rotation in *O* through the given arc

(b)

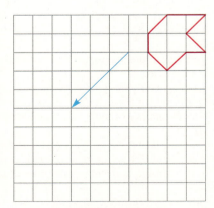

A translation, as pictured

(c)

2. For each of the following figures, construct the image of △*ABC*.

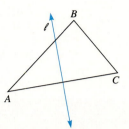

Through a reflection in ℓ

(a)

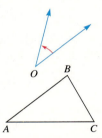

Through the given rotation in *O*

(b)

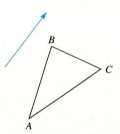

Through the translation arrow pictured

(c)

3. Determine how many lines of symmetry, if any, each of the following figures has.

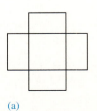

(a)   (b)

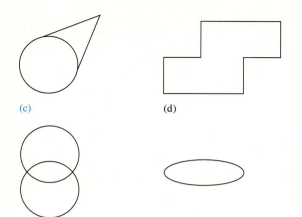

(c)   (d)

(e)   (f)

4. For each of the following figures, identify the types of symmetry (line, rotational, or point) it possesses.

(a)   (b)

(c)

5. Determine how many planes of symmetry each of the following has.
   a. A ball
   b. A right cylindrical water pipe
   c. A box that is a right rectangular prism but not a cube
   d. A cube
6. What type of symmetry (line, rotational, or point) does each of the lowercase letters of the printed English alphabet have?
7. Two towns at *A* and *B* in the following figure plan to pipe water from a river represented by the line *r* as shown. The towns decided to build a single pumping station along the river so that the total length of the pipe is as short as possible.

   a. Construct the point *S* on *r* on which the station should be built.
   b. From *A* and *B*, perpendiculars to *r* are drawn intersecting *r* at *O* and *P*, respectively. If $AO = 4$ mi, $BP = 3$ mi, and $OP = 15$ mi, find how far the pumping station *S* is from *O*.
8. In the following figure, $\triangle A'B'C'$ is the image of $\triangle ABC$ under a size transformation.

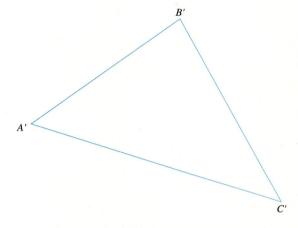

Locate points *A*, *B*, and *C* such that *A'* is the center of the size transformation and $BC = \frac{1}{2}B'C'$.

9. Given that *STAR* in the following figure is a parallelogram, describe a sequence of isometries to show the following.
   a. $\triangle STA \cong \triangle ARS$
   b. $\triangle TSR \cong \triangle RAT$

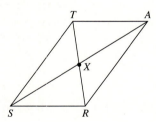

10. Given that *BEAUTY* in the following figure is a regular hexagon, describe a sequence of isometries that will transform the following.
   a. *BEAU* into *AUTY*
   b. *BEAU* into *YTUA*

11. Given that △*SNO* ≅ △*SWO* in the following figure, describe one or more isometries that will transform △*SNO* into △*SWO*.

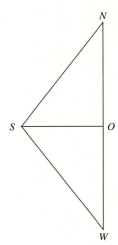

12. Show that △*SER* in the following figure is the image of △*HOR* under a succession of isometries with a size transformation.

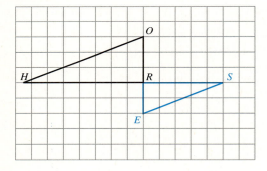

13. The triangle *A′B′C′* with *A′*(0, 7.91), *B′*(⁻5, ⁻4.93), *C′*(4.83, 0) is the image of triangle *ABC* under the translation $(x, y) \rightarrow (x + 3, y - 5)$. Find the coordinates of *A*, *B*, and *C*.

14. Show that △*TAB* in the following figure is the image of △*PIG* under a succession of isometries with a size transformation:

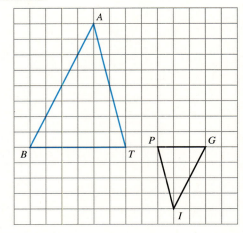

* **15.** Explain why a regular octagon cannot tessellate the plane.
 16. Write a Logo procedure called RHOMSTRIP that will draw a vertical strip of rhombuses.

SELECTED BIBLIOGRAPHY

Bannon, T. "Fractals and Transformations." *Mathematics Teacher* 84 (February 1991): 178–185.

Bidwell, J. "Using Reflections to Find Symmetric and Asymmetric Patterns." *Arithmetic Teacher* 34 (March 1987): 10–15.

Billstein, R., S. Libeskind, and J. Lott. *Logo: MIT Logo for the Apple.* Menlo Park, Calif.: Benjamin/Cummings (1985).

DeTemple, D. "Reflection Borders for Patchwork Quilts." *Mathematics Teacher* 80 (February 1986): 138–143.

Eddins, S. et al. "Geometric Transformations — Part 1." *Mathematics Teacher* 87 (March 1994): 177–180.

Eddins, S. et al. "Geometric Transformations — Part 2." *Mathematics Teacher* 87 (April 1994): 258–260.

Gardner, M. "On Tessellating the Plane with Convex Polygonal Tiles." *Scientific American* (July 1975): 112–117.

Lappan, G., and R. Even. "Research into Practice: Similarity in the Middle Grades." *Arithmetic Teacher* 35 (May 1988): 32–35.

May, B. "Reflections on Miniature Golf." *Mathematics Teacher* 78 (May 1985): 351–353.

Ranucci, E., and J. Teeters. *Creating Escher-type Drawings.* Palo Alto, Calif.: Creative Publications (1977).

Reesink, C. "Crystals: Through the Looking Glass with Planes, Points, and Rotational Symmetry." *Mathematics Teacher* 80 (May 1987): 377–388.

Rice, M., and D. Schattschneider. "The Incredible Pentagonal Versatile." *Mathematics Teaching* 93 (1980): 133–144.

Sanok, G. "Living in a World of Transformations." In Jane Hill, Ed. *Geometry for Grades K–6: Readings from the Arithmetic Teacher.* Reston, Va: NCTM (1987).

Senk, S. L., and D. B. Hirschhorn. "Multiple Approaches to Geometry: Teaching Similarity." *Mathematics Teacher* 83 (April 1990): 274–280.

Shilgalis, T. "Symmetries for Irregular Polygons." *Mathematics Teacher* 85 (May 1992): 342–344.

Shyers, J. "Reflective Paths to Minimum-Distance Solutions." *Mathematics Teacher* 79 (March 1986): 174–177, 203.

Sicklick, F., B. Turkel, and F. R. Curcio. "The Transformation Game." *Arithmetic Teacher* 36 (October 1988): 37–41.

Walter, M. *The Mirror Puzzle Book.* New York: Parkwest Publications (1985).

Willcutt, B. "Triangular Tiles for Your Patio." *Arithmetic Teacher* 34 (May 1987): 43–45.

Woods, J. "Let the Computer Draw the Tessellations That You Design." *Mathematics Teacher* 81 (February 1988): 138–141.

Zaslavsky, C. "Symmetry in American Folk Art." *Arithmetic Teacher* 37 (January 1990): 6–12.

Appendix I

Logo Turtle Graphics

Introducing the Turtle

Turtle graphics, implemented using the computer language Logo, are especially suited for studying geometry. Students can draw geometric figures by giving instructions to a **turtle,** a triangular figure on the display screen. Different versions of Logo exist and commands may vary depending on the version used. Most commands given in this discussion are for MIT Logo, with commands for the LCSI version mentioned in parentheses. You may need to consult your user's manual if commands do not function exactly the same way for the Logo version you are using. If an abbreviation can be used in place of a command, then it is given in parentheses immediately after the command when the command is introduced.

HISTORICAL NOTE

The computer language Logo was developed in 1967 at Bolt, Beranek, and Newman, Inc. of Cambridge, Massachusetts, and the Massachusetts Institute of Technology (MIT) by Daniel Bobrow, Wallace Feurzeig, and Seymour Papert. The name "Logo" is derived from the Greek word for "thought." The developers of Logo were influenced by the field of artificial intelligence, the computer language LISP, and the theories of Jean Piaget. The tradition of calling the display creature a turtle can be traced to early experiments involving robot-like creatures referred to as "tortoises." When computer graphics were implemented, the screen creature inherited the turtle terminology. In some versions, the figure on the screen actually appears as a turtle.

---

draw mode/DRAW

After Logo is loaded into the computer, a question mark called a *prompt* and a flashing *cursor* appear as the computer waits for instructions. To execute turtle graphics commands, enter **draw mode** by typing **DRAW** *(in the LCSI version, CLEARSCREEN (CS))* and pressing RETURN or ENTER . In the draw mode, the turtle appears in the center of the screen, as shown in Figure AI-1. The turtle's position in the center of the screen is called "home."

Figure AI-1

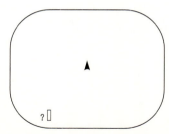

Moving the Turtle

FORWARD (FD)
BACK (BK)

To make the turtle change position, we use the primitives **FORWARD (FD)** and **BACK (BK),** *followed by a space* and a numerical input. The numerical input tells the turtle how far to move. For example, after the DRAW command is executed, typing FORWARD 100 or FD 100 and pressing ⌐RETURN⌐ causes the turtle to move 100 "turtle units" in the direction it is pointing. Figure AI-2 shows a series of directions and drawings at each stage when the turtle starts at home pointing upwards. Similarly, the BACK command may be used with a numerical input. For example, BACK 75 or BK 75 causes the turtle to move backwards 75 units. Giving the turtle too great an input causes the turtle to "wrap around" the screen. To explore how the turtle wraps, try FD 250 and observe what happens.

Figure AI-2

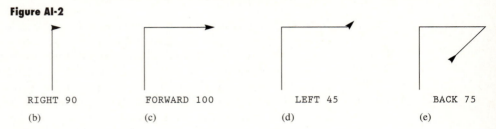

| DRAW FORWARD 100 | RIGHT 90 | FORWARD 100 | LEFT 45 | BACK 75 |
| (a) | (b) | (c) | (d) | (e) |

Turning the Turtle

RIGHT (RT) • LEFT (LT)

To make the turtle change direction, we used the commands **RIGHT (RT)** and **LEFT (LT).** The RIGHT and LEFT commands, along with numerical inputs, cause the turtle to turn in place the specified number of degrees. For example, typing RIGHT 90 or RT 90 and pressing ⌐RETURN⌐ causes the turtle to turn 90° to the right of the direction it previously pointed. A sequence of moves illustrating these commands is given in Figure AI-2.

Logo accepts a sequence of commands written on one line. For example, Figure AI-2(e) could be drawn by typing the following and pressing ⌐RETURN⌐:

```
DRAW FD 100 RT 90 FD 100 LT 45 BK 75
```

(In LCSI, replace DRAW with CLEARSCREEN.)

PENUP (PU)
PENDOWN (PD)
HIDETURTLE (HT)
SHOWTURTLE (ST)
HOME

To move the turtle without leaving a trail, we use the command **PENUP (PU).** To make the turtle leave a trail again, type **PENDOWN (PD).** It is possible to hide the turtle by typing **HIDETURTLE (HT).** To make the turtle reappear, type **SHOWTURTLE (ST).**

To return the turtle to the center of the screen with heading 0, type the command **HOME.** However, a trail to the center of the screen will be drawn from the position the turtle occupied before HOME was typed unless the command PENUP is used before HOME.

To start a new drawing with a clear screen, we type DRAW *(in LCSI, replace DRAW with CLEARSCREEN (CS)).* This returns the turtle to its initial position and direction in the center of the screen and clears the screen. Any time the turtle points straight north (up), we say it has heading 0. A heading of 90 is directly east, 180 is directly south, and 270 is directly west. The screen could be marked as shown in Figure AI-3.

Figure AI-3

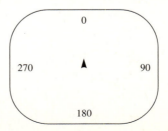

HEADING

PRINT (PR)

To learn the turtle's heading, we use HEADING. **HEADING** needs no inputs; typing HEADING in the draw mode and pressing RETURN causes the computer to output the turtle's heading. To have the computer print only the value of the heading, we use **PRINT (PR)** along with HEADING, as in PRINT HEADING. For example, if the turtle is at home with heading 0 and we type RT 45 PR HEADING, then 45 will be displayed. If we execute RT 45 PR HEADING again, then 90 will be displayed.

SETHEADING (SETH)

The command **SETHEADING (SETH)** requires one input and can be used to turn the turtle in a direction from the 0 heading. For example, SETH 100 turns the turtle so that it has a heading of 100. This command can be used no matter where the turtle is located or what its heading is at the time. Figure AI-4 gives an example of the use of the SETH and HOME commands. A summary of commands introduced thus far is shown in Table AI-1.

Table AI-1

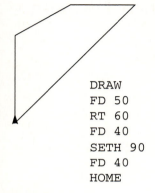

```
DRAW
FD 50
RT 60
FD 40
SETH 90
FD 40
HOME
```

Figure AI-4

Command	Abbreviation	Example
BACK	BK	BK 60
DRAW*		
FORWARD	FD	FD 50
HEADING		PR HEADING
HIDETURTLE	HT	
HOME		
LEFT	LT	LT 45
PENDOWN	PD	
PENUP	PU	
PRINT	PR	PR "LOGO
RIGHT	RT	RT 90
SETHEADING	SETH	SETH 270
SHOWTURTLE	ST	

*The command in *LCSI* is CLEARSCREEN (CS).

Creating Figures

People studying Logo are encouraged to "play turtle" and act out their commands. For example, to act out drawing a square, we may walk around the square by moving forward 50 units, turning right 90°, moving forward 50 units, turning right 90°, moving forward 50 units, turning right 90°, and finally moving forward 50 units. The sequence of commands for these moves is summarized in Figure AI-5(a), with the resulting square and final position of the turtle shown in Figure AI-5(b).

Figure AI-5

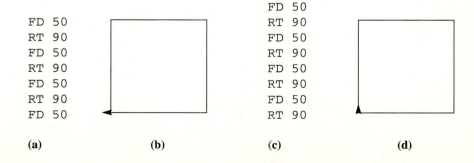

```
FD 50
RT 90
FD 50
RT 90
FD 50
RT 90
FD 50
```
(a)

(b)

```
FD 50
RT 90
FD 50
RT 90
FD 50
RT 90
FD 50
RT 90
```
(c)

(d)

The turtle's final position in Figure AI-5(b) is the same as its initial position, but its heading is different. When drawing a figure, you will often find it convenient to have the turtle's final state be the same as its initial state. When this happens, we say that the set of commands is **state transparent.** To return the turtle shown in Figure AI-5(b) to its initial state, we turn it right 90° by adding the line RT 90 at the end of the sequence of commands in Figure AI-5(a). The new sequence of commands is given in Figure AI-5(c), with the resulting square and turtle position shown in Figure AI-5(d).

state transparent

The sequence of commands in Figure AI-5(c) contains the instructions FD 50 and RT 90 repeated four times. Logo allows us to use the REPEAT command to repeat a list of instructions. For example, to draw the square in Figure AI-5(d), we would type the following:

```
REPEAT 4 [FD 50 RT 90]
```

REPEAT

In general, **REPEAT** takes two inputs: a number and a list of commands. The commands in the brackets are repeated the designated number of times.

• • •

Example AI-1

Predict the results of each of the following, indicating the initial and final turtle states. Then, check your answers with a computer. In each case, assume the turtle starts at home with heading 0.

a. FD 100
   RT 135
   FD 100
   RT 45
   FD 100
   RT 135
   FD 100
   RT 45
b. REPEAT 2 [FD 100 RT 135 FD 100 RT 45]
c. REPEAT 8 [FD 50 RT 45]
d. BK 100 SETH 270 FD 100 HOME
e. SETH 90 REPEAT 5[FD 10 PU FD 5 PD]

Solution The results are depicted in Figure AI-6.

Figure AI-6

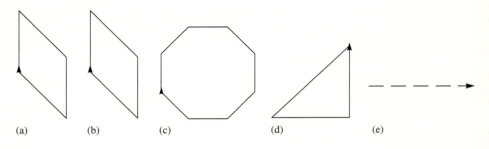

(a)　　　　(b)　　　　(c)　　　　(d)　　　　(e)

• • •

Defining Procedures

The sequence of commands in Figure AI-5(c) instructed the turtle to draw a square. If the screen is cleared, the figure is lost. To redraw the square, the entire sequence of commands

procedure

must be retyped. Fortunately, with Logo, it is possible to store instructions in the computer's memory by creating a procedure. A **procedure** is a group of one or more instructions to the computer that the computer can store to be used later.

TO

To create a procedure in MIT Logo, we type **TO,** followed by the name we wish to call the procedure, and then press RETURN . *(In LCSI, we type EDIT (ED), followed by a double quotation mark and the procedure name, for example, ED "TRIANGLE.)* When RETURN is pressed, the computer enters **edit mode,** or the teaching mode. In this mode, the lines that follow are not executed but may be stored in memory under the given name. The name must be a sequence of symbols with no spaces, and it may not be the name of a **primitive,** a word that is part of the Logo language. For example, to create a procedure called SQUARE1 to draw a square, the following is entered.

edit mode

primitive

```
TO SQUARE1
  REPEAT 4 [FD 50 RT 90]
END
```

END

To signify the end of a procedure, we type **END** as the last line of the procedure. Typing END at the end of a procedure is necessary if you intend to define another procedure without leaving edit mode.

In Logo, one procedure can call another, as shown in Example AI-2. *Note:* If the SQUARE1 procedure has not been defined on your computer, be sure to define it before working the example. In the rest of this section, we assume that the SQUARE1 procedure and all subsequent procedures are stored in the computer's memory and can be reused.

Example AI-2

Predict the figures that will be drawn by defining and executing each of the following procedures. Assume the turtle starts at home with heading 0.

a. `TO SQUARE2`
  `RT 90`
  `SQUARE1`
`END`

b. `TO SQUARESTACK`
  `SQUARE1`
  `RT 90`
  `SQUARE1`
`END`

c. `TO STAIR`
  `SQUARE1`
  `RT 180`
  `SQUARE1`
`END`

d. `TO TURNSQUARE`
  `SQUARE1`
  `RT 45`
  `SQUARE1`
`END`

Solution   The results are depicted in Figure AI-7.

Figure AI-7

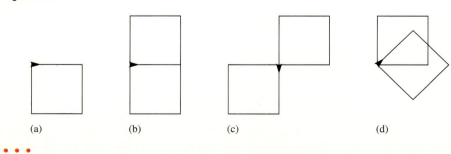

(a)   (b)   (c)   (d)

Problem 1

Write a procedure for drawing a triangle whose sides each have length of 50 turtle steps and whose angles each have measure of 60°. This type of triangle is an *equilateral triangle*.

Understanding the Problem.   We are to write a procedure to draw a triangle with all sides of length 50 turtle units and all angles of measure 60°. We can start at any position with any heading.

Devising a Plan.   It is helpful to sketch the triangle to determine the angle the turtle needs to turn at each vertex. Suppose the turtle starts at point *A* with heading 0 and moves 50 turtle steps to point *B*, as shown in Figure AI-8. This can be done by telling the turtle to move FD 50. At point *B*, the turtle still has heading 0. To walk on $\overrightarrow{BC}$, the turtle must turn 120° to the right. Thus the next command should be RT 120. The triangle has three sides of equal length, so three turns are necessary to achieve the turtle's initial heading. Repeating the sequence FD 50 RT 120 three times should cause the turtle to walk around the triangle and finish in its original position with its original heading.

Figure AI-8

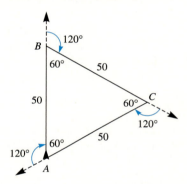

Carrying Out the Plan.   A procedure called TRIANGLE1 based on the preceding discussion follows:

```
TO TRIANGLE1
 REPEAT 3 [FD 50 RT 120]
END
```

Looking Back.   Executing the TRIANGLE1 procedure yields the desired figure. Additional investigations include writing a procedure to draw the same type of triangle by turning left instead of right or writing a procedure to draw a triangle with one horizontal side. Procedures for drawing other polygons could also be explored.

• • •

One of the great advantages of Logo is its ability to use procedures to define new procedures. Consider the following problem.

Problem 2

Write a procedure to draw the "house" shown in Figure AI-9.

Understanding the Problem.   The top of the house appears to be a triangle similar to the one in Problem 1, and the bottom appears to be a square. We must write a super procedure

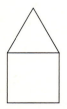

Figure AI-9

in which procedures for drawing a square and a triangle will be incorporated to draw the house.

Devising a Plan.   One way to solve the problem is to break down the problem of drawing a house into *simpler problems,* that of drawing the bottom of the house (the square) and that of drawing the roof (the triangle). The type of programming that starts with a general idea and breaks down the problem into smaller parts is **top-down programming.** We have a procedure SQUARE1 for drawing a square of length 50 units and a procedure TRIANGLE1 for drawing a triangle of length 50 units. If we use these two procedures, then we should be able to draw the house.

top-down programming

Carrying Out the Plan.   If the turtle has heading 0, it may seem that typing SQUARE1 followed by TRIANGLE1 would draw the desired house. The result of this effort is shown in Figure AI-10(a). Why did it not produce the desired figure?

Figure AI-10

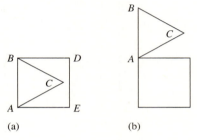

(a)   (b)

To draw the roof in proper position, we need the turtle to be at the upper-left vertex of the square. This can be achieved by typing SQUARE1 FD 50. But, if we now type TRIANGLE1, we obtain the shape in Figure AI-10(b), which is still not the desired house.

After we type SQUARE1 and FD 50, the turtle is at point *A* with heading 0. For it to form the roof shown in Figure AI-11(a), and to walk on $\overline{AB}$, the turtle needs to turn right by 90° − 60°, or 30°. With the turtle's having this heading, our typing TRIANGLE1 should cause the turtle to draw the desired roof. The complete procedure, called HOUSE, is shown in Figure AI-11(b).

Figure AI-11

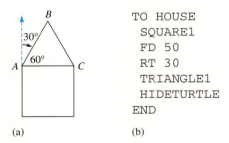

```
TO HOUSE
   SQUARE1
   FD 50
   RT 30
   TRIANGLE1
   HIDETURTLE
END
```

(a)   (b)

Looking Back.   If the HOUSE procedure is executed, the desired figure is obtained. Alternative techniques for drawing the figure could also be explored. Houses of other sizes could be drawn, and windows and doors could be added.

• • •

As Problem 2 shows, trial and error helps the user to get acquainted with the problem and eventually to find the correct solution. This process of rewriting a program that does not do what we want it to do is called *debugging*. Making mistakes is accepted in Logo. Being able to experiment with Logo is part of its power. Students need to understand that "bugs" will not break the computer and that sometimes bugs or experimentation can lead to unexpected results or pictures that are sometimes better than what was intended.

To help you understand how Logo works when a procedure calls another procedure, a telescoping model of the HOUSE procedure in Problem 2 is given in Figure AI-12.

Figure AI-12

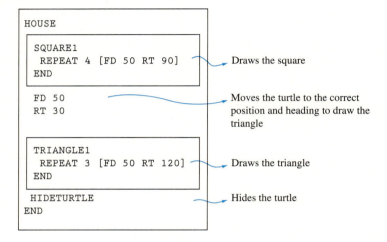

When HOUSE is run, it encounters the call for SQUARE1. At this point, all the lines of SQUARE1 are inserted. After SQUARE1 has been completed, control is returned to the procedure that called it, namely, HOUSE. Now, HOUSE continues where it left off and executes FD 50 RT 30. Then it calls the TRIANGLE1 procedure. After TRIANGLE1 has been executed, control returns to HOUSE, which hides the turtle and encounters its own END statement. (Remember to clear the screen before trying HOUSE again.)

In working through the HOUSE procedure, we went through several steps. These are summarized next. They might be useful in solving a variety of problems presented in this text.

1. Sketch your drawing on paper (preferably graph paper) to get an idea of the scale to be used and of how the final picture should look.
2. Divide the drawing into parts that are repeated, that you already know how to draw, or that are smaller parts of the whole. Separate procedures for drawing each individual part are easier to debug than a single procedure for the whole drawing.
3. Decide how your individual procedures are going to fit together to form the complete picture. Some procedures might be necessary just to move the turtle to the right position for drawing the individual parts.
4. Write your procedures. One approach for doing this is to write individual procedures for separate pieces, make sure they work, and then try to put them all together to form the complete picture. Another approach is to fit the procedures together as they are completed. Either approach is an acceptable problem-solving strategy, and each has advantages in different situations.

We demonstrate in Problem 3 how these steps can be used in a problem-solving format.

Problem 3

Write a procedure to draw the figure sketched on the graph paper in Figure AI-13.

Figure AI-13

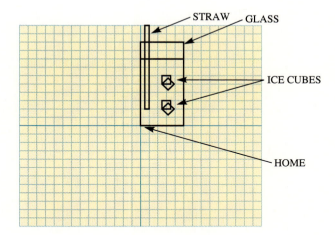

Understanding the Problem. We are to write a procedure to draw a figure similar to the one shown in Figure AI-13. Each length of a side of a small square on the grid paper represents 10 turtle steps.

Devising a Plan. The figure can be broken into three separate parts: the glass, the straw, and the ice cubes. Using top-down programming, we can write a procedure called DRINK that draws the figure.

```
TO DRINK
  GLASS
  ICE.CUBES
  ICE.CUBES
  STRAW
  HT
END
```

To complete the problem, we must write procedures for each portion of the DRINK procedure.

Carrying Out the Plan. First, we design a procedure called GLASS for drawing the glass. If the turtle starts at home with heading 0, one possible procedure and its output are given in Figure AI-14.

Figure AI-14

```
TO GLASS
  REPEAT 2 [FD 100 RT 90 FD 50 RT 90]
  FD 80 RT 90
  FD 50 BK 50
  LT 90 BK 80
END
```

Likewise, procedures called STRAW and ICE.CUBES can be designed to draw the other two parts, as shown in Figure AI-15(a) and (b).

Figure AI-15

```
TO STRAW
 REPEAT 2 [FD 100 RT 90 FD 5 RT 90]
END

TO ICE.CUBES
 SQUARE3
 RT 45
 SQUARE3
 LT 45
END

TO SQUARE3
 REPEAT 4 [FD 10 RT 90]
END
```

(a)

(b)

If we now execute DRAW *(CS in LSCI)* and attempt to execute the DRINK procedure as defined, the result is as shown in Figure AI-16.

Figure AI-16

To correct the DRINK procedure so that it will draw the desired figure, we must keep track of the turtle's position and heading. Sometimes, it is convenient to move the turtle to the required positions and headings by using a set of procedures. The following procedures —SETUP.CUBES1, SETUP.CUBES2, and SETUP. STRAW—move the turtle to the correct position and heading to draw each part. Notice the use of PU and PD to keep the transitions invisible.

```
TO SETUP.CUBES1
 PU FD 50 RT 90 FD 25 LT 90 PD
END

TO SETUP.CUBES2
 PU BK 30 PD
END

TO SETUP.STRAW
 PU LT 90 FD 20 RT 90 PD
END
```

If we edit DRINK and add these new procedures, we obtain the procedures and figure shown in Figure AI-17.

Figure AI-17

```
TO DRINK
  GLASS
  SETUP.CUBES1
  ICE.CUBES
  SETUP.CUBES2
  ICE.CUBES
  SETUP.STRAW
  STRAW
  HT
END
```

Looking Back. When the DRINK procedure is executed, it yields the desired figure. The procedure could have been written in many different ways. Although various strategies could be used to develop the procedure, we see that the top-down strategy can be very useful. One advantage of this strategy is that it is easier to debug smaller portions of the figure rather than to try to do the complete figure all at one time.

• • •

Writing Procedures with Variables

The SQUARE1 procedure in this section allowed us to draw only squares of side length 50. If we want to draw smaller or larger squares, we must write a new procedure. It would be more convenient if we could write one procedure that would work for a square of any size. This can be accomplished in Logo by using a variable as input, rather than a fixed number such as 50 in FD 50. To use variable input in Logo, we need to warn the computer that the "thing" we are going to type is a variable. We do this by using a colon before the variable name. For example, a variable input to the SQUARE1 procedure might be called :SIDE, where :SIDE stands for the length of a side of the square. Note that there is no space between the colon and the word SIDE. We define a new SQUARE procedure with variable input :SIDE and place the name of the variable in the title line.

```
TO SQUARE :SIDE
 REPEAT 4 [FD :SIDE RT 90]
END
```

If we want the turtle to draw a square of size 40, we type SQUARE 40. Notice that we do not type SQUARE :40 because 40 is not a variable. Investigate what happens if SQUARE is typed with no inputs.

REMARK   We call the new variable square procedure SQUARE instead of SQUARE1. If we attempt to enter the edit mode to define a new SQUARE1 procedure and the old procedure has not been erased, the computer will display the old SQUARE1 procedure on the screen for us to edit. Consult your Logo manual for directions on how to edit procedures.

A procedure may have more than one input. In the following procedure, two variables are used so that two inputs can be accepted.

```
TO RECTANGLE :HEIGHT :WIDTH
 REPEAT 2 [FD :HEIGHT RT 90 FD :WIDTH RT 90]
END
```

Figure AI-18 shows rectangles drawn by the RECTANGLE procedure with different inputs for the sides.

Figure AI-18

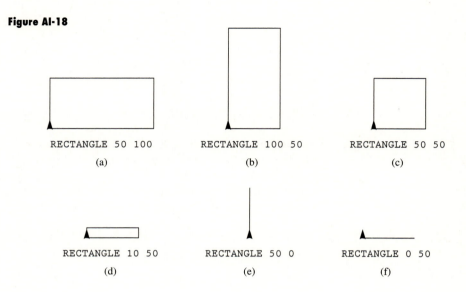

RECTANGLE 50 100
(a)

RECTANGLE 100 50
(b)

RECTANGLE 50 50
(c)

RECTANGLE 10 50
(d)

RECTANGLE 50 0
(e)

RECTANGLE 0 50
(f)

Logo Recursion

recursion **Recursion** is the process of a procedure's calling a copy of itself. As a first example of recursion, we write a procedure called CIRC for drawing a "turtle-type" circle. This could be done by having the turtle move forward "a little," then turn right "a little," and then continuing this process until a closed figure is obtained. Thus we could start the procedure with FD 1 RT 1 and then have the turtle start the procedure anew each time the instruction is executed. Such a procedure follows:

```
TO CIRC
  FD 1 RT 1
  CIRC
END
```

To stop the procedure, press ⌞CTRL⌟ ⌞G⌟. (This key sequence will vary depending on the version of Logo.) To understand how CIRC works and, in general, what happens when a procedure calls itself, we use the telescoping model in Figure AI-19.

Figure AI-19

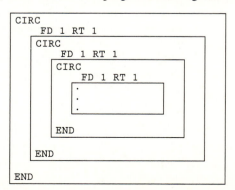

When CIRC is executed, FD 1 RT 1 causes the turtle to move forward one unit and then turn right 1°. CIRC then calls a copy of the CIRC procedure, which again executes FD 1 RT 1 and in turn calls another copy of CIRC, and so on. The process continues because we have made CIRC one of the instructions in the CIRC procedure. The END statement is never reached, and the instruction FD 1 RT 1 is executed indefinitely.

tail-end recursion

The repetitive process shown in the CIRC procedure occurs in the type of recursion called **tail-end recursion.** In tail-end recursion, only one recursive call is made within the body of the procedure, and it is the final step before the END statement.

INVESTIGATION AI — 1

● Write a procedure called CIRCLE1 that uses a REPEAT command rather than recursion to draw a Logo-type circle similar to the one drawn by the CIRC procedure. ●

Recursion is particularly valuable when we do not know how many times to repeat a set of instructions to accomplish some goal. For example, consider the shapes that can be drawn by repeating the instruction "Go forward some fixed distance and turn right some fixed angle." A recursive procedure called POLY that does this is as follows:

```
TO POLY :SIDE :ANGLE
 FD :SIDE RT :ANGLE
 POLY :SIDE :ANGLE
END
```

To execute the POLY procedure, we need two numerical inputs, one for :SIDE and the other for :ANGLE. Figure AI-20 shows shapes drawn by POLY with different inputs. The drawings were stopped using CTRL-G.

Figure AI-20

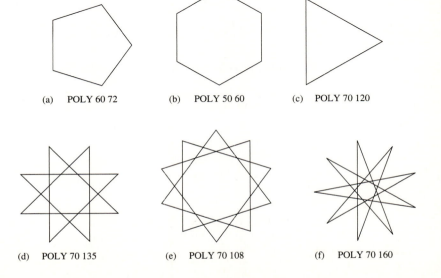

(a)   POLY 60 72   (b)   POLY 50 60   (c)   POLY 70 120

(d)   POLY 70 135   (e)   POLY 70 108   (f)   POLY 70 160

The POLY procedure draws regular polygons (polygons that have congruent sides and congruent angles), as in Figure AI-20(a), (b), and (c), and also star shapes as in Figure AI-20(d), (e), and (f). Try other executions of POLY, such as POLY 50 180, POLY 50 181, POLY 60 288, POLY 6000 300, and POLY 7000 135. Try to predict which inputs produce regular polygons and which produce star shapes.

All the figures drawn by the POLY procedure in Figure AI-20 are closed; that is, they can be drawn by starting and stopping at the same point. Will all figures drawn by POLY be closed? We can also ask the following questions:

1. Given the value of :ANGLE in the POLY procedure, is it possible to predict (before the figure is drawn) how many vertices the figure will have?
2. If we wish the POLY procedure to draw a figure with a given number of vertices, can we determine what the correct angle input should be?

With the help of recursion, we can accomplish tasks that cannot be done easily with just the REPEAT command, especially if we do not know how many times to repeat a sequence of instructions. Consider drawing a square-type spiral as shown in Figure AI-21.

Figure AI-21

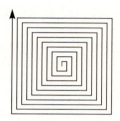

Suppose each side of the figure is five units longer than the preceding side. If the turtle starts at home, the figure can be drawn by telling the turtle to move forward a certain length :LEN, turn right 90°, move forward five units more than the previous value of :LEN, and so on. A recursive procedure called SQSPI shows how this can be done.

```
TO SQSPI :LEN
 FD :LEN RT 90
 SQSPI :LEN + 5
END
```

Each time SQSPI calls itself, the length of :LEN is increased by five units. When SQSPI is run, the sides grow too large to fit on the screen. Rather than stopping SQSPI with CTRL-G, we can write a "stop" instruction in the procedure. This can be done with the IF and STOP primitives. **IF** is a primitive that tests one of three conditions: equal (=), less than (<), or greater than (>). The IF primitive is used in the following form:

IF

IF *(Condition)   (Action to be taken if condition is true)*

The parentheses should not be typed. *(In LCSI, the format is IF (Condition) [Action to be taken if condition is true], where the square brackets must be typed.)*

For example, if we do not want the turtle to draw any segment longer than 100 units, we insert the following instruction:

IF :LEN > 100 STOP

(In LSCI, IF :LEN > 100 [STOP].) When this line is inserted into a procedure, the IF statement causes the computer to check whether the value of :LEN is greater than 100. If it is, **STOP**   the procedure stops; if not, the next line is executed. The **STOP** primitive causes the cur-

rent procedure to stop and returns control to the calling procedure, if there is one. An edited form of the SQSPI procedure is as follows:

```
TO SQSPI :LEN
 IF :LEN > 100 STOP
 FD :LEN RT 90
 SQSPI :LEN + 5
END
```

(In LCSI, replace STOP with [STOP].)

The SQSPI procedure can be generalized to draw other spiral-type figures. Investigate the following POLYSPI procedure for various inputs:

```
TO POLYSPI :SIDE :ANGLE
 IF :SIDE > 100 STOP
 FD :SIDE RT :ANGLE
 POLYSPI :SIDE + 5 :ANGLE
END
```

(In LCSI, replace STOP with [STOP].)

What inputs should be given to POLYSPI in order to achieve the same effect that SQSPI does? Also, investigate what happens when :ANGLE, rather than :SIDE, is incremented each time the recursive call is made.

Summary of Commands

BACK (BK)	Takes one input. Positive input moves the turtle backwards the number of turtle units that are input. For example, BK 40 moves the turtle backwards 40 units.
DRAW*	Needs no input. It sends the turtle home and clears the graphics screen.
END	Used at the end of a procedure. Tells the computer that there are no more instructions to be given in the procedure.
FORWARD (FD)	Takes one input. Positive input moves the turtle forward (in the direction the turtle is facing) the number of turtle units that are input. For example, FD 20 moves the turtle forward 20 units.
HEADING	Needs no input. In draw mode, it outputs the turtle's heading.
HIDETURTLE (HT)	Needs no input. It causes the turtle to disappear.
HOME	Needs no input. It returns the turtle to the center of the screen and sets its heading to 0. If the pen is down, it leaves a track from the turtle's present location to the home position.
IF†	Takes two inputs. The first must be either true or false. The second contains instructions that are carried out if, and only if, the first is true.
LEFT (LT)	Takes one input. Positive input turns the turtle left from its present heading the number of degrees that are input. For example, LT 90 turns the turtle left 90°.
PENDOWN (PD)	Needs no input. In graphics mode, it causes the turtle to leave a track.

*In *LCSI*, this command is CLEARSCREEN (CS).

†In *LCSI*, the second input must be enclosed in brackets, for example, IF :SIDE > 100 [STOP].

Summary of Commands *continued*

PENUP (PU)	Needs no input. In graphics mode, it enables the turtle to move without leaving a track.
PRINT (PR)	Takes one input. It causes the input to be printed on the screen and moves the cursor to the next line.
REPEAT	Takes a number and a list as input. It executes the instructions in the list the designated number of times.
RIGHT (RT)	Takes one input. Positive input turns the turtle right from its present heading the number of degrees that are input. For example, RT 90 turns the turtle right 90°.
SETHEADING (SETH)	Takes one input. It turns the turtle to the heading indicated by the input.
SHOWTURTLE (ST)	Needs no input. It causes the turtle to reappear.
STOP	Takes no inputs. It causes the current production to stop and then returns control to the calling procedure.
TO‡	Takes the name of a procedure as input and causes Logo to enter edit mode.

‡In *LCSI*, this command is EDIT (ED).

Ongoing Assessment A-I

1. Sketch figures drawn by the turtle using each of the following sets of instructions. Check your sketches by executing the instructions on a computer. Type DRAW *(CS in LCSI)* after each lettered part.

   a. FD 50
   RT 90
   FD 50
   RT 45
   FD 50
   RT 135
   FD 50

   b. FD 50
   RT 90
   BK 50
   RT 60
   FD 50

   c. FD −50 FD 50
   d. LT −90 BK −50 RT 40 PR HEADING
   e. RT 360 PR HEADING
   f. SETH 30 REPEAT 3[FD 50 RT 120]
   g. FD 100/2 RT 5*6 BK 100 + 20

2. Experiment with the turtle to find the dimensions of the screen.

3. Predict what the turtle will draw with the following sets of instructions. Check your answers by executing the instructions on the computer. (SQUARE1 and TRIANGLE1 are defined in the text.)

   a. REPEAT 8 [SQUARE1 RT 45]
   b. REPEAT 6 [TRIANGLE1 RT 60]
   c. REPEAT 36 [SQUARE1 RT 10]

4. Write procedures to draw figures similar to each of the following:

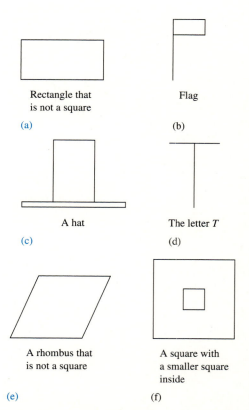

Rectangle that
is not a square
(a)

Flag
(b)

A hat
(c)

The letter *T*
(d)

A rhombus that
is not a square
(e)

A square with
a smaller square
inside
(f)

5. Write a procedure to draw the following:

6. Use any procedures in this section to write new procedures that will draw each of the following figures:

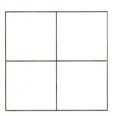

(a)

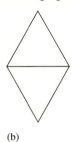

(b)

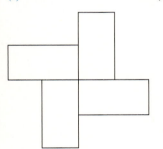

(c)

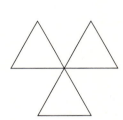

(d)

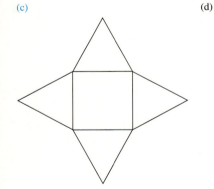

(e)

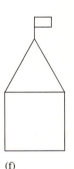

(f)

7. Write procedures to draw figures similar to each of the following:

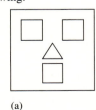

(a)

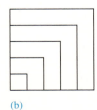

(b)

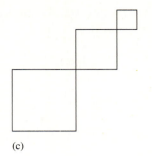

(c)

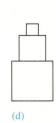

(d)

8. Use top-down programming to write a procedure called DOG to draw a figure similar to the following:

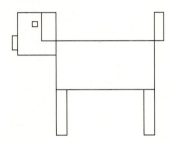

9. Use top-down programming to write a procedure called KITE to draw a figure similar to the following:

10. Write procedures to draw figures similar to those in Problem 4, but of variable size.

11. Write a procedure called BLADES to draw a figure similar to the following, but of variable size:

12. Write a procedure called RECTANGLES to draw a figure similar to the following, but of variable size:

13. Predict the shapes that will be drawn by the following procedures and then check your predictions on the computer. The SQUARE and TRIANGLE procedures are defined as follows. *(In LCSI, replace STOP with [STOP] in (b), (d), (e), and (f).)*

```
TO TRIANGLE :SIDE
 REPEAT 3 [FD :SIDE RT 120]
END
TO SQUARE :SIDE
 REPEAT 4 [FD :SIDE RT 90]
END
```

a.
```
TO FIGURE :SIDE
  TRIANGLE :SIDE
  RT 10
  FIGURE :SIDE
END
```

b.
```
TO FIGURE1 :SIDE
  IF :SIDE < 5 STOP
  TRIANGLE :SIDE
  RT 10
  FIGURE1 :SIDE − 5
END
```

c.
```
TO TOWER :SIDE
  SQUARE :SIDE
  FD :SIDE
  TOWER :SIDE * 0.5
END
```

d.
```
TO TOWER1 :SIDE
  IF :SIDE < 2 STOP
  SQUARE :SIDE
  FD :SIDE
  TOWER1 :SIDE * 0.5
END
```

e.
```
TO SQ :SIDE
  IF :SIDE < 2 STOP
  SQUARE :SIDE
  SQ :SIDE − 5
END
```

f.
```
TO SPIRAL :SIDE
  IF :SIDE > 50 STOP
  FD :SIDE
```
```
  RT 30
  SPIRAL :SIDE + 3
END
```

14. Given the following NEWPOLY, POLYSPIRAL, and INSPI procedures, predict the shapes that will be drawn by each and then check your predictions on the computer:

```
TO NEWPOLY :SIDE :ANGLE
 FD :SIDE RT :ANGLE
 FD :SIDE RT :ANGLE * 2
 NEWPOLY :SIDE :ANGLE
END
TO POLYSPIRAL :SIDE :ANGLE :INC
 FD :SIDE RT :ANGLE
 POLYSPIRAL (:SIDE + :INC) :ANGLE :INC
END
TO INSPI :SIDE :ANGLE :INC
 FD :SIDE RT :ANGLE
 INSPI :SIDE (:ANGLE + :INC) :INC
END
```

a. NEWPOLY 50 30
b. NEWPOLY 50 144
c. NEWPOLY 50 125
d. POLYSPIRAL 2 85 3
e. POLYSPIRAL 1 119 2
f. POLYSPIRAL 1 100 5
g. INSPI 10 2 20
h. INSPI 2 0 10
i. INSPI 10 5 10

15. Write recursive procedures to draw figures similar to the following six figures. Use the STOP command in your procedures.

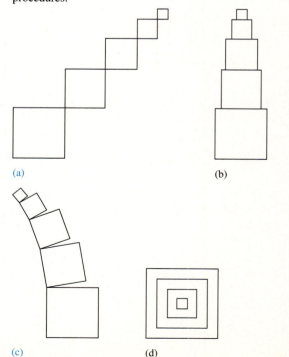

(a)

(b)

(c)

(d)

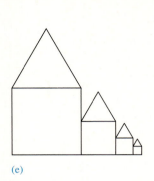

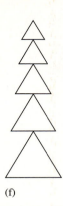

(e)   (f)

16. Write a recursive procedure with a STOP command to draw a figure similar to the following:

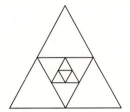

17. Write a procedure called SPIN.SQ that uses recursion and a STOP command to spin a variable-sized square while "shrinking" its size, as shown in the following figure:

18. Write a recursive procedure with a STOP statement that draws the following variable-sized figure made of squares:

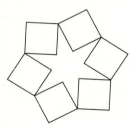

Appendix II

Graphing Calculators

In the *Teaching Standards* (p. 52), we find the following:

▲ *Teachers should also help students learn to use calculators, computers, and other techno-logical devices as tools for mathematical discourse. Given the range of mathematical tools available, teachers should often allow and encourage students to select the means they find most useful for working on or discussing a particular mathematical problem.*

In this appendix, we introduce many features of the graphing calculator by working through problems in various ways to show how students might attack a problem by using a graphing calculator. One advantage of the graphing calculator is its large screen, which can display not only graphs but also many lines of text. With this feature, computations and answers can be viewed, various methods can be compared, and changes can be easily made.

Graphing calculators are now being marketed for the middle-school level. In this appendix, we assume your calculator has at least the capabilities of the Texas Instruments TI–80 middle-school graphing calculator. The features that are mentioned are also present on the TI–82, TI–83, and TI–85. If other calculators are used, you will have to determine whether those features are available on them. (The following discussion is based on ideas presented in a workshop presented by Chuck Vonder Embse of Central Michigan University.)

Problem 1

Molly belongs to a club that sells CDs by mail. The CDs sell for $12.95 each, and she can order as many as she wants each month. Each order has a shipping charge of $5.00 no matter how many CDs are ordered. She would like to be able to develop a table that tells her how much money she owes when she orders from 1 to 10 CDs. Develop such a table.

This problem is worked using a variety of techniques to show some of the capabilities of the graphing calculator.

Using the Replay Feature

Suppose we want to solve Problem 1 using paper and pencil to build a table and using the calculator to perform the computations. First, we must realize that the cost for any number of CDs is given by multiplying the number of CDs by $12.95 and adding $5.00. To find the cost of one CD using this process, enter the following:

$$1 \times 12.95 + 5$$

and press $\boxed{\text{ENTER}}$. The answer, 17.95, is displayed. This number can then be recorded in a table. It is important for elementary-school students to see the whole problem as well as the answer. This allows students to check visually whether they have entered their numbers and operations correctly.

replay feature   To find the cost for other quantities of CDs, we use the **replay feature** of the calculator. To activate this feature, press $\boxed{\text{2nd}}$ $\boxed{\text{ENTRY}}$; the previous entry is displayed. We then use the left arrow to move the cursor over the first 1 and replace it with a 2. When ENTER is pressed, the next answer, 30.90, is displayed. We could shorten the left arrow strokes even further by pressing 2nd followed by the left arrow; the cursor will go to the beginning of the line. If we continue in this manner, as shown in Figure AII-1, we could find the cost of any number of CDs and enter these costs into a table.

Figure AII-1

```
1*12.95+5
              17.95
2*12.95+5
               30.9
3*12.95+5
              43.85
4*12.95+5
```

Using Data Lists

CLRLIST

Many graphing calculators can work with lists. To clear any existing lists, press STAT and choose the CLRLIST feature with the name of the list as input. For example, to clear list 1 (2nd L1), we enter CLRLIST L1 and press ENTER. A message is displayed telling us that the list is cleared. Other lists are cleared in the same way.

EDIT

We use L1 to represent the number of CDs and then use L2 to represent the total cost for the CDs. To enter the values for L1, we press STAT and choose the EDIT feature. We then press ENTER, and the lists are shown in columns as in Figure AII-2(a). On the bottom edit line where L1(1) = is displayed, the numeral 1 is typed followed by ENTER. A 1 will appear as the first entry in L1, as shown in Figure AII-2(a).

Figure AII-2

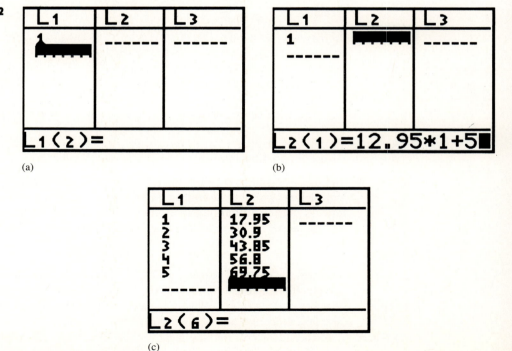

(a)

(b)

(c)

By pressing the right arrow, we move to list L2. The first entry in L2 can be entered directly or it can be computed by entering the expression L2(1) = 12.95 × 1 + 5 in the edit line at the bottom of the screen, as shown in Figure AII-2(b). When ENTER is pressed, 17.95 appears as the first entry in L2. We next use the left and down arrows to return to the second entry in L1 and enter 2. The remainder of the table as shown in Figure AII-2(c) can be completed to 10 entries by using the same method.

This method using lists is a hard way to complete the table. An easier method for finding the total costs is to define a general pattern and have the calculator do all the computations at once. To do this, enter the numbers 1 through 10 in L1. Move the cursor to the top of L3 so that L3 is highlighted. When L3 is highlighted, anything that is done in the edit line on the bottom will happen to every element in L3. In the edit line, enter L3 = 12.95L1 + 5, as shown in Figure AII-3(a), and press ENTER. The entire list in L3 is then computed based on the entries in L1 and the rule given in the edit line (see Fig. AII-3b). Lists L2 and L3 should be the same even though they were obtained in two different ways.

Figure AII-3

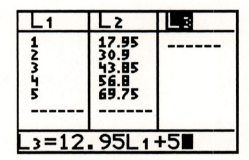

(a)   (b)

Using Lists on the Home Screen

Computations involving lists can be done on the home screen using the braces { and } located above the parentheses keys. A list can be entered by using a left brace, followed by the list, with each element separated by a comma. Figure AII-4(a) shows a list representing the number of possible CDs ordered: {1, 2, 3, 4, 5, 6, 7, 8, 9, 10}. We then multiply each element in this list by 12.95 and add 5 to the result; the answers are given on the screen (see Fig. AII-4b). To see the entire list of answers, scroll to the right using the right arrow key.

Figure AII-4

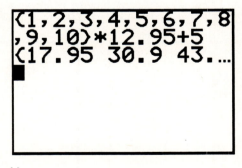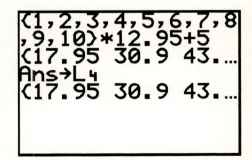

(a)   (b)

The list of answers can be stored in one of the list memories by using STO and the list number you choose. If we press STO L4, the answers are stored in L4. The list of answers still appears on the home screen, as shown in Figure AII-4(b), even though the answers are stored in L4. If we press STAT , select EDIT, and use the right arrow to move to the L4 column, we can see that the list of answers has been stored in L4. Notice that this list matches the ones in L2 and L3.

Using STAT Plot Graphing Capabilities

Next we investigate how Problem 1 could be solved using a graphical representation. Before we do any graphing, we need to set an appropriate graphing window. We must decide how large a window is required in this particular problem. If we plot the number of CDs ordered on the x-axis and the total cost on the y-axis, we need only look at our lists to determine appropriate values. The number of CDs ranges from 1 to 10, and the cost ranges from \$12.95 to \$134.50. We have several choices. If we press WINDOW , then we can enter the choices, as shown in Figure AII-5(a). After we select WINDOW , we can enter the minimum and maximum values for the x- and y-axes and the scale that gives the distance between the marks on each axis.

Figure AII-5

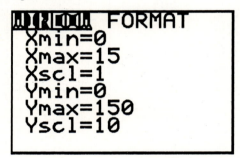

(a)

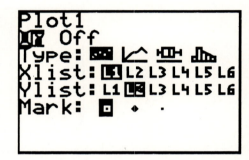

(b)

We can plot these points by using 2nd to choose STAT PLOT and then select Plot1, as shown in Figure AII-5(b). We see in Figure AII-5(b) that Plot1 is on, the first choice of a scatterplot is chosen, the x-values come from L1, and the y-values come from L2. We can choose 5 different plots and each plot can be a scatterplot, a line graph, a box-and-whisker plot, or a histogram.

By pressing GRAPH , we obtain the graph shown in Figure AII-6(a). If we then press TRACE and use the right and left arrow keys, we can see the trace cursor move along the dots, displaying the x- and y-values at each point, as shown in Figure AII-6(b).

Figure AII-6

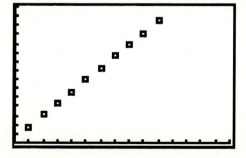

(a)

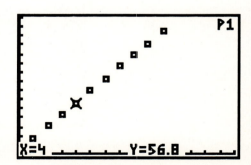

(b)

INVESTIGATION AII-1

a. How are the values that are displayed using the Trace feature related to L1 and L2?

b. Why are just the points shown rather than a line containing the points?

c. What pattern is shown in the graphical representation that is not shown when working with only numbers or lists?

d. Use the graph to approximate the cost of 12 CDs.

Connecting Graphing and Algebra

Earlier in this appendix, we generated a mathematical rule for computing the total cost for any number of CDs. The rule was to multiply the number of CDs by 12.95 and add 5. We can enter this rule as a function by pressing $\boxed{Y =}$. We can enter the rule for Y_1 using x to represent the number of calculators. The variable x has a separate key, either $\boxed{X, T}$ or $\boxed{X, T, \theta}$. Figure AII-7(a) shows the function, and Figure AII-7(b) shows the graph obtained when $\boxed{GRAPH}$ is pressed.

Figure AII-7

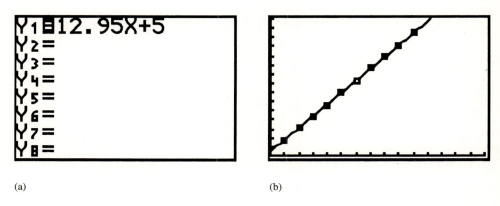

(a)   (b)

Press $\boxed{TRACE}$ and a P1 (Plot1) appears in the upper-right corner. The P1 indicates that the STAT PLOT (P1) is being traced. The values that appear are the same as those we generated earlier when we built the cost tables. If we press the up arrow, a 1 appears in the corner. This indicates that the line Y_1 from the $\boxed{Y =}$ menu is being traced. You can toggle back and forth between the two graphs by pressing the up arrow.

When the line Y_1 is being traced, the x-values can be nonintegers. The graph of the line Y_1 is not really an appropriate graph for this problem because the data in this case are not continuous, that is, the y-values exist only for nonnegative integer values of x. There is no such thing as a cost for 1.5 CDs as implied by the graph. However, the graph can be used to find values of y (costs) when x is a nonnegative integer.

I N V E S T I G A T I O N   A I I - 2

a. How are the two graphs in Figure AII-7 the same, and how are they are different?

b. Can you obtain the cost of 12 CDs from either graph? How?

Using Tables

We can build a table based on the algebraic rule that we developed for Problem 1. To do this, we press 2nd to choose TblSet and set the table menu, as shown in Figure AII-8(a). The TblMin set at 1 starts the table at 1 and the $\triangle$Tbl setting of 1 sets the increment between x-values at 1. If we next press 2nd to select TABLE , we see the table of values generated by the rule $y = 12.95x + 5$. Notice that the x-values are incremented by 1 in each case because this is what we selected in the TblSet menu. Also notice that if we use the up and down arrow keys, we can continue to obtain y-values for any integer x-value, as shown in Figure AII-8(b). From the result in Figure AII-8(b), determine the cost of 15 CDs.

Figure AII-8

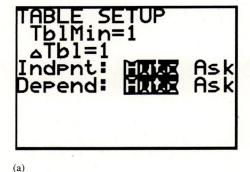

(a)

(b)

Problem 2

Another company is advertising CDs for $7.95 per CD with no shipping charge. However, they charge a processing fee of $20 for each order. Molly is considering switching companies. Compare the prices of the two companies and discuss who has the better price.

The rule for computing the cost under the second plan is $Y_2 = 7.95x + 20$. If we enter this rule as Y_2 in the Y= menu, as shown in Figure AII-9(a), we can compare the two plans using tables. If we keep the same table setup as in the earlier problem, then Figure AII–9(b) shows a comparison of the two rules. (On the TI-80, the right arrow key must be used, since only two columns are displayed at a time.) It follows that the first plan is better if we order either one or two CDs. If we order three CDs, it makes no difference which plan we use. If we order more than three CDs, then the second plan is better.

Figure AII-9

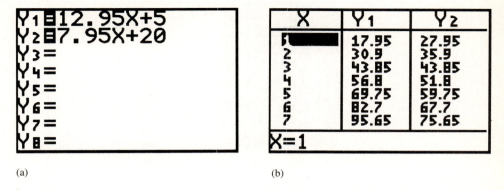

(a)   (b)

We can compare the two plans graphically by pressing $\boxed{\text{GRAPH}}$. The two graphs are shown in Figure AII-10(a). The same comments that were made about continuous data are also true in this case. If $\boxed{\text{TRACE}}$ and the arrow keys are used, then we see in Figure AII-10(b) that the two lines intersect at point (3, 43.85), which is the point on which the two plans match. After $x = 3$, we see that the second line illustrates the less expensive cost.

Figure AII-10

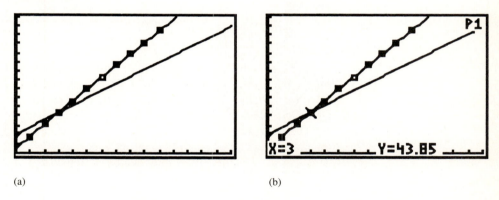

(a)   (b)

Using ZOOM

We can use various zoom features to adjust the viewing window to see more of the features of the graph. If we press $\boxed{\text{ZOOM}}$, we see the menu shown in Figure AII-11(a). The first item on the menu, ZBox, lets us use the cursor to select opposite corners of a box to define a new viewing window. To use this feature, we move the zoom cursor to any point on the screen on which we want to locate a corner of the box and then press $\boxed{\text{ENTER}}$. As we move the cursor away from the selected point, we see a small square dot indicating the selected corner. We then move the cursor to the diagonal corner of the box we want to define. As we use the arrow keys to move the cursor, we see the box change on the screen. When we get the box where we want it, as shown in Figure AII-11(b), we press $\boxed{\text{ENTER}}$ to re-plot the graph as shown in Figure AII-11(c). The TRACE feature can now be used to find values of various points. We can cancel ZBox at any time by pressing $\boxed{\text{CLEAR}}$ before pressing $\boxed{\text{ENTER}}$.

Figure AII-11

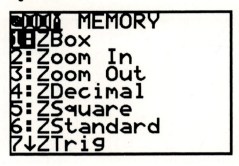

(a)

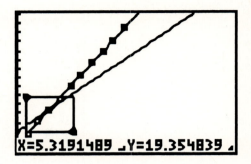

X=5.3191489 ⌐Y=19.354839 ⌐

(b)

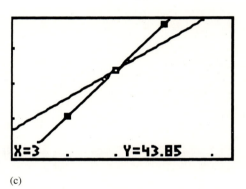

X=3   .   . Y=43.85   .

(c)

There are other zoom features in the ZOOM menu. For example, we can select Zoom In from the menu and then press ENTER . We then can move the cursor to the point on which we want the center of the new viewing window to be and press ENTER . The graph will be re-plotted. We can also select Zoom Out in a similar manner.

These are only a few of the features available on a graphing calculator. Many other important features are contained in menus under keys such as MATH . Consult your user's manual to see how these other tools can be used in solving mathematical problems.

Ongoing Assessment A-II

1. Use trial and error to determine when $1000 invested at 6% annual compounded interest will double in value. (*Hint:* The value after 10 yr is given by 1000×1.06^{10}.)

2. Given the sequence 3, 6, 9, 12, 15, 18, . . . , use the TABLE feature to find the 32nd term by entering the appropriate equation using the Y = menu.

3. Enter $y = 3x^2 + 5x + 7$ in the Y = menu and use the TABLE feature to evaluate the function at 10 and ⁻10.

4. Set the WINDOW to graph on each axis from ⁻10 to 10 with increments of 1 unit, then graph each of the following, and answer the questions that follow:

   i. $y = x + 3$ **ii.** $y = 2x + 3$
   iii. $y = 3x + 3$ **iv.** $y = 4x + 3$

   a. What do the graphs have in common?
   b. How do they differ?
   c. How does changing the slope, m, change the shape of the graph in the equation $y = mx + b$?

5. Leave the WINDOW the same as it was in Problem 4, graph each of the following, and answer the questions that follow:

   i. $y = x + 3$ **ii.** $y = x + 4$
   iii. $y = x + 5$ **iv.** $y = x + 6$

   a. What do the graphs have in common?
   b. How do they differ?
   c. How does changing the value, b, in the equation $y = mx + b$ change the shape of the graph?

6. Graph the following system. Make sure to choose an appropriate window. Use [ZOOM] and [TRACE] features to find the point of intersection to two decimal places.

$$y = 2x - 3$$
$$y = {}^{-}7x + 8$$

7. The distance from Missoula to Billings is 350 mi. To investigate how long it takes to drive this distance, Joan entered the following equations for Y = .

$$Y_1 = 50x, \quad Y_2 = 60x, \quad Y_3 = 70x, \quad Y_4 = 350$$

She set the window for Xmin = 0, Xmax = 10, Xscl = 1, Ymin = ⁻100, Ymax = 600, and Yscl = 20 and then graphed the functions.

   a. How could she tell the time it takes to make the trip traveling at 50, 60, and 70 mph?
   b. How much time is saved traveling at 70 mph rather than 50 mph?

8. a. Evaluate the function $y = x^2 - 5x + 4$ at each integer value between ⁻10 and 10. How many sign changes are there in this range, and where do they occur?
   b. Set the window from ⁻10 to 10 on the x-axis and ⁻10 to 10 on the y-axis with increments of 1 and graph the equation.
   c. Use the [TRACE] feature to examine where the function crosses the x-axis.

9. Linda has 33 coins in dimes and quarters. The value of the coins is $5.55. Determine how many of each coin she has.

Appendix III

Using a Geometry Drawing Utility

Introduction

In the time of Plato, the use of only a compass and straightedge became the norm for classical geometry. Today's world demands that we consider other tools. In this appendix, we present a series of problems appropriate for use with a computer geometry utility. Most geometry utilities, such as *The Geometer's Sketchpad, Cabri,* and *Geometry Inventor,* allow both drawing and construction. Some educators have noted the difference between the two methods. In a drawing, an "eyeballing" approach is used to place a figure to look as it should, but the figure may not be constrained by elements of its geometric properties. For example, a segment may be drawn in a circle to look like a diameter, as in Figure AIII-1(a). However, if it is not constructed to pass through the center of the circle and one moves the circle as in Figure AIII.1(b), the segment may no longer move with the circle and may not appear to be a diameter.

The constraint of having the diameter pass through the center was not used. If the segment is constructed as a chord to contain the center as a part of the construction, then when the circle is moved, the segment moves accordingly (as a diameter should). For most purposes in this appendix, we are using constructions with all the geometric constraints applied.

In the Ongoing Assessment in this appendix, the problems are roughly arranged in the order they might be used with the geometry chapters of the book. But they may be used independently if the teacher provides the language and definitions as needed.

About a Geometry Utility

Figure AIII-2 is an example of a drawing window with the Toolbox and Menu Bar shown from *The Geometer's Sketchpad (GSP)*. Other utilities have different windows, but *GSP* is used for illustrations in this appendix.

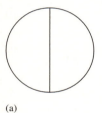

(a)

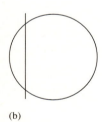

(b)

Figure AIII–1

Figure AIII-2

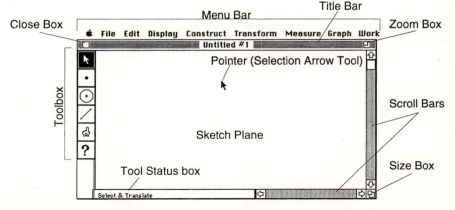

The Menu bar of Figure AIII-2 shows the following menu options:

- **File,** for opening, closing, saving, and printing documents
- **Edit,** for selecting objects and editing drawings and scripts
- **Display,** for changing the appearance of drawings and setting preferences
- **Construct,** for constructing figures
- **Transform,** for translating, rotating, dilating, and reflecting figures
- **Measure,** for displaying measurements and making calculations
- **Work,** for options with open sketches and scripts

In the Toolbox, located along the left side (see Figure AIII–2), are the following tools:

Selection tool for choosing objects and translating, rotating and dilating them. This tool is used for clicking on an object by using the mouse and moving it about the screen by dragging the object and then clicking the mouse again when the desired location is reached.

Point tool, for creating points. We click on this tool and move the mouse pointer to a desired location of a point on the screen and then click the mouse again to place a point on the screen at that location.

Circle tool (also called the Compass *tool) for creating circles.* This tool does exactly what the title suggests. By clicking this tool and moving the mouse pointer about the screen, we can draw circles.

Segment tool, for creating segments, rays, and lines. When you click on this tool, a small box appears at the left of the tool to allow you to choose either a segment, a ray, or a line. After the choice is made, we may move the mouse pointer on the screen to decide on the placement of the desired object.

Text tool, for creating labels and captions for drawings

Information tool, for inspecting and altering characteristics of a selection. This tool is used to show information about an object or group of objects in a drawing.

In this appendix, a series of investigations or problem constructions are suggested that are to be used to try out features of *GSP*. Both types of activities are labeled as investigations. Both include suggested steps for the drawing or construction using *GSP*.

Investigation AIII-1: Regions of a Circle

A problem from Chapter 1 dealt with the maximum number of regions into which a circle could be separated by chords that were drawn by connecting given points on the circle. A geometry utility is a convenient tool for examining this problem because segments or chords can be easily moved without recreating the picture. Study this problem by drawing sketches with a geometry utility.

Steps to Proceed

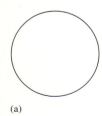

(a)

1. Use the Circle tool to draw a large circle, as in Figure AIII–3(a).
2. We know that one point does not separate the circular region into any other regions. We begin recording the information as in Table AIII-1. (A table could be created on *GSP*, but for our purposes record the information in a table on paper.)

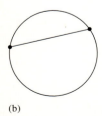

(b)

Figure AIII-3

Table AIII-1

Number of Points	Number of Regions
1	1
2	2

3. Place two points on the circle as in Figure AIII-3(b) using the *Point* tool and then draw the segment connecting the points. Record the information in the table.
4. Continue the process by adding more points on the circle, determining the number of regions, and recording the maximum number of regions of the circle determined by connecting the points.
5. Predict how many regions are determined with *n* points on the circle.
6. Does your record help to verify the formula

$$\frac{n(n-1)(n-2)(n-3)}{24} + \frac{n(n-1)}{2} + 1$$

for the maximum number of regions? If not, reexamine your drawings.

Extension: Duplicate the investigation for any simple closed figure. Are your results the same?

Investigation AIII-2: Inscribing a Circle in a Triangle

This investigation is built in stages, with the construction of a bisector of an angle of a triangle first.

Steps to Proceed

1. Construct any triangle by following these steps:
   a. Choose the *Point* tool.
   b. Move the mouse pointer to the screen and click anywhere. This chooses the first vertex.
   c. The *Point* tool is still active, so move to another point on the screen and click to choose the second vertex.
   d. Choose the *Segment* tool. Move the mouse until the crosshair pointer is centered on one of the points. Press the mouse button down and hold it down. Drag the mouse pointer to the second point until the crosshair pointer is centered over the second point. Release the mouse pointer, and the segment is drawn.
   e. Repeat the process to choose the third vertex and to complete the triangle.
2. Construct a bisector of one angle of the triangle. First, click on the Construct menu in the menu bar, as shown in Figure AIII-4. Next pull down the menu and choose *Angle Bisector*.

Figure AIII-4

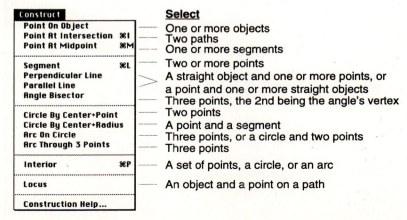

To use this construction tool, we must first highlight three points, which determine the angle with the vertex as the second point chosen. To highlight the three points, click on the first point and hold down $\boxed{\text{Shift}}$ as you click on each of the other points in order. (This process is used when naming a series of objects needed for a construction.) With the three points highlighted, you can then use the *Angle Bisector* construction.

3. Choose any point on the angle bisector with the Construct menu item *Point on Object.* Construct perpendicular segments from the point to the sides of the angle using the *Perpendicular Line* selection on the Construct menu.

4. To identify the perpendicular segments constructed, we use the Construct menu item *Point at Intersection* to find the points on which the perpendiculars intersect the sides of the angle.

5. Measure the lengths of the perpendicular segments using the Measure menu shown in Figure AIII-5.

Figure AIII-5

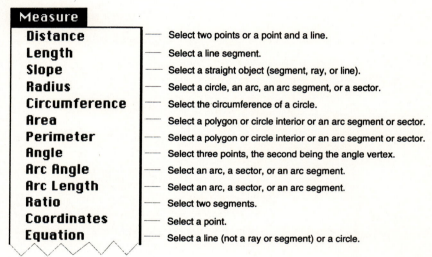

Measure	
Distance	Select two points or a point and a line.
Length	Select a line segment.
Slope	Select a straight object (segment, ray, or line).
Radius	Select a circle, an arc, an arc segment, or a sector.
Circumference	Select the circumference of a circle.
Area	Select a polygon or circle interior or an arc segment or sector.
Perimeter	Select a polygon or circle interior or an arc segment or sector.
Angle	Select three points, the second being the angle vertex.
Arc Angle	Select an arc, a sector, or an arc segment.
Arc Length	Select an arc, a sector, or an arc segment.
Ratio	Select two segments.
Coordinates	Select a point.
Equation	Select a line (not a ray or segment) or a circle.

6. Move the point along the angle bisector by clicking the mouse pointer on it and dragging it along the bisector. As the point is dragged, consider the measures shown.

7. Make a conjecture about any observed results.

incircle of the triangle
8. Construct the **incircle of the triangle.** The incircle is the circle that is inside the triangular region and is tangent to each of the sides of the triangle. The point at which the three angle bisectors intersect is the center of the incircle. The radius is the length of the perpendicular segment from the center to one of the sides.

Investigation AIII-3: Circumscribing a Circle about a Triangle

This investigation is built in stages, beginning with the construction of a perpendicular bisector of a side of a triangle.

Steps to Proceed

1. Construct any triangle using the process in Investigation AIII-2.

2. Construct the midpoint of the sides of the triangles and then construct the perpendicular bisector of one side of the triangle using the Construct menu item *Perpendicular Line.*

3. Choose any point on the perpendicular bisector using the Construct menu item *Point of Object* and draw segments connecting the point to the endpoints of the original side of the triangle.
4. Measure the lengths of the segments drawn in (3) using the Measure menu.
5. Move the point along the perpendicular bisector (in the same manner we moved a point along the angle bisector in Investigation AIII-2), observing the measurements of the segments as in (4).
6. Make a conjecture about any observed results.
7. Construct the **circumscribed circle** (a circle containing each of the vertices of the triangle) about the triangle by constructing all the perpendicular bisectors of the sides. Then find the point on which they intersect — the **circumcenter of the circle** — and use the distance from the circumcenter to one of the vertices as the radius of the circle.

circumscribed circle

circumcenter of the circle

Extension: Suppose the triangle being circumscribed is a right triangle. Where is the center of the circumscribed circle located?

Investigation AIII-4: The Pythagorean Theorem

The Pythagorean Theorem is a classic theorem of Euclidean geometry. It is probably the most useful of all geometry theorems.

Steps to Proceed

1. Construct any right triangle *ABC* with the right angle at vertex *C*. To do this, we may construct perpendicular segments using the Construct menu.
2. Construct a square on each side of the triangle, again using items from the Construct menu. (We may use a combination of constructions using the items *Perpendicular Line* and *Parallel Line*.)
3. Find the areas of the squares using the Measure menu. To do this, we will need to identify a polygon by clicking on the vertices in order while holding down Shift. Then use the Construct menu item *Polygon Interior*. With the polygon interior defined, the area can be found using the Measure menu.
4. Find the sum of the areas of the smaller squares and compare this sum to the area of the largest square. To compute the sums, we may want to use the *Calculate* feature under the Measure menu. To use this feature, highlight the measurement items we want to use in the calculations. Then when the *Calculate* feature is chosen, we may use any highlighted items and the calculator shown on the screen.
5. Change the sizes of the right triangle by moving around any vertex.
6. Make a conjecture about the results. (Note that the use of a geometry utility allows us to make conjectures. Verifying a conjecture with a drawing or a series of drawings does not constitute a proof of the conjecture.)

Extension: Construct any similar figures, for example, equilateral triangles or semicircles, on the sides of the original triangle. Use an entire side as a side of each similar figure. Perform steps similar to (3), (4), (5), and (6). Again make a conjecture based upon the results.

Investigation AIII-5: Angles in Circles

Some angles with vertices on a circle may be related to angles with vertices at the circle's center. This investigation explores such a relationship.

Steps to Proceed

1. Construct any circle, marking its center by using the Construct menu item *Circle by Center + Point.*
2. Construct a central angle (one whose vertex is at the center of the circle).
3. Measure the angle and its intercepted arc by using the Measure menu item *Arc Length.*
4. Draw any inscribed angle whose vertex is a point of the circle and whose sides intersect the circle in the same points as the central angle.
5. Measure the inscribed angle by using the Measure menu item *Arc Angle.*
6. Move the vertex of the inscribed angle and make a conjecture about the relationship between the measure of an inscribed and the central angle intercepting the same arc.

Extension: If the points of intersection of the sides of the inscribed angle intersect the circle at the ends of a diameter, what is the measure of the inscribed angle?

Investigation AIII-6: Finding the Area of a Figure

In Chapter 12, areas are estimated using the grid method. Another technique for doing this involves both similar figures and the use of a geometry utility.

Steps to Proceed

1. Draw any two-dimensional shape on the screen for which the area is desired.
2. Click on a point on the boundary of the shape. Then hold down Shift to identify points in a sequence and continue to trace around the shape, outlining it as closely as possible with a polygon by clicking on successive points and then returning to the starting point. Use the Construct menu to construct the *Polygon Interior.*
3. Find the area of the polygon using the Measure menu item *Area.* This process allows the approximation of the area of the shape.

Extension: Draw on transparent paper any shape smaller than your computer screen. Tape the drawing to the screen. Draw a polygon on the screen that approximates the shape by clicking on successive points around the shape while holding down Shift and finally returning to the point on which you started. Then measure as before.

Consider how to use a copy machine, a transparency, the process described in the extension and properties of similar figures to determine the area of any-sized shape.

Investigation AIII-7: Slopes and Trigonometry

This investigation explores the relationship between slopes and the tangent ratio.

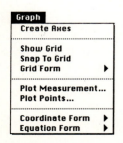

Figure AIII-6

Steps to Proceed

1. Use the Graph menu items *Create Axes* and *Show Grid* as seen in Figure AIII-6 to construct a coordinate system.
2. On the coordinate grid, construct any nonvertical line through the origin O and passing through the first and third quadrants.
3. Choose any point P not on the axes and construct a perpendicular segment $\overline{PX}$ to point X on the *x*-axis. (Follow the construction procedure outlined in Investigation AIII-3.)
4. Measure $\overline{OX}$, $\overline{PX}$, and $\overline{OP}$.
5. Record the following ratios in a chart: $\dfrac{OX}{OP}, \dfrac{PX}{OP}, \dfrac{OP}{OX}$.

6. Move point *P* up and down the line. What happens to the ratios?

7. Describe the ratios in terms of trigonometry and slope.

Extension: Drag the original line about the origin while continuing to find the ratios. What are the maximum and minimum values, if any, for the ratios?

Investigation AIII-8: Symmetry

The *GSP* can be used to design a logo for a company or for fun.

Steps to Proceed

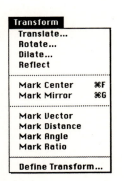

Figure AIII-7

1. Use the *Segment* tool to draw a line on the computer screen.

2. Use any *GSP* construction tools to design half of a logo on one side of the line.

3. Use the Transform menu item *Reflect*, shown in Figure AIII-7, to mark a mirror (reflecting line).

4. Select the object (the half of the design created) to be reflected.

5. Select the *Reflect* item from the Transform menu again, and *GSP* will construct the reflected image to complete the design.

Extension: Try other features of the Transform menu to design a logo with three turn or rotational symmetries. Construct one third of the design on the drawing utility and use the *Rotate* transformation to create the rest of the design.

Ongoing Assessment A-III

The following items are suggested for further investigation using a geometry drawing utility. Note that some parts of the assessment items may be directions for completing the investigations and not separate problems.

1. Study the relationship between the areas of a rectangle and a parallelogram, both with the same base and height.

2. Study the relationship between the areas of a triangle and a parallelogram, both with the same base and height.

3. Draw any two similar figures. Find the ratio of the corresponding sides and the ratios of the corresponding areas of the figures. Make a conjecture. Check the conjectures for several similar figures.

4. **a.** Construct any regular polygon inscribed in a circle.
   b. Connect vertices to the center.
   c. Find the height of one of the triangles formed by a side and the center of the circle.
   d. Find the area of each triangle formed.
   e. Find the area of the regular polygon.
   f. Find the perimeter of the regular polygon.
   g. What is the ratio of the area in (e) to the height in (c)? (To find this, you may want to investigate the *Calculate* item on the Measurement menu.)

5. **a.** Draw any circle.
   b. Inscribe a regular polygon in the circle.

   c. Find the measure of the longest diagonal of the polygon and the perimeter of the polygon. Find the ratio of the perimeter to the length of the diagonal.
   d. Repeat the process using a polygon with twice as many sides.
   e. Find the ratio again.
   f. Repeat the process in (d) two more times. What do you expect the ratio to be? Why?

6. **a.** Inscribe a circle in a square. Find the percent of the area in the square not covered by the circular region.
   b. Inscribe a square in a circle. Find the percent of the area of the circle not covered by the square region.
   c. Use the answers from (a) and (b) to determine whether a square peg might fit better into a round hole or a round peg might fit better in a square hole.

7. **a.** Draw a rectangle with two circles inside, pictured as follows:

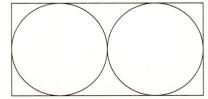

Find the percent of the area of the rectangle not covered by the circular regions.

b. Repeat the process in (a) using four circles.

c. Make a conjecture about the percent of the area of any rectangle not covered by circular regions when constructed in this manner.

8. a. Draw any shape with the utility.

b. Draw any line and move the line through the shape.

c. Stop moving the line when you estimate the shape is divided into two equal areas.

d. Find the areas of the shapes to check the estimate.

e. Repeat (a) through (d) to practice your area estimation skills.

9. a. Draw any rectangle and a segment, shown as follows:

b. Move the segment across the rectangle and estimate when 60% of the area is to the right of the segment.

c. Measure the areas to check.

d. Repeat steps (a) through (c) to practice area estimation skills with other percents.

Appendix IV

Using a Spreadsheet

Introduction

spreadsheet

An electronic **spreadsheet** is a table of rows and columns in which each cell may contain a value that can be operated on and changed at any time. A spreadsheet has the capacity to allow a change in one cell to be reflected in any other cell that relies on the data in that original cell. A simple example of a nonelectronic spreadsheet is seen in Table AIV-1, which depicts certain values for the function $f(x) = x^2$.

In Table AIV-1, each item in the $f(x)$ column depends on the value in the x column. A spreadsheet, as it might appear on a computer, is shown in Table AIV-2, depicting the information in Table AIV-1. (The labels x and $f(x) = x$^2 are for headings only.)

x	$f(x)$
1	1
2	4
3	9
4	16
5	25

Table AIV-1

Table AIV-2

	A	B	C	D	E	F
1	x	f(x) = x^2				
2	1	1				
3	2	4				
4	3	9				
5	4	16				
6	5	25				

In Table AIV-2, an index column down the left-hand side numbers the rows of the table. Across the top, an index row of letters identifies the columns. In the table, the value 3 is in column A and row 4. As a result, the value 3 could be identified by the label A4, where A is the column heading and 4 is the row number. The labels can be used to write formulas for the values of column B in terms of column A. For example, the value in B2 could be written as A2 times A2, or in computer language as A2^2, where the symbol ^ represents raising A2 to the power 2. Similarly, the value in B5 could be written as A5^2. In Table AIV-2, the items in row 1 are used as headings to indicate what the table is depicting.

The user bars on an opening of the *Microsoft Excel* spreadsheet are shown in Figure AIV-1.

Figure AIV-1

Menu bar
Toolbars
Formula bar

In the figure, three bars are depicted: a Menu bar, a Standard toolbar, and a Formula bar. The Menu bar offers such options as File, Edit, Formula, and so on. For example, as a beginning user you might choose to click on File and choose *New* to obtain a new worksheet on the screen. The standard Toolbar shows different options available to the user, including file folder, disk, and printing options on the left along with other types of options, such as **B** for bold type and the *I* for italics on the right. The Formula bar is for entry of items in a worksheet and is discussed later in this appendix.

Developing a Spreadsheet

To create the spreadsheet in Table AIV-2, we first open a new worksheet and then type the entries in cells A1 and B1 by typing x and $f(x) = x$^2, respectively, in the entry line (also known as the Formula bar) and pressing RETURN after each. These are simply headings for our reference.

1. To create the column of values listed under x in the A column, we enter the first item as 1 in A2 and press RETURN . Then we use a formula to create the value for A3 by assigning the values for A3 using a formula. We tell the spreadsheet that a formula is being used by highlighting the cell to be filled and typing = in the entry line followed by the formula we wish to use. In this case, we want A3 to have the value A2 + 1. We signal this by highlighting cell A3, typing = A2 + 1, and pressing RETURN . That done, the value 2 appears in A3, as shown in Table AIV-3. (Near the Formula bar are two boxes, one containing an X and one containing a tic mark. The X is used to cancel any changes you have made in a formula. The tic is used in the same way as the RETURN key.)

Table AIV-3

	A	B	C	D	E	F
1	x	f(x) = x^2				
2	1					
3	2					

2. To complete the column under A, we use the *Fill Down* command by first highlighting A3 and all the cells to be filled and then using the *Fill Down* command in the Menu bar normally found under the Edit menu. The *Fill Down* command fills successive cells in Column A by adapting the created formula to accommodate the cell number. For example, the entry in A4 is automatically created as the value of A3 + 1, and so on. The *Fill Down* command will fill all highlighted cells. If the cells A3 through A6 are highlighted, the result is seen in Table AIV-4. (If there is no data in a cell to create other cells, the program assumes that the value in the cell is 0.)

Table AIV-4

	A	B	C	D	E	F
1	x	f(x) = x^2				
2	1					
3	2					
4	3					
5	4					
6	5					

3. To complete the column under the heading B and $f(x) = x^2$, we highlight cell B2, type $= A2^2$, and press ⌗RETURN⌗ . This should cause a 1 to be placed in cell B2. We then highlight cell B2 and the rest of the column through row 6 and use the *Fill Down* command to complete column B.

REMARK   Most spreadsheets also have a *Fill Right* command to fill in cells in rows as well as columns.

To clear a table or a set of values in *Excel*, highlight the desired values to be deleted and pull down the Edit menu. If we choose *Clear,* then we are asked about clearing *All, Formats, Formulas,* or *Notes.* To clear all highlighted values, choose *All* and press ⌗RETURN⌗ .

Most spreadsheets allow the use of various functions, including $+$, $-$, $\div$, $\cdot$, $\wedge$, trigonometric functions, square roots and absolute values. To determine what your spreadsheet can do, consult the software manual. (Note that many graphing calculators have the capability of acting like a spreadsheet.)

Graphing with a Spreadsheet

In addition to allowing the use of arithmetic operations, most spreadsheets can create graphs of the data presented in a table. For example, to create a graph of the data in Table AIV-2, we follow these steps:

1. Highlight the information to be graphed. In the graph in Figure AIV-2, the data from rows A2 through A6 and columns B2 through B6 were highlighted. After the data is highlighted, then we choose the *Graph* icon from the Toolbar. (On some spreadsheets, when you choose the *Graph* icon, you can size the graph as you want; other spreadsheets will do this automatically for you.) In *Excel,* clicking on the icon once causes the highlighted information to be placed in a flashing dashed rectangle. If we move the mouse pointer on the worksheet, we see a $+$ symbol. Click the mouse, and drag it while holding the mouse button down to size the graph. Once the graph is sized, most spreadsheets will ask for a variety of information, such as what you want for the *x*-values, what you want for the *y*-values, what legends you want, and what maximum and minimum values you want. Because each spreadsheet is different, we suggest that you consult your user's manual to see what features are available. For example, in *Excel* the first question is about the range of data. With the data we are graphing, the range is written as $A2:B6 automatically. We can change or accept this range. The A2 indicates that the first values from our table to be used in the graph start at A2 and this will not change in the graph; B6 tells the computer that cell B6 contains the last value of the graph.

REMARK   The $ is used before and after a variable to indicate that the variable is fixed and does not change in this application. This feature is particularly useful when we want to use a specific value of a variable over and over in an application. An example is seen in Ongoing Assessment Problem 4, where we use the calculated mean of a set of data over and over to find the standard deviation of the set of data.

---

2. Because the range from A2 to B6 contains the values we intend to graph, we move to the next screen, where we must select a chart type, usually from several options. *Excel* presents these options in icon form. Figure AIV-2 was created as a scatterplot. (See Chapter 9.) Once we choose the scatterplot style, by double-clicking on an icon, the next screen asks about the type of scatterplot desired. Again, in *Excel,* the choices are presented as icons. We chose the connected scatterplot (option (2)), after which a graph is drawn. But there are other options to consider. To use the data as ordered pairs with the *x* data as the first column, we are using the data series in columns. Finally, we are asked if we want to use the first row as a legend or as data. Because we started with A2, we want this as the first value of *x* data. Next, we are asked if we want to add a legend to the graph. Figure AIV-2 shows the data from Table AIV-2 as a connected scatterplot. Using a title of Chart 1, we see a finished product with the $f(x)$ values and *x*-values labeled along the axes.

Figure AIV-2

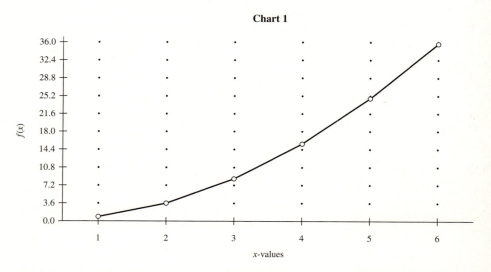

The same information could be depicted as a bar graph, as shown in Figure AIV-3, by using other graph icons.

Figure AIV-3

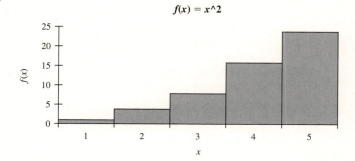

Many spreadsheets allow the options of using scatterplots, line plots, bar graphs, stem and leaf plots, and three-dimensional plots. Again, check the user's manual to see what is available for your spreadsheet.

Explicit and Recursive Formulas

When using a spreadsheet as in the previous paragraphs, most users discover they need to know the difference between explicit and recursive formulas. In Table AIV-4, a recursive formula was used — a value in a cell was determined by the value in the cell immediately above it. For example, the value in cell A5 is 1 plus the value in cell A4. Whenever a value in any cell is expressed in terms of a value in a previous cell (or cells), we say that the expression is a **recursive expression** or **formula.** Recursive formulas are typically used by most young students to describe patterns. For example, most students would describe the following pattern as adding 3, meaning that to find the next item, a person would add 3 to the previous term:

recursive expression or formula

$$3, 6, 9, 12, 15, 18, 21, 24, \ldots$$

On a spreadsheet, the pattern could be depicted using two columns. Row A may serve to count the numbers of the terms, as seen in Table AIV-5. (Note that column A serves the same purpose as the index column, but we can use the numbers in the A cells to create the terms in the B column.)

Table AIV-5

	A	B
1	1	3
2	2	6
3	3	9
4	4	12
5	5	
6	6	

To fill in additional rows, we can highlight cell B5 and type $= B4 + 3$ in the entry line and then use the *Fill Down* command by highlighting the number of entries needed. Clearly, the value of a cell is determined by the cell immediately above it.

If we decided to write a formula to describe a cell value using the number of the term (as in Chapter 1), then we would need to look at the number of the term and the values in column B to see how they are related. In this example, the values in column B are multiples of 3. If n is the term number, then the corresponding value is $3n$. The expression $3n$ is an **explicit formula** for finding the value of an expression as a function of the number of the term n.

explicit formula

To use the explicit formula $3n$ to create the entries in column B, we use the formula $= 3*A:A$ to fill in the entry in B1 and then use the *Fill Down* command to fill all highlighted cells of column B where there is a corresponding A entry. The use of :A at the end of the formula tells the spreadsheet to use column A to fill column B entries.

Other Features of a Spreadsheet

Spreadsheets can act as simple calculators. For example, a problem in Chapter 1 is to determine the number of handshakes at a party that 25 people attended. Each person shook hands with each other person, and no one shook hands with himself. This problem can be solved using a spreadsheet. We consider a *simpler case* whereby there is first only one person in the room, in which case there are no handshakes. Then another person enters for a total of two persons, and so one handshake occurs. When a third person enters the room, two more handshakes take place, and so on. This could be recorded as in Table AIV-6, in which column A records the number of people in the room and is developed by using the *Fill Down* command and the formula = A2 + 1. Column B depicts the number of additional handshakes when another person enters the room. Column B is 1 less than the number in column A and can be set up using the formula = A2 − 1.

Table AIV-6

	A	B
1	No. people	No. of additional handshakes
2	1	0
3	2	1
4	3	2
5	4	3
6		
. . .	. . .	. . .
26	25	24
27		300

To find the total number of handshakes, we need to find the total number of handshakes in column B. The spreadsheet does this when we highlight the cell in which we want the total, in this case B27, and then click on the Σ button. (On some spreadsheets, you may need to use the *SUM* feature.) When we click on Σ, the spreadsheet surrounds the numbers immediately above the highlighted cell with a flashing rectangle to show what will be added. (In some cases, we may have to click and drag a rectangle around the numbers that are to be added. This is especially true if there is an empty cell among the other cells to be added.) When the $\boxed{\text{RETURN}}$ or $\boxed{\text{ENTER}}$ key is pressed, the total appears in the highlighted cell. As Table AIV-6 shows, the total is 300 handshakes for the 25 people.

Many other features are available on most spreadsheets but are not discussed here. We suggest that you consult the user's manual that comes with your spreadsheet program and try the following problems.

Ongoing Assessment A-IV

1. **a.** Write any arithmetic sequence.
   b. In column A of your spreadsheet, list the number of the term of the arithmetic sequence.
   c. What formula did you use to fill down the column?
   d. List the first 25 terms of the arithmetic sequence in column B.

   e. What formula could be used to fill in the terms in column B?
   f. Find the sum of the first 25 terms in the arithmetic sequence. Describe how that was done with a spreadsheet.

g. Plot the number of the terms of the arithmetic sequence versus the actual terms using the graphing or chart option of your spreadsheet. Describe the graph of the arithmetic sequence.

2. a. Write any geometric sequence.
   b. In column A of your spreadsheet, list the number of the term of the geometric sequence.
   c. List the first 25 terms of the geometric sequence in column B.
   d. What formula could be used to fill in the terms of column B?
   e. Find the sum of the first 25 terms of the geometric sequence. Describe how that was done by using a spreadsheet.
   f. Plot the number of the terms of the geometric sequence versus the actual terms using the graphing or chart option of your spreadsheet. Describe the graph of the geometric sequence.

3. Given the following set of data, use a spreadsheet to find the arithmetic mean:

   23, 45, 67, 78, 98, 54, 36, 76, 75, 24, 43, 54, 100, 99

4. Use the data in Problem 3 to develop a spreadsheet to find the standard deviation of the data. Use the columns of the spreadsheet to represent the number of the term, the term, and the difference of the mean and the term. Then find the square of each of the differences, the sum of those squares, and the quotient of the sum and n, where n is the number of terms. Finally, find the square root of the quotient.

5. Businesspeople use spreadsheets for the calculation of interest on loans or outstanding bills. Consider a debt of $1000 with payments of $40 per month, which includes 1.5% interest per month on the unpaid balance. Develop a spreadsheet that shows the number of the month the payment was made, the amount of payment in each month, and the outstanding balance. If no other debts accrue, how many months will it take to pay off the debt?

6. Use a spreadsheet to show the first 100 multiples of 13. Explain all steps in developing this spreadsheet.

7. Develop a spreadsheet for finding your college grade-point average. Explain all steps used in developing the spreadsheet.

8. The sequence of Fibonacci numbers is 1, 1, 2, 3, 5, 8, ..., where each successive term after the first two is the sum of the two preceding terms.
   a. Develop a spreadsheet to find the first 25 Fibonacci numbers.
   b. Extend your spreadsheet to find the square of each term of the Fibonacci sequence and the sum of those squares. Make a conjecture about the sum of the squares of the first n terms of the sequence.
   c. To examine the updating feature of your spreadsheet, change the first two terms of the Fibonacci sequence and observe how each cell that was written based on these terms is changed. Does the conjecture in (b) still hold?

9. Develop a spreadsheet for finding $n!$. Explain the steps used to develop the spreadsheet.

Answers to Selected Problems

CHAPTER 1

Ongoing Assessment 1-1

1. (a)

   (c)

2. (a) 11, 13, 15; arithmetic (c) 96, 192, 384; geometric
   (e) 33, 37, 41; arithmetic
4. 2, 7, 12
5. (a) Answers vary. For example, one possibility is to notice that the sum of the first n odd numbers is given by n^2, that is, $1 + 3 + 5 + 7 = 4^2 = 16$. Or, to find the sum, you could square the sum of the average of the first and last terms, that is, $1 + 3 + 5 + 7 = [(1 + 7)/2]^2 = 4^2 = 16$.
7. (a) 12, 14
8. (b) 10,100
10. (a) 41
11. (a) 10,000
12. (a) 42
14. 15 L
16. (a) $1660 (c) 103 mo
18. 23rd year
20. (a) 299, 447, 644 (b) 56, 72, 90
21. (a) 101 (d) 87
22. (a) 3, 6, 11, 18, 27 (c) 9, 99, 999, 9,999, 99,999
23. (a) 1, 1, 2, 3, 5, 8, 13, 21, 34, 55, 89, 144, . . . (c) 143
25. The sequence in (b) becomes greater than the sequences in (a) on the twelfth term.
27. 64, 128, 256

Communication

29. (a) You must produce at least one rectangle that does not have diagonals that are perpendicular. Any nonsquare rectangle will do. (b) You must find two even numbers whose sum is not divisible by 4. For example, $2 + 4 = 6$ and 6 is not divisible by 4.

32. (a) Yes. The difference between the terms in the new sequence is the same as in the old sequence because a fixed number was added to each number in the sequence.

Open-ended

33. Answers vary. For example, two more patterns are shown here:

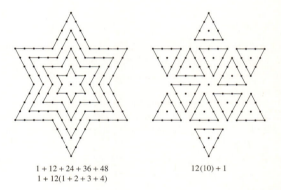

$1 + 12 + 24 + 36 + 48$
$1 + 12(1 + 2 + 3 + 4)$

$12(10) + 1$

36. (a) 27 (b) 13

Brain Teaser (p. 15)

(a) N, T, E (Rule: One, Two, Three, Four, Five, Six, Seven, Eight, Nine, Ten, Eleven) (b) Letters composed of only line segments go above the line. Letters with curves go below the line.

Technology Corner (p. 18)

Following are the rules for the columns:

Column	Rule
B	$x + y$
C	$y - x$
D	$x \cdot y$
E	$2(x + 3)$
F	$2x + y$
G	$xy + 1$

Ongoing Assessment 1-2

1. **(a)** 4950   **(c)** 251,001
2. **(b)** 5
4. 12
6. Dandy, Cory, Alababa, Bubba
8. 18
10. 12
13. $2.45
14. 16 days
16. **(a)** 10,500 squares   **(b)** $n^2 + 5n$ squares
18. width = 230 ft, length = 310 ft
21. Yes. She can use the $8\frac{1}{2}$-inch side twice to get 17 in. and then use the 11-in. side to get back to 6 in.
22. **(a)** 260,610   **(c)** 20,503
23. **(a)** 204 squares
24. **(a)** If both numbers were less than or equal to 9, then their product would be less than or equal to $9 \cdot 9 = 81$, which is not greater than 82.

Communication

27. Answers vary, but the discussion should point out that the two methods give the same answer and that the advantage of this method is that it works with an even or odd number of terms.
29. **(a)** Answers vary. For example, you could weigh 4 marbles against 4 marbles and then pick the heavier side. You could then weigh 2 marbles against 2 marbles and pick the heavier side. Finally, you could weigh 1 marble against 1 marble; the heavier one would be the one sought.

Open-ended

35. 35 moves. This can be solved by using the strategy of examining simpler cases and looking for a pattern. If one person is on each side, 3 moves are necessary. If two people are on each side, 8 moves are necessary. With 3 people on each side, 15 moves are necessary. If n people are on both sides, $(n + 1)^2 - 1$ moves are required.
36. **(a)** 21, 24, 27   **(b)** 243, 2, 729
37. $22 + (n - 1)10$ or $10n + 12$
38. 21 terms
39. 903
40. **(a)** The digits in the product always sum to 9. The 10s digit in the answer is always one less than the number that is multiplied by 9. This pattern works for the other exercises presented.   **(b)** The pattern can be used to check if you remembered the product of a digit and 9 correctly.

Brain Teaser (p. 38)

Thursday

Ongoing Assessment 1-3

1. **(a)** **(i)** 541×72 **(ii)** divide 754 by 12
3. $3.99 + $5.87 + $6.47 = $16.33
5. 17 terms
6. 275,000,000
8. **(a)** Answers vary. For example: **(i)** Add $500 + 200 + 56 + 100 + 60 + 20 + 3$.   **(ii)** Subtract 31 from 155 until there is a remainder of less than 31. Count the number of times 31 was subtracted.
9. **(a)** $(6 \times 7) + 8 = 50$
11. $5,256,000
13. 625
15. **(a)** If the product were *abcd*, then $a + c = 9$ and $b + d = 9$.
17. **(a)** $2^6 - 1$

Communication

20. **(a)** **(i)** $37 \times 18 = 666$, **(ii)** $37 \times 21 = 777$, **(iii)** $37 \times 24 = 888$ **(b)** 999. Answers vary. For example, notice that the numbers multiplied by 37 are all multiples of 3 and that $3 \times 37 = 111$. Therefore $37 \times 27 = 37 \times (3 \times 9) = (37 \times 3) \times 9 = 111 \times 9 = 999$. Because this can be done with multiples of 3, the pattern of answers in parts (a) and (b) is possible.
21. **(a)** 53×103

Cooperative Learning

25. **(a)** Play second and make sure that the sum showing when you hand the calculator to your opponent is a multiple of 3. **(c)** Play first and press 3. After that, make sure that each time you hand the calculator to your opponent, it displays three more than a multiple of 10.   **(e)** Play second. Make sure the calculator displays a multiple of 4 each time you hand it to your opponent.
26. **(a)** 35, 42, 49   **(b)** 1, 16, 1
27. $20n - 8$
28. 21 terms
29. 9 ways

Brain Teaser (p. 46)

Christmas (Notice that there is no L (NOEL) in the display.)

Chapter 1 Review

1. **(a)** 15, 21, 28   **(c)** 400, 200, 100   **(e)** 17, 20, 23 **(g)** 16, 20, 24
3. **(a)** $3n + 2$ **(c)** 3^n
4. **(b)** 2, 6, 12, 20, 30, . . .
5. **(a)** 10,100
6. **(a)** 123,456, 1,234,567, 12,345,678, . . .
8. 89 yr
9. The worm will climb out on the tenth day.

12. 21 posts
15. 44,000,000 rotations
17. 39 boxes
19. 9 hr
21. There will be 96,000 ants on the seventh day and 192,000 ants on the eighth day, so it will certainly be full.
22. 4 questions

CHAPTER 2

Ongoing Assessment 2-1

1. (a) $\{m, a, t, h, e, i, c, s\}$ **(c)** $\{x \mid x$ is a natural number, and $x > 20\}$ or $\{21, 22, 23, \ldots\}$
2. (b) $\{1, 2\} \subset \{1, 2, 3, 4\}$
3. (d) No
4. (b) 720
5. (a) 24
7. (b) 11   **(d)** 3
9. (a) 7
11. (c) $\notin$ **(e)** $\notin$
14. (a) True   **(d)** False. Consider $A = \{1\}$ and $B = \{1, 2\}$.
16. (a) $2^6 - 1$ or 63

Communication

18. (a) This set is not well defined, since we do not know what is meant by "wealthy."   **(b)** This set is not well defined, since we do not know what is meant by "great."   **(c)** This set is well defined. Given a number, we can easily tell whether it is a natural number greater than 100.   **(d)** This set is well defined. We could just list them all.   **(e)** This set is not well defined, since we do not know what is meant by "$\neq$." (We cannot assume that x refers to a number.)
21. No, the empty set is not a proper subset of itself, since it equals itself.
23. (b) $\overline{B} \subset \overline{A}$

Open-ended

24. (a) Let A be the set of all numbers not equal to 1. Then $\overline{A} = \{1\}$ is finite.   **(b)** Let A be the set of even natural numbers. Its complement, $\overline{A}$, is the set of odd natural numbers and so is infinite. (Here U is the set of natural numbers.)

Cooperative Learning

27. (a) There are $2^{64} \doteq 1.84 \cdot 10^{19}$ subsets of $\{1, 2, 3, \ldots, 64\}$. If a computer can list one every millionth of a second, then it would take

$$1.84 \cdot 10^{19} \cdot 000001 \text{ sec} \cdot \frac{1 \text{ year}}{31,536,000 \text{ sec}} \doteq$$

580,000 yr to list all the subsets.

Ongoing Assessment 2-2

1. (a) Yes   **(e)** Yes
2. (b) False. Let $A = \{a, b, c\}$ and $B = \{a, b\}$. Then $A - B = \{c\}$, but $B - A = \varnothing$.   **(e)** True   **(f)** False. Let $A = \{1, 2, 3\}$, $B = \{3, 4, 5\}$, and $U = \{1, 2, 3, \ldots, 10\}$. Then $(A \cup B) - A = \{1, 2, 3, 4, 5\} - \{1, 2, 3\} = \{4, 5\} \neq B$.
3. (a) $A \cap B = B$
4. (a)

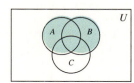

(b)

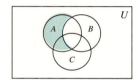

(h)

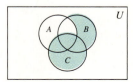

5. (a) $S \cup \overline{S} = U$ **(f)** $\overline{\varnothing} = U$ **(i)** $U \cap \overline{S} = \overline{S}$
6. (a) $A - B = A$ **(b)** $A - B = \varnothing$
7. (c) $(A \cap B) - C$ **(d)** $A \cap C$
8. (a)

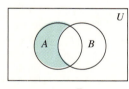

$A \cap \overline{B}$

9. (a) False

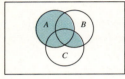 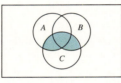

$A \cup (B \cap C)$ $(A \cup B) \cap C$

10. (a) $A \cap B \cap C \subseteq A \cap B$
11. (a) (i) 5; (ii) 2; (iii) 2; (iv) 3
12. (a) 15, 6
14. $A = B$
16. (a) The set of all Paxson eighth graders who are members of the band but not the choir   **(b)** The set of all Paxson eighth graders who are members of both the band and the choir
(c) The set of all Paxson eighth graders who are members of the choir but not the band   **(d)** The set of all Paxson eighth graders who are members of neither the band nor the choir
18. 4
20. (c) 10
21. (b) False. Let $A = B$.   **(c)** False. Let $A = \{1, 2, 3\}$ and $B = \{1, 2, 3, 4\}$.
23. (a) $A \times B = \{(x, a), (x, b), (x, c), (y, a), (y, b), (y, c)\}$
(d) $(A \cup B) \times C = \{(x, 0), (y, 0), (a, 0), (b, 0), (c, 0)\}$
24. (a) $C = \{a\}, D = \{b, c, d, e\}$
26. (a) 0   **(b)** 0
29. (a) Always true. This is a special case of (b).
30. 30

Communication

32. (a) Yes. $A \cap B \subseteq A \subseteq A \cup B$.
34. The following Venn diagram indicates only 490 cardholders are accounted for:

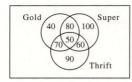

So either there is some other type of credit card the remaining 10 people could have, or else the editor was right.
36. 3. Using the following Venn diagram and the fact that the set of people who are O-negative is $100 - n (A \cup B \cup C)$ we see that the answer is 3.

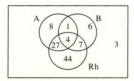

Review Problems

41. (a) These are all the subsets of $\{2, 3, 4\}$. There are $2^3 = 8$ such subsets.   **(b)** There are 8 subsets that contain the number 1. Every subset either contains 1 or it does not. So exactly half of the $2^4 = 16$ subsets contain 1.   **(c)** Twelve subsets contain 1 or 2 (or both). There are 4 subsets of $\{3, 4\}$. We can form subsets that contain 1 or 2 or both by adding 1 to each, 2 to each, or 1 and 2 to each. By the Fundamental Counting Principle then, there are $3 \cdot 4 = 12$ possibilities. (It's also not hard to list them.)   **(d)** Four subsets contain neither 1 nor 2, since 12 subsets do contain 1 or 2.   **(e)** B has $2^5 = 32$ subsets. Half contain 5 and half do not.   **(f)** Every subset of A is a subset of B. The others can be listed by adding the number 5 to each subset of A. So there are twice as many subsets of B as subsets of A ($2^5 = 32$).
42. (a) A and B are equal.   **(b)** C is a proper subset of A and a proper subset of B, since $C = \{4, 8, 12, 16, \ldots\}$.
43. Answers vary.

Ongoing Assessment 2-3

1. (a) Double the input number.   **(d)** Square the input number and add 1.
2. (a) This is not a function, since the input 1 is paired with 2 outputs (a and d).   **(d)** This is not a function, since the input 1 is paired with several outputs.
4. (c)

x	$f(x)$
0	1
1	3
2	5
3	7
4	9

5. (b) This is a function.   **(e)** This is a function.
7.

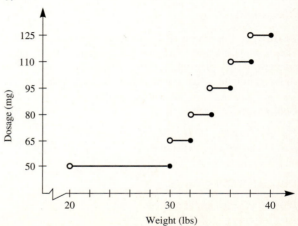

9. **(a)** 8 dollars
10. **(c)** $L(n) = n(n + 1)$
11. **(a)** $7 + 4 = 11$ **(b)** 55
12. **(b)** 3^n
13. **(c)** 65
14. **(c)** 2, 12, 2550
15. **(a)** $2 \cdot 1 + 2 \cdot 7 = 16; 2 \cdot 2 + 2 \cdot 6 = 16; 2 \cdot 6 + 2 \cdot 2 = 16;$
$2 \cdot 5 + 2 \cdot 5 = 20$
16. **(b)** The third and the fourth
17. **(b)** Between 6 and 6:30 A.M. **(c)** 0
19. **(a)** $H(2) = 192; H(6) = 192$
$H(3) = 240; H(5) = 240$. Some of the heights
correspond to the ball's going up and some to the ball's
coming down.
(b)

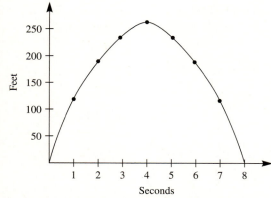

At $t = 4$ sec, the ball's height is 256 feet above the ground.
(c) 8 sec **(d)** $0 \le t \le 8$ **(e)** $0 \le H(t) \le 256$
(approximately, from graph)
20. **(a)** $A(x) = x \cdot \frac{1}{2}(900 - x)$
21. **(a) (a)** 4, 12, 24, 40 **(b)** 4, 10, 22, 38 **(c)** 4, 10,
16, 22
(b) (a) $S(n) = 2n(n + 1)$ **(b)** 4 when $n = 1; 2n(n + 1) - 2$
when $n \ge 2$ **(c)** $S(n) = 6n - 2$
23. **(b)** $\{(A, B), (A, C), (A, D), (C, A), (C, B), (C, D), (D, A),$
$(D, B), (D, C), (F, G), (G, F), (I, J)\}$
24. **(a)** Function **(b)** Relation, but not a function
26. **(a)** None **(f)** Reflexive and symmetric **(g)** Transitive

Communication

28. Yes, since each element of A is paired with exactly 1
element of B.
30. **(a)** This is not a function, since a faculty member may
teach more than one class. **(b)** This is a function (assuming
only 1 teacher per class).

Review Problems

39. **(a)** These are equivalent, since each has 500 elements.
(b) Not equivalent. The function $f(x) = 3x - 2$ sets up a

correspondence where the second set is the domain set. But
then nothing corresponds to 3001. In other words, the first set
has 1001 elements and the second 1000. **(c)** These are
equivalent, since the function $f(x) = x + 1$ establishes a one-to-
one correspondence between the 2 sets (with the first set as
domain). **(d)** These are equivalent, since the function
$f(x) = 2x$ establishes a one-to-one correspondence between the
2 sets (with the first set as domain).
40. **(a)** True. $A - (B \cup C) = A \cap \overline{B \cup C} = A \cap (\overline{B} \cap \overline{C}) =$
$A \cap \overline{B} \cap \overline{C} = (A \cap \overline{B}) \cap (A \cap \overline{C}) = (A - B) \cap (A - C)$
(b) True. $A \subseteq A \cup B = B$ **(c)** True. $\overline{A} \cup \overline{B} = \overline{A \cap B} = \overline{\varnothing} = U$
(d) False. Let $A = \{1, 2, 3\}, B = \{2, 3, 4\}$, and $C = A$.
41. **(a)** 6 **(b)** 9
42. **(a)** False. Let $A = \{1, 2, 3\}, B = \{1, 2, 3, 4\}$, and $C = \{4\}$.
(b) False. Let $A = \{1, 2, 3\}, B = \{3, 4\}$, and $C = \{3\}$.
(c) False. Suppose $A = C$. **(d)** False. It is always true that
$A \times \varnothing = B \times \varnothing = \varnothing$, regardless of whether A and B are equal.
(e) True
43. 22
44. **(a)** 2200 **(b)** 500
45. **(a)** $\{2n \mid n$ is a natural number and $n > 6\}$ **(b)** $\{n \mid n$ is a
natural number and $n < 14\}$
46. **(a)** $A \cup \overline{B} = \{a, b, c\} \cup \{a, d\} = \{a, b, c, d\} = U$
(b) $\overline{A \cap B} = \overline{\{b, c\}} = \{a, d\}$ **(c)** $A \cap \varnothing = \varnothing$
(d) $B \cap C = \{b, c\} \cap \{d\} = \varnothing$ **(e)** $B - A = B \cap \overline{A} =$
$\{b, c\} \cap \{d\} = \varnothing$

Brain Teaser: The eleventh person was never accounted for.

Ongoing Assessment 2-4

1. **(a)** False statement **(e)** Not a statement **(h)** Not a
statement
2. **(a)** There exists a natural number x such that $x + 8 = 11$.
(b) For all $x, x + 0 = x$.
4. **(a)** The book does not have 500 pages. **(d)** No people
have blond hair. **(g)** Not all squares are rectangles, or some
squares are not rectangles.
6. **(c)** $\sim(q \wedge r)$ **(d)** $\sim q$
7. **(a)** False **(b)** True **(c)** True **(d)** False **(e)** False
(f) True **(g)** False **(h)** False **(i)** False **(j)** False
9. **(a)** Yes
(d) Yes
11. **(b)** Yesterday I either did not eat breakfast or did not
watch television.
13. **(a)** Converse: If you are good in sports, then you eat
Meaties.
Inverse: If you do not eat Meaties, then you are not good in
sports.
Contrapositive: If you are not good in sports, then you do not
eat Meaties.
(c) Converse: If you have cavities, then you do not use Ultra
Brush toothpaste.
Inverse: If you use Ultra Brush toothpaste, then you do not
have cavities.

Contrapositive: If you do not have cavities, then you use Ultra Brush toothpaste.
15. Only statement B.
17. (a) Valid   **(d)** Invalid
18. (a) Helen is poor.   **(b)** Some freshmen are intelligent.
19. (a) If a figure is a square, then it is a rectangle.   **(c)** If a figure has exactly 3 sides, then it may be a triangle.

Communication

20. (a) $\sim(p \vee q)$ is equivalent to $\sim p \wedge \sim q$, and $\sim(p \wedge q)$ is equivalent to $\sim p \vee \sim q$.
23. (a) Therefore we go shopping. (Going shopping is equivalent to getting a bonus.)   **(b)** Therefore the figure is not a rectangle. (Contrapositive)   **(c)** Let p be the statement "It is sunny," q the statement "We go hiking," and r the statement "It is freezing." Symbolically, $p \rightarrow q$ and $r \rightarrow \sim q$. The second statement gives $q \rightarrow \sim r$. So the Chain Rule tells us that $p \rightarrow \sim r$; that is, "if it is sunny, then it is not freezing."

Chapter 2 Review

1. $\{x \mid x$ is a letter of the Greek alphabet$\}$
2. $\varnothing$, $\{m\}$, $\{a\}$, $\{t\}$, $\{h\}$, $\{m, a\}$, $\{m, t\}$, $\{m, h\}$, $\{a, t\}$, $\{a, h\}$, $\{t, h\}$, $\{m, a, t\}$, $\{m, a, h\}$, $\{m, t, h\}$, $\{a, t, h\}$, $\{m, a, t, h\}$
4. (a) $A \cup B = A$ **(d)** $A \cap \overline{D} = \{r, v\}$
6. Assuming all 7 letters are different, 5040
8. It is not true that $A \cap (B \cup C) = (A \cap B) \cup C$ for all A, B, and C. The diagrams show why.

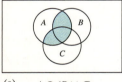
(a) $A \cap (B \cup C)$

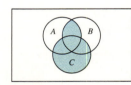
(b) $(A \cap B) \cup C$

10. (a) False. Consider the sets $\{a\}$ and $\{2\}$.   **(d)** False. This set is in one-to-one correspondence with the set of natural numbers.   **(g)** True
11. (a) 17
13. The first question might be, "Is the state or province one of the 48 contiguous states in the United States?" If the answer is yes, the second question could be, "Does it begin with a vowel?" The third question can then be, "Is it _____?" If the answer to the first question is no, the second question could be, "Is it in Canada?", and the third question could be the same as above.
15. (a) Yes   **(b)** No   **(c)** Yes
17. (a) range = $\{3, 4, 5, 6\}$ **(d)** range = $\{5, 9, 15\}$
18. (a) This is not a function, since 1 student can have 2 majors.   **(e)** This is a function. The range is N.
19. (c) After the ninth month, the cost exceeds $600.

20. (a) Yes   **(b)** Yes   **(c)** No   **(d)** Yes
21. (a) No women smoke.   **(b)** $3 + 5 \neq 8$ **(c)** Some heavy-metal rock is not loud, or not all heavy-metal rock is loud.   **(d)** Beethoven wrote some music that is not classical.
23. (c) Albertina passed Math 100.

CHAPTER 3

Ongoing Assessment 3-1

1. (a) $\overline{\overline{\text{MCDXXIV}}}$. The double bar over M represents $1000 \cdot 1000 \cdot 1000$.   **(b)** 46,032. The 4 in 46,032 represents 40,000, while the 4 in 4632 represents only 4000.   **(c)** $<$ ▼▼. The space in the latter number indicates $<$ is multiplied by $10 \cdot 60$ rather than by 10.   **(d)** The ⌀ represents 1000, while 9 represents only 100.   **(e)** ⊛ represents three groups of 20 plus zero 1s, while ⚏ represents three 5s and three 1s.
2. (a) MCML; MCMXLVIII   **(c)** M; CMXCVIII
(e) ⌀991; ⌀9   ∩∩∩∩∩ ⏐⏐⏐⏐⏐
                        ∩∩∩∩ ⏐⏐⏐⏐
4. (a) CXXI   **(c)** LXXXIX
5. (a) ∩∩∩∩∩ ⏐⏐   **(c)** ⌀ ⏐⏐⏐
6. (a) ▼ $<$ ▼▼ ; ∩∩∩∩∩∩∩⏐⏐ ; LXXII; ⫶⫶
(c) 1223; $<<$ $<<$ ▼▼▼ ; MCCXXIII; ⫶⫶
7. (a) Hundreds   **(c)** Thousands
8. (a) 3,004,005   **(c)** 3560
9. (a) 86
10. 811 or 910
12. 20
14. (a) 111_{two} **(c)** 999_{ten}
15. (a) ETE_{twelve}; $EE1_{twelve}$ **(c)** 554_{six}; 1000_{six}
(e) 444_{five}; 1001_{five}
16. (a) There is no numeral 4 in base four.   **(c)** There is no numeral T in base three.
17. (a) 3212_{five} **(c)** 12110_{four} **(e)** $1E3T4_{twelve}$
19. (a) 117   **(c)** 1331   **(e)** 157
21. 1 prize of $625, 2 prizes of $125, and 1 of $25
23. (a) 8 wk, 2 days   **(c)** 1 day, 5 hr
25. (a) 6   **(c)** nine
26. (a) 9 (4 quarters, 3 nickels, 2 pennies)
27. Above the bar are depicted 5s, 50s, 500s, and 5000s. Below the bar are 1s, 10s, 100s, and 1000s. Thus there are $1 \cdot 5000$, $1 \cdot 500$, $3 \cdot 100$, $1 \cdot 50$, $1 \cdot 5$, and $2 \cdot 1$ depicted for a total of 5857. The number 4869 could be depicted as follows:

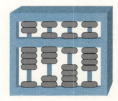

29. Assume an eight-digit display without scientific notation. **(a)** 98,765,432 **(c)** 99,999,999

Communication

32. Answers vary. Ben is incorrect. Zero is a placeholder in the Hindu-Arabic system. It is used among other things to differentiate between 54 and 504. If zero were nothing, then we could eliminate it without changing our number system. Zero is the cardinal number of the empty set.
34. This is primarily for readability. It has been proposed with the metric system to drop the commas and simply use spaces instead. The comma in a number symbol has different meanings in some countries.

Open-ended

37. The drawings of maize dolls, maize plants, flags, and blobs will certainly vary. With the depiction of 80, there should be four flags. With the depiction of 100, there should be five flags. With the depiction of 200, there should be 10 flags. With the depiction of 300, there should be 15 flags. With the depiction of 10,000, there should be 1 maize doll and 5 maize plants.

Cooperative Learning

40. 4; 1, 2, 4, 8; 1, 2, 4, 8, 16

Ongoing Assessment 3-2

1. (a) $k = 2$
2. No. If $k = 0$, we would have $k = 0 + k$, implying $k > k$.
4. (a) Yes **(c)** Yes **(e)** Yes
6. (b) $213 = x + 119$
7. (a) Commutative property of addition **(c)** Commutative property of addition
8. (a) 3820, 3802, 8023
9. (a) 33, 38, 43
10. (a) 9 **(c)** 3 **(e)** 5
11. (a) 1 **(c)** 8 or 9
12. 0
13. (a)

8	1	6
3	5	7
4	9	2

16. (a) 28
17. 5 mo
18. 45 points
23. 400
24. (a) Kent is shortest and Vera is the tallest.

Communication

25. An arrow starting at 0 and ending at 3 represents the same number as an arrow starting at 4 and ending at 7. One way to explain this to students is to make physical models of each and show by matching that the lengths are the same. Students will probably not understand the difference in free and fixed vectors, although teachers should.
26. In this situation, algebraic thinking might mean considering the missing addend as an unknown variable. The addition equation might be thought of as an equation in one unknown.
30. Answers vary. For example, students can think of $3 + 9$ as $9 + 3$ and use the "counting-on" method.

Open-ended

33. Answers vary. For example, let $A = \{a, b\}$ and $B = \{a, b, c, d\}$. Then $4 - 2 = n(B - A) = n(\{c, d\}) = 2$.

Cooperative Learning

36. Students may use number-line models to illustrate how the addition facts for base five may be found. The facts are shown in the following table:

+	0	1	2	3	4
0	0	1	2	3	4
1	1	2	3	4	10
2	2	3	4	10	11
3	3	4	10	11	12
4	4	10	11	12	13

Review Problems

37. (a) CMLIX **(b)** XXXVIII
38. There are fewer symbols to remember and place value is used.
39. $5 \cdot 10^3 + 2 \cdot 10^2 + 8 \cdot 10^1 + 6 \cdot 1$

Ongoing Assessment 3-3

1. $35
2. (b) 4
3. Each possible pairing of two of the sets is disjoint.
5. (a) Yes **(c)** Yes **(e)** Yes
6. (a) No, $2 + 3 = 5$ **(b)** Yes
7. (a) $ac + ad + bc + bd$ **(d)** $x^2 + 2xy + xz + y^2 + yz$
8. (a) $(4 + 3) \cdot 2 = 14$ **(c)** $(5 + 4 + 9) \div 3 = 6$
10. (a) 6 **(c)** 4

11. (b)

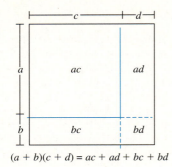

$$(a + b)(c + d) = ac + ad + bc + bd$$

12. (a) $40 = 8 \cdot 5$ **(c)** $48 = x \cdot 16$
14. (a) $2 \div 1 \neq 1 \div 2$ **(c)** $8 \div (2 + 2) \neq (8 \div 2) + (8 \div 2)$
16. 2; 3 left
18. A possible answer follows:

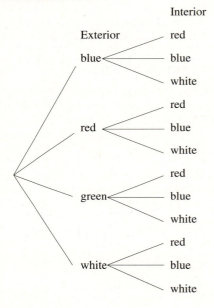

19. 30
21. (a) 3 **(c)** 2 **(e)** 4
22. (b) For example, $4 \cdot 4 - (4 \div 4) - (4 \div 4) - (4 \div 4)$.
23. (a) is the solution showing that each adult ticket costs $17 and a student ticket costs $15.
24. (a) Subtract 18. **(c)** Add 11 and 48.
26. This is the case when x is either 0 or 1.
28. (a) A/π **(c)** $60h$

Communication

30. The distributive property works with two operations. Only one operation is used in this example. Multiplication is not distributive over multiplication. Sue needs to look again at the associative property of multiplication.
33. This can be done, but many students may not believe it. Because the empty set has no elements, the Cartesian product of 2 empty sets has no elements and thus is empty.

Open-ended

36. Division is not a binary operation on the set of whole numbers because the set is not closed over division. For example, $\frac{3}{5}$ has no solution.
38. (a) Yes **(c)** Yes; a

Review Problems

39. (a) ∩∩∩∩∩∩∩|||| **(b)** LXXV **(c)** ▼ <▼▼▼▼
40. The points of the graph lie along a line.
41. An addition pattern is to find a term; then 5 is added to a previous term. A multiplication pattern is that the sequence is the set of multiples of 5.
42. $3 \cdot 10^4 + 5 \cdot 10^3 + 2 \cdot 10^2 + 0 \cdot 10^1 + 6$
43. For example, $\{0, 1\}$.
44. No. For example, $5 - 2 \neq 2 - 5$.
45.

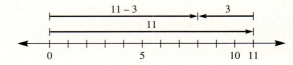

Ongoing Assessment 3-4

1. (a) 981 **(c)** 1,069
  $+ 421$ 2,094
  1402   9,546
           9,003
          $+ 7,064$
           28,776

2. (a) 87693 **(c)** 383
  $- 46414$ $- 159$
  41279   224

3. (a) One possibility: 863
            $+ 752$
            1615

4. Only if positive numbers are used:
  (a) 876
     $- 235$
     641

6. (a) 34, 39, 44
8. No, not all at dinner; he can have either the steak or the salad.
10. 3428
    $+ 5631$
    9059

11. (a) (i) No, not clustered; (ii) yes, clustered around 500
13. (a) About 121 wk **(c)** Answers vary.
15. (a) (i) 1236; (ii) 1032
16. Answers may vary. For example, **(a)** There is no carry.
(c) The lesser number is subtracted from the greater.
17. 1 hr 34 min 15 sec

18. (a) 121_{five} **(c)** 1010_{five} **(e)** 1001_{two}
20. (b) 1 hr 39 min 40 sec
21. (a) 2 qt, 1 pt, 0 c, or 1 half gallon, 0 qt, 1 p, 0 c
(c) 2 qt, 1 pt, 1 c
22. $2\frac{1}{2}$ so buy 3 gal

23. (a) The method produces a palindrome.
25. $8 + 8 + 8 + 88 + 888$
26. (a)

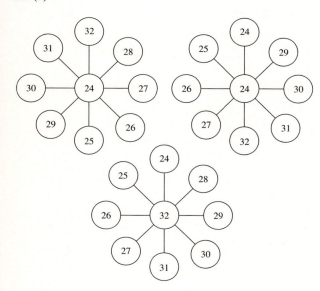

27. It is doubling the second number in the operation
28. (a) 34, 34, 34   **(c)** 34   **(e)** Yes
29. (b)
$$\begin{array}{r} 3\cancel{3}2 \\ 1\cancel{7}_0 \\ 22 \\ \cancel{4}_3\cancel{7}_0 \\ \cancel{7}_03 \\ \underline{1\,\cancel{7}_0} \\ 3\,1\,0_{\text{five}} \end{array}$$

30. (a) 3 gro 10 doz 9 ones
31. (a) 22 students on Tuesday
32. (a) 70
34. (a)
$$\begin{array}{r} 230_{\text{five}} \\ -\,22_{\text{five}} \\ \hline 203_{\text{five}} \end{array}$$

Communication

35. Yes, the front-end estimate considers only the value of the leading digit to estimate the sum.
38. Answers vary. For example, the diagram shows that an exact answer can be found by paper and pencil, calculator, or computer. In each case, estimation is recommended.

Open-ended

40. Examples include the number of people in a state, the amount of the national debt, and the number of hairs on a head.

Review Problems

44. This will be studied in detail in later chapters. However, with the meter as a basic unit of length, we have 10 meters = 1 decameter, 10 decameters = 1 hectometer, 10 hectometers = 1 kilometer.
45. $5280 = 5 \cdot 10^3 + 2 \cdot 10^2 + 8 \cdot 10 + 0 \cdot 1$
46. For example: $2 + (3 + 4) = (2 + 3) + 4$
$$2 + 7 = 5 + 4$$
$$9 = 9$$
47.

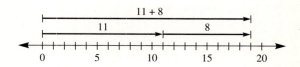

48. 1,000,410
49. (a) $a(x + 1)$ **(b)** $(3 + a)(x + y)$
50. 15

Ongoing Assessment 3-5

1. (a)

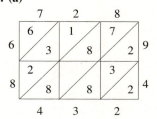

3. (a)
$$\begin{array}{r} 426 \\ \times\ 783 \\ \hline 1278 \\ 3408 \\ \underline{2982} \\ 333558 \end{array}$$

5. (a) 5^{19} **(c)** 10^{313}
6. (a) 2^{100}
8. (c)
$$\begin{array}{r} 363 \\ \times 84 \\ \hline 2904 \\ \underline{1452} \\ 30492 \end{array}$$

10. (a) 21   **(c)** 304
11. (a) 22   **(c)** 7
12. (a) $15 \cdot (10 + 2) = 150 + 30 = 180$

14. (a) 1332   **(c)** Maurice, 96 more calories
16. $60
18. (a) $3 \overline{)876}$
19. (a) Monthly payments are more expensive.
21. 3
22. 8 cars (remember the match)
23.

2	11
4	15
0	7
6	19
12	31

25. (b) $(10a + b)(10c + d) = (10b + a)(10d + c)$ implies $100ac + 10bc + 10ad + bd = 100bd + 10ad + 10bc + ac$ or $99ac = 99bd$, which implies that $ac = bd$.
26. 3 hr
29. 21 wk
30. 58 buses needed, not all full
33. (a) (i) $70; (ii) $10
34. (a) 233_{five} **(c)** 2144_{five} **(e)** 67_{eight} **(g)** 110_{two}
35. (a) Nine   **(c)** Six
37. (a)

$$763$$
$$\underline{\times 8}$$
$$6104$$

38. (a)

$$762$$
$$\underline{\times 83}$$
$$63{,}246$$

40. (a)

$$37$$
$$\underline{\times 43}$$
$$111$$
$$\underline{1480}$$
$$1591$$

41. (a) 1; 121; 12,321; 1,234,321
43. 19

Communication

46. The base sixteen, or hexadecimal, system has 16 symbols, while the base ten system has only 10. The hexadecimal system has uses in computer science because of its relationship to base two.
48. The result is always 4. Let the original number be x. The operation appears as follows:

$$[(2x)3 + 24]/6 - x = 4.$$

Open-ended

51. Answers will vary depending on student opinion. Students could read the list of topics with decreased emphasis in the *Standards*.

Cooperative Learning

52. The sliding rulers work much in the same way that arrows are used with a number line to show addition.

Review Problems

53. 999999∩∩∩∩∩∩∩IIII
54. 300,260
55. For example, $3 + 0 = 3 = 0 + 3$.
56. (a) $x(a + b + 2)$ **(b)** $(3 \times x)(a + b)$
57. 6979 mi
58. 724

Chapter Review

1. (a) 400,044   **(c)** 1704   **(e)** 1448
2. (a) CMXCIX   **(c)** $\overset{\bullet}{\underset{\bullet\bullet\bullet}{}}$ **(e)** 11011_{two}
3. (a) 3^{17} **(c)** 3^5
4. (a) Distributive property for multiplication over addition
   (c) Identity property for multiplication
   (e) Commutative property for multiplication
5. (a) $3 < 13$ because $3 + 10 = 13$
6. $1000 \cdot 483 = 10^3(4 \cdot 10^2 + 8 \cdot 10 + 3)$
$$= 4 \cdot 10^5 + 8 \cdot 10^4 + 3 \cdot 10^3$$
$$= 4 \cdot 10^5 + 8 \cdot 10^4 + 3 \cdot 10^3 + 0 \cdot 10^2 + 0 \cdot 10^1$$
$$+ 0 \cdot 1$$
$$= 483{,}000$$
8. 60,074
9. (a) 5 remainder 243   **(c)** 120_{five} remainder 2_{five}
11. (a) Tens   **(c)** Hundreds
12. (a) 10, 11, 12, 13, 14, 15   **(c)** All whole numbers
13. (a) $15a$ **(c)** $xa + xb + xy$
15. $395
17. 2600
19. 40 cans
21. 26
23. $6000
25. $214
28. Selling pencils by the units, dozens, and gross is an example of the use of the base twelve.

CHAPTER 4

Ongoing Assessment 4-1

1. (b) 5   **(f)** $^{-}a + {}^{-}b$ or $^{-}(a + b)$
3. (a) 5   **(d)** $^{-}5$
4. (a)

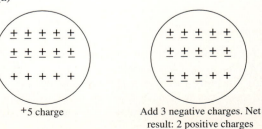

+5 charge

Add 3 negative charges. Net result: 2 positive charges

(d)

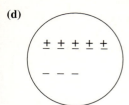

−3 charge on the field

Add 2 negative charges. Net result: 5 negative charges

7. (a) ⁻7   **(d)** ⁻$150

9. (c)

−3 charge on field

Take away 2 negative charges. Net result: 1 negative charge on the field

11. (b) $3 - 1 = 2; 2 - 1 = 1; 1 - 1 = 0; 0 - 1 = ⁻1; ⁻1 - 1 = ⁻2; ⁻2 - 1 = ⁻3$

13. (b) 3   **(e)** ⁻13

15. 33 points

16. (c) 192°F

18. ⁻4 lb

19. (a) 10W–40 or 10W–30
(c) 10W–40, 5W–30, or 10W–30
(e) 10W–30 or 10W–40

20. (b) $2x + y$

21. (b) All positive integers   **(e)** There are none.
(g) There are none.

23. (a) I **(c)** $I - \{0\}$ **(e)** ∅   **(g)** $\{0\}$ **(i)** I

24.

2	⁻13	8
5	⁻1	⁻7
⁻10	⁻11	⁻4

Other answers are possible.

26. (a) 0   **(c)** 1

27. (c) 0 or 2

29. (b) 19   **(c)** 19

31. (a) ⁻3; . . . , ⁻12, ⁻15, . . .   **(c)** ⁻y; . . . , $x - 2y, x - 3y$ . . .

32. (b) 3775

34. (b) True   **(c)** True   **(e)** False; let $x = ⁻1$

35. The smaller gear rotates 28 times in the opposite direction of the larger gear.

37. (b) ⁻106   **(d)** 22   **(f)** 2   **(h)** 23

38. (b) 516   **(c)** 10,894

Communication

41. He could have driven 12 mi in either direction from milepost 68. Therefore his location could be either at the $68 - 12 = 56$ milepost or at the $68 + 12 = 80$ milepost.

42. (a) $(a + b) + (⁻a + ⁻b) = a + b + ⁻a + ⁻b = a + ⁻a + b + ⁻b = (a + ⁻a) + (b + ⁻b) = 0 + 0 = 0$

Ongoing Assessment 4-2

3. If you are now at 0 moving west at 4 km/hr, you will be at 8 km west of 0 2 hr from now.

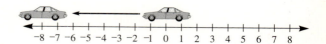

4. (a) ⁻20 · 4   **(c)** ⁻20n

5. (b) ⁻13   **(d)** 0   **(f)** Impossible; division by 0 is not defined.

6. (a) ⁻10   **(d)** ⁻10   **(e)** a; if $b \neq 0$ **(j)** ⁻4
(k) Impossible   **(n)** ⁻2

7. (b) 0°C + 25 · (4°C)   **(d)** 25°C − 20 · (3°C)
(f) 20°C − m · (d°C)

8. (b) ⁻66 divided by 11 = ⁻6. He lost 6 yd. per play.

10. (b) ⁻3(⁻3 + 2) = ⁻3(⁻1) = 3; (⁻3)(⁻3) + (⁻3)(2) = 9 + ⁻6 = 3

11. (b) 16   **(d)** 81   **(f)** ⁻1   **(h)** ⁻1

12. (a) 12   **(c)** ⁻5   **(f)** ⁻9   **(g)** ⁻13   **(h)** ⁻8

13. (b), (c), (g), (h) are always positive; (a), (f) are always negative.

15. (a) Commutative property of multiplication
(d) Distributive property of multiplication over addition

16. (b) $2xy$ **(e)** $x + 2y$ **(f)** b

17. (b) 2   **(d)** ⁻6   **(f)** 6   **(h)** All integers except 0
(j) 3 or ⁻3   **(l)** All integers except 0   **(n)** All integers

18. (b) $⁻2x + 2y$ **(d)** $⁻x^2 + xy$ **(f)** $⁻x^2 + xy + 3x$
(i) $⁻x^4 + 3x^2 - 2$

19. (b) $25 - 10,000 = ⁻9975$ **(d)** $4 - 9x^2$
(f) $(213 + 13)(213 - 13) = 226 · 200 = 45,200$

20. (a) $8x$ **(e)** $x(x + y)$ **(h)** $x(3x + y - 1)$ **(j)** $(a + b)c$
(m) $(2x + 5y)(2x - 5y)$

22. (b) True   **(d)** True

23. (a) The sums are 9 times the middle number.

24. (b) ⁻8, ⁻11, $d = ⁻3$, nth term is ⁻3n + 13   **(d)** ⁻128, 256, $r = ⁻2$, nth term is $(⁻2)^n$

26. (a) ⁻9, ⁻6, ⁻1, 6, 15   **(e)** ⁻1, 4, ⁻9, 16, ⁻25,
(f) 2, ⁻8, 24, ⁻64, 160

27. 7, 2

29. (a) ⁻81   **(c)** ⁻2

Communication

30. No, it is not of the form $(a - b)(a + b)$.

33. ⁻$(a + b) = (⁻1)(a + b)$ by the first part of Problem 32.
$= (⁻1)a + (⁻1)b$ by the distributive property
$= ⁻a + ⁻b$ by the first part of Problem 32.

Review Problems

40.

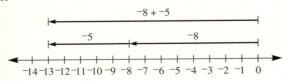

41. (a) 5 **(b)** $^-7$ **(c)** 0

42. (a) 14 **(b)** 21 **(c)** $^-4$ **(d)** 22

43. 400 lb

Ongoing Assessment 4-3

1. (b) True **(d)** True **(f)** False; 6 is a factor of 30, not a multiple of 30.

2. (a) Yes **(c)** Yes **(e)** Yes

3. (b) 2, 3, 6, 9 **(d)** 2, 4 **(f)** None of them

4. (a) No, $17|34000$ and $17\nmid 15$, so $17\nmid 34{,}015$.

(c) No, $19|19000$ and $19\nmid 31$, so $19\nmid 19{,}031$.

(e) No, $5|2 \cdot 3 \cdot 5 \cdot 7$ and $5\nmid 1$, so $5\nmid (2 \cdot 3 \cdot 5 \cdot 7) + 1$.

5. (a) True by Theorem 4-1 **(c)** None

(e) True by Theorem 4-1

6. (a) True **(c)** False **(e)** True **(g)** True

8. (a) A number is divisible by 16 if, and only if, the last 4 digits form a number divisible by 16. **(b)** A number is divisible by 25 if, and only if, the number formed by the last 2 digits is divisible by 25.

10. (a) 7 **(c)** 6

11. (a) Any digit 0–9 **(c)** 1, 3, 5, 7, 9 **(e)** 7

13. Each bar costs 19¢.

14. (a) Yes **(c)** Yes

15. (a) 1, 2, 4, 5, 8, 11 **(c)** 5 field goals

16. (a) 4 4 4 **(c)** 3 12 3 **(e)** 2 20 2

17. (a) $12{,}343 + 4546 + 56 = 16{,}945$
$$4 + 1 + 2 = 7$$

(c) $10{,}034 + 3004 + 400 + 20 = 13{,}458$
$$8 + 7 + 4 + 2 = 21$$ has a remainder 3 when divided by 9, as does $1 + 3 + 4 + 5 + 8$.

(e) $1003 - 46 = 957$
$$4 - 1 = 3$$ has remainder 3 when divided by 9, as does $9 + 5 + 7 = 21$ **(g)** Answers vary.

18. (a) False; $2|4$, but $2\nmid 1$ and $2\nmid 3$ **(c)** False; $12|72$ but $12\nmid 8$ and $12\nmid 9$ **(e)** True **(g)** False. If $a = 5$ and $b = {}^-5$, then $a|b$ and $b|a$, but $a \neq b$. **(i)** False; $2\nmid 3$ and $2\nmid 9$ but $2|(3 + 9)$ **(k)** False; $50\nmid 10$, but $50|100$

21. Let $n = a \cdot 10^4 + b \cdot 10^3 + c \cdot 10^2 + d \cdot 10 + e$
$$a \cdot 10^4 = a \cdot (10{,}000) = a \cdot (9999 + 1) = a \cdot 9999 + a$$
$$b \cdot 10^3 = b \cdot (1000) = b \cdot (999 + 1) = b \cdot 999 + b$$
$$c \cdot 10^2 = c \cdot (100) = c \cdot (99 + 1) = c \cdot 99 + c$$
$$d \cdot 10 = d \cdot (10) = d \cdot (9 + 1) = d \cdot 9 + d$$
Thus $n = (a \cdot 9999 + b \cdot 999 + c \cdot 99 + d \cdot 9) + (a + b + c + d + e)$. Because $9|9$, $9|99$, $9|999$, $9|9999$, it follows that $9|[(a \cdot 9999 + b \cdot 999 + c \cdot 99 + d \cdot 9) + (a + b + c + d + e)]$;

that is, $9|n$. If, on the other hand, $9\nmid (a + b + c + d + e)$ it follows that $9\nmid n$.

22. (a) The result is always 9. **(c)** Let the number be $a \cdot 10 + b$. The number with the digits reversed is $b \cdot 10 + a$. Now, $a \cdot 10 + b - (b \cdot 10 + a) = a \cdot 10 + b - b \cdot 10 - a$
$$= a \cdot 10 - a + b - b \cdot 10$$
$$= 9a - 9b$$
$$= 9(a - b)$$
Thus the difference is a multiple of 9.

23. 6,868,395 is divisible by 15 because it is divisible by both 3 and 5. The last digit is 5 and the sum of the digits is 45, which is divisible by 3.

Communication

24. No. For the 6¢ and 15¢ stamps to be used for the exact postage, 286 must be divisible by 6 or by 15 or by both. Both 6 and 15 are multiples of 3 and 286 is not divisible by 3, so 286 is not divisible by either 6 or 15.

29. (a) Yes, $4|52{,}832$, so 4 divides anything times 52,832. Therefore 4 divides $52{,}832 \cdot 324{,}518$, which is the area.

32. (a) No. If $5\nmid d$ for any integer d, then there is no integer m such that $5m = d$. If we assume $10|d$, this means there exists n such that $10n = d$ or $5(2n) = d$. This contradicts the original assumption that d is not divisible by 5.

36. 243. Yes. Consider any number n of the form $abcabc$. Then we have the following:
$$n = (a \cdot 10^5) + (b \cdot 10^4) + (c \cdot 10^3) + (a \cdot 10^2) + (b \cdot 10^1) + c$$
$$= a(10^5 + 10^2) + b(10^4 + 10^1) + c(10^3 + 1)$$
$$= a(100{,}000 + 100) + b(10{,}000 + 10) + c(1001)$$
$$= a(1001 \cdot 100) + b(1001 \cdot 10) + c(1001)$$
$$= (1001)[(a \cdot 100) + b(10) + c(1)]$$
$$= (7 \cdot 11 \cdot 13)[(a \cdot 100) + b(10) + c(1)]$$
Therefore $7|n$, $11|n$, and $13|n$.

Ongoing Assessment 4-4

1. (a) Prime **(c)** Prime **(e)** Prime

2. 73

3. (a)

```
        504
       /   \
      2    252
          /   \
         2    126
             /   \
            2     63
                 /  \
                3    21
                    /  \
                   3    7
```
$504 = 2^3 \cdot 3^2 \cdot 7$

(c)

```
        11250
       /    \
      2     5625
           /    \
          3     1875
               /    \
              3     625
                   /   \
                  5    125
                      /   \
                     5     25
                          /  \
                         5    5
```
$11250 = 2 \cdot 3^2 \cdot 5^4$

6. **(a)** $1 \cdot 48, 2 \cdot 24, 3 \cdot 16, 4 \cdot 12$ **(b)** Only one: $1 \cdot 47$
8. **(a)** 3, 5, 15, 29 people   **(b)** 145 committees of 3; 87 committees of 5; 29 committees of 15; 15 committees of 29
9. **(a)** 1, 2, 3, 4, 6, 9, 12, 18, or 36   **(c)** 1 or 17
10. 27,720
12. **(a)** The Fundamental Theorem of Arithmetic says that n can be written as a product of primes in one and only one way. Since $2|n$ and $3|n$ and 2 and 3 are both prime, they must be included in the unique factorization.
That is, $2 \cdot 3 \cdot p_1 \cdot p_2 \cdot \ldots \cdot p_m = n$.
Therefore $(2 \cdot 3)(p_1 \cdot p_2 \cdot \ldots \cdot p_m) = n$.
Thus $6|n$.
14. 101, 103, 107, 109, 113, 127, 131, 137, 139, 149, 151, 157, 163, 167, 173, 179, 181, 191, 193, 197, 199
15. 3, 5; 5, 7; 11, 13; 17, 19; 29, 31; 41, 43; 59, 61; 71, 73; 101, 103; 107, 109; 137, 139; 149, 151; 179, 181; 191, 193; 197, 199
16. **(b)** Let $n = 41a$, where $a \in N$. Then $n^2 - n + 41 = (41a)^2 - 41a + 41 = 41(41a^2 - a + 1)$.
17. Every number would have its "usual" factorization $1(p_1 \cdot p_2 \cdot p_3 \cdot \ldots \cdot p_n)$, along with infinitely many such other factorizations, because $1^n = 1$; n may be any natural number.
19. No, because 5^z has no factors of either 2 or 3.
20. **(a)** 4, 6, 8, 0   **(c)** 23, 29, 31, 37, 53, 59, 71, 73, 79
21. There are infinitely many composites of the form 1, 11, 111, 1111, 11111, 111111 . . . , since every third member of this sequence will be divisible by 3.
23. None of the primes 2, 3, 5 . . . , p divides N because if any one of the primes were to divide N, then it would also have to divide 1, which is impossible.
24. If $2N = 2^6 \cdot 3^5 \cdot 5^4 \cdot 7^3 \cdot 11^7$, then $N = 2^5 \cdot 3^5 \cdot 5^4 \cdot 7^3 \cdot 11^7 = (2 \cdot 3 \cdot 5 \cdot 7 \cdot 11)(2^4 \cdot 3^4 \cdot 5^3 \cdot 7^2 \cdot 11^6)$, which implies that $(2 \cdot 3 \cdot 5 \cdot 7 \cdot 11)$ is a factor of N.
26. **(a)** $3 \cdot 5 \cdot 7 \cdot 11 \cdot 13$ is composite because it is divisible by 3, 5, 7, 11, and 13.   **(c)** $(3 \cdot 5 \cdot 7 \cdot 11 \cdot 13) + 5 = 5((3 \cdot 7 \cdot 11 \cdot 13) + 1)$, and so it is composite.   **(e)** $10! + k$ can be factored as in (d) depending on the value of k, and so it is composite.

Communication

28. To check if 173 is prime, we must check only for divisibility by primes whose squares are less than 173. In this case, we must check for divisibility by 2, 3, 5, 7, 11, and 13.
34. The multiples of 4, 8, and 10 were crossed out with the multiples of 2. The multiples of 6 were crossed out when the multiples of 2 and 3 were crossed out. The multiples of 9 were crossed out when the multiples of 3 were crossed out. All composite numbers less than 100 must have a factor less than or equal to 10 and these are all accounted for. Therefore the remaining numbers that have not been crossed out are prime.

Review Problems

41. **(a)** False   **(b)** True   **(c)** True   **(d)** True

42. **(a)** 2, 3, 6   **(b)** 2, 3, 5, 6, 9, 10
43. If $12|n$, there exists an integer a such that $12a = n$:
$$(3 \cdot 4)a = n$$
$$3(4a) = n$$
Thus $3|n$.
44. Yes, among 8 people. Each would get $422.

Ongoing Assessment 4-5

1. **(a)** $D_{18} = \{1, 2, 3, 6, 9, 18\}$
$D_{10} = \{1, 2, 5, 10\}$
GCD$(18, 10) = 2$
$M_{18} = \{18, 36, 54, 72, 90 \ldots\}$
$M_{10} = \{10, 20, 30, 40, 50, 60, 70, 80, 90, \ldots\}$
LCM$(18, 10) = 90$
   (c) $D_8 = \{1, 2, 4, 8\}$
$D_{24} = \{1, 2, 3, 4, 6, 8, 12, 24\}$
$D_{52} = \{1, 2, 4, 13, 26, 52\}$
GCD$(8, 24, 52) = 4$
$M_8 = \{8, 16, 24, 32, 40, 48, 56, 64, 72, 80, 88, 96 \ldots\}$
$M_{24} = \{24, 48, 72, 96, 120, 144, 168, 192, 216, 240, 264, 288, 312 \ldots\}$
$M_{52} = \{52, 104, 156, 208, 160, 312 \ldots\}$
LCM$(8, 24, 52) = 312$
2. **(a)** $132 = 2^2 \cdot 3 \cdot 11$
$504 = 2^3 \cdot 3^2 \cdot 7$
GCD$(132, 504) = 2^2 \cdot 3 = 12$
LCM$(132, 504) = 2^3 \cdot 3^2 \cdot 7 \cdot 11 = 5544$
   (c) $96 = 2^5 \cdot 3$
$900 = 2^2 \cdot 3^2 \cdot 5^2$
$630 = 2 \cdot 3^2 \cdot 5 \cdot 7$
GCD$(96, 900, 630) = 2 \cdot 3 = 6$
LCM$(96, 900, 630) = 2^5 \cdot 3^2 \cdot 5^2 \cdot 7 = 50,400$
   (e) $63 = 3^2 \cdot 7$
$147 = 3 \cdot 7^2$
GCD$(63, 147) = 3 \cdot 7 = 21$
LCM$(63, 147) = 3^2 \cdot 7^2 = 441$
3. **(a)** GCD $(2924, 220) = $ GCD$(220, 64) = $ GCD$(64, 28) = $ GCD$(28, 8) = $ GCD$(8, 4) = $ GCD$(4, 0) = 4$
(c) GCD$(123,152, 122,368) = $ GCD$(122,368, 784) = $ GCD $(784, 64) = $ GCD $(64, 16) = $ GCD$(16, 0) = 16$
4. **(a)** 72   **(c)** 630
5. **(a)** $220 \cdot 2924/4$ or 160,820   **(c)** $123,152 \cdot 122,368/16$ or 941,866,496
7. **(a)** LCM$(15, 40, 60) = 120$ min $= 2$ hr, so the clocks' alarms go off together again at 8:00 A.M.
9. **(a)** $60   **(c)** 30
11. 24 nights
13. After $7\frac{1}{2}$ hr, or 2:30 A.M.
15. **(a)** ab **(c)** GCD$(a^2, a) = a$; LCM$(a^2, a) = a^2$
(e) GCD$(a, b) = 1$; LCM$(a, b) = ab$ **(g)** $b|a$
16. **(a)** True. If a and b are even, then GCD$(a, b) > 2$.
(c) False. The GCD could be a multiple of 2; for example,

$GCD(8, 12) = 4.$ **(e)** True, by Theorem 4-9. **(g)** True. If
$LCM (a, b) < a$, then the LCM could not be a multiple.
17. $GCD(120, 75) = 15$; $GCD(15, 105) = 15$; $GCD(120, 75, 105) = 15$
18. (a) $4 = 2^2$. Since 97,219,988,751 is odd, it has no prime
factors of two. Consequently, 1 is their only common divisor
and they are relatively prime.
20. $48
22. 2 packages of plates, 4 packages of cups, and 3 packages
of napkins
23. 12 revolutions
25. (a)

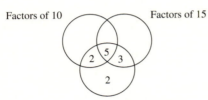

Factors of 10   Factors of 15

Factors of 60

26. $1, p,$ and p^2
27. $\{1, 2, 3, 4, 6, 7, 8, 9, 11, 12, 13, 14, 16, 17, 18, 19, 21, 22, 23, 24\}$

Communication

29. No. The set of common multiples is infinite; therefore
there could be no greatest common multiple.

Review Problems

35. $x = 15,625; y = 64$
36. (a) 83,151; 83,451; 83,751 **(b)** 86,691 **(c)** 10,396
37. $17 \cdot 183 = 3111$; thus 3111 is not prime.
38. Answers may vary. $30,030 = 2 \cdot 3 \cdot 5 \cdot 7 \cdot 11 \cdot 13$
39. 27,720
40. 43

Ongoing Assessment 4-6

1. 2:00 P.M.
3. (a) 3 **(c)** 6 **(e)** 3 **(g)** Does not exist
4. (a) 2 **(c)** 2 **(e)** 2 **(g)** 2
5. (a)

$\oplus$	1	2	3	4	5	6	7
1	2	3	4	5	6	7	1
2	3	4	5	6	7	1	2
3	4	5	6	7	1	2	3
4	5	6	7	1	2	3	4
5	6	7	1	2	3	4	5
6	7	1	2	3	4	5	6
7	1	2	3	4	5	6	7

(c) Every subtraction problem can be written as an addition
problem, which can always be performed.

6. (a)

$\otimes$	1	2	3	4	5	6	7
1	1	2	3	4	5	6	7
2	2	4	6	1	3	5	7
3	3	6	2	5	1	4	7
4	4	1	5	2	6	3	7
5	5	3	1	6	4	2	7
6	6	5	4	3	2	1	7
7	7	7	7	7	7	7	7

(c) Yes. Division by numbers different from 7 is possible,
since each row and column in the table contains every element
1 through 6.
7. (a) 10 **(c)** 7 **(e)** 1
8. (a) 2, 9, 16, 30 **(c)** $366 \equiv 2(\text{mod}7)$; Wednesday
9. (a) 4 **(c)** 0
10. (a) $8|(81 - 1)$ **(c)** $13|(1000 - (^-1))$
(e) $10^2 = 1(\text{mod } 11)$ implies $(10^2)^{50} \equiv 1^{50}(\text{mod } 11)$
12. (a) $24 \equiv 0(\text{mod } 8)$ **(c)** $n \equiv 0(\text{mod } n)$
13. (a) $x = 2k$, where k is an integer. **(c)** $x - 3 = 5k$ implies
$x = 3 + 5k$, where k is an integer.
14. (a) 1 **(c)** 10
16. Wednesday
18. For example, $2 \cdot 11 \equiv 1 \cdot 11(\text{mod } 11)$, but $2 \equiv 1(\text{mod } 11)$
is false.

Chapter Review

1. (a) $^-3$ **(e)** $x - y$ **(g)** 32
2. (a) $^-7$ **(d)** 0 **(e)** 8
3. (a) 3 **(c)** Any integer except 0 **(e)** $^-41$
5. (a) $10 - 5 = 5$ **(b)** $1 - (^-2) = 3$
6. (a) $(x - y)(x + y) = (x - y)x + (x - y)y$
$$= x^2 - yx + xy - y^2$$
$$= x^2 - xy + xy - y^2$$
$$= x^2 - y^2$$
(b) $4 - x^2$
7. (a) ^-x **(c)** $3x - 1$ **(f)** $^-x^2 - 6x - 9$
8. (a) ^-2x **(b)** $x(x + 1)$ **(e)** $5(1 + x)$ **(f)** $(x - y)x$
9. (a) False. It is not positive for $x = 0$.
(c) False, if $b < 0$.
(e) False. It is equal to ab.
10. (b) $3 - (4 - 5) \neq (3 - 4) - 5$ **(d)** $8/(4 - 2) \neq 8/4 - 8/2$
11. $^-7°C$
13. (a) False **(c)** True **(e)** False; 9, for example
14. (a) False; 7|7 and $7 \nmid 3$, yet $7|3 \cdot 7$ **(c)** True **(e)** True
15. (a) Divisible by 2, 3, 4, 5, 6, 8, 9, 11
16. If 10,007 is prime, $17 \nmid 10,007$. We know $17|17$, so
$17 \nmid (10,007 + 17)$ by Theorem 4-2(b).
17. (a) 87$\underline{2}$4; 86$\underline{5}$4; 87$\underline{8}$4 **(c)** 87,$\underline{1}$74; 87,$\underline{4}$64; 87,$\underline{7}$54
18. (a) Composite
19. Check for divisibility by 3 and 8, 24|4152.
20. (a) 4
21. (a) $2^4 \cdot 5^3 \cdot 7^4 \cdot 13 \cdot 29$
22. Answers vary; for example, 16. To obtain 5 divisors, we
raise a prime (2) to the $(5 - 1)$ power.
23. 1, 2, 3, 4, 6, 8, 9, 12, 16, 18, 24, 36, 48, 72, 144

24. (a) $2^2 \cdot 43$ **(c)** $2^2 \cdot 5 \cdot 13$
25. 15 min
26. \$.31
27. 9:30 A.M.

CHAPTER 5

Ongoing Assessment 5-1

1. (a) The solution to $8x = 7$ is 7/8.   **(c)** The ratio of boys to girls is 7 to 8.
2. (a) 1/6   **(c)** 2/6 or 1/3   **(e)** 5/16
3. (a) 2/3   **(c)** 6/9 or 2/3
4. (a)

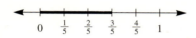

(c)

(e)

5. (a) 9/24 or 3/8   **(c)** 4/24 or 1/6
6. (a) 4/18, 6/27, 8/36   **(c)** 0/1, 0/2, 0/4
7. (a) 52/31   **(c)** ⁻5/7   **(e)** 144/169
9. (a) Undefined   **(c)** 0   **(e)** Cannot be simplified
(g) 5/3
10. (a) 1   **(c)** $a/1$ **(e)** $1/(3 + b)$
11. (a) Equal   **(c)** Equal
12. (a) Not equal   **(c)** Equal
13. Yes, 1/32 in.
15. 36/48
17.

18. (a) $2\frac{7}{8}$ in.   **(c)** $1\frac{3}{8}$ in.
20. (a) 32/3   **(c)** x is any rational number except 0.
21. (a) $a = b, c \neq 0$
22. (a) Not equal   **(c)** Equal
23. (a) True   **(c)** False   **(e)** True
24. Bren's class.
25. (a) >   **(c)** <   **(e)** =
26. (a) $\frac{11}{13}, \frac{11}{16}, \frac{11}{22}$
27. (a) A positive fraction less than 1 is greater than its square.   **(c)** If a fraction is greater than 1, it is less than its square.
28. $\frac{a}{b} < 1$ and $\frac{c}{d} > 0$ imply $\frac{a}{b} \cdot \frac{c}{d} < 1 \cdot \frac{c}{d}$, or $\frac{a}{b} \cdot \frac{c}{d} < \frac{c}{d}$
30. We need to show that $\frac{n}{n+1} < \frac{n+1}{n+2}$. This inequality is equivalent to $n^2 + 2n < n^2 + 2n + 1$, or $0 < 1$.
31. (a) There is no whole number between 3 and 4, for example.
32. Answers vary. The following are possible answers:
(a) $\frac{10}{21}, \frac{11}{21}$ **(c)** $\frac{997}{1200}, \frac{998}{1200}$
33. (a) 1   **(c)** The ratios are the same. To show this, let x equal the top circled number. Then the sum of the circled numbers is $x + (x + 12) + (x + 19) + (x + 31) = 4x + 62$. The sum of the four interior numbers is $(x + 10) + (x + 11) + (x + 20) + (x + 21) = 4x + 62$. Here the ratio is always 1.
34. 456 mi
36. 100 yd = 300 ft. The estimate should be between 13 and 14 sec, but closer to 13 sec.

Communication

37. It is less than either factor. If $\frac{a}{b} < 1$ and $\frac{c}{d} < 1$, then by multiplying the first inequality by $\frac{c}{d}$, we have $\frac{ac}{bd} < \frac{c}{d}$.

Similarly, multiplying the second inequality by $\frac{a}{b}$ yields $\frac{ca}{db} < \frac{a}{b}$.
39. No, the answer depends on the context of problem.
40. Answers vary.   **(a)** Suppose the rational numbers are $\frac{2}{16}$ and $\frac{1}{4}$. $\frac{1}{4} \cdot \frac{1}{4} > \frac{2}{16}$. Iris is incorrect.
41. The points determined by the coordinates lie along a line. Students will not realize this yet, but essentially they are graphing points along the line with slope 1/3.

Open-ended

43. Frequently in recipes, measurements are found in fractional parts of cups, teaspoons, and tablespoons. For example, a recipe might call for 1/2 tsp of salt and 2/3 c of flour.

Cooperative Learning

45. In this assessment, students must work together to determine the heights and to order the people according to height. Once that is done, the students may decide how many are in the class — for example, 24 — and then number the people in the class from 1/24 to 24/24, or 1. Many other rational numbers may be used.

Ongoing Assessment 5-2

1. (a)

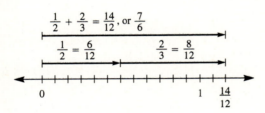

(c) $\frac{-4}{12}$, or $\frac{-1}{3}$ **(e)** $\frac{-9y + 5x + 42y^2}{6x^2y^2}$

(g) $\frac{71}{24}$, or $2\frac{23}{24}$ **(i)** $\frac{-23}{3}$, or $-7\frac{2}{3}$

2. (a) $18\frac{2}{3}$ **(c)** $-2\frac{93}{100}$

3. (a) $\frac{27}{4}$ **(c)** $\frac{-29}{8}$

5. (a) 1/3; high   **(c)** 3/4; low
6. (a) Beavers   **(c)** Bears   **(e)** Lions
8. (a) 1/2; high   **(c)** 3/4; high   **(e)** 1; low   **(g)** 3/4; low
9. (a) 2   **(c)** 0
10. (a) No
11. (a) 1/4   **(c)** 0
12. (a) A   **(c)** T
13. (a) $\frac{3 + 3}{3} \neq \frac{3}{3} + 3$ **(c)** $\frac{ab + c}{a} \neq \frac{\not{a}b + c}{\not{a}}$

(e) $\frac{a + c}{b + c} \neq \frac{a + \not{c}}{b + \not{c}}$

14. $\frac{1}{4}$

15. (a) $\frac{1}{30}$ **(c)** $\frac{1}{60}$

16. $6\frac{7}{12}$ yd

18. $2\frac{5}{6}$ yd

20. (a) Team 4; $76\frac{11}{16}$ lb

21. (a) $\frac{1}{2} + \frac{3}{4} \in Q$ **(c)** $\left(\frac{1}{2} + \frac{1}{3}\right) + \frac{1}{4} = \frac{1}{2} + \left(\frac{1}{3} + \frac{1}{4}\right)$

22. (a) $\frac{6}{4}, \frac{7}{4}$, 2; arithmetic, $\frac{1}{2} - \frac{1}{4} = \frac{3}{4} - \frac{1}{2} = 1 - \frac{3}{4} = \frac{5}{4} - 1$

(c) $\frac{17}{3}, \frac{20}{3}, \frac{23}{3}$; arithmetic, $\frac{5}{3} - \frac{2}{3} = \frac{8}{3} - \frac{5}{3} = \frac{11}{3} - \frac{8}{3} = \frac{14}{3} - \frac{11}{3}$
24. (a) 622/985   **(c)** 24/985
25. (a) Afghanistan
27. (a) (i) $\frac{3}{4}$;   **(ii)** $\frac{25}{12}$, or $2\frac{1}{12}$;   **(iii)** 0

28. (a) $f(0) = {}^-2$ **(c)** $f({}^-5) = \frac{1}{2}$

29. (b) $\frac{1}{n} = \frac{1}{n + 1} + \frac{1}{n(n + 1)}$

Communication

30. Although they are not whole quantities, they still may add up to whole quantities. A single fractional part may be far from negligible if the mixed number is small. For example, consider 1 7/8.
32. No. Because 4/5 is a proper fraction, there is no equivalent that can be improper.
33. (a) Yes. If *a, b, c,* and *d* are integers, then $\frac{a}{b} - \frac{c}{d} =$

$\frac{ad - bc}{bd}$ is a rational number.   **(c)** No. For example,

$\frac{1}{2} - \left(\frac{1}{4} - \frac{1}{8}\right) \neq \left(\frac{1}{2} - \frac{1}{4}\right) - \frac{1}{8}$.   **(e)** No. Since there is no

identity, an inverse cannot be defined.
34. (a) Like digits are being canceled.   **(c)** Numerators and denominators of fractional portions are both being subtracted.

Open-ended

35. (a) It is feasible to add the numbers in the table for Montana and Russia to determine the population density of the combined country and state because the population density is the number of people per square mile in each case. In terms of rational numbers, the denominator in each case is 1 mi^2.
(c) Answers vary. For example, one question might be "If the population of Montana is removed from that of the United States, is the population density of the remaining portion of the United States 62?"

Cooperative Learning

37. Depending on the people interviewed, students may hear an answer like the following from a teacher:
   I use fractions in determining total grades for my classes. For example, if a paper is 1/2 of the grade and a test is another 1/3 of the grade, I need to know what fractional part of the grade is yet to be determined.

Review Problems

38. (a) The triangles created will vary.   **(b)** The ratio of the directed segments is always 1/1.   **(c)** The conjecture should be that all triangles created in this manner will have sides in the ratio of 1/1. This ratio of change in *y*-coordinates to change in *x*-coordinates is the slope of the line created.

39. (a) $\frac{2}{3}$ **(b)** $\frac{13}{17}$ **(c)** $\frac{25}{49}$ **(d)** $\frac{a}{1}$ or *a* **(e)** Reduced

40. (a) Equal **(b)** Not equal **(c)** Equal **(d)** Not equal

41. (a) February **(b)** The answer depends on whether the year is a leap year. If it is a leap year, the answer is 183/366; if not, the answer is 184/365. **(c)** Most people consider there are 365 1/4 days in a year. As an improper fraction, this number is 1461/4.

42. $0 < \frac{a}{b} < \frac{c}{d}$ so that $0 < \frac{1}{2} \cdot \frac{a}{b} < \frac{1}{2} \cdot \frac{c}{d}$. Also, $0 < \frac{a}{b} = \frac{1}{2} \cdot \frac{a}{b} +$

$\frac{1}{2} \cdot \frac{a}{b} < \frac{1}{2} \cdot \frac{a}{b} + \frac{1}{2} \cdot \frac{c}{d} = \frac{1}{2}\left(\frac{a}{b} + \frac{c}{d}\right)$. Similarly, $\frac{1}{2}\left(\frac{a}{b} + \frac{c}{d}\right) < \frac{c}{d}$,

and therefore $0 < \frac{a}{b} < \frac{1}{2}\left(\frac{a}{b} + \frac{c}{d}\right) < \frac{c}{d}$.

43. We are considering $\frac{a}{b}$ and $\frac{a+x}{b+x}$ when $a < b$. $\frac{a}{b} < \frac{a+x}{b+x}$ because $ab + ax < ab + bx$; $ax < bx$; $x > 0$; $a < b$ which is true.

Ongoing Assessment 5-3

1. (a) $\frac{1}{4} \cdot \frac{1}{3} = \frac{1}{12}$

2. (a)

(c)

3. (a) $\frac{1}{5}$ **(c)** $\frac{za}{x^2 y}$ **(e)** $\frac{44}{3}$ or 14 2/3

4. (a) $10\frac{1}{2}$ **(c)** $24{,}871\frac{1}{20}$

5. (a) $^-3$ **(c)** $\frac{y}{x}$

6. (a) 26 **(c)** 92 **(e)** 6 **(g)** 9

7. (a) 20 **(c)** 2

8. (a) 18 **(c)** 7

9. (a) Less than 1 **(c)** Greater than 2 **(e)** Greater than 4

10. (c)

11. $\frac{29}{36}$

13. 400

15. (a) 39 uniforms

16. $240

17. (a) $121,000 **(c)** $300,000

18. 1/4

20. $225

21. (a) Peter, 30 min; Paul, 25 min; Mary, 20 min

22. (a) $89\frac{3}{5}$ °F

23. $2253\frac{1}{8}$

25. The arithmetic is not true. There are 3600 sec in an hour, so 2264/3600 ≠ 1 1/2.

27. 120 1/4 lb

28. (a) $2S = 2\left(\frac{1}{2} + \frac{1}{2^2} + \ldots + \frac{1}{2^{64}}\right) = 1 + \frac{1}{2} + \frac{1}{2^2} + \ldots + \frac{1}{2^{63}}$

29. (a) $1\frac{49}{99}$

31. (a) $n(n+1) + \left(\frac{1}{2}\right)^2$

32. (a) (i) $\frac{^-4}{5}$; **(ii)** $\frac{^-26}{17}$; **(iii)** $\frac{^-14}{33}$ **(c)** $\frac{5}{4}$

33. (a) First 3, second 4, third 5. Guess 6. The guess is correct since

$$\left(1 + \frac{1}{1}\right)\left(1 + \frac{1}{2}\right)\left(1 + \frac{1}{3}\right)\left(1 + \frac{1}{4}\right)\left(1 + \frac{1}{5}\right) = 5\left(1 + \frac{1}{5}\right) = 6$$

(c) $n + 2$

Communication

34. Never less than *n*.

36. One estimate might be 5 1/2 because 1/7 of 35 is 5 and 1/7 of 42 is 6; and 39 is approximately halfway between 35 and 42. Another reasonable estimate might be found by finding 1/13 of 39 to be 3 and then using 2 of these as 6. 2/13 is reasonably close to 2/14 or 1/7.

38. The plumber needs 10 5/8 ft of pipe. It can be cut from the 12-ft section. With no waste in cutting, there is 1 3/8 ft of pipe left.

40. Mentally might be better if commutativity of multiplication is used.

41. (a) $2 \div 1 \neq 1 \div 2$ **(c)** There is no rational number *a* such that $2 \div a = a \div 2 = 2$.

42. Answers will vary about class use; 7 oz

Cooperative Learning

44. The answers here may vary depending on the size of bricks and the size of the joints. The measurements likely will be made in fractions of inches for the size of the joints. The size of the bricks may be measured in inches or, alternatively, in centimeters. In any event, all measurements are approximate and some rounding or estimation may occur.

Review Problems

45. (a) 17 min after the experiment started   **(b)** $^-108°C$

46. (a) $\dfrac{25}{16}$, or $1\dfrac{9}{16}$ **(b)** $\dfrac{25}{18}$ or $1\dfrac{7}{18}$ **(c)** $\dfrac{5}{216}$ **(d)** $\dfrac{259}{30}$ or

$8\dfrac{19}{30}$ **(e)** $\dfrac{37}{24}$ or $1\dfrac{13}{24}$ **(f)** $\dfrac{-39}{4}$ or $-9\dfrac{3}{4}$

47. 120 students

Chapter Review

1. (a)

(c)

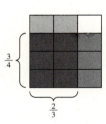

3. (a) $\dfrac{6}{7}$ **(c)** $\dfrac{0}{1}$ **(e)** $\dfrac{b}{1}$

4. (a) $=$ **(c)** $>$

5. (a) $^-3, \dfrac{1}{3}$ **(c)** $\dfrac{-5}{6}, \dfrac{6}{5}$

7. 17 pieces; $\dfrac{11}{6}$ yd left

8. (a) 15   **(c)** 4

9. $\dfrac{a}{b} \div \dfrac{c}{d} = x$ if, and only if, $\dfrac{a}{b} = \dfrac{c}{d} \cdot x.\ x = \dfrac{d}{c} \cdot \dfrac{a}{b}$ is the solution

of the equation because $\dfrac{c}{d} \cdot \left(\dfrac{d}{c} \cdot \dfrac{a}{b}\right) = \dfrac{a}{b}$.

11. 76/100, 78/100, but answers may vary.

13. $333\dfrac{1}{3}$ calories

14. 752 times

16. It is not reasonable to say that the University won 3/4 + 5/8 of its basketball games. One way for this to be reasonable is to make sure the men and women play the same number of games. That is not known.

18. You should show him that the given fraction could be written as an integer over an integer. In this case, the result is 8/9.

20. The minute hand points directly at a numeral only 1 min out of the entire hour, or 1/60 of an hour.

21. $^-12/10$ is greater than $^-11/9$ because $^-12/10 - (^-11/9)$ is a positive number.

CHAPTER 6

Ongoing Assessment 6-1

1. (e) $1/(^-5)^2$ or $1/5^2$ **(h)** $1/a$

2. (c) $(2/3)^9$

3. (e) False. $(2 + 3)^2 \neq 2^2 + 3^2$ **(f)** False.

$(2 + 3)^{-2} \neq \dfrac{1}{2^2} + \dfrac{1}{3^2}$

4. (e) 0   **(f)** 15

6. (b) $x \leq 1$ **(d)** $x \geq 1$

7. (b) $\left(\dfrac{3}{4}\right)^8$ **(d)** $\left(\dfrac{4}{5}\right)^{10}$

8. (b) $10^{10} \cdot \left(\dfrac{6}{5}\right)^2 = 1.44 \cdot 10^{10} = 14.4$ billion

9. (a) $\dfrac{3}{4}$ **(c)** $\dfrac{3}{128}$

11. (a) 32^{50}, since $32^{50} = (2^5)^{50} = 2^{250}$ and $4^{100} = (2^2)^{100} = 2^{200}$

14. (b) 3.008

16. (a), (b), (c), (d), (e), (f), and (h), can be represented as terminating decimals.

18. (a) 13.492, 13.49199, 13.4919, 13.49183

20. (b) $5.797 \cdot 10^6$

22. (c) $2 \cdot 10^2$

24. $100,000^3 = 1000^5$ and these are the greatest. To see this, write the numbers in scientific notation. Then it is easy to compare them.

$$100,000^3 = (1 \cdot 10^5)^3 = 1 \cdot 10^{15}$$
$$1000^5 = (1 \cdot 10^3)^5 = 1 \cdot 10^{15}$$
$$100,000^2 = (1 \cdot 10^5)^2 = 1 \cdot 10^{10}$$

Communication

26. Let $m = n$. Then $1 = \dfrac{a^m}{a^m} = a^{m-m} = a^0$.

27. If the exponent is an odd number, the result is negative. If the exponent is even, the result is positive. Explanations will vary. For example, let $a > 0$ and $n > 0$. Then $(^-a)^{-n} = \dfrac{1}{(^-a)^n}$

$= \dfrac{1}{[(^-1)a]^n} = \dfrac{1}{(^-1)^n a^n}$. If n is odd then $(^-1)^n = ^-1$, and if n is even then $(^-1)^n = 1$. Because $a^n > 0$, then $(^-1)^n a^n$ is negative if n is odd, and positive if n is even.

Ongoing Assessment 6-2

1. $231.24

4. $8.00

6. (a) 6390.955 cubic cm

11. No, the bank is over $7.74.

13. (a) 200   **(c)** 204

15. (c) 7/5   **(e)** $^-211/90$

18. (a) 0.45

21. $2.35 \cdot 10^{13}$

23. (a) $0.\overline{446355}$; 6

24. (d) $(1.001)^{10^6} = ((1.001)^{100,000})^{10} \doteq 1.2 \cdot 10^{434}$
26. (b) $619.75

Communication

31. Because $1/99 = .0101010101 \ldots$,
then $51/99 = 51(1/99) = 51(0.0101010101 \ldots)$
$= 0.5151515151 \ldots$. However, $x/99$ behaves differently if
$x > 99$.

Cooperative Learning

35. (a) $3^9 = 19683$

Review Problems

37. (a) True **(b)** False **(c)** False **(d)** False **(e)** False
(f) False
38. a. $x = 9$ is the greatest. **(b)** $x = -10$ is the greatest.
(c) $x = 3$ is the smallest. **(d)** $x = -5$ is the greatest.
39. (a) $(a^4)^5 = a^4 \cdot a^4 \cdot a^4 \cdot a^4 \cdot a^4 = a^{4+4+4+4+4} = a^{4 \cdot 5}$
(b) $(a^{-4})^{-5} = 1/(a^{-4})^5 = 1/a^{-4} \cdot a^{-4} \cdot a^{-4} \cdot a^{-4} \cdot a^{-4} = 1/a^{5(-4)}$
$= a^{-[5(-4)]} = a^{(-5)(-4)}$
40. (a) 49,736.5281 **(b)** 41,235.6789
41. $22,761.95

Ongoing Assessment 6-3

3. $0.\overline{9}, 0.9\overline{8}, 0.98\overline{8}, 0.9, 0.\overline{898}$
7. (b) False; $\overline{-\sqrt{2} + \sqrt{2}}$ **(d)** False; $\sqrt{2} - \sqrt{2}$
10. (a) R **(c)** Q
12. (c) $^-64$ **(e)** All real numbers greater than zero
13. 6.4 ft
14. (b) 2.007 sec
16. (b) $\sqrt{363} = 11\sqrt{3}$
17. (d) $^-3$
18. (b) $2, 2\sqrt[4]{1/2}, 2\sqrt[4]{1/4}, 2\sqrt[4]{1/8}, 1$
19. (a) 2^{10}
20. (a) $\sqrt{3}$
22. (c) $^-4/7$
25. (a) Rational **(b)** Rational
26. (b)

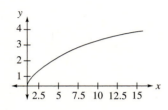

Communication

31. False: $\sqrt{64 + 36} \neq \sqrt{64} + \sqrt{36}$.
35. (d) Sometimes (if $a + b \geq 0$) **(e)** Sometimes (if $a \geq 0$)
38. (a) Yes; $z = (\sqrt{x} + \sqrt{y})^2$.

Review

43. (a) 21.6 lbs **(b)** 48 lbs
44. $22,761.95
45. (a) 418/25 **(b)** 3/1000 **(c)** $^-507/100$ **(d)** 123/1000
46. (a) $4.\overline{9}$ **(b)** $5.0\overline{9}$ **(c)** $0.4\overline{9}$
47. 3/12,500
48. $4.09, 4.09\overline{1}, 4.099, 4.0\overline{9}$
49. 8/33
50. (a) 208,000 **(b)** 0.00038
51. (a) $2^n + 2^{n+1} = 2^n + 2 \cdot 2^n = (1 + 2)2^n = 3 \cdot 2^n$
(b) $3^n + 3^{n+1} = 4 \cdot 3^n$
52. (a) False; $2^1 + 2^2 \neq 2^3$ **(b)** False; $1^2 \cdot 3^4 \neq 3^6$
(c) False; 0^{-13} is undefined. **(d)** True;
$(a^{-m})^{-n} = a^{(-m)(-n)} = a^{mn}$. Also $1/a^{-mn} = \dfrac{1}{1/a^{mn}} = 1 \cdot a^{mn}/1 = a^{mn}$.
53. (a) 800 parts per million **(b)** $C(n) = 25 \times 2^{n/5}$ parts per
million **(c)** Use guess and check strategy: The least n for
which $2^n > 400^5 = 1.024 \cdot 10^{13}$ is $n = 44$.

Chapter Review

1. (a) $1/2^{11}$ **(b)** $1/5^{20}$ **(c)** $(3/2)^{28}$ **(d)** 3^{18}
4. 8
7. (b) 307.6 **(d)** 300
10. (c) $3.24 \cdot 10^{-4}$
13. (a) $11\sqrt{2}$ **(d)** $3\sqrt[3]{6}$
14. (b) Approximately $1.62 \cdot 10^{13}$
15. (c) The least integer is 10. **(d)** The greatest integer is 9.
16. $1.451\overline{9}, 1.45\overline{19}, 1.4\overline{519}, 1.4519, 0.134\overline{01}, 0.13401, 0.134$
17. (d) $10\sqrt[5]{10}, 10\sqrt[5]{100}, 10\sqrt[5]{1000}, 10\sqrt[5]{10,000}$

CHAPTER 7

Ongoing Assessment 7-1

1. (b) $20 + 25x$ **(c)** $175d$ **(d)** $3x + 3$
2. (a) $P = 0.04E$ **(c)** 6 lbs
3. (b) $d = 1.647g$
4. (a) 220
7. (b) $C = K - 273.15$
8. (c) $P = 20 + 10t$ **(e)** $C = 30 + 0.35m$
9. (i) $x = \dfrac{1234}{224} \doteq 5.51$ **(l)** $x \leq 1$
10. (c) $x \geq \sqrt{7}$ or $x \leq {}^-\sqrt{7}$ **(e)** $x = 2.\overline{6}$ or $\dfrac{8}{3}$.
11. (c) $x = {}^-28$ **(d)** $x = {}^-56/5$ **(e)** $x = 13$
13. If x is any number, then the teacher's instructions were
$\left(\dfrac{3x + 49}{7} - 7\right) \div 3$. This expression is equivalent to
$\left(\dfrac{3x + 49}{7} - 7\right) \div 3 = \dfrac{3x}{7} \cdot \dfrac{1}{3} = \dfrac{x}{7}$. Thus to tell the value of x,
the teacher multiplies the answer $\dfrac{x}{7}$ by 7.

Communication

16. Both are correct. For the first student, x is the first of the three consecutive integers. The second chose x to be the second of the three consecutive integers.
19. Answers vary for example: $x + 3 > x + 2$, $x^2 + 1 > 0$, $(x + 1)^2 \geq 0$

Ongoing Assessment 7-2

1. $^-5$
3. Factory A produces 2800 cars per day, Factory B 1400 cars per day, and Factory C 3100 cars per day.
5. 78, 79, 80
8. Eldest, $30,000; middle, $24,000; youngest, $10,000
10. 400   **12.** 9600
14. (b) $90,000   **16.** 246
18. Work backwards: 600 students got a C. This is three fourths of the number of students who received a B or a C. We solve $600 = (3/4)x$ to see that $x = 800$ students received either a B or a C. This is four fifths of the overall total. So we solve $800 = (4/5)y$ to see there are $y = 1000$ students in the school.
19. In the first experiment, the total temperature change in 5 min was $28 - (^-12) = 40$ degrees. Thus the rate of change is 8 degrees per minute. The temperature of the reaction is given by $T_1 = 28 - 8t$, where t is the number of minutes since the reaction began. In the second experiment, the temperature is given by $T_2 = ^-57 - 3t$. Solve $28 - 8t = ^-57 - 3t$: $t = 17$ min. The common temperature was $^-108°C$.

Communication

21. No. A solution is $x = 0$. (One can divide by x only under the stipulation that $x \neq 0$.)

Review Problems

26. (a) $6x$ **(b)** $10 + 2(t - 1)$ or $2t + 8$
27. (a) $x = 1$ **(b)** $x > \dfrac{1}{6}$ **(c)** x is any real number (the solution set is R).

Ongoing Assessment 7-3

2. For every x, the point on $y = mx + 3$ is 3 units higher than the point on $y = x$. Consequently the graph of $y = mx + 3$ contains the point $(0, 3)$, and is parallel to the line $y = mx$. Similarly the graph of $y = mx - 3$ contains the point $(0, ^-3)$ and is parallel to $y = mx$.

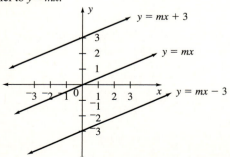

3. (d)   **(e)**

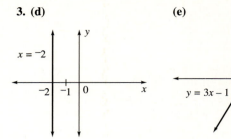

6. (c) $y = ^-4x/3 + 4$ **(d)** $y = (3/4)x + 7/4$
7. (a) $y = ^-x - 1$ **(b)** $y = (1/2)x$ **(d)** $x = 2$
8. Answers vary.
9. (a) $x = ^-2$; y is any real number.
11. (b) $y = ^-2$
13. (a) Answers vary. One possible answer is $y = 1.97x + 6.13$.
(b) Approximately 203.1.

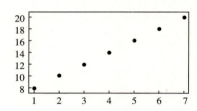

15. (a) $(2, 5)$, unique solution   **(f)** $(4/11, 1/11)$; unique solution
17. 4000 gal of gasoline and 1000 gal of kerosene
18. (a) $2000   **(b)** 6% annual interest or 5% per month
19. 17 quarters, 10 dimes

Communication

24. Lines with undefined slopes are vertical lines and hence parallel.

Review Problems

30. 25 yr
31. 253, 255, 257, 259
32. 110 ft × 330 ft

Ongoing Assessment 7-4

2. (a) 30   **(b)** $^-3\dfrac{1}{3}$
4. 2469
6. 270 mi
8. 72 min for 30 in.
10. 500 ft × 900 ft
12. $77 and $99
14. (a) 5/7
16. 8 days
17. (a) 27

19. 312 lbs

20. (a) $2:5$. Because the ratio is $2:3$, there are $2x$ boys and $3x$ girls; hence, the ratio of boys to all students is $2x/(2x + 3x) = 2/5$.

21. (a) 2/3 tsp mustard seeds, 1 c scallions, $2\frac{1}{6}$ c beans

(b) 2/3 tsp mustard seeds, 2 c tomato sauce, $2\frac{1}{6}$ c beans

(c) 7/13 tsp mustard seeds, $1\frac{8}{13}$ c tomato sauce, $\frac{21}{26}$ c scallions

23. (a) 1/3 **(b)** 10 lb **(c)** $A = 7.5$, $B = 2.5$ lbs

25. 74.6 cm

27. 3 ft

28. (b) $WL = 10$ **(c)** Inverse

29. (a) (i) $d = 15t$ **(ii)** direct **(iii)**

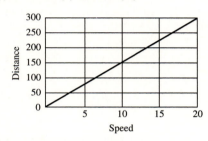

(d) (i) $W = 100 - L$ **(ii)** neither **(iii)**

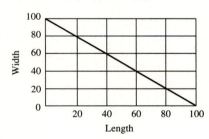

30. (b) directly
(e) neither

31. (b) Let $\dfrac{a}{b} = \dfrac{c}{d} = \dfrac{e}{f} = r$. Then $a = br$, $c = dr$, and $e = fr$. So $a + c + e = br + dr + fr$. Thus $a + c + e = r(b + d + f)$, $r = \dfrac{a + c + e}{b + d + f}$.

Communication

33. (a) 40/700 or 4/70 or 2/35 **(c)** For the first set, $\dfrac{\text{footprint length}}{\text{thighbone length}} = \dfrac{40}{100} = \dfrac{20}{50}$, i.e., a 50 cm thighbone would correspond to a 20 cm footprint. Thus it is not likely that the 50 cm thighbone is from the animal which left the 30 cm footprint. $\left(\text{Notice that } \dfrac{20}{50} \neq \dfrac{30}{50}.\right)$

35. The ratio between the mass of the gold in the ring and the mass of the ring is 18/24. If x is the number of ounces of pure gold in the ring that weighs 0.4 oz we have $18/24 = x/0.4$.

Hence $x = (18 \cdot 0.4)/24$ or 0.3 oz. Consequently the price of the gold in the ring is $0.3 \cdot \$300$ or \$90.

37. (b) Yes, because $d = t/c = (1/c) \cdot t$ and $1/c$ is a constant.

40. (a) 57.6 lb/in.^{2}

Review Problems

43. The sum is $x + (x + 2) + (x + 4) = 3x + 6$, and $(3x + 6 - 6)/3 = x$.

44. (a) $x = 0$ **(b)** $x = 15.5$ **(c)** $x = -0.019$ **(d)** 4
(e) $x < 6/5$ **(f)** $x \geq \sqrt{2}$, or $x \leq {}^{-}\sqrt{2}$

Ongoing Assessment 7-5

1. (b) 3.2% **(g)** 12.5% **(l)** 2.5%
2. (f) 1.25 **(h)** 0.0025
5. (a) 2.04 **(d)** 3.43 **(f)** 40
6. 63 boxes
8. \$14,500
10. 20%
12. 18.4%
14. 100%
16. \$5.10
18. \$336
20. \$3200
22. Approximately 23.5%.
23. \$10.37 per hour
25. \$440
27. Approximately \$9207.58
29. (a) 4% **(b)** 32% **(c)** 64%
33. 20%
34. 20%
36. (a) 4% **(b) (i)** 44 **(ii)** 8.8%
37. \$82,644.63
39. \$399,375

Communication

41. Let x be the amount invested. The first stock option will yield $(1.15x) \cdot 0.85$ after two years. The second stock will yield $(0.85x) \cdot 1.15$. Because each yield equals $(1.15 \cdot 0.85)x$ the investments are equally good.

Review Problems

46. Approximately 873 sq ft
47. They are the same.
48. Boys: approximately 42.9%; girls: approximately 57.1%.

Ongoing Assessment 7-6

2. \$5,460.00
3. \$24.45
6. \$64,800
8. \$1944
10. Approximately \$2.53.
12. Approximately \$3592.89.

14. Approximately $7.026762 \cdot 10^8$.

16. $81,628.83

18. $10,935

Communication

19. Let a be the original value of the house. Because it depreciates 10% each year for the first three years, using compound depreciation the price after 3 years will be $a(1 - 0.10)^3$ or $a \cdot 0.9^3$. Because of compound appreciation, after another 3 years the value of the house will be $a(0.9^3) \cdot 1.1^3$ or $a(0.9^3 \cdot 1.1^3)$, which equals approximately $a \cdot 0.9703$. Because $a \cdot 0.9703 < a$, the value of the house decreased after 6 years.

Open-ended

22. (b) Let P be the initial amount which depreciates at the rate r per period (compound depreciation). Let A be the amount at the end of the n-th period. If the amount at the beginning of any period is x, then because of depreciation, at the end of that period the new amount is $x - xr = x(1 - r)$. Thus to find the amount at the end of any period, we need only to multiply the amount at the beginning of the period (that is the end of the previous period) by $1 - r$. Because the amount at the end of the first period is $P(1 - r)$, the amounts at the end of each period form the following geometric sequence: $P(1 - r)$, $P(1 - r)^2$, $P(1 - r)^3$, ..., $P(1 - r)^n$. Hence $A = P(1 - r)^n$.

Chapter Review

1. (c) In cents, $C = 0.6(0.14t) = 0.084t$ **(e)** $V = (88/100)m$

3. 35 1-kg packages, 115 2-kg packages

6. 42 gal

7. $16/9$ oz $= 1.\overline{7}$ oz.

8. (a) 6 mi   **(b)** 5.2 mi

9. 560 fish

12. Hoover, 15,957,537; Roosevelt, 22,521,525

13. (b) $x = {}^-3$

14. (a) $x = 4.2$, $y = {}^-0.6$ **(b)** $x = \dfrac{10}{9}$, $y = \dfrac{4}{3}$ **(c)** There is no solution because the lines are parallel.

15. (b) 192   **(d)** 20%

17. (a) 0.60   **(b)** $0.00\overline{6}$

19. $3.\overline{3}\%$

21. $5750

23. $80

24. $15,000

CHAPTER 8

Ongoing Assessment 8-1

2. (a) $\{0, 1, 2, 3, 4, 5, 6, 7, 8, 9\}$ **(c)** $\{1, 3, 5, 7, 9\}$

3. (a) 3/8   **(c)** 4/8, or 1/2   **(e)** 0   **(g)** 1/8

4. (a) 26/52, or 1/2   **(c)** 28/52, or 7/13   **(e)** 48/52, or 12/13   **(g)** 3/52

5. (a) 4/12, or 1/3   **(c)** 0

7. 0.8

8. (a) 1/6

9. (a) 8/36, or 2/9   **(c)** 24/36, or 2/3   **(e)** 0   **(g)** 10 times

11. (a) 18/38, or 9/19   **(c)** 26/38, or 13/19

13. (a) No   **(c)** Yes   **(e)** No   **(g)** No

15. (a) 2/4, or 1/2   **(c)** 3/4

16. 350/1380, or 35/138

18. (a) 20/52, or 5/13   **(c)** 0

19. The answers may vary depending on how the 6, 7, and 9 are formed. The following answers are based on a Casio digital watch: **(b)** 8/10   **(d)** 10/10, or 1

20. (a) The probability of students' taking algebra or chemistry   **(c)** This represents 1 minus the probability of a student's taking chemistry or the probability of a student's not taking chemistry.

21. 0.7

22. (a) 45/80, or 9/16   **(c)** 60/80, or 3/4

Communication

24. Bobbie's reasoning is not correct unless her theoretical probability of making a basket is really 1/2. The outcomes of making a basket or missing it are probably not equally likely, so this definition does not apply. To calculate her experimental probability of making a free throw, divide the number of shots made by the number attempted.

25. Joe's conjecture is incorrect. Each of the numbers 1 through 4 has probability 1/4 of occurring because each angle where the arrow is located measures 90 degrees and the spinner has the same chance of landing in any of the regions.

Open-ended

29. Answers vary. For example, event A is an impossible event, such as rolling a 10 on a single roll of a standard die. Event B has low probability, such as the chance of rain being 20%. Event C is around 0.5, so this might be something like obtaining a head when tossing a fair coin. Event D has a high probability of happening, but it is not certain; for example, tossing a number less than 6 on a toss of a standard die. Event E has probability 1, so it has to happen; for example, tossing either head or a tail on the toss of a fair coin. Event F has probability greater than 1. This cannot happen, so no event is possible.

Cooperative Learning

30. This will depend on the number of each color cube in the bag. The experimental probability of drawing each color can be obtained by finding the number of times a color is drawn

and dividing this number by 50. We can then use this
probability to guess the number of cubes of each color. For
example, if 20/50 of the draws were red, then a guess for the
number of red is (20/50)(8) = 3.2, or 3.
31. (b) 1 and 2 and then 0 and 3.

Ongoing Assessment 8-2

1. (a)

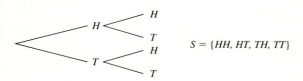

$S = \{HH, HT, TH, TT\}$

2. (a) {(1, 1), (1, 2), (1, 3), (2, 1), (2, 2), (2, 3)}   **(c)** {(1, 2),
(2, 1), (2, 2), (2,3)}
3. (a) 1/216
4. (a) 1/24   **(c)** 1/84
6. (a) Box 1, with probability 1/3 (box 2 has probability 1/5)
7. (a) 64/75
9. (a) 1/5   **(c)** 11/15
11. 1/16
12. (a) 1/4   **(c)** 1/8
13. (a) 8/20, or 2/5
14. 2/16, or 1/8
15. (a) 1/320   **(c)** 0
16. 1/32
18. 1/256
20. (a) 1/25   **(c)** 16/25
21. (a) 100 sq units   **(c)** 1/625
22. 0.7
25. 2/5
26. 25/30, or 5/6
28. 69/3000, or 23/1000
29. Billie-Bobby-Billie because the probability of winning two
in a row is greater this way. Note, it does not say win two out
of three.

Communication

31. If the die is fair, the probability that Jim will roll a 3 on the
next roll is 1/6, which is the same probability of rolling any
one of the other numbers. The results of the first 3 rolls should
have no effect on the next roll.

Cooperative Learning

39. (a) The game is not fair. You should choose spinner *A*.

Review Problems

40. (a) v   **(b)** iii   **(c)** ii   **(d)** i   **(e)** iv
41. (a) 1/30   **(b)** 0   **(c)** 19/30

Ongoing Assessment 8-3

1. Answers vary. For example, a black card might represent
the birth of a boy and a red card might represent the birth of a
girl. Choose a card to represent a birth.
2. (a) Answers vary. For example, you could use a random-
digit table. The numbers 1 through 9 could represent rain and 0
could represent no rain.   **(c)** Approximately 0.52
4. (a) Let 1, 2, 3, 4, 5, and 6 represent the numbers of the
die. Ignore the numbers 0, 7, 8, and 9.   **(c)** Represent red by
the numbers 0, 1, 2, 3, and 4; green by the numbers 5, 6, and 7;
yellow by the number 8; and white by the number 9.
6. To simulate Monday, let the digits 1 through 8 represent
rain and 0 and 9 represent no rain. If rain occurred on Monday,
repeat the same process for Tuesday. If it did not rain on
Monday, let the digits 1 through 7 represent rain and 0, 8, and
9 represent dry. Repeat a similar process for the rest of the
week.
7. Answers may vary. For example, mark off blocks of 2
digits and let the digits 00, 01, 02, . . . , 13, 14 represent
contracting the disease and 15 to 99 represent no disease. Mark
off blocks of 6 digits to represent the 3 children. If at least one
of the numbers is in the range 00 to 14, then this represents a
child in the 3-child family having strep.
9. 1200 fish
10. (a) 7
15. Answers may vary. For example, use a random-digit table.
Let the digits 1–8 represent a win and the digits 0 and 9
represent losses. Mark off blocks of 3. If only the digits 1–8
appear, then this represents 3 wins in a row.
16. Let the 10 ducks be represented by the digits 0, 1, 2,
3, . . . , 8, 9. Then pick a starting point in the table and mark
off 10 digits to simulate at which ducks the hunters shoot.
Count how many of the digits 0 through 9 are not in the
10 digits; this represents the ducks that escaped. Do this
experiment many times and take the average to determine an
answer. See how close your simulation comes to 3.49 ducks.

Cooperative Learning

17. (d) The probability of 2 boys and 2 girls is 6/16, or 3/8.
18. (d) $(1/2)^{10} = 1/1024$

Review Problems

21. No, you will win about 6/16, or 3/8, of the games.
22. (a) 1/4   **(b)** 1/52   **(c)** 48/52, or 12/13   **(d)** 3/4
(e) 1/2   **(f)** 1/52   **(g)** 16/52, or 4/13   **(h)** 1
23. (a) 15/19   **(b)** 56/361   **(c)** 28/171

Ongoing Assessment 8-4

1. (a) 12 to 40, or 3 to 10
3. 15 to 1
4. (a) 1/2   **(c)** 1023 to 1

6. 1 to 1

7. 4 to 6, or 2 to 3

9. 1/27

10. 3 hr

11. $E = 1/6 (10) + 5/6 (^-2) = 10/6 + (^-10/6) = 0$. Therefore, if you play a long time, you should come out about even.

12. (a) 1/38   **(c)** $^-2/38$, or $^-1/19$ dollars

14. $10,000

15. (a) Because Al's probability of winning at this point was 3/4 and Betsy's was 1/4, Al should get $75 and Betsy should get $25.   **(b)** 3 to 1

17. No

Communication

18. Odds are determined from probabilities. The *odds in favor* of an event, E, are determined by $P(E)/P(\overline{E})$. The *odds against* an event are determined by $P(\overline{E})/P(E)$.

19. Don't believe it. If the odds of getting AIDS are 68,000 to 1, then the probability of getting AIDS is 68,000/68,001. Therefore the probability of getting AIDS is almost certain. The article should have talked about the odds against getting AIDS.

Review Problems

23. (a) {1, 2, 3, 4}   **(b)** {Red, Blue}   **(c)** {(1, Red), (1, Blue), (2, Red), (2, Blue), (3, Red), (3, Blue), (4, Red), (4, Blue)}   **(d)** {(Blue, 1), (Blue, 2), (Blue, 3), (Blue, 4), (Blue 5), (Blue, 6), (Red, 1), (Red, 2), (Red, 3), (Red, 4), (Red, 5), (Red, 6)}   **(e)** {(1, 1), (1, 2), (1, 3), (1, 4), (2, 1), (2, 2), (2, 3), (2, 4), (3, 1), (3, 2), (3, 3), (3, 4), (4, 1), (4, 2), (4, 3), (4, 4)}   **(f)** {(Red, Red), (Red, Blue), (Blue, Red), (Blue, Blue)}

24. The Blue section must have 300°; the Red has 60 °.

25. 25/676

Ongoing Assessment 8-5

2. 224

3. 32

5. 1352 with 3-letter call letters; 35,152 with 4-letter call letters

7. (a) True   **(c)** False   **(e)** True   **(g)** True

9. 15

10. (a) 12   **(c)** 3360   **(e)** 3780

11. (a) 24,360

13. 1/120

15. 1260

16. (a) 6

18. (a) 1/13

19. 2,598,960 different 5-card hands (order within the hand is not important)

21. 1/25,827,165

23. 13,440/59,049, or approximately 0.228

24. 3840

Communication

25. Answers vary. For example, the Fundamental Counting Principle says that to find the number of ways of making several decisions in a row, multiply the number of choices that can be made for each decision. The Principle can be used to find the number of permutations. A permutation is an arrangement of things in a definite order. A combination is a selection of things in which the order is not important. We could find the number of combinations by using the Principle and then dividing by the number of ways in which the things can be arranged.

Open-ended

28. (a) 10^6, or 1,000,000

Cooperative Learning

29. (c) The sums of the numbers in the rows are 1, 2, 4, 8, 16, 32, 64. The sum in the tenth row is $2^{10} = 1024$.   **(d)** Yes, a similar relationship holds in all the rows for the entries in Pascal's triangle.

Review Problems

30. (a) 396/2652, or 33/221   **(b)** 1352/2652, or 26/51

31. 3/36, or 1/12

32. $E = \$0$, so the game is fair.

Chapter Review

1. (a) {Monday, Tuesday, Wednesday, Thursday, Friday, Saturday, Sunday}   **(c)** 2/7

2. There's at least 1 other colored bean besides red and blue. There are 800 blue ones and 125 red ones.

3. (a) Approximately 0.501   **(c)** 34,226,731 to 34,108,157

4. (a) 5/12   **(c)** 5/12   **(e)** 0

5. (a) 13/52, or 1/4   **(c)** 22/52, or 11/26

6. (a) 64/729

7. 6/25

8. 14/80, or 7/40

9. 7/45

10. 4 to 48, or 1 to 12

12. 3/8

13. $.30

15. 900

17. 5040

18. 2/20, or 1/10

19. (a) $5 \cdot 4 \cdot 3$, or 60   **(c)** 1/60

20. 15/36

22. 0.027

23. 63/80

24. (a) Answers vary.

25. (a) 1/8   **(c)** 1/16

26. 8/20, or 2/5

CHAPTER 9

Ongoing Assessment 9-1

2. (a) 225 million   **(c)** 550 million

3.

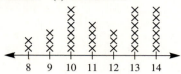

4. (a) 72, 74, 81, 81, 82, 85, 87, 88, 92, 94, 97, 98, 103, 123, 125   **(c)** 125 lbs

5.

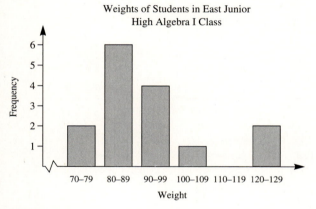

7. (b) 50 cm

8. (a)

```
Ages of HKM Employees
6 | 332
5 | 8224
4 | 8561511
3 | 474224          3 | 4 represents
2 | 14333617301365396    34 yr old
1 | 898
```

(c) 20

9. (a) Approximately 3800 km

11.

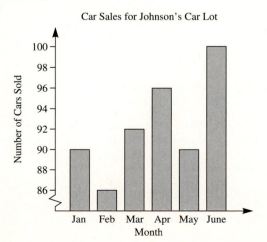

13. (b)

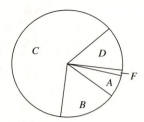

Course Grades for Elementary Teachers

14. (b)

Fall Textbook Costs

Classes	Tally	Frequency
$15–19	I	1
$20–24	II	2
$25–29		0
$30–34	II	2
$35–39	IIIII	5
$40–44	IIII	4
$45–49	III	3
$50–54	IIII	4
$55–59	I	1
$60–64	III	3
		25

(c)-(d) Frequency polygon and histogram on same graph.

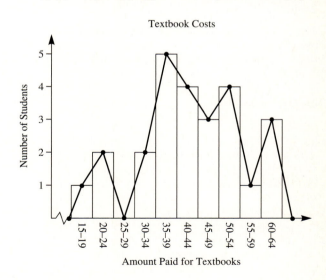

15. (a) Chicken   **(c)** Cheetah
16. (a) Women   **(c)** Approximately 7.5 yr
17. (a) Approximately $8400   **(c)** Approximately $7000
18. (a) Asia   **(c)** It is about $\frac{2}{3}$ as large.   **(e)** 5:16

19. (a)

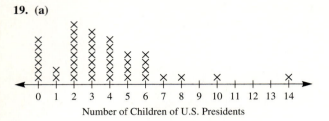

Number of Children of U.S. Presidents

(c) 2

20. (b) The number of deaths in 1992 is significantly greater than the number of deaths in each age category in 1985.

Communication

21. Answers may vary. However, a circle graph would be more appropriate when emphasizing proportions is desired.

23. Answers may vary. However, a stem-and-leaf plot is more informative when exact data are needed.

24. Answers may vary. The line graph is more helpful, since we can approximate the point midway between 8:00 A.M. and 12:00 noon and then draw a vertical line upward until it hits the line graph. An approximation for the 10:00 A.M. temperature can be obtained from the vertical line.

Open-ended

26. Answers may vary. The federal budget is usually depicted as a circle graph. This is probably to show the proportion of total budget each category has for funding.

Cooperative Learning

29. Answers will vary. Students may not be able to make definitive decisions other than for their class. You may want to check in department stores to see if they can determine the desired size.

Ongoing Assessment 9-2

1. (a) Mean = 6.625, median = 7.5, mode = 8
(c) Mean $\doteq$ 19.9, median = 18, modes = 18 and 22
(e) Mean = 5.8$\overline{3}$, median = 5, mode = 5
2. (a) The mean, median, and mode are all 80.
3. 1500
5. 78.$\overline{3}$
6. (a) $\overline{x}$ = 18.4 yr   **(c)** 28.4 yr
8. Approximately 2.59
10. $1880
11. (a) $41,275   **(c)** $38,000
12. (a) Balance beam: Olga (9.575); uneven bars: Lisa (9.85); Floor: Lisa (9.925)
14. 30 mph
16. 58 yr old
17. (a) A   **(c)** C
19. (a) $s = 0$

20. (a) Approximately 76.8   **(c)** 71   **(e)** Approximately 12.5
22. 96, 90, and 90
24.

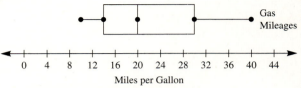

Miles per Gallon

25. (a) A: $25, B: $50   **(c)** $80 at B
27. (a)

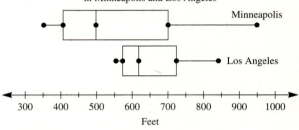

Height of 10 Tallest Buildings in Minneapolis and Los Angeles

(b) There are no outliers.
28. (a) (i) Increase by $1000   (ii) Increase by $1000
(iii) Increase by $1000   (iv) Increase by $1000   (v) Stays the same
29. (a) (i) $\overline{x}$ = 5, median = 5   (ii) $\overline{x}$ = 100, median = 100
(iii) $\overline{x}$ = 307, median = 307
30. One might use the mode. If you collect the data of all states and consider the most common age at which a person could get a license, that would be the mode. Both the mean and median might be decimals, and no state would worry about a decimal age for a driver's license.
32. The government probably uses the mean of data collected over a period of time.

Communication

33. (a) Mean: 90; median: 90; mode: 90   **(c)** Mean
35. No. To find the average speed, we divide the distance traveled by the time it takes to drive it. The first part of the trip took $\frac{5}{30}$, or $\frac{1}{6}$, hr. The second part of the trip took $\frac{5}{50}$, or $\frac{1}{10}$, hr.

Therefore, to find the average speed, we compute $\dfrac{10}{\dfrac{1}{6} + \dfrac{1}{10}}$ to obtain 37.5 mph.

36. The mean increases by the number that has been added. The standard deviation remains the same.

Open-ended

38. Answers will vary depending on student choice. Probably a good choice might be a box plot with the 2 sets of data depicted so that comparisons could be easily seen.

Cooperative Learning

40. Answers will vary. To do this problem, the class will have to be divided in such a way that the choices of newspapers do not overlap. A teacher may want to discuss how one might do a random sampling of newspapers.

Review Problems

41. Most of the equipment probably would be exercise walking equipment for females and both swimming and fishing equipment for males. Arguments could be made for other types of equipment as well.
42. (a) Education: 191°; General Fund: 97°; Cities: 25°; Senior Citizen Programs: 25°; Other 25°   **(b)** Students should recognize that the graph depicts more than 100% of the distribution of state lottery proceeds.
43. (a) Everest, approximately 8500 m   **(b)** Aconcagua, Everest, McKinley
44. (a)

History Test Scores

5	5
6	48
7	2334679
8	0255567889
9	00346

7 | 2 represents a score of 72

(b)

History Test Scores

Class	Tally	Frequency
55–59	I	1
60–64	I	1
65–69	I	1
70–74	IIII	4
75–79	III	3
80–84	II	2
85–89	IIII III	8
90–94	IIII	4
95–99	I	1

(c)

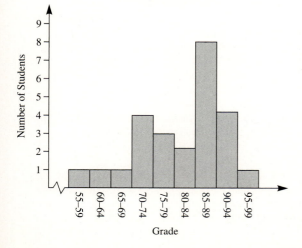

(d)

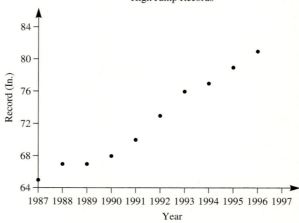

(e) Approximately 115°

Ongoing Assessment 9-3

1. (a) 1020   **(c)** 1.5, so 1 or 2 people
3. 0.68
4. (a) Verbal, 0.6; quantitative, 0.8$\overline{3}$; logical reasoning, 1
5. 16%
6. (a) 47.5%
7. (a) 1.07%   **(c)** 2.27%
8. 1.4%
10. 8
12. Between 60.5 in. and 70.5 in.
14. 1600
15. (a)

(b) Positive
16. (a) Negative   **(c)** 22 yr old

Communication

18. Answers may vary. For example, in reality the curve is not smooth. If we are showing student scores, then the graph should be a series of points, not a continuous curve.
19. Answers may vary. For example, the Central Limit Theorem may be interpreted as follows: As the size of the data increases, the closer the normal curve comes to approximating the data.

Open-ended

20. (a) Two different normal curves depicting scores on a nationally standardized test have the same mean, but one test has twice as many students taking it as the other. Then on the same graph, the height of the normal curve for the test with the most students taking it should be greater than the height of the curve for the other test.   **(c)** The percents under the curves will not change, but the standard deviations in the two curves will not be placed exactly in the same places.

Cooperative Learning

22. This problem is a take-off on the problem of deciding from a sample of writing what letter is used most in the English language. This one is somewhat easier than that one, however. One thing that might be observed is that individual students may have strange data, but the entire collection should be more typical of the population.

Review Problems

23. (a) 74.17   **(b) 75**   **(c)** 65   **(d)** 237.97   **(e)** 15.43
24. 27.74
25. 76.$\overline{6}$
26.

```
          Men's Olympic
          100-m Run Times
            1896–1964
       10 | 023334568888
       11 | 00
       12 | 0            10 | 0 represents
                            10.0 sec
```

27.

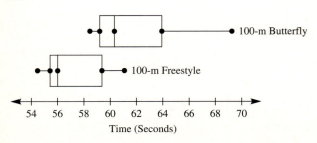

Time (Seconds)

From examining the box plot, we can see that the times on the 100-m butterfly are much greater (relatively speaking) than are the times on the 100-m freestyle.

Ongoing Assessment 9-4

1. Answers may vary for all parts of this question.   **(a)** A question to ask is whether the car is running. If it is not, then there is no sound and the car would be quieter.   **(c)** 11% more fruit solids than 10% is very little.   **(e)** "Up to" is very indefinite and the conditions under which the 30 was obtained.   **(g)** How many dentists responded?   **(i)** A question to ask is whether there is another airline flying to the city.
3. She could have taken a different number of quizzes during the first part of the quarter than in the second.
4. When the radius of a circle is doubled, the area is quadrupled, which is misleading, since the population has only doubled.
5. The horizontal axis does not have uniformly-sized intervals and both the horizontal axis and the graph are not labeled.
7. It could very well be that most of the pickups sold in the last 10 yr were actually sold during the last 2 yr. Then most of the pickups have been on the road for only 2 yr. Therefore the given information would not imply that the average life of a pickup is around 10 yr.
9. The three-dimensional drawing distorts the graph. The result of doubling the radius and the height of the can is to increase the volume by a factor of 8.
10. There are no labels so that we can compare actual sales. Also, there is no scale on the vertical axis.
12. (a) False. Prices vary only by $30.   **(c)** True
13. (a) This bar graph could have perhaps 20 accidents as the point where the scale starts. Then 38 in 1996 would appear to be almost double the 24 of 1988, when in fact it is only 58% higher.
14. Answers may vary, but one such would be 5, 5, 5, 5, 5, 5, 100, 100. The mean would be 28.75 and the median 5.
15. You could not automatically conclude correctly that the population of the coastal west has increased since 1970. However, based on the westward movement of the mean center of population, there would be a strong suspicion that that was the case.
17. Answers will vary. One such line has equation $y = ^-0.017x + 44.164$.
(a) If we use the linear regression, the expectation in 1992 is 10.3. That is truly unexpected from looking at the data.
(c) We use the previous equation to see that the expectation is $^-6.77$ sec in 2996.
19. A student would need to know the highest possible score that a person could make. Also the scores of other students would be important.
21. You could report the mode of a selected number of spots if enough spots were chosen at random. It is also possible that

the mode would not exist. A median might be misleading depending on the number of data points given. Also the mean would not be sufficient. A report of the mean, median, and standard deviation would be the most helpful of all "averages" studied.

23. Answers may vary. A sample size is needed. One way to pick a random sample of adults in the town is to use the telephone book or a voter registration list. These methods will not result in a list of all adults in the town, but this information is probably the most accessible sets of data. To pick the sample, one might roll a die and consider the number *n* that appears on it. Then starting at some point in the adult list, choose every *n*th person after the start on the list.

25. Answer may vary. The writers of the *Standards* may have based the statement only on their own interactions with students. They may also have observed magazines and television show ratings, for example.

Chapter Review

1. If the average is 2.41 children, then the mean is being used. If the average is 2.5, then the mean or the median might have been used.

3. (a) Mean = 30, median = 30, mode = 10

5. (a)

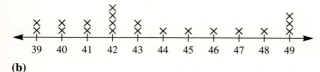

Miss Rider's Class
Masses in Kilograms

(b)

Miss Rider's Class
Masses in Kilograms

```
3 | 99
4 | 001122223345678999      4 | 0 represents
                                  40 kg
```

(c)

Miss Rider's Class
Masses in Kilograms

Mass	Tally	Frequency
39	II	2
40	II	2
41	II	2
42	IIII	4
43	II	2
44	I	1
45	I	1
46	I	1
47	I	1
48	I	1
49	III	3
		20

(d)

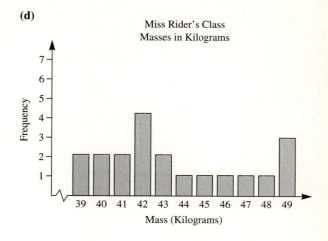

Miss Rider's Class
Masses in Kilograms

6. (a)

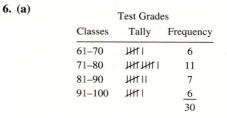

Test Grades

Classes	Tally	Frequency
61–70	ⅢⅢ I	6
71–80	ⅢⅢ ⅢⅢ I	11
81–90	ⅢⅢ II	7
91–100	ⅢⅢ I	6
		30

(b) and **(c)** are on the same graph.

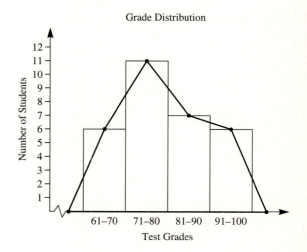

Grade Distribution

8. The widths of the bars are not uniform and the graph has no title.

9. $2840

11. (a)

Life Expectancies
of Males and Females

Females		Males
	67	1446
	68	28
	69	156
	70	0049
	71	0223458
	72	
	73	
7	74	
9310	75	
86	76	
88532	77	
54332211	78	
7 |74| represents	79	|67| 1 represents
74.7 years old		67.1 years old

(b)

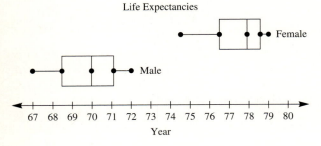

Life Expectancies

67 68 69 70 71 72 73 74 75 76 77 78 79 80
Year

12. Larry was correct because his average was $3.2\overline{6}$, while Marc's was $2.7\overline{3}$.

13. (a) 360 **(c)** 350

14. (a) 67

(c)

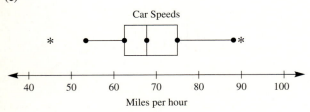

Car Speeds

40   50   60   70   80   90   100
Miles per hour

(e) 30%

15. (a) 25 **(c)** 0.16

17. $1.\overline{6}$

19. (a) Positive **(c)** 67 **(e)** 50

22. Answers will vary. If your state is one of the darkest regions, then you would probably want to use this type of graph because it shows that your state has greater than 105% of the national average for hourly earnings.

23. One way to obtain the line labeled "Total" is to sum the "y-values" for corresponding points on the other graphs and to plot the sum as the y-value on the "Total" line.

24. The advertisement is not reasonable. One would expect the snow to be okay for skiing but with reports like those given, there is little information about the snow in the middle of the mountain. If the weather is cold enough for 23 in. of snow at the bottom of a hill, one would expect there to be snow all the way to the top. However, if the bottom and the top of the hill are shaded, then there could be much variation if a part of the hill was sunny.

CHAPTER 10

Ongoing Assessment 10-1

2. (a) For example: $\overleftrightarrow{BC}$ and $\overleftrightarrow{DH}$ or $\overleftrightarrow{AE}$ and $\overleftrightarrow{BD}$ **(e)** Point H

4. 20 pairs

6. (a) 110° **(d)** 130°

8. (a) i. 41°31′10″ **(b) i.** 54′

9. (b) 52° 30′

10. 2:27

12. (c) 10

16. $b, d, e,$ and g

Communication

21. (a) No. If $\angle BCD$ were a right angle, then both $\overleftrightarrow{BD}$ and $\overleftrightarrow{BC}$ would be perpendicular to $\overleftrightarrow{DC}$ and thus be parallel.

Cooperative Learning

24.

Points	Lines	Planes
3	3	1
4	6	4
5	10	10
n	$\dfrac{n(n-1)}{2}$	$\dfrac{n(n-1)(n-2)}{6}$

Ongoing Assessment 10-2

1. (a) 1, 2, 5, 6, 7, 8, 10 **(b)** 1, 6, 7, 8 **(c)** 1, 2, 5, 6, 7, 8
(d) 1, 6, 7, 8 **(e)** 6, 7 **(f)** 1, 8

4. A concave polygon

7. (a) 35

9. (a) represents rhombuses and rectangles.

10. (a) *T, Q, R, H, G, I, F, J*
12. (b) Answers vary; for example:

```
TO RECTANGLE :WIDTH :LENGTH
   REPEAT 2 [FD :WIDTH RT 90 FD
      :LENGTH RT 90]
END
```

Cooperative Learning

16. (a) 4

Review Problems

17. (a) 45   **(b)** $n(n-1)/2$
18. Ø, 1 point, 2 points, ray
19. (a) False. A ray has only one endpoint.   **(b)** True
(c) False. Skew lines cannot be contained in the single plane.
(d) False. $\overrightarrow{MN}$ has endpoint *M* and extends in the direction of
point *N*; $\overrightarrow{NM}$ has endpoint *N* and extends in the direction of
point *M*.   **(e)** True   **(f)** False. Their intersection is a line.

Ongoing Assessment 10-3

2. (b) 14,400   **(d)** 31
7. (a) 0.35, 350   **(b)** 163, 1630   **(c)** 0.035, 3.5
(d) 0.1, 10   **(e)** 200, 2000
9. 6 m, 5218 mm, 245 cm, 700 mm, 91 mm, 8 cm
12. (a) 1 cm   **(c)** 3000 m   **(j)** 5130 cm
17. (a) Answers vary.   **(b)** 8 squares
19. (b) $3/\pi$ m   **(d)** 46 cm
20. (d) $6\pi^2$ cm
22. πr
23. (d) 2495 hr, or about 104 days
27. Answers vary.

Open-ended

31. (a) Answers vary; for example: 1-1-1 and 2-2-1 work,
while 2-3-6 and 1-2-3 do not.

Review Problems

34. (a) Yes, because $\overleftrightarrow{BC}$ and $\overleftrightarrow{EH}$ are parallel and determine the
shaded plane shown below.   **(b)** Yes, every three points
labeled are not collinear and hence, determine a unique plane.
(c) No, because *C* is not in the unique plane determined by *E,
H,* and *G*.

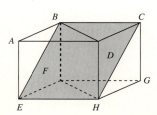

Ongoing Assessment 10-4

3. (a) 60°   **(d)** 60°
4. (c) Yes. A pair of alternate interior angles are 40° each.
6. (a) 20   **7. (a)** 70°   **(b)** 70°
8. (c) $x = 50°$ and $y = 60°$ **9. (b)** 90°
10. (a) 360°   **13.** 90°   **14.** 111°   **16.** 135°   **18. (a)** 100°

Communication

20. (d) No. It may have an obtuse or right angle as well.
22. (a) Five triangles will be constructed in which the sum of
the angles of each triangle is 180°. The sum of the measures of
the angles of all the triangles equals 5(180°), from which we
subtract 360° (the sum of all the measures of the angles of the
triangles with vertex *P*). Thus $5(180°) - 360° = 540°$.
25. (a) Divide the quadrilateral into 2 triangles: $\triangle ABC$ and
$\triangle ACD$. The sum of the measures of the interior angles of each
triangle is 180°, so the sum of the measures of the interior
angles of the quadrilateral is 2(180°), or 360°.
26. No. Regular hexagons fit because the measure of each
vertex angle is 120°, 3 hexagons fit to form 360°, and the plane
can be filled. For a regular pentagon, the measure of each
vertex angle is 108°, so pentagons cannot be placed together
to form 360° (360 is not divisible by 108) and the plane cannot
be filled.
28. Answers vary for example:
(a)

```
TO PARALLELOGRAM :L :W :A
   REPEAT 2 [FD :L RT 180- :A FD :W RT :A]
END
```

(b)

```
TO RECTANGLE :L :W
   PARALLELOGRAM :L :W 90
END
```

(c)

```
TO RHOMBUS :L :A
   PARALLELOGRAM :L :L :A
END
```

Review Problems

33. (a) 10 cm   **(b)** 104 mm   **(c)** 0.35 m   **(d)** 40 mm
(e) 8000 m   **(f)** 6.504 km
34. (a) $(2\pi + 4)$ mm   **(b)** $(5\pi + 6)$ mm
35.

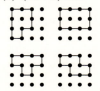

36. (a) All angles must be right angles, and all diagonals are
the same length.   **(b)** All sides are the same length, and all
angles are right angles.   **(c)** This is impossible because all
squares are parallelograms.

Ongoing Assessment 10-5

2. (d) $\{R\}$
4. (a) 5 **(b)** 4
5. (e) False **(h)** True
9. (b) Quadrilateral (square) pyramid
10. (a) iv
12.

Prism	Vertices per Base	Diagonals per Vertex	Total Number of Diagonals
Quadrilateral	4	1	4
Pentagonal	5	2	10
Hexagonal	6	3	18
Heptagonal	7	4	28
Octagonal	8	5	40
.	.	.	.
.	.	.	.
.	.	.	.
n-gonal	n	$(n-3)$	$n(n-3)$

15. (d)

Right pentagonal prism
This intersection is a pentagon.

16. (a) Rectangle, square, triangle
17. (a) $10 + 7 - 15 = 2$ **(b)** $9 + 9 - 16 = 2$
19.

	Pyramid	Prism
(a)	$n+1$	$n+2$
(b)	$n+1$	$2n$
(c)	$2n$	$3n$

Communication

20. (a) Yes. A prism with bases that are 11-gons will have exactly 33 edges because there are 11 edges on each of the bases and 11 edges that connect each vertex of the top base to each vertex of the bottom base.

Review Problems

29. Yes because the sum of the angles of a triangle is 180°.
30. $m(\angle BCD) = 60°$
31. 140°
32. (a) True **(b)** True **(c)** True

33. Lines in the same plane and perpendicular to the same line are parallel. This is because corresponding angles are right angles and hence are congruent.

Ongoing Assessment 10-6

1. All the networks other than (d), (f), and (i) are traversable. Networks (a) and (j) are Euler circuits.
(a)

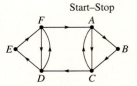

Path:
ABCACDEFDFA;
any point can be a starting point.

(b)

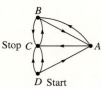

Yes. It has all even vertices.

Path:
DACDCBABC;
Only points *C* and *D* can be starting points.

(c)

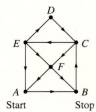

Yes. It has exactly 2 odd vertices; all others are even.

Path:
ABCFAEDCEFB;
only points *A* and *B* can be starting points.

(e)

Yes. It has exactly 2 odd vertices; both of the others are even.

Path:
ABCBDCAD;
only points *A* and *D* can be starting points.

(g)

Yes. It has exactly 2 odd vertices; all others are even.

Start   Stop

Path:
FADABCBGFEDCHEHG;
only points *F* and *G*
can be starting points.

(h)

Yes. It has exactly 2 odd vertices; both of the others are even.

Path:
ACBCDCDAB;
only points *A* and *B*
can be starting points.

(j)

Path:
EFHKLNABDFGHLMNBCDE;
any point can be a
starting point.

3.

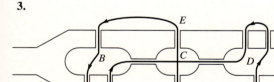

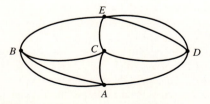

Path: *CEBABCADEDC*; any point can be a starting point.

4. (b) Network (i) is not traversable because it has 4 odd vertices. Network (ii) has 2 odd vertices, so it is traversable, as shown in the following figure:

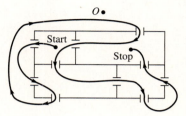

6. It is not possible.

8.

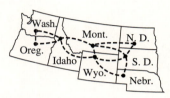

All vertices are even, so the trip is possible. It makes no difference where she starts.

Communication

9. Answers vary. Possibilities are as follows:

(a)
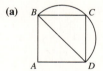

(b)

Chapter Review

2. (b) $\overrightarrow{BA}$ and $\overrightarrow{BC}$ **(d)** $\overrightarrow{AB}$
3. (c) $\overleftrightarrow{AQ}$
5. (b) No. The sum of the measures of the 4 angles in a parallelogram must be 360°. If all the angles are acute, the sum would be less than 360°.
7. (b) 90 sides
10. $m(\angle 3) = m(\angle 4) = 45°$
11. 35°8′ 35″
12. (c) 120°
13. (a) The sum of the measures of the angles in a triangle is 180°. Also the fact that the measure of an exterior angle of a triangle equals the sum of the measures of the 2 other angles that are not supplementary to the exterior angle.
14. (b) Not possible because $q + r = p$.
15. (a) 16 2/3 yd   **(c)** 3960 ft
18. 8

20. (a) (i), (ii), and (iv)

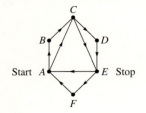

Path:
ABCDEFACEA;
any point can be used
as a starting point.

(i)

Path:
ABCDAEDBE;
points *A* and *E* are
possible starting points.

(ii)

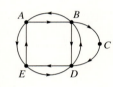

Path:
BDEABAEDBCD;
points *B* and *D* are
possible starting points.

(iv)

CHAPTER 11

Ongoing Assessment 11-1

1. (b) The side of greater length is opposite the angle of greater measure.
2. (c) Scalene right   **(d)** No triangle is possible.
4. 22 triangles
5. (a) Yes; SAS   **(c)** No
7. The lengths of the wires must be the same because they are congruent parts of the congruent triangles formed.
11. (b) Because $\triangle ABC \cong \triangle BCA$, $\angle A \cong \angle B$ and $\angle B \cong \angle C$. Hence, $\angle A \cong \angle B \cong \angle C$.
13. (a) One method of placing the six points on the circle is to use a compass with an opening the length of the circle's radius. **(c)** The triangles are congruent by SSS. The sides are the same length as a radius of the circle.
14. (a) F is the midpoint of both diagonals. We can show $\triangle ABD \cong \triangle CBD$ by SSS and then $\angle BDC \cong \angle BDA$ by CPCTC. $\triangle AFD \cong \triangle CFD$ by SAS, so $\overline{AF} \cong \overline{FC}$, thus F is the midpoint of $\overline{AC}$. A similar argument will show $\overline{BF} \cong \overline{FD}$.
15. (a) A parallelogram. Let $ABCD$ be the quadrilateral, with E the intersection point of its diagonals. Show that $\triangle AED \cong \triangle CEB$ and that $\triangle BEA \cong \triangle DEC$. Use congruent alternate interior angles to show $\overline{BC} \parallel \overline{AD}$ and $\overline{AB} \parallel \overline{CD}$. **(c)** Rhombus
16. (a) The angles formed by the diagonals of a rhombus are right angles.
17. A parallelogram. In quadrilateral $ABCD$, let $\overline{AB} \cong \overline{CD}$ and $\overline{BC} \cong \overline{AD}$. Prove that $\triangle ABC \cong \triangle CDA$ and conclude that

$\overline{BC} \parallel \overline{AD}$. Similarly, show that $\triangle ABD \cong \triangle DCB$ and conclude that $\overline{AB} \parallel \overline{DC}$.
19. The side of one cube is congruent to a side of the other cube.
21. (a) 6   **(c)** $n(n-1)(n-2) \cdot \ldots \cdot 3 \cdot 2 \cdot 1$
23. The perimeters are equal because the sides are congruent, thus making measures equal.
24. Answers vary; for example:
```
TO EQUITRI :SIDE
  REPEAT 3 [FD :SIDE RT 120]
END
```
26. (a) A triangle is constructed because the computer does not know the difference in an angle measure and a compass heading.   **(c)** Add the following:
```
IF NOT (:ANGLE < 180) PRINT [NO TRIANGLE IS
POSSIBLE.] STOP
```

Communication

27. Two triangles can be proved to be similar using SSS and SAS type of properties. If the corresponding sides of two triangles are proportional, the triangles are similar. Also, if the corresponding sides of two triangles are proportional and the included angles are congruent, the triangles are similar.
29. A brick wall of a building might be considered a rep-tile if the wall is similar to a brick in the wall and the wall is used to construct larger walls also similar to the brick.

Open-ended

31. Answers vary. One possible pattern is the stamp-block quilt, that is, a quilt constructed entirely of squares.

Cooperative Learning

33. Answers vary. Without the correspondence among vertices, students can have selected congruent sides and all congruent angles and have similar figures that are not necessarily congruent.

Ongoing Assessment 11-2

1. (d) Infinitely many triangles are possible.
3. (a) Yes; ASA   **(c)** No. SSA does not assure congruence.
4. When the parallel ruler is open at any setting, the distance $BC = BC$. It is given that $AB = DC$ and $AC = BD$. So $\triangle ABC \cong \triangle DCB$ by SSS. Hence, $\angle ABC \cong \angle DCB$ by CPCTC. Because these angles are alternate interior angles formed by lines $\overleftrightarrow{AB}$ and $\overleftrightarrow{CD}$ with transversal line $\overleftrightarrow{BC}$, then $\overline{AB} \parallel \overline{DC}$.
5. (a) Parallelogram   **(c)** None   **(e)** Rhombus
(g) Parallelogram
7. The third angles of the triangles must also be congruent because the sum of the measures of the three angles of a triangle must be 180°.

8. (a) If one leg and an acute angle of one right triangle are congruent respectively to a leg and an acute angle of another right triangle, the triangles are congruent.

Also, if the hypotenuse and an acute angle of a right triangle are congruent respectively to the hypotenuse and an acute angle of another right triangle, the triangles are congruent.

9. (a) True **(c)** True **(e)** True **(g)** True **(i)** False. A square is a trapezoid.

10. (c) No. Any parallelogram with a pair of right angles must have right angles as its other pair of angles and hence must be a rectangle.

12. The quadrilateral formed must be a rhombus because all the sides are congruent.

14. The minimal conditions are that the measures of the central angles of the sectors must be the same.

16. (a) $\triangle ABC \cong \triangle ADC$ by SSS. Hence, $\angle BAC \cong \angle DAC$ and $\angle BCM \cong \angle DCM$ by CPCTC. Therefore, $\overleftrightarrow{AC}$ bisects $\angle A$ and $\angle C$.

17. (a) The sides opposite congruent angles in an isosceles trapezoid are congruent.

19. (a) Rhombus **(c)** Parallelogram **(e)** Parallelogram

20. (b) The lengths of the sides of two perpendicular sides of the rectangles must be equal.

21. (a) Use the definition of a parallelogram and ASA to prove that $\triangle ADB \cong \triangle CDB$ and $\triangle ADC \cong \triangle CBA$.
(c) *Hint:* Prove that $\triangle ABF \cong \triangle CDF$.

22. (b) (i) Two intersecting line segments **(ii)** Three segments that do not close into a triangle

23. (a) Answers vary.
```
TO RHOMBUS :SIDE :ANGLE
  REPEAT 2 [FD :SIDE RT (180-:ANGLE)
    FD :SIDE RT :ANGLE]
END
```
(c)
```
TO SQ.RHOM :SIDE
  RHOMBUS :SIDE 90
END
```

Communication

25. Mathematical congruence is exact. Two objects are congruent if they have exactly the same size and shape. In manufacturing, the best that can happen is that two items are congruent if they are within some tolerance of each other.

27. One way is to make both legs of the ironing board the same length and fasten them together with a hinge at their centers. If one of these legs is attached to the board at a fixed spot and the other leg can be attached at various spots, then the height of the ironing board can be adjusted. Since the legs form the diagonals of a rectangle, the board will always be parallel to the floor. (It can be shown that a quadrilateral whose diagonals are the same length and bisect each other is a rectangle.) In most commercially available ironing boards, the legs are designed to form diagonals of a trapezoid. The fact that the surface is always parallel to the floor follows from properties of similar triangles discussed in Section 11-4.

Open-ended

28. (a) All rolls of wallpaper are not congruent. They come in different widths and lengths. Typically, with the same pattern, they are congruent.

29. The United States Postal Service tries to make all of a single variety of stamps congruent. However, there have been some notable examples of stamps of one type not being congruent. Probably the most famous of the noncongruent stamps was the upside down "flying jenny." There have been others. The anomalies are rare and become very expensive collector's items.

Cooperative Learning

30. (c) The definition used in this text allows for a structure among the quadrilaterals that does not exist with the definition in (a), namely the subset relationships among the quadrilaterals. The definition in this text does cause some difficulty in the definition of an isosceles trapezoid, which must be defined in terms of its base angles, not its sides.

Review Problems

31. The triangles that are congruent to triangle *ABC* are triangles *AED* and *CDE*. They are all congruent by SAS. Students may need to cut these triangles out and compare shapes.

32.-33. Constructions.

34. (a) Yes; SAS **(b)** Yes; SSS **(c)** No

Ongoing Assessment 11-3

2. Constructions. The advantages and disadvantages of each may be discussed. The Mira is easy to use when the paper on which the constructions are to be performed may not be altered. The compass and straightedge is the classical way to do constructions. Paperfolding adds a tactile approach to the problem. The geometric drawing utility demands that exact measurements be used on the screen unless you want similar figures.

3. (b) The altitude of the triangle is along the cable.

4. (a) The perpendicular bisectors of the sides of an acute triangle meet inside the triangle. **(c)** The perpendicular bisectors of the sides of an obtuse triangle meet outside the triangle.

5. (a) The point on the perpendicular bisector of a segment is equidistant from the endpoints of the segment.

7. (a) The distances are equal.

8. (a) The perpendicular bisector of a chord of a circle contains the center of the circle. **(c)** *Hint:* Construct two nonparallel chords and find their perpendicular bisectors. The intersection of the perpendicular bisectors is the center of the circle.

12. (a) $\overrightarrow{PQ}$ is the perpendicular bisector of $\overline{AB}$.   **(c)** $\overrightarrow{PQ}$ is the angle bisector of $\angle APB$; $\overrightarrow{QC}$ is the angle bisector of $\angle AQB$.

14. (b) Construct two perpendicular segments that bisect each other and are congruent to the given diagonal.   **(d)** Without the angle between the sides being given, there is no unique parallelogram.   **(f)** This is impossible because the sum of the measures of the angles would be greater than 180°.   **(h)** The kite would not be unique without knowing the lengths of some sides.   **(j)** Consider $\triangle ABC$ and the angle bisector $\overline{CD}$. Since $\overline{AC} \cong \overline{BC}$, then $\overline{CD} \perp \overline{AB}$. It is possible to construct $\triangle ADC$, since $\overline{AD}$ is half as long as the base and $m(\angle DAC) = 90° - 1/2\ m\ (\angle ACB)$.

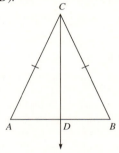

17. (a) Since the triangles are congruent, the acute angles formed by the hypotenuse and the line are congruent. Since the corresponding angles are congruent, the hypotenuses are parallel (the line formed by the top of the ruler is the transversal).

19. Connecting the points with the center of the circle forms six congruent equilateral triangles. Thus all interior angles of the polygon may be proved congruent, and all the sides are congruent. The polygon is a regular hexagon.

20. An equilateral triangle may be formed by connecting every other vertex of the regular hexagon.

23. *Hint:* Bisect the angles formed by the diagonals of the square. The angle bisectors, if extended, intersect the circle in four of the vertices. The other vertices are the vertices of the square.

24. Answers vary.

```
TO ALTITUDES
  REPEAT 3 [RT 30 FD 60 RT 90 FD 110 BK
    130 FD 20 LT 90 FD 60 RT 90]
END
```

Communication

26. Fold the circle onto itself along two diameters. The intersection of the diameters is the center of the circle. Using a Mira, reflect the circle onto itself using two different diameters as the reflecting lines.

28. The lines along the side of the highway appear to intersect, and the middle line appears to bisect the angle formed.

Open-ended

30. Most students will say that there are more perpendiculars from a point to a line using the North Pole as a point and the equator as a line. All lines of longitude intersect at the North Pole and all are perpendicular to the equator.

31. There are no parallels on a sphere. All great circles (that represent lines) intersect in two points.

Cooperative Learning

33. The three classical problems of antiquity are to duplicate a cube (or construct a cube with twice the volume of a given cube), to square a circle (or to construct a square and a circle with equal areas), and to trisect any angle. Descriptions of these problems are given in most geometry books and in any encyclopedia.

Review Problems

34. $\triangle ABC \cong \triangle DEC$ by ASA. ($\overline{BC} \cong \overline{CE}$, $\angle ACB \cong \angle ECD$ as vertical angles, and $\angle B \cong \angle E$ as alternate interior angles formed by the parallels $\overline{AB}$ and $\overline{ED}$ and the transversal $\overleftrightarrow{EB}$.) $\overline{AC} \cong \overline{DC}$ by CPCTC.

35. Construction

36. (a) No   **(b)** (1) $\triangle LYC \cong \triangle UCY$ by SAS. $\overline{LY} \cong \overline{UC}$ is given; $\overline{YC} \cong \overline{CY}$. To show $\angle LYC \cong \angle UCY$, construct $\overline{UV} \parallel \overline{LY}$. Now $\angle UVY$ is a parallelogram; $\overline{UV} \cong \overline{LY}$ and, by transivity, $\overline{UV} \cong \overline{UC}$. $\angle LYC \cong \angle UVC$ (corresponding angles formed by $\overline{LY} \parallel \overline{UV}$ and transversal YC.) $\angle UVC \cong \angle UCV$ (base angles of isosceles triangle UVC). $\angle LYC \cong \angle UCY$ by transitive property. (2) $\triangle ULY \cong \triangle LUC$ by SAS; $\overline{LY} \cong \overline{UC}$ is given, $\overline{UL} \cong \overline{LU}$. To show $\triangle ULY \cong \triangle LUC$, use supplementary pairs of angles $\angle ULY$ and $\angle LYC$, $\angle LUC$ and $\angle UCY$ and $\angle LYC$ and $\angle UCY$ from part (1)   (3) $\triangle LOY \cong \triangle UOC$ by SAS. $\overline{LY} \cong \overline{UC}$ is given. $\angle YLC \cong \angle CUY$ by CPCTC from part (1). $\angle LYU \cong \angle UCL$ by CPCTC from part (2).

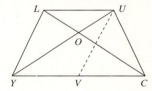

37. $\overline{AB}$

38. $\angle ABC$

39. If $\angle A$ is not the right angle, the triangles are congruent. If $\angle A$ is the right angle, the triangles are not necessarily congruent.

Ongoing Assessment 11-4

1. (a) Yes; AAA   **(c)** No   **(e)** Yes. Radii are proportional. **(g)** Yes. Sides are proportional, and angles are congruent.

3. (c) The triangles are similar if the corresponding sides are proportional.

4. (c) The triangles are similar if, for example, in $\triangle ABC$ and $\triangle DEF$, we have $\dfrac{AB}{DE} = \dfrac{AC}{DF}$ and $\angle A \cong D$.

5. Answers vary.   **(a)** Two rectangles; one is a square and the other is not.

7. (b) (i) 2/3   (ii) 1/2   (iii) 3/4   (iv) 3/4

8. **(a)** 7 **(c)** 3

10. **(b)** (1) $\frac{AC}{AB} = \frac{CD}{CB} = \frac{AD}{AC}$ (2) $\frac{CB}{AB} = \frac{CD}{AC} = \frac{DB}{CB}$

(3) $\frac{AC}{CB} = \frac{AD}{CD} = \frac{CD}{DB}$

12. 15 m

13. 9 m

15. 232.6 in. or 19.4 ft

17. **(a)** 1/3 **(c)** 0 **(e)** 20,000

18. **(a)** $y - 3 = \left(\frac{1}{3}\right)(x - 4)$ **(b)** $y - 1 = \left(\frac{1}{9}\right)(x + 4)$ **(c)** $y = 2$

(d) $x = {}^-3$ **(e)** $y - 12 = 20,000(x - 1.0001)$ **(f)** $y = x$

19. Answers vary. **(a)** $({}^-3, 2), (5, 2), \ldots$ **(c)** $(2, 0),$ $(4, 0), \ldots$ **(e)** $(3, 3), (2, 2), \ldots$

21. The perimeters have ratios $1/k$ because all sides are in this proportion. The sum must be in the same proportion.

23. The answer is no. The cross-sections may be circular if cut parallel to bases, but they could also be oval or elliptical.

24. Answers vary.

(a)
```
TO RECTANGLE :LEN :WID
  REPEAT 2[FD :LEN RT 90 FD :WID RT 90]
END
TO SIM.RECT :LEN :WID
  RECTANGLE :LEN*2 :WID*2
END
```

25. Answers vary.

(a)
```
TO TRISECT :LEN
  REPEAT 3 [MARK FD :LEN/3]
END
TO MARK
  RT 90 FD 5
  BK 5 LT 90
END
```

Communication

26. Any two cubes are similar because they have the same shape.

28. Lay the licorice diagonally on the paper so that it spans a number of spaces equal to the number of children. (See the figure.) Cut on the lines. Equidistant parallel lines will divide any transversal into congruent segments.

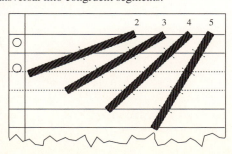

Open-ended

30. Babies and adults are not similar in body shape. Student answers may vary though.

Cooperative Learning

31. **(a)-(b)** The following are two different size triangles with the given data. The triangles are similar but not congruent. (The ratio of the corresponding sides is $\frac{80}{100}$, or $\frac{4}{5}$.) Hence, the surveyor and the architect could both have been correct in their conclusions.

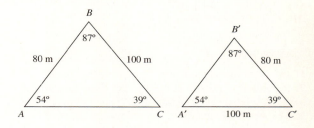

Review Problems

32. No. The image is two-dimensional, while the original person is three-dimensional.

33. Construction

34. Construction

35. Answers vary. Students may suggest that angles of measure 45° be constructed with the endpoints of the hypotenuse as vertices of the 45° angles and the hypotenuse as one of the sides of the angles. Both angles need to be constructed on the same side of the hypotenuse.

36. Yes. Use the vertical angles to justify this result.

37. Answers vary.
```
TO TR130 :HYPOT
  DRAW
  FD :HYPOT/2 RT 120
  FD :HYPOT RT 120
  HOME
END
```
(In LCSI Logo, replace DRAW with CLEARSCREEN.)

38. Answers may vary.
```
TO RTISOS :HYPOT
  DRAW
  FD :HYPOT RT 135
  CHECK
END
```
(In LCSI Logo, replace DRAW with CLEARSCREEN.)
```
TO CHECK
  FORWARD 1
  SETHEADING TOWARDS 00
  IF ABS (HEADING -225) < 2 HOME STOP
```

```
   SETHEADING -135
   CHECK
END
```
(In LCSI Logo, replace SETHEADING TOWARDS 00 with SETHEADING TOWARDS [0 0] and IF ABS (HEADING-225) < 2 HOME STOP with IF ABS (HEADING-225 < 2) [HOME STOP].)
```
TO ABS :VALUE
   IF :VALUE < 0 OUTPUT -:VALUE ELSE
      OUTPUT :VALUE
END
```
(In LCSI Logo, replace IF :VALUE < 0 OUTPUT -:VALUE ELSE OUTPUT :VALUE with IF :VALUE < 0 [OUTPUT -:VALUE] [OUTPUT :VALUE].)

Ongoing Assessment 11-5

1. (a) 13.12 m   **(c)** 9.53 m
3. Regardless of the size of the tile, (*sin* 45° is equal to the *cos* 45° is approximately equal to 0.707; *tan* 45° is 1.)
5. The vertical component is approximately 8.62 lb; the horizontal component is approximately 11.03 lb.
6. (a) The angle should be approximately 35.7°.
7. Approximately 63.9 ft
9. Approximately 41.4 ft
11. (a) Decimals are rounded at three places.

Angle Measure	Sine	Cosine	Square of Sine	Square of Cosine	Sum of Columns 4 and 5
10°	0.174	0.985	0.030	0.970	1
20°	0.342	0.940	0.117	0.884	1.01
30°	0.500	0.866	0.250	0.750	1
40°	0.643	0.766	0.413	0.587	1
50°	0.766	0.643	0.587	0.413	1
60°	0.866	0.500	0.750	0.250	1
70°	0.940	0.342	0.884	0.117	1.01
80°	0.985	0.174	0.970	0.030	1

(b) The sum of the squares of the sines and cosines of various angles is 1.
13. The tangent is the rise over the run. The tangent is also related to the slope of a line.
15. Approximately 63.59 ft horizontally and approximately 101.77 ft vertically
16. (a) 121.8°   **(c)** 1.68 m
17. (a) 0.669   **(c)** 0.900
18. The program draws a square with one diagonal.

Chapter Review

1. (a) $\triangle ADB \cong \triangle CDB$ by SAS   **(c)** $\triangle ABC \cong \triangle EDC$ by AAS   **(e)** $\triangle ABD \cong \triangle CBD$ by ASA or by SAS   **(g)** $\triangle ABD \cong \triangle CBE$ by SSS
2. A parallelogram. $\triangle ADE \cong \triangle CBF$ by SAS. Hence, $\angle DEA \cong \angle CFB$. $\angle DEA \cong \angle EAF$ (alternate interior angles between the parallels $\overleftrightarrow{DC}$ and $\overleftrightarrow{AB}$ and the transversal $\overleftrightarrow{AE}$), so it follows that $\angle EAF \cong \angle CFB$. Consequently, $\overline{AE} \cong \overline{AE}$. Also, $\overline{EC} \cong \overline{EC}$ (why?), and therefore $AECF$ is a parallelogram.
4. (a) $x = 8$ cm; $y = 5$ cm
6. $\dfrac{a}{b} = \dfrac{c}{d}$ because $\dfrac{a}{b} = \dfrac{x}{y}$ and $\dfrac{x}{y} = \dfrac{c}{d}$
8. (a) $\triangle ACB - \triangle DEB$ by AA. $x = \dfrac{24}{5}$ in.
9. (a) False; A chord has its endpoints on the circle.
10. 12 m high
11. (a) (iii) and (iv)
12. 6 m
13. $\dfrac{256}{5}$ m
15. (a) $y - 1 = \left(\dfrac{-4}{3}\right)(x + 1)$
16. There is no single line through the points with the given coordinates because by using two of the points, we get slope $\dfrac{-4}{7}$.
17. Approximately 5.20 cm
19. We might draw an altitude of the triangle forming two right triangles, one of which has an acute angle measuring 72°. Then we can measure sides and find the ratio to approximate the sine.
20. Approximately 3.46 cm
21. The measures of the angles of elevation and depression are equal because they are alternate interior angles formed by a transversal cutting parallel lines.

CHAPTER 12

Ongoing Assessment 12-1

1. (a) cm^2, in.^{2} **(c)** cm^2, in.^{2} **(e)** m^2, yd^2
3. (a) 0.0588 m^2, 58,800 mm^2 **(c)** 15,000 cm^2, 1,500,000 mm^2 **(e)** 0.0005 m^2, 500 mm^2
4. (a) 444.$\overline{4}$ yd^2 **(c)** 6400 A
5. (a) 4900 m^2 **(c)** 0.98 ha
6. (a) 3 sq. units   **(c)** 2 sq. units   **(e)** 6 sq. units
8. (a) 20 cm^2 **(c)** 7.5 m^2 **(e)** 600 cm^2
9. (a) 9 cm^2 **(c)** $(2\sqrt{21} - 2\sqrt{5})$ cm^2, or approximately 4.69 cm^2 **(e)** 84 cm^2
10. (a) (i) 1.95 km^2 (ii) 195 ha
11. (a) True   **(c)** Don't know

12. $(1/2)ab$

13. (a) \$405.11

14. (a) 25π cm^2 **(c)** $(18/5)\pi$ cm^2 **(e)** 100 cm^2

15. 1200 tiles

17. (a) $24\sqrt{3}$ cm^2

19. (a) 16π cm^2

20. (a) 2π cm^2 **(c)** 2π cm^2 **(e)** $(1/4)\pi r^2$ **(g)** $(1/16)\pi r^2$

22. (a) 48 cm

23. (a) The area is quadrupled.

24. (a) The area is quadrupled.   **(c)** The area is increased by a factor of 9.

26. The first is a better buy at 10 ft^2 per dollar versus 9.375 ft^2 per dollar for the second one.

27. $(320 + 64\pi)$ m^2

30. (a)

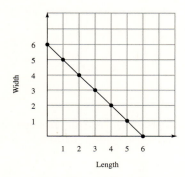

31. The area of the cross-hatched portion is the same as the area of the shaded region: 9π in.^{2}.

32. (a)

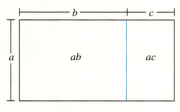

$a(b + c) = ab + ac$

33. (a) $4:9$; $A_1/A_2 = S_1^2/S_2^2$, and $S_1/S_2 = 2/3$. Hence, $A_1/A_2 = (2/3)^2 = 4/9$

34. (a) $4:1$

35. (a) The ratio of the areas of the two screens is $20^2 : 27^2$, or $400:729$. This ratio is less than $400:600$, so the larger set is the better buy.

Communication

38. (a) The area of the 10-in. pizza is 25π in.^{2}. The area of the 20-in. pizza is 100π in.^{2}. Because the area of the 20-in. pizza is four times as great, this pizza might cost four times as much, or \$40. However, this is not the case because other factors are considered in addition to the area of the pizza.

39. The area of each triangle is 10 cm^2 because the base of each triangle is $\overline{AB}$ and the height of each triangle is the perpendicular distance between the two lines. Because each triangle has the same base and height, the areas of the triangles are the same.

41. After the rotations, a rectangle is formed. The area of the rectangle is length times width. In the case of the parallelgram, this is the same as the base times the height.

Open-ended

42. Answers vary; for example, a rectangle that is 3 cm × 4 cm has perimeter 14 cm and area 12 cm^2. A rectangle that is 5 cm × 2 cm also has perimeter 14 cm, but it has area 10 cm^2.

44. (a) 5 sq. units   **(b)** 12 units

45. (a) (i) 12, 10 (ii) 14, 10 (iii) 62, 22   **(c)** $2(n + 1)$

Ongoing Assessment 12-2

1. (a) No. For the figure to be a square, the sides must be the same length and the angles must be right angles. The sides are of different lengths.   **(c)** The length of the diagonal is doubled.

2. (a) 6   **(c)** 12   **(e)** 9   **(g)** $2\sqrt{2}$ **(i)** $3\sqrt{3}$

4. (a) No   **(c)** Yes   **(e)** Yes

5. $\sqrt{450}$, or $15\sqrt{2}$

7. $\sqrt{125}$, or about 11.2, mi

9. 9.8 m approximately

10. (a) $(s^2\sqrt{3})/4$

11. (a) $x = 8, y = 2\sqrt{3}$

13. 12.5 cm; 15 cm

14. 8 cm

16. $90\sqrt{2}$, or about 127.28, ft

19. $\triangle ACD \sim \triangle ABC$; $AC/AB = AD/AC$ implies $b/c = x/b$, which implies $b^2 = cx$; $\triangle BCD \sim \triangle ABC$. $AB/CB = CB/DB$ implies $c/a = a/y$, which implies $a^2 = cy$; $a^2 + b^2 = cx + cy = c(x + y) = cc = c^2$.

20. $\sqrt{10}$, or approximately 3.16 m

22. Approximately 99.5 ft

23. Approximately 10.6 mi

24. The area of the trapezoid is equal to the sum of the areas of the three triangles. Thus

$$1/2(a + b)(a + b) = (1/2)ab + (1/2)ab + (1/2)c^2$$
$$1/2(a^2 + 2ab + b^2) = ab + (1/2)c^2$$
$$a^2/2 + ab + b^2/2 = ab + c^2/2.$$

Subtracting ab from both sides and multiplying both sides by 2, we have $a^2 + b^2 = c^2$. The reader should also verify that the angle formed by the two sides of length c has measure $90°$.

26. Yes

28. (a) 4   **(c)** $2\sqrt{13}$ **(e)** 5

29. $10 + \sqrt{10}$

31. The side lengths are 5, $7\sqrt{2}$, and 5 and so the triangle is isosceles.

32. $x = 9$ or $^-7$

Communication

34. (a) Let the length of the side of the square be s. Draw the diagonal of the square and make the new square have side lengths equal to the diagonal. Then the area is $(\sqrt{2}\,s)^2 = 2s^2$.
37. Yes. She had a right triangle because the converse of the Pythagorean Theorem implies that if $13^2 = 12^2 + 5^2$, then the triangle is a right angle. Because this is true, she has a right triangle and therefore a right angle.

Open-ended

40. (b) Yes. We know that if a-b-c is a Pythagorean triple, then $a^2 + b^2 = c^2$. This implies that $4(a^2 + b^2) = 4c^2$ and that $(2a)^2 + (2b)^2 = (2c)^2$.

Cooperative Learning

43. 0.032 km, 322 cm, 3.2 m, 3.020 mm
44. (a) 33.25 cm^2 **(b)** 30 cm^2 **(c)** 32 m^2
45. (a) 10 cm, 10π cm, 25π cm^2 **(b)** 12 cm, 24π cm, 144π cm^2 **(c)** $\sqrt{17}$ m, $2\sqrt{17}$ m, $2\pi\sqrt{17}$ m **(d)** 10 cm, 20 cm, 100π cm^2
46. $25/\pi$ m^2

Ongoing Assessment 12-3

1. (a) 96 cm^2 **(c)** 236 cm^2 **(e)** 24π cm^2 **(g)** 1500π ft^2
3. 2688π mm^2
5. 4:9
6. (a) They have equal lateral surface areas.
8. Approx. 32.97 in.^{2}
10. Approx. 91.86 ft^2
11. $l = 11$ cm, $w = 8$ cm, $h = 4$ cm
12. (a) The surface area is multiplied by 4.
(c) The surface area is multiplied by k^2.
13. (a) The lateral area is multiplied by 3.
(c) The lateral area is multipled by 9.
14. (a) The surface area is multiplied by 4.
16. (a) 44
17. (a) 1.5π m^2
18. (a) $100\pi(1 + \sqrt{5})$ cm^2 **(c)** 2250π cm^2
19. (a) Approximately 42 cm
21. 375π cm^2

Communication

22. The ice cubes would melt faster because they have a greater surface area that is exposed to the air.
23. She would need 4 times as much cardboard. If each face is doubled, then the area of each face is increased by a factor of 4, that is, $A_1 = lw = A_2 = (2l)(2w) = 4lw = 4A_1$. Because this is true for all faces, the surface area is multiplied by 4.

Open-ended

26. (a) 2%

Review Problems

29. (a) 100,000 **(b)** 1.3680 **(c)** 500 **(d)** 2,000,000
(e) 1 **(f)** 1,000,000
30. $10\sqrt{5}$ cm
31. $20\sqrt{5}$ cm
32. (a) 240 cm; 2400 cm^2 **(b)** $(10\sqrt{2} + 30)$ cm, 75 cm^2
33. Length of side $= 25$ cm; diagonal $\overline{BD} = 30$ cm

Ongoing Assessment 12-4

1. (a) 8000 **(c)** 0.000675 **(e)** 7 **(g)** 0.00857 approx.
(i) 345.6
2. 32.4 L
3. (a) 64 cm^3 **(c)** 216 cm^3 **(e)** 21π cm^2
(g) $(4000/3)\pi$ cm^3 **(i)** $(20,000/3)\pi$ ft^3 **(k)** $(256/3)\pi$ cm^3
4. (a) 2000, 2, 2000 **(c)** 1500, 1.5, 1500 **(e)** 0.75, 0.75, 750
5. (a) 200.0 **(c)** 1.0
6. 1680π mm^3
8. It is multiplied by 8.
9. (a) 2,000, 2, 2 **(c)** 2 dm, 4000, 4
10. $253,500\pi$ L
12. 1.62 L
14. π mL
15. (a) It is multiplied by 8. **(b)** It is multiplied by 27.
16. The Great Pyramid has the greater volume, approximately 25.12 times greater.
19. Approximately 35.34 L
21. $\frac{1}{8}$ of the cone is filled.
23. 260,810,575,168 m^3
25. 33 1/3% air
26. About 21.5%
28. They are equal.
30. No, it is only $\frac{1}{3}$ of the volume for $\frac{1}{2}$ the price.
32. The larger is the better buy. The volume of the larger melon is 1.728 times that of the smaller, but it is only 1.5 times as expensive.
34. $(2/3)\sqrt{2/(5\sqrt{5})}$ m^3, or approximately 0.28 m^3
35. (a) 512,000 cm^3
36. Approx. 45.90 in.^{2}
37. It won't hold the cream at 10 cm tall; it would have to be 20 cm tall.

Communication

39. (a) Doubling the height will only double the volume. Doubling the radius will multiply the volume by 4. This happens because the value of the radius is squared after it is doubled.

Review Problems

47. (a) 15,600 cm^2 **(b)** $(100 + 200\sqrt{2})$ cm^2
(c) $(1649 + (81\sqrt{3})/2)$ m^2, or about 1719.1 m^2

48. (a) 340 cm **(b)** 6000 cm^2
49. $2\sqrt{2}$ m^2
50. 62 cm

Ongoing Assessment 12-5

1. (a) Kilograms or tons **(c)** Grams **(e)** Grams
(g) Tons **(i)** Grams or kilograms
2. (a) Milligrams **(c)** Milligrams **(e)** Grams
3. (a) 15 **(c)** 36 **(e)** 4.230 **(g)** 5750 **(i)** 30
(k) 1.5625 **(m)** 60.8
4. (a) No **(c)** Yes **(e)** Yes
5. 16 kg
7. 2¢
9. ⁻12°C **(c)** ⁻1°C **(e)** 100°C
10. (a) No **(c)** No **(e)** No **(g)** Yes **(i)** Hot
11. (a) 50°F **(c)** 86°F **(e)** 414°F
13. (a) 200,000 L
14. Approximately 145.52 lb

Communication

17. The air temperature increases by more than 10 degrees on the Celsius scale because every time the air temperature increases 1 degree Celsius, it increases 1 4/5 degrees Fahrenheit.

Review

21. (a) $(20 + 6\pi)$ cm; $(48 + 18\pi)$ cm^2 **(b)** 40π cm; 100π cm^2
(c) 50 m; 80 m^2
22. (a) 35 **(b)** 0.16 **(c)** 400,000 **(d)** 5,200,000
(e) 5200 **(f)** 0.0035
23. (a) Yes **(b)** No **(c)** Yes **(d)** No
24. $\sqrt{61}$ km
25. (a) $12,000\pi$ cm^3; 2400π cm^2 **(b)** 42,900 cm^3;
$(6065 + 40\sqrt{5314})$ cm^2

Chapter Review

1. 16
2. (a) $8\frac{1}{2}$ cm^2 **(c)** 7 cm^2
4. (a) The pieces of the trapezoid are rearranged to form a rectangle with width $\frac{h}{2}$ and length $(b_2 + b_1)$. The area is $A = h/w \, (b_2 + b_1)$, which is the area of the initial trapezoid.
5. (a) $54\sqrt{3}$ cm^2
6. (a) 12π cm^2 **(c)** 24 cm^2 **(e)** 178.5 m^2
8. (a) $S.A. = 32(2 + \sqrt{13})$ cm^2; Volume = 128 cm^3
(c) $S.A. = 100\pi$ m^2; Volume = $(500\pi)/3$ m^3
(e) $S.A. = 304$ m^2; Volume = 320 m^3
9. 65π m^3
11. (a) Metric tons **(c)** 1 g **(e)** 25 L **(g)** 51,800
(i) 50,000 **(k)** 25,000 **(m)** 52.813

13. (a) 6000 kg
14. (a) L **(c)** g **(e)** kg **(g)** mL
15. (a) Unlikely **(c)** Unlikely **(e)** Unlikely
16. (a) 2000 **(c)** 3 **(e)** 0.0002

CHAPTER 13

Ongoing Assessment 13-1

2. Reverse the translation so that the image completes a slide from X' to X (to what is called its pre-image). Then check by carrying out the given motion in the "forward" direction; that is, see if $\overline{AB}$ goes to $\overline{A'B'}$.

(a)

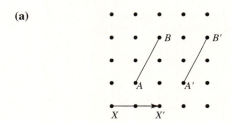

4. (a) $(3, ⁻4)$ **(d)** $(10, 10)$
5. (b) $(0, 0)$ **(d)** $(10, 10)$
6. (b)

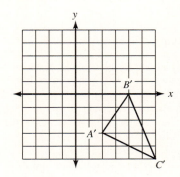

7. (a)

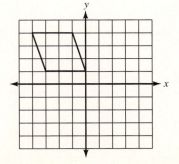

10. Reverse the rotation (to the counterclockwise direction) to locate $\overline{AB}$, that is, the pre-image.

(a)

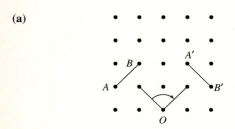

14. (a) ($^-4$, 0) **(e)** (2, 4)

17. (a) (i) $A'(^-2, 3)$ **(ii)** $A'(^-3, ^-2)$ **(iii)** $A'(2, 3)$

19. Construct the image m' of m under a half-turn about P. Point A is the intersection of m' and ℓ. The intersection of $\overrightarrow{AP}$ with m is B.

22.
```
TO ROTATE :A :SIDE
   SQUARE :SIDE
   RIGHT :A
   SQUARE :SIDE
END

TO SQUARE :SIDE
   REPEAT 4[FORWARD :SIDE RIGHT 90]
END
```

Communication

25. (a) Yes. If a point P and its image P' are known, the translation is determined by the slide arrow from P to P'.
(b) No. If A and B are 2 points and A' and B' are their respective images, then the center of the rotation must be on the perpendicular bisector of $\overline{AA'}$ as well as on the perpendicular bisector of $\overline{BB'}$. If $\overline{AA'}$ and $\overline{BB'}$ are not parallel, then the perpendicular bisectors intersect. The point of intersection is the center of the rotation, and $\angle AOA'$ is the angle of rotation. However, if $\overline{AA'}$ and $\overline{BB'}$ are parallel the center of the rotation cannot be determined.

27. (a) A parallelogram. Under a half-turn, the image of a line is parallel to the line. Thus $\overline{AB} \parallel \overline{CD}$ and $\overline{AC} \parallel \overline{DB}$; therefore $ABCD$ is a parallelogram.

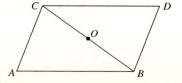

Cooperative Learning

31. (a) The path will look like the one shown in the following figure. Such a path traced by P on the circle is called a *cycloid*.

(b) Rotation about the center of the circle and translation by the slide arrow from A to B
(c) The path is not an arc of a circle. The perpendicular bisectors of all the chords (segments connecting 2 points on the arc) do not intersect in a single point.
(d) The length $\overline{AB}$ is the circumference of the circle.

Ongoing Assessment 13-2

4. Reflecting lines are described for each. **(a)** All diameters (infinitely many) **(b)** Perpendicular bisector of the segment **(c)** The line containing the ray **(d)** Perpendicular bisectors of the sides and lines containing the diagonals **(e)** Perpendicular bisectors of pairs of parallel sides **(f)** None **(g)** Perpendicular bisector of the side that is not congruent to the other two **(h)** Perpendicular bisectors of each side **(i)** None **(j)** Perpendicular bisector of parallel sides **(k)** Perpendicular bisector of the chord connecting the endpoints of the arc **(l)** The line containing the diagonal determined by vertices of the noncongruent angles **(m)** The lines containing the diagonals **(n)** Perpendicular bisectors of parallel sides and three diameters determined by vertices on the circumscribed circle **(o)** There will be n reflecting lines in all. If n is even the lines are determined like in part (n). If n is odd the lines are the perpendicular bisectors of the sides.
5. The original figure.
9. (a) Examples include MOM, WOW, TOOT, and HAH.
12. Reflect A in road 1 to locate A' and B in road 2 to locate B'. Connect A' and B' to locate P and Q. Reflecting A and B creates the straight-line (i.e., shortest) path $A'B'$, which by construction is equal to the distance $(AP + PQ + QB)$ for the actual roads.
14. (a) $A'(3, ^-4)$, $B'(2, 6)$, $C'(^-2, ^-5)$ **(d)** $A'(^-3, ^-4)$, $B'(^-2, 6)$, $C'(2, ^-5)$

Communication

16. Find A' the image of A under reflection in $\overline{EH}$ and B', the image of B under reflection in $\overline{GH}$. Mark the intersections of $\overline{A'B'}$ with $\overline{EH}$ and $\overline{GH}$, respectively, by C and D. The player should aim the ball at A towards the point C. The ball will hit D, bounce off, and hit B. To justify the answer, we need to show that the path A-C-D-B is such that $\angle 1 \cong \angle 3$ and $\angle 4 \cong \angle 6$. Notice that $\angle 1 \cong \angle 2$ and $\angle 6 \cong \angle 5$ because the image of an angle under reflection is congruent to the original angle. Also $\angle 2 \cong \angle 3$ and $\angle 4 \cong \angle 5$ as each pair constitutes a vertical angle. Consequently, $\angle 1 \cong \angle 3$ and $\angle 4 \cong \angle 6$.

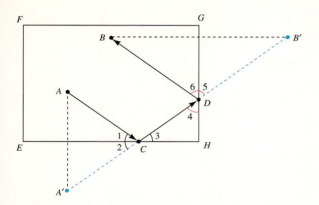

18. (b) Equilateral triangles. Each side could be considered a base.   **(d)** All lines containing diameters will satisfy this situation. Diameters divide a circle into two congruent semicircles.

Cooperative Learning

23. (a) Constructions will vary.   **(b)** The outgoing ray is parallel to the incoming ray.

Review Exercises

25. For a rotation of 360°, all letters. For 180°, see Problem 26. No other rotations result in the original letter.
26. H, I, N, O, S, Z
27. A half-turn about the center of the letter O.
28. (a) A rotation by any angle about the center of the circle will result in the same circle.   **(b)** Reflections about lines containing diameters
29. (a) Rectangle   **(b)** It equals the area of △*ABC*.
(c) Because a half-turn preserves angle measure, the angles at *P′* and *Q′* are right angles and hence *PP′Q′Q* is a rectangle. Notice that △*ABC* and the rectangle *PP′Q′Q* both contain the pentagon *MANQP*. Because △*CMP* ≅ △*AMP′* and △*AQ′N* ≅ △*BQN*, each pair of triangles has the same area. We mark the equal areas by I and II. We mark the area of the pentagon by III and obtain the following:

$$\text{Area } \triangle ABC = \text{I} + \text{III} + \text{II}$$
$$\text{Area of } PP'Q'Q = \text{I} + \text{II} + \text{III}$$

Hence, the areas are equal.

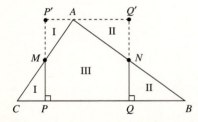

30. Construct $\overline{BE}$ perpendicular to $\overline{AD}$ as shown. Next translate △*BAE* by the slide arrow from *B* to *C*. The image

of △*ABE* is △*DCE′*. The rectangle *BCE′E* is the required rectangle.

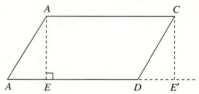

Ongoing Assessment 13-3

3. (a) Translation taking *B* to *B′* followed by a size transformation with center *B′* (and scale factor 2)
(d) Half-turn about *C* followed by a size transformation with center *C* and scale factor $\dfrac{3}{2}$

4. (b) $x = 98/15$, $y = 90/7$
5. (c) 120 mm
6. (a) Scale factor 3, $x = 12$, $y = 10$

Communication

9. (a) It does change. For example, consider the segment whose endpoints are $(0, 0)$ and $(1, 1)$ and has length 1. Under the size transformation with center at $(0, 0)$ and scale factor 2, the image of the segment is a segment whose endpoints are $(0, 0)$ and $(2, 2)$. That segment has length 2.
11. (a) A single size transformation with center *O* and scale factor $\dfrac{1}{2} \cdot \dfrac{1}{3}$, or $\dfrac{1}{6}$. Let *P* be any point and *P′* its image under the first size transformation and *P″* the image of *P′* under the second size transformation. Then $OP'/OP = \dfrac{1}{2}$ and $OP''/OP' = \dfrac{1}{3}$. Consequently, $(OP'/OP) \cdot (OP''/OP') = \dfrac{1}{2} \cdot \dfrac{1}{3}$ or $OP''/OP = \dfrac{1}{2} \cdot \dfrac{1}{3}$. Thus *P′* can be obtained from *P* by a size transformation with center *O* and scale factor $\dfrac{1}{2} \cdot \dfrac{1}{3}$.

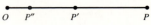

13. Yes. Suppose the size transformation with center *O* has a scale factor *r*. The image of any point *P* on the circle with radius *d* is *P′* such that $OP'/OP = r$. Thus $OP' = r(OP)$ or $OP' = rd$. This means that the image of every point on the circle is at the same distance *rd* from *O* and hence on a circle with radius *rd*.

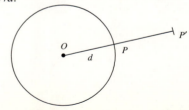

Cooperative Learning

15. (a) If p is the perimeter of the figure and p' the perimeter of the image, then $p' = 3p$.

Review Problems

17. (a) The translation given by slide arrow from N to M.
(b) A counterclockwise rotation of 75° about O **(c)** A clockwise rotation of 45° about A **(d)** A reflection in m and translation from B to A **(e)** A second reflection in n
18. (a) $(4, 3)$ reflects in m to $(4, 1)$; $(4, 1)$ reflects in n to $(2, 1)$.
(b) $(0, 1) \rightarrow (0, 3) \rightarrow (6, 3)$ **(c)** $(^-1, 0) \rightarrow (^-1, 4) \rightarrow$
$(7, 4)$ **(d)** $(0, 0) \rightarrow (0, 4) \rightarrow (6, 4)$

Ongoing Assessment 13-4

3. Reflect the given portions about ℓ.
(b)

4. (a) (i) Four lines of symmetry; the diagonals and horizontal or vertical lines through the center.   (ii) No lines of symmetry.   (iii) Two lines of symmetry; horizontally and vertically through the center.   (iv) One line of symmetry; vertically through the center.
5. (a) 6

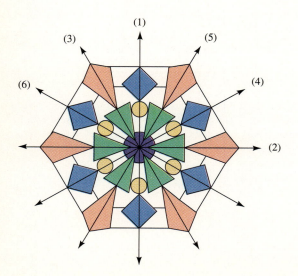

7. (a)

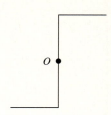

8. (c) Seven; three through the vertices, three through the faces, and one perpendicular to the others through the width of the figure
10. (a) Execute   `TURN.SY 50 6 60`

Communication

11. (a) Yes. The definition of point symmetry is that it is rotational symmetry of 180°.   **(b)** No. It may have rotational symmetry of other than 180°; an equilateral triangle is an example.

Cooperative Learning

17. Answers vary; for example, consider a rectangle. You would report that your figure has 2 line symmetries and a rotational symmetry of 180°.

Review Problems

18. One method is to trace over the figure. Then fold at ℓ and trace along the figure as seen through the paper.
19. Find the images of the vertices.

Ongoing Assessment 13-5

2. (a) Perform half-turns about the midpoints of all sides.
5. (a) The dual is another tessellation of squares (congruent to those given).   **(b)** A tessellation of equilateral triangles.
6. (a)

```
TO TESSELSQUARE
    PENUP BACK 70 PENDOWN
    REPEAT 9 [SQUARE 20 FORWARD 20]
    PENUP BACK 180 RIGHT 90
    FORWARD 20 LEFT 90 PENDOWN
    REPEAT 9 [SQUARE 20 FORWARD 20]
END
TO SQUARE :SIDE
    REPEAT 4 [FORWARD :SIDE RIGHT 90]
END
```

8. (a) The image $ABCD$ under a half-turn in M (the midpoint of $\overline{CD}$) is the following trapezoid $FEDC$. Because the trapezoids are congruent, $ABFE$ is a parallelogram. The area of the parallelogram is $AE \cdot h$ or $(a + b) \cdot h$. The parallelogram is the union of two nonoverlapping congruent trapezoids. The area of each trapezoid is $(a + b) \cdot h/2$.

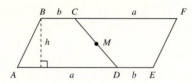

Open-ended

12. Answers vary. For example, a right rectangular prism, as well as a tetrahedron, will tile the space but a cylinder of square pyramid will not.

Cooperative Learning

14. (a) Four copies of the figure will generate a figure similar to the original figure. Then use 4 copies of the new figure and so on. Alternately, two copies of the original figure can be arranged to form a parallelogram, and parallelograms tessellate the plane.   **(c)** Answers vary. For example, the following figure is a rep-tile.

Chapter Review

  3. (a) Four; two diagonals, one each horizontal and vertical
(b) One; the diagonal bisecting the central angle
(c) One; the bisector of the point angle
  4. (a) Rotational (120° and 240°)
  5. (b) Infinitely many   **(c)** Three; each cutting the length, width, and height in half
  7. (b) 60/7 mi or approximately 8.57 mi
  9. (a) Half-turn about X
10. (b) A reflection about the perpendicular bisector of $\overline{BY}$ (and $\overline{AU}$) will complete the desired transformation.
11. Reflection about $\overline{SO}$
12. Let $\triangle H'O'R'$ be the image of $\triangle HOR$ under a half turn about R. Then $\triangle SER$ is the image of $\triangle H'O'R'$ under a size transformation with center R and scale factor $\frac{2}{3}$. Thus $\triangle SER$ is the image of $\triangle HOR$ under the half turn about R followed by the size tranformation described above.
14. Rotate $\triangle PIG$ 180° (half-turn) about the midpoint of $\overline{PT}$, then perform a size transformation with scale factor 2 and center P' ($= T$).

APPENDIX I

Ongoing Assessment AI

  1. (a)

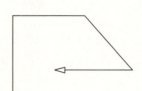

  (c)

  (e) ◁   **(g)**

  3. (a)

  (c)

  4. Answers may vary.
  (a) `TO RECT`
     `REPEAT 2 [FORWARD 30 RIGHT 90`
     `FORWARD 60 RIGHT 90]`
     `END`
  (c) `TO HAT`
     `REPEAT 2 [FORWARD 60 RIGHT 90`
     `FORWARD 30 RIGHT 90]`

```
      PENUP LEFT 90 FORWARD 30 PENDOWN
      REPEAT 2[LEFT 90 FORWARD 6
       LEFT 90 FORWARD 90]
      END
(e) TO RHOMBUS
      RIGHT 20
      REPEAT 2[FD 40 RT 70 FD 40
       RT 110]
      END
```

6. Answers may vary

```
TO SQUARE1
 REPEAT 4[FORWARD 50 RIGHT 90]
END
TO TRIANGLE1
 REPEAT 3[FORWARD 50 RIGHT 120]
END
(a) TO SQUARE.PILE
      REPEAT 4[SQUARE1 RIGHT 90]
      END
(c) TO RECT1
      REPEAT 2[FORWARD 60 RIGHT 90
       FORWARD 30 RIGHT 90]
      END
      TO RECT.SWIRL
       RIGHT 30
       REPEAT 4[RECT1 LEFT 90]
      END
(e) TO STAR
      RIGHT 30
      REPEAT 4[TRIANGLE1 RIGHT 60
       FORWARD 50 RIGHT 30]
      END
```

7. Answers may vary.

```
(b) TO BUILD.SQR :S
      SQUARE :S
      SQUARE :S + 10
      SQUARE :S + 20
      SQUARE :S + 30
      SQUARE :S + 40
      END
(d) TO TOWER :S
      SQUARE :S
      FORWARD :S RIGHT 90
      FORWARD :S/4 LEFT 90
      SQUARE :S/2
      FORWARD :S/2 RIGHT 90
      FORWARD :S/8 LEFT 90
      SQUARE :S/4
      END
```

9.
```
TO KITE
 LEFT 45
 REPEAT 4[FORWARD 40 RIGHT 90]
 RIGHT 45
 REPEAT 3[BACK 20 K.TAIL RIGHT 60]
```

```
 BACK 20
END
TO K.TAIL
 RIGHT 60
 REPEAT 3[FORWARD 10 RIGHT 120]
 LEFT 120
 REPEAT 3[FORWARD 10 LEFT 120]
END
```

12.
```
TO RECTANGLES :S
 LEFT 90
 REPEAT 4[RECTANGLE :S/3 :S RIGHT 90
  FORWARD :S/3]
END
TO RECTANGLE :S1 :S2
 REPEAT 2[FORWARD :S1 RIGHT 90
  FORWARD :S2 RIGHT 90]
END
```

15. Answers may vary.

```
(a) TO STRETCH :S
      IF :S < 5 STOP
      SQUARE :S
      FORWARD :S RIGHT 90
      FORWARD :S LEFT 90
      STRETCH :S- 10
      END
```
(In LCSI, replace IF :S < 5 STOP with IF :S < 5 [STOP])

```
(c) TO PISA :S :A
      IF :S < 5 STOP
      SQUARE :S
      FORWARD :S LEFT :A
      PISA :S*0.75 :A
      END
```
(In LCSI, replace IF :S < 5 STOP with IF: S < 5 [STOP])

```
(e) TO ROW.HOUSE :S
      IF :S < 5 STOP
      HOUSE :S
      SETUP :S
      ROW.HOUSE :S/2
      END
```
(In LCSI, replace IF :S < 5 STOP with IF :S < 5 [STOP])
```
      TO HOUSE :S
       SQUARE :S
       FORWARD :S
       RIGHT 30 TRIANGLE :S
       LEFT 30
      END
      TO SETUP :S
       BACK :S RIGHT 90
       FORWARD :S LEFT 90
      END
```

16.
```
TO NEST.TRI :S
  IF :S < 10 STOP
  RIGHT 30 TRIANGLE :S
  FD :S/2 RIGHT 30
  NEST.TRI :S/2
END
```
(In LCSI, replace IF :S < 10 STOP with IF :S < 10 [STOP])
```
TO TRIANGLE :S
  REPEAT 3 [FORWARD :S RIGHT 120]
END
```
17. Answers may vary.
```
TO SPIN.SQ :S
  IF :S < 5 STOP
  SQUARE :S
  RIGHT 20
  SPIN.SQ :S-5
END
```
(In LCSI, replace IF :S < 5 STOP with IF :S < 5 [STOP])
```
TO SQUARE :S
  REPEAT 4[FORWARD :S RIGHT 90]
END
```

APPENDIX II

Ongoing Assessment A-II

1. Approximately 11.896, or 11.9, yr
3. ($^-$10, 257) and (10, 357)
4. (a) The graphs all pass through the point (0, 3), and all are linear.   **(c)** As the slope becomes greater, the graph becomes steeper. The lines have slopes of 1, 2, 3, and 4, respectively.
5. (b) They cross the y-axis at different points.
6. Approximately (1.22, $^-$0.55)
7. (a) She needs to find the intersection points of Y_1, Y_2, and Y_3 with Y_4.
8. (a) Sign changes occur at $x = 1$ and $x = 4$.   **(c)** The graphs cross at $x = 1$ and $x = 4$.

APPENDIX III

Ongoing Assessment A-III

1. The areas of a rectangle and a parallelogram, both with the same base and height, are the same.
3. The ratio of the areas of 2 similar figures is the square of the ratio of 2 corresponding sides of the similar figures.

6. (a) The percent of area in the square not covered by the circle is approximately 21%.   **(b)** The percent of area in the circle not covered by the square is approximately 36%.
(c) The answers in (a) and (b) suggest that the circular peg will fit better in the square hole than vice versa.
7. (a) Approximately 21%   **(b)** Approximately 21%
(c) The answer doesn't change
9. This exercise can be used to practice estimation of areas and the estimation of percentages.

APPENDIX IV

Ongoing Assessment A-IV

1. Answers will vary; for example: **(a)** 5, 9, 13, 17, 21, . . .
(b) Column A should contain the numbers 1, 2, 3, 4, 5, 6, ...
(c) The formula =A1+1 should be used to find A2 and then to fill down the rest of the column.   **(d)** Column B for this example will start with 5, and each successive term is 4 more than the previous one.   **(e)** The formula =B1+4 could be used here.   **(f)** The Σ key should be used when the cell in which the sum is wanted is highlighted.   **(g)** In an arithmetic sequence, no matter which one was used the data should lie along a line.
3. If all the data is listed in the first 14 cells of column A, the Σ key can be used to find the sum of all the data, and the sum can be placed in cell A15. The formula =A15/14 can be used to place the mean in cell A16.
6. The first step is to create column A that is the number of the term by placing 1 in cell A1 and using the formula =A1+1 to fill down for a total of 100 cells in column A. Next, we could use the formula =13*A:A and fill down for a total of 100 cells in column B.
7. Answers may vary depending on the method used for computing grade-point averages at your college. In general, you may use 4 quality points for each hour of A, 3 quality points for each hour of B, 2 for each hour of C, 1 for each hour of D, and 0 for each hour of F. After multiplying each hour by the respective number of quality points, find the total of all quality points and then divide by the total number of hours.
9. Column A can be created by entering 1 in cell A1 and using the formula =A1+1 and the Fill Down feature to fill as many cells as wanted. Column B can be created by entering =A1 in cell B1 and using =B1*A2 with the Fill Down feature to complete the wanted cells.

Index

The Cover Solution

Wheels 1, 3, 4, 6, 11, and 12 have rotational symmetry.
Wheels 2 and 5 have reflective symmetry.
Wheels 7, 8, and 10 have both reflective and rotational symmetry.
Wheel 9 has no symmetry.

Wheel 1 is from a 1991 Eagle Premier
Wheel 2 is from a 1992 Chevrolet Corsica LT
Wheel 3 is from a 1992 Mercury Capri
Wheel 4 is from a 1991 Oldsmobile Custom Cruiser
Wheel 5 is from a 1991 Pontiac Grand Am
Wheel 6 is from a 1992 Dodge Stealth
Wheel 7 is from a 1993 Jeep Cherokee
Wheel 8 is from a 1991 Pontiac Grand Prix
Wheel 9 is from a 1992 Chevrolet Cavalier
Wheel 10 is from a 1991 Chrysler Le Baron
Wheel 11 is from a 1992 Dodge Shadow
Wheel 12 is from a 1992 Chevrolet Lumina Coupe